Anarchy and the Law

Independent Studies in Political Economy

THE ACADEMY IN CRISIS
The Political Economy of Higher Education
Edited by John W. Sommer
Foreword by Nathan Glazer

AMERICAN HEALTH CARE
Government, Market Processes, and the Public Interest
Edited by Roger D. Feldman
Foreword by Mark V. Pauly

ANARCHY AND THE LAW
The Political Economy of Choice
Edited by Edward P. Stringham

CUTTING GREEN TAPE
Toxic Pollutants, Environmental Regulation, and the Law
Edited by Richard L. Stroup and Roger E. Meiners
Foreword by W. Kip Viscusi

MONEY AND THE NATION STATE
The Financial Regulation, Government, and the World Monetary System
Edited by Kevin Dowd and Richard H. Timberlake Jr.

PRIVATE RIGHTS & PUBLIC ILLUSIONS
Tibor R. Machan
Foreword by Nicholas Rescher

STREET SMART
Competition, Entrepreneurship, and the Future of Roads
Edited by Gabriel Roth
Foreword by Mary E. Peters

TAXING CHOICE
The Predatory Politics of Fiscal Discrimination
Edited by William F. Shughart II
Foreword by Paul W. McCracken

WRITING OFF IDEAS
Taxation, Foundations, and Philanthropy in America
Randall G. Holcombe

Anarchy and the Law

The Political Economy of Choice

Edward P. Stringham, editor

Transaction Publishers
New Brunswick (U.S.A.) and London (U.K.)

Second printing 2009

This book is printed on acid-free paper that meets the American National Standard for Permanence of Paper for Printed Library Materials.

Library of Congress Catalog Number: 2005054852
ISBN: 978-0-7658-0330-6 (cloth); 978-1-4128-0579-7 (paper)
Printed in the United States of America

Library of Congress Cataloging-in-Publication

Anarchy and the law : the political economy of choice / Edward P. Stringham, editor.

p. cm.

Includes bibliographical references and index.

ISBN 0-7658-0330-5 (cloth : alk. paper)—ISBN 1-4128-0579-1 (pbk. : alk. paper)

1. Anarchism. 2. Libertarianism. 3. State, The. 4. Social choice. I. Stringham, Edward..

HX833.A5864 2006
340'.115—dc22 2005054852

Contents

Section II: Debate

Section III: History of Anarchist Thought

Section IV: Historical Case Studies of Non-Government Law Enforcement

Acknowledgments

Chapter 2 from Murray Rothbard, "Police, Law, and the Courts," in *For a New Liberty: Libertarian Manifesto* (San Francisco: Fox and Wilkes, 1996 [1973]), pp. 214-241. Copyright © 1973, 1978 by Murray N. Rothbard. Reprinted with permission of the Ludwig von Mises Institute, Auburn, Alabama 36832.

Chapter 3 from David Friedman, *The Machinery of Freedom: Guide to a Radical Capitalism*, second edition (La Salle, IL: Open Court, 1989), pp. 111-134. Reprinted by permission of Open Court Publishing Company, a division of Carus Publishing Company, Peru, IL, copyright © 1989.

Chapter 4 from Morris and Linda Tannehill, *Market for Liberty* (Lansing, MI: Morris and Linda Tannehill, 1970); reprinted as *Society without Government* (New York: Arno Press, 1972), pp. 88-108. Reprinted with permission of the publisher, Laissez Fair Books, from *Market for Liberty*. Copyright © 1970 by Morris and Linda Tannehill.

Chapter 5 from Randy Barnett, "Pursuing Justice in a Free Society: Part II, Crime Prevention and the Legal Order," *Criminal Justice Ethics* 5, 1 (Winter/Spring 1986): 30-53. Reprinted by permission of The Institute for Criminal Justice Ethics, 555 West 57th Street, Suite 607, New York, NY, 10019-1029.

Chapter 6 from Hans Hoppe, "Capitalist Production and the Problem of Public Goods," in *A Theory of Socialism and Capitalism* (Boston: Kluwer, 1989), pp. 199-210. Reprinted with permission of the author.

Chapter 7 from Jeffrey Rogers Hummel and Don Lavoie, "National Defense and the Public-Goods Problem," in Robert Higgs, ed., *Arms, Politics, and the Economy* (New York: Holmes & Meier Publishers, 1990), pp. 37-60. Reprinted with permission of the Independent Institute, Oakland, California 94621.

Chapter 8 from Roderick Long, "Defending a Free Nation," *Formulations* II, 6 (1994). Reprinted with permission of the author.

Chapter 9 from John Hasnas, "The Myth of the Rule of Law," *Wisconsin*

Law Review (1995): 199-233. Copyright © 1995 by The Board of Regents of the University of Wisconsin System. Reprinted by permission of the *Wisconsin Law Review.*

Chapter 10 from Robert Nozick, "The State," in *Anarchy, State, & Utopia* (New York: Basic Books, 1974), pp. 88-119. From ANARCHY STATE & UTOPIA by ROBERT NOZICK, ISBN: 0465097200, copyright © 1974 by Basic Books, reprinted by permission of BASIC BOOKS, a member of Perseus Books, L.L.C. Territory Granted: WORLD RIGHTS.

Chapter 11 from Roy A. Childs, Jr., "The Invisible Hand Strikes Back," *Journal of Libertarian Studies* 1 (1977): 22-33. Reprinted with permission of the Ludwig von Mises Institute, Auburn, Alabama 36832.

Chapter 12 from Murray Rothbard, "Robert Nozick and the Immaculate Conception of the State," *Journal of Libertarian Studies* 1 (1977): 45-57. Reprinted with permission of the Ludwig von Mises Institute, Auburn, Alabama 36832.

Chapter 13 from Roy A. Childs, Jr., "Objectivism and the State: An Open Letter to Ayn Rand," in Joan Kennedy Taylor, ed., *Liberty Against Power: Essays by Roy A. Childs, Jr.* (San Francisco: Fox & Wilkes, 1994), pp. 145-156. Copyright © 1969 by the International Society for Individual Liberty. All rights reserved. Reprinted with permission.

Chapter 14 from Alfred G. Cuzan, "Do We Ever Really Get Out of Anarchy?" *Journal of Libertarian Studies* 3 (1979): 151-158. Reprinted with permission of the Ludwig von Mises Institute, Auburn, Alabama 36832.

Chapter 15 from Tyler Cowen, "Law as a Public Good: The Economics of Anarchy," *Economics and Philosophy* 8 (1992): 249-267. Copyright © 1992 Cambridge University Press. Reprinted with the permission of Cambridge University Press.

Chapter 16 from David Friedman, "Law as a Private Good: A Response to Tyler Cowen on the Economics of Anarchy," *Economics and Philosophy* 10 (1994): 319-327. Copyright © 1994 Cambridge University Press. Reprinted with the permission of Cambridge University Press.

Chapter 17 from Tyler Cowen, "Rejoinder to David Friedman on the Economics of Anarchy," *Economics and Philosophy* 10 (1994): 329-332. Copyright © 1994 Cambridge University Press. Reprinted with the permission of Cambridge University Press.

Chapter 18 from Bryan Caplan and Edward Stringham, "Networks, Law, and the Paradox of Cooperation," *Review of Austrian Economics* 16, 4 (2003): 309-326. Copyright © 2003 Kluwer Academic Publishers. Reprinted with kind permission from Spriner Science and Business Media.

Chapter 19 from Tyler Cowen and Daniel Sutter, "Conflict, Cooperation and Competition in Anarchy," *Review of Austrian Economics* 18 (2005): 109-115. Copyright © 2005 Springer Science + Business Media, Inc. Reprinted with kind permission from Spriner Science and Business Media.

Chapter 20 from Anthony de Jasay, "Conventions: Some Thoughts on the Economics of Ordered Anarchy," in *Against Politics: On Government, Anarchy, and Order* (UK: Routledge, 1997), pp. 192-121. Copyright © 1997 Routledge. Reproduced by permission of Taylor & Francis Books UK.

Chapter 21 from Andrew Rutten, "Can Anarchy Save Us from Leviathan?" *The Independent Review* 3, 4 (Spring 1999): 581-593. Reprinted with permission of the Independent Institute, Oakland, California 94621.

Chapter 22 from Randall G. Holcombe, "Government: Unnecessary but Inevitable," *The Independent Review* 8, 3 (Winter 2004): 325-342. Reprinted with permission of the Independent Institute, Oakland, California 94621.

Chapter 23 from Peter Leeson and Edward Stringham, "Is Government Inevitable? Comment on Holcombe's Analysis," *The Independent Review* 9, 4 (2005): 543-549. Reprinted with permission of the Independent Institute, Oakland, California 94621.

Chapter 24 from David Hart, portions of the three-part essay "Gustave de Molinari and the Anti-statist Liberal Tradition," *Journal of Libertarian Studies* (1981/1982), 5: 263-273, 399-400, 402; 6: 83-88. Reprinted with permission of the Ludwig von Mises Institute, Auburn, Alabama 36832.

Chapter 25 from Edmund Burke, *Vindication of Natural Society*, edited by Frank N. Pagano (Indianapolis: Liberty Fund, 1982 [1757]), pp. 38-96. Public domain.

Chapter 26 from Gustave de Molinari, "The Production of Security," translated by J. Huston McCulloch (New York: The Center for Libertarian Studies, 1977 [1849]). Reprinted with permission of the Ludwig von Mises Institute, Auburn, Alabama 36832.

Chapter 27 from Murray Rothbard, "Individualist Anarchism in the U.S.: Origins," *Libertarian Analysis* 1, 1 (Winter 1970): 14-28. Reprinted with permission of the Ludwig von Mises Institute, Auburn, Alabama 36832.

Chapter 28 from Voltairine de Cleyre, "Anarchism and American Traditions," *Mother Earth* 3, 10-11 (December 1908/January 1909). Public domain.

Chapter 29 from David Lipscomb, *Civil Government: Its Origin, Mission, and Destiny, and the Christian's Relation to It* (Nashville: McQuiddy Printing Company, 1913 [1889]), pp. 133-147. Public domain.

Chapter 30 from Lysander Spooner, "No Treason: The Constitution of No Authority" (1869). Public domain.

Chapter 31 from Lysander Spooner, "Trial by Jury" (1852). Public domain.

Chapter 32 from Benjamin Tucker, "Relation of the State to the Individual," *Liberty*, November 15, 1890. Public domain.

Chapter 33 from David Osterfeld, *Freedom, Society, and the State: An Investigation Into the Possibility of Society without Government* (Lanham, MD: University Press of America, 1983), pp. 1-49. Published by Cobden Press, San Francisco, 1986 and reprinted with permission.

Chapter 34 from Bruce Benson, "Are Public Goods Really Common Pools? Considerations of the Evolution of Policing and Highways in England," *Economic Inquiry* XXXII (April 1994): 249-271. Copyright © Western Economic Association International. Reprinted with permission of Oxford University Press and the Western Economic Association International.

Chapter 35 from Joseph R. Peden, "Property Rights in Celtic Irish Law," *Journal of Libertarian Studies* 1 (1977): 81-95. Reprinted with permission of the Ludwig von Mises Institute, Auburn, Alabama 36832.

Chapter 36 from David Friedman, "Private Creation and Enforcement of Law—A Historical Case," *Journal of Legal Studies* 8 (1979): 399-415. Copyright © 1979 by the University of Chicago. All rights reserved. Reprinted with permission of the *Journal of Legal Studies*, the University of Chicago, and the author.

Chapter 37 from Paul Milgrom, Douglass North, and Barry Weingast, "The Role of Institutions in the Revival of Trade: The Law Merchant, Private Judges, and the Champagne Fairs," *Economics and Politics* 2 (1990): 1-23. Reprinted with permission of Blackwell Publishing.

Chapter 38 from Bruce Benson, "Legal Evolution in Primitive Societies," *Journal of Institutional and Theoretical Economics* 144, 5 (1988): 772-788. Reprinted with permission of the author.

Chapter 39 from Terry L. Anderson and P. J. Hill, "An American Experiment in Anarcho-Capitalism: The *Not* So Wild, Wild West," *The Journal of Libertarian Studies* (1979): 9-29. Reprinted with permission

1

Introduction

Edward P. Stringham

"Political economy has disapproved equally of monopoly and communism in the various branches of human activity, wherever it has found them. Is it not then strange and unreasonable that it accepts them in the industry of security?"—Gustave de Molinari (1849)

Is government necessary? Private-property anarchism—also known as anarchist libertarianism, individualist anarchism, or anarcho-capitalism—is a political philosophy and set of economic arguments that says that just as markets provide bread, so too should markets provide law. If someone agued that because food is so important it must be supplied by government, most would respond that government provision of food would be a disaster. Private-property anarchism applies the same logic to law and argues that because protecting property rights is so important, it is the last thing that should be left to the state. Under private-property anarchy, individual rights and market forces would reign supreme; there would just be no state. Security would be provided privately as it is at colleges, shopping malls, hotels, and casinos, and courts would be provided privately, as they are with arbitration and mediation today.

The current volume brings together a sampling of the major essays explaining, debating, and giving historical examples of stateless orders. Led by economists and political theorists such as Murray Rothbard and David Friedman, the authors in this volume emphasize the efficacy of markets and the shortfalls of government. To the libertarian, the state and its enforcement apparatus is not a benign force in society—but where limited government libertarians argue in favor of political constraints, anarchist libertarians argue that the only way to check government against abuse is to eliminate it completely.

Today, more and more scholars and general readers see private-property anarchism as a viable and worthy alternative to the monopolistic and coercively funded state. Individualist anarchism has a long history but most of the early writing was published anonymously or in obscure places. Today, in contrast,

I thank Walter Block, Mark Brady, Bryan Caplan, David Hart, Jeffrey Rogers Hummel, Benjamin Powell, Alex Tabarrok, and David Theroux for helpful comments and suggestions. Andrew Neumann provided excellent research assistance.

private-property anarchism is now discussed in top economics journals such as the *Journal of Political Economy* (Hirshleifer, 1995; Dowd, 1997) and in 2002 George Mason University economist Vernon Smith became the first private-property anarchist to win the Nobel Prize (Smith, 2003, pp. 484-6). In addition to being a potentially important normative position, anarchist research helps explain events and trends of historical and contemporary relevance. Consider, for example, that private security guards now outnumber the public police, and private arbitration—the so-called "rent-a-judge" business—is booming. Private-property anarchism also sheds light on nineteenth-century Britain, where private prosecution agencies tracked down criminals long before the public police existed. Similarly, trade in Medieval Europe, like international trade today, was governed for hundreds of years under competing systems of law.

The works in this volume are influential, yet many were published in relatively obscure publications and are often difficult to track down. This editor knows this first hand, having written a doctoral dissertation, and before that a college senior thesis, on the topic. In college my professor liked my proposed topic but he doubted whether enough material on the subject had been published. Luckily, another economics professor was well read in private-property anarchism, and he compiled a list of books and articles for me. Only through that guidance, and a number of interlibrary loan requests, was I able to get a representative overview of the subject. Many of these articles are reprinted here. By compiling all of these important articles in one place, these works are now accessible to more than just a handful of experts or fortunate students.

This book reprints articles about anarchism from many libertarian points of view rather than attempt to present a unified vision of anarchy. Although all anarchists agree that the state is unnecessary, many of the specifics are still debated. For example, some authors support anarchy using arguments about consequences, while others support anarchy using arguments about rights. Some authors highlight how markets can function with private law enforcement, while others highlight how markets can function without any formal law at all. The articles in this volume will give the reader a sampling of some of the more important works on the subject.

The book's articles are organized in four categories: Section I presents the major theoretical works that argue in favor of private-property anarchism; Section II contains writings that debate the viability of private-property anarchism, presenting articles and responses from the classical liberal and anarchist perspectives; Section III contains some of the early works in individualist anarchism, as well as modern articles on the history of individualist anarchist thought and the different types of anarchism; Section IV presents case studies and historical examples of societies that functioned without public law enforcement. The chapters need not be read in order so one can skip around depending on one's interests. For example, if one wants an overview of the differences between libertarian and non-libertarian anarchism, one can skip directly to the chapter by Osterfeld.

I. Theory of Private Property Anarchism

The articles in this first section criticize arguments for government law enforcement and discuss how the private sector can provide law. They critique the very notion that a government monopoly over the use of force is needed. How will a competitive system function? How will the provision of public goods or the problem of free riders be dealt with under anarchy? Not all private-property anarchists agree but many of the chapters in this section offer speculative visions about how various problems might be solved. Reading the articles in this section will give an overview of some of the major anarchist visions.

The first chapter in Section I is Murray Rothbard's important "Police, Law, and the Courts," from *For a New Liberty* (1973). Jerome Tuccille (1971) once wrote a book about libertarianism entitled *It Usually Begins with Ayn Rand* indicating how many libertarians became interested in freedom by reading Ayn Rand. If one were to write a book about anarchist libertarianism one might entitle it *It Usually Begins with Murray Rothbard*. In the late 1940s, Murray Rothbard decided that that private-property anarchism was the logical conclusion of free-market thinking and published his first work on it in 1954. Rothbard was the first to merge modern economic thinking with nineteenth-century anarchists' distaste for the state (Powell and Stringham, forthcoming). Rothbard wrote dozens of articles on anarchy but this, one of his most concise pieces, is reprinted here. Rothbard argues that the way to figure out how much protection there should be is to have a market for law enforcement. This chapter provides a speculative account of how police and courts could be provided on the market and it offers possible ways that people who subscribe to different protection agencies could settle disputes. Under Rothbard's vision each protection agency would be held accountable to respect individual rights.

Along with Murray Rothbard, David Friedman is one of the founders of anarcho-capitalist thinking. Friedman, too, has written many articles on this subject but his earliest work on the subject appeared in his *The Machinery of Freedom* (1973). This chapter reprints a portion of the second edition (1989) of that book. Not content to believe that convincing people of anarchism requires changing their moral precepts, Friedman argues that even non-libertarians can embrace anarchism out of pure self-interest. Where Rothbard argues for anarchism based on rights, Friedman argues for anarchism based on efficiency. Friedman's vision differs from that of Rothbard because Friedman believes that anarchist laws need not be libertarian. Under a market for law people would be free to choose any rules they wish and the resulting outcome would be determined by net willingness to pay. Friedman describes how multiple police might operate in each area and how they would have incentives to settle disputes through bargaining rather than violence.

Another early work that provides many details on how a competitive system might function was self-published by Morris and Linda Tannehill in 1970 and reprinted by Arno Press in 1972.[1] This book certainly had less circulation than

Rothbard (1973) or Friedman (1973) but it clearly had influence on subsequent writers such as Friedman, who refers to a fictional defense agency as Tannehelp, Inc. These authors are concerned with any monopoly of the use of force (regardless of whether it is agreed to) and so they offer a system where multiple agencies compete in each geographic area. Some of the Tannehills' discussion may appear as science fiction or less worked out than subsequent writing, but their book deserves a place as being one of the pioneering pieces to ponder how private police might work.

Subsequent writers have been able to expand or refine some of the early anarchist arguments. Boston University Law Professor Randy Barnett has contributed much to the subject (Barnett, 1998) and this volume reprints his 1986 article "Pursuing Justice in a Free Society: Crime Prevention and the Legal Order." Barnett discusses how much of our current crime is caused by the fact that streets are publicly owned and not privately policed. Instead of having government incarcerate people to produce order, Barnett argues that simple exclusion would do much of the job. Once government monopoly is abolished Barnett believes that competing police could pick up any remaining slack. He offers a vision of how multiple law enforcers would operate in each geographic area and how they might deal with unfair renegade enforcers of law.

The next chapter, "Capitalist Production and the Problem of Public Goods," is by Hans-Hermann Hoppe, a colleague of Rothbard who edited of the *Journal of Libertarian Studies* from 1995-2005. Hoppe's subsequent books, such as *Democracy—The God That Failed* (2001), have had a much wider circulation, but this chapter from *A Theory of Socialism and Capitalism* (1989) contains one of Hoppe's original contributions on the subject. Hoppe questions the public goods justifications for government altogether by arguing that that police and courts are excludable, rivalrous, and must be allocated in certain areas. They are not abstract public goods as commonly presented in textbooks. The government needs to decide whether to hire one judge and one policeman or 100,000 of each, but without a market mechanism the government has little way of figuring out how to allocate resources. Like authors before him, Hoppe describes arrangements that competing protection agencies might use to enforce laws, and Hoppe emphasizes the importance of public ideology towards maintaining liberty.

What about international conflict under anarchy? Jeffrey Rogers Hummel and Don Lavoie address the issue in "National Defense and the Public-Goods Problem." Hummel and Lavoie have two responses to those who believe that government militaries are necessary. First, they question whether creating a national military actually solves the free-rider problem, and second, they question the extent to which the military is defending the public rather than defending the state. Most supporters of national defense assume that the interests of the public and the government coincide but Hummel and Lavoie question this assumption. In fact, militaries often pose the greatest threats to the public. Hummel and Lavoie believe that the true public good is defending liberty and they argue that this does not depend on the state. The important constraint against government must always be resistance on the part of the public.[2]

Roderick Long also discusses the problem of national defense in "Defending a Free Nation." Like Hummel and Lavoie, Long argues that a nationalized military actually provides more of a threat than a defense. Long discusses that decentralized defense could be provided in at least four ways: first, by for-profit firms that act in consortium to defend their clients; second, by private firms that raise money through charitable means; third, by an armed populace who defend themselves without centralization; or fourth, defense by civilians who use non-violent resistance. Long discusses the possible benefits and possible shortcomings of each and argues that defending a free society would require some combination of all of the above.

The final chapter in Section I is by John Hasnas, who takes a different approach than anarchist predecessors such as the Tannehills, Rothbard, Friedman, or Barnett. Where earlier theorists attempt to create a blueprint of how the market would handle law, this legal philosopher argues that the law will evolve in ways we cannot predict. He argues that there is no one right way to settle disputes and we should not attempt to centrally plan the law. Attempting to create blueprints of how all problems will be solved might even be counterproductive because the blueprints will necessarily be incomplete. Hasnas argues that we need not have a crystal ball yet we should be confident that market solutions will be discovered.

II. Debate

After presenting some of the arguments in favor of private-property anarchism, the volume gets to the debate. The authors in this section are all libertarians, although some support anarchism while others support limited government. Early critics of anarchism argue that the only system consistent with individual rights is a system with a government monopoly on the use of force (Rand, 1964; Nozick, 1974). Later critics of anarchy often accept anarchy as being morally superior yet they express doubts in the viability of the system (Cowen, 1992; Rutten, 1999; Holcombe, 2004; Cowen and Sutter, 2005). All of these authors argue that special characteristics of law enforcement make a competitive system unlikely or impossible. This section includes some of the major criticisms of anarchy and some anarchist responses.

Robert Nozick provided one of the most famous critiques of private-property anarchism in *Anarchy, State, and Utopia*, which ended up winning the 1975 National Book Award for Philosophy and Religion. Nozick was a Harvard philosopher who had become a libertarian after meeting one of Rothbard's colleagues, and later Rothbard, in the early 1960s (Raico, 2002). Still, Nozick was unconvinced of anarchist libertarianism, so he devoted the first third of his treatise arguing against Rothbard's views on law. Nozick attempts to rebut the anarchist claim that all governments violate rights by positing an invisible hand theory of government. He argues that out of a state anarchy, a dominant protection agency would be justified in protecting their customers from potentially risky firms and this dominant protection agency would be justified in becoming a state. Even though the government would use force to prohibit competition, Nozick argues that the government would not violate rights provided it compensated those who wished to have an alternative arrangement. The best way of compensating those injured parties, according to Nozick, would be to provide them with free police.

Not all libertarians were convinced. The inaugural issue of the *Journal of Libertarian Studies* was devoted to analyzing Nozick's theory of government; two of the responses are reprinted here. Roy Childs takes on Nozick's defense of government in "The Invisible Hand Strikes Back" (1977). Childs criticizes Nozick for arguing that smaller protection agencies might be risky but the dominant protection agency would not. It might be the case that the government is the riskiest agency of all. Nozick gives no reason for us expect that this government would not become abusive itself. Childs also questions Nozick's proposed compensation for those who do not wish to have government. He writes, "What is he willing to offer us as compensation?… He is generous to a fault. He will give us nothing less than *the State*." Does Nozick really believe that compensating those who dislike police with more police will return them to their original indifference curve?

In "Robert Nozick and the Immaculate Conception of the State," Rothbard argues that even if Nozick were correct in his logical reasoning, he fails to provide a justification for any existing government. Because no government was ever formed according to Nozick's process or acts in a way that Nozick wishes, Rothbard argues that Nozick should join the anarchists in opposing government. At a more fundamental level, Rothbard questions Nozick's logical justification for government. Where Nozick argues that prohibiting risky behavior is just, Rothbard argues that such a position would lead to numerous authoritarian laws. Many people have the potential to engage in dangerous behavior, but that does not justify prohibiting them from acting or locking them up. Rothbard deals with many of Nozick's claims, and in the end concludes: "[E]very step of Nozick's invisible hand process is invalid."

Another famous supporter of minimal government was Ayn Rand. In "The Nature of Government," published in 1964, Rand argued that society requires a respect for individual rights and argues that the government must enforce those rights. She argued that the use of force—even in self-defense—cannot be left to the discretion of individuals. Rand criticized libertarian anarchy by saying that a system with private police would lack objective laws and will result in conflict. She offered a hypothetical scenario where two neighbors hire different police and then get in a dispute. According to Rand, the only result under anarchy would be for the two parties to resort to arms and the only solution is to have a government monopoly on the use of force.

Roy Childs first criticized her on this topic in "Objectivism and the State: An Open Letter to Ayn Rand." Childs argued that if one supports liberty one should oppose the state in all forms. Although Rand says she is against the initiation of the use of force, Childs points out that any government necessarily initiates force when it prevents people from defending themselves. In this letter, Childs takes on Rand's specific claims maintaining that many of her arguments are not as logical as Rand implies. He argues that just because people in society should abide by objective rules it does not follow that a government monopoly is necessary. Her argument is equivalent to saying that because one must follow objective procedures to produce a ton of steel, government steel production is necessary. Childs points out that Rand simply assumes that competing police will act violently and she assumes that her benevolent government will not. Economists call this the Nirvana fallacy. An upset Rand never wrote a written response and had Child's subscription to *The Objectivist* cancelled. Child's letter made its rounds and, according to Jeffrey Rogers Hummel, was one of the most influential writings in convincing Rand-influenced libertarians to become full-fledged anarchists.

As the 1970s progressed, the number of people writing about anarchism increased exponentially. In 1977 Murray Rothbard founded the *Journal of Libertarian Studies*, which printed many articles on anarchy. One exemplary article from an early issue is "Do We Ever Really Get Out of Anarchy?" by Alfred Cuzan. In this article he questions some of the basic assumptions of government advocates such as Rand. If a third party is required to settle disputes between individuals, who settles a dispute between individuals and the state? Cuzan argues that creating government is simply replacing one form of anarchic relations with another. Unenforceable relations between people or governments will always exist, so Cuzan questions whether creating a government hierarchy is desirable.

Later critics of anarchy do not posit that the state is necessary or that the state is just as in Rand or Nozick. Nevertheless, these critics of anarchy argue that the state might be inevitable. In one of the more sophisticated criticisms of libertarian anarchy, Tyler Cowen argues that a system with competing courts will devolve into coercive government because law enforcement is a network industry where firms must be interdependent on each other. Cowen's article, "Law as a Public Good: The Economics of Anarchy," includes "Public Good" in the title, not because the government is providing a good but because Cowen believes that a legal system must apply to everyone in a geographic area. He argues that if firms are able to cooperate to settle disputes that same mechanism will enable them to cooperate to collude. Even if multiple firms exist, Cowen argues the result will be a de facto monopoly that can use force to exact taxes just like government.

David Friedman responds to Cowen in "Law as a Private Good." He agrees that firms would have relationships with other firms, but he disagrees that the industry must be a network industry that facilitates a cartel. He argues that a situation with bilateral contracts between firms is quite different from a situation with one industry-wide contract. If the only relationships in the industry are between pairs of firms, these relationships do nothing to enhance their ability to collude. Friedman argues that the situation is akin to the contractual relationships between grocery stores and suppliers. Cowen's "Rejoinder to

David Friedman on the Economics of Anarchy" (1994) provides a brief response arguing that analogies from regular industries do not apply. Cowen argues that competing firms must cooperate to enforce laws and he argues that they will be able to use force against those who do not comply. The number of firms is unimportant because even though the world has many different police forces and local governments they still collude. Cowen believes that often governments do terrible things, but he is pessimistic that libertarian anarchy offers a viable alternative.

Caplan and Stringham, in "Networks, Law and the Paradox of Cooperation" (2004), question Cowen's argument that network industries facilitate collusion. Although enforcement of law across multiple agencies would require some cooperation, the ability to cooperate does not guarantee they will be able to collude. Law enforcement may require some cooperation but the network need not be all-powerful. They distinguish between self-enforcing and non-self-enforcing agreements and argue that collusive agreements between firms would be harder to enforce. For example, if firms attempt to collude to raise prices, each firm would have an incentive to break the agreement. On the other hand, if firms coordinate to boycott a bad business risk, each firm has an incentive to follow the agreement lest it be cheated itself. Caplan and Stringham give historical examples of network industries, such as banks and credit card companies, that have been able to facilitate coordination but have been unable to facilitate collusion.

Cowen and Sutter reply in "Conflict, Cooperation and Competition in Anarchy" (2005), arguing that Caplan and Stringham's analysis underestimates the importance of the use of force. Cowen and Sutter argue that the interaction between firms is a coordination game with multiple equilibria, not all of which are libertarian. Although a situation of armed conflict may not occur, firms might end up backing down to a coercive firm rather than defending their clients' rights. Because membership in a network is valuable, the incumbents may be able to exercise their market power at the expense of others. Such a situation will enable members of an arbitration network to enact non-libertarian rules and then refuse to deal with new entrants who do not agree. This sows the seeds for the creation of government whether we like it or not. Perhaps the Hobbesian dilemma may never be solved.

One economist who accepts many of the Hobbesian arguments yet still supports anarchy is Anthony de Jasay. In one of his many works on the subject, "Conventions: Some Thoughts on the Economics of Ordered Anarchy" (1997), de Jasay addresses the possibility that suboptimal outcomes will result in an anarchist world. First de Jasay criticizes the advocates of limited government who argue that the state has the ability to eliminate these suboptimal outcomes. Just because a problem exists does not mean that government has the ability to solve it. De Jasay argues that under anarchy individuals would have an incentive to internalize some of the negative externalities that would result from conflict. The key is to find market solutions to potential problems. He also addresses the claim that people need government once people want to interact outside small groups. He says that although any given transaction may appear to be a prisoners' dilemma, transactions take place in the complex web of society where repeated transactions and reputation create incentives for cooperation.

Andrew Rutten addresses de Jasay's arguments in "Can Anarchy Save Us from Leviathan?" (1999). Although Rutten accepts most of de Jasay's criticisms of government, he is unconvinced that anarchy, or any other system for that matter, can eliminate the problem of force. Rutten accepts the argument that government will always abuse its power and that constitutions are of little use; he also accepts the argument prisoners' dilemmas problems are not as ubiquitous in the market as most supporters of government believe. Nevertheless, Rutten argues that anarchists may be too optimistic in their outlook because the incentive to abuse power and expropriate property will still remain. Anarchists, just like governments, will have an incentive to act against the wishes of others. According to this pessimistic anarchist, property rights may never be secure.

Another author who holds a pessimistic view towards anarchism is Randall Holcombe. In "Government: Unnecessary but Inevitable" (2004), Holcombe agrees with libertarian anarchists that government is coercive and unnecessary for public goods, but he maintains that nothing can be done to prevent its existence. Like Rutten, he argues that incentives for opportunistic behavior will always exist and he argues that libertarian anarchy would either internally devolve into government or be overtaken by force. Holcombe points out that the world is ruled by governments, which shows that anarchy is not an option. Instead of advocating government abolition, Holcombe argues that libertarians should seek to find ways to make government as small as possible. Holcombe maintains that the best course of action is preemptively creating a limited government that will still expropriate, but will expropriate less than less limited governments.

Leeson and Stringham question Holcombe's account in "Is Government Inevitable?" (2005), maintaining that Holcombe is too pessimistic about the possibility of stateless orders and too optimistic about the possibility of limited government. They point to many historical examples of anarchist societies, including modern-day Somalia, and argue that the evidence that most nations are currently controlled by states says nothing about the long-term prospects for anarchy. They also question the idea that society can create a more benign government if all governments are created for the benefit of their creators. If Holcombe's Hobbesian assumptions are correct then nothing stops limited government from becoming unlimited government. Leeson and Stringham argue that limiting government ultimately depends on ideological opposition to the state, and argue that if limited government is possible so too is anarchy.

III. History of Anarchist Thought

The next section contains a sampling of early anarchist works as well as modern commentary on the history of anarchist thought. Two chapters are by eighteenth- and nineteenth-century Europeans, five chapters are by nineteenth-century Americans, and three chapters are by contemporary writers who provide overviews of anarchist thought. Anarchist sentiment has a long history but its explicit formulation only came within the past couple centuries with the vast majority of the work coming in the past three decades. How does private property anarchism relate to other political philosophies and how did anarchists arrive at their views?

David Hart provides an excellent history of how private-property anarchism evolved. This chapter reprints portions of Hart's three-part essay, "Gustave de Molinari and the Anti-statist Liberal Tradition." David Hart sees private-property anarchism as originating from classical liberal philosophy, which focused the importance private property rights and the need to constrain the state. Eighteenth- and nineteenth-century anarchists and quasi-anarchists ended up advancing the view to the logical extreme, concluding that government is not needed at all. Private property anarchism was most explicitly spelled out starting in the nineteenth century by authors such as Gustav de Molinari. David Hart discusses the influence of these writers and how their ideas were passed on to the anarchists who exist today.

One of the earliest works that is clearly anarchist is Edmund Burke's "Vindication of Natural Society." Burke, who is often considered the father of new conservatism, published this essay anonymously as a letter by "a late noble writer" in 1757. Burke later had political aspirations, so when people discovered he was the author Burke claimed that the piece was a satire. The issue is debated in Pagano (1982), but Murray Rothbard (1958, p. 114) believed, "Careful reading reveals hardly a trace of irony or satire. In fact, it is a very sober and earnest treatise, written in his characteristic style." Burke's piece is a scathing attack on government. He discusses how governments have killed millions through wars and have enslaved their citizens. It does not matter if governments are despotic, aristocratic, or democratic; they are still tyrannical. Are not government laws created to protect the weak? Burke responds, "surely no Pretence can be so ridiculous." We may never know Burke's true motivation but this piece is an all time anarchist classic.

The first person to explicitly advocate competitive law enforcement was Belgian economist Gustave de Molinari, who wrote "The Production of Security" in 1849. Molinari argues that, because competition better serves the interests of consumers, there should be competition in all areas, including law. He maintains that all monopolies are coercive and argues that the natural consequence of monopoly over security is war. Governments war only because they wish to wrest the monopoly over the use of force; if the monopoly over the use of force could be eliminated so too would the incentives for aggression. Molinari proposes letting individuals be clients of any enforcement agency of their choice and provides a brief description of how such a system might work. He believes that law enforcement would likely be territorially based but he says that individuals should be able go to another protection agency in case of abuse. The article was revolutionary in its day and can be considered the first piece to explain how a system with private police might function.

In America, although the colonists were not writing economics treatises on private-property anarchism, Murray Rothbard argues that anarchist sentiment has a long history. In "Individualist Anarchism in the United States: The Origins," Rothbard describes how many seventeenth-century colonists opposed taxation or any form of government, often on religious grounds. Rothbard discusses such people as Anne Hutchinson, who left Massachusetts and ended up setting up communities that operated without a state. In seventeenth-century Pennsylvania, William Penn did not intend to create an anarchist colony, but it ended up being de facto anarchy for some years. Many of the Quakers believed that any participation in government was a violation of Quaker principles, and when Penn tried to impose a tax he was met with strong resistance. Eventually Penn and others created government but the legacy of anarchist sentiment lived on.

Voltairine de Cleyre lived from 1866–1912 and wrote that the principles of the American Revolution were anarchist. De Cleyre was one of the many nineteenth-century individualist anarchists in America and she wrote "Anarchism and American Traditions" in 1908. In this chapter de Cleyre makes the case that the principles of the American Revolution need to be reawakened. She outlines the commonalities between the revolutionaries and the individualist anarchists in their mistrust of government and their goal to create equal liberty for all. Unfortunately, after the Revolution the government has grown and the public has not done enough to stop it. In the early 1800s Americans were concerned about having a standing army of 3,000 and in de Cleyre's day she was outraged that the number had grown to 80,000. (In 2005 the U.S. government has a standing army of over 1.4 million people![3]) Wishful thinking notwithstanding, the Constitution appears to be ineffective against the growth of government.

Nineteenth-century Boston anarchist Lysander Spooner provides a scathing analysis of the U.S. Constitution in "No Treason: The Constitution of No Authority." This chapter reprints a portion of his 1869 attack on the federal government of the United States. How the times have changed: Whereas in modern times defenders of Constitution are considered defenders of small government, in the nineteenth century defenders of the Constitution were considered defenders of big government! Spooner argues that the Constitution is an illegitimate social contract because neither he nor anyone he knows actually signed the Constitution. Just because thirty-nine men signed the Constitution in 1787 does not mean that it should hold any moral weight on the other 3 million Americans at the time or the 300 million Americans living today. Spooner likens the government to a highway robber but argues that government is worse. After stealing your money the highway robber is too much of a gentleman to follow you around and say he is protecting you!

Nineteenth-century Tennessee preacher David Lipscomb is also critical of the idea that government is created for moral reasons. His 1889 *Civil Government:*

Its Origin, Mission, and Destiny, and the Christian's Relation to It provides an in-depth analysis of the morality government and a portion of this work is reprinted here. He says that government is founded upon force and that moral people should have nothing to do with it. He says that government only tries to appear as if it is a force for good, but government's tactics are deceitful like those of the devil. He argues that Christianity and government are at odds, and that supporters of the state are not true followers of God. He argues that Christians should not participate in politics, vote, work in government administration, or participate on juries. The methods of all government institutions including courts are nothing more than the use of force.

Lysander Spooner also criticizes the government legal system in "Trial by Jury" (1852). Spooner, a lawyer by training, wrote volumes defending liberty. He argues that trial by jury was created so laws would be judged by citizens rather than by government. He describes how government courts corrupt this institution by creating the laws of evidence, deciding who will serve on juries, and dictating the laws juries are to enforce. The government co-opts this bulwark for liberty and replaces it with a trial by government. Spooner maintains that a government legal system cannot be trusted because it is allowed to determine the legality of its own acts. He argues that juries should be able to judge any law to be illegitimate regardless of what government says.

Another nineteenth-century Boston anarchist was Benjamin Tucker, who published the periodical *Liberty* from 1881–1908 (McElroy, 2003). Tucker wrote many small contributions on anarchy and he also delved into philosophy and economics. Subsequent writers, such as Rothbard (1974/2000), have criticized Tucker for his old-fashioned economic views (and many libertarians will find he also had some odd views on ethics), but Tucker was strong on the question of anarchy. In his "Relation of the State to the Individual"[4] (1890), Tucker argues that people will be better off by cooperating without government. He says that if one opposes the initiation of the use of force one must oppose the state in all forms. He argues that defense is not an essential component of the state but aggression is; defense was just an afterthought. In addition to violating liberty, the state adds insult to injury by making its victims pay. These words ring true today.

The final chapter in this section puts private-property anarchism into perspective by comparing it to other political and economic philosophies. David Osterfeld gives a "Political and Economic Overview," which is reprinted from his book *Freedom, Society, and State: An Investigation of the Possibility of Society Without Government.* He outlines how on the political spectrum one can be anywhere from an anarchist to a hyperarchist and on the economic spectrum one can be anywhere from a capitalist to a socialist. Osterfeld distinguishes between the various types of anarchism, from socialist to capitalist: anarcho-communism, anarcho-collectivism, anarcho-syndicalism, mutualism, Godwinism, egoism, philosophical anarchism, and individualist anarchism. Many mistakenly lump all anarchists together, which might be one reason why some conservatives and classical liberals get scared if they hear the suggestion to get rid of government police. In addition, Osterfeld distinguishes between the capitalist systems, from statist to anarchist: conservatism, classical liberalism, objectivism, evolutionary individualist anarchism, minarchism, ultraminarchism, and individualist anarchism. Many people mistakenly lump all forms of capitalism together, which might be one reason some critics of crony state capitalism believe they must oppose capitalism altogether. Osterfeld's chapter provides a useful roadmap for thinking about the relationships between different political and economic philosophies.

IV. Historical Case Studies of Non-Government Law Enforcement

The chapters in this section show that the idea that markets can function without government law enforcement is not just science fiction. Theories or speculative accounts about how an anarchist society might function are well and good, but many people remain unconvinced until they see something in practice. As the chapters in this section demonstrate, the world is replete with examples of private law enforcement or markets that function without formal law enforcement at all.[5] These studies range from historical episodes from hundreds of years ago to often-overlooked situations in modern society. Many of these research articles have appeared in top ranked economics journals and they show that research on private-property anarchism can be more than pure theorizing.

Bruce Benson has two books and dozens of articles on private law enforcement; two of his articles are included here. The first, "Are Public Goods Really Common Pools? Considerations of the Evolution of Policing and Highways in England," appeared in *Economic Inquiry* and documents how private parties in medieval England solved disputes without relying on government. The system was largely restitution based, so wrongdoers would have to compensate their victims. Even though law enforcement requires coordination between many people, Benson describes how people joined groups of one hundred to police and settle disputes. The Anglo-Saxon kings, however, began centralizing the law once they realized that they could use the legal system to collect revenue. By declaring private torts to be violations of the king's peace as well, they could require wrongdoers to pay restitution to the king in addition to the actual victim. By the time of the Norman invasion, the king declared that all of the restitution must go directly to the king. Predictably, this eliminated the incentive for private law enforcement and then created the "need" for public law enforcement. The article shows that government law enforcement was not created to deal with market failure and instead was created to enhance revenue for the state!

Another article that shows that government law enforcement is unnecessary is Joseph Peden's "Property Rights in Celtic Irish Law." Peden's article is important because, along with Friedman (1979) and Anderson and Hill (1979), it was one of the first to document how a system of private law enforcement actually functioned. In medieval Ireland disputes were settled by private jurists called brehons and law relied on the use of sureties rather than government coercion. The legal system was based on restitution rather than punishment and people could pledge property or their own personal labor as a bond. Peden provides many specific details about the property rights system, which shows that our contemporary government law enforcement system is not the only one.

Another historical case study of medieval times is David Friedman's "Private Creation and Enforcement of Law—A Historical Case" (1979), which documents how Iceland had a system of competing law enforcement for over three hundred years. People had a choice of law enforcing bodies and they could join another coalition at will. If someone committed an offense he would pay restitution unless he wanted to be deemed an outlaw. Victims were given the right of compensation or they could transfer that right to another party who was more likely to collect the fine. Because people would have to pay if they committed a wrong, the system created incentives to reduce conflict. Friedman argues that this competitive system created relatively efficient law and it led to a murder rate that was lower than in the current United States.

In addition to providing systems of criminal or tort law, private legal systems provided contract law as well. In the middle ages most disputes between merchants were settled privately in courts developed by the merchants themselves. Paul Milgrom, Douglass North, and Barry Weingast document how this system functioned in "The Role of Institutions in the Revival of Trade: The Law Merchant, Private Judges, and the Champagne Fairs."[6] Milgrom, North, and Weingast represent this situation using game theory, so for those interested in formalizing some of the anarchist theories this paper offers a model. These authors explain how merchants would bring their disputes to private courts, and if a merchant refused listen to the court he would be blacklisted by the remaining merchants. These private courts show that laws of commerce can be enforced without resorting to government or the use of force.

Examples of non-government law enforcement occur throughout the globe. Bruce Benson, in "Legal Evolution in Primitive Societies" (1988), documents how many societies use voluntary customary law rather than government imposed law. If a legal rule is beneficial people will have an incentive to adopt it and it need not be imposed by the state. He describes the legal system of the Kapauku Papuans of West New Guinea in the twentieth century who had no formal government yet had a private legal system that evolved to meet ongoing needs. The Kapauku created reciprocal legal arrangements based on kinship and based on the reputation of tonowi (wealthy men) who they trusted to assist in legal matters. The legal system was mostly based on restitution or public reprimand rather than punishment, and the system had a large respect for individual property rights.

Non-government legal systems also have a history in America as Terry Anderson and P. J. Hill document in "American Experiment in Anarcho-Capitalism:

The Not So Wild, Wild West" (1979). Governments were unestablished in much of the frontier in nineteenth-century America, yet it turns out that the frontier system was much more peaceful than the depictions in movies. Anderson and Hill describe the enforcement methods in the West: Land clubs enabled people to establish property rights even though the federal government had yet to survey the territory; cattlemen's associations helped enforce property rights in the open range, which had millions of cattle and lacked government police; mining camps established ways of settling mining claims without the use of lawyers; and wagon trains dealt with enforcement issues once people traveling West left the jurisdiction of the federal government. Many think of systems of private law enforcement as completely foreign to the American experience; Anderson and Hill show otherwise. Anderson and Hill (1975) developed these ideas further in the *Journal of Law and Economics* and a book published by Stanford in 2004, but this 1979 *Journal of Libertarian Studies* article is a classic.

Another study of the American West is done by Yale University law professor Robert Ellickson. This time, however, the study is about contemporary society. This chapter reprints part of Ellickson's *Order Without Law*, which shows that examples of non-government law enforcement are alive and well today. While many theorists assume that individuals respect property rights only because of the threat of law, Ellickson's case study of farmers and ranchers in rural Shasta County, California shows nothing of the sort. Ellickson studied the official laws to figure out how cattle trespass disputes "should" be settled, and then he went to Shasta County to ask people how the disputes were actually settled. Ellickson found that ranchers and farmers (and even town lawyers!) had little idea what the laws actually said. Instead of relying on legalistic methods of dealing with disputes, the ranchers and farmers relied on notions of what they considered right. Because their norms often differed significantly from the law, their system of property rights and means of settling disputes is clearly not a product of government.

Summary

The state has worked for years attempting to indoctrinate people of the necessity of government law enforcement. The chapters in this volume suggest that this government wisdom is wrong. Just because monopolization of law was a convenient way for government to enhance revenue and exert control does not mean that government law is necessary. The articles in this volume are important from two perspectives. From an academic perspective they show that anarchism might be a useful lens to help us analyze the world. Do people only cooperate because of the threat of government law? Perhaps the answer is no. By taking a more realistic perspective, the anarchists have the potential to shed light on many situations that others cannot explain. The articles in this book, especially in the case study section, represent the tip of the iceberg of possible articles about anarchy. Like the farmers and ranchers in Shasta County, self-governance is all around us, and this presents a tremendous opportunity for academic research.

From a normative perspective private-property anarchism may be important for promoting liberty in both the short and long run. For those interested in marginal change in the short run, private-property anarchism has practical policy implications today. For example, should individuals be able to opt for arbitration (if all parties agree), or should government regulate and overturn arbitration decisions as it does today? Likewise, should landowners be allowed to create gated communities with private security, or should government make their streets open to the public and patrol them with government police? Private-property anarchism sheds light on these issues.

Private-property anarchism is also important for the long-run prospects for liberty. Markets have been a blessing wherever they have been implemented and government has been a calamity wherever it has been implemented. Instead of advocating a system that we know does not work, why not advocate a system that might? Limited government appears to be inherently unstable and anarchism might offer the libertarian the only alternative. In the past 250 years the world has successfully thrown off the yoke of monarchism and in the past twenty-five years the world has successfully thrown off the yoke of communism. Why not continue and throw off the bonds of all government?

Notes

1. The 1972 volume also reprinted Wollstein's (1969) short monograph *Society Without Coercion*, which advocates anarchism but goes in less depth than the Tannehills.
2. These arguments are elaborated in greater detail in Hummel (1990) and Hummel (2001).
3. From 1800 to 2005 the American population has increased fifty fold whereas the number of people in the U.S. military has increased almost 500 fold.
4. This chapter reprints the majority of his article but leaves off the last few pages, most of which is a long quote from Proudhon.
5. A lot of research analyzes private police or courts that operate within the context of a government system (Foldvary, 1994; Mahoney, 1997; Romano, 1998; Stringham, 1999, 2002; and 2003), but the examples in this section focus on case studies where government police and courts are largely absent.
6. Between these authors, two have appointments at Stanford and one has a Nobel Prize and the article was published in a highly ranked journal. The article demonstrates that anarchist research may have a place in mainstream outlets.

References

Anderson, Terry and Hill, P. J. (1975) "The Evolution of Property Rights: A Study of the American West." *Journal of Law and Economics* 18: 163-79.

Anderson, Terry and Hill, P. J. (2004) *The Not So Wild, Wild West: Property Rights on the Frontier*. Stanford, CA: Stanford University Press.

Barnett, Randy (1998) *The Structure of Liberty: Justice and the Rule of Law*. Oxford: Clarendon Press.

Cowen, Tyler (1992) "Law as a Public Good: The Economics of Anarchy." *Economics and Philosophy* 8: 249-267.

Cowen, Tyler, and Sutter, Daniel (2005) "Conflict, Cooperation and Competition in Anarchy." *Review of Austrian Economics* 18: 109-115.

Dowd, Kevin (1997) "Anarchy, Warfare, and Social Order: Comment on Hirshleifer." *Journal of Political Economy* 105: 648-51.

Foldvary, Fred (1994) *Public Goods and Private Communities: The Market Provision of Social Services*. Aldershot, UK: Edward Elgar Publishing.

Friedman, David (1979) "Private Creation and Enforcement of Law—A Historical Case." *Journal of Legal Studies* 8: 399-415.

Hirshleifer, Jack (1995) "Anarchy and its Breakdown." *Journal of Political Economy* 103: 26-52.

Holcombe, Randall (2004) "Government: Unnecessary but Inevitable." *The Independent Review* 8: 325-42.

Hoppe, Hans-Hermann (2001) *Democracy—The God That Failed: The Economic and Politics of Monarchy, Democracy, and Natural Order*. New Brunswick, NJ: Transaction Publishers.

Hummel, Jeffrey Rogers (1990) "National Goods Versus Public Goods: Defense, Disarmament, and Free Riders." *Review of Austrian Economics* 4: 88-122.

Hummel, Jeffrey Rogers (2001) "The Will to Be Free: The Role of Ideology in National Defense." *Independent Review* 5: 523–537.

Mahoney, Paul (1997) "The Exchange as Regulator." *Virginia Law Review* 83: 1453-1500.

McElroy, Wendy (2003) *The Debates of Liberty: An Overview of Individualist Anarchism, 1881–1908*. Lanham, Md.: Rowman and Littlefield.

Nozick, Robert (2004) *Anarchy, State, and Utopia*. New York: Basic Books.

Pagano, Frank (1982) "Introduction," in Frank Pagano (ed.), *A Vindication of Natural Society*. Indianapolis: Liberty Classics.

Powell, Benjamin and Stringham, Edward (forthcoming) "Economics in Defense of Liberty: The Contribution of Murray Rothbard," in Steven Horwitz (ed.), *Biographical Dictionary of Austrian Economists*. Cheltenham, UK: Edward Elgar Publishing.

Raico, Ralph (2002) "Robert Nozick: A Historical Note." *LewRockwell.com* February 5, 2002.

Rand, Ayn (1964) *The Virtue of Selfishness*. New York: New American Library.

Romano, Roberta (1998) "Empowering Investors: A Market Approach to Securities Regulation." *Yale Law Journal* 107: 2359-2430.

Rothbard, Murray (1958) "A Note on Burke's Vindication of Natural Society." *Journal of the History of Ideas* 19: 114-118.

Rothbard, Murray (1974/2000) "The Spooner-Tucker Doctrine: An Economist's View," pp. 205-219 in *Egalitarianism as a Revolt Against Nature*. Auburn, AL: Mises Institute.

Rutten, Andrew (1999) "Can Anarchy Save Us from Leviathan?" *The Independent Review* 3: 581-593.

Smith, Vernon (2003) "Constructivist and Ecological Rationality in Economics." *American Economic Review* 93: 465-508.

Stringham, Edward (1999) "Market Chosen Law." *Journal of Libertarian Studies* 14: 53-77.

Stringham, Edward (2002) "The Emergence of the London Stock Exchange as a Self-Policing Club." *Journal of Private Enterprise* 17:1-19.

Stringham, Edward (2003) "The Extralegal Development of Securities Trading in Seventeenth Century Amsterdam." *Quarterly Review of Economics and Finance* 43: 321-344.

Tuccille, Jerome (1971) *It Usually Begins with Ayn Rand*. San Francisco: Fox & Wilkes.

Wollstein, Jarret (1969) *Society without Coercion: A New Concept of Social Organization*. Silver Spring, MD: Society for Individual Liberty.

2

Police, Law, and the Courts

Murray Rothbard

Police Protection

The market and private enterprise do exist, and so most people can readily envision a free market in most goods and services. Probably the most difficult single area to grasp, however, is the abolition of government operations in the service of protection: police, the courts, etc.—the area encompassing defense of person and property against attack or invasion. How could private enterprise and the free market possibly provide such service? How could police, legal systems, judicial services, law enforcement, prisons—how could these be provided in a free market? We have already seen how a great deal of police protection, at the least, could be supplied by the various owners of streets and land areas. But we now need to examine this entire area systematically.

In the first place, there is a common fallacy, held even by most advocates of laissez-faire, that the government must supply "police protection," as if police protection were a single, absolute entity, a fixed quantity of something which the government supplies to all. But in actual fact there is no absolute commodity called "police protection" any more than there is an absolute single commodity called "food" or "shelter." It is true that everyone pays taxes for a seemingly fixed quantity of protection, but this is a myth. In actual fact, there are almost infinite degrees of all sorts of protection. For any given person or business, the police can provide everything from a policeman on the beat who patrols once a night, to two policemen patrolling constantly on each block, to cruising patrol cars, to one or even several round-the-clock personal bodyguards. Furthermore, there are many other decisions the police must make, the complexity of which becomes evident as soon as we look beneath the veil of the myth of absolute "protection." How shall the police allocate their funds, which are, of course, always limited as are the funds of all other individuals, organizations, and agencies? How much shall the police invest in electronic equipment? fingerprinting equipment? detectives as against uniformed police? patrol cars as against foot police, etc.?

The point is that the government has no rational way to make these allocations. The government only knows that it has a limited budget. Its allocations of funds are then subject to the full play of politics, boondoggling, and bureaucratic inefficiency, with no indication at all as to whether the police department is serving the consumers in a way responsive to their desires or whether it is doing so efficiently. The situation would be different if police services were supplied on a free, competitive market. In that case, consumers would pay for whatever degree of protection they wish to purchase. The consumers who just want to see a policeman once in a while would pay less than those who want continuous patrolling, and far less than those who demand twenty-four-hour bodyguard service. On the free market, protection would be supplied in proportion and in whatever way that the consumers wish to pay for it. A drive for efficiency would be insured, as it always is on the market, by the compulsion to make profits and avoid losses, and thereby to keep costs low and to serve the highest demands of the consumers. Any police firm that suffers from gross inefficiency would soon go bankrupt and disappear.

One big problem a government police force must always face is: what laws really to enforce? Police departments are theoretically faced with the absolute injunction, "enforce all laws," but in practice a limited budget forces them to allocate their personnel and equipment to the most urgent crimes. But the absolute dictum pursues them and works against a rational allocation of resources. On the free market, what would be enforced is whatever the customers are willing to pay for. Suppose, for example, that Mr. Jones has a precious gem he believes might soon be stolen. He can ask, and pay for, round-the-clock police protection at whatever strength he may wish to work out with the police company. He might, on the other hand, also have a private road on his estate he doesn't want many people to travel on—but he might not care very much about trespassers on that road. In that case, he won't devote any police resources to protecting the road. As on the market in general, it is up to the consumer—and since all of us are consumers this means each person individually decides how much and what kind of protection he wants and is willing to buy.

All that we have said about landowners' police applies to private police in general. Free-market police would not only be efficient, they would have a strong incentive to be courteous and to refrain from brutality against either their clients or their clients' friends or customers. A private Central Park would be guarded efficiently in order to maximize park revenue, rather than have a prohibitive curfew imposed on innocent—and paying—customers. A free market in police would reward efficient and courteous police protection to customers and penalize any falling off from this standard. No longer would there be the current disjunction between service and payment inherent in all government operations, a disjunction which means that police, like all other government agencies, acquire their revenue, not voluntarily and competitively from consumers, but from the taxpayers coercively.

In fact, as government police have become increasingly inefficient, consumers have been turning more and more to private forms of protection. We have already mentioned block or neighborhood protection. There are also private guards, insurance companies, private detectives, and such increasingly sophisticated equipment as safes, locks, and closed-circuit TV and burglar alarms. The President's Commission on Law Enforcement and the Administration of Justice estimated in 1969 that government police cost the American public $2.8 billion a year, while it spends $1.35 billion on private protection service and another $200 million on equipment, so that private protection expenses amounted to over half the outlay on government police. These figures should give pause to those credulous folk who believe that police protection is somehow, by some mystic right or power, necessarily and forevermore an attribute of State sovereignty.[1]

Every reader of detective fiction knows that private insurance detectives are far more efficient than the police in recovering stolen property. Not only is the insurance company impelled by economics to serve the consumer—and thereby try to avoid paying benefits—but the major focus of the insurance company is very different from that of the police. The police, standing as they do for a mythical "society," are primarily interested in catching and punishing the criminal; restoring the stolen loot to the victim is strictly secondary. To the insurance company and its detectives, on the other hand, the prime concern is recovery of the loot, and apprehension and punishment of the criminal is secondary to the prime purpose of aiding the victim of crime. Here we see again the difference between a private firm impelled to serve the customer-victim of crime and the public police, which is under no such economic compulsion.

We cannot blueprint a market that exists only as an hypothesis, but it is reasonable to believe that police service in the libertarian society would be supplied by the landowners or by insurance companies. Since insurance companies would be paying benefits to victims of crime, it is highly likely that they would supply police service as a means of keeping down crime and hence their payment of benefits. It is certainly likely in any case that police service would be paid for in regular monthly premiums, with the police agency—whether insurance company or not—called on whenever needed.

This supplies what should be the first simple answer to a typical nightmare question of people who first hear about the idea of a totally private police: "Why, that means that if you're attacked or robbed you have to rush over to a policeman and start dickering on how much it will cost to defend you." A moment's reflection should show that no service is supplied in this way on the free market. Obviously, the person who wants to be protected by Agency A or Insurance Company B will pay regular premiums rather than wait to be attacked before buying protection. "But suppose an emergency occurs and a Company A policeman sees someone being mugged; will he stop to ask if the victim has bought insurance from Company A?" In the first place, this sort of street crime will be taken care of, as we noted above, by the police hired by whoever owns the street in question. But what of the unlikely case that a neighborhood does not have street police, and a policeman of Company A happens to see someone being attacked? Will he rush to the victim's defense? That, of course, would be up to Company A, but it is scarcely conceivable that private police companies would not cultivate goodwill by making it a policy to give free aid to victims in emergency situations and perhaps ask the rescued victim for a voluntary donation afterward. In the case of a homeowner being robbed or attacked, then of course he will call on whichever police company he has been using. He will call Police Company A rather than "the police" he calls upon now.

Competition insures efficiency, low price, and high quality, and there is no reason to assume a priori, as many people do, that there is something divinely ordained about having only one police agency in a given geographical area. Economists have often claimed that the production of certain goods or services is a "natural monopoly," so that more than one private agency could not long survive in a given area. Perhaps, although only a totally free market could decide the matter once and for all. Only the market can decide what and how many firms, and of what size and quality, can survive in active competition. But there is no reason to suppose in advance that police protection is a "natural monopoly." After all, insurance companies are not; and if we can have Metropolitan, Equitable, Prudential, etc., insurance companies coexisting side by side, why not Metropolitan, Equitable, and Prudential police protection companies? Gustave de Molinari, the nineteenth-century French free-market economist, was the first person in history to contemplate and advocate a free market for police protection.[2] Molinari estimated that there would eventually turn out to be several private police agencies side by side in the cities, and one private agency in each rural area. Perhaps—but we must realize that modern technology makes much more feasible branch offices of large urban firms in even the most remote rural areas. A person living in a small village in Wyoming, therefore, could employ the services of a local protection company, or he might use a nearby branch office of the Metropolitan Protection Company.

"But how could a poor person afford private protection he would have to pay for instead of getting free protection, as he does now?" There are several answers to this question, one of the most common criticisms of the idea of totally private police protection. One is: that this problem of course applies to any commodity or service in the libertarian society, not just the police. But isn't protection necessary? Perhaps, but then so is food of many different kinds, clothing, shelter, etc. Surely these are at least as vital if not more so than police protection, and yet almost nobody says that therefore the government must nationalize food, clothing, shelter, etc., and supply these free as a compulsory monopoly. Very poor people would be supplied, in general, by private charity, as we saw in our chapter on welfare. Furthermore, in the specific case of police there would undoubtedly be ways of voluntarily supplying free police protection to the indigent—either by the police companies themselves for goodwill (as hospitals and doctors do now) or by special "police aid" societies that would do work similar to "legal aid" societies today. (Legal aid societies voluntarily supply free legal counsel to the indigent in trouble with the authorities.)

There are important supplementary considerations. As we have seen, police service is not "free"; it is paid for by the taxpayer, and the taxpayer is very often the poor person himself. He may very well be paying more in taxes for police now than he would in fees to private, and far more efficient, police companies. Furthermore, the police companies would be tapping a mass market; with the economies of such a large-scale market, police protection would undoubtedly be much cheaper. No police company would wish to price itself out of a large chunk of its market, and the cost of protection would be no more prohibitively expensive than, say, the cost of insurance today. (In fact, it would tend to be much cheaper than current insurance, because the insurance industry today is heavily regulated by government to keep out low-cost competition.)

There is a final nightmare which most people who have contemplated private protection agencies consider to be decisive in rejecting such a concept. Wouldn't the agencies always be clashing? Wouldn't "anarchy" break out, with perpetual conflicts between police forces as one person calls in "his" police while a rival calls in "his"?

There are several levels of answers to this crucial question. In the first place, since there would be no overall State, no central or even single local government, we would at least be spared the horror of interState wars, with their plethora of massive, superdestructive, and now nuclear, weapons. As we look back through history, isn't it painfully clear that the number of people killed in isolated neighborhood "rumbles" or conflicts is as nothing to the total mass devastation of interState wars? There are good reasons for this. To avoid emotionalism let us take two hypothetical countries: "Ruritania" and "Walldavia." If both Ruritania and Walldavia were dissolved into a libertarian society, with no government and innumerable private individuals, firms, and police agencies, the only clashes that could break out would be local, and the weaponry would necessarily be strictly limited in scope and devastation. Suppose that in a Ruritanian city two police agencies clash and start shooting it out. At worst, they could not use mass bombing or nuclear destruction or germ warfare, since they themselves would be blown up in the holocaust. It is the slicing off of territorial areas into single, governmental monopolies that leads to mass destruction—for then if the single monopoly government of Walldavia confronts its ancient rival, the government of Ruritania, each can wield weapons of mass destruction and even nuclear warfare because it will be the "other guy" and the "other country" they will hurt. Furthermore, now that every person is a subject of a monopoly government, in the eyes of every other government he becomes irretrievably identified with "his" government. The citizen of France is identified with "his" government, and therefore if another government attacks France, it will attack the citizenry as well as the government of France. But if Company A battles with Company B, the most that can happen is that the respective customers of each company may be dragged into the battle—but no one else. It should be evident, then, that even if the worst happened, and a libertarian world would indeed become a world of "anarchy," we would still be much better off than we are now, at the mercy of rampant, "anarchic" nation-states, each possessing a fearsome monopoly of weapons of mass destruction. We must never forget that we are all living, and always have lived, in a world of "international anarchy," in a world of coercive nation-states unchecked by any overall world government, and there is no prospect of this situation changing.

A libertarian world, then, even if anarchic, would still not suffer the brutal wars, the mass devastation, the A-bombing, that our State-ridden world has suffered for centuries. Even if local police clash continually, there would be no more Dresdens, no more Hiroshimas.

But there is far more to be said. We should never concede that this local "anarchy" would be likely to occur. Let us separate the problem of police clashes into distinct and different parts: honest disagreements, and the attempt of one or more police forces to become "outlaws" and to extract funds or impose their rule by coercion. Let us assume for a moment that the police forces will be honest, and that they are only driven by honest clashes of opinion; we will set aside for a while the problem of outlaw police. Surely one of the very important aspects of protection service the police can offer their respective customers is quiet protection. Every consumer, every buyer of police protection, would wish above all for protection that is efficient and quiet, with no conflicts or disturbances. Every police agency would be fully aware of this vital fact. To assume that police would continually clash and battle with each other is absurd, for it ignores the devastating effect that this chaotic "anarchy" would have on the business of all the police companies. To put it bluntly, such wars and conflicts would be bad—very bad—for business. Therefore, on the free market, the police agencies would all see to it that there would be no clashes between them, and that all conflicts of opinion would be ironed out in private courts, decided by private judges or arbitrators.

To get more specific: in the first place, as we have said, clashes would be minimal because the street owner would have his guards, the storekeeper his, the landlord his, and the homeowner his own police company. Realistically, in the everyday world there would be little room for direct clashes between police agencies. But suppose, as will sometimes occur, two neighboring home owners get into a fight, each accuses the other of initiating assault or violence, and each calls on his own police company, should they happen to subscribe to different companies. What then? Again, it would be pointless and economically as well as physically self-destructive for the two police companies to start shooting it out. Instead, every police company, to remain in business at all, would announce as a vital part of its service, the use of private courts or arbitrators to decide who is in the wrong.

The Courts

Suppose, then, that the judge or arbitrator decides Smith was in the wrong in a dispute, and that he aggressed against Jones. If Smith accepts the verdict, then, whatever damages or punishment is levied, there is no problem for the theory of libertarian protection. But what if he does not accept it? Or suppose another example: Jones is robbed. He sets his police company to do detective work in trying to track down the criminal. The company decides that a certain Brown is the criminal. Then what? If Brown acknowledges his guilt, then again there is no problem and judicial punishment proceeds, centering on forcing the criminal to make restitution to the victim. But, again, what if Brown denies his guilt?

These cases take us out of the realm of police protection and into another vital area of protection: judicial service, i.e., the provision, in accordance with generally accepted procedures, of a method of trying as best as one can to determine who is the criminal, or who is the breaker of contracts, in any sort of crime or dispute. Many people, even those who acknowledge that there could be privately competitive police service supplied on a free market, balk at the idea of totally private courts. How in the world could courts be private? How would courts employ force in a world without government? Wouldn't eternal conflicts and "anarchy" then ensue?

In the first place, the monopoly courts of government are subject to the same grievous problems, inefficiencies, and contempt for the consumer as any other government operation. We all know that judges, for example, are not selected according to their wisdom, probity, or efficiency in serving the consumer, but are political hacks chosen by the political process. Furthermore, the courts are monopolies; if, for example, the courts in some town or city should become corrupt, venal, oppressive, or inefficient, the citizen at present has no recourse. The aggrieved citizen of Deep Falls, Wyoming, must be governed by the local Wyoming court or not at all. In a libertarian society, there would be many courts, many judges to whom he could turn. Again, there is no reason to assume a "natural monopoly" of judicial wisdom. The Deep Falls citizen could, for example, call upon the local branch of the Prudential Judicial Company.

How would courts be financed in a free society? There are many possibilities. Possibly, each individual would subscribe to a court service, paying a monthly premium, and then calling upon the court if he is in need. Or, since courts will probably be needed much less frequently than policemen, he may pay a fee whenever he chooses to use the court, with the criminal or contract-breaker eventually recompensing the victim or plaintiff. Or, in still a third possibility, the courts may be hired by the police agencies to settle disputes, or there may even be "vertically integrated" firms supplying both police and judicial service: the Prudential Judicial Company might have a police and a judicial division. Only the market will be able to decide which of these methods will be most appropriate.

We should all be more familiar with the increasing use of private arbitration, even in our present society. The government courts have become so clogged, inefficient, and wasteful that more and more parties to disputes are turning to private arbitrators as a cheaper and far less time-consuming way of settling their disputes. In recent years, private arbitration has become a growing and highly successful profession. Being voluntary, furthermore, the rules of arbitration can be decided rapidly by the parties themselves, without the need for a ponderous, complex legal framework applicable to all citizens. Arbitration therefore permits judgments to be made by people expert in the trade or occupation concerned. Currently, the American Arbitration Association, whose motto is "The Handclasp is Mightier than the Fist," has 25 regional offices throughout the country, with 23,000 arbitrators. In 1969, the Association conducted over 22,000 arbitrations. In addition, the insurance companies adjust over 50,000 claims a year through voluntary arbitration. There is also a growing and successful use of private arbitrators in automobile accident claim cases.

It might be protested that, while performing an ever greater proportion of judicial functions, the private arbitrators' decisions are still enforced by the courts, so that once the disputing parties agree on an arbitrator, his decision becomes legally binding. This is true, but it was not the case before 1920, and the arbitration profession grew at as rapid a rate from 1900 to 1920 as it has since. In fact, the modern arbitration movement began in full force in England during the time of the American Civil War, with merchants increasingly using the "private courts" provided by voluntary arbitrators, even though the decisions were not legally binding. By 1900, voluntary arbitration began to take hold in the United States. In fact, in medieval England, the entire structure of merchant law, which was handled clumsily and inefficiently by the government's courts, grew up in private merchants' courts. The merchants' courts were purely voluntary arbitrators, and the decisions were not legally binding. How, then, were they successful?

The answer is that the merchants, in the Middle Ages and down to 1920, relied solely on ostracism and boycott by the other merchants in the area. In other words, should a merchant refuse to submit to arbitration or ignore a decision, the other merchants would publish this fact in the trade, and would refuse to deal with the recalcitrant merchant, bringing him quickly to heel. Wooldridge mentions one medieval example:

> Merchants made their courts work simply by agreeing to abide by the results. The merchant who broke the understanding would not be sent to jail, to be sure, but neither would he long continue to be a merchant, for the compliance exacted by his fellows, and their power over his goods, proved if anything more effective than physical coercion. Take John of Homing, who made his living marketing wholesale quantities of fish. When John sold a lot of herring on the representation that it conformed to a three-barrel sample, but which, his fellow merchants found, was actually mixed with "sticklebacks and putrid herring," he made good the deficiency on pain of economic ostracism.[3]

In modern times, ostracism became even more effective, and it included the knowledge that anyone who ignored an arbitrator's award could never again avail himself of an arbitrator's services. Industrialist Owen D. Young, head of General Electric, concluded that the moral censure of other businessmen was a far more effective sanction than legal enforcement. Nowadays, modern technology, computers, and credit ratings would make such nationwide ostracism even more effective than it has ever been in the past.

Even if purely voluntary arbitration is sufficient for commercial disputes, however, what of frankly criminal activities: the mugger, the rapist, the bank robber? In these cases, it must be admitted that ostracism would probably not be sufficient—even though it would also include, we must remember, refusal of private street owners to allow such criminals in their areas. For the criminal cases, then, courts and legal enforcement become necessary.

How, then, would the courts operate in the libertarian society? In particular, how could they enforce their decisions? In all their operations, furthermore, they must observe the critical libertarian rule that no physical force may be used against anyone who has not been convicted as a criminal—otherwise, the users of such force, whether police or courts, would be themselves liable to be convicted as aggressors if it turned out that the person they had used force against was innocent of crime. In contrast to statist systems, no policeman or judge could be granted special immunity to use coercion beyond what anyone else in society could use.

Let us now take the case we mentioned before. Mr. Jones is robbed, his hired detective agency decides that one Brown committed the crime, and Brown refuses to concede his guilt. What then? In the first place, we must recognize that there is at present no overall world court or world government enforcing its decrees; yet while we live in a state of "international anarchy" there is little or no problem in disputes between private citizens of two countries. Suppose that right now, for example, a citizen of Uruguay claims that he has been swindled by a citizen of Argentina. Which court does he go to? He goes to his own, i.e., the victim's or the plaintiff's court. The case proceeds in the Uruguayan court, and its decision is honored by the Argentinian court. The same is true if an American feels he has been swindled by a Canadian, and so on. In Europe after the Roman Empire, when German tribes lived side by side and in the same areas, if a Visigoth felt that he had been injured by a Frank, he took the case to his own court, and the decision was generally accepted by the Franks. Going to the plaintiff's court is the rational libertarian procedure as well, since the victim or plaintiff is the one who is aggrieved, and who naturally takes the case to his own court. So, in our case, Jones would go to the Prudential Court Company to charge Brown with theft.

It is possible, of course, that Brown is also a client of the Prudential Court, in which case there is no problem. The Prudential's decision covers both parties, and becomes binding. But one important stipulation is that no coercive subpoena power can be used against Brown, because he must be considered innocent until he is convicted. But Brown would be served with a voluntary subpoena, a notice that he is being tried on such and such a charge and inviting him or his legal representative to appear. If he does not appear, then he will be tried in absentia, and this will obviously be less favorable for Brown since his side of the case will not be pleaded in court. If Brown is declared guilty, then the court and its marshals will employ force to seize Brown and exact whatever punishment is decided upon—a punishment which obviously will focus first on restitution to the victim.

What, however, if Brown does not recognize the Prudential Court? What if he is a client of the Metropolitan Court Company? Here the case becomes more difficult. What will happen then? First, victim Jones pleads his case in the Prudential Court. If Brown is found innocent, this ends the controversy. Suppose, however, that defendant Brown is found guilty. If he does nothing, the court's judgment proceeds against him. Suppose, however, Brown then takes the case to the Metropolitan Court Company, pleading inefficiency or venality by Prudential. The case will then be heard by Metropolitan. If Metropolitan also finds Brown guilty, this too ends the controversy and Prudential will proceed against Brown with dispatch. Suppose, however, that Metropolitan finds Brown innocent of the charge. Then what? Will the two courts and their arms-wielding marshals shoot it out in the streets?

Once again, this would clearly be irrational and self-destructive behavior on the part of the courts. An essential part of their judicial service to their clients is the provision of just, objective, and peacefully functioning decisions—the best and most objective way of arriving at the truth of who committed the crime. Arriving at a decision and then allowing chaotic gunplay would scarcely be considered valuable judicial service by their customers. Thus, an essential part of any court's service to its clients would be an appeals procedure. In short, every court would agree to abide by an appeals trial, as decided by a voluntary arbitrator to whom Metropolitan and Prudential would now turn. The appeals judge would make his decision, and the result of this third trial would be treated as binding on the guilty. The Prudential court would then proceed to enforcement.

An appeals court! But isn't this setting up a compulsory monopoly government once again? No, because there is nothing in the system that requires any one person or court to be the court of appeal. In short, in the United States at present the Supreme Court is established as the court of final appeal, so the Supreme Court judges become the final arbiters regardless of the wishes of plaintiff or defendant alike. In contrast, in the libertarian society the various competing private courts could go to any appeals judge they think fair, expert, and objective. No single appeals judge or set of judges would be foisted upon society by coercion.

How would the appeals judges be financed? There are many possible ways, but the most likely is that they will be paid by the various original courts who would charge their customers for appeals services in their premiums or fees.

But suppose Brown insists on another appeals judge, and yet another? Couldn't he escape judgment by appealing ad infinitum? Obviously, in any society legal proceedings cannot continue indefinitely; there must be some cutoff point. In the present statist society, where government monopolizes the judicial function, the Supreme Court is arbitrarily designated as the cutoff point. In the libertarian society, there would also have to be an agreed-upon cutoff point, and since there are only two parties to any crime or dispute—the plaintiff and the defendant—it seems most sensible for the legal code to declare that a decision arrived at by any two courts shall be binding. This will cover the situation when both the plaintiff's and the defendant's courts come to the same decision, as well as the situation when an appeals court decides on a disagreement between the two original courts.

The Law and the Courts

It is now clear that there will have to be a legal code in the libertarian society. How? How can there be a legal code, a system of law without a government to promulgate it, an appointed system of judges, or a legislature to vote on statutes? To begin with, is a legal code consistent with libertarian principles?

To answer the last question first, it should be clear that a legal code is necessary to lay down precise guidelines for the private courts. If, for example, Court A decides that all redheads are inherently evil and must be punished, it is clear that such decisions are the reverse of libertarian, that such a law would constitute an invasion of the rights of redheads. Hence, any such decision would be illegal in terms of libertarian principle, and could not be upheld by the rest of society. It then becomes necessary to have a legal code which would be generally accepted, and which the courts would pledge themselves to follow. The legal code, simply, would insist on the libertarian principle of no aggression against person or property, define property rights in accordance with libertarian principle, set up rules of evidence (such as currently apply) in deciding who are the wrongdoers in any dispute, and set up a code of maximum punishment for any particular crime. Within the framework of such a code, the particular courts would compete on the most efficient procedures, and the market would then decide whether judges, juries, etc., are the most efficient methods of providing judicial services.

Are such stable and consistent law codes possible, with only competing judges to develop and apply them, and without government or legislature? Not only are they possible, but over the years the best and most successful parts of our legal system were developed precisely in this manner. Legislatures, as well as kings, have been capricious, invasive, and inconsistent. They have only introduced anomalies and despotism into the legal system. In fact, the government is no more qualified to develop and apply law than it is to provide any other service; and just as religion has been separated from the State, and the economy can be separated from the State, so can every other State function, including police, courts, and the law itself!

As indicated above, for example, the entire law merchant was developed, not by the State or in State courts, but by private merchant courts. It was only much later that government took over mercantile law from its development in merchants' courts. The same occurred with admiralty law, the entire structure of the law of the sea, shipping, salvages, etc. Here again, the State was not interested, and its jurisdiction did not apply to the high seas; so the shippers themselves took on the task of not only applying, but working out the whole structure of admiralty law in their own private courts. Again, it was only later that the government appropriated admiralty law into its own courts.

Finally, the major body of Anglo-Saxon law, the justly celebrated common law, was developed over the centuries by competing judges applying time-honored principles rather than the shifting decrees of the State. These principles were not decided upon arbitrarily by any king or legislature; they grew up over centuries by applying rational—and very often libertarian—principles to the cases before them. The idea of following precedent was developed, not as a blind service to the past, but because all the judges of the past had made their decisions in applying the generally accepted common law principles to specific cases and problems. For it was universally held that the judge did not make law (as he often does today); the judge's task, his expertise, was in finding the law in accepted common law principles, and then applying that law to specific cases or to new technological or institutional conditions. The glory of the centuries-long development of the common law is testimony to their success.

The common law judges, furthermore, functioned very much like private arbitrators, as experts in the law to whom private parties went with their disputes. There was no arbitrarily imposed "supreme court" whose decision would be binding, nor was precedent, though honored, considered as automatically binding either. Thus, the libertarian Italian jurist Bruno Leoni has written:

> ...courts of judicature could not easily enact arbitrary rules of their own in England, as they were never in a position to do so directly, that is to say, in the usual, sudden, widely ranging and imperious manner of legislators. Moreover, there were so many courts of justice in England and they were so jealous of one another that even the famous principle of the binding precedent was not openly recognized as valid by them until comparatively recent times. Besides, they could never decide anything that had not been previously brought before them by private persons. Finally, comparatively few people used to go before the courts to ask from them the rules deciding their cases.[4]

And on the absence of "supreme courts":

> ...it cannot be denied that the lawyers' law or the judiciary law may tend to acquire the characteristics of legislation, including its undesirable ones, whenever jurists or judges are entitled to decide ultimately on a case.... In our time the mechanism of the judiciary in certain countries where "supreme courts are established results in the imposition of the personal views of the members of these courts, or of a majority of them, on all the other people concerned whenever there is a great deal of disagreement between the opinion of the former and the convictions of the latter. But...this possibility, far from being necessarily implied in the nature of lawyers' law or of judiciary law, is rather a deviation from it....[5]

Apart from such aberrations, the imposed personal views of the judges were kept to a minimum: (a) by the fact that judges could only make decisions when private citizens brought cases to them; (b) each judge's decisions applied only to the particular case; and (c) because the decisions of the common-law judges and lawyers always considered the precedents of the centuries. Furthermore, as Leoni points out, in contrast to legislatures or the executive, where dominant majorities or pressure groups ride roughshod over minorities, judges, by their very position, are constrained to hear and weigh the arguments of the two contending parties in each dispute. "Parties are equal as regards the judge, in the sense that they are free to produce arguments and evidence. They do not constitute a group in which dissenting minorities give way to triumphant majorities...." And Leoni points out the analogy between this process and the free-market economy: "Of course, arguments may be stronger or weaker, but the fact that every party can produce them is comparable to the fact that everybody can individually compete with everybody else in the market in order to buy and sell."[6]

Professor Leoni found that, in the private law area, the ancient Roman judges operated in the same way as the English common law courts:

> The Roman jurist was a sort of scientist; the objects of his research were the solutions to cases that citizens submitted to him for study, just as industrialists might today submit to a physicist or to an engineer a technical problem concerning their plants or their production. Hence, private Roman law was something to be described or to be discovered, not something to be enacted—a world of things that were there, forming part of the common heritage of all Roman citizens. Nobody enacted that law; nobody could change it by any exercise of his personal will.... This is the long-run concept or, if you prefer, the Roman concept, of the certainty of the law.[7]

Finally, Professor Leoni was able to use his knowledge of the operations of ancient and common law to answer the vital question: In a libertarian society, "who will appoint the judges...to let them perform the task of defining the law?" His answer is: the people themselves, people who would go to the judges with the greatest reputation of expertise and wisdom in knowing and applying the basic common legal principles of the society:

> In fact, it is rather immaterial to establish in advance who will appoint the judges, for, in a sense, everybody could do so, as happens to a certain extent when people resort to private arbiters to settle their own quarrels.... For the appointment of judges is not such a special problem as would be, for example, that of "appointing" physicists or doctors or other kinds of learned and experienced people. The emergence of good professional people in any society is only apparently due to official appointments, if any. It is, in fact, based on a widespread consent on the part of clients, colleagues, and the public at large—a consent without which no appointment is really effective. Of course, people can be wrong about the true value chosen as being worthy, but these difficulties in their choice are inescapable in any kind of choice.[8]

Of course, in the future libertarian society, the basic legal code would not rely on blind custom, much of which could well be antilibertarian. The code would have to be established on the basis of acknowledged libertarian principle, of nonaggression against the person or property of others; in short, on the basis of reason rather than on mere tradition, however sound its general outlines. Since we have a body of common law principles to draw on, however, the task of reason in correcting and amending the common law would be far easier than trying to construct a body of systematic legal principles de novo out of the thin air.

The most remarkable historical example of a society of libertarian law and courts, however, has been neglected by historians until very recently. And this was also a society where not only the courts and the law were largely libertarian, but where they operated within a purely state-less and libertarian society. This was ancient Ireland—an Ireland which persisted in this libertarian path for roughly a thousand years until its brutal conquest by England in the seventeenth century. And, in contrast to many similarly functioning primitive tribes (such as the Ibos in West Africa, and many European tribes), preconquest Ireland was not in any sense a "primitive" society: it was a highly complex society that was, for centuries, the most advanced, most scholarly, and most civilized in all of Western Europe.

For a thousand years, then, ancient Celtic Ireland had no State or anything like it. As the leading authority on ancient Irish law has written: "There was no legislature, no bailiffs, no police, no public enforcement of justice.... There was no trace of State-administered justice."[9]

How then was justice secured? The basic political unit of ancient Ireland was the tuath. All "freemen" who owned land, all professionals, and all craftsmen, were entitled to become members of a tuath. Each tuath's members formed an annual assembly which decided all common policies, declared war or peace on other tuatha, and elected or deposed their "kings." An important point is that, in contrast to primitive tribes, no one was stuck or bound to a given tuath, either because of kinship or of geographical location. Individual members were free to, and often did, secede from a tuath and join a competing tuath. Often, two or more tuatha decided to merge into a single, more efficient unit. As Professor Peden states, "the tuath is thus a body of persons voluntarily united for socially beneficial purposes and the sum total of the landed properties of its members constituted its territorial dimension."[10] In short, they did not have the modern State with its claim to sovereignty over a given (usually expanding) territorial area, divorced from the landed property rights of its subjects; on the contrary, tuatha were voluntary associations which only comprised the landed properties of its voluntary members. Historically, about 80 to 100 tuatha coexisted at any time throughout Ireland.

But what of the elected "king"? Did he constitute a form of State ruler? Chiefly, the king functioned as a religious high priest, presiding over the worship rites of the tuath, which functioned as a voluntary religious, as well as a social and political, organization. As in pagan, pre-Christian, priesthoods, the kingly function was hereditary, this practice carrying over to Christian times. The king was elected by the tuath from within a royal kin-group (the derbfine), which carried the hereditary priestly function. Politically, however, the king had strictly limited functions: he was the military leader of the tuath, and he presided over the tuath assemblies. But he could only conduct war or peace negotiations as agent of the assemblies; and he was in no sense sovereign and had no rights of administering justice over tuath members. He could not legislate, and when he himself was party to a lawsuit, he had to submit his case to an independent judicial arbiter.

Again, how, then, was law developed and justice maintained? In the first place, the law itself was based on a body of ancient and immemorial custom, passed down as oral and then written tradition through a class of professional jurists called the brehons. The brehons were in no sense public, or governmental, officials; they were simply selected by parties to disputes on the basis of their reputations for wisdom, knowledge of the customary law, and the integrity of their decisions. As Professor Peden states:

> ...the professional jurists were consulted by parties to disputes for advice as to what the law was in particular cases, and these same men often acted as arbitrators between suitors. They remained at all times private persons, not public officials; their functioning depended upon their knowledge of the law and the integrity of their judicial reputations.[11]

Furthermore, the brehons had no connection whatsoever with the individual tuatha or with their kings. They were completely private, national in scope, and were used by disputants throughout Ireland. Moreover, and this is a vital point, in contrast to the system of private Roman lawyers, the brehon was all there was; there were no other judges, no "public" judges of any kind, in ancient Ireland.

It was the brehons who were schooled in the law, and who added glosses and applications to the law to fit changing conditions. Furthermore, there was no monopoly, in any sense, of the brehon jurists; instead, several competing schools of jurisprudence existed and competed for the custom of the Irish people.

How were the decisions of the brehons enforced? Through an elaborate, voluntarily developed system of "insurance," or sureties. Men were linked together by a variety of surety relationships by which they guaranteed one another for the righting of wrongs, and for the enforcement of justice and the decisions of the brehons. In short, the brehons themselves were not involved in the enforcement of decisions, which rested again with private individuals linked through sureties. There were various types of surety. For example, the surety would guarantee with his own property the payment of a debt, and then join the plaintiff in enforcing a debt judgment if the debtor refused to pay. In that case, the debtor would have to pay double damages: one to the original creditor, and another as compensation to his surety. And this system applied to all offences, aggressions and assaults as well as commercial contracts; in short, it applied to all cases of what we would call "civil" and "criminal" law. All criminals were considered to be "debtors" who owed restitution and compensation to their victims, who thus became their "creditors." The victim would gather his sureties around him and proceed to apprehend the criminal or to proclaim his suit publicly and demand that the defendant submit to adjudication of their dispute with the brehons. The criminal might then send his own sureties to negotiate a settlement or agree to submit the dispute to the brehons. If he did not do so, he was considered an "outlaw" by the entire community; he could no longer enforce any claim of his own in the courts, and he was treated to the opprobrium of the entire community.[12]

There were occasional "wars," to be sure, in the thousand years of Celtic Ireland, but they were minor brawls, negligible compared to the devastating wars that racked the rest of Europe. As Professor Peden points out, "without the coercive apparatus of the State which can through taxation and conscription mobilize large amounts of arms and manpower, the Irish were unable to sustain any large scale military force in the field for any length of time. Irish wars...were pitiful brawls and cattle raids by European standards."[13]

Thus, we have indicated that it is perfectly possible, in theory and historically, to have efficient and courteous police, competent and learned judges, and a body of systematic and socially accepted law—and none of these things being furnished by a coercive government. Government—claiming a compulsory monopoly of protection over a geographical area, and extracting its revenues by force—can be separated from the entire field of protection. Government is no more necessary for providing vital protection service than it is necessary for providing anything else. And we have not stressed a crucial fact about government: that its compulsory monopoly over the weapons of coercion has led it, over the centuries, to infinitely more butcheries and infinitely greater tyranny and oppression than any decentralized, private agencies could possibly have done. If we look at the black record of mass murder, exploitation, and tyranny levied on society by governments over the ages, we need not be loath to abandon the Leviathan State and...try freedom.

Outlaw Protectors

We have saved for the last this problem: What if police or judges and courts should be venal and biased—what if they should bias their decisions, for example, in favor of particularly wealthy clients? We have shown how a libertarian legal and judicial system could work on the purely free market, assuming honest differences of opinion—but what if one or more police or courts should become, in effect, outlaws? What then?

In the first place, libertarians do not flinch from such a question. In contrast to such utopians as Marxists or left-wing anarchists (anarchocommunists or anarcho-syndicalists), libertarians do not assume that the ushering in of the purely free society of their dreams will also bring with it a new, magically transformed Libertarian Man. We do not assume that the lion will lie down with the lamb, or that no one will have criminal or fraudulent designs upon his neighbor. The "better" that people will be, of course, the better any social system will work, in particular the less work any police or courts will have to do. But no such assumption is made by libertarians. What we assert is that, given any particular degree of "goodness" or "badness" among men, the purely libertarian society will be at once the most moral and the most efficient, the least criminal and the most secure of person or property.

Let us first consider the problem of the venal or crooked judge or court. What of the court which favors its own wealthy client in trouble? In the first place, any such favoritism will be highly unlikely, given the rewards and sanctions of the free market economy. The very life of the court, the very livelihood of a judge, will depend on his reputation for integrity, fair-mindedness, objectivity, and the quest for truth in every case. This is his "brand name." Should word of any venality leak out, he will immediately lose clients and the courts will no longer have customers; for even those clients who may be criminally inclined will scarcely sponsor a court whose decisions are no longer taken seriously by the rest of society, or who themselves may well be in jail for dishonest and fraudulent dealings. If, for example, Joe Zilch is accused of a crime or breach of contract, and he goes to a "court" headed by his brother-in-law, no one, least of all other, honest courts will take this "court's" decision seriously. It will no longer be considered a "court" in the eyes of anyone but Joe Zilch and his family.

Contrast this built-in corrective mechanism to the present-day government courts. Judges are appointed or elected for long terms, up to life, and they are accorded a monopoly of decision-making in their particular area. It is almost impossible, except in cases of gross corruption, to do anything about venal decisions of judges. Their power to make and to enforce their decisions continues unchecked year after year. Their salaries continue to be paid, furnished under coercion by the hapless taxpayer. But in the totally free society, any suspicion of a judge or court will cause their customers to melt away and their "decisions" to be ignored. This is a far more efficient system of keeping judges honest than the mechanism of government.

Furthermore, the temptation for venality and bias would be far less for another reason: business firms in the free market earn their keep, not from wealthy customers, but from a mass market by consumers. Macy's earns its income from the mass of the population, not from a few wealthy customers. The same is true of Metropolitan Life Insurance today, and the same would be true of any "Metropolitan" court system tomorrow. It would be folly indeed for the courts to risk the loss of favor by the bulk of its customers for the favors of a few wealthy clients. But contrast the present system, where judges, like all other politicians, may be beholden to wealthy contributors who finance the campaigns of their political parties.

There is a myth that the "American System" provides a superb set of "checks and balances," with the executive, the legislature, and the courts all balancing and checking one against the other, so that power cannot unduly accumulate in one set of hands. But the American "checks and balances" system is largely a fraud. For each one of these institutions is a coercive monopoly in its area, and all of them are part of one government, headed by one political party at any given time. Furthermore, at best there are only two parties, each one close to the other in ideology and personnel, often colluding, and the actual day-to-day business of government headed by a civil service bureaucracy that cannot be displaced by the voters. Contrast to these mythical checks and balances the real checks and balances provided by the free-market economy! What keeps A&P honest is the competition, actual and potential, of Safeway, Pioneer, and countless other grocery stores. What keeps them honest is the ability of the consumers to cut off their patronage. What would keep the free-market judges and courts honest is the lively possibility of heading down the block or down the road to another judge or court if suspicion should descend on any particular one. What would keep them honest is the lively possibility of their customers cutting off their business. These are the real, active checks and balances of the free-market economy and the free society.

The same analysis applies to the possibility of a private police force becoming outlaw, of using their coercive powers to exact tribute, set up a "protection racket" to shake down their victims, etc. Of course, such a thing could happen. But, in contrast to present-day society, there would be immediate checks and balances available; there would be other police forces who could use their weapons to band together to put down the aggressors against their clientele. If the Metropolitan Police Force should become gangsters and exact tribute, then the rest of society could flock to the Prudential, Equitable, etc., police forces who could band together to put them down. And this contrasts vividly with the State. If a group of gangsters should capture the State apparatus, with its monopoly of coercive weapons, there is nothing at present that can stop them—short of the immensely difficult process of revolution. In a libertarian society there would be no need for a massive revolution to stop the depredation of gangster-States; there would be a swift turning to the honest police forces to check and put down the force that had turned bandit.

And, indeed, what is the State anyway but organized banditry? What is taxation but theft on a gigantic, unchecked, scale? What is war but mass murder on a scale impossible by private police forces? What is conscription but mass enslavement? Can anyone envision a private police force getting away with a tiny fraction of what States get away with, and do habitually, year after year, century after century?

There is another vital consideration that would make it almost impossible for an outlaw police force to commit anything like the banditry that modern governments practice. One of the crucial factors that permits governments to do the monstrous things they habitually do is the sense of legitimacy on the part of the stupefied public. The average citizen may not like—may even strongly object to—the policies and exactions of his government. But he has been imbued with the idea—carefully indoctrinated by centuries of governmental propaganda—that the government is his legitimate sovereign, and that it would be wicked or mad to refuse to obey its dictates. It is this sense of legitimacy that the State's intellectuals have fostered over the ages, aided and abetted by all the trappings of legitimacy: flags, rituals, ceremonies, awards, constitutions, etc. A bandit gang—even if all the police forces conspired together into one vast gang—could never command such legitimacy. The public would consider them purely bandits; their extortions and tributes would never be considered legitimate though onerous "taxes," to be paid automatically. The public would quickly resist these illegitimate demands and the bandits would be resisted and overthrown. Once the public had tasted the joys, prosperity, freedom, and efficiency of a libertarian, State-less society, it would be almost impossible for a State to fasten itself upon them once again. Once freedom has been fully enjoyed, it is no easy task to force people to give it up.

But suppose—just suppose—that despite all these handicaps and obstacles, despite the love for their newfound freedom, despite the inherent checks and balances of the free market, suppose anyway that the State manages to reestablish itself. What then? Well, then, all that would have happened is that we would have a State once again. We would be no worse off than we are now, with our current State. And, as one libertarian philosopher has put it, "at least the world will have had a glorious holiday." Karl Marx's ringing promise applies far more to a libertarian society than to communism: In trying freedom, in abolishing the State, we have nothing to lose and everything to gain.

National Defense

We come now to what is usually the final argument against the libertarian position. Every libertarian has heard a sympathetic but critical listener say: "All right, I see how this system could be applied successfully to local police and courts. But how could a libertarian society defend us against the Russians?"

There are, of course, several dubious assumptions implied in such a question. There is the assumption that the Russians are bent upon military invasion of the United States, a doubtful assumption at best. There is the assumption that any such desire would still remain after the United States had become a purely libertarian society. This notion overlooks the lesson of history that wars result from conflicts between nation-states, each armed to the teeth, each direly suspicious of attack by the other. But a libertarian America would clearly not be a threat to anyone, not because it had no arms but because it would be dedicated to no aggression against anyone, or against any country. Being no longer a nation-state, which is inherently threatening, there would be little chance of any country attacking us. One of the great evils of the nation-state is that each State is able to identify all of its subjects with itself; hence in any inter-State war, the innocent civilians, the subjects of each country, are subject to aggression from the enemy State. But in a libertarian society there would be no such identification, and hence very little chance of such a devastating war. Suppose, for example, that our outlaw Metropolitan Police Force has initiated aggression not only against Americans but also against Mexicans. If Mexico had a government, then clearly the Mexican government would know full well that Americans in general were not implicated in the Metropolitan's crimes, and had no symbiotic relationship with it. If the Mexican police engaged in a punitive expedition to punish the Metropolitan force, they would not be at war with Americans in general—as they would be now. In fact, it is highly likely that other American forces would join the Mexicans in putting down the aggressor. Hence, the idea of inter-State war against a libertarian country or geographical area would most likely disappear.

There is, furthermore, a grave philosophical error in the very posing of this sort of question about the Russians. When we contemplate any sort of new system, whatever it may be, we must first decide whether we want to see it brought about. In order to decide whether we want libertarianism or communism, or left-wing anarchism, or theocracy, or any other system, we must first assume that it has been established, and then consider whether the system could work, whether it could remain in existence, and just how efficient such a system would be. We have shown, I believe, that a libertarian system, once instituted, could work, be viable, and be at once far more efficient, prosperous, moral, and free than any other social system. But we have said nothing about how to get from the present system to the ideal; for these are two totally separate questions: the question of what is our ideal goal, and of the strategy and tactics of how to get from the present system to that goal. The Russian question mixes these two levels of discourse. It assumes, not that libertarianism has been established everywhere throughout the globe, but that for some reason it has been established only in America and nowhere else. But why assume this? Why not first assume that it has been established everywhere and see whether we like it? After all, the libertarian philosophy is an eternal one, not bound to time or place. We advocate liberty for everyone, everywhere, not just in the United States. If someone agrees that a world libertarian society, once established, is the best that he can conceive, that it would be workable, efficient, and moral, then let him become a libertarian, let him join us in accepting liberty as our ideal goal, and then join us further in the separate—and obviously difficult—task of figuring out how to bring this ideal about.

If we do move on to strategy, it is obvious that the larger an area in which liberty is first established the better its chances for survival, and the better its chance to resist any violent overthrow that may be attempted. If liberty is established instantaneously throughout the world, then there will of course be no problem of "national defense." All problems will be local police problems. If, however, only Deep Falls, Wyoming, becomes libertarian while the rest of America and the world remain statist, its chances for survival will be very slim. If Deep Falls, Wyoming, declares its secession from the United States government and establishes a free society, the chances are great that the United States—given its historical ferocity toward secessionists—would quickly invade and crush the new free society, and there is little that any Deep Falls police force could do about it. Between these two polar cases, there is an infinite continuum of degrees, and obviously, the larger the area of freedom, the better it could withstand any outside threat. The "Russian question" is therefore a matter of strategy rather than a matter of deciding on basic principles and on the goal toward which we wish to direct our efforts.

But after all this is said and done, let us take up the Russian question anyway. Let us assume that the Soviet Union would really be hell-bent on attacking a libertarian population within the present boundaries of the United States (clearly, there would no longer be a United States government to form a single nation-state). In the first place, the form and quantity of defense expenditures would be decided upon by the American consumers themselves. Those Americans who favor Polaris submarines, and fear a Soviet threat, would subscribe toward the financing of such vessels. Those who prefer an ABM system would invest in such defensive missiles. Those who laugh at such a threat or those who are committed pacifists would not contribute to any "national" defense service at all. Different defense theories would be applied in proportion to those who agree with, and support, the various theories being offered. Given the enormous waste in all wars and defense preparations in all countries throughout history, it is certainly not beyond the bounds of reason to propose that private, voluntary defense efforts would be far more efficient than government boondoggles. Certainly these efforts would be infinitely more moral.

But let us assume the worst. Let us assume that the Soviet Union at last invades and conquers the territory of America. What then? We have to realize that the Soviet Union's difficulties will have only just begun. The main reason a conquering country can rule a defeated country is that the latter has an existing State apparatus to transmit and enforce the victor's orders onto a subject population. Britain, though far smaller in area and population, was able to rule India for centuries because it could transmit British orders to the ruling Indian princes, who in turn could enforce them on the subject population. But in those cases in history where the conquered had no government, the conquerors found rule over the conquered extremely difficult. When the British conquered West Africa, for example, they found it extremely difficult to govern the Ibo tribe (later to form Biafra) because that tribe was essentially libertarian, and had no ruling government of tribal chiefs to transmit orders to the natives. And perhaps the major reason it took the English centuries to conquer ancient Ireland is that the Irish had no State, and that there was therefore no ruling governmental structure to keep treaties, transmit orders, etc. It is for this reason that the English kept denouncing the "wild" and "uncivilized" Irish as "faithless," because they would not keep treaties with the English conquerors. The English could never understand that, lacking any sort of State, the Irish warriors who concluded treaties with the English could only speak for themselves; they could never commit any other group of the Irish population.[14]

Furthermore, the occupying Russians' lives would be made even more difficult by the inevitable eruption of guerrilla warfare by the American population. It is surely a lesson of the twentieth century—a lesson first driven home by the successful American revolutionaries against the mighty British Empire—that no occupying force can long keep down a native population determined to resist. If the giant United States, armed with far greater productivity and firepower, could not succeed against a tiny and relatively unarmed Vietnamese population, how in the world could the Soviet Union succeed in keeping down the American people? No Russian occupation soldier's life would be safe from the wrath of a resisting American populace. Guerrilla warfare has proved to be an irresistible force precisely because it stems, not from a dictatorial central government, but from the people themselves, fighting for their liberty and independence against a foreign State. And surely the anticipation of this sea of troubles, of the enormous costs and losses that would inevitably follow, would stop well in advance even a hypothetical Soviet government bent on military conquest.

Notes

1. See William C. Wooldridge, *Uncle Sam the Monopoly Man* (New Rochelle, NY: Arlington House), pp. 111ff.
2. Cf. Gustave de Molinari, *The Production of Security* (New York: Center for Libertarian Studies, 1977).
3. Wooldridge, op. cit., p. 96. Also see pp. 94–110.
4. Bruno Leoni, *Freedom and the Law* (Los Angeles: Nash Publishing Co., 1972), p. 87.
5. Ibid., pp. 23–24.
6. Ibid., p. 188.
7. Ibid., pp. 84–85.
8. Ibid., p. 183.
9. Quoted in the best introduction to ancient, anarchistic Irish institutions, Joseph R. Pedea, "Property Rights in Celtic Irish Law," *Journal of Libertarian Studies* I (Spring 1977), p. 83; see also pp. 81–95. For a summary, see Peden, "Stateless Societies: Ancient Ireland," *The Libertarian Forum* (April 1971), pp. 3–4.
10. Peden, "Stateless Societies," p. 4.
11. Ibid.
12. Professor Charles Donahue of Fordham University has maintained that the secular part of ancient Irish law was not simply haphazard tradition; that it was consciously rooted in the Stoic conception of natural law, discoverable by man's reason. Charles Donahue, "Early Celtic Laws" (unpublished paper, delivered at the Columbia University Seminar in the History of Legal and Political Thought, Autumn, 1964), pp. 13ff.
13. Peden, "Stateless Societies," p. 4.
14. Peden, "Stateless Societies," p. 3; also see Kathleen Hughes, introduction to A. Jocelyn Otway-Ruthven, *A History of Medieval Ireland* (New York: Barnes & Noble, 1968).

3

The Machinery of Freedom: Guide to a Radical Capitalism (excerpt)

David Friedman

> *Is Government, then, useful and necessary? So is a doctor. But suppose the dear fellow claimed the right every time he was called in to prescribe for a bellyache or a ringing in the ears, to raid the family silver, use the family toothbrushes, and execute the droit de seigneur upon the housemaid?*
> *—H.L. Mencken*

> *Anarchism: the theory that all forms of government are undesirable.—Webster's New World Dictionary of the American Language*

In Part 1, I described myself as an anarchist and asserted that government has no legitimate functions. In this part, I shall attempt to justify that statement. Conceivably I could do so by listing all the things the government does and explaining why each either should not be done or could be done better by private individuals cooperating voluntarily. Unfortunately, paper and ink are scarce resources; the list alone would fill this book. Instead, I will discuss in the next few chapters how private arrangements could take over the most fundamental government functions—police, courts, and national defense. When I finish, some readers will object that the institutions that provide these "governmental" functions are by definition governments, that I am therefore not an anarchist at all. I merely want a different kind of government.

They will be wrong. An anarchist is not, except in the propaganda of his enemies, one who desires chaos. Anarchists, like other people, wish to be protected from thieves and murderers. They wish to have some peaceful way of settling disagreements. They wish, perhaps even more than other people, to be able to protect themselves from foreign invasion. What, after all, is the point of abolishing your own government if it is immediately replaced by someone else's? What anarchists do not want is to have these useful services—the services now provided by police, courts and national defense—provided by the kind of institution that now provides them: government.

Before I proceed with my argument, I must define what I mean by "government." A government is an agency of legitimized coercion. I define "coercion," for the purposes of this definition, as the violation of what people in a particular society believe to be the rights of individuals with respect to other individuals.

For instance, people in this society believe that an individual has the right to turn down a job offer; the denial of that right is a form of coercion called enslavement. They believe that an individual has the right to turn down a request for money or an offered trade. The denial of that right is called robbery or extortion.

Government is an agency of legitimized coercion. The special characteristic that distinguishes governments from other agencies of coercion (such as ordinary criminal gangs) is that most people accept government coercion as normal and proper. The same act that is regarded as coercive when done by a private individual seems legitimate if done by an agent of the government.

If I yell "Stop, thief!" at a stickup man escaping with my wallet, the bystanders may or may not help, but they will at least recognize the reasonableness of my act. If I yell "Stop, thief!" at an employee of the Internal Revenue Service, leaving my house after informing me that he has just frozen my bank account, my neighbors will think I'm crazy. Objectively, the IRS is engaged in the same act as the thief. It seizes my resources without my permission. True, it claims to provide me with services in exchange for my taxes, but it insists on collecting the taxes whether or not I want the services. It is, perhaps, a fine point whether that is robbery or extortion. In either case, if it were the act of a private party, everyone would agree that it was a crime.

Suppose that a private employer, offering low wages for long hours of unpleasant work, failed to find enough workers and solved the problem by picking men at random and threatening to imprison them if they refused to work for him. He would be indicted on charges of kidnapping and extortion and acquitted on ground of insanity. This is exactly how the government hires people to fight war or sit on a jury.

It is often argued that government, or at least some particular government, is not merely legitimized but legitimate, that its actions only appear to be coercive. Such arguments often involve social contract theories—claims that the citizen is somehow contractually bound to obey the government. To those interested in that argument and its refutation I recommend "No Treason: The Constitution of No Authority" by Lysander Spooner.

Government is distinguished from other criminal gangs by being legitimized. It is distinguished from legitimate nongovernmental groups which may serve some of the same functions by the fact that it is coercive. Governments build roads. So, occasionally, do private individuals. But the private individuals must first buy the land at a price satisfactory to the seller. The government can and does set a price at which the owner is forced to sell.

Government is an agency of legitimized coercion. If the institutions which replace government perform their functions without coercion, they are not governments. If they occasionally act coercively but, when they do so, their actions are not regarded as legitimate, they are still not governments.

Police, Courts, and Laws—On the Market

How, without government, could we settle the disputes that are now settled in courts of law? How could we protect ourselves from criminals?

Consider first the easiest case, the resolution of disputes involving contracts between well-established firms. A large fraction of such disputes are now settled not by government courts but by private arbitration of the sort described in Chapter 18. The firms, when they draw up a contract, specify a procedure for arbitrating any dispute that may arise. Thus they avoid the expense and delay of the courts.

The arbitrator has no police force. His function is to render decisions, not to enforce them. Currently, arbitrated decisions are usually enforceable in the government courts, but that is a recent development; historically, enforcement came from a firm's desire to maintain its reputation. After refusing to accept an arbitrator's judgment, it is hard to persuade anyone else to sign a contract that specifies arbitration; no one wants to play a game of "heads you win, tails I lose."

Arbitration arrangements are already widespread. As the courts continue to deteriorate, arbitration will continue to grow. But it only provides for the resolution of disputes over preexisting contracts. Arbitration, by itself, provides no solution for the man whose car is dented by a careless driver, still less for the victim of theft; in both cases the plaintiff and defendant, having different interests and no prior agreement, are unlikely to find a mutually satisfactory arbitrator. Indeed, the defendant has no reason to accept any arbitration at all; he can only lose—which brings us to the problem of preventing coercion.

Protection from coercion is an economic good. It is presently sold in a variety of forms—Brinks guards, locks, burglar alarms. As the effectiveness of government police declines, these market substitutes for the police, like market substitutes for the courts, become more popular.

Suppose, then, that at some future time there are no government police, but instead private protection agencies. These agencies sell the service of protecting their clients against crime. Perhaps they also guarantee performance by insuring their clients against losses resulting from criminal acts.

How might such protection agencies protect? That would be an economic decision, depending on the costs and effectiveness of different alternatives. On the one extreme, they might limit themselves to passive defenses, installing elaborate locks and alarms. Or they may take no preventative action at all, but make great efforts to hunt down criminals guilty of crimes against their clients. They might maintain foot patrols or squad cars, like our present government police, or they might rely on electronic substitutes. In any case, they would be selling a service to their customers and would have strong incentive to provide as high a service as possible, at the lowest possible cost. It is reasonable to suppose that the quality of service would be higher and the cost lower than with the present governmental protective system.

Inevitably, conflicts would arise between one protective agency and another; how might they be resolved?

I come home one night and find my television set missing. I immediately call my protection agency, Tannahelp Inc., to report the theft. They send an agent. He checks the automatic camera which Tannahelp, as part of their service, installed in my living room and discovers a picture of one Joe Bock lugging the television set out the door. The Tannahelp agent contacts Joe, informs him that Tannahelp has reason to believe he is in possession of my television set, and suggests he return it, along with an extra ten dollars to pay for Tannahelp's time and trouble in locating Joe. Joe replies that he has never seen my television set in his life and tells the Tannahelp agent to go to hell.

The agent points out that until Tannahelp is convinced there has been a mistake, he must proceed on the assumption that the television set is my property. Six Tannahelp employees, all large and energetic, will be at Joe's door next morning to collect the set.

Joe, in response, informs the agent that he also has a protection agency, Dawn Defense, and that his contract with them undoubtedly requires them to protect him if six goons try to break into his house and steal his television set.

The stage seems set for a nice little war between Tannahelp and Dawn Defense. It is precisely such a possibility that has led some libertarians who are not anarchists, most notably Ayn Rand, to reject the possibility of competing free-market protection agencies.

But wars are very expensive, and Tannahelp and Dawn Defense are both profit-making corporations, more interested in saving money than face. I think the rest of the story would be less violent than Miss Rand supposed.

The Tannahelp agent calls up his opposite number at Dawn Defense. "We've got a problem...." After explaining the situation, he points out that if Tannahelp sends six men and Dawn eight, there will be a fight. Someone might even get hurt. Whoever wins, by the time the conflict is over it will be expensive for both sides. They might even have to start paying their employees higher wages to make up for the risk. Then both firms will be forced to raise their rates. If they do, Murbard Ltd., an aggressive new firm which has been trying to get established in the area, will undercut their prices and steal their customers. There must be a better solution.

The man from Tannahelp suggests that the better solution is arbitration. They will take the dispute over my television set to a reputable local arbitration firm. If the arbitrator decides that Joe is innocent, Tannahelp agrees to pay Joe and Dawn Defense an indemnity to make up for their time and trouble. If he is found guilty, Dawn Defense will accept the verdict; since the television set is not Joe's, they have no obligation to protect him when the men from Tannahelp come to seize it.

What I have described is a very makeshift arrangement. In practice, once anarcho-capitalist institutions were well established, protection agencies would anticipate such difficulties and arrange contracts in advance, before specific conflicts occurred, specifying the arbitrator who would settle them.

In such an anarchist society, who would make the laws? On what basis would the private arbitrator decide what acts were criminal and what their punishments should be? The answer is that systems of law would be produced for profit on the open market, just as books and bras are produced today. There could be competition among different brands of law, just as there is competition among different brands of cars.

In such a society there might be many courts and even many legal systems. Each pair of protection agencies agrees in advance on which court they will use in case of conflict. Thus the laws under which a particular case is decided are determined implicitly by advance agreement between the protection agencies whose customers are involved. In principle, there could be a different court and a different set of laws for every pair of protection agencies. In practice, many agencies would probably find it convenient to patronize the same courts, and many courts might find it convenient to adopt identical, or nearly identical, systems of law in order to simplify matters for their customers.

Before labeling a society in which different people are under different laws chaotic and unjust, remember that in our society the law under which you are judged depends on the country, state, and even city in which you happen to be. Under the arrangements I am describing, it depends instead on your protective agency and the agency of the person you accuse of a crime or who accuses you of a crime.

In such a society law is produced on the market. A court supports itself by charging for the service of arbitrating disputes. Its success depends on its reputation for honesty, reliability, and promptness and on the desirability to potential customers of the particular set of laws it judges by. The immediate customers are protection agencies. But the protection agency is itself selling a product to its customers. Part of that product is the legal system, or systems, of the courts it patronizes and under which its customers will consequently be judged. Each protection agency will try to patronize those courts under whose legal system its customers would like to live.

Consider, as a particular example, the issue of capital punishment. Some people might feel that the risk to themselves of being convicted, correctly or incorrectly, and executed for a capital crime outweighed any possible advantages of capital punishment. They would prefer, where possible, to patronize protection agencies that patronized courts that did not give capital punishment. Other citizens might feel that they would be safer from potential murderers if it were known that anyone who murdered them would end up in the electric chair. They might consider that safety more important than the risk of ending up in the electric chair themselves or of being responsible for the death of an innocent accused of murder. They would, if possible, patronize agencies that patronized courts that did give capital punishment.

If one position or the other is almost universal, it may pay all protection agencies to use courts of the one sort or the other. If some people feel one way and some the other, and if their feelings are strong enough to affect their choice of protection agencies, it pays some agencies to adopt a policy of guaranteeing, whenever possible, to use courts that do not recognize capital punishment. They can then attract anti-capital-punishment customers. Other agencies do the opposite.

Disputes between two anti-capital-punishment agencies will, of course, go to an anti-capital-punishment court; disputes between two pro-capital-punishment agencies will go to a pro-capital-punishment court. What would happen in a dispute between an anti-capital-punishment agency and a pro-capital-punishment agency? Obviously there is no way that if I kill you the case goes to one court, but if you are killed by me it goes to another. We cannot each get exactly the law we want.

We can each have our preferences reflected in the bargaining demands of our respective agencies. If the opponents of capital punishment feel more strongly than the proponents, the agencies will agree to no capital punishment; in exchange, the agencies that want capital punishment will get something else. Perhaps it will be agreed that they will not pay court costs or that some other disputed question will go their way.

One can imagine an idealized bargaining process, for this or any other dispute, as follows: Two agencies are negotiating whether to recognize a pro- or anti-capital-punishment court. The pro agency calculates that getting a pro-capital-punishment court will be worth $20,000 a year to its customers; that is the additional amount it can get for its services if they include a guarantee of capital punishment in case of disputes with the other agency. The anti-capital-punishment agency calculates a corresponding figure of $40,000. It offers the pro agency $30,000 a year in exchange for accepting an anti-capital-punishment court. The pro agency accepts. Now the anti-capital-punishment agency can raise its rates enough to bring in an extra $35,000. Its customers are happy, since the guarantee of no capital punishment is worth more than that. The agency is happy; it is getting an extra $5,000 a year profit. The pro agency cuts its rates by an amount that costs it $25,000 a year. This lets it keep its customers and even get more, since the savings is more than enough to make up to them for not getting the court of their choice. It, too, is making $5,000 a year profit on the transaction. As in any good trade, everyone gains.

If you find this confusing, it may be worth the trouble of going over it again; the basic principle of such negotiation will become important later when I discuss what sort of law an anarcho-capitalist society is likely to have.

If, by some chance, the customers of the two agencies feel equally strongly, perhaps two courts will be chosen, one of each kind, and cases allocated randomly between them. In any case, the customer's legal preference, his opinion as to what sort of law he wishes to live under, will have been a major factor in determining the kind of law he does live under. It cannot completely determine it, since accused and accuser must have the same law.

In the case of capital punishment, the two positions are directly opposed. Another possibility is that certain customers may want specialized law, suited to their special circumstances. People living in desert areas might want a system of law that very clearly defines property rights in water. People in other areas would find such detailed treatment of this problem superfluous at best. At worst, it might be the source of annoying nuisance suits. Thus the desert people might all patronize one protection agency, which had a policy of always going to a court with well-developed water law. Other agencies would agree to use that court in disputes with that agency but use other courts among themselves.

Most differences among courts would probably be more subtle. People would find that the decisions of one court were prompter or easier to predict than those of another or that the customers of one protection agency were better protected than those of another. The protection agencies, trying to build their own reputations, would search for the "best" courts.

Several objections may be raised to such free-market courts. The first is that they would sell justice by deciding in favor of the highest bidder. That would be suicidal; unless they maintained a reputation for honesty, they would have no customers—unlike our present judges. Another objection is that it is the business of courts and legislatures to discover laws, not create them; there cannot be two competing laws of gravity, so why should there be two competing laws of property? But there can be two competing theories about the law of gravity or the proper definition of property rights. Discovery is as much a productive activity as creation. If it is obvious what the correct law is, what rules of human interaction follow from the nature of man, then all courts will agree, just as all architects agree about the laws of physics. If it is not obvious, the market will generate research intended to discover correct laws.

Another objection is that a society of many different legal systems would be confusing. If this is found to be a serious problem, courts will have an economic incentive to adopt uniform law, just as paper companies have an incentive to produce standardized sizes of paper. New law will be introduced only when the innovator believes that its advantages outweigh the advantages of uniformity.

The most serious objection to free-market law is that plaintiff and defendant may not be able to agree on a common court. Obviously, a murderer would prefer a lenient judge. If the court were actually chosen by the disputants after the crime occurred, this might be an insuperable difficulty. Under the arrangements I have described, the court is chosen in advance by the protection agencies. There would hardly be enough murderers at any one time to support their own protective agency, one with a policy of patronizing courts that did not regard murder as a crime. Even if there were, no other protective agency would accept such courts. The murderers' agency would either accept a reasonable court or fight a hopeless war against the rest of society.

Until he is actually accused of a crime, everyone wants laws that protect him from crime and let him interact peacefully and productively with others. Even criminals. Not many murderers would wish to live under laws that permitted them to kill—and be killed.

The Stability Problem

Anyone with a little imagination can dream up a radical new structure for society, anarcho-capitalist or otherwise. The question is, will it work? Most people, when they hear my description of anarcho-capitalism for the first time, immediately explain to me two or three reasons why it won't. Most of their arguments can be reduced to two: The system will be at the mercy of the mafia, which can establish its own "protection agency" or take over existing ones and convert them into protection rackets. Or else the protection agencies will realize that theft is more profitable than business, get together, and become a government.

The main defensive weapon of organized crime is bribery. It works because policemen have no real stake in doing their job well and their "customers" have no standard of comparison to tell them if they are getting their money's worth. What is the cost to the chief of a police department of letting his men accept bribes to permit crime? In most cases, nothing. The higher crime rate might even persuade the voters to vote more money and higher salaries to the police department.

If the employees of a private protection agency accept such bribes, the situation is rather different. The worse the job the protection agency does, the lower the fee it can charge. If the customers of one agency find they lose, on average, ten dollars a year more to thieves than the customers of another, they will continue to do business with the inferior agency only if it is at least ten dollars a year cheaper. So every dollar stolen from the customer comes, indirectly, out of the revenue of the protection agency. If the agency is one that guarantees performance by insuring its customers against losses, the connection is more direct. Either way, it is very much in the interest of the men running a protection agency to see that their employees do not take bribes. The only bribe it would pay the agency to take would be one for more than the value of the goods stolen—a poor deal for the thief.

This does not mean that employees of protection agencies will never take bribes. The interests of the employee and of the agency are not identical. It does mean that the men running the agencies will do their best to keep their men honest. That is more than you can say for a police force. Organized crime, if it continues to exist under anarcho-capitalism, should be in a much weaker position than it now is. In addition, as I shall argue later, most of the things that organized crime now makes money on would be legal in an anarcho-capitalist society. Thus both its size and its popularity would be greatly reduced.

What about the possibility of the mafia getting its own protection agency? In order for such a firm to provide its clients with the service they want—protection against the consequences of their crimes—it must either get the other protection agencies to agree to arbitration by a court that approves of crime or refuse to go to arbitration at all. In order to do the first, it must offer the other agencies terms so good that their customers are willing to be stolen from; as in the previous case, this reduces to the thief bribing the victim by more than the amount stolen, which is improbable. If it refuses to accept arbitration, then the mafia's protection agency finds itself constantly in conflict with the other protection agencies. The victims of theft will be willing to pay more to be protected than the thieves will pay to be able to steal (since stolen goods are worth less to the thief than to the victim). Therefore the noncriminal protection agencies will find it profitable to spend more to defeat the criminal agency than the criminal agency could spend to defeat them. In effect, the criminals fight a hopeless war with the rest of society and are destroyed.

Another and related argument against anarcho-capitalism is that the "strongest" protection agency will always win, the big fish will eat the little fish, and the justice you get will depend on the military strength of the agency you patronize.

This is a fine description of governments, but protection agencies are not territorial sovereigns. An agency which settles its disputes on the battlefield has already lost, however many battles it wins. Battles are expensive—also dangerous for clients whose front yards get turned into free-fire zones. The clients will find a less flamboyant protector.

No clients means no money to pay the troops. Perhaps the best way to see why anarcho-capitalism would be so much more peaceful than our present system is by analogy. Consider our world as it would be is the cost of moving from one country to another were zero. Everyone lives in a housetrailer and speaks the same language. One day, the president of France announces that because of troubles with neighboring countries, new military taxes are being levied and conscription will begin shortly. The next morning the president of France finds himself ruling a peaceful but empty landscape, the population having been reduced to himself, three generals, and twenty-seven war correspondents.

We do not all live in housetrailers. But if we buy our protection from a private firm instead of from a government, we can buy it from a different firm as soon as we think we can get a better deal. We can change protectors without changing countries.

The risk of private protection agencies throwing their weight—and lead—around is not great, provided there are lots of them. Which brings us to the second and far more serious argument against anarcho-capitalism.

The protection agencies will have a large fraction of the armed might of the society. What can prevent them from getting together and using that might to set themselves up as a government?

In some ultimate sense, nothing can prevent that save a populace possessing arms and willing, if necessary, to use them. That is one reason I am against gun-control legislation.

But there are safeguards less ultimate than armed resistance. After all, our present police departments, national guard, and armed forces already possess most of the armed might. Why have they not combined to run the country for their own benefit? Neither soldiers nor policemen are especially well paid; surely they could impose a better settlement at gunpoint.

The complete answer to that question comprises nearly the whole of political science. A brief answer is that people act according to what they perceive as right, proper, and practical. The restraints which prevent a military coup are essentially restraints interior to the men with guns.

We must ask, not whether an anarcho-capitalist society would be safe from a power grab by the men with the guns (safety is not an available option), but whether it would be safer than our society is from a comparable seizure of power by the men with the guns. I think the answer is yes. In our society, the men who must engineer such a coup are politicians, military officers, and policemen, men selected precisely for the characteristic of desiring power and being good at using it. They are men who already believe that they have a right to push other men around—that is their job. They are particularly well qualified for the job of seizing power. Under anarcho-capitalism the men in control of protection agencies are selected for their ability to run an efficient business and please their customers. It is always possible that some will turn out to be secret power freaks as well, but it is surely less likely than under our system where the corresponding jobs are labeled "non-power freaks need not apply."

In addition to the temperament of potential conspirators, there is another relevant factor: the number of protection agencies. If there are only two or three agencies in the entire area now covered by the United States, a conspiracy among them may be practical. If there are 10,000 then when any group of them start acting like a government, their customers will hire someone else to protect them against their protectors.

How many agencies there are depends on what size agency does the most efficient job of protecting its clients. My own guess is that the number will be nearer 10,000 than 3. If the performance of present-day police forces is any indication, a protection agency protecting as many as one million people is far above optimum size.

My conclusion is one of guarded optimism. Once anarcho-capitalist institutions are established with widespread acceptance over a large area, they should be reasonably stable against internal threats.

Are such institutions truly anarchist? Are the private protection agencies I have described actually governments in disguise? No. Under my definition of government—which comes closer than any other, I think, to describing why people call some things governments and not others—they are not governments! They have no rights which individuals do not have, and they therefore cannot engage in legitimized coercion.

Most people, myself included, believe that an individual has the right to use force to prevent another from violating his rights—stealing from him, say, or murdering him. Most agree that the victim has a right to take back what the thief has stolen and to use force to do so. Social contract theories start from the premise that individuals have these rights and delegate them to the government. In order for such a government to be legitimate, it must be established by unanimous consent, otherwise it has no special rights over those who refuse to sign the "social contract." Under a system of private protection agencies, the actual agencies, like the ideal government, are merely acting as agents for willing clients who have employed the agencies to enforce their own rights. They claim no rights over non-clients other than the right to defend their clients against coercion—the same right every individual has. They do nothing that a private individual cannot do.

This does not mean that they will never coerce anyone. A protection agency, like a government, can make a mistake and arrest the wrong man. In exactly the same way, a private citizen can shoot at what he thinks is a prowler and bag the postman instead.

In each case, coercion occurs, but it occurs by accident and the coercer is liable for the consequences of his acts. The citizen can be indicted for postman-slaughter and the protection agency sued for false arrest. Once the facts that make an act coercive are known, it is no longer regarded as having been legitimate.

This is not true of government actions. In order to sue a policeman for false arrest I must prove not merely that I was innocent but that the policeman had no reason to suspect me. If I am locked up for twenty years and then proven innocent, I have no legal claim against the government for my lost time and mental anguish. It is recognized that the government made a mistake, but the government is allowed to make mistakes and need not pay for them like the rest of us. If, knowing that I am innocent, I try to escape arrest and a policeman shoots me down, he is entirely within his rights and I am the criminal. If, to keep him from, shooting me, I shoot him in self-defense, I am guilty of murder, even after it is proved that I was innocent of the theft and so doing no more than defending myself against the government's (unintentional) coercion.

This difference between the rights claimed by a private protection agency and those claimed by a government affects more than the semantic question of what is or is not anarchy. It is one of the crucial reasons why a government, however limited, can more easily grow into a tyranny than can a system of private protection agencies. Even the most limited government has the sort of special rights I have described; everything I said in the previous paragraph was true of this country in its earliest and (for white males) freest days.

Such special rights allow a government to kill off its opponents and then apologize for the mistake. Unless the evidence of criminal intent is very clear, the murderers are immune from punishment. Even when the evidence is overwhelming, as in the case of the 1969 Chicago Black Panther raid, there is no question of trying those responsible for their actual crime. The Cook County state attorney responsible for the raid, in which two men were killed, and the police officers who executed it, were eventually charged not with conspiracy to commit murder but with obstruction of justice—not, in other words, with killing people but with lying about it afterwards.

This is not an isolated instance of the miscarriage of justice; it is the inevitable result of a system under which the government has certain special rights, above and beyond the rights of ordinary individuals—among them the right not to be held responsible for its mistakes. When these rights are taken away, when the agent of government is reduced to the status of a private citizen and has the same rights and responsibilities as his neighbors, what remains is no longer a government.

> *...a policeman...is protected by the legislative and judicial arms in the peculiar rights and prerogatives that go with his high office, including especially the right to judge the laity at his will, to sweat and mug them, and to subdue their resistance by beating out their brains.—H.L. Mencken,* Prejudices

(State attorney Hanrahan and his codefendants were eventually acquitted, but in 1982, thirteen years after the raid, a civil case by the survivors and the mothers of the two men who were killed was settled for $1.85 million, paid by the city, county, and federal governments.)

Is Anarcho-Capitalism Libertarian?

> *A man who wants protection will fire patrolmen who waste their time harassing minorities... No private policeman has ever spent many hours at a restroom peephole in hopes of apprehending deviates.*
> *—William Woodldridge*

I have described how a private system of courts and police might function, but not the laws it would produce and enforce; I have discussed institutions, not results. That is why I have used the term anarcho-capitalist, which describes the institutions, rather than libertarian. Whether these institutions will produce a libertarian society—a society in which each person is free to do as he likes with himself and his property as long as he does not use either to initiate force against others—remains to be proven.

Under some circumstances they will not. If almost everyone believes strongly that heroin addiction is so horrible that it should not be permitted anywhere under any circumstances, anarcho-capitalist institutions will produce laws against heroin. Laws are being produced for a market, and that is what the market wants.

But market demands are in dollars, not votes. The legality of heroin will be determined, not by how many are for or against but by how high a cost each side is willing to bear in order to get its way. People who want to control other people's lives are rarely eager to pay for the privilege; they usually expect to be paid for the "services" they provide for their victims. And those on the receiving end—whether of laws against drugs, laws against pornography, or laws against sex—get a lot more pain out of the oppression than their oppressors get pleasure. They are willing to pay a much higher price to be left alone than anyone is willing to pay to push them around. For that reason the laws of an anarcho-capitalist society should be heavily biased toward freedom.

So compulsory Puritanism—"crimes without victims"—should be much rarer under anarcho-capitalism than under political institutions. We can get some idea of how rare by considering the costs such laws now impose on their victims and the value of such laws to their supporters. If the value of a law to its supporters is less than its cost to its victims, that law, by the logic of the previous chapter, will not survive in an anarcho-capitalist society.

Heroin addicts pay over $2 billion a year for heroin. If heroin were legal, its cost would be very low. Almost all of the $2 billion now spent for heroin is the cost of the law, not the habit; addicts bear additional costs in prison sentences, overdoses caused by the poor quality control typical of illegal products, and other side effects of the laws against heroin. Heroin addicts would therefore be willing, if necessary, to bear a cost of $2 billion or more in order to have the drug legal. It would cost the nonaddicts about ten dollars per capita or forty dollars per family, per year, to match that.

If the choice had to be made on an all-or-nothing basis, public opinion is probably so strongly against heroin that people would be willing to bear that cost. But one of the advantages of a market system of laws is its ability to tailor its product to its customers geographically, as well as in other ways. If the maximum return comes from having heroin illegal in some places and legal in others, that is what will happen.

Most of the population lives in areas where there are very few heroin addicts. For those people the cost of having heroin made illegal locally would be very small; there would be no one on the other side bidding to have it legal, except perhaps a few New York addicts who wanted to vacation away from the big city and bring their habit with them. In those areas protection agencies would accept arbitration agencies that viewed using or selling heroin as a crime. But people in those areas would have little to gain by paying a much higher price to have heroin illegal in New York as well.

That leaves 8 million New York nonaddicts bidding against 100,000 New York addicts, raising the cost to the nonaddicts of keeping heroin illegal in New York to over $100 a year per person. I predict that, if anarcho-capitalist institutions appeared in this country tomorrow, heroin would be legal in New York and illegal in most other places. Marijuana would be legal over most of the country.

By now the reader may be getting confused. This is natural enough; I am describing lawmaking in economic terms, and you are used to thinking of it in political terms. When I talk of bidding for one law or another, I do not mean that we will have a legislature that literally auctions off laws. I mean that each person's desire for the kinds of laws he believes in will be reflected in the different rates he is willing to pay his protection agency according to how good a job it does of getting him the law he wants. This set of "demands" for laws will be reconciled through the sort of bargaining described in the previous chapter. The process is analogous to the way you and I "bid" to have a piece of private land used the way we want it used. Our demands—for the food that can be grown on it, the buildings that can be built on it, possible recreational uses, or whatever—determine how it eventually gets used.

What I have been saying is that, just as the market allocates resources to producing illegal drugs in response to the demands of those who want to use them, it would make use of those drugs legal in response to the same demand. The obvious question is why the same argument does not hold for making murder legal. The answer is that murder hurts someone, and it is worth much more to the victim not to be shot than to the murderer to shoot him. There is a market demand from me for a law saying that you cannot kill me. "Crimes without victims" do not hurt anyone, except in the vague sense of arousing moral indignation in people upset over their neighbors' sins. There is little market demand for laws against them.

The same geographical effect that I described for drug laws would apply to other laws as well. Under present institutions the areas over which laws apply are determined by historical accident. If a majority of the population of a state supports one kind of law, everyone in the state gets it. Under anarcho-capitalism, insofar as it would be possible, everyone would have his own law. Diversity of law cannot be unlimited, since the same law must cover both parties to a dispute. But it is possible to have much more diversity than our present system allows. Where the majority and minority, or minorities, are geographically separate, the majority is mainly concerned with having the laws it wants for itself; it is only our political system that imposes those laws on the minority as well.

At this point in the argument, the question of poor people is often raised. Since dollars vote, won't the poor lose out?

Yes and no. The more money you are willing to spend for protection, the better quality you can get and the better you will be able to get the details of law the way you want them. This is notoriously true now. Our political system of police and courts provides much better service to those with higher incomes. Here, as elsewhere, although the market will not bring equality, it will greatly improve the position of the poor.

Why? Because the market allows people to concentrate their resources on what is most important to them. I discussed this point earlier, in the context of the poor man buying a necessity outbidding the rich man who wants the same good for a luxury. Protection from crime is not a luxury.

Currently, government expenditures on police and courts run about forty dollars a year per capita. According to Friedman's law, that means that private protection of the same average quality would cost about twenty dollars. There are many inhabitants of the ghetto who would be delighted to pay twenty dollars a year if in exchange they actually got protection; many of them have more than that stolen every year as a result of the lousy protection they get from our government-run protection system. They would be even happier if at the same time they were relieved of the taxes that pay for the protection that the government police do not give them.

In spite of popular myths about capitalism oppressing the poor, the poor are worst off in those things provided by government, such as schooling, police protection, and justice. There are more good cars in the ghetto than good schools. Putting protection on the market would mean better protection for the poor, not worse.

And, as a Free Bonus

> *If I was running for office, I'd change me name, and have printed on me cards: "Give him a chanst; he can't be worse."—Mr. Doodley*

A system of private courts and police has certain special advantages over our present government system, advantages associated with the political issues of freedom and stability discussed in the previous two chapters. Private courts and police have, in addition, the same advantages over the corresponding government institutions that market arrangements usually have over socialist arrangements.

When a consumer buys a product on the market, he can compare alternative brands. In the case of protection, he can compare how good a job different agencies do and their prices. His information is imperfect, as it is in making most decisions; he may make a mistake. But at least alternatives exist; they are there to be looked at. He can talk with neighbors who patronize different protection agencies, examine the contracts and rates they offer, study figures on the crime rates among their customers.

When you elect a politician, you buy nothing but promises. You may know how one politician ran the country for the past four years, but not how his competitor might have run it. You can compare 1968 Fords, Chryslers, and Volkswagens, but nobody will ever be able to compare the Nixon administration of 1968 with the Humphrey and Wallace administrations of the same year. It is as if we had only Fords from 1920 to 1928, Chryslers from 1928 to 1936, and then had to decide what firm would make a better car for the next four years. Perhaps an expert automotive engineer could make an educated guess as to whether Ford had used the technology of 1920 to satisfy the demands of 1920 better than Chrysler had used the technology of 1928 to satisfy the demands of 1928. The rest of us might just as well flip a coin. If you throw in Volkswagen or American Motors, which had not made any cars in America but wanted to, the situation becomes still worse. Each of us would have to know every firm intimately in order to have any reasonable basis for deciding which we preferred.

In the same way, in order to judge a politician who has held office, one must consider not only how his administration turned out but the influence of a multitude of relevant factors over which he had no control, ranging from the makeup of Congress to the weather at harvest time. Judging politicians who have not yet held office is still more difficult.

Not only does a consumer have better information than a voter, it is of more use to him. If I investigate alternative brands of cars or protection, decide which is best for me, and buy it, I get it. If I investigate alternative politicians and vote accordingly, I get what the majority votes for. The chance that my vote will be the deciding factor is negligible.

Imagine buying cars the way we buy governments. Ten thousand people would get together and agree to vote, each for the car he preferred. Whichever car won, each of the ten thousand would have to buy it. It would not pay any of us to make any serious effort to find out which car was best; whatever I decide, my car is being picked for me by the other members of the group. Under such institutions, the quality of cars would quickly decline.

That is how I must buy products on the political marketplace. I not only cannot compare the alternative products; it would not be worth my while to do so even if I could. This may have something to do with the quality of the goods sold on that market. Caveat emptor.

Socialism, Limited Government, Anarchy, and Bikinis

Most varieties of socialism implicitly assume unanimous agreement on goals. Everyone works for the glory of the nation, the common good, or whatever, and everyone agrees, at least in some general sense, on what that goal means. The economic problem, traditionally defined as the problem of allocating limited resources to diverse ends, does not exist; economics is reduced to the "engineering" problem of how best to use the available resources to achieve the common end. The organization of a capitalist society implicitly assumes that different people have different ends and that the institutions of the society must allow for that difference.

This is one of the things behind the socialist claim that capitalism emphasizes competition whereas socialism emphasizes cooperation; it is one of the reasons why socialism seems, in the abstract, to be such an attractive system. If we all have different ends, we are, in a certain sense, in conflict with each other; each of us wishes to have the limited resources available used for his ends. The institution of private property allows for cooperation within that competition; we trade with each other in order that each may best use his resources to his ends, but the fundamental conflict of ends remains. Does this mean that socialism is better? No more than the desirability of sunny weather means that women should always wear bikinis or that men should never carry umbrellas.

There is a difference between what institutions allow and what they require. If in a capitalist society everyone is convinced of the desirability of one common goal, there is nothing in the structure of capitalist institutions to prevent them from cooperating to attain it. Capitalism allows for a conflict of ends; it does not require it. Socialism does not allow for it. This does not mean that if we set up socialist institutions everyone will instantly have the same ends.

The experiment has been tried; they do not. It means rather that a socialist society will work only if people do have the same ends. If they do not it will collapse or, worse, develop, as did the Soviet Union, into a monstrous parody of socialist ideals. The experiment has been done many times on a more modest scale in this country. Communes that survive start with a common end, whether provided by a strong religion or a charismatic leader. Others do not.

I have encountered precisely the same error among libertarians who prefer limited government to anarcho-capitalism. Limited government, they say, can guarantee uniform justice based on objective principles. Under anarcho-capitalism, the law varies from place to place and person to person, according to the irrational desires and beliefs of the different customers that different protection and arbitration agencies must serve.

This argument assumes that the limited government is set up by a population most or all of whose members believe in the same just principles of law. Given such a population, anarcho-capitalism will produce that same uniform, just law; there will be no market for any other. But just as capitalism can accommodate to a diversity of individual ends, so anarcho-capitalism can accommodate to a diversity of individual judgments about justice.

An ideal objectivist society with a limited government is superior to an anarcho-capitalist society in precisely the same sense that an ideal socialist society is superior to a capitalist society. Socialism does better with perfect people than capitalism does with imperfect people; limited government does better with perfect people than anarcho-capitalism with imperfect. And it is better to wear a bikini with the sun shining than a raincoat when it is raining. That is no argument against carrying an umbrella.

4

Market for Liberty (excerpt)

Morris and Linda Tannehill

Throughout history, the means of dealing with aggression (crime) has been punishment. Traditionally, it has been held that when a man commits a crime against society, the government, acting as the agent of society, must punish him. However, because punishment has not been based on the principle of righting the wrong but only of causing the criminal "to undergo pain, loss, or suffering," it has actually been revenge. This principle of vengeance is expressed by the old saying, "An eye for an eye, a tooth for a tooth," which means: "When you destroy a value of mine, I'll destroy a value of yours." Present day penology no longer makes such demands; instead of the eye or the tooth, it takes the criminal's life (via execution), or a part of his life (via imprisonment), and/or his possessions (via fines). As can be readily seen, the principle—vengeance—is the same, and it inevitably results in a compound loss of value, first the victim's, then the criminal's. Because destroying a value belonging to the criminal does nothing to compensate the innocent victim for his loss but only causes further destruction, the principle of vengeance ignores, and in fact opposes, justice.

When an aggressor causes the loss, damage, or destruction of an innocent man's values, justice demands that the aggressor pay for his crime, not by forfeiting a part of his life to "society," but by repaying the victim for his loss, plus all expenses directly occasioned by the aggression (such as the expense of apprehending the aggressor). By destroying the victim's values, the aggressor has created a debt which he owes to the victim and which the principle of justice demands must be paid. With the principle of justice in operation, there is only one loss of value; and, while this loss must initially be sustained by the victim, ultimately it is the aggressor—the one who caused the loss—who must pay for it.

There is a further fallacy in the belief that when a man commits a crime against society, the government, acting as the agent of society, must punish him. This fallacy is the assumption that society is a living entity and that, therefore, a crime can be committed against it. A society is no more than the sum of all the individual persons of which it is composed: it can have no existence apart from, or in contradistinction to, those individual persons. A crime is always committed against one or more persons; a crime cannot be committed against that amorphous non-entity known as "society." Even if some particular crime injured every member of a given society, the crime would still have been committed against individuals, not society, since it is only the individuals who are distinct, separate, independent, living entities. Since a crime can only be committed against individuals, a criminal cannot be rationally regarded as "owing a debt to society"; nor can he "pay his debt to society": the only debt he owes is to the injured individual(s).

Every dispute is between aggressor(s) and victim(s): neither society nor its members as a group have any direct interest in the matter. It is true that all honest members of a society have a general interest in seeing aggressors brought to justice in order to discourage further aggression. This interest, however, applies not to specific acts of aggression but to the total social structure which either encourages or discourages acts of aggression. An interest in maintaining a just social structure does not constitute a direct interest in the solution of any particular dispute involving aggression.

Because crimes cannot be committed against society, it is fallacious to regard government as an agent of society for the punishment of crime. Nor can government be considered be the agent of the individual members of society, since these individuals have never signed a contract naming the government as their agent. There is, therefore, no valid reason for government officials to be designated the arbiters of disputes and rectifiers of injustice.

Granted, we are used to the governmental punishment-of-crime, so that to many people it seems "normal" and "reasonable," and any other means of dealing with aggression seems suspicious and strange; but an unbiased examination of the facts shows that this governmental system is actually traditional rather than rational.

Since neither "society" nor government can have any rational interest in bringing a specific aggressor to justice, who is interested? Obviously, the victim—and secondarily, those to whom the victim's welfare is a value, such as his family, friends, and business associates. According to the principle of justice, those who have suffered the loss from an aggressive act should be compensated (at the aggressor's expense), and, therefore, it is those who have suffered the loss who have an interest in seeing the aggressor brought to justice.

The steps which the victim may morally take to bring the aggressor to justice and exact reparations from him rest on the right to property, which, in turn, rests on the right to life. A man's property is his property, and this fact of ownership is not changed if the property comes into the possession of an aggressor by means of an act of force. The aggressor may be in possession of the property, but only the owner has a moral right to it. To illustrate: Suppose that as you come out of a building you see a stranger in the driver's seat of your car, preparing to drive it away. Would you have the moral right to push him out and thus regain possession of your car by force? Yes, since the thief's temporary possession does not alter the fact that it is your property. The thief used a substitute for initiated force when he attempted to steal your car, and you are morally justified in using retaliatory force to regain it.

Suppose that instead of catching the thief immediately you are forced to chase him and your car for two blocks and only catch up with him as he's stopped by a train. Do you still have the right to push him out and regain your car? Yes, since the passage of time does not erode your right to possess your property.

Suppose instead that the thief gets away, but that two months later you spot him downtown getting out of your car. You verify by serial number that it is, indeed, your car. Do you have the moral right to drive it away? Yes; again the passage of time makes no difference to your property rights.

Suppose that instead of yourself it is the detective you have hired to recover the car who spots the thief getting out of it. The detective, acting as your agent, has the right to repossess your car, just as you would.

You find that a front fender and headlight of your car are smashed in, due to the aggressor's careless driving. Repairs cost you $150. Do you have the right to collect this amount from the aggressor? Yes, you were the innocent victim of an act of aggression; it is the thief, not the victim, who is morally obligated to pay all costs occasioned by his aggression.

To summarize: the ownership of property is not changed if the property is stolen, nor is it eroded by the passage of time. The theft, damage, or destruction of another person's property constitutes an act of coercion, and the victim has a moral right to use retaliatory force to repossess his property. He also has a right to collect from the aggressor compensation for any costs occasioned by the aggression. If he wishes, the victim may hire an agent or agents to perform any of these actions in his place.

It should be noted that aggression often harms not only the victim but also those who are closely associated with him. For example, when a man is assaulted and seriously injured, his family may be caused expense, as well as anxiety. If he is a key man in his business, his employer or his partners and/or his company may suffer financial loss. All this destruction of value is a direct result of the irrational behavior of the aggressor and, since actions do have consequences, the aggressor has the responsibility of making reparations for these secondary losses, as well as for the primary loss suffered by the victim. There are practical limits to the amount of these secondary reparations. First, no one would bother to make such a claim unless the reparations he hoped to be paid were substantial enough to offset the expense, time, and inconvenience of making the claim. Second, the total amount of reparations which can be collected is limited by the aggressor's ability to pay, and first consideration goes to the victim. For the sake of simplicity, only the victim's loss will be dealt with here, but all the principles and considerations which apply to him apply as well to any others who have suffered a direct and serious loss as a result of the aggression.

In the process of collecting from the aggressor, the victim (or his agents) may not carelessly or viciously destroy values belonging to the aggressor or take more from him than the original property (or an equivalent value) plus costs occasioned by the aggression. If the victim does so, he puts himself in debt to the aggressor (unless, of course, the aggressor has made the destruction inevitable by refusing to give up the victim's property without a fight).

If the accused aggressor claims he is innocent or that the amount of reparations claimed by the victim is excessive, a situation of dispute exists between them which may require arbitration. The conditions of such arbitration, the forces impelling both parties to accept it as binding, and the market guarantees of its justice will now be examined.

In a laissez-faire society, insurance companies would sell policies covering the insured against loss of value by aggression (the cost of the policy based on the worth of the values covered and the amount of risk). Since aggressors would, in most instances, pay the major costs of their aggression, the insurance companies would lose only when the aggressor could not be identified and/or apprehended, when he died before making full reparations, or when the reparations were too great for him to be able to pay in his lifetime. Since the companies would recover most of their losses and since aggression would be much less common in a free-market society, costs of aggression insurance would be low, and almost all individuals could afford to be covered. For this reason, we shall deal primarily with the case of an insured individual who becomes the victim of aggression.

Upon suffering the aggression (assuming that immediate self-defense was either impossible or inappropriate), the victim would, as soon as possible, call his insurance company. The company would immediately send an investigator to determine the validity of his claim and the extent of the loss. When the amount was ascertained, the company would fully compensate the victim within the limits of the terms of the insurance policy. It would also act where feasible to minimize his inconvenience—e.g., lend him a car until his stolen one is recovered or replaced—in order to promote customer good will and increase sales (anyone ever heard of a government police department doing this?).

When the terms of the policy had been fulfilled, the insurance company, exercising its right of subrogation, would attempt to identify and apprehend the aggressor in order to recover its losses. At this point, the victim would be relieved of any further responsibilities in the case, except possibly appearing as a witness at any arbitration hearings.

If necessary, the insurance company would use detectives to apprehend the aggressor. Whether it used its own company detectives or hired an independent defense service would depend on which course was more feasible under the circumstances. Obviously, a competitive private enterprise defense agency, whether an auxiliary of a particular insurance company or an independent firm hired by several insurance companies (as are some claims adjusting companies today) would be far more efficient at the business of solving crimes and apprehending aggressors than are the present governmental police departments. In a free market, competition impels toward excellence.

Upon apprehending the aggressor, the insurance company's representatives would present him with a bill covering all damages and costs. Their first approach would be as peaceful as the situation permitted, since force is a non-productive expenditure of energy and resources and is, therefore, avoided by the market whenever possible. First, the insurance company's representatives would attempt a voluntary settlement with the accused aggressor. If he was obviously guilty and the amount of reparations requested was just, it would be in his interest to agree to this settlement and avoid involving an arbitration agency, since the cost of any arbitration would be added on to his bill if he lost in his attempt to cheat justice.

If the accused aggressor claimed innocence or wished to contest the amount of the bill and he and the insurance company's representatives could come to no agreement, the matter would have to be submitted to binding arbitration, just as would a contractual dispute. Legislation forcing the parties to submit to binding arbitration would be unnecessary, since each party would find arbitration to be in his own self-interest. Nor would it be necessary to have legal protection for the rights of all involved, because the structure of the market situation would protect them. For example, the insurance company would not dare to bring charges against a man unless it had very good evidence of his guilt, nor would it dare to ignore any request he made for arbitration. If the insurance company blundered in this manner, the accused, especially if he were innocent, could bring charges against the company, forcing it to drop its original charges and/or billing it for damages. Nor could it refuse to submit to arbitration on his charges against it, for it would do serious damage to its business reputation if it did; and in a free-market context, in which economic success is dependent on individual or corporate reputation, no company can afford to build a reputation of carelessness, unreliability, and unfairness.

It is worthy of note here that the notion of always presuming a man innocent until he is proved guilty by a jury trial can be irrational and sometimes downright ridiculous. For instance, when a man commits a political assassination in plain sight of several million television viewers, many of whom can positively identify him from the films of the incident, and is arrested on the spot with the gun still in his hand, it is foolish to attempt to ignore the facts and pretend he is innocent until a jury can rule on the matter. Though the burden of proof always rests on the accuser and the accused must always be given the benefit of the doubt, a man should be presumed neither innocent nor guilty until there is sufficient evidence to make a clear decision, and when the evidence is in he should be presumed to be whatever the facts indicate he is. An arbiter's decision is necessary only when the evidence is unclear and/or there is a dispute which cannot be resolved without the help of an unbiased third party.

The accused aggressor would desire arbitration if he wanted to prove his innocence or felt that he was being overcharged for his aggression, since without arbitration the charges against him would stand as made and he would have to pay the bill. By means of arbitration, he could prove his innocence and thus avoid paying reparations or if guilty he would have some say about the amount of reparations.

If innocent, he would be especially eager for arbitration, not only to confirm his good reputation, but to collect damages from the insurance company for the trouble it had caused him (and thereby rectify the injustice against him).

A further guarantee against the possibility of an innocent man being railroaded is that every individual connected with his case would be fully responsible for his own actions, and none could hide behind legal immunity as do governmental police and jailers. If you knew that a prisoner put into your custody to work off his debt could, if innocent, demand and get reparations from you for holding him against his will, you would be very reluctant to accept any prisoners without being fully satisfied as to their guilt.

Thus, the unhampered market would, in this area as in any other, set up a situation in which irrationality and injustice were automatically discouraged and penalized without any resort to statutory law and government.

The insurance company and the accused aggressor, as disputing parties, would mutually choose an arbitration agency (or agencies, in case they wished to provide for an appeal) and contractually bind themselves to abide by its decision. In the event they were unable to agree on a single arbitration agency, each could designate his own agency preference and the two agencies would hear the case jointly, with the prior provision that if they disagreed on the decision they would submit the case to a third agency previously selected by both for final arbitration. Such a course might be more expensive.

The insurance company could order its defense agency to incarcerate the accused aggressor before and during arbitration (which would probably be only a matter of a few days, since the market is always more efficient than the bumbling government), but in doing so they would have to take two factors into consideration. First, if the accused were shown to be innocent, the insurance company and defense agency would owe him reparations for holding him against his will. Even if he were judged guilty, they would be responsible to make reparations if they had treated him with force in excess of what the situation warranted; not being government agents, they would have no legal immunity from the consequences of their actions. Second, holding a man is expensive—it requires room, board, and guards. For these reasons, the defense company would put the accused aggressor under no more restraint than was deemed necessary to keep him from running off and hiding.

It would be the job of the arbitration agency to ascertain the guilt or innocence of the accused and to determine the amount of reparations due. In settling the reparations payment, the arbiters would operate according to the principle that justice in a case of aggression consists of requiring the aggressor to compensate the victim for his loss insofar as is humanly possible. Since each case of aggression is unique—involving different people, actions, and circumstances, reparations payments would be based on the circumstances of each case, rather than on statutory law and legal precedent. Although cases of aggression vary widely, there are several expense factors which, in varying combinations, determine the amount of loss and, thus, the size of the reparations.

A basic expense factor is the cost of any property stolen, damaged, or destroyed. The aggressor would be required to return any stolen property still in his possession. If he had destroyed a replaceable item, such as a television set, he would have to pay the victim an amount of money equal to its value so that the victim could replace it. If the aggressor had destroyed an item which couldn't be replaced but which had a market value (for example, a famous art work like the Mona Lisa), he would still have to pay its market value, even though another one couldn't be bought. The principle here is that, even though the value can never be replaced, the victim should at least be left no worse off financially than if he had sold it instead of losing it to a thief. Justice requires the aggressor to compensate the victim insofar as is humanly possible, and replacing an irreplaceable value is impossible.

In addition to the basic expense of stolen and destroyed property, an act of aggression may cause several additional costs, for which the aggressor would be responsible to pay. An aggressor who stole a salesman's car might cause the salesman to lose quite a bit of business—an additional financial cost. A rapist who attacked and beat a woman would be responsible not only for paying medical bills for all injuries he had caused her and reparations for time she might lose from work, but he would also owe his victim compensation for her pain and suffering, both mental and physical. Besides all debts owed to the primary victim, the aggressor might also owe secondary reparations to others who had suffered indirectly because of his actions (for example, the victim's family). In addition to these expenses, occasioned by the aggression itself, the aggressor would also be responsible for any reasonable costs involved in apprehending him and for the cost of arbitration (which would probably be paid by the loser in any case).

Since the arbitration agency's service would be the rendering of just decisions, and since justice is the basis on which they would compete in the market, the arbiters would make every attempt to fix reparations at a fair level, in accordance with market values. For instance, if the defense company had run up an excessively high bill in apprehending the aggressor, the arbiters would refuse to charge the aggressor for the excessive expense. Thus, the defense company would be forced to pay for its own poor business practices instead of "passing the buck" to someone else.

In case the reparations amounted to more than the aggressor could possibly earn in his lifetime (for example, an unskilled laborer who set a million dollar fire), the insurance company and any other claimants would negotiate a settlement for whatever amount he could reasonably be expected to pay over time. This would be done because it would be no profit to them to set the reparations higher than the aggressor could ever hope to pay and thus discourage him from working to discharge his obligation. It is worth noting here that quite a large percentage of a worker's pay can be taken for a long period of time without totally removing his incentive to live and work. At present the average American pays out well over a third of his income in taxes and expects to do so for the rest of his life, yet those who go on the government "welfare" dole are still in the minority.

Many values which can be destroyed or damaged by aggression are not only irreplaceable, they are also non-exchangeable—that is, they can't be exchanged in the market, so no monetary value can be placed on them. Examples of non-exchangeable values are life, a hand or eye, the life of a loved one, the safety of a kidnapped child, etc. When confronted with the problem of fixing the amount of reparations for a non-exchangeable value, many people immediately ask, "But how can you set a price on a human life?" The answer is that when an arbitration agency sets the reparations for a loss of life it isn't trying to put a monetary price on that life, any more than is an insurance company when it sells a $20,000 life insurance policy. It is merely trying to compensate the victim (or his survivors) to the fullest extent possible under the circumstances.

The problem in fixing reparations for loss of life or limb is that the loss occurred in one kind of value (non-exchangeable) and repayment must be made in another kind (money). These two kinds of values are incommensurable—neither can be measured in terms of the other. The value which has been destroyed not only can't be replaced with a similar value, it can't even be replaced with an equivalent sum of money, since there is no way to determine what is equivalent. And yet, monetary payment is the practical way to make reparations.

It is useful to remember here that justice consists of requiring the aggressor to compensate his victims for their losses insofar as is humanly possible, since no one can be expected to do the impossible. Even a destroyed item which has a market value can't always be replaced (e.g., the Mona Lisa). To demand that justice require the impossible is to make justice impossible. To reject the reparations system because it can't always replace the destroyed value with an equivalent value is like rejecting medicine because the patient can't always be restored to as good a state of health as he enjoyed before his illness. Justice, like medicine, must be contextual—it must not demand what is impossible in any given context. The question, then, is not how arbiters can set a price on life and limb; it is, rather, "How can they see that the victim is fairly compensated, insofar as is humanly possible, without doing injustice to the aggressor by requiring overcompensation?"

In attempting to reach a fair compensation figure, the arbitration agency would act, not as a judge handing down a sentence, but as a mediator resolving a conflict which the disputants can't settle themselves. The highest possible limit on the amount of reparations is, obviously, the aggressor's ability to pay, short of killing his incentive to live and earn. The lowest limit is the total amount of economic loss suffered (with no compensation. for such non-exchangeables as anxiety, discomfort, and inconvenience). The reparations payment must be set somewhere in the broad range between these two extremes. The function of the arbitration agency would be to aid the disputants in reaching a reasonable figure between these extremes, not to achieve the impossible task of determining the monetary value of a non-exchangeable.

Although the limits within which the reparations payment for a non-exchangeable would be set are very broad, the arbitration agency could not capriciously set the amount of reparations at any figure it pleased. An arbitration agency would be a private business competing in a free market, and the action of the market itself would provide guidelines and controls regarding the "price" of aggression, just as it does with any other price. Any free-market business, including an arbitration agency, can survive and prosper only as customers choose to patronize it instead of its competitors. An arbitration agency must be chosen by both (or all) disputants in a case, which means that its record of settling previous disputes of a similar nature must be more satisfactory, to both complainant and defendant, than the records of its competitors. Any agency which consistently set reparations too high or too low in the opinion of the majority of its customers and potential customers would lose business rapidly. It would have to either adjust its payments to fit consumer demand...or go out of business. In this way, arbitration agencies whose levels of reparation displeased consumers would be weeded out (as would any other business which failed to satisfy customers). Arbitration agencies which wanted to stay in business would adjust reparation levels to meet consumer demand. In a relatively short time, reparations payments for various non-exchangeable losses would become pretty well standardized, just as are charges for various kinds and amounts of insurance protection.

The manner in which the amount of reparations for a non-exchangeable value would be set by the action of the free market is very similar to the way in which the market sets any price. No good or service has an intrinsic monetary value built into it by the nature sellers are willing to take for it. "Value" means value to the people who trade that commodity in the market. All the traders determine what the price will be. In a similar way, the people who bought the services of arbitration agencies would determine the levels of reparations payments—the levels they considered just and fair compensation for various kinds of losses. It is impossible for us to foresee, in advance of the actual market situation, just where these levels would be set. But we can see, from a knowledge of how a free market operates, that the market would determine them in accordance with consumer desires.

Each reparation claim would be a complex combination of compensations for losses of various kinds of exchangeable and non-exchangeable values. For example, if a hoodlum beat a man and stole \$100 from him, the aggressor would be required not only to return the \$100 but also to pay the victim's medical bills, his lost earnings, compensation for pain and suffering, and reparations for any permanent injuries sustained. If the victim were a key man in his business, the aggressor would also have to pay the business for the loss of his services. Each reparation claim is also a highly individual matter, because the destruction of the same thing may be a much greater loss to one man than to another. While the loss of a finger is tragic for anyone, it is a much more stunning blow to a professional concert pianist than to an accountant. Because of the complexity and individuality of reparations claims, only a system of competing free-market arbitration agencies can satisfactorily solve the problem of what constitutes just payment for losses caused by aggression.

Murder poses a special problem in that it constitutes an act of aggression which, by its very nature, renders the victim incapable of ever collecting the debt owed by the aggressor. Nevertheless, the aggressor did create a debt, and the death of the creditor (victim) does not cancel this debt or excuse him from making payment. This point can be easily seen by supposing that the aggressor did not kill, but only critically injured the victim, in which case the aggressor would owe reparations for injuries sustained, time lost from work, physical disability, etc. But if the victim then died from his injuries before the debt could be paid, the debtor obviously would not be thereby released from his obligation.

In this connection, it is useful to recall what a debt actually is. A debt is property which morally belongs to one person but which is in the actual or potential possession of another. Since the debt occasioned by the attack on the victim would have been his property had he survived that attack, his death places it, together with the rest of his property, in his estate to become the property of his heirs. In addition to the primary debt owed to the estate of the victim, the aggressor also owes debts to all those whom the victim's death has caused a direct and major loss of value (such as his family), even though such people may also be his heirs. (Not to pay reparations to heirs simply because they will also inherit the reparations which would have been paid the victim had he survived, would be like refusing to pay them because they would inherit any other part of the victim's property.)

But suppose an aggressor murdered a grouchy old itinerant fruit picker who had neither family, friends, nor aggression insurance. Would the aggressor "get off scott free" just because his victim was of value to no one but himself and left no heirs to his property? No, the aggressor would still owe a debt to the fruit picker's estate, just as he would if there were an heir. The difference is that, without an heir, the estate (including the debt occasioned by the aggression) becomes unowned potential property. In our society, such unowned potential property is immediately expropriated by the government, as is much other unowned wealth. Such a practice can be justified only if one assumes that the government (or "the public") is the original and true owner of all property, and that individuals are merely permitted to hold property by the grace and at the pleasure of the government. In a free-market society, unowned wealth would belong to whatever person first went to the trouble of taking possession of it. In regard to the debt owed by an aggressor to the estate of his victim, this would mean that anyone who wished to go to the trouble and expense of finding the aggressor and, if necessary, proving him guilty before professional arbiters, would certainly deserve to collect the debt. This function could be performed by an individual, by an agency specially constituted for this purpose (though it seems unlikely that there would be enough situations of this nature to support such an agency), or by a defense agency or an insurance company. Insurance companies would be most likely to take care of this kind of aggression in order to deter violence and gain customer good will.

Before taking up the means by which an aggressor would be forced to pay reparations (if force were necessary), the position of an uninsured victim of aggression will be examined briefly. Whenever a demand for a service exists, the market moves to fill it. For this reason, a man who was uninsured would also have access to defense services and arbitration agencies. But, although he would have a similar recourse to justice, the uninsured man would find that his lack of foresight had put him at a disadvantage in several ways. The uninsured victim would not receive immediate compensation but would have to wait until the aggressor paid reparations (which might involve a span of years if the aggressor didn't have the money to discharge the debt immediately and had to pay it off in installments). Similarly, he would run the risk of being forced to forgo all or most of his compensation if the aggressor were not caught, died before being able to complete payment, or had incurred a debt too large to pay during his life. Also, the uninsured victim would have to bear all costs of apprehending the aggressor and, if necessary, of arbitration, until the aggressor was able to pay them back.

In addition to these monetary disadvantages, he would be put to extra inconvenience. If he wished to collect reparations, he would have to detect and apprehend the aggressor himself or (more likely) hire a defense agency to do it for him. He would also have to make his own arrangements for arbitration. Taking everything into consideration, a man would find aggression insurance well worth the expense, and there is little doubt that most people would have it.

* * *

Since aggression would be dealt with by forcing the aggressor to repay his victim for the damage caused (whenever the use of force was required), rather than by destroying values belonging to the aggressor, the free market would evolve a reparations-payment system vastly superior to and different from the present governmental prisons.

If the aggressor had the money to make his entire reparations payment immediately or could sell enough property to raise the money, he would do so and be free to go his way with no more than a heavy financial loss. Situations of this kind, however, would probably be very rare, because aggression is expensive. Even a small theft or destruction can quickly pile up a fairly large debt when related expenses, secondary payments to others who suffered because of the victim's loss, cost of defense and arbitration, etc., are taken into account. In a totally free society, men tend to be financially successful according to their merit. Few successful men would desire to commit aggression. Few unsuccessful men could afford to make immediate payment for it.

Assuming the aggressor could not make immediate payment of his entire debt, the method used to collect it would depend on the amount involved, the nature of the aggression, the aggressor's past record and present attitude, and any other pertinent variables. Several approaches suggest themselves.

If the aggression was not of a violent nature and the aggressor had a record of trustworthiness, it might be sufficient to leave him free and arrange a regular schedule of payments, just as would be done for any ordinary debt. If the aggressor could not be trusted to make regular payments, a voluntary arrangement could be made between the insurance company, the aggressor, and his employer, whereby the employer would be compensated for deducting the reparations payment from the aggressor's earnings each pay period.

If the aggressor were unable to find or hold a job because employers were unwilling to risk hiring him, he might have to seek employment from a company which made a practice of accepting untrustworthy workers at lower than market wages. (In an economy of full employment, some companies would be motivated to adopt such a practice in order to reach new sources of labor. Although the price of their product would remain close to that of their competitors, as prices are determined by supply and demand, the wages they paid would necessarily be lower to compensate for the extra risk involved in hiring employees of dubious character.) If the facts indicated that the aggressor was of an untrustworthy and/or violent nature, he would have to work off his debt while under some degree of confinement. The confinement would be provided by rectification companies—firms specializing in this field, who would maintain debtors workhouses (use of the term "prison" is avoided here because of the connotations of value-destruction attached to it). The labor of the men confined would be furnished to any companies seeking assured sources of labor, either by locating the debtors workhouses adjacent to their plants or by transporting the debtors to work each day. The debtors would work on jobs for wages, just as would ordinary employees, but the largest part of their earnings would be used to make reparations payments, with most of the rest going for their room and board, maintenance of the premises, guards, etc. To insure against refusal to work, the reparations payment would be deducted from each pay before room and board costs, so that if a man refused to work he would not eat, or at most would eat only a very minimal diet. There would be varying degrees of confinement to fit various cases. Many debtors workhouses might provide a very minimum amount of security, such as do a few present-day prison farms where inmates are told, "There are no fences to keep you here; however, if you run away, when you are caught you will not be allowed to come back here but will be sent to a regular prison instead." Such workhouses would give the debtor a weekly allowance out of his pay, with opportunities to buy small luxuries or, perhaps, to rent a better room. Weekend passes to visit family and friends, and even more extended vacations, might be arranged for those who had proved themselves sufficiently trustworthy.

Other workhouses would provide facilities of greater security, ranging up to a maximum security for individuals who had proved themselves extremely violent and dangerous. A man whose actions had forced his confinement in such a workhouse would find himself at a disadvantage in several ways. He would find he had less liberty, less luxuries, limited job opportunities, and a longer period of confinement because, with more of his earnings spent on guards and security facilities, it would take him longer to pay off his debt. Since there will be cases of mental imbalance even in the most rational of cultures, it is probable that there will be an occasional individual who will refuse to work and to rehabilitate himself, regardless of the penalties and incentives built into the system. Such an individual would be acting in a self-destructive manner and could properly be classified as insane. Obviously, neither the rectification company, the defense service that brought him to justice, nor the insurance company or other creditor has any obligation to go to the expense of supporting him (as victims are forced through taxation to do today). Nor would they wish to turn him loose to cause further destruction. And if they allowed him to die, they would cut off all hope of recouping the financial loss he had caused. What, then, could they do?

One solution that suggests itself is to sell his services as a subject of study by medical and psychiatric doctors who are doing research on the causes and cures of insanity. This should provide enough money to pay for his upkeep, while at the same time advancing psychological knowledge and ultimately offering hope of help for this aggressor and his fellow sufferers. If such an arrangement were made, it would be in the interests of all concerned to see that the aggressor received no ill treatment. In a rational culture, severe mental illness would be much rarer than it is in ours, and the medical-psychiatric team would not wish to damage such a valuable specimen. The rectification company in charge of the aggressor would be even more eager to protect him from harm, since no arbitration agency could afford the reputation of sending aggressors to a debtors workhouse where there was ill treatment of the inmates. This free-market system of debtors workhouses would have numerous practical advantages over the Dark Ages barbarity of the present governmental prison system. These advantages are a necessary consequence of the fact that the system would be run for profit—from the standpoint of both the insurance companies and the rectification companies operating the workhouses. In a laissez-faire economy, it is impossible to make consistent profits over a long-range period unless one acts with maximum rationality, which means: with maximum honesty and fairness.

A practical example of this principle can be seen in the results of the insurance company's desire to recoup its loss quickly. Because it would be in the insurance company's interest to have the aggressor's reparations installments as large as possible, it would have him confined to no greater degree than his own actions made necessary, since closer confinement means greater expense, which means less money left for reparations payments. Thus, it would be the aggressor himself who would determine, by his character and his past and present behavior, the amount of freedom he would lose while repaying his debt, and, to a certain degree, the length of time it would take him to pay it. Furthermore, at any time during his confinement, should the aggressor-debtor show himself to be a good enough risk, the insurance company would find it in their interest to gradually decrease his confinement—an excellent incentive to rational behavior.

Because both the insurance companies and the rectification companies would want to run their businesses profitably, it would be in their interest to have debtors be as productive as possible. In an industrialized society, a laborer's productivity depends not on his muscles but on his mind, his skills. So the debtor would be allowed to work in an area as close to the field of his aptitudes as possible and encouraged to develop further productive skills by on-the-job training, night school courses, etc. All this would help prepare him for a productive and honest life once his debt was paid. Thus, the application of free-market principles to the problem of aggression provides a built-in rehabilitation system. This is in sharp contrast to government-run prisons, which are little more than "schools for crime," where young first offenders are caged with hardened criminals and there is no incentive or opportunity for rehabilitation.

A system of monetary repayment for acts of aggression would remove a great deal of the "profit" incentive for aggressors. A thief would know that if he were caught he would have to part with all his loot (and probably quite a bit of his own money, too). He could never just stash the booty, wait out a five-year prison term, and come out a rich man.

The insurance company's desire for speedy repayment would be the aggressor-debtor's best guarantee against mistreatment. Earning power depends on productivity, and productivity depends on the use of the mind. But a man who is physically mistreated or mentally abused will be unwilling and even unable to use his mind effectively. A mistreated man is good for little more than brute physical labor—a situation of prohibitively low productivity.

Another strong guarantee of good treatment for the aggressor-debtor is that, in a laissez-faire society, every man would be fully responsible for his own actions. No guard in a debtors workhouse could beat a debtor and get away with it. The mistreated debtor could complain to a defense service agent or to the insurance company to whom he was making reparations. If he could prove his assertion of mistreatment, the guilty guard would soon find himself paying a debt to his former prisoner. Furthermore, the guard's employers would never dare to support their guard if the debtor had a good case, because if they knowingly permitted the guard's sadism the debtor could bring charges against them, too.

A guard in a government prison can treat the prisoners as less than animals and never be brought to account for it, because he is protected by his status as part of the policing arm of the government. But a guard in a debtors workhouse couldn't hide behind the skirts of the rectification company which employed him, the way the prison guard hides behind the skirts of the government. The debtors workhouse guard would be recognized as an individual, responsible for his own actions. If he mistreated a debtor in his custody, he would be held personally responsible, and he couldn't wriggle out of it by putting the blame on "the system."

A free-market system of dealing with aggression would operate with a maximum of justice precisely because it was based on the principle of self-interest. The entirety of a man's self-interest consists of rational thought and action and the rewards of such behavior; the irrational is never in man's self-interest. As long as a man is behaving rationally, he cannot intentionally harm any other noncoercive person. One of the reasons for the success of a laissez-faire society is that the free-market system impels men to act in their own rational self-interest to the extent that they wish to successfully participate in it. It thus rewards honesty and justice and penalizes dishonesty and the initiation of force. This principle would work just as well if the market were free to deal with the problem of aggression as it does when the market deals with the supply of food or the building of computers.

There have been several questions and objections raised concerning the proposal that payment for aggression be made in monetary terms. For instance, it has been objected that a thief could "get off the hook" simply by voluntarily returning the stolen item. But this is to overlook two important facts—additional expenses and loss of reputation. First, as long as the thief held the item in his possession he would be causing its owner inconvenience and expense, plus the ever-mounting cost involved in the owner's attempt to recover the item, all of which would be part of the debt created by the thief's act of aggression. In aggressive acts of any seriousness at all, it would be almost impossible for the aggressor to return the stolen item quickly enough to avoid incurring additional costs. For example, suppose a man stole $20,000 at gunpoint from a bank, but regretting his action a few minutes later, came back and returned the money. Could he get by without paying any further reparations? No, because his irrational actions interrupted the bank's business and may have caused a financial loss, for which he is directly responsible. In order to get the money, he had to threaten force against the teller and possibly other bank employees and customers, so he would owe them reparations for endangering their lives and safety. Also, as soon as he left the bank, the teller undoubtedly tripped an alarm, summoning the bank's defense agency, so the aggressor is responsible for paying the cost of the defense agency's coming to answer the call, plus any other related expenses.

But the second factor, loss of reputation, would be even more damaging to the aggressor. Just as specialized companies would keep central files, listing poor contractual risks, they would also list aggressors so that anyone wishing to do business with a man could first check his record. Insurance companies in particular would make use of this service. So our bank robber would find insurance companies listing him as a very poor risk and other firms reluctant to enter into contracts with him. Thus, if a man were foolish enough to engage in such a whim-motivated action as this bank robbery, he would find that he had caused himself considerable expense and loss of valuable reputation but had gained absolutely nothing.

In a similar vein, it has been objected that a very rich man could afford to commit any number of coercive acts, since all he would lose would be a little of his vast fortune. It is a bit difficult to imagine such a mentally ill person being able to continue existing uncured and unchallenged in a predominantly rational culture, but, assuming that he did, he would immediately find that money was hardly the only loss his actions cost him. As soon as his career of aggression was recognized for what it was, no honest man would take the chance of having anything to do with him. The only individuals who would not avoid him like the Plague would be those who felt they were tougher or craftier than he, and their only purpose in risking an association with him would be to part him from as large a share of his money as possible. Furthermore, he would run an immense risk of being killed by some victim acting in self-defense. Considering his reputation for aggression, a man would probably be justified in shooting him for any threatening gesture. So, in spite of his ability to pay, his life would be miserable and precarious, and his fortune would probably dwindle rapidly.

Again, it has been said that if a man confined himself to thefts so petty that the recoverable amount would be smaller than the cost of recovering it, thus making prosecution of the case economically unfeasible, he could get away with a career of aggression (of sorts). But such a "bubblegum thief' would lose much more than he could possibly gain, because he would lose his good reputation as his acts of aggression were discovered and recorded.

In each of these incidents, it is obvious that the aggressor's loss of reputation would be at least as damaging as his financial loss and that his lost reputation could not be regained unless he made reparations for his aggressive act and showed a determination to behave more reasonably in the future. He might shrug off the financial loss, but the loss of a good reputation would force him to live a substandard life, cut off from insurance protection, credit, reputable business dealings, and the friendship of all honest persons.

All the foregoing objections to a monetary payment assume that it would not be sufficiently costly to deter aggression, or, in other words, that it is severity of punishment which deters aggression. The untruth of this assumption should be evident from an examination of such historical eras as Elizabethan England, in which punishments of extreme severity prevailed, including physical mutilation and hanging for petty theft. Yet in spite of the great loss of value imposed on criminals, crime rates were very high. The reason for this is that it is not severity, but justice, which deters aggression. To punish the aggressor with more severity than his actions warrant—that is, to impose on him a greater loss of value than that which is necessary for him to make reasonable reparations to the victim—is to commit an injustice against him. Injustice cannot be a deterrent to injustice.

The aggressor who is treated with such excessive severity feels, quite rightly, that he has been victimized. Seeing little or no justice in his punishment, he feels a vast resentment, and often forms a resolve to "get even with society" as soon as possible. Thus, in dealing with aggression, excessive severity, as much as excessive laxity, can provoke further aggressive acts. The only valid answer to injustice, is justice. Justice cannot be served by excessive severity or by taking revenge against the aggressor, or by pacifism, but only by requiring the aggressor to pay the debt which he has created by his coercive action.

Dealing with a man justly helps him to improve himself and his life by inducing him to act in his own self-interest. In the case of an aggressor, justice induces him to want to, and be able to, live a productive, honest, non-coercive life, both while he is paying the debt he owes to his victim, and afterwards. Justice helps a man get on the right track by sending him the right signals. It penalizes him for his misdeeds—but only as much as he actually deserves. It also rewards him when he does the right thing. Injustice sends out incorrect signals which lead men astray. The injustice of letting an aggressor get away without paying for his aggressions teaches him to believe that "crime pays," which induces him to commit more and bigger crimes. The injustice of punishing an aggressor by making him pay more than he really owes the victim teaches the aggressor that he can't expect justice from others, so there's little point in his trying to treat them justly. He concludes that this is a dog-eat-dog world and that his best course is to "do it unto others before they do it unto him." Only justice sends the aggressor the right signals, so only justice can be a satisfactory deterrent to aggression.

It may be objected that some men will attempt to take advantage of a free-market system of dealing with aggression. This is true, as it is true of any other social system. But the big advantage of any action of the free market is that errors and injustices are self-correcting. Because competition creates a need for excellence on the part of each business, a free-market institution must correct its errors in order to survive. Government, on the other hand, survives not by excellence but by coercion; so an error or flaw in a governmental institution can (and usually will) perpetuate itself almost indefinitely, with its errors usually being "corrected" by further errors. Private enterprise must, therefore, always be superior to government in any field, including that of dealing with aggressors.

* * *

Some opponents of a laissez-faire society have contended that, because a governmentless society would have no single, society-wide institution able to legitimately wield superior force to prevent aggression, a state of gang warfare between defense agencies would arise. Then (as they argue), brute force, rather than justice, would prevail and society would collapse in internecine conflict. This contention assumes that private defense service entrepreneurs would find it to their advantage, at least in some circumstances, to use coercive, rather than market, means to achieve their ends. There is a further, unstated assumption that governmental officials would not only prevent coercion but would themselves consistently refrain from initiating force (or that the force they initiated would be somehow preferable to the chaos it is feared would result from an unhampered market).

The second of these assumptions is obviously groundless, since (as was shown in Chapter 4) government is a coercive monopoly which must initiate force in order to survive, and which cannot be kept limited. But what of the first assumption? Would a free-market system of value-protection lead to gang warfare between the competing defense companies?

The "gang warfare" objection has been raised in regard to theories advocating a system of competing governments. When applied to any type of governments, the objection is a valid one. A government, being a coercive monopoly, is always in the position of initiating force simply by the fact of its existence, so it is not surprising that conflicts between governments frequently take the form of war. Since a government is a coercive monopoly, the notion of more than one government occupying the same area at the same time is ridiculous. But a laissez-faire society would involve, not governments, but private businesses operating in a free market.

5

Pursuing Justice in a Free Society: Crime Prevention and the Legal Order

Randy Barnett

In the first installment of this article,[1] the substantive rights and remedies of the Liberty Approach were identified and evaluated. The substantive rights of individuals involve claims they make on the use of resources in the world, beginning with their bodies and ending in the use of external resources. Those claims which are justified are called property rights. Adherents to a Liberty Approach contend that each individual has moral and legal jurisdiction over his or her person and possessions. This means that they have discretion as to how their property is used unless this use threatens to violate the rights of another. Should someone interfere with the use and enjoyment of another's property or threaten to do so, the person whose rights are being violated or threatened may justifiably employ self-defense and also is entitled to restitution[2] for the forced appropriation of rights that has occurred.

What remains to be discussed, in this second installment, is the form that a legal order should take to secure these rights and remedies without itself infringing upon them. Before considering this question, however, it is important to see how the Liberty Approach can deal with the problem of crime in ways that do not directly involve the legal system.

Preventing Crime in a Free Society

It may be argued that in a society governed solely by the individual rights of the Liberty Approach, coupled with self-defense actions and a restitutive remedy for those rights violations that occur, there would be "too much" crime. Three observations need to be made before directly responding to this criticism.

First, the criticism assumes that a quantitative scale of evaluation exists by which we can assess how much crime is too much. No one believes that any legal system will eliminate all crime. Moreover, we know that we might have far less crime today, except for the value we place on features of a free society that would be lost in the unbridled pursuit of lower crime rates. Unless the critic who raises this point is more specific (and few ever are), we cannot know what it would take to satisfy the criticism. Just how much crime need we demonstrate will exist in a free society to rebut the claim that it will be "too much"?

Second, it would be improper to compare a society governed by the Liberty Approach against some absolute scale of perfection, assuming one was offered by the critic. No society is or ever will be perfect, and I have been careful to avoid criticizing the Power Principle for simply being imperfect.[3] The relevant method of comparison is, therefore, a comparative one.[4] The likely practical effects of a Liberty Approach need to be compared with the practical effects of the known alternatives—particularly the form of legal system we have today—to see which approach is likely to prevent crime more effectively.

Third, and perhaps most important, in comparing the Power Principle with a Liberty Approach, it would be improper simply to compare the respective remedies of each approach—for example, punishment vs. restitution—while controlling for all other social variables. Each remedy is but a component of a comprehensive legal approach to social problem solving. In other words, when either approach is actually adopted, the form or severity of the remedy for criminal conduct would never be the only variable that would account for differential rates of crime.

For example, the severity of a remedy affects the certainty of its imposition.[5] The more severe you make a penalty, the more resistance is offered against its imposition, and the more reluctant are people to impose it. Similarly, punishment requires government prosecutions and government penitentiaries, which in turn require taxes to be levied and heads of government bureaus somehow to be selected and reselected. Each of these institutions and practices has its own effects on crime prevention efforts. It is, therefore, highly misleading to evaluate in isolation the respective severity of two remedies while assuming that all other variables—such as the certainty of imposition or the legal structure needed for implementation—remain constant. Instead, we need to compare as best we can the social structure of a society governed by a Liberty Approach (including restitutive criminal sanctions) with one governed by a Power Principle (including punitive sanctions).

Crime Prevention as a Social Goal

The goal of crime prevention must be viewed in the same light as all other important social goals, such as health, education, and economic well-being. For a society to survive and flourish, it must strive to achieve each of these goals, but not every means can be permitted in this quest. Individual rights, the prerequisite of individual survival and fulfillment, must at all times be recognized and respected. Rights are what Nozick calls "side-constraints" on our pursuit of various social (and other) goals.[6] These constraints do not evaporate simply because the ultimate goal is the protection of individual rights themselves.

Any failure to adequately define or respect individual rights in organizing law enforcement institutions has three adverse effects. First, the example of community leaders disregarding individual rights in pursuit of goals thought to be socially desirable encourages the violation of rights by others in pursuit of their goals. Second, a principal benefit of respecting property rights is that it makes possible a free market in goods and services with its unique ability to efficiently allocate resources.[7] In the next section, we shall see that when property rights are overridden in pursuit of crime prevention, this vital social mechanism is unavailable to allocate resources in the most efficient manner. Finally, to the extent that we place security and the "defense of a free society" above individual rights, we may obtain the security we seek, but we are unlikely to preserve the freedom that makes security worth having.

Law Enforcement as a "Commons" Problem

When property rights are ill-defined, misallocations of resources will occur. If a particular resource is thought to be held in common—that is, if all are thought to have an equal right to exploit the use of this property—then no person has the right to exclude others from using the resource. Without the right to exclude, it is unlikely that the benefits accruing to persons who privately invest in the care or improvement of a resource will exceed the costs of their efforts. Indeed, the overriding incentive for resource users lacking a right to exclude others is to maximize their own consumption lest others consume the resource first. For this reason, commonly held resources are typically overused and undermaintained.

The depletion of vital resources in the face of a universal consensus as to the importance of their continued maintenance is known as the "tragedy of the commons."[8] In the case of grazing land, for example, the historical solution to the problem of depletion is to recognize property rights in land. This does not prevent all depletion, nor would the prevention of all depletion be desirable.[9] It does, however, permit the owner of the land to benefit enough from any effort to conserve the usefulness of the land to make conservation worthwhile. In this way, when the benefits of conservation exceed those of the alternative uses available for a particular piece of land, there exists a powerful incentive to conserve.

While this analysis of the use and consumption of farmland and other resources is well known, it has seldom been applied to the problem of crime prevention. If the traditional economic assessment of the "commons" problem is valid, it is reasonable to suggest that at least part of the problem of "crime in the streets" may stem from the belief that the streets must be owned in common. The fact that public parks and streets are held in common adversely affects crime prevention in two important ways.

First, when little incentive exists for individuals to commit their private resources to prevent rights-violating conduct on so-called "public" property, there appears no choice but to create an inherently inefficient coercive monopoly to provide "public" police protection. Second, when property is owned and administered by a central government, constitutional constraints on the government's power to exclude citizens from using public property is needed to minimize abuses of power. Such unavoidable limitations on the proper management of public property can be shown to seriously inhibit crime prevention.

1. Some Inefficiencies of Public Law Enforcement. Just as a parent will not invest in playground equipment to be put in a public park for the use of his children, neither will individuals voluntarily pay for private security patrols to protect themselves or their children while they use the public parks and streets unless, as is sometimes the case, the provision of this service can be limited to those who are paying for it. Security guards may be hired to patrol a government owned street if conditions become so dangerous that most residents of that street are induced to contribute. Or guards may be employed to escort a sufficiently valuable shipment of property that is being conveyed on public streets if the risk of loss is great enough to justify the costs.

Normally, however, because private investors in protective services on public property cannot adequately benefit from their investment, such services are unlikely to be privately provided. As a result, all responsibility for such protection must fall upon the governmental agency that has assumed jurisdiction over the property in question. Taxes must be raised and government employees hired to protect the users of the property. Here, as elsewhere, defining a package of goods and services—in this case protective services—as a "public good" and then attempting to provide that good by government agencies is inherently less responsive to the needs and demands of consumers than defining property rights in such a manner as to allow both private investment and consumption.

The reasons for this need not be elaborated here. It should suffice to say that the practical accountability of government law enforcement agencies to the consumer will at best be indirect and at worst nonexistent. Government police agencies, especially those in large cities, are beholden first to the political establishment that dictates their funding, and second—if at all—to individual members of the general public. Tax-financed government agencies are protected from competition and need not obtain the actual consent of their "customers." Unlike market institutions, which must rely on consensual agreements and payments, government police agencies lack both the motivation and the ability to discover and respond to shifting and diverse consumer preferences.[10] They are plagued by what has been called the "knowledge problem."[11] Ever inefficient, often counterproductive, and occasionally abusive, police services are among the more easily anticipated results of such an approach.

2. Public Property and the Right to Exclude. The unwillingness and inability of public law enforcement to allocate resources so as to efficiently respond to the needs of consumers is only part of the problem. Perhaps the defining characteristic of private property is the right of a property owner to control its use. You need not admit into your house any person who knocks on your door; nor must you wait for a guest on your property to commit an aggressive act before you may ask that person to leave. Being a private property owner gives you the right to consent to its use by others, and such a right is meaningless unless you have the right to withhold consent as well.[12]

When governments assume control over streets, parks, and other common resources, they are acting in the capacity of property owners. For sound theoretical and practical reasons, however, governments in a free society will be denied many of the rights accorded private individuals and institutions. Democratic theory specifies that government exists at the pleasure and for the benefit of the general public. Public property is said to belong to all the people and is merely "held in trust" by the government. A governmental right to limit the access of citizens to public property without some acceptable reason would be inconsistent with this theoretical premise. As a practical matter, a free society would not remain free for long if its government, which coercively maintained its monopoly control over all streets, sidewalks, and parks, were accorded the same rights and discretion enjoyed by private property owners.

For these reasons, governments must be prevented by constitutional constraints from denying access to public property, which is (in theory) held for the use and benefit of all citizens, unless good cause can be shown. But restricting the right of governments to control public property unavoidably creates intractable problems of "social" control. Requiring only a mere suspicion or "reasonable belief" that someone might commit a crime to justify governmental exclusion would not adequately protect citizens from government abuses. Such a standard would be too easy for the government to meet and too hard for the citizen to contest. But requiring probable cause before government can arrest a suspect, and proof beyond a reasonable doubt before it can use incarceration to deny access to public areas by those who have already committed crimes leaves considerable opportunity for criminal profit.

Any society that chooses to be organized by the Power Principle is therefore faced with what might be called a dilemma of vulnerability. Since governments enjoy privileges denied their citizens and are subject to few of the economic constraints of private institutions, their citizens are forever vulnerable to governmental tyranny. Therefore, freedom can only be preserved by denying government police agencies the right to regulate public property with the same discretion accorded private property owners. Yet steps taken to protect society from the government also serve to make citizens more vulnerable to criminally inclined persons by providing such persons with a greater opportunity for a safe haven on the public streets and sidewalks and in the public parks.

The Power Principle's dilemma of vulnerability creates an ever-present temptation to trade liberty for security—that is, to compensate for the inefficiency of government—provided law enforcement by unjustly restricting individual rights in one of two ways: by prior restraints on conduct (preventive detention) or by increasing the punishment of those few criminals who are caught in the hopes of deterring the many whom the government police cannot catch or the government courts cannot convict. Either tactic risks the serious consequences of "overpunishment." And, as was just discussed, to compensate for the inefficiency of monopoly law enforcement and public property by increasing the severity of punishment decreases still further the certainty of its imposition. In this manner, pursuing the social goal of crime prevention by means of the Power Principle creates a serious social instability that is always threatening a free society from within.

3. Comparing Private and Public Property. In those areas where private property rights are well defined or where government officials can act much like private owners, crime problems are reduced.[13]

In relatively well-to-do areas, where large shopping centers and office complexes are the most common forms of commercial activity, roads, parking lots, sidewalks, and security patrols are all privately provided. In contrast to governmentally administered shopping districts in big cities, the owners of private developments can control access to the common areas between stores and offices. Any failure to effectively curtail criminal conduct will carry with it serious economic costs since increased crime causes rent receipts to decline. By the same token, discourtesy and overly restrictive crime control efforts can also cause lost business and bad will. These consumer-oriented incentives also exist for owners of larger private residential developments. These incentives impel law enforcement efforts that are responsive to the needs of both the property owner and the consumer to whom the property owner is attempting to appeal.

Similarly, in smaller communities where values are relatively homogeneous, informal social pressure is more effective in inhibiting disapproved behavior and government officials can more easily exert control over governmental police agencies and public property akin to the control of private property owners. Consequently, the problem of crime control will be diminished in these settings for much the same reason that it is on truly private property.[14]

The brunt of today's crime problem occurs in older, predominantly poor areas, where commercial, residential, and recreational activity must depend most heavily on traditional forms of public property management, and in those places where the diversity of the population prevents a monopolistic system from approximating a market solution (as might be achieved in smaller, more insular, and more homogeneous communities). It is not surprising, then, to find the problem of "crime in the streets" at its worst where property rights are the least well defined. If the reliance on public property and public law enforcement is reduced, those who cannot now afford the benefits of private property and efficient law enforcement will obtain access to the types of services presently confined to other segments of society.

4. The Role of Imprisonment. Thinking of the provision of law enforcement as a "public good" that must be provided by "society" can lead some to view society as a rights-bearing entity. Crimes may, in this view, be seen as offenses against society or the "state." The victim's right to reparations is thought to be civil in nature and, in practice, is treated as secondary to a criminal charge (the sanction for which is rarely reparations to the victim). By subordinating individual rights to "the rights of society," this "organistic" conception of society undermines both justice and crime prevention.

The practice of incarcerating criminals in public prisons stems directly from the twin imperatives of the Power Principle: to punish offenders and to exclude them from public property. Imprisonment effectively deprives victims of their right to reparations in those cases where the greatest rights violations have occurred. Victims of the most serious crimes and their families are thereby twice victimized: once by the rights violator and again by the enforcement agencies that require victims to participate at some considerable risk and cost while denying to them any effective ability to obtain reparations from the offender.

Public prisons as they now exist are both unjust to victims and largely unnecessary to accomplish any other purpose. Imprisonment can at best be viewed as a crude approximation of a market response to criminal conduct. Just as private citizens may individually or collectively ban others from their property, the government uses the penitentiary system to keep dangerous individuals out of public (and private) property. But public imprisonment has several significant drawbacks.

First, because a complete deprivation of liberty is such a severe sanction, one must be proved guilty beyond a reasonable doubt of a most serious crime before imprisonment is permitted. Many guilty persons, therefore, escape the sanction and remain free. Second, imprisonment is a blunt instrument. Although sentence lengths can vary, you are either in prison or you are out. As a result criminal sanctions for many offenders admit of only two degrees of severity: onerous or virtually nonexistent. Third, imprisonment is expensive. While scarce resources are expended to confine, prisoners are prevented from producing anything of value to others.

Finally, because only the worst offenders are incarcerated, prisons become very dangerous places. Dangerousness is thereby added to the deprivation of liberty to heighten still further the severity of imprisonment. As a result, judges become even more reluctant to sentence a person to prison for fear of a very real risk of overpunishment. Where they have discretion, judges become even more inclined to give even serious felons the benefit of the doubt by sentencing them to a period of probation until they have established a sufficiently serious criminal record. Actions speak louder than words, and repeat offenders soon come to rely upon the legal system's reluctance to incarcerate them. No one is more surprised than they are when the prison gates finally close behind them for the first time. By this time it is too late for deterrence.

The Logic of Public Crime Prevention

Most people—including most criminal justice professionals—adhere to the Power Principle, and for this reason they cannot see any fundamental alternative to the "public" approach to crime prevention. Their vision is limited to ad hoc "reforms" of the present system that fail to address the fundamental obstacles placed in the path of crime prevention by public property, public law enforcement, and public imprisonment. Each of these institutions results from the internal logic of the Power Principle.

Step one: start with public streets, sidewalks, and parks where every citizen must be permitted unless proved guilty of a crime. Step two: rely on an inherently inefficient public bureaucracy to catch, prosecute, and try those criminals against whom enough evidence of guilt exists. Step three: should they be convicted, subject them to the dangerous and sometimes uncontrollable setting of public prisons to prevent them from engaging in further misconduct. Step four: periodically release most prisoners back into the community and then return to step one and repeat the cycle. Each step follows from the preceding step, and each step unavoidably leaves considerable room for criminal conduct to thrive. If we set out deliberately to design a system that encouraged criminal conduct and nurtured hardened career criminals, we could hardly do a better job. (And I have omitted any discussion of the bizarre legal system which attempts to deal with those criminals who are defined as "juveniles.")

A Liberty Approach promises a way to break free of this vicious cycle. Private social control and crime prevention become feasible as the institution of public property is supplanted by a more extensive recognition of private property rights. Such a shift promises significantly more effective law enforcement efforts. First, private efforts can be truly preventative. In contrast to the public response, which must await the commission of a crime before taking action,[15] private owners who will directly suffer from a crime can directly benefit from truly preventative measures. Their interest is in seeing that the crime not take place at all. Second, as was discussed above, ownership rights and free contracts both enable and compel private law enforcement agencies to allocate their resources more efficiently than public police departments do.

Third, in contrast to a penitentiary system, where one is either in prison or out, exclusion from private property is a far more decentralized process of individual decisions. Suspicious persons can be excluded from some "public" places and not others, resulting in a far more gradated response to the threat of crime than imprisonment. Fourth, in a society where the rights of victims to restitution were fully protected, any firm which confined convicted criminals would be legally obliged to provide them with productive work at market wages (reflecting their productivity) in a secure environment. Prisoners might even engage in collective bargaining. Their wages would be used to pay for their living costs and to make reparations to their victims, and they would be released only when full restitution had been made or when it was adjudged that reparations could more quickly be made by unconfined employment.[16]

Other Factors Influencing Criminal Conduct

Of course, other factors contribute to the problem of crime besides those discussed here. For example, governmentally enforced restrictions on the labor market and on entrepreneurial activity have prevented "classes" of people from escaping their dependence on government assistance or on criminal conduct. To the extent that persons are principally motivated to commit crimes (usually property crimes) by genuine financial need, a freer and more prosperous society where more economic opportunities were available to those who are willing to work should significantly reduce this incentive.

Moreover, statutes against victimless activities of all kinds have created lucrative black markets which provide enormous profits to those persons who are willing to break these "laws." Such "criminal" activity will inevitably undermine whatever respect for law a person engaged in such conduct may once have had. In such a setting, it is unrealistic to expect most black marketeers, whose livelihood is earned by providing goods and services that are deemed to be illegal, to observe the fine line between violating such statutes and violating the genuine rights of others—particularly when their black market activities are denied the protection of recognized legal institutions and they must routinely resort to self help.

Victimless crime laws not only breed victim crimes, but the huge premiums that result from making certain highly desired transactions illicit create powerful financial incentives for criminals to organize into groups which in effect purchase the "rights" to engage in criminal conduct by corrupting law enforcement agents at all levels.[17] Where legal constraints on exchanges between consenting adults are eliminated by a Liberty Approach, the source of the artificially inflated profits earned by those who are willing to accept the substantial risks of doing business on the black market would also be eliminated. Without these profits, the other sordid side effects of these statutes would also be rapidly and markedly diminished.

Unanswered Questions about a Liberty Approach

No approach to any serious problem is without difficulty. By now, several important questions about a Liberty Approach are likely to have occurred to most readers: How would private law enforcement services be paid for, especially by the poor? How would private owners be able to coordinate their preventative activities? How would injustice by private owners be held in check? How could enforcement agencies be prevented from banding together and recreating a monopoly system? Is law enforcement a "public good" that for economic reasons cannot be provided on a market?

Answers to some of these questions will be offered in an exploratory fashion in the next section. Other questions must be left unanswered for now because of space limitations. A Liberty Approach will not, however, be taken seriously by reformers if the problem of providing services to the poor is not discussed. So let us turn our attention briefly to this important issue.

Those who are unable to pay for private law enforcement services (and other privately provided goods and services) may receive them in one of four ways. Such services might be voluntarily provided to poor persons without charge (pro bono) by private firms, or people concerned about the well-being of others can voluntarily give to private agencies who will pay for private law enforcement services for the poor.[18] Or law enforcement agencies can be forced to service those who cannot afford to pay their fees, or some people can be forced to contribute their money to those agencies who serve the poor. These alternatives need not be evaluated here, for whether one favors or opposes forced redistribution to the poor, a Liberty Approach is far superior to a system based on the Power Principle and its regime of public crime prevention.

Supposing (as most people do) that some degree of forced redistribution of wealth to poor persons is justified, there is no reason why an inferior system of public property, public law enforcement, and public imprisonment must be created or preserved just to service those who are not wealthy enough to pay for private law enforcement. Either direct cash payments or "vouchers" (which are money payments with use restrictions) can be provided to the poor to pay for those privately provided services that are now governmentally provided.

Giving the poor recreational, law enforcement, and judicial services "in kind" makes as much sense as creating a governmental food production and distribution monopoly for everyone to ensure that the poor have food. Instead, vouchers—called "food stamps"—are given so that the poor can buy food from private sources. Had the private food production and distribution system been supplanted by a government system at some distant point in our history, exactly the same criticisms would probably be made of a Liberty Approach to food production as are made in opposition to extensions of a Liberty Approach to areas where our history has been less fortunate and the Power Principle has prevailed.

Despite whatever serious problems they may be experiencing, most people have a natural conservative instinct to accept that which exists as inevitable and right. The truth is, however, that imposing a retrogressive public system of law enforcement on everyone solely to benefit those who are poor is unnecessary, foolish, and wrong.

A Nonmonopolistic Legal Order

> A possible...objection to the view [of law] taken here is that it permits the existence of more than one legal system governing the same population. The answer is, of course, that such multiple legal systems do exist and have in history been more common than unitary systems.[19]

What kind of legal order is consistent with the rights and remedies described in Part One of this article?[20] Two constraints on our choices immediately present themselves.

First, the legal order must be financed by noncoercive means. The confiscation or extortion of one person's rightful possessions to finance the defense of that person's rights or those of another is itself a rights invasion.[21] Second, the jurisdiction of each court system cannot be a legal monopoly. It would be inconsistent with the rights and remedies of the Liberty Approach to impose legal sanctions on someone solely because he has attempted to provide judicial services in competition with another person or group since such an attempt would itself violate none of the rights specified by the Liberty Approach.[22] I shall consider each of these constraints in turn.

Noncoercive Sources of Funding

There is no reason why either a law enforcement agency or a court system cannot charge for its services, in much the same way as do other "essential" institutions, such as hospitals, banks, and schools.[23] Each business requires expertise and integrity, and institutions engaged in such activities must earn the trust of the consumer. Hospitals, banks, and schools, however, rely primarily on fees charged their customers, though payment of these charges can be made in a variety of different ways.

The very large and largely unanticipated expenditures for emergency hospital care are financed by insurance arrangements, by conventional credit, and, of course, by cash payments. Banks raise the bulk of their revenue from the difference between the interest they charge borrowers and the interest they pay depositors, and where this differential is narrow, service charges may be imposed as well. Schools which do not receive tax receipts rely largely on tuition payments made by parents and students out of savings or from the proceeds of long-term loans. A significant portion of both educational and health services is subsidized by private charitable contributions.[24]

It takes no great imagination to envision competitive law enforcement agencies providing police protection to paying subscribers—especially in a society where streets, sidewalks, and parks are privately owned. (Park and road owners could, for example, bundle the provision of protective services with their other transportation and recreational services.) Such a system[25] would probably include agreements between agencies to reimburse each other if they provide services in an emergency to another firm's client.[26] Competitive court systems could utilize many of the same techniques as hospitals to fund their services: insurance, credit, cash, and charity. Prepaid legal service plans or other forms of legal insurance are also possible and, where permitted, sometimes are available even today.

In addition, court systems could profit by selling the written opinions of their judges to law firms (or to the various retrieval services on which lawyers rely). Such opinions would be of value to lawyers and yield a profit to the court system which sold them only to the extent that they are truly useful to predict the future actions of these judges. So to fully profit from such publications, each court system would have to monitor and provide internal incentives to encourage its judges both to write and to follow precedential decisions.

At present, attorneys bill clients by the hour or collect a percentage of the damage awards they succeed in obtaining. They also work pro bono—that is, they donate their services in the interests of justice. Except in unusual cases, however, those who successfully bring or defend lawsuits in the United States today cannot recover their legal fees from those persons who either violated their rights or who wrongfully brought suit against them.

In contrast a Liberty Approach requires restitution to compensate as completely as possible for all the determinable expenses which result from a rights violation. Therefore, in a legal system that adheres to a Liberty Approach, the loser of a lawsuit must be liable (at least prima facie) for the full legal costs of the prevailing party. In the absence of such a rule, the innocent party would be made to absorb some of the costs of the other party's wrongdoing. And such a legal rule would also serve both to protect innocent persons from the expense and injustice of baseless lawsuits by increasing the costs of losing weak cases, and to help pay for meretricious winning lawsuits brought by people who could not otherwise afford the legal costs.

Moreover, it is important to note that consumers using such institutions as hospitals, schools, and banks must now pay both for the services of doctors, bankers, and teachers and for the overhead of the facility (the hospital, the bank, or the school) where these professionals practice. With the legal profession, however, we are accustomed to privately paying for lawyers, while providing the capital and labor used by lawyers—courts and court personnel—by tax receipts. This "public good" arrangement encourages overuse by some until court backlogs and overcrowding create queues that substitute for prices or fees to clear the market.

Some people worry that allocating court resources by means of a market price mechanism will unfairly reward the rich. But the system as it now exists rewards those litigants who are better able to wait out the imposed delays and penalizes those who for any reason require a fast decision.[27] Who is more likely to be in each group, the wealthy or the poor, a company or an injured consumer, the guilty or the innocent? Remember also that in a Liberty Approach, the loser would have to reimburse the prevailing party for court costs, including costs caused by delaying tactics.[28] The most likely result of adopting a competitive legal order with market-based pricing is that all legal costs would be greatly reduced from their present level, and successful litigants would be able to keep a higher proportion of whatever damages awards they recovered.

In short, the financing of legal services is neither a very different nor a more serious problem than the financing of many other public services that rely only minimally, if at all, on tax revenues and that sometimes even now must compete against tax subsidized competition to survive. Whatever problems may exist in providing indigents with legal and judicial services exist as well with hospitals and schools. But such problems do not justify taxation as a means of providing these services to everyone, whether indigent or not, nor, as was suggested above,[29] must these services be provided in kind.[30]

No Jurisdictional Monopoly

The argument that law enforcement and adjudication are so important that they must be provided by a coercive monopoly is ironic. If one had to identify a service that is really fundamental to social well-being, it would be the provision of food. Yet no one (in this country) seriously suggests that this service is "too important" to be left to private firms subject to the market competition.[31] On the contrary, both theory and history demonstrate that food production is too important to be left to a coercive monopoly.

The more vital a good or service is, the more dangerous it is to let it be produced by a coercive monopoly. A monopoly post office does far less harm than monopoly law enforcement and court systems. And a coercive monopoly might go largely unnoticed if it were limited to making paper clips—that is, the inferior and/or costly paper clips inevitably produced by such a monopoly might not bother us too much. It is when something really important is left to a coercive monopoly that we face potential disaster.

Moreover, upon closer examination the seemingly radical proposal to end the geographical monopoly of legal systems is actually a rather short step from the competitive spirit to which we have been, and to some extent still are, accustomed. In the long history of English law, royal courts competed with merchant courts; courts of law competed with courts of equity.[32] "The very complexity of a common legal order containing diverse legal systems contributed to legal sophistication."[33] Even today, the federal system in the United States preserves a degree of competition between state and federal courts. We are accustomed to the idea of "checks and balances" among governmental power centers that is said to be embodied in the constitutional framework.[34] And private adjudication and arbitration organizations routinely compete with government courts for commercial business.

In evaluating the merits of a nonmonopolistic legal order we must be careful always to take a comparative approach. It is tempting but ultimately fruitless to compare any proposal to an ideal that no other possible legal order could more closely achieve.[35] When comparing the realistic prospects of a legal order made up of diverse legal systems with those of a monopoly legal system, the advantages can readily be seen.

Without a coercive monopoly, actual or potential competition provides genuine checks and balances. In a competitive legal order, an individual excluded from or oppressed by one legal system can appeal to another; an individual shut out of a monopoly legal system cannot.[36] People are extremely reluctant to "vote with their feet" by leaving a country because doing so means abandoning one's friends, family, culture, and career. And yet people do so if things get bad enough. By having the choice to shift one's legal affiliation without having to incur the substantial costs of expatriation means that things do not have to get nearly so bad before a change in affiliation occurs.

Contrary to contemporary preferences for a unitary legal system, it is the pluralism of the Western legal order that has been, or once was, a source of freedom. A serf might run to the town court for protection against his master. A vassal might run to the king's court for protection against his lord. A cleric might run to the ecclesiastical court for protection against the king.[37]

Law will remain supreme in a society if, and only if, a unitary legal system does not develop.

Perhaps the most distinctive characteristic of the Western legal tradition is the coexistence and competition within the same community of diverse jurisdictions and diverse legal systems. It is this plurality of jurisdictions and legal systems that makes the supremacy of law both necessary and possible.[38]

The modern monopolistic conception of a unitary legal system threatens this vital diversity.[39]

Moreover, while we are accustomed to thinking about a single agency with a geographical monopoly—such as county government—providing both the judicial system and the police agency to enforce its orders, in a competitive legal order no such combination is either likely or desirable. Wholly different skills and resources are needed to efficiently render just decisions than are needed to efficiently enforce such decisions as are rendered by a court.

For instance, an efficient judicial system must accumulate and organize the historical information and legal analysis needed to do justice between contending parties, and it must also demonstrate to the relevant social group that justice is being done. A successful court system must fulfill at least two distinct functions: the justice function and the fairness function. The justice function consists of devising and implementing reliable means of accurately determining facts and law. The fairness function consists of convincing the practicing bar who must recommend where to initiate lawsuits, the litigants who must suffer the consequences of this choice, and the general public who must acquiesce to the enforcement of legal judgments in their midst that the procedures it has employed have produced justice. A legal system will not provide a service worth paying for if it fails to fulfill either function. Additionally, some kinds of procedural safeguards may be mandated not only by market demands but by principles of justice as well.[40]

Efficient law enforcement, on the other hand, involves the least costly use of coercion (a) to protect people from harm, (b) to seize and sell property in satisfaction of judgments by a "recognized" court, or (c) to administer a system of productive enterprises where persons who are either unable or unwilling to make payments from regular earnings can be employed under controlled conditions and paid market wages from which reparations are deducted until their debt to the victim is satisfied.[41] It is implausible that a single agency would provide any two of these services. The fact that an institution performs one of these functions well would seem to be unrelated to its ability to effectively perform any of the others. It is even more implausible that a successful law enforcement agency would also most efficiently supply judicial services.

As important as the balance maintained by a competitive legal order are the constraints provided by the requirement that legal systems contract with their clientele. Deprived of the power to tax and the power to coercively impose their services upon consumers, legal systems which must depend upon market-based fees and prepaid insurance would have to be comparatively more responsive to the needs and desires of their consumers than agencies with the right to collect their revenues at gun point. The fact that individuals and firms respond to the incentives provided by competition is acknowledged to be true in every other area of human endeavor. Human nature does not suddenly change when one gets a job providing law enforcement and judicial services.

Where opportunities for better service are perceived by entrepreneurs, the capital markets permit enormous amounts of money to be raised in a short period of time, either to purchase existing firms which are mismanaged, to start a new firm, or to diversify from one area of law enforcement into another. Each legal system would be constrained by the knowledge that alternative systems exist, in much the same way that individual states in a federal system are constrained in how they make corporation law by the knowledge that it is always possible for companies to reincorporate in another state without moving their assets.[42] Even a rumor of unreliability can be expected to shake the biggest of companies.

In short, there is an increased likelihood that a competitive legal order would be far more responsive to the consumer than a coercive monopoly. In fact, when one seriously compares the potential responsiveness of each system, many readers may concede the point and offer the opposite objection: Competing jurisdictions would most likely be too responsive to their customers, and this would inevitably lead to injustice and serious conflicts among agencies, creating serious social disruption. What is to prevent one judicial organization from fighting with or ignoring the rulings of another? Why should any organization heed the call of another? These are serious questions deserving serious answers, but first some perspective is needed.

We now have fifty (state) court systems in the United States, each with its own hierarchical structure, plus twelve Federal Circuit Courts of Appeals. There is no general right to appeal from the decision of any one of them to the Supreme Court of the United States. (With few exceptions, the Supreme Court of the United States must choose to accept a petition for review.) And the situation is, in fact, still more diverse. For within each state, there are often numerous appellate court jurisdictions from whose judgment one has no general right to appeal to the supreme court of that state. (Again, with few exceptions, the supreme courts of each state must choose to accept a petition for review.) Moreover, the federal as well as many state appellate court districts are divided into "panels" of judges, who are randomly assigned to hear cases arising from the same jurisdiction. Add to this diversity the many municipal court systems and courts of limited jurisdiction—such as bankruptcy courts—and the image of a unitary court system begins to blur.

The abolition of geography-based jurisdictional monopolies would mean only that jurisdictional conflicts would arise between persons who had chosen different court systems by contract, rather than as now between persons who have decided to live in different places.[43] Where two disputants have chosen the same court system, no jurisdictional conflict is presented. Where individuals have chosen different court systems, conflicts between the two disputants would be governed by the same type of preexisting agreements between the court systems that presently exists between the court systems of states and nations.

Extended conflict between competing court systems is quite unlikely. It is simply not in the interest of repeat players (and most of their clients) to attempt to obtain short-run gains at the cost of long-run conflict. Where they have the opportunity to cooperate, in even the most intense conflicts—warfare, for example—participants tend to evolve a "live and let live" philosophy.[44] Most successful lawyers do not today go to any lengths to pursue a given client's interests: they must live to fight another day and to preserve their ability to effectively defend other clients. Likewise, it is not in the interest of any judge or court system to use or threaten force to resolve a legal or jurisdictional conflict in any but the most serious of circumstances.

Courts and judges have, therefore, traditionally found peaceful ways to resolve the two questions most likely to lead to conflict when multiple legal jurisdictions exist: Which court system is to hear the case when more than one might do so? And which law is to be applied when more than one law might be applied? Much of the court-made law of "civil procedure" addresses the first question,[45] and an entire body of law—called the conflict of laws—has arisen spontaneously (that is, it was not imposed by a higher authority) to provide a means of resolving the second of these two questions. As one commentator wrote:

> What is the subject matter of the conflict of laws? A fairly neutral definition…is that the conflict of laws is the study of whether or not and, if so, in what way, the answer to a legal problem will be affected because the elements of the problem have contacts with more than one jurisdiction.[46]

How much greater the incentive to cooperate would be if competing judicial services did not have access to a steady stream of coercively obtained revenue—that is, by taxation. Those contemplating such a conflict would know that the resources available to fight would not exceed those on hand and those which people were freely willing to contribute to the fight. Unlike national governments, they could not obtain by coercion—that is by draft—personnel to enforce their judgment.

A "renegade" judicial system or law enforcement firm, no matter how financially well endowed it might be as compared with any single rival, would undoubtedly be dwarfed by the capital market as a whole. Imagine the Cook County Sheriff's Office fighting all the other sheriff's offices in the region, state, or country with only the resources it had on hand. (Actually, the jurisdictional dispersion of a nonmonopolistic legal order makes McDonald's declaring war on Wendy's and Burger King a far more apt analogy.)

The argument that we need court systems with geography-based jurisdictional monopolies does not stop at the border of a nation-state. Any such argument suggests the need for a single world court system with one Super-Supreme Court to decide international disputes and its own army to enforce its decisions. After all, the logic of the argument against a competitive legal order applies with equal force to autonomous nations.[47] Yet, although governments do go to war against one another—of course, they can tax their populations and draft soldiers[48]—few people favor the coercive monopoly "solution" to the most serious problem of war. Rather than invoking the Power Principle that would mandate the creation of a hierarchy, most people favor the use of "treaties" or agreements—contracts, if you will—between nations to settle their conflicts. That is precisely how a nonmonopolistic legal order should and would resolve their conflicts as well.

To better understand the case for a nonmonopolistic legal order and the deficiencies of a monopolistic system, posit what most people fear would happen if a unitary international "one-world" court system and police force were adopted. The same fears should apply with equal force to a national monopoly court system, except for the fact that some people have the ability to flee if a single country becomes too tyrannical. The abolition of geography-based jurisdictional monopolies would simply strengthen the constraints on tyranny by making alternative legal systems available without leaving home.

In sum, conflicts between court systems whose jurisdictions geographically overlap present no huge practical problem. It is more reasonable to expect a never-ending series of "little" problems around the edges. Information must be shared; duplicated efforts avoided; minor conflicts settled amicably; and profit margins preserved. As with any other organization, the normal problems confronting business and political rivals—who must constantly strike a balance between competition and cooperation—would have to be managed. How these edges would be smoothed would sometimes require ingenuity. There is no good reason, however, to refrain from seriously pursuing this alternative to the Power Principle.

Imagining a Nonmonopolistic Legal Order

It is no easier to predict the formal organization and division of labor of a future legal order than it is to predict the formal organization of the personal computer market ten years from now. (Of course, ten years ago the challenge would have been to predict the very existence of a personal computer market.) Difficulties of prediction notwithstanding, some speculation is needed, for without a conception of what such a legal order would look like, few will be inspired to move in the direction of a Liberty Approach. However, rather than attempt the impossible task of comprehensively assessing the limitless possibilities that freedom makes possible, let us instead imagine that somewhere today there exists the legal order that I shall now describe.[49]

In this hypothetical world, the vast majority of people who work or who have spouses or parents who work are covered by health insurance arrangements (like those provided in our world by such companies as Blue Cross/Blue Shield). In return for a monthly fee, if they are ever sick they receive medical attention by simply presenting their membership card to an approved doctor or hospital. In this hypothetical world, many people also carry a Blue Coif/Blue Gavel card ("Don't get caught without it!") as well. If they ever need legal services, they present their card to an approved lawyer and court system. Of course, as with medical insurance, not all kinds of legal actions are covered and there may be limits to some kinds of coverage; and not everyone makes use of this type of system.

Others belong to a "Rights Maintenance Organization" (or "R.M.O."). These firms keep lawyers on staff as salaried employees (rather than as partners) providing "preventative" legal services. Costs created by needless or hopeless litigation are said to be more tightly controlled than is possible with conventional legal insurance arrangements, and this permits an R.M.O. to offer more coverage for a lower premium. Legal disputes between members of the same R.M.O. are very expeditiously handled internally. And when it is necessary to go to an outside court, the R.M.O. will pay the court fee (having arranged group discounts for its members in advance). On the other hand, the freedom to pick your own lawyer within an R.M.O. is necessarily limited, and this feature will not satisfy everyone. Another drawback is the fact that the client is more dependent on the R.M.O.'s determination that a lawsuit is cost-justified than is a client who has coverage by Blue Coif/Blue Gavel.

Large retailers (like Sears) who sell insurance (Allstate), investment (Dean Witter), and real estate (Caldwell Banker) services also sell legal services, as do some bank and trust companies. Most offer in-house revolving charge accounts as an alternative to insurance and other kinds of credit arrangements. Law firm franchises dot the landscape with well-lit (some think garish) "Golden Scales of Justice" signs prominently displayed at streetside. Located in shopping malls and along busy streets, these firms advertise nationally and specialize in high volume (some say homogenized) practices, handling routine legal matters at standardized fees. (They accept Blue Coif/Blue Gavel and major credit cards.)

Such mass merchandising is not for everyone. Many clients still prefer the personal touch and custom tailored work of solo practitioners who thrive by providing a more individualized approach. Some of these independent lawyers offer more specialized expertise than the chains; others try to be "generalists" and claim that they can spot interrelated legal problems that the lawyers who only handle certain kinds of less complicated legal matters often miss. Most large companies with commercial legal problems prefer the elegance, prestige, and economies of scale of large, traditionally organized high-rise law firms. (Some things never change.)

Other means of financing lawsuits besides insurance are also available. A few credit card companies offer extended payment plans when used for legal services. Contingency-fee-based entrepreneurs (who, like everyone else, can and do advertise widely) serve many who cannot or choose not to advance the money for legal services. (However, to help minimize the number of improvident lawsuits, some court systems have established rules restricting such practices in a manner similar to the rules established in our world by private stock and mercantile exchanges.) Such legal entrepreneurs are a bit more risk averse than they are in our legal system since, if they lose, their clients will be liable for the full legal expenses of the other side. Still, they provide an important service to many who could not otherwise afford legal services.[50]

The judicial order mirrors the diversity of the legal profession as a whole. There are well-known and well-advertised national judicial centers, with regional and local offices, that handle the bulk of routine commercial practice. (These firms sometimes attempt to satisfy the fairness function by hiring lay jurors to decide simple factual matters.) There are small firms that handle specialized legal matters like maritime cases and patent or mineral disputes. (These firms almost never use lay jurors, but rely instead on panels of professional experts who receive retainers from the company.[51]) And there are thousands of individual judges who hang out a shingle in neighborhoods after registering with the National Register of Judges and Justices of the Peace, which requires of its members a minimum (some say minimal) level of legal education and experience. Many of these judges share the ethnic heritage of the community where their offices are located. Many of these judges are multilingual.

Individuals and businesses tend to avoid judges and judicial systems which lack some significant certification of quality. The Harvard Law School Guide to the American Judiciary, for example, is one useful source of information (but it is occasionally accused of being somewhat elitist). Who's Who in the American Judiciary, published by a nonacademic publishing firm, is another. Others prefer the annual guide published by the Consumers Union (it accepts no advertising). Still others prefer the Whole Earth Catalog of Judges (though it usually is a bit out of date). The Michelin Guide to International Law Judges uses a five-star rating system. Even with all of these publications providing information about the legal system that is unavailable to us in our world, newspapers and television "news magazines" never seem to tire of stories about judicial corruption. Such exposes sometimes lead to reforms by the various rating agencies.

To attract business most judges obtain enforcement of their judgments by subscribing to services offered by police companies. Otherwise only the moral authority of their rulings would induce compliance. Since all law enforcement agencies are legally liable to those who can prove to the satisfaction of a special appellate system that an erroneous judgment had been imposed upon them,[52] no enforcement company will long maintain a relationship with an unreliable judicial agency or an unregistered judge. (Some judges even advertise to law enforcement firms and the general public: "Judgment affirmed or your money back!") Until a few years ago, several large judicial agencies owned their own police company (more on this development in a moment).

Surprisingly, however, not every judge utilizes the services of an enforcement agency. The American Association of Adjudicators (AAA) does not promise enforcement but only a fair and just decision. All parties must contractually agree to binding adjudication in a form recognized as enforceable by other courts who do have enforcement arrangements and who will only on rare occasions fail to summarily honor an AAA adjudicator's decision. Other judges don't rely even indirectly on law enforcement agencies. In some discrete communities—like the diamond trading community in our world whose judges apply a variant of Jewish law—social sanctions are all that are required to effectively enforce judgments.

The enforcement agencies themselves tend to specialize in what we call criminal and civil cases. The distinction between these areas is not considered to be a theoretical matter, but turns instead on the differing enforcement problems that necessitate a division of labor. Those firms specializing in "criminal" matters either catch criminals or provide work to those who may not be able to earn enough to satisfy the judgment against them if left on their own. The "civil" agencies must be adept at sorting through paper arrangements to locate assets that can be legitimately seized and sold to satisfy judgments. Occasionally, when a civil agency is done with a convicted defendant, the case must be turned over to a criminal agency to collect the balance. To be sure, conflicts between enforcement agencies have arisen. Most have been quickly resolved by the agencies themselves. Some have required other agencies to intervene.

In addition, all law enforcement agencies subscribe to one of two competing computer networks that gather and store information about individuals who have been convicted of offenses (in much the same manner as government police departments and private credit rating agencies share information in our world). Such services provide their clients with near instantaneous information about individuals and firms that they might be contemplating doing business with (something like the information that local Better Business Bureaus in our world claim to provide) and persons whom they might consider excluding from their property.

While it does not directly concern the legal order, some may be interested to learn that most common areas in this world are as accessible as private shopping centers and other commercial and residential developments are in ours. Smaller parks, however, tend to be for the exclusive use of those neighborhood residents and their guests who pay annual fees; larger parks issue single admission tickets and season passes. People who do not use the parks at all are free to spend their money on other goods and services.

Intercity highways charge tolls. Urban commuter highways issue license plates that vary in price (and color) depending on whether or not they can be used during "rush hours." (Price rationing has eliminated regular traffic jams. For example, as with long distance phone service, usage between 8:00 p.m.

and 6:00 a.m. is heavily discounted.) Tourists can obtain temporary permits at outlying tollbooths. Some firms in this world are now experimenting with electronic systems that monitor highway usage—with rates that can more precisely reflect such factors as distance, time, and day—and send monthly bills to users. With road use subject to market pricing, competing private train and bus firms seem to do better in this world than in ours, where road use is rationed by gas prices and a queue.

All new commercial and residential developments must build their own roads, and all leases and land titles include both contractual rights of access and stipulated maintenance fees. Ownership of formerly public streets has been assigned to road companies. Stock in these companies belongs to those who own commercial or residential property adjacent to the streets, and these property owners also receive contractual rights of access and egress. These companies have continued to merge and break up with one another until their sizes and configurations are economically efficient.

(Aside: What now follows is a worse case scenario offered only to show the stability of such a legal order. What makes the story particularly unlikely to occur in a nonmonopolistic legal order is that its ending would be so easily foreseeable.)

Some years ago, one quite serious problem with the legal system did develop, however. About ten years after the monopoly legal system was ended, "TopCops," one of the country's largest law enforcement agencies (commanding about one-third of the national market in protective services) merged with Justice, Inc., one of the largest court systems. Many observers were quite disturbed by this development, and the other judicial companies and law enforcement agencies also became concerned. Since the merger violated no one's rights, no legal action against this new institution could be taken. The fears, however, turned out to be well founded.

Initially the operation of this organization appeared to be unobjectionable, but after a time rumors began to circulate that when subscribers to TopCops came into conflict with subscribers to other agencies, Justice, Inc., sided with TopCops in some highly questionable decisions. In response to these rumors, both the Chief Judge of Justice, Inc., and the corporate president of TopCops denied that any lack of fairness existed, and they publicly promised an internal investigation. Still the rumors persisted and took a new turn. Officers of TopCops were said to have been accused of committing crimes, but Justice, Inc., rarely if ever found for their accusers.

Unbeknownst to the general public, in response to these rumors a secret task force was formed by a consortium of major rival enforcement agencies and court systems to devise a strategy to deal with the problem. (It was thought at the time that secrecy was important so as not to shake the faith of the general public in the legal structure as a whole.) The following policies were quietly adopted and implemented:

First, no subscriber of a court system belonging to the consortium would submit to the sole jurisdiction of Justice, Inc. This had not been the usual practice formerly because avoiding duplicate legal actions saved costs for both sides.

Second, all decisions of Justice, Inc., that were in conflict with a decision of a court belonging to the consortium were to be automatically appealed to a third court system according to the appellate structure established by the Cambridge Convention (of which Justice, Inc., was a member).

Finally, no decision of Justice, Inc., that conflicted with that of a member court would be recognized and enforced by a member law enforcement agency.

Smaller court systems and law enforcement agencies quickly got wind of the new policy and began emulating it. The immediate consequence of these actions was a drastic increase in the adjudication and enforcement costs incurred by Justice, Inc., and TopCops. A backlog of cases began to develop, and the rates of both companies eventually had to be raised. As a result, subscribers began switching to alternative services. A major faction of the board of directors of TopCops resigned when the board refused to adopt any significant reforms. Instead, the remainder of the board voted to sever their affiliation with the Cambridge Convention and began to search for alliances with other companies. (The true reason for this apparently irrational behavior was discovered only later.)

Several small enforcement companies and even one medium size company were induced to affiliate with TopCops, forming the Confederation of Enforcement Agencies. It was rumored that some had been intimidated to affiliate. These alliances, however, did little more than make up for the steady drop in both subscribers and revenues. At its zenith, the entire Confederation controlled about a third of the enforcement market—about the same share of the market that TopCops alone had previously controlled.

In response, the Cambridge Convention formally severed relations with the members of the Confederation and went public with its factual findings. Notwithstanding the Confederation's public protests, its already jittery subscribers began to repudiate their contracts in large numbers. The Confederation first announced that it would no longer give pro rata refunds for subscription fees. When resignations nonetheless persisted, the Confederation announced that because they were a result of "unfounded panic," it would not recognize them as valid until the "rumormongering" of the "Cambridge Cartel" ceased.

Then a new and frightening story broke. It was learned that the board members of TopCops who had pioneered these developments were secretly affiliated with members of the remnants of the old "organized crime syndicate." Since all victimless crimes—crimes involving drugs, gambling, prostitution, pornography, and so on—had long ago been abolished, the syndicate's power and income had drastically declined. It obtained what income it received primarily from organizing and attempting to monopolize burglary, auto theft, and extortion activities. Of course, even these activities were not as profitable as they had once been because preventative law enforcement efforts had greatly increased, and the corruption of law enforcement officers had become much more difficult. Hence the scheme to infiltrate TopCops was hatched.

A search by independent investigative journalists of the court records made available by the consortium revealed that the syndicate-affiliated criminals had received unjustifiably favorable treatment by Justice, Inc. With this news, the Cambridge Convention communicated the following extraordinary order to all law enforcement agencies and to the general public:

No order of Justice, Inc. is to be recognized or obeyed. Free protection is to be extended to any subscriber of TopCops who is threatened in any way. Any victim of a burglary or auto theft whose case had been adversely decided by Justice, Inc., is entitled to a re-hearing, and all previously acquitted defendants in such cases are subject to immediate re-arrest and re-trial. All TopCops employees are to be placed under immediate surveillance.

With this action, Justice, Inc., was forced to close its operations because of lack of business. The remainder of TopCops' honest subscribers repudiated their affiliation, and scores of burglars and auto thieves were placed under arrest. (Several of TopCops' employees turned out to have been acquitted burglary and auto theft defendants.) Without a cash flow, and with the risk of personal liability now present, TopCops' employees began quitting the company in very large numbers. Since TopCops had been a national organization, it did not have a single location that was strategically defensible, so there was little armed resistance to the law enforcement actions of the consortium members. In most instances, TopCops facilities were within a few blocks of other agencies. Within a matter of weeks, the TopCops organization had been disbanded and its assets auctioned off to provide funds to partially reimburse persons whose rights it had violated. Soon, offices formerly operated by TopCops were reopened for business as new branches of other established companies.

The entire unhappy episode had taken not quite six months to unfold, but some important lessons were learned. First, the initial euphoria surrounding the abolition of the archaic monopoly legal system was tempered. People realized that a nonmonopolistic legal order was no panacea for the problems of law enforcement and adjudication. Diligence was still required to prevent injustice and tyranny from recurring. Second, the Cambridge Convention announced that in the future it would not recognize any court system created or purchased by a law enforcement agency. Court systems were still able to administer a small enforcement contingent, but strict guidelines were formulated for such arrangements. Third, organized burglary, auto theft, and extortion rings had been dealt a serious financial blow. (They still persist, however.)

Finally, after all the turmoil and talk of "crisis" had subsided, most people came to realize that their new legal order was far more stable than many of the "old guard" who had grown up under the ancient regime had expected it to be. The entire unhappy incident had unfolded in a matter of months and had been successfully and largely peacefully resolved. And this realization extended to members of the law enforcement community as well, making any future forays into aggressive activities much less likely than ever before.

Conclusion: Beyond Justice in a Free Society

We are now in a position to provide new answers to the three problems of power that were posed in the first installment:[53]

Who gets the power? Those court systems whose jurisdiction people agree to accept and those law enforcement agencies to which people are willing to subscribe.

How do you keep power in the hands of the good? By permitting people to withdraw their consent and their financial support from those who are perceived to be corrupt or to be advantage-takers and letting them shift their support to others who are perceived to be better. The potentially rapid swing of resources and the ability of law-abiding organizations to organize their resistance to aggression can help assure that swift preventative measures will be smoothly implemented.

How do you prevent holders of power from receiving undue legitimacy? No nonmonopolistic court would have any special legal privileges. Stripped of the legitimacy traditionally accorded rulers, private court systems would be constantly scrutinized to detect any self-serving behavior. Their legitimacy would depend solely on their individual reputations. While a tradition of integrity would heavily shape a reputation, an effective court system would need to ensure that its current practices and policies did not jeopardize its reputation in any way.

Two final questions remain to be addressed. First, how can we expect that the substantive rights and remedies suggested by a Liberty Approach will be the law adopted by a nonmonopolistic legal order? After all, these rights go far beyond the simple abolition of monopolistic legal jurisdictions.[54] As a practical matter the answer is quite simple. It is hard to imagine a society that did not adhere to some version of the rights and remedies prescribed by a Liberty Approach ever accepting a nonmonopolistic legal order in the first instance. In other words, a societal consensus supporting these rights and remedies would seem to be a precondition forever ending the monopolistic aspect of our legal system. Moreover, the inherent stability of a competitive system is likely to preserve this initial consensus. In the last analysis, where no consensus about liberty and individual rights exists, it is unlikely that a coercive monopoly of power will do much to prevent violations of these rights violations from occurring.[55]

Second, while acknowledging that only a summary description of a Liberty Approach has been presented here, even the most open-minded reader is likely to have a lingering doubt. There may remain a sense that a Liberty Approach—even if it operated as advertised—may somehow not be enough; that to achieve the kind of society to which we aspire requires more than the rights, duties, and legal order of a Liberty Approach.

In an important respect, I think that such a doubt is entirely justified. A Liberty Approach alone is not enough to ensure that a good society will be achieved—a world with culture, with learning, with wisdom, with generosity, with manners, with respect for others, with integrity, with a sense of humor, and much more. A Liberty Approach neither includes such values in its prescriptions nor seems to assure that by adhering to its prescriptions such a world will be attained. So what does a Liberty Approach have to offer to those who share these values?

Lon Fuller once distinguished between two moralities—the morality of aspiration and the morality of duty:

> The morality of aspiration...is the morality of the Good Life, of excellence, of the fullest realization of human powers. [A] man might fail to realize his full capabilities. As a citizen or as an official, he might be found wanting. But in such a case he was condemned for failure, not for being recreant to duty; for shortcoming, not for wrongdoing....
>
> Where the morality of aspiration starts at the top of human achievement, the morality of duty starts at the bottom. It lays down the basic rules without which an ordered society is impossible, or without which an ordered society directed toward certain specific goals must fail of its mark.... It does not condemn men for failing to embrace opportunities for the fullest realization of their powers. Instead, it condemns them for failing to respect the basic requirements of social living.[56]

A Liberty Approach, if correct, is a morality of duty. It purports to specify what justice is and how it may best be pursued. It is not an entire ethical system for achieving a good society. Adherents to a Liberty Approach seek to identify "the basic rules without which an ordered society is impossible." They believe that to legally require any more than this—to attempt to enforce a morality of aspiration as we would a morality of duty—will ultimately undermine both projects. They do not deny that more than justice is important. Nor do they deny that the pursuit of justice will be influenced by the extent to which people adhere to a morality of aspiration. But they believe no less firmly that the framework of justice provided by a Liberty Approach offers humankind the best opportunity to pursue both virtue and justice.

If the morality of aspiration is not enforced by a coercive monopoly in a Liberty Approach, then what kind of institutions would enforce it? In a society that rigorously adhered to a Liberty Approach, the so-called "intermediate" institutions that have traditionally bridged the gap between individual and State—schools, theaters, publishers, clubs, neighborhood groups, charities, religious and fraternal groups, and other voluntary associations—would continue to serve their vital function of developing and inculcating values. But in a completely free society, they would do so unburdened by the forcible interference of third parties that is made possible by an adherence to the Power Principle. Because they are noncoercive, these institutions—like the market process—are inadequately appreciated by many. But it is no coincidence that totalitarian regimes invariably strive to regulate, co-opt, subvert, and ultimately to completely destroy these institutions.

Are such voluntary institutions enough? We have no way of being sure. But, as I have repeatedly stressed here, a system based on the Power Principle offers no guarantees either. Even an ideally wielded coercive monopoly of power is only as "good" as the persons wielding the power. But power corrupts those who wield it, and virtue is its first victim. Our values come not from coercion but from the exhortations and examples set by countless individuals and groups.

The rights, remedies, and legal order specified by a Liberty Approach will not end all injustice. There will always be injustice, just as there will always be corruption and advantage-taking. But although a Liberty Approach offers no guarantees, it does enable us to better pursue justice in a free society by providing a clear idea of what we are pursuing and how we may best pursue it without undermining our precious freedom in the process. For those who believe in liberty and justice for all, a Liberty Approach may be an idea whose time has come.

Notes

1. Barnett, "Pursuing Justice in a Free Society: Power vs. Liberty," 4 *Crim. Just. Ethics* 50-72 (Summer/Fall 1985).
2. As discussed in Barnett, supra note 1, at 63-67, some within a Liberty Approach would favor punishment in addition to restitution. While I briefly discussed, id. at 65-66, the feasibility and justice of obtaining punishment within a Liberty Approach, more could and probably should be said about this dispute among adherents to a Liberty Approach than is possible in this space.
3. The Power Principle is the belief that there must exist somewhere in society a "coercive monopoly of power." See Barnett, supra note 1, at 50-52. 1 have suggested that certain features inherent in the Power Principle render it a counterproductive and inappropriate means of solving the problems it is supposedly devised to solve. Id. at 52-56.
4. Harold Demsetz's distinction between two types of economic policy analysis—the nirvana approach and the comparative institution approach—could be usefully applied to legal policy discussions as well. See Demsetz, "Information and Efficiency: Another Viewpoint," 12 *J. Law & Econ.* 1 (1969):

   In practice, those who adopt the nirvana viewpoint seek to discover discrepancies between the ideal and the real and if discrepancies are found, they deduce that the real is inefficient. Users of the comparative institution approach attempt to assess which alternative real institutional arrangement seems best able to cope with the economic problem; practitioners of this approach may use an ideal norm to provide standards from which divergences are assessed for all practical alternatives of interest and select as efficient that alternative which seems most likely to minimize the divergence.
5. See Barnett, supra note 1, at 63-64.
6. See R. Nozick, *Anarchy, State and Utopia* 28-35 (1974). See also Introduction to *Assessing the Criminal: Restitution, Retribution, and the Legal Process* 1-25 (R. Barnett and J. Hagel III, eds., 1977) (discussing the relationship between social goals and individual rights in the context of criminal justice).
7. See Furubotn and Pejovich, "Property Rights and Economic Theory: A Survey of recent Literature," 10 *J. of Econ. Literature* 1137 (1972) (discussing the literature analyzing property rights structures and the connection between ownership rights, incentives, and behavior).
8. See Hardin, "The Tragedy of the Commons," 161 *Sci.* 1243 (1968). For the view of a state supreme court judge that the present court system is an example of a

commons problem, see R. Neely, *Why Courts Don't Work* 164 (1983). ("Since the courts are available free of charge, they are overused, and the result is justice-defying delays.")

9. Even those who place an inordinately high value on protecting resources for the benefit of future generations must still place some value on the benefits resources can provide for presently living human beings.
10. See Barnett, supra note 1, at 58-59. See, e.g., Demsetz, "The Exchange and Enforcement of Property Rights," 7 *J. of Law & Econ.* 11, 18 (1964) (private property is useful "in revealing the social values upon which to base solutions to scarcity problems.... This valuation function is related to but distinct from the incentives to work provided by a property system.........); Demsetz, "Some Aspects of Property Rights," 9 *J. of Law & Econ.* 61, 65-68 (1966) ("insisting on voluntary consent tends to produce information accuracy when many costs and benefits are known only by the individuals affected.... The marginal cost and benefit curves associated with a prospective realignment of resources is not known to the government.... The primary problem of the government is the estimation problem.")
11. See D. Lavoie, *National Economic Planning: What is Left?* 51-87 (1985) (describing the "knowledge problem" facing nonmarket institutions).
12. See, e.g., Demsetz, "Some Aspects of Property Rights," supra note 10, at 62 ("A private property right system requires the prior consent of 'owners' before their property can be affected by others").
13. See B. Benson, *The Enterprise of Law: Justice without the State* (San Francisco: Pacific Research Institute for Public Policy, 1990) (describing contemporary and historical instances of private law enforcement).
14. However, minorities and strangers may suffer in such settings far more than they would in a regime of private property. Neither a Liberty Approach nor the Power Principle can guarantee that irrational prejudice will not make some worse off than they would otherwise be. In either system, if a critical mass of persons persists in hating certain persons or groups, these groups can be expected to suffer. However, even persecuted minorities fare far better in a regime of individual private property rights for two reasons. First, they may own private property and reap the many benefits of such ownership. Throughout history, Jews were prevented by the governments of many countries from owning land. Slavery and apartheid are two governmentally enforced systems that also restrict property ownership. Slavery goes so far as to legally enforce the claims of some persons to own others. Nonmonopolistic law enforcement of a complete range of property rights can only increase the well being of such persecuted groups. Second, a free market permits those members of the majority who treat minorities fairly to profit from such transactions, thereby always ensuring that powerful economic incentives exist to erode any barriers that prejudice may erect.
15. Ask yourself whether a smart public policeman who saw a suspected burglar (in a public alley behind your house) would stop him before he entered the house—that is, before a crime had been committed—or would he wait instead until after the burglary was in progress? Is it not perverse that public law enforcement makes standing by until a crime is being committed the smart way to prevent crime?
16. But see Barnett, supra note 1, at 71 n.45 (citing adherents to a Liberty Approach who would extend legal sanctions beyond restitution).
17. For more on the harmful effects of illegalizing victimless conduct, see Barnett, "Public Decisions and Private Rights," 3 *Crim. Just. Ethics* 50 (Summer/Fall 1984). The analysis of drug laws and victimless crimes presented there is greatly expanded in Barnett, "Curing the Drug Law Addiction: The Hidden Side Effects of Legal Prohibitions," in *Dealing with Drugs* (R. Hamowy, ed., 1987).

18. See infra note 24.
19. L. Fuller, *The Morality of Law* 123 (rev. ed. 1969).
20. See Barnett, supra note 1, at 56-67.
21. The philosophical claim that "taxation is theft" is, of course, controversial. The attempt to refute this claim by pointing to circumstances where the seizure and even the destruction of private property is allegedly justified to prevent a disaster from occurring is inapt. It is one thing to attempt to justify the destruction of a house to save a town from burning down. It is quite another to attempt to justify the systematic extortion of money to provide a "service" of police protection. The former describes a state of emergency. The latter does not. Normal rights theory is determined with normal social conditions in mind. Fortunately we do not live in a constant state of emergency. If we truly did, if life were really a perpetual "lifeboat situation," social order based on individual rights would probably be impossible. Happily, this is not the case.
22. Not all advocates of the Liberty Approach are in agreement on this point or on the analysis presented in the balance of this article. Robert Nozick, for example, devoted the first part of *Anarchy State and Utopia* (1974) to an attempt to show how a monopoly legal system—the so-called night watchman state—could arise without violating anyone's rights. For refutations of his argument that are consistent with the Liberty Approach presented here, see M. Rothbard, *The Ethics of Liberty* 229 (1982); Barnett, "Whither Anarchy? Has Robert Nozick Justified the State?" 1 *J. Libertarian Stud.* 15 (1977); Childs, "The Invisible Hand Strikes Back," 1 *J. Libertarian Stud.*
23. It is assumed here that law enforcement and judicial services are not, as some have argued, "public goods"—a category of goods and services that for technical economic reasons are said to be unobtainable in a free market. See, e.g., J. Buchanan, *The Limits of Liberty* 109 (1975) ("'law' of the sort analyzed here qualifies as a pure collective consumption or public good"). I plan to address this issue in a future essay.
24. Some might argue that charitable donations are induced by their being deductible from income taxes. The argument is largely implausible. Even people in the 50 percent tax bracket have to spend $1.00 to save 50 cents on their tax bills. This is hardly a profitable enterprise for most donors. And large gifts other than to charity are subject to a gift tax. Moreover, at no time in our history was there more philanthropy than prior to the enactment of an income tax when most of our private colleges and hospitals were founded. This only stands to reason. When people believe that the money taken from them by taxation is caring for the truly needy, they will feel much less inclined to give more than that amount.

    Two vitally important features of private giving militate for keeping charity voluntary, even if it were certain that less giving would take place. First, private charity will tend to be far more efficient in assisting the needy than government charity. Private charities have to answer directly to their donors. If they fail to adhere to the donors' Intentions, their contributions will dry up. By comparison, government "welfare" agencies have little or no such incentives. Second, the donor as well as the donee benefits from voluntary giving. Choosing to give to others gives satisfaction to the donor and, if such acts become habitual, can permanently improve the donor's character. Coerced giving, by contrast, breeds resentment toward the donee and can lead to class division and conflict. Ultimately, we risk undermining the charitable instincts that motivated political support for forced giving programs. Were this ever to happen, forced giving programs would not long survive.

We have witnessed an analogous development with the increasing public support for a "good faith" exception to the exclusionary rule. The exclusionary rule creates an unnecessary conflict between the protection of individual rights and public safety. See Barnett, "Resolving the Dilemma of the Exclusionary Rule: An Application of Restitutive Principles of justice," 32 *Emory L. J.* (1983) (describing this conflict and evaluating the deterrent effects of a restitutive remedy for police misconduct). Unyielding proponents of the exclusionary rule have, by forcing a choice between procedural rights and personal security, seriously undetermined popular support for the former.

25. There is no room here to consider the argument that any such system is a "natural monopoly." Suffice it to say that there is a big difference between a natural monopoly and a coercive monopoly. With the latter, even the threat of competition does not exist.
26. Some motor clubs, for example, now offer reimbursement for the expense of road repairs that were needed when club-provided services were unavailable.
27. See R. Neely, supra note 8, at 164-186; B. Bensen, supra note 13. Judge Neely endorses the Liberty Approach to court systems for "specialized users" but ultimately rejects a complete abolition of the monopoly court system, largely for economic reasons. He revealingly analogizes government courts to government schools. "Litigation, like education, serves a public function, and that function cannot be impaired by relegation [sic] it to the private sector where it cannot attract a sufficiently broad-based support to ensure its continued availability." Id. at 173n. Would that Judge Neely had thought about the problems of education as carefully as he has the problems of a legal system. For a contrary view of the necessity and desirability of government schools, see *The Public School Monopoly* (R. Everhart, ed. 1982).
28. See supra text accompanying notes 26 and 27.
29. See supra text accompanying note 18.
30. The public schools and the post office demonstrate the ineffectiveness of providing vital services in kind. Many students and parents opt out of the public school system, even though this means that they will have to pay for two school systems at the same time. The premiums charged by the burgeoning express package delivery industry indicate a similar failure of governmentally provided services. With legal services, however, most people do not have the option of (lawfully) paying a premium for better service. Where the stakes are high enough and the parties knowledgeable enough, however, many large companies insist on private arbitration clauses in their commercial contracts. Cf. R. Neely supra note 8, at 172n.
31. Even the age-old legislative efforts to assist failing farmers is no longer defended in terms of social necessity or efficiency. Rather, appeals are made to preserving the lifestyle of the "family farms" and to the "unfairness" of penalizing farmers for what are alleged to be the effects of government monetary and fiscal policy
32. H. Berman, *Law and Revolution* 10 (1983): "Legal pluralism originated in the differentiation of the ecclesiastical polity from the secular polities. The church declared its freedom from secular control, its exclusive jurisdiction in some matters, and its concurrent jurisdiction in other matters.... Secular law itself was divided into various competing types, including royal law, feudal law, manorial law, urban law, and mercantile law. The same person might be subject to the ecclesiastical courts in one type of case, the king's courts in another, his lord's courts in a third, the manorial courts in a fourth, a town court in a fifth, a merchant's court in a sixth."
33. Id. at 10. Consistent with this distinction the phrase "legal order" will be used when speaking of the entire legal structure and the phrase "legal system" when

speaking of one court or other dispute resolution system within the larger order. A nonmonopolistic legal order, then, would be likely to consist of several legal systems.

34. See also Barnett, supra note 1, at 54-55 (discussing the anemic nature of this form of "checks and balances").
35. See supra note 4.
36. Yet such appeals do occasionally take place now when citizens of one state or country flee to another and then contest (with occasional success) their extradition.
37. H. Berman, supra note 32, at 10.
38. H. Berman, supra note 32, at 10.
39. See H. Berman, supra note 32, at 38-39: "The source of supremacy of law in the plurality of legal jurisdictions and legal systems within the same legal order is threatened in the twentieth century by the tendency within each country to swallow up all the diverse jurisdictions and systems in a single central program of legislation and administrative regulation.... Blackstone's concept of two centuries ago that we live under a considerable number of different legal systems has hardly any counterpart in contemporary legal thought."
40. See Smith, "Justice Entrepreneurship in a Free Market," 4 *J. Libertarian Stud.* 405 (1979); Smith, "Justice Entrepreneurship Revisited: A Reply to Critics," 4 *J. Libertarian Stud.* 453 (1979); See also Barnett, supra note 1, at 71 n.48.
41. Such facilities have, for example, recently used prison labor to manufacture computer disk drives and as telephone operators to take reservations for a hotel chain. Confinement need not be synonymous with nonproductivity. And productivity is not synonymous with chain gangs.
42. Federal Appeals Court Judge Ralph Winter favors a limited expansion of the law-making competition that presently exists among the various states in the corporate law area into other areas such as secured transactions, sales, and landlord/tenant law. See Winter, "Private Goals and Competition Among State Legal Systems," 6 *Harv. J. of Law & Pub. Policy* 127, 128-29 (1982). ("With Delaware leading this race, you no longer have to worry about what the right law is. As long as Delaware is competing, there will be a race to the top. There will be a race to establish the optimal corporation code.... The system I am talking about is peculiar because it is the one area of the law in which the contracting parties can choose from among the law of fifty states") (emphasis added).
43. The reality is likely to be somewhat less open-ended than the text suggests. To minimize the costs of transacting in such a legal order, many kinds of property will undoubtedly be sold with jurisdictions over at least some legal issues specified in advance, as condominiums are sold today. When you buy a condominium, you buy the rules, procedures, and jurisdiction of the condominium association along with it. This does not guarantee that jurisdictional problems will not arise. It just minimizes their occurrence and severity.
44. See R. Axelrod, *The Evolution of Cooperation* 3 (1984) (presenting a theory of cooperation that can be used to discover what is necessary for cooperation to emerge "in a world of egoists without central authority").
45. The following describes the present legal system: "If the defendant does not want to submit to the jurisdiction of the court, he plainly would not authorize his attorney to enter a general appearance. If he is confident that jurisdiction over his person is lacking, he may, in theory at least, simply ignore the lawsuit entirely. To illustrate: P commences an action against D in State X for an alleged tort committed by D in State Y, seeking money for damages. D resides in State Y and has never set foot in or had any connection with State X and has no property there. P delivers process

to D in State Y. State X has not acquired jurisdiction over D's person. If judgment on D's default is entered against him, and an attempt made to enforce the judgment in State Y or elsewhere by an action in which proper service is made upon D, he can set up the invalidity of the judgment. But D may wish to contest State X's jurisdiction over his person in the courts of the State; he may be in genuine doubt whether State X has acquired jurisdiction over him, or he may not relish the prospect of an over-hanging judgment against him even though he is convinced it is invalid...[in which case] the defendant would file a notice that he was appearing solely for the purpose of challenging jurisdiction and/or submitting generally to the jurisdiction of the court." R. Field And B. Kaplan, *Civil Procedure* 199-200 (3d ed. 1973). The impetus for developing this elaborate set of rules, principles, and theories was simply to resolve the inevitable conflicts between geography-based jurisdictions.

46. R. Weintraub, *Commentary on the Conflicts Of Laws* 1 (1971). See also Chaetham and Willis, "Choice of the Applicable Law," 52 *Colum. L. Rev.* 959 (1952) (discussing the various policies to be weighed in deciding choice of law problems).
47. John Locke noted that national rulers are "independent" in the relevant sense. See Locke, "An Essay Concerning the True Original Extent and End of Civil Government" as it appears in *35 Great Books of the Western World* 28 (1980) ("All princes and rulers of 'independent' governments all through the world are in a state of Nature...whether they are, or are not, in league with others; for it is not every compact that puts an end to the state of Nature between men, but only this one of agreeing together mutually to enter into one community, and make one body politic; other promises and compacts men may make one with another, and still be in a state of Nature."). See also M. Rothbard, *For a New Liberty* 221 (rev. ed. 1978) ("We must never forget that we are all living in a world of 'international anarchy,' in a world of coercive nation-states unchecked by any world government, and there is no prospect of this situation changing").
48. There is another important reason why governments go to war against each other: they can hope to gain by obtaining the "surrender" of the other government. Governments start wars in large part to expropriate the wealth (both labor and resources) of the population ruled by another government. (Another popular motive is to distract the attention of their citizens from domestic problems.) If the total destruction of a society were necessary to bring a land area under the domination of an aggressor, then any prospective gain to be realized from war would be greatly reduced. When societies are organized in hierarchical monopolies, however, you do not have to conquer a whole people to win a war. You need only put enough pressure on the indigenous monopoly to cause its surrender. Then the conquering government puts its own people at the head of the monopoly apparatus already in place (being careful not to disrupt the existing bureaucracy) and begins extracting the wealth from the population by the same means that the native rulers did: by taxation, conscription, and condemnation.

    This indicates that one way to greatly reduce the incentives for war—as well as the incentives to develop and use weapons of mass destruction—is to end all monopoly legal (and political) systems and sufficiently intermix the competitive legal systems that supplant them so that there is no "over there" to conquer and no one has the authority to surrender for anyone else.
49. Another approach would be to examine historical examples of nonmonopolistic legal systems. See, e.g., Friedman, "Private Creation and Enforcement of Law: A Historical Case," 8 *J. of Legal Stud.* 399 (1979) (describing the ancient Icelandic legal system); Peden, "Property Rights in Celtic Law," I *J. Libertarian Stud.* 81

(1977) (describing the ancient Irish legal system); Bensen, "The Lost Victim and Other Failures of the Public Law Experiment," 9 *Harv. J. of Law & Pub. Policy* 2, 399-427 (1986) (discussing several historical examples of private legal systems in American territories); B. Benson, supra note 13 (expanding to include descriptions of other systems). Because of the vast cultural and technological differences between such remote cultures and our own and sometimes limited historical evidence, any such study can only partially assist an understanding of how a nonmonopolistic system would work in our day and age.

50. See J. Auerbach, *Unequal Justice* 45 (1976) (describing the historical controversy over "contingent fee" arrangements and the high costs to the legal system of such practices, but conceding that they served to "enable some workers to secure otherwise unobtainable legal services").
51. Cf. *Fed. R. Evid.* (1984) 706 (giving federal trial judges the power to appoint and compensate expert witnesses to testify in a trial); E. Cleary, *Mccormick On Evidence* §17 (3d ed. 1984) (describing the history of and recent proposals for court appointed experts). Some of these practices and proposals come close to letting panels of experts serve not as witnesses but as the fact finder. See id. at 45. But not all "expert" testimony is of equal value to a court. See, e.g., J. Ziskin, *Coping with Psychiatric and Psychological Testimony* (2d. ed. 1975) (forcefully arguing that psychiatric and psychological evidence should not be admitted in a court of law and, if admitted, should be given little or no weight).
52. See Barnett, supra note 24 (discussing the deterrent effect of a system of restitution to victims of police misconduct).
53. See Barnett, supra note 1, at 52-54.
54. See Barnett, supra note 1, at 56-67. This question is briefly discussed in D. Friedman, *The Machinery of Freedom* 172 (1973) ("I have described how a private system of courts and police might function, but not the laws it would produce and enforce; I have discussed institutions, not results.... Whether these institutions will produce a libertarian society—a society in which each person is free to do as he likes with himself and his property as long as he does not use either to initiate force against others—remains to be proven").
55. See, e.g., *Korematsu v. United States*, 323 U.S. 214, 223 (1944) (upholding the internment of citizens of Japanese descent "because we are at war with the Japanese Empire, because the properly constituted military authorities feared an invasion of our West Coast and felt constrained to take proper security measures, because they decided that the military urgency of the situation demanded that all citizens of Japanese ancestry be segregated from the West Coast temporarily, and finally, because Congress, reposing its confidence in this time of war in our military leaders—as inevitably it must—determined that they should have the power to do just this").
56. L. Fuller, supra note 19, at 5-6.

6

Capitalist Production and the Problem of Public Goods (excerpt)

Hans Hoppe

[N]owadays it is almost impossible to find a single economic textbook that does not make and stress the vital importance of the distinction between private goods, for which the truth of the economic superiority of a capitalist order of production is generally admitted, and public goods, for which it is generally denied. Certain goods or services, and among them, security, are said to have the special characteristic that their enjoyment cannot be restricted to those persons who have actually financed their production. Rather, people who have not participated in their financing can draw benefits from them, too. Such goods are called public goods or services (as opposed to private goods or services, which exclusively benefit those people who actually paid for them). And it is due to this special feature of public goods, it is argued, that markets cannot produce them, or at least not in sufficient quantity or quality, and hence compensatory state action is required. The examples given by different authors for alleged public goods vary widely. Authors often classify the same good or services differently, leaving almost no classification of a particular good undisputed. This clearly foreshadows the illusory character of the whole distinction. Nonetheless, some examples that enjoy particularly popular status as public goods are the fire brigade that stops a neighbor's house from catching fire, thereby letting him profit from my fire brigade, even though he did not contribute anything to financing it; or the police that by walking around my property scare away potential burglars from my neighbor's property as well, even if he did not help finance the patrols; or the lighthouse, a particularly dear example to economists, that helps ships find their way, even though they did not contribute a penny to its construction or upkeep.

Before continuing with the presentation and critical examination of the theory of public goods let us investigate how useful the distinction between private and public goods is in helping decide what should be produced privately and what by the state or with state help. Even the most superficial analysis could not fail to point out that using this alleged criterion, rather than presenting a sensible solution, would get one into deep trouble. While at least at first glance it seems that some of the state-provided goods and services might indeed qualifies public goods, it certainly is not obvious how many of the goods and services that are actually produced by states could come under the heading of public goods. Railroads, postal services, telephone, streets, and the like seem to be gold whose usage can be restricted to the persons who actually finance them, and hence appear to be private goods. And the same seems to be the case regarding many aspects of the multidimensional good "security": everything for which insurance could be taken out would have to qualify as a private good. Yet this does not suffice. Just as a lot of state-provided goods appear to be private goods, so many privately produced goods seem to fit in the category of a public good. Clearly my neighbors would profit from my well-kept rose garden—they could enjoy the sight of it without ever helping me garden. The same is true of all kinds of improvements that I could make on my property that would enhance the value of neighboring property as well. Even those people who do not throw money in his hat could profit from a street musician's performance. Those fellow travelers on the bus who did not help me buy it profit from my deodorant. And everyone who ever comes into contact with me would profit from my efforts, undertaken without their financial support, to turn myself into a most lovable person. Now, do all these goods—rose gardens, property improvements, street music, deodorants, personality improvements—since they clearly seem to possess the characteristics of public goods, then have to be provided by the state or with state assistance?

As these latter examples of privately produced public goods indicate, there is something seriously wrong with the thesis of public goods theorists that these goods cannot be produced privately but instead require state intervention. Clearly they can be provided by markets. Furthermore, historical evidence shows us that all of the alleged public goods which states now provide had at some time in the past actually been provided by private entrepreneurs or even today are so provided in one country or another. For example, the postal service was once private almost everywhere; streets were privately financed and still are sometimes; even the beloved lighthouses were originally the result of private enterprise; private police forces, detectives, and arbitrators exist; and help for the sick, the poor, the elderly, orphans, and widows has been a traditional field for private charity organizations. To say, then, that such things cannot be produced by a pure market system is falsified by experience one hundredfold.

Apart from this, other difficulties arise when the public-private goods distinction is used to decide what to leave to the market and what not. What, for instance, if the production of so-called public goods did not have positive but negative consequences for other people, or if the consequences were positive for some and negative for others? What if the neighbor whose house was saved from burning by my fire brigade had wished (perhaps because he was overinsured) that it had burned down, or my neighbors hate roses, or my fellow travelers find the scent of my deodorant disgusting? In addition, changes in the technology can change the character of a given good. For example, with the development of cable TV, a good that was formerly (seemingly) public has become private. And changes in the laws of property—of the appropriation of property—can have the very same effect of changing the public-private character of a good. The lighthouse, for instance, is a public good only insofar as the sea is publicly (not privately) owned. But if it were permitted to acquire pieces of the ocean as private property, as it would be in a purely capitalist social order, then as the lighthouse only shines over a limited territory, it would clearly become possible to exclude nonpayers from the enjoyment of its services.

Leaving this somewhat sketchy level of discussion and looking into the distinction between private and public goods more thoroughly, it turns out to be a completely illusory distinction. A clear-cut dichotomy between private and public goods does not exist, and this is essentially why there can be so many disagreements on how to classify given goods. All goods are more or less private or public and can—and constantly do—change with respect to their degree of privateness/publicness with people's changing values and evaluations, and with changes in the composition of the population. They never fall, once and for all, into either one or the other category. In order to recognize this, one must only recall what makes something a good. For something to be a good it must be realized and treated as scarce by someone. Something is not a good—as such—that is to say, but goods are goods only in the eyes of the beholder. Nothing is a good without at least one person subjectively evaluating it as such. But then, since goods are never goods—as such—no physico-chemical analysis can identify something as an economic good—there is clearly no fixed, objective criterion for classifying goods as either private or public. They can never be private or public goods as such. Their private or public character depends on how few or how many people consider them to be goods, with the degree to which they are private or public changing as these evaluations change, and ranging from one to infinity. Even seemingly completely private things like the interior of my apartment or the color of my underwear thus can become public goods as soon as somebody else starts caring about them. And seemingly public goods, like the exterior of my house or the color of my overalls, can become extremely private goods as soon as other people stop caring about them. Moreover, every good can change its characteristics again and again; it can even turn from a public or private good to a public or private bad and vice versa, depending solely on the changes in this caring or uncaring. However, if this is so, no decision whatsoever can be based on the classification of goods as private or public. In fact, to do so it would not only become necessary to ask virtually every individual person with respect to every single good whether or not he happened to care about it, positively or negatively and perhaps to what extent, in order to determine who might profit from what and should hence participate in its financing (and how could one know if they were telling the truth?!); it would also become necessary to monitor all changes in such evaluations continually, with the result that no definite decision could ever be made regarding the production of anything, and as a consequence of a nonsensical theory all of us would be long dead.

But even if one were to ignore all these difficulties, and were willing to admit for the sake of argument that the private-public good distinction did hold water, even then the argument would not prove what it is supposed to. It neither provides conclusive reasons why public goods—assuming that they exist as a separate category of goods—should be produced at all, nor why the state rather than private enterprises should produce them. This is what the theory of public goods essentially says, having introduced the above-mentioned conceptual distinction: The positive effects of public goods for people who do not contribute anything to their production or financing proves that these goods are desirable. But evidently, they would not be produced, or at least not in sufficient quantity and quality, in a free, competitive market, since not all of those who would profit from their production would also contribute financially to make the production possible. So in order to produce these goods (which are evidently desirable, but would not be produced otherwise), the state must jump in and assist in their production. This sort of reasoning, which can be found in almost every textbook on economics (Nobel laureates not excluded) is completely fallacious, and fallacious on two counts.

For one thing, to come to the conclusion that the state has to provide public goods that otherwise would not be produced, one must smuggle a norm into one's chain of reasoning. Otherwise, from the statement that because of some special characteristics of theirs certain goods would not be produced, one could never reach the conclusion that these goods should be produced. But with a norm required to justify their conclusion, the public goods theorists clearly have left the bounds of economics as a positive, wertfrei science. Instead they have transgressed into the field of morals or ethics, and hence one would expect to be offered a theory of ethics as a cognitive discipline in order for them to legitimately do what they are doing and to justifiably derive the conclusion that they actually derive. But it can hardly be stressed enough that nowhere in the public goods theory literature can there be found anything that even faintly resembles such a cognitive theory of ethics. Thus it must be stated at the outset, that the public goods theorists are misusing whatever prestige they might have as positive economists for pronouncements on matters on which, as their own writings indicate, they have no authority whatsoever. Perhaps, though, they have stumbled on something correct by accident, without supporting it with an elaborate moral theory? It becomes apparent that nothing could be further from the truth as soon as one explicitly formulates the norm that would be needed to arrive at the above-mentioned conclusion about the state's having to assist in the provision of public goals. The norm required to reach the above conclusion is this: whenever it can somehow be proven that the production of a particular goal or service has a positive effect on someone but would not be produced at all, or would not be produced in a definite quantity or quality unless others participated in its financing, then the use of aggressive violence against these persons is allowed, either directly or indirectly with the help of the state, and these persons maybe forced to share in the necessary financial burden. It does not need much comment to show that chaos would result from implementing this rule, as it amounts to saying that everyone can aggress against everyone else whenever he feels like it. Moreover, it should be sufficiently clear from the discussion of the problem of the justification of normative statements (Chapter 7) that this norm could never be justified as a fair norm. For to argue in that way and to seek agreement for this argument must presuppose, contrary to what the norm says, that everyone's integrity as a physically independent decision-making unit is assured.

But the public goals theory breaks down not just because of the faulty moral reasoning implied in it. Even the utilitarian, economic reasoning contained in the above argument is blatantly wrong. As the public goods theory states, it might well be that it would be better to have the public goods than not to have them, though it should not be forgotten that no a priori reason exists that this must be so of necessity (which would then end the public goods theorists' reasoning right here). For it is clearly possible, and indeed known to be a fact, that anarchists exist who so greatly abhor state action that they would prefer not having the so-called public goods at all to having them provided by the state! In any case, even if the argument is conceded so far, to leap from the statement that the public goods are desirable to the statement that they should therefore be provided by the state is anything but conclusive, as this is by no means the choice with which one is confronted. Since money or other resources must be withdrawn from possible alternative uses to finance the supposedly desirable public goods, the only relevant and appropriate question is whether or not these alternative uses to which the money could be put (that is, the private goods which could have been acquired but now cannot be bought because the money is being spent on public goods instead) are more valuable—more urgent— than the public goods. And the answer to this question is perfectly clear. In terms of consumer evaluations, however high its absolute level might be, the value of the public goods is relatively lower than that of the competing private goods, because if one had left the choice to the consumers (and had not forced one alternative upon them), they evidently would have preferred spending their money differently (otherwise no force would have been necessary). This proves beyond any doubt that the resources used for the provision of public goods are wasted, as they provide consumers with goods or services which at best are only of secondary importance. In short, even if one assumed that public goods which can be distinguished clearly from private goods existed, and even if it were granted that a given public good might be useful, public goods would still compete with private goods. And there is only one method for finding out whether or not they are more urgently desired and to what extent, or, mutatis mutandis, if, and to what extent, their production would take place at the expense of the nonproduction or reduced production of more urgently needed private goods: by having everything provided by freely competing private enterprises. Hence, contrary to the conclusion arrived at by the public goods theorists, logic forces one to accept the result that only a pure market system can safeguard the rationality, from the point of view of the consumers, of a decision to produce a public good. And only under a pure capitalist order could it be ensured that the decision about how much of a public good to produce (provided it should be produced at all) is rational as well. No less than a semantic revolution of truly Orwellian dimensions would be required to come up with a different result. Only if one were willing to interpret someone's "no" as really meaning "yes," the "nonbuying of something" as meaning that it is really "preferred over that which the nonbuying person does instead of nonbuying," of "force" really meaning "freedom," of "non-contracting" really meaning "making a contract" and so on, could the public goods theorists' point be "proven." But then, how could we be sure that they really mean what they seem to mean when they say what they say, and do not rather mean the exact opposite, or don't mean anything with a definite content at all, but are simply babbling? We could not! M. Rothbard is thus completely right when he comments on the endeavors of the public goods ideologues to prove the existence of so-called market failures due to the non-production or a quantitatively or qualitatively "deficient" production of public goods. He writes, "...such a view completely misconceives the way in which economic science asserts that free-market action is ever optimal. It is optimal, not from the standpoint of the personal ethical views of an economist, but from the standpoint of free, voluntary actions of all participants and in satisfying the freely expressed needs of the consumers. Government interference, therefore, will necessarily and always move away from such an optimum."

Indeed, the arguments supposedly proving market failures are nothing short of being patently absurd. Stripped of their disguise of technical jargon all they prove is this: a market is not perfect, as it is characterized by the nonaggression principle imposed on conditions marked by scarcity, and so certain goods or services which could only be produced and provided if aggression were allowed will not be produced. True enough. But no market theorist would ever dare deny this. Yet, and this is decisive, this "imperfection" of the market can be defended, morally as well as economically, whereas the supposed "perfections" of markets propagated by the public goods theorists cannot. It is true enough, too, that a termination of the state's current practice of providing public goods would imply some change in the existing social structure and the distribution of wealth. And such a reshuffling would certainly imply hardship for some people. As a matter of fact, this is precisely why there is widespread public resistance to a policy of privatizing state functions, even though in the long run overall social wealth would be enhanced by this very policy. Surely, however, this fact cannot be accepted as a valid argument demonstrating the failure of markets. If a man had been allowed to hit other people on the head and is now not permitted to continue with this practice, he is certainly hurt. But one would hardly accept that as a valid excuse for upholding the old (hitting) rules. He is harmed, but harming him means substituting a social order in which every consumer has an equal right to determine what and how much of anything is produced, for a system in which some consumers have the right to determine in what respect other consumers are not allowed to buy voluntarily what they want with the means justly acquired by them and at their disposal. And certainly, such a substitution would be preferable from the point of view of all consumers as voluntary consumers.

By force of logical reasoning, then, one must accept Molinari's above-cited conclusion that for the sake of consumers, all goods and services be provided by markets. It is not only false that clearly distinguishable categories of goods exist, which would render special amendments to the general thesis of capitalism's economic superiority necessary; even if they did exist, no special reason could be found why these supposedly special public goods should not also be produced by private enterprises since they invariably stand in competition with private goods. In fact, in spite of all the propaganda from the side of the public goods theorists, the greater efficiency of markets as compared with the state has been realized with respect to more and more of the alleged public goods. Confronted daily with experience, hardly anyone seriously studying these matters could deny that nowadays markets could produce postal services, railroads, electricity, telephone, education, money, roads and so on more effectively, i.e., more to the liking of the consumers, than the state. Yet people generally shy away from accepting in one particular sector what logic forces upon them: in the field of the production of security. Hence, the rest of this chapter will explain the superior functioning of a capitalist economy in this particular area—a superiority whose logical case has already been made, but which shall be rendered more persuasive once some empirical material is added to the analysis and it is studied as a problem in its own right.

How would a system of nonmonopolistic, competing producers of security work? It should be clear from the outset that in answering this question one is leaving the realm of purely logical analysis and hence the answers must necessarily lack the certainty, the apodictic character of pronouncements on the validity of the public goods theory. The problem faced is precisely analogous to that of asking how a market would solve the problem of hamburger production, especially if up to this point hamburgers had been produced exclusively by the state, and hence no one could draw on past experience. Only tentative answers could be formulated. No one could possibly know the exact structure of the hamburger industry—how many competing companies would come into existence, what importance this industry might have compared to others, what the hamburgers would look like, how many different sorts of hamburgers would appear on the market and perhaps disappear again because of a lack of demand, and so on. No one could know all of the circumstances and the changes which would influence the very structure of the hamburger industry that would take place over time—changes in demand of various consumer groups, changes in technology, changes in the prices of various goods that affect the industry directly or indirectly, and so on. It must be stressed that all this is no different when it comes to the question of the private production of security. But this by no means implies that nothing definitive can be said on the matter. Assuming certain general conditions of demand for security services which are known to be more or less realistic by looking at the world as it presently is, what can and will be said is how different social orders of security production, characterized by different structural constraints under which they have to operate, will respond differently. Let us first analyze the specifics of monopolistic, state-run security production, as at least in this case one can draw on ample evidence regarding the validity of the conclusions reached, and then turn to comparing this with what could be expected if such a system were replaced by a nonmonopolistic one.

Even if security is considered to be a public good, in the allocation of scarce resources it must compete with other goods. What is spent on security can no longer be spent on other goods that also might increase consumer satisfaction. Moreover, security is not a single, homogeneous good, but rather consists of numerous components and aspects. There is not only prevention, detection, and enforcement but there is also security from robbers, rapists, polluters, natural disasters, and so on. Moreover, security is not produced in a "lump, "but can be supplied in marginal units. In addition, different people attach different importance to security as a whole and also to different aspects of the whole thing, depending on their personal characteristics, their past experiences with various factors of insecurity, and the time and place in which they happen to live. Now, and here we return to the fundamental economic problem of allocating scarce resources to competing uses, how can the state—an organization which is not financed exclusively by voluntary contributions and the sales of its products, but rather partially or even wholly by taxes—decide how much security to produce, how much of each of its countless aspects, to whom and where to provide how much of what? The answer is that it has no rational way to decide this question. From the point of view of the consumers its response to their security demands must thus be considered arbitrary. Do we need one policeman and one judge, or 100,000 of each? Should they be paid $100 a month, or $10,000? Should the policemen, however many we might have, spend more time patrolling the streets, chasing robbers, recovering stolen loot, or spying on participants in victimless crimes such as prostitution, drug use, or smuggling? And should the judges spend more time and energy hearing divorce cases, traffic violations, cases of shoplifting, murder, or antitrust cases? Clearly, all of these questions must be answered somehow because as long as there is scarcity and we do not live in the Garden of Eden, the time and money spent on one thing cannot be spent on another. The state must answer these questions, too, but whatever it does, it does it without being subject to the profit-and-loss criterion. Hence, its action is arbitrary and thus necessarily involves countless wasteful misallocations from the consumer's viewpoint. Independent to a large degree of consumer wants, the state-employed security producers instead do, as everyone knows, what they like. They hang around instead of doing anything, and if they do work they prefer doing what is easiest or work where they can wield power rather than serve consumers. Police officers drive around a lot in cars, hassle petty traffic violators, and spend huge amounts of money investigating victimless crimes which a lot of people (i.e., nonparticipants) do not like, but which few would be willing to spend their money on to fight, as they are not immediately affected by it. Yet with respect to the one thing those consumers want most urgently—the prevention of hardcore crime (i.e., crimes with victims), the detection and effective punishment of hardcore criminals, the recovery of loot, and the securement of compensation to victims of crimes from the aggressors—they are notoriously inefficient, in spite of ever higher budget allocations.

Further, and here I return to the problem of a lowered quality of output (with given allocations), whatever state-employed police or judges happen to do (arbitrary as it must be), since their income is more or less independent of the consumers' evaluations of their respective services, they will tend to do poorly. Thus one observes police arbitrariness and brutality and the slowness in the judicial process. Moreover, it is remarkable that neither the police nor the judicial system offers consumers anything even faintly resembling a service contract in which it is laid down in unambiguous terms what procedure the consumer can expect to be set in motion in a specific situation. Rather, both operate in a contractual void which over time allows them to change their rules of procedure arbitrarily, and which explains the truly ridiculous fact that the settlement of disputes between police and judges on the one hand and private citizens on the other is not assigned to an independent third party, but to another police or judge who shares employers with one party—the government—in the dispute.

Third, anyone who has seen state-run police stations and courts, not to mention prisons, knows how true it is that the factors of production used to provide us with such security are overused, badly maintained, and filthy. There is no reason for them to satisfy the consumers who provide their income. And if, in an exceptional case, this happens not to be so, then it has only been possible at costs that are comparatively much higher than those of any similar private business.

Without a doubt, all of these problems inherent in a system of monopolistic security production would be solved relatively quickly once a given demand for security services was met by a competitive market with its entirely different incentive structure for producers. This is not to say that a "perfect" solution to the problem of security would be found. There would still be robberies and murders; and not all loot would be recovered nor all murderers caught. But in terms of consumer evaluations the situation would improve to the extent that the nature of man would allow this. First, as long as there is a competitive system, i.e., as long as the producers of security services depend on voluntary purchases, most of which probably take the form of service and insurance contracts agreed to in advance of any actual "occurrence" of insecurity or aggression, no producer could increase its income without improving services or quality of product as perceived by the consumers. Furthermore, all security producers taken together could not bolster the importance of their particular industry unless, for whatever reason, consumers indeed started evaluating security more highly than other goods, thus ensuring that the production of security would never and nowhere take place at the expense of the non- or reduced production of, let us say, cheese, as a competing private good. In addition, the producers of security services would have to diversify their offerings to a considerable degree because a highly diversified demand for security products among millions and millions of consumers exists. Directly dependent on voluntary consumer support, they would immediately be hurt financially if they did not appropriately respond to the consumers' various wants or changes in wants. Thus, every consumer would have a direct influence, albeit small, on the output of goods appearing on or disappearing from the security market. Instead of offering a uniform "security packet" to everyone, as is characteristic of state production policy, a multitude of service packages would appear on the market. They would be tailored to the different security needs of different people, taking account of different occupations, different risk-taking behavior, different things to be protected and insured, and different geographical locations and time constraints.

But that is far from all. Besides diversification, the content and quality of the products would improve, too. Not only would the treatment of consumers by the employees of security enterprises improve immediately, the "I could care less" attitude, the arbitrariness and even brutality, the negligence and tardiness of the present police and judicial systems would ultimately disappear. Since they then would be dependent on voluntary consumer support, any maltreatment, impoliteness, or ineptitude could cost them their jobs. Further, the above-mentioned peculiarity—that the settlement of disputes between a client and his service provider is invariably entrusted to the latter's judgment—would almost certainly disappear from the books, and conflict arbitration by independent parties would become the standard deal offered by producers of security. Most importantly, though, in order to attract and retain customers the producers of such services would have to offer contracts which would allow the consumer to know what he was buying and enable him to raise a valid, intersubjectively ascertainable complaint if the actual performance of the security producer did not live up to its obligations. And more specifically, insofar as they are not individualized service contracts where payment is made by the customers for covering their own risks exclusively, but rather insurance contracts proper which involve pooling one's own risks with those of other people, contrary to the present statist practice, these contracts most certainly would no longer contain any deliberately built-in redistributive scheme favoring one group of people at the expense of another. Otherwise, if anyone had the feeling that the contract offered to him involved his paying for other people's peculiar needs and risks—factors of possible insecurity, that is, that he did not perceive as applicable to his own case—he would simply reject signing it or discontinue his payments.

Yet when all this is said, the question will inevitably surface, "Wouldn't a competitive system of security production still necessarily result in permanent social conflict, in chaos and anarchy?" There are several points to be made regarding this alleged criticism. First, it should be noted that such an impression would by no means be in accordance with historical, empirical evidence. Systems of competing courts have existed at various places, such as in ancient Ireland or at the time of the Hanseatic league, before the arrival of the modern nation-state, and as far as we know they worked well.

Judged by the then existent crime rate (crime per capita), the private police in the Wild West (which incidentally was not as wild as some movies insinuate) was relatively more successful than today's state-supported police. And turning to contemporary experience and examples, millions and millions of international contacts exist even now—contacts of trade and travel—and it certainly seems to be an exaggeration to say, for instance, that there is more fraud, more crime, more breach of contract there than in domestic relations. And this is so, it should be noted, without there being one big monopolistic security producer and lawmaker. Finally it is not to be forgotten that even now in a great number of countries there are various private security producers alongside to the state: private investigators, insurance detectives, and private arbitrators. Regarding their work, the impression seems to confirm the thesis that they are more, not less, successful in resolving social conflicts than their public counterparts.

However, this historical evidence is greatly subject to dispute, in particular regarding whether any general information can be derived from it. Yet there are systematic reasons, too, why the fear expressed in the above criticism is not well-founded. Paradoxical as it may seem at first, this is because establishing a competitive system of security producers implies erecting an institutionalized incentive structure to produce an order of law and law-enforcement that embodies the highest possible degree of consensus regarding the question of conflict resolution, and hence will tend to generate less rather than more social unrest and conflict than under monopolistic auspices! In order to understand this it is necessary to take a closer look at the only typical situation that concerns the skeptic and allows him to believe in the superior virtue of a monopolistically organized order of security production. This is the situation when a conflict arises between A and B, both are insured by different companies and the companies cannot come to an immediate agreement regarding the validity of the conflicting claims brought forward by their respective clients. (No problem would exist if such an agreement were reached, or if both clients were insured by one and the same company—at least the problem then would not be different in any way from that emerging under a statist monopoly!) Wouldn't such a situation always result in an armed confrontation? This is highly unlikely. First, any violent battle between companies would be costly and risky, in particular if these companies had reached a respectable size which would be important for them to have in order to appear as effective guarantors of security to their prospective clients in the first place. More importantly though, under a competitive system with each company dependent on the continuation of voluntary consumer payments, any battle would have to be deliberately supported by each and every client of both companies. If there were only one person who withdrew his payments because he was not convinced the battle was necessary in the particular conflict at hand, there would be immediate economic pressure on the company to look for a peaceful solution to the conflict. Hence, any competitive producer of security would be extremely cautious about his dedication to engaging in violent measures in order to resolve conflicts. Instead, to the extent that it is peaceful conflict-resolution that consumers want, each and every security producer would go to great lengths to provide such measures to its clients and to establish in advance, for everyone to know, to what arbitration process it would be willing to submit itself and its clients in case of a disagreement over the evaluation of conflicting claims. And as such a scheme could only appear to the clients of different firms to be really working if there were agreement among them regarding such arbitrational measures, a system of law governing relations between companies which would be universally acceptable to the clients of all of the competing security producers would naturally evolve. Moreover, the economic pressure to generate rules representing consensus on how conflicts should be handled is even more far-reaching. Under a competitive system the independent arbitrators who would be entrusted with the task of finding peaceful solutions to conflicts would be dependent on the continued support of the two disagreeing companies insofar as they could and would select different judges if either one of them were sufficiently dissatisfied with the outcome of their arbitration work. Thus, these judges would be under pressure to find solutions to the problems handed over to them which, this time not with respect to the procedural aspects of law, but its content, would be acceptable to all of the clients of the firms involved in a given case as a fair and just solution. Otherwise one or all of the companies might lose some of their customers, thus inducing those firms to turn to a different arbitrator the next time they were in need of one.

But wouldn't it be possible under a competitive system for a security producing firm to become an outlaw company—a firm, that is, which, supported by its own clients, started to aggress against others? There is certainly no way to deny that this might be possible, though again it must be emphasized that here one is in the realm of empirical social science and no one could know such a thing with certainty. And yet the tacit insinuation that the possibility of a security firm becoming an outlaw company would somehow indicate a severe deficiency in the philosophy and economics of a pure capitalist social order is fallacious. First, it should be recalled that any social system, a statist-socialist order no less than a pure market economy, is dependent for its continued existence on public opinion, and that a given state of public opinion at all times delimits what can or cannot occur, or what is more or less likely to occur in a given society. The current state of public opinion in West Germany, for instance, makes it highly unlikely or even impossible that a statist-socialist system of the present-day Russian type could be imposed on the West German public. The lack of public support for such a system would doom it to failure and make it collapse. And it would be even more unlikely that any such attempt to impose a Russian-type order could ever hope to succeed among Americans, given American public opinion. Hence, in order to see the problem of outlaw companies correctly, the above question should be phrased as follows: How likely is it that any such event would occur in a given society with its specific state of public opinion? Formulated in this way, it is clear that the answer would have to be different for different societies. For some, characterized by socialist ideas deeply entrenched in the public, there would be a greater likelihood of the reemergence of aggressor companies, and for other societies there would be a much smaller chance of this happening. But then, would the prospect of a competitive system of security production in any given case be better or worse than that of the continuation of a statist system? Let us look, for instance, at the present-day United States. Assume that by a legislative act the state had abolished its right to provide security with tax funds, and a competitive system of security production were introduced. Given the state of public opinion, how likely would it then be that outlaw producers would spring up, and what if they did? Evidently, the answer would depend on the reactions of the public to this changed situation. Thus, the first reply to those challenging the idea of a private market for security would have to be: what about you? What would your reaction be? Does your fear of outlaw companies mean that you would then go out and engage in trade with a security producer that aggressed against other people and their property, and would you continue supporting it if it did? Certainly the critic would be much muted by this counterattack. But more important than this is the systematic challenge implied in this personal counterattack. Evidently, the described change in the situation would imply a change in the cost-benefit structure that everyone would face once he had to make his decisions. Before the introduction of a competitive system of security production it had been legal to participate in and support (state) aggression. Now such an activity would be an illegal activity. Hence, given one's conscience, which makes each of one's own decisions appear more or less costly, i.e., more or less in harmony with one's own principles of correct behavior, support for a firm engaging in the exploitation of people unwilling to deliberately support its actions would be more costly now than before. Given this fact, it must be assumed that the number of people—among them even those who otherwise would have readily lent their support to the state—who would now spend their money to support a firm committed to honest business would rise, and would rise everywhere this social experiment was tried. In contrast, the number of people still committed to a policy of exploitation, of gaining at the expense of others, would fall. How drastic this effect would be would, of course, depend on the state of public opinion. In the example at hand—the United States, where the natural theory of property is extremely widespread and accepted as a private ethic, the libertarian philosophy being essentially the ideology on which the country was founded and that let it develop to the height it reached —the above-mentioned effect would naturally be particularly pronounced. Accordingly, security-producing firms committed to the philosophy of protecting and enforcing libertarian law would attract the greatest bulk of public support and financial assistance. And while it may be true that some people, and among them especially those who had profited from the old order, might continue their support of a policy of aggression, it is very unlikely that they would be sufficient in number and financial strength to succeed in doing so. Rather, the likely outcome would be that the honest companies would develop the strength needed—alone or in a combined effort and supported in this effort by their own voluntary customers—to check any such emergence of outlaw producers and destroy them wherever and whenever they came into existence. And if against all odds the honest security producers should lose their fight to retain a free market in the production of security and an outlaw monopoly reemerged, one would simply have a state again.

In any case, implementing a pure capitalist social system with private producers of security—a system permitting freedom of choice—would necessarily be better than what one has now. Even if such an order should then collapse because too many people were still committed to a policy of aggression against and exploitation of others, mankind would at least have experienced a glorious interlude. And should this order survive, which would seem to be the more likely outcome, it would be the beginning of a system of justice and unheard-of economic prosperity.

Notes

1. Cf. for instance, W. Baumol and A. Blinder, *Economics, Principles and Policy* (New York, 1979), Chapter 31.
2. Another frequently used criterion for public goods is that of "non-rivalrous consumption." Generally, both criteria seem to coincide: when free riders cannot be excluded, nonrivalrous consumption is possible; and when they can be excluded, consumption becomes rivalrous, or so it seems. However, as public goods theorists argue, this coincidence is not perfect. It is, they say, conceivable that while the exclusion of free riders might be possible, their inclusion might not be connected with any additional cost (the marginal cost of admitting free riders is zero, that is), and that the consumption of the good in question by the additionally admitted free rider will not necessarily lead to a subtraction in the consumption of the good available to others. Such a good would be a public good, too. And since exclusion would be practiced on the free market and the good would not become available for nonrivalrous consumption to everyone it otherwise could—even though this would require no additional costs—this, according to statist-socialist logic, would prove a market failure, i.e., a suboptimal level of consumption. Hence, the state would have to take over the provision of such goods. (A movie theater, for instance, might only

be half-full, so it might be "costless" to admit additional viewers free of charge, and their watching the movie also might not affect the paying viewers; hence the movie would qualify as a public good. Since, however, the owner of the theater would be engaging in exclusion, instead of letting free riders enjoy a "costless" performance, movie theaters would be ripe for nationalization.) On the numerous fallacies involved in defining public goods in terms of nonrivalrous consumption cf. notes 8 and 12 below.

3. Cf. on this W. Block, "Public Goods and Externalities," in *Journal of Libertarian Studies*, 1983.
4. Cf. for instance, J. Buchanan, *The Public Finances* (Homewood, 1970), p.23; P. Samuelson, *Economics* (New York, 1976), p.160.
5. Cf. R. Coase, "The Lighthouse in Economics," in *Journal of Law and Economics*, 1974.
6. Cf. for instance, the ironic case that W. Block makes for socks being public goods in "Public Goods and Externalities," in *Journal of Libertarian Studies*, 1983.
7. To avoid any misunderstanding here, every single producer and every association of producers making joint decisions can, at any time, decide whether or not to produce a good based on an evaluation of the privateness or publicness of the good. In fact, decisions on whether or not to produce public goods privately are constantly made within the framework of a market economy. What is impossible is to decide whether or not to ignore the outcome of the operation of a free market based on the assessment of the degree of privateness or publicness of a good.
8. In fact, then, the introduction of the distinction between private and public goods is a relapse into the presubjectivist era of economics. From the point of view of subjectivist economics no good exists that can be categorized objectively as private or public. This, essentially, is why the second proposed criterion for public goods, i.e., permitting nonrivalrous consumption (cf. note 6 above), break down too. For how could any outside observer determine whether or not the admittance of an additional free rider at no charge would not indeed lead to a reduction in the enjoyment of a good by others?! Clearly, there is no way that he could objectively do so. In fact, it might well be that one's enjoyment of a movie or driving on a road would be considerably reduced if more people were allowed in the theater or on the road. Again, to find out whether or not this is the case one would have to ask every individual—and not everyone might agree. (What then?) Furthermore, since even a good that allows nonrivalrous consumption is not a free good, as a consequence of admitting additional free riders "crowding" would *eventually* occur, and hence everyone would have to be asked about the appropriate "margin." In addition, my consumption may or may not be affected, depending on *who* it is that is admitted free of charge, so I would have to be asked about this, too. And finally, everyone might change his opinion on all of these questions over time. It is thus in the same way impossible to decide whether or not a good is a candidate for state (rather than private) production based on the criterion of nonrivalrous consumption as on that of nonexcludability (cf. also note 16 below).
9. Ct. P. Samuelson, "The Pure Theory of Public Expenditure," in *Review of Economics and Statistics*, 1954; and *Economics* (New York, 1976), Chapter 8; M. Friedman, *Capitalism and Freedom* (Chicago, 1962), Chapter 2; F. A. Hayek, *Law, Legislation and Liberty*, vol. 3 (Chicago, 1979), Chapter 14.
10. In recent years economists, in particular of the so-called Chicago school, have been increasingly concerned with the analysis of property rights (cf. H. Demsetz, "The Exchange and Enforcement of Property Rights," in *Journal of Law and Economics*, 1964; and "Toward a Theory of Property Rights," in *American Economic Review*,

1967; R. Coase, "The Problem of Social Cost," in *Journal of Law and Economics*, 1960; A. Alchian, *Economic Forces at Work* (Indianapolis, 1977), part 2; R. Posner, Economic Analysis of Law (Boston, 1977). Such analyses, however, have nothing to do with ethics. On the contrary, they represent attempts to substitute economic efficiency considerations for the establishment of justifiable ethical principles (on the critique of such endeavors cf. M. N. Rothbard, *The Ethics of Liberty* (Atlantic Highlands, 1982), Chapter 26; W. Block, "Coase and Demsetz on Private Property Rights," in *Journal of Libertarian Studies*, 1977; R. Dworkin, "Is Wealth a Value," in *Journal of Legal Studies*, 1980; M. N. Rothbard, "The Myth of Efficiency," in M. Rizzo (ed.), *Time, Uncertainty, and Disequilibrium* (Lexington, 1979). Ultimately, all efficiency arguments are irrelevant because there simply exists no nonarbitrary way of measuring, weighing, and aggregating individual utilities or disutilitles that result from some given allocation of property rights. Hence, any attempt to recommend some particular system of assigning property rights in terms of its alleged maximization of "social welfare" is pseudo-scientific humbug (see in particular, M. N. Rothbard, "Toward a Reconstruction of Utility and Welfare Economics," Center for Libertarian Studies, Occasional Paper No.3 New York, 1977; also, L Robbins, "Economics and Political Economy," in *American Economic Review*, 1981).

The "Unanimity Principle" which J. Buchanan and G. Tullock, following K Wicksell (*Flnanztheoretlsche Untersuchungen* [Jena, 1896]), have repeatedly proposed as a guide for economic policy is also not to be confused with an ethical principle proper. According to this principle only such policy changes should be enacted which can find unanimous consent—and that surely sounds attractive; but then, mutatis mutandis, it also determines that the status quo be preserved if there is less than unanimous agreement or any proposal of change—and that sounds far less attractive because it implies that any given, present state of affairs regarding the allocation of property rights must be legitimate either as a point of departure or as a to-be-continued state. However, the public choice theorists offer no justification in terms of a normative theory of property rights for this daring claim as would be required. Hence, the unanimity principle is ultimately without ethical foundation. In fact, because it would legitimize any conceivable status quo, the Buchananites' most favored principle is no less than outrightly absurd as a moral criterion (cf. on this also M. N. Rothbard, *The Ethics of Liberty* [Atlantic Highlands, 1982], Chapter 26; arid "The Myth of Neutral Taxation," in *Cato Journal*, 1981, p. 549f). Whatever might still be left for the unanimity principle, Buchanan and Tullock, following the lead of Wicksell again, then give away by reducing it in effect to one of "relative" or "quasi" unanimity.

11. Cf. on this argument M. N. Rothbard, "The Myth of Neutral Taxation," in *Cato Journal*, 1981, p. 533. Incidentally, the existence of one single anarchist also invalidates all references to Pareto-optimality as a criterion for economically legitimate state action.
12. Essentially the same reasoning that leads one to reject the socialist statist theory built on the allegedly unique character of public goods as defined by the criterion of nonexcludability, also applies when instead, such goods are defined by means of the criterion of nonrivalrous consumption (cf. notes 2 and 8 above). For one thing, in order to derive the normative statement that they *should* be so offered from the statement of fact that goods which allow nonrivalrous consumption would *not* be offered on the free market to as many consumers as could be, this theory would face exactly the same problem of requiring a justifiable ethics. Moreover, the utilitarian reasoning is blatantly wrong, too. To reason, as the public goods theorists do, that the free-market practice of excluding free riders from the enjoyment of

goods which would permit nonrivalrous consumption at zero marginal costs would indicate a suboptimal level of social welfare and hence would require compensatory state action is faulty on two related counts. First, cost is a subjective category and can never be objectively measured by any outside observer. Hence, to say that additional free riders could be admitted at no cost is totally inadmissible. In fact, if the subjective costs of admitting more consumers at no charge were indeed zero, the private owner-producer of the good in question would do so. If he does not do so, this reveals that to the contrary, the costs for him are *not* zero. The reason for this may be his belief that to do so would reduce the satisfaction available to the other consumers and so would tend to depress the price for his product; or it may simply be his dislike for uninvited free riders as, for instance, when I object to the proposal that I turn over my less-than-capacity filled living room to various self-inviting guests for nonrivalrous consumption. In any case, since for whatever reason the cost cannot be assumed to be zero, it is then fallacious to speak of a market failure when certain goods are not handed out free of charge. On the other hand, welfare losses would indeed become unavoidable if one accepted the public goods theorists' recommendation of letting goods that allegedly allow for nonrivalrous consumption to be provided free of charge by the state. Besides the insurmountable task of determining what fulfills this criterion, the state, independent of voluntary consumer purchases as it is would first face the equally insoluble problem of rationally determining *how much* of the public good to provide. Clearly, since even public goods are not free goods but are subject to "crowding" at some level of use, there is no stopping point for the state, because at any level of supply there would still be users who would have to be excluded and who, with a larger supply, could enjoy a free ride. But even if this problem could be solved miraculously, in any case the (necessarily inflated) cost of production and operation of the public goods distributed free of charge for nonrivalrous consumption would have to be paid for by taxes. And this then, i.e., the fact that consumers would have been coerced into enjoying their free rides, again proves beyond any doubt that from the consumers' point of view these public goods, too, are inferior in value to the competing private goods that they now no longer can acquire.

13. The most prominent modem champions of Orwellian double talk are J. Buchanan and G. Tullock (cf. their works cited above). They claim that government is founded by a "constitutional contract" in which everyone "conceptually agrees" to submit to the coercive powers of government with the understanding that everyone else is subject to it, too. Hence, government is only seemingly coercive but really voluntary. There are several evident objections to this curious argument. First, there is no empirical evidence whatsoever for the contention that any constitution has ever been voluntarily accepted by everyone concerned. Worse, the very idea of all people voluntarily coercing themselves is simply inconceivable, much in the same way that it is inconceivable to deny the law of contradiction. For if the voluntarily accepted coercion as voluntary, then it would have to be possible to revoke one's subjection to the constitution and the state would be no more than a voluntarily joined club. If, however, one does not have the "right to ignore the state"—and that one does not have this right is, of course, the characteristic mark of a state as compared to a club—then it would be logically inadmissible to claim that one's acceptance of state coercion is voluntary. Furthermore, even if all this were possible, the constitutional contract could still not claim to bind anyone except the original signers of the constitution.

How can Buchanan and Tullock come up with such absurd ideas? By a semantic trick. What was "inconceivable" and "no agreement" in pre-Orwellian talk is for them "conceptually possible" and a "conceptual agreement." For a most instructive short exercise in this sort of reasoning in leaps and bounds cf. J. Buchanan, "A Contractarian Perspective on Anarchy," in *Freedom in Constitutional Contract* (College Station, 1977). Here we learn (p. 17) that even the acceptance of the 55 m.p.h. speed limit is possibly voluntary (Buchanan is not quite sure), since it ultimately rests on all of us conceptually agreeing on the constitution, and that Buchanan is not really a statist, but in truth an anarchist (p. 11).

14. M. N. Rothbard, *Man, Economy and State* (Los Angeles, 1970), p. 887.
15. This, first of all, should be kept in mind whenever one has to assess the validity of statist-interventionist arguments such as the following, by J. M. Keynes ("The End of Laissez Faire," in J. M. Keynes, *Collected Writings* [London 1972], vol. 9, p. 291): "The most important Agenda of the state relate not to those activities which private individuals are already fulfilling but to those functions which fall outside the sphere of the individual, to those decisions which are made by *no one* if the state does not make them. The important thing for government is not to do things which individuals are doing already and to do them a little better or a little worse; but to do those things which are not done at all." This reasoning not only *appears* phony, it truly is.
16. Some libertarian minarchists object that the existence of a market presupposes the recognition and enforcement of a common body of law, and hence a government as a monopolistic judge and enforcement agency. (Cf., for instance, J. Hospers, *Libertarianism* [Los Angeles, 1971]; T. Machan, *Human Rights and Human Liberties* [Chicago, 1975].) Now, it is certainly correct that a market presupposes the recognition and enforcement of those rules that underlie its operation. But from this it does not follow that this task must be entrusted to a monopolistic agency. In fact, a common language or sign-system is also presupposed by the market; but one would hardly think it convincing to conclude that hence the government must ensure the observance of the rules of language. Just as the system of language then, the rules of market behavior emerge spontaneously and can be enforced by the "invisible hand" of self-interest. Without the observance of common rules of speech people could not reap the advantages that communication offers, and without the observance of common rules of conduct, people could not enjoy the benefits of the higher productivity of an exchange economy based on the division of labor. In addition, as I have demonstrated in Chapter 7, independent of any government, the rules of the market can be defended a priori as just. Moreover, as I will argue in the conclusion of this chapter, it is precisely a competitive system of law administration and law enforcement that generates the greatest possible pressure to elaborate and enact rules of conduct that incorporate the highest degree of *consensus* conceivable. And, of course, the very rules that do just this are those that a priori reasoning establishes as the logically necessary presupposition of argumentation and argumentative agreement.
17. Incidentally, the same logic that would force one to accept the idea of the production of security by private business as economically the best solution to the problem of consumer satisfaction also forces one, as far as moral ideological positions are concerned, to abandon the political theory of classical liberalism and take the small but nevertheless decisive step (from there) to the theory of libertarianism, or private property anarchism. Classical liberalism, with L. v. Mises as its foremost representative in this century, advocates a social system based on the fundamental rules of the natural theory of property. And these are also the rules that libertarianism advocates. But classical liberalism then wants to have these laws enforced by a monopolistic agency (the government, the state)—an organization, that is, which

is not exclusively dependent on voluntary, contractual support by the consumers of its respective services, but instead has the right to unilaterally determine its own income, i.e., the taxes to be imposed on consumers in order to do its job in the area of security production. Now, however plausible this might sound, it should be clear that it is inconsistent. Either the principles of the natural property theory are valid, in which case the state as a privileged monopolist is immoral, or business built on and around aggression—the use of force and of no contractual means of acquiring resources—is valid, in which case one must toss out the first theory. It is impossible to sustain both contentions and not be inconsistent unless, of course, one could provide a principle that is more fundamental than both the natural theory of property and the state's right to aggressive violence and from which both, with the respective limitations regarding the domain, in which they are valid, can be logically derived. However, liberalism never provided any such principle, nor will it ever be able to do so, since, as demonstrated in Chapter 7, to argue in favor of anything presupposes one's right to be free of aggression. Given the fact then that the principles of the natural theory of property cannot be argumentatively contested as morally valid principles without implicitly acknowledging their validity, by force of logic one is committed to abandoning liberalism and accepting instead its more radical child: libertarianism, the philosophy of pure capitalism, which demands that the production of security be undertaken by private business too.

18. Cf. on the problem of competitive security production G. de Molinari, "The Production of Security," Center for Libertarian Studies, Occasional Paper No. 2, New York, 1977; M. N. Rothbard, *Power and Market* (Kansas City, 1977), Chapter 1; and *For A New Liberty* (New York, 1978), Chapter 12; also, W. C. Wooldridge, *Uncle Sam the Monopoly Man* (New Rochelle, 1970), Chapters 5-6; M. and L. Tannehill, *The Market for Liberty* (New York, 1984), Part 2.
19. Cf. M. Murck, *Soziologie der oeffentlichen Sicherheit* (Frankfurt/M., 1980).
20. On the deficiencies of democratically controlled allocation decisions cf. above, Chapter 9, n. 4.
21. Sums up Molinari ("Production of Security," Center for Libertarian Studies, Occasional Paper No. 2, New York, 1977, pp. 13-14): "If...the consumer is not free to buy security wherever he pleases, you forthwith see open up a large profession dedicated to arbitrariness and bad management. Justice becomes slow and costly, the police vexatious, individual liberty is no longer respected, the price of security is abusively inflated and inequitably apportioned, according to the power and influence of this or that class of consumers."
22. Cf. the literature cited in note 17 above; also, B. Leoni, *Freedom and the Law* (Princeton, 1961); J. Peden, "Property Rights in Celtic Irish Law," in *Journal of Libertarian Studies*, 1977.
23. Cf. T. Anderson and P. J. Hill, "The American Experiment in Anarcho-Capitalism: The Not So Wild, Wild West," in *Journal of Libertarian Studies*, 1980.
24. Ct. on the following H. H. Hoppe, *Eigentum, Anarchier und Staat* (Opladen 1987), Chapter 5.
25. Contrast this with the state's policy of engaging in battles without having everyone's deliberate support because it has the right to tax people; and ask yourself if the risk of war would be lower or higher if one had the right to stop paying taxes as soon as one had the feeling that the state's handling of foreign affairs was not to one's liking.
26. And it may be noted here again that norms that incorporate the highest possible degree of consensus are, of course, those that are presupposed by argumentation and whose acceptance makes consensus on anything at all possible, as shown in Chapter 7.

27. Again, contrast this with state-employed judges who, because they are paid from taxes and so are relatively independent of consumer satisfaction, can pass judgments which are clearly not acceptable as fair by everyone; and ask yourself if the risk of not finding the truth in a given case would be lower or higher if one had the possibility of exerting economic pressure whenever one had the feeling that a judge who one day might have to adjudicate in one's own case had not been sufficiently careful in assembling and judging the facts of a case, or simply was an outright crook.
28. Cf. on the following in particular, M. N. Rothbard, *For a New Liberty* (New York, 1978), pp. 233ff.
29. Cf. B. Bailyn, *The Ideological Origins of the American Revolution* (Cambridge, 1967); J. T. Main, *The Anti-Federalists: Critics of the Constitution* (Chapel Hill, 1961); M. N. Rothbard, *Conceived in Liberty*, 4 vols. (New Rochelle, 1975-1979).
30. Naturally, insurance companies would assume a particularly important role in checking the emergence of outlaw companies. Note M. and L. Tannehill: "Insurance companies, a very important sector of any totally free economy, would have a special incentive to dissociate themselves from any aggressor and, in addition, to bring all their considerable business influence to bear against him. *Aggressive violence causes value loss*, and the insurance industry would suffer the major cost in most such value losses. An unrestrained aggressor is a walking liability, and no insurance company, however remotely removed from his original aggression, would wish to sustain the risk that he might aggress against one of its own clients next. Besides, aggressors and those who associate with them are more likely to be involved in situations of violence and are, thus, bad insurance risks. An insurance company would probably refuse coverage to such people out of a foresighted desire to minimize any future losses which their aggressions might cause. But even if the company were not motivated by such foresight, it would still be forced to raise their premiums up drastically or cancel their coverage altogether in order to avoid carrying the extra risk involved in their inclination to violence. In a competitive economy, no insurance company could afford to continue covering aggressors and those who had dealings with aggressors and simply pass the cost on to its honest customers; it would soon lose these customers to more reputable firms which could afford to charge less for their insurance coverage.

    What would loss of insurance coverage mean in a free economy? Even if [the aggressor] could generate enough force to protect itself against any aggressive or retaliatory force brought against it by any factor or combination of factors, it would still have to go completely without several economic necessities. It could not purchase insurance protection against auto accidents, natural disasters, or contractual disputes. It would have no protection against damage suits resulting from accidents occurring on its property. It is very possible that [it] would even have to do without the services of a fire extinguishing company, since such companies are natural outgrowths of the fire insurance business.

    In addition to the terrific penalties imposed by the business ostracism which would naturally follow its aggressive act [it] would have trouble with its employees... [For] if a defense service agent carried out an order which involved the intentional initiation of force, both the agent and the entrepreneur or manager who gave him the order, as well as any other employees knowledgeably involved, would be liable for any damages caused" (M. and L. Tannehill, *The Market for Liberty* [New York, 1984], pp. 110-111).
31. The process of an outlaw company emerging as a state would be even further complicated, since it would have to reacquire the "ideological legitimacy" that marks the existence of the presently existing states and which took them centuries of relentless propaganda to develop. Once this legitimacy is lost through the experience with a pure free market system, it is difficult to imagine how it could ever be easily regain.

7

National Defense and the Public-Goods Problem

Jeffrey Rogers Hummel and Don Lavoie[1]

National defense, according to the popular ideal, is a service provided by the state to its citizens.[2] It entails protection from aggressors outside the state's jurisdiction, usually foreign states. The most sophisticated theoretical justification for government provision of this service is the public-goods argument. Roughly stated, this argument claims that the incentive to free ride inhibits people from providing enough protection from foreign aggression voluntarily. Thus, it is in people's best interests to coerce themselves. Taxation is necessary to ensure sufficient military expenditures.

Many opponents of arms control treat the public-goods problem as if it alone were sufficient to discredit any radical reduction in military spending. We, however, will challenge this presumption. This chapter will not question the validity, realism, or relevance of the public-goods concept.[3] Indeed, we think that the core service within national defense—safety from violence and aggression—captures the essence of a public good more fully than economists have appreciated. But this essential feature, rather than providing a solid justification for heavy military expenditures, offers one of the most powerful objections to such a government policy.

We will first reexamine the nature of national defense in order to clarify the underlying goal of military spending. The presumption that the state's military establishment automatically provides safety from aggression needs careful scrutiny. The taxation necessary to fuel military expansion often generates more public-goods problems than it circumvents. This leads us to the more general question of how the free-rider incentive is ever overcome, despite theoretical predictions to the contrary. Public-goods theory seems to misunderstand human nature, by exaggerating the importance of narrow self-interest and confining attention to artificially static Prisoners' Dilemmas. A more social and dynamic model of human action is better able to account for the observed fact that free-rider problems are overcome in the real world all the time.

What is a Public Good?

Economists have called many things public goods and then endlessly debated whether the label really applies, but national defense has remained the quintessential public good. Although rarely discussed in detail, it is universally invoked as the classic representative of the public-goods category.[4]

Two characteristics distinguish a pure public good from a private good, and both are exhibited by the case of national defense. The first is nonrival consumption. One customer's consumption of a marginal unit of the good or service does not preclude another's consumption of the same unit. For example, in an uncrowded theater, two patrons' enjoyment of the same movie is nonrival. The second characteristic is nonexcludability. The good or service cannot be provided to an individual customer without simultaneously providing it to others. The owner of a dam, for example, cannot provide flood control separately to the individual farmers residing downstream.[5]

Although these two characteristics frequently come in conjunction with each other, they do not necessarily have to. Nonexcludability from the dam's flood-control services is accompanied by nonrival consumption of the services among the various farmers, but the owner of a nearly empty theater can still exclude additional patrons. Yet, according to the public-goods argument, either characteristic alone causes "market failure"—that is, an allocation of resources that is less than Pareto optimal. Thus, either can be sufficient to justify state intervention.[6]

Even national defense is not a pure public good. Americans in Alaska and Hawaii could very easily be excluded from the U.S. government's defense perimeter, and doing so might enhance the military value of at least conventional U.S. forces to Americans in the other forty-eight states. But, in general, an additional ICBM in the U.S. arsenal can simultaneously protect everyone within the country without diminishing its services. In that respect, consumption of national defense is nonrival. Moreover, a technique that defends just a single American from the Soviet state without necessarily defending his or her entire community and perhaps the entire nation is difficult to visualize. That makes national defense nonexcludable as well.

We are going to focus, however, only upon nonexcludability. If consumption of a service is nonrival, but businessmen and entrepreneurs can exclude those who do not pay for it, then they still have strong incentives to provide the service. The most serious "market failure" that is alleged to result is underutilization of the service. Some people will be prevented from benefiting from the quantity of the service that has been produced, even though permitting them to do so costs nothing. Furthermore, even this imperfection will dissipate if the market permits discriminatory pricing.[7]

On the other hand, nonexcludabillty creates opportunities for free riders, who will pay for the service only if doing so is absolutely necessary to receive it. From the perspective of economic self-interest, every potential customer has an incentive to try to be a free rider. If enough of them act on this incentive, the service will not be produced at all, or at least not enough of it.

Another way to think about nonexcludability is as a positive externality in its purest form. Many goods and services generate additional benefits for people other than those who directly consume and pay for them. There is often no way for the producers of these goods to charge those who receive these external benefits. A nonexcludable good or service is one where the positive externalities are not just an incidental by-product but rather constitute the major benefit of the good or service.[8]

Clearly, the justification for the state's provision of national defense does not stem from any major concern that in its absence protection services would be produced but underutilized. Rather, it stems from the assumption that, unless taxation or some other coercive levy forces people to contribute, national defense will be inadequately funded and therefore its core service of safety from aggression will be underproduced. It is this widely held but rarely examined assumption that we wish to question.

What is National Defense?

Before we can explore the free-rider dynamics of the state's military establishment, we must clarify the meaning of the term "national defense." The public-goods justification for military expenditures rests upon a fundamental equivocation over exactly what service national defense entails. When economists discuss national defense, the core service they usually have in mind, explicitly or implicitly, is protection of people's lives, property, and liberty from foreign aggressors. This also appears to be what people have in mind when they fear foreign conquest, particularly in the case of the American fear of Soviet conquest. People throughout the world believe that their own government, no matter how disagreeable, defends them from foreign governments, which they think would be even more oppressive.

This defense of the people is not synonymous with another service that goes under the same "national defense" label: protection of the state itself and its territorial integrity. Historically, the state has often embarked on military adventures unrelated to the defense of its subjects. If this were not the case, people would require no protection from foreign states in the first place. Many Americans seriously doubt that the U.S. bombing of North Vietnam and Cambodia had very much to do with protecting their liberty. One defense-budget analyst, Earl Ravenal, contends that nearly two-thirds of U.S. military expenditures goes toward the defense of wealthy allied nations in Europe and Asia and has little value for the defense of Americans.[9]

The distinction between the two meanings of national defense does not apply only when the state engages in foreign intervention or conquest. Even during unambiguously defensive wars, the state often systematically sacrifices the defense of its subjects to the defense of itself. Such universal war measures as conscription, confiscatory taxation, rigid economic regulation, and suppression of dissent aggress against the very citizens whom the state is presumably protecting. People believe the state defends their liberty; in fact, many end up surrendering much of their liberty to defend the state.

People of course may consider some tradeoff worth it. They may accept the costs and risks of the state's protection in order to reduce the risks and costs of foreign conquest. But in most discussions of national defense, the aggressive acts taken by the government against its own subjects are arbitrarily excluded from the discussion. It is this frequently overlooked cost which is suggested in Randolph Bourne's famous observation: "War is the health of the State."[10]

In other words, the national interest and the public good do not automatically coincide. We do not deny the possibility of an incidental relationship between the defense of the state and the defense of the people. But in the next section, we will present general reasons why we think this relationship is not as strong as usually supposed. Before we can do that, we, must fully expose the conceptual gulf between the two meanings of national defense.

The pervasive doctrine of nationalism obscures this fundamental distinction. Nationalism treats nations as collective entities, applying principles drawn from the analysis of individual interaction to the international level. In a war between two nations, the nationalist model focuses on essentially two parties: nation A and nation B. As in fights between individuals, one of these two nations is the aggressor, whereas the other is the defender. As a result, the model axiomatically equates protecting the state with protecting its subjects.

The basic flaw in the nationalist model is its collectivist premise. Although the model informs many of the formal economic analyses of international relations, it represents a glaring example of the fallacy of composition. The state simply is not the same thing as its subjects. Democracies are sometimes referred to as "governments of the people," but this is, at best, rhetorical sloppiness. The state and the people interpenetrate one another and in complex ways, but they clearly do not have exactly the same purposes or interests.

Consequently, any conflict between two nations involves not just two parties, but at least four: the state governing nation A, the state governing nation B, the people with the (mis)fortune to live under state A, and the people with the (mis)fortune to live under state B. Whatever the merits of a dispute between states A and B, the dispute need not divide a significant portion of people A from people B.[11]

Abandoning this collectivist identification of the state with its subjects exposes the critical insight about the national-defense service. If one is truly concerned about defense of peoples' lives, property, and liberty, then the transfer of their capital city from one location to another is not intrinsically significant. In some cases it might even be thought an improvement. Many Americans are convinced that the territory constituting Russia is in a very real sense already conquered—by the Soviet government. Some even believe that the Soviet people would fare better with Washington, D.C. as their capital city. What ultimately matters is whether transferring the capital city brings the citizens a net loss or gain.

The danger therefore is not foreign conquest per se, but the amount of power the conquering government can successfully wield. In the final analysis, protection from foreign states is not a unique service. It is a subset of a more general service: protection from aggression by anyone—or any state. Whether we formally label an oppressive state "foreign" or "domestic" becomes a secondary consideration.

People admittedly may highly value their own state's preservation and glorification, in and of itself. Their government's military establishment may directly enter their utility functions, the same way their favorite baseball or football team does. But nationalism is not just a subjective preference. It is also a positive social theory, as legitimately subject to criticism for its policy recommendations as any other. The military's coercive funding unfortunately prevents people from revealing their true preferences about national defense directly and unambiguously. Some citizens may still want a huge and expensive military establishment even if they discover that it gives them less protection than they thought. But meanwhile, an examination of whether military expansion truly does defend people's lives, property, and liberty is still in order.[12]

The Free-Rider Dynamics of Government Intervention

When Paul Samuelson first formalized public-goods theory, many economists unreflectively subscribed to what Harold Demsetz has called the nirvana approach to public policy. Demonstrating some "market failure" with respect to an abstract optimum was considered sufficient to justify state action. Economists assumed that the costless, all-knowing, and benevolent state could simply and easily correct any failure.

Since then, economists have become far more realistic. Public-goods theory has advanced to the point where it is now an exercise in comparative institutions. Demonstrating "market failure" is no longer sufficient. One must compare the market with the state, not as one wishes the state would behave in some ideal realm, but as it must behave in the real world. To justify state action, one must show that the agents of government have the capacity and the incentive to do a better job than participants in the market. Can the state provide the public good without costs that exceed the benefits? And is there some incentive structure that would conceivably ensure that it do so?[13]

Economists within the field of public choice have done some of the most important work on the comparative capabilities of the state—by applying public-goods insights to political action itself. They have come to the realization that the free-rider incentive does not only arise for market enterprises. As Mancur Olson has demonstrated, the free-rider incentive can arise for any group, especially political groups wanting to influence state policy. This imparts an inherent public-goods character to all political decisions.[14]

Assume that one of us wishes to change some state policy that we personally find particularly onerous—for instance, to repeal a tax. We are members of a fairly large group that will benefit if the tax is repealed. If enough of us contribute money, time, or other resources to bringing about the tax's repeal, we will succeed and all be better off. The money we save in taxes will more than reimburse us for our effort. Once the tax is repealed, however, even those who did not join our campaign will no longer have to pay it. We cannot exclude them from the benefits of the tax's repeal. They will be free riders on our political efforts.

Just as in the case of a nonexcludable good in the market, every potential beneficiary of the tax repeal has an incentive, from the perspective of economic self-interest, to try to be a free rider. If enough of them act according to this incentive, the tax will never be repealed. Public choice economists call this result "government failure," completely analogous the "market failure" caused by nonexcludability.

Of course, this example grossly oversimplifies the problem. Under democratic states, people do not directly purchase changes in state policy; they vote for them. Or more precisely, some of them vote for representation who then vote on and bargain over state policy. If the tax repeal example were completely accurate, nearly every intentional benefit provided by the state would be a pure private good, similar to the current salaries of politicians and bureaucrats. With voting, political entrepreneurs and vote maximizing firms (which are called political parties) have some incentive to provide us with our tax repeal, even if we do not politically organize, in order to entice us to vote for them.[15]

This incentive, however, is not very great. First of all, voting itself gives rise to a public good. An individual must expend time and other resources to vote, but he or she can avoid these expenditures by free riding on the voting of others. Only in the very remote case where the voter anticipates that a single vote will decide the election's outcome does this incentive to free ride disappear. Consequently, the political entrepreneur must have some reason to expect that we will vote at all. And if we do in fact vote, he must in addition have some reason to expect that the tax repeal, among all the other competing issues, will affect how we vote. Our forming a political organization to repeal the tax gives him reason to believe both these things.[16]

In short, unorganized groups have some influence upon the policies of a democratic state. But other things being equal, groups that organize and campaign for policies have a significant advantage. That is presumably why they organize and campaign. It strains credulity to suppose that all the people who pour vast sums of money into political lobbying are utterly mistaken in the belief that they thereby gain some leverage on policy. The common observation that special interests have inordinate influence upon a democratic state is without doubt empirically well founded.

Two variables affect the likelihood that a group will overcome the free-rider problem and successfully organize. These variables operate whether the group is trying to attain nonexcludable benefits on the market or from the state. The first is the size of the group. The smaller the group, *ceteris paribus*, the more likely the members are to organize successfully. The larger the group, the more difficult it is to involve enough of them to secure the public good.

The second variable is the difference between the value of the public good to the members of the group and the cost to them. The greater this difference, *ceteris paribus*, the more likely they are to organize successfully. Indeed, if this difference is great enough, one single member might benefit enough to be willing to pay the entire cost and let all the other members of the group free ride. The smaller this difference, on the other hand, the more essential becomes the contribution of each potential member.[17]

The democratic state therefore makes it much easier to enact policies that funnel great benefits to small groups than to enact policies that shower small benefits on large groups. Because of this free-rider-induced "government failure," the state has the same problem in providing nonexcludable goods and services as the market—with one crucial difference. When a group successfully provides itself a public good through the market, the resources it expends pay directly for the good. In contrast, when a group successfully provides itself a public good through the state, the resources it expends pay only the overhead cost of influencing state policy. The state then finances the public good through taxation or some coercive substitute.

Moreover, the group that campaigned for the state-provided public good will not in all likelihood bear very much of the coerced cost of the good. Otherwise, they would have had no incentive to go through the state, because doing so then costs more in total than simply providing themselves the good voluntarily. Instead, the costs will be widely distributed among the poorly organized large group, who may not benefit at all from the public good.

This makes it possible for organized groups to get the state to provide bogus public goods, goods and services which in fact cost much more than the beneficiaries would be willing to pay even if exclusion were possible and they could not free ride. In this manner, the state generates externalities, and ones that are negative. Rather than overcoming the free-rider problem, the state benefits freeloaders, who receive bogus public goods at the expense of the taxpayers. Provision of these goods and services moves the economy away from, not toward, Pareto optimality. When the bogusness of such public goods is obvious enough, economists call them transfers.

What is the upshot of this "government failure" for national defense? In the case of defending the state itself, we are dealing quite clearly with a service that the state has enormous incentives to provide. If this is a nonexcludable good or service at all, then it is a public good that benefits small groups very highly. But in the case of defending the people, we are talking about, in the words of David Friedman, "a public good...with a very large public." The benefits, although potentially great, are dispersed very broadly.[18]

Thus, to the extent that the free-rider obstacle inhibits market protection of liberty, it raises an even more difficult obstacle to the state's ever undertaking that vital service. The state has strong incentives to provide national defense that protects itself and its prerogatives, but it has very weak incentives to provide national defense that protects its subjects' lives, property, and liberty. This explains the common historical divergence between defending the state and defending the people.

Furthermore, there is a perverse inverse relationship between the people's belief that the state defends them and the reality. To the extent that they accept this nationalistic conclusion, their political resistance against the domestic state's aggression, however weak because of the public-goods problem to begin with, decreases further. This is most noticeable during periods of actual warfare. The belief of the state's subjects that it provides protection actually reduces the amount of protection they enjoy, at least against the domestic state.

Nationalism thus results in an ironic paradox. It views the state as a protection agency, but this very view contributes to the possibility that the state will take on the literal role of a protection racket. Those who decline to pay for the state's protection become its victims. This in turn gives the state an added incentive to find foreign enemies. For without a foreign threat, the justification for the state's protection becomes far less persuasive.[19]

Our remarks have thus far been confined to the democratic state. They apply, however, even more strikingly to the undemocratic state, insofar as there is any significant difference between the political dynamics of the two types. We believe that many economists have overemphasized the operative significance of formal voting. Both types of states are subject to the influence of groups that marshal resources in order to affect policy. Formal voting only makes it possible for some changes to manifest themselves faster and less painfully.

Our argument does not rule out the possibility that the state might actually defend its subjects. Whereas the difference between the political dynamics of democratic and undemocratic states is overdrawn, states do differ markedly in the amount of aggression they commit against their own subjects. If we automatically assume that a conquering government can wield as much power over foreign populations as it does over its domestic subjects, then a relatively less oppressive government will, in the process of defending itself, provide some protection for its subjects. But this is often only an unintended positive externality.

Moreover, a military policy designed primarily to defend the state's prerogatives will generally differ from what would be sufficient for the protection of its subjects. This difference may unnecessarily involve the people in dangerous military commitments and adventures. Their lives, liberty, and property, beyond being sacrificed to the interests of the domestic state, will then be at greater risk from foreign governments as well. Even when countering oppressive governments, national defense therefore generates negative externalities that may more than offset the possible positive externality.

Above all, the value of this defense hinges entirely upon the assumption that conquering governments can oppress a foreign population more fully and easily than can that population's domestic government. But this assumption is highly simplistic. It treats the power of the state as exogenously determined. Yet, if our concern is for the protection of people's lives, property, and liberty from *any* state, then a state's oppressiveness becomes the most critical variable of all. One state's military policy might not only directly affect the liberty of its own subjects, but it might also indirectly influence the power of opposing states. Only a more sophisticated understanding of oppression's fundamental determinants can tell us how best to ward off foreign aggression.

The Free-Rider Dynamics of Social Consensus

To this point, our conclusions have been somewhat pessimistic, justifying Earl Brubaker's observation that the free-rider assumption makes economics a dismal science.[20] Based on that assumption, neither the market nor the state has much incentive to provide any direct protection of peoples lives, property, and liberty. To the extent that historical accident has resulted in marked differences in the power of various states over their own subjects, some such protection might be produced as an unintended externality of the state's effort to protect its own territorial integrity. But that very effort at self-protection will also have a significant countervailing negative impact on the degree to which the state aggresses against its own subjects.

Attributing a difference to historical accident, however, is simply another way of saying that the difference is unexplained. Not until we explain the marked differences in domestic power of the world's states will we fully comprehend the relationship between protecting the state and protecting the people.

One naive explanation common among economists is the public-goods theory of the state. This theory often rests upon a sharp dichotomy between two types of states, usually democratic and undemocratic. Undemocratic states according to this theory are little better than criminal gangs, run by single despots or small groups of oligarchs essentially for their own personal ends. The subjects of these states suffer under their rulers but can do very little about their plight. Any effort on their part to change the situation, whether through violent revolution or other means, produces an outcome that is a public good; again, we are caught in the free-rider trap.[21]

Democratic states, in contrast, are the result of social contracts. According to the public-goods theory of the state, people create democratic states to solve the free-rider problem. At some obscure moment in the past, they drew up constitutional rules in which they agreed to be coerced in order to provide public goods for themselves. Over time, because the free-rider problem generates "government failure," democratic states have a tendency to fall under the influence of special interests. Perhaps better constitutional decision rules could alleviate this decay. Nonetheless, democratic states always retain vestiges of their public-goods origin. That is why they aggress against their own subjects far less than do undemocratic states.[22]

We do not have to turn to the readily accessible historical evidence to refute this naive theory about the origin of democratic states. The theory's proponents quite often do not literally believe it. Instead, they view the theory as merely explaining the conceptual nature rather than the concrete origin of the democratic state. Either way, however, the theory has an inner contradiction. Creating a democratic state of this nature is a public good itself. A very large group must in some manner have produced it. Because of the free-rider problem, they have no more incentive to do that than to revolt against an undemocratic state or to provide themselves any other nonexcludable benefit.[23]

A more realistic alternative to the public-goods theory of the state is what we can call the social-consensus theory of the state. All states are legitimized monopolies on coercion. The crucial word is "legitimized." This legitimization is what differentiates states from mere criminal gangs. Any society in which people refrain from regularly killing each other enjoys some kind of social consensus. No government rules through brute force alone, no matter how undemocratic. Enough of its subjects must accept it as necessary or desirable for its rule to be widely enforced and observed. But the very consensus which legitimizes the state also binds it.[24]

The social consensus bears little resemblance to the mythical social contract of public-goods theory. Whereas the social contract is generally conceived of as an *intentional* political agreement, agreed upon explicitly at some specific moment, the social consensus is an *unintended* societal institution, like language, evolving implicitly over time. Sometimes, the evolution of the social consensus can be very violent. Often, particular individuals or even fairly large groups will strongly disagree with certain features of their society's consensus. But at all times, members of society are socialized into the consensus in ways that they only dimly grasp, if at all.[25]

Consider a classroom filled with average American citizens. Ask for a show of hands on the following question: how many would pay their taxes in full if no penalties resulted from nonpayment? Very few would raise their hands. This shows that taxation is involuntary. Then ask the group a second question: how many think taxes are necessary or just? This time, nearly every hand would go up. This shows that taxation is legitimized.[26]

Of course, one of the reasons Americans generally view taxation as legitimate is because they think it is necessary in order to provide public goods. All this proves, however, is that, although the public-goods theory of the state is utterly worthless as an objective description of the state's origin or nature, it is very valuable as an ideological rationalization for the state's legitimization. It performs a function analogous to that performed by the divine right of kings under monarchical states or by Marxist dogma under communist states.

The social-consensus theory of the state suggests that if you conducted the same survey about taxation upon a group of average Russians living within the Soviet Union, or a group of average Iranians living under the Ayatollah (and you could guarantee them complete immunity regardless of how they answered), you would get similar results. These foreign and "evil" undemocratic states are not exogenous and alien institutions imposed on their subjects by sheer terror. They are complex products of the culture, attitudes, preferences, and ideas, whether explicit or implicit, that prevail within their societies.[27]

The vast ideological and cultural differences among the peoples of the world are what explain the marked differences in the domestic power of their states. The consensual constraints upon states differ in content, but all states face them. The Soviet leaders fully realize this, which is why they devote so many resources to domestic and foreign propaganda. The shifting social consensus also explains the many changes in the form and power of the state over time. Although professional economists tend to ignore the ideological and cultural components of social dynamics, professional historians give these factors the bulk of their attention.

History records that in the not-so-distant past the world was entirely in the grip of undemocratic states, which permitted their subjects very little liberty. Democratic states evolved from undemocratic states. States that now must tolerate a large degree of liberty emerged from states that did not have to do so. Public-goods theory is in the awkward position of theoretically denying that this could have happened. It raises an across-the-board theoretical obstacle to every conceivable reduction in state power that benefits more than a small group of individuals.[28] The social-consensus theory, in contrast, attributes this slow progress, sometimes punctuated with violent revolutions and wars, to ideological changes within the social consensus.

Thus, history is littered with drastic changes in state power and policy that resulted from successful ideological surmountings of the free-rider obstacle. The Minutemen volunteers who fought at Concord Bridge could not even come close to charging all the beneficiaries of their action. They produced tremendous externalities from which Americans are still benefiting today. The Abolitionist movement produced such a cascade of positive externalities that chattel slavery—a labor system that was one of the world's mainstays no less than two hundred years ago, and had been so for millennia—has been rooted out everywhere across the entire globe. We could multiply the examples endlessly.[29]

Indeed, the existence of any voluntary ethical behavior at all faces a free-rider obstacle. Society is much more prosperous if we all cease to steal and cheat, but the single individual is better off still if everyone else behaves ethically while he or she steals and cheats whenever able to get away with it. Thus, everyone has a powerful personal incentive to free ride on other people's ethical behavior. If we all succumbed to that incentive, society would not be possible at all.

We must avoid the mistaken impression that the government's police forces and courts are what prevents most stealing and cheating. To begin with, the initial creation of such a police and court system (at least under government auspices) is another public good. But far more important, the police and courts are only capable of handling the recalcitrant minority, who refuse voluntarily to obey society's norms. A cursory glance at varying crime rates, over time and across locations, clearly indicates that the total stealing and cheating in society is far from solely a function of the resources devoted to the police and the courts. Certain neighborhoods are less safe, making an equal unit of police protection less effective, because they contain more aspiring ethical free riders. If all members of society or even a substantial fraction became ethical free riders, always stealing and cheating whenever they thought they could get away with it, the police and court system would collapse under the load.[30]

In short, every humanitarian crusade, every broad-based ideological movement, every widely practiced ethical system, religious and non-religious, is a defiant challenge hurled at the neoclassical economist's justification for state provision of public goods. The steady advance of the human race over the centuries is a series of successful surmountings of the free-rider obstacle. Civilization itself would be totally impossible unless people had somehow circumvented the public-goods problem.[31]

Beyond the Free-Rider Incentive

If what we have been saying so far is even partly correct, there must be a serious flaw in public-goods theory. Howard Margolis points out that "no society we know could function" if all its members actually behaved as the free-rider assumption predicts they will. He calls this theoretical failure free-rider "overkill."[32]

Despite this flaw, public-goods theory explains a great deal, which is why it remains so popular among economists. It explains why so many eligible voters do not waste their time going to the polls. But it fails to explain why so many of them still do go. (We think an interesting empirical study would be to determine what percentage of economists who accept public-goods theory violate their theoretical assumptions about human behavior by voting.) It explains why the progress of civilization has been so painfully slow. But it fails to explain why we observe any progress at all.

Before we work out the implications of this theoretical flaw for the issue of national defense, let us digress briefly and try to identify it. It must involve some weakness in the theory's assumption about human behavior. We make no pretensions, however, to being able fully to resolve the weakness. Because this very issue sits at the conjunction of public-goods theory and game theory, it has become one of the most fertile areas of inquiry within economics and political science over the last decade. All we can do is modestly offer some tentative thoughts about the sources of the weakness.

Two possibilities suggest themselves. Either people do not consistently pursue the ends that the free-rider assumption predicts they will pursue, or they pursue those ends but using means inconsistent with the assumption.

We will take up both of these possibilities in order:

1. Do people consistently pursue their self-interest, as the free-rider assumption defines self-interest? Public-goods theorists have offered not one but two motives that should cause a person to behave in accordance with the free-rider assumption. The most obvious is narrow economic self-interest. This end does provide a sufficient reason to free ride, but visualizing someone choosing a different end is quite easy. Simple altruism is not the only alternative that will violate this narrow assumption. People may desire social improvements—liberty, justice, peace, etc.—not simply for their material benefits, but as ends in and of themselves, independently present within their utility functions. Patrick Henry may have been engaging in political hyperbole when he exclaimed "Give me liberty or give me death!", but he was still expressing a willingness to pay more for attaining liberty than its narrow economic returns would cover. Perhaps this

willingness should be called ideological; no matter what we call it, it appears to be quite common in human history.[33]

Mancur Olson is the most prominent public-goods theorist to argue that a second motive beyond narrow economic self-interest justifies the free-rider assumption. This second motive applies even to the individual with ideological ends—*if* the group is large enough. He contends that only rationality in the pursuit of whatever end the individual chooses is strictly necessary. The individual will still choose to free ride, because for a public good requiring a large group his meager contribution will have no perceptible effect on attaining the end.[34]

We could object that an individual's contribution to a cause is often not contingent in any way upon the cause's overall success. Consequently, how much the individual thinks his action will affect the probability of success is often irrelevant. Some people refuse to litter, for instance, fully aware that their refusal will have no perceptible impact on the quantity of litter. Such individuals gain satisfaction from doing what they believe is proper, regardless of its macro-impact. In addition to a sense of righteousness, ideological movements can offer their participants a sense of solidarity, of companionship in a cause that keeps many loyal no matter how hopeless the cause.[35]

But this objection concedes far too much to Olson. As philosopher Richard Tuck has cogently pointed out, Olson's notion of "rationality" if consistently obeyed precludes some everyday activities. It does not just apply to an individual's contribution to the effort of a large group; it applies just as forcefully to the cumulative actions of a single person on a large individual project. Olson's "rationality" is simply a modern variant of the ancient philosophical paradox of the Sorites. In one version, the paradox argues that there can never be a heap of stones. One stone does not constitute a heap, nor does the addition of one stone to something that is not already a heap. Therefore, no matter how many stones are added, they will never constitute a heap. (Of course, in the other direction, this paradox argues that there can never be anything but a heap of stones.)

One more dollar will not make a perceptible difference in a person's life savings. One day's exercise will not make a perceptible difference in a person's health. If the fact that the individual's imperceptible contribution goes toward a group rather than an individual effort is what is decisive, then we are simply back again at the motive of narrow self-interest. No doubt, this type of "rationality" does influence some people not to undertake some actions under some circumstances. But just how compelling people find it is demonstrated by the millions who vote in presidential elections, despite the near certainty that the outcome will never be decided by one person's vote.[36]

2. Do people pursue their self-interest but in a manner inconsistent with the free-rider assumption? Olson, again, has suggested one way that individuals might effectively organize despite the free-rider obstacle. Groups can link their efforts at achieving nonexcludable benefits with excludable by-products. Such by-products include low group-rate insurance and professional journals. The incentive provided by these by-products helps counteract the incentive to be a free rider.[37]

One intriguing aspect of the by-product theory is the easy method it seems to offer for providing national defense without a state. Why couldn't the purchase of national defense be linked to some excludable by-product that everyone wants, such as protection insurance or contract enforcement? Indeed, most of those advocating voluntary funding of national defense have hit upon some such scheme.[38]

But this solution is too easy. If the excludable by-product is really what people want, then a competitor who does not link it with the nonexcludable good or service can sell it at a lower price. Only if the group has a legal monopoly on marketing its by-product can it really counteract the free-rider incentive. Every really successful example of groups relying upon by-products that Olson discusses involves some sort of legal monopoly. But the group's initial attainment of this legal monopoly remains an unexplained surmounting of the public-goods problem.[39]

Far more promising than the by-product theory for explaining the empirical weakness of the free-rider assumption is some of the recent dynamic analysis being done in game theory. As many scholars have pointed out, the free-rider problem in public-goods theory is identical to the famous Prisoner's Dilemma in game theory.[40]

The Prisoner's Dilemma derives its name from an archetypal situation where two prisoners are being held for some crime. The prosecutor separately proposes the same deal to both prisoners, because he only has sufficient evidence to convict them of a minor crime with a light sentence. Each is told that if he confesses, but the other does not, he will get off free, while the other will suffer the full penalty, unless the other also confesses. If they both confess, they both will be convicted of the more serious crime, although they both will receive some small leniency for confessing. This deal gives each prisoner an incentive independently to confess, because by doing so he individually will be better off regardless of what the other does. Consequently, they both confess, despite the fact that they both collectively would have had much lighter sentences if they both refused to confess.

The public-goods problem is essentially a Prisoner's Dilemma with many prisoners. We cannot delve into the details here of the recent work, both theoretical and empirical, of such game theorists as Michael Taylor, Russell Hardin, and Robert Axelrod, but essentially they have explored the Prisoner's Dilemma within a dynamic rather than static setting. Their conclusion: Whereas in a static single Prisoner's Dilemma, cooperation is never rational, in dynamic iterated Prisoner's Dilemmas, with two or more people, cooperation frequently becomes rational for even the most narrowly self-interested individual. What this work implies is that in many real-world dynamic contexts, ideological altruism or some similar motive beyond narrow self-interest may not be necessary at all to counterbalance the free-rider incentive.[41]

Conclusion

We have seen that putting domestic limitations upon the power of the state is a public-goods problem, but nonetheless one that in many historical instances for whatever reason has been solved. We have also seen that national defense, in the sense of protecting the people from a foreign state, is a subset of the general problem of protecting them from any state, domestic or foreign.

Because of "government failure," the domestic military establishment itself can become the greatest threat to the lives, property, and liberty of the state's subjects. The danger from military expansion, moreover, is not confined to its domestic impact. By threatening the opposing nation, it cannot even unambiguously guarantee greater international safety. The same threat that deters can also provoke the opposing side's military expansion.

Perhaps the factors that already provide protection from the domestic state are the very factors to which we should turn for protection from foreign states. The same social consensus that has voluntarily overcome the free-rider obstacle to make the United States one of the freest, if not the freest, nation may be able to overcome the free-rider obstacle to protect American freedom from foreign states.

Nearly all of us desire a world in which all states have been disarmed. Of course, most of the formal economic models of international relations are not very sanguine about this eventuality. Yet our analysis points to two possible shortcomings in such models and suggests at least a glimmer of hope. First, they are generally built upon a static formulation of the Prisoner's Dilemma, whereas dynamic formulations are more realistic and more likely to yield cooperative outcomes. Second, they generally commit the nationalistic fallacy of composition, ignoring the interactions of the state with its own and foreign populations. Like the public-goods theory they emulate, these models are very good at explaining the cases where disarmament fails. They do not do so well at explaining the cases where it succeeds—as for instance, along the U.S.-Canada border since 1871.[42]

The domestic production of disarmament is itself a public good, confronting the same free-rider obstacle that confronts every nonexcludable good and service. Should a majority in any one nation come to endorse this policy, the narrow—or not so narrow—special interests who benefit from an armed state would undoubtedly be willing to commit vast resources to keeping a huge military establishment. Thus, like all significant gains in the history of civilization, the disarming of the state could only be accomplished by a massive ideological surge that surmounts the free-rider obstacle.

Notes

1. We wish to acknowledge the invaluable assistance of Williamson M. Evers and Joe Fuhrig in working out the themes of this paper. Tyler Cowen, David Friedman, Marshall Fritz, M. L. Rantala, David Ramsay Steele, Richard H. Timberlake, Jr., David J. Theroux, and Lawrence H. White all gave us helpful comments upon earlier

drafts. They do not necessarily share our conclusions, however, and we alone are responsible for any remaining errors.

2. By "the state" we mean government. We use the two terms interchangeably, unlike many political scientists, who use the term the "state" either for what we are calling the "nation," i.e., the government plus its subjects, or for some vague intermediate entity which is less than the entire nation but more than just the government. We recognize that the state and its subjects can often be intricately interwoven into a complex web of mixed institutions, but the distinction is still fundamental.
3. Although we will not take up these issues here, some economists suggest that the characteristics that make something a public good are almost never physically inherent in the good or service but are rather nearly always a consequence of choosing one out of many feasible methods for producing the good or service. See Tyler Cowen, "Public Goods Definitions and Their Institutional Context: A Critique of Public Goods Theory," *Review of Social Economy* 43 (April 1985): 53-63; Tom G. Palmer, "Infrastructure: Public or Private?" *Policy Report* 5 (May 1983): 1-5, 11; Walter Block, "Public Goods and Externalities: The Case of Roads," *Journal of Libertarian Studies* 7 (Spring 1983): 1-34; Murray Rothbard, "The Myth of Neutral Taxation," *Cato Journal* 1 (Fall 1981): 532-46; Kenneth D. Goldin, "Equal Access vs. Selective Access: A Critique of Public Goods Theory," *Public Choice* 29 (Spring 1977): 53-71; and Earl Brubaker, "Free Ride, Free Revelation, or Golden Rule," *Journal of Law and Economics* 18 (April 1975): 147-61.
4. Examples of economists treating national defense as the quintessential public good include Paul A. Samuelson, *Economics*, 10th ed. (with Peter Temin) (New York: McGraw-Hill, 1976), p. 159; James M. Buchanan and Marilyn R. Flowers, *The Public Finances: An Introductory Textbook*, 4th ed. (Homewood, Ill.: Richard D. Irwin, 1975), p. 27; and John G. Head and Carl S. Shoup, "Public Goods, Private Goods, and Ambiguous Goods," *Economic Journal* 79 (September 1969): 567.

   Among the few attempts of economists to look in any detail at national defense as a public good are Earl A. Thompson, "Taxation and National Defense," *Journal of Political Economy* 82 (July/August 1974): 755-82; and R. Harrison Wagner, "National Defense as a Collective Good," in *Comparative Public Policy: Issues, Theories, and Methods*, eds. Craig Liske, William Loehr, and John McCamant (New York: John Wiley & Sons, 1975), pp. 199-221.
5. Paul A. Samuelson's two classic articles, "The Pure Theory of Public Expenditure," *Review of Economics and Statistics* 36 (November 1954): 387-89, and "Diagrammatic Exposition of a Theory of Public Expenditure," ibid. 37 (November 1955): 350-56, are generally credited as being the first formal statements of modern public-goods theory.

   Important further developments in public-goods theory include Paul A. Samuelson, "Aspects of Public Expenditure Theories," *Review of Economics and Statistics* 40 (November 1958): 332-38; Richard A. Musgrave, *The Theory of Public Finance: A Study in Public Economy* (New York: McGraw-Hill, 1959); James M. Buchanan and M. Z. Kafoglis, "A Note on Public Good Supply," *American Economic Review* 53 (January 1963): 403-14; Harold Demsetz, "The Exchange and Enforcement of Property Rights," *Journal of Law and Economics* 7 (October 1964): 11-26; Jora R. Minasian, "Television Pricing and the Theory of Public Goods," ibid., 71-80; William J. Baumol, *Welfare Economics and the Theory of the State*, 2nd ed. (Cambridge, Mass.: Harvard University Press, 1965); R. N. McKean and Jora R. Minasian, "On Achieving Pareto Optimality—Regardless of Cost," *Western Economic Journal* 5 (December 1966): 14-23; Otto Davis and Andrew Winston, "On the Distinction Between Public and Private Goods," *American Economic Review* 57 (May1967): 360-73; James M. Buchanan, *The Demand and Supply of Public Goods* (Chicago: Rand McNally, 1968); E. J. Mishan, "The Relationship Between Joint Products,

Collective Goods, and External Effects," *Journal of Political Economy* 77 (May/June 1969): 329-48; Head and Shoup, "Public Goods, Private Goods, and Ambiguous Goods"; John G. Head, *Public Goods and Public Welfare* (Durham, N.C.: Duke University Press, 1974); and Duncan Snidal, "Public Goods, Property Rights, and Political Organizations," *International Studies Quarterly* 23 (December 1979): 532-66.

6. Much of the literature has conceded that, strictly speaking, very few actual goods or services exhibit either of the public-good characteristics in its polar form. Instead, in the real world we encounter a range of goods and services for which the potential capacity and quality of nonrival consumption is increasing or for which the costs of exclusion are increasing.
7. We have slightly understated the supposed "market failure" from nonrival consumption with excludability. The quantity of the public good could also be nonoptimal. There is a vast economic literature debating the intricacies of nonrival consumption. Some of the highlights include Paul A. Samuelson, "Contrast Between Welfare Conditions for Joint Supply and for Public Goods," *Review of Economics and Statistics* 51 (February 1969): 26-30; Harold Demsetz, "The Private Production of Public Goods," *Journal of Law and Economics* 13 (October 1970): 293- 306; Earl A. Thompson, "The Perfectly Competitive Production of Collective Goods," *Review of Economics and Statistics* 50 (February 1968): 1-12; Robert B. Ekelund and Joe R. Hulett, "Joint Supply, the Taussig-Pigou Controversy, and the Competitive Provision of Public Goods," *Journal of Law and Economics* 16 (October 1973): 369-87; Harold Demsetz, "Joint Supply and Price Discrimination," ibid., 389-405; William H. Oakland, "Public Goods, Perfect Competition and Underproduction," *Journal of Political Economy* 82 (September/October 1974): 927-39; Dwight R. Lee, "Discrimination and Efficiency in the Pricing of Public Goods," *Journal of Law and Economics* 20 (October 1977): 403-20; Thomas Borcherding, "Competition, Exclusion, and the Optimal Supply of Public Goods," ibid. 21 (April 1978): 111-32; and Michael E. Burns and Cliff Walsh, "Market Provision of Price-Excludable Public Goods: A General Analysis," *Journal of Political Economy* 89 (February 1981): 166-91.
8. On the relationship of public goods and externalities, see Paul Samuelson, "Pure Theory of Public Expenditure and Taxation," in *Public Economics: An Analysis of Public Production and Consumption and their Relations to the Private Sectors*, ed. J. Margolis and H. Guitton (London: Macmillan, 1969), pp. 98-123; Buchanan, *Demand and Supply of Public Goods*, p. 75; John G. Head, "Externality and Public Policy," in *Public Goods and Public Welfare*, pp. 184-213; and Mishan, "The Relationship Between Joint Products, Collective Goods, and External Effects."
9. Earl G. Ravenal, *Defining Defense: The 1985 Military Budget* (Washington: Cato Institute, 1984). See also Bruce M. Russett, *What Price Vigilance? The Burdens National Defense* (New Haven: Yale University Press, 1970), pp. 91-126.
10. Randolph Bourne, "The State," in *War and the Intellectuals: Essays by Randolph Bourne, 1915-1919*, ed. Carl Resek (New York: Harper & Row, 1964), pp. 65-104. A general substantiation (or refutation) of Bourne's observation has so far not attracted the professional energies of any historian, perhaps because they feel no need to belabor the obvious. There are lots of studies showing the growth of state power in particular countries during particular wars, but very few that even treat a single country during more than one war, or more than a single country during one war. A few exceptions that have come to our attention include: Clinton Rossiter, *Constitutional Dictatorship: Crisis Government in the Modern Democracies* (Princeton: Princeton University Press, 1948); Arthur A. Ekirch, Jr., *The Civilian and the Military: A History of the American Antimilitarist Tradition* (New York: Oxford University Press, 1956); Robert Higgs, *Crisis and Leviathan: Critical*

Episodes in the Growth of American Government (New York: Oxford University Press, 1987); Charles Tilly, ed., *The Formation of National States in Western Europe* (Princeton: Princeton University Press, 1975); Tilly, "War Making and State Making as Organized Crime," in *Bringing the State Back In*, ed. Peter B. Evans, Dietrich Rueschemeyer, and Theda Skocpol (Cambridge: Cambridge University Press, 1985); and J. R. Hale, *War and Society in Renaissance Europe, 1450-1620* (New York: St. Martin's Press, 1985).

11. We cite examples of economic models exhibiting the nationalistic fallacy of composition below. One of the very few written challenges to the nationalistic model is Murray N. Rothbard, "War, Peace and the State," in Rothbard, *Egalitarianism as a Revolt Against Nature: And Other Essays* (Washington: Libertarian Review Press, 1974), pp. 70-80. We have profited greatly from this path-breaking essay.
12. For a purely formal approach to people's utility functions with regard to national defense, see Wagner, "National Defense as a Collective Good."
13. Demsetz makes the comparison between the "nirvana" and "comparative institutions" approaches in "Information and Efficiency: Another Viewpoint," *Journal of Law and Economics* 12 (April 1969): 1-3. See also Ronald Coase, "The Problem of Social Cost," ibid. 3 (October 1960): 1-44; James M. Buchanan, "Politics, Policy, and the Pigovian Margins," *Economica*, 2nd ser., 29 (February 1962): 17-28; and Ralph Turvey, "On the Divergences between Social Cost and Private Cost," ibid. 30 (August 1963): 309-13.
14. Anthony Downs, *An Economic Theory of Democracy* (New York: Harper & Row, 1957); James M. Buchanan and Gordon Tullock, *The Calculus of Consent: Logical Foundations of Constitutional Democracy* (Ann Arbor: University of Michigan Press, 1962); Mancur Olson, *The Logic of Collective Action: Public Goods and the Theory of Groups*, 2nd ed. (Cambridge, Mass.: Harvard University Press, 1971); William A. Niskanen, Jr., *Bureaucracy and Representative Government* (Chicago: AI Dine Atherton, 1971); Gordon Tullock, *Toward a Mathematics of Politics* (Ann Arbor: University of Michigan Press, 1967); Albert Breton, *The Economic Theory of Representative Government* (Chicago: Aldine, 1974); and Gary Becker, "A Theory of Competition among Pressure Groups for Political Influence," *Quarterly Journal of Economics* 98 (August 1983): 372-80.
15. Richard E. Wagner, "Pressure Groups and Political Entrepreneurs: A Review Article," *Papers on Non-Market Decision Making* 1 (1966): 161-70; and Norman Frohlich, Joe A. Oppenheimer, and Oran R. Young, *Political Leadership and Collective Goods* (Princeton: Princeton University Press, 1971), stress the political-entrepreneur thesis. Olson responds briefly in the second edition of *The Logic of Collective Action*, pp. 174-75. Brian Barry, *Sociologists, Economists and Democracy* (Chicago: University of Chicago Press, 1978), pp. 37-40, and Russell Hardin, *Collective Action* (Baltimore: Johns Hopkins University Press, 1982), pp. 35-37, go into the weakness of this thesis in greater detail.
16. Extended discussions of the outcome of voting as a public good include Yoram Barzel and Eugene Silberberg, "Is the Act of Voting Rational?" *Public Choice* 16 (Fall 1973): 51-58; Paul E. Meehl, "The Selfish Voter Paradox and the Throw-Away Vote Argument," *American Political Science Review* 71 (March 1977): 11-30; James M. Buchanan and G. Brennan, "Voter Choice: Evaluating Political Alternatives," *American Behavioral Scientist* 29 (November/December 1984): 185-201; and Barry, *Sociologists, Economists and Democracy*, pp. 13-19.
17. One of the clearest expositions of these factors appears in David Friedman's neglected *The Machinery of Freedom: Guide to a Radical Capitalism* (New York: Harper & Row, 1973), pp. 185-88. See also his *Price Theory: An Intermediate Text* (Cincinnati: South-Western, 1986), pp. 440-47. Olson's taxonomy of groups—privileged (small), intermediate, and latent (large)—in *The Logic of Collective Action*

treats the two factors—group size and relative cost of the public good—simultaneously and thereby slightly confuses the issue. Hardin, *Collective Action*, pp. 38-42, clarifies Olson's taxonomy, correctly pointing out that a privileged group (one in which a single member values the public good enough to pay its entire cost) could theoretically be quite large.

Admittedly, there is some ambiguity about which *cetera* remain *pares* when group size is varied. Some scholars have consequently challenged the claim that larger groups have greater difficulty overcoming the free-rider incentive. See Norman Frohlich and Joe A. Oppenheimer, "I Get By with a Little Help from My Friends," *World Politics* 23 (October 1970): 104-20;John Chamberlin, "Provision of Public Goods as a Function of Group Size," *American Political Science Review* 68 (June 1974): 707-16; and Martin C. McGuire, "Group Size, Homogeneity, and the Aggregate Provision of a Pure Public Good under Cournot Behavior," *Public Choice* 18 (Summer 1974): 107-26. The best resolution of these questions is Hardin, *Collective Action*, pp. 42-49, 125-37.

18. Friedman, *The Machinery of Freedom*, p. 189. Dwight R. Lee, "The Soviet Economy and the Arms Control Delusion," *Journal of Contemporary Studies* 8 (Winter/Spring 1985): 46, makes the same observation about the political production of national defense, but because he does not recognize the distinction between defending the state and defending the people, he arrives at a much different conclusion: viz., democratic states will underproduce military defense relative to undemocratic states.
19. A similar point is made by Kenneth E. Boulding, "The World War Industry as an Economic Problem," in the collection he coedited with Emile Benoit, *Disarmament and the Economy* (New York: Harper & Row, 1963), pp. 3-27. He refers to the world's competing military organizations as "milorgs" and insists that, in contrast to any other social enterprise (including police protection), military organizations generate their own demand. "The only justification for the existence of a milorg is the existence of another milorg in some other place.... A police force is not justified by the existence of a police force in another town, that is, by another institution of the same kind" (p. 10).
20. Brubaker, "Free Ride, Free Revelation, or Golden Rule," p. 153.
21. For the argument that revolution is a public good, see Gordon Tullock, "The Paradox of Revolution," *Public Choice* 9 (Fall1971): 89-99, which became with minor alterations one of the chapters of his book, *The Social Dilemma: The Economics of War and Revolution* (Blacksburg, Va.: University Publications, 1974). Tullock distinguishes between what he calls "exploitative" and "cooperative" governments, rather than democratic and undemocratic, but the two classifications are almost identical.
22. The public-goods theory of the democratic state is still stated best in Baumol, *Welfare Economics and the Theory of the State*, p. 57.
23. Joseph P. Kalt, "Public Goods and the Theory of Government," *Cato Journal* 1 (Fall1981): 565-84, pinpoints the contradiction in the public-goods theory of the state. The still devastating, classic, point-by-point refutation of the social contract remains Lysander Spooner, *No Treason: The Constitution of No Authority* (1870; reprint ed., Larkspur, Colo.: Pine Tree Press, 1966). See also Williamson M. Evers, "Social Contract: A Critique," *Journal of Libertarian Studies* (Summer 1977): 185-94, which traces the literal notion of a social contract all the way back to Socrates.
24. Since the definition of the state (or government) is something political scientists cannot even agree upon, ours will obviously be controversial. By "legitimized" (a positive adjective), we of course do not mean "legitimate" (a normative adjective). Most economists should have no difficulty conceiving of the state as a monopo-

listic coercive institution, but noneconomists might balk. Members of the general public appear to have a bifurcated definition of the state, depending on whether it is domestic or foreign. They view hostile foreign states as simply monopolies on coercion, just like criminal gangs, which is why they fear foreign conquest. They overlook the legitimization of these states. On the other hand, that is the only element they seem to recognize about the domestic state, overlooking or at least deemphasizing the coercive element. This dichotomy is only a cruder version of the distinction made by public-goods theory between democratic and undemocratic states. For an extended defense of the implications of our universal definition, see Murray N. Rothbard, "The Anatomy of the State," in *Egalitarianism as a Revolt Against Nature*, pp. 34-53.

25. One of the earliest observations that a social consensus *always* legitimizes the state is Etienne de la Boetie, *The Politics of Obedience: The Discourse of Voluntary Servitude* (1574; reprint ed., New York: Free Life Editions, 1975). Other writers who have since put forward a social-consensus theory of the state include David Hume, "Of the First Principles of Government," in *Essays, Moral, Political, and Literary* (1741-42; reprint ed. London: Oxford University Press, 1963), pp. 29-34; Ludwig von Mises, *Human Action: A 'Treatise on Economics*, 3rd rev. ed. (Chicago: Henry Regnery, 1966), pp. 177-90; and Gene Sharp, *The Politics of Nonviolent Action* (Boston: Porter Sargent, 1973).
26. We are confident about the empirical results, having conducted the test ourselves many times.
27. Victor Zaslavsky, *The Neo-Stalinist State* (New York: Oxford University Press, 1983), has actually conducted fairly reliable surveys among Soviet subjects, which indicate quite unambiguously that the Soviet state is legitimized. Good single-volume histories that impart an appreciation for the domestic sources of the Soviet state are Robert V. Daniels, *Russia: The Roots of Confrontation* (Cambridge: Harvard University Press, 1985), and Geoffrey Hosking, *The First Socialist Society: A History of the Soviet Union from Within* (Cambridge: Harvard University Press, 1985). An introduction to the various interpretations of Soviet history by American scholars, written from a revisionist slant, is Stephen E Cohen, *Rethinking the Soviet Experience: Politics and History since 1917* (New York: Oxford University Press, 1985).
28. This awkward position is clearest in Tullock's *Social Dilemma.* The new Society for Interpretive Economics, codirected by Don Lavoie and Arjo Klamer (Economics Department, George Mason University) is a welcome exception to the general neglect among economists of cultural and ideological dynamics. We also cite some specific exceptions below.
29. The premier work on the role of ideas in the American Revolution is Bernard Bailyn, *Ideological Origins of the American Revolution* (Cambridge: Harvard University Press, 1967), while a work that explores the international repercussions of the revolution is Robert R. Palmer, *The Age of Democratic Revolution: A Political History of Europe and America, 1760-1899*, 2 vols. (Princeton: Princeton University Press, 1959-64). A magisterial survey of the international history of chattel slavery is David Brion Davis, *Slavery and Human Progress* (New York: Oxford University Press, 1984). On the emergence of the international abolitionist movement, see his *The Problem of Slavery in the Age of Revolution, 1770-1823* (Ithaca: Cornell University Press, 1975).
30. Among the economists who recognize the public-goods nature of ethical behavior are James M. Buchanan, in "Ethical Rules, Expected Values, and Large Numbers," *Ethics* 76 (October 1965): 1-13, and *The Limits of Liberty: Between Anarchy and Leviathan* (Chicago: University of Chicago Press, 1975), pp. 123-29; Richard B. McKenzie, in "The Economic Dimensions of Ethical Behavior," *Ethics* 87 (April

1977): 208-21; and Douglass C. North, in *Structure and Change in Economic History* (New York: W.W. Norton, 1981), pp. 11-12, 18-19, 45-46. See also Dereck Parfit, *Reasons and Persons* (Oxford: Clarendon Press, 1984).

31. Rothbard, "The Myth of Neutral Taxation," 545, makes a similar observation: "Thus the free-rider argument proves far too much. After all, civilization itself is a process of all of us free-riding on the achievements of others. We all free-ride, every day, on the achievements of Edison, Beethoven, or Vermeer."
32. Howard Margolis, *Selfishness, Altruism, and Rationality: A Theory of Social Choice* (Cambridge: Cambridge University Press, 1982), p. 6. See also John McMillan, "The Free Rider Problem: A Survey," *The Economic Record* 55 (June 1979): 95-107; Vernon L. Smith, "Experiments with a Decentralized Mechanism for Public Good Decisions," *American Economic Review* 70 (September 1980): 584-99 and Friedrich Schneider and Werner W. Pommerehne, "Free Riding and Collective Action: An Experiment in Public Microeconomics," *Quarterly Journal of Economics* 91 (November 1981): 689-704.
33. Several scholars are moving in this direction. For instance, Robyn M. Dawes, "Social Dilemmas," *Annual Review of Psychology* 31 (1980): 169-93; Earl R Brubaker, "Demand Disclosures and Conditions on Exclusion," *Economic Journal* 94 (September 1984): 536-53; Barry, *Sociologists, Economists, and Democracy*; Higgs, *Crisis and Leviathan*, chapter 3; and North, *Structure and Change in Economic History*, chapter 5. Even Mancur Olson suggests this approach in "Economics, Sociology, and the Best of All Possible Worlds," *Public Interest* 12 (Summer 1968): 96-118, which contrasts economics, the study of rational action, with sociology, the study of socialization. But the most ambitious effort along these lines is Margolis's *Selfishness Altruism, and Rationality*, which is summarized in his journal article, "A New Model of Rational Choice," *Ethics* 91 (January 1981): 265-79.

    We should note that we attach the adjective "narrow" to the term "self-interest" to indicate the usage that involves seeking particular, usually selfish, goals. This is to distinguish it from the broader usage of the term, which can encompass any goal, including altruism. Whether individuals do in fact pursue their narrow self-interest is a question subject to empirical verification or falsification, but individuals by definition always pursue their broad self-interest.
34. Olson, *The Logic Of Collective Action*, pp. 64-65.
35. Higgs, *Crisis and Leviathan*, chapter 3, heavily emphasizes the role of ideological solidarity. James S. Coleman, "Individual Interests and Collective Action," *Papers on Non-Market Decision Making* 1 (1966): 49-62, postulates an individual's psychic investment in collective entities. Buchanan and Brennan, "Voter Choice: Evaluating Political Alternatives," think that this symbolic identification is the major motivation behind voting.
36. Richard Tuck, "Is There a Free-Rider Problem, and if so, What Is It?" in *Rational Action: Studies in Philosophy and Social Science*, ed. Ross Harrison (Cambridge: Cambridge University Press, 1979), pp. 147-56.

    We can salvage Olsonian "rationality" under two strict conditions. When (1) a threshold level of resources is necessary before any of the public good becomes available whatsoever, *and* (2) people end up paying whatever resources they contribute, irrespective of whether they reach the threshold or not, it becomes rational not to contribute *if* a person predicts that the threshold will not be reached. In that special case, he or she would simply be throwing away resources for nothing. Notice that these two conditions apply more frequently to obtaining public goods through politics—which is often a win-or-lose, all-or-nothing, situation—than to obtaining public goods on the market. In particular, it applies to voting. Hardin, *Collective Action*, pp. 55-61, analyzes the first of these conditions, for which he employs the term "step goods."

37. Olson, *The Logic of Collective Action*, pp. 132-68. Olson also refers to excludable "by-products" as "selective incentives." Looked at another way the by-product theory converts a full public good into a positive externality of a private good.
38. Those advocating voluntary funding of national defense through the sale of excludable by-products include Ayn Rand, "Government Financing in a Free Society," in *The Virtue of Selfishness: A New Concept of Egoism* (New York: New American Library, 1964), pp. 157-63; Jarret B. Wollstein, *Society without Coercion: A New Concept of Social Organization* (Silver Springs, Md.: Society for Individual Liberty, 1969), pp. 35-38; Morris and Linda Tannehill, *The Market for Liberty* (Lansing: Tannehill, 1970), pp. 126-35; and Tibor R. Machan, "Dissolving the Problem of Public Goods," in *The Libertarian Reader* (Totowa, N.J.: Rowman and Littlefield, 1982), pp. 201-8. For a telling critique of the by-product theory as applied to national defense, see Friedman, *The Machinery of Freedom*, pp. 192-93.
39. Hardin, *Collective Action*, pp. 31-34, criticizes the by-product theory.
40. The book that launched mathematical game theory was John von Neumann and Oskar Morgenstern, *The Theory of Games and Economic Behavior*, 3rd ed. (Princeton: Princeton University Press, 1953), the first edition of which appeared in 1944.According to Hardin, *Collective Action*, p. 24, the Prisoner's Dilemma itself was first discovered in 1950 by Merril Flood and Melvin Dresher. A. W. Tucker, a game theorist at Princeton University, later gave the Prisoner's Dilemma its name. For the personal reminiscences of one of the early researchers who worked on the Prisoner's Dilemma, coupled with a survey of the studies of the dilemma up to the mid-seventies, see Anatol Rapoport, "Prisoner's Dilemma—Recollections and Observations," in *Game Theory as a Theory of Conflict Resolution* (Dordrecht: D. Reidel, 1974), pp. 17-34.
41. R. Hardin, "Collective Action as an Agreeable n-Prisoners' Dilemma," *Behavioral Science* 16 (September 1971): 472-81; Michael Taylor, *Anarchy and Cooperation* (London: John Wiley & Sons, 1976); Hardin, *Collective Action*; and Robert Axelrod, *The Evolution of Cooperation* (New York: Basic Books, 1984). Axelrod confines himself to two-person dynamic Prisoner's Dilemmas, while both Taylor and Hardin consider n-person iterated games. For a good review of the growing literature on n-person games, see Dawes, "Social Dilemmas."
42. Britain and the United States demilitarized the Great Lakes in the Rush Bagot Treaty of 1817. The process of disarming the entire border was not complete until 1871, however. Both Philip Noel-Baker, *The Arms Race: A Programme for World Disarmament* (London: Atlantic Books, 1958), and Boulding, "The World War Industry as an Economic Problem," appreciate the significance of this example.

    Economic studies of international relations that share these weaknesses include Lee, "The Soviet Economy and the Arms Control Delusion" and Tullock, *The Social Dilemma.* Most of the economic work in these areas has focused upon alliances. See for instance Mancur Olson, Jr. and Richard Zeckhauser, "An Economic Theory of Alliances," *Review of Economics and Statistics* 48 (August 1966): 266-79; Olson and Zeckhauser, "Collective Goods, Comparative Advantage, and Alliance Efficiency," in *Issues in Defense Economics*, ed. Roland N. McKean (New York: National Bureau of Economic Research, 1967), pp. 25-63; Todd Sandler, "The Economic Theory of Alliances: Realigned," in *Comparative Public Policy*, ed. Liske, Loehr, and McCamant, pp. 223-39; and Todd M. Sandler, William Loehr, and John T. Cauley, *The Political Economy of Public Goods and International Cooperation* (Denver: University of Denver Press, 1978).

8

Defending a Free Nation

Roderick Long

Defense: How?

How should a free nation defend itself from foreign aggression?

Defense: Why?

This question presupposes a prior question: Would a free nation need to defend itself from foreign aggression? Some would answer no: the rewards of cooperation outweigh the rewards of aggression, and so a nation will probably not be attacked unless it first acts aggressively itself.

On the other hand, if this were true, conflicts would never occur—since no one would make the first aggressive move. It's true that the rewards for cooperation are evident enough that most people do cooperate most of the time. That's what makes human society possible. If people weren't basically cooperative, no government could make them so—since the people in government would have as much difficulty working together as all the rest of us.

Still, a small but troublesome minority obviously do believe they're better off not cooperating: we call them criminals. Maybe they do tend to lose out in the long run—but on the way to that long run they cause a heck of a lot of damage to the rest of us.

More importantly, governments face different incentives from those faced by private individuals. Under a government, the people who make the decision to go to war are not the same people as those who bear the greatest burden of the costs of the war; and so governments are much more likely than private individuals to engage in aggression. Thus it's a mistake to model a nation-state as if it were a single individual weighing costs against benefits. It's more like a split personality, where the dominant personality reaps the benefits but somehow manages to make the repressed personality bear the costs. (Hence the superiority of private protection agencies: a protection agency that chooses to resolve its disputes with other agencies through war rather than arbitration will have to charge constantly rising premiums, and so will lose customers to nicer agencies.)

That doesn't mean governments are completely isolated from the bad effects of war. Certainly the people in power will suffer if they lose the war, especially if their country is conquered by the enemy. And they can also share in the prosperity that peace and free trade bring. But the disincentives for war are much weaker for governments than for individuals—which means that it's a dangerous world out there, so a free nation needs a defense.

Why Not a Government Military?

Most societies, at least in this century, handle the problem of national defense by having a large, well-armed, permanent military force, run by a centralized government, funded by taxation, and often (though not always) manned by conscription. Is this a solution that a free nation can or should follow?

I don't think so. First of all, I don't think there should be a centralized government. My reasons for this position have been set out in some detail both in FNF Forums and in recent issues of *Formulations*, so I'll just summarize the main points briefly:

First, government is unjust. Government, by definition, requires its citizens to delegate to the ruler all or part of their right to self-defense. (An institution that does not require this is no government, but something else.) But to "delegate" a right involuntarily is no delegation at all; the right has simply been obliterated. And I do not see how this can be justified. By what right does one group of people, calling itself a government, arrogate to itself the right to take away the rights of others? (As for taxation and conscription, I can't see that these are anything more than fancy words for theft and slavery.)

Second, government is impractical. Government is a monopoly: it prohibits competition and obtains its revenues by force. It thus faces far less market pressure, and its customers are not free to take their money elsewhere. As a result, governments have little incentive to cut costs or to satisfy their customers. Hence governments are, unsurprisingly, notorious for inefficiency, wastefulness, and abuse of power.

So, since I don't want a government, I obviously don't want a government military. However, even in societies that do have a government, I think it's still a good idea not to have a government military. A government which has an army that it can turn against its own citizens is a lot more dangerous than a government that doesn't. That's why so many of this country's Founders were so adamantly opposed to a standing army, seeing it as a threat to domestic liberty (see, e.g., the Virginia Declaration of Rights, drafted by George Mason). (A standing navy worried them less because it's harder to impose martial law on land by means of sea power! If the United States had been an archipelago of islands, they might have thought differently.) In this country today, U.S. soldiers are reportedly being asked whether they would be willing to shoot American citizens! A free nation needs to find a less dangerous way of protecting its citizens.

The Dangers of Centralization

Centralized government poses yet another threat to a nation's liberty. The more that control over a society is centralized in a single command center, the easier it is for an invading enemy to conquer the entire nation simply by conquering that command center. Indeed, invaders have historically done just that, simply taking over the power structure that already existed.

By contrast, a society in which power is decentralized lacks a command center whose defeat or surrender can deliver the entire nation into bondage. For example, during the American Revolution the British focused their energies on conquering Philadelphia, at that time the nominal capital of the United States, on the assumption that once the capital had fallen the rest of the country would be theirs as well. What the British failed to realize was that the United States was a loose-knit confederation, not a centralized nation-state, and the government in Philadelphia had almost no authority. When Philadelphia fell, the rest of the country went about its business as usual; Americans were not accustomed to living their lives according to directives from Philadelphia, and so the British troops ended up simply sitting uselessly in the occupied capital, achieving nothing. Hence Benjamin Franklin, when he heard that the British army had captured Philadelphia, is said to have replied, "Nay, I think Philadelphia has captured the British army."

The Dangers of Decentralization?

Having pointed out how excessive centralization can make a nation more vulnerable to foreign domination, let me also point out a respect in which extreme decentralization might seem to pose a similar threat.

In the fourth century B.C., the mass murderer we fondly remember as Alexander the Great conquered nearly all of the area we know today as the Middle East. If you want to read a terrifying story, put down the latest Stephen King novel and pick up Arrian's *Campaigns of Alexander*, which in dry and matter-of-fact style records how this erratic psychopath and his tired and aging army somehow swept like lightning across the shattered remnants of the Persian Empire, conquering city after city after city after city after city...

Now if the various cities had organized some sort of collective defense, and attacked Alexander simultaneously, they would have destroyed his army. Hundreds of thousands of lives would have been saved, and hundreds of cities would have kept their freedom. Instead, the cities faced Alexander one by one, each confident of its own unassailability. And one by one they fell.

This might seem to show that some sort of centralized defense is needed in order to provide effective security. But I don't think it shows exactly that. It does show the need for organization—for collective, concerted, cooperative action. But not all organization should be viewed in terms of a top-down hierarchical model in which a central authority issues directives and imposes order on the lower ranks. The key to defending a free nation is to have a system of security decentralized enough to lack a command center the enemy can capture, but organized enough so that the invader must face a united collective defense, not a series of individual skirmishes.

In other words, the key is: ORGANIZATION WITHOUT CENTRALIZATION.

Organization Without Centralization, then, is the goal. How to realize that goal is, of course, another matter.

An Encouraging Note

It is admittedly a difficult balance to strike. Before we despair, however, we should notice that the goal we are trying to achieve is relatively modest. The defense of a free nation will be limited to just that: defense. No military interventions around the globe, no imperialism, no foreign adventuring, no gunboat diplomacy. Which means that a free nation's defense budget will be much cheaper than those of its potential enemies. If we put that fact together with the fact that a free nation is also likely to have a much more prosperous economy than its enemies have, we can see some reason for optimism.

Let the Market Take Care of It

Most libertarians have heard the joke: "How many libertarians does it take to change a light bulb?" "None, the market will take care of it."

Perhaps we can give the same answer to worries about national defense. As students of Austrian economics (see, e.g., the writings of F. A. Hayek) we know that the free market, by coordinating the dispersed knowledge of market actors, has the ability to come up with solutions that no individual could have devised. So why not let a solution to the problem of national defense emerge through the spontaneous order of the market, rather than trying to dictate ahead of time what the market solution must be?

In a sense I think that is the answer; but it's incomplete. As students of Austrian economics (see, e.g., the writings of Israel Kirzner), we also know that the efficiency of markets depends in large part on the action of entrepreneurs; and on the Austrian theory entrepreneurs do not passively react to market prices (as they do in neoclassical economics), but instead are actively alert to profit opportunities and are constantly trying to invent and market new solutions. I see our role in the Free Nation Foundation as that of intellectual entrepreneurs; our coming up with solutions is part of (though by no means the whole of) what it means for the market to come up with solutions. We are the market.

The light bulb joke captures the Hayekian side of libertarian economics, and Hayek's insight is an important one. But before following Hayek in a tirade against the evils of "constructive rationalism," we should remember to balance the Hayekian insight against the equally important Kirznerian insight that the working of the market depends on the creative ingenuity of individuals.

I would thus suggest a different ending to the joke: "How many libertarians does it take to change a light bulb?" "I'll do it, for a dollar."

The Three Economies

In short, then, although we cannot hope to predict precisely what solutions the market will come up with, it's worth trying to figure out what could work—and indeed, like good entrepreneurs, try to influence the market process in the direction of the solutions we like. (In any case, we'll have an easier time getting people to join the free nation movement if we have something to tell them about how we propose to defend the nation we hope to found!)

In attempting to devise solutions to the problem of national defense, we need to make sure that we're not limiting our search to an excessively narrow range of options. In this context I find extremely useful a distinction that was first explained to me by Phil Jacobson. Jacobson pointed out that one can distinguish three kinds of economy: the Profit Economy, the Charity Economy, and the Labor Economy.[1] (I'm not sure I'm using Jacobson's exact terminology, but never mind.) In the Profit Economy, the people who want some good or service X can obtain X by paying someone else to provide it. In the Charity Economy, the people who want X can obtain it by finding someone who will give it to them for free. In the Labor Economy, the people who want X can obtain it by producing it themselves. As Jacobson notes, when free-market anarchists start looking for voluntary private alternatives to government, they tend to think primarily in terms of the Profit Economy—while left-wing anarchists, on the other hand, tend to think primarily in terms of the Labor Economy. Yet in any real-world market system, all three economies coexist and interact, in different combinations depending on culture and circumstances.

Suppose, for example, that a family emergency arises, and I need more money than my regular income supplies. How can I get the extra money?

I might take a second job, or get a loan. Both of these solutions are available through the Profit Economy; if I take the job, I am paying for the money with my labor; if I get a loan, I am paying for the loan through interest payments. In either case, I solve my problem by finding someone who will help me in exchange for some good or service I can offer.

Or I might appeal to a private charity, or to a government welfare program—or obtain an interest-free loan from a friend. In this way, I would be getting my money through the Charity Economy: I find someone who will help me for free.

Or I might cut down on expenses by growing my own food in my garden; or perhaps I could draw on the pooled resources of a mutual-aid organization like those I have described in "How Government Solved the Health Care Crisis: Medical Insurance that Worked—Until Government 'Fixed' It" (*Formulations*, Vol. I, No. 2 [Winter 1993-94]) and "Anarchy in the U.K.: The English Experience With Private Protection" (*Formulations*, Vol. II, No. 1 [Autumn 1994]). This solution involves the Labor Economy: I find some way of helping myself (perhaps in concert with others who are helping themselves).

In looking for free-market approaches to national defense, then, we should be sure to consider ways in which each of Jacobson's "three economies" might be able to help.

Defense via the Profit Economy

In the literature of market anarchism, the most commonly offered solution to the problem of domestic security is the private protection agency. (I shall assume general familiarity with this theory. For more details, see, e.g., David Friedman's *Machinery of Freedom*, Murray Rothbard's *For A New Liberty*, and Bruce Benson's *Enterprise of Law*.) In this context, the most obvious solution to the problem of national security is simply to have the protection agencies (or some of them, or a consortium of them) offer to sell protection against foreign invaders as well as domestic criminals.

Some market anarchists, like David Friedman, are sympathetic to this solution, but pessimistic about its viability. The difficulty is that national security poses a much greater public goods problem than domestic security, because it is much harder to exclude non-contributors from the benefits of national security—and if non-contributors can't be excluded, there's no incentive to contribute, and so the agencies selling this protection can't gain enough revenue to make it worth their while.

In previous issues I have explained why I do not regard the public goods problem as a terribly serious difficulty. ("The Nature of Law, Part I: Law and Order Without Government," *Formulations*, Vol. I, No. 3 [Spring 1994]; "Funding Public Goods: Six Solutions," *Formulations*, Vol. II, No. 1 [Autumn 1994].) So I won't say much about it here.

There are other problems associated with a Profit Economy solution. A united military defense seems to require some degree of centralization in order to be effective, and there is the danger that a consortium of protection agencies selling national security might evolve into a government, as the Anglo-Saxon monarchs in the Middle Ages, thanks to the pressure of constant Viking invasions, were able to evolve from military entrepreneurs providing national defense in exchange for voluntary contributions, to domestic dictators with the power to tax and legislate.

This danger might be especially pressing if the consortium's soldiers are more loyal to the consortium than to the clients. Political authors from Livy to Machiavelli have warned against the use of foreign mercenaries rather than citizen soldiers, because it is easier for a government to turn foreign mercenaries against its own citizens. A vivid example of this was seen during the Polish government's attempt to crack down on the Solidarity movement in the 1980s; when a crowd had to be crushed and beaten, the government used Russian troops, because they feared Polish troops might be divided in their loyalties. (This perhaps gives us some reason to view with alarm the increasing use of multinational U.N. forces by Western governments.)

But the problem is perhaps not insuperable. A consortium of defense agencies would lack the mantle of legitimacy and authority available to a king or government, which would make a power grab more difficult. Moreover, the citizens of a free nation would presumably be armed; and the freedom of any people against an encroaching government rests, in the final analysis, on their possession of arms and their willingness to use them. (Hence governments bent on consolidating their power have generally followed Cardinal Richelieu's advice to the French monarchs: disarm the people, disband local militias, and monopolize access to weapons in the hands of the central government. But Machiavelli advised the opposite, since he saw an armed populace as an integral part of national defense; thus, like such earlier political thinkers as Xenophon, he would have regarded today's advocates of gun control as unwisely weakening their nation's security against invasion.[2] In any case, whether a government or would-be government can succeed in disarming the people ultimately depends on the vigilance of the people themselves; and for this I know no automatic formula.)

Defense via the Charity Economy

People donate money all the time to causes they care about. And the more prosperous they are, the more they donate. Unless libertarian economics is hopelessly wrong—in which case we might as well give up now—people in a free nation would be extremely prosperous. And they would presumably care about national security. So we can predict that a great deal of money could be collected for purposes of national defense by charity alone. Since, as mentioned above, the financial needs of a truly defensive national defense are relatively modest, charity could easily be a major source of defense funds.

Let me mention two problems that occur to me. First, there's the matter of determining the appropriate recipient of these donations. How could such a recipient be prevented from misusing the weapons it purchases? In essence this is simply the problem of a consortium turning into a government, which was discussed above. The subject of how to prevent libertarian anarchy from evolving into government again—and perhaps a worse government than the one the anarchist system displaced—is a vitally important issue, but one too vast to consider in depth here. (I think this would be an excellent subject for a future FNF Forum.)

The second, related difficulty is this: As I mentioned in "Funding Public Goods: Six Solutions" (*Formulations*, Vol. II, No. 1 [Autumn 1994]), large companies will have a motive—namely, good publicity—to donate large sums to national defense (just as they now improve their image by donating to environmental causes, etc.). That's the good news. But the bad news, seemingly, is that these contributions might enable such companies to skew national security decisions in their favor (analogous to large corporations like United Fruit/United Brands getting the U.S. military to intervene to promote corporate interests in Guatemala—or oil companies getting the CIA to oust Mossadegh in Iran; for details, see Jonathan Kwitny's *Endless Enemies*).

But I think this would be much less of a problem in a market anarchist society than it is today. Government magnifies the influence of the rich, because government decision-makers do not own the money they control, and so are willing to spend a larger sum to promote corporate interests than they actually receive from those interests in the way of bribes and campaign contributions. Private protection agencies' costs would be internalized, and so the corporate class would be deprived of this crucial lever. (This would not make it utterly ineffective; for my worries on this score, see my article "Can We Escape the Ruling Class?" (*Formulations*, Vol. II, No. 1 [Autumn 1994]). But it would significantly decrease its power.)

Defense via the Labor Economy: An Armed Populace

I think both the Profit Economy and the Charity Economy are viable as providers of defense services. There are admittedly problems about trusting the providers of those services, but I think those problems may be soluble.

But to the extent that it is dangerous to delegate the power of national defense, perhaps a significant degree of self-help should be an important ingredient in any national security package. As mentioned above, an armed populace is the ultimate safeguard of a nation's liberties, against threats both foreign and domestic.

A possible drawback to a heavy reliance on armed civilian-based defense is that it cannot take effect until the enemy has already entered the country—at which point it might seem that the cause is hopeless. But Machiavelli, in his *Discourses on Livy*, argues persuasively that it is better to meet the enemy on your own home ground rather than his—if, he adds, you have an armed populace. If your populace is not armed, he warns, you should engage the enemy as far from your own soil as possible.

I have often heard it said that it takes roughly three times as many troops to invade a country as to defend it; the defender knows the territory better, does not face hostile locals, and has a much shorter and so less vulnerable supply line. Many military theorists have argued that the South might have won the Civil War if they had stayed put and relied on sniping and guerilla warfare against the invader instead of marching forward to meet the Northern troops on equal terms, in regular battle array. The armed citizenry of Switzerland has long posed a powerful deterrent against potential invaders, enabling that country to maintain peace and freedom for what in comparative terms is an amazingly long time. (Of course, having your country surrounded by Alps doesn't hurt!)

An armed populace, then, may be a viable defense. But recall the lesson of Alexander: unless an armed defense is organized, an invader can simply pick off individual armed neighborhoods one at a time. What is needed, then, is some kind of citizens' militia. But a militia called up and directed by a centralized government poses difficulties we've mentioned already. The key, remember, is: ORGANIZATION WITHOUT CENTRALIZATION.

The best kind of militia, then, might be one organized along the following lines. Begin with a number of local neighborhood militias, run by their members on a democratic basis—the military equivalent of the mutual-aid societies discussed in previous issues of *Formulations*. A number of these local militias get together to form a county militia, which in turn combines with others to form a statewide militia, and so forth—so the ultimate National Militia would be organized as an "association of associations" (the French anarchist Proudhon's formula for what should replace the state), with power and authority running from bottom to top rather than top to bottom. (As for manpower, although many militias have traditionally relied on conscription, this seems unnecessary; if a nation is genuinely under attack—as opposed to engaging in foreign interventions—there is never a shortage of volunteers. And where the populace is used to bearing and handling arms, the training period required for new recruits would be shorter.) Members of each militia would elect their commanding officers (as American soldiers did during the Revolutionary War), and so on up to the commander-in-chief of the National Militia. This bottom-up approach, replacing the top-down approach of a traditional military, would make it much more difficult for the supreme military leader to seize power. Such a militia might well be able to achieve the goal of organization without centralization.[3]

This model might have to be changed somewhat in order to be adapted to a minarchist rather than an anarchist society; we would need to think about whether or not to make the commander-in-chief of the militia subordinate to the libertarian government. Both a yes and a no seem to pose dangers. I welcome suggestions on this topic.

Defense via the Labor Economy: Nonviolent Resistance

Another possible form of organized self-help against an invader is the strategy of nonviolent resistance. This may sound impractical; yet sustained and widespread nonviolent resistance ultimately drove the British out of India, the French and Belgians out of the Ruhr, the Kapp Putschists out of power in Weimar Germany, and racial segregation out of the United States. Nonviolent resistance—"the secession of the plebs"—was also used effectively in ancient Rome by the plebeians against the Senate; and nonviolent resistance by war protestors in this country played an important role in ending the Vietnam War. Nonviolent resistance also had a significant impact against the British in the early phase of the American Revolution, and more recently against totalitarian governments during the Fall of Communism.

Nonviolent resistance often fails, of course, as the blood of Tiananmen should remind us. But violent resistance often fails, too. It's worth considering whether, to what extent, and under what circumstances nonviolent resistance could be an effective tool of national defense.

Many theorists of nonviolent resistance—e.g., Tolstoy, Gandhi, LeFevre—advocate it primarily on ethical grounds, because they view the use of violence as immoral even in self-defense. I do not share this view. (For my reasons, see my article "Punishment vs. Restitution: A Formulation," in *Formulations*, Vol. I, No. 2 [Winter 1993-94].) But a recent article by Bryan Caplan ("The Literature of Nonviolent Resistance and Civilian-Based Defense," *Humane Studies Review*, Vol. 9, No. 1 [1994]) defends the superiority of nonviolent resistance on purely strategic grounds:

> The ability of the government to use violence greatly exceeds that of the rebels. Indeed, violent rebellion often strengthens oppressive regimes which can plausibly claim that rebel violence necessitates repression. Government's comparative advantage lies in violent action. The comparative advantage of the people, in contrast, lies in their ability to deny their cooperation without which it is nearly impossible for government to persist. Consider the deadliness to a government of tax strikes, boycotts, general strikes, and widespread refusal to obey the law. While these tactics are nonviolent, their universal and unyielding use should terrify any government. Nonviolence has other advantages as well. Because it seems less dangerous and radical than violence, it more easily...wins broad public support. The costs of participation are lower, so more people are likely to participate. Traditional non-combatants like children, women, and the old can effectively participate in nonviolent struggle. It is more likely to convert opponents and produce internal disagreement within the ruling class. It generally leads to far fewer casualties and material losses than violence. And since it is more decentralized than violent action, it is less likely to give rise to an even more oppressive state if it succeeds. (Caplan, p. 6)

To those who object that an oppressive government can simply mow down such defenseless dissenters, making nonviolent resistance impractical, Caplan replies that

> ...ideology and consent—whether grudging or enthusiastic—rather than brute force are the ultimate basis of political power. If a large enough segment of the population refuses to comply with the government, it will lose its ability to rule. Merely the threat of non-compliance is often serious enough to provoke the government to redress grievances. Moreover, when governments use violence against protesters who are clearly committed to nonviolence, they undermine their ideological foundations and often make uncontested rule even more difficult.... [T]he very fact that the protesters remain committed to nonviolence even as the government turns to repression to combat them tends to win over previously neutral groups, and inspire and involve other members of persecuted groups. [Gene Sharp] refers to this as "political jiu-jitsu"—jiu-jitsu being a style of martial art that uses an opponent's aggressiveness and ferocity against him.... [I]nsofar as it succeeds, it usually does so by converting opponents, making repression too costly to maintain, and threatening the very ability of the government to maintain power. (Caplan, pp. 4-5)

The rise of Christianity might be a good example of what Caplan is talking about; through their nonviolent resistance to persecution, the tiny sect won the sympathy and admiration of many Romans, and ultimately secured their conversion. (Unfortunately, after the Christians gained power, their attachment to nonviolence waned...)

Caplan extends the idea of nonviolent resistance to the arena of national defense:

> ...deterrents are not limited to standard military ones. Rather, it is merely necessary to make occupation so difficult that the costs of conquest exceed the benefits. Massive tax resistance, boycotts, incitement of desertion, and strikes might accomplish this. And, if a would-be conqueror realized that nonviolent techniques might make the costs of occupation skyrocket, he might be deterred from trying. (Caplan, p. 7)

Nonviolent resistance to foreign invasion has had a surprisingly strong history of success, and Caplan cites many fascinating examples. He also notes that nonviolent resistance has sometimes been effective, at least in a limited way, even against the most brutal and totalitarian of invaders: "The nations which nonviolently resisted National Socialist racial persecutions [e.g., Norway, Denmark, Belgium] saved almost all of their Jews, while Jews in other Nazi-controlled nations were vastly more likely to be placed in concentration camps and killed" (p. 10). But he stresses that nonviolent resistance could be far more effective through organization:

> ...since most nonviolence has historically been sporadic and unorganized, it might be possible to increase its effectiveness through training and strategic and tactical planning.... What would happen if countries spent as much energy preparing for a nonviolent struggle as they do for a military struggle? (Caplan, p. 6)

Among possible stratagems for increasing the effectiveness of nonviolent resistance, Caplan suggests

> general education and training in the techniques of nonviolence, as well as a "West Point" for training specialists; the wide-spread dissemination of publishing and broadcasting equipment to prevent invaders from seizing all of the means of communication; and local stockpiles...to ease the pain of a general strike. (Caplan, p. 7)

Caplan's main source for the ideas he discusses is Gene Sharp, who has devoted his career to investigating how the techniques of nonviolent resistance might be applied to the problem of national defense. Among the works by Sharp cited by Caplan are: *The Politics of Nonviolent Action*; *Exploring Nonviolent Resistance*; *Gandhi as a Political Strategist*; *Social Power and Political Freedom: Making Europe Unconquerable*; *National Security Through Civilian-Based Defense*; and *Civilian-Based Defense: A Post-Military Weapons System*. Caplan also cites dozens of other works on the subject; I shall simply mention two of the ones that sounded most interesting: *Civilian Resistance as a National Defense* by Adam Roberts, and *War Without Weapons* by Anders Boserup and Andrew Mack. I have not read any of these books, but I intend to.

I can also recommend two delightful science-fiction novels that illustrate these ideas: Eric Frank Russell's *The Great Explosion* and James Hogan's *Voyage From Yesteryear*. In *The Great Explosion*, a very funny and satirical book, bureaucrats and military brass from Earth attempt to reestablish Earth's control over the planet Gand, a world of anarcho-pacifists who successfully apply the techniques of nonviolent resistance to frustrate and/or win over the would-be invaders. In *Voyage From Yesteryear*, a less satirical, more realistic work, the basic plot is the same, except that the anarchist planet (now Chiron, not Gand)[4] is not pacifist, and its inhabitants are willing and able to use violence to defend their freedom. They do not rely on violence alone, however, but successfully blend violent with nonviolent techniques to frustrate and/or win over the invaders, with the same result as in Russell's book. (On a rather different note, Vernor Vinge's novel *Across Realtime* tells the story of a government whose invasion of an anarchist society fails because rich crackpots holed up in the anarchist wilderness turn out to have been stockpiling privately owned nuclear weapons! Different strokes for different folks, I guess. All three books are well worth reading.)

I am, I suspect, somewhat less optimistic than Bryan Caplan is about the effectiveness of a purely nonviolent approach to national defense. I'm still inclined to rely on an armed populace, private protection agencies, and an organized but decentralized militia. (For a more cautious assessment than Caplan's of the effectiveness of nonviolent techniques, see Ted Galen Carpenter's "Resistance Tactics: A Review of *Strategic Nonviolent Conflict: The Dynamics of People Power in the Twentieth Century* by Peter Ackerman and Christopher Kruegler," in *Reason*, January 1995.) But Caplan's suggestions deserve our serious consideration. Perhaps the best solution would be one that, rather than either rejecting nonviolence altogether or relying on nonviolence alone, managed to integrate aspects of nonviolent resistance into a violent-if-necessary militia framework (thus following the example of Chiron rather than of Gand).[5]

In any case, I strongly endorse Caplan's closing plea for further research by libertarians into this area:

> Despite their distrust of state power and interventionist foreign policy, classical liberals have had a difficult time envisioning specific alternatives to violence to combat tyranny. The literature of nonviolent resistance is filled with penetrating insights in this area. And, while classical liberals frequently long for alternatives to both electoral politics and violence, specific suggestions have been sparse. These are merely a few gaps that the nonviolence literature may fill. On a more aesthetic note, many of the historical examples of nonviolence are beautiful illustrations of the power of voluntary institutions to supplement or replace the role of the state. (Caplan, p. 12)

Who Will Defend Against the Defenders?

On surveying the options, then, I would argue that as libertarians we have reason to place confidence—albeit cautious confidence—in a three-pronged strategy for defending our free nation, should we be fortunate enough to get one.

- First prong: a regular high-tech military defense, supported by paying customers and charitable contributions alike.
- Second prong: an armed citizenry, organized into a decentralized militia.
- Third prong: organized nonviolent resistance.

These prongs might well be combined into a single fearful scimitar: a militia, collecting dues from its combatant members and contributions from noncombatants or nonmembers, and coordinating violent and nonviolent resistance through one and the same democratic structure.

This would be an impressive military force, I think. And it makes me wonder: What will protect other nations from us? As I read more and more ancient and mediæval history, I come to realize that anarchic, decentralized, egalitarian, individualistic societies are not necessarily peaceful societies. The Celtic and Viking societies we admire so much as libertarian models were among the most effective raiders and conquerors in history. What is to prevent our free nation from itself becoming a threat to the security of other nations (and thus ultimately a threat to its own security, as those nations are provoked into attacking us)?

This worry might be reinforced by reading Machiavelli's *Discourses on Livy*, a book I have already cited several times now—and a much more interesting and important book, I think, then his more famous (or notorious) work *The Prince*. (The *Discourses on Livy* is not a libertarian book by any means; but it contains much for libertarians to ponder. What strikes a libertarian in reading it is the odd way in which Machiavelli manages to combine the political insight and perspicacity of an Isabel Paterson—with the economic insight of a log.)

Machiavelli argues that a free nation is the greatest possible threat to the freedom of other nations:

- free nations are more prosperous, and thus better armed;
- they are more politically stable, and thus harder to defeat through treachery;
- there is higher morale among their citizens, thus making them better soldiers;
- equal opportunity and free competition among citizens tend to reward, and thus to foster, what Machiavelli calls virtù (by which he means, not "virtue" in our sense, but a combination of self-discipline, boldness, and ingenuity—which are nice things to have in your own nation, but can be dangerous traits in a vigorous and aggressive nation next door);
- and the high standard of living enjoyed by free nations leads to an increase in population, thus creating a pressure to expand into the territory of their neighbors.

Machiavelli cites Rome and Athens as instances (see also the account of Athens in Thucydides' *History of the Peloponnesian War*, in particular comparing Pericles' panegyric to Athenian libertarianism at II. 34-46 with the Corinthian speech on the restless energy and virtù of Athenian imperialism at I. 68-71); today Machiavelli might add the United States. Of course there are counterexamples: Switzerland, for instance. And despite Machiavelli's brilliance, he seems to have little understanding of the free market; his notion of a free society thus does not appear to include the concept of free trade, which nineteenth-century classical liberals favored in part because of its tendency to create ties of mutual dependence that discouraged war. Still, it is true that freedom, together with the technological progress that freedom brings in its train, has the effect of increasing people's options; and one goal one can better pursue when one's options have increased, is the decreasing of one's neighbors' options.

But maybe the solution is that the free nation's neighbors had better become free nations themselves!

Notes

1. Jacobson, Philip, "Three Voluntary Economies," *Formulations* Vol. 2, No. 1: 405-409.
2. Though Machiavelli may not be consistent on this point. He insists that it weakens a nation militarily to have a disarmed populace; but he also insists that it's dangerous in peacetime to have an armed populace—since, in the absence of an external enemy, they might turn their arms against the government. (Oh no!) But I suspect Machiavelli's solution would be to keep the nation constantly at war—since his model of an ideal nation is the Roman Republic, which Machiavelli praises precisely for its policy of permanent war, whereby it constantly and unceasingly expanded and gobbled up other people's territory. That way, since pesky peacetime never arrives, you get all the advantages of an armed populace with none of the disadvantages. Since my aims are rather different from Machiavelli's (I want to discourage imperialism and encourage resistance to government, not the other way around), I can accept his analysis without sharing his precise recommendations!
3. Phil Jacobson has pointed out to me that volunteer fire departments have historically succeeded in coordinating their activities with one another without centralized control; an unusually large fire in town A will bring in fire departments from towns B, C, and D as well. This example makes me wonder whether an association-of-associations militia would need a commander-in-chief at all.
4. Gand is named, of course, after Gandhi. The significance of the name Chiron is harder to guess. In Greek mythology, Chiron was the centaur who tutored Achilles, and Hogan's use of the name may be a reference to the fact that the first generation of his Chironians were reared by robots rather than humans. Another hypothesis (somewhat less likely given Hogan's militant antipathy toward Christianity) is that Chiron is a pun on Chi-Rho, the traditional Greek abbreviation for Christ, signifying that the Chironians embody the true essence of Christianity.
5. As this issue goes to press, the secessionist rebels in Chechnya are having a surprising, though sadly limited, degree of success in employing a mixture of violent and nonviolent techniques against Russian troops.

9

The Myth of the Rule of Law

John Hasnas

Commitment to the rule of law is one of the core values of a liberal legal system. The adherents of such a system usually regard the concept of a "government of laws and not people" as the chief protector of the citizens' liberty. This article argues that such is not the case. It begins with what is intended as an entertaining reprise of the main jurisprudential arguments designed to show that there is, in fact, no such thing as a government of laws and not people and that the belief that there is constitutes a myth that serves to maintain the public's support for society's power structure. It then suggests that the maintenance of liberty requires not only the abandonment of the ideal of the rule of law, but the commitment to a monopolistic legal system as well. The article concludes by suggesting, in a somewhat fanciful way, that the preservation of a truly free society requires liberating the law from state control to allow for the development of a market for law.

I.

Stop! Before reading this Article, please take the following quiz.

The First Amendment to the Constitution of the United States provides, in part: "Congress shall make no law...abridging the freedom of speech, or of the press;..."[1] On the basis of your personal understanding of this sentence's meaning (not your knowledge of constitutional law), please indicate whether you believe the following sentences to be true or false.

1) In time of war, a federal statute may be passed prohibiting citizens from revealing military secrets to the enemy.
2) The President may issue an executive order prohibiting public criticism of his administration.
3) Congress may pass a law prohibiting museums from exhibiting photographs and paintings depicting homosexual activity.
4) A federal statute may be passed prohibiting a citizen from falsely shouting "fire" in a crowded theater.
5) Congress may pass a law prohibiting dancing to rock and roll music.
6) The Internal Revenue Service may issue a regulation prohibiting the publication of a book explaining how to cheat on your taxes and get away with it.
7) Congress may pass a statute prohibiting flag burning.

Thank you. You may now read on.

In his novel *1984*, George Orwell created a nightmare vision of the future in which an all-powerful Party exerts totalitarian control over society by forcing the citizens to master the technique of "doublethink," which requires them "to hold simultaneously two opinions which cancel[] out, knowing them to be contradictory and believing in both of them."[2] Orwell's doublethink is usually regarded as a wonderful literary device, but, of course, one with no referent in reality since it is obviously impossible to believe both halves of a contradiction. In my opinion, this assessment is quite mistaken. Not only is it possible for people to believe both halves of a contradiction, it is something they do every day with no apparent difficulty.

Consider, for example, people's beliefs about the legal system. They are obviously aware that the law is inherently political. The common complaint that members of Congress are corrupt, or are legislating for their own political benefit or for that of special interest groups demonstrates that citizens understand that the laws under which they live are a product of political forces rather than the embodiment of the ideal of justice. Further, as evidenced by the political battles fought over the recent nominations of Robert Bork and Clarence Thomas to the Supreme Court, the public obviously believes that the ideology of the people who serve as judges influences the way the law is interpreted.

This, however, in no way prevents people from simultaneously regarding the law as a body of definite, politically neutral rules amenable to an impartial application which all citizens have a moral obligation to obey. Thus, they seem both surprised and dismayed to learn that the Clean Air Act might have been written, not to produce the cleanest air possible, but to favor the economic interests of the miners of dirty burning West Virginia coal (West Virginia coincidentally being the home of Robert Byrd, who was then chairman of the Senate Appropriations Committee) over those of the miners of cleaner-burning western coal.[3] And, when the Supreme Court hands down a controversial ruling on a subject such as abortion, civil rights, or capital punishment, then, like Louis in Casablanca, the public is shocked, shocked to find that the Court may have let political considerations influence its decision. The frequent condemnation of the judiciary for "undemocratic judicial activism" or "unprincipled social engineering" is merely a reflection of the public's belief that the law consists of a set of definite and consistent "neutral principles"[4] which the judge is obligated to apply in an objective manner, free from the influence of his or her personal political and moral beliefs.

I believe that, much as Orwell suggested, it is the public's ability to engage in this type of doublethink, to be aware that the law is inherently political in character and yet believe it to be an objective embodiment of justice, that accounts for the amazing degree to which the federal government is able to exert its control over a supposedly free people. I would argue that this ability to maintain the belief that the law is a body of consistent, politically neutral rules that can be objectively applied by judges in the face of overwhelming evidence to the contrary, goes a long way toward explaining citizens' acquiescence in the steady erosion of their fundamental freedoms. To show that this is, in fact, the case, I would like to direct your attention to the fiction which resides at the heart of this incongruity and allows the public to engage in the requisite doublethink without cognitive discomfort: the myth of the rule of law.

I refer to the myth of the rule of law because, to the extent this phrase suggests a society in which all are governed by neutral rules that are objectively applied by judges, there is no such thing. As a myth, however, the concept of the rule of law is both powerful and dangerous. Its power derives from its great emotive appeal. The rule of law suggests an absence of arbitrariness, an absence of the worst abuses of tyranny. The image presented by the slogan "America is a government of laws and not people" is one of fair and impartial rule rather than subjugation to human whim. This is an image that can command both the allegiance and affection of the citizenry. After all, who wouldn't be in favor of the rule of law if the only alternative were arbitrary rule? But this image is also the source of the myth's danger. For if citizens really believe that they are being governed by fair and impartial rules and that the only alternative is subjection to personal rule, they will be much more likely to support the state as it progressively curtails their freedom.

In this article, I will argue that this is a false dichotomy. Specifically, I intend to establish three points: 1) there is no such thing as a government of law and not people, 2) the belief that there is serves to maintain public support for society's power structure, and 3) the establishment of a truly free society requires the abandonment of the myth of the rule of law.

II.

Imagine the following scene. A first-year contracts course is being taught at the prestigious Harvard Law School. The professor is a distinguished scholar with a national reputation as one of the leading experts on Anglo-American contract law. Let's call him Professor Kingsfield. He instructs his class to research the following hypothetical for the next day.

A woman living in a rural setting becomes ill and calls her family physician, who is also the only local doctor, for help. However, it is Wednesday, the doctor's day off and because she has a golf date, she does not respond. The woman's condition worsens and because no other physician can be procured in time, she dies. Her estate then sues the doctor for not coming to her aid. Is the doctor liable?

Two of the students, Arnie Becker and Ann Kelsey, resolve to make a good impression on Kingsfield should they be called on to discuss the case. Arnie is a somewhat conservative, considerably egocentric individual. He believes that doctors are human beings, who like anyone else, are entitled to a day off, and that it would be unfair to require them to be at the beck and call of their patients. For this reason, his initial impression of the solution to the hypothetical is that the doctor should not be liable. Through his research, he discovers the case of *Hurley v. Eddingfield*,[5] which establishes the rule that in the absence of an explicit contract, i.e., when there has been no actual meeting of the minds, there can be no liability. In the hypothetical, there was clearly no meeting of the minds. Therefore, Arnie concludes that his initial impression was correct and that the doctor is not legally liable. Since he has found a valid rule of law which clearly applies to the facts of the case, he is confident that he is prepared for tomorrow's class.

Ann Kelsey is politically liberal and considers herself to be a caring individual. She believes that when doctors take the Hippocratic oath, they accept a special obligation to care for the sick, and that it would be wrong and set a terrible example for doctors to ignore the needs of regular patients who depend on them. For this reason, her initial impression of the solution to the hypothetical is that the doctor should be liable. Through her research, she discovers the case of *Cotnam v. Wisdom*,[6] which establishes the rule that in the absence of an explicit contract, the law will imply a contractual relationship where such is necessary to avoid injustice. She believes that under the facts of the hypothetical, the failure to imply a contractual relationship would be obviously unjust. Therefore, she concludes that her initial impression was correct and that the doctor is legally liable. Since she has found a valid rule of law which clearly applies to the facts of the case, she is confident that she is prepared for tomorrow's class.

The following day, Arnie is called upon and presents his analysis. Ann, who knows she has found a sound legal argument for exactly the opposite outcome, concludes that Arnie is a typical privileged white male conservative with no sense of compassion, who has obviously missed the point of the hypothetical. She volunteers, and when called upon by Kingsfield criticizes Arnie's analysis of the case and presents her own. Arnie, who knows he has found a sound legal argument for his position, concludes that Ann is a typical female bleeding-heart liberal, whose emotionalism has caused her to miss the point of the hypothetical. Each expects Kingsfield to confirm his or her analysis and dismiss the other's as the misguided bit of illogic it so obviously is. Much to their chagrin, however, when a third student asks, "But who is right, Professor?" Kingsfield gruffly responds, "When you turn that mush between your ears into something useful and begin to think like a lawyer, you will be able to answer that question for yourself" and moves on to another subject.

What Professor Kingsfield knows but will never reveal to the students is that both Arnie's and Ann's analyses are correct. How can this be?

III.

What Professor Kingsfield knows is that the legal world is not like the real world and the type of reasoning appropriate to it is distinct from that which human beings ordinarily employ. In the real world, people usually attempt to solve problems by forming hypotheses and then testing them against the facts as they know them. When the facts confirm the hypotheses, they are accepted as true, although subject to reevaluation as new evidence is discovered. This is a successful method of reasoning about scientific and other empirical matters because the physical world has a definite, unique structure. It works because the laws of nature are consistent. In the real world, it is entirely appropriate to assume that once you have confirmed your hypothesis, all other hypotheses inconsistent with it are incorrect.

In the legal world, however, this assumption does not hold. This is because unlike the laws of nature, political laws are not consistent. The law human beings create to regulate their conduct is made up of incompatible, contradictory rules and principles; and, as anyone who has studied a little logic can demonstrate, any conclusion can be validly derived from a set of contradictory premises. This means that a logically sound argument can be found for any legal conclusion.

When human beings engage in legal reasoning, they usually proceed in the same manner as they do when engaged in empirical reasoning. They begin with a hypothesis as to how a case should be decided and test it by searching for a sound supporting argument. After all, no one can "reason" directly to an unimagined conclusion. Without some end in view, there is no way of knowing what premises to employ or what direction the argument should take. When a sound argument is found, then, as in the case of empirical reasoning, one naturally concludes that one's legal hypothesis has been shown to be correct, and further, that all competing hypotheses are therefore incorrect.

This is the fallacy of legal reasoning. Because the legal world is comprised of contradictory rules, there will be sound legal arguments available not only for the hypothesis one is investigating, but for other, competing hypotheses as well. The assumption that there is a unique, correct resolution, which serves so well in empirical investigations, leads one astray when dealing with legal matters. Kingsfield, who is well aware of this, knows that Arnie and Ann have both produced legitimate legal arguments for their competing conclusions. He does not reveal this knowledge to the class, however, because the fact that this is possible is precisely what his students must discover for themselves if they are ever to learn to "think like a lawyer."

IV.

Imagine that Arnie and Ann have completed their first year at Harvard and coincidentally find themselves in the same second-year class on employment discrimination law. During the portion of the course that focuses on Title VII of the Civil Rights Act of 1964,[7] the class is asked to determine whether section 2000e-2(a)(1), which makes it unlawful "to fail or refuse to hire or to discharge any individual, or otherwise to discriminate against any individual with respect to his compensation, terms, conditions, or privileges of employment, because of such individual's race, color, religion, sex, or national origin," permits an employer to voluntarily institute an affirmative action program giving preferential treatment to African-Americans. Perhaps unsurprisingly, Arnie strongly believes that affirmative action programs are morally wrong and that what the country needs are color-blind, merit-based employment practices. In researching the problem, he encounters the following principle of statutory construction: When the words are plain, courts may not enter speculative fields in search of a different meaning, and the language must be regarded as the final expression of legislative intent and not added to or subtracted from on the basis of any extraneous source.[8] In Arnie's opinion, this principle clearly applies to this case. Section 2000e-2(a)(1) prohibits discrimination against any individual because of his race. What wording could be more plain? Since giving preferential treatment to African-Americans discriminates against whites because of their race, Arnie concludes that section 2000e-2(a)(1) prohibits employers from voluntarily instituting affirmative action plans.

Perhaps equally unsurprisingly, Ann has a strong belief that affirmative action is moral and is absolutely necessary to bring about a racially just society. In the course of her research, she encounters the following principle of statutory construction: "It is a familiar rule, that a thing may be within the letter of a statute and yet not within the statute because not within its spirit, nor within the intention of its makers";[9] and that an interpretation which would bring about an end at variance with the purpose of the statute must be rejected.[10] Upon checking the legislative history, Ann learns that the purpose of Title VII of the Civil Rights Act is to relieve "the plight of the Negro in our economy" and "open employment opportunities for Negroes in occupations which have been traditionally closed to them."[11] Since it would obviously contradict this purpose to interpret section 2000e-2 to make it illegal for employers to voluntarily institute affirmative action plans designed to economically benefit African-Americans by opening traditionally closed employment opportunities, Ann concludes that section 2000e-2 does not prohibit such plans.

The next day, Arnie presents his argument for the illegality of affirmative action in class. Since Ann has found a sound legal argument for precisely the opposite conclusion, she knows that Arnie's position is untenable. However, having gotten to know Arnie over the last year, this does not surprise her in the least. She regards him as an inveterate reactionary who is completely unprincipled in pursuit of his conservative (and probably racist) agenda. She believes that he is advancing an absurdly narrow reading of the Civil Rights Act for the purely political end of undermining the purpose of the statute. Accordingly, she volunteers, and when called upon, makes this point and presents her own argument demonstrating that affirmative action is legal. Arnie, who has found a sound legal argument for his conclusion, knows that Ann's position is untenable. However, he expected as much. Over the past year he has come to know Ann as a knee-jerk liberal who is willing to do anything to advance her mushy-headed, left-wing agenda. He believes that she is perversely manipulating the patently clear language of the statute for the purely political end of extending the statute beyond its legitimate purpose.

Both Arnie and Ann know that they have found a logically sound argument for their conclusion. But both have also committed the fallacy of legal reasoning by assuming that under the law there is a uniquely correct resolution of the case. Because of this assumption, both believe that their argument demonstrates that they have found the objectively correct answer, and that therefore, the other is simply playing politics with the law.

The truth is, of course, that both are engaging in politics. Because the law is made up of contradictory rules that can generate any conclusion, what conclusion one finds will be determined by what conclusion one looks for, i.e., by the hypothesis one decides to test. This will invariably be the one that intuitively "feels" right, the one that is most congruent with one's antecedent, underlying political and moral beliefs. Thus, legal conclusions are always determined by the normative assumptions of the decision-maker. The knowledge that Kingsfield possesses and Arnie and Ann have not yet discovered is that the law is never neutral and objective.

V.

I have suggested that because the law consists of contradictory rules and principles, sound legal arguments will be available for all legal conclusions, and hence, the normative predispositions of the decision-makers, rather than the law itself, determine the outcome of cases. It should be noted, however, that this vastly understates the degree to which the law is indeterminate. For even if the law were consistent, the individual rules and principles are expressed in such vague and general language that the decision-maker is able to interpret them as broadly or as narrowly as necessary to achieve any desired result.

To see that this is the case, imagine that Arnie and Ann have graduated from Harvard Law School, gone on to distinguished careers as attorneys, and later in life find, to their amazement and despair, that they have both been appointed as judges to the same appellate court. The first case to come before them involves the following facts:

A bankrupt was auctioning off his personal possessions to raise money to cover his debts. One of the items put up for auction was a painting that had been in his family for years. A buyer attending the auction purchased the painting for a bid of $100. When the buyer had the painting appraised, it turned out to be a lost masterpiece worth millions. Upon learning of this, the seller sued to rescind the contract of sale. The trial court granted the rescission. The question on appeal is whether this judgment is legally correct.

Counsel for both the plaintiff seller and defendant buyer agree that the rule of law governing this case holds that a contract of sale may be rescinded when there has been a mutual mistake concerning a fact that was material to the agreement. The seller claims that in the instant case there has been such a mistake, citing as precedent the case of *Sherwood v. Walker*.[12] In *Sherwood*, one farmer sold another farmer a cow which both farmers believed to be sterile. When the cow turned out to be fertile, the seller was granted rescission of the contract of sale on the ground of mutual mistake.[13] The seller argues that Sherwood is exactly analogous to the present controversy. Both he and the buyer believed the contract of sale was for an inexpensive painting. Thus, both were mistaken as to the true nature of the object being sold. Since this was obviously material to the agreement, the seller claims that the trial court was correct in granting rescission.

The buyer claims that the instant case is not one of mutual mistake, citing as precedent the case of *Wood v. Boynton*.[14] In *Wood*, a woman sold a small stone she had found to a jeweler for one dollar. At the time of the sale, neither party knew what type of stone it was. When it subsequently turned out to be an uncut diamond worth $700, the seller sued for rescission claiming mutual mistake. The court upheld the contract, finding that since both parties knew that they were bargaining over a stone of unknown value, there was no mistake.[15] The buyer argues that this is exactly analogous to the present controversy. Both the seller and the buyer knew that the painting being sold was a work of unknown value. This is precisely what is to be expected at an auction. Thus, the buyer claims that this is not a case of mutual mistake and the contract should be upheld.

Following oral argument, Arnie, Ann, and the third judge on the court, Bennie Stolwitz, a non-lawyer appointed to the bench predominantly because the governor is his uncle, retire to consider their ruling. Arnie believes that one of the essential purposes of contract law is to encourage people to be self-reliant and careful in their transactions, since with the freedom to enter into binding arrangements comes the responsibility for doing so. He regards as crucial to his decision the facts that the seller had the opportunity to have the painting appraised and that by exercising due care he could have discovered its true value. Hence, he regards the contract in this case as one for a painting of unknown value and votes to overturn the trial court and uphold the contract. On the other hand, Ann believes that the essential purpose of contract law is to ensure that all parties receive a fair bargain. She regards as crucial to her decision the fact that the buyer in this case is receiving a massive windfall at the expense of the unfortunate seller. Hence, she regards the contract as one for an inexpensive painting and votes to uphold the trial court's decision and grant rescission. This leaves the deciding vote up to Bennie, who has no idea what the purpose of contract law is, but thinks that it just doesn't seem right for the bankrupt guy to lose out, and votes for rescission.

Both Arnie and Ann can see that the present situation bodes ill for their judicial tenure. Each believes that the other's unprincipled political manipulations of the law will leave Bennie, who is not even a lawyer, with control of the court. As a result, they hold a meeting to discuss the situation. At this meeting, they both promise to put politics aside and decide all future cases strictly on the basis of the law. Relieved, they return to court to confront the next case on the docket, which involves the following facts:

A philosophy professor who supplements her academic salary during the summer by giving lectures on political philosophy had contracted to deliver a lecture on the rule of law to the Future Republicans of America (FRA) on July 20, for $500. She was subsequently contacted by the Young Socialists of America, who offered her $1000 for a lecture to be delivered on the same day. She thereupon called the FRA, informing them of her desire to accept the better offer. The FRA then agreed to pay $1000 for her lecture. After the professor delivered the lecture, the FRA paid only the originally stipulated $500. The professor sued and the trial court ruled she was entitled to the additional $500. The question on appeal is whether this judgment is legally correct.

Counsel for both the plaintiff professor and defendant FRA agree that the rule of law governing this case holds that a promise to pay more for services one is already contractually bound to perform is not enforceable, but if an existing contract is rescinded by both parties and a new one is negotiated, the promise is enforceable. The FRA claims that in the instant case, it had promised to pay more for a service the professor was already contractually bound to perform, citing *Davis & Co. v. Morgan*[16] as precedent. In Davis, a laborer employed for a year at $40 per month was offered $65 per month by another company. The employer then promised to pay the employee an additional $120 at the end of the year if he stayed with the firm. At the end of the year, the employer failed to pay the $120, and when the employee sued, the court held that because he was already obligated to work for $40 per month for the year, there was no consideration for the employer's promise; hence, it was unenforceable.[17] The FRA argues that this is exactly analogous to the present controversy. The professor was already obligated to deliver the lecture for $500. Therefore, there was no consideration for the FRA's promise to pay an additional $500 and the promise is unenforceable.

The professor claims that in the instant case, the original contract was rescinded and a new one negotiated, citing *Schwartzreich v. BaumanBasch, Inc.* [18] as precedent. In Schwartzreich, a clothing designer who had contracted for a year's work at $90 per week was subsequently offered $115 per week by another company. When the designer informed his employer of his intention to leave, the employer offered the designer $100 per week if he would stay and the designer agreed. When the designer sued for the additional compensation, the court held that since the parties had simultaneously rescinded the original contract by mutual consent and entered into a new one for the higher salary, the promise to pay was enforceable.[19] The professor argues that this is exactly analogous to the present controversy. When the FRA offered to pay her an additional $500 to give the lecture, they were obviously offering to rescind the former contract and enter a new one on different terms. Hence, the promise to pay the extra $500 is enforceable.

Following oral argument, the judges retire to consider their ruling. Arnie, mindful of his agreement with Ann, is scrupulously careful not to let political considerations enter into his analysis of the case. Thus, he begins by asking himself why society needs contract law in the first place. He decides that the objective, nonpolitical answer is obviously that society needs some mechanism to ensure that individuals honor their voluntarily undertaken commitments. From this perspective, the resolution of the present case is clear. Since the professor is obviously threatening to go back on her voluntarily undertaken commitment in order to extort more money from the FRA, Arnie characterizes the case as one in which a promise has been made to pay more for services which the professor is already contractually bound to perform, and decides that the promise is unenforceable. Hence, he votes to overturn the trial court's decision. Ann, also mindful of her agreement with Arnie, is meticulous in her efforts to ensure that she decides this case purely on the law. Accordingly, she begins her analysis by asking herself why society needs contract law in the first place. She decides that the objective, nonpolitical answer is obviously that it provides an environment within which people can exercise the freedom to arrange their lives as they see fit. From this perspective, the resolution of the present case is clear. Since the FRA is essentially attempting to prevent the professor from arranging her life as she sees fit, Ann characterizes the case as one in which the parties have simultaneously rescinded an existing contract and negotiated a new one, and decides that the promise is enforceable. Hence, she votes to uphold the trial court's decision. This once again leaves the deciding vote up to Bennie, who has no idea why society needs contract law, but thinks that the professor is taking advantage of the situation in an unfair way and votes to overturn the trial court's ruling.

Both Arnie and Ann now believe that the other is an incorrigible ideologue who is destined to torment him or her throughout his or her judicial existence. Each is quite unhappy at the prospect. Each blames the other for his or her unhappiness. But, in fact, the blame lies within each. For they have never learned Professor Kingsfield's lesson that it is impossible to reach an objective decision based solely on the law. This is because the law is always open to interpretation and there is no such thing as a normatively neutral interpretation. The way one interprets the rules of law is always determined by one's underlying moral and political beliefs.

VI.

I have been arguing that the law is not a body of determinate rules that can be objectively and impersonally applied by judges; that what the law prescribes is necessarily determined by the normative predispositions of the one who is interpreting it. In short, I have been arguing that law is inherently political. If you, my reader, are like most people, you are far from convinced of this. In fact, I dare say I can read your thoughts. You are thinking that even if I have shown that the present legal system is somewhat indeterminate, I certainly have not shown that the law is inherently political. Although you may agree that the law as presently constituted is too vague or contains too many contradictions, you probably believe that this state of affairs is due to the actions of the liberal judicial activists, or the Reaganite adherents of the doctrine of original intent, or the self-serving politicians, or the (feel free to fill in your favorite candidate for the group that is responsible for the legal system's ills). However, you do not believe that the law must be this way, that it can never be definite and politically neutral. You believe that the law can be reformed; that to bring about an end to political strife and institute a true rule of law, we merely need to create a legal system comprised of consistent rules that are expressed in clear, definite language.

It is my sad duty to inform you that this cannot be done. Even with all the good will in the world, we could not produce such a legal code because there is simply no such thing as uninterpretable language. Now I could attempt to convince you of this by the conventional method of regaling you with myriad examples of the manipulation of legal language (e.g., an account of how the relatively straightforward language of the Commerce Clause giving Congress the power to "regulate Commerce...among the several States"[20] has been interpreted to permit the regulation of both farmers growing wheat for use on their own farms[21] and the nature of male-female relationships in all private businesses that employ more than fifteen persons[22]). However, I prefer to try a more direct approach. Accordingly, let me direct your attention to the quiz you completed at the beginning of this article. Please consider your responses.

If your response to question one was "True," you chose to interpret the word "no" as used in the First Amendment to mean "some."

If your response to question two was "False," you chose to interpret the word "Congress" to refer to the President of the United States and the word "law" to refer to an executive order.

If your response to question three was "False," you chose to interpret the words "speech" and "press" to refer to the exhibition of photographs and paintings.

If your response to question four was "True," you have underscored your belief that the word "no" really means "some."

If your response to question five was "False," you chose to interpret the words "speech" and "press" to refer to dancing to rock and roll music.

If your response to question six was "False," you chose to interpret the word "Congress" to refer to the Internal Revenue Service and the word "law" to refer to an IRS regulation.

If your response to question seven was "False," you chose to interpret the words "speech" and "press" to refer to the act of burning a flag.

Unless your responses were: 1) False, 2) True, 3) True, 4) False, 5) True, 6) True, and 7) True, you chose to interpret at least one of the words "Congress," "no," "law," "speech," and "press" in what can only be described as something other than its ordinary sense. Why did you do this? Were your responses based on the "plain meaning" of the words or on certain normative beliefs you hold about the extent to which the federal government should be allowed to interfere with citizens' expressive activities? Were your responses objective and neutral or were they influenced by your "politics"?

I chose this portion of the First Amendment for my example because it contains the clearest, most definite legal language of which I am aware. If a provision as clearly drafted as this may be subjected to political interpretation, what legal provision may not be? But this explains why the legal system cannot be reformed to consist of a body of definite rules yielding unique, objectively verifiable resolutions of cases. What a legal rule means is always determined by the political assumptions of the person applying it.[23]

VII.

Let us assume that I have failed to convince you of the impossibility of reforming the law into a body of definite, consistent rules that produces determinate results. Even if the law could be reformed in this way, it clearly should not be. There is nothing perverse in the fact that the law is indeterminate. Society is not the victim of some nefarious conspiracy to undermine legal certainty to further ulterior motives. As long as law remains a state monopoly, as long as it is created and enforced exclusively through governmental bodies, it must remain indeterminate if it is to serve its purpose. Its indeterminacy gives the law its flexibility. And since, as a monopoly product, the law must apply to all members of society in a one-size-fits-all manner, flexibility is its most essential feature.

It is certainly true that one of the purposes of law is to ensure a stable social environment, to provide order. But not just any order will suffice. Another purpose of the law must be to do justice. The goal of the law is to provide a social environment which is both orderly and just. Unfortunately, these two purposes are always in tension. For the more definite and rigidly-determined the rules of law become, the less the legal system is able to do justice to the individual. Thus, if the law were fully determinate, it would have no ability to consider the equities of the particular case. This is why even if we could reform the law to make it wholly definite and consistent, we should not.

Consider one of the favorite proposals of those who disagree. Those who believe that the law can and should be rendered fully determinate usually propose that contracts be rigorously enforced. Thus, they advocate a rule of law stating that in the absence of physical compulsion or explicit fraud, parties should be absolutely bound to keep their agreements. They believe that as long as no rules inconsistent with this definite, clearly-drawn provision are allowed to enter the law, politics may be eliminated from contract law and commercial transactions greatly facilitated.

Let us assume, contrary to fact, that the terms "fraud" and "physical compulsion" have a plain meaning not subject to interpretation. The question then becomes what should be done about Agnes Syester.[24] Agnes was "a lonely and elderly widow who fell for the blandishments and flattery of those who" ran an Arthur Murray Dance Studio in Des Moines, Iowa.[25] This studio used some highly innovative sales techniques to sell this 68-year-old woman 4,057 hours of dance instruction, including three life memberships and a course in Gold Star dancing, which was "the type of dancing done by Ginger Rogers and Fred Astaire only about twice as difficult,"[26] for a total cost of $33,497 in 1960 dollars. Of course, Agnes did voluntarily agree to purchase that number of hours. Now, in a case such as this, one might be tempted to "interpret" the overreaching and unfair sales practices of the studio as fraudulent[27] and allow Agnes to recover her money. However, this is precisely the sort of solution that our reformed, determinate contract law is designed to outlaw. Therefore, it would seem that since Agnes has voluntarily contracted for the dance lessons, she is liable to pay the full amount for them. This might seem to be a harsh result for Agnes, but from now on, vulnerable little old ladies will be on notice to be more careful in their dealings.

Or consider a proposal that is often advanced by those who wish to render probate law more determinate. They advocate a rule of law declaring a handwritten will that is signed before two witnesses to be absolutely binding. They believe that by depriving the court of the ability to "interpret" the state of mind of the testator, the judges' personal moral opinions may be eliminated from the law and most probate matters brought to a timely conclusion. Of course, the problem then becomes what to do with Elmer Palmer, a young man who murdered his grandfather to gain the inheritance due him under the old man's will a bit earlier than might otherwise have been the case.[28] In a case such as this, one might be tempted to deny Elmer the fruits of his nefarious labor despite the fact that the will was validly drawn, by appealing to the legal principle that no one should profit from his or her own wrong.[29] However, this is precisely the sort of vaguely-expressed counter-rule that our reformers seek to purge from the legal system in order to ensure that the law remains consistent. Therefore, it would seem that although Elmer may spend a considerable amount of time behind bars, he will do so as a wealthy man. This may send a bad message to other young men of Elmer's temperament, but from now on the probate process will be considerably streamlined.

The proposed reforms certainly render the law more determinate. However, they do so by eliminating the law's ability to consider the equities of the individual case. This observation raises the following interesting question: If this is what a determinate legal system is like, who would want to live under one? The fact is that the greater the degree of certainty we build into the law, the less able the law becomes to do justice. For this reason, a monopolistic legal system composed entirely of clear, consistent rules could not function in a manner acceptable to the general public. It could not serve as a system of justice.

VIII.

I have been arguing that the law is inherently indeterminate, and further, that this may not be such a bad thing. I realize, however, that you may still not be convinced. Even if you are now willing to admit that the law is somewhat indeterminate, you probably believe that I have vastly exaggerated the degree to which this is true. After all, it is obvious that the law cannot be radically indeterminate. If this were the case, the law would be completely unpredictable. Judges hearing similar cases would render wildly divergent decisions. There would be no stability or uniformity in the law. But, as imperfect as the current legal system may be, this is clearly not the case.

The observation that the legal system is highly stable is, of course, correct, but it is a mistake to believe that this is because the law is determinate. The stability of the law derives not from any feature of the law itself, but from the overwhelming uniformity of ideological background among those empowered to make legal decisions. Consider who the judges are in this country. Typically, they are people from a solid middle- to upper-class background who performed well at an appropriately prestigious undergraduate institution; demonstrated the ability to engage in the type of analytical reasoning that is measured by the standardized Law School Admissions Test; passed through the crucible of law school, complete with its methodological and political indoctrination; and went on to high-profile careers as attorneys, probably with a prestigious Wall Street-style law firm. To have been appointed to the bench, it is virtually certain that they were both politically moderate and well-connected, and, until recently, white males of the correct ethnic and religious pedigree. It should be clear that, culturally speaking, such a group will tend to be quite homogeneous, sharing a great many moral, spiritual, and political beliefs and values. Given this, it can hardly be surprising that there will be a high degree of agreement among judges as to how cases ought to be decided. But this agreement is due to the common set of normative presuppositions the judges share, not some immanent, objective meaning that exists within the rules of law.

In fact, however, the law is not truly stable, since it is continually, if slowly, evolving in response to changing social mores and conditions. This evolution occurs because each new generation of judges brings with it its own set of "progressive" normative assumptions. As the older generation passes from the scene, these assumptions come to be shared by an ever-increasing percentage of the judiciary. Eventually, they become the consensus of opinion among judicial decision-makers, and the law changes to reflect them. Thus, a generation of judges that regarded "separate but equal" as a perfectly legitimate interpretation of the Equal Protection Clause of the Fourteenth Amendment[30] gave way to one which interpreted that clause as prohibiting virtually all governmental actions that classify individuals by race, which, in turn, gave way to one which interpreted the same language to permit "benign" racial classifications designed to advance the social status of minority groups. In this way, as the moral and political values conventionally accepted by society change over time, so too do those embedded in the law.

The law appears to be stable because of the slowness with which it evolves. But the slow pace of legal development is not due to any inherent characteristic of the law itself. Logically speaking, any conclusion, however radical, is derivable from the rules of law. It is simply that, even between generations, the range of ideological opinion represented on the bench is so narrow that anything more than incremental departures from conventional wisdom and morality will not be respected within the profession. Such decisions are virtually certain to be overturned on appeal, and thus, are rarely even rendered in the first instance.

Confirming evidence for this thesis can be found in our contemporary judicial history. Over the past quarter-century, the "diversity" movement has produced a bar, and concomitantly a bench, somewhat more open to people of different racial, sexual, ethnic, and socioeconomic backgrounds. To some extent, this movement has produced a judiciary that represents a broader range of ideological viewpoints than has been the case in the past. Over the same time period, we have seen an accelerated rate of legal change. Today, long-standing precedents are more freely overruled, novel theories of liability are more frequently accepted by the courts, and different courts hand down different, and seemingly irreconcilable, decisions more often. In addition, it is worth noting that recently, the chief complaint about the legal system seems to concern the degree to which it has become "politicized." This suggests that as the ideological solidarity of the judiciary breaks down, so too does the predictability of legal decision-making, and hence, the stability of the law. Regardless of this trend, I hope it is now apparent that to assume that the law is stable because it is determinate is to reverse cause and effect. Rather, it is because the law is basically stable that it appears to be determinate. It is not rule of law that gives us a stable legal system; it is the stability of the culturally shared values of the judiciary that gives rise to and supports the myth of the rule of law.

IX.

It is worth noting that there is nothing new or startling about the claim that the law is indeterminate. This has been the hallmark of the Critical Legal Studies movement since the mid-1970s. The "Crits," however, were merely reviving the earlier contention of the legal realists who made the same point in the 1920s and '30s. And the realists were themselves merely repeating the claim of earlier jurisprudential thinkers. For example, as early as 1897, Oliver Wendell Holmes had pointed out:

> The language of judicial decision is mainly the language of logic. And the logical method and form flatter that longing for certainty and for repose which is in every human mind. But certainty generally is illusion, and repose is not the destiny of man.

> Behind the logical form lies a judgment as to the relative worth and importance of competing legislative grounds, often an inarticulate and unconscious judgment, it is true, and yet the very root and nerve of the whole proceeding. You can give any conclusion a logical form.[31]

This raises an interesting question. If it has been known for 100 years that the law does not consist of a body of determinate rules, why is the belief that it does still so widespread? If four generations of jurisprudential scholars have shown that the rule of law is a myth, why does the concept still command such fervent commitment? The answer is implicit in the question itself, for the question recognizes that the rule of law is a myth and, like all myths, it is designed to serve an emotive, rather than cognitive, function. The purpose of a myth is not to persuade one's reason, but to enlist one's emotions in support of an idea. And this is precisely the case for the myth of the rule of law; its purpose is to enlist the emotions of the public in support of society's political power structure.

People are more willing to support the exercise of authority over themselves when they believe it to be an objective, neutral feature of the natural world. This was the idea behind the concept of the divine right of kings. By making the king appear to be an integral part of God's plan for the world rather than an ordinary human being dominating his fellows by brute force, the public could be more easily persuaded to bow to his authority. However, when the doctrine of divine right became discredited, a replacement was needed to ensure that the public did not view political authority as merely the exercise of naked power. That replacement is the concept of the rule of law.

People who believe they live under "a government of laws and not people" tend to view their nation's legal system as objective and impartial. They tend to see the rules under which they must live not as expressions of human will, but as embodiments of neutral principles of justice, i.e., as natural features of the social world. Once they believe that they are being commanded by an impersonal law rather than other human beings, they view their obedience to political authority as a public-spirited acceptance of the requirements of social life rather than mere acquiescence to superior power. In this way, the concept of the rule of law functions much like the use of the passive voice by the politician who describes a delict on his or her part with the assertion "mistakes were made." It allows people to hide the agency of power behind a facade of words; to believe that it is the law which compels their compliance, not self-aggrandizing politicians, or highly capitalized special interests, or wealthy white Anglo-Saxon Protestant males, or (fill in your favorite culprit).

But the myth of the rule of law does more than render the people submissive to state authority; it also turns them into the state's accomplices in the exercise of its power. For people who would ordinarily consider it a great evil to deprive individuals of their rights or oppress politically powerless minority groups will respond with patriotic fervor when these same actions are described as upholding the rule of law.

Consider the situation in India toward the end of British colonial rule. At that time, the followers of Mohandas Gandhi engaged in nonviolent civil disobedience by manufacturing salt for their own use in contravention of the British monopoly on such manufacture. The British administration and army responded with mass imprisonments and shocking brutality. It is difficult to understand this behavior on the part of the highly moralistic, ever-so-civilized British unless one keeps in mind that they were able to view their activities not as violently repressing the indigenous population, but as upholding the rule of law.

The same is true of the violence directed against the nonviolent civil rights protestors in the American South during the civil rights movement. Although much of the white population of the southern states held racist beliefs, one cannot account for the overwhelming support given to the violent repression of these protests on the assumption that the vast majority of the white Southerners were sadistic racists devoid of moral sensibilities. The true explanation is that most of these people were able to view themselves not as perpetuating racial oppression and injustice, but as upholding the rule of law against criminals and outside agitators. Similarly, since despite the '60s rhetoric, all police officers are not "fascist pigs," some other explanation is needed for their willingness to participate in the "police riot" at the 1968 Democratic convention, or the campaign of illegal arrests and civil rights violations against those demonstrating in Washington against President Nixon's policies in Vietnam, or the effort to infiltrate and destroy the sanctuary movement that sheltered refugees from Salvadorian death squads during the Reagan era or, for that matter, the attack on and destruction of the Branch Davidian compound in Waco. It is only when these officers have fully bought into the myth that "we are a government of laws and not people," when they truly believe that their actions are commanded by some impersonal body of just rules, that they can fail to see that they are the agency used by those in power to oppress others.

The reason why the myth of the rule of law has survived for 100 years despite the knowledge of its falsity is that it is too valuable a tool to relinquish. The myth of impersonal government is simply the most effective means of social control available to the state.

X.

During the past two decades, the legal scholars identified with the Critical Legal Studies movement have gained a great deal of notoriety for their unrelenting attacks on traditional, "liberal" legal theory. The modus operandi of these scholars has been to select a specific area of the law and show that because the rules and principles that comprise it are logically incoherent, legal outcomes can always be manipulated by those in power to favor their interests at the expense of the politically "subordinated" classes. The Crits then argue that the claim that the law consists of determinate, just rules which are impartially applied to all is a ruse employed by the powerful to cause these subordinated classes to view the oppressive legal rulings as the necessary outcomes of an objective system of justice. This renders the oppressed more willing to accept their socially subordinated status. Thus, the Crits maintain that the concept of the rule of law is simply a facade used to maintain the socially dominant position of white males in an oppressive and illegitimate capitalist system.

In taking this approach, the Crits recognize that the law is indeterminate, and thus, that it necessarily reflects the moral and political values of those empowered to render legal decisions. Their objection is that those who currently wield this power subscribe to the wrong set of values. They wish to change the legal system from one which embodies what they regard as the hierarchical, oppressive values of capitalism to one which embodies the more egalitarian, "democratic" values that they usually associate with socialism. The Crits accept that the law must be provided exclusively by the state, and hence, that it must impose one set of values on all members of society. Their contention is that the particular set of values currently being imposed is the wrong one.

Although they have been subjected to much derision by mainstream legal theorists,[32] as long as we continue to believe that the law must be a state monopoly, there really is nothing wrong, or even particularly unique, about the Crits' line of argument. There has always been a political struggle for control of the law, and as long as all must be governed by the same law, as long as one set of values must be imposed upon everyone, there always will be. It is true that the Crits want to impose "democratic" or socialistic values on everyone through the mechanism of the law. But this does not distinguish them from anyone else. Religious fundamentalists want to impose "Christian" values on all via the law. Liberal Democrats want the law to ensure that everyone acts so as to realize a "compassionate" society, while conservative Republicans want it to ensure the realization of "family values" or "civic virtue." Even libertarians insist that all should be governed by a law that enshrines respect for individual liberty as its preeminent value.

The Crits may believe that the law should embody a different set of values than liberals, or conservatives, or libertarians, but this is the only thing that differentiates them from these other groups. Because the other groups have accepted the myth of the rule of law, they perceive what they are doing not as a struggle for political control, but as an attempt to depoliticize the law and return it to its proper form as the neutral embodiment of objective principles of justice. But the rule of law is a myth, and perception does not change reality. Although only the Crits may recognize it, all are engaged in a political struggle to impose their version of "the good" on the rest of society. And as long as the law remains the exclusive province of the state, this will always be the case.

XI.

What is the significance of these observations? Are we condemned to a continual political struggle for control of the legal system? Well, yes; as long as the law remains a state monopoly, we are. But I would ask you to note that this is a conditional statement while you consider the following parable.

A long time ago in a galaxy far away, there existed a parallel Earth that contained a nation called Monosizea. Monosizea was remarkably similar to the present-day United States. It had the same level of technological development, the same social problems, and was governed by the same type of common law legal system. In fact, Monosizea had a federal constitution that was identical to that of the United States in all respects except one. However, that distinction was quite an odd one. For some reason lost to history, the Monosizean founding fathers had included a provision in the constitution that required all shoes manufactured or imported into Monosizea to be the same size. The particular size could be determined by Congress, but whatever size was selected represented the only size shoe permitted in the country.

As you may imagine, in Monosizea, shoe size was a serious political issue. Although there were a few radical fringe groups which argued for either extremely small or extremely large sizes, Monosizea was essentially a two-party system with most of the electorate divided between the Liberal Democratic party and the Conservative Republican party. The Liberal Democratic position on shoe size was that social justice demanded the legal size to be a large size such as a nine or ten. They presented the egalitarian argument that everyone should have equal access to shoes, and that this could only be achieved by legislating a large shoe size. After all, people with small feet could still use shoes that were too large (even if they did have to stuff some newspaper into them), but people with large feet would be completely disenfranchised if the legal size was a small one. Interestingly, the Liberal Democratic party contained a larger than average number of people who were tall. The Conservative Republican position on shoe size was that respect for family values and the traditional role of government required that the legal size be a small size such as a four or five. They presented the moralistic argument that society's obligation to the next generation and government's duty to protect the weak demanded that the legal size be set so that children could have adequate footwear. They contended that children needed reasonably well-fitting shoes while they were in their formative years and their feet were tender. Later, when they were adults and their feet were fully developed, they would be able to cope with the rigors of barefoot life. Interestingly, the Conservative Republican party contained a larger than average number of people who were short.

Every two years as congressional elections approached, and especially when this corresponded with a presidential election, the rhetoric over the shoe size issue heated up. The Liberal Democrats would accuse the Conservative Republicans of being under the control of the fundamentalist Christians and of intolerantly attempting to impose their religious values on society. The Conservative Republicans would accuse the Liberal Democrats of being misguided, bleeding-heart do-gooders who were either the dupes of the socialists or socialists themselves. However, after the elections, the shoe size legislation actually hammered out by the President and Congress always seemed to set the legal shoe size close to a seven, which was the average foot size in Monosizea. Further, this legislation always defined the size in broad terms so that it might encompass a size or two on either side, and authorized the manufacture of shoes made of extremely flexible materials that could stretch or contract as necessary. For this reason, most averaged-sized Monosizeans, who were predominantly politically moderate, had acceptable footwear.

This state of affairs seemed quite natural to everyone in Monosizea except a boy named Socrates. Socrates was a pensive, shy young man who, when not reading a book, was often lost in thought. His contemplative nature caused his parents to think of him as a dreamer, his schoolmates to think of him as a nerd, and everyone else to think of him as a bit odd. One day, after learning about the Monosizean Constitution in school and listening to his parents discuss the latest public opinion poll on the shoe size issue, Socrates approached his parents and said: "I have an idea. Why don't we amend the constitution to permit shoemakers to manufacture and sell more than one size shoe. Then everyone could have shoes that fit and we wouldn't have to argue about what the legal shoe size should be anymore."

Socrates' parents found his naive idealism amusing and were proud that their son was so imaginative. For this reason, they tried to show him that his idea was a silly one in a way that would not discourage him from future creative thinking. Thus, Socrates' father said: "That's a very interesting idea, son, but it's simply not practical. There's always been only one size shoe in Monosizea, so that's just the way things have to be. People are used to living this way, and you can't fight city hall. I'm afraid your idea is just too radical."

Although Socrates eventually dropped the subject with his parents, he was never satisfied with their response. During his teenage years, he became more interested in politics and decided to take his idea to the Liberal Democrats. He thought that because they believed all citizens were entitled to adequate footwear, they would surely see the value of his proposal. However, although they seemed to listen with interest and thanked him for his input, they were not impressed with his idea. As the leader of the local party explained: "Your idea is fine in theory, but it will never work in practice. If manufacturers could make whatever size shoes they wanted, consumers would be at the mercy of unscrupulous business people. Each manufacturer would set up his or her own scale of sizes and consumers would have no way of determining what their foot size truly was. In such a case, profit-hungry shoe sales people could easily trick the unwary consumer into buying the wrong size. Without the government setting the size, there would be no guarantee that any shoe was really the size it purported to be. We simply cannot abandon the public to the vicissitudes of an unregulated market in shoes."

To Socrates' protests that people didn't seem to be exploited in other clothing markets and that the shoes manufactured under the present system didn't really fit very well anyway, the party leader responded: "The shoe market is unique. Adequate shoes are absolutely essential to public welfare. Therefore, the ordinary laws of supply and demand cannot be relied upon. And even if we could somehow get around the practical problems, your idea is simply not politically feasible. To make any progress, we must focus on what can actually be accomplished in the current political climate. If we begin advocating radical constitutional changes, we'll be routed in the next election."

Disillusioned by this response, Socrates approached the Conservative Republicans with his idea, explaining that if shoes could be manufactured in any size, all children could be provided with the well-fitting shoes they needed. However, the Conservative Republicans were even less receptive than the Liberal Democrats had been. The leader of their local party responded quite contemptuously, saying: "Look, Monosizea is the greatest, freest country on the face of the planet, and it's respect for our traditional values that has made it that way. Our constitution is based on these values, and it has served us well for the past 200 years. Who are you to question the wisdom of the founding fathers? If you don't like it in this country, why don't you just leave?"

Somewhat taken aback, Socrates explained that he respected the Monosizean Constitution as much as they did, but that did not mean it could not be improved. Even the founding fathers included a process by which it could be amended. However, this did nothing to ameliorate the party leader's disdain. He responded: "It's one thing to propose amending the constitution; it's another to undermine it entirely. Doing away with the shoe size provision would rend the very fabric of our society. If people could make whatever size shoes they wanted whenever they wanted, there would be no way to maintain order in the industry. What you're proposing is not liberty, it's license. Were we to adopt your proposal, we would be abandoning the rule of law itself. Can't you see that what you are advocating is not freedom, but anarchy?"

After this experience, Socrates came to realize that there was no place for him in the political realm. As a result, he went off to college where he took up the study of philosophy. Eventually, he got a Ph.D., became a philosophy professor, and was never heard from again.

So, what is the point of this outlandish parable? I stated at the beginning of this section that as long as the law remains a state monopoly, there will always be a political struggle for its control. This sounds like a cynical conclusion because we naturally assume that the law is necessarily the province of the state. Just as the Monosizeans could not conceive of a world in which shoe size was not set by the government, we cannot conceive of one in which law is not provided exclusively by it. But what if we are wrong? What if, just as Monosizea could eliminate the politics of shoe size by allowing individuals to produce and buy whatever size shoes they pleased, we could eliminate the politics of law by allowing individuals to adopt whatever rules of behavior best fit their needs? What if law is not a unique product that must be supplied on a one-size-fits-all basis by the state, but one which could be adequately supplied by the ordinary play of market forces? What if we were to try Socrates' solution and end the monopoly of law?

XII.

The problem with this suggestion is that most people are unable to understand what it could possibly mean. This is chiefly because the language necessary to express the idea clearly does not really exist. Most people have been raised to identify law with the state. They cannot even conceive of the idea of legal services apart from the government. The very notion of a free market in legal services conjures up the image of anarchic gang warfare or rule by organized crime. In our system, an advocate of free market law is treated the same way Socrates was treated in Monosizea, and is confronted with the same types of arguments.

The primary reason for this is that the public has been politically indoctrinated to fail to recognize the distinction between order and law. Order is what people need if they are to live together in peace and security. Law, on the other hand, is a particular method of producing order. As it is presently constituted, law is the production of order by requiring all members of society to live under the same set of state-generated rules; it is order produced by centralized planning. Yet, from childhood, citizens are taught to invariably link the words "law" and "order." Political discourse conditions them to hear and use the terms as though they were synonymous and to express the desire for a safer, more peaceful society as a desire for "law and order."

The state nurtures this confusion because it is the public's inability to distinguish order from law that generates its fundamental support for the state. As long as the public identifies order with law, it will believe that an orderly society is impossible without the law the state provides. And as long as the public believes this, it will continue to support the state almost without regard to how oppressive it may become.

The public's identification of order with law makes it impossible for the public to ask for one without asking for the other. There is clearly a public demand for an orderly society. One of human beings' most fundamental desires is for a peaceful existence secure from violence. But because the public has been conditioned to express its desire for order as one for law, all calls for a more orderly society are interpreted as calls for more law. And since under our current political system, all law is supplied by the state, all such calls are interpreted as calls for a more active and powerful state. The identification of order with law eliminates from public consciousness the very concept of the decentralized provision of order. With regard to legal services, it renders the classical liberal idea of a market-generated, spontaneous order incomprehensible.

I began this article with a reference to Orwell's concept of doublethink. But I am now describing the most effective contemporary example we have of Orwellian "newspeak," the process by which words are redefined to render certain thoughts unthinkable.[33] Were the distinction between order and law well understood, the question of whether a state monopoly of law is the best way to ensure an orderly society could be intelligently discussed. But this is precisely the question that the state does not wish to see raised. By collapsing the concept of order into that of law, the state can ensure that it is not, for it will have effectively eliminated the idea of a non-state generated order from the public mind. Under such circumstances, we can hardly be surprised if the advocates of a free market in law are treated like Socrates of Monosizea.

XIII.

I am aware that this explanation probably appears as initially unconvincing as was my earlier contention that the law is inherently political. Even if you found my Monosizea parable entertaining, it is likely that you regard it as irrelevant. You probably believe that the analogy fails because shoes are qualitatively different from legal services. After all, law is a public good which, unlike shoes, really is crucial to public welfare. It is easy to see how the free market can adequately supply the public with shoes. But how can it possibly provide the order-generating and maintaining processes necessary for the peaceful coexistence of human beings in society? What would a free market in legal services be like?

I am always tempted to give the honest and accurate response to this challenge, which is that to ask the question is to miss the point. If human beings had the wisdom and knowledge-generating capacity to be able to describe how a free market would work, that would be the strongest possible argument for central planning. One advocates a free market not because of some moral imprimatur written across the heavens, but because it is impossible for human beings to amass the knowledge of local conditions and the predictive capacity necessary to effectively organize economic relationships among millions of individuals. It is possible to describe what a free market in shoes would be like because we have one. But such a description is merely an observation of the current state of a functioning market, not a projection of how human beings would organize themselves to supply a currently non-marketed good. To demand that an advocate of free market law (or Socrates of Monosizea, for that matter) describe in advance how markets would supply legal services (or shoes) is to issue an impossible challenge. Further, for an advocate of free market law (or Socrates) to even accept this challenge would be to engage in self-defeating activity since the more successfully he or she could describe how the law (or shoe) market would function, the more he or she would prove that it could be run by state planners. Free markets supply human wants better than state monopolies precisely because they allow an unlimited number of suppliers to attempt to do so. By patronizing those who most effectively meet their particular needs and causing those who do not to fail, consumers determine the optimal method of supply. If it were possible to specify in advance what the outcome of this process of selection would be, there would be no need for the process itself.

Although I am tempted to give this response, I never do. This is because, although true, it never persuades. Instead, it is usually interpreted as an appeal for blind faith in the free market, and the failure to provide a specific explanation as to how such a market would provide legal services is interpreted as proof that it cannot. Therefore, despite the self-defeating nature of the attempt, I usually do try to suggest how a free market in law might work.

So, what would a free market in legal services be like? As Sherlock Holmes would regularly say to the good doctor, "You see, Watson, but you do not observe." Examples of non-state law are all around us. Consider labor-management collective bargaining agreements. In addition to setting wage rates, such agreements typically determine both the work rules the parties must abide by and the grievance procedures they must follow to resolve disputes. In essence, such contracts create the substantive law of the workplace as well as the workplace judiciary. A similar situation exists with regard to homeowner agreements, which create both the rules and dispute settlement procedures within a condominium or housing development, i.e., the law and judicial procedure of the residential community. Perhaps a better example is supplied by universities. These institutions create their own codes of conduct for both students and faculty that cover everything from academic dishonesty to what constitutes acceptable speech and dating behavior. In addition, they not only devise their own elaborate judicial procedures to deal with violations of these codes, but typically supply their own campus police forces as well. A final example may be supplied by the many commercial enterprises that voluntarily opt out of the state judicial system by writing clauses in their contracts that require disputes to be settled through binding arbitration or mediation rather than through a lawsuit. In this vein, the variegated "legal" procedures that have recently been assigned the sobriquet of Alternative Dispute Resolution (ADR) do a good job of suggesting what a free market in legal service might be like.[34]

Of course, it is not merely that we fail to observe what is presently all around us. We also act as though we have no knowledge of our own cultural or legal history. Consider, for example, the situation of African-American communities in the segregated South or the immigrant communities in New York in the first quarter of the twentieth century. Because of prejudice, poverty, and the language barrier, these groups were essentially cut off from the state legal system. And yet, rather than disintegrate into chaotic disorder, they were able to privately supply themselves with the rules of behavior and dispute-settlement procedures necessary to maintain peaceful, stable, and highly structured communities. Furthermore, virtually none of the law that orders our interpersonal relationships was produced by the intentional actions of central governments. Our commercial law arose almost entirely from the Law Merchant, a non-governmental set of rules and procedures developed by merchants to quickly and peacefully resolve disputes and facilitate commercial relations. Property, tort, and criminal law are all the products of common law processes by which rules of behavior evolve out of and are informed by the particular circumstances of actual human controversies. In fact, a careful study of Anglo-American legal history will demonstrate that almost all of the law which facilitates peaceful human interaction arose in this way. On the other hand, the source of the law which produces oppression and social division is almost always the state. Measures that impose religious or racial intolerance, economic exploitation, one group's idea of "fairness," or another's of "community" or "family" values virtually always originate in legislation, the law consciously made by the central government. If the purpose of the law really is to bring order to human existence, then it is fair to say that the law actually made by the state is precisely the law that does not work.

Unfortunately, no matter how suggestive these examples might be, they represent only what can develop within a state-dominated system. Since, for the reasons indicated above, it is impossible to out-think a free market, any attempt to account for what would result from a true free market in law would be pure speculation. However, if I must engage in such speculation, I will try to avoid what might be called "static thinking" in doing so. Static thinking occurs when we imagine changing one feature of a dynamic system without appreciating how doing so will alter the character of all other features of the system. For example, I would be engaging in static thinking were I to ask how, if the state did not provide the law and courts, the free market could provide them in their present form. It is this type of thinking that is responsible for the conventional assumption that free market legal services would be "competing governments" which would be the equivalent of organized gang warfare. Once this static thinking is rejected, it becomes apparent that if the state did not provide the law and courts, they simply would not exist in their present form. This, however, only highlights the difficulty of describing free market order-generating services and reinforces the speculative nature of all attempts to do so.

One thing it seems safe to assume is that there would not be any universally binding, society-wide set of "legal" rules. In a free market, the law would not come in one-size-fits-all. Although the rules necessary to the maintenance of a minimal level of order, such as prohibitions against murder, assault, and theft, would be common to most systems, different communities of interest would assuredly adopt those rules and dispute-settlement procedures that would best fit their needs. For example, it seems extremely unlikely that there would be anything resembling a uniform body of contract law. Consider, as just one illustration, the differences between commercial and consumer contracts. Commercial contracts are usually between corporate entities with specialized knowledge of industrial practices and a financial interest in minimizing the interruption of business. On the other hand, consumer contracts are those in which one or both parties lack commercial sophistication and large sums do not rest upon a speedy resolution of any dispute that might arise. In a free market for legal services, the rules that govern these types of contracts would necessarily be radically different.

This example can also illustrate the different types of dispute-settlement procedures that would be likely to arise. In disputes over consumer contracts, the parties might well be satisfied with the current system of litigation in which the parties present their cases to an impartial judge or jury who renders a verdict for one side or the other. However, in commercial disputes, the parties might prefer a mediational process with a negotiated settlement in order to preserve an ongoing commercial relationship or a quick and informal arbitration in order to avoid the losses associated with excessive delay. Further, it is virtually certain that they would want mediators, arbitrators, or judges who are highly knowledgeable about commercial practice, rather than the typical generalist judge or a jury of lay people.

The problem with trying to specify the individuated "legal systems" which would develop is that there is no limit to the number of dimensions along which individuals may choose to order their lives, and hence no limit to the number of overlapping sets of rules and dispute resolution procedures to which they may subscribe. An individual might settle his or her disputes with neighbors according to voluntarily adopted homeowner association rules and procedures, with coworkers according to the rules and procedures described in a collective bargaining agreement, with members of his or her religious congregation according to scriptural law and tribunal, with other drivers according to the processes agreed to in his or her automobile insurance contract, and with total strangers by selecting a dispute resolution company from the yellow pages of the phone book. Given the current thinking about racial and sexual identity, it seems likely that many disputes among members of the same minority group or among women would be brought to "niche" dispute resolution companies composed predominantly of members of the relevant group, who would use their specialized knowledge of group "culture" to devise superior rules and procedures for intra-group dispute resolution.[35]

I suspect that in many ways a free market in law would resemble the situation in Medieval Europe before the rise of strong central governments in which disputants could select among several fora. Depending upon the nature of the dispute, its geographical location, the parties' status, and what was convenient, the parties could bring their case in either village, shire, urban, merchant, manorial, ecclesiastical, or royal courts. Even with the limited mobility and communications of the time, this restricted market for dispute-settlement services was able to generate the order necessary for both the commercial and civil advancement of society. Consider how much more effectively such a market could function given the current level of travel and telecommunication technology. Under contemporary conditions, there would be an explosion of alternative order-providing organizations. I would expect that, late at night, wedged between commercials for Veg-o-matic and Slim Whitman albums, we would find television ads with messages such as, "Upset with your neighbor for playing rock and roll music all night long? Is his dog digging up your flowerbeds? Come to Acme Arbitration Company's grand opening two-for-one sale."

I should point out that, despite my earlier disclaimer, even these suggestions embody static thinking since they assume that a free market would produce a choice among confrontational systems of justice similar to the one we are most familiar with. In fact, I strongly believe that this would not be the case. The current state-supplied legal system is adversarial in nature, pitting the plaintiff or prosecution against the defendant in a winner-take-all, loser-get-nothing contest. The reason for this arrangement has absolutely nothing to do with this procedure's effectiveness in settling disputes and everything to do with the medieval English kings' desire to centralize power. For historical reasons well beyond the scope of this article, the Crown was able to extend its temporal power relative to the feudal lords as well as raise significant revenue by commanding or enticing the parties to local disputes to bring their case before the king or other royal official for decision.[36] Our current system of adversarial presentation to a third-party decision-maker is an outgrowth of these early "public choice" considerations, not its ability to successfully provide mutually satisfactory resolutions to interpersonal disputes.

In fact, this system is a terrible one for peacefully resolving disputes and would be extremely unlikely to have many adherents in a free market. Its adversarial nature causes each party to view the other as an enemy to be defeated, and its winner-take-all character motivates each to fight as hard as he or she can to the bitter end. Since the loser gets nothing, he or she has every reason to attempt to reopen the dispute, which gives rise to frequent appeals. The incentives of the system make it in each party's interest to do whatever he or she can to wear down the opponent while being uniformly opposed to cooperation, compromise, and reconciliation. That this is not the kind of dispute-settlement procedure people are likely to employ if given a choice is evidenced by the large percentage of litigants who are turning to ADR in an effort to avoid it.

My personal belief is that under free-market conditions, most people would adopt compositional, rather than confrontational, dispute settlement procedures, i.e., procedures designed to compose disputes and reconcile the parties rather than render third party judgments. This was, in fact, the essential character of the ancient "legal system" that was replaced by the extension of royal jurisdiction. Before the rise of the European nation-states, what we might anachronistically call judicial procedure was chiefly a set of complex negotiations between the parties mediated by the members of the local community in an effort to reestablish a harmonious relationship. Essentially, public pressure was brought upon the parties to settle their dispute peacefully through negotiation and compromise.

The incentives of this ancient system favored cooperation and conciliation rather than defeating one's opponent.[37]

Although I have no crystal ball, I suspect that a free market in law would resemble the ancient system a great deal more than the modern one. Recent experiments with negotiated dispute-settlement have demonstrated that mediation 1) produces a higher level of participant satisfaction with regard to both process and result, 2) resolves cases more quickly and at significantly lower cost, and 3) results in a higher rate of voluntary compliance with the final decree than was the case with traditional litigation.[38] This is perhaps unsurprising, given that mediation's lack of a winner-take-all format encourages the parties to seek common ground rather than attempt to vanquish the opponent and that, since both parties must agree to any solution, there is a reduced likelihood that either will wish to reopen the dispute. Given human beings' manifest desire to retain control over their lives, I suspect that, if given a choice, few would willingly place their fate in the hands of third-party decision-makers. Thus, I believe that a free market in law would produce a system that is essentially compositional in nature.

XIV.

In this article, I have suggested that when it comes to the idea of the rule of law, the American public is in a state of deep denial. Despite being surrounded by evidence that the law is inherently political in nature, most people are nevertheless able to convince themselves that it is an embodiment of objective rules of justice which they have a moral obligation to obey. As in all cases of denial, people participate in this fiction because of the psychological comfort that can be gained by refusing to see the truth. As we saw with our friends Arnie and Ann, belief in the existence of an objective, non-ideological law enables average citizens to see those advocating legal positions inconsistent with their values as inappropriately manipulating the law for political purposes, while viewing their own position as neutrally capturing the plain meaning immanent within the law. The citizens' faith in the rule of law allows them to hide from themselves both that their position is as politically motivated as is their opponents' and that they are attempting to impose their values on their opponents as much as their opponents are attempting to impose their values on them. But, again, as in all cases of denial, the comfort gained comes at a price. For with the acceptance of the myth of the rule of law comes a blindness to the fact that laws are merely the commands of those with political power, and an increased willingness to submit oneself to the yoke of the state. Once one is truly convinced that the law is an impersonal, objective code of justice rather than an expression of the will of the powerful, one is likely to be willing not only to relinquish a large measure of one's own freedom, but to enthusiastically support the state in the suppression of others' freedom as well.

The fact is that there is no such thing as a government of law and not people. The law is an amalgam of contradictory rules and counter-rules expressed in inherently vague language that can yield a legitimate legal argument for any desired conclusion. For this reason, as long as the law remains a state monopoly, it will always reflect the political ideology of those invested with decision-making power. Like it or not, we are faced with only two choices. We can continue the ideological power struggle for control of the law in which the group that gains dominance is empowered to impose its will on the rest of society, or we can end the monopoly.

Our long-standing love affair with the myth of the rule of law has made us blind to the latter possibility. Like the Monosizeans, who after centuries of state control cannot imagine a society in which people can buy whatever size shoes they wish, we cannot conceive of a society in which individuals may purchase the legal services they desire. The very idea of a free market in law makes us uncomfortable. But it is time for us to overcome this discomfort and consider adopting Socrates' approach. We must recognize that our love for the rule of law is unrequited, and that, as so often happens in such cases, we have become enslaved to the object of our desire. No clearer example of this exists than the legal process by which our Constitution was transformed from a document creating a government of limited powers and guaranteed rights into one which provides the justification for the activities of the all-encompassing super-state of today. However heart wrenching it may be, we must break off this one-sided affair. The time has come for those committed to individual liberty to realize that the establishment of a truly free society requires the abandonment of the myth of the rule of law.

Notes

1. U.S. Const. amend. I.
2. George Orwell, *1984*, at 32 (Commemorative 1984 ed., The New Am. Library 1983 [1949]).
3. See Iain McLean, *Public Choice* 71-76 (1987)
4. See Herbert Wechsler, "Toward Neutral Principles of Constitutional Law," 73 *Harv. L. Rev.* 1 (1959).
5. 59 N.E. 1058 (Ind. 1901).
6. 104 S.W. 164 (Ark. 1907).
7. 42 U.S.C. section 2000e-2 (1988).
8. See *United Steelworkers v. Weber*, 443 U.S. 193, 228 n.9 (1979) (Rehnquist, J., dissenting).
9. Id. at 201 (quoting *Holy Trinity Church v. United States*, 143 U.S. 457, 459 (1892)).
10. Id. at 202.
11. 110 Cong. Rec. 6548 (1964).
12. 33 N.W. 919 (Mich. 1887).
13. Id. at 923-24.
14. 64 Wis. 265, 25 N.W. 42 (1885).
15. Id. at 45.
16. 43 S.E. 732 (Ga. 1903).
17. Id. at 733.

18. 131 N.E. 887 (N.Y. 1921).
19. Id. at 890.
20. U.S. Const. art. I, section 8, cl. 3.
21. See *Wickard v. Filburn*, 317 U.S. 111, 128-29 (1942).
22. The federal government regulates sexual harassment in the workplace under Title VII of the Civil Rights Act of 1964, 42 U.S.C. section 2000e(b) (1988), which was enacted pursuant to the Commerce Clause.
23. On this point, it may be relevant to observe that as I write these words, the President and Congress of the United States are engaged in a vigorous debate over what percentage of the American public must have health insurance for there to be universal coverage.
24. The facts of the case being described are drawn from *Syester v. Banta*, 133 N.W.2d 666 (Iowa 1965).
25. Id. at 668.
26. Id. at 671.
27. As the court did in the actual case. Id. at 674-75.
28. See *Riggs v. Palmer*, 22 N.E. 188 (N.Y. 1889).
29. As the court did in the actual case. Id. at 191.
30. U.S. Const. amend. XIV, section 1.
31. Oliver Wendell Holmes, "The Path of the Law," 10 *Harv. L. Rev*. 457, 465-66 (1897).
32. The Crits have been accused of being intellectual nihilists and attacked for undermining the commitment to the rule of law that is necessary for the next generation of lawyers to engage in the principled, ethical practice of law. For this reason, their mainstream critics have suggested that the Crits have no business teaching in the nation's law schools. See, e.g., Paul D. Carrington, "Of Law and the River," 34 *J. Legal Educ*. 222, 227 (1984).
33. See Orwell, supra note 2, at 46.
34. The *National Law Journal* has noted, "Much of corporate America is creating its own private business 'courts' that are far removed from the public courthouses." William H. Schroder Jr., "Private ADR May Offer Increased Confidentiality," *Nat'l L.J.*, July 25, 1994, at C14.
35. I am fairly confident that the parties to such disputes will not choose to have them resolved by a panel composed almost exclusively of White Anglo-Saxon Protestants as is the case today.
36. The story of how royal jurisdiction came to supplant all others and why the adversarial system of litigation replaced the earlier methods of settling disputes is fascinating one, but one which obviously cannot be recounted here. Those interested in pursuing it may wish to consult Harold J. Berman, *Law and Revolution* (1983); Leonard W. Levy, *Origins of the Fifth Amendment* (1986).
37. Once again, any extended account of the roots of our legal system is beyond the scope of this article. For a useful general description, see Berman, supra note 36, at 49-84.
38. See Joshua D. Rosenberg, "Court Studies Confirm That Mandatory Mediation Works," *Nat'l L.J.*, Apr. 11, 1994, at C7

10

The State

Robert Nozick

Prohibiting Private Enforcement of Justice

An independent might he prohibited from privately exacting justice because his procedure is known to be too risky and dangerous—that is, it involves a higher risk (than another procedure) of punishing an innocent person or over-punishing a guilty one—or because his procedure isn't known not to be risky. (His procedure would exhibit another mode of unreliability if its chances were much greater of not punishing a guilty person, but this would not be a reason for prohibiting his private enforcement.)

Let us consider these in turn. If the independent's procedure is very unreliable and imposes high risk on others (perhaps he consults tea leaves), then if he does it frequently, he may make all fearful, even those not his victims. Anyone, acting in self-defense, may stop him from engaging in his high-risk activity. But surely the independent may be stopped from using a very unreliable procedure, even if he is not a constant menace. If it is known that the independent will enforce his own rights by his very unreliable procedure only once every ten years, this will *not* create general fear and apprehension in the society. The ground for prohibiting his widely intermittent use of his procedure is not, therefore, to avoid any widespread uncompensated apprehension and fear which otherwise would exist.[1]

If there were many independents who were all liable to punish wrongly, the probabilities *would* add up to create a dangerous situation for all. Then, others would be entitled to group together and prohibit the *totality* of such activities. But how would this prohibition work? Would they prohibit *each* of the individually non-fear-creating activities? Within a state of nature by what procedure can they pick and choose which of the totality is to continue, and what would give them the right to do this? No protective association, however dominant, would have this right. For the legitimate powers of a protective association are merely the *sum* of the individual rights that its members or clients transfer to the association. No new rights and powers arise; each right of the association is decomposable without residue into those individual rights held by distinct individuals acting alone in a state of nature. A combination of individuals may have the right to do some action C, which no individual alone had the right to do, if C is identical to D and E, and persons who individually have the right to do D and the right to do E combine. If some rights of individuals were of the form "You have the right to do A provided 51 percent or 85 percent or whatever of the others agree you may," then a combination of individuals would have the right to do A, even though none separately had this right. But no individual's rights are of this form. No person or group is entitled to pick who in the totality will be allowed to continue. *All* the independents might group together and decide this. They might, for example, use some random procedure to allocate a number of (sellable?) rights to continue private enforcement so as to reduce the total danger to a point below the threshold. The difficulty is that, if a large number of independents do this, it will be in the interests of an individual to abstain from this arrangement. It will be in his interests to continue his risky activities as he chooses, while the others mutually limit theirs so as to bring the totality of acts including his to below the danger level. For the others probably would limit themselves some distance away from the danger boundary, leaving him room to squeeze in. Even were the others to rest adjacent to the line of danger so that his activities would bring the totality across it, on which grounds could *his* activities be picked out as the ones to prohibit? Similarly, it will be in the interests of any individual to refrain from otherwise unanimous agreements in the state of nature: for example, the agreement to set up a state. Anything an individual can gain by such a unanimous agreement he can gain through separate bilateral agreements. Any contract which really needs almost unanimity, any contract which is essentially joint, will serve its purpose whether or not a given individual participates; so it will be in his interests not to bind himself to participate.

"The Principle of Fairness"

A principle suggested by Herbert Hart, which (following John Rawls) we shall call the *principle of fairness*, would be of service here if it were adequate. This principle holds that when a number of persons engage in a just, mutually advantageous, cooperative venture according to rules and thus restrain their liberty in ways necessary to yield advantages for all, those who have submitted to these restrictions have a right to similar acquiescence on the part of those who have benefited from their submission. Acceptance of benefits (even when this is not a giving of express or tacit undertaking to cooperate) is enough, according to this principle, to bind one. If one adds to the principle of fairness the claim that the others to whom the obligations are owed or their agents may *enforce* the obligations arising under this principle (including the obligation to limit one's actions), then groups of people in a state of nature who agree to a procedure to pick those to engage in certain acts will have legitimate rights to prohibit "free riders." Such a right may be crucial to the viability of such agreements. We should scrutinize such a powerful right very carefully, especially as it seems to make *unanimous* consent to coercive government in a state of nature *unnecessary*! Yet a further reason to examine it is its plausibility as a counterexample to my claim that no new rights emerge at the group level, that individuals in combination cannot create new rights which are not the sum of preexisting ones. A right to enforce others' obligation to limit their conduct in specified ways might stem from some special feature of the obligation or might be thought to follow from some general principle that all obligations owed to others may be enforced. In the absence of argument for the special enforcement-justifying nature of the obligation supposedly arising under the principle of fairness, I shall consider first the principle of the enforceability of all obligations and then turn to the adequacy of the principle of fairness itself. If either of these principles is rejected, the right to enforce the cooperation of others in these situations totters. I shall argue that *both* of these principles must be rejected.

Herbert Hart's argument for the existence of a natural right[2] depends upon particularizing the principle of the enforceability of all obligations: someone's being under a special obligation to you to do A (which might have arisen, for example, by their promising to you that they would do A) gives you, not only the right that they do A, but also the right to force them to do A. Only against a background in which people may not force you to do A or other actions you may promise to do can we understand, says Hare, the *point* and purpose of special obligations. Since special obligations do have a point and purpose, Hare continues, there is a natural right not to be forced to do something unless certain specified conditions pertain; this natural right is built into the background against which special obligations exist.

This well-known argument of Hart's is puzzling. I may release someone from an obligation not to force me to do A. ("I now release you from the obligation not to force me to do A. You now are free to force me to do A.") Yet so releasing them does *not* create in me an obligation to them to do A. Since Hart supposes that my being under an obligation to someone to do A gives him (entails that he has) the right to force me to do A, and since we "have seen the converse does not hold, we may consider that component of being under an obligation to someone to do something over and above his having the right to force you to do it. (May we suppose there is this distinguishable component without facing the charge of "logical atomism"?) An alternative view which rejects Hart's inclusion of the right to force in the notion of being owed an obligation might hold that this additional component is the *whole* of the content of being obligated to someone to do something. If I don't do it, then (all things being equal) I'm doing something wrong; control over the situation is in his hands; he has the power to release me from the obligation unless he's promised to someone else that he won't; and so on. Perhaps all this looks too *ephemeral* without the additional presence of rights of enforcement. Yet rights of enforcement are themselves merely *rights*; that is, permissions to do something and obligations on others not to interfere. True, one has the right to enforce these further obligations, but it is not clear that including *rights* of enforcing really shores up the whole structure if one assumes it to be insubstantial to begin with. Perhaps one must merely take the moral realm seriously and think one component amounts to something even without a connection to enforcement. (Of course, this is not to say that this component *never* is connected with enforcement!) On this view, we can explain the point of obligations without bringing in rights of enforcement and hence without supposing a general background of obligation not to force from which this stands out. (Of course, even though Hart's argument does not demonstrate the existence of such an obligation not to force, it may exist nevertheless.)

Apart from these general considerations against the principle of the enforceability of all special obligations, puzzle cases can be produced. For example, if I promise to you that I will not murder someone, this does not *give* you the right to force me not to, for you already have this right, though it does create a particular obligation *to you.* Or, if I cautiously insist that you first promise to me that you won't force me to do A before I will make my promise to you to do A, and I do receive this promise from you first, it would be implausible to say that in promising I give you the right to force me to do A. (Though consider the situation which results if I am so foolish as to release you unilaterally from your promise to me.)

If there were cogency to Hart's claim that only against a background of required nonforcing can we understand the point of special rights, then there would seem to be equal cogency to the claim that only against a background of *permitted* forcing can we understand the point of *general* rights. For according to Hart, a person has a general right to do A if and only if for all persons P and Q, Q may not interfere with P's doing A or force him not to do A, unless P has acted to give Q a special right to do this. But not every act can be substituted for "A"; people have general rights to do only particular types of action. So, one might argue, if there is to be a point to having general rights, to having rights to do a particular type of act A, to other's being under an obligation not to force you not to do A, then it must be against a contrasting background, in which there *is no* obligation on people to refrain from forcing you to do, or not to do, things, that is, against a background in which, for actions generally, people do *not* have a general right to do them. If Hart can argue to a presumption against forcing from there being a point to particular rights, then it seems he can equally well argue to the absence of such a presumption from there being a point to general rights.[3]

An argument for an enforceable obligation has two stages: the first leads to the existence of the obligation, and the second, to its enforceability. Having disposed of the second stage (at least insofar as it is supposed generally to follow from the first), let us turn to the supposed obligation to cooperate in the joint decisions of others to limit their activities. The principle of fairness, as we stated it following Hart and Rawls, is objectionable and unacceptable. Suppose some of the people in your neighborhood (there are 364 other adults) have found a public address system and decide to institute a system of public entertainment. They post a list of names, one for each day, yours among them. On his assigned day (one can easily switch days) a person is to run the public address system, play records over it, give news bulletins, tell amusing stories he has heard, and so on. After 138 days on which each per son has done his part, your day arrives. Are you obligated to take your turn? You *have* benefited from it, occasionally opening your window to listen, enjoying some music or chuckling at someone funny story. The other people *have* put themselves out. But must you answer the call when it is your turn to do so? As it stands surely not. Though you benefit from the arrangement, you may know all along that 364 days of entertainment supplied by other will not be worth your giving up *one* day. You would rather not have any of it and not give up a day than have it all and spend one of your days at it. Given these preferences, how can it be that you are required to participate when your scheduled time comes? It would be nice to have philosophy readings on the radio to which one could tune in at any time, perhaps late at night when tired. But it may not be nice enough for you to want to give up or whole day of your own as a reader on the program. Whatever you want, can others create an obligation for you to do so by going ahead and starting the program themselves? In this case you can choose to forgo the benefit by not turning on the radio; in other cases the benefits may be unavoidable. If each day a different person on your street sweeps the entire street, must you do so when your time comes? Even if you don't care that much about a clean street? Must you imagine dirt as you traverse the street, so as not to benefit as a free rider? Must you refrain from turning on the radio to hear the philosophy readings? Must you mow your front lawn as often as your neighbors mow theirs?

At the very least one wants to build into the principle of fairness the condition that the benefits to a person from the actions of the others are greater than the costs to him of doing his share. How are we to imagine this? Is the condition satisfied if you do enjoy the daily broadcasts over the PA system in your neighborhood but would prefer a day off hiking, rather than hearing these broadcasts all year? For you to be obligated to give up your day to broadcast mustn't it be true, at least, that there is nothing you could do with a day (with that day, with the increment in any other day by shifting some activities to that day) which you would prefer to hearing broadcasts for the year? If the only way to get the broadcasts was to spend the day participating in the arrangement, in order for the condition that the benefits outweigh the costs to be satisfied, you would have to be willing to spend it on the broadcasts rather than to gain *any* other available thing.

If the principle of fairness were modified so as to contain this very strong condition, it still would be objectionable. The benefits might only barely be worth the costs to you of doing your share, yet others might benefit from *this* institution much more than you do; they all treasure listening to the public broadcasts. As the person least benefited by the practice, are you obligated to do an equal amount for it? Or perhaps you would prefer that all cooperated in *another* venture, limiting their conduct and making sacrifices for *it*. It is true, *given* that they are not following your plan and thus limiting what other options are available to you, that the benefits of their venture *are* worth to you the costs of your cooperation. However, you do not wish to cooperate, as part of your plan to focus their attention on your alternative proposal which they have ignored or not given, in your view at least, its proper due. (You want them, for example, to read the Talmud on the radio instead of the philosophy they are reading.) By lending the institution (their institution) the support of your cooperating in it, you will only make it harder to change or alter.[4]

On the face of it, enforcing the principle of fairness is objectionable. You may not decide to give me something, for example a book, and then grab money from me to pay for it, even if I have nothing better to spend the money on. You have, if anything, even less reason to demand payment if your activity that gives me the book also benefits you; suppose that your best way of getting exercise is by throwing books into people's houses, or that some other activity of yours thrusts books into people's houses as an unavoidable side effect. Nor are things changed if your inability to collect money or payments for the books which unavoidably spill over into others' houses makes it inadvisable or too expensive for you to carryon the activity with this side effect. One cannot, whatever one's purposes, just act so as to give people benefits and then demand (or seize) payment. Nor can a group of persons do this. If you may not charge and collect for benefits you bestow without prior agreement, you certainly may not do so for benefits whose bestowal costs you nothing, and most certainly people need not repay you for costless-to-provide benefits which yet *others* provided them. So the fact that we partially are "social products" in that we benefit from current patterns and forms created by the multitudinous actions of a long string of long-forgotten people, forms which include institutions, ways of doing things, and language (whose social nature may involve our current use depending upon Wittgensteinian matching of the speech of others), does not create in us a general Boating debt which the current society can collect and use as it will.

Perhaps a modified principle of fairness can be stated which would be free from these and similar difficulties. What seems certain is that any such principle, if possible, would be so complex and involuted that one could not combine it with a special principle legitimating *enforcement* within a state of nature of the obligations that have arisen under it. Hence, even if the principle could be formulated so that it was no longer open to objection, it would not serve to obviate the need for other persons *consenting* to cooperate and limit their own activities.

Procedural Rights

Let us return to our independent. Apart from other nonindependents' fear (perhaps they will not be so worried), may not the person about to be punished defend himself? Must he allow the punishment to take place, collecting compensation afterwards if he can show that it was unjust? But show to whom? If he knows he's innocent, may he demand compensation immediately and enforce *his* rights to collect it? And so on. The notions of procedural rights, public demonstration of guilt, and the like, have a very unclear status within state-of-nature theory.

It might be said that each person has a right to have his guilt determined by the least dangerous of the known procedures for ascertaining guilt, that is, by the one having the lowest probability of finding an innocent person guilty. There are well-known maxims of the following form: better m guilty persons go free than n innocent persons be punished. For each n, each maxim will countenance an upper limit to the ratio m/n. It will say: better m, but not better $m + 1$. (A system may pick differing upper limits for different crimes.) On the greatly implausible assumption that we know each system of procedures' precise probability of finding an innocent person guilty,[5] and a guilty person innocent, we will opt for those procedures whose long-run ratio of the two kinds of errors comes closest, from below, to the highest ratio we find acceptable. It is far from obvious where to set the ratio. To say it is better that any number of guilty go free rather than that one innocent person be punished presumably would require *not* having any system of punishment at all. For any system we can devise which sometimes does actually punish someone will involve some appreciable risk of punishing an innocent person, and it almost certainly will do so as it operates on large numbers of people. And any system S can be transformed into one having a lower probability of punishing an innocent person, for example, by conjoining to it a roulette procedure whereby the probability is only 1 that anyone found guilty by S actually gets punished. (This procedure is iterative.)

If a person objects that the independent's procedure yields too high a probability of an innocent person's being punished, how can it be determined what probabilities are too high? We can imagine that each individual goes through the following reasoning: The greater the procedural safeguards, the less my chances of getting unjustly convicted, and also the greater the chances that a guilty person goes free; hence the less effectively the system deters crime and so the greater my chances of being a victim of a crime. That system is most effective which minimizes the expected value of unearned harm to me, either through my being unjustly punished or through my being a victim of a crime. If we simplify *greatly* by assuming that penalties and victimization costs balance out, one would want the safeguards at that most stringent point where any lowering of them would increase one's probability of being unjustly punished more than it would lower (through added deterrence) one's vulnerability to being victimized by a crime; and where any increasing of the safeguards would increase one's probability of being victimized by a crime (through lessened deterrence) more than it would lessen one's probability of being punished though innocent. Since utilities differ among persons, there is no reason to expect individuals who make such an expected value calculation to converge upon the identical set of procedures. Furthermore, some persons may think it important in itself that guilty people be punished and may be willing to run some increased risks of being punished themselves in order to accomplish this. These people will consider it more of a drawback, the greater the probability a procedure gives guilty people of going unpunished, and they will incorporate this in their calculations, apart from its effects on deterrence. It is, to say the least, very doubtful that any provision of the law of nature will (and will be known to) settle the question of how much weight is to be given to such considerations, or will reconcile people's different assessments of the seriousness of being punished when innocent as compared to being victimized by a crime (even if both involve the same physical thing happening to them). With the best will in the world, individuals will favor differing procedures yielding differing probabilities of an innocent person's being punished.

One could not, it seems, permissibly prohibit someone from using a procedure solely because it yields a marginally higher probability of punishing an innocent person than does the procedure you deem optimal. After all, your favorite procedure also will stand in this relation to that of someone else. Nor are matters changed by the fact that many other persons use your procedure. It seems that persons in a state of nature must tolerate (that is, not forbid) the use of procedures in the "neighborhood" of their own; but it seems they may forbid the use of far more risky procedures. An acute problem is presented if two groups each believe their own procedures to be reliable while believing that of the other group to be very dangerous. No *procedure* to resolve their disagreement seems likely to work; and presenting the nonprocedural principle that the group which is right should triumph (and the other should give in to it) seems unlikely to produce peace when each group, firmly believing itself to be the one that is right, acts on the principle.

When sincere and good persons differ, we are prone to think they must accept some procedure to decide their differences, some procedure they both agree to be reliable or fair. Here we see the possibility that this disagreement may extend all the way up the ladder of procedures. Also, one sometimes will refuse to let issues stay settled by the adverse decision of such a procedure, specifically when the wrong decision is worse even than the disruption and costs (including fighting) of refusing to accept it, when the wrong decision is worse than conflict with those on the other side. It is dismaying to contemplate situations where both of the opposed parties feel that conflict is preferable to an adverse decision by any procedure. Each views the situation as one in which he who is right must act, and the other should give in. It will be of little avail for a neutral party to say to both, "Look, you both *think* you're right, so on that principle, as you will apply it, you'll fight. Therefore you must agree to some procedure to decide the matter." For they each believe that conflict *is* better than losing the issue.[6] And one of them may be right in this. *Shouldn't* he engage in the conflict? Shouldn't *he* engage in the conflict? (True, both of them will think the one is themselves.) One might try to avoid these painful issues by a commitment to procedures, come what may. (May one possible result of applying the procedures be that they themselves are rejected?) Some view the state as such a device for shifting the ultimate burden of moral decision, so that there never comes to be that sort of conflict among individuals. But what sort of individual could so abdicate? Who could turn every decision over to an external procedure, accepting whatever results come? The possibility of such conflict is part of the human condition. Though this problem in the state of nature is an unavoidable one, given suitable institutional elaboration it need be no more pressing in the state of nature than under a state, where it also exists.[7]

The issue of which decisions can be left to an external binding procedure connects with the interesting question of what moral obligations someone is under who is being punished for a crime of which he knows himself to be innocent. The judicial system (containing no procedural unfairness, let us suppose) has sentenced him to life imprisonment, or death. May he escape? May he harm another in order to escape? These questions differ from the one of whether someone wrongfully attacking (or participating in the attack of) another may claim self-defense as justifying his killing the other when the other, in self-defense, acts so as to endanger his own attacker's life. Here the answer is, "No." The attacker should not be attacking in the first place, nor does someone else's threatening him with death unless he does attack make it permissible for him to do so. His job is to get out of that situation; if he fails to do so he *is* at a moral disadvantage. Soldiers who know their country is waging an aggressive war and who are manning antiaircraft guns in defense of a military emplacement may *not* in self-defense fire upon the planes of the attacked nation which is acting in self-defense, even though the planes are over their heads and are about to bomb *them*. It is a soldier's responsibility to determine if his side's cause is just; if he finds the issue tangled, unclear, or confusing, he may not shift the responsibility to his leaders, who will certainly tell him their cause is just. The selective conscientious objector may be right in his claim that he has a moral duty not to fight; and if he is, may not another acquiescent soldier be punished for doing what it was his moral duty not to do? Thus we return to the point that some bucks stop with each of us; and we reject the morally elitist view that some soldiers cannot be expected to think for themselves. (They are certainly not encouraged to think for themselves by the practice of absolving them of all responsibility for their actions within the rules of war.) Nor do we see why the political realm is special. Why, precisely, is one specially absolved of responsibility for actions when these are performed jointly with others from political motives under the direction or orders of political leaders?[8]

We thus far have supposed that you know that another's procedure of justice differs from your own for the worse. Suppose now that you have no reliable knowledge about another's procedure of justice. May you stop him in self-defense and may your protective agency act for you, solely because you or it does not know whether procedure is reliable? Do you have the right to have your guilt, innocence, and punishment, determined by a system known to be reliable and fair? Known to whom? Those wielding it may know it to be reliable and fair. Do you have a right to have your guilt or innocence, and punishment, determined by a system *you* know to be reliable and fair? Are someone's rights violated if he thinks that only the use of tea leaves is reliable or if he is incapable of concentrating on the description of the system others use so that he doesn't know whether it's reliable, and so on? One may think of the state as the authoritative settler of doubts about reliability and fairness. But of course there is no guarantee that it *will* settle them (the president of Yale didn't think Black Panthers could get a fair trial), and there is no reason to suppose it will manage to do so more effectively than another scheme. The natural-rights tradition offers little guidance on precisely what one's procedural rights are in a state of nature, on how principles specifying how one is to act have knowledge built into their various clauses, and so on. Yet persons within this tradition do not hold that there are no procedural rights; that is, that one may not defend oneself against being handled by unreliable or unfair procedures.

How May the Dominant Agency Act?

What then may a dominant protective association forbid other individuals to do? The dominant protective association may reserve for itself the right to judge any procedure of justice to be applied to its clients. It may announce, and act on the announcement, that it will punish anyone who uses on one of its clients a procedure that it finds to be unreliable or unfair. It will punish anyone who uses on one of its clients a procedure that it already knows to be unreliable or unfair, and it will defend its clients against the application of such a procedure. May it announce that it will punish anyone who uses on one of its clients a procedure that it has not, at the time of punishment, already approved as reliable and fair? May it set itself up as having to pass, in advance, on any procedure to be used on one of its clients, so that anyone using on one of its clients any procedure that has not already received the protective association's seal of approval will be punished? Clearly, individuals themselves do not have this right. To say that an individual may punish anyone who applies to him a procedure of justice that has not met his approval would be to say that a criminal who refuses to approve anyone's procedure of justice could legitimately punish anyone who attempted to punish him. It might be thought that a protective association legitimately can do this, for it would not be partial to its clients in this manner. But there is no guarantee of this impartiality. Nor have we seen any way that such a new right might arise from the combining of individuals' preexisting rights. We must conclude that protective associations do not have this right, including the sole dominant one. Every individual does have the right that information sufficient to show that a procedure of justice about to be applied to him is reliable and fair (or no less so than other procedures in use) be made publicly available or made available to him. He has the right to be shown that he is being handled by some reliable and fair system. In the absence of such a showing he may defend himself and resist the imposition of the relatively unknown system. When the information is made publicly available or made available to him, he is in a position to know about the reliability and fairness of the procedure.[9] He examines this information, and if he finds the system within the bounds of reliability and fairness he must submit to it; finding it unreliable and unfair he may resist. His submission means that he refrains from punishing another for using this system. He may resist the imposition of its particular decision though, on the grounds that he is innocent. If he chooses not to, he need not participate in the process whereby the system determines his guilt or innocence. Since it has not yet been established that he is guilty, he may not be aggressed against and forced to participate. However, prudence might suggest to him that his chances of being found innocent are increased if he cooperates in the offering of some defense.

The principle is that a person may resist, in self-defense, if others try to apply to him an unreliable or unfair procedure of justice. In applying this principle, an individual will resist those systems which after all conscientious consideration he finds to be unfair or unreliable. An individual may empower his protective agency to exercise for him his rights to resist the imposition of any procedure which has not made its reliability and fairness known, and to resist any procedure that is unfair or unreliable. In Chapter 2 we described briefly the processes that would lead to the dominance of one protective association in a given area, or to a dominant federation of protective associations using rules to peacefully adjudicate disputes among themselves. This dominant protective association will prohibit anyone from applying to its members any procedure about which insufficient information is available as to its reliability and fairness. It also will prohibit anyone from applying to its members an unreliable or unfair procedure; which means, since *they* are applying the principle and have the muscle to do so, that others are prohibited from applying to the protective association's members any procedure the protective association deems unfair or unreliable. Leaving aside the chances of evading the system's operation, anyone violating this prohibition will be punished. The protective association will publish a list of those procedures it deems fair and reliable (and perhaps of those it deems otherwise); and it would take a brave soul indeed to proceed to apply a known procedure not yet on its approved list. Since an association's clients will expect it to do all it can to discourage unreliable procedures, the protective association will keep its list up-to-date, covering all publicly known procedures.

It might be claimed that our assumption that procedural rights exist makes our argument too easy. Does a person who *did* violate another's rights himself have a right that this fact be determined by a fair and reliable procedure? It is true that an unreliable procedure will too often find an innocent person guilty. But does applying such an unreliable procedure to a *guilty* person violate any right of his? May he, in self-defense, resist the imposition of such a procedure upon himself? But what would he be defending himself against? Too high a probability of a punishment he deserves? These questions are important ones for our argument. If a guilty person may not defend himself against such procedures and also may not punish someone else for using them upon him, then may his protective agency defend him against the procedures or punish someone afterwards for having used them upon him, independently of whether or not (and therefore even if) he turns out to be guilty? One would have thought the agency's only rights of action are those its clients transfer to it. But if a guilty client has no such right, he cannot transfer it to the agency.

The agency does not, of course, *know* that its client is guilty, whereas the client himself does know (let us suppose) of his own guilt. But does this difference in knowledge make the requisite difference? Isn't the ignorant agency required to investigate the question of its client's guilt, instead of proceeding on the assumption of his innocence? The difference in epistemic situation between agency and client *can* make the following difference. The agency may under some circumstances defend its client against the imposition of a penalty while promptly proceeding to investigate the question of his guilt. If the agency knows that the punishing party has used a reliable procedure, it accepts its verdict of guilty, and it cannot intervene on the assumption that its client is, or well might be, innocent. If the agency deems the procedure unreliable or doesn't know how reliable it is, it need not presume its client guilty, and it may investigate the matter itself. If upon investigation it determines that its client is guilty, it allows him to be punished. This protection of its client against the actual imposition of the penalty is relatively straightforward, except for the question of whether the agency must compensate the prospective punishers for any costs imposed upon them by having to delay while the protective agency determines to its satisfaction its own client's guilt. It would seem that the protective agency does have to pay compensation to users of relatively unreliable procedures for any disadvantages caused by the enforced delay; and to the users of procedures of unknown reliability it must pay full compensation if the procedures are reliable, otherwise compensation for disadvantages. (Who bears the burden of proof in the question of the reliability of the procedures?) Since the agency may recover this amount (forcibly) from its client who asserted his innocence, this will be something of a deterrent to false pleas of innocence.[10]

The agency's temporary protection and defense against the infliction of the penalty is relatively straightforward. Less straightforward is the protective agency's appropriate action after a penalty has been inflicted. If the punisher's procedure was a reliable one, the agency does not act against the punisher. But may the agency punish someone who punishes its client, acting on the basis of an unreliable procedure? May it punish that person independently of whether or not its client *is* guilty? Or must it investigate, using its own reliable procedure, to determine his guilt or innocence, punishing his punishers *only* if it determines its client innocent? (Or is it: if it fails to find him guilty?) By what right could the protective agency announce that it will punish anyone using an unreliable procedure who punishes its clients, independently of the guilt or innocence of the clients?

The person who uses an unreliable procedure, acting upon its result, imposes risks upon others, whether or not his procedure misfires in a particular case. Someone playing Russian roulette upon another does the same thing if when he pulls the trigger the gun does not fire. The protective agency may treat the unreliable enforcer of justice as it treats any performer of a risky action. We distinguished in Chapter 4 a range of possible responses to a risky action, which were appropriate in different sorts of circumstances: prohibition, compensation to those whose boundaries are crossed, and compensation to all those who undergo a risk of a boundary crossing. The unreliable enforcer of justice might either perform actions others are fearful of, or not; and either might be done to obtain compensation for some previous wrong, or to exact retribution.[11] A person who uses an unreliable procedure of enforcing justice and is led to perform some *unfeared* action will not be punished afterwards. If it turns out that the person on whom he acted was guilty and that the compensation taken was appropriate, the situation will be left as is. If the person on whom he acted turns out to be innocent, the unreliable enforcer of justice may be forced fully to compensate him for the action.

On the other hand, the unreliable enforcer of justice may be forbidden to impose those consequences that would be feared if expected. Why? If done frequently enough so as to create general fear, such unreliable enforcement may be forbidden in order to avoid the general uncompensated-for fear. Even if done rarely, the unreliable enforcer may be punished for imposing this feared consequence upon an innocent person. But if the unreliable enforcer acts rarely and creates no general fear, why may he be punished for imposing a feared consequence *upon a person who is guilty*? A system of punishing unreliable punishers for their punishment of guilty persons would help deter them from using their unreliable system upon anyone and therefore from using it upon innocent people. But not everything that would aid in such deterrence may be inflicted. The question is whether it would be legitimate in this case to punish after the fact the unreliable punisher of someone who turned out to be guilty.

No one has a right to use a relatively unreliable procedure in order to decide whether to punish another. Using such a system, he is in no position to know that the other deserves punishment; hence he has no right to punish him. But how can we say this? If the other has committed a crime, doesn't *everyone* in a state of nature have a right to punish him? And therefore doesn't someone who doesn't know that this other person has committed the crime? Here, it seems to me, we face a terminological issue about how to merge epistemic considerations with rights. Shall we say that someone doesn't have a right to do certain things unless he knows certain facts, or shall we say that he does have a right but he does wrong in exercising it unless he knows certain facts? It may be neater to decide it one way, but we can still say all we wish in the other mode; there is a simple translation between the two modes of discourse.[12] We shall pick the latter mode of speech; if anything, this makes our argument look *less* compelling. If we assume that anyone has a right to take something that a thief has stolen, then under this latter terminology someone who takes a stolen object from a thief, without knowing it had been stolen, had a right to take the object; but since he didn't know he had this right, *his* taking the object was wrong and impermissible. Even though no right of the first thief is violated, the second didn't know this and so acted wrongly and impermissibly.

Having taken this terminological fork, we might propose an epistemic principle of border crossing: If doing act A would violate Q's rights unless condition C obtained, then someone who does not know that C obtains may not do A. Since we may assume that all know that inflicting a punishment upon someone violates his rights unless he is guilty of an offense, we may make do with the weaker principle: If someone *knows* that doing act A would violate Q's rights unless condition C obtained, he may not do A if he does not know that C obtains. Weaker still, but sufficient for our purposes, is: If someone knows that doing act A would violate Q's rights unless condition C obtained, he may not do A if he has not ascertained that C obtains through being in the best feasible position for ascertaining this. (This weakening of the consequent also avoids various problems connected with epistemological skepticism.) Anyone may punish a violator of this prohibition. More precisely, anyone has the right so to punish a violator; people may do so only if they themselves don't run afoul of the prohibition, that is, only if they themselves have ascertained that another violated the prohibition, being in the best position to have ascertained this.

On this view, what a person may do is *not* limited only by the rights of others. An unreliable punisher violates no right of the guilty person; but still he may not punish him. This extra space is created by epistemic considerations. (It would be a fertile area for investigation, if one could avoid drowning in the morass of considerations about "subjective-ought" and "objective-ought.") Note that on this construal, a person does not have a right that he be punished only by use of a relatively reliable procedure. (Even though he may, if he so chooses, give another permission to use a less reliable procedure on him.) On this view, many procedural rights stem not from rights of the person acted upon, but rather from moral considerations about the person or persons doing the acting.

It is not clear to me that this is the proper focus. Perhaps the person acted upon does have such procedural rights against the user of an unreliable procedure. (But what is a *guilty* person's complaint against an unreliable procedure? That it is too likely to mispunish him? Would we have the user of an unreliable procedure compensate the guilty person he punished, for violating his right?) We have seen that our argument for a protective agency's punishing the wielder of the unreliable procedure for inflicting a penalty upon its client would go much more smoothly were this so. The client merely would authorize his agency to act to enforce his procedural right. For the purposes of our subargument here, we have shown that our conclusion stands, even without the facilitating assumption of procedural rights. (We do not mean to imply that there aren't such rights.) In either case, a protective agency may punish a wielder of an unreliable or unfair procedure who (against the client's will) has punished one of its clients, independently of whether or not its client actually is guilty and therefore even if its client is guilty.

The De Facto Monopoly

The tradition of theorizing about the state we discussed briefly Chapter 2 has a state claiming a monopoly on the use of force. Has any monopoly element yet entered our account of the dominant protective agency? *Everyone* may defend himself against unknown or unreliable procedures and may punish those who use or attempt to use such procedures against him. As its client's agent, the protective association has the right to do this for its clients. It grants that every individual, including those *not* affiliated with the association, has this right. So far, no monopoly is claimed. To be sure, there is a universal element in the content of the claim: the right to pass on *anyone's* procedure. But it does not claim to be the possessor of this right; everyone has it. Since no claim is made that there is some right which it and only it has, no monopoly is claimed. With regard to its own clients, however, it applies and enforces these rights which it grants that everyone has. It deems its own procedures reliable and fair. There will be a strong tendency for it to deem all other procedures, or even the "same" procedures run by others, either unreliable or unfair. But we need not suppose it excludes *every* other procedure. Everyone has right to defend against procedures that are in fact not, or known to be, both reliable and fair. Since the dominant protective association judges its own procedures to be both reliable and fair, and believes this to be generally known, it will not allow anyone to defend against *them*; that is, it will punish anyone who does so. The dominant protective association will act freely on its own understanding of the situation, whereas no one else will be able to so with impunity. Although no monopoly is claimed, the dominant agency does occupy a unique position by virtue of its power. It, and it alone, enforces prohibitions on others' procedures of justice, as it sees fit. It does not claim the right to prohibit others arbitrarily; it claims only the right to prohibit anyone's using actually defective procedures on its clients But when it sees itself as acting against actually defective procedures, others may see it as acting against what it thinks are defective procedures. It alone will act freely against what it thinks are defective procedures, whatever anyone else thinks. As the most powerful applier of principles which it grants everyone the right to apply *correctly*, it enforces its will, which, from the inside, it thinks *is* correct. From its strength stems its actual position as the ultimate enforcer and the ultimate judge with regard to its own clients. Claiming only the universal right to act correctly, it acts correctly by its own lights. It alone is in a position to act solely by its own lights.

Does this unique position constitute a monopoly? There is no right the dominant protective association claims uniquely to possess. But its strength leads it to be the unique agent acting across the board to enforce a particular right. It is not merely that it *happens* to be the only exerciser of a right it grants that all possess; the nature of the right is such that once a dominant power emerges, it alone will actually exercise that right. For the right includes the right to stop others from wrongfully exercising the right, and only the dominant power will be able to exercise this right against all others. Here, if anywhere, is the place for applying some notion of a *de facto* monopoly: a monopoly that is not *de jure* because it is not the result of some unique grant of exclusive right while others are excluded from exercising a similar privilege. Other protective agencies, to be sure, can enter the market and attempt to wean customers away from the dominant protective agency. They can attempt to replace it as the dominant one. But being the already dominant protective agency gives an agency a significant market advantage in the competition for clients. The dominant agency can offer its customers a guarantee that no other agencies can match: "Only those procedures *we* deem appropriate will be used on our customers."

The dominant protective agency's domain does *not* extend to quarrels of nonclients *among themselves*. If one independent is about to use his procedure of justice upon another independent, then presumably the protective association would have no right to intervene. It would have the right we all do to intervene to aid an unwilling victim whose rights are threatened. But since it may not intervene on paternalistic grounds, the protective association would have no proper business interfering if both independents were satisfied with *their* procedure of justice. This does not show that the dominant protective association is not a state. A state, too, could abstain from disputes where all concerned parties chose to opt out of the state's apparatus. (Though it is more difficult for people to opt out of the state in a limited way, by choosing some other procedure for settling a particular quarrel of theirs. For that procedure's settlement, and their reactions to it, might involve areas that not all parties concerned have removed voluntarily from the state's concern.) And shouldn't (and mustn't) each state allow that option to its citizens?

Protecting Others

If the protective agency deems the independents' procedures for enforcing their own rights insufficiently reliable or fair when applied to its clients, it will prohibit the independents from such self-help enforcement. The grounds for this prohibition are that the self-help enforcement imposes risks of danger on its clients. Since the prohibition makes it impossible for the independents credibly to threaten to punish clients who violate their rights, it makes them unable to protect themselves from harm and seriously disadvantages the independents in their daily activities and life. Yet it is perfectly possible that the independents' activities including self-help enforcement could proceed without anyone's rights being violated (leaving aside the question of procedural rights). According to our principle of compensation given in Chapter 4, in these circumstances those persons promulgating and benefiting from the prohibition must compensate those disadvantaged by it. The clients of the protective agency, then, must compensate the independents for the disadvantages imposed upon them by being prohibited self-help enforcement of their own rights against the agency's clients. Undoubtedly, the least expensive way to compensate the independents would be to *supply* them with protective services to cover those situations of conflict with the paying customers of the protective agency. This will be less expensive than leaving them unprotected against violations of their rights (by not punishing any client who does so) and then attempting to pay them afterwards to cover their losses through having (and being in a position in which they were exposed to having) their rights violated. If it were *not* less expensive, then instead of buying protective services, people would save their money and use it to cover their losses, perhaps by jointly pooling their money in an insurance scheme.

Must the members of the protective agency *pay* for protective services (vis-à-vis its clients) for the independents? Can they insist that the independents purchase the services themselves? After all, using self-help procedures would not have been without costs for the independent. The principle of compensation does not require those who prohibit an epileptic from driving to pay his full cost of taxis, chauffeurs, and so on. If the epileptic were allowed to run his own automobile, this too would have its costs: money for the car, insurance, gasoline, repair bills, and aggravation. In compensating for disadvantages imposed, the prohibitors need pay only an amount sufficient to compensate for the disadvantages of the prohibition *minus* an amount representing the costs the prohibited party would have borne were *it* not for the prohibition. The prohibitors needn't pay the complete costs of taxis; they must pay only the amount which when combined with the costs to the prohibited party of running his own private automobile *is* sufficient for taxis. They may find it less expensive to compensate in kind for the disadvantages they impose than to supply monetary compensation; they may engage in some activity that removes or partially lessens the disadvantages, compensating in money only for the net disadvantages remaining.

If the prohibitor pays to the person prohibited monetary compensation equal to an amount that covers the disadvantages imposed *minus* the costs of the activity where it permitted, this amount may be insufficient to enable the prohibited party to overcome the disadvantages. If his costs in performing the prohibited action would have been monetary, he can combine the compensation payment with this money unspent and purchase the equivalent service. But if his costs would not have been directly monetary but involve energy, time, and the like, as in the case of the independent's self-help enforcement of rights, then this monetary payment of the difference will not by itself enable the prohibited party to overcome the disadvantage by purchasing the equivalent of what he is prohibited. If the independent has other financial resources he can use without disadvantaging himself, then this payment of the difference will suffice to leave the prohibited party undisadvantaged. But *if* the independent has no such other financial resources, a protective agency may *not* pay him an amount *less* than the cost of its least expensive protective policy, and so leave him only the alternatives of being defenseless against the wrongs of its clients or having to work in the cash market to earn sufficient funds to total the premium on a policy. For this financially pressed prohibited individual, the agency must make up the difference between the *monetary* costs to him of the unprohibited activity and the amount necessary to purchase an overcoming or counterbalancing of the disadvantage imposed. The prohibitor must completely supply enough, in money or in kind, to overcome the disadvantages. No compensation need be provided to someone who would not be disadvantaged by buying protection for himself. For those of scanter resources, to whom the unprohibited activity had no monetary costs, the agency must provide the difference between the resources they can spare without disadvantage and the cost of protection. For someone for whom it had some monetary costs, the prohibitor must supply the additional monetary amount (over and above what they can spare without disadvantage) necessary to overcome the disadvantages. If the prohibitors compensate in kind, they may *charge* the financially pressed prohibited party for this, up to the monetary costs to him of his unprohibited activity provided this amount is not greater than the price of the good.[13] As the only effective supplier, the dominant protective agency must offer in compensation the difference between its own fee and monetary costs to this prohibited party of self-help enforcement. It almost always will receive this amount back in partial payment for the purchase of a protection policy. It goes without saying that these dealings and prohibitions apply only to those using unreliable or unfair enforcement procedures.

Thus the dominant protective agency must supply the independents—that is, everyone it prohibits from self-help enforcement against its clients on the grounds that their procedures of enforcement are unreliable or unfair—with protective services against its clients; it may have to provide some persons services for a fee that is less than the price of these services. These persons may, of course, choose to refuse to pay the fee and so do without these compensatory services. If the dominant protective agency provides protective services in this way for independents, won't this lead people to leave the agency in order to receive its services without paying? Not to any great extent, since compensation is paid only to those who would be disadvantaged by purchasing protection for themselves, and only in the amount that will equal the cost of an unfancy policy when added to the sum of the monetary costs of self-help protection plus whatever amount the person comfortably could pay. Furthermore, the agency protects these independents it compensates only against its own paying clients on whom the independents are forbidden to use self-help enforcement. The more free riders there are, the more desirable it is to be a client always protected by the agency. This factor, along with the others, acts to reduce the number of free riders and to move the equilibrium toward almost universal participation.

The State

We set ourselves the task, in Chapter 3, of showing that the dominant protective association within a territory satisfied two crucial necessary conditions for being a state: that it had the requisite sort of monopoly over the use of force in the territory, and that it protected the rights of everyone in the territory, even if this universal protection could be provided only in a "redistributive" fashion. These very crucial facets of the state constituted the subject of the individualist anarchists' condemnation of the state as immoral. We also set ourselves the task of showing that these monopoly and redistributive elements were themselves morally legitimate, of showing that the transition from a state of nature to an ultraminimal state (the monopoly element) was morally legitimate and violated no one's rights and that the transition from an ultraminimal to a minimal state (the "redistributive" element) also was morally legitimate and violated no one's rights.

A protective agency dominant in a territory does satisfy the two crucial necessary conditions for being a state. It is the only generally effective enforcer of a prohibition on others using unreliable enforcement procedures (calling them as it sees them), and it oversees these procedures. And the agency protects those nonclients in its territory whom it prohibits from using self-help enforcement procedures on its clients, in their dealings with its clients, even if such protection must be financed (in apparent redistributive fashion) by its clients. It is morally required to do this by the principle of compensation, which requires those who act in self-protection in order to increase their own security to compensate those they prohibit from doing risky acts which might actually have turned out to be harmless[14] for the disadvantages imposed upon them.

We noted in beginning Chapter 3 that whether the provision of protective services for some by others was "redistributive" would depend upon the reasons for it. We now see that such provision need not be redistributive since it can be justified on other than redistributive grounds, namely, those provided in the principle of compensation. (Recall that "redistributive" applies to reasons for a practice or institution, and only elliptically and derivatively to the institution itself.) To sharpen this point, we can imagine that protective agencies offer two types of protection policies: those protecting clients against risky private enforcement of justice and those not doing so but protecting only against theft, assault, and so forth (provided these are not done in the course of private enforcement of justice). Since it is only with regard to those with the first type of policy that others are prohibited from privately enforcing justice, only they will be required to compensate the persons prohibited private enforcement for the disadvantages imposed upon them. The holders of only the second type of policy will not have to pay for the protection of others, there being nothing they have to compensate these others for. Since the reasons for wanting to be protected against private enforcement of justice are compelling, almost all who purchase protection will purchase this type of protection, despite its extra costs, and therefore will be involved in providing protection for the independents.

We have discharged our task of explaining how a state would arise from a state of nature without anyone's rights being violated. The moral objections of the individualist anarchist to the minimal state are overcome. It is not an unjust imposition of a monopoly; the *de facto* monopoly grows by an invisible-hand process and *by morally permissible means*, without anyone's rights being violated and without any claims being made to a special right that others do not possess. And requiring the clients of the *de facto* monopoly to pay for the protection of those they prohibit from self-help enforcement against them, far from being immoral, is morally required by the principle of compensation adumbrated in Chapter 4.

We canvassed, in Chapter 4, the possibility of forbidding people to perform acts if they lack the means to compensate others for possible harmful consequences of these acts or if they lack liability insurance to cover these consequences. Were such prohibition legitimate, according to the principle of compensation the persons prohibited would have to be compensated for the disadvantages imposed upon them, and they could use the compensatory payments to purchase the liability insurance! Only those disadvantaged by the prohibition would be compensated: namely, those who lack other resources they can shift (without disadvantaging sacrifice) to purchase the liability insurance. When these people spend their compensatory payments for liability insurance, we have what amounts to public provision of special liability insurance. It is provided to those unable to afford it and covers only those risky actions which fall under the principle of compensation—those actions which are legitimately prohibited when uncovered (provided disadvantages are compensated for), actions whose prohibition would seriously disadvantage persons. Providing such insurance almost certainly would be the least expensive way to compensate people who present only normal danger to others for the disadvantages of the prohibition. Since they then would be insured against the eventuation of certain of their risks to others, these actions then would not be prohibited to them. Thus we see how, if it were legitimate to prohibit some actions to those uncovered by liability insurance, and were this done, another *apparent* redistributive aspect of the state would enter by solid libertarian moral principles! (The exclamation point stands for *my* surprise.)

Does the dominant protective agency in a given geographical territory constitute the *state* of that territory? We have seen in Chapter 2 how the notion of a monopoly on the use of force is difficult to state precisely so that it does not fall before obvious counterexamples. This notion, as usually explained, cannot be used with any confidence to answer our question. We should accept a decision yielded by the precise wording of a definition in some text only if that definition had been devised for application to cases as complicated as ours and had stood up to tests against a range of such cases. No classification, in passing, by accident can answer our question in any useful manner.

Consider the following discursive description by an anthropologist:

> The concentration of all physical force in the hands of the central authority is the primary function of the state and is its decisive characteristic. In order to make this clear, consider what may not be done under the state form of rule: no one in the society governed by the state may take another's life, do him physical harm, touch his property, or damage his reputation save by permission of the state. The officers of the state have powers to take life, inflict corporal punishment, seize property as fine or by expropriation, and affect the standing and reputation of a member of the society.
>
> This is not to say that in societies without the state one may take life with impunity. But in such societies (e.g., among Bushmen, Eskimo, and the tribes of central Australia) the central authority that protects the household against wrongdoers is nonexistent, weak, or sporadic, and it was applied among the Crow and other Indians of the western Plains only as situations arose. The household or the individual is protected in societies without the state by nonexplicit means, by total group participation in suppression of the wrongdoer, by temporarily or sporadically applied force that is no longer needed (and so no longer used) when the cause for its application is past. The state has means for the suppression of what the *society* considers to be wrongs or crimes: police, courts of law, prisons, institutions which explicitly and specifically function in this area of activity. Moreover, these institutions are stable within the frame of reference of the society, and permanent.
>
> When the state was formed in ancient Russia, the ruling prince asserted the power to impose fines and to wreak physical pain and death, but allowed no one else to act thus. He asserted once again the monopolistic nature of the state power by withholding its power from any other person or body. If harm was done by one subject to another without the prince's express permission, this was a wrong, and the wrongdoer was punished. Moreover, the prince's power could only be explicitly delegated. The class of subject thus protected was thereby carefully defined, of course; by no means were all those within his realm so protected.
>
> No one person or group can stand in place of the state; the state's acts can only be performed directly or by express delegation. The state if delegating its power makes its delegate an agent (organ) of the state. Policemen, judges, jail guards derive their power to coerce, according to the rules of the society, directly from the central authority; so do the tax-collectors, the military, frontier guards, and the like. The authoritative function of the state rests on its command of these forces as its agents.[15]

The writer does not claim that the features he lists all are necessary features of the state; divergence in one feature would not serve to show that the dominant protective agency of a territory was not a state. Clearly the dominant agency has almost all of the features specified; and its enduring administrative structures, with full-time specialized personnel, make it diverge greatly—in the direction of a state—from what anthropologists call a stateless society. On the basis of the many writings like that quoted, one would call it a state.

It is plausible to conclude that the dominant protective association in a territory is its state, only for a territory of some size containing more than a few people. We do not claim that each person who, under anarchy, retains a monopoly on the use of force on his quarter acre of property is its state; nor are the only three inhabitants of an island one square block in size. It would be futile, and would serve no useful purpose, to attempt to specify conditions or the size of population and territory necessary for a state to exist. Also, we speak of cases where almost all of the people in the territory are clients of the dominant agency and where independent are in a subordinate power position in conflicts with the agency and its clients. (We have argued that this will occur.) Precisely what percentage must be clients and how subordinate the power position of the independents must be are more interesting questions, but concerning these I have nothing especially interesting to say.

One additional necessary condition for a state was extracted from the Weberian tradition by our discussion in Chapter 2: namely, that it claims to be the sole authorizer of violence. The dominant protective association makes no such claim. Having described the position of the dominant protective association, and having seen how closely it fits anthropologists' notions, should we weaken the Weberian necessary condition so that it includes a *de facto* monopoly which is the territory's sole effective judge over the permissibility of violence, having a right (to be sure, one had by all) to make judgments on the matter and to act on correct ones? The case is very strong for doing so, and it is wholly desirable and appropriate. We therefore conclude that the protective association dominant in a territory, as described, *is* a state. However, to remind the reader of our slight weakening of the Weberian condition, we occasionally shall refer to the dominant protective agency as "a statelike entity," instead of simply as "a state."

The Invisible-Hand Explanation of the State

Have we provided an invisible-hand explanation (see Chapter 2) of the state's arising within a state of nature; have we given an invisible-hand explanation of the state? The *rights* possessed by the state are already possessed by each individual in a state of nature. These rights, since they are already contained whole in the explanatory parts, are *not* provided an invisible-hand explanation. Nor have we provided an invisible-hand explanation of how the state acquires rights unique to it. This is fortunate; for since the state has no special rights, there is nothing of that sort to be explained.

We have explained how, without anyone having this in mind, the self-interested and rational actions of persons in a Lockean state of nature will lead to single protective agencies dominant over geographical territories; each territory will have either one dominant agency or a number of agencies federally affiliated so as to constitute, in essence, one. And we have explained how, without claiming to possess any rights uniquely, a protective agency dominant in a territory will occupy a unique position. Though each person has a right to act correctly to prohibit others from violating rights (including the right not to be punished unless shown to deserve it), only the dominant protective association will be able, without sanction, to enforce correctness as it sees it. Its power makes it the arbiter of correctness; *it* determines what, for purposes of punishment, counts as a breach of correctness. Our explanation does not assume or claim that might makes right. But might does make enforced prohibitions, even if no one thinks the mighty have a *special* entitlement to have realized in the world their own view of which prohibitions are correctly enforced.

Our explanation of this *de facto* monopoly is an invisible-hand explanation. If the state is an institution (1) that has the right to enforce rights, prohibit dangerous private enforcement of justice, pass upon such private procedures, and so forth, and (2) that effectively is the *sole wielder* within a geographical territory of the right in (1), then by offering an invisible-hand explanation of (2), though not of (1), we have partially explained in invisible-hand fashion the existence of the state. More precisely, we have partially explained in invisible-hand fashion the existence of the *ultraminimal* state. What is the explanation of how a *minimal* state arises? The dominant protective association with the monopoly element is morally required to compensate for the disadvantages it imposes upon those it prohibits from self-help activities against its clients. However, it actually might fail to provide this compensation. Those operating an ultraminimal state are morally required to transform it into a minimal state, but they might choose not to do so. We have assumed that generally people will do what they are morally required to do. Explaining how a state could arise from a state of nature without violating anyone's rights refutes the principled objections of the anarchist. But one would feel more confidence if an explanation of how a state *would* arise from a state of nature also specified reasons why an ultraminimal state would be transformed into a minimal one, in addition to moral reasons, if it specified incentives for providing the compensation or the causes of its being provided in addition to people's desire to do what they ought. We should note that even in the event that no nonmoral incentives or causes are found to be sufficient for the transition from an ultraminimal to a minimal state, and the explanation continues to lean heavily upon people's moral motivations, it does not specify people's objective as that of establishing a state. Instead, persons view themselves as providing particular other persons with compensation for particular prohibitions they have imposed upon them. The explanation remains an invisible-hand one.

Notes

1. Herbert Hart, "Are There Any Natural Rights?" *Philosophical Review*, 1955; John Rawls, *A Theory of Justice* (Cambridge, Mass.: Harvard University Press, 1971), sect. 18. My statement of the principle stays close to Rawls'. The argument Rawls offers for this principle constitutes an argument only for the narrower principle of fidelity (bona fide promises are to be kept). Though if there were no way to avoid "can't get started" difficulties about the principle of fidelity (p. 349) other than by appealing to the principle of fairness, it *would* be an argument for the principle of fairness.

2. Hart, "Are There Any Natural Rights?"
3. I have formulated my remarks in terms of the admittedly vague notion of there being a "point" to certain kinds of rights because this, I think, gives Hart's argument its most plausible construction.
4. I have skirted making the institution one that you didn't get a fair say in setting up or deciding its nature, for here Rawls would object that it doesn't satisfy his two principles of justice. Though Rawls does not require that every microinstitution satisfy his two principles of justice, but only the basic structure of the society, he seems to hold that a microinstitution must satisfy these two principles if it is to give rise to obligations under the principle of fairness.
5. The acceptability of our procedures to us may depend on our not knowing this information. See Lawrence Tribe, "Trial by Mathematics," *Harvard Law Review*, 1971.
6. Must their calculation about which is better include their chances of success? There is some temptation to define this area of conflict as one where such chances of wrong are for certain purposes thought to be as bad as the wrong for sure. A theory of how probability interacts with the moral weight of wrongs is sorely needed.

   In treating the question as one of whether the benefits of conflict outweigh costs, the text seriously oversimplifies the issue. Instead of a simple cost-benefit principle, the correct principle requites for an act to be morally permissible, not merely that its moral benefits outweigh its moral costs, but that there is no other alternative action available with less moral cost, such that the additional moral cost of the contemplated action over the alternative outweighs its additional moral benefit. (For a detailed discussion of these issues see my "Moral Complications and Moral Structures," *Natural Law Forum*, 1968, pp. 1-5, especially the discussion of Principle VII.) One would be in a position to advance the discussion of many issues if one combined such a principle with a theory of the moral weight of harms or wrongs with certain specified probabilities, to get an explicitly probabilified version of this principle. I mention only one application here that might not spring to mind. It is often assumed that the only pacifist position which is a moral position absolutely forbids violent action. Any pacifist position that considers the effectiveness of pacifist techniques is labeled tactical rather than moral. But if a pacifist holds that because certain techniques of significant effectiveness are available (civilian resistance, nonviolent defense, satyagraha, and so on) it is *morally* wrong to wage or prepare for war, he is putting forth a comprehensible position that is a *moral* one, and which does require appeal to facts about the effectiveness of pacifist techniques. Given the lack of certainty about the effects of various actions (wars, pacifist techniques) the principle to govern the moral discussion of whether nonpacifist actions are morally permitted is a probabilified version of the principle (Principle VII) described briefly above.
7. It is a consequence of Locke's view that each citizen is in a state of nature with respect to the highest appeal procedure of the state, since there is no further appeal. Hence he is in a state of nature with respect to the state as a whole. Also, citizens have "a liberty to appeal to Heaven, whenever they judge the cause of sufficient moment. And therefore, though the people cannot be judge, so as to have by the constitution of that society any superior power, to determine and give effective sentence in the case; yet they have, by a Law antecedent and paramount to all positive laws of men, reserved that ultimate determination to themselves, which belongs to all mankind, where there lies no appeal on earth, viz. to judge whether they have just cause to make their appeal to Heaven. And this judgment they cannot part with...." *Two Treatises of Government*, ed. Peter Laslett (New York: Cambridge

University Press, 1967), II, sect. 168; see also sects. 20, 21, 90-93, 176, 207, 241, 242.

8. The considerations of this paragraph, though I find them powerful, do not completely remove my uneasiness about the position argued in the text. The reader who wishes to claim, against this book, that special moral principles emerge with regard to the *state* might find this issue a fruitful one to press. Though if I do make a mistake here, it may be one concerning responsibility rather than concerning the state.
9. May someone in a position to know say that he hasn't gotten around to examining the information, and so he will defend himself against anyone's now coming to apply the procedure to him? Presumably not, if the procedure is well known and not of recent origin. But even here, perhaps, a *gift* of some extra time may be made
10. Clients no doubt would empower their agency to proceed as described in the text, if the client himself is unable to say whether he is guilty or innocent, perhaps because he is unconscious, agreeing to replace any compensating amount the agency must pay to the prospective punisher.

    This deterrent to false pleas of innocence might act also to deter some innocent people against whom the evidence is overwhelming from protesting their innocence. There will be few such cases, but it may be to avoid this undesirable deterrence that a person who is found guilty beyond a reasonable doubt after having pleaded innocent is not also penalized for perjury.
11. The category of feared exaction of compensation will be small but nonempty. Exacting compensation may involve activities people fear because it involves compelling them to do compensatory forced labor; might it even be the direct imposition of a feared consequence, because only this can raise the victim to his previous indifference curve?
12. Gilbert Harman proposes simple intertranslatability as a criterion of merely verbal difference in "Quine on Meaning and Existence," *Review of Metaphysics*, 21, no. 1 (September 1967). *If* we wish to say that two persons with the same beliefs who speak different languages differ only verbally, then Harman's criterion will include as "simple," translations as complex as those between languages. Whatever is to be decided about such cases, the criterion serves in the present instance.
13. May the prohibitors charge the prohibited party for the other costs to him of performing the activity were it unprohibited, such as time, energy, and so on?
14. Here, as at all other places in this essay, "harm" refers only to border crossings.
15. Lawrence Krader, *Formation of the State* (Englewood Cliffs, N.J.: Prentice-Hall, 1968), pp. 21-22.

11

The Invisible Hand Strikes Back

Roy A. Childs, Jr.

Surely one of the most significant occurrences on the intellectual scene during the past few years has been the emergence of a professor of philosophy at Harvard University as an eloquent and forceful spokesman for the doctrine of Libertarianism. Indeed, so much attention and praise has been lately showered upon the man, Robert Nozick, and his National Book-Award-winning treatise, *Anarchy, State and Utopia*, that all who uphold the doctrine of human liberty have been cheered.

If they have been cheered by the reception given to the book, however, and to the new concern of portions of the intellectual establishment with libertarianism, they have not been equally cheered by the content of the book itself. For amidst the book's subtle and wide ranging critiques of doctrines such as Marx's theory of exploitation, egalitarianism, and John Rawls' theory of justice (so hailed by intellectuals in recent years), appears an argument so central to Nozick's thinking that it dominates the first third of the treatise itself: a defense of the "minimal State" against the claims and arguments of anarchism.

Part of the consternation caused by this section is due to the fact that Nozick's argument is often of brain-cracking complexity, using against the reader all of the techniques and tools of contemporary philosophy—with not a few other technical insights from other fields, such as economics, thrown in for good measure—giving the reader oftentimes the feeling of being on a merry-go-round moving at a dizzying pace, changing speed and direction in unpredictable ways.

But part of the consternation is caused equally by the nature of the arguments themselves, with their seemingly anti-libertarian bent; arguments resting on notions such as the "compensation principle," the principle of "risk," and the alleged "right" to prohibit certain risky activities of others.

It is no accident, then, that *Anarchy, State, and Utopia* has raised a storm of controversy in Libertarian circles. While the media and the intellectual world in general have focused, appropriately enough, on Nozick's persuasive critiques of the conventional wisdom, particularly the section devoted to examining Rawls' theory of justice, and to Nozick's defense of "capitalist acts between consenting adults," Libertarians have focused more on Nozick's frame of reference, the absence of a theory of rights (upon which much of the book tacitly rests its case), and the attack on anarchism.

It is obvious that any persuasive and comprehensive critique of this profound and complex work would have to be as long as the hook itself. We aspire to no such grandiose heights here. What we shall do instead is to attempt to answer Nozick's main argument in defense of the "minimal state." Nozick begins with the Lockeian "state-of-nature" to show how, by means of a series of "invisible hand" processes which violate the rights of no one, a legitimate "minimal state" may arise. We shall, on the contrary, maintain that, beginning with a "minimal state," and moving through a series of stages (which process violates the rights of no one), we may properly arrive back at a state of anarchy. In short, we shall maintain that the only good minimal state is a dead minimal state, one which avows those processes to operate which would, if continued over a period of time, dissolve the minimal state into anarchism.

In clarifying this, we shall have to discuss Nozick's concept of "risk," his principle of "compensation," and his view that the explanation offered for the origin of the state is an "invisible hand" explanation. We shall see that, on the contrary, there is instead a very *visible* hand: in fact, a veritable iron fist. Professor Nozick's defense of the minimal state unfolds in three stages. Firstly, he argues that, "given" an anarchistic system of competing protective associations within a free market, one *dominant agency* will emerge, through market procedures and by economic necessity. This "dominant agency" will in turn "evolve" into an *"ultraminimal state"* by an invisible hand process in a morally permissible way which violates the rights of no one. This "ultraminimal state" differs from the dominant agency in that it maintains a monopoly on force in a given geographical area (except that necessary in immediate self-defense). It therefore "excludes private (or agency) retaliation for wrong and exaction of compensation; but it provides protection and enforcement services only to those who purchase its protection and enforcement policies." Professor Nozick then shows how this ultraminimal state evolves into a *minimal* state, which is "equivalent to the ultraminimal state conjoined with a (clearly redistributive) Friedmanesque voucher plan, financed from tax revenues. Under this plan all people, or some (for example, those in need) are given tax-funded vouchers that can be used only for their purchase of a protection policy from the ultraminimal state." Professor Nozick holds that "the operators of the ultraminimal state are morally obligated to produce the minimal state," since "it would be morally impermissible for persons to maintain the monopoly in the ultraminimal state without providing protective services for all..."

This last is, of course, especially interesting. The successful transformation of the ultraminimal state into the minimal state is dependent upon the ultraminimal state's allegiance to Professor Nozick's principle of compensation. The ultraminimal state is obligated to "compensate" those whose risky activities they forcibly prohibit. Adequate compensation is taken to be, quite without reason, as we shall see, the provision of protective services. Professor Nozick grants that the ultraminimal state "might fail to provide this compensation," but he assumes that "generally people will do what they are morally required to do." This assumption, unfortunately, is *only* made by Professor Nozick in considering the actions of the state apparatus, not in pausing to consider the actions of competing protective associations. This naiveté is charming indeed, but not very heartwarming, reassuring or realistic. That such an assumption should find its way to make a crucially important bridge in Professor Nozick's argument is, in many ways, symptomatic of the book, and much of contemporary philosophical discussion of the state.

Why must one "dominant agency" develop, within the free market system of competing protection agencies? "Initially," Professor Nozick writes, "several different protective associations or companies will offer their services in the same geographical area. What will happen when there is a conflict between clients of different agencies?" We learn that "only three possibilities are worth considering":

1. In such situations the forces of the two agencies do battle. One of the agencies always wins such battles. Since the clients of the losing agency are ill protected in conflicts with clients of the winning agency, they leave their agency to do business with the winner.
2. One agency has its power centered in one geographical area, the other in another. Each wins the battles fought close to its center of power, with some gradient being established. People who deal with one agency but live under the power of the other either move closer to their own agency's home headquarters or shift their patronage to the other protective agency...
3. The two agencies fight evenly and often. They win and lose about equally, and their interspersed members have frequent dealings and disputes with each other. Or perhaps without fighting or after only a few skirmishes the agencies realize that, such battling will occur continually in the absence of preventive measures. In any case, to avoid frequent, costly and wasteful battles the two agencies, perhaps through their executives, agree to resolve peacefully those cases about which they reach differing judgments. They agree to set up, and abide by the decisions of, some third judge or court to which they can turn when their respective judgments differ. (Or they might establish rules determining which agency has jurisdiction under which circumstances.) Thus emerges a system of appeals courts and agreed upon rules about jurisdiction, and the conflict of laws. Though different agencies operate, there is one unified federal judicial system of which they are components.

What is the significance of this? "In each of these cases," we are told, "all the persons in a geographical area are under some common system that judges between their competing claims and enforces their rights."

> Out of anarchy, pressed by spontaneous groupings, mutual-protection associations, division of labor, market pressures, economics of scale, and rational self-interest there arises something very much resembling a minimal state or a group of geographically distinct minimal states.

According to Professor Nozick, then, if competing protection associations make arrangements between themselves to settle disputes, we have a type of "federal judicial system," a variant of government. This is surely metaphorical and unjustified. Surely, if we take all the protective devices in use in a given society and lump them together, then the total has what some might call a "monopoly" on protection. Similarly, all farmers taken collectively have a "monopoly" on growing food. But this is tautological.

The real point which Professor Nozick wishes to make is that if either of these alternative courses result, then we have a "legal system" resulting. Now, no one has ever denied that there would indeed be a "legal system" under anarchism. Many prominent anarchists have claimed that they advocate that structures and processes (even content, in some cases), be *separated from* the state, and the state abolished entirely. If one is going to term *any* "legal system" in this broad sense a "state," then there is little point in pursuing the matter.

Discussion may proceed along more productive lines if we distinguish between two radically different *types* of legal systems: a "market legal system" and a "state legal system." A "market legal system" could be designated as a system of rules and enforcement procedures which arises from the processes of the market economy: competition, bargaining, legal decisions, and so forth; a legal system whose order is "spontaneous" in the Hayekian sense. A "state legal system" on the other hand, could be designed as a system of rules and enforcement procedures which are designed by the state apparatus, as a result of political procedures, and imposed by force upon the rest of society.

In a society with a "market legal system," the shape of the legal system is determined by the processes set in motion by the actions of a number of independent agencies whose plans may conflict, and therefore cause some adjustment in the means-ends structure of themselves and others. Independent agencies, then, can make agreements, reach decisions, set precedents, bargain and so forth, producing a legal "order" which is not designated by anyone. The resulting system is not a "federal system" in the traditional manner: we may have *ad hoc* decisions for individual disputes, procedures agreed upon in advance, such as drawing the names of arbitrators out of a hat, alternating arbitrators chosen by each agency, *ad infinitum.* We need not suppose that any *permanent*, distinct, appeals system has been erected. (If one had, it would not change our essential argument.) Anarchism, then, can have a legal system, a "market legal system" as opposed to a "state legal system." The analogy is to the distinction drawn between state-economic systems and unhampered market economic systems. Both are *systems*, but not of the same sort; they are built on different principles of organization and are the manifestations of different processes altogether. What we shall conclude, then, is that if the third of Professor Nozick's three alternatives results, then there will *not* be a state apparatus as the result.

Several other objections to this reasoning arise here; Professor Nozick's argument that "maximal competing protective services cannot coexist" lacks force, because he merely assumes that violent conflicts between agencies will be the norm. Now, if such conflicts do begin to develop, economics gives us every reason to assume that it will be more in the interest of competing parties to develop a means of arbitrating disputes rather than to engage in violent actions. Finally, there is no reason to regard the concept of "protective services" with holistic awe. An infinite variety of institutions can develop in society, concerned with as many different aspects of protection. Some institutions may patrol the neighborhood block, some might focus on copyrights, some on violations of contracts, some merely on insuring against crime, rather than on apprehending criminals (for cases where customers in society do not think that retribution or punishment is justified or worthwhile). Here again, there is no reason to expect a single agency to dominate the field.

The "invisible hand" has indeed gotten itself entangled in a very strong web. Let us examine the process by which the "dominant agency" would evolve into an "ultraminimal state," which is in turn morally obliged to become the "minimal state."

> "An ultraminimal state," writes Nozick, "maintains a monopoly over all use of force except that necessary in immediate self-defense, and so excludes private (or agency) retaliation for wrong and exaction of compensation; but it provides protection and enforcement services only to those who purchase its protection and enforcement policies.
>
> "The minimal (night watchman) state," on the other hand is, as he writes, "equivalent to the ultraminimal state conjoined with a (clearly redistributive) Friedmanesque voucher plan, financed from tax revenues. Under this plan all people, or some (for example, those in need), are given tax-funded vouchers that can be used only for their purchase of a protection policy from the ultraminimal state."

Professor Nozick assumes the existence of a dominant protection agency in a field of competitors, and shows how it might evolve into the ultraminimal state, which is in turn morally obligated to become the minimal state. The key question to ask is: how may the dominant agency act towards independents? To answer this, we must briefly consider the notions of risk, prohibition, and the principle of compensation.

In Professor Nozick's view, one is morally justified in prohibiting certain acts, provided one compensates those who are so prohibited. What actions may be prohibited? In *Anarchy, State, and Utopia*, there is no clear and unambiguous line drawn between classes of human actions which one may justifiably prohibit, and those which one may not. One class can be identified, however: we may prohibit certain *risky* actions, providing those so prohibited are compensated. Which risky actions? It is not too clear, but the answer seems to be: those presenting "too high" a probability of harm to others. The dominant agency may justifiably prohibit enforcement procedures of independent agencies, by this reasoning, since these risk harming others, whether by punishing wrongly, using unreliable procedures, or anything else. In asking the question "How may the dominant agency act?" or "What...may a dominant protective association forbid other individuals to do?" Professor Nozick answers:

> The dominant protective association may reserve for itself the right to judge any procedure of justice to be applied to its clients. It may announce, and act on the announcement, that it will punish anyone who uses on one of its clients a procedure that it finds to be unreliable or unfair.

This is based in turn on the notion of "procedural rights." "The person who uses an unreliable procedure, acting upon its results," he writes, "imposes risks upon others, whether or not his procedure misfires in a particular case." Nozick articulates the general principle that "*everyone* may defend himself against the unknown or unreliable procedures and may punish those who use or attempt to use such procedures against him," and does not in principle reserve this "right" to a monopoly agency. *However*:

> Since the dominant protective association judges it, own procedures to be both reliable and fair and believes this to be generally known, it will not allow anyone to defend against *them*; that is, it will punish anyone who does so. The dominant protective association will act freely on its own understanding of the situation, whereas no one else will be able to do so with impunity. *Although no monopoly is chimed*, the dominant agency does occupy a unique position by virtue of its power... It is not merely that it happens to be the only exerciser *of* a right it grants that all possess; the nature of the right is such that once a dominant power emerges, it alone will actually exercise that right. (my emphasis)

Hence: a *de facto* monopoly. Ergo: the ultraminimal state.

It is at this point that the principle of compensation rears its ugly head.

Professor Nozick has stated that one has a right to prohibit certain excessively risky actions of others *provided they are compensated*. What constitutes "compensation"?

> Something fully compensates a person for a loss if and only if it makes him no worse off than he other wise would have been; it compensates person X for person Y's action if X is no worse off receiving it, Y having done A, than X would have been without receiving it if Y had not done A. (In the terminology of economists, something compensates X for Y's act if receiving it leaves X on at least as high an indifference curve as he would have been on, without it, had Y not so acted.)

Professor Nozick then proceeds to "shamelessly" ignore certain key questions surrounding the central issues concerning the meaning of "compensation." His final formulation is as follows:

> Y is required to raise X above his actual position (on a certain indifference curve I) by an amount equal to the difference between his position on I and his original position. Y compensates X for how much worse off Y's action would have made a reasonably prudent acting X.

This is the meaning, then, of "compensation." "The principle of compensation requires that people be compensated for having certain risky activities prohibited to them." What "risky" activities does Professor Nozick wish to prohibit? The enforcement procedures of the non-dominant protection agencies. That is, he wishes to prohibit us from turning to any of a number of competing agencies, other than the dominant protection agency.

What is he willing to offer us as *compensation* for being so prohibited? He is generous to a fault. He will give us nothing less than *the State*.

Should one wish to reject this admittedly generous offer, it would be responded that he *cannot* reject it. It is foisted upon one whether one likes it or not, whether one is *willing* to accept the State as compensation or not. It is *this* which should give us pause, and lead us to think a bit. Let us consider the nature of Professor Nozick's State, and then consider a few of the weak links in the chain of arguments which will, in the end, bind us to the State. With a good yank or two, perhaps we can snap some of these weak links, and save ourselves from what some of us, at least, regard as certain doom. In the meantime, though, let it be realized that we have arrived at the minimal state. The ultraminimal state arose when non-dominant agencies were prohibited from certain activities. The minimal state was reached when the ultraminimal state was combined with the extension of protective services to those who were so prohibited.

(We should note that the only thing binding the minimal state to pay such compensation is a moral principle. Professor Nozick "assumes" in this case, that they [those in the ultraminimal state] will act as they ought, even though they might not acknowledge this moral obligation.)

Consider the nature of the Nozickian state itself. The Randian "limited government" has a rather interesting economic form: it is in essence a consumer's co-op, with all coming under its power being "consumers," having the right to vote, and so on. *But Professor Nozick's State is private property.* It was, one recalls, a private firm, an agency, which developed by a series of specifiable steps, into a State. It remains private property, then, since nothing was done to change matters. Since it was once upon a time ago a dominant agency, and got that way through the free market, one is justified in assuming that its owners, the board of directors (stockholders or whatever) are aggressive businessmen, driving towards "expansion" of their business. There is no question of a constitution, of course, merely the contracts with its clients, which in case of conflicts it alone can judge and interpret. There is no voting. There is no separation of powers, no checks and balances, and no longer any market checks and balances, either. There is merely a private agency, now with a monopoly on power, on the use of physical force to attain its ends.

This, we are told, is an agency which is going to follow certain moral principles and (a) extend protection to those whose risky activities are prohibited (or whose agencies were prohibited from functioning), and (b) stop with the functions of a "minimal state." What is to check its power? What happens in the event of its assuming even more powers? Since it has a monopoly, any disputes over its functions are solved exclusively by itself. Since careful prosecution procedures are costly, the ultraminimal state may become careless without competition. Nevertheless, only the ultraminimal state may judge the legitimacy of its own procedures, as Professor Nozick explicitly tells us.

One might find Nozick's argument as to why *this* should be taken as a less "risky" situation than that of competing agencies, less than totally convincing. Let us take up some of those weak links in the chain of reasoning, and see if they can be snapped.

The fact that, as we saw, we cannot reject the State's "protection" as justifiable "compensation" for being prohibited from patronizing competing agencies, should lead us to question Professor Nozick's view of compensation. A similar critical glance will lead us to reexamine his view of risk as well.

We are justified in prohibiting the actions of competing agencies because they are alleged to be "risky." How "risky" does an action have to be before it can be prohibited? Professor Nozick does not say. Nor does he give us any indication of how risk of the kind he deals with can be calculated. As Murray Rothbard wrote in *Man, Economy and State*:

> "Risk" occurs when an event is a member of a class of a large number of homogeneous events and there is fairly certain knowledge of the frequency of occurrence of this class of events.

In his masterwork *Risk, Uncertainty and Profit*, Frank Knight uses the term "risk" to designate cases of *measurable uncertainty*. As applied to human action, this becomes very dubious indeed. In fact, it involves us in innumerable difficulties.

As Professor Knight writes, "We live only by knowing *something* about the future; while the problems of life, or of conduct, at least, arise from the fact that we know so little." This is why we cannot calculate the risks from future human actions. (We shall restrict the concept of "risk" to the cases of the probability of harm resulting from certain actions.) In dealing with questions of probability of consequences of human actions, our calculations must of necessity be vague and inexact. While in some cases, certainly, we can say that a probability is greater or less, a *quantitative* calculation is impossible. Not dealing with homogeneous units, or with accidents distributed throughout a large number of cases with some frequency, we lack the preconditions of quantitative calculation. This is particularly the case with such institutions as "competing protection agencies," since they may differ vastly in scope of activities, procedures, or any number of other attributes. If Nozick provided a criterion of what degree of "risk" was permissible, and what not, then we might be able to separate those agencies which are "too risky" from those which are not, prohibiting only the former. No criterion is given, however. Moreover, Nozick is not even simply concerned with "harm," but extends his concern to a much more subjective element, namely, *fear*. How much "fear" justifies what response is not discussed. It is very difficult, then, to see how one can arrive at any objective cut-off level. Not only can "fear" not be calculated or measured, it is so subjective that it cannot even be said to be a simple response to any one set of objective conditions. There may be psychological and ideological factors, as well. For instance, the person in question might at one time have had to live under a State apparatus, and that experience might have left deep fears in his subconscious.

Since man anticipates the future without knowing what will happen, since he modifies his plans and actions continually as new knowledge accumulates, how can anyone predict that competing agencies will automatically and inevitably supersede any given level of "risk" in society? Uncertainty and fear on some level seem to be an essential (or at least central) part of the human condition; Professor Nozick has given us no reason to believe that any one category of uncertainty, such as the risk of unjustifiable punishment, or unreliable enforcement procedures, should morally lead us to establish one set of institutions over another. Why isn't fear of tyranny an equally valid reason for prohibiting something? And who is to say that the procedures of the dominant protection agency are not among the most *unreliable*? Only *given* the assumption of reliability can we even begin to consider as "morally justifiable" any judgment and prohibition of the activities of others. Certainly a dominant agency whose procedures were among the least reliable would be in the same position as one with reliable procedures with respect to its *power* to prohibit other procedures and agencies. But we would not defend the *moral permissibility* of this prohibition. In the absence of criteria, Professor Nozick has given us few guides here.

Moreover, while there is an extent to which people can correctly anticipate the future in human actions, including the risk of harm, there is no means of objectively discovering, in the present, which people will *correctly* anticipate the future, and which not. The best chance we have of picking those whose expectations are likely to be most in harmony with future reality, in the area of "risk of harm," would be to look at objective tests. But in the realm of human action, the closest we can come is not any science of risk-calculation, but through a record of profit-making, that their expectations have been historically more in harmony with reality than those of other market participants. Entrepreneurship is the general category of such risk-taking in the area of producing goods and services in society. But even in the case of entrepreneurs, there is no way of predicting that those whose abilities in forecasting the future *have been* historically more accurate, *will be* more accurate in the future.

If we are concerned with risk and uncertainty, there is therefore no reason to focus our attention on the political channel of attaining ends. If, in a free society, there were sufficient concern with the risk imposed by some actions of members of a market economy (or market processes or market institutions), institutions would be developed to deal with and alleviate the fear and the risk. The insurance firm is one such institution. We know from market analyses that prices are more stable in those areas where futures markets exist than when they do not. Now "prices" are merely exchange ratios between buyers and sellers of a given commodity. Thus, insurance markets, and futures markets in related fields, would in an unhampered market economy most probably provide the greatest stability of the level of risk in a society, that is: risk as seen through the eyes of a participant of the market economy. Moreover, an unhampered market economy would provide for the optimal degree of present provision for future risk in society. Any intervention by a minimal state would, therefore, *increase* risk, and lead to a sub-optimal allocation devoted to provision for risk. It would lead to a shift *away from* the optimum societal provision for risk. The minimal state would thus create *discoordination* of resources in the vitally important market of provision for risk.

What we have seen here is that risk-calculation cannot be quantitative, but only qualitative: indeed, even then the concept is vague when we deal with the *possible* consequences of precisely *unknown future actions*. Moreover, insofar as there can be calculation of risks, entrepreneurs and other market participants are the only ones we have a right to expect to be successful in their expectations. The unhampered market economy is the only means of setting institutions and processes in society free, to deal effectively with risk and fear. Any movement away from the purely free market, from the choices and decisions of market participants, each with limited know ledge, learning through market processes, is a shift *away from* an optimal situation in the area of expectations of and provision for risk of future harm. In short, in the very process of forming a network of competing market agencies, differentiating each from the other, risk would be provided for tacitly, by the preferences and choices of market participants.

All of this gives us reason to believe that any attempt to prohibit certain actions of independent agencies is *not* morally permissible, and cannot be motivated by any concern with risk or fear.

The problems with the principle of compensation are much more difficult.

Professor Nozick's notion of compensation rests upon the concept of an "indifference curve." The "indifference curve" is one of the saddest plagues to hit economic science since the concept of "macroeconomics" first reared its ugly head. Indifference curve analysis is based on interviewing people about their relative preferences between two or more alternatives. Points of "indifference" between different quantities of certain goods or services are placed on a "map." When many such points of indifference are reached, all placed neatly on a map, the noble indifference curve analyst connects the points by a line, and applies the techniques of mathematics to analyzing varying things.

Very little of this has anything to do with reality. A person's value scale is a constantly fluctuating thing, ranks shifting constantly, sometimes violently. Even if some useful information were imparted by interviewing people in this way, it could not be the basis of any action or expectation on our part. We need not go into this further. Professor Nozick is a new Platonist or Rousseauean, and is really developing a new version of "real" or "rational" interests or values, to supplant our "actual" or concrete interests.

To "compensate" someone, we must place him, according to this view, at a point on his indifference curve at least as high as he would have been without any interference. The point should be made that we are talking about the individual's own view of things, about his evaluations, not any objective state of affairs. It is therefore not possible to judge what would constitute full compensation merely by looking at such states of affairs. We must look at the value hierarchies of the individuals involved.

Professor Nozick, however, does not look at the actual evaluations of individuals. Instead, he *assumes* that everyone prohibited from taking certain risky actions *may be compensated in the same way*, namely, by providing protective services for them through the minimal state. The basis for this assumption is hard to determine. *Why* does provision of protection constitute full compensation? Apparently, because Nozick thinks that it comes close to "copying" the initial situation (objective), where the oppressed victim of the minimal state could still buy alternative protection from independent agencies. But this is entirely unjustified.

What this actually amounts to is saying that *we* are to judge what makes a person "at least as well off," rather than the person himself, through choosing and acting. But this is *paternalism*, which Professor Nozick rejects elsewhere in *Anarchy, State, and Utopia*.

If we take the point of view of the person whose actions are prohibited, then we can concern ourselves only with his own value scale. This places matters in a different light.

The only ways in which we could tell if someone was justly compensated then would be:

4. If they will accept A in exchange for B, i.e. if they exchange one for the other on a free market. This exchange, if it occurs, tells us that A was worth at least as much as B to the relevant party. Obviously, this exchange needs to be made in the absence of force, violence, aggression, or threats of either.
5. If, after the relevant agent has been aggressed against, he agrees to accept A as compensation from an aggressor or aggressor's agent. Again, this acceptance must be in the absence of force, violence, aggression or the threats of them.

Apart from these, there are *no* objective means of measuring justifiable or "full" compensation. The minimal state however makes both of these impossible, for it does threaten such violence or punishment. Moreover, the argument rests on a variant of the "just price" doctrine, applied to compensation. But this is not justified anywhere.

Let us see if we can arrive at the minimal state by some legitimate method of "compensation." In a market society, anyone would have the right to approach anyone who is a client of an independent agency, and buy him off, strike some sort of a bargain with him. A certain number, no doubt, would go along with this. But what of those who will not? We may see the problem by considering a supply and demand chart. In this case, let "S" represent the supply of a given service, namely, foregoing the use of independent agencies and accepting state protection instead. Let "D" represent the demand for this service. Consider that portion of a supply-and-demand chart below the point where exchanges of these sorts would occur. In this situation, *there is no exchange.* The suppliers (those who subscribe to independent agencies) are not willing to settle for anything the demanders (the dominant agency) are willing to offer. Ergo, there is no point of contact between them at which compensation would be both offered and accepted. Even in the absence of threats of force, there would be no settlement. Since there is nothing which the "S's" would accept *before* prohibition, why should one assume that compensation is possible *after* prohibition? If the supply and demand curves have not shifted, the dominant agency cannot offer more (or the non-dominant agencies accept less), than was offered before, and still there can be no meeting of the minds. How, then, can those whose risky activities are prohibited be compensated? How can they be raised to a situation equal in their eyes (on their own value scales) to that in which they would have found themselves without prohibition? It appears that we have reached a dead end.

(We should add that Professor Nozick makes things no less difficult by talking about compensating only those "disadvantaged" by the prohibition. The problems of compensation remain, and there is, to boot, no theory of "disadvantage" offered in *Anarchy, State, and Utopia.*)

There are, in addition, other arguments which might be made against the principle of compensation. Professor Nozick does not deal with the problem of compensating those for whom the creation of the minimal state would be a vast moral and psychic trauma. What just compensation could be offered in *this* case? How could they be raised to a position equal to the situation they were in *before* the creation of the minimal state? Moreover, consider the case of the clients of the dominant agency, A. They may very well benefit (or perceive themselves as benefiting) from the existence of agencies B, C, D..., which they may perceive as a *probable check* on A's activities, fearing that A might supersede its contractual functions in the absence of B, C, D.... Must A, in the transition from dominant agency to minimal state, compensate its own clients after taking those actions which eliminate this benefit? If so, what compensation? If not, why not? Why aren't they as "disadvantaged" as anyone else?

If we cannot assume that providing protection[1] to clients of independent agencies constitutes full compensation, but suppose instead that compensation can be arrived at, perhaps, through higher costs to the agency, then consider the chain of events which begins.

If the minimal state must protect everyone, even those who cannot pay, and if it must compensate those others for prohibiting their risky actions, then this must mean that it will charge its original customers *more* than it would have in the case of the ultraminimal state. But this would, *ipso facto*, increase the number of those who, because of their demand curves, *would have chosen* non-dominant agencies B, C, D... over dominant agency-turned ultraminimal state-turned minimal state. Must the minimal state then protect *them* (or subsidize them) at no charge, or compensate them for prohibiting them from turning to other agencies?

If so, then once again, it must either increase the cost of its service to its remaining customers, or decrease its services. In either case, this *again* produces those who, given the nature and shape of their demand curves, *would have* chosen the non-dominant agencies over the dominant agency. Must *these* then be compensated? If so, then the process leads on, to the point where no one but a few wealthy fanatics advocating a minimal state would be willing to pay for greatly reduced "services" of government. If this happened, there is reason to believe that very soon the minimal state would be thrown into the invisible dustbin of history, which it would richly deserve.

What would more likely happen is that the state would turn instead to its old friend, robbery—otherwise known as "taxation" (which is, incidentally, treated altogether too slightly in Professor Nozick's tome). Hence, one sees the sinister invisible hand leading us from a defense agency...to a dominant agency...to an ultra-minimal state...to a minimal state...to the first trappings of tyranny. Moreover, it is a *private* tyranny, since the agency is privately owned. This being so, what can be our protection against a private company's monopoly on force in society? Surely the objective risks here are immensely greater than those which led to the hesitant creation of the minimal state.

The compensation principle, then, as is presently formulated, leads us into difficulties. Let us then make our remaining points quickly.

Is the process which led to the creation of a minimal state an "invisible hand" process? We maintain that it is not. The reason is that while the state may not be *intended* as the end result, the *state-like action* of prohibiting competition is still the outcome of a *specific decision.* The dominant agency must *decide* to prohibit the actions, and punish offenders. At each step lies an insidious but rather explicit decision. If this is an "invisible hand," it nonetheless packs a mean wallop, threatening to crush liberty in its grasp.

Finally, before we turn the Professor's argument around, what, in our view, *is* the dominant agency justified in doing? Nothing more than punishing those who can be shown to have initiated violence against its citizens or clients, and this only after the fact. Risks of harm in the case of human agencies cannot be calculated except by observing the actions of men (such as those who constitute competing protection agencies) over some considerable period of time. It is by means of their *policies* that we judge the reliability of their procedures, the threat that they do or do not constitute to innocent people, and thus decide how to respond to irresponsible or criminal agencies. There are difficult problems here, but there are more problems in assuming that a dominant agency is more virtuous, more reliable in its procedures or even, of all things, less threatening to the safety and liberty of the people than other agencies. Professor Nozick cannot even prove that those agencies which employ *reliable* procedures should be prohibited from acting along with those which do *not* employ such procedures.

But if that is the case, then the invisible hand returns:

Assume the existence of the minimal state. An agency arises which copies the procedures of the minimal state, allows the state's agents to sit in on its trials, proceedings, and so forth. Under this situation, it *cannot* be alleged that this agency is any more "risky" than the state. If it is still too risky, then we are also justified in saying that the state is too risky, and in prohibiting its activities, providing we compensate those who are disadvantaged by such prohibition. If we follow this course, the result is *anarchy.*

If we do not, then the dominant-agency-turned-minimal-state finds itself competing against an admittedly watched-over competing agency.

But wait: the competing, legally subordinate, spied upon, oppressed second agency finds that it can charge a lower price for its services, since the minimal state is guaranteeing "risk" and has to compensate those who would have patronized agencies using risky procedures. It also has to pay the costs of spying on the new agency, which constitutes a greater capital expenditure.

Since it is only *morally* bound to provide such compensation, it is likely to cease doing so under competitive pressure. This sets two processes in motion: those formerly compensated because they would have chosen agencies other than the state, rush to subscribe to the maverick agency, thus partially reasserting their old preferences.

Alas, another fateful step has also been taken: the once proud minimal state, having ceased compensation, reverts to a mere ultraminimal state.

But the process cannot be stopped. The maverick agency must and does establish a good record, to win clients away from the mere ultraminimal state. It offers a greater variety of services, toys with different prices, and generally becomes a more attractive alternative, all the time letting the state spy on it, bugging its offices, checking its procedures, processes and decisions. Other noble entrepreneurs follow suit. Soon, the once mere ultraminimal state becomes a lowly dominant agency. It finds that the other agencies have established noteworthy records, with safe, non-risky procedures, and stops spying on them, preferring less expensive arrangements instead. Its executives have, alas, grown fat and placid without competition; their calculations of who to protect, how, by what allocation of resources to what ends (gathering information, courts, buildings, prisons, cops, etc.) are adversely affected, since they have taken themselves out of a truly competitive market price system. The dominant agency grows inefficient, when compared to the dynamic, new, improved agencies.

Soon—lo! and behold!—the lowly dominant protection agency becomes simply one agency among many in a market legal system, or disappears altogether. The sinister minimal state is reduced, by a series of morally permissible steps which violate the rights of no one, to at best merely one agency among many. The evil black State apparatus dissolves into the utopia of anarchy. In short, the invisible hand strikes back. Justice is triumphant, and everyone lives happily ever after.

I should like to end with one quotation, from Benjamin R. Tucker, and one paraphrase, from Karl Marx, which express most clearly my own attitudes toward the matters we have been discussing. Tucker pointed to the anarchist definition of the State as the "embodiment of the principle aggression."

> "...we see," he said, "that the State is antagonistic to society; and, society being essential to individual life and development, the conclusion leaps to the eyes that the relation of the State to the individual and of the individual to the State must be one of hostility, enduring till the State shall perish."

And, paraphrasing Marx, we may say that "traditional political philosophers have sought only to explain and justify the State. The point, however, is to abolish it."

Note

1. It is not clear whether this protection will be offered without cost or if the former customers will be forced to pay for it. My interpretation is that the "minimal state" can force clients to pay up to what they would have with another agency (what problems this raises in a world of shifting prices!). "Compensation" would then consist of picking up the tab for the *difference* between the cost with another agency and its own "price."

12

Robert Nozick and the Immaculate Conception of the State

Murray Rothbard

Robert Nozick's *Anarchy, State, and Utopia* (New York: Basic Books, 1974) is an "invisible hand" variant of a Lockean contractarian attempt to justify the State, or at least a minimal State confined to the functions of protection. Beginning with a free-market anarchist state of nature, Nozick portrays the State as emerging, by an invisible hand process that violates no one's rights, first as a dominant protective agency, then to an "ultraminimal state," and then finally to a minimal state.

Before embarking on a detailed critique of the various Nozickian stages, let us consider several grave fallacies in Nozick's conception itself, *each of which* would in itself be sufficient to refute his attempt to justify the State.

First, despite Nozick's attempt (6-9) to cover his tracks, it is highly relevant to see whether Nozick's ingenious logical construction has ever indeed occurred in historical reality: namely, whether any State, or most or all States, have *in fact* evolved in the Nozickian manner. It is a grave defect in itself, when discussing an institution all too well grounded in historical reality, that Nozick has failed to make a single mention or reference to the history of actual States. In fact, there is no evidence whatsoever that any State was founded or developed in the Nozickian manner. On the contrary, the historical evidence cuts precisely the other way: for every State where the facts are available originated by a process of violence, conquest and exploitation: in short, in a manner which Nozick himself would have to admit violated individual rights. As Thomas Paine wrote in *Common Sense*, on the origin of kings and of the State:

> Could we take off the dark covering of antiquity and trace them to their first rise, we should find the first of them nothing better than the principal ruffian of some restless gang; whose savage manners or preeminence in subtlety obtained him the title of chief among plunder as; and who by increasing in power and extending his depredations, overawed the quiet and defenceless to purchase their safety by frequent contributions.[1]

Note that the "contract" involved in Paine's account was of the nature of a coerced "protection racket" rather than anything recognizable to the libertarian as a voluntary agreement.

Since Nozick's justification of existing States—provided they are or become minimal—rests on their alleged immaculate conception, and since no such State exists, then none of them *can* be justified, *even* if they should later become minimal. To go further, we can say that, *at best*, Nozick's model can *only* justify a State which indeed did develop by his invisible hand method. Therefore it is incumbent upon Nozick to join anarchists in calling for the abolition of all existing States, and *then* to sit back and wait for his alleged invisible hand to operate. The only minimal State, then, which Nozick *at best* can justify is one that will develop out of a future anarcho-capitalist society.

Secondly, *even if* an existing State had been immaculately conceived, this would *still* not justify its present existence. A basic fallacy is endemic to all social contract theories of the State, namely, that *any* contract based on a promise is binding and enforceable. If, then, *everyone*—in itself of course a heroic assumption—in a state of nature surrendered all or some of his rights to a State, the social contract theorists consider this promise to be binding forevermore. A correct theory of contracts, however, termed by Williamson Evers the "title transfer" theory, states that the only valid (and therefore binding) contract is one that surrenders what is, in fact, philosophically *alienable*, and that *only* specific titles to property are so alienable, so that their ownership can be ceded to someone else. While, on the contrary, *other* attributes of man: specifically, his self-ownership over his own will and body, and the *rights* to person and property which stem from that self-ownership, are "inalienable" and therefore cannot be surrendered in a binding contract. If no one, then, can surrender his own will, his body, or his rights in an enforceable contract, *a fortiori* he cannot surrender the persons or the rights of his posterity. This is what the Founding Fathers meant by the concept of rights as being "inalienable," or, as George Mason expressed it in his Virginia Declaration of Rights:

> ...all men are by nature equally free and independent, and have certain inherent natural rights, of which when they enter into a state of society, they cannot, by any compact, deprive or divest their posterity.[2]

Or, as Evers writes, "all philosophical defenses of human rights to life, liberty, and estates...are founded upon the natural fact that each human is the proprietor of his own will. To take rights like those of property and contractual freedom that are based on a foundation of the absolute self-ownership of the will and then to use those derived rights to destroy their own foundation is philosophically invalid."[3]

Thus, we have seen (1) that no existing State has been immaculately conceived—quite the contrary; (2) that therefore the only minimal State that could *possibly* be justified is one that would emerge *after* a free-market anarchist world had been established; (3) that therefore Nozick, on his own grounds, should become an anarchist and then wait for the Nozickian invisible hand to operate afterward, and finally (4) that *even* if any State had been founded immaculately, the fallacies of social contract theory would mean that no present State, even a minimal one, would be justified.

Let us now proceed to examine the Nozickian stages, particularly the alleged necessity as well as the morality of the ways in which the various stages develop out of the preceding ones. Nozick begins by assuming that each anarchist protective agency acts morally and non-aggressively, that is, "attempts in good faith to act within the limits of Locke's law of Nature" (17).

First, Nozick assumes that each protective agency would require that each of its clients renounce the right of private retaliation against aggression, by refusing to protect them against counter-retaliation (15). Perhaps, perhaps not. This would be up to the various protection agencies, acting on the market, and is certainly not self-evident. It is certainly possible if not probable that they would be out competed by other agencies that do not restrict their clients in that way.

Nozick then proceeds to discuss disputes between clients of different protection agencies. He offers three scenarios, on how they might proceed. But two of these scenarios (and part of the third) involve physical battles between the agencies. In the first place, these scenarios contradict Nozick's own assumption of good-faith, non-aggressive behavior *by each of* his agencies, since, in any combat, clearly at least one of the agencies would be committing aggression. Furthermore, economically, it would be absurd to expect that the protective agencies would battle each other physically; such warfare would alienate clients and be highly expensive to boot. It is absurd to think that, on the market, protective agencies would fail to agree in advance on private appeals courts or arbitrators whom they would turn to, in order to resolve any dispute. Indeed, a vital part of the protective or judicial service which a private agency or court would offer to its clients would be that it had agreements to turn disputes over to a certain appeals court or a certain arbitrator or group of arbitrators.

Let us turn then to Nozick's crucial scenario 3, in which he writes that "the two agencies...agree to resolve peacefully those cases about which they reach differing judgments. They agree to set up, and abide by the decisions of, some third judge or court to which they can turn when their respective judgments differ. (Or they might establish rules determining which agency has jurisdiction under which circumstances.)" (16) So far so good. But then comes a giant leap: "Thus emerges a system of appeals courts and agreed upon rules... Though different agencies operate, there is one unified federal judicial system of which they are all components." I submit that the "thus" is totally illegitimate, and that the rest is a *non sequitur*. The fact that every protective agency will have agreements with every other to submit disputes to particular appeals courts or arbitrators does not imply "one unified federal judicial system." On the contrary, there may well be, and probably would be, hundreds, even thousands, of arbitrators or appeals judges who would be selected, and there is no need to consider them part of one "judicial system." There is no need, for example, to envision or to establish one unified Supreme Court to decide upon disputes. Since every dispute involves only two parties, there need be only one third party appeals judge or arbitrator; there are in the United States, at the present time, for example, over 23,000 professional arbitrators, and presumably there would be many thousands more if the present government court system were to be abolished. Each one of these arbitrators could serve an appeals or arbitration function.

Nozick claims that out of anarchy there would inevitably emerge, as by an invisible hand, one *dominant* protection agency in each territorial area, in which "almost all the persons" in that area are included. But we have seen that his major support for that conclusion is totally invalid. Nozick's other arguments for this proposition are equally invalid. He writes, for example, that "unlike other goods that are comparatively evaluated, maximal competing protective services cannot exist" (17). Why *cannot*, surely a strong term? First, because "the nature of the service brings different agencies...into violent conflict with each other" rather than just competing for customers. But we have seen that this conflict assumption is incorrect, first, on Nozick's own grounds of each agency acting non-aggressively, and, second, on his own scenario 3, that each will enter into agreements with the others for peaceful settlement of disputes. Nozick's second argument for this contention is that "since the worth of the less than maximal product declines disproportionately with the number who purchase the maximal product, customers will not stably settle for the lesser good, and competing companies are caught in a declining spiral." But *why?* Nozick is here making statements about the economics of a protection market which are totally unsupported. *Why* is there such an "economy of scale" in the protection business that Nozick feels will lead inevitably to a near-natural monopoly in each geographical area? This is scarcely self-evident. On the contrary, all the facts—and here the empirical facts of contemporary and past history are again directly relevant—cut precisely the other way. There are, as was mentioned above, tens of thousands of professional arbitrators in the U.S.; there are also tens of thousands of lawyers and judges, and a large number of private protection agencies that supply guards, night-watchmen, etc. with no sign whatsoever of a geographical natural monopoly in any of these fields. Why then for protection agencies under anarchism?

And, if we look at approximations to anarchist court and protective systems in history, we again see a great deal of evidence of the falsity of Nozick's contention. For hundreds of years, the fairs of Champagne were the major international trade mart in Europe; a number of courts, by merchants, nobles, the Church, etc. competed for customers; not only did no one dominant agency ever emerge, but they did not even feel the need for appeals courts. For a thousand years ancient Ireland, until the Cromwellian conquest, enjoyed a system of numerous jurists and schools of jurists, and numerous protection agencies, which competed within geographical areas without any one becoming dominant. After the fall of Rome, various coexisting barbarian tribes peacefully adjudicated their disputes *within* each area, with each tribesman coming under his own law, and with agreed-upon peaceful adjudications between these courts and laws. Furthermore, in these days of modern technology and low-cost transportation and communication, it would be even easier to compete across geographical boundaries; the "Metropolitan,"

"Equitable," and "Prudential" protection agencies, for example, could easily maintain branch offices over a large geographical area.

In fact, there is a far better case for *insurance* being a natural monopoly than protection, since a large insurance pool would tend to reduce premiums; and yet, it is clear that there is a great deal of insurance competition and that there would be more if it were not restricted by state regulation.

The Nozick contention that a dominant agency would develop in each geographical area, then, is an example of an illegitimate *a priori* attempt to decide what the free market would do, and it is an attempt that flies in the face of concrete historical and institutional knowledge. Certainly, a dominant protective agency *could conceivably* emerge in a particular geographical area, but it is not very likely. And, as Roy Childs points out in his critique of Nozick, even if it did, it would not likely be a "unified federal system." Childs also correctly points out that it is no more legitimate to lump all protective services together and call it a unified monopoly, than it would be to be to lump all the food growers and producers on the market together and say that they have a collective "system" or "monopoly" of food production.[4]

Furthermore, law and the State are both conceptually and historically separable, and law would develop in an anarchistic market society without any form of State. Specifically, the concrete *form* of anarchist legal institutions—judges, arbitrators, procedural methods for resolving disputes, etc.—would indeed grow by a market-invisible hand process, while the basic Law Code (requiring that no one invade any one else's person and property) would have to be agreed upon by all the judicial agencies, just as all the competing judges once agreed to apply and extend the basic principles of the customary or common law.[5] But the latter, again, would imply no unified legal system or dominant protective agency. Any agencies that transgressed the basic libertarian code would be open outlaws and aggressors, and Nozick himself concedes that, lacking legitimacy, such outlaw agencies would probably not do very well in an anarchist society (17).

Let us now assume that a dominant protective agency has come into being, as unlikely as that may be. How then do we proceed, without violation of anyone's rights, to Nozick's ultraminimal state? On pages 55-56 Nozick writes of the plight of the dominant protective agency who sees the independents, with their unreliable procedures, rashly and unreliably retaliating against its own clients. Shouldn't the dominant agency have the right to defend its clients against these rash actions? Nozick claims that the dominant agency *has* a right to prohibit risky procedures against its clients, and that this prohibition *thereby* establishes the ultraminimal state," in which one agency coercively prohibits all other agencies from enforcing the rights of individuals.

There are two problems here at the very beginning. In the first place, what has happened to the peaceful resolution of disputes that marked scenario 3? Why can't the dominant agency and the independents agree to arbitrate or adjudicate their disputes, preferably in advance? Ahh, but here we encounter

Nozick's curious "thus" clause, which incorporated such voluntary agreements into one "unified federal judicial system": In short, if every time that the dominant agency and the independents work out their disputes in advance, Nozick then *calls this* "one agency," then by definition he precludes the peaceful settlement of disputes *without* a move onward to the compulsory monopoly of the ultraminimal state.

But suppose, for the sake of continuing the argument, that we grant Nozick his question-begging definition of "one agency." Would the dominant agency still be justified in outlawing competitors? Certainly not, even if it wishes to preclude fighting. For what of the many cases in which the independents are enforcing justice for their *own* clients, and have nothing to do with the clients of the dominant agency? By what conceivable right does the dominant agency step in to outlaw peaceful arbitration and adjudication between the independents' own clients, with no impact on *its* clients? The answer is no right whatsoever, so that the dominant agency, in outlawing competitors, is aggressing against their rights, and against the rights of their actual or potential customers. Furthermore, as Roy Childs emphasizes, this decision to enforce their monopoly is scarcely the action of an invisible hand; it is a *conscious*, highly visible decision, and must be treated accordingly.[6]

The dominant agency, Nozick claims, has the right to bar "risky" activities engaged by independent. But what then of the independents? Do *they* have right to bar the risky activities of the dominant? And must not a war of all against all again ensue in violation of scenario 3 and also necessarily engaging in some aggression against rights along the way? Where, then, are the moral activities of the state of nature assumed by Nozick all along? Furthermore, as Childs points out, what about the risk involved in having a compulsory monopoly protection agency? As Childs writes: "What is to check its power? What happens in the event of its assuming even more powers? Since it has a monopoly, any disputes over its functions are solved and judged exclusively by itself. Since careful prosecution procedures are costly there is every reason to assume that it will become less careful without competition and, again, only it can judge the legitimacy of its own procedures, as Nozick explicitly tells us."[7]

Competing agencies, whether the competition be real or potential, not only insure high-quality protection at the lowest cost, as compared to a compulsory monopoly, but they also provide the genuine checks and balances of the market against any one agency yielding to the temptations of being an "outlaw," that is, of aggressing against the persons and properties of its clients or non-clients. If one agency among many becomes outlaw, there are others around to do battle against it on behalf of the rights of their clients; but who is there to protect anyone against the State, whether ultraminimal or minimal? If we may be permitted to return once more to the historical record, the grisly annals of the crimes and murders of the State throughout history give one very little confidence in the non-risky nature of *its* activities. I submit that the risks of State tyranny are far greater than the risks of worrying about one or two unreliable procedures of competing defense agencies.

But this is scarcely all. For once it is permitted to proceed beyond defense against an overt act of actual aggression, once one can use force against someone because of his "risky" activities, then the sky is the limit, in short there is then virtually no limit to aggression against the rights of others. Once permit someone's "fear" of the "risky" activities of others to lead to coercive action, then *any* tyranny becomes justified, and Nozick's "minimal" state quickly becomes the "maximal" State. I maintain, in fact, that there is no Nozickian stopping point from his ultraminimal state to the maximal, totalitarian state. There is no stopping point to so-called preventive restraint or detention. Surely Nozick's rather grotesque suggestion of "compensation" in the form of "resort detention centers" is scarcely sufficient to ward off the specter of totalitarianism (142 ff). A few examples: Perhaps the largest criminal class in the United States today are teenage black males. The risk of this class committing crime is far greater than any other age, gender, or color group. Why not, then, lock up all teenage black males until they are old enough for the risk to diminish? And then I suppose we could compensate them by giving them healthful food, clothing, playgrounds, and teaching them a useful trade in the "resort" detention camp. If not, why not? Example: the most important argument for Prohibition was the undoubted fact that people commit significantly more crimes, more acts of negligence on the highways, when under the influence of alcohol than when cold sober. So why not prohibit alcohol, and thereby reduce risk and fear, perhaps "compensating" the unfortunate victims of the law by free, tax-financed supplies of healthful grape juice? Or the infamous Dr. Arnold Hutschneker's plan of "identifying" allegedly future criminals in the grade schools, and then locking them away for suitable brainwashing? If not, why not? In each case, I submit that there is only one why not, and this should be no news to libertarians who presumably believe in inalienable individual rights: namely that no one has the *right* to coerce anyone not himself directly engaged in an *overt* act of aggression against rights. Any loosening of this criterion, to include coercion against remote "risks," is to sanction impermissible aggression against the rights of others. Any loosening of this criterion furthermore, is a passport to unlimited despotism. Any state founded on *these* principles has been conceived, not immaculately without interfering with anyone's rights, but by a savage act of rape.

Thus, even if risk were measurable, even if Nozick could provide us with a cutoff point of when activities are "too" risky, his rite of passage from dominant agency to ultraminimal state would still be aggressive, invasive, and illegitimate. But, furthermore, as Childs has pointed out, there is no way to measure (the probability of) such "risk," let alone the fear, both of which are purely subjective.[8] The only risk that can be measured is in those rare situations—such as a lottery or a roulette wheel—where the individual events are strictly homogeneous, and repeated a very large number of times. In almost all cases of actual human action, this condition does not apply, and so there is no measurable cutoff point of risk.

This brings us to Williamson Evers' extremely useful concept of the "proper assumption of risk." We live in a world of ineluctable and unmeasurable varieties of uncertainty and risk. In a free society, possessing full individual rights, the proper assumption of risk is by each individual over his own person and his justly owned property. No one, then, can have the right to coerce anyone else into reducing *his* risks; such coercive assumption is aggression and invasion to be properly stopped and punished by the legal system. Of course, in a free society, anyone may take steps to reduce risks that do not invade someone else's rights and property; for example, by taking out insurance, hedging operations, performance bonding, etc. But all of this is voluntary, and none involves either taxation or compulsory monopoly. And, as Roy Childs states, any coercive intervention in the market's provision for risk shifts the societal provision for risk *away from* the optimal, and hence *increases* risk to society.[9]

One example of Nozick's sanctioning aggression against property rights is his concern (55*n*) with the private landowner who is surrounded by enemy landholders who won't let him leave. To the libertarian reply that any rational landowner would have first purchased access rights from surrounding owners, Nozick brings up the problem of being surrounded by such a set of numerous enemies that he *still* would not be able to go anywhere. But the point is that this is not simply a problem of landownership. Not only in the free society, but even now, suppose that one man is so hated by the whole world that no one will trade with him or allow him on their property. Well, then, the only reply is that this is his own proper assumption of risk. Any attempt to break that voluntary boycott by physical coercion is illegitimate aggression against the boycotters' rights. This fellow had better find some friends, or at least purchase allies, as quickly as possible.

How then does Nozick proceed from his "ultraminimal" to his "minimal" State? He maintains that the ultraminimal state is morally bound to "compensate" the prohibited, would-be purchasers of the services of independents by supplying them with protective services—and *hence* the "night watchman" or minimal state. In the first place, this decision too is a conscious and visible one, and scarcely the process of an invisible hand. But, more importantly, Nozick's principle of compensation is in even worse philosophical shape, if that is possible, than his theory of risk. For, first, compensation, in the theory of punishment, is simply a method of trying to recompense the victim of crime; it must in no sense be considered a moral sanction for crime itself. Nozick asks (57) whether property rights mean that people are permitted to perform invasive actions "provided that they compensate the person whose boundary has been crossed?" In contrast to Nozick, the answer must be no, in every case. As Randy Barnett states, in his critique of Nozick, "Contrary to the principle of compensation, all violations of rights are prohibited. That's what rights means." And, "while voluntarily paying a purchase price makes an exchange permissible, compensation does not make an aggression permissible or justified."[10] Rights must not be transgressed, period, compensation being simply one method of restitution or punishment after the fact; I must not be permitted to cavalierly invade someone's home and break his furniture, simply because I am prepared to "compensate" him afterward.[11]

Secondly, there is no way of knowing, in any case, what the compensation is supposed to be. Nozick's theory depends on people's utility scales being constant, measurable, and knowable to outside observers, none of which is the case.[12] Austrian subjective value theory shows us that people's utility scales are always subject to change, and that they can neither be measured nor known to any outside observer. If I buy a newspaper for 15 cents, than *all* we can say about my value-scale is that, at the moment of purchase the newspaper was worth more to me than the 15 cents, and that is all. That valuation can change tomorrow, and no other part of my utility scale is knowable to others at all. (A minor point: Nozick's pretentious use of the "indifference curve" concept is not even necessary for his case, and it adds still further fallacies: namely, that indifference is *never* by definition exhibited in action, in actual exchanges, and is therefore unknowable and objectively meaningless, and because an indifference curve postulates two commodity axes—and *what* are the axes to Nozick's alleged curve?)[13] But if there is no way of knowing what will make a person as well off as before any particular change, then there is no way for an outside observer, such as the minimal state, to discover how much compensation is needed. The Chicago School tries to resolve this problem by simply assuming that a person's utility loss is measured by the money-price of the loss; so if someone slashes my painting, and outside appraisers determine that I could have sold it for $2000 then that is my proper compensation. But first, no one really knows what the market price would have been, since tomorrow's market may well differ from yesterday's, and second and more important, my psychic attachment to the painting may he worth far more to me than the money price, and there is *no way* for anyone to determine what that psychic attachment might he worth: *asking* is invalid since there is nothing to prevent me from lying grossly in order to drive up the "compensation."[14]

Moreover, Nozick says nothing about the dominant agency compensating *its* clients for the shutting down of *their* opportunities in being able to shift their purchases to competing agencies. Yet their opportunities are shut off by compulsion, and furthermore, they may well perceive themselves as benefiting from the competitive check on the possible tyrannical impulses of the dominant agency. But *how* is the extent of such compensation to be determined? Furthermore, if compensation to the deprived clients of the dominant agency is forgotten by Nozick, what about the dedicated anarchistic state of nature? What about their trauma at seeing the far from immaculate emergence of the State? Are *they* to he compensated for their horror at seeing the State emerge? And *how much* are they to he paid? In fact, the existence of only *one* fervent anarchist who *could not* be compensated for the psychic trauma inflicted on him by the emergence of the State, is enough by itself to scuttle Nozick's allegedly non-invasive model for the origin of the minimal state. For that absolutist anarchist, no amount of compensation would suffice to assuage his grief.

This brings us to another flaw in the Nozickian scheme: the curious fact that the compensation paid by the dominant agency is paid, not in cash, hut in the extension of its sometimes dubious services to the clients of other agencies. And yet, advocates of the compensation principle have demonstrated that *cash*—which leaves the recipients free to buy whatever they wish—is far better from their point of view than any compensation in kind. Yet, Nozick, in postulating the extension of protection as the form of compensation, never considers the cash payment alternative. In fact, for the anarchist, this form of "compensation"—the institution of the State itself—is a grisly and ironic one indeed. As Childs forcefully points out: Nozick "wishes to prohibit us from turning to any of a number of competing agencies, other than the dominant protection agency. What is he willing to offer us as *compensation* for being so prohibited? He is generous to a fault. He will give us nothing less than *the State.* Let me be the first to publicly reject this admittedly generous offer. But...the point is, we can't reject it. It is foisted upon us whether we like it or not, whether we are willing to accept the state as compensation or not."[15]

Furthermore, there is no warrant whatever, even on Nozick's own terms, for the minimal state's compensating every one uniformly, as he postulates; surely, there is no likelihood of everyone's value-scales being identical. But then *how* are the differences to be discovered and differential compensation paid?

Even confining ourselves to Nozick's compensated people—the former or current would-be clients of competing agencies: who are they? How can they be found? For, on Nozick's own terms, only such actual or would-be competing clients need compensation. But how does one distinguish, as proper compensation must, between those who have been deprived of their desired independent agencies and who therefore deserve compensation, and those who wouldn't have patronized the independents anyway and who therefore don't need compensation? By not making such distinctions, Nozick's minimal state doesn't even engage in proper compensation on Nozick's own terms.

Childs raises another excellent point on Nozick's own prescribed form of compensation—the dire consequences for the minimal state of the fact that the payment of such compensation will necessarily raise the costs, and therefore the prices charged, by the dominant agency. As Childs states:

> If the minimal state must protect everyone, even those who cannot pay, and if it must compensate those others for prohibiting their risky actions, then this must mean that it will charge its original customers *more* than it would have in the case of the ultraminimal state. But this, would, ipso facto, increase the number of those who,

> because of their demand curves *would have chosen* non-dominant agencies...over dominant agency-turned ultraminimal state-turned minimal state. Must the minimal state then protect *them* at no charge, or compensate them for prohibiting them from turning to the other agencies? If so, then once again it must either increase its price to its remaining customers, or decrease its services. In either case this again produces those who, given the nature and shape of their demand curves, *would have* chosen the non-dominant agencies over the dominant agency. Must *these* then be compensated? If so, then the process leads on, to the point where no one but a few wealthy fanatics avoiding a minimal state would be willing to pay for greatly reduced services. If this happened there is reason to believe that very soon the minimal state would be thrown into the invisible dustbin of history, which it would, I suggest, richly deserve.[16]

A tangential but important point on compensation: adopting Locke's unfortunate "proviso," on homesteading property rights in unused land, Nozick declares that no one may appropriate unused land if the remaining population who desire access to land are "worse off" (178 ff.). But again: how do we know if they are worse off or not? In fact, Locke's proviso may lead to outlawry of *all* private ownership of land, since one can always say that the reduction of available land leaves everyone else, who could have appropriated the land, worse off. In fact, there is no way of measuring or knowing when they are worse off or not. And even if they are, I submit that that, too, is their proper assumption of risk. Everyone should have the right to appropriate as his property previously unowned land or other resources. If latecomers are worse off, well then that is their proper assumption of risk in this free and uncertain world. There is no more vast frontier in the United States, and there is no point in crying over the fact. In fact, we can generally achieve as much "access" as we want to these resources by paying a market price for them, but even if the owners refused to sell or rent, that should be their right in a free society. Even Locke could nod once in a while.[17]

We come now to another crucial point: that Nozick's presumption that he can outlaw risky activities upon compensation rests on his contention that no one has the right to engage in "non-productive" (including risky) activities or exchanges, and that therefore they can legitimately be prohibited.[18] For Nozick concedes that if the risky activities of others were legitimate, then prohibition and compensation would not be valid, and that we would then be "required instead to negotiate or contract with them whereby they agree not to do the risky act in question. Why wouldn't we have to offer them an incentive, or hire them, or bribe them, to refrain from doing the act?" (83-84). In short, if not for Nozick's fallacious theory of illegitimate "non-productive" activities, he would have to concede people's rights to engage in such activities, the prohibition of risk and compensation principles would fall to the ground, and neither Nozick's ultraminimal nor his minimal state could be justified.

And here we come to what we might call Nozick's "drop dead" principle. For his criterion of a "productive" exchange is one where each party is better off than if the other did not exist at all; whereas a "non-productive" exchange is one where one party would be better off if the other dropped dead. Thus: "If I pay you for not harming me, I gain nothing from you that I wouldn't posses if either you didn't exist at all or existed without having anything to do with me" (84). Nozick's "principle of compensation" maintains that a "non-productive" activity can be prohibited provided that the person is compensated by the benefit he was forced to forego from the imposition of the prohibition.

Let us then see how Nozick applies his "non-productive" and compensation criteria to the problem of blackmail. Nozick tries to rehabilitate the outlawry of blackmail by asserting that "non-productive" contracts should be illegal, and that a blackmail contract is non-productive because a blackmailee is worse off because of the blackmailer's very existence (84-86). In short, if blackmailer Smith dropped dead, Jones (the blackmailee) would be better off. Or, to put it another way, Jones is paying not for Smith's making him better off, but for *not* making him *worse off.* But surely the latter is *also* a productive contract, because Jones is still better off making the exchange than he *would have been* if the exchange were not made.

But this theory gets Nozick into very muddy waters indeed, some, though by no means all of which, he recognizes. He concedes, for example, that his reason for outlawing blackmail would force him also to outlaw the following contract: Brown comes to Green, his next-door neighbor, with the following proposition: I intend to build such-and-such a pink building on my property (which he knows that Green will detest). I *won't* build this building, however, if you pay me *x* amount of money. Nozick concedes that this, too, would have to be illegal in his schema, because Green would be paying Brown for not being worse off, and hence the contract would be "non- productive." In essence, that Green would be better off if Brown dropped dead. It is difficult, however, for a libertarian to square such outlawry with any plausible theory of property rights. In analogy with the blackmail example above, furthermore, Nozick concedes that it *would* be legal, in his schema, for Green, on finding out about Brown's projected pink building, to come to Brown and offer to pay him not to go ahead. But why would such an exchange *be* "productive" just because Green made the offer?[19] What difference does it make *who* makes the offer in this situation? Wouldn't Green *still* be better off if Brown dropped dead? And again, following the analogy, *would* Nozick make it illegal for Brown to refuse Green's offer and *then* ask for more money? Why? Or, again, would Nozick make it illegal for Brown to subtly let Green know about the projected pink building and then let nature take its course: say, by advertising in a newspaper about the building and sending Green the clipping? Couldn't this be taken as an act of courtesy? And why should merely *advertising* something be illegal? Clearly, Nozick's case becomes ever more flimsy as we consider the implications.

Furthermore, Nozick has not at all considered the manifold implications of his "drop dead" principle. If he is saying, as he seems to, that A is illegitimately "coercing" B if B is better off should A drop dead, then consider the following case: Brown and Green are competing at auction for the same painting which they desire. They are the last two customers left. Wouldn't Green be better off if Brown dropped dead? Isn't Brown therefore illegally coercing Green in some way, and therefore shouldn't Brown's participation in the auction be outlawed? Or, *per contra*, isn't Green coercing Brown in the same manner and shouldn't *Green's* participation in the auction be outlawed? If not, why not? Or, suppose that Brown and Green are competing for the hand of the same girl; wouldn't each be better off if the other dropped dead, and shouldn't either or both's participation in the courtship therefore be outlawed? The ramifications are virtually endless.

Nozick, furthermore, gets himself into a deeper quagmire when he adds that a blackmail exchange is not "productive" because outlawing the exchange makes one party (the blackmailee) no worse off. But that of course is not true: as Professor Block has pointed out, outlawing a blackmail contract means that the blackmailer has no further incentive *not* to disseminate the unwelcome, hitherto secret information about the blackmailed party. However, after twice asserting that the victim would be "no worse off" from the outlawing of the blackmail exchange, Nozick immediately and inconsistently concedes that "people value a blackmailer's silence, and pay for it." In that case, if the blackmailer is prohibited from charging for his silence, he need not maintain it and hence the blackmail—payer would indeed be worse off because of the prohibition! Nozick adds, without supporting the assertion, that "his being silent is not a productive activity." Why not? Apparently because "His victims would be as well off if the blackmailer did not exist at all..." Back again to the "drop dead" principle. But then, reversing his field once more, Nozick adds—inconsistently with his own assertion that the blackmailer's silence is not productive—that "On the view we take here, a seller of such silence could legitimately charge only for what he forgoes by silence...includ(ing) the payments others would make to him to reveal the information." Nozick adds that while a blackmailer may charge the amount of money he would have received for revealing the information, "he may not charge the best price he could get from the purchaser of his silence" (85-86).

Thus, Nozick, waffling inconsistently between outlawing blackmail and permitting only a price that the blackmailer could have received from selling the information, has mired himself into an unsupportable concept of a "just price." *Why* is it only licit to charge the payment foregone? Why *not* charge whatever the blackmailee is willing to pay? In the first place, both transactions are voluntary, and within the purview of both parties' property rights. Secondly, *no one knows*, either conceptually or in practice, what price the blackmailer could have gotten for his secret on the market. No one can predict a market price in advance of the actual exchange. Thirdly, the blackmailer may not only be gaining money from the exchange; he also possibly gains psychic satisfaction—he may dislike the blackmailee, or he may enjoy selling secrets and therefore he may "earn" from the sale to a third party more than just a monetary return. Here, in fact, Nozick gives away the case by conceding that a blackmailer "who *delights* in selling secrets may charge differently" (86n). But, in that case, what outside legal enforcement agency will ever be able to discover *to what extent* the blackmailer delights in revealing secrets and therefore what price he may legally charge to the "victim"? More broadly, it is conceptually impossible ever to discover the existence or the extent of his subjective delight or of any other psychic factors that may enter into his value-scale and therefore into his exchange.

And fourthly, suppose that we take Nozick's worst case, a blackmailer who could not find any monetary price for his secret. But, if blackmail were outlawed either totally or in Nozick's "just price" version, the thwarted blackmailer would simply disseminate the secrets for free—would *give away* the information (Block's "gossip or blabbermouth"). In doing so, the blackmailer would simply be exercising his right to use his body, in this case his freedom of speech. There can be no "just price" for restricting this right, for it has no objectively measurable value.[20] Its value is subjective to the blackmailer, and his right may not be justly restricted. And furthermore, the "protected" victim is, in this case, surely worse off as a result of the prohibition against blackmail.[21]

We must conclude, then, with modern, post-medieval economic theory, that the *only* "just price" for any transaction is the price voluntarily agreed upon by the two parties. Furthermore and more broadly, we must also join modern economic theory in labeling *all* voluntary exchanges as "productive," and as making both parties better off from making the exchange. Any good or service voluntarily purchased by a user or consumer benefits him and is therefore "productive" from his point of view. Hence, all of Nozick's attempts to justify either the outlawing of blackmail or the setting of some sort of just blackmail price (as well as for any other contracts that sell someone's inaction) fall completely to the ground. But this means, too, that his attempt to justify the prohibition of *any* "non-productive" activities—including risk—fails as well, and hence fails, on *this ground alone*, Nozick's attempt to justify his ultraminimal (as well as his minimal) state.

In applying his theory to the risky, fear inducing "non-productive" activities of independent agencies which allegedly justify the imposition of the coercive monopoly of the ultraminimal state, Nozick concentrates on his asserted "procedural rights" of each individual, which he states is the "right to have his guilt determined by the least dangerous of the known procedures for ascertaining guilt, that is, by the one having the lowest probability of finding an innocent party guilty" (96). Here Nozick adds to the usual *substantive* natural rights—to the use of one's person and justly acquired property unimpaired by violence—alleged "procedural rights," or rights to certain procedures for determining innocence or guilt. But one vital distinction between a genuine and a spurious "right" is that the former requires no positive action by anyone except non-interference.

Hence, a right to person and property is not dependent on time, space or the number or wealth of other people in the society; Crusoe can have such a right against Friday as can anyone in an advanced industrial society. On the other hand, an asserted right "to a living wage" is a spurious one, since fulfilling it requires positive action on the part of other people; as well as the existence of enough people with a high enough wealth or income to satisfy such a claim. Hence such a "right" cannot be independent of time, place, or the number or condition of other persons in society. But surely a "right" to a less risky procedure requires positive action from enough people of specialized skills to fulfill such a claim; hence it is not a genuine right. Furthermore, such a right cannot be deduced from the basic right of self-ownership. On the contrary, everyone has the absolute right to defend his person and property against invasion. The criminal has no right, on the other hand, to defend his ill-gotten gains. But what *procedure* will be adopted by any group of people to defend their rights—whether, for example, personal self-defense, or the use of courts or arbitration agencies—depends on the knowledge and skill of the individuals concerned. Presumably, a free market will tend to lead to most people choosing to defend themselves with those private institutions and protection agencies whose procedures will attract the most agreement from people in society. People who will be willing to abide by their decisions as the most practical way of approximating the determination of *who*, in particular cases, are innocent and who are guilty. But these are matters of utilitarian discovery on the market as to the most efficient means of arriving at self-defense, and do not imply any such fallacious concepts as "procedural rights."[22]

Finally, in a scintillating *tour de force*, Roy Childs, after demonstrating that each of Nozick's stages to the State is accomplished by a visible decision rather than by an "invisible hand," stands Nozick on his head by demonstrating that the invisible hand, *on Nozick's own terms*, would lead straight back from his minimal State to anarchism. Childs writes:

> Assume the existence of the minimal state. An agency arises which copies the procedures of the minimal state, allows the state to sit in on its trials, proceedings, and so forth. Under this situation, it cannot be alleged that this agency is any more "risky" than the state. If it is still too risky, then we are also justified in saying that the state is too risky, and in prohibiting its activities, providing we compensate those who are disadvantaged by such prohibition. If we follow this course, the result is anarchy.
>
> If not, then the "dominant agency"-turned minimal state finds itself competing against an admittedly watched-over competing agency. But wait: the competing, spied upon, oppressed second agency finds that it can charge a lower price for its services, since the minimal state has to compensate those who would have patronized agencies using risky procedures. It also has to pay the costs of spying on the new agency.
>
> Since it is only *morally* bound to provide such compensation, it is likely to cease doing so under severe economic pressure. This sets two processes in motion: those formerly compensated because they would have chosen other agencies over the state, rush to subscribe to the maverick agency, thus reasserting their old preferences. Also, another fateful step has been taken: the once proud minimal state, having ceased compensation, reverts to a lowly ultraminimal state.

> But the process cannot be slopped. The maverick agency must and does establish a good record, to win clients away from the ultraminimal state. It offers a greater variety of services, toys with different prices, and generally becomes a more attractive alternative, all the time letting the state spy on it, checking its processes and procedures. Other noble entrepreneurs follow suit. Soon, the once lowly ultraminimal state becomes a mere dominant agency, finding that the other agencies have established a noteworthy record, with safe, non-risky procedures, and stops spying on them, preferring less expensive agreements instead. Its executives have, alas!, grown fat and placid without competition; their calculations of who to protect, how by what allocation of resources to what ends...are adversely affected by their having formerly removed themselves out of a truly competitive market price system. The dominant agency grows inefficient, when compared to the new, dynamic, improved agencies.
>
> Soon—lo! and behold—the mere dominant protection agency becomes simply one agency among many in a market legal network. The sinister minimal state is reduced, by a series of morally permissible steps which violate the rights of no one, to merely one agency among many. In short, the invisible hand strikes back.[23]

Some final brief but important points. Nozick, in common with all other limited government, *laissez-faire* theorists, has no theory of taxation: of how much it shall be, of who shall pay it, of what kind it should be, etc. Indeed, taxation is scarcely mentioned in Nozick's progression of stages toward his minimal state. It would seem that Nozick's minimal state could only impose taxation on the clients it *would* have had before it became a state, and not on the would-be clients of competing agencies. But clearly, the existing State taxes *everyone*, with no regard whatever for who they *would* have patronized, and indeed it is difficult to see how they could try to find and separate these different hypothetical groups.

Nozick also, in common with his limited government colleagues, treats "protection"—at least when preferred by his minimal state—as one collective lump. But *how much* protection shall be supplied, and at what cost of resources? And what criteria shall decide? For after all, we can *conceive* of almost the entire national product being devoted to supplying each person with a tank and an armed guard; or, we can conceive of only one policeman and one judge in an entire country. Who decides on the degree of protection, and on what criterion? For, in contrast, all the goods and services on the *private* market are produced on the basis of relative demands and costs to the consumers on the market. But there is no such criterion for protection in the minimal or any other State.

Moreover, as Childs points out, the minimal State that Nozick attempts to justify is a State *owned* by a private, dominant firm. There is still no explanation or justification in Nozick for the modern form of voting, democracy, checks and balances, etc.[24]

Finally, a grave flaw permeates the entire discussion of rights and government in the Nozick volume: that, as a Kantian intuitionist, he *has no* theory of rights. Rights are simply emotionally intuited, with no groundwork in natural law—in the nature of man or of the universe. At bottom, Nozick has no real argument for the existence of rights.

To conclude: (1) no existing State has been immaculately conceived, and therefore Nozick, on his own grounds, should advocate anarchism and then wait for his State to develop; (2) even if any State had been so conceived, individual rights are inalienable and therefore no existing State could be justified; (3) every step of Nozick's invisible hand process is invalid: the process is all too conscious and visible, and the risk and compensation principles are both fallacious and passports to unlimited despotism; (4) there is no warrant, even on Nozick's own grounds, for the dominant protective agency to outlaw procedures by independents that do not injure its own clients, and therefore it cannot arrive at an ultraminimal state; (5) Nozick's theory of "non-productive" exchanges is invalid, so that the prohibition of risky activities and hence the ultraminimal state falls on that account alone; (6) contrary to Nozick, there are no "procedural rights," and therefore no way to get from his theory of risk and non-productive exchange to the compulsory monopoly of the ultraminimal state; (7) there is no warrant, even on Nozick's own grounds, for the minimal state to impose taxation; (8) there is no way, in Nozick's theory, to justify the voting or democratic procedures of any State; (9) Nozick's minimal state would, on his own grounds, justify a maximal State as well; and (10) the only "invisible hand" process, on Nozick's own terms, would move society from his minimal State back to anarchism.

Thus, the most important attempt in this century to rebut anarchism and to justify the State fails totally and in each if it's parts.

Notes

1. *The Complete Writings of Thomas Paine*, ed. P. Foner (New York: Citadel Press, L945), V.I., p. 13.
2. In Robert A. Rutland, *George Mason* (Williamsburg, Va.: Colonial Williamsburg, 1961), p. 111.
3. Williamson M. Evers, "Toward a Reformulation of the Law of Contracts" (unpublished MS.), p. 12. The great 17th-century English Leveller leader Richard Overton wrote, "To every individual in nature is given an individual property by nature, not to be invaded or usurped by any: for everyone as he is himself, so he hath a self propriety, else he could not be himself.... Mine and thine cannot be, except this be: No man hath power over my rights and liberties and I over no man's: I may be but an individual, enjoy myself and myself propriety." Quoted in Sylvester Petro, "Feudalism, Property, and Praxeology," in S. Blumenfeld, ed., *Property in a Humane Economy* (LaSalle, Ill.: Open Court. 1974). p. 162.
4. Roy Childs, "The Invisible Hand Strikes Back," *Journal of Libertarian Studies*, pp. 23-33.
5. Cf. Bruno Leoni, *Freedom and the Law* (Los Angeles: Nash Publishing, 1972) and F. A. Hayek, *Law, Legislation, and Liberty*, Vol. I (Chicago: University of Chicago Press, 1973).
6. Childs, "The Invisible Hand Strikes Back," pp. 23-33.
7. Ibid.
8. Ibid.
9. Ibid.

10. Randy Barnett. "Whither Anarchy? Has Robert Nozick Justified the State?" *The Libertarian Forum* (December 1975), p. 5.
11. Nozick, furthermore, compounds the burdens on the victim by compensating him only for actions that respond "adaptively" to the aggression (58).
12. Nozick explicitly assumes the measurability of utility (58).
13. I am indebted for this latter point to Mr. Roger Garrison of the economics department, University of Virginia.
14. Nozick also employs the concept of "transaction costs" and other costs in arriving at what activities may be prohibited with compensation. But this is invalid on the same grounds, i.e. that transaction and other costs are all subjective to each individual and not objective, and hence are unknowable by any outside observer.
15. Childs, "The Invisible Hand Strikes Back," pp. 23-33.
16. Ibid.
17. Nozick also reiterates Hayek's position on charging for the use of one's solitary waterhole (180).
18. See Barnett, "Whither Anarchy?" pp. 4-5
19. Nozick doesn't answer this crucial question; he only asserts that this "will be a productive exchange" (84, 340n16). Ironically, Nozick was apparently forced into this retreat—conceding the "productivity" of the exchange if Green makes the offer—by the arguments of Professor Ronald Hamowy: ironic because Hamowy has also delivered a devastating critique of a somewhat similar definition of coercion by Professor Hayek.
20. See Barnett, "Whither Anarchy?" pp. 4-5.
21. Nozick compounds his fallacies by going on to liken the blackmailer to a "protection racketeer," pointing out that, whereas protection is productive, selling someone "the racketeers' mere abstention from harming you" is not (86). But the "harm" threatened by the protection racketeer is not the exercise of free speech but aggressive violence, and the threat to commit aggressive violence is itself aggression. Here the difference is not the fallacies "productive vs. nonproductive" but between "voluntary" and "coercive" or "invasive"—the very essence of the libertarian philosophy. As professor Block points out, "In aggression, what is being threatened is aggressive violence, something that the blackmailer most certainly *does* have a right to do! To exercise his right of free speech, to gossip about our secrets…" Walter Block, "The Blackmailer as Hero," *Libertarian Forum* (December 1972), p. 3.
22. For an excellent and detailed critique of Nozick's concept of "procedural rights," see Barnett, "Whither Anarchy?" pp. 2-4. Professor Jeffrey Paul has also shown that any concept of "procedural rights" implies a "right" of some other procedure to arrive at such procedures, and this in turn implies another set of "rights" for methods of deciding on *those* procedures, and so on to an infinite regress. Paul, "Comment on Barnett" (unpublished MS.).
23. Childs, "The Invisible Hand Strikes Back," pp. 23-33.
24. Ibid.

13

Objectivism and the State: An Open Letter to Ayn Rand

Roy A. Childs, Jr.

Dear Miss Rand:

The purpose of this letter is to convert you to free market anarchism. As far as I can determine, no one has ever pointed out to you in detail the errors in your political philosophy. That is my intention here. I attempted this task once before, in my essay "The Contradiction in Objectivism," in the March 1968 issue of the Rampart Journal, but I now think that my argument was ineffective and weak, not emphasizing the essentials of the matter. I will remedy that here.

Why am I making such an attempt to convert you to a point of view which you have, repeatedly, publicly condemned as a floating abstraction? Because you are wrong. I suggest that your political philosophy cannot be maintained without contradiction, that, in fact, you are advocating the maintenance of an institution—the state—which is a moral evil. To a person of self-esteem, these area reasons enough.

There is a battle shaping up in the world—a battle between the forces of archy—of statism, of political rule and authority—and its only alternative—anarchy, the absence of political rule. This battle is the necessary and logical consequence of the battle between individualism and collectivism, between liberty and the state, between freedom and slavery. As in ethics there are only two sides to any question—the good and the evil—so too are there only two logical sides to the political question of the state: either you are for it, or you are against it. Any attempt at a middle ground is doomed to failure, and the adherents of any middle course are doomed likewise to failure and frustration—or the blackness of psychological destruction, should they blank out and refuse to identify the causes of such failure, or the nature of reality as it is.

There are, by your framework, three alternatives in political organization: statism, which is a governmental system wherein the government initiates force to attain its ends; limited government, which holds a monopoly on retaliation but does not initiate the use or threat of physical force; and anarchy, a society wherein there is no government, government being defined by you as "an institution that holds the exclusive power to enforce certain rules of social conduct in a given geographical area." You support a limited government, one which does not initiate the use or threat of physical force against others.

It is my contention that limited government is a floating abstraction which has never been concretized by anyone; that a limited government must either initiate force or cease being a government; that the very concept of limited government is an unsuccessful attempt to integrate two mutually contradictory elements: statism and voluntarism. Hence, if this can be shown, epistemological clarity and moral consistency demands the rejection of the institution of government totally, resulting in free market anarchism, or a purely voluntary society.

Why is a limited government a floating abstraction? Because it must either initiate force or stop being a government. Let me present a brief proof of this.

Although I do not agree with your definition of government and think that it is epistemologically mistaken (i.e., you are not identifying its fundamental, and hence essential, characteristics), I shall accept it for the purpose of this critique. One of the major characteristics of your conception of government is that it holds a monopoly on the use of retaliatory force in a given geographical area. Now, there are only two possible kinds of monopolies: a coercive monopoly, which initiates force to keep its monopoly, or a non-coercive monopoly, which is always open to competition. In an Objectivist society, the government is not open to competition, and hence is a coercive monopoly.

The quickest way of showing why it must either initiate force or cease being a government is the following: Suppose that I were distraught with the service of a government in an Objectivist society. Suppose that I judged, being as rational as I possibly could, that I could secure the protection of my contracts and the retrieval of stolen goods at a cheaper price and with more efficiency. Suppose I either decide to set up an institution to attain these ends, or patronize one which a friend or a business colleague has established. Now, if he succeeds in setting up the agency, which provides all the services of the Objectivist government, and restricts his more efficient activities to the use of retaliation against aggressors, there are only two alternatives as far as the "government" is concerned: (a) It can use force or the threat of it against the new institution, in order to keep its monopoly status in the given territory, thus initiating the use of threat of physical force against one who has not himself initiated force. Obviously, then, if it should choose this alternative, it would have initiated force. Q.E.D. Or: (b) It can refrain from initiating force, and allow the new institution to carry on its activities without interference. If it did this, then the Objectivist "government" would become a truly marketplace institution, and not a "government" at all. There would be competing agencies of protection, defense and retaliation—in short, free market anarchism.

If the former should occur, the result would be statism. It is important to remember in this context that statism exists whenever there is a government which initiates force. The degree of statism, once the government has done so, is all that is in question. Once the principle of the initiation of force has been accepted, we have granted the premise of statists of all breeds, and the rest, as you have said so eloquently, is just a matter of time.

If the latter case should occur, we would no longer have a government, properly speaking. This is, again, called free market anarchism. Note that what is in question is not whether or not, in fact, any free market agency of protection, defense or retaliation is more efficient than the former "government." The point is that whether it is more efficient or not can only be decided by individuals acting according to their rational self-interest and on the basis of their rational judgment. And if they do not initiate force in this pursuit, then they are within their rights. If the Objectivist government, for whatever reason, moves to threaten or physically prevent these individuals from pursuing their rational self-interest, it is, whether you like it or not, initiating the use of physical force against another peaceful, nonaggressive human being. To advocate such a thing is, as you have said, "to evict oneself automatically from the realm of rights, of morality, and of the intellect." Surely, then, you cannot be guilty of such a thing.

Now, if the new agency should in fact initiate the use of force, then the former "government"-turned-marketplace-agency would of course have the right to retaliate against those individuals who performed the act. But, likewise, so would the new institution be able to use retaliation against the former "government" if that should initiate force.

I shall cover some of your major "justifications" for government, pointing out your logical flaws, but first let us get one thing very clear: as far as I can determine, I have absolutely and irrefutably shown that government cannot exist without initiating force, or at least threatening to do so, against dissenters. If this is true, and if sanctioning any institution which initiates force is a moral evil, then you should morally withdraw all sanction from the U.S. government, in fact, from the very concept of government itself. One does not have an obligation to oppose all evils in the world, since life rationally consists of a pursuit of positives, not merely a negation of negatives. But one does, I submit, have a moral obligation to oppose a moral evil such as government, especially when one had previously come out in favor of such an evil.

Note also that the question of how free market anarchism would work is secondary to establishing the evil of government. If a limited government, i.e., a non-statist government, is a contradiction in terms, then it cannot be advocated—period. But since there is no conflict between the moral and the practical, I am obliged to briefly sketch how your objections to free market anarchism are in error.

I do not intend to undertake a full "model" of a free market anarchist society, since I, like yourself, truly cannot discuss things that way. I am not a social planner and again, like yourself, do not spend my time inventing Utopias. I am talking about principles whose practical applications should be clear. In any case, a much fuller discussion of the technical aspects of the operation of a fully voluntary, nonstatist society is forthcoming, in the opening chapter of Murray N. Rothbard's follow-up volume to his masterly two-volume economic treatise, Man, Economy, and State, to be entitled Power and Market, and in Morris and

Linda Tannehill's book, which will hopefully be published soon, to be entitled The Market for Liberty. The latter take sup the problem where Murray Rothbard leaves off, and discusses the problems in detail. A chapter from this book, incidentally, entitled "Warring Defense Agencies and Organized Crime," will appear in the Libertarian Connection #5, and a short statement of the authors' position is presented in their pamphlet "Liberty Via the Market."

To make consideration of your errors easier, I shall number them and present the outline of possible replies to your major, and hence essential, points, as presented in your essay, "The Nature of Government."

1. "If a society provided no organized protection against force, it would compel every citizen to go about armed, to turn his home into a fortress, to shoot any strangers approaching his door," etc.

This is a bad argument. One could just as easily assert that if "society" (subsuming whom?) provided no organized way of raising food, it would compel every citizen to go out and raise vegetables in his own backyard, or to starve. This is illogical. The alternative is most emphatically not either we have a single, monopolistic governmental food-growing program or we have each man growing his own food, or starving. There is such a thing as the division of labor, the free market—and that can provide all the food man needs. So too with protection against aggression.

2. "The use of physical force—even its retaliatory use—cannot be left at the discretion of individual citizens."

This contradicts your epistemological and ethical position. Man's mind—which means: the mind of the individual human being—is capable of knowing reality, and man is capable of coming to conclusions on the basis of his rational judgment and acting on the basis of his rational self-interest. You imply, without stating it, that if an individual decides to use retaliation, that that decision is somehow subjective and arbitrary. Rather, supposedly the individual should leave such a decision up to government which is—what? Collective and therefore objective? This is illogical. If man is not capable of making these decisions, then he isn't capable of making them, and no government made up of men is capable of making them, either. By what epistemological criterion is an individual's action classified as "arbitrary," while that of a group of individuals is somehow "objective"?

Rather, I assert that an individual must judge, and evaluate the facts of reality in accordance with logic and by the standard of his own rational self-interest. Are you here claiming that man's mind is not capable of knowing reality? That men must not judge, or act on the basis of their rational self-interest and perception of the facts of reality? To claim this is to smash the root of the Objectivist philosophy: the validity of reason, and the ability and right of man to think and judge for himself.

I am not, of course, claiming that a man must always personally use retaliation against those who initiate such against him—he has the right, though not the obligation, to delegate that right to any legitimate agency. I am merely criticizing your faulty logic.

3. "The retaliatory use of force requires objective rules of evidence to establish that a crime has been committed and to prove who committed it, as well as objective rules to define punishments and enforcement procedures."

There is indeed a need for such objective rules. But look at the problem this way: there is also a need for objective rules in order to produce a ton of steel, an automobile, an acre of wheat. Must these activities, too, therefore be made into a coercive monopoly? I think not. By what twist of logic are you suggesting that a free market would not be able to provide such objective rules, while a coercive government would? It seems obvious that man needs objective rules in every activity of his life, not merely in relation to the use of retaliation. But, strange as it may seem, the free market is capable of providing such rules. You are, it seems to me, blithely assuming that free market agencies would not have objective rules, etc., and this without proof. If you believe this to be the case, yet have no rational grounds for believing such, what epistemological practice have you smuggled into your consciousness?

4. "All laws must be objective (and objectively justifiable): Men must know clearly, and in advance of taking an action, what the law forbids them to do (and why), what constitutes a crime and what penalty they will incur if they commit it."

This is not, properly speaking, an objection to anarchism. The answer to this problem of "objective laws" is quite easy: all that would be forbidden in any voluntary society would be the initiation of physical force, or the gaining of a value by any substitute thereof, such as fraud. If a person chooses to initiate force in order to gain a value, then by his act of aggression, he creates a debt which he must repay to the victim, plus damages. There is nothing particularly difficult about this, and no reason why the free market could not evolve institutions around this concept of justice.

5. We come to the main thrust of your attack on free market anarchism on pages 112-113 of the paperback edition of The Virtue of Selfishness, and I will not quote the relevant paragraph here.

Suffice it to say that you have not proven that anarchy is a naive floating abstraction, that a society without government would be at the mercy of the first criminal to appear—(which is false, since market protection agencies could perform more efficiently the same service as is supposedly provided by "government"), and that objective rules could not be observed by such agencies. You would not argue that since there are needs for objective laws in the production of steel, therefore the government should take over that activity. Why do you argue it in the case of protection, defense and retaliation? And if it is the need for objective laws which necessitates government, and that alone, we can conclude that if a marketplace agency can observe objective laws, as can, say, marketplace steel producers, then there is, in fact, really no need for government at all.

We "younger advocates of freedom," incidentally, are not "befuddled" by our anarchist theory. The theory which we advocate is not called "competing governments," of course, since a government is a coercive monopoly. We advocate competing agencies of protection, defense, and retaliation; in short, we claim that the free market can supply all of man's needs—including the protection and defense of his values. We most emphatically do not accept the basic premise of modern statists, and do not confuse force and production. We merely recognize protection, defense and retaliation for what they are: namely, scarce services which, because they are scarce, can be offered on a market at a price. We see it as immoral to initiate force against another to prevent him from patronizing his own court system, etc. The remainder of your remarks in this area are unworthy of you. You misrepresent the arguments of Murray Rothbard and others, without even identifying them by name so that those who are interested can judge the arguments by going to their source. Since we understand the nature of government, we advocate no such thing as competing governments; rather, we advocate the destruction or abolition of the state, which, since it regularly initiates force, is a criminal organization. And, incidentally, the case for competing courts and police has been concretized—by the individualist anarchist Benjamin R. Tucker, over 80 years ago, by Murray Rothbard, and by a host of other less prominent theorists.

Let us take up your example of why competing courts and police supposedly cannot function.

Suppose Mr. Smith, a customer of Government A, suspects that his next-door neighbor, Mr. Jones, a customer of Government B, has robbed him; a squad of Police A proceeds to Mr. Jones' house and is met at the door by a squad of Police B, who declare that they do not accept the validity of Mr. Smith's complaint and do not recognize the authority of Government A. What happens then? You take it from there.

Unfortunately, though this poses as a convincing argument, it is a straw man, and is about as accurate a picture of the institutions pictured by free market anarchists as would be my setting up Nazi Germany as an historical example of an Objectivist society.

The main question to ask at this point is this: do you think that it would be in the rational self-interest of either agency to allow this to happen, this fighting out conflicts in the streets, which is what you imply? No? Then what view of human nature does it presuppose to assume that such would happen anyway?

One legitimate answer to your allegations is this: since you are, in effect, asking "what happens when the agencies decide to act irrationally?" allow me to ask the far more potent question: "What happens when your government acts irrationally?"—which is at least possible. And which is more likely, in addition, to occur: the violation of rights by a bureaucrat or politician who got his job by fooling people in elections, which are nothing but community-wide opinion-mongering contests (which are, presumably, a rational and objective manner of selecting the best people for a job), or the violation of rights by a hard-nosed businessman, who has had to earn his position? So your objection against competing agencies is even more effective against your own "limited government."

Obviously, there are a number of ways in which such ferocious confrontations can be avoided by rational businessmen: there could be contracts or "treaties" between the competing agencies providing for the peaceful ironing out of disputes, etc., just to mention one simplistic way. Do you see people as being so blind that this would not occur to them?

Another interesting argument against your position is this: there is now anarchy between citizens of different countries, i.e., between, say, a Canadian citizen on one side of the Canadian-American border and an American citizen on the other. There is, to be more precise, no single government which presides over both of them. If there is a need for government to settle disputes among individuals, as you state, then you should look at the logical implications of your argument: is there not then a need for a super-government to resolve disputes among governments? Of course the implications of this are obvious: theoretically, the ultimate end of this process of piling government on top of government is a government for the entire universe. And the practical end, for the moment, is at the very least world government.

Also, you should be aware of the fact that just as conflicts could conceivably arise between such market agencies, so could they arise between governments—which is called war, and is a thousand times more terrible. Making a defense agency a monopoly in a certain area doesn't do anything to eliminate such conflicts, of course. It merely makes them more awesome, more destructive, and increases the number of innocent bystanders who are harmed immensely. Is this desirable?

Suffice it to say that all of your arguments against free market anarchism are invalid; and hence, you are under the moral obligation, since it has been shown that government cannot exist without initiating force, to adopt it. Questions of how competing courts could function are technical questions, not specifically moral ones. Hence, I refer you to Murray Rothbard and Morris G. Tannehill, who have both solved the problem.

In the future, if you are interested, I will take up several other issues surrounding your political philosophy, such as a discussion of the epistemological problems of definition and concept formation in issues concerning the state, a discussion of the nature of the U.S. Constitution, both ethically and historically, and a discussion of the nature of the Cold War. I believe that your historical misunderstanding of these last two is responsible for many errors in judgment, and is increasingly expressed in your commentaries on contemporary events.

Finally, I want to take up a major question: why should you adopt free market anarchism after having endorsed the political state for so many years? Fundamentally, for the same reason you gave for withdrawing your sanction from Nathaniel Branden in an issue of The Objectivist: namely, you do not fake reality and never have. If your reputation should suffer with you becoming a total voluntarist, a free market anarchist, what is that compared with the pride of being consistent—of knowing that you have correctly identified the facts of reality, and are acting accordingly? A path of expedience taken by a person of self-esteem is psychologically destructive, and such a person will find himself either losing his pride or committing that act of philosophical treason and psychological suicide which is blanking out, the willful refusal to consider an issue, or to integrate one's knowledge. Objectivism is a completely consistent philosophical system you say—and I agree that it is potentially such. But it will be an Objectivism without the state.

And there is the major issue of the destructiveness of the state itself. No one can evade the fact that, historically, the state is a bloodthirsty monster, which has been responsible for more violence, bloodshed and hatred than any other institution known to man. Your approach to the matter is not yet radical, not yet fundamental: it is the existence of the state itself which must be challenged by the new radicals. It must be understood that the state is an unnecessary evil, that it regularly initiates force, and in fact attempts to gain what must rationally be called a monopoly of crime in a given territory. Hence, government is little more, and has never been more, than a gang of professional criminals. If, then, government has been the most tangible cause of most of man's inhumanity to man, let us, as Morris Tannehill has said, "identify it for what it is instead of attempting to clean it up, thus helping the statists to keep it by preventing the idea that government is inherently evil from becoming known.... The 'sacred cow' regard for government (which most people have) must be broken! That instrument of sophisticated savagery has no redeeming qualities. The free market does; let's redeem it by identifying its greatest enemy—the idea of government (and its ramifications)."

This is the only alternative to continuing centuries of statism, with all quibbling only over the degree of the evil we will tolerate. I believe that evils should not be tolerated—period. There are only two alternatives, in reality: political rule, or archy, which means: the condition of social existence wherein some men use aggression to dominate or rule another, and anarchy, which is the absence of the initiation of force, the absence of political rule, the absence of the state. We shall replace the state with the free market, and men shall for the fist time in their history be able to walk and live without fear of destruction being unleashed upon them at any moment—especially the obscenity of such destruction being unleashed by a looter armed with nuclear weapons and nerve gases. We shall replace statism with voluntarism: a society wherein all man's relationships with others are voluntary and uncoerced. Where men are free to act according to their rational self-interest, even if it means the establishment of competing agencies of defense.

Let me then halt this letter by repeating to you those glorious words with which you had John Galt address his collapsing world: "Such is the future you are capable of winning. It requires a struggle; so does any human value.

All life is a purposeful struggle, and your only choice is the choice of a goal. Do you wish to continue the battle of your present, or do you wish to fight for my world?... Such is the choice before you. Let your mind and your love of existence decide."

Let us walk forward into the sunlight, Miss Rand. You belong with us.

Yours in liberty,

R.A. Childs, Jr.

cc: Nathaniel Branden, Leonard Peikoff, Robert Hessen, Murray N. Rothbard

P.S. I would like to thank Murray Morris and Joe Hoffman for their advice and suggestions.—R.A.C., Jr.

14

Do We Ever Really Get Out of Anarchy?[1]

Alfred G. Cuzán

Introduction

A major point of dispute among libertarian theorists and thinkers today as always revolves around the age-old question of whether man can live in total anarchy or whether the minimal state is absolutely necessary for the maximization of freedom. Lost in this dispute is the question of whether man is *capable* of getting out of anarchy at all. Can we really abolish anarchy and set up a Government in its place? Most people, regardless of their ideological preferences, simply assume that the abolition of anarchy is possible, that they live under Government, and that anarchy would be nothing but chaos and violence.[2]

The purpose of this paper is to question this venerated assumption and to argue that the escape from anarchy is impossible, that we always live in anarchy, and that the real question is what kind of anarchy we live under, market anarchy or non-market (political) anarchy.[3] Further, it is argued that political anarchies are of two types—hierarchical or plural. The more pluralist political anarchy is, the more it resembles market anarchy. The performance of hierarchical and plural anarchies is evaluated in terms of their ability to minimize the level of force in society. It is shown that plural anarchies are much less violent than hierarchical anarchies. We conclude that the real question libertarians must solve is not whether minimalism or anarchy, but which type of anarchy, market or political, hierarchical or plural, is most conducive to the maximization of freedom.

I

Anarchy is a social order without Government, subject only to the economic laws of the market.[4] Government is an agent external to society, a "third party" with the power to coerce all other parties to relations in society into accepting its conceptions of those relations. The idea of Government as an agent external to society is analogous to the idea of God as an intervener in human affairs. For an atheist, a good analogy might be to assume that omnipotent Martians fill the role we usually ascribe to Government, i.e., an external designer and enforcer of rules of behavior by which everyone subject to those rules *must* abide.[5]

However, that the idea of Government exists is no proof of its empirical existence.[6] Few of us would be convinced by an argument such as: "I believe the idea of God is possible, therefore God exists." Yet such is the structure of the argument which underlies all assumptions about the existence of Government. That societies may have some form of organization they call the "government" is no reason to conclude that those "governments" are empirical manifestations of the *idea* of Government.

A closer look at these earthly "governments" reveals that they do not get us out of anarchy at all. They simply replace one form of anarchy by another and hence do not give us real Government. Let's see how this is so.

Wherever earthly "governments" are established or exist, anarchy is officially prohibited for all members of society, usually referred to as subjects or citizens. They can no longer relate to each other on their own terms—whether as merchants at a port or a vigilante unit and its prey in the open desert or the streets of Newark, N.J. Rather, all members of society must accept an external "third party"—a government—into their relationships, a third party with the coercive powers to enforce its judgments and punish detractors.

For example, when a thief steals my wallet at a concert, I am legally required to rely on the services of members of a third party to catch him (policemen), imprison him (jailers), try him (prosecutors, judges, even "public" defenders), judge him (trial by a group of individuals coerced into jury duty by the courts), and acquit or punish him (prisons, hangmen). At most, I am legally authorized to catch him, but I am prohibited from settling the account myself. Such prohibitions have reached tragi-comic proportions, as when government punishes victims of crime for having defended themselves beyond the limits authorized by "law."[7] In short, I or any other citizen or subject must accept the rulings of government in our relations with others. We are required to abide by the law of this "third party."

However, such a "third party" arrangement for society is non-existent among those who exercise the power of government themselves. In other words, there is no "third party" to make and enforce judgments among the individual members who make up the third party itself. The rulers still remain in a state of anarchy *vis-à-vis* each other. They settle disputes *among themselves*, without regard for a Government (an entity outside themselves). Anarchy still exists. Only whereas without government it was market or natural anarchy, it is now a *political* anarchy, an anarchy inside power.[8] Take, for example, the rulers of our own Federal government. It is a group composed of congressmen, judges, a president and a vice-president, top level bureaucrats in civilian and military agencies, and their armies of assistants who together oversee the work of the millions of public employees who man the several Federal bureaucracies. These individuals together make and enforce laws, edicts, regulations and vast arrays of orders of all kinds by which all members of society must abide.

Yet, in their relations among each other, they remain largely "lawless." Nobody *external to the group* writes and enforces rules governing the relations among them. At most, the rulers are bound by flexible constraints imposed by a "constitution" which they, in any case, interpret and enforce among and upon themselves. The Supreme Court, after all, is only a *branch* of the government, composed of people appointed by and subjected to pressures from other members of the government. Moreover, their decisions are enforced by some *other* branch of the government, the executive, over whom the judges have no power, only authority. Further, the Congress, through vocal pressures and the manipulation of budgetary allocations to the judiciary, also exercises pressures which the judges must contend with. Similarly, congressmen have no "third party" arbiters either among themselves or in their relations with the executive. Furthermore, even the various federal bureaucracies and all their component parts are without a "third party" to govern their relations, internally or externally. In short, looking *inside* the government reveals that the rulers remain in a state of anarchy among themselves. They live in a political anarchy.[9]

The anarchic relations of government officials can be illustrated in the following example: Suppose that a congressman manages to divert streams of moneys from the government's flows to his private estate. This is a crime, theft, the stealing of money. But from whom? From you or me? Only in the sense that we were coerced into contributing to the public treasury which the congressman viewed as booty. It was no longer ours; it belonged to someone else. But who? Why, the members of the government who have the power to allocate those flows of resources.

In short, the congressman stole from *other* government officials, congressmen, bureaucrats, a president, etc. But what is done about the crime? Is the congressman publicly accused, indicted, and tried for his crime like an ordinary citizen who steals from another citizen? Sometimes; but what usually happens is a flurry of political maneuverings at high levels; mutual threats are delivered behind closed doors and forces marshaled against each other; occasional battles take place in which either reputations are destroyed, money changes hands, or resource flows or access to them are altered.

The hue and cry is soon forgotten, the congressman receives a "clean bill of health" by the prosecution, or the charges are dismissed or not pressed, and the congressman wins reelection at the polls. Occasionally, if the infractor was a weak or declining public figure, or one much hated by his colleagues, he is brought before the courts, tried, and given a minimal or even a suspended sentence. In most instances, small fish near the bottom of the bureaucracies are sacrificed for the crimes higher-ups directed, profited from or sanctioned. But make no mistake: no "third party," no Government, ever made or enforced a judgment. The rulers of the government themselves literally took the law into their own hands and produced what outside the government would be considered "vigilante justice."[10]

In short, society is *always* in anarchy. A government only abolishes anarchy among what are called "subjects" or "citizens," but among those who rule, anarchy prevails.

Figure 1 illustrates this situation. The circle on the left shows a state of true or market or natural anarchy, in which all members of society relate to each other in strictly bilateral transactions without third party intervention. The circle on the right shows the situation prevalent under government. In the higher compartment we see individuals whose relations among each other are no longer bilateral. All relations are legally "triangular," in that all members of society are forced to accept the rule of government in their transactions. However, in the lower compartment, inside the "government" itself, relations among the rulers remain in anarchy.[11]

Figure 1

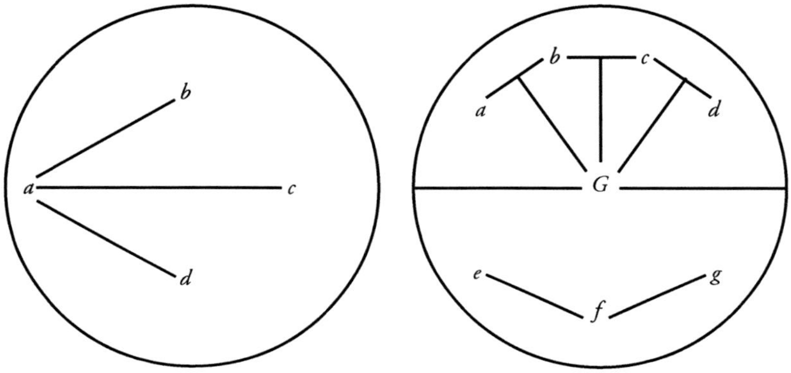

II

Having shown that anarchy is not completely abolished by government but reserved, so to speak, for the rulers only, among whom it is the prevailing condition, it is proper to inquire whether this is beneficial for society. Its proponents and defenders claim that without government society would be in a state of intolerable violence. Thus it is logical to inquire whether the effect of government is to increase, reduce, or in no way affect the level of violence in society.

Is political anarchy less violent than natural or market anarchy? Minimalists argue that it is, provided government is strictly confined to the role of acting as a third party in property disputes. While government necessarily involves the use of limited violence, minimalists say, the level of violence in a minimal state would he lower than that in natural anarchy.

Figure 2 illustrates the minimalist idea. By providing the amount of government of the minimal state, the level of violence in society drops below the level in natural anarchy. Presumably, judging from the vociferous anti-interventionist stand of the minimalists, if government grows beyond the size of a limited state, either there are no further gains in reducing violence—and thus more government is pointless and costly in other ways—and/or beyond a certain size the level of violence in society rises to meet or perhaps surpass the amount of natural violence. (See Figure 3.)

Figure 2

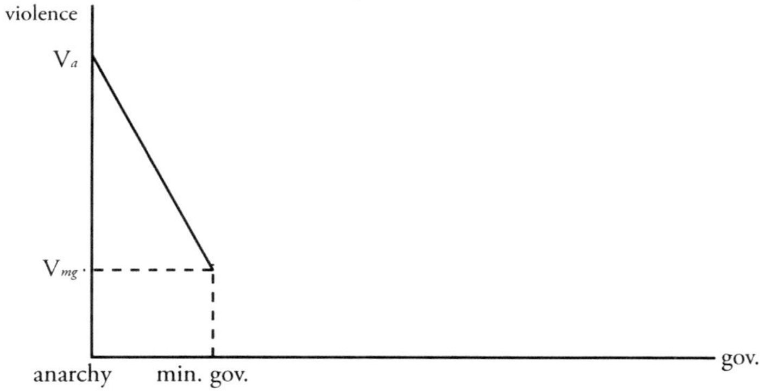

Figure 3*

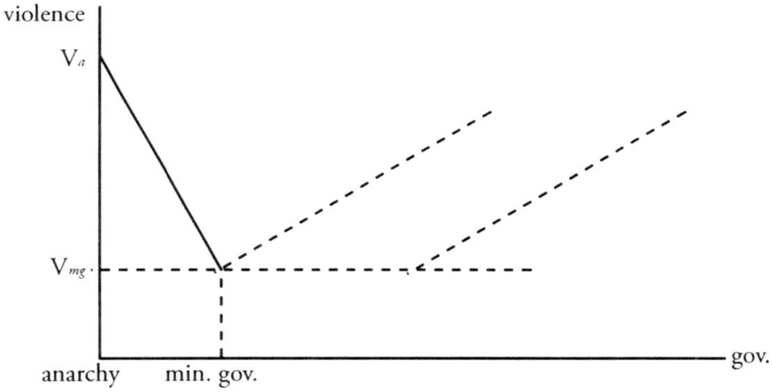

*Broken lines represent possible effects on violence from enlarging government beyond the minimal state.

That violence under political anarchy might exceed the violence of market anarchy is not inconceivable.[12] Hitler's concentration camps and Stalin's Gulags are evidence of violence in such proportions that one could hardly venture to say that natural anarchy would be *worse* than that. Similarly, the political anarchy of nation-states has produced interstate violence on such a scale that it must give pause even to the most devoted disciple of Hobbes.[13]

A third view is possible and theoretically the most interesting. This view says that the relation between government (the substitution of political for market anarchy) and violence, is qualified by a third element, the *structure* of the government, measured along a centralization dimension. The more authoritative powers are dispersed among numerous political units, the more pluralistic the government. The more centralized the structure, i.e., the more authoritative powers are concentrated, the more hierarchical the government. Note that the more hierarchical the government, the more government is run on the assumption of an ultimate arbiter. In other words, the more centralized the structure, the greater the effort to *create* a single "third party" inside the government itself in the form of a God-like figure such as a Hitler, Stalin, Mao or Castro. Such a "third party," however, remains in complete anarchy from the rest of his countrymen and the rest of the world.[14]

The more plural the politics of a country, the more the rulers behave without any reference to a "third party" and thus the more society resembles natural anarchy. The less plural or more hierarchical the politics of a country, the more society appears to be ruled by a truly "external" element, a god-like figure sent from the heavens of history, religion or ideology.

A cursory glance at contemporary societies and recent history shows that, empirically, it is precisely those societies ruled by such earthly personifications of Government where the level of violence in the form of political repression, coercion and intimidation is highest. In contrast, violence is lowest in societies with highly pluralistic politics, such as Switzerland. This is true even in the "communist" world: the more pluralistic communist politics of Poland or Yugoslavia are less violent than the more hierarchical politics of the Soviet Union. Similarly, in the Western world, the more pluralistic politics of the United States are less violent than those of Italy, where politics are much more hierarchical.[15]

But why would the degree of centralization determine whether political anarchy is violent in hierarchical states such as China or Cuba, and relatively peaceful in pluralist states such as India and Costa Rica? The answer may simply lie in the fact that centralized states are more likely to make mistakes than decentralized states.[16] Political mistakes are in the form of *wrong* or *false* conceptions about the nature of bilateral relations in society and in politics, such as conceptions held about the relation between worker and capitalist in communist states. If judgments are wrong, they are not voluntarily accepted by one or both of the parties to the transactions. Under those conditions, the only way for the rulers to enforce their "third party" conceptions is to use force, which, under different conditions, will or will not be resisted by the opposition.

In a pluralist government, wrong conceptions about bilateral relations in society are less likely to occur. This is because there are numerous units independently interacting with each other and with the citizens and subjects, so that more and better information about the effect of these judgments on bilateral relations exist. Moreover, wrong conceptions are more easily checked as various autonomous political units, each capable of marshaling political resources of their own, confront each other in a successive series of political transactions.

In a hierarchical government, however, not even the members of the government are permitted to settle disputes among themselves. *All* relations are subjected to the judgment of some supreme leader. Such a leader must maintain a vast network of spies and enforcers to accomplish such a superhuman feat. Of course, one man's ability to control the behavior of others is quite limited, and so even in Hitler's Germany, truly Machiavellian, feudalistic deals were made right under the Fuhrer's nose. Naturally, such arrangements were prohibited so everyone lived in a state of fearful insecurity, not knowing when his enemies would succeed in turning Hitler against him.[17]

Whether this explanation is a good one or not, we still have with us the *explanandum*, i.e., the fact that hierarchical politics are more violent than pluralist politics. But if society with a pluralist political anarchy experiences less violence than societies with a hierarchical or "governed" government, isn't it logical to inquire whether natural anarchy is less violent than political anarchy? Why should the relation between government and violence be curvilinear? Isn't it possible that it is upward sloping *all* the way, so that government always produces more violence than the market?[18]

Summary and Conclusion

We have shown that anarchy, like matter, never disappears—it only changes form. Anarchy is either market anarchy or political anarchy. Pluralist, decentralized political anarchy is less violent than hierarchical political anarchy. Hence, we have reason to hypothesize that market anarchy could be less violent than political anarchy. Since market anarchy can be shown to outperform political anarchy in efficiency and equity *in all other respects*,[19] why should we expect anything different now? Wouldn't we be justified to expect that market anarchy produces less violence in the enforcement of property rights than political anarchy? After all, the market is the best economizer of all—wouldn't it also economize on violence better than government does, too?[20]

Notes

1. 2006 addition: It's been almost three decades since I wrote this essay. A couple of years ago, when he was still editor of *The Journal of Libertarian Studies*, Hans-Hermann Hoppe invited me to revisit it. His successor renewed the invitation. But the pursuit of other interests and the fulfillment of other obligations have stood in the way. In lieu of that task, which I hope to accomplish some day, I take this opportunity to insert a few reflections in the footnotes. Also, I have found passages in Locke's *Second Treatise* and Hobbes' *Leviathan* that are consistent with the idea that the escape from anarchy is illusory, and these have been inserted in footnotes, as well.
2. Even Gordon Tullock writes, "If, as I believe is correct, people under anarchy are every bit as selfish as they are now, we would have the Hobbesian jungle...." From the point of view of this paper, it is interesting that in the very next sentence he adds: "...we would be unable to distinguish a fully corrupt government from no government." Gordon Tullock, "Corruption and Anarchy," in Gordon Tullock (ed.) *Further Explorations in the Theory of Anarchy* (Blacksburg, Virginia: University Publications, 1974).
3. 2006 addition: In the original essay I used "market anarchy" and "natural anarchy" interchangeably. Today I would consistently use the latter term, which is equivalent to what Hobbes and Locke called "the state of nature."
4. 2006 addition: As well as market laws, anarchy would be subject to whatever other sociological laws govern (in the naturalistic sense) interpersonal or intergroup relations. For example, the outbreak of violent conflict in the state of nature could be a function of the distribution of capabilities for exerting force among individuals or groups, much like the onset of interstate war may well be at least partly a function of the dyadic or systemic distribution of military power among nations.

5. 2006 addition: Perhaps the closest approximation to the idea of Government is found in Hobbes' *Leviathan.* See below.
6. Paul Craig Roberts, in *Alienation and the Soviet Economy* (Albuquerque: University of New Mexico Press, 1971), argues similarly that to be able to conceive of central planning is no proof of its empirical possibility. Roberts shows that formally planned economies like the Soviet Union are not centrally planned at all, but are plural economies guided by *non*-market signals. Roberts' conclusion that central planning does not exist is analogous to my own conclusion that Government does not exist either. I am grateful to Murray Rothbard for pointing out the parallels in the two arguments.

   While the body of this paper was being typed, I read Michael Bakunin *God and the State* (New York: Dover Publications, 1970), and was struck by the similarities between Bakunin's argument against God and my argument against Government. This is not surprising, since many assumptions used to justify government refer to man's evil nature. It's as if government took God's place on earth to keep evil humans in line. That governments are themselves made up of ordinary human beings who remain in a state of anarchy among themselves seems to have escaped those who adhere to this view.
7. 2006 addition: John Locke argues that when quitting the state of nature for what he calls civil society, man surrenders the right to punish while reserving a qualified right of self-defense. See *Second Treatise on Government* (Indianapolis: Hackett Publishing Company, 1980), 67.
8. Of course, the rulers of any government have as their power base interest groups in and *out* of government. The leaders of non-governmental interest groups often hold the key to the political survival of even the mast powerful politicians. Hence, the strict dichotomy between governmental and non-governmental members of society breaks down. Around the edges of government, many private individuals live in a state of anarchy vis-à-vis government officials. George Meany is probably as good an example as any. I am indebted to my colleague Cal Clark for pointing this out.

   Also living in anarchy vis-à-vis government officials are all those members of underground criminal organizations which supply consumers with a vast array of illegal goods and services. That the CIA made deals with top gangsters to carry out some of its missions should not come as a surprise. Most police departments probably have similar relations with local crime chiefs.
9. 2006 addition: That there can be no government within the government was made plain by Hobbes, who rejected the doctrine that the sovereign is subject to the laws on the grounds that "to be subject to laws, is to be subject to the commonwealth, that is to the sovereign representative, that is to himself; which is not subjection, but freedom from the laws. Which error, because it setteth the laws above the sovereign, setteth also a judge above him, and a power to punish him; which is to make a new sovereign; and again for the same reason a third, to punish the second; and so continually without end, to the confusion, and dissolution of the commonwealth." See *Leviathan* (London: The Crowell-Collier Publishing Company), 240.
10. 2006 addition: This and the previous two paragraphs may be overly cynical about what happens to miscreant public officials in America and other countries where the rule of law, a civic culture, and a vigorous public opinion exert their salutary influence. It is an empirical question whether public officials in different political regimes are punished more or less severely than their private counterparts convicted of equivalent crimes.

11. 2006 addition: In his discussion of executive prerogative, Locke recognized this. He wrote: "The old question will be asked in this matter of *prerogative*, But *who shall be judge* when this power is made a right use of? I answer: between an executive power in being, with such a prerogative, and a legislative that depends upon his will for their convening, there can be no *judge on earth*; as there can be none between the legislative and the people, should either the executive, or the legislative, when they have got the power in their hands, design, or go about to enslave or destroy them" (*Second Treatise*, 87; italics in original). That members of the political elite lack a third party to settle their disputes highlights the importance for avoiding civil war of a culture of self-restraint and what used to be called "gentlemen's agreements." The problem is that when elite opinion becomes polarized over a set of issues, such restraints go out the window. The English, American, and Spanish civil wars are cases in point.

    Hobbes, for whom anarchy meant a war of "every man, against every man," was also aware of this, and argued therefore against dividing the powers of government: "For what is it to divide the power of the commonwealth, but to dissolve it; for powers divided mutually destroy each other" (*Leviathan*, 100, 240). The passage previously quoted from the *Leviathan* on the impossibility of setting up a government within the government is also pertinent.
12. 2006 addition: Locke argues that while a properly limited civil society is preferable to the state of nature, tyranny would be worse (*Second Treatise*, 113).
13. This is an argument which Murray Rothbard makes and which implies that true archists should logically favor a single world government in order to abolish anarchy among nation-states. Yet few of them do. (Murray Rothbard, in letter to the author, September 21, 1978; and Walter Block, in letter to the author, October 26, 1978.)
14. 2006 addition: As Locke puts it, "such a man [i.e., the tyrant]...is as much *in the state of nature*, with all under his dominion, as he is with the rest of mankind...." (*Second Treatise*, 48-49; italics in the original).
15. 2006 addition: I am not sure why I contrasted Italy with the United States. I may have been thinking of the violence associated with the Mafia and the Red Brigades, which were wreaking mayhem at the time. According to an entry in the Wikipedia, consulted on April 25, 2006, "Throughout the 1970's the Red Brigades were credited with 14,000 acts of violence." Interestingly, in the 1980s Italy underwent a decentralization of government whose effects are traced by Robert Putnam in *Making Democracy Work* (Princeton University Press, 1993).
16. See Gordon Tullock, *The Politics of Bureaucracy* (Washington, D.C.: The Public Affairs Press, 1965), for a full theoretical development of this idea.
17. See Albert Speer, *Inside the Third Reich* (New York: Avon Books, 1970), Part II.
18. 2006 addition: That is, the state of nature.
19. Murray Rothbard, *Power and Market* (Kansas City: Sheed Andrews and McMeel, Inc., 1970). 2006 addition: I am less sure of the truth of this claim than I used to be. Be that as it may, this has no bearing on the central proposition of the essay.
20. 2006 addition: The logic of the argument leads to the raising of these questions. The answers, however, are elusive and may never be found. There must be a reason why there is no society without government. Locke no less than Hobbes concluded that a properly constituted government is at least convenient. There may very well be a social law that drives men into civil society, that is, into substituting political anarchy for the natural kind. That it turns into an ill bargain for many subjects of tyrannical regimes is a terrible tragedy. But that does not mean that the remedy lies in natural anarchy. A decentralized political anarchy bounded by a culture of sober self-restraint on the part of the members of the political elite is probably a safer bet.

15

Law as a Public Good: The Economics of Anarchy

Tyler Cowen

1. Introduction

Various writers in the Western liberal and libertarian tradition have challenged the argument that enforcement of law and protection of property rights are public goods that must be provided by governments. Many of these writers argue explicitly for the provision of law enforcement services through private market relations.[1]

When protection services are purchased through markets, I refer to this situation as anarchy, or libertarian anarchy. Libertarian anarchy is to be contrasted with the "crude anarchy" of Hobbes's state of nature. Unlike crude anarchy, libertarian anarchy has organized institutions responsible for the provision of public order and prevention of crime. By examining institutions that attempt to provide governmental services without actually being governments, we may learn what, if anything, makes government necessary, special, or important.[2]

I do not offer a single, all-purpose definition of government. However, I treat finance through taxation, claim of sovereignty, ultimate decision-making authority, and prohibitions on competitive entry as features that characterize government. In contrast, libertarian private protection agencies allow the right of secession, finance themselves through sale of product, and compete with other agencies within a given geographical area.

I argue that libertarian anarchy is not a stable equilibrium. For the purposes of this paper, I accept the premise that the absence of government will not lead to crude anarchy. The same factors that create the potential for orderly anarchy, however, also imply that anarchy will reevolve into government.

The claims of libertarian anarchists have received critical scrutiny from several quarters. Robert Nozick focuses upon whether a state could arise from a state of nature ("anarchy") without violating individual rights. He examines how private protection agencies *could* behave to give rise to a state in a just

The author wishes to thank Jerry Ellig, Fred Foldvary, Jeffrey Rogers Hummel, Gregory Kavka, Daniel Klein, David Levy, Jeremy Shearmur, Sterios Skaperdas, Dan Sutter, Alex Tabarrok, and Carole Uhlaner for useful comments and discussions.

manner. In contrast, my focus is upon incentives and how private protection agencies actually *would* behave. Nonetheless, both Nozick and I focus upon the possibility that anarchy would evolve into government because individuals prefer to participate in a common legal system.[3]

The "Virginia School" political economy considers the incentive to engage in predation when governmental rule of law is not present. These writers, however, do not examine systematically the provision of law enforcement through markets. Instead, they focus upon whether markets will come into existence in the first place. The focus of the Virginia School literature is logically prior to my analysis; it considers whether a feasible transition is possible from a state of nature to markets without government protection of property rights. In contrast I focus upon the stability of an anarchist equilibrium.[4]

The literature on libertarianism considers several kinds or varieties of anarchism. First, private defense agencies may offer competing law codes (Friedman, 1989). Slander and libel, for instance, could be legal under some codes but illegal under others. Secondly, private defense agencies may offer the same law code and punishment standards, but compete across other quality dimensions, such as means of protection (Rothbard, 1978). Some agencies would place a patrolman on every block, whereas others would supply their clients with locks and burglar alarms. Different agencies need not offer exactly the same law codes, but could agree upon a common adjudication mechanism, or network, in case of interagency conflict.[5] A third scenario, following Nozick (1974), posits a dominant protection agency. Protection services are a natural monopoly, and market competition gives rise to one large agency. Conflicts among different law codes or agencies do not arise.

2. Assumptions

I treat individuals as rational, utility-maximizing agents. I do not defend this assumption on the grounds of realism, but rather as a simplifying maneuver, which highlights the role that incentives would play in anarchy. Behavior in accordance with rational self-interest and marketplace incentives is presumably an assumption that ought to favor the libertarian anarchist case.[6]

I combine the rationality assumption with three substantive restrictions upon individual preferences. First, individuals aggress against others only when they benefit directly by doing so. Persons do not enjoy aggression for its own sake. Second, once a well-functioning social order is in place, persons expect that others obey the law to some basic degree. When breaking the law, a person sees the remainder of society as siding with the established legal system, and not with himself. Without this assumption, it is difficult to explain why government edicts are obeyed in today's world, or why any set of political institutions has a stable core.

Third, libertarian ideology does not provide a safeguard against the emergence of government, if incentives based on self-interest dictate that government emerge. Reliance upon libertarian ideology alone to defend the continued survival of anarchy involves a *deus ex machina*. It is inconsistent to rely upon self-interest to motivate the basic workings of markets and then have a model in which supporting the underlying institutional structure behind markets is contrary to self-interest.[7]

More practically, if the stability of an anarchist society requires libertarian values of its citizens, it is likely to be short-lived. Anarchy might arise through evolutionary means or through the purposive behavior of individuals with non-libertarian motives. Ideologies also change over time. Anarchy might come about through libertarian ideology, but later be accompanied by other ideologies.[8]

The analysis of this paper focuses upon incentives, but in doing so, I ignore many issues in political philosophy necessary for a complete evaluation of anarchism. For instance, I treat power relations in society as transitive. If A has jurisdiction over B and B has jurisdiction over C, then A has jurisdiction over C. An alternative approach to political philosophy treats nontransitivity as the distinguishing feature of law and compares different systems of nontransitivity. I abstract from these complications.[9]

My arguments proceed as follows. I first consider the conditions under which the private provision of law enforcement services can overcome public goods and "free-rider" problems. In some cases, consumers can be induced to contribute funds toward the provision of property protection and law enforcement, once a stable system of private protection agencies is in place. I next examine whether a system of private protection agencies would evolve into government. The same conditions that allow private agencies potentially to overcome public goods problems also imply that these agencies will collude successfully.

I consider the different scenarios for anarchism discussed above. The first anarchist scenario, competing legal systems, is not stable unless private defense agencies develop a common means of mediating disputes, which will evolve into a single legal system. Stable versions of competing agencies thus resemble the second arbitration scenario with a single legal system. Once a single legal system is in place, the difference is small between cooperating agencies enforcing uniform laws and a single dominant protection agency. In each case, a single arbitration network possesses monopoly power, whether this network is composed of "separate" cooperating firms or a single firm.

I then analyze the behavior of private protection agencies when a single firm or dominant adjudication network is present. An anarchist dominant protection agency or network can produce public goods but will also have the incentive and ability to start behaving like a government. The same factors that allow anarchy to be stable may also allow the protection agencies to exercise monopoly power and collude. I present some reasons why a cartel of private protection agencies is likely to prove more stable than most private cartels, which have historically demonstrated instability.[10]

3. Anarchist Scenarios

The different possibilities for libertarian anarchy examined below share the common feature of offering protection services through private markets. In these scenarios, individuals find it in their self-interest to purchase protection services. Although protection has a public good component (the security of my property may enhance the security of property in general), the purchase of protection services also yields significant private benefits. Victims of criminal aggression incur psychic and pecuniary losses, and individuals are presumably willing to purchase protection to decrease or avoid these costs.[11]

The private-good component of protection services is demonstrated by expenditures in today's world. Private security, police, and protection services are commonplace. There are now twice as many private-sector police as public-sector police in the United States, despite the fact that public police are supplied free of charge to users (Benson, 1990, pp. 3-4). Not all protection services need be purchased by individuals on a subscription basis. Owners of condominiums, housing developments, and proprietary communities hire private security forces to protect their property and preserve property values. Shopping malls, museums, businesses, and universities all provide their own protection services.[12]

In anarchy, protection services can also be supplied by insurance agencies. Persons purchase home, property, and automobile insurance to protect their belongings against damage. Insurance companies might then find it profitable to form a consortium of security forces to protect the property they have insured (Tandy, 1896, p. 66). Similarly, private road owners are another possible source of protection services. Just as shopping mall owners provide protection and security for the "streets" and parking lots they offer, so could the owners of outdoor roads and streets.[13]

Funding the protection of property is not the most difficult problem in anarchy. The most difficult problems arise when disputes must be adjudicated between two or more institutions that claim to be protecting property. Adjudication and resolution of disputes involve at least two parties, and create a potential externalities problem. How individuals would resolve disputes over property rights is the issue to which I now turn.[14]

3.1 Competing Legal Systems

Under the anarchist scenario envisioned by David Friedman, consumers of protection services subscribe to the law code that best suits their preferences. Competing agencies offer different punishments, definitions of crime, and legal procedures. Friedman's scenario does not present particular problems when both plaintiff and defendant belong to the same agency. The agency enforces laws to which both parties have agreed. Difficulties arise when disputing parties subscribe to different agencies with conflicting law codes. What happens if the plaintiff's agency promises capital punishment for murder but the defendant's agency promises protection against capital punishment?

Agencies may go to war each time a dispute arises. This is the least favorable case for anarchy, as private protection agencies generate a war of all against all. Competing law codes do not prove feasible, as libertarian anarchy collapses into Hobbesian anarchy.[15]

Warfare, however, is not a certain outcome of competing law codes. Private protection agencies may find interagency warfare unprofitable and dangerous, and subscribe to a common arbitration mechanism for settling disputes. Economic forces may also encourage the consolidation of competing agencies either through conquest or simply because citizens of a territorial area join the strongest agency in that area. Each geographical area would possess a dominant protection agency. (Agencies, however, might skirmish at their borders, much like many governments.)

I am not suggesting that such mechanisms of consolidation and adjudication would triumph necessarily over Hobbesian anarchy. Instead, the argument is that Friedman's scenario is not an independent alternative. Competing law codes are stable only if they evolve into a dominant agency or arbitration network, possibilities to which I now turn.

3.2 Interagency Cooperation and Arbitration

Agencies might eschew warfare in favor of arbitration and interagency cooperation. Agencies would agree in advance how interagency conflicts will be settled. Common standards would be applied for criminality, punishment, and criminal procedures when disputes occur. Even when no specific resolution to a case has been agreed upon in advance, agencies could take disputes to an impartial, third-party arbitrator. Agencies could also apply the law of the party on whose territory the crime was committed. Today's governments use a similar procedure when citizens of one country aggress against citizens of another.[16]

A systematic arbitration network would arise to encourage the orderly application of law. Although intra-agency conflicts might be settled differently from interagency conflicts, society would possess effectively a single legal code. For any action committed by one person against another, agencies agree upon the principles to be applied. At the very least, agencies abide by higher-order arbitration. The arbitration literature stresses the importance of preexisting contractual relationships between disputing parties; such relationships would be instituted through subscription to agency policies.[17]

The arbitration network internalizes adjudication externalities by providing for systematic contractual relationships among disputing parties. Like governments, however, anarchist private protection agencies need not enforce a libertarian legal code. If a sufficient number of persons demand illiberal policies and are willing to pay for them, the legal code implemented by the network may be quite interventionist.

The arbitration network would punish defectors, or "outlaw" agencies. Member agencies who did not respect the decisions of the arbitration network would be ostracized, and their rulings, requests for extradition, and so on, would not be heeded. In extreme cases, the network could use force to rein in outlaws. Outlaws could also be excluded from interagency cooperative ventures, such as the use of databases to track down criminals or the negotiation of treaties with foreign countries. The ability of agency consumers to discontinue their subscriptions serves as a further check on outlaws. Organizing a revolt against an arbitration network is not necessarily easier than organizing a revolt against a government.

Outlaws would meet with success only if they could command a high degree of support from their fellow agencies. Perhaps half of the agencies would band together and attempt to conquer the other half. Such outcomes, however, are also possible under government. A large enough group of individuals and institutions, acting in concert, can impose their will upon any political system.

Revolutions do not continually occur, because they are prevented by such factors as free-rider problems, coordination difficulties, and fear of failure and retaliation. These forces would continue to operate under anarchy, just as they do in today's world of governments. The arbitration equilibrium is not necessarily less stable than a government or less stable than international relations between different governments. If the existing order is well-functioning and perceived as legitimate, I assumed (above) that individuals take the basic loyalty of others to the system as parametrically given.

Agency attempts to lead a revolution would be further discouraged by interagency collusion (discussed later). The presence of monopoly profits gives agencies a stake in the existing order and discourages radical actions that might endanger these profits. In contrast, a perfectly competitive protection industry with zero economic profit would imply that agencies have little to lose by risking their position in the industry.[18]

The motivating forces behind cooperative relations among agencies are well summarized by Tandy (1896, p. 69):

> Many people seem to fear that with the existence of several different protective associations in the same city, there will be incessant conflict between them. But as each will be endeavoring to get the largest possible number of patrons, each will endeavor to follow the policy that is most universally approved. The ordinary businessman does not lie awake in the small hours of the morning pining for civil war. So the probabilities are that protective associations will not attempt to place such an expensive commodity upon the market when there is no demand for it.

3.3. Dominant Protection Agency

Nozick (1974) develops a model for an "ultraminimal" state, which supplies only protection services and law enforcement. Property rights are enforced by a dominant protection agency, which Nozick considers a state because it does not admit competitors. Competing agencies are forbidden to operate by the dominant agency because their procedures are considered too risky. Nozick's ultraminimal state does not resort to taxation. Individuals have the option of not paying "fees" and taking their chances with criminals. These individuals, however, are subject to the dominant legal code if they commit a crime against agency members.[19]

Nozick's ultraminimal state differs from the network by degree only. Unlike Nozick's ultraminimal state, the network consists of more than one firm. These firms have separate shareholders and seek to maximize their own profit, rather than the profit of the entire network (nonprofits and mutuals are considered later). The importance of separate shareholders, however, is limited by the presence of network relations. The presence of a network gives rise to contractual relations that induce firms to behave cooperatively, as if they were one large firm. Whether the common arbitration network is "one big firm," or "many cooperating smaller firms" is primarily a matter of semantics. The network can just as well be considered a single firm with separate divisions that compete to some degree. Each division has its own set of residual claimants, but the behavior of divisions is constrained to favor the interests of the entire network.[20]

Nor can we use restrictions on competitors to differentiate Nozick's minimal state and the network. Nozick's ultraminimal state does not allow competitors to exist, but law enforcement entrants who subordinate their will to the state are allowed. Nozick's ultraminimal state does not rule out taking in new citizens through immigration or birth, government subcontracting to private agencies for certain tasks, or the absorption of new territories through annexation, discovery, or liberation, for instance.

The common arbitration network deals with potential competitors in similar fashion. Entrants who are willing to subordinate their will to the network are allowed to enter the market and "compete" with other network members for customers, just as states in a federal republic may compete for citizens. Challenges to the network itself, however, are not allowed. Entrant agencies who do not recognize the network as the ultimate decision-making authority are treated as outlaws and driven out of business.

4. Collusive Arbitration Networks with Monopoly Power

The presence of a common arbitration network is responsible for the orderly relations among private protection agencies. Rather than using force to settle disputes, agencies settle claims through mutual agreement and cooperation. This same arbitration network, however, allows agencies to exert private monopoly power collectively or perhaps even to become a government.

The existence of a common arbitration network creates a vehicle for protection agency collusion. Members of the network find it profitable to write a contract agreeing not to compete with each other. The agencies restrict output and raise prices, thus reaping monopoly profits. Network membership requires contractual acceptance of jointly determined prices and outputs, as well as legal procedures. The collusive contract can also include other monopolizing devices, such as exclusive territories. Finally, network shareholders can agree to impose taxation upon the populace.

The ability to collude successfully is inherent in the nature of the network. The network can internalize the externalities problem behind peaceful adjudication only by suspending quality competition—that is, by offering a uniform set of laws or higher-order adjudication procedures. The ability to engage successfully in quality collusion, however, implies that other kinds of collusion are possible also.[21]

Collusion is enforced when network members agree not to cooperate with potential entrants. We saw above that anarchy is orderly only under the condition that the network, can act collectively to prevent outlaw firms from gaining sizeable market share. If the network can implement successful sanctions against outlaws, however, the network can also implement successful sanctions against potential competitors. The network decides which agencies are outlaws, and profit maximization dictates labeling potential competitors as outlaws, even if these competitors do not threaten societal order. If punishing potential competitors is too costly, punishing outlaws is also too costly, and anarchy will collapse into the scenario where different agencies have conflicting law codes. Competing legal systems are either unstable or collapse into a monopoly agency or network.

Neither free entry nor defection from the cartel provides the usual protection against collusion that we find in most other markets. First, network members will retaliate against defectors, through sanctions, the use of force, or simply ignoring judgments rendered by defectors. This retaliation need not be costly for the network; the network can simply render systematically biased judgments against nonmembers. Such biased judgments will favor network interests. Second, membership in the common arbitration network is one of the most important services an agency can offer its members. Network membership implies that interagency disputes are settled without risk of force or radical uncertainty about the final outcome. Agency members will be loathe to defect and sacrifice both these privileges and their monopoly profits.

Although private cartels usually collapse of their own accord, most historical examples of cartel instability do not involve the benefits of joining a common network. The food that I buy from one supermarket is just as valuable to me regardless of whether this supermarket has friendly relations with its competitors; this independence does not hold with private protection agencies.

In response to the collusion argument, Friedman (1989, pp. 169-70) argues that the profitability of collusion requires small numbers of protection agencies:

> In addition to the temperament and incentives of potential conspirators, there is another relevant factor: the number of protection agencies. If there are only two or three agencies in the entire area now covered by the United States, a conspiracy among them may be practical. If there are 10,000, then when any group of them starts acting like a government, their customers will hire someone else to protect them against their protectors.

> How many agencies there are depends on what size agency does the most efficient job protecting its clients. My own guess is that there will be nearer 10,000 agencies than 3. If the performance of present-day police forces is any indication, a protection agency protecting as many as one million people is far above optimum size.

Several replies can be made to Friedman's argument. First, it illustrates the danger of making inferences about industry structure under anarchy from observed industry structures today. The number of private protection and detective agencies today is very large, but this does not imply that the number of independent firms would be very large in anarchy. Current private agencies and arbiters are not required to serve as *ultimate* arbitrators and enforcers in disputes. Government is available to settle disputes that might arise between different firms. In anarchy, the incentives that generate a monopoly firm or network arise from absence of this external final arbiter.

Second, Friedman's argument does not consider that even large numbers of protection agencies can collude through the network. The network itself overcomes the coordination problem of implementing and enforcing collusion. There are no legal obstacles to enforcing the collusive contract, and the network has a strong profit incentive to prevent shirking on the collusive agreement. Some forms of shirking on collusion, such as price shading, may survive, but the network will take great pains to ensure that the cartel does not break down altogether. A large number of potential competitors increases the benefits of successful collusion. We can even imagine the network implementing a perverse form of "antirust" law, which would enforce collusion rather than prevent it.

Private-sector experience demonstrates the feasibility of enforcing cooperative relationships across many firms that might otherwise be tempted to compete. Different franchises of McDonalds, for instance, enter into common relations through the parent company and agree not to compete with each other. The franchises abide by common quality standards and marketing practices and receive territorial rights to a market area. Franchises that deviate from their contract with the parent company are reprimanded and ultimately cut off, if disobedience persists. While different McDonald's franchises undoubtedly do compete across some margins in violation of their instructions, parent company attempts to discipline franchises are frequently successful in this regard.

It may still be possible that detecting and punishing competitive behavior is too costly for the network. If the network cannot monitor and control the behavior of member agencies, however, anarchy will not remain orderly. Agencies will favor the interests of their own customers, enforce their own preferred law codes, and treat the customers of other agencies poorly. We are effectively back to the case of competing outlaw agencies, even though these agencies belong nominally to the network. Orderly anarchy again implies collusive anarchy.

If collusion is successful, the protection network now holds the power to initiate coercion against customers. Like a government, the network's revenue is raised through taxation and becomes independent of consumer demand through markets. Taxpayers can exit only through death or emigration. Furthermore, consumers lose the influence over product mix that they have under normal market arrangements. The network is well on its way to becoming a full-fledged state. The state that evolved through anarchy would still be privately held through shareholders, unlike today's governments. In this respect, a residual difference would remain between modern states and the states that might evolve through anarchy. The decision-making apparatus in a shareholder-held state, for instance, differs from that of a constitutional democracy.[22] If the network does become a state, however, public trading of the network's shares may eventually cease. Trading the right to enforce and define contracts involves problems if network shares are traded in large, controlling blocks. After a person or consortium has purchased a controlling interest in the network, for instance, how do sellers require them to settle, or prevent them from seizing the funds received from sale of the network?

4.1. Extending Monopoly Power

Once the network obtains monopoly power over society's apparatus of adjudication and punishment, it can use this power to achieve monopolistic positions elsewhere in the economy. The network, for instance, could threaten to withhold protection from private entrepreneurs unless they sell out to the network. Even more baldly, the network might simply seize the desired resources and proclaim itself the rightful owner. The network can thus take control of communications and transportation systems or other industries in order to support its bid to maintain power. More generally, the network could implement policies at variance with free-market and libertarian principles.[23]

Nonetheless, a profit-maximizing network would not seize all of society's productive economic resources. A network that owned the entire economy would find itself in a position similar to that of a central planner. In the complete absence of competition, efficient resource allocation would be difficult, national product would fall, and the network's profits would decline. A rational network will preserve a significant amount of competition in the private sector of industries other than the adjudication industry.[24]

4.2. Anarchy and International Anarchy

The possibility of interagency collusion points to a disanalogy between competing defense agencies and the international "anarchy" that exists between different governments in today's world. Collusion among private protection agencies is more likely than collusion between governments for several reasons. First, protection agencies are owned by shareholders who wish to maximize profits; these shareholders favor successful collusion. The incentives and motives of governments are less clear. It is not obvious, for instance, that intergovernmental collusion significantly increases incumbents' chances of reelection.

Second, immigration and trade restrictions limit competition between nation-states for citizens and economic resources. Because competition is limited to begin with, the motivation to collude is weaker. Private protection agencies, in contrast, cannot prevent their clients from switching allegiance to other firms in the absence of collusion; the cost of changing one's subscription may be quite low. Since agencies do not have a natural lock on their market, the value of collusion is high.[25]

Third, international criminal and legal relations are a very small part of the activities of, say, the American and Canadian governments. The benefits of forming a world government to more profitably or efficiently deal with Americans who murder Canadians are relatively small. In the case of private protection agencies, interagency relations on issues of criminal law likely form large part of their business. The benefits of forming a single, overarching, collusive arbitration network are correspondingly larger.

5. How Might Anarchy Avoid Government?

In the above scenarios, the network becomes a government because network shareholders are able to exploit successfully conflicts between network profit maximization and the interests of the network consumers. If consumers are sufficiently far-sighted, they may prefer dealing with agencies that precommit to never becoming collusive or coercive. Consumers may attempt to control the network by owning the member firms; under this scenario, the protection agencies would become mutuals or cooperatives. Protection agencies could then be bound by democratic procedures, according to customer vote. Collusion could not occur unless approved by agency customers (shareholders).[26]

Notes

1. Arguments for provision of law enforcement through private markets originate with Tucker (1893/1972), de Molinari (1849/1977), and the Anglo-American "Voluntaryist" Movement (e.g. Francis Tandy [1896]). Today, anarchism is most commonly associated with segments of the libertarian movement. Libertarian economists such as Rothbard (1978), Friedman (1989), and Benson (1990), and libertarian legal theorist Barnett (1986) have endorsed the private provision of law enforcement services. Other writers sympathetic to the market provision of protection and law enforcement services include Morris and Linda Tannehill (1972), Wollstein (1972), Tador (1982), Osterfeld (1983), de Jasay (1989), Hummel (1990).,Christiansen (1990), and Sutter (1991). The *Journal of Libertarian Studies* contains many articles arguing in favor of anarchy, some of which are cited throughout the text. Landes and Posner (1979) provide a law and economics perspective on private courts. The profit-maximizing punishment strategies of private protection agencies are considered in Becker and Stigler (1974) and Friedman (1984).

   I do not consider many varieties of anarchism. "Left-wing" anarchists such as Proudhon, Kropotkin, and Bakunin consider anarchist societies in which law enforcement institutions are not necessary, usually because of changes in human nature. These writers devote little attention to whether their proposed reforms lead to incentive compatible outcomes.
2. Posner (1979, p. 323) explains a similar motivation: "What we ask in Part I is what would the world look like, in terms of judicial services, if there were no state? We don't ask this question because we are interested in privatizing judicial services. Our piece is not normative in its thrust. But it is frequently a useful approach to positive analysis to ask: What would be the problems if a service which has

traditionally been regarded as governmental were to be provided exclusively on a private basis?

3. See Nozick (1974). In addition to the authors mentioned in the text, critics of anarchy include French (1973), Hospers (1973), Kelley (1974), Rand (1961), Sampson (1984, chap. 8), Newman (1984), and Kavka (1986).
4. Some representative Virginia School writings on anarchy are Tullock (1972, 1974), Buchanan (1975), and Bush (1976). Gregory Kavka and I consider the prior issue of how markets could arise in Cowen and Kavka (1991). Kavka and I argue that monopoly power in law enforcement increases the likelihood that the public good of markets will evolve, just as this paper argues that monopoly power is associated with the sustenance of a stable law-and-order equilibrium.
5. I read the proposals of Rothbard (1978) as consistent with this approach. Hospers (1973) calls for a system where government enforces a single law code but private agencies compete to enforce this code. If enforcement power is in the hands of private agencies, this system is difficult to distinguish from anarchy.
6. Historical experience illustrates that stable anarchy is at the very least possible. Medieval Iceland and medieval Ireland are two examples of relatively stable anarchist societies. On Iceland, see Friedman (1979) and Solvason (1991). On Ireland, see Peden (1977).
7. The roll that I allow ideology to play can be expressed in the language of game theory. Ideology may be a factor in selecting among multiple equilibria. For instance, if each individual believes that others will cooperate with the established legal order, crude anarchy will be less likely; ideology may be responsible for such expectations. Given an equilibrium and set of mutual expectations, however, I do not invoke ideology to produce cooperation when aggression would serve self-interest.
8. Rothbard (1973) and Hummel (1990) assign a central roll to ideology in preventing the reemergence of government.
9. Neither anarchy nor government is likely to have fully transitive power relations. Various social institutions, such as churches, terrorist groups, and families, have their own spheres of jurisdiction that are not directly subject to political rule. The government or anarchist adjudication mechanism does not have a strict monopoly on the use of retaliatory violence or the initiation of violence. Even within a government, transitivity of power relations does not generally hold. Under a system with federalism and the separation of powers, different parts of government exist in a state of anarchy with respect to each other. There is no clearly defined transitive ordering of who has jurisdiction over whom. Similarly, the adjudication mechanisms in anarchy may not develop a clearly defined power ordering to cover all possible relationships and conflicts. Just as in the American system of government, the adjudication may consist of a coalition of forces, none of which has ultimate authority. The importance of nontransitivity for political philosophy is stressed by Cuzan (1979).
10. Of the critics of anarchy, only Kelley (1974, pp. 247-48) raises the issue of collusion. Some writers, such as Kavka (1986, p. 172), raise the distinct issue of natural monopoly. While natural monopoly will give rise to a dominant agency or network, collusion will produce a dominant network without requiring the cost structure traditionally associated with natural monopoly. Friedman (1989, pp. 169-70) argues that the protection industry is not characterized by natural monopoly. I discuss this issue in further detail later.
11. General arguments that markets can produce public goods, or that many supposed public goods are actually private goods, can be found in Cowen (1988); de Jasay (1989) and Schmidtz (1991) examine the market provision of law enforcement services.

12. McCallum (1970) emphasizes proprietary communities as a means of public goods provision through private markets.
13. I assume a closed economy by considering only protection services in general, and not protection against foreign aggressors. Protection against foreign aggressors presents a problem different in scope, but not different in kind from protection against domestic aggressors. Relatively small territories, whether governmental or anarchistic, may not be able to protect themselves against their more powerful neighbors. Anarchy may increase the significance of this problem at the margin, but government does not ensure its elimination. In any case, consideration or foreign conquest would only strengthen my argument that government is to be expected.
14. On adjudication, see Landes and Posner (1979). The purchase of private adjudication services through markets is widespread in the United States and other countries. On the punishment incentives of private law enforcement agencies, see Becker and Stigler (1974) and Friedman (1984).
15. We cannot rely upon the Coase theorem to prevent violent outcomes. First, individuals have an incentive to engage in threats and strategic behavior in small-numbers problems. Second, the Coase theorem takes the distribution or property rights as given and examines a small change in rights at the margin, such as the assignment of rights to a water stream, piece of land, or natural resource. The Coase theorem does not apply when the entire distribution of property is potentially up for grabs. We cannot argue that those who value rights the most will bid the highest for them; the distribution of property and thus bidding power itself is precisely what is being determined. Enforceable contracts are no longer present. Kuwait, for instance, could not bribe Iraq not to invade; Iraq could simply pocket the bribe and invade anyway. Cowen (1990) discusses these problems in further detail.
16. Agencies may agree not to punish too harshly convicted criminals who belong to other agencies. Furthermore, agencies might also agree to restrictions upon conflict resolution procedures among their own clients. Selling a law code that offers very harsh punishments for minor crimes, for instance, might offend members or other agencies with more lenient values. Or imposing lenient punishments for serious crimes, even within a single agency's members, may decrease the strength of other agencies' attempts at deterrence (criminals do not always know to which agency their potential victims belong). For these reasons agencies may collectively abide by common standards, even for intra-agency disputes.
17. On the prerequisites or arbitration, see Landes and Posner (1979, p. 246). The problem of individuals who do not join any agency is dealt with further below.
18. The effect of monopoly profits in firm behavior is considered in Klein and Leffler (1981).
19. Much of Nozick's argument is geared toward establishing that this monopolization of the market does not violate individual rights. I am discussing Nozick's "ultraminimal" state. Nozick's slightly larger "minimal" state provides protection services to noncontributors for free. These services are compensation for forbidding noncontributors from taking the law into their own hands.
20. Competing divisions are common in entities that are traditionally considered "single firms." The corporate structure of General Motors is one well-known example. Most economists agree that the difference between "firm" and "market" is one of degree rather than of kind. See Richardson (1972), Fama (1980), and Cheung (1983).
21. In the context of other markets, economists have argued that the presence of common relations between firms allows for incentive-compatible collusion even without an explicit collusive contract. See Bernheim and Whinston (1985).
22. This difference should not be overdrawn. Some monarchies, for instance, can be interpreted as privately held slates. Furthermore, a new state arising from anarchy

need not remain shareholder-owned. It is possible that managers could turn against shareholders and seize control of the network. Or some shareholders could stage a coup d'état and control the network exclusively. Under another scenario, the new state could offer democratic constraints upon its leaders. Fear of immigration, lower tax revenues, and popular revolt might encourage the new government to be democratic.

23. The dominant agency or collusive network can attempt to extend its monopoly power through several means. A dominant protection agency or agency network would find it profitable to offer tied sales of public goods, for instance. A protection agency with monopoly power can spread its monopoly successfully across goods that are produced at declining average cost (e.g., excludable public goods). For a demonstration of this proposition, see Mumy (1987). Whinston (1990) reaches similar conclusions.
24. On the consequences of centralized private ownership of all the means of production, see Cowen and Glazer (1991).
25. As resource mobility increases, we should expect to see increased regulatory collusion through international agencies. This is precisely the case in the European Community. Similarly, the U.S.-Canada free-trade agreement can be expected to increase collusion between these two governments. We should also expect states in a federal system to favor a larger role for the federal government as resource mobility increases.
26. In mutuals, the corporation's customers are also its owners. A mutual life insurance company, for instance, is owned by its policyholders, who serve as residual claimants. If the company makes money. the profits are refunded in the form of lower premiums; conversely, losses imply higher premiums. (Not all of the mutual's profits are rebated to customers, however, as managers retain perks for themselves.) In so far as mutual shareholders succeed in controlling their company, their dual roles as owners and customers diminish conflicts of interest. Policies that deliberately defraud customers, for instance, would not be approved by mutual shareholders. Shareholders of traditional corporations, in contrast, will maximize profits as the expense of consumer interests, when possible. Cooperatives and nonprofit organizations are other possible organizational forms for protection agencies. Although these forms differ from mutuals with respect to many details, they also eschew direct profit-maximization and allow managers to maximize the now of perks, although subject to different institutional constraints. See Rose-Ackerman (1986) on these alternative forms of organization.

References

Cheung, Steven S. 1983. "The Contractual Nature of the Firm." *Journal of Law Economics* 26: 1-22.

Christiansen, Gregory B. 1990. "Law as a Discovery Procedure." *Cato Journal* 9: 497-530.

Cowen Tyler. 1988. *The Theory of Market Failure: A Critical Examination*. Fairfax, Virginia: George Mason University Press.

———. 1990. "Economic Effects of a Conflict-Prone World Order." *Public Choice* 64: 121-34.

Cowen, Tyler and Amihai Glazer. 1991. "Why Do Firms Compete: Shareholder Diversification and Joint Profit Maximization." University of California, Irvine. Unpublished manuscript.

Cowen, Tyler. Amihai Glazer, and Henry MacMillan. 1991 "Rent-Seeking Promotes the Provision of Public Goods." Unpublished manuscript. University of California, Irvine.

Cowen, Tyler, and Gregory Kavka. 1991. "The Public Goods Rationale for Government and the Circulatory Problem." Unpublished Manuscript, George Mason University.

Cuzan, Alfred G. 1979. "Do We Ever Really Get Out of Anarchy?" *Journal of Libertarian Studies* 3: 151-58.

De Jasay, Anthony. 1989. *Social Contract, Free Ride*. Oxford: Clarendon Press.

De Molinari, Gustav. 1977 (first ed. 1849). *The Production of Security*. New York: Center for Libertarian Studies.

Fama, Eugene F. 1980. "Agency Problems and the Theory of the Firm." *Journal of Political Economy* 88: 288-307.

Fama, Eugene F., and Michael Jensen. 1983a : "Separation of Ownership and Control." *Journal of Law and Economics* 26: 327-49.

———. 1983b. "Agency Problems and Residual Claims." *Journal of Law and Economics* 26: 327-49.

Frech, III, H. E. 1973. "The Public Choice of Murray N. Rothbard, A Modern Anarchist." *Public Choice* 14: 143-54.

Friedman. David. 1989. *Tilt Machinery of Freedom: Guide to a Radical Capitalism*. 2nd ed. La Salle, IL: Open Court.

———. 1979. "Private Creation and Enforcement of law: A Historical Case." *Journal of Legal Studies* 8: 399-415.

———. 1984. "Efficient Institutions for the Private Enforcement of Law." *Journal of Legal Studies* 8: 379-97.

Hospers, John. 1973. "Will Rothbard's Free Market Justice Suffice?" *Reason* May: 18-23.

Hummel, Jeffrey Rogers. 1990. "National Goods Versus Public Goods: Defense Disarmament, and Free Riders." *Review of Austrian Economics* 4: 88-122.

Kavka, Gregory. 1986. *Hobbesian Moral and Political Theory*. Princeton: Princeton University Press.

Kelley, David. 1974. "The Necessity of Government." *The Freeman* 24: 243-18.

Klein, Benjamin, and Keith Leffler. 1981. "The Role of Market Forces in Assuring Contractual Performance." *Journal of Political Economy* 89: 615-41.

Landes, William M., and Richard A Posner. 1979. "Adjudication as a Private Good." *Journal of Legal Studies* 8: 235-84.

McCallum, Spencer Heath. 1970. *The Art of Community*. Menlo Park, California: Institute for Humane Studies.

Mumy, Gene E. 1987. "What Does Nozick's Minimal State Do?" *Economics and Philosophy* 3: 275-305.

Newman, Steven L. 1984. *Liberalism at Wit's End: The Libertarian Revolt Against the Modern State*. Ithaca, NY: Cornell University Press.

Nozick, Robert. 1974. *Anarchy, State, and Utopia*. New York: Basic Books.

Osterfeld, David 1983. *Freedom, Society and the State*. Lanham, Maryland: University Press of America.

Peden. Joseph. 1977. "Property Rights in Celtic Irish Law." *Journal of Libertarian Studies* 1: 81-95.

Posner, Richard A. 1979. "Discussion by Seminar Participants." *Journal of Legal Studies* 8: 323-98.

Rand, Ayn. 1961. *The Virtue of Selfishness*. New York: Signet.

Rasmusen, Eric. 1988. "Mutual Banks and Stock Banks." *Journal of Law and Economics* 31: 395-422.

Richardson, G. B. 1972. "The Organization of Industry." *Economic Journal* 82: 883-96.

Rose-Ackerman, Susan (editor). 1986. *The Economics of Non-Profit Institutions*. New York: Oxford University Press.
Rothbard, Murray. 1973. "Will Rothbard's Free-Market Justice Suffice? Yes." *Reason* May: 19-25.
———. 1978. *For a New Liberty*. New York: Collier Books.
Sampson, Geoffrey. 1984. *An End to Allegiance*. London: Temple Smith.
Schmidtz, David, 1991. *The Limits of Government: An Essay on Public Goods Argument.* Boulder, CO: Westview Press.
Solvason, Birgir Thor. 1991. "The Evolution of a Decentralized Legal Order in Medieval Iceland." Unpublished Manuscript. George Mason University.
Sutter, Daniel. 1992. "Contractual Freedom with Private Protection Agencies." Unpublished Manuscript. George Mason University.
Tandy, Francis. 1896. *Voluntary Socialism*. Denver Colorado: Francis Tandy Publisher.
Tannehill, Morris, and Linda Tannehill. 1972. *The Market for Liberty*. Reprinted in *Society Without Government*. New York: Arno Press and The New York Times.
Taylor, Michael. 1982. *Community, Anarchy, and Liberty*. Cambridge: Cambridge University Press.
Tucker, Benjamin R. 1972 (first ed. 1893). *Instead of a Book*. New York Arno Press.
Tullok, Gordon (editor). 1972. *Explorations in the Theory of Anarchy*. Blacksburg VA: Center for the Study of Public Choice.
———. 1974. *The Social Dilemma: The Economics of War and Revolution*. Blacksburg VA: University Publications.
Whinston, Michael D. 1990. "Tying, Foreclosure, and Exclusion." *American Economic Review* 80: 837-59.
Wollstein, Jarret B. 1972. *Society Without Coercion*. Reprinted in *Society Without Government*. New York: Arno Press and The New York Times.

16

Law as a Private Good: A Response to Tyler Cowen on the Economics of Anarchy

David Friedman

In "Law as a Public Good" Tyler Cowen argues that an anarcho-capitalist system of private protection agencies of the sort proposed by myself and others is unworkable. I believe he is mistaken. In explaining why, I will start with a brief explanation of how I believe that such a system would work, then summarize Professor Cowen's arguments and attempt to show why they are wrong.

Imagine a society with no government. Individuals purchase protection of themselves and their property from private firms. Each such firm faces the problem of possible conflicts with other firms. Private policemen working for the protection agency that I employ may track down the burglar who stole my property only to discover, when they try to arrest him, that he too employs a protection agency.

There are three ways in which this problem might be dealt with. The most obvious and least likely is direct violence—a mini-war between my agency, attempting to arrest the burglar, and his agency attempting to defend him from arrest. A somewhat more plausible scenario is negotiation. Since warfare is expensive, agencies might include in the contracts they offer their customers a provision under which they are not obliged to defend customers against legitimate punishments for their actual crimes. When a conflict occurs, it would then be up to the two agencies to determine whether the accused customer of one will or will not be deemed guilty and turned over to the other.

A still more attractive and more likely solution is advance contracting between the agencies. Under this scenario, any two agencies that faced a significant probability of such clashes would agree on an arbitration agency to settle them—a private court. Implicit or explicit in their agreement would be the legal rules under which such disputes were to be settled.

Under these circumstances, both law enforcement and law are private goods produced on a private market. Law enforcement is produced by enforcement agencies and sold directly to their customers. Law is produced by arbitration agencies and sold to the protection agencies, who resell it to their customers as one characteristic of the bundle of services they provide.

One attractive feature of such a system is that the usual economic arguments for the efficiency of market outcomes apply to the legal system and the rules it generates. To see why, imagine that there is some change in the legal rules currently prevailing between two enforcement agencies which would yield net benefits to their customers. If it benefits both sets of customers, then it is in the interest of the protection agencies either to persuade their arbitration agency to make the change or to shift to one that follows the superior set of rules. If it benefits the customers of one agency but imposes costs on the customers of the other, with net costs smaller than net benefits, then it is in the interest of the two agencies to agree to make the change, with the loser compensated either directly or by some other change elsewhere in the legal rules. In practice, since it is the arbitration agencies that specialize in legal rules, we would expect them to try to develop superior legal codes in the process of competing for customers. The result should be a set of legal codes that are economically efficient in the conventional sense.[1]

While this argument implies an efficient set of legal codes, it does not tell us which efficient set. Legal rules have distributional as well as allocational consequences. Imagine, for example, that agency X and agency Y represent customers with different tastes in legal rules. Perhaps the customers of X support the death penalty and the customers of Y oppose it. The argument of the previous paragraph implies that whichever group most values its preferred legal rule will get it. But it does not tell us which agency will have to pay the other in order to get its way in disputes between their customers. Will X have to pay Y to get its agreement to a pro-death penalty court for disputes between their customers, or will Y have to pay X if it wants an anti-death penalty court? I have described the logic of the bargaining, but not the starting point—the default rules from which mutually beneficial changes will be made.[2]

The answer is that the distributional starting point is the solution to a bilateral monopoly bargaining game between the agencies. Each agency can threaten to refuse to agree to any arbitrator, subjecting both to the costs of occasional violence, or at least ad hoc negotiation to avoid violence. Each knows that the other would prefer even a rather unfavorable set of legal rules to no agreement at all. The situation is analogous to a union management negotiation or the negotiations determining borders, trade policies, and the like between neighboring countries. While there is no good theoretical account of exactly what determines the outcome of bilateral monopoly bargaining, experience suggests that some reasonably efficient equilibrium usually exists. Most unionized firms manage to settle their differences without lengthy strikes, and most nations are at peace with most of their neighbors most of the time.[3]

So we may imagine the market for law as starting out with a set of default rules between each pair of protection agencies, representing the result of bargaining backed by threats of refusal to agree on an arbitrator. From there, the agencies bargain to an efficient set of rules. Where the change benefits both, it may occur without side payments. Where the change is preferred by only one agency, it must pay the other enough to obtain its agreement. The distributional outcome is the result of an implicit threat game between the agencies; the allocational outcome is the result of a (logically subsequent) bargaining game to move from the starting point to the Pareto frontier.

Experience suggests that there is enormous inertia in mutual threat games of this sort. National boundaries do not move half a mile one way or the other each time one nation becomes a little richer or a little more powerful. In practice, an anarcho-capitalist society will probably be built not so much on an ongoing mutual threat game as on a mutual threat game played out in the distant past. That suggests that, once the initial equilibrium has been established, the success of a protection agency will be based mainly on its ability to produce protection for its customers, not its ability to defeat rivals in open warfare.

While it is always possible for one firm to threaten to withdraw from its arbitration agreement with another unless the terms are renegotiated de novo, such threats are unlikely to be either common or successful. Other agencies have a strong incentive to insist on basing their bargaining on the existing rules, in order to prevent the costs of continual renegotiation and the costs of violence when negotiations break down.

I have now described anarcho-capitalism as I believe it would function in a modern society.[4] What are Cowen's reasons for believing that such institutions would be unstable?

Cowen (1992) writes:

> ...the argument is that Friedman's scenario is not an independent alternative. Competing law codes are stable only if they evolve into a dominant agency or arbitration network....
>
> Agencies might eschew warfare in favor of arbitration and interagency cooperation. Agencies would agree in advance how interagency conflicts will be settled. Common standards would be applied for criminality, punishment, and criminal procedures when disputes occur....
>
> A systematic arbitration network would arise to encourage the orderly application of law. Although intra-agency conflicts might be settled differently from interagency conflicts, society would possess effectively a single legal code.... At the very least, agencies abide by higher-order arbitration....

So far I agree with Cowen,[5] provided that the accent is put on the final sentence and that it is recognized that what is described is an equilibrium, not a constraint. Firms almost always abide by arbitration because it is almost always in their interest to do so. Describing this as a single legal code is, however, somewhat misleading, since there may be as many legal codes as there are pairs of agencies.[6]

The distinction between a market equilibrium and a constraint is not merely a verbal one. Consider the analogous case of an ordinary competitive market. Economic theory tells us that firms selling identical goods will all charge the same price. That does not mean that firms are not free to change their price if they wish, nor that a change by one firm will somehow force every other firm to make an identical change. On the contrary, the analysis of what the price will be depends on the assumption that each firm is free to set whatever price it wishes, and deduces both the existence and level of the common price from that assumption. Similarly, protection firms under anarcho-capitalism will agree on arbitrators to settle disputes between them, but that is a consequence of their profit maximizing behavior, not a constraint upon it. The fact that they are free to refuse to agree to arbitration is one of the elements that determine what the actual terms of arbitration will be.

Cowen then writes:

> Unlike Nozick's ultraminimal state, the network consists of more than one firm.... The presence of a network gives rise to contractual relations that induce firms to behave cooperatively, as if they were one large firm. Whether the common arbitration network is "one big firm," or "many cooperating smaller firms" is primarily a matter of semantics. The network can just as well be considered a single firm with separate divisions that compete to some degree. Each division has its own set of residual claimants, but the behavior of divisions is constrained to favor the interests of the entire network.

So far as I can tell, this final assertion is nowhere justified, and I believe it to be false. What Cowen describes as a "network" is simply a set of private firms—protection and arbitration agencies—linked by a large number of contracts. Each pair of protection agencies has a contract specifying an arbitrator for disputes between their customers, and each protection agency has contracts with one or more arbitration agencies specifying the terms on which they will arbitrate its disputes with specified other protection agencies.

Nothing in this situation requires or implies a single firm controlling the whole, nor anything analogous to one. The network as I have described it has no decision-making body. Its "decisions," the set of legal codes it enforces, are the outcome of independent profit-making decisions by the individual firms and bargaining between pairs of firms. Nothing in the logic of the market for protection and arbitration implies that the outcome will maximize the summed profits of the firms, as Cowen seems to assert. Indeed, ordinary economic theory suggests that in equilibrium this market, like any competitive market, will yield zero profit to the firms that make it up.

Consider Cowen's argument applied to a less exotic industry—groceries. As a practical matter, any grocery that wishes to stay in business must have contracts with a number of large suppliers, such as Kraft and General Mills, either directly or through distributors that function as intermediaries. Thus all grocery stores are linked together by contracts with common intermediaries. The whole collection of firms—grocery stores, producers, wholesalers—could be described as a network in the same sense in which Cowen describes the protection agency as a network.[7] Does it follow that, in the grocery industry, "contractual relations...induce firms to behave cooperatively, as if they were one large firm?" Is there any reason to believe that the behavior of the separate firms "is constrained to favor the interests of the entire network?"

Grocery stores and protection agencies are indeed constrained, but it is not their own interest that they are constrained to follow. Grocery stores are constrained to follow policies that maximize the welfare of their customers, and protection agencies are constrained to enforce legal codes that maximize the welfare of their customers, for essentially analogous reasons. In both cases the constraint is only approximate, due to the familiar problems of imperfect competition, imperfect knowledge, externalities, and the like. But nothing in the logic of either market leads to maximization of the interests of the industry.

Having asserted that the protection industry is in effect a single firm, the next step in Cowen's argument is straightforward.

> The existence of a common arbitration network creates a vehicle for protection agency collusion. Members of the network find it profitable to write a contract agreeing not to compete with each other. The agencies restrict output and raise prices, thus reaping monopoly profits. Network membership requires contractual acceptance of jointly determined prices and outputs, as well as legal procedures....

Let us see how this works—remembering that the "network" is not a firm but a set of contracts among a large number of firms. Firm A announces that it will only agree to arbitration agreements with other firms that agree to restrict output and raise price. Firm B treats this offer like any other move in its negotiations with firm A—it accepts it if the agreement, along with any compensation offered by firm A for agreeing, makes it better off, otherwise it insists on sticking to the old terms.

But firm B could have raised prices and restricted output without any demand from firm A. The reason it did not was that doing so would have lowered its profits. It will accept A's demand only if A is willing to pay enough to make up for the resulting losses. The situation is no different than in any industry (without antitrust laws) where one firm attempts to create a cartel. As in any industry, it is possible to have a profitable cartel if all of the firms can somehow agree to and abide by a cartel agreement, while keeping out new entrants. One reason that is difficult, here as elsewhere, is that if some subgroup of the industry forms a cartel it is in the interest of all the non-members to undercut the members.

Cowen seems to imagine the collusion occurring not at the level of the firm but at the level of the network. He writes:

> The ability to collude successfully is inherent in the nature of the network. The network can internalize the externalities problem behind peaceful adjudication only by suspending quality competition—that is, by offering a uniform set of laws or higher-order adjudication procedures. The ability to engage successfully in quality collusion, however, implies that other kinds of collusion are possible also.

But, as we have already seen, nothing in the logic of the system requires either uniform laws or any single body determining such laws. It is, of course, possible that there will be one or more bodies offering model legal codes, and that many firms may adopt such codes in order to reduce the costs of legal diversity. To the extent that reasonably uniform standards prevail, collusion will be somewhat easier since there will be fewer dimensions on which the collusive agreement must be defined and adherence to it monitored. But a standard setting body does not, as Cowen seems to assume, provide an enforcement mechanism for a cartel. Non-member firms can abide by non-price standards while chiseling on the cartel's price.

Cowen also argues that "anarchy is orderly only under the condition that the network can act collectively to prevent outlaw firms from gaining sizable market share. If the network can implement successful sanctions against outlaws, however, the network can also implement successful sanctions against potential competitors."

Here again, he is misinterpreting the anarcho-capitalist system, or at least the version of it that I proposed and he earlier cites. In a system of a hundred agencies of equal size, one of which is an outlaw, each of the ninety-nine others settles ninety-nine percent of its conflicts by arbitration and one percent by violence. The outlaw agency settles a hundred percent of its conflicts by violence. Since violence is much more expensive than arbitration, the outlaw's costs are much higher than the costs of its competitors. Agencies that are unwilling to sign arbitration agreements acceptable to most other agencies with which they are likely to come in conflict are prevented from gaining market share not by some collective action by "the network" but by the difficulty of selling a product when your production cost is much higher than your competitors'.

There is, it is true, one special feature of this market which might make cartelization easier. If all the existing firms do agree on a common anti-competitive policy, they may well have the physical force necessary to enforce it by keeping new firms from forming. I discussed this possibility at some length in Friedman (1989), where I wrote:

> The protection agencies will have a large fraction of the armed might of the society. What can prevent them from getting together and using that might to set themselves up as a government?
>
> ...our present police departments, national guard, and armed forces already possess most of the armed might. Why have they not combined to run the country for their own benefit? Neither soldiers nor policemen are especially well paid; surely they could impose a better settlement at gunpoint.
>
> ... A brief answer is that people act according to what they perceive as right, proper, and practical. The restraints which prevent a military coup are essentially restrains interior to the men with guns.
>
> We must ask, not whether an anarcho-capitalist society would be safe from a power grab by the men with the guns (safety is not an available option), but whether it would be safer than our society is from a comparable seizure of power by the men with the guns. I think the answer is yes. In our society, the men who must engineer such a coup are politicians, military officers, and policemen, men selected precisely for the characteristic of desiring power and being good at using it. They

are men who already believe that they have a right to push other men around—that is their job. They are particularly well qualified for the job of seizing power. Under anarcho-capitalism the men in control of protection agencies are selected for their ability to run an efficient business and please their customers. It is always possible that some will turn out to be secret power freaks as well, but it is surely less likely than under our system where the corresponding jobs are labeled "non-power freaks need not apply."

In addition to the temperament of potential conspirators, there is another relevant factor: the number of protection agencies. If there are only two or three agencies in the entire area now covered by the United States, a conspiracy among them may be practical. If there are 10,000, then when any group of them starts acting like a government, their customers will hire someone else to protect them against their protectors.

How many agencies there are depends on what size agency does the most efficient job of protecting its clients. My own guess is that the number will be nearer 10,000 than 3. If the performance of present-day police forces is any indication, a protection agency protecting as many as one million people is far above optimum size.

My conclusion is one of guarded optimism. (pp. 123-124).

Notes

1. This conclusion is qualified, for this market as for other markets, by the possibility of the usual sorts of market failure. In particular, since the legal rule applying between A and B is negotiated on their behalf by their protection agencies, the decision will not take account of effects on C. Consider the case of intellectual property. When B agrees to respect A's intellectual property, the result is an increased incentive for A to produce such property, which may benefit others who use it. Such benefits will not be taken into account in the negotiations that determine whether or not B makes such an agreement. Similar problems will arise with pollution law, where A's right to sue B for polluting his air results in a reduction of B's emissions and thus an external benefit for A's neighbor C.

   This problem is not part of the argument Cowen offers for why anarcho-capitalism is unworkable, and I have therefore not discussed it in the body of this article. Its implication is that the legal rules generated by anarcho-capitalism will not be perfectly efficient. That is not, however, a reason to prefer the rules generated by other institutions, unless we have some reason to expect them to generate efficient rules. Arguments for the efficiency of the legal rules generated by ordinary political processes are, however, weak or nonexistent. For an attempt to argue that the common law tends to generate efficient law, but not, in my view, a convincing one, see Posner (1992, pp. 254-255, 535-536).
2. This omission was pointed out in a perceptive review of *The Machinery of Freedom* by James Buchanan (1974).
3. For one approach to understanding how the solution to such conflicts is determined and maintained, see Friedman (1994).
4. For a description of a historical society with some, although not perfect, similarity to what I have described, see Friedman (1979).
5. It is unclear to me whether Cowen, in this part of his discussion, intends to describe the institutions proposed in Friedman (1989) or a different set of institutions that he believes they would evolve into.
6. There will be some market pressure towards legal uniformity, since there are costs to a system where the legal rules applying to a transaction vary widely according to who you happen to be transacting with. There will also be some pressure towards

diversity, designed to satisfy the different legal needs of different segments of the population. It seems likely that the result, as in the U.S. states, will be a small number of basic legal systems, but variations in detail among the legal rules followed by different arbitrators. See Friedman (1989, p. 120).

7. Of course, the structure of the two networks is not the same. Protection agencies will typically have contracts with both other protection agencies and arbitrators. Grocery stores may have contracts with other grocery stores providing for joint purchasing, or lobbying efforts, or whatever, but the essential contracts are with suppliers. Perhaps Cowen can show that the particular structure of contracts in the former case somehow leads to an industry that acts like a single firm—but so far as I can tell, he has not done so anywhere in this article.

References

Buchanan, James M. 1974. Review of *The Machinery of Freedom: Guide to a Radical Capitalism* by David D. Friedman, *Journal of Economic Literature* XII, 3 (September): 914-915.

Cowen, Tyler. 1992. "Law as a Public Good: The Economics of Anarchy," *Economics and Philosophy* 8: 249-267.

Friedman, David. 1994. "A Positive Account of Property Rights," *Social Philosophy and Policy* 11, 2 (Summer).

Friedman, David. 1979. "Private Creation and Enforcement of Law—A Historical Case." *Journal of Legal Studies* 8 (March): 399-415.

Friedman, David. 1989. *The Machinery of Freedom, Guide to a Radical Capitalism*, 2nd ed. (La Salle, IL: Open Court).

Posner, Richard. 1992. *Economic Analysis of Law*, 4th ed. (Boston: Little Brown).

17

Rejoinder to David Friedman on the Economics of Anarchy

Tyler Cowen

The received wisdom once stated that anarcho-capitalism would collapse into Hobbes's state of nature, with life nasty, short, and brutish. The problem of competing governments is the problem of externality par excellence. But David Friedman, among others, has argued persuasively that privately financed arbitration agencies can overcome the basic externalities problems behind social order.

Unfortunately the matter is not so simple, because the state—a coercive monopoly on the use of force—may reemerge. Like most advocates of libertarian anarchy, Friedman wishes to have it both ways. Private protection agencies are supposed to be able to produce public goods by cooperating. But somehow collusion, which is a public good for the firms in question (if not for all of society), is supposed to be impossible or unstable.

My initial piece argued that the same mechanisms that encourage interagency cooperation also would allow agency collusion. Friedman's comment has not changed my mind about the soundness of this conclusion.[1]

The industry for protection services is particularly vulnerable to collusion because it is what I call a network industry. Specifically, the industry is characterized by the following features:

1. Firms that do not have friendly, cooperative relations with the other firms in the same industry cannot capture market share. Private protection agencies under anarchy differ from Friedman's example of the grocery industry. I do not mind patronizing a Safeway that is having a price war with another rival supermarket, but I do mind patronizing a protection agency whose decisions are ignored by other agencies. This means that if there is a dominant protection cartel, customers will patronize the cartel, not the lower-price upstarts.
2. Protection firms with differing law codes must offer a form of quality collusion that provides a common product (a final decision) to their respective customers when interests clash. The firms must have contractual agreements to cooperate when potential conflict of interest is present.

3. A cooperating network of protection service agencies could use aggressive force to enforce its market domination (Friedman does concede this point, although he doubts its likelihood).
4. The adjudication network is stable only if it can use force to put down outlaw agencies that do not accept its higher-order arbitration decisions. Such a network also could use force to put down firms that do not adhere to the collusive agreement.

The adjudication network could divide the market into exclusive territories and institute taxation. Each firm belonging to the network would agree not to deal with upstart firms, or with firms that violated against the common agreement to monopolize. Under this agreement the forces that usually break down cartels—new entrants and renegade colluders—cannot obtain market share.

What Happens to Noncooperating Firms Under Anarchy?

Friedman assumes that the adjudication network need not implement violence or the threat of violence against noncooperators. They can simply let these firms, which supposedly must settle their conflicts with violence, go out of business.

Friedman and I agree that outlaw firms will not prosper but we have different reasons for holding this belief; these reasons lead to different conclusions about the likelihood of collusion. Friedman thinks that outlaw firms will lose customers because of competitive market forces. But competitive forces could conceivably favor such firms. How would competitive market forces alone prevent an outlaw firm from increasing its business by promising never to turn over its guilty customers for imprisonment or trial?[2]

I think this kind of outlaw firm will fail, but not because customers will automatically stop patronizing it. The threat of violence from the network can enforce compliance, or the network could brand such firms renegades and cut off all relations with them. Nonconforming firms will lose market share and go out of business because they cannot promise peaceful adjudication. But we should not be so quick to jump on the anarchist bandwagon. The disciplinary actions of the network that put down these outlaws are precisely the actions that could enforce collusion as well.

Friedman also thinks that an anarcho-capitalist society would be safer from a power grab than a government. He cites ideology as the relevant constraint in both cases—"The restraints which prevent a military coup are essentially restraints interior to the men with guns." Friedman portrays government officials as more power-hungry than businessmen and thus more dangerous. I did not deal with this issue in my original piece, but I am nonetheless skeptical about Friedman's argument.

Businessmen and government officials differ little with respect to temperament. Electing businessmen to political office, even average ones (opposed to those who deliberately seek election), would not change the tyranny of government much. In addition, businessmen, if in a position to engineer a coup through the network, might prove more efficient and cost-effective than their public-sector counterparts. A privately owned network holds out the possibility of residual claimancy and profits, which makes the likelihood of a coup through the network might prove more efficient and cost-effective than their public-sector counterparts. A privately owned network holds out the possibility of residual claimancy and profits, which makes the likelihood of a coup through the network greater.

Finally, Friedman thinks that there will be a very large number of protection agencies, thus making collusion more difficult. But today there are a very large number of police forces and local governments, yet they still collude. In the network the number of truly independent sources of power is likely to be small. It is not the number of police forces that matters; it is the number of sources for final-order arbitration.

Perhaps Friedman has in mind a world where the number of independent protection agencies is initially so large that a collusive network cannot get off the ground. But if collusion, one public good among agencies, cannot be provided, neither can the punishment of renegades be provided, another public good among agencies. We cannot have it both ways.

Furthermore, a large number of small agencies implies only that the resulting pools of collusion will be geographically limited. Rather than a united Europe, we will have the Swiss confederacy. A smaller government may or may not be a better government, but it is a government nonetheless. And over time, we can expect some amount of consolidation among these groups of small governments, just as we have seen throughout world history.

Governments often do terrible things, but the reason we observe them so frequently is because they are the predominant form that a stable equilibrium takes. If getting rid of a geographic monopoly of coercive power is our goal, my conclusion, unfortunately, is one of guarded pessimism.

Notes

1. See Cowen (1992). I refer interested readers also to Caplan (1993), another (unpublished) critical comment on my original piece. Caplan argues that anarcho-capitalist protection firms need only bilateral relations, not a network, and that bilateral relations would not imply collusion.
2. Friedman seems to assume that an outlaw firm can only take the form of a firm that settles all disputes by brute force.

References

Caplan, Bryan. 1993. "Comment on Tyler Cowen's 'The Economics of Anarchy.'" Unpublished manuscript. Princeton University, Department of Economics.

Cowen, Tyler. 1992. "Law as a Public Good: The Economics of Anarchy." *Economics and Philosophy* 8: 249-67.

18

Networks, Law, and the Paradox of Cooperation

Bryan Caplan and Edward P. Stringham

Abstract

There is a tension between libertarians' optimism about private supply of public goods and skepticism of the viability of voluntary collusion (Cowen 1992, Cowen and Sutter 1999). Playing off this asymmetry, Cowen (1992) advances the novel argument that the "free market in defense services" favored by anarcho-capitalists is a network industry where collusion is especially feasible. The current article dissolves Cowen's asymmetry, showing that he fails to distinguish between self-enforcing and non-self-enforcing interaction. Case study evidence on network behavior before and after antitrust supports our analysis. Furthermore, libertarians' joint beliefs on public goods and collusion are, contrary to Cowen and Sutter (1999), theoretically defensible.

1. Introduction

Cowen and Sutter (1999) argue that libertarian doubts about the viability of collusion are inconsistent. How, they ask, can free-market economists be simultaneously optimistic about the private production of public goods, but skeptical about collusion? Collusion is, after all, a public good vis-à-vis competing firms. Cowen and Sutter's challenge may be dubbed the Paradox of Cooperation: Laissez-faire can cope with either the monopoly or the public good problem, but not both.[1] Libertarians who dismiss concerns about collusion are at best over-confident.

Cowen (1992) goes further by claiming that in so-called network industries, libertarians are not just over-confident, but wrong: Laissez-faire leads to monopoly, not competition. Although his network industry argument poses a challenge for more moderate libertarians too, Cowen primarily employs it to expose the fundamental weakness of the radical anarcho-capitalist position (Rothbard 1978, Friedman 1989): An excellent example of a network industry is the very free market in defense services that anarcho-capitalists favor. In consequence, anarcho-capitalists are sorely mistaken about the consequences of their ideas if tried.

We maintain that these critiques are thought-provoking but wrong. The dilemmas that Cowen (1992) and Cowen and Sutter (1999) put forward are artificial. Cowen's (1992) network industry argument neglects the deep contrast between prisoners' dilemmas and coordination games; voluntary solutions are self-enforcing for the latter but not the former. Cowen and Sutter's (1999) Paradox of Cooperation likewise glosses over major dissimilarities between collusion and traditional public goods. Empirically, moreover, there is little evidence that modern network industries have the collusive powers Cowen ascribes to them. Even before antitrust laws could have deterred collusive behavior, voluntary efforts to restrict competition in network industries were not noticeably more successful than in other areas of the economy. The paper has the following structure: Section 2 explains Cowen's (1992) network industry argument in depth and discusses responses that take his challenge at face value. Section 3 critiques Cowen's position: There are deep strategic reasons why socially beneficial standardization is easier to orchestrate than socially harmful collusion. Section 4 provides supporting empirical evidence from industry case studies, both before and after the rise of modern antitrust enforcement. Section 5 deconstructs Cowen and Sutter's (1999) Paradox of Cooperation, arguing that libertarians' beliefs about monopoly and public goods can be grounded in sound economic analysis. Section 6 concludes.

2. Network Industries and Collusion

2.1. Cowen's Argument

The underpinning of Cowen's (1992) critique of anarcho-capitalism is the notion of network industries. In such industries, the value of the good increases as the number of users increases (Katz and Shapiro 1985, 1994, Liebowitz and Margolis 1994). ATM cards, telephones, and software are standard examples. ATM cards grow more useful when the number of ATM machines rises; ATM machines become more profitable to set up as the number of ATM cards in circulation expands. The whole point of owning a phone, similarly, is to call other phone-owners and talk to them. Software file formats are less attractive if no one else can open them.

In a network industry, decentralized provision runs two risks. The best-known is product convergence that locks in a sub-optimal standard (Liebowitz and Margolis 1994). A potentially more destructive problem, though, is proliferation of incompatible products. It would be a serious drawback if a phone produced by one firm could not interface with a competitor's phone, to take a mundane example. Similarly, in an anarcho-capitalist defense services market, it would be disastrous if firms' products were "incompatible"; that is, if competing suppliers shared no procedures for resolving disputes between their respective clients. As Cowen puts it, "The food that I buy from one supermarket is just as valuable to me regardless of whether this supermarket has friendly relations with its competitors; this independence does not hold with private protection agencies" (1992:260).

Monopoly is one way around lock-in and compatibility dilemmas. But there is an attractive alternative remedy: Set up an industry "club" or network. Competing firms could then work together, not only to make their products mutually compatible, but to overcome lock-in problems as they arose. Phone companies would agree to interconnect, competing defense firms to peacefully arbitrate disputes using mutually acceptable rules. Proponents of anarcho-capitalism have forcefully maintained that any sensible businessman would do precisely that (Rothbard 1978, Friedman 1989, Benson, 1990). An "outlaw" firm that refused to arbitrate—or recognize unwelcome verdicts—would be reduced to unending warfare with its competitors.

While Cowen recognizes the benefits of networks, he emphasizes their serious downside. The networks that prod their members towards product compatibility are, as a corollary, well-structured to promote price collusion (Bernheim and Whinston 1985). Voluntary cartels may be notoriously ineffective due to cheating and entry, but networks have a special ability to short-circuit the usual market checks.

Why? A network can punish non-colluders by expelling them from the club, and exclude new entrants by refusing to admit them. Outsiders cannot undercut the network by selling the same product for less, because services provided outside the network cease to be the same. A phone company with which other companies refuse to connect, or a defense service with which competing suppliers refuse to arbitrate, cannot offer the product consumers want. As Cowen elaborates: "[M]embership in the common arbitration network is one of the most important services an agency can offer its members. Network membership implies that interagency disputes are settled without risk of force or radical uncertainty about the final outcome" (1992:259-260). Firms may remain de jure "independently owned and operated," but for practical purposes there is but one: "In the network the number of truly independent sources of power is likely to be small" (Cowen 1994:331; emphasis added). The transaction costs of enforcing collusion might be prohibitively high. But if so, it hardly means that laissez-faire works well. When transaction costs preclude collusion, they also rule out simple standardization. After all, why should transactions costs be greater for the former than the latter? The alternative to the orderly cartel is therefore cacophonous competition.

Thus, Cowen (1992) amounts to a virtual impossibility theorem for the efficiency of network industries under laissez-faire. When applied to an anarcho-capitalist defense industry, moreover, his impossibility theorem looks particularly menacing. Low transaction costs in this market lead to far worse than garden-variety monopoly. Since the defense industry, taken as a whole, has a near-monopoly on force, the entire society would be in danger if collusion worked. "Pay the monopoly price or live unprotected" would be a softball threat; a defense cartel could up the ante to "Pay the monopoly price or be reduced to slavery." Anarchy could easily morph into a state of the worst sort. High transaction costs, conversely, would engender not just consumer frustration, but interminable violent conflict between competing suppliers. Cowen's impossibility theorem, as applied to the defense industry, implies that anarcho-capitalism decays into either Hobbes' despotic Leviathan or Hobbes' brutish anarchy.

2.2. Competition for the Network and Competition between Networks

Before turning to the deeper flaws in Cowen's analysis, it is worth considering two less fundamental replies. The first is to appeal to the notion of contestability. Just because a network is the only visible seller does not mean it will act monopolistically. It may be fully constrained by fear of potential competition from a new network. For defense, though, this claim is unpersuasive. However over-rated the link between competition and number of competitors usually is, the link in an anarcho-capitalist defense industry is very real. Once a group of defense firms earned a large enough market share, they could credibly threaten would-be replacement networks with violence.[2] Entrants would not swarm into the industry as soon as price rose above average cost. They would wait until expected monopoly profits exceeded expected costs of an initial period of warfare. In other words, contestability assumes a legally protected right of entry. A dominant network in the defense industry is in a strong position to suppress this right. Entry remains a lingering threat, but leaves ample leeway for an incumbent network to impose a Hobbesian despotism. A second reply is that a network industry can often support a number of competing networks. Just because consumers put some value on mutual compatibility does not mean the market will deliver full compatibility. Consumers may value diversity as well as uniformity. Moreover, as Liebowitz and Margolis (1998) point out, diseconomies of scale can outweigh the pressure for a single network. The Windows and Macintosh operating systems coexist. So do multiple languages. Why not multiple anarcho-capitalist defense networks? Cowen specifically mentions the case of McDonald's restaurants, observing that "Different franchises of McDonald's, for instance, enter into common relations through the parent company and agree not to compete with each other" (1992:261). But McDonald's is only one fast-food franchise out of hundreds! Even if chain restaurants controlled 100% of the market, the chains would still compete with each other.

Unfortunately, competing defense networks, if viable, appear to run once again into Cowen's impossibility theorem. Disputes between networks' respective clients will inevitably arise. If transactions costs are low, the rival networks will reach mutually acceptable procedures for resolution. But once again, why stop there? Why not go further and strike deals to suppress price competition and scare off prospective entrants? In contrast, if transaction costs are high, this means chaos, not ordered anarchy. Finding negotiation too costly, the competing networks resort to violence.

2.3. Friedman's Reply

David Friedman (1994) raises a simple but critical doubt about the link between network goods and collusion. Suppose there are N firms in a network industry. Then even a complete set of N(N-1)/2 bilateral contracts between competitors is not equivalent to one N-firm multilateral contract. Each bilateral contract maximizes the joint profits of the two signatories, ignoring the interests of the other (N-2) firms. The signatories have a mutual interest in avoiding conflict with each other, so we should expect their contracts to handle dispute resolution. But they have almost no incentive to write collusive contracts, because virtually all of its benefits spill over onto the other (N-2) firms. As Friedman explains: Nothing in this situation requires or implies a single firm controlling the whole, nor anything analogous to one. The network as I have described it has no decision-making body. Its "decisions," the set of legal codes it enforces, are the outcome of independent profit making decisions by the individual firms and bargaining between pairs of firms.

Nothing in the logic of the market for protection and arbitration implies that the outcome will maximize the summed profits of the firms, as Cowen seems to assert (1994:323). Friedman undercuts any claim Cowen might have to an impossibility theorem. But one could retreat to the more moderate position that a single N-firm multilateral contract would probably have lower transactions costs than N(N-1)/2 bilateral contracts. One centralized clearinghouse may cost less than N(N-1)/2 bilateral bank clearing contracts, and one centralized arbitration network may cost less than N(N-1)/2 arbitration contracts. If so, an unregulated market delivers one N-firm contract and, as per Cowen's argument, endogenously moves to the collusive outcome. The next section tries to meet this claim head-on by arguing that even if the market delivers one N-firm contract, the resulting network would focus on standardization, not collusion.

3. The Limits of Networks: Self-Enforcing Agreements and Beyond

Two jointly exhaustive inferences form the backbone of Cowen's thesis. First, "If the network can implement successful sanctions against outlaws, however, the network can also implement successful sanctions against potential competitors"; second, "If punishing potential competitors is too costly, punishing outlaws is also too costly" (1992:259). The underlying premise is that outlaws and potential competitors are equally costly to punish. Initially, this looks highly plausible. How could it be wrong? Consider one of the most frequently invoked sanctions: the boycott (Rothbard 1978, Benson 1990). Can the nature of a boycott's target affect the costliness of making it work? Absolutely. Let us distinguish two kinds of boycotts: self-enforcing and non-self-enforcing (Telser 1980). A good example of the former is a boycott against a crooked businessman. To maintain it, publicity alone is likely to suffice; no one wants to continue dealing with a known cheat[3] (Veitch 1986, Greif 1993, Benson 1993, Greif, Milgrom and Weingast 1994, Stringham 2003). Note further that the business community does not need to carefully monitor its members to enforce such a boycott. The cheater's former victims think, in effect, "Fool me once, shame on you; fool me twice; shame on me"; but those with no prior dealings with the cheater similarly reason, "Fool him once, shame on you; fool me once, shame on me." If defense firm A reneges on an arbitration bargain with defense firm B, it alienates not just B, but its full array of actual and potential trading partners. By breaking the rules, cheaters ipso facto reduce the profitability of trading with them. Other businesses punish them not out of sympathy with the victim, but from their proverbial regard to their own self-interest.

On the other hand, a good example of a non-self-enforcing boycott would be a refusal to deal with redheads. As long as "being a redhead" is uncorrelated with "being a bad business risk," it is more profitable for an individual merchant to break the boycott than keep it. Hatred of redheads is likely to be heterogeneously distributed; but more fundamentally, even if anti-redhead preferences were equally intense, boycotting them would be a public good. Simple publicity about the existence of redheads consequently falls on deaf ears. It would take more drastic measures to sustain the boycott: mutual monitoring to detect profit-driven violations of the boycott, "courts" to weigh evidence, and secondary boycotts to punish those "found guilty."

So the nature of a boycott's target matters. It is cheap to orchestrate self-enforcing boycotts of the dishonest, but expensive to orchestrate non-self-enforcing boycotts of redheads. In fact, incentives parallel those for statistical versus taste-based discrimination (Coate and Loury 1993). Cowen's line of reasoning could easily lead us to think that: "If the market can sustain discrimination against contract-breakers, however, the market can also sustain discrimination against redheads. If discriminating against redheads is too costly, discriminating against contract-breakers is too costly." This overlooks the interaction between the nature of the target and the costliness of discrimination. Competitive pressure reinforces statistical discrimination based on real group differences: People who broke contracts in the past are more likely to break them in the future. But competitive pressure dissolves purely taste-based discrimination (Sowell 1994): Redheads' dollars are as good as anyone's. Unregulated markets are neither generically "discriminatory" nor "non-discriminatory." One form thrives, the other withers.

The same point holds for networks; it is easy to reach some types of cooperation, even as the cost of others remains prohibitive. Consider the classic contrast between prisoners' dilemmas and coordination games. Every industry faces a prisoners' dilemma: Firms within an industry can earn more profits if they all collude, yet individual firms earn more if they continue to compete. Coordination problems are less ubiquitous. They surface when consumers want compatibility: DVDs that play in their DVD players, ATM cards that work in unfamiliar ATM machines, or a defense firm that subscribes to a common body of procedures for dispute resolution.

The difficulty of solving the two classes of problems hinges on self-enforcement. In coordination games, maintaining a cooperative outcome is fairly simple. If other banks issue ATM cards of standard dimensions, an oddball bank that refuses to conform hurts only itself. The reverse holds in prisoners' dilemmas.

The temptation to defect actually rises with the expected extent of cooperative play.[4] If all of the other banks collude to charge exorbitant fees, profits of the deviant bank that undercuts them go up. True, the banking network might offset incentives to defect with extensive monitoring and punishment; but solving coordination problems is far easier.

It is worth pursuing this point at length because Cowen maintains that networks' ability to standardize products is ipso facto evidence of their ability to collude: The ability to collude is inherent in the nature of the network. The network can internalize the externalities problem behind peaceful adjudication only by suspending quality competition—that is, by offering a uniform set of laws or higher-order adjudication procedures. The ability to engage successfully in quality collusion, however, implies that other kinds of collusion are possible also (1992:259). Cowen here conflates two radically different sorts of business cooperation under the generic heading of "collusion." Standardizing products is essentially a coordination game, fixing prices a prisoners' dilemma. As long as consumers want a uniform product, adhering to industry standards is self-enforcing. As long as consumers prefer to pay less rather than more, price-fixing is not. Ability to reach the cooperative outcome in the former in no way "implies" ability to reach it in the latter.[5]

Cowen makes the strong claim that it is inconsistent to believe in only one: "But if collusion, one public good among agencies, cannot be provided, neither can the punishment of renegades be provided, another public good among agencies. We cannot have it both ways" (1994:331). This inconsistency is illusory: When firms peacefully resolve disputes and ostracize renegades, it is selfishly optimal behavior in a coordination game, not civic-minded production of a public good.

Cowen conflates standardization and collusion in a second way. By labeling product uniformity "quality collusion" he makes it sound as if the goal is to hold product quality down. But isn't uniformity better seen as an aspect of quality? Consumers' preference for standardized products is the motive to have a network in the first place (Liebowitz and Margolis 1995).

On reflection, Cowen would probably acknowledge this, but retreat to the position that network formation remains a "Faustian bargain": Centralization raises product quality by sacrificing the familiar benefits of competition. But this Faustian tradeoff may not even exist, because coordination problems are, compared to prisoners' dilemmas, readily solved. Any network strong enough to enforce collusion will be at least strong enough to realize the benefits of uniformity. The reverse is not true: Ability to standardize—to overcome mere coordination problems—hardly indicates ability to suppress ordinary competition. Stepping back, imagine graphing—in the spirit of Cowen and Sutter (1999)—the feasible extent of cooperation as a function of its cost. Cowen effectively partitions this graph into two regions (Figure 1). If the costs of cooperation are low, as in Region 1, bargains of all sorts flourish—including some with large negative externalities. If the costs of cooperation are high, as in Region 2, mutually beneficial interaction is impossible. There is a collapse into chaos.

The distinction between coordination games and prisoners' dilemmas—more generally, self-enforcing versus non-self-enforcing interaction—highlights a better way to conceive the relationship between cooperation and its cost. Imagine splitting the graph into three regions rather than two (Figure 2). In Region 1, the costs of cooperation are extremely low. It is cheap to reach and enforce agreements—even collusive agreements that require numerous actors to fix prices or attack new entrants. In Region 3, the costs of cooperation are extremely high. Elementary forms of coordination, like language and measurement, fail to arise. But Cowen (1992) and Cowen and Sutter (1999) neglect Region 2, where the costs of cooperation are intermediate: High enough to prevent collusion, low enough to permit coordination. The remainder of the paper argues that this intermediate case is not only logically possible but empirically dominant.

Figure 1
The Cost and Extent of Feasible Cooperation

Region 1	Region 2
Cooperation Can Overcome Both Coordination Problems and Prisoners' Dilemmas	*Cooperation Can Overcome Neither Coordination Problems nor Prisoners' Dilemmas*

0 ——————————————————— ∞

cost of cooperation

Figure 2
The Cost and Extent of Feasible Cooperation

Region 1	Region 2	Region 3
Cooperation Can Overcome Both Coordination Problems and Prisoners' Dilemmas	*Cooperation Can Overcome Coordination Problems but not Prisoners' Dilemmas*	*Cooperation Can Overcome Neither Coordination Problems nor Prisoners' Dilemmas*

0 ——————————————————— ∞

cost of cooperation

4. Evidence from Network Industries

Cowen's case is almost wholly theoretical. The usual historical evidence on collusion under laissez-faire, he maintains, cannot be credibly extended to network industries: "Although private cartels usually collapse of their own accord, most historical examples of cartel instability do not involve the benefits of joining a common network" (1992:260). But Cowen provides little in the way of empirical counter-examples to support his belief that networks industries are different.[6]

This section takes a preliminary look at modern and historical network industries. While they definitely standardize products in beneficial ways, there is little evidence that network industries are more prone to collusion than non-network industries. Instances of attempted and temporarily successful collusion do surface. But collusive efforts in network industries appear neither more common nor more successful than in other sectors of the economy (Dewing 1914). A full-blown comparative history of collusion in network and non-network industries is beyond the scope of this paper. On Cowen's account, however, the contrast should be too large to miss.

The exercise remains probative, we maintain, in spite of the special potential for anticompetitive violence in the defense industry. Once a single network reaches the collusive outcome, it might be able to enforce collusion and deter entry with the threat of violence. The critical question, though, is whether decentralized firms can bootstrap themselves into this dominant position. This is Tullock's (1974) "paradox of revolution" in another guise. After a violent movement gets off the ground, it can use violence to reinforce its position by extorting help from fence-straddlers. The hard part is getting a violent movement off the ground in the first place. In other words, saying that violence solves the free-rider problem begs the question: Violent threats are only credible after the free-rider problem has been non-violently solved to a moderate degree. While the potential for violence under anarcho-capitalism raises special issues, these will probably not materialize unless it is abnormally easy for networks to peacefully collude first.

4.1. Modern Networks: The Credit Card Industry

The market for credit cards has all the defining characteristics of a network industry (Carlton and Frankel 1995a, 1995b, Economides 1995, Evans and Schmalensee 1995, 1999). The value of a credit card increases with the number of participating consumers, merchants, and banks. As Evans and Schmalensee (1999:138) observe, "[P]ayment cards are provided through a network industry in which participants are linked economically in unusual ways. Payment cards are useless to consumers unless merchants accept them, but merchants have no reason to accept cards unless consumers carry them and want to use them." Consumers value widely accepted payment cards more, so issuers typically belong to large networks. But competition persists (Stringham 1999, Zywicki 2000). The market sustains inter-network competition between networks owned by member banks, such as Visa and MasterCard, proprietary networks like Discover and American Express, and store-specific cards. What is more striking is the scope of intra-network competition. Visa and MasterCard, the two leading networks, are non-profit membership corporations with thousands of member firms. They provide infrastructure and a large network of users, and finance their services with membership fees (Hausman et al. 1999, Carlton and Frankel 1995:646). Despite strong network features, there is vigorous intra-network competition (Rochet and Tirole 2000). Evans and Schmalensee (1995:889) note that:

> Given the inherent interdependency of transactions, how—if at all—should the costs, risk, and income from the "two sides" of the business be shared? In theory, the problem could be addressed by having the organization (e.g., Visa) establish the terms (i.e., interest, annual fee, special features) for all Visa cards issued by any member as well as the discount rate to be paid by the merchants... Such an approach, however, would be far more restrictive on competition at the intrasystem level than is desirable (or, perhaps, even legal). Therefore, neither Visa nor MasterCard regulates the amount charged to cardholders by its various issuers or the amount of discounts paid by merchants.

Though one might expect the network to impose monolithic restrictions, member firms have a lot of autonomy. Members cooperate to make the product more convenient, not to stop them from stealing each other's customers. Visa founder Dee Hock (1999) explains that Visa was deliberately designed to allow intra-network competition. According to Evans and Schmalensee (1995:865–866):

> Competition for consumers takes place between issuers of Visa and MasterCard... Nationally, there are approximately 7,300 Visa issuers, each of which sets its own interest rates, fees, features, and marketing strategy for its cards. Although many payment cards are marketed locally, there are also nearly 100 national issuers, including all the largest Visa and MasterCard issuing members... Competition to enroll merchants to take a Visa or MasterCard brand and to service these merchants took place among approximately 250 acquirer organizations.

The benefits of network membership are great. But this hardly induces the networks to "squeeze" aspiring members, or subject them to draconian restrictions. Broad membership is what makes it valuable to join in the first place. The natural way for networks to build and maintain such a membership base is a "big tent" approach, where affiliating is cheap and low-hassle. If one network's rules create a lot of outsiders, a more inclusive network comes along to take advantage of the situation. In the fifties, Diners Club created the first charge card network among Manhattan restaurants (Evans and Schmalensee 1999:62). Visa originated in 1966 when the Bank of America licensed its card nationally and shortly spun off its franchise system to create a nonstock membership corporation (Evans and Schmalensee 1999:66). MasterCard has similar origins. It was a cooperative effort to induce many banks, merchants, and consumers to jointly adopt the new card. Decades later, alongside a handful of existing networks, Sears leveraged its store card to create Discover. Following the "big tent" approach, Discover offered such attractive rates that it became as widely accepted as American Express shortly after its creation, turning profitable three years later after a $300 million investment (Evans and Schmalensee 1999:232). The credit card industry thus provides little support for Cowen's fears. But while evidence from modern examples can hardly be dismissed, antitrust is a troubling confounding variable. The checkered history of antitrust makes us doubt that the Department of Justice deserves credit for the accomplishments of the credit card industry[7] (McChesney and Shughart 1995). Still, perhaps Visa and MasterCard permit intra-network competition because they must. It is therefore in many respects more probative to examine networks during the era prior to modern antitrust enforcement.

4.2. Networks Before Antitrust: Clearinghouses

Banking is a good example of a nineteenth-century network industry. Competing banks formed clearinghouses to enhance the value of their product. As Timberlake (1984:2-3) explains, "Instead of each bank establishing a transactional relationship with all other banks, every bank sends a representative to one place—the clearinghouse—where its debit items are cleared against its credit items." Gorton (1985), Gorton and Mullineaux (1987), and Calomiris (1990) emphasize another function: Since the leading reasons for bank failure were fraud and conflict of interest (Calomiris and Kahn 1991), banks needed a way to signal honesty. One good signal was joining a banking network liable for member obligations, conditional on adherence to its rules. As Calomiris puts it, banks used "self-regulation, made credible by mutual liability" (1990:283).

In the pre-antitrust U.S. banking industry, then, networks known as clearinghouses arose to reduce transactions costs and bolster reputations. "An essential feature of the banking industry was the endogenous development of the clearinghouse, a governing association of banks to which individual banks voluntarily abrogated certain rights and powers normally held by firms" (Gorton 1985:277). Membership requirements and monitoring enhanced the public's trust in the redeemability of members' bank notes and the overall soundness of their business practices. As Gorton and Mullineaux (1987:461) explain:

> The clearinghouse required, for example, that member institutions satisfy an admissions test (based on certification of adequate capital), pay an admissions fee, and submit to periodic exams (audits) by the clearinghouse. Members who failed to satisfy [commercial-bank clearinghouse] regulations were subject to disciplinary actions (fines) and, for extreme violations, could be expelled. Expulsion from the clearinghouse was a clear negative signal concerning the quality of the bank's liabilities.

Did the threat of expulsion from the clearinghouse lead to a blatant pattern of industry-wide collusion? No; as Dowd (1994:298) puts it, "Nor is there any strong evidence, populist views about banking power notwithstanding, that banks were able to cartelize the market successfully." Banks that tried to set rates found it difficult to punish cheating and provoked fierce competition.

Consider the case of the New York Clearinghouse, which decreed, in 1873, that "No bank shall pay, or procure to be paid, interest upon deposits" (Sprague 1910:102). Things did not play out as expected. As Sprague (1910:104) recounts:

> The report of the clearinghouse committee seems to have been received with general approval, both by bankers and by the public, but it led to no immediate change in banking methods. It was considered at a meeting of the banks...and the adoption of its principal recommendation, that interest on its deposits be prohibited, was favored by about three-fourths of the banks. It was felt, however, that a unanimous agreement was necessary to secure its effective adoption.

In 1884, American Exchange National Bank president George Coe complained, "This subject has upon several occasions in years past been under consideration, and its total abolition has been almost unanimously agreed to among banks by written contract. Yet by the refusal of one or more members it has failed to become a binding obligation" (Sprague 1910:375). Rate-fixing banks would lose out to those offering competitive rates. Expelling rate-cutters would have been legal, but apparently members saw it as imprudent. Excluding financially impeccable members would dilute the network's reputation for financial probity. Far better to keep transactions costs low by sticking to an inclusive, "big tent" approach.

In another scheme a clearinghouse tried to fix rates of exchange. This too was unsuccessful:

> But the formation of new banks finally played havoc with the uniform-rate system. While it lasted, it was obligatory upon every [member] bank, but in 1891 the newly organized banks began to cut on rates. The clearing-house members endeavored to induce the new banks to join the association, but did not at first succeed. It was regarded as unjust to the member banks to hold them to the existing agreement when their competitors were free, and accordingly, in June, 1891, the schedule of rates was made no longer obligatory (Cannon 1910:15).

An additional check against collusion was banks' credible threat to withdraw from the network or refuse to join. As Dowd recounts:

> A good example of banks "voting with their feet" even when the market could only support one clearinghouse is provided by the demise of the Suffolk system. The Suffolk system was a club managed by the Suffolk Bank of Boston, but some members found the club rules too constraining and there were complaints about the Suffolk's highhanded attitude toward members. Discontent led to the founding of a rival, the Bank of Mutual Redemption (BMR), and when the latter opened in 1858 many of the Suffolk's clients defected to it (Dowd 1994:295).

Despite the benefits of participation, then, a dominant clearinghouse hardly had a stranglehold on uppity members. Since one of a clearinghouse's main selling points is breadth of membership, they mostly stuck to issues where member banks could broadly agree.[8] Expelling financially unstable firms makes the network more attractive for consumers; expelling up-and-coming firms makes it less attractive. Conditioning membership on factors other than financial honesty dilutes the value of the name brand of the network.

So clearinghouses took a soft-line on some issues, like cutting rates. But they took a hard-line on others. They had no qualms about ousting insolvent banks. Calomiris (1990:288) explains that, "The Indiana insurance system relied on bankers themselves to make and enforce laws and regulations through a Board of Directors and, importantly, gave the board authority when to close a bank. Unlimited mutual liability provided bankers the incentive to regulate and enforce properly." Because consumers knew that unreliable banks would be penalized, it raised "the public's perception of the quality of the 'average' bank" (Gorton and Mullineaux 1987:463). Thus, clearinghouses were bad at orchestrating some forms of cooperation, but good at others.

During banking panics, the power of clearinghouses expanded. But this was temporary by design:

> Suppose that once the more hierarchical form of organization had been adopted during the panic, the [clearinghouse] did not revert back to its more limited form. Then individual banks, knowing that the loan certificates were available, would have an incentive to make riskier loans since each would believe that the risk could be spread over the other members through the loan certificate process. Clearly, this would not be viable... Only by reverting back to the more limited organizational form did individual banks have the incentives to monitor each other (Gorton and Mullineaux 1987:466).

For Gorton (1985:283), "the existence of the clearinghouse suggests that private agents can creatively respond to market failure." At the same time, the historical evidence disconfirms Cowen's belief that a new—and perhaps worse—market failure accompanies each of the market's "creative responses."

4.3. The Sports League Anomaly

There are numerous other examples of competitive network industries: ATM machines, computer software, computer hardware, fax machines, financial exchanges,[9] the Internet, television, telecommunications, and more. Geddes (2000) surveys utilities and network industries such as airlines, cable television, railroads, telecommunications, and trucking, and concludes that laissez-faire outperforms state control.[10] There is however one cluster of network industries where collusion has been fairly effective: professional and college sports[11] (Boal and Ransom 1997, Salop and White 1991).

The rules of sports leagues are often expansive. They address salaries, player mobility, television contracts, revenue sharing, location, and more. The underlying threat is expulsion of disobedient teams (NCAA Division I Manual 2000–2001: Article 19). High-profile defiance does surface: In *NCAA v. Board of Regents*, for instance, a group of large schools negotiated their own television contracts in spite of NCAA rules. Nevertheless, Cowen's pessimistic scenario for network industries is often consistent with economic histories of sport (Noll 1974). Leagues impose collusive rules and teams take sanctions for noncompliance seriously.

There is however an alternative explanation for their successful collusion: Professional sports are superstar markets (Rosen 1981). A vital characteristic of their product, for many fans, is that the contending teams are "the best." While there is obviously a market for minor league games, college sports, and so on, consumer interest declines rapidly with the quality of play.

Given these consumer preferences, collusion gets a lot easier. The supply of good players is elastic, but the supply of "the best" players is extremely inelastic almost by definition. A league where a moderate number of teams employ almost all of the "best" players is like a natural resource cartel. This does not make it any less laborious to initially reach a collusive agreement. But it multiplies the present value of success, because the monopoly profits of natural resource cartels are so persistent. There is little need to worry about entry. As long as demand to watch the sport's best players endures, a cartel can earn monopoly profits indefinitely.

If this hypothesis is correct, the effectiveness of collusion in professional sports is no cause for concern about network industries in general.[12] Network industries might function poorly when they also happen to be superstar markets. But this is a rare combination. Few consumers care much if their bank or credit card company is "the best." Networks in these industries are accordingly unlikely to successfully jump from coordination to collusion.

Would anarcho-capitalist defense services turn out to be a superstar market? Conceivably so: Free-market defense, like legal representation in the current world, would be a positional good to some degree. Consumers might feel safer with the best firm standing behind them. This pushes the market in a superstar direction. But the effect is probably slight: Few people today see the need to hire "the best" law firm, in spite of the positional nature of legal representation.[13] Similarly, many consumers opt for low-quality, low-cost security in today's marketplace, despite the positional aspects of protection (Benson 1998).

5. The Paradox of Cooperation Resolved

Let us now return to Cowen and Sutter's paradox:

> Free market economists typically express confidence in the ability of markets to produce public goods… At the same time, free market economists tend to be pessimistic about the stability of cartels in an unregulated market. If markets successfully produce local public goods, however, why are stable cartels not more prevalent? (1999:168)

So far, our implicit response has been: Yes, it is hard for markets to produce public goods, but private provision of defense services functions well as long as free markets possess the humbler ability to solve coordination problems. In other words, the externalities of social order are infra-marginal. If farmers grew no food, or if defense providers failed to develop procedures for dispute resolution, society would collapse into chaos. Yet these dire situations are unlikely at the laissez-faire level of output.

On reflection, though, this response is too pessimistic. Common sense tells us, and experimental studies verify, that voluntary production of public goods is a reality (Schmidtz 1991, Smith 1980). What makes this possible? There are two critical variables we would advance: (a) the effectiveness of partial participation, and (b) ideological appeal. Furthermore, along both dimensions, voluntary provision of traditional public goods like clean air usually has a decisive advantage over voluntary collusion.

First consider the effectiveness of partial participation. Voluntary collaboration never yields unanimity. But how injurious is the shortfall? This hinges on the elasticity of outsiders' behavior. Suppose that 50% of all firms in an industry join a cartel to restrict production. They will be unable to raise prices much because outsiders' supply curves will typically be elastic. Firms that refuse to join the cartel increase their output to exploit the situation. Indeed, if outsiders' supply is perfectly elastic, strict unanimity is crucial; any departure from 100% participation renders the cartel impotent. In contrast, if 50% of all people who benefit from clean air decide to "do their part" by buying low-pollution cars, they can make a significant dent in the problem. As long as the outsiders already pollute to the selfishly optimal point, an improvement in the level of air quality has no effect on their marginal incentive to pollute. Half of the drivers pollute less; half pollute the same; air quality improves. Of course, neither the cartel nor the clean air movement fully solves its public good problem. The point is that voluntary pollution abatement is a partial success, whereas the voluntary cartel is a full failure.

Admittedly, outsiders' supply of a product is occasionally less elastic: A natural resource cartel may be moderately effective in spite of partial participation, at least in the short-term. Similarly, outsiders' response to altruism might be more elastic: Donations to relieve world hunger could elicit a Malthusian population response, leaving the level of starvation insensitive to charitable giving. We can also imagine a crowding out of altruism, so that if some people give more, others offset it by giving less; or, even more perversely, charities might have conflicting goals (e.g. socialist and libertarian think tanks). But for most purposes, we should expect outsider elasticity to be high for products but low for causes. After all, the more successful a cartel is, the more profitable it becomes to break it; but increases in charity rarely make it more profitable to exacerbate the very ills the donations were intended to alleviate.

The effectiveness of partial participation warrants optimism only if participation rises above the selfishly optimal level—none—in the first place. This is where ideological appeal makes it entrance. Empirically, people typically are—to a minor extent—willing to make tradeoffs between their narrow self-interest and their ideological beliefs (Tullock 1981). In spite of their diversity, moreover, ideological commitments are not random. This gives rise to the second asymmetry between cartels and more familiar public goods: While many people willingly sacrifice to help the environment, combat world hunger, expel foreign oppressors, or promote human liberty, few want to crusade for the maximization of their industry's total profits. Investors have occasionally heeded calls to forego profit for a public-spirited cause, from turnpike construction in the 19th century (Klein 1990) to "social investing" in the 21st.[14] Exhortations to forego profit for the benefit of fellow investors do not have the same moral resonance. A general account of why some causes—but not others—elicit charity is beyond the scope of this paper. But there can be little doubt that this contrast is real.

Cowen and Sutter (1999) wonder how free market economists can be optimistic about voluntary public good provision, but skeptical about the prospects of voluntary cartels. A natural explanation is wishful thinking. We argue, in contrast, that both beliefs are reasonable. Cartels are unlikely to work with partial participation, and in any case enjoy little ideological loyalty. More familiar public goods, in contrast, cope better with partial participation, and are, due to ideological appeal, more able to win voluntary support.

6. Conclusion: Public Opinion as a Public Good

Cowen and Sutter put forward a final, more challenging, paradox: "[L]ibertarians believe that voluntary institutions do not necessarily produce the public good of mobilizing public opinion against excess government intervention" (1999:169). This point must be granted. But it impinges only on the difficulty of establishing a libertarian society. It does not show that it would be unstable once established. It does not even show that the costs of transition outweigh the benefits. By itself, the paradox practically amounts to, "It is a good idea, but it will never be." Maybe so, but it is worth pointing out the endogeneity: If widely accepted, this paradox would seem to be self-defeating. Once enough people see something as a good idea, it generally happens.

Acknowledgment

We would like to thank Peter Boettke, Tyler Cowen, Robin Hanson, John Hasnas, Dan Sutter, and two anonymous referees for numerous helpful comments and suggestions. Scott Beaulier provided excellent research assistance. The standard disclaimer applies.

Notes

1. It is worth mentioning that Cowen and Sutter (1999) critique a wide spectrum of political positions, and find comparable inconsistencies in a variety of non-libertarian viewpoints.
2. Sutter (1995) makes a stronger version of this claim. In his model of the "Protection Racket Game," firms can credibly threaten violence even when there are no network externalities and the market for defense services is highly decentralized. While we doubt that the bad equilibria in Sutter's model would be focal, developing this argument must be left for future research.
3. The boycott victim could naturally offer, instead, to compensate prospective business partners for the extra risk of trading with a known cheat. But the incentive structure is essentially the same: Publicity alone leads the business community to make cheaters worse off.

4. Entry amplifies the contrast between coordination games and prisoners' dilemmas. The existence of common standards does not spur entry, and new entrants have every reason to adhere to prevailing standards. The opposite holds for price collusion. Artificially high prices raise the incentive to enter, and new entrants' standard strategy is to upset preexisting industry practices by under-pricing incumbent firms.
5. There is a standard list of factors that make collusion easier to achieve. Some of these are likely to make coordination easier as well: most obviously, a small number of firms and ease of communication. Others probably make little difference: legal restriction of entry makes collusion easier, but probably has little effect on coordination. Unless incumbents have "locked-in" an inferior standard, a new entrant has a clear incentive to make its products compatible with those already on the market.
6. Cowen (1994:331) observes that "[T]he reason we observe [governments] so frequently is because they are the predominant form that a stable equilibrium takes." But this hardly counts as empirical evidence for Cowen's network industry hypothesis. The ubiquity of government is equally consistent with virtually every account of its origin. For example, one might argue that government universally exists because the public supports it existence, and policy tends to match public opinion.
7. There have been several major antitrust challenges in the credit card industry, though their connection to "competition" is questionable. In 1975, the US DOJ forced Visa and MasterCard to permit dual membership, or "duality." But in 1998 the DOJ initiated a suit to forbid duality (Hausman et al. 1999). A recent lawsuit by Discover against Visa and MasterCard focuses on interchange fees (Carlton and Frankel 1995a, 1995b). Visa and MasterCard maintain that their fee structure is necessary to cover the costs of running the networks and discourage free riding (Evans and Schmalensee 1995, Allen 2000, Hanft, 2000).
8. With identical firms, of course, strict collusive rules can enjoy unanimous support. But in the real world, the benefits of collusion are far from uniform; up-and-coming firms, for example, tend to lose out (Libecap and Wiggins 1984).
9. The evidence on financial exchanges' ability to effectively fix commission rates is more ambiguous than the other cases and demands further research. From their beginnings, exchanges in London and New York faced competition from other exchanges and brokers who were not members of any exchange (Stringham 2002, Banner 1998). In 1792, a handful of New York brokers agreed to fix commission rates with the Buttonwood Tree Agreement. The attempt failed, but common rates became the norm in 1817, and continued through the 1934 inception of the SEC. In London fixed commission rates eventually fell apart on their own. Perhaps fixed rates lasted so long in New York (Mahoney 1997) because they differentiated members from less reputable bucket-shops.
10. See also Lal (1997). Gabel (1994) points to government regulation as a major reason that competing telephone networks ended in monopoly. Mahoney (1997) likewise argues that the SEC propped up brokerage commissions above market rates.
11. Cowen has raised this point in several informal exchanges.
12. Indeed, the effectiveness of collusion in professional sports may actually be efficiency enhancing. Most obviously, league rules increase the entertainment value of sporting events by creating more evenly-matched teams (Neale 1964, Fort and Quirk 1995).
13. Perhaps the relevant positional variable, though, is not absolute quality, but size. Consumers might feel safer with the largest firm protecting them, instead of the tenth largest. Empirically, again, this does not seem like a big factor. Larger auto insurers, for instance, have more legal resources to defend their clients than small

insurers, but purchasers of insurance rarely care about firms' relative size. The reason, presumably, is that large firms also have proportionally more demands on their resources. The threat of bringing the totality of their resources to bear on a single case is not credible.

14. We would like to thank an anonymous referee for bringing the first example to our attention.

References

Allen, P. (2000) "Prepared Testimony of Mr. Paul Allen." Senate Banking Committee, Subcommittee on Financial Institutions, Hearing on Competition and Innovation in the Credit Card Industry at the Consumer and Network Level, May 25, 2000.

Banner, S. (1998) "The Origin of the New York Stock Exchange, 1791–1860." *Journal of Legal Studies*, 27:113-140.

Benson, B. (1990) *The Enterprise of Law*. San Francisco: Pacific Research Institute for Public Policy.

Benson, B. (1993) "The Impetus for Recognizing Private Property and Adopting Ethical Behavior in a Market Economy: Natural Law, Government Law, or Evolving Self-Interest." *Review of Austrian Economics*, 6: 43-80.

Benson, B. (1998) T*o Serve and Protect: Privatization and Community in Criminal Justice*. New York: New York University Press.

Bernheim, D. and Whinston, M. (1985) "Common Marketing Agencies as a Device for Facilitating Collusion." *Rand Journal of Economics*, 16: 269-281.

Boal, W. and Ransom, M. (1997) "Monopsony in the Labor Market." *Journal of Economic Literature*, 35: 86-112.

Calomiris, C. and Kahn, C. (1991) "The Role of Demandable Debt in Structuring Optimal Banking Arrangements." *American Economic Review*, 81: 497-513.

Calomiris, C. (1990) "Is Deposit Insurance Necessary? A Historical Perspective." *Journal of Economic* History, 50: 283-295.

Cannon, J. G. (1910) *Clearing Houses*. Washington, Govt. Print. Off.

Carlton, D. and Frankel, A. (1995a) "The Antitrust Economics of Payment Card Networks." *Antitrust Law Journal*, 63: 643-668.

Carlton, D. and Frankel, A. (1995b) "The Antitrust Economics of Payment Card Networks: Reply to Evans and Schmalensee Comment." *Antitrust Law Journal*, 63: 903–915.

Coate, S. and Loury, G. (1993) "Will Affirmative-Action Policies Eliminate Negative Stereotypes?" *American Economic Review*, 83: 1220-1240.

Cowen, T. (1992) "Law as a Public Good: The Economics of Anarchy." *Economics and Philosophy*, 8: 249-267.

Cowen, T. (1994) "Rejoinder to David Friedman on the Economics of Anarchy." *Economics and Philosophy*, 10: 329-332.

Cowen, T. and Sutter, D. (1999) "The Costs of Cooperation." *Review of Austrian Economics*, 12: 161-173.

Dewing, A. (1914) *Corporate Promotions and Reorganizations*. Cambridge, MA: Harvard University Press.

Dowd, K. (1994) "Competitive Banking, Bankers' Clubs, and Bank Regulation." *Journal of Money, Credit and Banking*, 26: 289-308.

Economides, N. (1995) "Commentary on 'Antitrust Economics of Credit Card Networks'." *Federal Reserve Bank of St. Louis Review*, Nov.-Dec. 1995: 60-63.

Evans, D. and Schmalensee, R. (1995) "Economic Aspects of Payment Card Systems and Antitrust Policy Toward Joint Ventures." *Antitrust Law Journal*, 63: 861-901.

Evans, D. and Schmalensee, R. (1999) *Paying with Plastic: The Digital Revolution in Buying and Borrowing*. Cambridge, MA: MIT Press.

Fort, R. and Quirk, J. (1995) "Cross-Subsidization, Incentives, and Outcomes in Professional Sports Leagues." *Journal of Economic Literature*, 33: 1265-1299.
Friedman, D. (1989) *The Machinery of Freedom: Guide to Radical Capitalism*, 2nd ed. La Salle, IL: Open Court.
Friedman, D. (1994) "Law as a Private Good: A Response to Tyler Cowen on the Economics of Anarchy." *Economics and Philosophy*, 10: 319-327.
Gabel, D. (1994) "Competition in a Network Industry: The Telephone Industry, 1894-1910." *Journal of Economic History*, 54: 543-572.
Geddes, R. (2000) "Public Utilities." In: *Encyclopedia of Law and Economics, Vol. III. The Regulation of Contracts*. Cheltenham, UK: Edward Elgar, pp. 1162-1205.
Goodhart, C. (1988) *The Evolution of Central Banks*. Cambridge, MA: MIT Press.
Gorton, G. (1985) "Clearinghouses and the Origin of Central Banking in the United States." *Journal of Economic History*, 45: 277-283.
Gorton, G. and Mullineaux, D. (1987) "The Joint Production of Confidence: Endogenous Regulation and Nineteenth Century Commercial-Bank Clearinghouses." *Journal of Money, Credit and Banking*, 19: 457-468.
Greif, A. (1993) "Contract Enforceability and Economic Institutions in Early Trade: The Maghribi Traders' Coalition." *American Economic Review*, 83: 525-548.
Greif, A., Milgrom, P., and Weingast, B. R. (1994) "Coordination, Commitment, and Enforcement: The Case of the Merchant Guild." *Journal of Political Economy*, 102: 745-776.
Hanft, N. (2000) "Prepared Testimony of Mr. Noah Hanft." Senate Banking Committee, Subcommittee on Financial Institutions, Hearing on Competition and Innovation in the Credit Card Industry at the Consumer and Network Level, May 25, 2000.
Hausman, J., Leonard, G., and Tirole, J. (1999) "The Impact of Duality on Productive Efficiency and Innovation." Working paper, MIT.
Hock, D. (1999) *Birth of the Chaordic Age*. San Francisco: Berrett-Koehler Pub.
Katz, M. and Shapiro, C. (1985) "Network Externalities, Competition, and Compatibility." *American Economic Review*, 75: 424-440.
Katz, M. and Shapiro, C. (1994) "Systems Competition and Network Effects." *Journal of Economic Perspectives*, 8: 93-115.
Klein, D. (1990) "The Voluntary *Provision of Public Goods? The Turnpike Companies of Early America." Economic* Inquiry, 28: 788-812.
Lal, D. (1997) "From Planning to Regulation: Toward a New Dirigisme?" *Cato Journal*, 17: 211-227.
Libecap, G. and Wiggins, S. (1984) "Contractual Responses to the Common Pool: Prorationing of Crude Oil Production." *American Economic Review*, 74: 87-98.
Liebowitz, S. J. and Margolis, S. (1994) "Network Externality: An Uncommon Tragedy." *Journal of Economic Perspectives*, 8: 133-150.
Liebowitz, S. J. and Margolis, S. (1995) "Are Network Externalities a New Source of Market Failure?" *Research in Law and Economics*, 17: 1-22.
Liebowitz, S. J. and Margolis, S. (1998) "Network Effects and Externalities." In: *The New Palgrave Dictionary of Economics and the Law*, pp. 671-675. London: MacMillan.
Mahoney, P. (1997) "The Exchange as Regulator." *Virginia Law Review*, 83: 1453-1500.
McChesney, F. and Shughart, W. (1995) *The Causes and Consequences of Antitrust: The Public-Choice Perspective*. Chicago: University of Chicago Press.
National Collegiate Athletic Association (2000) *NCAA Division I Manual 2000-2001*. Overland Park, KS: NCAA.
National Collegiate Athletic Association v. Board of Regents of the University of Oklahoma et al. (1984) 468 U.S. 85.

Neale, W. (1964) "The Peculiar Economics of Professional Sports." *Quarterly Journal of Economics*, 78: 1-14.
Noll, R. (Ed.) (1974) *Government and the Sports Business*. Washington, DC: The Brookings Institution.
Rochet, J. C. and Tirole, J. (2000) "Cooperation among Competitors: The Economics of Payment Card Associations." Working paper, IDEI, Toulouse.
Rosen, S. (1981) "The Economics of Superstars." *American Economic Review*, 71: 845-858.
Rothbard, M. N. (1978) *For a New Liberty: The Libertarian Manifesto*. NY: Libertarian Review Foundation.
Salop, S. and White, L. J. (1991) "Policy Watch: Antitrust Goes to College." *Journal of Economic Perspectives*, 5: 193-202.
Schmidtz, D. (1991) *The Limits of Government: An Essay on the Public Goods Argument*. Boulder: Westview Press.
Smith, V. L. (1980) "Experiments with a Decentralized Mechanism for Public Good Decisions." *American Economic Review*, 70: 584-599.
Sowell, T. (1994) *Race and Culture*. NY: Basic Books.
Sprague, O.M.W. (1910/1977) *History of Crisis Under the National Banking System*. Fairfield, NJ: Augustus M. Kelly Publishers.
Stringham, E. (1999) "Market Chosen Law." *Journal of Libertarian Studies*, 14: 53-77.
Stringham, E. (2002) "The Emergence of the London Stock Exchange as a Self-Policing Club." *Journal of Private Enterprise*, 17: 1-19.
Stringham, E. (2003) "The Extralegal Development of Securities Trading in Seventeenth Century Amsterdam." *Quarterly Review of Economics and Finance*, 43: 321-344.
Sutter, D. (1995) "Asymmetric Power Relations and Cooperation in Anarchy." *Southern Economic Journal*, 61: 602-613.
Telser, L. (1980) "A Theory of Self-Enforcing Agreements." *Journal of Business*, 53: 27-44.
Timberlake, R. (1984) "The Central Banking Role of Clearinghouse Associations." *Journal of Money, Credit and Banking*, 16: 1-15.
Tullock, G. (1974) *The Social Dilemma: The Economics of War and Revolution*. Blacksburg, VA: University Publications.
Tullock, G. (1981) "The Rhetoric and Reality of Redistribution." *Southern Economic Journal*, 47: 895-907.
Veitch, J. (1986) "Repudiations and Confiscations by the Medieval State." *Journal of Economic History*, 46: 31-36.
Zywicki, T. (2000) "The Economics of Credit Cards." *Chapman Law Review*, 3: 79-172.

19

Conflict, Cooperation and Competition in Anarchy

Tyler Cowen and Daniel Sutter

Abstract

Caplan and Stringham (2002) attempt to rebut the "paradox of cooperation (Cowen and Sutter 1999) as it applies to libertarian anarchy. The paradox in the context of anarchy implies that if private defense agencies can cooperate to avoid conflict they can also collude to reestablish coercion. Caplan and Stringham argue that arbitration is self-enforcing while collusion requires solution of a prisoner's dilemma. We agree that collusion requires more cooperative efficacy than arbitration, but maintain that arbitration requires considerably more organization than a simple coordination game. If a network of protection agencies can organize sufficiently to arbitrate disputes, they can also create a barrier to entry by refusing to arbitrate with entrants.

* * *

Cowen and Sutter (1999) outlined a "paradox of cooperation." If civil society can use norms to enforce cooperative solutions, that same society will be prone to certain kinds of cartels. In other words, cooperation-enhancing social features will bring bad outcomes as well as good outcomes. To provide a simple example, the Nazis relied on cooperation in addition to their obvious coercive elements in perpetrating their crimes. The ability to organize therefore is a mixed blessing. In the context of libertarian anarchy, this argument implies that private defense agencies are likely to collude and reestablish coercion. We refer the reader to our original paper for the details of the argument (see also Cowen 1992, 1994).

Caplan and Stringham (2002) attempt to rebut the argument as it applies to libertarian anarchy. They maintain that inter-agency collusion requires solution of a prisoner's dilemma problem, while private defense agencies face only a coordination problem in resolving disputes peacefully through arbitration. They view membership in an arbitration network of agencies as self-enforcing and believe that such a network will not evolve into a cartel. Self-interested individuals will defect from a cartel in the absence of a sufficiently vigorous punishment mechanism. Private defense agencies supposedly have enough cooperative efficacy to overcome the coordination problem but cannot collude. Thus the arbitration network will not devolve into government.

Caplan and Stringham have advanced the debate on cooperation and anarchy. We accept their contention that collusion requires greater organization among network members than establishing a system of arbitration. We remain skeptical though about the likelihood of benevolent noncollusive anarchy. Establishing an arbitration mechanism we contend brings us closer to collusion than their arguments suggest. An arbitration scheme requires far more organization than a simple convention, like driving on the right hand side of the road, which significantly narrows the space between cooperation and collusion. An arbitration network should have sufficient organization to create a barrier to entry by refusing to arbitrate disputes with an entrant agency. Even if the network initially lacks the organization necessary to collude, entry barriers create conditions likely to lead to the evolution of government.

1. Confrontation Games, Equilibrium Selection and Arbitration.

Conflict is costly, and the desire of utility maximizing in individuals to control the cost of conflict creates the potential for ordered anarchy. Figure 1 presents the normal form of a confrontation game between two private protection agencies. Two protection agencies, Able and Baker, face a potential confrontation due to a dispute between clients of the two agencies. A customer of Able accuses a customer of Baker of violating her rights as entailed in her contract with Able. The customer seeks redress against the alleged perpetrator through Able. Each agency has two actions in the game, which we label for convenience Challenge and Backdown. Challenge for Able refers to aggressively pursuing their customer's claim, and using force if necessary to prosecute the offender. Challenge for Baker refers to aggressively defending their customer. The payoff matrix in Figure 1 presents utility payoffs for each agency, but we will only use the ordering of the outcomes from 4 (best) to 1 (worst). Conflict occurs if both agencies choose their Challenge action, and is costly. The most preferred outcome for each agency is to Challenge and have the other agency Backdown. The costs of conflict exceed the financial stake each agency has in this one interaction so each agency prefers to Backdown to Challenge when the other agency Challenges.[1]

The game in Figure 1 is a coordination game with two Nash equilibria in pure strategies, one where Able backs down to Baker's challenge and the second where Baker backs down to Able's challenge. The costs of conflict provide an incentive for a peaceful resolution of the confrontation (Rothbard 1978, Friedman 1989, Benson 1990), but do not determine which equilibrium will prevail. Nonetheless we can already see the potential for the evolution of government in the interests of some parties to the adjudication prevail over the interests of others.

We also can see that only one of these equilibria is libertarian (Sutter 1995). Both equilibria may be peaceful, but at least one equilibrium does not respect individual rights. For instance, Able (the victim) backing down is an equilibrium of the confrontation game. Caplan and Stringham (and other proponents

Figure 1
A Confrontation Game between Protection Agencies

		Baker	
		Challenge	Backdown
Able	Challenge	1,1	4,2
	Backdown	2,4	3,3

Payoffs are ordinal with 4 indicating agency's most preferred outcome and 1 its least preferred outcome.

of anarcho-capitalism) have not to our minds offered an argument why the competitive, libertarian equilibrium is likely to prevail.

The confrontation between the agencies is more than a pure coordination game. The agencies care about which equilibrium prevails; in other words, the game also involves division of a surplus. Repeated play of the confrontation game in Figure 1 increases the incentive of each agency to fight and attempt to establish the equilibrium in which they capture the gains of cooperatives. Anarchy might be peaceful after an initial conflict, but equilibrium selection then would depend on the relative strength of the agencies. If might makes right, as Umbeck (1981) argues, only by luck would the libertarian equilibrium prevail. And over time, an agency that consistently backs down would lose customers. Customers will patronize agencies that can win battles, and the protection market will become increasingly concentrated.

Arbitration could alter the game as portrayed above. We can imagine, for instance, that the agencies take turns backing down, as suggested by an arbitrator. If the arbitrator decides based on evidence of rights violation, libertarian rights would be respected and each agency could stay in business. Technically speaking, arbitration offers the hope of a libertarian outcome through a correlated equilibrium of the confrontation game, with the arbitrator's decision serving as the correlating signal. Establishing a correlated equilibrium, however, is more complicated than implementing a Nash equilibrium in a pure coordination game. For one thing the agencies' ignoring the signal and playing one of the Nash equilibria of the game in Figure 1 remains an equilibrium with arbitration. So the non-libertarian outcomes do not go away. Furthermore establishing a credible arbitrator and inducing the parties to follow the arbitrator's decision requires organization. The organization required for an arbitration network creates the potential for anti-competitive actions by the network; we now turn to this topic in more detail.

2. Arbitration, Barriers to Entry, and Collusion

Consider the decisions a group of defense agencies must make to arbitrate disputes arising between the agencies' clients. The network must have some means of determining which agencies are members, who will serve as arbitrators in disputes among the members, and the rules that will apply in resolving disputes. These decisions cannot be made once and for all; rather the network will need a procedure to determine membership. In a competitive protection market, new agencies might always arise, or clients of the network agencies might travel farther and encounter agencies not currently in the network. Agencies might fail to abide by an arbitrator's decision, so the network will also need a rule to expel or punish members. And since arbitrators retire, or may fail to apply the agreed on rules properly, the network will need a procedure for deciding acceptable arbitrators and rules for arbitration.

A network with this degree of organization could create a barrier to entry into the local protection market by refusing to arbitrate disputes with an entrant. Suppose Young Guns is a new agency trying to enter the market. The members of the network have a common interest in preventing new competition so the network votes to not admit Young Guns. The network then has a ruling requiring members not to arbitrate disputes with nonmember agencies.[2] Members are supposed to stand firm and demand that Young Guns back down in any dispute. Young Guns will then either have higher costs from constant conflict or be unable to effectively defend its customers' interests. This serves as a barrier to entry.

In this framework, consider the (implicit) argument of Caplan and Stringham. If Able has a dispute with Young Guns, it faces the Confrontation game in Figure 1 and has an incentive to defect from the network's decision to fight Young Guns to avoid the cost of conflict. In essence the network is relying on Able (and other members with disputes with Young Guns' customers) to bear the costs of conflict to drive the entrant out of the market. Able may be reluctant to provide this public good for the network without side compensation but may nonetheless stand firm against Young Guns.

Let us consider in more detail Able's decision to abide by the network's rule not to arbitrate disputes with nonmember agencies, as opposed to defecting from the network and cutting a separate and "reasonable" deal with Young Guns. The network could threaten expulsion against members who accommodate entrants. Membership in the network is valuable, so a credible threat of expulsion could make Able willing to stand firm. Furthermore, the network could extend the entry barrier contract to arbitrators, threatening to stop employing arbitrators who arbitrate disputes with non-network agencies. Normally cheating on a cartel is difficult for members to detect, but monitoring arbitrators might provide an easy way to detect cheating. Without arbitration Able faces the confrontation game from Figure 1 and the choice between the two pure strategy equilibria. The "division of the surplus" element of the confrontation game provides Able an additional incentive to stand firm; Able wants to induce selection of the equilibrium in which Young Guns backs down. Indeed, backing down against Young Guns could be particularly costly for Able, which could lose many of its customers to other agencies in the network willing to stand firm. Unlike the case of a price cartel, a member may not gain from defecting from an agreement to challenge entrants. Finally, the network may back up Able should its firm stand with Young Guns lead to a violent conflict; assistance from the network in a fight would share the cost of this collective good.

The network also might decide on the less extreme strategy of unfair arbitration with entrants—entrants might have to accept arbitration by one of the network's arbitrators with the arbitrator instructed to decide in favor of the network. The arbitrator might give Young Guns enough in his decision to prevent a violent conflict, but not enough to be fair. Although the reader might object that Young Guns would never agree to such biased arbitration, their only alternative is conflict in each dispute with the network. By construction of the example, the incumbent, not the entrant, has the first-mover advantage. Young Guns could avoid constant conflict only by backing down on a regular basis, which would render it an ineffective entrant.

The network could go one step further and force member agencies to change their laws. The network will have procedures for expelling member agencies. If say a two-thirds vote of members is necessary to expel a member, a super majority of agencies could demand changes of the laws of minority agencies. Suppose that one agency in the network allows its customers to grow, buy and use drugs, while all other agencies enforce drug prohibition. Customers of the prohibitionist agencies might object to nearby availability of drugs. The other network members could threaten the libertarian agency with expulsion if it does not prohibit drugs. Once expelled, the agency faces a situation parallel to that of the entrant discussed above. If the entry deterrent is credible, the expulsion threat may be credible as well.

The arbitration network may not be able to fix prices or establish a full cartel, at least not immediately. Although all current members of a network have a common interest in deterring entry by new rivals, all have the incentive to chisel on a price fixing agreement. And expelling members is costly for a network. Network members might be reluctant to expel cheaters, and the potential exists for defection of several agencies at once. Also, price-cutting may be difficult to observe. Thus we accept Caplan and Stringham's contention that collusion will require greater cooperation than establishing a network.

That being said, price competition still may disappear over time. If a core group of agencies manage to institute coercive taxation, the incentive for price shading will disappear. Governments may compete against each other with lower taxes, as we find in today's world as well, but the previous customers now have become tax payers, who must pay the price whether they like it or not. This part of the story is more speculative, but it shows how easily inter-agency cooperation can evolve into widespread coercion and indeed centralized government.

No doubt we can imagine other, non-coercive equilibria for the game. "Folk theorems" suggest most beneficial outcomes can be sustained as an equilibrium in a repeated games, provided agents hold the right conjectures and have long enough time horizons. Nonetheless we believe that our postulated process is at the very least plausible.

3. Empirics

We must take seriously the fact that governments exist all around the world, for better or worse. Even without further analysis, government appears to be the most likely equilibrium of a large number of political games. History shows that "cooperating to coerce" is relatively easy to establish, regardless of the exact path to that final state of affairs.[3]

Looking to more specific examples, the arbitration network of protection agencies is similar to the merchant guilds described in Grief, Milgrom and Weingast (1994). Merchant guilds arose to protect traveling merchants from expropriation by the princes of different cities. Caplan and Stringham cite the guilds in support of their claim that arbitrating interagency disputes is self-enforcing. Yet refusing to trade with princes who expropriate merchants' property was not self-enforcing. A boycott of a city that recently expropriated a merchant was vulnerable to defection and difficult to enforce. The volume of trading falls when a boycott is declared, so the marginal value to a city of a merchant rises and at a sufficiently low volume a prince's promise not to expropriate merchants becomes credible. Trading by only a few merchants could allow the city to defeat the boycott. Merchants needed the organization of the guild to generate a boycott effective enough to deter expropriation by princes; the guild threatened boycott-violating merchants with expulsion and membership in the guild had to offer benefits (Grief, Milgrom and Weingast 1994). Once organized to protect merchants, guilds often managed to restrict entry to benefit current members.

The National Collegiate Athletic Association (NCAA) provides another example of a network formed to help overcome a coordination problem but which has succeeded in cartel behavior. The NCAA was formed in the early 1900s to enforce rules to limit the violence in college football (Byers 1995). An organization was needed to write rules, schedule games and identify schools not complying with the rules. But the organization moved beyond the simple coordination tasks to perform as a cartel. The major cartel function of the NCAA has been of course to limit the compensation of student-athletes to tuition and room and board, despite the millions of dollars of revenues generated by major athletic programs each year (Fleisher, Goff and Tollison 1992). The organization created to enforce the rules also had the ability to adopt new rules, and in 1952 the NCAA approved measures to punish members who paid players; adoption of the punishment mechanism reduced the competitive balance of major college football (Eckard 1998). Caplan and Stringham suggest that competing networks might reduce the potential of a coordinating network to enforce a cartel, but the existence of a rival organization in college sports, the National Association of Intercollegiate Athletics (NAIA), has failed to limit the NCAA's cartel function.

4. Conclusion

We do not contend that an arbitration network will immediately begin colluding and become a government. The ability to deter entrants, however, begins the devolution toward government. Collusion by the member agencies is superior from their point of view. We thus continue to believe that a paradox of cooperation holds for the adjudication of legal disputes. Even the ordered, libertarian equilibrium in anarchy is likely to result in the reemergence of government. It makes us doubt the value of experimenting with anarchy, given the risk of chaos and the potential for a decidedly unlibertarian equilibrium.

Acknowledgment

We would like to thank Bryan Caplan, Eric Crampton and a referee for comments on an earlier draft.

Notes

1. If an agency backs down from a challenge in this instance, they might well lose their customer. The present value of profit from an individual customer over her expected term of patronage is plausibly small compared to the cost of even a moderately violent confrontation. If the costs of conflict are always relatively small, anarcho-capitalism is likely to be quite violent.
2. At least disputes arising among residents of the local area.
3. Caplan and Stringham do not take this global evidence seriously enough. Their comment considers numerous other supposed "network industries" (of their own choosing), but does not consider the universality of government in modern industrial society.

References

Benson, B. (1990) *The Enterprise of Law.* San Francisco: Pacific Research Institute.

Byers, W. and Hammer, C. (1995) *Unsportsmanlike Conduct: Exploiting College Athletes.* Ann Arbor: University of Michigan Press.

Caplan, B. and Stringham, E. (2002) "Networks, Law, and the Paradox of Cooperation." *Review of Austrian Economics*, 16: 309-326.

Cowen, T. (1992) "Law as a Public Good: The Economics of Anarchy." *Economics and Philosophy*, 8: 249-267.

Cowen, T. (1994) "Rejoinder to David Friedman on the Economics of Anarchy." *Economics and Philosophy*, 10: 329-332.

Cowen, T. and Sutter, D. (1999) "The Costs of Cooperation." *Review of Austrian Economics*, 12: 161-173.

Eckard, W. W. (1998) "The NCAA Cartel and Competitive Balance in College Football." *Review of Industrial Organization*, 13: 347-369.

Fleisher, A. A. III, Goff. B. L., and Tollison, R. D. (1992) *The National Collegiate Athletic Association* Chicago: University of Chicago Press.

Friedman, D. (1989) *The Machinery of Freedom*, 2nd ed. La Salle IL: Open Court.

Greif A., Milgrom, P., and Weingast, B. R. (1994) "Coordination, Commitment, and Enforcement: The Case of the Merchant Guild." *Journal of Political Economy*, 102: 745-776.

Rothbard, M. N. (1978) *For a New Liberty*, revised edition. Francisco: Fox, Wilkes.

Sutter, D. (1995) "Asymmetric Power Relations and Cooperation in Anarchy." *Southern Economic Journal*, 61: 602-613.

20

Conventions: Some Thoughts on the Economics of Ordered Anarchy

Anthony de Jasay

1

Theft, robbery, and default have robust attractions. Property and contract look fragile by comparison. On the whole and most of the time, they nevertheless prevail. This result borders on the counterintuitive, since it goes against palpable interests. Why is it that these interests nevertheless usually fail? It is far from self-evident that they should. An explanation is needed. The standard one is that property and contract prevail because the state enforces the laws that secure them. But unless cooperative behavior is for some reason first established, how can the state itself prevail?—since it is not obvious why it should. For it must stand up against the same robust, palpable interests as the very institutions it is supposed to protect, and must somewhere find the strength that property and contract need, but apparently cannot find in their own defense. Simply assuming that the state does uphold them, because after all this is what the facts are saying, is to my mind shallow, as well as potentially circular. Exploring the possibility of an endogenous theory may well permit a deeper insight into these institutions—even if the theory is no more than a coherent but counterfactual account of how they might have arisen, rather than a factual one of how they did arise.

It has become a commonplace that the application of such concepts as rational choice, maximization, efficiency, and equilibrium presupposes some institutional framework, within which the rules of property and contract have pride of place. On the specific content of this institutional framework depends the form that social cooperation takes in the division of labor and the allocation of other resources. Doesn't, however, the dependence go the other way, too, so that what we are really facing is interdependence?

Marx, as we may remember, maintained that it was the economic "infrastructure," the "forces of production" (by which he basically meant technology) that engendered the institutional "superstructure," the "relations of production" (by which he basically meant property relations). The standard view in contemporary thought is the exact opposite. It stands Marx on his head: legal and political institutions are the "infrastructure" that supports the economic "superstructure," without which some of the principal forms of social cooperation, notably the beneficial interaction of free agents in markets, would not even be possible. Here, the dependence goes from the legal and political to the economic: law and its enforcement are prior to market exchange.

However, even if no causal priority is imputed to institutions, it is standard practice to take them as exogenous data, rather than as part and parcel of a rational-choice explanation of social interaction. For example, in noncooperative game theory (or, as Schelling would have it, the theory of interdependent action), it is assumed that credible commitments do not exist; in cooperative game theory, it is assumed that they do. It is of course perfectly legitimate to make assumptions of this sort. But it does not help us to understand where contracts come from, and why they are credible. If they are "given," who gave them?

Lastly, what if was "given" is suddenly "taken away"? The recent collapse of the set of bizarrely contrived institutions that used to pass for the socialist system, and that looked as if it had been deliberately designed to breed the most monstrous and perverse principal-agent problems, drives home the recognition that such a far-fetched question can confront us in real life. Even if it were just idle speculation, it would behoove scholarship to explore it. The recent (late 1980s, 1990s) historical accident that "took away" a set of socialist institutions painfully erected on a gigantic scale over seventy years argues that conducting such thought experiments is not a wholly idle pursuit.

2

Lest my purpose be misunderstood, before going on I should like to come to terms with a class of theories that I believe are misdirected, seeking as they do to explain institutions endogenously by demonstrating their efficiency. Harold Demsetz, in his justly admired papers on the emergence of property rights (esp. Demsetz, 1964 and 1967), contrary to most economists who tend to take property rights as an initial datum, puts forward a theory of why and how they came into being. For him, they evolved to fulfill a function, namely to let property users internalize externalities when the gains from doing so exceeded the costs. With hunting grounds in seventeenth-century Quebec used by the Indian inhabitants as a common pool, over-hunting was the predictable result. This imposed a negative externality on hunters as a whole. The rise in the value of furs with the advent of the organized fur trade has increased the potential benefit from "privatizing" the hunting grounds, with access to a given area reserved to a given family. As the sole owner of this piece of hunting ground, the family could fully internalize the net benefit from stopping the over-hunting. The same cause produced the same effect in the late nineteenth-century American West (Anderson and Hill, 1975). Open range ranching led to overgrazing. When the value of cattle increased as transport to Eastern markets became cheaper, the gain from preventing overgrazing came to exceed the cost of fencing in portions of the range and reserving its use to a single rancher. In either case, internalizing all the positive and negative effects from hunting or grazing removed the previous difference between maximizing the total net benefit from a given area of land, and maximizing the net benefit accruing to a particular user of that land. Only when there is a single (personal or corporate) user, entitled to all residual benefits after bearing all costs, can he maximize *his* returns by maximizing the "social" return, that is by adopting the most efficient hunting or grazing practice. Multiple users have overriding, "dominant" free-rider incentives to abuse resources at each other's expense.

It also follows that if resource use has become more efficient in private ownership, the people who used to have free access while the resource was in common pool must now be better *off as a group*. But it does not follow that *some* of them are not worse off, absolutely or at least relatively. The distribution of the benefit remains problematical. This is where functional theories of institutions, destined to evolve toward ever more efficient solutions, must watch their step. For, contrary to central command-obedience systems, an individual incentive-based system is not teleological. It has no identifiable purpose and is not seeking out efficient solutions (Streit, 1992). If it evolves and grows particular institutions, it is not because social benefit is maximized thereby, but because free agents adopt courses of individual action that seem best to them, and never mind whether their action promotes or on the contrary frustrates social efficiency. If it promotes it, it will do so as pure happenstance.

For take Rancher Smith whose cattle are now excluded by Rancher Jones's fence from part of the range. He has lost something. It is true that he will also gain something, and probably more than he has lost, if he follows Jones's example and fences in another part of the range, stopping all strange cattle from grazing there. But it is surely even better for him both to get this gain, and also to stop Jones from inflicting any loss on him. Fairness and reasonableness need have nothing to do with what he thinks is the best outcome for him if he can get it. He may well try to tear down the fence Jones has put up, and the cost to Jones of internalizing the grazing externality of the open range is not the cost of putting up a fence, but also that of permanently guarding it from Smith, or of buying off Smith's intrusions. "Normally," Jones and Smith ought to reach a mutually profitable bargain over the division and enclosure of the range they formerly shared. But this might fail to come about or fail to work for a number of reasons. One of them is the possibility that Smith will no sooner shake hands on a bargain with Jones than he will break it, cutting Jones's fence while protecting his own. Jones will have little choice but to adopt symmetrical tactics. Only if there is literally boundless open range left for the cattle of both, will Smith and Jones have no rational reason to contest each other's attempt to "privatize" any part of it. If there is only a finite area of open range left, however vast, any diminution of it by enclosure increases the probability that some future act of additional enclosure will cause an opportunity loss (a forgone gain) to Smith, Jones, or both. This is just another way of saying that Locke's proviso for legitimate first occupation, i.e., that "enough and as good is left to others," is inconsistent with finite resources.[1]

However, since strictly speaking even the most unreasonable and wild fence-cutting, agreement-refusing, or agreement-breaking tactics to oppose enclosure and exclusive occupation by others can be rational, satisfaction of the Lockean proviso (assuming it could be satisfied) might still not suffice to assure the passage from common to private property. Showing that the passage is beneficial to a group *as a whole* is not the same as showing that the institution of private property will in fact emerge, and will not be effectively opposed by a strong enough subgroup within the group. The more stringent condition of Pareto-superiority, i.e., that the group as a whole would gain from it and no individual within it would lose, looks more promising; but even this condition fails to rule out successful opposition by the envious or the egalitarian who will not stand for some members of the group gaining more than he does. Unless we are prepared to call ends irrational, we cannot simply sweep acts of envy aside as irrational, and it would not help if we did. The fact that it would be collectively beneficial to privatize certain resources does not permit us to predict that they will in fact be privatized. What it does is to alert us to a latent distribution problem: will the collective benefit be shared among the members or will it fail to be realized due to a failure to settle the question of how it is to be distributed? Clearly, the share (if any) each can successfully claim will bear some relation to his bargaining power, which in turn is a matter of his capacity to stop everybody else from getting anything, by spoiling the privatization attempt altogether. It is difficult to say more than this in a first approximation.[2]

For these reasons, social or collective benefit and functional superiority do not prove much. To say, as Demsetz does of private property (1964/1988, p. 136) that "its existence is probably due in part to [its capacity to reveal] social values upon which to base solutions to scarcity problems" appears to take a teleological view, assigning high purposes to institutions and explaining their emergence by their capacity to fulfill them. Yet nobody in his story of the common hunting grounds, or in the story of the open range, is concerned one way or the other about the high purpose and valuable signaling function of private property. To listen to Mandeville, this is perhaps just as well.

3

Consider next the problem of stability once some solution has been reached for the distribution of a common pool resource among the "hunters" or "ranchers." For argument's sake, let us take it that a tacit convention to respect private property has been widely adopted. If everybody continues to adhere to it, property is secure. There is no need to incur "enclosure costs" to exclude from it all others whose access is not authorized by the owner. There need be no fences, no locks; houses can be left open with valuables lying about. Armed guards, fingerprint data banks, and criminal courts are superfluous. There is, then, a strong incentive, created by the very confidence in established convention, to deviate from it and steal with both hands. Even if many continue to adhere to it and do not become opportunistic thieves, there is a sense in which the convention has broken down if a large enough fraction of individuals concerned deviates from it and steals when the risk-reward relation tempts it. The convention, in other words, is not self-enforcing, and is liable to break down. A certain expenditure of resources is needed to keep noncompliance (theft, trespass, etc.) down to a level at which the convention is still usefully functioning. The optimum level of expenditure (current cost or investment) is one where the marginal cost of enforcement is equal to the marginal benefit from the increased security of property. Somebody, however, must bear this enforcement cost. Paying it generates externalities: it is possible to benefit from the greater safety of property in general without contributing to its general costs. It is perhaps best if my neighbor contributes to the cost and I do not. My neighbor, of course, is symmetrically placed and may take the same view, in which case neither of us will contribute, and the convention will not be enforced.

Beneficial conventions that are not self-enforcing are logically equivalent to noncooperative games whose equilibrium solutions are Pareto inferior; technically, they work as prisoners' dilemmas. The players are condemned to a suboptimal outcome, failing to maximize the available game sum—unless they transform the game, or it is transformed for them, into one where their reciprocal commitments not to adopt the "dominant" noncooperative strategy can be made credible to each other. Under most standard rationality assumptions, the commitment will be credible if it is "common knowledge" (all players know, and each knows that the other knows that he knows that the other knows, and so on) that the dominant strategy will bring down adverse extra-game consequences on the player's head that outweigh its intra-game advantage. This is typically the case if the dominant noncooperative strategy is likely to be severely punished after the game, i.e., if the nonself-enforcing convention is enforced.

There may be a secondary convention, as it were, a satellite of the primary one, whose sole function is to enforce the latter. The classic example of such a combination is the convention of queuing: the primary convention is to wait one's turn in the queue, and the secondary or satellite convention among the more civic-minded queuers is to shout at, menace, and push and pull back into line, any queue jumpers, always provided there are not too many of those. Enforcement and the level of noncompliance are in an equilibrium which may be unstable over some ranges, stable over others.

In the queuing example, nothing enforces the enforcing convention; no tertiary norm stands behind the secondary one. Hence, if it functions, it must be self-enforcing. However, there is no prima facie reason to believe that all or most other nonself-enforcing conventions will be backed up by a satellite convention among civic-minded adherents that will be self-enforcing. In fact, there is a prima facie reason for holding the contrary.

Punishment of noncompliance is in general costly, as are other measures of enforcement. Punishment and some, perhaps most, measures of enforcement create strong externalities: anybody can benefit from the enforcement of a useful convention whether or not he bears any part of the cost. If and to the extent that this is so enforcement is not selfenforcing, but is itself enforcement dependent. For all we know, we may be facing a series of successively higher-degree enforcing conventions, each depending on the next-higher one. No matter how high one goes, there is never a highest convention that is no longer enforcement dependent. The normal way of dealing with this kind of logical mischief is to lose patience and postulate an arbitrary stopping point, beyond which we simply refuse to carry on the argument. In the present case, the stopping point is the state.

Conceived as an entity of an altogether different kind from the individuals and organizations that are subordinated to it, the state does not maximize its own utility, profit, or wealth; it does not respond to incentives, but seeks to carry out society's mandate, or rather its own reading of the variety of signs and noises emitted by society that must be interpreted by politicians, judges, and high officials in order to know what society's mandate really is. The state, then, is society's agent. Some even view it as an agent that is in some metaphysical way exempt from the principal-agent problem that in every other case we regard as intrinsic, logically inseparable from the agency relation. On reflexion, this is a strange view to take, but it is necessary to support the assignment to the state of the role of stopping point, of ultimate enforcer. For only then can we say that its contract with society, under which it acts as its enforcing agency, is not itself in need of enforcement, lest it should breed parasitism, extortion, sloth, bureaucracy, partiality, and other familiar vices.

This stopping point, then, acts as a *deus ex machina* postulate: for if it is impossible to deduce, by way of individual rational choice theory, a cooperative solution to the ordinary first-degree enforcement problem, then how is it possible, with the aid of the same premises, to deduce the state as the cooperative solution to any nth degree enforcement problem? It can, of course, always be introduced as an exogenous datum. But that, so to speak, is where we came in.

4

James Buchanan (1979, p. 282), in implicitly making the very existence of crucial institutions depend on the state as last-resort enforcer, claims support by both Hobbes and history: "Institutions matter. The libertarian anarchists who dream of markets without states are romantic fools who have read neither Hobbes nor history." Reading history, however conducive to wisdom and understanding, is a notoriously inconclusive way of reaching specific conclusions about such vast, amorphous and diffuse features of the past as markets, states, and their interdependence. Buchanan reads one lesson from history; I for one would read a rather different one, and the chances are that neither of our readings is very near the mark.[3]

Let us, however, read Hobbes by all means. In *Leviathan*, he marks off two alternative "models" of the conflict over property, one producing stalemate at the status quo, the other permanent trespass and the continuous overturning of any status quo. The first model applies when, or perhaps because, force is just matched by equal force; the second and contrary model when, or because, attack gathers more force than defense.

To establish the first alternative, Hobbes lays down that "the difference between man, and man, is not considerable...the weakest has strength enough to kill the strongest, either by secret machination, or by confederacy with others" (Hobbes 1651/1968, p. 113) and "the fear of coercive power...where all men are equal...cannot possibly be supposed" (ibid., p. 196). In such a configuration of equal opposing forces, unless technology is biased in favor of attack, a given distribution of property can, and among rational men will, always be successfully defended by the incumbent. If one individual seeks to change the property status quo by excluding from it another, the other has just enough force to resist (kill) him; in case of unequal forces, the weaker can have recourse to a "confederacy" strong enough to resist. The important point is that in this model, coalition forming has the object of equalizing the opposing forces. Consequently, whether the property status quo is efficient or inefficient, it cannot be altered by way of a stronger coalition forming on the side of the efficient change (or indeed of *any* change, whether efficient or not), and imposing it on the weaker one.

The second alternative, by contrast, stipulates that the role of "confederacy" is to create force inequality in favor of the attacker: "...if one plant, sow, build, or possess a convenient Seat, others may probably be expected to come *with forces united to dispossess*, and deprive him. (ibid., p. 184, my italics). Since the attacker, being "probably" a coalition of united forces "hath no more to fear, than another man's *single power*" (ibid., my italics), the attack is generally successful. A new status quo is created, and by the logic of the model becomes the new target of attack by a new coalition. It is this second model that Hobbes and all his intellectual descendants implicitly invoke when they argue the impossibility of contract and order in anarchy, and the imperative necessity of "a common power set over them both, with right and force sufficient" (Hobbes, ibid., p. 196).

Nobody has, to my knowledge, bothered to ask the obvious question: why in a Hobbesian world should coalitions form only for attack and never for defense? What happens if, in any conflict over property, both the attacker and the defender are free to attract allies? Why can't we make the commonsense assumption that the force of the coalition gathered to back a given side in the conflict will be proportional to the "payoff" (gain or avoided loss) the side would get if it won the conflict? To meet the objection that this would amount to a doubtfully rational "maximax" strategy guided only by the best possible outcome and taking no account of intermediate or worst-possible alternatives, the assumption could be recast in terms of the mathematical expectation of utility payoffs. However, the essential point would, as far as I can see, remain intact: incentives work both ways, they may attract coalitions on both sides of a conflict, and the tacit supposition of an asymmetry, giving a natural advantage to the attacking coalition, must be justified. Failing that, it must be rejected.

5

How to justify the supposed asymmetry? If a given population is free to form coalitions, prior to the emergence of institutions (such as a convention to respect property, contract, or both, since the two will almost certainly come or go together), the resulting interaction will in effect be an n-person "distribution game," whose game sum is the aggregate property of the *n* players. Let there be, for simplicity, only three players, each equally "strong." Their "strength" (muscle, arms, economic power, political influence) can be employed with equal effectiveness to defend the property status quo, or to change it to one's advantage; technology is neutral between attack and defense, and there are constant returns to scale. Defense, then, wins against attack of equal or lesser strength. Attack, to win, must have greater strength. (A special case of this distribution game is democracy, where "strength," instead of having a quite general significance, is reduced to "number of votes," and a simple or qualified majority wins.) Whatever the status quo before the game, the solution of the game is a distribution of property decided by the winner, and the stronger coalition necessarily wins.

Evidently, since players are equally strong, in a three-person game, if any two players can agree on how to divide all property between them, that division will be the solution of the game and the third player will be left propertyless.[4] If he tried to obstruct this outcome, he would incur some cost, only to be defeated; therefore if he is rational, he will not try. The winning coalition knows this; therefore it will not negotiate with the loser. (However, if they believed the loser was irrational, or precommitted to a costly defense unless bought off, the winners might be prepared to buy him off.)

Of the two members of the winning coalition, one, the "poorer," now has less property than the other, the "richer" (in the limiting case, they will have equal property; but the reasoning below holds in the limiting case as well). The "poorer" and the propertyless "poorest" can now improve their joint payoff by forming a new coalition that, being stronger than the solitary "richer," can dispossess him. One of the new winners will now be the "richer," the other the "poorer." The latter can again improve his payoff at the new "richer's" expense by forming a coalition with the new "poorest" and dispossessing the "richer." The solution, in other words, will always remain unstable. It will rotate round and round, always superseded by another of the same form and the same instability. Only the members of the winning and losing coalitions will be changing places cyclically. The mechanism by which strength (including, in a democracy, voting strength) is attracted by prospective payoffs and produces a certain distribution of the game sum (i.e., in the present example, of property) is analogous to other well-known social-choice cycles (Arrow, Sen). There is no distribution of property to which at least one other is not "preferred" by a stronger coalition, leading to a perpetual cycle of redistribution.

This, I think, goes some way to justify the strange asymmetry in what I called (in section 4) Hobbes's second "model," where coalition always produces an imbalance of force in favor of attacking the status quo and dispossessing the possessor. But it only goes some way, and not a very long way either. For it is clear that while the unstable solution of each round of the distribution game is the direct consequence of each player acting rationally, a perpetual cycle of dispossession and redistribution is *not* going to be the solution of indefinitely repeated rounds of the same game. The players will soon see new costs and new incentives appearing, which will alter their view of expected payoffs and of the rational strategy they must choose to maximize them.

Over any three rounds of this game, each player takes turns to be once "richer," once "poorer," and once "poorest." The statistical average return to each is one-third of the property available for redistribution. The players can improve their joint return from the game by forming a coalition, and having taken all property, refusing to desert the alliance despite the availability of an even higher payoff to the deserter in the next round. This refusal to quit a coalition in order to join a new one imposes a stable solution on the game, i.e., it "stops" it from rotating. However, is it rational for the "poorer" player not to desert his richer partner?

By deserting, he can only hope to improve his position from "poorer" to "richer" for a single round. In the round after that, he must expect his partner to desert him, causing him to fall all the way from "richer" to propertyless "poorest." Therefore standing fast, respecting his richer coalition partner's property, and accepting that his position is permanently poorer, would be his best strategy provided the poorer position represents, in the worst case, not much less than a one-third share of the property to be divided. This is so because, if the game is not stabilized and redistribution continues indefinitely, he can statistically expect to average out with a share of one-third, *less* the cost and disutility of periodic dispossession. He will want to do no worse than this (settling for less would be irrational), but anything better is a bonus.

Note that the decision to "stop the game," stand fast, and not desert, is the poorer partner's alone: if he is prepared to accept his roughly one-third share, the richer partner cannot permanently improve his own position, and will be happy to stabilize his share at around two-thirds, rather than revert to the cyclical average of one-third. The propertyless has no choice if the coalition of the propertied holds.

Note also that while a three-person game under the very abstract conditions stipulated here produces a stable distribution of about two-thirds or less to the first player, about one-third or more to the second, and nothing or next to nothing to the third, an n-person game under less neat and artificial conditions would probably produce a solution that was messier, less structured, and more like real-life distributions of wealth, the more so as real-life distributions are influenced by many more elements in addition to coalition forming to produce concentrations of force, influence, or voting strength.

What I have just attempted to demonstrate was that on full reflexion it is reasonable to expect private property to emerge, and to prevail over the temptations that threaten it, as a product of the same robust incentives that we would, perhaps a little hastily, expect to provoke, not respect for property, but theft, robbery, dispossession, and default instead. This result, let me add, owes nothing to decency, sympathy, a sense of fairness, and a desire for mutual accommodation. Such motives, residing in our better nature, are almost certainly important in human conduct, but it seems to me gratifying that we can find an explanation that is at least coherent whether or not it is right, for a crucial institution of the social order, property, from the most elementary assumptions of rationality, without having recourse to any special motivation springing, not from human nature *tout court*, but from our *better* nature.

The logic of the "distribution game" rests, not on any collective quest for efficient solutions for a whole group, but on individual maximizing behavior. The resulting game solution implies an escape from the costly, futile, and sterile "churning" of repeated redistribution; it stabilizes a set of property relations. If this is socially efficient, it is so as an almost accidental by-product of each individual doing the best he can for himself.

Any regard he has for the interests of others serves only to help foresee their likely reactions to his alternative strategies, in order to let him choose the best one given that others will also choose their best ones. This, in other words, is still a Hobbesian world of every man for himself, except that it produces property relations that are stable and orderly, instead of being precarious and chaotic.

How is this world, where property relations are merely facts of life upheld by forces that are mightier than the forces that would overthrow them, transformed into one where they are respected as parts of the legitimate interests of others? How does the convention of respect for property—not for one's own, but for yours, his, and hers—arise and take root? How does *any* convention arise and take root whose operation favors some more than others? There is little doubt that Hume is right: The passage of time lends legitimacy to almost any stable state of affairs that is not downright vicious or stupidly inefficient. Original occupation, exclusion, the forcible enclosure of previously accessible common resources, and their taking into private property, gradually recede into the distant past; passage of title from the original occupiers and "finders" to new owners by sale, gift, or bequest comes into the foreground and promotes a sense of legitimacy.

This is not to suggest that the passage of time alone can bring into being a convention of property that is self-enforcing because everybody's best policy is to respect and never to violate it. Property no doubt needs a secondary convention for its enforcement, protection, and deterrence of violations. Such a secondary convention may be self-enforcing (a sufficiently large and strong body of property-owners supporting it in spontaneous cooperation) or not; in the latter case, it needs the support of binding contractual arrangements for the provision of resources devoted to enforcement. It is to contracts, and their enforceability, the pivotal problem in the social order, that we must finally turn.

While property is best understood as an n-person, and in its most elementary form a three-person, game, the essence of contract, i.e., a promised exchange, is a two-person game where the two available pure strategies consist of performance of the promise or default. The contract is optimally efficient if the value of the two performances is equal at the margin to each party. If it were unequal for one party, it would pay him to increase or reduce the contract sum, and if this were not consistent with equal marginal value of performances for the other party, they could both improve their expected gain from the contract by changing the relative price of the performances to be exchanged until marginal equality was established. This maximization condition is naturally subject to the budget constraints of the parties, and to any indivisibilities.

Like the property distribution game, the key to the solution of the contract game is coalition forming to create an inequality between the forces favoring rival solutions: the larger payoff attracts the stronger coalition that can impose its payoff-maximizing strategy on the weaker one. In the property game, the stronger coalition secures the larger payoff by overriding the status quo. Once secured, it preserves its larger payoff by stabilizing the new status quo. Where, however, is the larger payoff in the contract game; how does one get it; and how can stronger and weaker coalitions be formed in a game that has only two players?

Assuming the gains from trade promised in the contract are maximized, the value of the two performances is equal at the margin. Let performances be nonsimultaneous. The player who is meant to move first can choose to perform or not to perform as promised. In the former case, the second player will default, because he can make no further gain from the contract by performing what he promised. In the latter case, he will try to force the first player to perform. In each of these possible configurations, each party would gain a payoff equal to the contract sum if he succeeded to make the defaulting party perform; and each defaulting party would save the contract sum if he successfully resisted the attempt. A rational player would be willing to employ his strength, or otherwise spend resources up to, but not exceeding, the contract sum to force the other party to perform.[5] Neither side can gain more than this by frustrating or subduing the other side; hence no side would be willing to spend more than this to enforce the other side's performance. Whether the players act alone, or find extra-game allies to form coalitions, they have (at least in the ideal contract) strictly offsetting incentives, and would lose even from successful enforcement if they incurred enforcement costs in excess of the contract sum. The solution of the game, then, is stalemate: whatever the status quo (whether neither side performs or one side performs), it can be effectively protected and will not be overturned by enforcement. The plaintiff will never subdue the defendant.

This conclusion, reached after telling the first and most Hobbesian half of the contract story, is preliminary. It seems strongly to support the standard belief that contracts, to be binding, require a third-party enforcer who stands outside the particular contract, and whose capacity and willingness to incur enforcement expenditure is not limited by the incentives the contract offers. But what incentives motivate the third-party enforcer? We have seen that the standard belief runs into nasty obstacles. Third-party enforcement is to let the genie out of the bottle without knowing however to put it back. It has every chance to breed a dangerous principal-agent problem, whose putative solution is either an infinite regress of ever higher-order enforcers, or a *deus ex machina* final power, exogenous and unexplained. However, all this is perhaps no great matter, for the preliminary conclusion, namely that contracts are per se unenforceable, is wrong.

8

To get it right, the story of the contract must be told to the end. First, let us recall that the problem of enforceability impinges primarily, if not exclusively, on contracts with nonsimultaneous performances, such as credit transactions. It is a fair guess that such contracts are found indispensable as social cooperation becomes complex and sophisticated,[6] but they are nonetheless only one kind of contract among two. Second, and more important, the apparently dominant strategy in such contracts, to "take the money and run," is seldom really dominant in real life among contracting parties who can calculate.

Running off with the money nearly always involves heavy costs in terms of rebuilding a life elsewhere, replacing lost goodwill and regaining the status of an acceptable contract party. It will pay if the runaway leaves little of value behind, and if the contract sum was big enough; but for understandable reasons these two conditions tend to be mutually exclusive. He who has no valuable life to regret, little reputation and goodwill to lose, seldom gets to make contracts that leave him with big money to run away with. For default to be definitely a dominant strategy, it is best if the defaulter is anonymous and transient; yet who will willingly perform first, face to an anonymous and transient second performer? The usual game theory assumption of anonymous (interchangeable) players, for all its helpful effect to clarify the logic of a given game, must not be allowed to confuse a situation where it is plainly not applicable. Anonymity predictably produces default, but anonymity deprives the party to a contract of the opportunity to lay his hands on the money that would make defaulting worthwhile. This point has obvious relevance to the so called "large group problem," which I hope to address later (section 9).

Take a two-person contract game witnessed with a minimum of attention by a nonplaying group of indeterminate size. Members of this "kibitzer" group, however, have been, are now, and expect in the future to be playing in other contract games. The first player performs his obligation under the contract, the second defaults, and the fact comes to be known by some "kibitzers" in the surrounding group, who in turn can pass this knowledge along if they deem it worth doing so. The first player as plaintiff now recruits a coalition to help him enforce the contract,[7] offering it a reward up to but not exceeding the contract sum in case of success, nothing in case of failure. This coalition, however, may find that it would pay it to incur enforcement expenditure in excess of the contract sum. The reason for this apparent extravagance is that the maximum payoff it can expect is not simply the contract sum, but also the value of some positive externality or "spillover" upon those other contracts to which members of the coalition are or can expect to be parties. There is a degree of payoff interdependence: first performers to certain contracts benefit from the enforcement of the claims of other first performers in other contracts. Such spillover effects enhance the reputation of the enforcers who came to the aid of the plaintiff, teach a lesson to the defendant and other would-be defaulters, and discourage their potential coalition partners. As such, they reduce enforcement costs throughout the group. This gain, a positive externality, is probably more perceptible in the close "neighborhood" (the same locality, the same line of business, the same peer group) than at distant points near the edges of the group: hence it is more likely to be internalized.

The defendant, for reasons symmetrical to the plaintiffs, will also recruit a coalition to oppose enforcement, holding out as reward some sum up to, but not exceeding, the contract sum he would save if he could get away with default. His coalition, however, assuming it is formed, can only hope for a best-case payoff equal to the reward offered by the defendant *less* negative spillover effects on future contracts the coalition members expect to wish to conclude. The most important negative spillover effect is likely to be the reduced willingness of third parties to enter into contracts with a defaulter's coalition partners. Members of both coalitions, if they calculate (however crudely and with however large a margin of error, as long as the error is not systematically biased), will internalize the positive and negative spillovers created by coalition action, which would help determine their willingness to enter, or abstain from, a given coalition.

Internalizing the neighborhood spillover effects increases the coalition payoff from enforcement, and decreases that from default, relative to their common benchmark, the contract sum. The asymmetry between the two, reflected in an asymmetry between the resources either side could rationally spend in order to win, obviously improves the odds that the enforcing coalition will win. Consequently, in the limit it will not pay at all, but merely entail useless expenditure, to oppose such a coalition; and the consequence of *that*, in turn, is that where potential enforcement is powerful, actual enforcement cost under moderately favorable conditions may be reduced to vanishing point: if the defendant's coalition will not form, it is hardly necessary for the plaintiff's coalition to form as long as it is common knowledge that the incentives are present for it to form as occasion demands.

At this stage we are, it seems to me, fairly entitled to two deductions: (a) default will normally fail to find coalition support, and (b) enforcing coalitions will form readily, and will tend to be sufficiently powerful.

In sections 5 and 6, I have advanced a reason why, among rationally maximizing individuals, "common pool" resources would pass into private property, and why a certain, no doubt unequal distribution of property would be finally stabilized, ultimately giving rise to a convention of respect for property. I have not tried to prove that the convention would be self-enforcing. Lack of space forbids the marshalling of arguments or against, but on the whole I think they are inconclusive: whether a group or an entire society can make its property convention into a complex self-enforcing one depends on contingencies, including its history, and there can be no certitude about the matter on a priori grounds. It is this uncertainty that makes a self-enforcing contract convention particularly critical for the orderly functioning of society: if contracts can be relied on, any other convention can be made enforceable, for compliance can be contracted for, and if not, protection from noncompliance and for its punishment can be.

9

My argument that successful enforcement generates positive, default negative externalities; that prospective coalition partners internalize them; and that consequently enforcement will attract the support of the stronger coalition, is for all its simplicity not decisive. Challengers of the theory of ordered anarchy have a last-resort objection to it, the Large Group problem. This objection enjoys more generous credit than its intellectual content deserves; but in the present context it cannot be bypassed. It must be dealt with, if only to show why the credit it is accorded is excessive.

In the large group, individuals are alleged to lack the incentives that would lead them to choose cooperative solutions in the same kind of repeated, game-like interactions that take place in small groups. This belief is based on a putative analogy between social groups with many members and n-person indefinitely repeated prisoners' dilemmas where *n* is a large number, or the players are anonymous, or both. This analogy is almost totally false, and based on elementary mistakes. The subject is large and cannot be done full justice here, but a few pointers should suffice.

Unlike the abstract large-number supergame where all players are alike, homogeneous for the purposes of the game, and all play only in the same game and in no other, the large group in society is always eterogeneous. It is the sum of small groups, which, in turn, are only homogeneous for some purposes and heterogeneous for most others; their heterogeneity is often relevant for the game. All players do not play in one and the same game. The characteristic configuration is that small groups, their subgroups, and in the vast majority of cases (i.e., in the most frequent form of social cooperation, the contract of exchange) pairs of players, each play in a different game, or in other words are parties to a different contract. Some, probably many, of the same players take part in different games, running parallel or with a time lead or time lag; and most of these games are repeated with the participation of some previous players and some new ones. Hence there is a complex and dense web of communication in which it is both easy to send[8] and profitable to receive information about prospective players (contract partners). Consequently, the play of a player is rapidly translated into a reputation that influences his chances of being invited or admitted to other games, and the terms he can hope to get. In all these respects, far from an analogy, there is an almost total contrast between the real-life large group and the n-person game where *n* is large. Lastly, there is some, albeit weak, analogy between the real-life *large* group with its numerous small subgroups (down to the two-person group made up of the two parties to one contract) and the *n*-person game where *n* is *small* rather than large. This weak analogy concerns the vulnerability of cooperative small-group solutions to the probability that the next game in a repeated series is going to be the last, beyond which by definition nothing matters, hence the noncooperative strategy becomes dominant. A contract between two parties who will never deal again with one another is in this sense a "last game." But unless neither will ever deal with *anybody else* either, the consequences of the noncooperative strategy in *their* last contract carry over into contracts with *others*, where they continue to matter. Contracting continues in the same and connected localities, trades, and communities as long as society keeps functioning.

In transposing the "large group" objection from game theory to transactions cost economics, the objectors claim that economies of scale impose mass markets, hence a great multitude of "impersonal transactions" between unknown parties[9]: thus they bring the faceless, nameless player back into play. It is no doubt true that there are proportionately more "impersonal" transactions in a modern economy than in earlier times. Many supermarket customers are unknown to the checkout girl. But they pay before rolling out their trolley. If not, they produce a credit card; and the credit card company is not unknown. It is equally true that where performances are not simultaneous or are incompletely defined in the contract (cf. Hart, 1991), serious precautions are generally taken to ensure that the second performer, far from being impersonal, is thoroughly known, vouched for, and has a reputation to lose.[10] It is this that raises entry costs in industries where quality and service are important, difficult to define and to litigate.

Under these conditions, the invocation of "impersonal exchanges" is hardly intelligible, as is the claim that third-party enforcement makes such exchanges possible—for there *are* no such exchanges, with or without third-party enforcement. They are imaginary constructs, except in the world of cash-and-carry—a world to which enforcement of any kind is irrelevant.

10

One object of the present paper was to prove that, contrary to James Buchanan's verdict, it is possible for romantic fools *both* to see coherence and good sense in a theory of ordered anarchy *and* to read Hobbes. In fact, I find Hobbes a positive help to drawing the outlines of such a theory.

Why, then, is it that states are ubiquitous? The inference is universally drawn that just as a mammal must have a lung or a brain, a normal developed society must have a state as a requirement of organic completeness, without which it cannot function properly; the state as a superior form of social organization is imposed by the processes of cultural selection no less inexorably than the lung is by natural selection.

The answer to this type of wide-eyed social determinism had, once again, best be a Human one. As he remarks with some asperity in the *Treatise* (1739/1978), governments "arise from quarrels, not among men of the same society, but among those of different societies" (p. 540). An anarchic society may not be well equipped to resist military conquest by a command-directed one. But this is a less general claim, less decisive and different from the one underlying practically all received theory of political and economic institutions, namely that the state is a necessary prior condition of social order in, general, of property and contract in particular, so that it would be needed and wanted even in the absence of any threat of foreign attack. To listen to Hume again, "the stability of possession, its translation by consent, and the performance of promises...are...antecedent to government" (p. 541).

The weight of arguments seems to me decisive that whatever causes states to be everywhere and ordered anarchy nowhere, it is not some kind of utility-maximizing logic, some putative economic necessity due to which property and contract cannot exist without being enforced by the state. The reasoning, leading from the *prevalence* of centralized, sovereign third-party enforcement to its *necessity* is manifestly a mistake of inference, a *non sequitur*.

A more modest claim holds that while ordered anarchy, based on conventions, with their enforcement "made or bought" by the directly interested parties themselves, may well be feasible, it would be inefficient. Among its tools, violence must figure: and violence is an industry that operates under increasing returns to scale.[11] It is, for this and perhaps other reasons, a "natural" monopoly.[12] A corollary of the increasing returns thesis is that the state, using the threat of violence, reduces transactions costs below what they would be under private contract enforcement. Both these proposition run into intrinsic difficulties. How will monopoly enforcement affect the distribution of income between the monopolist and its customers? Will transaction costs really be lower if they must provide monopoly rent to the enforcer?—and so on.[13] Such difficulties, however, are as nothing next to a blunter and more powerful objection. It is that we have not the faintest idea whether the state is or is not an efficient enforcer, whether statute laws are efficient substitutes for the conventions of property and contract, and whether the existence of a state over a territory, or of several states across territories, raises or lowers transactions costs. Any assertion that it does one or the other is almost entirely a matter of guesswork based on practically no evidence. In fact, valid, *ceteris paribus* evidence is impossible to produce, since comparisons of public and private enforcement regimes that cannot coexist are impossible. No one can pretend to know what a place at a time would be like if the omnipresent state with its monopolistic claims were absent, and had been absent from Day One, rather than present one day, crumbling the next, and leaving its moral footprints and material debris on the ground. The anxious conviction that anarchy is chaos and mayhem, exemplified by postcolonial Africa, Lebanon in the 1980s, or the ex-Soviet Union in the 1990s, springs from a misunderstood and misplaced empiricism that confuses historical experience with experiment.

Notes

1. Nozick (1974, p. 176) uses a different route to demonstrate the same result, i.e., the internal inconsistency of the Lockean proviso in a world of finite resources.
2. Libecap (1989), suggests that the higher the ratio of benefit to cost, the more likely it is that a solution will be found.
3. Douglass North, reading with the eyes of the professional historian, wonders whether "voluntary cooperation can exist without…a coercive state to create cooperative solutions?" He thinks the answer is contingent on circumstances, and "the jury is still out" (North, 1990, p. 14, citing North, 1981). He adds (1990, p. 58): "If we cannot do without the state, we cannot do with it either." The truth of the matter is no doubt the obverse: we can live with it if we must, *and* also without it if we must. Neither is always comfortable, and both must be learnt by practice.
4. In an even more extreme solution, two players might actually enslave the third. For this to be an equilibrium solution, the economics of slavery have to be more favorable than the economics of wage labor. A similar consideration may influence the choice between leaving the third player wholly propertyless, or letting him have some property.
5. There is a parallel between this somewhat absurd situation, where the two parties taken together spend twice as much as their greatest possible gain which only one of the two can gain, and the economics of thieving as depicted by Gary Becker (1992, p. 8). In his Nobel lecture, he relates that in his earlier work (1968, n.3), looking for a way to impute social cost to crime against property, which, at first sight, looks like a pure transfer from owners to thieves, he has put the social costs of thieving at approximately equal to the aggregate dollar value stolen, since "rational criminals would be willing to spend up to that amount on their crimes." He then remembers that potential victims would also be willing to spend resources to protect their property against crime, therefore one should add this expenditure to the resource cost the thieves incur, to get total social cost. He does not say whether protective expenditure is equal, greater or less than thieving expenditure, but the two together are implicitly estimated to exceed, perhaps by a great deal, the aggregate sum stolen.
6. In fact, such contracts have apparently *always* been an integral part of exchange. Primitive tribes bartered with other, strange tribes by leaving their surplus goods at some conspicuous midway spot. The foreign tribesmen came, picked them up and left their own surplus goods on the spot. It must be added that although the parties did not personally know each other, both sides knew perfectly well whom they were dealing with—which is why the deal, where one party performed first,

despite the risk that the other party might default and just walk off with the goods, became a reasonable proposition.

7. An enforcing coalition may use a range of costly self-help measures, from threats of discrimination and actual ostracism, to violence to compel performance and to punish. But it may just as well provide money to hire enforcement services. A trade association may have a budget for such purposes, just as long-distance traders in antiquity, medieval, and even more recent times used to hire (subsidize) foreign potentates to protect their interests against brigands, debtors, and interlopers. The choice between enforcing and hiring enforcement is basically the same as the classic "make-or-buy" choice, well known from the theory of the firm.
8. In a given line of business, the spread of information about the quality and reputation of a person or firm spreads like wildfire, and knows no frontiers. Information is "cheap" to send and "cheap" to obtain, for the less than respectable reason that businessmen are like idle old women in one respect: in their delight to spread and to listen to gossip.
9. To quote Douglass North (1990, pp. 55-8) again, third-party enforcement (by the state) is hard to do without, because self-enforcing solutions require that the game be played indefinitely between the same parties who must have "perfect information," but "[i]n a world of *impersonal* exchange, we are exchanging with multiple individuals and can acquire very little information about them" (p. 58, my italics). To a practicing businessman, the idea of dealing with nameless unknowns must be nigh incomprehensible. Whatever the economies of scale he wished to realize, he would simply see no possible occasion to deal with unknown parties otherwise than in self-enforcing contracts; least of all would he deal on credit. He would always place identified parties, banks, brokers, bondsmen, wholesalers, quality inspectors, and so on, between himself and the "nameless" credit customer. Cash customers, of course, need no enforcement and may even remain nameless for all the difference it makes.
10. William Niskanen, one-time chief economist of the Ford Motor Company, relates that in his day the company had hundreds of component suppliers who had no written contract whatsoever, which did not hurt either Ford or the suppliers.
11. If this argument were taken really seriously, it would be hard to explain why there are many states instead of one world state (perhaps returns do not go on increasing on *that* scale?); why the number of states, instead of steadily diminishing, waxes and wanes unpredictably, with some large states breaking up, some small ones trying to unite. The easy answer, of course, is that when states are getting larger, returns to scale must be increasing, when states are getting smaller, they are diminishing. This defense effectively empties the thesis of all possible empirical content.
12. A summary and lucid critique of the family of explanations of the state's monopoly, advanced by Engels, Kropotkin, Max Weber, Norbert Elias, and Robert Nozick, is found in Green (1988, pp.78-82).
13. An intriguing public-choice type problem in this respect concerns the incidence of a given aggregate burden of transactions costs. Borne by parties having interests in contracts, they are internalized. Borne by the general public via direct and indirect taxation, as is the case for the part of enforcement costs assumed by the state, they are externalized, and no longer impinge on contract parties. This is inefficient, as is all divorce between the incidence of a benefit and of the cost incurred to secure it. However, this would not stop the business community cheering as enforcement costs were shifted to the state and transaction costs were seemingly lowered. However, their real social cost might have been actually increased by the shift to the state, for reasons the public choice literature can liberally provide.

References

Anderson, Terry L. and Hill, P. J. (1975) "The Evolution of Property Rights: A Study of the American West," *Journal of Law and Economics*, vol. XVIII, 1.

Becker, Gary S. (1968) "Crime and Punishment: An Economic Approach," *Journal of Political Economy*, 76.

———. (1992) "The Economic Way of Looking at Life," Stockholm, The Nobel Foundation.

Buchanan, James M. (1979) *What Should Economists Do?* Indianapolis: Liberty Press.

Cowen, Tyler (ed.) (1988) *The Theory of Market Failure*. Fairfax, Va: George Mason University Press.

Demsetz, Harold (1964) "The Exchange and Enforcement of Property Rights," *Journal of Law and Economics*, 7, repro in Cowen, 1988.

———. (1967) "Toward a Theory of Property Rights," *American Economic Review*, Proceedings Issue.

Green, Leslie (1988) *The Authority of the State*. Oxford: Clarendon Press.

Hart, Oliver D. (1991) "Incomplete Contracts and the Theory of the Firm," in Williamson and Winter, 1991.

Hobbes, Thomas (1651, 1968) *Leviathan*, ed. by C. B. Macpherson. Harmondsworth: Penguin.

Hume, David (1739/1978) *A Treatise of Human Nature*, 2nd ed. by P. H. Nidditch. Oxford: Clarendon Press.

Libecap, Gary D. (1989) *Contracting for Property Rights*. Cambridge: Cambridge University Press.

North, Douglass C. (1981) *Structure and Change in Economic History*. New York: W.W. Norton.

———. (1990) *Institutions, Institutional Change and Economic Performance*. Cambridge: Cambridge University Press.

Nozick, Robert (1974) *Anarchy, State, and Utopia*. Oxford: Blackwell.

Streit, Manfred E. (1992) "Economic Order, Private Law and Public Policy: The Freiburg School of Law and Economics in Perspective," *Journal of Institutional and Theoretical Economics*, vol. 148, 4.

Williamson, Oliver E. and Stanley G. Winter (eds.) (1991) *The Nature of the Firm*. New York: Oxford University Press.

21

Can Anarchy Save Us from Leviathan?

Andrew Rutten

These days, it seems that anarchy is everywhere. Its fans range from Yale law professors (Ellickson 1991) to pulp novelists (Ferrigno 1996; Mosley 1998). Last fall, it even showed up in the *New Yorker*, where it was touted it as "the next big thing" in law enforcement (Rosen 1997).

At first glance, it is hard to understand this fascination. Most of us equate anarchy—literally, "the absence of the state"—with chaos and mayhem. Following Hobbes, we reason that without the state to enforce rights, venality would reign and society would lapse into the war of all against all, making our lives "solitary, poor, nasty, brutish and short." Who, except the most depraved sociopath, would want such a condition?

The advocates of anarchy would answer "not us." The theme of their work is that Hobbes, Locke, and almost everyone else are wrong about anarchy. The advocates point to the growing body of theory and evidence that life in anarchy isn't at all as most people imagine it. Whether we look at businessmen in Wisconsin, diamond merchants in New York, or farmers in Sri Lanka, we find that "order without law" is not just a slogan but a way of life (Macaulay 1963; Bernstein 1992; Ostrom 1990). Those anarchies work because, *contra* Hobbes, they do not lack an enforcer of rights.[1] Or rather, instead of a single enforcer—the centralized monopolist we call the state—anarchies have a variety of decentralized enforcers, such as markets, firms, and communities. Thus, anarchies avoid chaos by providing lots of folks with an incentive to pitch in and punish deviants.

For a small but growing group of anarchists, rehabilitating anarchy is only the first step toward reconstructing liberal political theory. For them, liberal theory errs by treating the state as a necessary evil, rather than an unnecessary one. The anarchists argue that the state is evil because it invariably abuses its power, violating the rights of some for the benefit of others, and that it is unnecessary because even without it we would still have social order and respect for each other's rights. From their perspective, "limited government" is a contradiction in terms, a project that simply cannot succeed. Thus, for them, the job of the political economist is not to tame the state but to teach us how to do without it.

In the essays in *Against Politics*, one of our leading anarcho-liberals, Anthony de Jasay, argues the case against the state with flair and insight. He claims that the only consistent liberal is an anarcho-liberal. He takes his inspiration from Edmund Burke, who wrote, "In vain you tell me that Artificial Government is good, but that I fall out only with the abuse. The Thing, the Thing itself is the Abuse" (p. vii). In explaining why government "itself is the Abuse," de Jasay ranges widely, giving us essays on topics from contractarian theories of the state to multiculturalism and rights. He arranges the essays into two broad sections. In the first, called "Excuses," he examines carefully a variety of arguments for government. Whether we think of the state as necessary (the third party that is essential to keep us from each other's throats) or merely convenient (a better way to keep us from each other's throats) or fixable (a basically good idea that has been corrupted by bad people or rules), de Jasay wants us to see that we are wrong. For him, the analyses that underlie such accounts, whether set in the state of nature, behind the veil of ignorance, or in the shadow of the prisoners' dilemma, are just happy fictions designed to hide an unhappy truth: "States are an imposition, sometimes useful, sometimes a millstone, always costly, never legitimate, and never a necessity for binding agreements" (p. 36). In the second part of the book, called "Emergent Solutions," he expands on the claim that a successful liberal society—one in which people's rights are secured against all aggressors—doesn't need a state. Against the orthodox view of anarchy as chaos and mayhem, he argues that anarchy need not be so bad, and usually is much better. We find that argument novel only because we've heard Hobbesian jeremiads against anarchy so often that we treat them as established fact.

De Jasay makes serious charges. If they are true, then much of what we think we know about good government is wrong. Unfortunately, even sympathetic readers may find it hard to go all the way with him. Such readers will almost certainly agree with his critiques of existing theories of the state, whether descriptive or prescriptive. They are also likely to agree that anarchy has gotten short shrift in the modern world, that far too many of us unthinkingly toe the party line on the benefits of the state. But before accepting the claim that anarchy is always superior to the state, they will want more. They will want an explicit comparison, so they can see for themselves that anarchy actually is better. Without such a comparison, readers must worry that they are making the very mistake of which de Jasay accuses his statist foes: simply asserting that their favorite would win the Hobbesian horse race, rather than proving it would. Although de Jasay's accusation may be an understandable response to three hundred years of statist mendacity, it isn't good political economy.

At this point, readers may be tempted to conclude that my argument with de Jasay amounts to arid pedantry, a sectarian tempest in a libertarian teapot. That would be a mistake. As noted earlier, anarchy is all the rage among those who find contemporary interest-group politics sordid and ineffective. Because de Jasay has thought longer and harder about anarchy and the state than most other anarcho-liberals, taking him seriously allows us to better understand their arguments as well.

But close examination shows that anarchy needn't be as happy as de Jasay implies. If we treat his defense of anarchy the way he treats liberal analyses of the state, asking what incentive people have to comply with its rules, we will not necessarily reach his conclusions. The reason is simple: even in anarchy, some have power over others. And they can abuse that power, using it to benefit themselves at the expense of others. Thus, to show that some anarchic arrangement would be superior to the state, we need to show that it wouldn't be the sort of anarchy in which people abuse their power. De Jasay doesn't consider this issue directly, but examples ranging from Bosnia to the mafia suggest that he should, that anarchy is not automatically liberal.

Despite this lacuna in his argument, serious liberals ignore de Jasay at their own risk. Even the reader who agrees with everything I say here would benefit from reading de Jasay for himself. Obviously, I can touch on only a few of the themes of his book. But, more important, my own essay is fundamentally de Jasian, asking of him the same question he asks of traditional liberals: "This sounds nice, but how will it really work?" Thus, even skeptical readers will learn much from him. They may even find themselves persuaded.

The Liberal Case for the State: Anarchy Is Intolerable

When asked for their political creed, most liberals would say that they want a government that protects the rights of its citizens against predators. If pressed further, most of them would identify that government with a state, an institution with a monopoly on the legitimate use of violence. They would base their argument for the state on a comparative institutional analysis, one that examines the extent of social order provided by various governance institutions.

Most such comparisons are fairly abstract, based on stick-figure renderings of life under the available alternatives. Since Hobbes, the comparisons have usually begun by considering a society of people living in the state of nature, that is, without a state. Nowadays, that society is modeled as some sort of social dilemma, such as the well-known prisoners' dilemma.[2] The dilemmas arise whenever people are more productive working with others than working alone, but individually best off shirking rather than working, no matter what others do. In such situations, rational people would always shirk, because shirking is the best response to whatever others do. Of course, when everyone reasons that way, nobody works and they end up back where they started, in autarky. Thus, acting rationally leads them to forgo any of the gains from cooperation. This outcome is both individually sensible (nobody could do better by behaving differently on his own) *and* wasteful (if only they would cooperate, each would be better off).

This sorry outcome confronts the members of society with a dilemma: given the choice between everyone working and everyone shirking, everyone prefers that they all work; yet given the incentives they face, none of them will work. They will not work even if they sign a contract promising to do so. Such promises would not be, in the jargon of game theory, "credible." Because each knows that when it comes time to act, everybody will have an incentive to go back on his word, everyone will treat a promise to work as what it is—empty talk. Moreover, this situation poses a true social dilemma, because it is rooted in their strategic circumstance, not their psychology.[3]

At this point, liberal theorists introduce the state. They do so by asking why people who are giving up obvious gains don't get together and find some way to resolve the dilemma. The traditional liberal answer is that they would do so. And when they got together, people would adopt a social contract creating a third party empowered to force them to do what they cannot do themselves: enforce contracts and other rights. By punishing those who do not respect rights, the state changes the incentives. With the addition of that threat, people no longer face social dilemmas. Instead, they face trivial coordination games, in which the only rational course is to cooperate and reap the gains from trade. Under those conditions, nobody cheats, cooperation flourishes, and everyone is better off.

For most liberals, recognizing the need for a state is only the first step toward a sound political economy. After all, there are many different social contracts, or ways of organizing governments. Should the rulers be chosen from one family, a group of families, or the general citizenry? And under what terms should they rule? For life? Until the next election? Or until the revolution? Liberals want answers to these questions because *how* a society makes choices—the specific decision rule that it uses—usually determines *what* it chooses. The same group of people using different rules might choose different policies—often, radically different policies.

The recognition that institutional rules influence outcomes has revived interest in constitutional design among fans of limited government. In the past few decades, liberal scholars from James Buchanan to Robert Nozick to Richard Epstein have investigated the consequences of a variety of different rules, always with the hope of finding a rule that, if obeyed, leads to better choices than the rules we now use. The proposed solutions range from heightened judicial review to term limits to balanced-budget amendments. In spite of their differences, each analyst traces inferior policy choices directly to the political structure. In this view, politicians do not choose the policies because they are less civic-minded than others; they choose them because the political system gives them both a motive and an opportunity to do so. A structural ailment requires a structural cure. Of course, the specific solution depends on the particular problem to be solved.

The Liberal Case against the State: Let's Take the Con Out of Constitutional Political Economy

For de Jasay, standard liberal theory is fine as far as it goes, but it does not go nearly far enough. In particular, he notes that it says nothing about the incentives of politicians to actually obey any particular set of rules. That omission is hardly a trivial one. After all, to do its job, the state must be strong enough to force any other group in society to obey its commands. And, because it consists of people with their own interests, the state will often have an incentive to abuse its power by violating the rights of citizens for its own benefit. As a result, it seems that the liberal simply replaces one problem (how to get citizens to respect each other's rights) with another (how to get the sovereign to respect the rights of citizens). Although some argue that anarchy is so bad that any state, even an abusive one, would be better, not everyone agrees. Many liberals side with John Locke, who doubted that "men are so foolish that they take care to avoid what mischiefs may be done them by pole-cats or foxes; but are content, nay, think it safety, to be devoured by lions" ([1690] 1980, 50).

Classical liberal theorists of the eighteenth and nineteenth centuries took Locke's observation seriously. They worried that the people who make up the government wouldn't obey constitutional rules unless doing so was in their interest. That worry led them to examine the incentives created by the constitutional rules, to see whether they were strong enough to force politicians (and others) to obey the rules. If the incentives were not compatible with the rules, a constitution would be, in the words of James Madison, merely "a parchment barrier" (Madison, Hamilton, and Jay [1788] 1987, 309). To strengthen the barrier, many liberals argued for such institutions as separated powers, federalism, and an independent judiciary. They wanted those institutions for prudential, rather than ethical, reasons. Such institutional arrangements, they believed, would give even the most narrowly self-interested politicians an incentive to serve the public interest.

Modern liberals agree that the classical liberal institutions failed because the constitutional rules that they established did not channel self-interest effectively enough to restrain predation. For them, that failure can be corrected by restructuring the government, changing the rules so as to provide better incentives. Yet, as de Jasay points out, when asking what new rules we should adopt, liberals tend to ignore issues of constitutional politics, that is, of how the constitution will be chosen and maintained. They do not try "to find the conditions, if there are any, under which [constitutions] would be likely to be adopted, respected and left intact for long enough to do any good" (p. 53). Instead, contemporary advocates of limited government implicitly assume that constitutional politics differs radically from ordinary politics. They justify that assumption by invoking devices such as the veil of ignorance, behind which people have very little idea how their decisions will affect them, or unanimous consent, which effectively gives everyone a veto. Under such conditions, decisions about constitutions are depoliticized, and therefore people choose constitutions with special features.

But as de Jasay points out, the liberals' neglect of constitutional politics is problematic precisely because the analysis of ordinary politics underlying their critiques of existing constitutions is so convincing. That analysis assumes that people will do whatever is economic to get outcomes they want. If achieving their objectives requires altering or overturning the constitution rather than ordinary politics, they will not be deterred. They will want a constitution that leads politicians to adopt policies that favor them. Their ability to actually get the preferred constitution will depend on what others want, and on how *they* choose. In the United States, constitutions are normally chosen and amended using representative methods. Nor are constitutions enforced in an institutional vacuum. In the United States, courts decide whether or not the acts of the other branches of government are consistent with the constitutional mandate. The judges who make those decisions are chosen by politicians. Taken together, the foregoing conditions make it seem likely that real constitutions will be susceptible to venal considerations, contrary to the assumption of liberal theorists.

These considerations lie at the heart of de Jasay's critique of liberal constitutionalism. He begins by taking on the idea that a constitution is a social contract, adopted in the state of nature. "If," he asks, "contracts require an enforcer, how could there be a social contract creating an enforcer without *its* enforcement being assured by a meta-enforcer created by a meta-social contract, and so on in an infinite regress?" (p. 5). In other words, is it consistent to assert that people who could not enforce private contracts could enforce a social contract? Given the complexity of the social contract, the obvious answer is that they could not. The contradiction leads de Jasay to label this part of the liberal project "Self-Contradictory Contractarianism" (chap. 1).

He goes on to argue that showing that a particular constitution *could* improve policy does not prove that it would in fact do so. We must also show that any particular constitution would be chosen and enforced. We need to ask, in the jargon of economics, whether it is incentive compatible. When it comes time to enforce the rules, who will do the dirty work? Will those who are supposed to enforce the rules have any incentive to do so? De Jasay points out that this problem parallels the one faced by private contractors in the state of nature: how to create a self-enforcing agreement. As he so charmingly puts it, the constitution is like "a chastity belt whose key is always within reach" (p. 3), because the very people against whom the constitution is supposed to be enforced are the ones who are supposed to enforce it. In a chapter entitled "Is Limited Government Possible?" he points out that the logic of democratic politics, in which coalitions are notoriously unstable, makes it seem likely that compliance will be fleeting (p. 56). Most of those who lose when the constitution is enforced will be able to bribe away enough of the complying coalition to form their own, noncomplying, winning coalition.

The lesson that de Jasay draws from this analysis (and from others) is that the self-seeking by our fellow citizens creates worse problems than are predicted by the standard liberal creed. In particular, he argues that liberals are overly optimistic about their ability to design institutions that will channel self-interest in public-regarding directions. If he is right, it seems that we must choose between anarchy, in which we are impoverished by the depredations of our fellow citizens, and tyranny, in which we are impoverished by the depredations of the sovereign. Either way, our prospects look bleak.

The Case for Anarchy: Repeated Prisoners' Dilemmas Are Not Prisoners' Dilemmas

At this point, de Jasay makes his most radical claim. He tells us that despite the failure of the liberal constitutional program, our prospects aren't so bad. On the contrary, they are actually pretty good. This is so because it turns out that we have neglected an option: anarchy. We have limited our options because we have misunderstood the incentives created by life in anarchy. When we understand anarchy correctly, we see that it can protect us from each other.

The major difference between the Hobbesian and the de Jasian view of anarchy is that de Jasay, like other anarcho-liberals, takes into account a central fact of social life: not everyone is a stranger. Whether at work or at play, most of us find ourselves dealing again and again with the same people. This fact makes a huge difference for strategic behavior. Put crudely, the knowledge that we will see people again gives us a powerful incentive to be nice to them, because if we are not, they may not be nice to us in the future. Facing that threat, even the most narrowly self-interested, brutally calculating egotist might find that it pays to act like Mother Teresa. Because this account is central to de Jasay's claims, and because he touches on it only briefly, it is worthwhile to explore the underlying logic of the rational-choice account of anarchy in some detail.

Stripped to its core, the argument for anarcho-liberalism is that the Hobbesians mischaracterize anarchy when they treat it as a series of isolated two-person deals. Doing so ignores the obvious fact that most of our dealings with others are embedded in a rich web of social relations. In game-theoretic terms, that embeddedness moves society from one-shot games to repeated games. And, as is now well known, cooperation is rational in repeated games. It is rational not because dealing with each other again and again changes peoples' preferences or because it allows them to learn who is honest and thus trustworthy. Rather, people cooperate in repeated games because doing so pays them more than not cooperating. It pays more because, as long as the future value of the relationship exceeds the onetime gain from cheating, people can punish each other by not cooperating in the future.

Thus, in the shadow of the future, people can make what economists call *implicit* or *self-enforcing* contracts, agreements that bind them without the help of any third parties. Such a contract exemplifies an *equilibrium institution*, a set of rules obeyed because everyone finds it in his interest to obey. Of course, besides following the rules about their own behavior in the social games they play with each other, people must also follow the rules about monitoring compliance and punishing deviants.

The idea of a self-enforcing contract, if not the terminology, lies behind much of the empirical literature on "order without law." For example, few business arrangements resemble the classic arms-length agreements enforced by courts that used to populate textbooks in economics and law. Instead, in many instances real contracts are better thought of as *relational contracts*, deals between people who expect to have a long (and prosperous) relationship. Moreover, in the shadow of the future, people can sustain cooperation even with strangers. They can do so because, even though we may not deal with any one person often, we do deal with the same group of people repeatedly. Even in the modern world, many of our relationships take place in communities, groups of people who have overlapping relations. We can use those communities to enforce cooperation by expanding the terms of cooperation, so that we respond not just to our own history but to everyone else's history as well. In that way, people who belong to a community can use the other members as third parties to enforce their agreements (Greif 1993; Kreps 1990).

In a very real sense, communal enforcement allows one to offer his reputation as a bond to guarantee his behavior. The reputation embodies the future value of cooperation with other members of the community. Extending repeated games from dyads to communities brings the models much closer to what we usually think of when we think of anarchic institutions such as communities and norms. Most descriptions of norms stress the importance of reputations and of communal, third-party enforcement. For example, Robert Ellickson argues that ranchers and farmers in Shasta County, California, do not rely solely on self-help to enforce norms. They also rely on the threat that other members of the community will not cooperate with defectors.

The use of reputations to induce cooperation among the members of a community increases the level of cooperation, but at a cost. For communal reputations to work, people need much more information than they have in the repeated two-person prisoners' dilemma. Instead of knowing just their own history, they need to know everyone else's history as well. Eventually, the costs of gathering and disseminating that information may become so large that they exceed all of the gains from cooperation. If people cannot contain those costs, then the communal reputation mechanism will destroy itself.

Throughout history, people have developed a variety of methods to economize on the flow of information needed to support reputations. One common method is to empower some citizens to hear and resolve disputes, leaving enforcement of the decision to the general citizenry. Thus, in medieval Europe, long-distance merchants often brought their disputes to judges at trade fairs (Milgrom, North, and Weingast 1990). The judges would investigate and then announce their decision. Losers who did not pay in accordance with a judge's ruling faced the threat that other merchants would not trade with them. Similarly, in East Africa, disputes over cattle were traditionally settled by an official known as the Leopard Chief, an ordinary citizen with absolutely no enforcement power (Bates 1981). Yet, once his decision had been announced, both parties to the dispute abided by it. They did so not only out of respect for his abilities and wisdom but also because of the threat that others would punish them if they did not.

This brief tour of repeated games shows why de Jasay and others invoke it to argue against the Hobbesian understanding of life without the state. The repeated-game approach to anarchy has several noteworthy features. First, it treats the institutions that support cooperation as equilibria that must provide all parties, including enforcers, with incentives to do their jobs. Second, it treats anarchic institutions, such as norms, not in isolation but as part of the fabric of daily life. Like Hobbes, anarcho-liberals start with people in a state of nature and show how they can build effective institutions. As a result, the incentives to conform to anarchic institutions must come from the games of daily life among the citizens; those games are literally the only source of rewards. Finally, notwithstanding their origin in a Hobbesian state of nature, none of the institutions that arise are Hobbesian. Even those that rely on a central authority to collect information rely on decentralized methods to enforce the rules.

The Case against Anarchy: Anarchists Too Will Abuse Their Power

So far, the story of anarchy seems happy: when people deal with each other repeatedly, as they usually do, they have an effective method of punishing those who do not respect the rights of others. Thus, it seems that Hobbes was wrong, that anarchy *can* work. However, this account must answer an obvious question: If anarchy is so wonderful, why did so many people believe the Hobbesians? Were they just blind to the anarchic alternative, or is anarchy perhaps more complicated than the optimists suggest? Could it be, as suggested by my own survey, that anarchy promises no particular outcome and that the provision of social order outside the state may take many forms? For example, we might buy our justice on the market, as people do when they hire private guards or arbitrators. Or we might rely on a community for enforcement, as people do in all traditional societies.

However we conceive of anarchy, we don't have to look far to see it being abused. Those who invoke anarcho-capitalism, complete with buying and selling protection on the market, need look no farther than the mafia, a private institution that both provides justice and preys on its clients. (Indeed, it uses its power to force even the unwilling to become its clients; often, the predator it protects against is itself!) Many anarcho-capitalists argue that in the market for justice, as in the market for cars, competition will limit rent collection. That argument ignores some rather obvious opportunities for collusion among anarchists. With more than one firm providing justice, the firms will have to work together when their clients have claims against each other. Without more detail, it is hard to see why such cooperation won't sometimes lead to collusion against weaker clients (Cowen 1992). (For a thorough discussion of real-world examples, see Benson 1998.) It is also hard to see why the competition among such firms will be any more effective than that among politicians, political parties, and jurisdictions in modern democracies. Yet the anarcho-liberals all agree that existing political competition does not provide sufficient threat to prevent abuse of power.

Anarchic governance through communities faces similar problems. Throughout history, most communities have been the setting for various sorts of oppression. For example, communal enforcement is easier when the community is ethnically or religiously homogenous, and many communities treat outsiders badly. Nor are all insiders treated equally well. For example, traditional societies often impose heavy burdens on women, among others. Finally, most traditional societies have enforced harsh norms of equality, often forcibly redistributing wealth (Cook and Miller 1998). Given the relatively great inequalities in the distribution of wealth in modern capitalist societies, it is hard to be sanguine that modern communities will resist the redistributionist urge. Certainly, the record of small towns opposing "threats" such as Wal-Mart suggests otherwise.

Those familiar with the theory of repeated games will not find these sad stories surprising. The happy results discussed earlier are only a part of the story of repeated games. Contrary to the claims of many of its popularizers, that theory does not show that cooperation is the only rational strategy. Rather, it shows that in repeated games, many outcomes, including cooperation, are rational. The reason is simple, and illuminating: there is no single natural or unique way to distribute the surplus generated by cooperation. As long as all players get more than they would under feasible alternatives, they will go along. Thus, the proper interpretation of the theory of repeated games is that repeated play raises a new question: Among the many different outcomes, all of which distribute the gains from cooperation differently, which should be chosen? In other words, as de Jasay points out, repetition turns social dilemmas into coordination games, in which people want to cooperate, but on terms favorable to them. Whether any particular anarchy ends up with a liberal outcome, with rights enforced against all parties, depends on which of the many feasible outcomes the anarchy "chooses." Without more information about the choice process, we have no reason to suppose that, in general, anarchy is more liberal that the state.

The lesson here is not that de Jasay is wrong about anarchy and that we can comfortably return to our traditional statist-liberal verities. No doubt, he and other anarcho-liberals have shown that anarchic order is both theoretically and factually robust. Given the weight of that reasoning and evidence, it would be foolish to argue for a return to the Hobbesian status quo. However, it would also be foolish to ignore the contrary evidence and to argue that anarchy is so good that surely we can do without the state. What we need is an anarchic constitutional political economy, a study of what life would be like under the various possible anarchic institutions.

The Poetry of Power

In many ways, the preceding criticisms miss the most important lesson of de Jasay's book, which is the importance of the poetry of power, that is, of the way we talk about governance. Again and again, he urges that we resist seduction by the easy analogies of liberal statists and refuse to accept as proved what has merely been asserted. Instead, he would have us join him in going behind such metaphors as "consent," "social contract," and "state of nature" to ask what is really going on in any particular society. Querying metaphors, we find that they do not always illuminate; instead, they often lead us to skip over crucial details that analyses such as de Jasay's expose and emphasize.

After reading de Jasay, one appreciates that much of the appeal of the Hobbesian program lies in its congruity with common sense. All of us rely on some model of what makes people tick to guide us through the social world. For most of us, that model resembles what philosophers call "folk psychology" and includes an ample allowance for self-interest and venality. Starting from that bleak picture of human nature, we easily conclude that Hobbes was right and that life in the state of nature, where order comes from anarchic institutions, would be terrible. From that perspective, cooperation without the state seems an unattainable ideal, a goal that only the most saintly might seek. It seems perverse or naive to suggest that we rely on anything but the state to protect us.

De Jasay's account suggests that this presumption is not well founded. Moreover, the counter-account does not reject folk psychology but embraces it wholeheartedly. From its perspective, ordered anarchy is not an unattainable ideal but part of the web of institutions, simply one more way that people order their social world. And, like other governance institutions such as firms, markets, and states, anarchic institutions can (and should) be treated as an incentive system that can be understood only by close examination of the incentives and opportunities it presents to individuals.

To implement that approach, de Jasay (along with many others) builds models in which rational egoists confront a much richer strategic environment than they do in the simple models, such as the prisoners' dilemma, that generate Hobbesian outcomes. Even the richer models remain sparse and abstract. Nevertheless, as my brief tour shows, their minimal enrichment of the environment suffices to overturn completely the Hobbesian account of anarchy. In these models, as in reality, anarchy can work.

When performed carefully, rational-choice analysis suggests that anarchy is far more complicated than either de Jasay or his Hobbesian foes make it out to be. Anarchy's foes err by asserting that it is inconsistent with social order; both theory and evidence show that the richness of social relations may lead even the most brutal egoists to cooperate rationally. And anarchy's friends, like de Jasay, err by asserting that its lack of hierarchy is equivalent to a lack of coercion or that anarchic institutions are accepted in ways that statist institutions are not. The social order in anarchy often rests on appeals to the basest sort of self-interest. That anarchic institutions are equilibria implies that self-interest will lead people to "accept" any outcome that gives them more than they could get in autarky. Hence, compliance need not imply consent in any ethically interesting fashion. Because people will try to attain those anarchic institutions that favor them, anarchy is likely to be subject to the same crass considerations that guide ordinary politics and will not automatically offer an alternative superior to the state.

Despite these caveats, the evidence shows that de Jasay is right at the most basic level: *it is time to throw off the Hobbesian yoke.* For too long, Hobbes's claim that anarchy was so bad that anything would be better has limited the imagination of institutional designers. Seduced by that false inference, they have ruled out some important options on the grounds that they could not be effective. But we know too much about both Leviathan and its alternatives to accept such a view.

Notes

1. For explicit models of anarchic order, see Benson 1990; Klein 1997; Taylor 1982, 1987, and 1996; or the survey in Rutten 1997.
2. For discussion of the extent to which modern game theory captures the approach of the classics, see Hampton 1986; Kavka 1986; and Taylor 1987.
3. That is why the game is better called the prisoners' dilemma than the prisoner's dilemma.

References

Bates, Robert. 1981. "The Preservation of Order in Stateless Societies: A Reinterpretation of Evans Pritchards' 'The Nuer.'" In *Essays in the Political Economy of Rural Africa.* New York: Cambridge University Press.

Benson, Bruce. 1990. *The Enterprise of Law: Justice without the State.* San Francisco: Pacific Research Institute.

———. 1998. *To Serve and Protect: Privatization and Community in Criminal Justice.* New York: New York University Press.

Bernstein, Lisa. 1992. "Opting Out of the Legal System: Extralegal Contractual Relations in the Diamond Industry." *Journal of Legal Studies* 21 (January): 115-57.

Cook, Kathleen, and Gary Miller. 1998. "Leveling and Leadership in States and Firms." In *New Institutionalisms: Institutions and Social Order*, edited by Karol Soltan, Virginia Haufler, and Eric Uslaner. Ann Arbor: University of Michigan Press.

Cowen, Tyler. 1992. "Law as a Public Good: The Economics of Anarchy." *Economics and Philosophy* 8: 249-67.

De Jasay, Anthony. 1997. *Against Politics: On Government, Anarchy and Order.* London: Routledge.

Ellickson, Robert. 1991. *Order without Law: How Neighbors Resolve Disputes.* Cambridge: Harvard University Press.

Ferrigno, Robert. 1996. *Dead Silent.* New York: Putnam.

Greif, Avner. 1993. "Contract Enforceability and Economic Institutions in Early Trade: The Maghribi Traders' Coalition." *American Economic Review* 83 (June): 528-48.

Hampton, Jean. 1986. *Hobbes and the Social Contract Tradition.* New York: Cambridge University Press.

Kavka, Gregory. 1986. *Hobbesian Moral and Political Theory.* Princeton: Princeton University Press.

Klein, Daniel, ed. 1997. *Reputation: Studies in the Voluntary Elicitation of Good Conduct.* Ann Arbor: University of Michigan Press.

Kreps, David. 1990. "Corporate Culture and Economic Theory." In *Perspectives on Positive Political Theory*, edited by James Alt and Kenneth Shepsle. New York: Cambridge University Press.

Locke, John. [1690] 1980. *The Second Treatise of Government.* Edited by C. B. McPherson. Indianapolis: Hackett.
Macaulay, Stewart. 1963. "Non-contractual Relations in Business: A Preliminary Study." *American Sociological Review* 28 (June): 55-67.
Madison, James, Alexander Hamilton, and John Jay. [1788] 1987. *The Federalist Papers.* Edited by Isaac Kramnick. London: Penguin Books.
Milgrom, Paul, Douglass North, and Barry Weingast. 1990. "The Role of Institutions in the Revival of Trade: The Law Merchant, Private Judges, and the Champagne Fairs." *Economics and Politics* 2 (March): 1-23.
Mosley, Walter. 1998. *Always Outnumbered, Always Outgunned.* New York: Norton.
Ostrom, Elinor. 1990. *Governing the Commons: The Evolution of Institutions for Collective Action.* New York: Cambridge University Press.
Rosen, Jeffrey. 1997. "The Next Crimebuster: The Social Police." *New Yorker,* Oct. 20 and 27, 170-81.
Rutten, Andrew. 1997. "Anarchy, Order, and the Law: A Post-Hobbesian View." *Cornell Law Review* 82: 1150-64.
Taylor, Michael. 1982. *Community, Anarchy, and Liberty.* New York: Cambridge University Press.
———. 1987. *The Possibility of Cooperation.* New York: Cambridge University Press.
———. 1996. "Good Government: On Hierarchy, Social Capital, and the Limitations of Rational Choice Theory." *Journal of Political Philosophy* 4 (March): 1-28.

22

Government: Unnecessary but Inevitable

Randall G. Holcombe

Ludwig von Mises, Friedrich Hayek, and Milton Friedman, perhaps the best-known twentieth-century academic defenders of liberty, envisioned a role for limited government in protecting liberty.[1] Friedman's (1962) defense of freedom includes proposals for a negative income tax and school vouchers; Hayek (1960) advocates limited government to enforce the rule of law despite his concern about excessive government;[2] and Ludwig von Mises, who also warns of the dangers of big government,[3] states, "the task of the state consists solely and exclusively in guaranteeing the protection of life, health, liberty, and private property against violent attacks" (1979, 52). In contrast, by the end of the twentieth century, many libertarians, guided by the work of Murray Rothbard and others, viewed orderly anarchy as a desirable and potentially achievable state of affairs and—some would argue—the only state of affairs consistent with a libertarian philosophy.[4] My purpose in this article is to examine that proposition critically and to defend and extend the classical liberal idea of limited government. My conclusions align more with those theorists, such as Hayek and Mises, who see a need for limited government than with those who see the libertarian ideal as an orderly anarchy.

The debate over limited government versus orderly anarchy typically turns on the effectiveness of government versus private means to achieve certain ends. Government's defenders argue that markets cannot provide certain goods and services as efficiently as government can—in some cases, markets may be completely unable to provide certain desired goods—whereas the advocates of orderly anarchy argue that private contractual arrangements can provide every good and service more effectively and can do so without the coercion inherent in government activity. I maintain, however, that the effectiveness of government versus that of private arrangements to produce goods and services is irrelevant to the issue of the desirability of government in a libertarian society. Governments are not created to produce goods and services for citizens. Rather, they are created and imposed on people by force, most often for the purpose of transferring resources from the control of those outside government to the control of those within it.

Without government—or even with a weak government—predatory groups will impose themselves on people by force and create a government to extract income and wealth from these subjects. If people create their own government preemptively, they can design a government that may be less predatory than the one that outside aggressors otherwise would impose on them.[5]

Anarchy as an Alternative to Government

One strand of the libertarian anarchist argument is the claim that everything the government does, the market can do better, and therefore the government should be eliminated completely.[6] A second strand is the proposition that government is unethical because of its use of force.[7] Murray Rothbard has been the leading proponent of both arguments, and his 1973 book *For a New Liberty* is his most direct defense of orderly anarchy. Rothbard illustrates how the private sector can undertake more effectively all government activities, including national defense. All of Rothbard's arguments are persuasive, but his national-defense argument is worth reviewing here because it has direct relevance to my thesis.

Rothbard argues first that national defense is needed only because the governments of some countries have differences with the governments of others. Wars occur between governments, not between the subjects of those governments. Without a government to provoke outsiders, outside governments would have no motivation to attack, so a group of people living in anarchy would face a minimal risk of invasion from a foreign government. An auxiliary line of reasoning is that if a government does try to use military force to take over an area with no government, such a takeover would be very difficult because the aggressor would have to conquer each individual in the anarchistic area. If those people have a government, a foreign country has only to induce the other country's head of state to surrender in order to take over that other country, but in taking over a country without a government an aggressor faces the much more daunting task of getting everyone to surrender, going from house to house and from business to business, a formidable and perhaps impossible undertaking.[8]

Jeffrey Rogers Hummel offers an interesting extension of Rothbard's arguments regarding defense. Hummel (1990) argues that national defense against foreign aggression is a subset of the problem of protecting people from any state, domestic or foreign, and Hummel (2001) notes that if people can design institutions to protect themselves from domestic government, those same institutions should suffice to protect them from foreign governments. In this line of reasoning, the private production of defense services would occur as a byproduct of the elimination of domestic government by an orderly anarchy.

These arguments regarding national defense show the flavor of the argument that people would be better off without government. Orderly anarchy would eliminate the need for government provision of national defense because the risks of invasion would be lower and because the private sector can supply any defense services people want. By considering each activity the government now undertakes, a substantial literature shows that in each case a superior private-sector alternative exists or might be created. Private arrangements can provide public goods, law, and order at any scale. A substantial mainstream academic literature on the inefficiencies of government production and regulation further buttresses the case against government. Thus, the libertarian anarchist position rests heavily on the argument that anything the government does, the private sector can do more effectively and less coercively.

Why Do Governments Exist?

The argument that people should do away with government because everything the government does the private sector can do better would be persuasive if governments were created, as their rationales suggest, to improve their subjects' well-being. In fact, governments are not created to improve the public's well-being. In most cases, governments have been imposed on people by force, and they maintain their power by force for the purpose of extracting resources from subjects and transferring the control of those resources to those in government. Sometimes foreign invaders take over territory and rule the people who live there; more commonly, people already subject to a government overthrow it and establish a new government in its place. Whether government is more or less effective in producing public goods or in protecting property is irrelevant.

A possible exception to this claim is the formation of the U.S. government, which was established to overthrow British rule in the colonies and to replace it with a new government designed to protect the liberty of its citizens. Much of the Declaration of Independence consists of a list of grievances against the king of England, and the American founders wanted to replace what they viewed as a predatory government with one that would protect their rights. One can dispute this story,[9] but for present purposes the point is that even in what appears to be the best real-world case in which government was designed for the benefit of its citizens, it was not designed to produce public goods or to control externalities or to prevent citizens from free riding on a social contract. Its underlying rationale had nothing to do with any of the common economic or political rationales given for government.

The point here is straightforward: despite many theories justifying government because its activities produce benefits to its citizens, no government was ever established to produce those benefits. Governments were created by force to rule over people and extract resources from them. Thus, the argument that citizens would be better off if they replaced government activities with private arrangements and market transactions is irrelevant to the issue of whether an orderly anarchy would be a desirable—or even feasible—replacement for government. The real issue is whether a group of people with no government can prevent predators both inside and outside their group from using force to establish a government.

Protection and the State

Without government, people would be vulnerable to predators and therefore would have to find ways to protect themselves. In the anarchy Hobbes described, life is a war of all against all—nasty, brutish, and short. The strong overpower the weak, taking everything the victims have, but the strong themselves do not prosper in Hobbesian anarchy because there is little for them to take. Nobody produces when the product will surely be taken away from them. Even under more orderly conditions than Hobbesian anarchy, predation has a limited payoff because people who have accumulated assets forcibly resist those who try to plunder them, and the ensuing battles consume both predators' and victims' resources.[10]

Disorganized banditry produces Hobbesian anarchy in which nobody prospers because nobody has an incentive to be productive. If the predators can organize, they may evolve into little mafias that can offer their clients some protection. This evolution will create a more productive society, with more income for both the predators and their prey, but the mafias will have to limit their take in order for this outcome to arise. If the mafia can assure its clients that in exchange for payment they will be protected from other predators and allowed to keep a substantial portion of what they produce, output will increase, and everybody's income can rise. Losses from rivalries among mafias will continue to be borne, however, because competing mafias have an incentive to plunder individuals who do not contract with them.

If the mafias become even better organized, they can establish themselves as a state. Predators have every incentive to move from operating as bandits to operating as states because bandits cannot guarantee themselves a long-term flow of income from predation and because if banditry is rampant, people have little incentive to produce wealth. States try to convince citizens that they will limit their take and that they will protect their citizens in order to provide an incentive for those citizens to produce. Governments receive more income than bandits because governments can remain in one place and receive a steady flow of income rather than snatching once and moving on (Usher 1992). In such a situation, citizens gain, too (Holcombe 1994).

Nozick (1974) describes this process in more benign terms. Nozick's protection agencies establish monopolies and evolve into a minimal state, but the evolutionary process is the same. The evolution of predatory bandits into mafias (protection firms) and thence into governments may be inevitable. If not inevitable, it is desirable because governments have an incentive to be less predatory than bandits or mafias. Citizens will be more productive, creating more for predators to take and more for citizens themselves to keep. The predators gain because they need only threaten to use force in order to induce the victims to surrender their property. Citizens benefit because they need not devote resources to using force in defense of their property—the government protects property, except for the share it takes for itself.[11]

Successful predation of this type requires a particular institutional arrangement in which government makes a credible promise to limit its take and to protect its citizens from other predators. Only then do citizens have an incentive to produce much. Government has an incentive to protect citizens in order to protect its own source of income.

The contractarian literature of Rawls (1971), Buchanan (1975), and especially Tullock (1972, 1974) is related to the argument presented here, but it differs in a significant respect. Noting the problems that exist for citizens in Hobbesian anarchy, these writers argue that citizens can gain by forming a government to protect property rights and to enforce contracts. Government is a result of the contract, not a party to it. The argument here is not that government will be created because everyone's welfare will be enhanced by an escape from anarchy, but rather that anarchy will not persist because those with the power to create a government will do so regardless of the desires of those outside of government. The creation of government may enhance everyone's welfare because government has an incentive to protect the source of its income—its citizens' productive capacity—but the "contract" that creates government is not made because everyone agrees to it or because everyone will benefit. Rather, it springs from the capacity of those in government to force their rule on others.

A Potential Problem with Protection Firms

In an orderly anarchy, potential victims of predation can hire protective firms to help them protect their assets, and these protective firms may try to cooperate with each other, as Rothbard (1973) argues. However, with many competing protective firms, potential problems arise. Firms might prey on their competitors' customers, as competing mafia groups do, to show those customers that their current protective firm is not doing the job and thus to induce them to switch protection firms. This action seems to be a profit-maximizing strategy; hence, protection firms that do not prey on noncustomers may not survive. The problem is even more acute if Nozick is correct in arguing that there is a natural monopoly in the industry. In that case, firms must add to their customer base or lose out to larger firms in the competition.

Cowan (1992, 1994) argues that this tendency toward natural monopoly is accentuated because for protection firms to cooperate in the adjudication of disputes, a single arbitration network is required. This network might be established through the creation of a monopoly protection agency, as Nozick suggests, but even if many firms participate, the result will be a cartel whose members have an incentive to act anticompetitively. For the network to work, it must sanction outlaw firms that try to operate outside the network. The power to sanction competitors reinforces its monopoly position. As Adam Smith notes, "People of the same trade seldom meet together, even for merriment and diversion, but the conversation ends in a conspiracy against the public" ([1776] 1937, 128). The reasonable argument that protection firms would cooperate to avoid violence and produce justice thus evolves into the argument that such firms would cartelize to use their power for their benefit in a conspiracy against the public.

A more general and therefore more serious threat is that using the assets of a protective firm for both plunder and protection might prove most profitable.[12] A protection firm might use armored vehicles, guns, investigative equipment, and other assets to protect its clients and to recover stolen property or to extract damages from people who violated its clients' rights. The firm might find it more profitable, however, to use its investigative capacity also to locate assets that can be stolen and to use guns and other weapons to rob people who are not its clients. The mafia, for example, does offer protection for a fee, but it also uses its resources for predation. Profit-maximizing firms with these kinds of assets can be expected to employ them in the dual roles of protection and predation. Otherwise, they would not be maximizing their profits, and they would lose market share to firms that do use their resources in this profit-maximizing way.

Much of the time protection firms must have excess capacity in their role as protectors because they need to be able to respond to violations of their clients' rights with sufficient force to return stolen property, collect restitution, and otherwise deal with predators. Most of the time they will need to use their resources only to guard and monitor their clients' property, leaving some of their assets idle.[13] Absent government, protection firms might want to display their excess capacity to use violence conspicuously, in part to reassure their customers and in part to deter aggressors. They also might use these resources, however, in a predatory manner against nonclients.

This line of reasoning further bolsters Nozick's argument that the production of protection is a natural monopoly, and it bolsters Cowan's argument that even if many protection firms remained in anarchy, they would be pushed to cartelize, creating the same result as a monopoly protection firm. If potential customers have to be concerned not only with how well a firm will protect property, but also with the threat that protection firms they do not contract with may take their property, they have even more reason to patronize the largest and most powerful firm. Protection firms do not necessarily offer an escape from Hobbesian anarchy.[14]

The Special Case of Protection Services

As noted earlier, one conclusion of the libertarian literature on government production is that private providers can provide more effectively all of the goods and services that government now supplies. This conclusion applies to protection services as much as to any government-provided good or service. As with other goods and services, though, it applies to the market provision of protection services within an economy in which government enforces its rules on all market participants, including protection firms. Economic analysis that shows the effectiveness of markets in allocating resources does so within a framework that assumes that property rights are protected and that exchange is voluntary.[15] Economic theorists from Samuelson (1947) to Rothbard (1962) make the assumption that market exchange arises from mutual agreement, without theft or fraud. In the analysis of protection firms, this assumption of voluntary exchange amounts to an assumption that the industry's output is already being produced—as a prerequisite for showing that it can be produced by the market! As a simple matter of logic, one cannot assume a conclusion to be true as a condition for showing that it is true. This problem makes the production of protection services a special case from the standpoint of economic analysis.

The noncoercive nature of market exchange allows competing firms to enter at any time, regardless of incumbents' market share or market power. Protection firms, however, cannot be analyzed on this assumption because they themselves provide the protection that is assumed to exist in a free market and that underlies the ability to enter the market. If they can protect themselves, the assumption is met; if not, the assumption is violated. In the previous section, I explained why the assumption is likely to be violated. The use of force is an integral part of these firms' business activities, and protection firms have an incentive to use their resources for predatory purposes, which includes keeping competitors from entering the market.[16]

In a world dominated by government, how protection firms might behave in the absence of government is a matter of speculation, but in examining the turf wars fought by different mafia families and by rival city gangs, we see a tendency for nongovernmental groups to use force to try to eliminate competitors from the market. Some protection firms might shy away from such activity, but, as noted in the previous section, using the firm's resources for predatory as well as protective activities is a profit-maximizing strategy, and protection firms that are not predatory will tend to lose out in the competition with those that are. If protection firms use predatory means to keep competitors from entering, then one of the fundamental (and usually unstated) institutional assumptions underlying the demonstration of the efficiency of market activity is violated. This problem makes the provision of protection services different from the provision of most services.

In most industries, firms with market power exercise that power through their pricing decisions, marketing strategies (such as bundling), contractual means (such as exclusive contracts), or other means that involve only voluntary activity on the part of everyone involved. Firms with market power in the protection industry are uniquely in a position to use force to prevent competitors from entering the market or to encourage people to become their customers, simply as a result of the nature of their business.[17] Nozick presents a relatively benign description of how private protective firms might evolve into a minimal state, but in a business where those who are best at using coercion are the most successful, the actual evolution of protection firms into a state may result in a very predatory state.

Government Is Inevitable

In the foregoing arguments, I have maintained that although government may not be desirable, it is inevitable because if no government exists, predators have an incentive to establish one. From a theoretical standpoint, Nozick's argument—that competing protection firms will evolve into a monopoly that then becomes the state—represents one form of the general argument that government is inevitable. Because of the prominence of Nozick's work, I offer no further theoretical defense of it here. More significant, however, as de Jasay notes, "Anarchy, if historical precedent is to be taken as conclusive, does not survive" (1989, 217). Every place in the world is ruled by government. The evidence shows that anarchy, no matter how desirable in theory, does not constitute a realistic alternative in practice, and it suggests that if government ever were to be eliminated anywhere, predators would move in to establish themselves as one by force.[18] One can debate the merits of anarchy in theory, but the real-world libertarian issue is not whether it would more be desirable to establish a limited government or to eliminate government altogether. Economist Bruce Benson notes, "When a community is at a comparative disadvantage in the use of violence it may not be able to prevent subjugation by a protection racket such as the state" (1999, 153). Libertarian philosopher Jan Narveson writes, "Why does government remain in power? Why, in fact, are there still governments? The short answer is that governments command powers to which the ordinary citizen is utterly unequal" (2002, 199-200). Government is inevitable, and people with no government—or even with a weak government—will find themselves taken over and ruled by predatory gangs who will establish a government over them.[19] As de Jasay observes, "An anarchistic society may not be well equipped to resist military conquest by a command-directed one" (1997, 200). People may not need or want government, but inevitably they will find themselves under government's jurisdiction.[20]

Some Governments Are More Predatory Than Others

All governments were established by force and retain their power by force, but some are more predatory than others. Governments can take more from their citizens than can bandits or mafias because of their superior organization, but their advantage in part requires them to be less predatory. Bandits can plunder everything people have, but then nothing more will be left to take, and people will have little incentive to produce more if they believe that another complete plunder awaits them. Bandits must move from victim to victim, using resources to find victims and forcing them to surrender their wealth. Governments can remain in one place, continually taking a flow of wealth from the same people, often with their victims' cooperation and assistance. If governments nurture their citizens' productivity, the amount of their takings can continue to increase over time. It then becomes increasingly important for government to protect its source of income from outside predators, so the production of protection serves the self-interest of those in government as well as the interest of the mass of citizens.

The longer the government's time horizon, the less predatory it will be.[21] If a government takes over by force but believes that it will rule for only a limited time before another gang of predators forces it out, then it has an incentive to take everything it can while it still has the power to do so. This incentive will obtain especially if the rulers are unpopular with the citizens and therefore cannot count on the citizens for support. Governments imposed on people from the outside are likely to be especially predatory, which gives citizens an incentive to form their own government preemptively to prevent outsiders from taking over.

If a group of outside predators establishes itself as a government, it will have every reason to keep most of the surplus for itself, in part because the people in the predatory group care more about their own welfare than they do about the welfare of the people they rule. Moreover, the conquered group probably will resist takeover by the predators, creating ill will between the conquerors and the conquered. If government is inevitable, and if some governments are better than others, then citizens have an incentive to create and maintain preemptively a government that minimizes predation and is organized to preserve, as much as possible, its citizens' liberty (Holcombe forthcoming).

Can Government Preserve Liberty?

The arguments developed here frame a challenge to the idea that a minimal state can be designed to preserve liberty. If government is simply a matter of the strong forcing themselves on the weak, it should not matter whether citizens want to create a limited government to protect their rights because in the end those who have the most power will take over and rule for their own benefit. That threat is real, and a brief examination of political history shows many examples. One example is the 1917 Russian Revolution that created the Soviet Union. Other examples include China and Eastern Europe after World War II and many African nations at the beginning of the twenty-first century. Likewise, limited governments such as the U.S. government created in 1776 and the British government in the nineteenth century became less libertarian and more predatory in the twentieth century. Limited governments may not remain limited, and any government constitutes a standing threat to liberty. A challenge to advocates of a minimal state is to explain how people can create and sustain preemptively a liberty-preserving government.

The historical record also offers some basis for optimism that government's predatory impulses can be controlled. History shows that oppressive governments can be overthrown, as they were in Eastern Europe after the collapse of the Berlin Wall in 1989, and that even when they are not overthrown, pressures from their citizens can result in less-predatory states. One would not want to hold Russia and China up as examples of libertarian governments, but they do exemplify governments that have reduced their oppression and increased individual liberty. Governments can become less predatory. Even though the U.S. government has been firmly entrenched for two centuries, it is less oppressive than many other governments, notwithstanding that it has become more predatory over time. Thus, the evidence is that the worst thugs do not always seize and maintain power, and even when they do, reversals toward liberty are possible. In light of this experience, it should be possible to identify the factors that make governments less predatory. Such factors fall into two general categories: economic and ideological.

The economic incentives are relatively straightforward. There are net gains from establishing a less-predatory government. Gwartney, Holcombe, and Lawson (1998) have shown that countries with lower levels of government spending have higher incomes and faster economic growth, and in examining economic freedom more broadly Gwartney, Lawson, and Holcombe (1999) have shown that less government interference in all areas of an economy leads to greater prosperity. Olson (2000) examines the political conditions under which less-predatory governments can be established, and a substantial body of work follows up on Olson's ideas to promote less-predatory and more market-oriented governments (Azfar and Cadwell 2003; Knack 2003). If less-predatory governments mean more production, then potentially everyone can gain from replacing more-predatory government with less-predatory government.

Leaders of predatory governments, however, may do better by preserving the status quo, and they may generate sufficient political support by promoting a national ideology (Edelman 1964; North 1981, 1988) or by intimidating potential rivals (Lichbach 1995; Kurrild-Klitgaard 1997) in order to maintain power. As Olson (1965) explains, even if most people believe that they would be better off with a less-predatory government, they have an incentive to free ride on others' revolutionary activities, which limits the possibilities for change. Kurrild-Klitgaard (1997) notes, however, that some incentives for revolutionary action remain. Moreover, revolution is not the only option. Just as government in the United States has grown by small steps, a gradual contraction of government's scope and power also may be brought about. The demise of the Eastern European dictatorships after the collapse of the Berlin Wall in 1989 shows that changes can happen with surprising speed. This development points toward the second factor: ideology.

In a famous passage of *The General Theory of Employment, Interest, and Money*, John Maynard Keynes emphasizes the power of ideas: "Indeed, the world is ruled by little else. Practical men, who believe themselves to be quite exempt from any intellectual influences, are usually the slaves of some defunct economist. Madmen in authority, who hear voices in the air, are distilling their frenzy from some academic scribbler of a few years back. I am sure that the power of vested interests is vastly exaggerated compared with the gradual encroachment of ideas" (1936, 383). The American Revolution of 1776 was strongly supported by an ideology of freedom (Bailyn 1992; Holcombe 2002a), as was the fall of the European eastern bloc dictatorships after 1989. At the beginning of the twenty-first century, citizens of governments throughout the world are increasingly coming to accept the libertarian ideas of Mises, Hayek, Friedman, Rothbard, and others.

Together, economic and ideological forces are now creating an environment more conducive to the advance of liberty than the environment of the twentieth century. From an economic standpoint, the connection between freedom and prosperity has become universally recognized. Through most of the twentieth century, the conventional wisdom held that a government-controlled economy would be more productive than a market economy, an idea that persisted until the collapse of the Berlin Wall in 1989. Economic realities have not changed, but the generally accepted economic view of freedom has. In the twentieth century, the conventional wisdom held that more freedom came at the cost of a less-productive economy. In the twenty-first century, the generally accepted view is that freedom brings prosperity. From an ideological standpoint, the academic scribbler who had the largest influence on the twentieth century was probably Karl Marx, whereas at the beginning of the twenty-first century the ideas of Mises, Hayek, and Friedman have found greater popular acceptance.

A minimal libertarian state would require strong ideological support from its citizens, and both economic and ideological factors are turning in the direction of liberty. As Jeffrey Rogers Hummel says of libertarian ideology, "Although we may never abolish all states, there is little doubt that we can do better at restraining their power if only we can motivate people with the will to be free" (2001, 535).

Government and Liberty

History has shown not only that anarchy does not survive, but also that some governments are better than others. Therein lies the libertarian argument for a limited government. People benefit from an institutional mechanism to prevent their being taken over by a predatory gang. They can provide this mechanism by preemptively establishing their own limited government, in a form they themselves determine, not on the terms forced upon them by outside predators. A government created by the people themselves can be designed to produce the protection they desire while returning to them the bulk of the surplus owing to peaceful cooperation rather than allowing the state to retain it.

Is it really possible to design a limited government that will protect people's liberty? Despite the challenges, it is well known that some institutional arrangements do a better job of securing liberty and creating prosperity than others. Nations that have protected property rights and allowed markets to work have thrived, whereas nations that have not done so have remained mired in poverty.[22] A libertarian analysis of government must go beyond the issue of whether government should exist. Some governments are more libertarian than others, and it is worth studying how government institutions can be designed to minimize their negative impact on liberty. This proposition is obviously true if one believes that government is inevitable, but even advocates of orderly anarchy should have an interest in understanding how government institutions can be designed to maximize their protection of liberty.

Many writers have noted that limited governments usually tend to expand their scope once established, perhaps suggesting that limited governments, once established, cannot be controlled (Olson 1982, 2000; Higgs 1987; Holcombe 2002a). Nevertheless, in the real world, some governments are less oppressive and closer to the libertarian ideal than others. The United States, with one of the oldest governments in the world, remains one of the freest nations, so clearly it is possible to preserve a degree of liberty, even if the situation does not approach the libertarian ideal. In any event, if government is inevitable, there is no real-world libertarian alternative but to work to make government more libertarian. Although ideas have been advanced as to how institutions might be redesigned to lessen government's coercive activities (for example, by Tucker 1990; Anderson and Leal 1991; Holcombe 1995; Holcombe and Staley 2001), there may be no final answer to the question of how to design the ideal government because any innovations in government designed to protect the rights of individuals may prompt offsetting innovations by those who want to use government for predatory purposes. The preservation of liberty will remain a never-ending challenge.

My argument may convince some readers that limited government is necessary to preserve liberty—to protect citizens from being taken over and ruled by a predatory government much worse for their liberty than a government they design themselves. Others may believe, despite the arguments presented here, that libertarian anarchy remains a feasible and desirable alternative. In any event, my arguments point to a different direction for the debate between libertarian anarchists and libertarian minarchists.[23] Both groups agree that government is not necessary to produce public goods or to correct externalities or to get people to cooperate for the public good—that private parties can undertake voluntarily and more effectively all of the activities undertaken in the public sector. The libertarian issue regarding government is whether a society with no government has the means to prevent predators from establishing one by force.

Rothbard (1973) argues that an anarchistic society can resist such predators, whereas Nozick (1974) and de Jasay (1989, 1997) argue that anarchy will not survive. However, most of the arguments supporting a libertarian anarchy have been framed in terms of whether private arrangements can replace government activities. Whether private arrangements are superior to government activity, however, is largely irrelevant.[24] Government is not created to produce public goods, to control externalities, or to enforce social cooperation for the good of all. It is created by force for the benefit of its creators. The libertarian argument for a minimal government is not that government is better than private arrangements at doing anything, but that it is necessary to prevent the creation of an even more predatory and less-libertarian government.

Notes

1. I refer only to academic defenders of liberty because other libertarians need not be so rigorous in their analysis of alternatives to the status quo. H. L. Mencken, for example, could offer trenchant critiques of government without having to offer an alternative. Ayn Rand, a novelist, did not need to offer alternatives but did offer them, and she also belongs to the limited-government camp. The Libertarian Party in the United States runs candidates for political office, a few of whom are elected. Although some people view libertarianism as consistent with only the elimination of all government, many people who call themselves libertarians see a role for limited government.
2. Hayek argues for limited government despite his reservations (for example, in Hayek [1944]) about the expansion of government.
3. See, for example, Mises (1998), 715-16, for a discussion of the role of government. Elsewhere, Mises (1945) expresses his reservations about government.

4. Rothbard (1973) explains how private arrangements effectively can replace all of government's functions, and Rothbard (1982) gives an ethical argument for the complete elimination of government.
5. Robert Higgs has written, "Without government to defend us from external aggression, preserve domestic order, define and enforce property rights, few of us could achieve much" (1987, 1). He recently reevaluated his position, however, and now declares, "When I was younger and even more ignorant that I am today, I believed that government...performs an essential function—namely, the protection of individuals from the aggressions of others.... Growing older, however, has given me an opportunity to reexamine the bases of my belief in the indispensability of the protective services of government.... As I have done so, I have become increasingly skeptical, and I now am more inclined to disbelieve the idea than to believe it" (2002, 309). In this more recent article, Higgs does not deal with the argument that private protective services work under the umbrella of the state and that without the state to check their power they might evolve into organizations more predatory than a constitutionally limited state. In my view, Higgs's earlier position retains merit.
6. In Holcombe forthcoming, I discuss some of this literature. See, for example, the critiques by de Jasay (1989), Foldvary (1994), and Holcombe (1997) of the public-goods rationale for government, and by Berman (1983), Foldvary (1984), D. Friedman (1989), Benson (1989, 1990, 1998), Stringham (1998-99), and Tinsley (1998-99) on how law can exist without the state, how property rights can be defined, and how externalities can be internalized through private arrangements. Rothbard (1973) and D. Friedman (1989) more generally describe how the private sector can handle better all activities the state currently undertakes. Another justification for the state is the social contract theory that goes back at least to Hobbes ([1651] 1950) and appears in the work of Rawls (1971) and Buchanan (1975). De Jasay (1985, 1997) and Yeager (1985) present extensive critiques of the social contract theory, and Axelrod (1984), Foldvary (1984), de Jasay (1989), Rothbard (1973), D. Friedman (1989), Benson (2001), and many others have shown how private arrangements can overcome the prisoners' dilemma problem. In Holcombe (2002b), I note that the actual activities of government do not correspond with the social contractarian framework.
7. See, for example, Rothbard (1982). Rothbard (1956) lays a foundation for both the ethical and economic arguments against government by reformulating welfare economics to show that market activity is welfare enhancing, whereas government activity, which relies on coercion, is not. Along these lines, Brewster (2002) argues that the state cannot exist if by *state* one means an organization acting in the public interest. People act in their own interests, Brewster argues, and the state is merely designed to appear as if it acts in the public interest. Edelman (1964) lays an interesting foundation for this point of view.
8. This argument is developed further in Hoppe (1998-99), which argues that in the absence of government, insurance companies can provide defense services. This argument is interesting, but it should be noted that companies that offer fire insurance or theft insurance do not provide home security or fire protection services even in areas where such services are not available from government. Note also that typical insurance policies often exclude losses owing to war, even though government provides defense services. In the absence of government, if companies offered insurance against losses from foreign invasion, they might find it cheaper to pay their policyholders for their losses than to provide defense services to protect them.
9. See, for example, Beard (1913), which argues that the U.S. Constitution was written to further its authors' interests.

10. See Tullock (1967), an article titled "The Welfare Costs of Tariffs, Monopolies, and Theft," which is focused on the welfare cost of monopolies and tariffs, but whose arguments about theft apply here. See also Usher (1992) for a Hobbesian view of life in anarchy. See Bush (1972) for a formal model of the costliness of anarchy and how it leads to government.
11. Not surprisingly, some people prefer even more protection services, so they hire private protection services to augment the government's. Many people, however, rely entirely on the state's protection of their persons and assets.
12. Sutter (1995) argues that in anarchy, power would be biased in favor of protection agencies, which might degenerate into exploitative gangs. Rutten (1999) argues that an orderly anarchy may not always be very liberal because some people or groups might abuse the power they have over others, as the mafia does.
13. Private protection firms under the umbrella of government do not need as much excess capacity because when they detect a violation, their normal response is to call the police to marshal the additional force needed to respond to rights violations.
14. Note also Rutten's (1999) more general argument that protection firms would tend to abuse their power, much like the mafia, sacrificing liberty in any event.
15. Sutter (1995) shows how asymmetric power can lead to the exploitation of some people in this situation. See also Rutten (1999) on this point.
16. Those who argue that private protection firms would negotiate among themselves to settle disputes are in effect arguing that competitors would not enter the market unless they also entered the dispute-resolution cartel.
17. Of course, other types of firms might try to use force as a competitive tool—for example, by saying, "If you don't deal exclusively with us, we will burn your house down." Such actions, however, lie outside the type of market activity normally incorporated into economic analysis, whereas the use of force is an integral part of a protection firm's business activity.
18. Perhaps the most recent examples of areas effectively without government were Bosnia, Somalia, and Afghanistan in the 1990s, which fell well short of being anarchistic utopias.
19. Much has been made in libertarian literature of the case of Iceland from about A.D. 800 to 1262. For the historical details, see D. Friedman (1979). Yet this example ended nearly 750 years ago, and it existed in a world much different from the modern one. Iceland was remote, given the transportation technology of the day, it was poor, and it had an undesirable climate, making it an undesirable target for predators. Nevertheless, a government was eventually established from the inside.
20. This argument is aimed at libertarians and takes a libertarian perspective. Libertarians should keep in mind, however, that the overwhelming majority of people, if given the choice, would choose government over anarchy, and a substantial number of people would like a bigger and more powerful government than they have today.
21. Levi (1988) discusses the effect of the rulers' time horizon and other factors on the degree to which they act in a predatory manner. Hoppe (2001) argues that monarchy is superior to democracy because political leaders have a longer time horizon.
22. Landes (1998) considers the historical evidence and makes a powerful case for this connection.
23. Although I argue that libertarian anarchy is not a viable alternative, I do not mean to suggest that the libertarian anarchist literature has no merit. In fact, this literature has made valuable contributions in two broad ways. First, it has shown the viability of market institutions in areas where the mainstream literature argues the necessity of government, thus making significant advances in our understanding of both markets and government. Second, it helps promote the libertarian ideology required to rein in the power of predatory government.

24. My argument also suggests that claims that government is immoral (as in Rothbard [1982]) are not relevant to the issue of whether people should have government. If government is inevitably imposed on them by force, they have no choice.

References

Anderson, Terry L., and Donald Leal. 1991. *Free Market Environmentalism.* San Francisco: Pacific Research Institute for Public Policy.

Axelrod, Robert. 1984. *The Evolution of Cooperation.* New York: Basic.

Azfar, Omar, and Charles A. Cadwell. 2003. *Market-Augmenting Government.* Ann Arbor: University of Michigan Press.

Bailyn, Bernard. 1992. *The Ideological Origins of the American Revolution.* Enlarged ed. Cambridge, Mass.: Belknap.

Beard, Charles A. 1913. *An Economic Interpretation of the Constitution of the United States.* New York: MacMillan.

Benson, Bruce L. 1989. "The Spontaneous Evolution of Commercial Law." *Southern Economic Journal* 55, no. 3 (January): 644-61.

———. 1990. *The Enterprise of Law: Justice Without the State.* San Francisco: Pacific Research Institute for Public Policy.

———. 1998. *To Serve and Protect: Privatization and Community in Criminal Justice.* New York: New York University Press.

———. 1999. "An Economic Theory of the Evolution of Governance and the Emergence of the State." *Review of Austrian Economics* 12, no. 2: 131-60.

———. 2001. "Knowledge, Trust, and Recourse: Imperfect Substitutes as Sources of Assurance in Emerging Economies." *Economic Affairs* 21, no. 1 (March): 12-17.

Berman, Harold J. 1983. *Law and Revolution: The Formation of Western Legal Tradition.* Cambridge, Mass.: Harvard University Press.

Brewster, Leonard. 2002. "The Impossibility of the State." *Journal of Libertarian Studies* 16, no. 3 (summer): 19-34.

Buchanan, James M. 1975. *The Limits of Liberty: Between Anarchy and Leviathan.* Chicago: University of Chicago Press.

Bush, Winston C. 1972. "Individual Welfare in Anarchy." In *Explorations in the Theory of Anarchy*, edited by Gordon Tullock, 5-18. Blacksburg, Va.: Center for the Study of Public Choice.

Cowan, Tyler. 1992. "Law as a Public Good." *Economics and Philosophy* 8, no. 2 (October): 249-67.

———. 1994. "Rejoinder to David Friedman on the Economics of Anarchy." *Economics and Philosophy* 10, no. 2 (October): 329-32.

de Jasay, Anthony. 1985. *The State.* New York: Basil Blackwell.

———. 1989. *Social Contract, Free Ride: A Study of the Public Goods Problem.* Oxford: Clarendon.

———. 1997. *Against Politics: On Government, Anarchy, and Order.* London: Routledge.

Edelman, Murray. 1964. *The Symbolic Uses of Politics.* Urbana: University of Illinois Press.

Foldvary, Fred. 1994. *Public Goods and Private Communities: The Market Provision of Social Services.* Brookfield, Vt.: Edward Elgar.

Friedman, David. 1979. "Private Creation and Enforcement of Law: A Historical Case." *Journal of Legal Studies* 8 (March): 399-415.

———. 1989. *The Machinery of Freedom: Guide to a Radical Capitalism.* 2d ed. La Salle, Ill.: Open Court.

Friedman, Milton. 1962. *Capitalism and Freedom.* Chicago: University of Chicago Press.

Gwartney, James, Randall Holcombe, and Robert Lawson. 1998. "The Scope of Government and the Wealth of Nations." *Cato Journal* 18, no. 2 (fall): 163-90.

Gwartney, James, Robert Lawson, and Randall Holcombe. 1999. "Economic Freedom and the Environment for Economic Growth." *Journal of Institutional and Theoretical Economics* 155, no. 4 (December): 643-63.

Hayek, Friedrich A. 1944. *The Road to Serfdom.* Chicago: University of Chicago Press.

———. 1960. *The Constitution of Liberty.* Chicago: University of Chicago Press.

Higgs, Robert. 1987. *Crisis and Leviathan: Critical Episodes in the Growth of American Government.* New York: Oxford University Press.

———. 2002. "Government Protects Us?" *The Independent Review* 7, no. 2 (fall): 309-13.

Hobbes, Thomas. [1651] 1950. *Leviathan.* New York: E. P. Dutton.

Holcombe, Randall G. 1994. *The Economic Foundations of Government.* New York: New York University Press.

———. 1995. *Public Policy and the Quality of Life.* Westport, Conn.: Greenwood.

———. 1997. A Theory of the Theory of Public Goods. *Review of Austrian Economics* 10, no. 1: 1-22.

———. 2002a. *From Liberty to Democracy: The Transformation of American Government.* Ann Arbor: University of Michigan Press.

———. 2002b. "Political Entrepreneurship and the Democratic Allocation of Economic Resources." *Review of Austrian Economics* 15, nos. 2-3 (June): 143-59.

———. Forthcoming. "Why Government?" In *Ordered Anarchy: Jasay and His Surroundings*, edited by Hardy Buillon and Hartmut Kliemt.

Holcombe, Randall G., and Samuel R. Staley. 2001. *Smarter Growth: Market-Based Strategies for Land-Use Planning in the 21st Century.* Westport, Conn.: Greenwood.

Hoppe, Hans-Hermann. 1998-99. "The Private Production of Defense." *Journal of Libertarian Studies* 14, no. 1 (winter): 27-52.

———. 2001. *Democracy—The God That Failed: The Economics and Politics of Monarchy, Democracy, and Natural Order.* New Brunswick, N.J.: Transaction.

Hummel, Jeffrey Rogers. 1990. "National Goods Versus Public Goods: Defense, Disarmament, and Free Riders." *Review of Austrian Economics* 4, no. 1: 88-122.

———. 2001. "The Will to Be Free: The Role of Ideology in National Defense." *The Independent Review* 5, no. 4 (spring): 523-37.

Keynes, John Maynard. 1936. *The General Theory of Employment, Interest, and Money.* New York: Harcourt, Brace.

Knack, Stephen, ed. 2003. *Democracy, Governance, and Growth.* Ann Arbor: University of Michigan Press.

Kurrild-Klitgaard, Peter. 1997. *Rational Choice, Collective Action, and the Paradox of Rebellion.* Copenhagen: University of Copenhagen, Institute of Political Science.

Landes, David S. 1998. *The Wealth and Poverty of Nations: Why Some Are So Rich, and Others So Poor.* New York: W. W. Norton.

Levi, Margaret. 1988. *Of Rule and Revenue.* Berkeley and Los Angeles: University of California Press.

Lichbach, Mark Irving. 1995. *The Rebel's Dilemma.* Ann Arbor: University of Michigan Press.

Mises, Ludwig von. 1945. *Omnipotent Government: The Rise of the Total State and Total War.* New Haven, Conn.: Yale University Press.

———. 1979. *Liberalism: A Socio-economic Exposition.* New York: New York University Press.

———. 1998. *Human Action: A Treatise on Economics.* Scholar's ed. Auburn, Ala.: Ludwig von Mises Institute.

Narveson, Jan. 2002. *Respecting Persons in Theory and Practice: Essays on Moral and Political Philosophy.* Lanham, Md.: Rowman and Littlefield.
North, Douglass C. 1981. *Structure and Change in Economic History.* New York: W.W. Norton.
———. 1988. "Ideology and Political/Economic Institutions." *Cato Journal* 8 (Spring-Summer): 15-28.
Nozick, Robert. 1974. *Anarchy, State, and Utopia.* New York: Basic.
Olson, Mancur. 1965. *The Logic of Collective Action.* New York: Shocken.
———. 1982. *The Rise and Decline of Nations.* New Haven, Conn.: Yale University Press.
———. 2000. *Power and Prosperity: Outgrowing Communist and Capitalist Dictatorships.* New York: Basic.
Rawls, John. 1971. *A Theory of Justice.* Cambridge, Mass.: Belknap.
Rothbard, Murray N. 1956. "Toward a Reconstruction of Utility and Welfare Economics." In *On Freedom and Free Enterprise: Essays in Honor of Ludwig von Mises*, edited by Mary Sennholz, 224-62. Princeton, N.J.: D. Van Nostrand.
———. 1962. *Man, Economy, and State.* Princeton, N.J.: Van Nostrand.
———. 1973. *For a New Liberty.* New York: Macmillan.
———. 1982. *The Ethics of Liberty.* Atlantic Highlands, N.J.: Humanities.
Rutten, Andrew. 1999. "Can Anarchy Save Us from Leviathan?" *The Independent Review* 3, no. 4 (Spring): 581-93.
Samuelson, Paul Anthony. 1947. *Foundations of Economic Analysis.* Cambridge, Mass.: Harvard University Press.
Smith, Adam. [1776] 1937. *The Wealth of Nations.* Modern Library ed. New York: Random House.
Stringham, Edward. 1998-99. "Market Chosen Law." *Journal of Libertarian Studies* 14, no. 1 (winter): 53-77.
Sutter, Daniel. 1995. "Asymmetric Power Relations and Cooperation in Anarchy." *Southern Economic Journal* 61, no. 3 (January): 602-13.
Tinsley, Patrick. 1998-99. "Private Police: A Note." *Journal of Libertarian Studies* 14, no. 1 (Winter): 95-100.
Tucker, William. 1990. *The Excluded Americans: Homelessness and Housing Policies.* Washington, D.C.: Regnery Gateway.
Tullock, Gordon. 1967. "The Welfare Costs of Tariffs, Monopolies, and Theft." *Western Economic Journal* 5 (June): 224-32.
———, ed. 1972. *Explorations in the Theory of Anarchy.* Blacksburg, Va.: Center for the Study of Public Choice.
———, ed. 1974. *Further Explorations in the Theory of Anarchy.* Blacksburg, Va.: University Publications.
Usher, Dan. 1992. *The Welfare Economics of Market, Voting, and Predation.* Ann Arbor: University of Michigan Press.
Yeager, Leland B. 1985. "Rights, Contract, and Utility in Policy Analysis." *Cato Journal* 5, no. 1 (summer): 259-94.

Acknowledgments: The author gratefully acknowledges helpful comments from Bruce Benson, Fred Foldvary, Gil Guillory, Robert Higgs, Hans Hoppe, and two anonymous reviewers of this journal. All arguments presented in the article and any of the article's remaining shortcomings remain the author's responsibility.

23

Is Government Inevitable? Comment on Holcombe's Analysis

Peter Leeson and Edward P. Stringham

Randall G. Holcombe's article "Government: Unnecessary but Inevitable" (2004) offers excellent insights into the sustainability of anarchy and the creation of government. Holcombe recognizes that "government was not created for the benefit of its citizens, it was created for the benefit of those who rule." Although he agrees that government is unnecessary for the provision of public goods, he believes that libertarian anarchists ignore more practical questions about the sustainability of anarchy. He argues that because the stronger individuals will always get their way and form a government, the relevant debate among advocates of liberty should be about how weaker individuals can "create and sustain preemptively a liberty-preserving government." The inevitability of the state forces society to decide between evils. Instead of advocating anarchy, Holcombe believes that libertarians should advocate the establishment of minimal governments that can prevent takeover by more tyrannical ones.

Inspired by Holcombe's discussion, we reconsider here some of his claims. Despite Holcombe's interesting hypothesis, we believe that his argument fails on two counts: he does not show, first, that anarchy must break down and, second, that limited government will remain limited. The arguments he uses against the viability of anarchy can be applied to the viability of limited government, and the arguments he uses for the viability of limited government can be applied to the viability of anarchy. In this comment, we discuss the problems of Holcombe's theoretical arguments and the historical evidence that shows he cannot have his cake and eat it too. Holcombe, who might be considered a pessimistic anarchist, is in our opinion too pessimistic about anarchy and too optimistic about government.

Some Observations Concerning the Sustainability of Anarchy

Building on earlier criticisms of anarchy (Tullock 1972, 1974; Nozick 1974; Cowen 1992), Holcombe argues that government is inevitable. Conventional wisdom is that stateless orders must be short-lived because of their susceptibility to outside forces. There may be truth in this claim, but we believe that the historical record calls it into question.

The ubiquity of government today causes us to forget that many societies were stateless for most of their histories and that many remained so well into the twentieth century. The historical presence of long-standing, primitive, anarchic societies spans the globe. Consider, for example, societies such as the Eskimo tribes of the North American Arctic, Pygmies in Zaire, the Yurok of North America, the Ifugao of the Philippines, the Land Dyaks of Sarawak, the Kuikuru of South America, the Kabyle Berbers of Algeria, the Massims of East Papua-Melanesia, and the Santals of India—none of which had governments (Leeson forthcoming).

Many stateless societies also populated precolonial Africa; a few encompassed significant numbers of people. Consider, for example, the Tiv, which included more than one million individuals; the Nuer, whose population has been estimated at four hundred thousand; or the Lugbara, with more than three hundred thousand members. In Africa, the Barabaig, Dinka, Jie, Karamojong, Turkana, Tiv, Lugbara, Konkomba, Plateau Tonga, and others long existed as stateless or near-anarchic orders as well. Today Somalia is essentially stateless and has remained effectively so since its government dissolved in 1991 despite predictions that a new government would emerge immediately (Little 2003).

More striking yet is that the world as a whole has operated and continues to operate as international anarchy (Cuzan 1979, 156). The continuing presence of numerous sovereigns creates massive ungoverned interstices for many of the interactions between the inhabitants of different nations as well for the interactions between sovereigns themselves (Stringham 1999). Many of the stateless orders mentioned earlier disappeared with the extension of colonial rule in the nineteenth century. However, the international sphere remains anarchic and shows few signs of coming under the rule of formal government soon.

Holcombe is correct, however, that no modern nation has what can be considered libertarian anarchy.[1] He believes that because anarchy is not practiced today, we should expect that it never will be practiced. He writes, "Every place in the world is ruled by government. The evidence shows that anarchy, no matter how desirable in theory, is not a realistic alternative in practice" (2004, 333). But this evidence does not prove his point. Suppose that someone had used the same argument against democracy in the year 1500: "Every place in the world is ruled by *monarchy*. The evidence shows that *democracy*, no matter how desirable in theory, is not a realistic alternative in practice." Over the past few centuries, political systems have changed dramatically. Just because monarchy was pervasive a half millennium ago does not mean that it was inevitable, as Holcombe's logic suggests. The rarity of democracy five hundred years ago does not "show" that democracy was "not realistic in practice." The evidence shows only that democracy was uncommon a half millennium ago and that anarchy is uncommon today. To show that government is inevitable, Holcombe must advance a theory that explains why anarchy is impossible, as Nozick (1974), Cowen (1992), and the contributors in Gordon Tullock's collection *Explorations in the Theory of Anarchy* (1972) have attempted to do.[2]

Is Government Truly Inevitable?

Building on the arguments of his professors James Buchanan (1972) and Gordon Tullock (1972), Holcombe gives some theoretical reasons in support of his claim that government is inevitable. He maintains that stronger agents will be tempted to use force against the weak and impose government on them. Because some agents are stronger than others, they will see that using force is cheaper than engaging in peaceful interaction, such as trade. Although parts of the argument may ring true, they do not establish the state's inevitability. Two special assumptions must be made if we are to arrive at Holcombe's conclusion.

First, strengths must be so disparate that the strong have little to lose by engaging in conflict with the weak. This assumption may be unrealistic. Imagine what would happen if everyone were of similar strengths. If one stood a 50 percent chance of losing any fight, then as long as fighting entails costs, the use of force would not be the income-maximizing strategy. Even if one has superior strength, the use of force may not be the income-maximizing strategy. As long as weaker parties can commit to injuring the stronger party in the course of fights, the stronger party who consistently "wins" may still be worse off by engaging in fighting (Friedman 1994b).

The critical question is not whether some are more powerful than others, but whether power is so lopsided that the strong face few risks by engaging in conflict. Consider again the state of global anarchy in which we find ourselves. Although some nations can win wars against others consistently, they would do so at significant cost. The use of guerilla warfare or terrorist tactics by others can make victory extremely costly for stronger powers. The ability of even small nations to inflict harm on larger nations may explain why violent confrontations between states are less common than confrontations between individuals in New York's Central Park. Thus, in discussing the anarchy of the international sphere, it would be inappropriate to assume that anarchy necessarily leads to the establishment of hegemony by one state over others. This remark is not to say that invasions never take place. It is merely to point out that the presence of asymmetric power is insufficient to prove the inevitability of world government.

The second assumption required for Holcombe's conclusion is that weaker individuals cannot find private solutions to transform the incentives of the strong to plunder. This assumption also can be questioned, as certain historical events suggest. For example, the environment in which individuals interacted in nineteenth-century West Central Africa satisfied the conditions that Holcombe describes for the inevitable emergence of the state. Traveling middlemen who made connections between the producers of exports in the remote interior of Africa and the European exporters on the coast of Angola were substantially stronger than the producers with whom they interacted. No formal authority policed the interactions between the members of these two groups—they interacted in the context of anarchy. The middlemen thus faced a strong incentive to steal the goods they desired rather than to obtain them by means of trade.

Holcombe's argument suggests that these middlemen would establish a government over the producers, but the historical record indicates that they did not do so. Why not? Producers devised several informal institutions, such as middleman credit, for transforming the stronger middlemen's incentive from banditry to exchange. Producers decided not to produce anything, so that if middlemen came to plunder their goods, nothing would be available for them to steal. After having incurred a costly trip to the interior to plunder producers, middlemen who approached producers and found nothing to take therefore faced two options. They could either go home empty handed, or they could agree to exchange with producers on credit. Because the former choice involved certain losses and the latter involved the prospect of profits, middlemen agreed to credit agreements with producers. Middlemen would pay up front, and producers would agree to harvest the goods and make them available at a future date. In order to repay the middlemen, producers had to be alive and healthy. This arrangement created a strong incentive for credit-offering middlemen to protect the producers from others who might try to harm or steal from them. Credit thus transformed producers from targets of plunder to valuable productive assets that the middlemen desired to protect (Leeson 2004).

This arrangement is just one of several such private mechanisms that producers employed to alter the relative payoffs of plunder versus trade faced by middlemen. We do not mean to suggest that introducing credit will prevent the emergence of government in all cases, but this example illustrates how weaker agents may be able to prevent predatory actions by stronger agents. Another example of a stateless society altering incentives to protect property rights is the potlatch system of the Kwakiutl Indians described by Johnsen (1986). If private mechanisms are devised that alter the cost-benefit structure of activities for stronger agents, the imposition of force need not be inevitable.

Would Preemptive Government Work?

Besides questioning the alleged inevitability of government, we also question Holcombe's belief in the viability of constitutional government. Holcombe claims that individuals can achieve a more limited state by forming a constitutional government preemptively. Let us assume for the moment that he is correct that anarchy must break down. Do his assumptions warrant his conclusion regarding preemptive state formation? It seems to us that the answer must be no. The reasons are straightforward.

According to Holcombe, individuals *can* achieve smaller government if "they design [it] themselves" (2004, 338). For this alternative to work, he points out, they must have a will and a desire for greater liberty. Except for revolutionary change, however, he fails to specify the process by which individuals might arrive at this government. This failure is a major problem because it leaves us wondering which individuals are to do the designing.

It seems uncontroversial that any such process must involve political agents, but once we admit political agents, these agents' self-interest enters the picture (Powell and Coyne 2003). In light of this ruler self-interest, coupled with the superior strength that Holcombe describes, does any hope remain for limits on government? Rather than creating the minimal state as Holcombe desires, these political actors will deliver much more than anyone bargained for. If we agree with Holcombe that government is created by force, why then would we assume that its creators will produce the minimal state?

Holcombe points to one way out of this dilemma: if citizens are strongly unified against the political agents' will, then those agents will be forced to consider the public's desires. Notice, however, that now Holcombe is relying on ideology, not constitutional constraints, as the main check on government. Yet if one accepts the hypothesis that ideology can trump government force, then anarchy becomes a sustainable socioeconomic organization, which is just the opposite of what Holcombe wants to argue. Ideology, after all, is what libertarian anarchists such as Hummel (1990, 2001) believe can stave off the violent formation of the state. If the public agrees on the principles of liberty and can act in concert to maintain the minimal state, the public can act in concert also to maintain libertarian anarchy. Just as the public can constrain the minimal state from becoming more coercive, the public can constrain private protection agencies from becoming more coercive.

The preemptive creation of limited government in Holcombe's argument faces another serious problem as well. If we assume that the stronger agents will always use their superior strength to overawe the weak, what prevents stronger authoritarian states that devote most of their resources to military buildup from taking over societies that have preemptively created limited governments? Unless we assume that the society that has designed this limited government also designs the strongest government, its people will again be confronted with the problem they faced in anarchy: being dominated by a stronger party.

Conclusions

Holcombe's argument represents an advance over the argument of public-choice economists who analyze the formation of government as a voluntary social contract. He introduces a more realistic view in which government is not created to solve public-goods problems. Holcombe's pessimistic anarchism, with its recognition that government is unnecessary, is a welcome improvement over the offerings of other advocates of limited government. Nevertheless, we believe that he is too pessimistic about anarchy and too optimistic about government as we know it. Although we recognize the important advances in Holcombe's discussion, we believe that his conclusions should be questioned.

Notes

1. Somalia may be a possible exception, although libertarians disagree.
2. Rothbard (1977) and Childs (1977) question Nozick's theories; Friedman (1994a) and Caplan and Stringham (2003) question Cowen's theories; and the contributors in Stringham forthcoming question the theories in Tullock 1972, arguing that Nozick, Cowen, and other contributors to this volume do not offer compelling reasons why anarchy must break down.

References

Buchanan, James. 1972. "Before Public Choice." In *Explorations in the Theory of Anarchy*, edited by Gordon Tullock, 27-38. Blacksburg, Va.: Center for the Study of Public Choice.

Caplan, Bryan, and Edward Stringham. 2003. "Networks, Law, and the Paradox of Cooperation." *Review of Austrian Economics* 16: 309-26.

Childs, Roy. 1977. "The Invisible Hand Strikes Back." *Journal of Libertarian Studies* 1: 23-33.

Cowen, Tyler. 1992. "Law as a Public Good: The Economics of Anarchy." *Economics and Philosophy* 8: 249-67.

Cuzan, Alfred. 1979. "Do We Ever Really Get Out of Anarchy?" *Journal of Libertarian Studies* 3: 151-58.

Friedman, David. 1994a. "Law as a Private Good: A Response to Tyler Cowen on the Economics of Anarchy." *Economics and Philosophy* 10: 319-27.

———. 1994b. "A Positive Account of Property Rights." *Social Philosophy and Policy* 11: 1-16.

Holcombe, Randall G. 2004. "Government: Unnecessary but Inevitable." *The Independent Review* 8, no. 3: 325-42.

Hummel, Jeffrey Rogers. 1990. "National Goods Versus Public Goods: Defense, Disarmament, and Free Riders." *Review of Austrian Economics* 4: 88-122.

———. 2001. "The Will to Be Free: The Role of Ideology in National Defense." *The Independent Review* 5, no. 4: 523-37.

Johnsen, D. B. 1986. "The Formation and Protection of Property Rights among the Southern Kwakiutl Indians." *Journal of Legal Studies* 15: 41-67.

Leeson, Peter. 2004. *Trading with Bandits.* Working Paper. Fairfax, Va.: George Mason University.

———. Forthcoming. "Cooperation and Conflict: Evidence on Self-Enforcing Arrangements and Heterogeneous Groups." *American Journal of Economics and Sociology.*

Little, Peter. 2003. *Somalia: Economy Without State.* Bloomington: Indiana University Press.

Nozick, Robert. 1974. *Anarchy, State, and Utopia.* New York: Basic.

Powell, Benjamin, and Christopher Coyne. 2003. "Do Pessimistic Assumptions about Human Behavior Justify Government?" *Journal of Libertarian Studies* 17: 17-38.

Rothbard, Murray. 1977. "Robert Nozick and the Immaculate Conception of the State." *Journal of Libertarian Studies* 1: 45-57.

Stringham, Edward. 1999. "Market Chosen Law." *Journal of Libertarian Studies* 14: 53-77.

———, ed. Forthcoming. *Anarchy, State, and Public Choice.* Cheltenham, United Kingdom: Edward Elgar.

Tullock, Gordon, ed. 1972. *Explorations in the Theory of Anarchy.* Blacksburg, Va.: Center for the Study of Public Choice.

———, ed. 1974. *Further Explorations in the Theory of Anarchy.* Blacksburg, Va.: Center for the Study of Public Choice.

Acknowledgments: The authors have benefited greatly from discussions with Bryan Caplan, Christopher Coyne, David Friedman, and Benjamin Powell.

24

Gustave de Molinari and the Anti-statist Liberal Tradition (excerpts)

David Hart

The Intellectual Origins of Liberal Anti-statism

1. Edmund Burke, William Godwin and Benjamin Constant

The origins of liberal anti-statism go back at least to the radical dissent of the Levellers in the English Revolution of the seventeenth century. Their efforts to defend themselves against the power of the state, which wanted to control or prohibit their religious practices, resulted in some of the earliest liberal defenses of property rights and the natural right of the individual to enjoy his liberty. One of the most thoroughgoing statements of the Leveller defense of natural rights in property and liberty is Richard Overton's "An Arrow Against All Tyrants," written from prison in 1646. In this tract, Overton was able to abstract the principles of natural rights from the more general question of religious liberty and was thus able to develop a secular theory of rights as a basis for political rights. He began his pamphlet with he following paragraph:

> To every individual in nature is given an individual property by nature, not to be invaded or usurped by any: for every one as he is himselfe, so he hath a selfe propriety, else could he not be himselfe, and on this no second may presume to deprive any of, without manifest violation and affront to the very principles of nature, and of the Rules of equity and Justice between man and man; mine and thine cannot be, except this be: No man hath power over my rights and. liberties, and I over no man's; I may be but an individual, enjoy my selfe and my selfe propriety, and may write my selfe no more [than] my selfe, or presume any further; if I doe, I am an encroacher and an invader upon another man's Right, to which I have no Right. For by natural birth, all men are equally and alike borne to like propriety, liberty and freedom, and as we are delivered of God by the hand of nature into this world, every one with a naturall, innate freedome and propriety (as it were writ in the table of every man's heart, never to be obliterated) even so are we to live, everyone equally and alike to enjoy his Birthright and privilege; even all whereof God by nature hath made him free.[1]

However, it was not until the eighteenth century that these liberal ideas of liberty and property were developed into a more comprehensive theory of the state. The young Edmund Burke, for example, in his *Vindication of Natural Society* written in 1756, extended the religious dissenter's criticism of "artificial," imposed religion to the institutions of government.[2] In what is probably the first individualist, liberal anarchist tract ever written, Burke condemned all forms of political society for being the main cause of war, suffering and misfortune.[3]

Making a distinction common to many anti-statist liberals, Burke divided society into two types. Natural society, "founded in natural appetites and instincts, and not in any positive institution," was not based on force and allowed individuals to freely exercise their God-given natural rights as their individual consciences directed. Artificial or political society, on the other hand, was based on the imposition of "artificial" laws and regulations, thus usurping the proper function of the individual to determine his own peaceful behavior.[4] Immediately, conflict arises from the division of society into two classes, the governed and the governors, the latter seeking to increase its power and wealth at the expense of the former. After cataloguing the political history of the world, a "history dyed in blood, and blotted and confounded by tumults, rebellions, massacres, assassinations, proscriptions,"[5] Burke squarely places the blame on political society of whatever kind.[6] He accused all states of being essentially the same, in that they are based on force and exist for the benefit of those privileged minorities who are powerful or influential enough to control them. He wrote:

> We have shown them [the three simple forms of artificial society: democracy, monarchy and aristocracy], however they may differ in name or in some slight circumstances, to be all alike in effect; in effect to be all tyrannies.... In vain you tell me that artificial government is good, but that I fall out only with the abuse. The thing! the thing itself is the abuse![7]

Burke recognized that even in "natural society" there would still exist the need for the protection of life, liberty and property because "[it] was observed that men had ungovernable passions, which made it necessary to guard against the violence they might offer to each other."[8] As Molinari was to argue later,[9] the "grand error"[10] that men made in attempting to solve this problem of how to protect themselves from aggression was to establish or accept a monopoly government with the powers to provide this service. Men now found themselves worse off than when they were without the state[11] because they now faced a nationally organized engine of oppression, whereas before they had faced only disorganized bandits or, at most, local feudal lords and their mercenaries. The perennial problem arose of who was to guard against the guardians.[12]

Burke's failure was in not being able to provide a positive view of the form his "natural society" would take. He limited himself to a bri1liant criticism of the basis of all political institutions from a natural rights' perspective and did not elaborate on "natural society" save for the assertion that "[in] a state of nature it is an inevitable law that a man's acquisitions are in proportion to his labours"[13] and that each individual would have the right to defend his person and property as he saw fit.[14] Burke did not have the tools at hand which were necessary to explain how an anarchist[15] society would function. He lacked the Smithian free-market economics that Molinari later used to explain how society could provide itself with defense services without resorting to the coercive monopoly of the state.

A similar problem was faced by William Godwin. Like Burke, he defended individualism and the right to property,[16] drawing considerably, in fact, from Burke's *Vindication* for his criticism of the state,[17] and he concluded that the state was an evil which had to be reduced in power if not eliminated completely.

> Above all we should not forget that government is, abstractly taken, an evil, an usurpation upon the private judgment and individual conscience of mankind; and that, however, we may be obliged to admit it as a necessary evil for the present, it behooves us, as the friends of reason and the human species, to admit as little of it as possible, and carefully to observe, whether, in the consequence of the gradual elimination of the human mind, that little may not hereafter be diminished.[18]

Godwin looked forward to the day when the entire state could be done away with completely.

> With what delight must every well-informed friend of mankind look forward to the auspicious period, the dissolution of political government, of that brute engine which has been the only perennial cause of the vices of mankind, and which, as has abundantly appeared in the present work, has mischief of various sorts incorporated with its substance, and no otherwise removable than by its utter annihilation![19]

But he still faced the difficult problem of adequately explaining how the stateless society which he envisioned could work in practice. Godwin's stateless society presupposed a sudden change in the behavior of the individuals comprising that society. He was convinced of the essential goodness of uncorrupted men and believed that when political institutions disappeared men would become "reasonable and virtuous."

> Simplify the social system in the manner which every motive but those of usurpation and ambition powerfully recommends; render the plain dictates of justice level to every capacity; remove the necessity of implicit faith; and we may expect the whole species to become reasonable and virtuous.[20]

Godwin's solution to the problem of aggression involved the use of juries which would act as advisory bodies in "adjusting controversies." These juries would reason with the offender, urging him to forsake his errors, and if this failed, could subject the offender to the criticism and ostracism of his peers.[21] But it is difficult to see how these juries could exercise this function without using force to capture criminals and, as Molinari was at pains to argue in *Les Soirées de Jarue Saint-Lazare*, how they could recompense the victims for any losses caused by the crime. Godwin's unreasonable optimism about the unaggressive nature of man in a stateless society unfortunately was common to many other anarchists, especially communist anarchist thinkers of the nineteenth and twentieth centuries.[22]

It is quite probable that Molinari was well aware of William Godwin's and, through him, Edmund Burke's anti-statism. Godwin's ideas were brought to France by Benjamin Constant among others. Constant had studied at the University of Edinburgh from 1783 to 1784 and was aware of English political thinking of this entire period. He corresponded with Godwin in 1795 and 1796 and expressed his desire to translate Godwin's *Enquiry Concerning Political Justice* into French. Godwin had even sent a copy to the French National Convention via John Fenwick on February 15, 1793, and his novel, *Caleb Williams*, had been reviewed in *La Decade* in January 1796. In 1799, Constant announced his forthcoming translation of the *Enquiry* but it never appeared due to the "political events then and in the future" which "caused the indefinite postponement of its publication."[23] However, Constant was able to popularize many of Godwin's anti-statist ideas through his writings and his speeches at the Tribunate. Only with the publication of Constant's *Oeuvres manuscrites de 1810* did 576 pages of translation appear, along with an essay on Godwin and his ideas.[24] Constant was influenced by Godwin to reject state intervention and coercion and to support all forms of voluntary and peaceful activity and he, in turn, influenced many of the laissez-faire liberals who worked with and influenced Molinari.[25]

2. Adam Smith and Jean-Baptiste Say

The other major intellectual current that influenced the anti-statism of the French laissez-faire liberals, and Molinari in particular, was the economic ideas of Adam Smith and Jean-Baptiste Say. Both these theorists described how society would operate in the absence of government control and intervention in the economy. Smith argued that government intervention was immoral, because it violated individuals' natural rights to property, and that it was generally inefficient. The selfish actions of individuals in the unhampered market promoted the general interest in spite of having no explicit intention of doing so:

> [E]very individual necessarily labours to render the annual revenue of the society as great as he can. He generally, indeed, neither intends to promote the public interest, nor knows how much he is promoting it...and by directing that industry in such a manner as its produce may be of the greatest value, he intends only his own gain, and he is in this, as in many other cases, led by an invisible hand to promote an end which was no part of his intention. Nor is it always the worse for the society that it was no part of it. By pursuing his own interest he frequently promotes that of society more effectively than when he really intends to promote it.[26]

In the stateless economy "the simple system of natural liberty" would prevail and this "spontaneous order"[27] of the market, rather than the imposed order of the state, would maximize wealth and ensure the uninterrupted use of each individual's justly acquired (whether by first use or by peaceful exchange) property. Thus:

> All systems of preference or restraint therefore being completely taken away, the obvious and simple system of natural liberty establishes itself of its own accord. Every map, as long as he does not violate the laws of justice, is left perfectly free to pursue his own interest his own way, and to bring both his industry and capital into competition with those of any other man, or order of men. The sovereign is completely discharged from a duty, in the attempting to perform which he must always be exposed to innumerable delusions, and for the proper performance of which no human wisdom or knowledge could ever be sufficient; the duty of superintending the industry of private people, and of directing it towards the employments most suitable to the interest of the society.[28]

Molinari was to use Smith's two concepts—the spontaneous order of the market and the system of natural liberty—to build his theory of extreme liberal anti-statism.

Jean-Baptiste Say popularized and extended Smith's ideas of the free market. He defended the right to property more rigorously than Smith and his conclusions had a greater influence on the anti-statism of Molinari. Say considered any barrier to the free use or abuse of property a violation of the individual's rights.[29] He condemned slavery and military conscription[30] and argued against taxes for the same reasons,[31] especially if they were in excess of the "minimum" necessary to protect the public. In that case

> it would be difficult indeed not to view this excess as a theft, a gratuitous sacrifice seized from individuals by force. I say "seized by force" even under representative governments, because even their authority may be so great as to brook no refusal.[32]

To a liberal like Say, force could never legitimize the activity of the state, even in so important a matter as taxation. Say, like Molinari, went to great pains to denounce the use of force in all human affairs, especially when used by the state or the privileged political classes.[33] The state was nothing more than a tool used by the politically privileged to maintain an "artificial order" which "endures only through force, and which can never be reestablished without injustice and violence."[34] It was because the state was an artificial body that it had to be limited in scope as much as possible. Say concluded that it must "never meddle in production" and, as a general principle, "[if] government intervention is an evil, a good government makes itself as unobtrusive as possible" because government "can unfortunately always rely upon the negligence, incompetence and odious condescensions of its own agents."[35]

The greatest enemies of the laissez-faire liberals were the monopolies, whether granted to privileged individuals or exercised by the state itself. Consistent with his defense of property rights and his general disdain for the state, Say made an initial attack on all government monopolies which Molinari was later to develop into his theory of free-market anarchism. Say argued:

> The government violates the property of each in his own person and faculties when it monopolizes certain professions such as those of bankers and brokers and sells to privileged elites these exclusive rights. It violates property even more seriously when, under the pretext of public security or simply that of the security of the state, it prevents a man from traveling or authorizes an officer or commissioner of police or judge to arrest him, so that no man is ever completely certain of the disposition of his time and faculties or of his ability to complete any enterprise. Could the public safety be any more effectively threatened by a criminal whom everyone is against and who is always so quickly caught?[36]

Not only was monopoly a violation of individual property rights but it was also inefficient. No central authority could know the needs of ail consumers because this information was dispersed throughout the economy.[37]

Say even made a tentative step towards Molinari's anarchism when he suggested that public services should be made competitive by having their coercive monopoly destroyed. His scheme was to "open all public services to free competition" in order to make them as cheap and efficient as other industries whose activities were regulated by the market.

> While recognizing the extreme difficulty involved in allowing the payment of public services to be regulated by the same principle of free competition which presides over the majority of all other social transactions, we must agree that the more this principle is applied to the administration of States, the better managed will be their interests.[38]

Like Molinari, Say quotes the important passage from Smith's *Wealth of Nations* which argues that the reason justice was so cheap in England was that the separate courts competed for clients by offering them the speediest service at the lowest price.[39] As a principle of justice, Say argued that those who consume a good or service should be the ones to pay for it.[40] When the production of security is monopolized by the state, the purchaser's rights are violated because the range of choice has been artificially limited and he thus is forced to pay a monopoly price. The excess of the monopoly price over the "necessary" or free-market price is equivalent to the theft of that amount of property from the consumer.[41] To overcome this problem, Say proposed to follow Smith's example in *Wealth of Nations* and allow competition in the pricing of court services. Each litigant would be free to choose the court and judge that best suited him. Fees would be made up of three components: a levy set by the province, a premium paid to the particular judge, and an honorarium proportional to the "values under litigation" which would be payable after the judgment had been given. In some cases, for example in criminal trials, the costs would be borne by the losing party.[42]

Anticipating Molinari by some twenty years, Say argued that only the competition provided by the free market could give the consumers of security a service that was "prompt, equitable and of reasonable cost." The market would encourage the courts and the judges to recognize the interests of the consumers since it would be their voluntary patronage that paid their salaries. In order to attract as many clients to their court as they could, the judges would be

> interested in being honest in order to garner a wide reputation for equity and be frequently called to sit in judgment. They would be motivated to end trials promptly in order to expedite the greatest number. Finally, the cost of litigation would not be out of proportion to the interests in question and there would be no useless costs.[43]

Molinari later added considerably to Say's early formulation of free-market anarchism by introducing the idea of paying for police services and protection by contracting individually with insurance companies. He was even to argue that national defense could be better supplied by competing companies on the free market and that small proprietary communities would gradually replace the leviathan state. It was with Molinari that the two different currents of anarchist thought converged: he combined the political anarchism of Burke and Godwin with the nascent economic anarchism of Adam Smith and Say to create a new form of anarchism that has been variously described as individualist anarchism, anarcho-capitalism, or free-market anarchism.

3. The Ideologues: Charles Comte and Charles Dunoyer

Both Comte and Dunoyer were influenced by the economic liberalism of Say. Together with Saint-Simon they developed the doctrine of *industrielisme* based on their class analysis of society in which the warrior class, with political privilege, and the industrial class, the result of the unhampered market, were in constant conflict. In their economic theories Comte and Dunoyer argued that the market, with all the voluntary exchanges that took place in it, was the antithesis of force. Thus the market, identified with society, was completely separate from the state and antagonistic towards it. As the historian Albert Schatz argued:

> Liberalism thus tends to create a fundamental antagonism between the individual and the State—an antagonism which does not exist in classical doctrine, one which views the individual and the State as two forces inversely proportional to one another. Consequently, there is a tendency in liberalism, at first potential, later active, to strip the State of any role in the economy. We will see this originate in Dunoyer's extension of classical doctrine and later result in a more or less disguised form of anarchism.[44]

There can be no question about the implicit anarchism of Comte's and Dunoyer's liberalism. Dunoyer, for example, thought that in the future the state would merely be an appendage of the market and would gradually wither and die as the market expanded.[45] Perfection would be reached when "everyone works and no one governs,"[46] and "the maintenance of public safety would no longer demand the intervention of a permanent, special force, the government to this extent disappears."[47] A colleague and fellow liberal, Augustin Thierry, echoed Dunoyer's sentiments when he wrote that "it was in losing their powers that the actions of governments [have] ameliorate[d]" and that, if given a choice between an oppressive state apparatus and "anarchy," he believed that "the excesses of the police are far more fatal than the absence of the police."[48] In Comte's words: "the less [government] makes itself felt, the more the people prosper."[49]

The anarchism of Comte and Dunoyer was dependent on their view of the evolution of societies. Like Molinari, they believed that "as we become more civilized, there is less need for police and courts."[50] The advance of *industrielisme* would dissolve the state until there was complete freedom to trade and move across national borders:

> These monstrous aggregations were formed and made necessary by the spirit of domination. The spirit of industry will dissolve them. One of its last, greatest and most salutary effects will be to municipalize the world.... Centers of actions will multiply and ultimately the vastest regions will contain but a single people composed of an infinite number of homogeneous groups bound together without confusion and without violence by the most complex and simplest of ties, the most peaceful and the most profitable of relationships.[51]

J. L. Talmon described the final stage of this gradual evolution of the industrial society of the liberals as a community where

> among themselves they would settle matters by way of contract, warranted by their own corporations and their laws and customs. Since the feudal-military-clerical State was in no position to render real assistance, but only to do harm, or worse, to extort ransom, the industrial classes developed almost a religion of non-interference by the State. Liberty became identified with the absence of government, individual freedom with isolationism. The experience of feudal-clerical rule was universalized into a philosophy teaching that *government as such is a natural enemy.*[52] (Emphasis added)

Comte and Dunoyer contributed to the *Journal des Economistes* (Dunoyer was in fact one of the founders of the *Société d'Économie Politique* in 1842), so the writings of these two theorists were well known in free trade Liberal circles.[53] Molinari acknowledged his debt to Comte in the *Dictionnaire* biography and admitted that he owed his insights into the application of economic analysis of state functions to Dunoyer.[54] A closer examination of Molinari's views will show how he adapted the insights of the political and economic anarchists to forge a new and ultimately more devastating critique of the state and its coercive monopolization of the production of security.

The above summary has attempted to show that Molinari was working within a tradition of liberal anti-statism that stretched back at least as far as the seventeenth century. The influence of Molinari's anti-statist ideas will be briefly examined in the discussion of the influence of Molinari's ideas, where it will be argued that a continuous thread of liberal anti-statist thought has existed until the present day, largely due to the pioneering work of Gustave de Molinari.[55]

Gustave de Molinari (1819-1912)

> Man appropriates to himself the sum total of elements and powers, both physical and moral, which make up his being. This appropriation is the result of an effort in discovering and recognizing these elements and powers and in their application for the satisfaction of his needs, in other words their utilization. This is self-ownership. Man appropriates and possesses himself. He also appropriates, by another effort in discovering and occupying, transforming and adapting, the earth, the material and powers of his immediate surroundings, as much as they can be appropriated. This is real and personal property. Man continually acts, under the impetus of his self-interest, to conserve and increase these elements and agents which he has appropriated in his person and in his immediate surroundings and which constitute values. He fashions them, transforms them, modifies them or exchanges them at will, as he deems it beneficial. This is liberty. Property and liberty are the two factors or components of sovereignty.
>
> What is the self-interest of the individual? It is to have absolute ownership of his person and the things that he has appropriated outside of his person, and to be able to dispose of them as he wishes. It is to be able to work alone or to freely combine his powers and other property, either wholly or in part, with that of others. It is to be able to exchange the products that he gets from the use of his private property, whether personal or real, or even to consume or conserve them. In one word, it is to possess in all its fullness "individual sovereignty."[56]

Molinari was not French by birth, for he was the son of Baron de Molinari, a former *officier supérieur* in Napoleon's Empire, who had subsequently settled in Liège as a physician. From the time of his birth on March 3, 1819, until he left Belgium for Paris in 1840, little is known of Molinari's life and upbringing. Like many others who wished to follow a *carrière de lettres*, he was attracted to Paris, the political and cultural center of the French-speaking world. As he hoped to establish himself in journalism, particularly in the new field of "economic propagandism," it is possible that he became associated with the *Société d'économie Politique* which had been established in 1842 and included in its membership some of the most active political economists in France. Like Michel Chevalier, who had already established himself as a political economist as Rossi's successor at the *Collège de France* in 1840,[57] Molinari took an early interest in the effect of railways on the industrialization which Europe was undergoing, and his first published essay dealt with that question.[58] In 1846 he became involved in the *Association pour la liberté des échanges* following a meeting of distinguished liberals in Paris at which he was invited to join the board of the newly formed association and be the *secrétaire adjoint*. Indeed, it is likely that Molinari had helped found the Paris free-trade association as it was only the second of its kind in France after Bordeaux. In addition, he became one of the editors of the association's journal, *Libre-Échange*.

In the mid-1840s, Molinari became increasingly active in the free-trade press in Paris, defending his ideas in the *Courrier français* (1846-47), the *Revue nouvelle*, *Commerce* (1848), the *Journal des Économistes* (of which he became an editor in 1847), and *La Patrie* (1849-51). He also published the first of his many books on economic and political themes. In 1846 appeared his *Études économiques: sur l'organisation de la liberté industrielle et l'abolition de l'esclavage* and, in the following year, the *Histoire du tarif: I. Les fers et les huiles; II. Les céréales.*[59] In 1848, he was commissioned to edit and annotate volume two of the *Mélanges d'Économie politique* in the *Collection des Principaux Économistes*. Molinari's most famous work appeared in 1849, *Les Soirées de la rue Saint-Lazare, entretiens sur les lois économiques et défense de la propriété*, in which he pushed to its ultimate limits his opposition to all state intervention in the economy. Arguing that the market could better satisfy the public's need for security than could the compulsory monopoly of the state, Molinari became the most consistent of the French free-trade liberal school, with his insistence that all spheres of human activity could be described and explained by economic law.

Molinari continued his argument in the October 1849 issue of the *Journal des Économistes* in the essay "De la Production de la Sécurité," which sparked a lively debate in the *Société d'Économie Politique*. Although his colleagues could not agree with his foray into economic anarchism, Molinari continued to elaborate his thesis on free-market security for fifty years until old age and pessimism overtook him. Nevertheless, Molinari must be credited with being the first person to solve the antistatists' problem of how to explain the functioning of a fully free society. Previously, anarchist or near-anarchist theorists had preferred to leave unexplained how their utopia would operate. They had simply asserted that the future society would not require a police force since mankind would no longer need protection; either there would no longer be property to steal or men would no longer want to steal, for public pressure would deter the criminal. Molinari was the first "free market proprietary anarchist"[60] who, working within the tradition of Adam Smith and the early nineteenth century French liberals Constant, Say, Comte and Dunoyer, combined antistatism with the political economist's understanding of the market and how it operated to satisfy the needs of consumers.

1. The Production of Security—1849

Molinari's most original contribution to political and economic thought is his thesis that the market can provide more cheaply and more efficiently the service of police protection of life, liberty and property. Hitherto, this had been considered to be the monopoly of the state, and it was Molinari's insight that the laws of political economy could and should be applied to the management of state functions.[61] His attempt to apply economic laws to the state led him to conclude that the market could in fact replace the state monopoly of police as well as the provision of roads, lighting, garbage collection, sewerage and education. Molinari argues, in summary, that if the market was more efficient in providing people with shoes or bread then, for exactly the same reasons, it would be better to hand over the monopoly-state functions to the market. Thus the argument is tacitly made that "proprietary anarchism"[62] is inherent in the logic of the free market and that consistency requires that one pursue the minimization of the state power to its logical conclusion, i.e., no government at all.

As far as it can be determined, Molinari's first efforts in applying the laws of political economy to the state were made in a short essay printed in the *Courrier français* in July 1846,[63] in which he likens the state to a grand mutual insurance company. In his ideal state, individuals would only form a society in order to guarantee their security from outside threats. Only those who consent to "take part in a society" would become members of the association. Only those who realized the benefits of organized society would be prepared to make the sacrifices necessary to sustain it. The individual members of the society would be required to "contribute to the maintenance of the government charged by society with the maintenance of security for the profit of all [its members]."[64] However, it is unclear whether Molinari accepted the idea that consent should be available to individuals who now compose the society (one of the major arguments of the anarchists) or whether this "act of incorporation" had taken place at one time in the past and was somehow binding on those living in the present. The latter thought seems to be implicit in this early essay, and it would not be until he published his essay "De la production de la sécurité" in 1849 that he would take the major step of abandoning the binding nature of the original social contract.

The inevitable consequence of subjecting state monopolies to the close scrutiny of political economy was to question the state's very right to have monopolies, and even to question the right of the state to exist at all. Between 1846, when he wrote "Le droit électoral," and 1849, when the result of his enquires into the nature of the state monopoly of protection was published in the *Journal des Économistes*, Molinari had been undergoing this revolution in his thought. Unfortunately, little is known about his activities during this period except for the fact that he had been giving some lectures at the *Athénée royal de Paris* in 1847 which were published in 1855 as his *Cours d'économie politique.* In the *Cours* Molinari deals at length with the problem of state monopolies, and it is possible that he felt compelled to push political economy to its logical, anarchist limits as he organized his material for the introductory lectures at the *Athénée royal.* As he rethought the role of competition in the free market and the acknowledged weakness of state-run enterprises, perhaps he was struck by the compelling logic that these universal, natural laws governing economic behavior should also apply to the state and its activities. The result was the historic 1849 essay "De la production de la sécurité."

So radical was Molinari's proposal that private, competitive insurance companies could and should replace that state for the provision of police protection of life and property, that the editor of the *Journal des Économistes*, Joseph Garnier, felt obliged to write a short defense of his decision to print the article. Although he criticized the article for "smacking of utopia in its conclusions," he praised the attempt to delineate more clearly the true function of the state, which "up till now has been treated in a haphazard manner."[65] Few political theorists then, as now, were prepared to analyze the assumptions upon which their defense of the state rested. It is to the credit of the *économistes* that at least some of then were willing to do just that and this was recognized by Garnier. Those who "exaggerated the essence and properties of government"[66] had been challenged by Molinari to justify and defend their position, and it is indeed unfortunate that more did not come to adopt his position.

The Influence of Molinari's Ideas

1. The Coincidence of Liberal Anti-statism: Herbert Spencer and Aubberon Herbert

Two years after Molinari has first proposed his theory of the "production of security," the English political philosopher, Herbert Spencer, independently pushed free-market liberalism to its anarchist limits in his book *Social Statics*.[67] Spencer argued that the state was not an "essential" institution and that it would not necessarily last forever.[68] As society progressed, government would inevitably become smaller and "decay" as voluntary market organizations replaced the coercive political institutions of the state.

Using arguments that Molinari was to borrow for his later works (especially his double work on the evolution of societies, *L'Évolution politique et la revolution* [1884] and *L'Évolution économique du XIXe siècle* [1880]), Spencer asserted that this evolution "always [tended] towards perfection...towards a complete development and a more unmixed good, subordinating in its universality all petty irregularities and fallings back, as the curvature of the earth subordinates mountains and valleys."[69]

Spencer deduced from the principle of equal liberty the individual's "right to ignore the state." In a chapter with the same name, which was deleted in later editions of *Social Statics* as Spencer drifted away from his radical anti-statism, he advocated the right of the individual to refuse to pay taxes to the state for the protection of his life and property. Spencer compared this right with the right claimed by the Dissenters to refuse to pay dues to the church and argued that if religious separation and independence was just, then this, "if consistently maintained, implies a right to ignore the state entirely."[70] By exercising their natural rights to property and uncoerced activity, the political protestant who refused to pay taxes to the state became a "voluntary outlaw" who merely had exercised his right to "drop connection with the state—to relinquish its protection and to refuse paying towards its support."[71] If the state refused to recognize this right to peacefully withdraw from the state, then "its acts must be essentially criminal."[72]

Spencer's alternative to the coercive monopoly of the state was to convert it into a "mutual-safety confederation"[73] which would provide protection to all who paid its "taxes." Those who decided to secede would be free to make their own arrangements for defense, but Spencer did not go as far as Molinari in arguing that "competing governments" would spring up to provide the security of those who withdrew. He did, however, hint that this would be the case with the statement that if,

> as was shown, every man has a right to secede from the state, and if, as a consequence, the state must be regarded as a body of men voluntarily associated, there remains nothing to distinguish it in the abstract from any other incorporated body.[74]

Spencer also hinted that this voluntary defense organization would be run on business principles. On several occasions he described it as a "mutual assurance," "insurance" or "joint-stock protection society confine[d]...to guaranteeing the rights of its members."[75] From Spencer's position it would be only a small step to the full free-market competing defense agencies as described by Molinari.

There is no evidence to connect the very similar views of the young Molinari and the young Spencer on the right of the individual to either compete with or withdraw from the monopoly of the state. In the absence of such evidence, it must be assumed that the two thinkers arrived at their positions independently of one another, suggesting that anti-statism is inherent in the logic of the free market. Both men were prepared to push their liberal ideas to their furthest logical extent, so long as they were consistent with the natural right of the individual to act freely and to enjoy the uncoerced use of his property.

Another "liberty philosopher" who was struck with the internal logic of liberty was a disciple of Herbert Spencer. Auberon Herbert was drawn to a similar anti-statist position. As he argued in 1885,

> They are...the necessary deductions from the great principle—that a man has inalienable rights over himself, over his own faculties and possessions—and those, who having once accepted this principle, who having once offered their allegiance to liberty, are prepared to follow her frankly and faithfully wherever she leads, will find, unless I am mistaken, that they are irresistibly drawn step by step to the same or to very similar conclusions.[76]

He was aware that there were few men who were prepared to "loyally submit themselves to a great principle" and accept the conclusion that "if the great principle justifies itself anywhere, it justifies itself everywhere."[77] Herbert, however, was such a man and he was prepared to go even further than Spencer in defending the right of the individual to refuse to pay taxes to a coercive government.

Like Molinari, Herbert believed that, if the market were given a chance to operate free from the restrictions of the state, "every want that we have will be satisfied by means of a voluntary combination."[78] He extended Spencer's idea of the joint-stock protection society and argued that a "system of insurance" would develop on the free market whereby "voluntary protective associations of every kind and form" would replace the monopoly of the state.[79] These protective associations would be financed by "voluntary taxes"—insurance premiums in Molinari's system—paid by those individuals who voluntarily placed themselves under the jurisdiction of each association. In this "deofficialized" fully voluntary society[80]

> the state should compel no services and exact no payments by force, but should depend entirely upon voluntary services and voluntary payments...it should be free to conduct many useful undertakings...but that it should do so in competition with all voluntary agencies, without employment of force, in dependence on voluntary payments, and acting with the consent of those concerned, simply as their friend and their adviser.[81]

The similarity of Herbert's ideas to those of Molinari is quite striking and, again, there is no evidence suggesting that he had ever read or even heard of Molinari. Neither Spencer nor Herbert went as far as Molinari's suggestion that these voluntary defense agencies would be fully professional business organizations whose prices would be determined on the market by competition. They merely limited themselves to criticizing the monopoly of the state and arguing that the individual had the right to organize freely.

Herbert faced the same problem that Molinari had with labeling his philosophy. Like Molinari, he rejected the term "anarchism," which he associated with the socialism of Proudhon and the terrorism of the "detestable bomb," even though he was quite tolerant of Tolstoy's and Benjamin Tucker's "most peaceful and reasonable forms."[82] Herbert argued that the "sane, peaceful and reasonable section of anarchists," Tucker for example, were mistaken in their rejection of "government." He argued, like Molinari, that even in a fully free society there would exist a need for protection from aggression. Any organization which provided this service was called a "government," even if it did not have monopoly; thus the protective associations of the anarchists merely provided a government decentralized "to the furthest point, [split] up into minute fragments of all sizes and shapes."[83] In Herbert's mind, a true "anarchist" wished to do away with all organized forms of protection and, since this was impossible given human nature, "anarchy, or 'no government,' is founded on a fatal mistake." Thus

> by the necessity of things, we are obliged to choose between regularly constituted government, generally accepted by all citizens for the protection of the individual, and irregularly constituted government, irregularly accepted, and taking its shape just according to the pattern of each group. Neither in the one case nor in the other case is government got rid of.[84]

However, unlike Molinari and Herbert, it has been argued in this paper that the second form of "government," the "irregularly constituted government" of Herbert and the "competitive governments" of Molinari, is in fact a new form of anarchism, since the most important aspect of the modern state, the monopoly of the use of force in a given area, is rejected in no uncertain terms by both men.

2. The Influence of Molinari on Benjamin Tucker

An (admittedly minor) figure who was probably influenced by Molinari was P. E. De Puydt. De Puydt wrote an essay in 1860 extolling the virtues of "Panarchy," a system very similar to Molinari's, where "governmental competition" would permit "as many regularly competing governments as have ever been conceived and will ever be invented" to exist simultaneously.[85] Governments would become political churches, only having jurisdiction over their congregations who had elected to become members of that particular denomination. Disputes between "governments" would be settled by "international" courts and an individual could change from one government to another, without leaving his home, by registering his decision, for a small fee, with a "Bureau of Political Membership."[86] De Puydt described his "panacea" as simply free competition in the business of government. Everyone has the right to look after his own welfare as he sees it, and to obtain security under his own conditions. On the other hand, this means progress through contest between governments forced to compete for followers. True, worldwide liberty is that which is not forced on anyone, being to each just what he wants for it; it neither suppresses nor deceives, and is always subject to a right of appeal. To bring about such a liberty, there would be no need to give up either national traditions or family ties, no need to learn to think in a new language, no need at all to cross rivers or seas, carrying the bones of one's ancestors. It is simply a matter of declaring before one's local political commission, for one to move from republic to monarchy, from representative government to autocracy, from oligarchy to democracy, or even to Mr. Proudhon's anarchy, without so much as removing one's dressing gown and slippers.[87]

Given the similarity of De Puydt's ideas to those of Molinari's and given the fact that De Puydt was familiar with the writings of the political economists,[88] it would be reasonable to conclude that De Puydt was influenced by Molinari's anti-statism, although giving it a new twist with his concept of "panarchy."

Benjamin Tucker, the American individualist anarchist, was not reluctant to call his own laissez-faire liberalism a variant of anarchism. In fact, Tucker argued that "the only true believers in laissez faire are the Anarchists"[89] and hailed Auberon Herbert as "a true anarchist in everything but name."[90] Tucker was definitely aware of Molinari's work and at least one of Molinari's books was reviewed in Tucker's magazine.[91] He shared Molinari's view that the production of security was an economic commodity which could be better supplied by the free and unhampered market, thus going beyond the criticism of Herbert and Spencer and, arguing with Molinari, that the market could offer a positive and practical alternative to state monopoly defense. These "political abolitionists"[92] argued that defense is a service like any other service; that it is labor both useful and desired, and therefore an economic commodity subject to the law of supply and demand; that in a free market this commodity would be furnished at the cost of production; that, competition prevailing, patronage would go to those who furnished the best article at the lowest price; that the production and sale of this commodity are now monopolized by the State; and that the State, like almost all monopolists, charges exorbitant prices;...and, finally, that the State exceeds all its fellow-monopolists in the extent of its villainy because it enjoys the unique privilege of compelling all people to buy its product whether they want it or not.[93]

The Modern Libertarian Movement

After the death of Molinari in 1912 and the political retirement of Tucker in 1908 when a fire destroyed his bookshop and publication office,[94] liberal anti-statism virtually disappeared until it was rediscovered by the economist Murray Rothbard in the late 1950s. As a political philosophy, it had led a precarious existence, emerging in seventeenth-century England, mixing with Smithian economic ideas in France in the early nineteenth century, and coming to an unsteady maturity simultaneously in mid-century England and France. Molinari was its most radical and original expositor and, for nearly fifty years, he defended and elaborated these ideas without assistance or support. Liberal anti-statism died out in both France and England during the twentieth century, but it was revived in the United States by a group of laissez-faire economists, Rothbard in particular,[95] who have combined a natural-law defense of property and the liberty of the individual with economic theory drawn from the Austrian rather than the classical school of economics.[96] A leading member of the Austrian school, Friedrich Hayek, who won the Nobel Prize for economics in 1974, has stated as recently as October 1976, in terms reminiscent of Molinari, that regional and local governments, limited by the same uniform laws with regard to the manner in which they could make their individual inhabitants contribute to their revenue, would develop into business-like corporations. They would compete with each other for citizens, who could "vote with their feet" for that corporation which offered the highest benefits compared with the price charged.[97]

Thus liberal anti-statism, seemingly an aberration in the development of laissez-faire and liberal ideas, has in fact been an adjunct of mainstream liberalism from its origin in the seventeenth century to the present. It is a tradition of thought which many adherents have claimed to be a logical extension of the classical liberal notions of the right to property and the freedom to exchange on the market. The importance of Molinari's contribution to this tradition was to put forward, for the first time, a theory of how the market could replace the state's monopoly of police, law courts and defense. He therefore deserves attention from scholars interested in the development of classical liberal as well as anarchist thought in order to explain, firstly, the interconnection between these two streams of thought and the rise of the modern nation-state, and, secondly, the continued interest expressed in these ideas in the present.

Notes

1. Richard Overton, "An Arrow Against All Tyrants and Tyranny, Shot from the Prison of Newgate into the Prerogative Bowels of the Arbitrary House of Lords, and all other Usurpers and Tyrants Whatsoever," in G. B. Aylmer, ed., *The Levellers in the English Revolution* (Ithaca, N.Y.: Cornell University Press, 1975), pp. 68-69. See also C. B. MacPherson, "The Levellers: Franchise and Freedom," *The Political Theory of Progressive Individualism* (Oxford: Oxford University Press, 1975), pp. 107-59.
2. Burke wrote: "the cause of artificial society is more defenseless even than that of artificial religion...the design [of this work] was to show that, without the extension of any considerable forces, the same engines which were employed for the destruction of religion might be employed with equal success for the subversion of government.... If you say that natural religion is a sufficient guide without the foreign aid or revelation, on what principle should political laws become necessary? Is not the same reason available in the theology and in politics? If the laws of nature are the laws of God, is it consistent with divine wisdom to prescribe rules to us, and leave the enforcement of them to the folly of human institutions? Will you follow truth but to a certain point?" (Edmund Burke, *A Vindication of Natural Society: Or a View of the Miseries and Evils Arising to Mankind from every Species of Artificial Society. In a Letter to Lord—by a late Nobel Writer*, in *The Works of the Right Honorable Edmund Burke* [1756; Oxford: Oxford University Press, 1906-1907], 1:53, 4, 53).
3. For the view that Burke's *Vindication of Natural Society* was not written as a satire, as is commonly believed, see Murray N. Rothbard, "A Note on Burke's *Vindication of Natural Society*," *Journal of the History of Ideas* (1958), pp. 114-18; Elie Halevy, *The Growth of Philosophical Radicalism* (London: Faber and Faber, 1952); and Isaac Kramnick, "Vindication Burke's *Vindication*," *The Rage of Edmund Burke: Portrait of an Ambivalent Conservative* (New York: Basic Books, 1977), pp. 88-93. The internal evidence suggests that Burke did not believe that he was able to state his real opinions openly because of the dangers faced by radical political theorists and other dissenting authors. "I have defended natural religion against a confederacy of atheists and divines. I now plead for natural society against politicians, and for natural reason against all three. When the world is in a fitter temper than it is at present to hear truth, or when I shall be more indifferent about its temper,

my thoughts may become more public. In the meantime, let them repose in my own bosom, and in the bosoms of such men as are fit to be initiated in the sober mysteries of truth and reason.... A man is allowed sufficient freedom of thought, provided he knows how to choose his subject properly. You may criticize freely upon the Chinese constitution, and observe with as much severity as you please upon the absurd tricks or destructive bigotry of the bonzees. But the scene is changed as you come homeward, and atheism or treason may be the names given in Britain to what would be reason and truth if asserted of China" (Burke, *A Vindication of Natural Society*, pp. 37,40-41).

4. Burke, *A Vindication of Natural Society*, p. 9. Political society he defined as "the usurpation of man" (ibid., p. 46).
5. Ibid., p. 16.
6. "I charge the whole of these effects on political society...political society is justly chargeable with much the greatest part of this destruction of the species.... I still insist in charging it to political regulations that these broils are so frequent, so cruel, and attended with consequences so deplorable" (ibid., pp. 20-21).
7. Ibid., pp. 35, 37.
8. Ibid., p. 37.
9. See the discussion of Molinari's "Production of Security" in Part II of the present essay, in the *Journal of Libertarian Studies*, no. 4.
10. Burke, *A Vindication of Natural Society*, p. 37.
11. Burke writes: "the greatest part of the governments on earth must be concluded tyrannies, impostures, violations of the natural rights of mankind, and worse than the most disorderly anarchies" (ibid., p. 28).
12. "They appointed governors over them for this reason (to defend themselves)! but a worse and more perplexing difficulty arises, how to be defended against the governors? *Quis custodiet ipsos custodes?*" (ibid., p. 37).
13. Ibid., p. 47.
14. "I am at full liberty to defend myself, or make reprisal by surprise or by cunning, or by any other way in which I may be superior to him" (ibid., p. 46).
15. "Anarchy" and "anarchic" are used in this paper in the sense of chaos, disorder and lawlessness. "Anarchism" or "anarchist," on the other hand, are used in the sense of a political theory which advocates the maximum amount of individual liberty, a necessary condition of which is the elimination of governmental or other organized force. The kind of anarchism developed by Molinari and others is not lawless or chaotic but depends on the observance of natural law and the market for the establishment of a just and peaceful economic order.
16. "I ought to appropriate such part of the fruits of the earth as by any accident comes into my possession, and is not necessary to my benefit, to the use of others; but they must obtain it from me by argument and expostulation, not by violence. It is in this principle that what is commonly called the right of property is founded. Whatever then comes into my possession, without violence to any other man, or to the institutions of society, is my property" (William Godwin, *Enquiry Concerning Political Justice and Its Influence on Modern Morals and Happiness*, ed. Isaac Kramnick [Harmondsworth: Penguin Classics, 1976], p. 199).
17. Godwin's footnote acknowledging his debt to Burke is in ibid., p. 88. See also F.E.L. Priestley's edition of *Enquiry Concerning Political Justice* (Toronto: University of Toronto Press, 1969), 3:39, 117, 125-26. Remaining references in this essay, however, are to the Kramnick edition.
18. Godwin, Enquiry Concerning Political Justice, p.408.
19. Ibid., p. 554.

20. Ibid., p. 553.
21. "It might then be sufficient for juries to recommend a certain mode of adjusting controversies, without assuming the prerogative of dictating that adjustment. It might then be sufficient for them to invite offenders to forsake their errors. If their expostulations proved, in a few instances, ineffectual, the evils arising out of this circumstance would be of less importance than those which proceed from the perpetual violation of the exercise of private judgment. But, in reality, no evils would arise: for, where the empire of reason was so universally acknowledged, the offender would either readily yield to the expostulations of authority; or, if he resisted, though suffering no personal molestation, he would feel so uneasy, under the equivocal disapprobation, and observant eye, of public judgment, as willingly to remove to a society more congenial to his errors" (ibid., pp. 553-54). On juries and the division of society into "parishes," exercising this function of social control by "banishment, " see ibid., pp. 545-46.
22. George Woodcock, *Anarchism: A History of Libertarian Ideas and Movements* (New York: Meridian, 971), p. 92.
23. Leonard P. Liggio, "Charles Dunoyer and French Classical Liberalism," *Journal of Libertarian Studies* 1, no. 3 (Summer 1977): 173. See also Elizabeth W. Schermerhorn, *Benjamin Constant: His Private Life and His Contribution to the Cause of Liberal Government in France, 1767-1830* (Boston: Houghton-Mifflin, 1924), pp. 179, 188.
24. Benjamin Constant, *Écrits et Discours politiques*. ed. O. Pozzo di Borgo (Paris: Chez Jean-Jacques Pauvert, 1964), 1:234-35; and idem, "De Godwin et de son ouvrage sur la justice politique," *Recueil d'Artides: Le Mercure t la Renommée*, ed. Ephraim Harpaz (Geneva: Droz, 1972), 1:214-26.
25. A short biographical sketch of Godwin was done for the *Dictionnaire de l'économie polilique* (ed. Coquelin and Guillaumin, 2 vols. [Paris: Guillaumin, 1852], 1:933), by Joseph Garnier, a friend and colleague of Molinari, which suggests the ideas of Godwin were known to the *économistes.*
26. Adam Smith, *The Wealth of Nations* (London: J. M. Dent and Sons, 1933), vol. 1, bk. 4, chap. 2, p. 400.
27. Adam Ferguson explained "spontaneous order" as "the result of human actions but not of human design," as quoted in F. A. Hayek, *Law, Legislation and Liberty*, 3 vols. (Chicago: University of Chicago Press, 1973-79), 1:20.
28. Smith, *Wealth of Nations*, vol. 2, bk. 4, chap. 9, p. 150.
29. "I will say that we can violate a man's property rights not only by seizing the products of his lands, capital and industry, but also by hindering him in the free use of these means of production. For the right to property as it is defined by the jurisconsults is the right to use, and even to abuse" (Jean-Baptiste Say, *Traité d'économie politique*, vol. 9, *Collections des Principaux Économistes*, ed. Horace Say (1841; reprint ed., Onsbruck: Otto Zeller, 1966), p. 134.
30. J.-B. Say describes slavery as that "which thus violates the most indisputable of properties" (ibid., p. 13). On conscription: "It is the most scandalous violation of property and of all natural rights" *(Cours d'économie politique*, vols. 10 and 11, *Collections des Principaux Économistes*, 11:64).
31. "Taxes, even when authorized by the public, are a violation of property…a theft" (J.-B. Say, *Traité d'économie politique*, p. 136).
32. J.-B. Say, *Cours d'économie politique*, 11:514.
33. J.-B. Say: "force never constitutes a right, even when it commands obedience" (ibid., 11:273).
34. Ibid., 10:555.

35. J.-B. Say, *Traité d'économie politique*, p. 198.
36. Ibid., p. 135.
37. "Under free competition, the better an industrious man defends his own interests, the better he serves the national wealth. The meddling interference of authority cannot comprehend these interests any better than the individual. Each regulation is fatal, because it can never take the place of the intelligence of producers and it hinders their actions, the principal means of their successes" (J .-B. Say, *Cours d'économie politique*, 10:555). For a modern statement of this argument, see Hayek, "Economics and Knowledge," *Individualism and Economic Order* (Chicago: Henry Regnery, 1972).
38. J.-B. Say, *Cours d'économie politique*, 11:62. "We see that it is not impossible to introduce into public service the principle of free competition from which we have reaped such happy consequences in productive activities" (ibid., 11:227).
39. J.-B Say, *Traité d'économie politique*, p. 222. The quote is from Smith, *Wealth of Nations*, vol. 2, bk. 4, chap. 7, p. 206ff., and can be found in the appendix to this essay, *Journal of Libertarian Studies* 6, no. 1.
40. "If equity commands that consumption be paid for by those who have enjoyed it, then in this respect the best administered countries are those where each class supports the cost of public expenses to the extent that they have benefited from them" (J.-B Say, *Traité d'économie politique*, p. 501).
41. "The price of goods based upon a monopoly is, by virtue of this privilege, higher than its cost of production and is to that extent an assault upon the property of the buyer. A tax which is raised higher than the cost necessary to procure the taxpayer the security he desires is likewise an assault upon the property of the taxpayer" (J .-B. Say, *Cours d'économie politique*, 11:389).
42. "Smith wished to have civil suits paid for by the parties involved. This idea would be even more practical if judgments were made not by officially chosen tribunals but by arbiters chosen by the parties from among those men singled out by public confidence. If these arbiters, acting as a jury of equity, were paid in proportion to the sum in dispute without regard to the length of the proceeding, they would be motivated to simplify and shorten the procedure in order to save their own time and to judge fairly in order to assure their continued employment" (J.-B. Say, *Traité d'économie politique*, pp. 501-502). "Arbiters would be paid by the parties, or perhaps by the losing party only, according to the importance of the interests in question not of the length of the trial. The parties would or would not employ the services of lawyers and advocates as they pleased. Thus, the honorarium of the judge would be composed: (1) of a fixed sum for each province, a very moderate sum paid simply to have a man keep himself at the disposition of the public, (2) an *ad hoc* premium when he is called to be an arbiter, and (3) an honorarium proportional to the value in dispute, payable after judgment" (J.-B. Say, *Cours d' économie politique*, 11:267-77).
43. Ibid., 11:276.
44. Albert Schatz, *L'Individualisme économique et sociale: Ses origines, son évolution, ses formes contemporaines* (Paris: Librairie Armand Colin, 1907), p. 197.
45. In a well ordered state, the government ought to be nothing more than an aid to production, a commission charged and paid for by producers to look after the safety of their persons and property while they work and to guard them against all parasites" (Charles Dunoyer, *Censeur européen*, 2:102; quoted in Edgar Allix, "La Déformation de l'économie politique liberale après J.-B. Say.: Charles Dunoyer," *Revue d'histoire des doctrines économiques et sociales* [1911], p. 118). Schatz observed of Dunoyer's ideas: "In this view, the functions of government would requite only a small number of agents. The mass of workers would remain available to increase

the sum of social utilities other than security. It is appropriate therefore to reduce the number of both public functions and public functionaries, employing the only effective means which is the reduction of their profits or salaries. The title of the company charged with the public safety is of little importance, be it monarchy or republic, provided that it costs little and does not interfere, and that it progressively realizes the ideal of a society so perfectly educated that the government might disappear altogether leaving the people to the full enjoyment of their time, their income and their liberty" (Schatz, *L'Individualisme*, pp. 210-11). Molinari was to show in *Les Soirées de la rue Saint-Lazare* (Paris: Guillaumin, 1849) that there was no need to assume that society or individuals would become progressively more educated before society could do without government monopoly security.

46. Dunoyer, *Censeur européen*, 2:102, quoted in Allix, "La Déformaltion de l'économie politique," p. 119.
47. Ibid., 7:92, quoted in Allix, "La Deformation de I'economie politique," p. 119.
48. Thierry, *Censeur européen*, 8:230, 241, quoted in Mark Weinburg, "The Social Analysis of Three Early 19th Century French liberals: Say, Comte, and Dunoyer," *Journal of Libertarian Studies* 2, no. 1 (Winter 1978): 54.
49. Charles Comte, *Traité de legislation*, 1:448,quoted in Weinburg, "The Social Analysis," p. 57.
50. Dunoyer, *Oeuvres de Charles Dunoyer* (Paris: Guillaumin, 1886), 1:297, quoted in Allix, "La Deformation de l'économie politique," p. 131.
51. Dunoyer, *L'lndustrie et la morale, considérées dans leurs rapports avec la liberté* (Paris: A. Sautelet, 1825), pp. 366-67.
52. J. L. Talmon, *Political Messianism: The Romantic Phase* (London: Seckar & Warburg, 1960), pp. 48-50, quoted in Liggio, "Charles Dunoyer and French Classical Liberalism," p. 171.
53. "Dunoyer," *Supplement du Nouveau Dictionnaire de l'éeonomie politique de M. Leon Say et Joseph Chailley-Bert* (Paris: Guillaumin, 1897), pp. 142-44; Obituary of Dunoyer, *Journal des Économistes* (henceforth *JDE*), 2nd ser. 36 (October-December 1862): 442. Gustave de Molinari wrote the biographical study of Charles Comte for the *Dictionnaire*, 1:446-47.
54. Molinari, *Cours d'économie politique*. 2nd ed. rev. and enl., 2 vols. (1855; Paris, Guillaumin, 1863), 1:186.
55. See Part II of the present essay, in *Journal of Libertarian Studies* 6, no. 1.
56. Molinari, *L'Evolution politique et la révolution* (Paris: C. Reinwald, 1884), p. 394.
57. See Emile Levasseur's address to the "Quarantieme anniversaire de la fondation de la Socciété Économie politique," *JDE*, 4th ser., 20 (1882), p. 297.
58. Molinari, "L'avenir des chemins de fer" (1843), first published in *La Nation*, then in *La Gazzette de France.*
59. This was the first of Molinari's books to be published by the great liberal publisher Guillaumin, who was to publish many of his later works and under whose impress appeared a large number of important and influential liberal works throughout the nineteenth century.
60. See Laurence S. Moss, "Private Property Anarchism: An American Variant," in *Further Explorations in the Theory of Anarchism* (Blacksburg, Va.: University Publications, 1974).
61. "We have been accustomed to believing that government—charged with a sublime mission—has nothing in common in its establishment and functioning with the multitude of other enterprises. Similarly, no one has ever thought that the laws which apply to it are the same as those which apply to the others" (Molinari, *Cours d'économie politique*, 2nd ed. rev. and enl., 2 vols. [1855; Paris: Guillaumin, 1863], 2:515, 521).

62. It will be argued in section 2, which follows, that there are two main kinds of anarchist thought: "left-wing" communist anarchism which denies the right of an individual to seek profit, charge rent or interest and to own property, and "right-wing" proprietary anarchism, which vigorously defends these rights.
63. Molinari, "Le droit électoral," *Courrier français*. July 23, 1846, reprinted in "La liberté de governement II," *Questions d'économie politique et de droit public*, 2 vols. (Brussels; Lacroix; Paris: Guillaumin. 1861), Set. 3.
64. Ibid.
65. Molinari, "De la production de la securite," *Journal des Économists* (henceforth *JDE*) 21 (1849): 277, n. 1. Reprinted in Molinari, *Questions d'économie politique*, 1:245; translated by J. Huston McCulloch. "The Production of Security," *Occasional Paper Series #2* (New York: Center for Libertarian Studies, 1977).
66. Ibid.
67. Herbert Spencer, *Social Statics* (1851; New York: Robert Schalkenbach Foundation, 1970).
68. Ibid., p. 13.
69. Ibid., p. 263.
70. Ibid., p. 191.
71. Ibid., p. 185.
72. Ibid., p. 189.
73. Ibid., p. 185.
74. Ibid., p. 224.
75. Ibid., pp. 241, 247.
76. Auberon Herbert, "The Right and Wrong of Compulsion by the State," in *The Right and Wrong of Compulsion of the State, and Other Essays*, ed. Eric Mack (Indianapolis, Ind.: Liberty Classics, 1978), pp. 176-77. Molinari did become aware of Auberon Herbert's views well after he had developed his free-market anarchism. Herbert's book, *A Politician in Trouble about His Soul*, was reviewed by Yves Guyot in the *Journal des Économists*, 4th ser. 30 (1885):246. In addition, many of Spencer's books were translated into French and reviewed in the *Journal des Économistes*, but, surprisingly, not *Social Statics*.
77. Herbert, "The Right and Wrong," pp. 177, 178.
78. Ibid., p. 185. Herbert argues for "Friendly voluntary cooperation, as free men and women, for all public wants and services" ("Mr. Spencer and the Great Machine," in *The Right and Wrong*, p. 303).
79. Herbert, "The Right and Wrong," pp. 186-88.
80. Herbert, "The Principles of Voluntaryism and Free Life," in *The Right and Wrong*, p. 378.
81. Ibid., p. 390.
82. Herbert, "Mr. Spencer," p. 311.
83. Herbert, "The Principles of Voluntaryism," p. 383.
84. Ibid.
85. P. E. De Puydt, "Panarchy," trans. Adrian Falk, in *An A.B.C. Against Nuclear War*, ed. John Zube (Berrima, N.S.W.: Peace Plans, 1975), p. 229; reprinted from *Revue Trimestrielle* (Brussels, July 1860).
86. "If a disagreement came about between subjects of different governments, or between one government and a subject of another, it would simply be a matter of observing the principles heretofore observed between neighboring peaceful states. Anything else would be the business of common courts of justice" (ibid., p. 227).
87. Ibid.

88. "It is from the works of the economists that I have derived the principle whereof I propose a new application, still farther reaching and no less logical than all others" (ibid., p. 223). It is most likely that De Puydt was aware of Molinari because Molinari was at that time living and teaching in Belgium and De Puydt quotes from a work of Charles de Brouckere, who had arranged for Molinari to teach at the Musee royal, the *Principes generaux d'économie politique* (1851). See also the obituary of de Brouckere, *Journal des Économistes*, 2nd ser. 26 (April-June 1860):265.
89. Benjamin R. Tucker, *Instead of a Book by a Man Too Busy to Write One: A Fragmentary Exposition of Philosophical Anarchism* (1897; New York: Haskell House, 1969), p. 371.
90. *Liberty* 15 (December 1906):16; quoted in Mack, *The Right and Wrong*, p.20.
91. Review of *The Society of Tomorrow* (1904), the English translation of Molinari's *Esquisse de L'organisation politique et économique de société future* (1899), in *Liberty* 14 (September 1904):2. Albert Schatz, the French historian of individualism, was struck by the similarity of Tucker's and Molinari's rejection of the state's monopoly of security. See his *L'Individualisme économique et social: Ses origines, son évolution, ses formes contemporaines* (Paris: Librairie Armand Colin, 1907), p. 514.
92. Tucker, *Instead of a Book*, p. 54.
93. Ibid., pp. 32-33, 14.
94. James J. Martin, *Men Against the State: The Expositors of Individualist Anarchism in America, 1827-1846* (Colorado Springs, Colo.: Ralph Myles, 1970), p. 273.
95. Murray N. Rothbard, *Man, Economy and State: A Treatise on Economic Principles* (Los Angeles: Nash Publishing, 1970), 2:884; idem, *Power and Market: Government and the Economy* (Menlo Park, Calif.: Institute for Humane Studies, 1910), esp. chap. 1, "Defense Services on the Free Market," pp. 1-7; and idem, *For a New Liberty: The Libertarian Manifesto* (rev. ed., New York: Collier Macmillan, 1978), esp. chap. 12, "The Public Sector, Ill: Police, Law and the Courts," pp. 215-4l.
96. See also Jarrett B. Wollstein, *Society without Coercion: A New Concept of Social Organization* (Society for Rational Individualism, 1969); reprinted in *Society without Government, The Right Wing Individualist Tradition in America*, ed. Murray N. Rothbard and Jerome Tuccille (New York: Arno Press and the New York Times, 1972); Morris and Linda Tannehill, *The Market for Liberty* (Lansing, Mich.: n.p., 1970); and Richard and Ernestine Perkins, *Precondition for Peace and Prosperity: Rational Anarchy* (Ontario: Phibbs, 1871). For a non-Austrian, neo-classical approach to the same concept, see David Friedman, *The Machinery of Freedom: Guide to a Radical Capitalism* (New York: Harper Colophon, 1973). For a discussion of market orders, economic and legal, see F. A. Hayek's magnum opus, *Law, Legislation and Liberty*, vol. I, *Rules and Order* (Chicago: University of Chicago Press, 1913); Bruno Leoni, *Freedom and the Law* (Los Angeles: Nash Publishing, 1972); and Lon Fuller, *The Morality of the Law* (New Haven: Yale University Press, 1964).
97. Hayek, "Whither Democracy," lecture given before the Institute of Public Affairs, Sydney, October 8, 1976, in *Social Justice, Socialism and Democracy: Three Australian Lectures* (Sydney: Centre for Independent Studies, 1979).

25

Vindication of Natural Society (excerpt)

Edmund Burke

I now come to shew, that Political Society is justly chargeable with much the greatest Part of this Destruction of the Species. To give the fairest Play to every side of the Question, I will own that there is a Haughtiness, and Fierceness in human Nature, which will cause innumerable Broils, place Men in what Situation you please; but owning this, I still insist in charging it to political Regulations, that these Broils are so frequent, so cruel, and attended with Consequences so deplorable. In a State of Nature, it had been impossible to find a Number of Men, sufficient for such Slaughters, agreed in the same bloody Purpose; or allowing that they might have come to such an Agreement, (an impossible Supposition) yet the Means that simple Nature has supplied them with, are by no means adequate to such an End; many Scratches, many Bruises undoubtedly would be received upon all hands; but only a few, a very few Deaths. Society, and Politicks, which have given us these destructive Views, have given us also the Means of satisfying them. From the earliest Dawnings of Policy to this Day, the Invention of Men has been sharpening and improving the Mystery of Murder, from the first rude Essays of Clubs and Stones, to the present Perfection of Gunnery, Cannoneering, Bombarding, Mining, and all these Species of artificial, learned, and refined Cruelty, in which we are now so expert, and which make a principal Part of what Politicians have taught us to believe is our principal Glory.[1]

How far mere Nature would have carried us, we may judge by the Examples of those Animals, who still follow her Laws, and even of those to whom she has given Dispositions more fierce, and Arms more terrible than ever she intended we should use. It is an incontestable Truth, that there is more Havock made in one Year by Men, of Men, than has been made by all the Lions, Tygers, Panthers, Ounces, Leopards, Hyenas, Rhinoceroses, Elephants, Bears, and Wolves, upon their several Species, since the Beginning of the World; though these agree ill enough with each other, and have a much greater Proportion of Rage and Fury in their Composition than we have. But with respect to you, ye Legislators, ye Civilizers of Mankind! ye Orpheuses, Moseses, Minoses, Solons, Theseuses, Lycurguses, Numas![2] with Respect to you be it spoken, your Regulations have done more Mischief in cold Blood, than all the Rage of the fiercest Animals in their greatest Terrors, or Furies, have ever done, or ever could do!

These Evils are not accidental. Whoever will take the pains to consider the Nature of Society, will find they result directly from its Constitution. For as Subordination, or in other Words, the Reciprocation of Tyranny, and Slavery, is requisite to support these Societies, the Interest, the Ambition, the Malice, or the Revenge, nay even the Whim and Caprice of one ruling Man among them, is enough to arm all the rest, without any private Views of their own, to the worst and blackest Purposes; and what is at once lamentable and ridiculous, these Wretches engage under those Banners with a Fury greater than if they were animated by Revenge for their own proper Wrongs.

It is no less worth observing, that this artificial Division of Mankind, into separate Societies, is a perpetual Source in itself of Hatred and Dissention among them. The Names which distinguish them are enough to blow up Hatred, and Rage. Examine History; consult present Experience; and you will find, that far the greater Part of the Quarrels between several Nations, had scarce any other Occasion, than that these Nations were different Combinations of People, and called by different Names;—to an Englishman, the Name of a Frenchman, a Spaniard, an Italian, much more a Turk, or a Tartar, raise of course Ideas of Hatred, and Contempt. If you would inspire this Compatriot of ours with Pity or Regard, for one of these, would you not hide that Distinction? You would not pray him to compassionate the poor Frenchman, or the unhappy German. Far from it; you would speak of him as a Foreigner, an Accident to which all are liable. You would represent him as a Man: one partaking with us of the same common Nature, and subject to the same Law. There is something so averse from our Nature in these artificial political Distinctions, that we need no other Trumpet to kindle us to War, and Destruction. But there is something so benign and healing in the general Voice of Humanity, that maugre all our Regulations to prevent it, the simple Name of Man applied properly, never fails to work a salutary Effect.

This natural unpremediated Effect of Policy on the unpossessed Passions of Mankind, appears on other Occasions. The very Name of a Politician, a Statesman, is sure to cause Terror and Hatred; it has always connected with it the Ideas of Treachery, Cruelty, Fraud and Tyranny; and those Writers who have faithfully unveiled the Mysteries of State-freemasonry, have ever been held in general Detestation, for even knowing so perfectly a Theory so detestable. The Case of Machiavelli seems at first sight something hard in that Respect. He is obliged to bear the Iniquities of those whose Maxims and Rules of Government he published. His Speculation is more abhorred than their Practice.

But if there were no other Arguments against artificial Society than this I am going to mention, methinks it ought to fall by this one only. All Writers on the Science of Policy are agreed, and they agree with Experience, that all Governments must frequently infringe the Rules of Justice to support themselves; that Truth must give way to Dissimulation; Honesty to Convenience; and Humanity itself to the reigning Interest.[3] The Whole of this Mystery of Iniquity is called the Reason of State. It is a Reason, which I own I cannot penetrate. What Sort of a Protection is this of the general Right, that is maintained by infringing the Rights of Particulars? What sort of Justice is this, which is inforced by Breaches of its own Laws? These Paradoxes I leave to be solved by the able heads of Legislators and Politicians. For my part, I say what a plain Man would say on such an Occasion. I can never believe, that any Institution agreeable to Nature, and proper for Mankind, could find it necessary, or even expedient in any Case whatsoever to do, what the best and worthiest Instincts of Mankind warn us to avoid. But no wonder, that what is set up in Opposition to the State of Nature, should preserve itself by trampling upon the Law of Nature.

To prove, that these Sort of policed Societies are a Violation offered to Nature, and a Constraint upon the human Mind, it needs only to look upon the sanguinary Measures, and Instruments of Violence which are every where used to support them. Let us take a Review of the Dungeons, Whips, Chains, Racks, Gibbets, with which every Society is abundantly stored, by which hundreds of Victims are annually offered up to support a dozen or two in Pride and Madness, and Millions in an abject Servitude, and Dependence. There was a Time, when I looked with a reverential Awe on these Mysteries of Policy; but Age, Experience, and Philosophy have rent the Veil; and I view this Sanctum Sanctorum, at least, without any enthusiastick Admiration. I acknowledge indeed, the Necessity of such a Proceeding in such Institutions; but I must have a very mean Opinion of Institutions where such Proceedings are necessary.

It is a Misfortune, that in no Part of the Globe natural Liberty and natural Religion are to be found pure, and free from the Mixture of political Adulterations. Yet we have implanted in us by Providence Ideas, Axioms, Rules, of what is pious, just, fair, honest, which no political Craft, nor learned Sophistry, can entirely expel from our Breasts. By these we judge, and we cannot otherwise judge of the several artificial Modes of Religion and Society, and determine of them as they approach to, or recede from this Standard.

The simplest form of Government is Despotism, where all the inferior Orbs of Power are moved merely by the Will of the Supreme, and all that are subjected to them, directed in the same Manner, merely by the occasional Will of the Magistrate. This Form, as it is the most simple, so it is infinitely the most general. Scarce any Part of the World is exempted from its Power. And in those few Places where Men enjoy what they call Liberty, it is continually in a tottering Situation, and makes greater and greater Strides to that Gulph of Despotism which at last swallows up every Species of Government. This Manner of ruling being directed merely by the Will of the weakest, and generally the worst Man in the Society, becomes the most foolish and capricious Thing, at the same time that it is the most terrible and destructive that well can be conceived. In a Despotism the principal Person finds, that let the Want, Misery, and Indigence of his Subjects, be what they will, he can yet possess abundantly of every thing to gratify his most insatiable Wishes. He does more. He finds that these Gratifications increase in proportion to the Wretchedness and Slavery of his Subjects. Thus encouraged both by Passion and Interest to trample on the publick Welfare, and by his Station placed above both Shame and Fear, he proceeds to the most horrid and shocking Outrages upon Mankind. Their Persons become Victims of his Suspicions. The slightest Displeasure is Death; and a disagreeable Aspect is often as great a Crime as High-treason. In the court of Nero a Person of Learning, of unquestioned Merit, and of unsuspected Loyalty, was put to Death for no other Reason than that he had a pedantick Countenance which displeased the Emperor.[4] This very Monster of Mankind appeared in the Beginning of his Reign to be a Person of Virtue. Many of the greatest Tyrants on the Records of History have begun their Reigns in the fairest Manner. But the Truth is, this unnatural Power corrupts both the Heart, and the Understanding. And to prevent the least Hope of Amendment, a King is ever surrounded by a Crowd of infamous Flatterers, who find their Account in keeping him from the least Light of Reason, till all Ideas of Rectitude and Justice are utterly erased from his Mind. When Alexander had in his Fury inhumanly butchered one of his best Friends, and bravest Captains; on the Return of Reason he began to conceive an Horror suitable to the Guilt of such a Murder. In this Juncture, his Council came to his Assistance. But what did his Council? They found him out a Philosopher who gave him Comfort. And in what Manner did this Philosopher comfort him for the Loss of such a Man, and heal his Conscience, flagrant with the Smart of such a Crime? You have the Matter at Length in Plutarch. He told him, "that let a Sovereign do what he will, all his actions are just and lawful, because they are his."[5] The Palaces of all Princes abound with such courtly Philosophers. The Consequence was such as might be expected. He grew every Day a Monster more abandoned to unnatural Lust, to Debauchery, to Drunkenness, and to Murder. And yet this was originally a great Man, of uncommon Capacity, and a strong Propensity to Virtue. But unbounded Power proceeds Step by Step, until it has eradicated every laudable Principle. It has been remarked, that there is no Prince so bad, whose Favourites and Ministers are not worse. There is hardly any Prince without a Favourite, by whom he is governed in as arbitrary a Manner as he governs the Wretches subjected to him. Here the Tyranny is doubled. There are two Courts, and two Interests; both very different from the Interests of the People. The Favourite knows that the Regard of a Tyrant is as unconstant and capricious as that of a Woman; and concluding his Time to be short, he makes haste to fill up the Measure of his Iniquity, in Rapine, in Luxury, and in Revenge. Every Avenue to the Throne is shut up. He oppresses, and ruins the People, whilst he persuades the Prince, that those Murmurs raised by his own Oppression are the Effects of Disaffection to the Prince's Government. Then is the natural Violence of Despotism inflamed, and aggravated by Hatred and Revenge. To deserve well of the State is a Crime against the Prince. To be popular, and to be a Traitor, are considered as synonimous Terms. Even Virtue is dangerous, as an aspiring Quality, that claims an Esteem by itself, and independent of the Countenance of the Court. What has been said of the chief, is true of the inferior Officers of this Species of Government; each in his Province exercising the same Tyranny, and grinding the People by an Oppression, the more severely felt, as it is near them, and exercised by base and subordinate Persons. For the Gross of the People; they are considered as a mere Herd of Cattle; and really in a little Time become no better; all Principle of honest Pride, all Sense of the Dignity of their Nature, is lost in their Slavery. The Day, says Homer, which makes a Man a Slave, takes away half his Worth;[6] and in fact, he loses every Impulse to Action, but that low and base one of Fear. In this kind of Government human Nature is not only abused and insulted, but it is actually degraded and sunk into a Species of Brutality. The Consideration of this made Mr. Locke say, with great Justice, that a Government of this kind was worse than Anarchy; indeed it is so abhorred, and detested by all who live under Forms that have a milder Appearance, that there is scarce a rational Man in Europe, that would not prefer Death to Asiatick Despotism. Here then we have the Acknowledgement of a great Philosopher, that an irregular State of Nature is preferable to such a Government; we have the Consent of all sensible and generous Men, who carry it yet further, and avow that Death itself is preferable; and yet this Species of Government,[7] so justly condemned, and so generally detested, is what infinitely the greater Part of Mankind groan under, and have groaned under from the Beginning. So that by sure and uncontested Principles, the greatest Part of the Governments on Earth must be concluded Tyrannies, Impostures, Violations of the Natural Rights of Mankind, and worse than the most disorderly Anarchies. How much other Forms exceed this, we shall consider immediately.

In all Parts of the World, Mankind, however debased, retains still the Sense of Feeling; the Weight of Tyranny, at last, becomes insupportable; but the Remedy is not so easy; in general, the only Remedy by which they attempt to cure the Tyranny, is to change the Tyrant. This is, and always was the Case for the greater Part. In some Countries however, were found Men of more Penetration; who discovered, "*that to live by one Man's Will, was the Cause of all Men's Misery*."[8] They therefore changed their former Method, and assembling the Men in their several Societies, the most respectable for their Understanding and Fortunes, they confided to them the Charge of the publick Welfare. This originally formed what is called an Aristocracy. They hoped, it would be impossible that such a Number could ever join in any Design against the general Good; and they promised themselves a great deal of Security and Happiness, from the united Counsels of so many able and experienced Persons. But it is now found by abundant Experience, that an Aristocracy, and a Despotism, differ but in Name; and that a People, who are in general excluded from any Share of the Legislative, are to all Intents and Purposes, as much Slaves, when twenty, independent of them, govern, as when but one domineers. The Tyranny is even more felt, as every Individual of the Nobles has the Haughtiness of a Sultan; the People are more miserable, as they seem on the Verge of Liberty, from which they are for ever debarred, this fallacious Idea of Liberty, whilst it presents a vain Shadow of Happiness to the Subject, binds faster the Chains of his Subjection. What is left undone, by the natural Avarice and Pride of those who are raised above the others, is compleated by their Suspicions, and their Dread of losing an Authority, which has no Support in the common Utility of the Nation. A Genoese, or a Venetian Republick, is a concealed Despotism; where you find the same Pride of the Rulers, the same base Subjection of the People, the same bloody Maxims of a suspicious Policy. In one respect the Aristocracy is worse than the Despotism. A Body Politick, whilst it retains its Authority, never changes its Maxims; a Despotism, which is this Day horrible to a Supreme Degree, by the Caprice natural to the Heart of Man, may, by the same Caprice otherwise exerted, be as lovely the next; in a Succession, it is possible to meet with some good Princes. If there have been Tiberiuses, Caligulas, Neros, there have been likewise the serener Days of Vespasians, Tituses, Trajans, and Antonines;[9] but a Body Politick is not influenced by Caprice or Whim; it proceeds in a regular Manner; its Succession is insensible; and every Man as he enters it, either has, or soon attains the Spirit of the whole Body. Never was it known, that an Aristocracy, which was haughty and tyrannical in one Century, became easy and mild in the next. In effect, the Yoke of this Species of Government is so galling, that whenever the People have got the least Power, they have shaken it off with the utmost Indignation, and established a popular Form. And when they have not had Strength enough to support themselves, they have thrown themselves into the Arms of Despotism, as the more eligible of the two Evils. This latter was the Case of Denmark, who sought a Refuge from the Oppression of its Nobility, in the strong Hold of arbitrary Power. Poland has at present the Name of Republick, and it is one of the Aristocratick Form; but it is well known, that the little Finger of this Government, is heavier than the Loins of arbitrary Power in most Nations. The People are not only politically, but personally Slaves, and treated with the utmost Indignity. The Republick of Venice is somewhat more moderate; yet even here, so heavy is the Aristocratick Yoke, that the Nobles have been obliged to enervate the Spirit of their Subjects by every Sort of Debauchery; they have denied them the Liberty of Reason, and they have made them amends, by what a base Soul will think a more valuable Liberty, by not only allowing, but encouraging them to corrupt themselves in the most scandalous Manner. They consider their Subjects, as the Farmer does the Hog he keeps to feast upon. He holds him fast in his Stye, but allows him to wallow as much as he pleases in his beloved Filth and Gluttony. So scandalously debauched a People as that of Venice, is to be met with no where else. High, Low, Men, Women, Clergy, and Laity, are all alike. The ruling Nobility are no less afraid of one another, than they are of the People; and for that Reason, politically enervate their own Body by the same effeminate Luxury, by which they corrupt their Subjects. They are impoverished by every Means which can be invented; and they are kept in a perpetual Terror by the Horrors of a State-inquisition; here you see a People deprived of all rational Freedom, and tyrannized over by about two thousand Men; and yet this Body of two thousand, are so far from enjoying any Liberty by the Subjection of the rest, that they are in an infinitely severer State of Slavery; they make themselves the most degenerate, and unhappy of Mankind, for no other Purpose than that they may the more effectually contribute to the Misery of an whole Nation. In short, the regular and methodical Proceedings of an Aristocracy, are more intolerable than the very Excesses of a Despotism, and in general, much further from any Remedy.

Thus, my Lord, we have pursued Aristocracy through its whole Progress; we have seen the Seeds, the Growth, and the Fruit. It could boast none of the Advantages of a Despotism, miserable as those Advantages were, and it was overloaded with an Exuberance of Mischiefs, unknown even to Despotism itself. In effect, it is no more than a disorderly Tyranny. This Form therefore could be little approved even in Speculation, by those who were capable of thinking, and could be less borne in Practice by any who were capable of feeling. However, the fruitful Policy of Man was not yet exhausted. He had yet another Farthing-candle to supply the Deficiencies of the Sun. This was the third Form, known by political Writers under the Name of Democracy. Here the People transacted all publick Business, or the greater Part of it, in their own Persons: their Laws were made by themselves, and upon any Failure of Duty, their Officers were accountable to themselves, and to them only. In all appearance, they had secured by this Method the Advantages of Order and good Government, without paying their Liberty for the Purchace. Now, my Lord, we are come to the Master-piece of Grecian Refinement, and Roman Solidity, a popular Government. The earliest and most celebrated Republic of this Model, was that of Athens. It was constructed by no less an Artist, than the celebrated Poet and Philosopher, Solon.[10] But no sooner was this political Vessel launched from the Stocks, than it overset, even in the Lifetime of the Builder. A Tyranny immediately supervened;[11] not by a foreign Conquest, not by Accident, but by the very Nature and Constitution of a Democracy. An artful Man became popular, the People had Power in their Hands, and they devolved a considerable Share of their Power upon their Favourite; and the only Use he made of this Power, was to plunge those who gave it into Slavery. Accident restored their Liberty, and the same good Fortune produced Men of uncommon Abilities and uncommon Virtues amongst them. But these Abilities were suffered to be of little Service either to their Possessors or to the State. Some of these Men, for whose Sakes alone we read their History, they banished; others they imprisoned; and all they treated with various Circumstances of the most shameful Ingratitude. Republicks have many Things in the Spirit of absolute Monarchy, but none more than this; a shining Merit is ever hated or suspected in a popular Assembly, as well as in a Court; and all Services done the State, are looked upon as dangerous to the Rulers, whether Sultans or Senators. The Ostracism at Athens was built upon this Principle. The giddy People, whom we have now under consideration, being elated with some Flashes of Success, which they owed to nothing less than any Merit of their own, began to tyrannize over their Equals, who had associated with them for their common Defence. With their Prudence they renounced all Appearance of Justice. They entered into Wars rashly and wantonly. If they were unsuccessful, instead of growing wiser by their Misfortune, they threw the whole Blame of their own Misconduct on the Ministers who had advised, and the Generals who had conducted those Wars; until by degrees they had cut off all who could serve them in their Councils or their Battles. If at any time these Wars had an happier Issue, it was no less difficult to deal with them on account of their Pride and Insolence. Furious in their Adversity, tyrannical in their Successes, a Commander had more Trouble to concert his Defence before the People, than to plan the Operations of the Campaign. It was not uncommon for a General, under the horrid Despotism of the Roman Emperors, to be ill received in proportion to the Greatness of his Services. Agricola is a strong Instance of this. No Man had done greater Things, nor with more honest Ambition. Yet on his Return to Court, he was obliged to enter Rome with all the Secrecy of a Criminal. He went to the Palace, not like a victorious Commander who had merited and might demand the greatest Rewards, but like an Offender who had come to supplicate a Pardon for his Crimes. His Reception was answerable: "Brevi osculo, & nullo sermone exceptus, turbæ servientium immistus est."[12] Yet in that worse Season of this worst of monarchical* Tyrannies, Modesty, Discretion, and a Coolness of Temper, formed some kind of Security even for the highest Merit. But at Athens, the nicest and best studied Behaviour was not a sufficient Guard for a Man of great Capacity. Some of their bravest Commanders were obliged to fly their Country, some to enter into the Service of its Enemies, rather than abide a popular Determination of their Conduct, lest, as one of them said, their Giddiness might make the People condemn where they meant to acquit; to throw in a black Bean, even when they intended a white one.

* *Sciant quibus moris illicita mirari, posse etiam sub malis principibus magnos viros, etc. See 42 to the End of it.*[13]

The Athenians made a very rapid Progress to the most enormous Excesses. The People under no Restraint soon grew dissolute, luxurious, and idle. They renounced all Labour, and began to subsist themselves from the publick Revenues. They lost all Concern for their common Honour or Safety, and could bear no Advice that tended to reform them. At this time Truth became offensive to those Lords the People, and most highly dangerous to the Speaker. The Orators no longer ascended the Rostrum, but to corrupt them further with the most fulsome Adulation. These Orators were all bribed by foreign Princes on the one Side or the other. And besides its own Parties, in this City there were Parties, and avowed ones too, for the Persians, Spartans, and Macedonians, supported each of them by one or more Demagogues pensioned and bribed to this iniquitous Service. The People, forgetful of all Virtue and publick Spirit, and intoxicated with the Flatteries of their Orators (these Courtiers of Republicks, and endowed with the distinguishing Characteristicks of all other Courtiers) this People, I say, at last arrived at that Pitch of Madness, that they coolly and deliberately, by an express Law, made it capital for any Man to propose an Application of the immense Sums squandered in publick Shows, even to the most necessary Purposes of the State. When you see the People of this Republick banishing or murdering their best and ablest Citizens, dissipating the publick Treasure with the most senseless Extravagance, and spending their whole Time, as Spectators or Actors, in playing, fiddling, dancing, and singing, does it not, my Lord, strike your Imagination with the Image of a sort of a complex Nero? And does it not strike you with the greater Horror, when you observe, not one Man only, but a whole City, grown drunk with Pride and Power, running with a Rage of Folly into the same mean and senseless Debauchery and Extravagance? But if this People resembled Nero in their Extravagance, much more did they resemble and even exceed him in Cruelty and Injustice. In the Time of *Pericles*,[14] one of the most celebrated Times in the History of that Commonwealth, a King of Egypt sent them a Donation of Corn. This they were mean enough to accept. And had the Egyptian Prince intended the Ruin of this City of wicked Bedlamites,[15] he could not have taken a more effectual Method to do it, than by such an ensnaring Largess. The Distribution of this Bounty caused a Quarrel; the Majority set on foot an Enquiry into the Title of the Citizens; and upon a vain Pretence of Illegitimacy, newly and occasionally set up, they deprived of their Share of the royal Donation no less than five thousand of their own Body. They went further; they disfranchised them; and having once begun with an Act of Injustice, they could set no Bounds to it. Not content with cutting them off from the Rights of Citizens, they plundered these unfortunate Wretches of all their Substance; and to crown this Masterpiece of Violence and Tyranny, they actually sold every Man of the five thousand as Slaves in the publick Market. Observe, my Lord, that the five thousand we here speak of, were cut off from a Body of no more than nineteen thousand; for the entire Number of Citizens was no greater at that Time. Could the Tyrant who wished the Roman People but one Neck; could the Tyrant Caligula himself have done, nay, he could scarcely wish for a greater Mischief, than to have cut off, at one Stroke, a fourth of his People? Or has the Cruelty of that Series of sanguine Tyrants, the Caesars, ever presented such a Piece of flagrant and extensive Wickedness? The whole History of this celebrated Republick is but one Tissue of Rashness, Folly, Ingratitude, Injustice, Tumult, Violence, and Tyranny, and indeed of every Species of Wickedness that can well be imagined. This was a City of Wisemen, in which a Minister could not exercise his Functions; a warlike People amongst whom a General did not dare either to gain or lose a Battle; a learned Nation, in which a Philosopher could not venture on a free Enquiry. This was the City which banished Themistocles, starved Aristides, forced into Exile Miltiades, drove out Anaxagoras, and poisoned Socrates.[16] This was a City which changed the Form of its Government with the Moon; eternal Conspiracies, Revolutions daily, nothing fixed and established. A Republick, as an ancient Philosopher has observed, is no one Species of Government, but a Magazine of every Species;[17] here you find every Sort of it, and that in the worst Form. As there is a perpetual Change, one rising and the other falling, you have all the Violence and wicked Policy, by which a beginning Power must always acquire its Strength, and all the Weakness by which falling States are brought to a complete Destruction.

Rome has a more venerable Aspect than Athens; and she conducted her Affairs, so far as related to the Ruin and Oppression of the greatest Part of the World, with greater Wisdom and more Uniformity. But the domestic Oeconomy of these two States was nearly or altogether the same. An internal Dissention constantly tore to Pieces the Bowels of the Roman Commonwealth. You find the same Confusion, the same Factions which subsisted at Athens, the same Tumults, the same Revolutions, and in fine, the same Slavery. If perhaps their former Condition did not deserve that Name altogether as well. All other Republicks were of the same Character. Florence was a Transcript of Athens. And the modern Republicks, as they approach more or less to the Democratick Form, partake more or less of the Nature of those which I have described.

We are now at the Close of our Review of the three simple Forms of artificial Society, and we have shewn them, however they may differ in Name, or in some slight Circumstances, to be all alike in effect; in effect, to be all Tyrannies. But suppose we were inclined to make the most ample Concessions; let us concede Athens, Rome, Carthage,[18] and two or three more of the ancient, and as many of the modern Commonwealths, to have been, or to be free and happy, and to owe their Freedom and Happiness to their political Constitution. Yet allowing all this, what Defence does this make for artificial Society in general, that these inconsiderable Spots of the Globe have for some short Space of Time stood as Exceptions to a Charge so general? But when we call these Governments free, or concede that their Citizens were happier than those which lived under different Forms, it is merely ex abundanti. For we should be greatly mistaken, if we really thought that the Majority of the People which filled these Cities, enjoyed even that nominal political Freedom of which I have spoken so much already. In reality, they had no Part of it. In Athens there were usually from ten to thirty thousand Freemen: This was the utmost. But the Slaves usually amounted to four hundred thousand, and sometimes to a great many more. The Freemen of Sparta and Rome were not more numerous in proportion to those whom they held in a Slavery, even more terrible than the Athenian. Therefore state the Matter fairly: The free States never formed, though they were taken all together, the thousandth Part of the habitable Globe; the Freemen in these States were never the twentieth Part of the People, and the Time they subsisted is scarce any thing in that immense Ocean of Duration in which Time and Slavery are so nearly commensurate. Therefore call these free States, or popular Governments, or what you please; when we consider the Majority of their Inhabitants, and regard the Natural Rights of Mankind, they must appear in Reality and Truth, no better than pitiful and oppressive Oligarchies.[19]

After so fair an Examen, wherein nothing has been exaggerated; no Fact produced which cannot be proved, and none which has been produced in any wise forced or strained, while thousands have, for Brevity, been omitted; after so candid a Discussion in all respects; what Slave so passive, what Bigot so blind, what Enthusiast so headlong, what Politician so hardened, as to stand up in Defence of a System calculated for a Curse to Mankind? a Curse under which they smart and groan to this Hour, without thoroughly knowing the Nature of the Disease, and wanting Understanding or Courage to apply the Remedy.

I need not excuse myself to your Lordship, nor, I think, to any honest Man, for the Zeal I have shewn in this Cause; for it is an honest Zeal, and in a good Cause. I have defended Natural Religion against a Confederacy of Atheists and Divines.[20] I now plead for Natural Society against Politicians, and for Natural Reason against all three. When the World is in a fitter Temper than it is at present to hear Truth, or when I shall be more indifferent about its Temper; my Thoughts may become more publick. In the mean time, let them repose in my own Bosom, and in the Bosoms of such Men as are fit to be initiated in the sober Mysteries of Truth and Reason. My Antagonists have already done as much as I could desire. Parties in Religion and Politics make sufficient Discoveries concerning each other, to give a sober Man a proper Caution against them all. The Monarchic, Aristocratical, and Popular Partizans have been jointly laying their Axes to the Root of all Government, and have in their Turns proved each other absurd and inconvenient. In vain you tell me that Artificial Government is good, but that I fall out only with the Abuse. The Thing! the Thing itself is the Abuse! Observe, my Lord, I pray you, that grand Error upon which all artificial legislative Power is founded. It was observed, that Men had ungovernable Passions, which made it necessary to guard against the Violence they might offer to each other. They appointed Governors over them for this Reason; but a worse and more perplexing Difficulty arises, how to be defended against the Governors? Quis custodiet ipsos custodes?[21] In vain they change from a single Person to a few. These few have the Passions of the one, and they unite to strengthen themselves, and to secure the Gratification of their lawless Passions at the Expence of the general Good. In vain do we fly to the Many. The Case is worse; their Passions are less under the Government of Reason, they are augmented by the Contagion, and defended against all Attacks by their Multitude.

I have purposely avoided the mention of the mixed Form of Government, for Reasons that will be very obvious to your Lordship. But my Caution can avail me but little. You will not fail to urge it against me in favour of Political Society. You will not fail to shew how the Errors of the several simple Modes are corrected by a Mixture of all of them, and a proper Ballance of the several Powers in such a State. I confess, my Lord, that this has been long a darling Mistake of my own; and that of all the Sacrifices I have made to Truth, this has been by far the greatest. When I confess that I think this Notion a Mistake, I know to whom I am speaking, for I am satisfied that Reasons are like Liquors, and there are some of such a Nature as none but strong Heads can bear. There are few with whom I can communicate so freely as with Pope.[22] But Pope cannot bear every Truth. He has a Timidity which hinders the full Exertion of his Faculties, almost as effectually as Bigotry cramps those of the general Herd of Mankind. But whoever is a genuine Follower of Truth, keeps his Eye steady upon his Guide, indifferent whither he is led, provided that she is the Leader. And, my Lord, if it be properly considered, it were infinitely better to remain possessed by the whole Legion of vulgar Mistakes, than to reject some, and at the same time to retain a Fondness for others altogether as absurd and irrational. The first has at least a Consistency, that makes a Man, however erroneously, uniform at least; but the latter way of proceeding is such an inconsistent Chimæra and Jumble of Philosophy and vulgar Prejudice, that hardly any thing more ridiculous can be conceived. Let us therefore freely, and without Fear or Prejudice, examine this last Contrivance of Policy. And without considering how near the Quick our Instruments may come, let us search it to the Bottom.

First then, all Men are agreed, that this Junction of Regal, Aristocratic, and Popular Power, must form a very complex, nice, and intricate Machine, which being composed of such a Variety of Parts, with such opposite Tendencies and Movements, it must be liable on every Accident to be disordered. To speak without Metaphor, such a Government must be liable to frequent Cabals, Tumults, and Revolutions, from its very Constitution. These are undoubtedly as ill Effects, as can happen in a Society; for in such a Case, the Closeness acquired by Community, instead of serving for mutual Defence, serves only to increase the Danger. Such a System is like a City, where Trades that require constant Fires are much exercised, where the Houses are built of combustible Materials, and where they stand extremely close.

In the second Place, the several constituent Parts having their distinct Rights, and these many of them so necessary to be determined with Exactness, are yet so indeterminate in their Nature, that it becomes a new and constant Source of Debate and Confusion. Hence it is, that whilst the Business of Government should be carrying on, the Question is, who has a Right to exercise this or that Function of it, or what Men have Power to keep their Offices in any Function. Whilst this Contest continues, and whilst the Ballance in any sort continues, it has never any Remission; all manner of Abuses and Villanies in Officers remain unpunished, the greatest Frauds and Robberies in the publick Revenues are committed in Defiance of Justice; and Abuses grow, by Time and Impunity, into Customs; until they prescribe against the Laws, and grow too inveterate often to admit a Cure, unless such as may be as bad as the Disease.

Thirdly, the several Parts of this Species of Government, though united, preserve the Spirit which each Form has separately. Kings are ambitious; the

Nobility haughty; and the Populace tumultuous and ungovernable. Each Party, however in appearance peaceable, carries on a Design upon the others; and it is owing to this, that in all Questions, whether concerning foreign or domestick Affairs, the Whole generally turns more upon some Party-Matter than upon the Nature of the Thing itself; whether such a Step will diminish or augment the Power of the Crown, or how far the Privileges of the Subject are like to be extended or restricted by it. And these Questions are constantly resolved, without any Consideration of the Merits of the Cause, merely as the Parties who uphold these jarring Interests may chance to prevail; and as they prevail, the Ballance is overset, now upon one side, now upon the other. The Government is one Day, arbitrary Power in a single Person; another, a juggling Confederacy of a few to cheat the Prince and enslave the People; and the third, a frantick and unmanageable Democracy. The great Instrument of all these Changes, and what infuses a peculiar Venom into all of them, is Party. It is of no Consequence what the Principles of any Party, or what their Pretensions are, the Spirit which actuates all Parties is the same; the Spirit of Ambition, of Self-Interest, of Oppression, and Treachery. This Spirit entirely reverses all the Principles which a benevolent Nature has erected within us; all Honesty, all equal Justice, and even the Ties of natural Society, the natural Affections. In a word, my Lord, we have all seen, and if any outward Considerations were worthy the lasting Concern of a wise Man, we have some of us felt, such Oppression from Party Government as no other Tyranny can parallel. We behold daily the most important Rights, Rights upon which all the others depend; we behold these Rights determined in the last Resort, without the least Attention even to the Appearance or Colour of Justice; we behold this without Emotion, because we have grown up in the constant View of such Practices; and we are not surprised to hear a Man requested to be a Knave and a Traitor, with as much Indifference as if the most ordinary Favour were asked; and we hear this Request refused, not because it is a most unjust and unreasonable Desire, but that this Worthy has already engaged his Injustice to another. These and many more Points I am far from spreading to their full Extent. You are sensible that I do not put forth half my Strength; and you cannot be at a Loss for the Reason. A Man is allowed sufficient Freedom of Thought, provided he knows how to chuse his Subject properly. You may criticise freely upon the Chinese Constitution,[23] and observe with as much Severity as you please upon the Absurd Tricks, or destructive Bigotry of the Bonzees. But the Scene is changed as you come homeward, and Atheism or Treason may be the Names given in Britain, to what would be Reason and Truth if asserted of China. I submit to the Condition, and though I have a notorious Advantage before me, I wave the Pursuit. For else, my Lord, it is very obvious what a Picture might be drawn of the Excesses of Party even in our own Nation. I could shew, that the same Faction has in one Reign promoted popular Seditions, and in the next been a Patron of Tyranny; I could shew, that they have all of them betrayed the publick Safety at all Times, and have very frequently with equal

Perfidy made a Market of their own Cause, and their own Associates. I could shew how vehemently they have contended for Names, and how silently they passed over Things of the last importance. And I could demonstrate, that they have had the Opportunity of doing all this Mischief, nay, that they themselves had their Origin and Growth from the Complex Form of Government which we are wisely taught to look upon as so great a Blessing. Revolve, my Lord, our History from the Conquest. We scarce ever had a Prince, who by Fraud, or Violence, had not made some Infringement on the Constitution. We scarce ever had a Parliament which knew, when it attempted to set Limits to the Royal Authority, how to set Limits to its own. Evils we have had continually calling for Reformation, and Reformations more grievous than any Evils. Our boasted Liberty sometimes trodden down, sometimes giddily set up, ever precariously fluctuating and unsettled; it has been only kept alive by the Blasts of continual Feuds, Wars, and Conspiracies. In no Country in Europe has the Scaffold so often blushed with the Blood of its Nobility. Confiscations, Banishments, Attainders, and Executions, make a large Part of the History of such of our Families as are not utterly extinguished by them. Formerly indeed Things had a more ferocious Appearance than they have at this Day. In these early and unrefined Ages, the jarring Parts of a certain chaotic Constitution supported their several Pretensions by the Sword. Experience and Policy have since taught other Methods.

Res vero nunc agitur tenui pulmone rubetæ.[24] But how far Corruption, Venality, the Contempt of Honour, the Oblivion of all Duty to our Country, and the most abandoned publick Prostitution, are preferable to the more glaring and violent Effects of Faction, I will not presume to determine. Sure I am that they are very great Evils.

I have done with the Forms of Government. During the Course of my Enquiry you may have observed a very material Difference between my Manner of Reasoning and that which is in Use amongst the Abetors of artificial Society. They form their Plans upon what seems most eligible to their Imaginations, for the ordering of Mankind.[25] I discover the Mistakes in those Plans, from the real known Consequences which have resulted from them. They have inlisted Reason to fight against itself, and employ its whole Force to prove that it is an insufficient Guide to them in the Conduct of their Lives. But unhappily for us, in proportion as we have deviated from the plain Rule of our Nature, and turned our Reason against itself, in that Proportion have we increased the Follies and Miseries of Mankind. The more deeply we penetrate into the Labyrinth of Art, the further we find ourselves from those Ends for which we entered it.[26] This has happened in almost every Species of Artificial Society, and in all Times. We found, or we thought we found, an Inconvenience in having every Man the Judge of his own Cause. Therefore Judges were set up, at first with discretionary Powers. But it was soon found a miserable Slavery to have our Lives and Properties precarious, and hanging upon the arbitrary Determination of any one Man, or Set of Men. We flew to Laws as a Remedy for this Evil. By these we persuaded ourselves we might know with some Certainty upon what Ground we stood. But lo! Differences arose upon the Sense and Interpretation of these Laws. Thus we were brought back to our old Incertitude. New Laws were made to expound the old; and new Difficulties arose upon the new Laws; as Words multiplied, Opportunities of cavilling upon them multiplied also. Then Recourse was had to Notes, Comments, Glosses, Reports, Responsa Prudentum, learned Readings: Eagle stood against Eagle: Authority was set up against Authority. Some were allured by the modern, others reverenced the ancient. The new were more enlightened, the old were more venerable. Some adopted the Comment, others stuck to the Text. The Confusion increased, the Mist thickened, until it could be discovered no longer what was allowed or forbidden, what Things were in Property, and what common. In this Uncertainty, (uncertain even to the Professors, an Ægyptian Darkness to the rest of Mankind) the contending Parties felt themselves more effectually ruined by the Delay than they could have been by the Injustice of any Decision. Our Inheritances are become a Prize for Disputation; and Disputes and Litigations are become an Inheritance.

The Professors of Artificial Law have always walked hand in hand with the Professors of Artificial Theology. As their End, in confounding the Reason of Man, and abridging his natural Freedom, is exactly the same, they have adjusted the Means to that End in a Way entirely similar. The Divine thunders out his Anathemas with more Noise and Terror against the Breach of one of his positive Institutions, or the Neglect of some of his trivial Forms, than against the Neglect or Breach of those Duties and Commandments of natural Religion, which by these Forms and Institutions he pretends to enforce. The Lawyer has his Forms, and his positive Institutions too, and he adheres to them with a Veneration altogether as religious. The worst Cause cannot be so prejudicial to the Litigant, as his Advocate's or Attorney's Ignorance or Neglect of these Forms. A Law-suit is like an ill-managed Dispute, in which the first Object is soon out of Sight, and the Parties end upon a Matter wholly foreign to that on which they began. In a Law-suit the Question is, Who has a Right to a certain House or Farm? And this Question is daily determined, not upon the Evidences of the Right, but upon the Observance or Neglect of some Forms of Words in use with the Gentlemen of the Robe, about which there is even amongst themselves such a Disagreement, that the most experienced Veterans in the Profession can never be positively assured that they are not mistaken.

Let us expostulate with these learned Sages, these Priests of the sacred Temple of Justice. Are we Judges of our own Property? By no means. You then, who are initiated into the Mysteries of the blindfold Goddess, inform me whether I have a Right to eat the Bread I have earned by the Hazard of my Life, or the Sweat of my Brow? The grave Doctor answers me in the Affirmative. The reverend Serjeant replies in the Negative; the learned Barrister reasons upon one side and upon the other, and concludes nothing. What shall I do? An Antagonist starts up and presses me hard. I enter the Field, and retain these three Persons to defend my Cause. My Cause, which two Farmers from the Plough could have decided in half an Hour, takes the Court twenty Years. I am however at the end of my Labour, and have in Reward for all my Toil and Vexation, a Judgment in my Favour. But hold—a sagacious Commander, in the Adversary's Army has found a Flaw in the Proceeding. My Triumph is turned into Mourning. I have used or, instead of and, or some Mistake, small in Appearance, but dreadful in its Consequences, and have the whole of my Success quashed in a Writ of Error. I remove my Suit; I shift from Court to Court; I fly from Equity to Law, and from Law to Equity; equal Uncertainty attends me every where: And a Mistake in which I had no Share, decides at once upon my Liberty and Property, sending me from the Court to a Prison, and adjudging my Family to Beggary and Famine. I am innocent, Gentlemen, of the Darkness and Uncertainty of your Science. I never darkened it with absurd and contradictory Notions, nor confounded it with Chicane and Sophistry. You have excluded me from any Share in the Conduct of my own Cause; the Science was too deep for me; I acknowledged it; but it was too deep even for yourselves: You have made the way so intricate, that you are yourselves lost in it: You err, and you punish me for your Errors.

The Delay of the Law is, your Lordship will tell me, a trite Topic, and which of its Abuses have not been too severely felt not to be often complained of? A Man's Property is to serve for the Purposes of his Support; and therefore to delay a Determination concerning that, is the worst Injustice, because it cuts off the very End and Purpose for which I applied to the Judicature for Relief. Quite contrary in Case of a Man's Life, there the Determination can hardly be too much protracted. Mistakes in this Case are as often fallen into as in any other, and if the Judgment is sudden, the Mistakes are the most irretrievable of all others. Of this the Gentlemen of the Robe are themselves sensible, and they have brought it into a Maxim. De morte hominis nulla est cunctatio longa.[27] But what could have induced them to reverse the Rules, and to contradict that Reason which dictated them, I am utterly unable to guess. A Point concerning Property, which ought, for the Reasons I just mentioned, to be most speedily decided, frequently exercises the Wit of Successions of Lawyers, for many Generations. Multa virum volvens durando sæcula vincit.[28] But the Question concerning a Man's Life, that great Question in which no Delay ought to be counted tedious, is commonly determined in twenty-four Hours at the utmost. It is not to be wondered at, that Injustice and Absurdity should be inseparable Companions.

Ask of Politicians the End for which Laws were originally designed; and they will answer, that the Laws were designed as a Protection for the Poor and Weak against the Oppression of the Rich and Powerful.[29] But surely no Pretence can be so ridiculous; a Man might as well tell me he has taken off my Load, because he has changed the Burthen.[30] If the poor Man is not able to support his Suit, according to the vexatious and expensive manner established in civilized

Countries, has not the Rich as great an Advantage over him as the Strong has over the Weak in a State of Nature? But we will not place the State of Nature, which is the Reign of God, in competition with Political Society, which is the absurd Usurpation of Man. In a State of Nature, it is true, that a Man of superior Force may beat or rob me; but then it is true, that I am at full Liberty to defend myself, or make Reprisal by Surprize or by Cunning, or by any other way in which I may be superior to him. But in Political Society, a rich Man may rob me in another way. I cannot defend myself; for Money is the only Weapon with which we are allowed to fight. And if I attempt to avenge myself, the whole Force of that Society is ready to complete my Ruin.

A good Parson once said, that where Mystery begins, Religion ends. Cannot I say, as truly at least, of human Laws, that where Mystery begins, Justice ends? It is hard to say, whether the Doctors of Law or Divinity have made the greater Advances in the lucrative Business of Mystery. The Lawyers, as well as the Theologians, have erected another Reason besides Natural Reason; and the Result has been, another Justice besides Natural Justice. They have so bewildered the World and themselves in unmeaning Forms and Ceremonies, and so perplexed the plainest Matters with metaphysical Jargon, that it carries the highest Danger to a Man out of that Profession, to make the least Step without their Advice and Assistance. Thus by confining to themselves the knowledge of the Foundation of all Men's Lives and Properties, they have reduced all Mankind into the most abject and servile Dependence. We are Tenants at the Will of these Gentlemen for every thing; and a metaphysical Quibble is to decide whether the greatest Villain breathing shall meet his Desserts, or escape with Impunity, or whether the best Man in the Society shall not be reduced to the lowest and most despicable Condition it affords. In a word, my Lord, the Injustice, Delay, Puerility, false Refinement, and affected Mystery of the Law are such, that many who live under it come to admire and envy the Expedition, Simplicity, and Equality of arbitrary Judgments. I need insist the less on this Article to your Lordship, as you have frequently lamented the Miseries derived to us from Artificial Law, and your Candor is the more to be admired and applauded in this, as your Lordship's noble House has derived its Wealth and its Honours from that Profession.

Before we finish our Examination of Artificial Society, I shall lead your Lordship into a closer Consideration of the Relations which it gives Birth to, and the Benefits, if such they are, which result from these Relations. The most obvious Division of Society is into Rich and Poor; and it is no less obvious, that the Number of the former bear a great Disproportion to those of the latter. The whole Business of the Poor is to administer to the Idleness, Folly, and Luxury of the Rich; and that of the Rich, in return, is to find the best Methods of confirming the Slavery and increasing the Burthens of the Poor. In a State of Nature, it is an invariable Law, that a Man's Acquisitions are in proportion to his Labours. In a State of Artificial Society, it is a Law as constant and as invariable, that those who labour most, enjoy the fewest Things; and that those who labour not at all, have the greatest Number of Enjoyments. A Constitution of Things this, strange and ridiculous beyond Expression. We scarce believe a thing when we are told it, which we actually see before our Eyes every Day without being in the least surprized. I suppose that there are in Great-Britain upwards of an hundred thousand People employed in Lead, Tin, Iron, Copper, and Coal Mines; these unhappy Wretches scarce ever see the Light of the Sun; they are buried in the Bowels of the Earth; there they work at a severe and dismal Task, without the least Prospect of being delivered from it; they subsist upon the coarsest and worst sort of Fare; they have their Health miserably impaired, and their Lives cut short, by being perpetually confined in the close Vapour of these malignant Minerals. An hundred thousand more at least are tortured without Remission by the suffocating Smoak, intense Fires, and constant Drudgery necessary in refining and managing the Products of those Mines. If any Man informed us that two hundred thousand innocent Persons were condemned to so intolerable Slavery, how should we pity the unhappy Sufferers, and how great would be our just Indignation against those who inflicted so cruel and ignominious a Punishment? This is an Instance, I could not wish a stronger, of the numberless Things which we pass by in their common Dress, yet which shock us when they are nakedly represented. But this Number, considerable as it is, and the Slavery, with all its Baseness and Horror, which we have at home, is nothing to what the rest of the World affords of the same Nature. Millions daily bathed in the poisonous Damps and destructive Effluvia of Lead, Silver, Copper, and Arsenic. To say nothing of those other Employments, those Stations of Wretchedness and Contempt in which Civil Society has placed the numerous Enfans perdus[31] of her Army. Would any rational Man submit to one of the most tolerable of these Drudgeries, for all the artificial Enjoyments which Policy has made to result from them? By no means. And yet need I suggest to your Lordship, that those who find the Means, and those who arrive at the End, are not at all the same Persons. On considering the strange and unaccountable Fancies and Contrivances of artificial Reason, I have somewhere called this Earth the Bedlam of our System. Looking now upon the Effects of some of those Fancies, may we not with equal Reason call it likewise the Newgate, and the Bridewell of the Universe.[32] Indeed the Blindness of one Part of Mankind co-operating with the Frenzy and Villainy of the other, has been the real Builder of this respectable Fabric of political Society: And as the Blindness of Mankind has caused their Slavery, in Return their State of Slavery is made a Pretence for continuing them in a State of Blindness; for the Politician will tell you gravely, that their Life of Servitude disqualifies the greater Part of the Race of Man for a Search of Truth, and supplies them with no other than mean and insufficient Ideas. This is but too true; and this is one of the Reasons for which I blame such Institutions.

In a Misery of this Sort, admitting some few Lenities, and those too but a few, nine Parts in ten of the whole Race of Mankind drudge through Life. It may be urged perhaps, in palliation of this, that, at least, the rich Few find a considerable and real Benefit from the Wretchedness of the Many. But is this so in fact? Let us examine the Point with a little more Attention. For this Purpose the Rich in all Societies may be thrown into two Classes. The first is of those who are Powerful as well as Rich, and conduct the Operations of the vast political Machine. The other is of those who employ their Riches wholly in the Acquisition of Pleasure. As to the first Sort, their continual Care, and Anxiety, their toilsome Days, and sleepless Nights, are next to proverbial. These Circumstances are sufficient almost to level their Condition to that of the unhappy Majority; but there are other Circumstances which place them in a far lower Condition. Not only their Understandings labour continually, which is the severest Labour, but their Hearts are torn by the worst, most troublesome, and insatiable of all Passions, by Avarice, by Ambition, by Fear and Jealousy. No part of the Mind has Rest. Power gradually extirpates from the Mind every humane and gentle Virtue. Pity, Benevolence, Friendship are Things almost unknown in high Stations. Varæ amicitiæ rarissime inveniuntur in iis qui in honoribus reque publica versantur, says Cicero.[33] And indeed, Courts are the Schools where Cruelty, Pride, Dissimulation, and Treachery are studied and taught in the most vicious Perfection. This is a Point so clear and acknowledged, that if it did not make a necessary Part of my Subject, I should pass it by entirely. And this has hindered me from drawing at full length, and in the most striking Colours, this shocking Picture of the Degeneracy and Wretchedness of human Nature, in that Part which is vulgarly thought its happiest and most amiable State. You know from what Originals I could copy such Pictures. Happy are they who know enough of them to know the little Value of the Possessors of such Things, and of all that they possess; and happy they who have been snatched from that Post of Danger which they occupy, with the Remains of their Virtue; Loss of Honours, Wealth, Titles, and even the Loss of one's Country, is nothing in Balance with so great an Advantage.

Let us now view the other Species of the Rich, those who devote their Time and Fortunes to Idleness and Pleasure. How much happier are they? The Pleasures which are agreeable to Nature are within the reach of all, and therefore can form no Distinction in favour of the Rich. The Pleasures which Art forces up are seldom sincere, and never satisfying. What is worse, this constant Application to Pleasure takes away from the Enjoyment, or rather turns it into the Nature of a very burthensome and laborious Business. It has Consequences much more fatal. It produces a weak valetudinary State of Body, attended by all those horrid Disorders, and yet more horrid Methods of Cure, which are the Result of Luxury on one hand, and the weak and ridiculous Efforts of human Art on the other. The Pleasures of such Men are scarcely felt as Pleasures; at the same time that they bring on Pains and Diseases, which are felt but too severely. The Mind has its Share of the Misfortune; it grows lazy and enervate, unwilling and unable to search for Truth, and utterly uncapable of knowing, much less of relishing real Happiness. The Poor by their excessive Labour, and the Rich by their enormous Luxury, are set upon a Level, and rendered equally ignorant of any Knowledge which might conduce to their Happiness. A dismal View of the Interior of all Civil Society. The lower Part broken and ground down by the most cruel Oppression; and the Rich by their artificial Method of Life bringing worse Evils on themselves, than their Tyranny could possibly inflict on those below them. Very different is the Prospect of the Natural State. Here there are no Wants which Nature gives, and in this State Men can be sensible of no other Wants, which are not to be supplied by a very moderate Degree of Labour; therefore there is no Slavery. Neither is there any Luxury, because no single Man can supply the Materials of it. Life is simple, and therefore it is happy.

I am conscious, my Lord, that your Politician will urge in his Defence, that this unequal State is highly useful. That without dooming some Part of Mankind to extraordinary Toil, the Arts which cultivate Life could not be exercised. But I demand of this Politician, how such Arts came to be necessary? He answers, that Civil Society could not well exist without them. So that these Arts are necessary to Civil Society, and Civil Society necessary again to these Arts. Thus running in a Circle, without Modesty, and without End, and making one Error and Extravagance an Excuse for the other. My Sentiments about these Arts and their Cause, I have often discoursed with my Friends at large. Pope has expressed them in good Verse, where he talks with so much Force of Reason and Elegance of Language in Praise of the State of Nature:

> Then was not Pride, nor Arts that Pride to aid, Man walk'd with Beast, Joint-tenant of the Shade.[34]

On the whole, my Lord, if Political Society, in whatever Form, has still made the Many the Property of the Few; if it has introduced Labours unnecessary, Vices and Diseases unknown, and Pleasures incompatible with Nature; if in all Countries it abridges the Lives of Millions, and renders those of Millions more utterly abject and miserable, shall we still worship so destructive an Idol, and daily sacrifice to it our Health, our Liberty, and our Peace? Or shall we pass by this monstrous Heap of absurd Notions, and abominable Practices, thinking we have sufficiently discharged our Duty in exposing the trifling Cheats, and ridiculous Juggles of a few mad, designing, or ambitious Priests? Alas! my Lord, we labour under a mortal Consumption, whilst we are so anxious about the Cure of a sore Finger. For has not this Leviathan of Civil Power[35] overflowed the Earth with a Deluge of Blood, as if he were made to disport and play therein? We have shewn, that Political Society, on a moderate Calculation, has been the Means of murdering several times the Number of Inhabitants now upon the Earth, during its short Existence, not upwards of four thousand Years in any Accounts to be depended on. But we have said nothing of the other, and perhaps as bad Consequence of these Wars, which have spilled such Seas of Blood, and reduced so many Millions to a merciless Slavery. But these are only the Ceremonies performed in the Porch of the political Temple. Much more horrid ones are seen as you enter it. The several Species of Government vie with each other in the Absurdity of their Constitutions, and the Oppression which they make their Subjects endure. Take them under what Form you please, they are in effect but a Despotism, and they fall, both in Effect and Appearance too, after a very short Period, into that cruel and detestable Species of Tyranny; which I rather call it, because we have been educated under another Form,[36] than that this is of worse Consequences to Mankind. For the free Governments, for the Point of their Space, and the Moment of their Duration, have felt more Confusion, and committed more flagrant Acts of Tyranny, than the most perfect despotic Governments which we have ever known. Turn your Eye next to the Labyrinth of the Law, and the Iniquity conceived in its intricate Recesses. Consider the Ravages committed in the Bowels of all Commonwealths by Ambition, by Avarice, Envy, Fraud, open Injustice, and pretended Friendship; Vices which could draw little Support from a State of Nature, but which blossom and flourish in the Rankness of political Society. Revolve our whole Discourse; add to it all those Reflections which your own good Understanding shall suggest, and make a strenuous Effort beyond the Reach of vulgar Philosophy, to confess that the Cause of Artificial Society is more defenceless even than that of Artificial Religion; that it is as derogatory from the Honour of the Creator, as subversive of human Reason, and productive of infinitely more Mischief to the human Race.

If pretended Revelations have caused Wars where they were opposed, and Slavery where they were received, the pretended wise Inventions of Politicians have done the same. But the Slavery has been much heavier, the Wars far more bloody, and both more universal by many Degrees. Shew me any Mischief produced by the Madness or Wickedness of Theologians, and I will shew you an hundred, resulting from the Ambition and Villainy of Conquerors and Statesmen. Shew me an Absurdity in Religion, I will undertake to shew you an hundred for one in political Laws and Institutions. If you say, that Natural Religion is a sufficient Guide without the foreign Aid of Revelation, on what Principle should Political Laws become necessary? Is not the same Reason available in Theology and in Politics? If the Laws of Nature are the Laws of God, is it consistent with the Divine Wisdom to prescribe Rules to us, and leave the Enforcement of them to the Folly of human Institutions?[37] Will you follow Truth but to a certain Point?

We are indebted for all our Miseries to our Distrust of that Guide, which Providence thought sufficient for our Condition, our own natural Reason, which rejecting both in human and divine Things, we have given our Necks to the Yoke of political and theological Slavery. We have renounced the Prerogative of Man, and it is no Wonder that we should be treated like Beasts. But our Misery is much greater than theirs, as the Crime we commit in rejecting the lawful Dominion of our Reason is greater than any which they can commit. If after all, you should confess all these Things, yet plead the Necessity of political Institutions, weak and wicked as they are, I can argue with equal, perhaps superior Force concerning the Necessity of artificial Religion; and every Step you advance in your Argument, you add a Strength to mine. So that if we are resolved to submit our Reason and our Liberty to civil Usurpation, we have nothing to do but to conform as quietly as we can to the vulgar Notions which are connected with this, and take up the Theology of the Vulgar as well as their Politics. But if we think this Necessity rather imaginary than real, we should renounce their Dreams of Society, together with their Visions of Religion, and vindicate ourselves into perfect Liberty.[38]

You are, my Lord, but just entering into the World; I am going out of it. I have played long enough to be heartily tired of the Drama. Whether I have acted my Part in it well or ill, Posterity will judge with more Candor than I, or than the present Age, with our present Passions, can possibly pretend to. For my part, I quit it without a Sigh, and submit to the Sovereign Order without murmuring. The nearer we approach to the Goal of Life, the better we begin to understand the true Value of our Existence, and the real Weight of our Opinions. We set out much in love with both; but we leave much behind us as we advance. We first throw away the Tales along with the Rattles of our Nurses; those of the Priest keep their Hold a little longer; those of our Governors the longest of all. But the Passions which prop these Opinions are withdrawn one after another; and the cool Light of Reason at the Setting of our Life, shews us what a false Splendor played upon these Objects during our more sanguine Seasons. Happy, my Lord, if instructed by my Experience, and even by my Errors, you come early to make such an Estimate of Things, as may give Freedom and Ease to your Life. I am happy that such an Estimate promises me Comfort at my Death.

FINIS

Notes

1. Compare Montesquieu, *The Persian Letters*, letters 105 and 106.
2. Each is an ancient lawgiver. Orpheus is a mystical figure who supposedly established the Greek orphic rites and their accompanying code. Moses is the lawgiver of Israel, Minos of Crete, Solon of democratic Athens, Theseus the founder of Athens, Lycurgus the lawgiver of Sparta, and Numa of Rome. The obvious contrast is with Machiavelli. See *The Prince*, ch. 6; and the *Discourses*, Bk. 1, ch. 1; Bk. 3, chs. 10 and 11. He stresses that the founders formed cities by good arms, that is, by force, and not by good laws. The noble writer blames the lawgivers and hence implies that they are more responsible for the formation of nations than the armed founders. His list also is weighted toward men who reputedly received their laws from a god or God.
3. This is a paraphrase of Machiavelli, *Discourses*, Bk. 1, ch. 3. "All those who have written upon civil institutions demonstrate (and history is full of examples to support them) that whoever desires to found a state and give it laws, must start with assuming that all men are bad and ever ready to display their vicious nature, whenever they may find occasion for it." *The Prince and the Discourses*, trans. Christian E. Oetmold, The Modem Library (New York: Random House, 1950), p. 117.

There are differences between the noble writer's and Machiavelli's perspectives. The former accepts Machiavelli's observation as accurate—legislators must assume all men are wicked—but he claims that this assumption, although necessary, is false and therefore unjust. There are good men, but laws are not made for them.

4. This may be an allusion to Nero's ordering the suicide of his tutor, the philosopher and poet, Seneca, for allegedly participating in a plot to disthrone the emperor. Nero's virtuous early reign may have been a result of Seneca's influence.
5. This is a reference to the murder of Cleitus by Alexander the Great during one of the king's banquets: After considerable drinking, Alexander joined some singing which mocked the older Macedonians. Cleitus responded by reminding Alexander that he saved the king's life and by criticizing Alexander's disowning of his father Philip and claiming descent from the God Ammon. In a drunken rage, Alexander slew Cleitus. The king lamented the deed for days. Two philosophers were sent for to soothe him: Callisthenes, the nephew of Aristotle, and Anaxarchus. The noble writer neglects to mention Callisthenes who did not justify the murder and who himself ultimately died in prison because he did not adore Alexander in the eastern fashion. Anaxarchus admittedly justified the deed. Still, the noble writer, whose apparent purpose is to defend philosophy, distorts the tale to philosophy's disadvantage. He also distorts Anaxarchus' speech. In Plutarch it reads, "Knowest thou not," said he, "That Zeus has Justice and Law seated beside him, in order that everything that is done may be lawful and just?" Bernadotte Perrin, trans., *Plutarch's Lives* (Cambridge, Mass.: Harvard University Press, 1958), 7:376-77. In fact the passage as quoted more resembles a statement in Hobbes's Leviathan than Anaxarchus' words. "Fourthly, because every Subject is by this Institution Author of all the Actions, and Judgments of the Soveraigne Instituted; it followes, that whatsoever he doth, it can be no injury to any of his Subjects; nor ought he to be by any of them accused of Injustice." Thomas Hobbes, *Leviathan* (New York: Dutton, 1965), p. 92. Bolingbroke criticized Hobbes for extending Anaxarchus' flatteries of Alexander to all despots. See *Philosophical Works*, 4:17.
6. See Odyssey, Bk. 17, lines 322-23.
7. John Locke (1632-1704) was an English political philosopher and the classic proponent of liberalism. For Locke's comparison of absolute monarchy (despotism) and the state of nature, see The Second Treatise of Government, sect. 13.
8. This quotation is nearly an exact reproduction of a line from *Of the Laws of Ecclesiastical Polity* by Richard Hooker (c. 1554-1600), an English theologian and political philosopher. The line in Hooker is, "that to live by one man's will became the cause of all men's misery." Bk. 1, sect. 10. Locke reproduces this line, along with the paragraph to which it belongs, in a footnote to section 94 of *The Second Treatise of Government.*
9. All were Roman emperors. The first set were members of Julius Caesar's family. The next six (there were three Antonines) reigned intermittently from 79 to 192.
10. Solon (c.639-c.559) reformed the Athenian laws and made them more democratic.
11. Pisistratus (c.605-527) was thrice tyrant of Athens apparently at the demand of the rural populace.
12. See n. 13.
13. "With the greeting of a hasty kiss and without conversation, he slipped away into the obsequious mob. [Let those whose way it is to admire only what is forbidden learn from him that great men can live even under bad rulers, etc.]" M. Hutton, rev. R.M. Ogilivie, trans., *Tacitus: Agricola, Germania, Dialogus* (Cambridge, Mass: Harvard University Press, 1970), 40 and 42. Looking at the sections following 42, especially 45, we find that there is some doubt that an upright man can live in cor-

rupt times. It is suggested that had Agricola not died, the emperor Dominan would eventually have killed him. Compare to n. 4 above.

14. Compare "Pericles," *The Lives of the Noble Grecians and Romans.*
15. See n. 32.
16. Whereas the oppression of outstanding men by despotisms is understated (see n. 13), these offenses are somewhat exaggerated. Themistocles (c.525-c.460), the strategic savior of the Greeks from the second Persian invasion, was ostracized, a regular institution used to preserve the democracy from the influence of great men, and then he was accused, apparently unjustly, of conspiring with the Persians against the Greeks. See Plutarch, "Themistocles," *The Lives of the Noble Grecians and Romans*. Aristides (d.c.468), called "the Just," was an Athenian general at Marathon and Salamis, when the Greeks twice repulsed the Persians. Athens did not starve him. He was poor, and it did not feed him perhaps by his own choice. See Plutarch, "Aristides," *The Lives of the Noble Grecians and Romans*. Miltiades (d. 489) was the commanding general at Marathon. He was fined and not exiled. Anaxagoras (c. 500-428) was a Greek philosopher who fled Athens because he claimed that the heavenly bodies were not gods. Socrates (469-399) was condemned to death partly as a result of his unyielding defense. See Plato, *The Apology of Socrates.*
17. Compare Plato, Republic, 557d-e.
18. The choice of these cities, Athens, a democracy, Rome, a mixture of aristocracy and democracy, and Carthage, according to Aristotle (*Politics*, 1272a-1273b), an oligarchy with elements of aristocracy and democracy, points to the superiority of mixed government.
19. The modern free commonwealths, like Venice, are not accused of having slavery. Although they have economic abuses, they appear to be an improvement over their ancient counterparts. Perhaps the modern condition has something to do with the spread of the doctrine of "the Natural Rights of Mankind"—a remarkable phrase to appear in Burke, and for the second time.
20. Compare Charles Montesquieu, *Defense* de l'Esprit des Lois (*Defense of*The Spirit of the Laws) ed. Roger Caillois, 2 vols. (Paris: Librairie Gallimard, 1951), 2:1134-36. In response to the tenth objection made to *The Spirit of the Laws*, Montesquieu defends himself in terms very similar to those of the noble writer. He cannot admit to disbelieving the doctrines of the Catholic religion, but in defending himself against this accusation, he does defend natural religion against believers and atheists.
21. Literally, "Who will guard the guardians?" This quotation is the first of three from Juvenal's (first to second centuries A.D.) *Satire VI*, lines 346-347. It satirizes women and the relations between the sexes. The guards referred to by Juvenal are those guarding women, presumably in a women's quarters. Men do not rely on the virtue of either the women or the guards but normally employ eunuchs. Juvenal parodies a question raised by Plato in the Republic (403e). Plato saw that even in the best regime with the best educated guardians of the law, there is still a problem insuring that the guardians themselves obey the law.

    The introduction of Juvenal indicates that the letter has become somewhat ironic. The Juvenalian quotations occur in the discussions of institutions related to England. See Montesquieu's prediction that England would give rise to many Juvenals before one Horace (*The Spirit of the Laws*, Bk. 19, ch. 27).
22. Alexander Pope (1688-1744) was an English poet, friend of Bolingbroke, and supposedly a major influence on Montesquieu when he wrote *The Spirit of the Laws.* See n. 20 and n. 34.
23. Compare Montesquieu, *The Spirit of the Laws*, Bk. 7, chs. 6, 7; Bk. 8, ch. 21; Bk. 9, ch. 8; and especially Bk. 19, chs. 10, 11, 12, 19, 20. Montesquieu praises the

Chinese for lying and formulates his famous axiom "that all political vices are not moral vices, and all moral vices are not political vices." Bk. 19, ch. 10.

24. "Whereas nowadays a slice of a toad's lung will do the business." Juvenal, *Satire VI* in *Juuenal and Persius*, trans. G.G. Ramsay (Cambridge, Mass.: Harvard University Press, 1957), line 659. The quotation is a reference to the invention and perfection by women of the art of poisoning.
25. Compare Machiavelli, *The Prince*, ch. 15, where he accuses Plato of establishing imaginary republics. The noble writer accuses all legislators, ancient and modern, of the same practice.
26. The whole discussion of law seems to be an attack on Locke's solution to the inconveniences of the state of nature. Compare *The Second Treatise of Government*, sects. 13 and 20, and ch. 9.
27. "No delay can be too long when a man's life is at stake," Juvenal, *Satire VI* in *Juvenal and Persius*, trans. G.G. Ramsay, line 221. This is a husband's reply to a wife who wants a slave crucified for apparently no good reason.
28. Many a generation, many an age of man rolls onward and [it] survives them all." Virgil, *Georgie II* in *The Poems of Virgil*, trans. James Rhoades, *The Great Books of the Western World* (Chicago: Encyclopaedia Britannica, 1952), line 295. Virgil describes a tree that is more enduring than men.
29. In Rousseau's *Second Discourse*, the speech that the founder of civil society makes to persuade others to join is essentially the same one that the noble writer here claims politicians make to justify civil society. See *The First and Second Discourses*, pp. 159-62.
30. Burden.
31. Lost children.
32. Bedlam was the popular name for Bethlehem Royal Hospital, Britain's oldest institution for the mentally ill. Newgate was a prison in London and originally part of the gatehouse of the west gate of London. Bridewell also was a prison.
33. "True friendships are very hard to find among those whose time is spent in office or in business of a public kind." W. A. Falconer, trans., *De amicitia in Cicero: De senectus, De amicitia, De divinatione* (Cambridge, Mass.: Harvard University Press, 1938), pp. xvii, 64. Cicero, throughout De amicitia, describes a friendship between two political men—Caius Laelius and Scipio Africanus.
34. Alexander Pope, *Essay on Man*, Epistle 3, lines 151-52. In the original it reads, "Pride then was not; nor Arts, that Pride to Aid: Man walk'd with beast, joint tenant of the shade."
35. Compare Thomas Hobbes, *Leviathan*, "The Introduction."
36. The noble writer almost at the last questions the adequacy of the scheme of governments used in the *Vindication*. It is clearly modern, that is, originating with Machiavelli (Discourses, Bk. 1, ch. 2, Bk. 2, ch. 2, Bk. 3, ch. 6). Locke uses tyranny to designate governments not protecting the natural rights of man. See *The Second Treatise of Government*, ch. 18. Montesquieu divides the rule of one into monarchy and despotism, calls the rule of more than one a republic, and divides republics into aristocracies, .the rule of the few, and democracies, the rule of the many. See *The Spirit of the Laws*, Bk. 2, chs. 2, 3.
37. Compare Pope, *Essay on Man*, Epistle 3, lines 144-50.
38. This is the only instance in the letter, apart from the title, where a form of the word, "vindication" appears. Compare Locke, *The Second Treatise of Government*, sects. 4-6.

26

The Production of Security

Gustave de Molinari

There are two ways of considering society. According to some, the development of human associations is not subject to providential, unchangeable laws. Rather, these associations, having originally been organized in a purely artificial manner by primeval legislators, can later be modified or remade by other legislators, in step with the progress of *social science*. In this system the government plays a preeminent role, because it is upon it, the custodian of the principle of authority, that the daily task of modifying and remaking society devolves.

According to others, on the contrary, society is a purely natural fact. Like the earth on which it stands, society moves in accordance with general, preexisting laws. In this system, there is no such thing, strictly speaking, as social science; there is only economic science, which studies the natural organism of society and shows how this organism functions.

We propose to examine, within the latter system, the function and natural organization of government.

The Natural Order of Society

In order to define and delimit the function of government, it is first necessary to investigate the essence and object of society itself.

What natural impulse do men obey when they combine into society? They are obeying the impulse, or, to speak more exactly, the instinct of sociability. The human race is essentially *sociable*. Like beavers and the higher animal species in general, men have an instinctive inclination to live in society.

Why did this instinct come into being?

Man experiences a multitude of needs, on whose satisfaction his happiness depends, and whose non-satisfaction entails suffering. Alone and isolated, he could only provide in an incomplete, insufficient manner for these incessant needs. The instinct of sociability brings him together with similar persons, and drives him into communication with them. Therefore, impelled by the *self-interest* of the individuals thus brought together, a certain *division of labor* is established, necessarily followed by *exchanges*. In brief, we see an organization emerge, by means of which man can more completely satisfy his needs than he could living in isolation.

This natural organization is called *society*.

The object of society is therefore the most complete satisfaction of man's needs. The division of labor and exchange are the means by which this is accomplished.

Among the needs of man, there is on particular type which plays an immense role in the history of humanity, namely the need for security.

What is this need?

Whether they live in isolation or in society, men are, above all, interested in preserving their existence and the fruits of their labor. If the sense of justice were universally prevalent on earth; if, consequently, each man confined himself to laboring and exchanging the fruits of his labor, without wishing to take away, by violence or fraud, the fruits of other men's labor; if everyone had, in one word, an instinctive horror of any act harmful to another person, it is certain that security would exist *naturally* on earth, and that no artificial institution would be necessary to establish it. Unfortunately this is not the way things are. The sense of justice seems to be the perquisite of only a few eminent and exceptional temperaments. Among the inferior races, it exists only in a rudimentary state. Hence the innumerable criminal attempts, ever since the beginning of the world, since the days of Cain and Abel, against the lives and property of individuals.

Hence also the creation of establishments whose object is to guarantee to everyone the peaceful possession of his person and his goods.

These establishments were called *governments*.

Everywhere, even among the least enlightened tribes, one encounters a government, so universal and urgent is the need for security provided by government. Everywhere, men resign themselves to the most extreme sacrifices rather than do without government and hence security, without realizing that in so doing, they misjudge their alternatives.

Suppose that a man found his person and his means of survival incessantly menaced; wouldn't his first and constant preoccupation be to protect himself from the dangers that surround him? This preoccupation, these efforts, this labor, would necessarily absorb the greater portion of his time, as well as the most energetic and active faculties of his intelligence. In consequence, he could only devote insufficient and uncertain efforts, and his divided attention, to the satisfaction of his other needs.

Even though this man might be asked to surrender a very considerable portion of his time and of his labor to someone who takes it upon himself to guarantee the peaceful possession of his person and his goods, wouldn't it be to his advantage to conclude this bargain?

Still, it would obviously be no less in his self-interest to procure his *security* at the lowest price possible.

Competition in Security

If there is one well-established truth in political economy, it is this:

> That in all cases, for all commodities that serve to provide for the tangible or intangible needs of the consumer, it is in the consumer's best interest that labor and trade remain free, because the freedom of labor and of trade have as their necessary and permanent result the maximum reduction of price.

And this:

> That the interests of the consumer of any commodity whatsoever should always prevail over the interests of the producer.

Now in pursuing these principles, one arrives at this rigorous conclusion:

> That the production of security should, in the interests of the consumers of this intangible commodity, remain subject to the law of free competition.

Whence it follows:

> That no government should have the right to prevent another government from going into competition with it, or to require consumers of security to come exclusively to it for this *commodity*.

Nevertheless, I must admit that, up until the present, one recoiled before this rigorous implication of the principle of free competition.

One economist who has done as much as anyone to extend the application of the principle of liberty, M. Charles Dunoyer, thinks "that the functions of government will never be able to fall into the domain of private activity."[1]

Now here is a citation of a clear and obvious exception to the principle of free competition.

This exception is all the more remarkable for being unique.

Undoubtedly, one can find economists who establish more numerous exceptions to this principle; but we may emphatically affirm that these are not *pure* economists. True economists are generally agreed, on the one hand, that the government should restrict itself to guaranteeing the security of its citizens, and on the other hand, that the freedom of labor and of trade should otherwise be whole and absolute.

But why should there be an exception relative to security? What special reason is there that the production of security cannot be relegated to free competition? Why should it be subjected to a different principle and organized according to a different system?

On this point, the masters of the science are silent, and M. Dunoyer, who has clearly noted this exception, does not investigate the grounds on which it is based.

Security an Exception?

We are consequently led to ask ourselves whether this exception is well founded, in the eyes of the economist.

It offends reason to believe that a well-established natural law can admit of exceptions. A natural law must hold everywhere and always, or be invalid. I cannot believe, for example, that the universal law of gravitation, which governs the physical world, is ever suspended in any instance or at any point of the universe. Now I consider economic laws comparable to natural laws, and I have just as much faith in the principle of the division of labor as I have in the universal law of gravitation. I believe that while these principles can be *disturbed*, they admit of no exceptions.

But, if this is the case, the production of security should not be removed from the jurisdiction of free competition; and if it is removed, society as a whole suffers a loss. Either this is logical and true, or else the principles on which economic science is based are invalid.

The Alternatives

It thus has been demonstrated *a priori*, to those of us who have faith in the principles of economic science, that the exception indicated above is not justified, and that the production of security, like anything else, should be subject to the law of free competition.

Once we have acquired this conviction, what remains for us to do? It remains for us to investigate how it has come about that the production of security has not been subjected to the law of free competition, but rather has been subjected to different principles.

What are those principles?

Those of *monopoly* and *communism*.

In the entire world, there is not a single establishment of the security industry that is not based on monopoly or on communism.

In this connection, we add, in passing, a simple remark.

Political economy has disapproved equally of monopoly and communism in the various branches of human activity, wherever it has found them. Is it not then strange and unreasonable that it accepts them in the security industry?

Monopoly and Communism

Let us now examine how it is that all known governments have either been subjected to the law of monopoly, or else organized according to the communistic principle.

First let us investigate what is understood by the words monopoly and communism.

It is an observable truth that the more urgent and necessary are man's needs, the greater will be the sacrifices he will be willing to endure in order to satisfy them. Now, there are some things that are found abundantly in nature, and whose production does not require a great expenditure of labor, but which, since they satisfy these urgent and necessary wants, can consequently acquire an exchange value all out of proportion with their natural value. Take salt for example. Suppose that a man or a group of men succeed in having the exclusive production and sale of salt assigned to themselves. It is apparent that this man or group could arise the price of this commodity well above its value, well above the price it would have under a regime of free competition.

One will then say that this man or this group possesses a monopoly, and that the price of salt is a monopoly price.

But it is obvious that the consumers will not consent freely to paying the abusive monopoly surtax. It will be necessary to compel them to pay it, and in order to compel them, the employment of force will be necessary.

Every monopoly necessarily rests on force.

When the monopolists are no longer as strong as the consumers they exploit, what happens?

In every instance, the monopoly finally disappears either violently or as the outcome of an amicable transaction. What is it replaced with?

If the roused and insurgent consumers secure the means of production of the salt industry, in all probability they will confiscate this industry for their own profit, and their first thought will be, not to relegate it to free competition, but rather to exploit it, *in common*, for their own account. They will then name a director or a directive committee to operate the saltworks, to whom they will allocate the funds necessary to defray the costs of salt production. Then, since the experience of the past will have made them suspicious and distrustful, since they will be afraid that the director named by them will seize production for his own benefit, and simply reconstitute by open or hidden means the old monopoly for his own profit, they will elect delegates, representatives entrusted with appropriating the funds necessary for production, with watching over their use, and with making sure that the salt produced is equally distributed to those entitled to it. The production of salt will be organized in this manner.

This form of the organization of production has been named communism.

When this organization is applied to a single commodity, the communism is said to be partial.

When it is applied to all commodities, the communism is said to be complete.

But whether communism is partial or complete, political economy is no more tolerant of it than it is of monopoly, of which it is merely an extension.

The Monopolization and Collectivization of the Security Industry

Isn't what has just been said about salt applicable to security? Isn't this the history of all monarchies and all republics?

Everywhere, the production of security began by being organized as a monopoly, and everywhere, nowadays, it tends to be organized communistically.

Here is why.

Among the tangible and intangible commodities necessary to man, none, with the possible exception of wheat, is more indispensable, and therefore none can support quite so large a monopoly duty.

Nor is any quite so prone to monopolization.

What, indeed, is the situation of men who need security? Weakness. What is the situation of those who undertake to provide them with this necessary security? Strength. If it were otherwise, if the consumers of security were stronger than the producers, they obviously would dispense with their assistance.

Now, if the producers of security are originally stronger than the consumers, won't it be easy for the former to impose a monopoly on the latter?

Everywhere, when societies originate, we see the strongest, most warlike races seizing the exclusive government of the society. Everywhere we see these races seizing a monopoly on security within certain more or less extensive boundaries, depending on their number and strength.

And, this monopoly being, by its very nature, extraordinarily profitable, everywhere we see the races invested with the monopoly on security devoting themselves to bitter struggles, in order to add to *the extent of their market*, the number of their *forced* consumers, and hence the amount of their gains.

War has been the necessary and inevitable consequence of the establishment of a monopoly on security.

Another inevitable consequence has been that this monopoly has engendered all other monopolies.

When they saw the situation of the monopolizers of security, the producers of other commodities could not help but notice that nothing in the world is more advantageous than monopoly. They, in turn, were consequently tempted to add to the gains from their own industry by the same process. But what did they require in order to monopolize, to the detriment of the consumers, the commodity they produced? They required force. However, they did not possess the force necessary to constrain the consumers in question. What did they do? They borrowed it, for a consideration, from those who had it. They petitioned and obtained, at the price of an agreed upon fee, the exclusive privilege of carrying on their industry within certain determined boundaries. Since the fees for these privileges brought the producers of security a goodly sum of money, the world was soon covered with monopolies. Labor and trade were everywhere shackled, enchained, and the condition of the masses remained as miserable as possible.

Nevertheless, after long centuries of suffering, as enlightenment spread through the world little by little, the masses who had been smothered under this nexus of privileges began to rebel against the privileged, and to demand *liberty*, that is to say, the suppression of monopolies.

This process took many forms. What happened in England, for example? Originally, the race which governed the country and which was militarily organized (the aristocracy), having at its head a hereditary leader (the king), and an equally hereditary administrative council (the House of Lords), set the price of security, which it had monopolized, at whatever rate it pleased. There was no negotiation between the producers of security and the consumers. This was the rule of *absolutism*. But as time passed, the consumers, having become aware of their numbers and strength, arose against the purely arbitrary regime, and they obtained the right to negotiate with the producers over the price of the commodity. For this purpose, they sent delegates to the *House of Commons* to discuss the level of taxes, the price of security. They were thus able to improve their lot somewhat. Nevertheless, the producers of security had a direct say in the naming of the members of the House of Commons, so that debate was not entirely open, and the price of the commodity remained above its natural value. One day the exploited consumers rose against the producers and dispossessed them of their industry. They then undertook to carry on this industry by themselves and chose for this purpose a director of operations assisted by a Council. Thus communism replaced monopoly. But the scheme did not work, and twenty years later, primitive monopoly was reestablished. Only this time the monopolists were wise enough not to restore the rule of absolutism; they accepted free debate over taxes, being careful, all the while, incessantly to corrupt the delegates of the opposition party. They gave these delegates control over various posts in the administration of security, and they even went so far as to allow the most influential into the bosom of their superior Council. Nothing could have been more clever than this behavior. Nevertheless, the consumers of security finally became aware of these abuses, and demanded the reform of Parliament. This long contested reform was finally achieved, and since that time, the consumers have won a significant lightening of their burdens.

In France, the monopoly on security, after having similarly undergone frequent vicissitudes and various modifications, has just been overthrown for the second time. [De Molinari was writing one year after the revolutions of 1848—Tr.] As once happened in England, monopoly for the benefit of one caste, and then in the name of a certain class of society, was finally replaced by communal production. The consumers as a whole, behaving like shareholders, named a director responsible for supervising the actions of the director and of his administration.

We will content ourselves with making one simple observation on the subject of this new regime.

Just as the monopoly on security logically had to spawn universal monopoly, so communistic security must logically spawn universal communism.

In reality, we have a choice of two things:

Either communistic production is superior to free production, or it is not.

If it is, then it must be for all things, not just for security.

If not, *progress* requires that it be replaced by free production.

Complete communism or complete liberty: that is the alternative!

Government and Society

But is it conceivable that the production of security could be organized other than as a monopoly or communistically? Could it conceivably be relegated to free competition? The response to this question on the part of *political* writers is unanimous: No.

Why? We will tell you why.

Because these writers, who are concerned especially with governments, know nothing about society. They regard it as an artificial fabrication, and believe that the mission of government is to modify and remake it constantly.

Now in order to modify or remake society, it is necessary to be empowered with an *authority* superior to that of the various individuals of which it is composed.

Monopolistic governments claim to have obtained from God himself this authority which gives them the right to modify or remake society according to their fancy, and to dispose of persons and property however they please. Communistic governments appeal to human reason, as manifested in the majority of the sovereign people.

But do monopolistic governments and communistic governments truly possess this superior, irresistible authority? Do they in reality have a higher authority than that which a free government could have? This is what we must investigate.

The Divine Right of Kings and Majorities

If it were true that society were not naturally organized, if it were true that the laws which govern its motion were to be constantly modified or remade, the *legislators* would necessarily have to have an immutable, sacred authority. Being the continuators of Providence on earth, they would have to be regarded as almost equal to God. If it were otherwise, would it not be impossible for them to fulfill their mission? Indeed, one cannot intervene in human affairs, one cannot attempt to direct and regulate them, without daily offending a multitude of interests. Unless those in power are believed to have a mandate from a superior entity, the injured interests will resist.

Whence the fiction of divine right.

This fiction was certainly the best imaginable. If you succeed in persuading the multitude that God himself has chosen certain men or certain races to give laws to society and to govern it, no one will dream of revolting against these appointees of Providence, and everything the government does will be accepted. A government based on divine right is imperishable.

On one condition only, namely that divine right is believed in.

If one takes the thought into one's head that the leaders of the people do not receive their inspirations directly from providence itself, that they obey purely human impulses, the prestige that surrounds them will disappear. One will irreverently resist their sovereign decisions, as one resists anything manmade whose *utility* has not been clearly demonstrated.

It is accordingly fascinating to see the pains theoreticians of the divine right take to establish the *superhumanity* of the races in possession of human government.

Let us listen, for example, to M. Joseph de Maistre:

> Man does not make sovereigns. At the very most he can serve as an instrument for dispossessing one sovereign and handing his State over to another sovereign, himself already a prince. Moreover, there has never existed a sovereign family traceable to plebeian origins. If this phenomenon were to appear, it would mark a new epoch on earth....

> It is written: *I am the Maker of sovereigns*. This is not just a religious slogan, a preacher's metaphor; it is the literal truth pure and simple; it is a law of the political world. God *makes* kings, word for word. He prepares royal races, nurtures them at the center of a cloud which hides their origins. Finally they appear, *crowned with glory and honor*; they take their places.[2]

According to this system, which embodies the will of Providence in certain men and which invests these chosen ones, these anointed ones with a quasi-divine authority, the *subjects* evidently have no rights at all. They must submit, *without question*, to the decrees of the sovereign authority, as if they were the decrees of Providence itself.

According to Plutarch, the body is the instrument of the soul, and the soul is the instrument of God. According to the divine right school, God selects certain souls and uses them as instruments for governing the world.

If men *had faith* in this theory, surely nothing could unsettle a government based on divine right.

Unfortunately, they have completely lost faith.

Why?

Because one fine day they took it into their heads to question and to reason, and in questioning, in reasoning, they discovered that their governors governed them no better than they, simply mortals out of communication with Providence, could have done themselves.

It was *free inquiry* that demonetized the fiction of divine right, to the point where the subjects of monarchs or of aristocracies based on divine right obey them only insofar as they think it *in their own self-interest* to obey them.

Has the communist fiction fared any better?

According to the communist theory, of which Rousseau is the high-priest, authority does not descend from on high, but rather comes up from below. The government no longer look to Providence for its authority, it looks to united mankind, to the *one, indivisible, and sovereign* nation.

Here is what the communists, the partisans of poplar sovereignty, assume. They assume that human reason has the power to discover the best laws and the organization which most perfectly suits society; and that, in practice, these laws reveal themselves at the conclusion of a free debate between conflicting opinions. If there is no unanimity, if there is still dissension after the debate, the majority is in the right, since it comprises the larger number of reasonable individuals. (These individuals are, of course, assumed to be equal, otherwise the whole structure collapses.) Consequently, they insist that the decisions of the majority must become *law*, and that the minority is obliged to submit to it, even if it is contrary to its most deeply rooted convictions and injures its most precious interests.

That is the theory; but, in practice, does the *authority* of the decision of the majority really have this irresistible, absolute character as assumed? Is it always, in every instance, respected by the minority? Could it be?

Let us take an example.

Let us suppose that socialism succeeds in propagating itself among the working classes in the countryside as it has already among the working classes in the cities; that it consequently becomes the majority in the country and that, profiting from this situation, it sends a socialist majority to the Legislative Assembly and names a socialist president. Suppose that this majority and this president, invested with sovereign authority, decrees the imposition of a tax on the rich of three billions, in order to organize the labor of the poor, as M. Proudhon demanded. Is it probable that the minority would submit peacefully to his iniquitous and absurd, yet legal, yet *constitutional* plunder?

No, without a doubt it would not hesitate to disown the *authority* of the majority and to defend its property.

Under this regime, as under the preceding, one obeys the custodians of authority only insofar as one thinks it in one's self-interest to obey them.

This leads us to affirm that the moral foundation of authority is neither as solid nor as wide, under a regime of monopoly or of communism, as it could be under a regime of liberty.

The Regime of Terror

Suppose nevertheless that the partisans of an *artificial organization*, either the monopolists or the communists, are right: that society is not naturally organized, and that the task of making and unmaking the laws that regulate society continuously devolves upon men, look in what a lamentable situation the world would find itself. The moral authority of governors rests, in reality, on the self-interest of the governed. The latter having a natural tendency to resist anything harmful to their self-interest, unacknowledged authority would continually require the help of physical force.

The monopolist and the communists, furthermore, completely understand this necessity.

If anyone, says M. de Maistre, attempts to detract from the authority of God's chosen ones, let him be turned over to the secular power, let the hangman perform his office.

If anyone does not recognize the authority of those chosen by the people, say the theoreticians of the school of Rousseau, if he resists any decision whatsoever of the majority, let him be punished as an enemy of the sovereign people, let the guillotine perform justice.

These two schools, which both take *artificial organization* as their point of departure, necessarily lead to the same conclusion: TERROR.

The Free Market for Security

Allow us now to formulate a simple hypothetical situation.

Let us imagine a newborn society: The men who compose it are busy working and exchanging the fruits of their labor. A natural instinct reveals to these men that their persons, the land they occupy and cultivate, the fruits of their labor, are their *property*, and that no one, except themselves, has the right to dispose of or touch this property. This instinct is not hypothetical; it exists. But man being an imperfect creature, this awareness of the right of everyone to his person and his goods will not be found to the same degree in every soul, and certain individuals will make criminal attempts, by violence or by fraud, against the persons or the property of others.

Hence, the need for an industry that prevents or suppresses these forcible or fraudulent aggressions.

Let us suppose that a man or a combination of men comes and says:

For a recompense, I will undertake to prevent or suppress criminal attempts against persons and property.

Let those who wish their persons and property to be sheltered from all aggression apply to me.

Before striking a bargain with this *producer of security*, what will the consumers do? In the first place, they will check if he is really strong enough to protect them.

In the second place, whether his character is such that they will not have to worry about his instigating the very aggressions he is supposed to suppress.

In the third place, whether any other producer of security, offering equal guarantees, is disposed to offer them this commodity on better terms.

These terms are of various kinds.

In order to be able to guarantee the consumers full security of their persons and property, and, in case of harm, to give them a compensation proportioned to the loss suffered, it would be necessary, indeed:

1. That the producer establish certain penalties against the offenders of persons and the violators of property, and that the consumers agree to submit to these penalties, in case they themselves commit offenses;
2. That he impose certain inconveniences on the consumers, with the object of facilitating the discovery of the authors of offenses;
3. That he regularly gather, in order to cover his costs of production as well as an appropriate return for his efforts, a certain sum, variable according to the situation of the consumers, the particular occupations they engage in, and the extent, value, and nature of their properties.

If these terms, necessary for carrying on this industry, are agreeable to the consumers, a bargain will be struck. Otherwise the consumers will either do without security, or else apply to another producer.

Now if we consider the particular nature of the security industry, it is apparent that the producers will necessarily restrict their clientele to certain territorial boundaries. They would be unable to cover their costs if they tried to provide police services in localities comprising only a few clients. Their clientele will naturally be clustered around the center of their activities. They would nevertheless be unable to abuse this situation by dictating to the consumers. In the event of an abusive rise in the price of security, the consumers would always have the option of giving their patronage to a new entrepreneur, or to a neighboring entrepreneur.

This option the consumer retains of being able to buy security wherever he pleases brings about a constant emulation among all the producers, each producer striving to maintain or augment his clientele with the attraction of cheapness or of faster, more complete and better justice.[3]

If, on the contrary, the consumer is not free to buy security wherever he pleases, you forthwith see open up a large profession dedicated to arbitrariness and bad management. Justice becomes slow and costly, the police vexatious, individual liberty is no longer respected, the price of security is abusively inflated and inequitably apportioned, according to the power and influence of this or that class of consumers. The protectors engage in bitter struggles to wrest customers from one another. In a word, all the abuses inherent in monopoly or in communism crop up.

Under the rule of free competition, war between the producers of security entirely loses its justification. Why would they make war? To conquer consumers? But the consumers would not allow themselves to be conquered. They would be careful not to allow themselves to be protected by men who would unscrupulously attack the persons and property of their rivals. If some audacious conqueror tried to become dictator, they would immediately call to their aid all the free consumers menaced by this aggression, and they would treat him as he deserved. Just as war is the natural consequence of monopoly, peace us the natural consequence of liberty.

Under a regime of liberty, the natural organization of the security industry would not be different from that of other industries. In small districts a single entrepreneur could suffice. This entrepreneur might leave his business to his son, or sell it to another entrepreneur. In larger districts, one company by itself would bring together enough resources adequately to carry on this important and difficult business. If it were well managed, this company could easily last, and security would last with it. In the security industry, just as in most of the other branches of production, the latter mode of organization will probably replace the former, in the end.

On the one hand this would be a monarchy, and on the other hand it would be a republic; but it would be a monarchy without monopoly and a republic without communism.

On either hand, this authority would be accepted and respected in the name of utility, and would not be an authority imposed by *terror*.

It will undoubtedly be disputed whether such a hypothetical situation is realizable. But, at the risk of being considered utopian, we affirm that this is not disputable, that a careful examination of the facts will decide the problem of government more and more in favor of liberty, just as it does all other economic problems. We are convinced, so far as we are concerned, that one day societies will be established to agitate for the *freedom of government*, as they have already been established on behalf of the freedom of commerce.

And we do not hesitate to add that after this reform has been achieved, and all artificial obstacles to the free action of the natural laws that govern the economic world have disappeared, the situation of the various members of society will become *the best possible*.[4]

Notes

1. In his remarkable book *De la liberté du travail (On the Freedom of Labor)*, Vol. III, p. 253. (Published by Guillaumin.)
2. *Du principe générateur des constitutions politiques (On the Generating Principle of Political Constitutions)*, Preface.
3. Adam Smith, whose remarkable spirit of observation extends to all subjects, remarks that the administration of justice gained much, in England, from the competition between the different courts of law:

> The fees of court seem originally to have been the principal support of the different courts of justice in England. Each court endeavoured to draw to itself as much business as it could, and was, upon that account, willing to take cognizance of many suits which were not originally intended to fall under its jurisdiction. The court of king's bench instituted for the trial of criminal causes only, took cognizance of civil suits; the plaintiff pretending that the defendant, in not doing him justice, had been guilty of some trespass or misdemeanor. The court of exchequer, instituted for the levying of the king's revenue, and for enforcing the payment of such debts only as were due to the king, took cognizance of all other contract debts; the plaintiff alleging that he could not pay the king, because the defendant would not pay him. In consequence of such fictions it came, in many case, to depend altogether upon the parties before what court they would chuse to have their cause tried; and each court endeavoured, by superior dispatch and impartiality, to draw to itself as many causes as it could. The present admirable constitution of the courts of justice in England was, perhaps, originally in a great measure, formed by this emulation, which anciently took place between their respective judges; each judge endeavouring to give, in his own court, the speediest and most effectual remedy, which the law would admit, for every sort of injustice.—*The Wealth of Nations* (New York: Modern Library, 1937; originally 1776), p. 679.

4. [This essay was] originally published as "De la production de la sécurité," in *Journal des Economistes* (February 1849), pp. 277-90. This translation was originally published as Gustave de Molinari, "The Production of Security," trans. J. Huston McCulloch, Occasional Papers Series #2 (Richard M. Ebeling, editor) (New York: The Center for Libertarian Studies, May 1977).

27

Individualist Anarchism in the U.S.: Origins

Murray Rothbard

Libertarians tend to fall into two opposing errors on the American past: the familiar "Golden Age" view of the rightwing that everything was blissful in America until some moment of precipitous decline (often dated 1933); and the deeply pessimistic minority view that rejects the American past root and branch, spurning all American institutions and virtually all of its thinkers except such late nineteenth-century individualist anarchists as Benjamin R. Tucker and Lysander Spooner. The truth is somewhere in between: America was never the golden "land of the free" of the conservative-libertarian legend, and yet managed for a very long time to be freer, in institutions and intellectual climate, than any other land.

Colonial America did not set out deliberately to be the land of the free. On the contrary, it began in a tangle of tyranny, special privilege, and vast land monopoly. Territories were carved out either as colonies subject directly to the English Crown, or as enormous land grabs for privileged companies or feudal proprietors. What defeated these despotic and feudal thrusts into the new territory was, at bottom, rather simple: the vastness of the fertile and uninhabited land that lay waiting to be settled. Not only relative freedom, but even outright anarchist institutions grew up early in the interstices between the organized, despotic English colonies.

Albemarle

There is a good possibility that for a couple of decades in the mid-seventeenth century, the coastal area north of Albemarle Sound in what is now northeastern North Carolina was in a quasi-anarchistic state. Technically a part of the Virginia colony but in practice virtually independent, the Albemarle area was a haven for persons chaffing under the despotic rule of the English Crown, the Anglican Church and the large planter aristocracy of Virginia. Roger Green led a Presbyterian group that left Virginia proper for Albemarle, and many Quakers settled in the area, which specialized in growing tobacco. This semi-libertarian condition came to an end in 1663, when the English Crown included Albemarle in the mammoth Carolina land grant bestowed on a group of eight feudal proprietors. Little is known of pre-1663 Albemarle, since historians display scant interest in stateless societies.[1]

"Rogue's Island"

Undoubtedly the freest colony in America, and the major source of anarchistic thought and institutions, was little Rhode Island, which originated as a series of more or less anarchic settlements founded by people fleeing from the brutal politico-religious tyranny of the Puritans of Massachusetts Bay (who referred to the new territory as "Rogue's Land"). Unsettled and untouched by the land grants or the Crown, the Rhode Island area provided a haven close to the Massachusetts Bay settlement.

Providence, the first refugee settlement, was founded in 1636 by the young Reverend Roger Williams. A political and especially a religious libertarian, Williams was close to the Levellers—that great group of English laissez-faire individualists who constituted the "extreme leftwing" of the republican side in the English Civil War. At first, the Williams settlement was virtually anarchistic. As Williams described it, "the masters of families have ordinarily met once a fortnight and consulted about our common peace, watch and plenty; and mutual consent have finished all matters of speed and pace." But this anarchistic idyll began to flounder in a tragically ironic trap that Williams had laid for himself and his followers. Williams had pioneered in scrupulously purchasing all the land from the Indians voluntarily—a method of land acquisition in sharp contrast to the brutal methods of extermination beloved by the Puritans of Massachusetts Bay. But the problem was that the Indians had erroneous theories of property. As collective tribes they laid claim to vast reaches of land on which they had only hunted. Not having transformed the land itself, they were not entitled to all of the land which they sold. Hence, Williams and his group, by purchasing all of this unsettled land, willy-nilly acquired these illegitimate land titles. Thinking that he had been generous, voluntaristic and libertarian, Williams (and his group) fell into the trap of becoming a feudalistic group of landowners. Instead of automatically acquiring the land in Providence which they homesteaded, later settlers had to purchase or rent the land from the original Williams claimants. The result was that Williams and his original colleagues, who had formed "The Fellowship," found themselves in the position of being oligarchic rulers of Providence as well as Providence's land "monopolists." Once again, as so many times in history, land-monopoly and government went hand in hand.

While a libertarian, Williams never became an explicit anarchist, even though he established an anarchistic community in Providence. The honor of being the first explicit anarchist in North America belongs to Williams' successor, a leading religious refugee from Massachusetts, Anne Hutchinson. Anne and her followers, who had become far more numerous a band of heretics than Williams had amassed, emigrated to the Rhode Island area in 1638 at the suggestion of Williams himself. There they purchased the island of Aquidneck from the Indians and founded the settlement of Pocasset (now Portsmouth). Anne soon became restive at Pocasset, seeing that her follower and major founder of the settlement, the wealthy merchant William Coddington, had quickly established his own theocratic rule over the infant colony. For Coddington, as "judge" of the settlement, based his decrees and rulings on the "word of God," as arbitrarily interpreted by himself.

Coddington, this time far more explicitly and consciously than Williams, founded his dictatorial power on his deed of purchase of the island from the Indians. Since his was the only name on the deed of purchase, Coddington claimed for himself all the "rights" of land monopolist and feudal lord, allotting no rights to homesteading settlers.

Anne Hutchinson, not yet an anarchist, now launched a political struggle against Coddington in early 1639 forcing him to give the entire body of freemen a veto over his actions. In April, Coddington was forced to agree to elections for his post as Governor, a position which he had expected to be his permanently by feudal right. Anne's husband, William Hutchinson, defeated Coddington in the elections, and Coddington and his followers left Pocasset to found a new settlement called New Port at the southern end of the island. The victorious Hutchinsonians adopted a new constitution, changing the name of the town to Portsmouth, and stating that 1) all male inhabitants were equal before the law; 2) Church and State were to be kept separate; and 3) trial by jury was to be established for all. Immediately thereafter Coddington declared war upon Portsmouth and at the end of a year of turmoil, the two groups agreed to unite the two settlements. Coddington was once more chosen as governor, but with democratic institutions and religious liberty guaranteed.

From the point of view of social philosophy, however, the important consequence of this struggle with Coddington was that Anne Hutchinson began to reflect deeply on the whole question of liberty. If, as Roger Williams had taught, there must be absolute religious liberty for the individual, than what right does government have to rule the individual at all? In short, Anne Hutchinson had come to the conclusion of the "unlawfulness of magistry government." As Anne's biographer Winifred Rugg put it: "She was supremely convinced that the Christian held within his own breast the assurance of salvation.... For such persons magistrates were obviously superfluous. As for the others, they were to be converted, not coerced."

Anne persuaded her husband to resign as one of Coddington's major assistants in the colony. In 1642, soon after his resignation, William Hutchinson died. Deprived of her husband and disgusted with all government, Anne left Rhode Island to settle at Pelham Bay, near New York City. There, in the late summer of 1643, Anne and her family were killed by a band of Indians, who had been set upon by the Dutch of New York.

But while Anne Hutchinson was dead, her ideas lived on. Some of her followers, headed by Anne's sister Mrs. Catherine Scott, headed the new Baptist movement in Rhode Island, which, as we shall see, was later to erupt as a highly important movement of Baptist anarchists.

One of the most interesting individualists of the American colonial period was Samuel Gorton. An English clothier, his libertarian political and religious views and individualistic spirit got him persecuted in every colony in New England, including Providence and Portsmouth. An opponent of theocracy, and indeed of all formal religious organizations, Gorton opposed all transgressions of government against the rights guaranteed by English common law. Fleeing Anglican England, Gorton successively had to escape from Massachusetts Bay, Plymouth, Portsmouth, and Providence. In the Providence incident Roger Williams began to display that totalitarian temperament, that impatience with anyone more individualistic than he, that was later to turn him sharply away from liberty and towards statism. Williams agreed to the expulsion of Gorton from Providence, declaring that Gorton was "bewitching and bemadding poor Providence…with his unclear and foul censures of all the ministers of this country…"

Accused of being "anarchists," denounced by Governor Winthrop of Massachusetts Bay as a "man not fit to live upon the face of the earth," Gorton and his followers were forced in late 1642 to found an entirely new settlement of their own: Shawomet (later Warwick) which he purchased from the Indians. There the little settlement was under continued threat of aggression by their mighty Massachusetts neighbor. While Gorton was not explicitly an anarchist, the little town of Shawomet lived in an anarchist idyll in the years that it remained a separate settlement. In the words of Gorton, for over five years the settlement "lived peaceably together, desiring and endeavoring to do wrong to no man, neither English nor Indian, ending all our differences in a neighborly and loving way of arbitration, mutually chosen amongst us." But in 1648, Warwick joined with the other three towns of Rhode Island to form the colony of the "Providence Plantation." From that time on Warwick was under a government, even though this was a government far more democratic and libertarian than existed anywhere else. As a respected leader of the new colony, now considered "fit to live" in Rhode Island, Gorton managed to abolish imprisonment for debt, lower the term of indentured service, and even to be the first to abolish slavery in America, even though abolition turned out to be a dead letter.

After two decades of struggle against the aggressions of Massachusetts, Roger Williams was finally able, in the mid-1650s, to win immunity for Rhode Island, by gaining the protection of the victorious republican revolutionaries of England. At the time of winning its protection from Massachusetts, Williams described the colony as having "long drunk of the cup of as great liberties as any people that we can hear of under the whole heaven." "Sir," Williams added, writing to his libertarian English friend Sir Henry Vane, "we have not known what an excise means; we have almost forgotten what tithes are, yea, or taxes either, to church or commonwealth."

Yet it was almost immediately after this triumph that Williams savagely turned on the liberty of the colony he had founded. Why the shift? Several reasons can be found: first, the inevitable corruptions of governmental power on even the most libertarian of rulers; and second, Williams' impatience with those even more libertarian than he. But a third reason has to do with the loss of liberty in England. For two decades, Roger Williams had worked closely with the most libertarian and individualistic groups in the revolutionary movement in England; but now, just as the laissez-faire, individualist "left" seemed to have triumphed, England suddenly moved precipitously rightward and stateward under the new dictatorship of the Independent Oliver Cromwell. The shift away from liberty in England was embodied in Cromwell's brutal suppression of the Levellers, the leaders of libertarianism in the Revolution. With the mother country sliding away from liberty and into dictatorship, the aging Williams undoubtedly lost much of his previously firm grip on libertarian principle.

Williams' shift from liberty was first revealed in 1655, when he suddenly imposed a system of compulsory military service on the people of Rhode Island. It was in reaction to this violation of all the libertarian traditions of Rhode Island that a vigorous opposition developed in the colony—an opposition that eventually polarized into outright individualistic anarchism. Heading this move toward anarchism was the bulk of the Baptists of Rhode Island. Led by the Reverend Thomas Olney, former Baptist minister of Providence, and including also John Field, John Throckmorton, the redoubtable William Harris, and Williams' own brother Robert. This group circulated a petition charging that "it was blood guiltiness, and against the rule of the gospel to execute judgment upon transgressors, against the private or pubic weal." In short, any punishment of transgressors and/or any bearing of arms was anti-Christian!

Williams' response was to denounce the petition as causing "tumult and disturbance." The anarchists thereupon rose in rebellion against Williams' government, but were put down by force of arms. Despite the failure of the revolt, the 1655 elections of a few months later elected Thomas Olney as an assistant to the inevitably reelected Williams, even though Olney himself had led the uprising.

Williams proceeded to aggrandize statism still further. The central government of the colony decided to bypass the home rule right of the individual towns to finance the colony, and appointed central officials to levy general taxes directly upon the people. Laws against "immorality" were also strengthened, with corporal punishment to be levied for such crimes as "loose living." The anti-immorality laws were probably a part of an attempt by Williams to curry favor with the puritanical Oliver Cromwell. Most ominously, after Cromwell had ordered Rhode Island to punish "intestinal commotions," the colony swiftly passed a law against "ringleaders of factions" who were thereafter to be sent to England for trial.

Baptist anarchism, however, continued to intensify in Rhode Island. One of the new adherents was none other than Catherine Scott, a leading Baptist preacher and the sister of Anne Hutchinson. In this way, Anne's lone pioneering in philosophical anarchism before her death had planted a seed that burst forth a decade and a half later. Also adopting anarchism were Rebecca Throckmorton, Robert West, and Ann Williams, wife of Robert. Finally, in March 1657, the crackdown on freedom of speech and dissent arrived. Williams hauled these four anarchist opponents into court, charging them with being "common opposers of all authority." After this act of intimidation, however, Williams relented and withdrew the charges. But Williams had accomplished the singular purpose of his repression: the frightened anarchist leaders lapsed into silence.

The formidable William Harris, however, could not be frightened so readily. Harris circulated a manuscript to all the towns of Rhode Island, denouncing all taxation and "all civil governments." He called upon the people to "cry out, No lords, No masters." Harris predicted that the State, which he called "the House of Saul," would inevitably grow weaker and weaker, while the "House of David" (namely Harris and his followers) would grow stronger and stronger. Harris also condemned all punishments and prisons, all officials and legislative assemblies.

William Harris was now hauled into court by the Williams administration. He was charged with "open defiance under his hand against our Charter, all our laws...Parliament, the Lord Protector [Cromwell] and all governments." Instead of quieting under repression as had Mrs. Scott and the others, Harris swore that he would continue to maintain his anarchism "with his blood." Persistently refusing to recant, Harris reiterated his interpretation of Scripture, namely that "he that can say it is his conscience ought not to yield subjection to any human order amongst men." The General Court found Harris guilty of being "contemptuous and seditious," and the evidence against Harris and his son was sent to England in preparation for a trial for treason.

The treason trial never materialized, because by good fortune the ship carrying the evidence to England was lost at sea. But Harris was finally sufficiently cowed to abandon his anarchism. He turned instead to a life-long harassment of the hated Roger Williams through endless litigation of land claims.[2]

Pennsylvania: The Holy Experiment

The third great example of anarchism in colonial America took place in Pennsylvania. This was William Penn's experiment for a Quaker colony that would provide "an example [that] may be set up to the nations." While religious liberty was guaranteed, and institutions were relatively libertarian, Penn never meant his new colony, founded in1681 to be anarchistic or anything of the like.[3] Curiously, Pennsylvania fell into living and functioning anarchism by happy accident. Lured by religious liberty and by cheap and abundant land, settlers, largely Quaker, poured into Pennsylvania in large numbers. At the end of eight years 12,000 people had settled in the new colony. The first touch of anarchy came in the area of taxation. While low excise and export duties had been levied by the Pennsylvania Assembly in 1683, Governor Penn set aside all taxes for a year to encourage rapid settlement. The next year, when Penn wanted to levy taxes for his own personal income, a group of leaders of the colony persuaded Penn to drop the tax, in return for them personally raising a voluntary gift for his own use.

William Penn returned to England in the fall of 1684, convinced that he had founded a stable and profitable colony. One of his major expectations was the collection of "quitrents" from every settler. This was to be in continuing payment for Penn's claim as feudal landlord of the entire colony, as had been granted by the Crown. But Penn, like the proprietors and feudal overlords in the other colonies, found it almost impossible to collect these quitrents. He had granted the populace a moratorium on quitrents until 1685, but the people insisted on further postponements, and Penn's threatened legal proceedings were without success. Furthermore, the people of Pennsylvania continued to refuse to vote to levy taxes. They even infringed upon the monopoly of lime production which Penn had granted to himself, by stubbornly opening their own lime quarries. William Penn found that deprived of feudal or tax income, his deficits from ruling Pennsylvania were large and his fortune was dissipating steadily. Freedom and a taxless society had contaminated the colonists. As Penn complained, "the great fault is, that those who are there, lose their authority one way or other in the spirits of the people and then they can do little with their outward powers."

When Penn returned to England, the governing of the colony fell in the Council of Pennsylvania. Although Penn had appointed Thomas Lloyd, a Welsh Quaker, to be president of the Council, the president had virtually no power, and could not make any decisions of his own. The Council itself met very infrequently, and no officials had the interim power to act. During these great intervals, Pennsylvania had no government at all—as indicated by the fact that neither quitrents nor axes were being levied in the colony.

Why did the Council rarely meet? For one thing because the Councilors, having little to do in that libertarian society and being unpaid, had their own private business to attend to. The Councilors, according to the laws of the colony, were supposed to receive a small stipend, but as was typical of this anarchistic colony, it proved almost impossible to extract these funds from the Pennsylvanian populace.

If the colonial government ceased to exist except for the infrequent days of Council meetings, what of local governments? Did they provide a permanent bureaucracy, a visible evidence of the continuing existence of the State apparatus? The answer is no; for the local courts met only a few days a year, and the county officials, too, were private citizens who devoted almost no time to upholding the law. To cap the situation the Assembly passed no laws after 1686, being in a continuing wrangle over the extent of its powers.

The colony of Pennsylvania continued in this *de facto* state of individualist anarchism from the fall of 1684 to the end of 1688: four glorious years in which no outcry arose from the happy citizens about "anarchy" or "chaos." No Pennsylvanian seemed to believe himself any the worse for wear.[4]

A bit of government came to Pennsylvania in 1685, in the person of William Dyer who was the appointed Collector of the King's Customs. Despite frantic appeals from William Penn to cooperate with Dyer, the Pennsylvanians persisted in their anarchism by blithely and consistently evading the Royal Navigation Laws.

It is no wonder that William Penn had the distinct impression that his "Holy Experiment" had slipped away from him, had taken a new and bewildering turn. Penn had launched a colony which he thought would quietly follow his dictates and yield him a handsome feudal profit. By providing a prosperous haven of refuge for Quakers, Penn expected in return the twin reward of wealth and power. Instead, he found himself without either. Unable to collect revenue from the free and independent-minded Pennsylvanians, he saw the colony slipping quietly and gracefully into outright anarchism—into a peaceful, growing and flourishing land of no taxes and virtually no State. Thereupon, Penn frantically tried to force Pennsylvania back into the familiar mold of the Old Order.

In February 1687 William Penn appointed five Pennsylvanians as commissioners of state, assigned to "act in the execution of the laws, as if I myself were there present." The purpose of this new appointment was "that there may be a more constant residence of the honorary and governing part of the government, for keeping all things in good order." Penn appointed the five commissioners from among the leading citizens of the colony, and ordered them to enforce the laws.

Evidently the colonists were quite happy about their anarchism, and shrewdly engaged in non-violent resistance toward the commission. In the first place, news about the commission was delayed for months. Then protests poured into Penn about the new commission. Penn soon realized that he had received no communication from the supposedly governing body.

Unable to delay matters any longer, the reluctant commissioners of state took office in February 1688. Three and one-half years of substantive anarchism were over. The State was back in its Heaven; once more all was right in William Penn's world. Typically, the gloating Penn urged the commissioners to conceal any differences among themselves, so as to deceive and overawe the public "Show your virtues but conceal your infirmities; this will make you awful and revered with ye people." He further urged them to enforce the King's duties and to levy taxes to support the government.

The commissioners confined themselves to calling the Assembly into session in the spring of 1688, and this time the Assembly did pass some laws, for the first time in three years. The most important bills presented to the Assembly by the Council and the Commissioners, however, was for the reimposition of taxes; and here the Assembly, at the last minute, heroically defied Penn and the government, and rejected the tax bills.

After a brief flurry of State activity in early 1688, therefore, the State was found wanting, taxes were rejected and the colony lapsed quickly back into a state of anarchism. Somehow, the commisioners, evidently exhausted by their task, failed to meet any further, and the Council fell back into its schedule of rare meetings.

In desperation, Penn acted to appoint a Deputy-Governor to rule Pennsylvania in his absence. Thomas Lloyd, president of the Council, refused the appointment, and as we saw from the reluctance of the commissioners, no one in happily anarchic Pennsylvania wanted to rule over others. At this point, Penn reached outside the colony to appoint a tough old non-Pennsylvanian and non-Quaker, the veteran Puritan soldier John Blackwell, to be Deputy-Governor of the colony. In appointing him, Penn made clear to Blackwell that his primary task was to collect Penn's quitrents and his secondary task to reestablish a government.

If John Blackwell had any idea that the Quakers were a meek people, he was in for a rude surprise. Blackwell was to find out quickly that a devotion to peace, liberty, and individualism in no sense implied an attitude of passive resignation to tyranny—quite the contrary.

Blackwell's initial reception as Deputy-Governor was an augur of things to come. Sending word ahead for someone to meet him upon his arrival in New York, Blackwell landed there only to find no one to receive him. After waiting in vain for three days, Blackwell went alone to the colony. When he arrived in Philadelphia on December 17, 1688, he found no escort, no parade, no reception committee. After having ordered the Council to meet him upon his arrival, Blackwell could find no trace of the Councilor of any other governmental officials. Instead he "found the Council room deserted and covered with dust and scattered papers. The wheels of government had nearly stopped turning."[5]

Only one surly escort appeared, and *he* refused to speak to his new Governor. And when Blackwell arrived at the empty Council room, his only reception was a group of boys of the neighborhood who gathered around to hoot and jeer.

The resourceful Pennsylvanians now embarked on a shrewd and determined campaign of non-violent resistance to the attempt to reimpose a State on a happy and stateless people. Thomas Lloyd, as Keeper of the Great Seal, insisted that none of Blackwell's orders or commissions were legally valid unless stamped with the Great Seal. And Lloyd, as Keeper, somehow stubbornly refused to do any stamping. Furthermore, David Lloyd, the clerk of the court and a distant relative of Thomas, absolutely refused to turn over the documents of any cases to Blackwell, even if the judges so ordered. For this act of defiance Blackwell declared David Lloyd unfit to serve as court clerk and dismissed him. Thomas promptly reappointed David by virtue of his power as Keeper of the Great Seal. Moreover, out of a dozen justices of the peace named by Blackwell, four bluntly refused to serve.

As the revolutionary situation intensified in Pennsylvania, the timid and short-sighted began to betray the revolutionary libertarian cause. All of the Council except two now sided with Blackwell. Leader of the pro-Blackwell clique was Griffith Jones, who had allowed Blackwell to live at his home in Philadelphia. Jones warned that "it is the king's authority that is opposed and [it] looks to me as if it were raising a force to rebel." On the Council, only Arthur Cook and Samuel Richardson continued to defy the Governor.

Blackwell was of course appalled at this situation. He wrote to Penn that the colonists were suffering from excessive liberty. They had eaten more of the "honey of your concessions than their stomachs can bear." Blackwell managed to force the Council to meet every week in early 1689, but he failed to force them to agree to a permanent and continuing Councilor from every county in Philadelphia. Arthur Cook led the successful resistance, pointing out that the "people were not able to bear the charge of constant attendance."

The climax in the struggle between Blackwell and the people of Pennsylvania came in April 1689, when the Governor introduced proceedings for the impeachment of Thomas Lloyd, charging him with high crimes and misdemeanors. In his address, Blackwell trumpeted to his stunned listeners that William Penn's powers over the colony were absolute. The Council, on his theory, existed not to represent the People but to be an instrument of Penn's will concluded his harangue by threatening to unsheathe and wield his sword against his insolent and unruly opponents.

Given the choice between the old anarchism or absolute rule by John Blackwell, even the trimmers and waverers rallied behind Thomas Lloyd. After Blackwell had summarily dismissed Lloyd, Richardson and others from the Council, the Council rebelled and demanded the right to approve of their own members. With the entire Council now arrayed against him, the disheartened Blackwell dissolved that body and sent his resignation to Penn. The Councilors, in turn, bitterly protested to Penn against his deputy's attempt to deprive them of their liberties. As for Blackwell, he considered the Quakers agents of the Devil, as foretold in the New Testament, men "who shall despise dominion and speak evil of dignities." These Quakers, Blackwell charged in horror, "have not the principles of government amongst them, nor will they be informed…"

Faced with virtually unanimous and determined opposition from the colonists Penn decided against Blackwell. For the rest of the year, Blackwell continued formally in office, but he now lost all interest in exerting his rule. He simply waited out his fading term of office. Penn in effect restored the old system by designating the Council as a whole as his "deputy governor." Replacing vinegar with honey Penn apologized for his mistake in appointing Blackwell, and asserted that "I have thought fit…to throw all into you hands, that you may all see the confidence I have in you."

Pennsylvania soon slipped back into anarchism. The Council, again headed by Thomas Lloyd, met but seldom. When a rare meeting was called it did virtually nothing and told William Penn even less. The Assembly also met but rarely. And when Secretary of the colony William Markham (a cousin of Penn, who had been one of the hated Blackwell clique) submitted a petition for the levying of taxes to provide some financial help for poor William Penn the Council totally ignored his request. Furthermore, when Markham asked for a governmental organization of militia to provide for military defense against a (non-existent) French and Indian threat, the Council preserved the anarchistic status of the colony by blandly replying that any people who are interested could provide for their defense *at their own expense*. Anarchism had returned in triumph to Pennsylvania. The determined non-violent resistance of the colony had won a glorious victory.

Penn, however, refused to allow the colony to continue in this anarchistic state. In 1691 he insisted that a continuing Deputy-Governor be appointed, although he would allow the colony to select a Governor. The colony, of course, chose their resistance hero Thomas Lloyd, who assumed his new post in April. After seven years of *de facto* anarchism (with the exception of a few months of Council meetings and several months of a Blackwellite attempt to rule), Pennsylvania now had a continuous, permanent head of government. "Archy" was back, but its burden was still negligible, for the Assembly and the Council still met but rarely and, above all, there was no taxation in the colony.

But the virus of power, the canker of archy, once let loose even a trifle, feeds upon itself. Suddenly, as a bolt from the blue, the Council in April 1692 passed a *new* bill for the reestablishment of taxation and the revered Governor Lloyd concurred in this betrayal. The question now reverted to the popularly elected Assembly, always the political stronghold of liberty in the province. Would they too succumb? The freemen of Philadelphia and of Chester sent the Assembly petitions strongly protesting the proposed imposition of taxation. They urged the Assembly to keep "their country free from bondage and slavery, and avoiding such ill methods, as may render themselves and posterity liable thereto." Heeding these protests, the Assembly refused to pass a tax law. *De facto* anarchy was still, though barely, alive.

Anarchy, however, was by now doomed, and governmental oppression, even without taxes, quickly returned to Pennsylvania. This new outcropping of statism was stimulated by opposition from a split-off from Quakerism headed by the scholarly Scottish Quaker George Keith, the outstanding Quaker minister of the middle colonies and the schoolmaster at Philadelphia. He was religiously more conservative than the bulk of the Quakers, leaning as he did toward Presbyterianism, but politically he was more individualistic. Stimulated by the anarchism he found in Pennsylvania, Keith quickly concluded logically from the Quaker creed that *all* participation in government ran counter to Quaker principles.

The return of Pennsylvania to government in the spring of 1691 especially provoked George Keith. How, he asked, could a Quaker minister like Thomas Lloyd, professing belief in non-violence, serve as a governmental magistrate at all, since the essence of government was the use of violence? A telling point: in short, Keith saw that Quaker non-violence logically implied, not only refusal to bear arms, but complete individualistic anarchism.

Finally, in the fall of 1692, the Keithian "Christian Quaker" faction was expelled from the body of Quakers. And to their shame, the main body of Quakers, after having been persecuted widely for their religious principles, reacted to a split in their *own* ranks in the very same way. Keithian pamphlets were confiscated and the printers arrested; Keith himself was ordered to stop making speeches and publishing pamphlets "that have a tendency to sedition, and disturbance of the peace, as also to the subversion of the present government." Three Keithian leaders, including Keith himself, were indicted for writing a book denouncing the magistrates, and the jury was packed with the friends of the Quaker rulers. Despite Keith's pleas that Quakers are duty-bound to settle all their disputes peacefully and voluntarily, and to never go to court, the men were convicted and fined (though the fines were never paid), and denied the right to appeal to the Council or to the provisional court. Government was back in Pennsylvania—with a vengeance.

Taxation would very soon be back too. William Penn, a close friend of the recently deposed King James II of England, was in deep political trouble at court. Angry at Penn, peeved at the anarchism and the pacifism of the colony, and anxious to weld the northern colonies into a fighting force for attacking the French in Canada, King William, in late 1692, named Benjamin Fletcher Governor of both New York and Pennsylvania. Pennsylvania, no longer under the proprietary of William Penn, was now a royal colony.

Governor Fletcher assumed the reins of government in April 1693. As in other royal colonies, the Council was now appointed by the Governor. Fletcher convened the Assembly in May, and was able to drive through a tax bill because of his and the Council's power to judge all the existing laws of Pennsylvania, and of a threat to annex the colony to New York. Taxes had arrived at last; archy was back in full force, and the glorious years of anarchism were gone.[6]

But a flurry of anarchism remained. In its 1694 session, the Pennsylvania Assembly decided to allocate almost half its tax revenue to the personal use of Thomas Lloyd and of William Markham, whom Fletcher had appointed as his Deputy-Governor. Infuriated, Fletcher dissolved the Assembly. After a year of imposition, taxes had again disappeared from Pennsylvania.

Disgusted, Fletcher lost interest in Pennsylvania, which after all these years was decidedly a poor place for raising tax revenue. The colony returned to its old quasi-anarchistic state, with no taxes and with a Council that did little and met infrequently. But, meanwhile, William Penn was campaigning energetically for returning to his feudal fiefdom. He abjectly promised the King that Pennsylvania would be good: that it would levy taxes, raise a militia, and obey royal orders. He promised to keep Fletcher's laws and to keep Markham as Governor. As a result the King restored Pennsylvania to the ownership of Penn in the summer of 1694, and by the spring of the following year, Markham was installed as Deputy-Governor under the restored Penn proprietary. But in the spring 1695 session, the now elected Council again refused to consider any tax bill.

The Assembly continued to refuse to pass a tax bill for another year and a half. With the exception of one year, Pennsylvania thus remained in a quasi-anarchist state of taxlessness from its founding in 1681 until the fall of 1696: fourteen glorious years. Governor Markham was only able to push through a tax bill at the end of 1696 by a naked usurpation of the powers of government, decreeing a new constitution of his own, including an appointed Council. Markham was able to purchase the Assembly's support by granting it the power to initiate legislation and also to raise the property requirement for voting in the towns, thus permitting the Quakers to exclude the largely non-Quaker urban poor from having the vote.

A libertarian opposition now gathered, led by Arthur Cook (Thomas Lloyd was now deceased). It included a coalition of former Keithians like Robert Turner and old Blackwell henchmen like Griffith Jones. The opposition gathered a mass petition in March 1697, signed by over a hundred, attacking the imposed constitution, the increase in suffrage requirements in the towns, and particularly the establishment of taxation. When the opposition Councilors and Assemblymen, elected as a protest under a separate set of votes under the old constitution, were summarily rejected, Robert Turner denounced this threat to "our ancient rights, liberties and freedom." Turner particularly denounced the tax bill of 1696, and urged that the tax money seized from its rightful owners "by that unwarranted, illegal and arbitrary act, be forthwith restored."

But all this was to no avail. Pennsylvania soon slipped into the same archic mould as all the other colonies. The "Holy Experiment" was over.

Bibliographical Note

None of this material has ever appeared in any work on the history of individualist anarchism in the United States. James J. Martin's excellent *Men Against the State* (DeKalb, Ill: Adrian Allen Associates, 1953) does not go back before the nineteenth century. In any case, Martin's methodology prevents him from acknowledging these men and women of the seventeenth century as anarchists, since he believes Christianity and anarchism to be incompatible. Neither Rudolf Rocker's *Pioneers of American Freedom* (Los Angeles: Rocker Publications Committee, 1949) nor Henry J. Silverman's (ed.) *American Radical Thought: The Libertarian Tradition* (Lexington, Mass.: D.C. Heath Co., 1970) touches on the colonial period.

The only history of individualist anarchism that deals with the colonial period is the pioneering work by Eunice Minette Schuster, *Native American Anarchism* (1932, rep. by New York: De Capo Press 1970). Schuster deals briefly with the religious views of Anne Hutchinson and the Quakers, but deals hardly at all with their political ideas nor with the institutions that they put into practice. Corinne Jacker's *The Black Flag of Anarchy* (New York: Charles Scribner's Sons, 1968) only sharply condenses Schuster.

Notes

1. The lack of record-keeping in stateless societies—since only government officials seem to have the time, energy and resources to devote to such activi-

ties—produce a tendency toward a governmental bias in the working methods of historians.

2. One of the original band that had helped Williams found Providence.
3. 1657 was the year that the first Quaker landed in Rhode Island from England. It is no surprise that within a decade this new individualistic sect had converted a majority of Rhode Islanders, including most of the former Baptists and Hutchinsonians.
4. Particularly remarkable was the treatment of the Indians by Penn and the Quakers. In striking contrast to the general treatment of Indians by white settlers the Quakers insisted on voluntary purchase of Indian land. They also dealt with the Indians as human beings, deserving of respect and dignity. As a consequence peace with the Indians was maintained for well over half a century; no drop of Quaker blood was shed by the Indians. Voltaire wrote rapturously of the Quaker achievement; for the Indians, he declared, "it was truly a new sight to see a sovereign William Penn to whom everyone said 'thou' and to whom one spoke with one's hat on one's head; a government without priests, a people without arms, citizens as the magistrates, and neighbors without jealousy."
5. Edwin B. Bronner, *William Penn's "Holy Experiment"* (New York: Temple University Publications, 1962), p.10a.
6. One reason for the failure of any Pennsylvania resistance to the new regime was that the unity of the colonists had foundered on the rock of the Keithian schism. One beneficial result of royal rule was the freeing of Keith and his friends. Keith, however, returned to England, and with his departure the Keithian movement soon fell apart. The final irony came in later years when Keith, now an ardent Anglican minister in America, his former Quakerish individualist anarchism totally forgotten, helped to impose a year's imprisonment on grounds of sedition against the established Anglican Church of New York, upon the Reverend Samuel Bownes of Long Island.

28

Anarchism and American Traditions

Voltairine de Cleyre

American traditions, begotten of religious rebellion, small self-sustaining communities, isolated conditions, and hard pioneer life, grew during the colonization period of one hundred and seventy years from the settling of Jamestown to the outburst of the Revolution. This was in fact the great constitution making epoch, the period of charters guaranteeing more or less of liberty, the general tendency of which is well described by Wm. Penn in speaking of the charter for Pennsylvania: "I want to put it out of my power, or that of my successors, to do mischief."

The Revolution is the sudden and unified consciousness of these traditions, their loud assertion, the blow dealt by their indomitable will against the counter force of tyranny, which has never entirely recovered from the blow, but which from then till now has gone on remolding and regrappling the instruments of governmental power, that the Revolution sought to shape and hold as defenses of liberty.

To the average American of today, the Revolution means the series of battles fought by the patriot army with the armies of England. The millions of school children who attend our public schools are taught to draw maps of the siege of Boston and the siege of Yorktown, to know the general plan of the several campaigns, to quote the number of prisoners of war surrendered with Burgoyne; they are required to remember the date when Washington crossed the Delaware on the ice; they are told to "Remember Paoli," to repeat "Molly Stark's a widow," to call General Wayne "Mad Anthony Wayne," and to execrate Benedict Arnold; they know that the Declaration of Independence was signed on the Fourth of July, 1776, and the Treaty of Paris in 1783; and then they think they have learned the Revolution…blessed be George Washington! They have no idea why it should have been called a "revolution" instead of the "English war," or any similar title: it's the name of it, that's all. And name-worship, both in child and man, has acquired such mastery of them, that the name "American Revolution" is held sacred, though it means to them nothing more than successful force, while the name "Revolution" applied to a further possibility, is a spectre detested and abhorred. In neither case have they any idea of the content of the word, save that of armed force. That has already happened, and long happened, which Jefferson foresaw when he wrote:

> The spirit of the times may alter, will alter. Our rulers will become corrupt, our people careless. A single zealot may become persecutor, and better men be his victims. It can never be too often repeated that the time for fixing every essential right, on a legal basis, is while our rulers are honest, ourselves united. From the conclusion of this war we shall be going down hill. It will not then be necessary to resort every moment to the people for support. They will be forgotten, therefore, and their rights disregarded. They will forget themselves in the sole faculty of making money, and will never think of uniting to effect a due respect for their rights. The shackles, therefore, which shall not be knocked off at the conclusion of this war, will be heavier and heavier, till our rights shall revive or expire in a convulsion.

To the men of that time, who voiced the spirit of that time, the battles that they fought were the least of the Revolution; they were the incidents of the hour, the things they met and faced as part of the game they were playing; but the stake they had in view, before, during, and after the war, the real Revolution, was a change in political institutions which should make of government not a thing apart, a superior power to stand over the people with a whip, but a serviceable agent, responsible, economical, and trustworthy (but never so much trusted as not to be continually watched), for the transaction of such business as was the common concern, and to set the limits of the common concern at the line where one man's liberty would encroach upon another's.

They thus took their starting point for deriving a minimum of government upon the same sociological ground that the modern Anarchist derives the no-government theory; viz., that equal liberty is the political ideal. The difference lies in the belief, on the one hand, that the closest approximation to equal liberty might be best secured by the rule of the majority in those matters involving united action of any kind (which rule of the majority they thought it possible to secure by a few simple arrangements for election), and, on the other hand, the belief that majority rule is both impossible and undesirable; that any government, no matter what its forms, will be manipulated by a very small minority, as the development of the State and United States governments has strikingly proved; that candidates will loudly profess allegiance to platforms before elections, which as officials in power they will openly disregard, to do as they please; and that even if the majority will could be imposed, it would also be subversive of equal liberty, which may be best secured by leaving to the voluntary association of those interested in the management of matters of common concern, without coercion of the uninterested or the opposed.

Among the fundamental likenesses between the Revolutionary Republicans and the Anarchists is the recognition that the little must precede the great; that the local must be the basis of the general; that there can be a free federation only when there are free communities to federate; that the spirit of the latter is carried into the councils of the former, and a local tyranny may thus become an instrument for general enslavement. Convinced of the supreme importance of ridding the municipalities of the institutions of tyranny, the most strenuous advocates of independence, instead of spending their efforts mainly in the general Congress, devoted themselves to their home localities, endeavoring to work out of the minds of their neighbors and fellow-colonists the institutions of entailed property, of a State-Church, of a class-divided people, even the institution of African slavery itself. Though largely unsuccessful, it is to the measure of success they did achieve that we are indebted for such liberties as we do retain, and not to the general government. They tried to inculcate local initiative and independent action. The author of the Declaration of Independence, who in the fall of '76 declined a re-election to Congress in order to return to Virginia and do his work in his own local assembly, in arranging there for public education which he justly considered a matter of "common concern," said his advocacy of public schools was not with any "view to take its ordinary branches out of the hands of private enterprise, which manages so much better the concerns to which it is equal"; and in endeavoring to make clear the restrictions of the Constitution upon the functions of the general government, he likewise said: "Let the general government be reduced to foreign concerns only, and let our affairs be disentangled from those of all other nations, except as to commerce, which the merchants will manage the better the more they are left free to manage for themselves, and the general government may be reduced to a very simple organization, and a very inexpensive one; a few plain duties to be performed by a few servants." This then was the American tradition, that private enterprise manages better all that to which it is equal. Anarchism declares that private enterprise, whether individual or co-operative, is equal to all the undertakings of society. And it quotes the particular two instances, Education and Commerce, which the governments of the States and of the United States have undertaken to manage and regulate, as the very two which in operation have done more to destroy American freedom and equality, to warp and distort American tradition, to make of government a mighty engine of tyranny, than any other cause save the unforeseen developments of Manufacture.

It was the intention of the Revolutionists to establish a system of common education, which should make the teaching of history one of its principal branches; not with the intent of burdening the memories of our youth with the dates of battles or the speeches of generals, nor to make of the Boston Tea Party Indians the one sacrosanct mob in all history, to be revered but never on any account to be imitated, but with the intent that every American should know to what conditions the masses of people had been brought by the operation of certain institutions, by what means they had wrung out their liberties, and how those liberties had again and again been filched from them by the use of governmental force, fraud, and privilege. Not to breed security, laudation, complacent indolence, passive acquiescence in the acts of a government protected by the label "home-made," but to beget a wakeful jealousy, a never-ending watchfulness of rulers, a determination to squelch every attempt of those entrusted with power to encroach upon the sphere of individual action—this was the prime motive of the revolutionists in endeavoring to provide for common education.

"Confidence," said the Revolutionists who adopted the Kentucky Resolutions, "is everywhere the parent of despotism; free government is founded in jealousy, not in confidence; it is jealousy, not confidence, which prescribes limited constitutions to bind down those whom we are obliged to trust with power; our Constitution has accordingly fixed the limits to which, and no further, our confidence may go.... In questions of power, let no more be heard of confidence in man, but bind him down from mischief by the chains of the Constitution."

These resolutions were especially applied to the passage of the Alien laws by the monarchist party during John Adams' administration, and were an indignant call from the State of Kentucky to repudiate the right of the general government to assume undelegated powers, for, said they, to accept these laws would be "to be bound by laws made, not with our consent, but by others against our consent—that is, to surrender the form of government we have chosen, and to live under one deriving its powers from its own will, and not from our authority." Resolutions identical in spirit were also passed by Virginia, the following month; in those days the States still considered themselves supreme, the general government subordinate.

To inculcate this proud spirit of the supremacy of the people over their governors was to be the purpose of public education! Pick up today any common school history, and see how much of this spirit you will find therein. On the contrary, from cover to cover you will find nothing but the cheapest sort of patriotism, the inculcation of the most unquestioning acquiescence in the deeds of government, a lullaby of rest, security, confidence—the doctrine that the Law can do no wrong, a Te Deum in praise of the continuous encroachments of the powers of the general government upon the reserved rights of the States, shameless falsification of all acts of rebellion, to put the government in the right and the rebels in the wrong, pyrotechnic glorifications of union, power, and force, and a complete ignoring of the essential liberties to maintain which was the purpose of the Revolutionists. The anti-Anarchist law of post-McKinley passage, a much worse law than the Alien and Sedition acts which roused the wrath of Kentucky and Virginia to the point of threatened rebellion, is exalted as a wise provision of our All-Seeing Father in Washington.

Such is the spirit of government-provided schools. Ask any child what he knows about Shays's rebellion, and he will answer, "Oh, some of the farmers couldn't pay their taxes, and Shays led a rebellion against the court-house at Worcester, so they could burn up the deeds; and when Washington heard of it he sent over an army quick and taught them a good lesson"—"And what was the result of it?" "The result? Why—why—the result was—Oh yes, I remember—the result was they saw the need of a strong federal government to collect the taxes and pay the debts." Ask if he knows what was said on the other side of the story, ask if he knows that the men who had given their goods and their health and their strength for the freeing of the country now found themselves cast into prison for debt, sick, disabled, and poor, facing a new tyranny for the old; that their demand was that the land should become the free communal possession of those who wished to work it, not subject to tribute, and the child will answer "No." Ask him if he ever read Jefferson's letter to Madison about it, in which he says

> Societies exist under three forms, sufficiently distinguishable. 1. Without government, as among our Indians. 2. Under government wherein the will of every one has a just influence; as is the case in England in a slight degree, and in our States in a great one. 3. Under government of force, as is the case in all other monarchies, and in most of the other republics. To have an idea of the curse of existence in these last, they must be seen. It is a government of wolves over sheep. It is a problem not clear in my mind that the first condition is not the best. But I believe it to be inconsistent with any great degree of population. The second state has a great deal of good in it.... It has its evils, too, the principal of which is the turbulence to which it is subject.... But even this evil is productive of good. It prevents the degeneracy of government, and nourishes a general attention to public affairs. I hold that a little rebellion now and then is a good thing.

Or to another correspondent: "God forbid that we should ever be twenty years without such a rebellion!... What country can preserve its liberties if its rulers are not warned from time to time that the people preserve the spirit of resistance? Let them take up arms.... The tree of liberty must be refreshed from time to time with the blood of patriots and tyrants. It is its natural manure." Ask any school child if he was ever taught that the author of the Declaration of Independence, one of the great founders of the common school, said these things, and he will look at you with open mouth and unbelieving eyes. Ask him if he ever heard that the man who sounded the bugle note in the darkest hour of the Crisis, who roused the courage of the soldiers when Washington saw only mutiny and despair ahead, ask him if he knows that this man also wrote, "Government at best is a necessary evil, at worst an intolerable one," and if he is a little better informed than the average he will answer, "Oh well, he was an infidel!" Catechize him about the merits of the Constitution which he has learned to repeat like a poll-parrot, and you will find his chief conception is not of the powers withheld from Congress, but of the powers granted.

Such are the fruits of government schools. We, the Anarchists, point to them and say: If the believers in liberty wish the principles of liberty taught, let them never intrust that instruction to any government; for the nature of government is to become a thing apart, an institution existing for its own sake, preying upon the people, and teaching whatever will tend to keep it secure in its seat. As the fathers said of the governments of Europe, so say we of this government also after a century and a quarter of independence: "The blood of the people has become its inheritance, and those who fatten on it will not relinquish it easily."

Public education, having to do with the intellect and spirit of a people, is probably the most subtle and far-reaching engine for molding the course of a nation; but commerce, dealing as it does with material things and producing immediate effects, was the force that bore down soonest upon the paper barriers of constitutional restriction, and shaped the government to its requirements. Here, indeed, we arrive at the point where we, looking over the hundred and twenty-five years of independence can see that the simple government conceived by the Revolutionary Republicans was a foredoomed failure. It was so because of (1) the essence of government itself; (2) the essence of human nature; (3) the essence of Commerce and Manufacture.

Of the essence of government, I have already said, it is a thing apart, developing its own interests at the expense of what opposes it; all attempts to make it anything else fail. In this Anarchists agree with the traditional enemies of the Revolution, the monarchists, federalists, strong government believers, the Roosevelts of to-day, the Jays, Marshalls, and Hamiltons of then—that Hamilton, who, as Secretary of the Treasury, devised a financial system of which we are the unlucky heritors, and whose objects were twofold: To puzzle the people and make public finance obscure to those that paid for it; to serve as a machine for corrupting the legislatures; "for he avowed the opinion that man could be governed by two motives only, force or interest;" force being then out of the question, he laid hold of interest, the greed of the legislators, to set going an association of persons having an entirely separate welfare from the welfare of their electors, bound together by mutual corruption and mutual desire for plunder. The Anarchist agrees that Hamilton was logical, and understood the core of government; the difference is, that while strong governmentalists believe this is necessary and desirable, we choose the opposite conclusion, NO GOVERNMENT WHATEVER.

As to the essence of human nature, what our national experience has made plain is this, that to remain in a continually exalted moral condition is not human nature. That has happened which was prophesied: we have gone down hill from the Revolution until now; we are absorbed in "mere money getting." The desire for material ease long ago vanquished the spirit of '76. What was that spirit? The spirit that animated the people of Virginia, of the Carolinas, of Massachusetts, of New York, when they refused to import goods from England; when they preferred (and stood by it) to wear coarse homespun cloth, to drink the brew of their own growths, to fit their appetites to the home supply, rather than submit to the taxation of the imperial ministry. Even within the lifetime of the Revolutionists the spirit decayed. The love of material ease has been, in the mass of men and permanently speaking, always greater than the love of liberty. Nine hundred and ninety-nine women out of a thousand are more interested in the cut of a dress than in the independence of their sex; nine hundred and ninety-nine men out of a thousand are more interested in drinking a glass of beer than in questioning the tax that is laid on it; how many children are not willing to trade the liberty to play for the promise of a new cap or a new dress? This it is which begets the complicated mechanism of society; this it is which, by multiplying the concerns of government, multiplies the strength of government and the corresponding weakness of the people; this it is which begets indifference to public concern, thus making the corruption of government easy.

As to the essence of Commerce and Manufacture, it is this: to establish bonds between every corner of the earth's surface and every other corner, to multiply the needs of mankind, and the desire for material possession and enjoyment.

The American tradition was the isolation of the States as far as possible. Said they: We have won our liberties by hard sacrifice and struggle unto death. We wish now to be let alone and to let others alone, that our principles may have time for trial; that we may become accustomed to the exercise of our rights; that we may be kept free from the contaminating influence of European gauds, pagents, distinctions. So richly did they esteem the absence of these that they could in all fervor write: "We shall see multiplied instances of Europeans coming to America, but no man living will ever see an instance of an American removing to settle in Europe, and continuing there." Alas! In less than a hundred years the highest aim of a "Daughter of the Revolution" was, and is, to buy a castle, a title, and a rotten lord, with the money wrung from American servitude! And the commercial interests of America are seeking a world-empire!

In the earlier days of the revolt and subsequent independence, it appeared that the "manifest destiny" of America was to be an agricultural people, exchanging food stuffs and raw materials for manufactured articles. And in those days it was written: "We shall be virtuous as long as agriculture is our principal object, which will be the case as long as there remain vacant lands in any part of America. When we get piled upon one another in large cities, as in Europe, we shall become corrupt as in Europe, and go to eating one another as they do there." Which we are doing, because of the inevitable development of Commerce and Manufacture, and the concomitant development of strong government. And the parallel prophecy is likewise fulfilled: "If ever this vast country is brought under a single government, it will be one of the most extensive corruption, indifferent and incapable of a wholesome care over so wide a spread of surface." There is not upon the face of the earth to-day a government so utterly and shamelessly corrupt as that of the United States of America. There are others more cruel, more tyrannical, more devastating; there is none so utterly venal.

And yet even in the very days of the prophets, even with their own consent, the first concession to this later tyranny was made. It was made when the Constitution was made; and the Constitution was made chiefly because of the demands of Commerce. Thus it was at the outset a merchant's machine, which the other interests of the country, the land and labor interests, even then foreboded would destroy their liberties. In vain their jealousy of its central power made them enact the first twelve amendments. In vain they endeavored to set bounds over which the federal power dare not trench. In vain they enacted into general law the freedom of speech, of the press, of assemblage and petition. All of these things we see ridden rough-shod upon every day, and have so seen with more or less intermission since the beginning of the nineteenth century. At this day, every police lieutenant considers himself, and rightly so, as more powerful than the General Law of the Union; and that one who told Robert Hunter that he held in his fist something stronger than the Constitution, was perfectly correct. The right of assemblage is an American tradition which has gone out of fashion; the police club is now the mode. And it is so in virtue of the people's indifference to liberty, and the steady progress of constitutional interpretation towards the substance of imperial government.

It is an American tradition that a standing army is a standing menace to liberty; in Jefferson's presidency the army was reduced to 3,000 men. It is

American tradition that we keep out of the affairs of other nations. It is American practice that we meddle with the affairs of everybody else from the West to the East Indies, from Russia to Japan; and to do it we have a standing army of 83,251 men.

It is American tradition that the financial affairs of a nation should be transacted on the same principles of simple honesty that an individual conducts his own business; viz., that debt is a bad thing, and a man's first surplus earnings should be applied to his debts; that offices and office-holders should be few. It is American practice that the general government should always have millions of debt, even if a panic or a war has to be forced to prevent its being paid off; and as to the application of its income, office-holders come first. And within the last administration it is reported that 99,000 offices have been created at an annual expense of $63,000,000. Shades of Jefferson! "How are vacancies to be obtained? Those by deaths are few; by resignation none." Roosevelt cuts the knot by making 99,000 new ones! And few will die—and none resign. They will beget sons and daughters, and Taft will have to create 99,000 more! Verily, a simple and a serviceable thing is our general government.

It is American tradition that the judiciary shall act as a check upon the impetuosity of Legislatures, should these attempt to pass the bounds of constitutional limitation. It is American practice that the Judiciary justifies every law which trenches on the liberties of the people and nullifies every act of the Legislature by which the people seek to regain some measure of their freedom. Again, in the words of Jefferson: "The Constitution is a mere thing of wax in the hands of the Judiciary, which they may twist and shape in any form they please." Truly, if the men who fought the good fight for the triumph of simple, honest, free life in that day, were now to look upon the scene of their labors, they would cry out together with him who said: "I regret that I am now to die in the belief that the useless sacrifice of themselves by the generation of '76 to acquire self-government and happiness to their country, is to be thrown away by the unwise and unworthy passions of their sons, and that my only consolation is to be that I shall not live to see it."

And now, what has Anarchism to say to all this, this bankruptcy of republicanism, this modern empire that has grown up on the ruins of our early freedom? We say this, that the sin our fathers sinned was that they did not trust liberty wholly. They thought it possible to compromise between liberty and government, believing the latter to be "a necessary evil," and the moment the compromise was made, the whole misbegotten monster of our present tyranny began to grow. Instruments which are set up to safeguard rights become the very whip with which the free are struck.

Anarchism says, Make no laws whatever concerning speech, and speech will be free; so soon as you make a declaration on paper that speech shall be free, you will have a hundred lawyers proving that "freedom does not mean abuse, nor liberty license"; and they will define and define freedom out of existence. Let the guarantee of free speech be in every man's determination to use it, and we shall have no need of paper declarations. On the other hand, so long as the people do not care to exercise their freedom, those who wish to tyrannize will do so; for tyrants are active and ardent, and will devote themselves in the name of any number of gods, religious and otherwise, to put shackles upon sleeping men.

The problem then becomes, Is it possible to stir men from their indifference? We have said that the spirit of liberty was nurtured by colonial life; that the elements of colonial life were the desire for sectarian independence, and the jealous watchfulness incident thereto; the isolation of pioneer communities which threw each individual strongly on his own resources, and thus developed all-around men, yet at the same time made very strong such social bonds as did exist—and, lastly, the comparative simplicity of small communities.

All this has mostly disappeared. As to sectarianism, it is only by dint of an occasional idiotic persecution that a sect becomes interesting; in the absence of this, outlandish sects play the fool's role, are anything but heroic, and have little to do with either the name or the substance of liberty. The old colonial religious parties have gradually become the "pillars of society," their animosities have died out, their offensive peculiarities have been effaced, they are as like one another as beans in a pod, they build churches and—sleep in them.

As to our communities, they are hopelessly and helplessly interdependent, as we ourselves are, save that continuously diminishing proportion engaged in all around farming; and even these are slaves to mortgages. For our cities, probably there is not one that is provisioned to last a week, and certainly there is none which would not be bankrupt with despair at the proposition that it produce its own food. In response to this condition and its correlative political tyranny, Anarchism affirms the economy of self-sustenance, the disintegration of the great communities, the use of the earth.

I am not ready to say that I see clearly that this will take place; but I see clearly that this must take place if ever again men are to be free. I am so well satisfied that the mass of mankind prefer material possessions to liberty, that I have no hope that they will ever, by means of intellectual or moral stirrings merely, throw off the yoke of oppression fastened on them by the present economic system, to institute free societies. My only hope is in the blind development of the economic system and political oppression itself. The great characteristic looming factor in this gigantic power is Manufacture. The tendency of each nation is to become more and more a manufacturing one, an exporter of fabrics, not an importer. If this tendency follows its own logic, it must eventually circle round to each community producing for itself. What then will become of the surplus product when the manufacturer shall have no foreign market? Why, then mankind must face the dilemma of sitting down and dying in the midst of it, or confiscating the goods.

Indeed, we are partially facing this problem even now; and so far we are sitting down and dying. I opine, however, that men will not do it forever; and when once by an act of general expropriation they have overcome the reverence and fear of property, and their awe of government, they may waken to the consciousness that things are to be used, and therefore men are greater than things. This may rouse the spirit of liberty.

If, on the other hand, the tendency of invention to simplify, enabling the advantages of machinery to be combined with smaller aggregations of workers, shall also follow its own logic, the great manufacturing plants will break up, population will go after the fragments, and there will be seen not indeed the hard, self-sustaining, isolated pioneer communities of early America, but thousands of small communities stretching along the lines of transportation, each producing very largely for its own needs, able to rely upon itself, and therefore able to be independent. For the same rule holds good for societies as for individuals—those may be free who are able to make their own living.

In regard to the breaking up of that vilest creation of tyranny, the standing army and navy, it is clear that so long as men desire to fight, they will have armed force in one form or another. Our fathers thought they had guarded against a standing army by providing for the voluntary militia. In our day we have lived to see this militia declared part of the regular military force of the United States, and subject to the same demands as the regulars. Within another generation we shall probably see its members in the regular pay of the general government. Since any embodiment of the fighting spirit, any military organization, inevitably follows the same line of centralization, the logic of Anarchism is that the least objectionable form of armed force is that which springs up voluntarily, like the minute-men of Massachusetts, and disbands as soon as the occasion which called it into existence is past: that the really desirable thing is that all men—not Americans only—should be at peace; and that to reach this, all peaceful persons should withdraw their support from the army, and require that all who make war shall do so at their own cost and risk; that neither pay nor pensions are to be provided for those who choose to make man-killing a trade.

As to the American tradition of non-meddling, Anarchism asks that it be carried down to the individual himself. It demands no jealous barrier of isolation; it knows that such isolation is undesirable and impossible; but it teaches that by all men's strictly minding their own business, a fluid society, freely adapting itself to mutual needs, wherein all the world shall belong to all men, as much as each has need or desire, will result.

And when Modern Revolution has thus been carried to the heart of the whole world—if it ever shall be, as I hope it will—then may we hope to see a resurrection of that proud spirit of our fathers which put the simple dignity of Man above the gauds of wealth and class, and held that to be an American was greater than to be a king.

In that day there shall be neither kings nor Americans—only Men; over the whole earth, MEN.

29

Civil Government: Its Origin, Mission, and Destiny, and the Christian's Relation to It (excerpt)

David Lipscomb

The civil power is founded on force, lives by it and it is its only weapon of offence or defence. Christians enter civil government, drink into its spirit, and carry that spirit with them into the church. All force in religious affairs is persecution. This spirit of force is antagonistic to the spirit of Christ. They cannot harmonize. They cannot dwell in the same bosom. "No man can serve two masters," or cherish two antagonistic spirits. The result of it is, that the spirit of Christ, the spirit of self-denial, of self-sacrifice, the forbearance and long suffering, the doing good for evil, so fully manifested in the life of and so fully taught by Jesus Christ and the apostles, are almost unknown to the Christian profession of this day. The sermon on the Mount, embraced in the fifth sixth and seventh chapters of Matthew, certainly contain the living and essential principles of the religion the Savior came to establish, those which must pervade and control the hearts and lives of men, without which no man can be a Christian. They are enforced by such expressions as these.

> Love your enemies, bless them that curse you, do good to them that hate you, and pray for them that despitefully use you, and persecute you; that ye may be the children of your Father which is in Heaven.

And again,

> Whosoever heareth these sayings of mine, and doeth them, I will liken him unto a wise man, which built his house upon a rock... Whoever heareth these sayings of mine, and doeth them not shall be likened unto a foolish man etc., which built his house upon the sand.

These sayings of mine, refer to the sayings presented in this sermon of Jesus, which constitute the laws that must control the lives of his subjects, and must rule in his kingdom. They are given as principles to be practices, without which we are not and cannot be children of our Father which is in heaven. Yet the religious world of to-day both Protestant and Romish, believes these principles not applicable at the present day. The laws and the spirit of civil government are more looked to, to guide the church and regulate the lives of its members, than the teaching of the Bible. Indeed it is usually regarded that the church member may do any thing the civil law allows and what it allows is not to be prohibited in the church. This comes from the members of the church going into the civil governments, imbibing their spirit, adopting their morality and bringing them both into the church of Christ. A man cannot cherish in his heart two spirits, one to rule his religious life, the other to rule his civil life. He cannot adopt two standards of morality, one for his church life, the other for his political life.

> A man cannot serve two masters, he will love the one, and hate the other, or he will cleave to one and despise the other.

That the political affairs, and the standard of general morality may be elevated by the affiliation, is possible, but the true spiritual life is destroyed by the affiliation. The antagonism between the principles laid down by Christ and those of civil government is so marked that in history, the statement, that they regulate their conduct by the sermon on the Mount, is equal to saying they take no part in civil affairs. The only people who claim to make the "sermon upon the Mount" their rule of life, are the small religious bodies, who take no part in civil affairs. Some bodies of Quakers, Mennonites, Nazarenes and Dunkards, and individuals among the larger brotherhoods.

But who can study the New Testament, the life of Christ, his teaching through his mission, the admonitions of the Holy Spirit speaking through the apostles and for a moment doubt, that Christ specially gave this sermon to regulate the hearts and lives of his followers. He gave it at the beginning of his ministry that all might understand the life, to which they were specifically called. The apostle Paul Romans xii: 19, reiterated the principles of this sermon on the Mount.

> Dearly beloved avenge not yourselves, but rather give place unto wrath: for it is written, Vengeance is mine, I will repay saith the Lord. Therefore if thine enemy hunger, feed him; if he thirst give him drink, for in so doing thou shalt heap coals of fire on his head. Be not overcome of evil, but overcome evil with good." 1 Peter ii: 19, "For this is thankworthy, if a man for conscience toward God endure grief, suffering wrongfully. For what glory is it, if, when ye be buffeted for your faults ye shall take it patiently? But if when ye do well, and suffer for it, ye take it patiently, this is acceptable with God. For even hereunto were called: because Christ also suffered for us, leaving us an example that ye should follow his steps: Who did no sin, neither was guile found in his mouth: Who, when he was reviled, reviled not again; when he suffered, he threatened not; but committed himself to him that judgeth righteously: Who his own self bare our sins in his own body on the tree, that we, being dead to sins, should live unto righteousness: by whose stripes we were healed.

The spirit of Christ is driven out of the church and the spirit of the world takes its abode in it by this affiliation.

So long as the idea prevails that it is allowable for Christians to enjoy the honors and emoluments, and engage in the contests for worldly glory and honor by managing the affairs of the civil or worldly governments, and yet enjoy the blessings of God, in this world and in that which is to come, so long will the young seek the service of the human rather than that of the Divine. While they are taught they can satisfy the flesh and still enjoy the blessings of spiritual life, they will follow the way of the flesh. Along with displacing the spirit of Christ, in the church, with the spirit of the world, the world absorbs the talent, the time the means that belong to the church, and leaves the church devoid of the spirit of Christ, stripped of its strength and talent and left without means.

Various difficulties are presented to the position here taken. Such as, "If Christian give the government up to sinners and those rejecting God, what will become of the world? What will become of Christians? If all were converted to the Christian religion, we would still need civil government. How would the mails be carried? How could the affairs of Railroads, Manufactures, and the many large corporations needful to the well-being of society be managed?"

To this last difficulty, it is responded, when all are converted to Christ, all dominion and power and rule on earth will be put down and destroyed, and the rule and the dominion and the kingdom under the whole heavens will be delivered up to God, the Father, that he may be all and in all. To the wisdom, and power and management, of him who created and rules the heavens we will cheerfully commit the adjustment and management of all things pertaining to the world, to man, and his well-being here or hereafter. And no true believer in God can have any apprehension of failure in ought that pertains to man's well-being here or hereafter.

God was an immediate and ever present ruler to man as he was first created and placed in Eden. Man refused to obey God, chose the devil as his ruler, and with himself carried the world into a state of rebellion against God. God ceased to be an immediate and present guide to man. "The voice of the Lord God" ceased to walk with, and guide him in his paths. The spirit of God forsook man and ceased to inspire his heart. Man's sin and rebellion separated between man and his God. But when man shall cease to sin—when man shall lay down the arms of his rebellion, when man shall come out of the earthly government of God, when "all rule and all authority and all power shall have been put down," then the kingdom shall be delivered up to God the Father, and he will be our God, the God of the human family, and of this earth—and shall again dwell there and they will be his children and walk under his guidance and direction. He will be all and in all.

As to the other objections, while God does not rule in, as a present guide to man in this world while in rebellion against him, he does overrule the affairs of earth so as that no evil shall come to him that trusts in the Lord, so that "all things shall work together for good to them that love the Lord," so that he "will keep him in perfect peace whose heart is stayed on the Lord, because he trusted in him." Isa. xxvi: 3, so that "when a man pleases the Lord, he maketh even his enemies to be at peace with him." Prov. xvi: 7. So that "He maketh the wrath of man praise him, and the remainder of wrath he will restrain." Ps. lxxvi: 10. Then again Christian men, as has been heretofore presented, cannot be governed by Christian principles in civil government. Civil government rests on force as its foundation. The weapons of the Christian are not carnal, but spiritual. A ruler or an officer in civil government cannot carry into the execution of these laws, the principles of the religion of Christ. To forgive his brother seventy times seven, on repentance, would destroy all authority in civil affairs. It is certainly true no Christian should go where he cannot carry the practice of the principles of the religion of Christ. The Savior presents the essential antagonism when he says, "ye know that the princes of the Gentiles exercise dominion over them (their subjects) and they that are great exercise authority upon them. But it shall not be so among you, but whosoever will be great among you, let him be your minister and whosoever would be chief let him be your servant: even as the son of man came not to be ministered unto, but to minister and to give his life a ransom for many."

A man cannot be a follower of Christ and a ruler in the governments of earth. Again, Christian men out of place are as liable to do wrong as others. The protection and security of the Christian, is, that while he is doing his duty as a Christian, in the walks God has appointed him, "God will not permit him to be tempted above that he is able to bear." But when he steps outside of the paths God has marked out for him, he loses this protection. Hence we find religious men often falling victims to the snares and temptations of the world as others. It is because they step outside of the limits of the Christian walk, and so forfeit the protection of God.

Again, the Christian spirit is a frank, open, unsuspecting one. A man that is suspicious of all, looking for evil in every one, is a poor Christian. An unsuspecting nature in political affairs will be imposed upon, taken advantage of and will be frequently used to carry out the aims and purposes of designing and corrupt partizans. There is but little doubt that Garfield's frank, confiding and unsuspecting nature, led him without evil intent, into connection with the Credit Mobilier, which was a reproach to him. The very nature that was an ornament to the Christian so laid him open to the designs of the designing and corrupt, that some of his nearest friends think it was to the credit of his administration that he died early. While we have Garfield up as an example, it is well-known that in early life he was a preacher. In later life he turned aside to politics, and war, both essential to the conduct of civil government.

After his experience through the war, it is said that he always refused to preach or to preside at the Lord's table. The reason was, his hands were stained in the blood of his fellowmen, and inasmuch as David was prohibited building in the material earthly temple on account of his hands being stained in blood, he could not take an active part in leading the hosts, or building up the spiritual temple of God. This shows a commendably sensitive conscience. But every man who voted to bring on or perpetuate that war, was just as guilty before God as the men who actively participated in it. Their souls were just as much stained in blood.[1] He heard that God's agent heard God. He that gave a cup of cold water to the least disciple of Christ in the name of Christ did it to Christ himself. This establishes fully what we do through another or cause another to do, we ourselves do and are responsible for.

Then again, he who maintains and supports an institution is responsible for the general results of that institution. The general and necessary results of human government are war and the use of carnal weapons to maintain the government. Every one then that actively supports human government, is just as responsible for the wars and bloodshed that grow out of its existence and maintenance as are the men who actively wage and carry on the war. Then every one who voted to bring about and carry on the war was just as much unfitted for service in the kingdom of God as was Gen. Garfield or any other soldier in the army. The same is true of every man that supports and maintains human government.

But religious men fail to make the best and fairest rulers in human government from other causes. The religious sentiment in man is the strongest, deepest, most permanent element of his nature. When this element is developed and cultivated and fully aroused it is uncompromising and unyielding. God never intended it should be aroused to use carnal weapons. Aroused and guided by the principles of love—and directed by the word of God, it is unyielding in self-sacrificing devotion to benefit and save man. But warped and perverted by the principles that control in civil governments and using the sword—it is implacable, unmerciful. In other words men with their religious natures developed, then perverted by personal ambition, as politicians, rulers and warriors, are the most intolerant, implacable and cruel of rulers.

The worst despots of earth have been those that have commingled religious fervor with the ambitions and strifes of political rulers. The bloodiest paths, the most cruel desolation made in our country during the late war, were made by preacher-warriors. The most intolerant of rulers—those slowest to end the bitterness and strifes of the war—are the religious bodies. The religious element in man is the permanent uncompromising enduring element of his nature. And the very qualities that make him a cruel and unrelenting despot with carnal weapons in his hand, make him the self-sacrificing, devoted servant of God, willing to endure all things to save his enemies when clothed with spiritual weapons. Saul the vindictive persecutor, haling men and women to prison, and giving his voice for their death, with carnal weapons in his hand, and the Apostle Paul dying daily and willing himself to be accursed to save his brethren the Jews, shows how differently the same person under the differing conditions, acts. This shows that religion and devotion are only good in the path and for the ends for which God has fitted them. They are not in place ruling with the sword.

Religious influence exerts a moralizing influence in society that benefits it and helps even civil government, but religion exerts its most benign effects as it influences persons and communities to adopt in their lives the precepts and principles of the religion of Christ Jesus and so leads the world to a higher standard of morality and virtue.

Officers and Employees

There are requirements sometimes made of persons by the government that they have difficulty in determining whether they violate the law of God in doing them. Among them is jury service. The rule determined in the preceding pages, is, the Christian should take no part in the administration or support of the government. Jury service is a part of its administration, and frequently lays on the juryman the duty of determining the life or death of his fellowman, and leads into affiliation with the agencies of government. Some anxious for office say, a postmaster is not a political office. Hence he may hold it, that clerkship in the executive offices are not political—but they are part of the essential elements of the civil administration, and make the holder a supporter of the government. Yet there are employments sometimes given in carrying on government operations that a Christian it seems to me might perform. The government builds a house. House building is no part of the administration of government. A mason or carpenter might do work on this building without other relation to the government than that of employee to the government. The government wishes a school taught. Teaching school is no part of the administration of the government. It seems to me a Christian might teach a government school as an employe without compromising his position. As a rule he may work as an employe of the government but may not be an officer or supporter. As a rule the government exacts an oath of its officers, to support the government but it does not of its employees. Its employes in building, in school teaching, in surveying, are frequently foreigners who do not owe allegiance to the government, in these a Christian it seems to me might work. This work constitutes no part of the government administration and requires no affiliation with or obligation to support the government....

All which means that the Christians came into the church with their whole hearts, and tolerated no divided fealty and service in its members. The service of God, the conforming their lives to the teachings of God's word, the building up of his church, the spread of his kingdom, the teachings of his holy word to the world, were the leading purposes and business of all Christians. To this one end, all who came into the church devoted their talents, their time, their means. Nothing counteracting this main work was tolerated. The man whose calling was not in harmony with this great work of the church, must give up that calling, or he could not be recognized as a member of the church of God. The consecration of all the powers of mind, body and soul, to the service of God on the part of every man, woman and child, was the rule of the church. A sedulous guarding against dividing the fealty and service with other institutions, and against the members remaining where they would imbibe a different spirit to bring into the church, is manifest. They sought first and only the kingdom of God and his righteousness. They were willing to sacrifice worldly honor, riches and glory, to the advancement of this work. Their children were trained for the service of God in the church.

When Christians thus consecrated themselves to the service of God and rendered to him an undivided fealty, the word of the Lord multiplied greatly. It ran and was glorified among men. Multitudes at home and abroad were converted to Christ.

The great weakness of the church to-day, is, when men are brought into the church they are not consecrated to the service of God and the upbuilding of his kingdom. The children of God devote more time, more talent to the service of earthly kingdoms and institutions than they do to the church of God. What they serve most they love best. They drink into the spirit of the earthly institutions and bring that spirit into the church of God. They bring the habits of thought—the reliance upon human wisdom, and devices and inventions of men—into the church of God. They drive out the spirit of God, substitute human wisdom and ways for the wisdom and power of God and in every way defile the church of God and work its ruin and the shame of our holy religion.

Questions of Practical Morality Considered

Questions come up in the workings of society and before the voters of a country that involve moral good to the community. Such are the questions regarding the restriction of the sale of intoxicants, the licensing of race courses and gambling houses and places of licentiousness. It is strongly denied in such cases that the government that restricts and prohibits sin can be of the devil, and hence it is claimed a Christian should vote on all such questions of morality.

To the first, it is replied, the devil has always been quite willing to compromise with Christians if he can induce them to divide their allegiance and to give the greater service to the upbuilding of his kingdom. He offered this compromise to the Savior when here on earth. He was quite willing the Savior should rule, and doubtless in his own way, and make things as moral and respectable as he desired them, if it only promoted the growth of his kingdom and extended and supported his rule and dominion. This very proffer that the Master rejected, his disciples accept and act upon in supporting human government.

> The Holy Spirit warned Christians, that, false prophets would transform themselves into prophets of God and the devil himself into an angel of light (2 Cor. xi: 13.)

There is no doubt the devil is willing to turn moral reformer and make the world moral and respectable, if thereby his rule and authority are established and extended. And it may be set down as a truth that all reformations that propose to stop short of a full surrender of the soul, mind, and body up to God, are of the devil.

To the claim that a Christian is bound to vote, when he has the privilege, for that which promotes morality, and to fail to vote for the restriction and suppression of evil is to vote for it, we have determined that, to vote or use the civil power is to use force and carnal weapons. Christians cannot use these. To do so is to do evil that good may come. This is specially forbidden to Christians. To do so is to fight God's battles with the weapons of the evil one. To do so is to distrust God. The effective way for Christians to promote morality in a community, is, to stand aloof from the political strifes and conflicts, and maintain a pure and true faith in God, which is the only basis of true morality, and is as a leaven in society, to keep alive an active sense of right. To go into political strife is to admit the leaven of evil into the church. For the church to remain in the world and yet keep itself free from the spirit of the world, is to keep alive an active leaven of morality in the world. If that leaven loses its leaven, wherewith shall the world be leavened? or if the salt lose its savor wherewith shall the earth be salted or saved? God has told his children to use the spiritual weapons, has warned them against appealing to the sword or force to maintain his kingdom or to promote the honor of God and the good of man. When they do as he directs them, and use his appointments, he is with them to fight their battles for them and to give them the victory. When they turn from his appointments to the human kingdoms and their weapons, they turn from God, reject his help, drive him out of the conflict and fight the battles for man's deliverance with their own strength and by their own wisdom.

Note

1. This statement was published in the WATCHMAN, Boston, Mass., soon after Garfield's death, after it was in type we learn through Elder F. D. Power, the preacher in Washington city, that Garfield did after the war preside at the Lord's table and exhort his brethren, though he never entered the pulpit.

30

No Treason: The Constitution of No Authority (excerpt)

Lysander Spooner

I.

The Constitution has no inherent authority or obligation. It has no authority or obligation at all, unless as a contract between man and man. And it does not so much as even purport to be a contract between persons now existing. It purports, at most, to be only a contract between persons living eighty years ago. And it can be supposed to have been a contract then only between persons who had already come to years of discretion, so as to be competent to make reasonable and obligatory contracts. Furthermore, we know, historically, that only a small portion even of the people then existing were consulted on the subject, or asked, or permitted to express either their consent or dissent in any formal manner. Those persons, if any, who did give their consent formally, are all dead now. Most of them have been dead forty, fifty, sixty, or seventy years. And the constitution, so far as it was their contract, died with them. They had no natural power or right to make it obligatory upon their children. It is not only plainly impossible, in the nature of things, that they could bind their posterity, but they did not even attempt to bind them. That is to say, the instrument does not purport to be an agreement between any body but "the people" then existing; nor does it, either expressly or impliedly, assert any right, power, or disposition, on their part, to bind anybody but themselves. Let us see. Its language is:

> We, the people of the United States [that is, the people then existing in the United States], in order to form a more perfect union, insure domestic tranquillity, provide for the common defense, promote the general welfare, and secure the blessings of liberty to ourselves and our posterity, do ordain and establish this Constitution for the United States of America.

It is plain, in the first place, that this language, as an agreement, purports to be only what it at most really was, viz., a contract between the people then existing; and, of necessity, binding, as a contract, only upon those then existing. In the second place, the language neither expresses nor implies that they had any right or power, to bind their "posterity" to live under it. It does not say that their "posterity" will, shall, or must live under it. It only says, in effect, that their hopes and motives in adopting it were that it might prove useful to their posterity, as well as to themselves, by promoting their union, safety, tranquillity, liberty, etc.

Suppose an agreement were entered into, in this form:

> We, the people of Boston, agree to maintain a fort on Governor's Island, to protect ourselves and our posterity against invasion.

This agreement, as an agreement, would clearly bind nobody but the people then existing. Secondly, it would assert no right, power, or disposition, on their part, to compel their "posterity" to maintain such a fort. It would only indicate that the supposed welfare of their posterity was one of the motives that induced the original parties to enter into the agreement.

When a man says he is building a house for himself and his posterity, he does not mean to be understood as saying that he has any thought of binding them, nor is it to be inferred that he is so foolish as to imagine that he has any right or power to bind them, to live in it. So far as they are concerned, he only means to be understood as saying that his hopes and motives, in building it, are that they, or at least some of them, may find it for their happiness to live in it.

So when a man says he is planting a tree for himself and his posterity, he does not mean to be understood as saying that he has any thought of compelling them, nor is it to be inferred that he is such a simpleton as to imagine that he has any right or power to compel them, to eat the fruit. So far as they are concerned, he only means to say that his hopes and motives, in planting the tree, are that its fruit may be agreeable to them.

So it was with those who originally adopted the Constitution. Whatever may have been their personal intentions, the legal meaning of their language, so far as their "posterity" was concerned, simply was, that their hopes and motives, in entering into the agreement, were that it might prove useful and acceptable to their posterity; that it might promote their union, safety, tranquillity, and welfare; and that it might tend "to secure to them the blessings of liberty." The language does not assert nor at all imply, any right, power, or disposition, on the part of the original parties to the agreement, to compel their "posterity" to live under it. If they had intended to bind their posterity to live under it, they should have said that their objective was, not "to secure to them the blessings of liberty," but to make slaves of them; for if their "posterity" are bound to live under it, they are nothing less than the slaves of their foolish, tyrannical, and dead grandfathers.

It cannot be said that the Constitution formed "the people of the United States," for all time, into a corporation. It does not speak of "the people" as a corporation, but as individuals. A corporation does not describe itself as "we," nor as "people," nor as "ourselves." Nor does a corporation, in legal language, have any "posterity." It supposes itself to have, and speaks of itself as having, perpetual existence, as a single individuality.

Moreover, no body of men, existing at any one time, have the power to create a perpetual corporation. A corporation can become practically perpetual only by the voluntary accession of new members, as the old ones die off. But for this voluntary accession of new members, the corporation necessarily dies with the death of those who originally composed it.

Legally speaking, therefore, there is, in the Constitution, nothing that professes or attempts to bind the "posterity" of those who established it.

If, then, those who established the Constitution, had no power to bind, and did not attempt to bind, their posterity, the question arises, whether their posterity have bound themselves. If they have done so, they can have done so in only one or both of these two ways, viz., by voting, and paying taxes.

II.

Let us consider these two matters, voting and tax paying, separately. And first of voting.

All the voting that has ever taken place under the Constitution, has been of such a kind that it not only did not pledge the whole people to support the Constitution, but it did not even pledge any one of them to do so, as the following considerations show.

1. In the very nature of things, the act of voting could bind nobody but the actual voters. But owing to the property qualifications required, it is probable that, during the first twenty or thirty years under the Constitution, not more than one-tenth, fifteenth, or perhaps twentieth of the whole population (black and white, men, women, and minors) were permitted to vote. Consequently, so far as voting was concerned, not more than one-tenth, fifteenth, or twentieth of those then existing, could have incurred any obligation to support the Constitution.

At the present time, it is probable that not more than one-sixth of the whole population are permitted to vote. Consequently, so far as voting is concerned, the other five-sixths can have given no pledge that they will support the Constitution.

2. Of the one-sixth that are permitted to vote, probably not more than two-thirds (about one-ninth of the whole population) have usually voted. Many never vote at all. Many vote only once in two, three, five, or ten years, in periods of great excitement.

No one, by voting, can be said to pledge himself for any longer period than that for which he votes. If, for example, I vote for an officer who is to hold his office for only a year, I cannot be said to have thereby pledged myself to support the government beyond that term. Therefore, on the ground of actual voting, it probably cannot be said that more than one-ninth or one-eighth, of the whole population are usually under any pledge to support the Constitution.

3. It cannot be said that, by voting, a man pledges himself to support the Constitution, unless the act of voting be a perfectly voluntary one on his part. Yet the act of voting cannot properly be called a voluntary one on the part of any very large number of those who do vote. It is rather a measure of necessity imposed upon them by others, than one of their own choice. On this point I repeat what was said in a former number,[1] viz.:

In truth, in the case of individuals, their actual voting is not to be taken as proof of consent, even for the time being. On the contrary, it is to be considered that, without his consent having even been asked a man finds himself environed by a government that he cannot resist; a government that forces him to pay money, render service, and forego the exercise of many of his natural rights, under peril of weighty punishments. He sees, too, that other men practice this tyranny over him by the use of the ballot. He sees further, that, if he will but use the ballot himself, he has some chance of relieving himself from this tyranny of others, by subjecting them to his own. In short, he finds himself, without his consent, so situated that, if he use the ballot, he may become a master; if he does not use it, he must become a slave. And he has no other alternative than these two. In self-defense, he attempts the former. His case is analogous to that of a man who has been forced into battle, where he must either kill others, or be killed himself. Because, to save his own life in battle, a man takes the lives of his opponents, it is not to be inferred that the battle is one of his own choosing. Neither in contests with the ballot—which is a mere substitute for a bullet—because, as his only chance of self-preservation, a man uses a ballot, is it to be inferred that the contest is one into which he voluntarily entered; that he voluntarily set up all his own natural rights, as a stake against those of others, to be lost or won by the mere power of numbers. On the contrary, it is to be considered that, in an exigency into which he had been forced by others, and in which no other means of self-defense offered, he, as a matter of necessity, used the only one that was left to him.

Doubtless the most miserable of men, under the most oppressive government in the world, if allowed the ballot, would use it, if they could see any chance of thereby meliorating their condition. But it would not, therefore, be a legitimate inference that the government itself, that crushes them, was one which they had voluntarily set up, or even consented to.

Therefore, a man's voting under the Constitution of the United States, is not to be taken as evidence that he ever freely assented to the Constitution, even for the time being. Consequently we have no proof that any very large portion, even of the actual voters of the United States, ever really and voluntarily consented to the Constitution, even for the time being. Nor can we ever have such proof, until every man is left perfectly free to consent, or not, without thereby subjecting himself or his property to be disturbed or injured by others.

As we can have no legal knowledge as to who votes from choice, and who from the necessity thus forced upon him, we can have no legal knowledge, as to any particular individual, that he voted from choice; or, consequently, that by voting, he consented, or pledged himself, to support the government. Legally speaking, therefore, the act of voting utterly fails to pledge any one to support the government. It utterly fails to prove that the government rests upon the voluntary support of anybody. On general principles of law and reason, it cannot be said that the government has any voluntary supporters at all, until it can be distinctly shown who its voluntary supporters are.

4. As taxation is made compulsory on all, whether they vote or not, a large proportion of those who vote, no doubt do so to prevent their own money being used against themselves; when, in fact, they would have gladly abstained from voting, if they could thereby have saved themselves from taxation alone, to say nothing of being saved from all the other usurpations and tyrannies of the government. To take a man's property without his consent, and then to infer

his consent because he attempts, by voting, to prevent that property from being used to his injury, is a very insufficient proof of his consent to support the Constitution. It is, in fact, no proof at all. And as we can have no legal knowledge as to who the particular individuals are, if there are any, who are willing to be taxed for the sake of voting, we can have no legal knowledge that any particular individual consents to be taxed for the sake of voting; or, consequently, consents to support the Constitution.

5. At nearly all elections, votes are given for various candidates for the same office. Those who vote for the unsuccessful candidates cannot properly be said to have voted to sustain the Constitution. They may, with more reason, be supposed to have voted, not to support the Constitution, but specially to prevent the tyranny which they anticipate the successful candidate intends to practice upon them under color of the Constitution; and therefore may reasonably be supposed to have voted against the Constitution itself. This supposition is the more reasonable, inasmuch as such voting is the only mode allowed to them of expressing their dissent to the Constitution.

6. Many votes are usually given for candidates who have no prospect of success. Those who give such votes may reasonably be supposed to have voted as they did, with a special intention, not to support, but to obstruct the execution of, the Constitution; and, therefore, against the Constitution itself.

7. As all the different votes are given secretly (by secret ballot), there is no legal means of knowing, from the votes themselves, who votes for, and who votes against, the Constitution. Therefore, voting affords no legal evidence that any particular individual supports the Constitution. And where there can be no legal evidence that any particular individual supports the Constitution, it cannot legally be said that anybody supports it. It is clearly impossible to have any legal proof of the intentions of large numbers of men, where there can be no legal proof of the intentions of any particular one of them.

8. There being no legal proof of any man's intentions, in voting, we can only conjecture them. As a conjecture, it is probable, that a very large proportion of those who vote, do so on this principle, viz., that if, by voting, they could but get the government into their own hands (or that of their friends), and use its powers against their opponents, they would then willingly support the Constitution; but if their opponents are to have the power, and use it against them, then they would not willingly support the Constitution.

In short, men's voluntary support of the Constitution is doubtless, in most cases, wholly contingent upon the question whether, by means of the Constitution, they can make themselves masters, or are to be made slaves.

Such contingent consent as that is, in law and reason, no consent at all.

9. As everybody who supports the Constitution by voting (if there are any such) does so secretly (by secret ballot), and in a way to avoid all personal responsibility for the acts of his agents or representatives, it cannot legally or reasonably be said that anybody at all supports the Constitution by voting. No

man can reasonably or legally be said to do such a thing as assent to, or support, the Constitution, unless he does it openly, and in a way to make himself personally responsible for the acts of his agents, so long as they act within the limits of the power he delegates to them.

10. As all voting is secret (by secret ballot), and as all secret governments are necessarily only secret bands of robbers, tyrants, and murderers, the general fact that our government is practically carried on by means of such voting, only proves that there is among us a secret band of robbers, tyrants, and murderers, whose purpose is to rob, enslave, and, so far as necessary to accomplish their purposes, murder, the rest of the people. The simple fact of the existence of such a band does nothing towards proving that "the people of the United States," or any one of them, voluntarily supports the Constitution.

For all the reasons that have now been given, voting furnishes no legal evidence as to who the particular individuals are (if there are any), who voluntarily support the Constitution. It therefore furnishes no legal evidence that anybody supports it voluntarily.

So far, therefore, as voting is concerned, the Constitution, legally speaking, has no supporters at all.

And, as a matter of fact, there is not the slightest probability that the Constitution has a single bona fide supporter in the country. That is to say, there is not the slightest probability that there is a single man in the country, who both understands what the Constitution really is, and sincerely supports it for what it really is.

The ostensible supporters of the Constitution, like the ostensible supporters of most other governments, are made up of three classes, viz.: 1. Knaves, a numerous and active class, who see in the government an instrument which they can use for their own aggrandizement or wealth. 2. Dupes—a large class, no doubt—each of whom, because he is allowed one voice out of millions in deciding what he may do with his own person and his own property, and because he is permitted to have the same voice in robbing, enslaving, and murdering others, that others have in robbing, enslaving, and murdering himself, is stupid enough to imagine that he is a "free man," a "sovereign"; that this is "a free government"; "a government of equal rights," "the best government on earth,"[2] and such like absurdities. 3. A class who have some appreciation of the evils of government, but either do not see how to get rid of them, or do not choose to so far sacrifice their private interests as to give themselves seriously and earnestly to the work of making a change.

III.

The payment of taxes, being compulsory, of course furnishes no evidence that any one voluntarily supports the Constitution.

1. It is true that the theory of our Constitution is, that all taxes are paid voluntarily; that our government is a mutual insurance company, voluntarily

entered into by the people with each other; that each man makes a free and purely voluntary contract with all others who are parties to the Constitution, to pay so much money for so much protection, the same as he does with any other insurance company; and that he is just as free not to be protected, and not to pay tax, as he is to pay a tax, and be protected.

But this theory of our government is wholly different from the practical fact. The fact is that the government, like a highwayman, says to a man: "Your money, or your life." And many, if not most, taxes are paid under the compulsion of that threat.

The government does not, indeed, waylay a man in a lonely place, spring upon him from the roadside, and, holding a pistol to his head, proceed to rifle his pockets. But the robbery is none the less a robbery on that account; and it is far more dastardly and shameful.

The highwayman takes solely upon himself the responsibility, danger, and crime of his own act. He does not pretend that he has any rightful claim to your money, or that he intends to use it for your own benefit. He does not pretend to be anything but a robber. He has not acquired impudence enough to profess to be merely a "protector," and that he takes men's money against their will, merely to enable him to "protect" those infatuated travelers, who feel perfectly able to protect themselves, or do not appreciate his peculiar system of protection. He is too sensible a man to make such professions as these. Furthermore, having taken your money, he leaves you, as you wish him to do. He does not persist in following you on the road, against your will; assuming to be your rightful "sovereign," on account of the "protection" he affords you. He does not keep "protecting" you, by commanding you to bow down and serve him; by requiring you to do this, and forbidding you to do that; by robbing you of more money as often as he finds it for his interest or pleasure to do so; and by branding you as a rebel, a traitor, and an enemy to your country, and shooting you down without mercy, if you dispute his authority, or resist his demands. He is too much of a gentleman to be guilty of such impostures, and insults, and villainies as these. In short, he does not, in addition to robbing you, attempt to make you either his dupe or his slave.

The proceedings of those robbers and murderers, who call themselves "the government," are directly the opposite of these of the single highwayman.

In the first place, they do not, like him, make themselves individually known; or, consequently, take upon themselves personally the responsibility of their acts. On the contrary, they secretly (by secret ballot) designate some one of their number to commit the robbery in their behalf, while they keep themselves practically concealed. They say to the person thus designated:

Go to A_____ B_____, and say to him that "the government" has need of money to meet the expenses of protecting him and his property. If he presumes to say that he has never contracted with us to protect him, and that he wants none of our protection, say to him that that is our business, and not his; that we choose to protect him, whether he desires us to do so or not; and that we demand pay, too, for protecting him. If he dares to inquire who the individuals are, who have thus taken upon themselves the title of "the government," and who assume to protect him, and demand payment of him, without his having ever made any contract with them, say to him that that, too, is our business, and not his; that we do not choose to make ourselves individually known to him; that we have secretly (by secret ballot) appointed you our agent to give him notice of our demands, and, if he complies with them, to give him, in our name, a receipt that will protect him against any similar demand for the present year. If he refuses to comply, seize and sell enough of his property to pay not only our demands, but all your own expenses and trouble beside. If he resists the seizure of his property, call upon the bystanders to help you (doubtless some of them will prove to be members of our band.) If, in defending his property, he should kill any of our band who are assisting you, capture him at all hazards; charge him (in one of our courts) with murder; convict him, and hang him. If he should call upon his neighbors, or any others who, like him, may be disposed to resist our demands, and they should come in large numbers to his assistance, cry out that they are all rebels and traitors; that "our country" is in danger; call upon the commander of our hired murderers; tell him to quell the rebellion and "save the country," cost what it may. Tell him to kill all who resist, though they should be hundreds of thousands; and thus strike terror into all others similarly disposed. See that the work of murder is thoroughly done; that we may have no further trouble of this kind hereafter. When these traitors shall have thus been taught our strength and our determination, they will be good loyal citizens for many years, and pay their taxes without a why or a wherefore.

It is under such compulsion as this that taxes, so called, are paid. And how much proof the payment of taxes affords, that the people consent to "support the government," it needs no further argument to show.

2. Still another reason why the payment of taxes implies no consent, or pledge, to support the government, is that the taxpayer does not know, and has no means of knowing, who the particular individuals are who compose "the government." To him "the government" is a myth, an abstraction, an incorporeality, with which he can make no contract, and to which he can give no consent, and make no pledge. He knows it only through its pretended agents. "The government" itself he never sees. He knows indeed, by common report, that certain persons, of a certain age, are permitted to vote; and thus to make themselves parts of, or (if they choose) opponents of, the government, for the time being. But who of them do thus vote, and especially how each one votes (whether so as to aid or oppose the government), he does not know; the voting being all done secretly (by secret ballot). Who, therefore, practically compose "the government," for the time being, he has no means of knowing. Of course he can make no contract with them, give them no consent, and make them no pledge. Of necessity, therefore, his paying taxes to them implies, on his part, no

contract, consent, or pledge to support them—that is, to support "the government," or the Constitution.

3. Not knowing who the particular individuals are, who call themselves "the government," the taxpayer does not know whom he pays his taxes to. All he knows is that a man comes to him, representing himself to be the agent of "the government"—that is, the agent of a secret band of robbers and murderers, who have taken to themselves the title of "the government," and have determined to kill everybody who refuses to give them whatever money they demand. To save his life, he gives up his money to this agent. But as this agent does not make his principals individually known to the taxpayer, the latter, after he has given up his money, knows no more who are "the government"—that is, who were the robbers—than he did before. To say, therefore, that by giving up his money to their agent, he entered into a voluntary contract with them, that he pledges himself to obey them, to support them, and to give them whatever money they should demand of him in the future, is simply ridiculous.

4. All political power, so called, rests practically upon this matter of money. Any number of scoundrels, having money enough to start with, can establish themselves as a "government"; because, with money, they can hire soldiers, and with soldiers extort more money; and also compel general obedience to their will. It is with government, as Caesar said it was in war, that money and soldiers mutually supported each other; that with money he could hire soldiers, and with soldiers extort money. So these villains, who call themselves governments, well understand that their power rests primarily upon money. With money they can hire soldiers, and with soldiers extort money. And, when their authority is denied, the first use they always make of money, is to hire soldiers to kill or subdue all who refuse them more money.

For this reason, whoever desires liberty, should understand these vital facts, viz.: 1. That every man who puts money into the hands of a "government" (so called), puts into its hands a sword which will be used against him, to extort more money from him, and also to keep him in subjection to its arbitrary will. 2. That those who will take his money, without his consent, in the first place, will use it for his further robbery and enslavement, if he presumes to resist their demands in the future. 3. That it is a perfect absurdity to suppose that any body of men would ever take a man's money without his consent, for any such object as they profess to take it for, viz., that of protecting him; for why should they wish to protect him, if he does not wish them to do so? To suppose that they would do so, is just as absurd as it would be to suppose that they would take his money without his consent, for the purpose of buying food or clothing for him, when he did not want it. 4. If a man wants "protection," he is competent to make his own bargains for it; and nobody has any occasion to rob him, in order to "protect" him against his will. 5. That the only security men can have for their political liberty, consists in their keeping their money in their own pockets, until they have assurances, perfectly satisfactory to themselves, that it will be used as they wish it to be used, for their benefit, and not for their injury. 6. That no government, so called, can reasonably be trusted for a moment, or reasonably be supposed to have honest purposes in view, any longer than it depends wholly upon voluntary support.

These facts are all so vital and so self-evident, that it cannot reasonably be supposed that any one will voluntarily pay money to a "government," for the purpose of securing its protection, unless he first make an explicit and purely voluntary contract with it for that purpose.

It is perfectly evident, therefore, that neither such voting, nor such payment of taxes, as actually takes place, proves anybody's consent, or obligation, to support the Constitution. Consequently we have no evidence at all that the Constitution is binding upon anybody, or that anybody is under any contract or obligation whatever to support it. And nobody is under any obligation to support it.

IV.

The constitution not only binds nobody now, but it never did bind anybody. It never bound anybody, because it was never agreed to by anybody in such a manner as to make it, on general principles of law and reason, binding upon him.

It is a general principle of law and reason, that a written instrument binds no one until he has signed it. This principle is so inflexible a one, that even though a man is unable to write his name, he must still "make his mark," before he is bound by a written contract. This custom was established ages ago, when few men could write their names; when a clerk—that is, a man who could write—was so rare and valuable a person, that even if he were guilty of high crimes, he was entitled to pardon, on the ground that the public could not afford to lose his services. Even at that time, a written contract must be signed; and men who could not write, either "made their mark," or signed their contracts by stamping their seals upon wax affixed to the parchment on which their contracts were written. Hence the custom of affixing seals, that has continued to this time.

The laws holds, and reason declares, that if a written instrument is not signed, the presumption must be that the party to be bound by it, did not choose to sign it, or to bind himself by it. And law and reason both give him until the last moment, in which to decide whether he will sign it, or not. Neither law nor reason requires or expects a man to agree to an instrument, until it is written; for until it is written, he cannot know its precise legal meaning. And when it is written, and he has had the opportunity to satisfy himself of its precise legal meaning, he is then expected to decide, and not before, whether he will agree to it or not. And if he do not then sign it, his reason is supposed to be, that he does not choose to enter into such a contract. The fact that the instrument was written for him to sign, or with the hope that he would sign it, goes for nothing.

Where would be the end of fraud and litigation, if one party could bring into court a written instrument, without any signature, and claim to have it enforced, upon the ground that it was written for another man to sign? that this other man had promised to sign it? that he ought to have signed it? that he had had the opportunity to sign it, if he would? but that he had refused or neglected to do so? Yet that is the most that could ever be said of the Constitution.[3] The very judges, who profess to derive all their authority from the Constitution—from an instrument that nobody ever signed—would spurn any other instrument, not signed, that should be brought before them for adjudication.

Moreover, a written instrument must, in law and reason, not only be signed, but must also be delivered to the party (or to some one for him), in whose favor it is made, before it can bind the party making it. The signing is of no effect, unless the instrument be also delivered. And a party is at perfect liberty to refuse to deliver a written instrument, after he has signed it. The Constitution was not only never signed by anybody, but it was never delivered by anybody, or to anybody's agent or attorney. It can therefore be of no more validity as a contract, than can any other instrument that was never signed or delivered.

V.

As further evidence of the general sense of mankind, as to the practical necessity there is that all men's important contracts, especially those of a permanent nature, should be both written and signed, the following facts are pertinent.

For nearly two hundred years—that is, since 1677—there has been on the statute book of England, and the same, in substance, if not precisely in letter, has been reenacted, and is now in force, in nearly or quite all the States of this Union, a statute, the general object of which is to declare that no action shall be brought to enforce contracts of the more important class, unless they are put in writing, and signed by the parties to be held chargeable upon them.[4]

The principle of the statute, be it observed, is, not merely that written contracts shall be signed, but also that all contracts, except for those specially exempted—generally those that are for small amounts, and are to remain in force for but a short time—shall be both written and signed.

The reason of the statute, on this point, is, that it is now so easy a thing for men to put their contracts in writing, and sign them, and their failure to do so opens the door to so much doubt, fraud, and litigation, that men who neglect to have their contracts—of any considerable importance—written and signed, ought not to have the benefit of courts of justice to enforce them. And this reason is a wise one; and that experience has confirmed its wisdom and necessity, is demonstrated by the fact that it has been acted upon in England for nearly two hundred years, and has been so nearly universally adopted in this country, and that nobody thinks of repealing it.

We all know, too, how careful most men are to have their contracts written and signed, even when this statute does not require it. For example, most men, if they have money due them, of no larger amount than five or ten dollars, are careful to take a note for it. If they buy even a small bill of goods, paying for it at the time of delivery, they take a receipted bill for it. If they pay a small balance of a book account, or any other small debt previously contracted, they take a written receipt for it.

Furthermore, the law everywhere (probably) in our country, as well as in England, requires that a large class of contracts, such as wills, deeds, etc., shall not only be written and signed, but also sealed, witnessed, and acknowledged. And in the case of married women conveying their rights in real estate, the law, in many States, requires that the women shall be examined separate and apart from their husbands, and declare that they sign their contracts free of any fear or compulsion of their husbands.

Such are some of the precautions which the laws require, and which individuals—from motives of common prudence, even in cases not required by law—take, to put their contracts in writing, and have them signed, and, to guard against all uncertainties and controversies in regard to their meaning and validity. And yet we have what purports, or professes, or is claimed, to be a contract—the Constitution—made eighty years ago, by men who are now all dead, and who never had any power to bind US, but which (it is claimed) has nevertheless bound three generations of men, consisting of many millions, and which (it is claimed) will be binding upon all the millions that are to come; but which nobody ever signed, sealed, delivered, witnessed, or acknowledged; and which few persons, compared with the whole number that are claimed to be bound by it, have ever read, or even seen, or ever will read, or see. And of those who ever have read it, or ever will read it, scarcely any two, perhaps no two, have ever agreed, or ever will agree, as to what it means.

Moreover, this supposed contract, which would not be received in any court of justice sitting under its authority, if offered to prove a debt of five dollars, owing by one man to another, is one by which—as it is generally interpreted by those who pretend to administer it—all men, women and children throughout the country, and through all time, surrender not only all their property, but also their liberties, and even lives, into the hands of men who by this supposed contract, are expressly made wholly irresponsible for their disposal of them. And we are so insane, or so wicked, as to destroy property and lives without limit, in fighting to compel men to fulfill a supposed contract, which, inasmuch as it has never been signed by anybody, is, on general principles of law and reason—such principles as we are all governed by in regard to other contracts—the merest waste of paper, binding upon nobody, fit only to be thrown into the fire; or, if preserved, preserved only to serve as a witness and a warning of the folly and wickedness of mankind.

VI.

It is no exaggeration, but a literal truth, to say that, by the Constitution—not as I interpret it, but as it is interpreted by those who pretend to administer it—the properties, liberties, and lives of the entire people of the United States are surrendered unreservedly into the hands of men who, it is provided by the Constitution itself, shall never be "questioned" as to any disposal they make of them.

Thus the Constitution (Art. I, Sec. 6) provides that, "for any speech or debate [or vote], in either house, they [the senators and representatives] shall not be questioned in any other place."

The whole law-making power is given to these senators and representatives (when acting by a two-thirds vote);[5] and this provision protects them from all responsibility for the laws they make.

The Constitution also enables them to secure the execution of all their laws, by giving them power to withhold the salaries of, and to impeach and remove, all judicial and executive officers, who refuse to execute them.

Thus the whole power of the government is in their hands, and they are made utterly irresponsible for the use they make of it. What is this but absolute, irresponsible power?

It is no answer to this view of the case to say that these men are under oath to use their power only within certain limits; for what care they, or what should they care, for oaths or limits, when it is expressly provided, by the Constitution itself, that they shall never be "questioned," or held to any responsibility whatever, for violating their oaths, or transgressing those limits?

Neither is it any answer to this view of the case to say that the men holding this absolute, irresponsible power, must be men chosen by the people (or portions of them) to hold it. A man is none the less a slave because he is allowed to choose a new master once in a term of years. Neither are a people any the less slaves because permitted periodically to choose new masters. What makes them slaves is the fact that they now are, and are always hereafter to be, in the hands of men whose power over them is, and always is to be, absolute and irresponsible.[6]

The right of absolute and irresponsible dominion is the right of property, and the right of property is the right of absolute, irresponsible dominion. The two are identical; the one necessarily implies the other. Neither can exist without the other. If, therefore, Congress have that absolute and irresponsible law-making power, which the Constitution—according to their interpretation of it—gives them, it can only be because they own us as property. If they own us as property, they are our masters, and their will is our law. If they do not own us as property, they are not our masters, and their will, as such, is of no authority over us.

But these men who claim and exercise this absolute and irresponsible dominion over us, dare not be consistent, and claim either to be our masters, or to own us as property. They say they are only our servants, agents, attorneys, and representatives. But this declaration involves an absurdity, a contradiction. No man can be my servant, agent, attorney, or representative, and be, at the same time, uncontrollable by me, and irresponsible to me for his acts. It is of no importance that I appointed him, and put all power in his hands. If I made him uncontrollable by me, and irresponsible to me, he is no longer my servant, agent, attorney, or representative. If I gave him absolute, irresponsible power over my property, I gave him the property. If I gave him absolute, irresponsible power over myself, I made him my master, and gave myself to him as a slave. And it is of no importance whether I called him master or servant, agent or owner. The only question is, what power did I put in his hands? Was it an absolute and irresponsible one? or a limited and responsible one?

For still another reason they are neither our servants, agents, attorneys, nor representatives. And that reason is, that we do not make ourselves responsible for their acts. If a man is my servant, agent, or attorney, I necessarily make myself responsible for all his acts done within the limits of the power I have entrusted to him. If I have entrusted him, as my agent, with either absolute power, or any power at all, over the persons or properties of other men than myself, I thereby necessarily make myself responsible to those other persons for any injuries he may do them, so long as he acts within the limits of the power I have granted him. But no individual who may be injured in his person or property, by acts of Congress, can come to the individual electors, and hold them responsible for these acts of their so-called agents or representatives. This fact proves that these pretended agents of the people, of everybody, are really the agents of nobody.

If, then, nobody is individually responsible for the acts of Congress, the members of Congress are nobody's agents. And if they are nobody's agents, they are themselves individually responsible for their own acts, and for the acts of all whom they employ. And the authority they are exercising is simply their own individual authority; and, by the law of nature—the highest of all laws—anybody injured by their acts, anybody who is deprived by them of his property or his liberty, has the same right to hold them individually responsible, that he has to hold any other trespasser individually responsible. He has the same right to resist them, and their agents, that he has to resist any other trespassers.

Notes

1. See *No Treason*, No. 2, pages 5 and 6.
2. Suppose it be "the best government on earth," does that prove its own goodness, or only the badness of all other governments?
3. The very men who drafted it, never signed it in any way to bind themselves by it, *as a contract*. And not one of them probably ever would have signed it in any way to bind himself by it, *as a contract*.
4. I have personally examined the statute books of the following States, viz.: Maine, New Hampshire, Vermont, Massachusetts, Rhode Island, Connecticut, New York, New Jersey, Pennsylvania, Delaware, Virginia, North Carolina, South Carolina, Georgia, Florida, Alabama, Mississippi, Tennessee, Kentucky, Ohio, Michigan, Indiana, Illinois, Wisconsin, Texas, Arkansas, Missouri, Iowa, Minnesota, Nebraska, Kansas, Nevada, California, and Oregon, and find that in all these States the English statute has been reenacted, sometimes with modifications, but generally enlarging its operations, and is now in force.

   The following are some of the provisions of the Massachusetts statute:

   "No action shall be brought in any of the following cases, that is to say:...

   "To charge a person upon a special promise to answer for the debt, default, or misdoings of another:...

   "Upon a contract for the sale of lands, tenements, hereditaments, or of any interest in, or concerning them; or

"Upon an agreement that is not to be performed within one year from the writing thereof:

"Unless the promise, contract, or agreement, upon which such action is brought, or some memorandum or note thereof, is in writing, and signed by the party to be charged therewith, or by some person thereunto by him lawfully authorized."

"No contract for the sale of goods, wares, or merchandise, for the price of fifty dollars or more, shall be good or valid, unless the purchaser accepts and receives part of the goods so sold, or gives something in earnest to bind the bargain, or in part payment; or unless some note or memorandum in writing of the bargain is made and signed by the party to be charged thereby, or by some person thereunto by him lawfully authorized."

5. And this two-thirds vote may be but two-thirds of a quorum—that is two-thirds of a majority—instead of two-thirds of the whole.
6. Of what appreciable value is it to any man, as an individual, that he is allowed a voice in choosing these public masters? His voice is only one of several millions.

31

Trial by Jury (excerpt)

Lysander Spooner

The Right of Juries to Judge the Justice of the Laws

Section I

For more than six hundred years—that is, since Magna Carta, in 1215—there has been no clearer principle of English or American constitutional law, than that, in criminal cases, it is not only the right and duty of juries to judge what are the facts, what is the law, and what was the moral intent of the accused; *but that it is also their right, and their primary and paramount duty, to judge of the justice of the law, and to hold all laws invalid, that are, in their opinion, unjust or oppressive, and all persons guiltless in violating, or resisting the execution of, such laws.*

Unless such be the right and duty of jurors, it is plain that, instead of juries being a "palladium of liberty"—a barrier against the tyranny and oppression of the government—they are really mere tools in its hands, for carrying into execution any injustice and oppression it may desire to have executed.

But for their right to judge of the law, *and the justice of the law*, juries would be no protection to an accused person, *even as to matters of fact*; for, if the government can dictate to a jury any law whatever, in a criminal case, it can certainly dictate to them the laws of evidence. That is, it can dictate what evidence is admissible, and what inadmissible, *and also what force or weight is to be given to the evidence admitted.* And if the government can thus dictate to a jury the laws of evidence, it can not only make it necessary for them to convict on a partial exhibition of the evidence rightfully pertaining to the case, but it can even require them to convict on any evidence whatever that it pleases to offer them.

That the rights and duties of jurors must necessarily be such as are here claimed for them, will be evident when it is considered what the trial by jury is, and what is its object.

"The trial by jury," then, is a "trial by the country"—that is by the people as distinguished from a trial the government.

It was anciently called "trial *per pais*" that is, "trial by the country." And now, in every criminal trial, the jury are told that the accused "has, for trial, put himself upon the *country*; which *country* you (the jury) are."

The object of this trial "by the country," or by the people, in preference to a trial by the government, is to guard against every species of oppression by the government. In order to effect this end, it is indispensable that the people, or "the country," judge of and determine their own liberties against the government; instead of the government's judging of and determining its own powers over the people. How is it possible that juries can do anything to protect the liberties of the people against the government, if they are not allowed to determine what those liberties are?

Any government, that is its own judge of, and determines authoritatively for the people, what are its own powers over the people, is an absolute government of course. It has all the powers that it chooses to exercise. There is no other—or at least no more accurate—definition of a despotism than this.

On the other hand, any people, that judge of, and determine authoritatively for the government, what are their own liberties against the government, of course retain all the liberties they wish to enjoy. *And this is freedom.* At least, it is freedom *to them*; because, although it may be theoretically imperfect, it, nevertheless, corresponds to *their* highest notions of freedom.

To secure this right of the people to judge of their own liberties against the government, the jurors are taken, (or must be, to make them lawful jurors,) from the body of the people, *by lot*, or by some process that precludes any previous knowledge, choice, or selection of them, on the part of the government. This is done to prevent the government's constituting a jury of its own partisans or friends; in other words, to prevent the government's *packing* a jury, with a view to maintain its own laws, and accomplish its own purposes.

It is supposed that, if twelve men be taken, *by lot*, from the mass of the people, without the possibility of any previous knowledge, choice, or selection of them, on the part of the government, the jury will be a fair epitome of "the country" at large, and not merely of the party or faction that sustain the measures of the government; that substantially all classes, of opinions, prevailing among the people, will be represented in the jury; and especially that the opponents of the government, (if the government have any opponents,) will be represented there, as well as its friends; that the classes, who are oppressed by the laws of the government, (if any are thus oppressed,) will have their representatives in the jury, as well as those classes, who take sides with the oppressor—that is, with the government.

It is fairly presumable that such a tribunal will agree to no conviction except such as *substantially the whole country* would agree to, if they were present, taking part in the trial. A trial by such a tribunal is, therefore, in effect, "a trial by the country." In its results it probably comes as near to a trial by the whole country, as any trial that it is practicable to have, without too great inconvenience and expense. And, as unanimity is required for a conviction, it follows that no one can be convicted, except for the violation of such laws as substantially the *whole* country wish to have maintained. The government can enforce none of its laws, (by punishing offenders, through the verdicts of juries,) except such as substantially the whole people wish to have enforced. The government, therefore, consistently with the trial by jury, can exercise no powers over the people, (or, what is the same thing, over the accused person, who represents the rights of the people,) except such as substantially the whole people of the country consent that it may exercise. In such a trial, therefore, "the country," or the people, judge of and determine their own liberties against the government, instead of the government's judging of and determining its own powers over the people.

But all this trial "by the country" would be no trial at all "by the country," but only a trial by the government, if the government could either declare who may, and who may not, be jurors, or could dictate to the jury anything whatever, either of law or evidence, that is of the essence of the trial.

If the government may decide who may, and who may not, be jurors, it will of course select only its partisans, and those friendly to its measures. It may not only prescribe who may, and who may not, be eligible to be drawn as jurors; but it may also question each person drawn as a juror, as to his sentiments in regard to the particular law involved in each trial, before suffering him to be sworn on the panel; and exclude him if he be found unfavorable to the maintenance of such a law.[1]

So, also, if the government may dictate to the jury *what laws they are to enforce*, it is no longer a trial "by the country," but a trial by the government; because the jury then try the accused, not by any standard of their own—by their own judgments of their rightful liberties—but by a standard dictated to them by the government. And the standard, thus dictated by the government, becomes the measure of the people's liberties. If the government dictates the standard of trial, it of course dictates the results of the trial. And such a trial is no trial by the country, but only a trial by the government; and in it the government determines what are its own powers over the people, instead of the people's determining what are their own liberties against the government. In short, if the jury have no right to judge of the justice of a law of the government, they plainly can do nothing to protect the people, against the oppressions of the government; for there are no oppressions which the government may not authorize by law.

The jury are also to judge whether the laws are rightly expounded to them by the court. Unless they judge on this point, they do nothing to protect their liberties against the oppressions that are cable of being practiced under cover of a corrupt exposition of the laws. If the judiciary can authoritatively dictate to a jury any exposition of the law, they can dictate to them the law itself, and such laws as they please; because laws are, in practice, one thing or another, according as they are expounded.

The jury must also judge whether there really be any such law, (be it good or bad,) as the accused is charged with having transgressed. Unless they judge on this point, the people are liable to have their liberties taken from them by brute force, without any law at all.

The jury must also judge of the laws of evidence. If the government can dictate to a jury the laws of evidence, it can not only shut out any evidence it pleases, tending to vindicate the accused, but it can require that any evidence whatever, that it pleases to offer, be held as conclusive proof of any offence whatever which the government chooses to allege.

It is manifest, therefore, that the jury must judge of and try the whole case, and every part and parcel of the case, free of any dictation or authority on the part of the government. They must judge of the existence of the law; of the true exposition of the law; *of the justice of the law*; and of the admissibility and weight of all the evidence offered; otherwise the government will have everything its own way; the jury will be mere puppets in the hands of the government; and the trial will be, in reality, a trial by the government, and not a "trial by the country." By such trials the government will determine its own powers over the people, instead of the people's determining their own liberties against the government; and it will be an entire delusion to talk, as for centuries we have done, of the trial by jury, as a "palladium of liberty," or as any protection to the people against the oppression and tyranny of the government.

The question, then, between trial by jury, as thus described, and trial by the government, is simply a question between liberty and despotism. The authority to judge what are the powers of the government, and what the liberties of the people, must necessarily be vested in one or the other of the parties themselves the government, or the people; because there is no third party to whom it can be entrusted. If the authority be vested in the government, the government is absolute, and the people have no liberties except such as the government sees fit to indulge them with. If, on the other hand, that authority be vested in the people, then the people have all liberties, (as against the government,) except such as substantially the whole people (through a jury) choose to disclaim; and the government can exercise no to power except such as substantially the whole people (through a jury) consent that it may exercise.

Section II

The force and justice of the preceding argument cannot be evaded by saying that the government is chosen by the people; that, in theory, it represents the people; that it is designed to do the will of the people; that its members are all sworn to observe the fundamental or constitutional law instituted by the people; that its acts are therefore entitled to be considered the acts of the people; and that to allow a jury, representing the people, to invalidate the acts of the government, would therefore be arraying the people against themselves.

There are two answers to such an argument.

One answer is, that, in a representative government, there is no absurdity or contradiction, nor any arraying of the people against themselves, in requiring that the statutes or enactments of the government shall pass the ordeal of any number of separate tribunals, before it shall be determined that they are to have the force of laws. Our American constitutions have provided five of these separate tribunals, to wit, representatives, senate, executive,[2] jury, and judges; and have made it necessary that each enactment shall pass the ordeal of all these separate tribunals, before its authority can be established by the punishment of those who choose to transgress it. And there is no more absurdity or inconsistency in making a jury one of these several tribunals, than there is in making the representatives, or the senate, or the executive, or the judges, one of them. There is no more absurdity in giving a jury a veto upon the laws, than there is in giving a veto to each of these other tribunals. The people are no more arrayed against themselves, when a jury puts its veto upon a statute, which the other tribunals have sanctioned, than they are when the same veto is exercised by the representatives, the senate, the executive, or the judges.

But another answer to the argument that the people are arrayed against themselves, when a jury hold an enactment of the government invalid, is, that the government, and all the departments of the government, *are merely the servants and agents of the people*; not invested with arbitrary or absolute authority to bind the people, but required to submit all their enactments to the judgment of a tribunal more fairly representing the whole people, before they carry them into execution by punishing any individual for transgressing them. If the government were not thus required to submit their enactments to the judgment of "the country," before executing them upon individuals; if, in other words, the people had reserved to themselves no veto upon the acts of the government, the government, instead of being a mere servant and agent of the people would be an absolute despot over the people. It would have all power in its own hands; because the power to *punish* carries all other powers with it. A power that can, of itself, and by its own authority, punish disobedience, can compel obedience and submission, and is above all responsibility for the character of its laws. In short, it is a despotism.

And it is of no consequence to inquire how a government carne by this power to punish, whether by prescription, by inheritance, by usurpation, or by delegation from the people. *If it have now but got it*, the government is absolute.

It is plain, therefore, that if the people have invested the government with power to make laws that absolutely bind the people, and to punish the people for transgressing those laws, the people have surrendered their liberties unreservedly into the hands of the government.

It is of no avail to say, in answer to this view of the case, that in surrendering their liberties into the hands of the government, the people took an oath from the government, that it would exercise its power within certain constitutional limits; for when did oaths ever restrain a government that was otherwise unrestrained? when did a government fail to determine that all its acts were within the constitutional and authorized limits of its power, if it were permitted to determine that question for itself?

Neither is it of any avail to say, that, if the government abuse its power, and enact unjust and oppressive laws, the government may be changed by the influence of discussion, and the exercise of the right of suffrage. Discussion can do nothing to prevent the enactment, or procure the repeal, of unjust laws, unless it be understood that the discussion is to be followed by resistance. Tyrants care nothing for discussions that are to end only in discussion. Discussions, which do not interfere with the enforcement of their laws, are but idle wind to them. Suffrage is equally powerless and unreliable. It can be exercised only periodically; and the tyranny must at least be borne until the time for suffrage comes. Besides, when the suffrage is exercised, it gives no guaranty for the repeal of existing laws that are oppressive, and no security against the enactment of new ones that are equally so. The second body of legislators are liable and likely to be just as tyrannical as the first. If it be said that the second body may be chosen for their integrity, the answer is, that the first were chosen for that very reason, and yet proved tyrants. The second will be exposed to the same temptations as the first, and will be just as likely to prove tyrannical. Who ever heard that succeeding legislatures were, on the whole, more honest than those that preceded them? What is there in the nature of men or things to make them so? If it be said that the first body were chosen from motives of injustice, that fact proves that there is a portion of society who desire to establish injustice; and if they were powerful or artful enough to procure the election of their instruments to compose the first legislature, they will be likely to be powerful or artful enough to procure the election of the same or similar instruments to compose the second. The right of suffrage, therefore, and even a change of legislators, guarantees no change of legislation—certainly no change for the better. Even if a change for the better actually comes, it comes too late, because it comes only after more or less injustice has been irreparably done.

But, at best, the right of suffrage can be exercised only periodically; and between the periods the legislators are wholly irresponsible. No despot was ever more entirely irresponsible than are republican legislators during the period for which they are chosen. They can neither be removed from their office, nor called to account while in their office, nor punished after they leave their office, be their tyranny what it may. Moreover, the judicial and executive departments of the government are equally irresponsible *to the people*, and are only responsible, (by impeachment, and dependence for their salaries), to these irresponsible legislators. This dependence of the judiciary and executive upon the legislature is a guaranty that they will always sanction and execute its laws, whether just or unjust. Thus the legislators hold the whole power of the government in their hands, and are at the same time utterly irresponsible for the manner in which they use it.

If, now, this government, (the three branches thus really united in one), can determine the validity of, and enforce, its own laws, it is, for the time being, entirely absolute, and wholly irresponsible to the people.

But this is not all. These legislators, and this government, so irresponsible while in power, can perpetuate their power at pleasure, if they can determine what legislation is authoritative upon the people, and can enforce obedience to it; for they can not only declare their power perpetual, but they can enforce submission to all legislation that is necessary to secure its perpetuity. They can, for example, prohibit all discussion of the rightfulness of their authority; forbid the use of the suffrage; prevent the election of any successors; disarm, plunder, imprison, and even kill all who refuse submission. If, therefore, the government (all departments united) be absolute for a day—that is, if it can, for a day, enforce obedience to its own law can, in that day, secure its power for all time—like the queen, who wished to reign but for a day, but in that day caused the king, her husband, to be slain, and usurped his throne. Nor will it avail to say that such acts would be unconstitutional, and that unconstitutional acts may be lawfully resisted; for everything a government pleases to do will, of course, be determined to be constitutional, if the government itself be permitted to determine the question of the constitutionality of its own acts. Those who are capable of tyranny, are capable of perjury to sustain it.

The conclusion, therefore, is, that any government, that can, *for a day*, enforce its own laws, without appealing to the people, (or to a tribunal fairly representing the people,) for their consent, is, in theory, an absolute government, irresponsible to the people, and can perpetuate its power at pleasure.

The trial by jury is based upon a recognition of this principle, and therefore forbids the government to execute any of its laws, by punishing violators, in any case whatever, without first getting the consent of "the country," or the people, through a jury. In this way, the people, at all times, hold their liberties in their own hands, and never surrender them, even for a moment, into the hands of the government.

The trial by jury, then, gives to any and every individual the liberty, at any time, to disregard or resist any law whatever of the government, if he be willing to submit to the decision of a jury, the questions, whether the law be intrinsically just and obligatory? and whether his conduct, in disregarding or resisting it, were right in itself? And any law, which does not, in such trial, obtain the unanimous sanction of twelve men, taken at random from the people, and judging according to the standard of justice in their own minds, free from all dictation and authority of the government, may be transgressed and resisted with impunity, by whomsoever pleases to transgress or resist it.[3]

The trial by jury authorizes all this, or it is a sham and a hoax, utterly worthless for protecting the people against oppression. If it do not authorize an individual to resist the first and least act of injustice or tyranny, on the part of the government, it does not authorize him to resist the last and the greatest. If it do not authorize individuals to nip tyranny in the bud, it does not authorize them to cut it down when its branches are filled with the ripe fruits of plunder and oppression.

Those who deny the right of a jury to protect an individual in resisting an unjust law of the government, deny him all legal defence whatsoever against oppression. The right of revolution, which tyrants, in mockery, accord to mankind, is no *legal* right *under* a government; it is only a *natural* right to overturn a government. The government itself never acknowledges this right. And the right is practically established only when and because the government no longer exists to call it in question. The right, therefore, can be exercised with impunity, only when it is exercised victoriously. All *unsuccessful* attempts at revolution, however justifiable in themselves, are punished as treason, if the government be permitted to judge of the treason. The government itself never admits the injustice of its laws, as a legal defence for those who have attempted a revolution, and failed. The right of revolution, therefore, is a right of no practical value, except for those who are stronger than the government. So long, therefore, as the oppressions of a government are kept within such limits as simply not to exasperate against it a power greater than its own, the right of revolution cannot be appealed to, and is therefore inapplicable to the case. This affords a wide field for tyranny; and if a jury cannot *here* intervene, the oppressed are utterly defenceless.

It is manifest that the only security against the tyranny of the government lies in forcible resistance to the execution of the injustice; because the injustice will certainly be executed, *unless it be forcibly resisted.* And if it be but suffered to be executed, it must then be borne; for the government never makes compensation for its own wrongs.

Since, then, this forcible resistance to the injustice of the government is the only possible means of preserving liberty; it is indispensable to all *legal* liberty that this *resistance* should be *legalized.* It is perfectly self-evident that where there is no *legal* right to resist the oppression of the government, there can be no *legal* liberty. And here it is all-important to notice, that, *practically speaking*, there can be no *legal* right to resist the oppressions of the government, unless there be some *legal* tribunal, other than the government, and wholly independent of, and *above*, the government, to judge between the government and those who resist its oppressions; in other words, to judge what laws of the government are to be obeyed, and what may be resisted and held for nought. The only tribunal known to our laws, for this purpose, is a jury. If a jury have not the right to judge between the government and those who disobey its laws, and resist its oppressions, the government is absolute, and the people, *legally speaking*, are slaves. Like many other slaves they may have sufficient courage and strength to keep their masters somewhat in check; but they are nevertheless *known to the law* only as slaves.

That this right of resistance was recognized as a common law right, when the ancient and genuine trial by jury was in force, is not only proved by the nature of the trial itself, but is acknowledged by history.[4]

This right of resistance is recognized by the constitution of the United States, as a strictly legal and constitutional right. It is so recognized, first by the provision that "the trial of all crimes, except in cases of impeachment, shall be by jury"—that is, by the country—and not by the government; secondly, by the provision that "the right of the people to keep and bear arms shall not be infringed." This constitutional security for "the right to keep and bear arms, implies the right to use themes much as a constitutional security for the right to buy and keep food would have implied the right to eat it. The constitution, therefore, takes it for granted that the people will judge of the conduct of the government, and that, as they have the right, they will also have the sense, to use arms, whenever the necessity of the case justifies it. And it is a sufficient and *legal* defence for a person accused of using arms against the government, if he can show, to the satisfaction of a jury, or *even any one of a jury*, that the law he resisted was an unjust one.

In the American *State* constitutions also, this right of resistance to the oppressions of the government is recognized, in various ways, as a natural, legal, and constitutional right. In the first place, it is so recognized by provisions establishing the trial by jury; thus requiring that accused persons shall be tried by "the country," instead of the government. In the second place, it is recognized by many of them, as, for example, those of Massachusetts, Maine, Vermont, Connecticut, Pennsylvania, Ohio, Indiana, Michigan, Kentucky, Tennessee, Arkansas, Mississippi, Alabama, and Florida, by provisions expressly declaring that, the people shall have the right to bear arms. In many of them also, as, for example, those of Maine, New Hampshire, Vermont, Massachusetts, New Jersey, Pennsylvania, Delaware, Ohio, Indiana, Illinois, Florida, Iowa, and Arkansas, by provisions, in their bills of rights, declaring that men have a natural, inherent, and inalienable right of "*defending* their lives and liberties." This, of course, means that they have a right to defend them against any injustice *on the part of the government*, and not merely on the part of private individuals; because the object of all bills of rights is to assert the rights of individuals and the people, *as against the government*, and not as against private persons. It would be a matter of ridiculous supererogation to assert, in a constitution of government, the natural right of men to defend their lives and liberties against private trespassers.

Many of these bills of rights also assert the natural right of all men to protect their property—that is, to protect it *against the government*. It would be unnecessary and silly indeed to assert, in a constitution of government, the natural right of individuals to protect their property against thieves and robbers.

The constitutions of New Hampshire and Tennessee also declare that "The doctrine of non-resistance against arbitrary power and oppression is absurd, slavish, and destructive of the good and happiness of mankind."

The legal effect of these constitutional recognitions of the right of individuals to defend their property, liberties, and lives, against the government, is to legalize resistance to all injustice and oppression, of every name and nature whatsoever, on the part of the government.

But for this right of resistance, on the part of the people, all governments would become tyrannical to a degree of which few people are aware. Constitutions are utterly worthless to restrain the tyranny of governments, unless it be understood that the people will, by force, compel the government to keep within the constitutional limits. Practically speaking, no government knows any limits to its power, except the endurance of the people. But that the people are stronger than the government, and will resist in extreme cases, our governments would be little or nothing else than organized systems of plunder and oppression. All, or nearly all, the advantage there is in fixing any constitutional limits to the power of a government, is simply to give notice to the government of the point at which it will meet with resistance. If the people are then as good as their word, they may keep the government within the bounds they have set for it; otherwise it will disregard them—as is proved by the example of all our American governments, in which the constitutions have all become obsolete, at the moment of their adoption, for nearly or quite all purposes except the appointment of officers, who at once become practically absolute, except so far as they are restrained by the fear of popular resistance.

The bounds set to the power of the government, by the trial by jury, as will hereafter be shown, are these—that the government shall never touch the property, person, or natural or civil rights of an individual, against his consent, (except for the purpose of bringing them before a jury for trial,) unless in pursuance and execution of a judgment, or decree, rendered by a jury in each individual case, upon such evidence, and such law, as are satisfactory to their own understandings and consciences, irrespective of all legislation of the government.

The Trial by Jury, as Defined by Magna Carta

That the trial by jury is all that has been claimed for it in the preceding chapter, is proved both by the history and the language of the Great Charter of English Liberties, to which we are to look for a true definition of the trial by jury, and of which the guaranty for that trial is the vital, and most memorable, part.

The History of Magna Carta

In order to judge of the object and meaning of that chapter of Magna Carta which secures the trial by jury, it is to be borne in mind that, at the time of Magna Carta, the king (with exceptions immaterial to this discussion, but which will appear hereafter) was, constitutionally, the entire government; the sole *legislative, judicial, and executive* power of the nation. The executive and judicial officers were merely his servants, appointed by him, and removable at his pleasure. In addition to this, "the king himself often sat in his court, which always attended his person. He there heard causes, and pronounced judgment; and though he was assisted by the advice of other members, it is not to be imagined that a decision could be obtained contrary to his inclination or opinion."[5] Judges were in those days, and afterwards, such abject servants of the king, that "we find that King Edward I (1272 to 1307) fined and imprisoned his judges, in the same manner as Alfred the Great, among the Saxons, had done before him, by the sole exercise of his authority."[6]

Parliament, so far as there was a parliament, was a mere *council* of the king.[7] It assembled only at the pleasure of the king; sat only during his pleasure; and when sitting had no power, so far as *general* legislation was concerned, beyond that of simply *advising* the king. The only legislation to which their assent was constitutionally necessary, was demands for money and military services for *extraordinary* occasions. Even Magna Carta itself makes no provisions whatever for any parliaments, except when the king should want means to carry on war, or to meet some other *extraordinary* necessity.[8] He had no need of parliaments to raise taxes for the *ordinary* purposes of government; for his revenues from the rents of the crown lands and other sources, were ample for all except extraordinary occasions. Parliaments, too, when assembled, consisted only of bishops, barons, and other great men of the kingdom, unless the king chose to invite others.[9] There was no House of Commons at that time, and the people had no right to be heard, unless as petitioners.[10]

Even when laws were made at the time of a parliament, they were made in the name of the king alone. Sometimes it was inserted in the laws, that they were made with the *consent or advice* of the bishops, barons, and others assembled; but often this was omitted. Their consent or advice was evidently a matter of no legal importance to the enactment or validity of the laws, but only inserted, when inserted at all, with a view of obtaining a more willing submission to them on the part of the people. The style of enactment generally was, either *"The King wills and commands,"* or some other form significant of the sole legislative authority of the king. The king could pass laws at any time when it pleased him. The presence of a parliament was wholly unnecessary. Hume says, "It is asserted by Sir Harry Spelman, as an undoubted fact, that, during the reigns of the Norman princes, every order of the king, issued with the consent of his privy council, had the full force of law."[11] And other authorities abundantly corroborate this assertion.[12]

The king was, therefore, constitutionally the government; and the only legal limitation upon his power seems to have been simply the *Common Law*, usually called *"the law of the land,"* which he was bound by oath to maintain; (which oath had about the same practical value as similar oaths have always had). This "law of the land" seems not to have been regarded at all by many of the kings, except so far as they found it convenient to do so, or were constrained to observe it by the fear of arousing resistance. But as all people are slow in making resistance, oppression and usurpation often reached a great height; and, in the case of John, they had become so intolerable as to enlist the nation almost universally against him; and he was reduced to the necessity of complying with any terms the barons saw fit to dictate to him.

It was under these circumstances, that the Great Charter of English Liberties was granted. The barons of England, sustained by the common people, having their king in their power, compelled him, as the price of his throne, to pledge himself that he would punish no freeman for a violation of any of his laws, unless with the consent of the peers—that is, the equals—of the accused.

The question here arises, Whether the barons and people intended that those peers (the jury) should be mere puppets in the hands of the king, exercising no opinion of their own as to the intrinsic merits of the accusations they should try, or the justice of the laws they should be called on to enforce? Whether those haughty and victorious barons, when they had their tyrant king at their feet, gave back to him his throne, with full power to enact any tyrannical laws he might please, reserving only to a jury ("the country") the contemptible and servile privilege of ascertaining, (under the dictation of the king, or his judges, as to the laws of evidence), the simple fact whether those laws had been transgressed? Was this the only restraint, which, when they had all power in their hands, they placed upon the tyranny of a king, whose oppressions they had risen in arms to resist? Was it to obtain such a charter as that, that the whole nation had united, as it were, like one man, against their king? Was it on such a charter that they intended to rely, for all future time, for the security of their liberties? No. They were engaged in no such senseless work as that. On the contrary, when they required him to renounce forever the power to punish any freeman, unless by the consent of his peers, they intended those peers should judge of, and try, the whole case on its merits, independently of all arbitrary legislation, or judicial authority, on the part of the king. In this way they took the liberties of each individual—and thus the liberties of the whole people—entirely out of the hands of the king, and out of the power of his laws, and placed them in the keeping of the people themselves. And this it was that made the trial by jury the palladium of their liberties.

The trial by jury, be it observed, was the only real barrier interposed by them against absolute despotism. Could this trial, then, have been such an entire farce as it necessarily must have been, if the jury had had no power to judge of the justice of the laws the people were required to obey? Did it not rather imply that the jury were to judge independently and fearlessly as to everything involved in the charge, and especially as to its intrinsic justice, and thereon give their decision, (unbiased by any legislation of the king,) whether the accused might be punished? The reason of the thing, no less than the historical celebrity of the events, as securing the liberties of the people, and the veneration with which the trial by jury has continued to be regarded, notwithstanding its essence and vitality have been almost entirely extracted from it in practice, would settle the question, if other evidences had left the matter in doubt.

Besides, if his laws were to be authoritative with the jury, why should John indignantly refuse, as at first he did, to grant the charter, (and finally grant it only when brought to the last extremity,) on the ground that it deprived him of all power, and left him only the name of a king? He evidently understood that the juries were to veto his laws, and paralyze his power, at discretion, by forming their own opinions as to the true character of the offences they were to try, and the laws they were to be called on to enforce; and that *"the king wills and commands*" was to have no weight with them contrary to their own judgments of what was intrinsically right.[13]

The barons and people having obtained by the charter all the liberties they had demanded of the king, it was further provided by the charter itself that twenty-five barons, should be appointed by the barons, out of their number, to keep special vigilance in the kingdom to see that the charter was observed, with authority to make war upon the king in case of its violation. The king also, by the charter, so far absolved all the people of the kingdom from their allegiance to him, as to authorize and require them to swear to obey the twenty-five barons, in case they should make war upon the king for infringement of the charter. It was then thought by the barons and people, that something substantial had been done for the security of their liberties.

This charter, in its most essential features, and without any abatement as to the trial by jury, has since been confirmed more than thirty times; and the people of England have always had a traditionary idea that it was of some value as a guaranty against oppression. Yet that idea has been an entire delusion, unless the jury have had the right to judge of the justice of the laws they were called on to enforce.

Notes

1. To show that this supposition is not an extravagant one, it may be mentioned that courts have repeatedly questioned jurors to ascertain whether they were prejudiced *against the government*—that is, whether they were in favor of, or opposed to, such laws of the government as were to be put in issue in the then pending trial. This was done (in 1851) in the United States District Court for the District of Massachusetts, by Peleg Sprague, the United States district judge, in panelling three several juries for the trials of Scott, Hayden, and Morris, charged with having aided in the rescue of a fugitive slave from the custody of the United States deputy marshal. This judge caused the following question to be propounded to all the jurors separately; and those who answered unfavorably for the purposes of the government, were excluded from the panel.

   "Do you hold any opinions upon the subject of the Fugitive Slave Law, so called, which will induce you to refuse to convict a person indicted under it, if the facts set forth in the indictment, *and constituting the offense*, are proved against him, and the court direct you that the law is constitutional?"

   The reason of this question was, that "the Fugitive Slave Law, so called," was so obnoxious to a large portion of the People, as to render a conviction under it hopeless, if the jurors were taken indiscriminately from among the people.

   A similar question was soon afterwards propounded to the persons drawn as jurors in the United States *Circuit* Court for the District of Massachusetts, by Benjamin R. Curtis, one of the Justices of the Supreme Court of the United States, in empanelling a jury for the trial of the aforesaid Morris on the charge before mentioned; and those who did not answer the question favorably for the government were again excluded from the panel.

   It has also been an habitual practice with the Supreme Court of Massachusetts, in empanelling juries for the trial of *capital* offences, to inquire of the persons drawn as jurors whether they had any conscientious scruples against finding verdicts of guilty in such cases; that is, whether they had any conscientious scruples against sustaining the law prescribing death as the punishment of the crime to be tried; and to exclude from the panel all who answered in the affirmative.

The only principle upon which these questions are asked, is this—that no man shall be allowed to serve as juror, unless he be ready to enforce any enactment of the government, however cruel or tyrannical it may be.

What is such a jury good for, as a protection against the tyranny of the government? A jury like that is palpably nothing but a mere tool of oppression in the hands of the government. A trial by such a jury is really a trial by the government itself—and not a trial by the country—because it is a trial only by men specially selected by the government for their readiness to enforce its own tyrannical measures.

If that be the true principle of the trial by jury, the trial is utterly worthless as a security to liberty. The Czar might, with perfect safety to his authority, introduce the trial by jury into Russia, if he could but be permitted to select his jurors from those who were ready to maintain his laws, without regard to their injustice.

This example is sufficient to show that the very pith of the trial by jury, as a safeguard to liberty, consists in the jurors being taken indiscriminately from the whole people, and in their right to hold invalid all laws which they think unjust.

2. The executive has a qualified veto upon the passage of laws, in most of our governments, and an absolute veto, in all of them, upon the execution of any laws which he deems unconstitutional; because his oath to support the constitution (as he understands it) forbids him to execute any law that he deems unconstitutional.
3. And if there be so much as a reasonable *doubt* of the justice of the laws, the benefit of that doubt must be given to the defendant, and not to the government. So that the government must keep its laws clearly within the limits of justice, if it would ask a jury to enforce them.
4. Hallam says, "The relation established between a lord and his vassal by the feudal tenure, far from containing principles of any servile and implicit obedience, permitted the compact to be dissolved in case of its violation by either party. This extended as much to the sovereign as to inferior lords. * * If a vassal was aggrieved, and if justice was denied him, he sent a defiance, that is, a renunciation of fealty to the king, and was entitled to enforce redress at the point of his sword. It then became a contest of strength as between two independent potentates, and was terminated by treaty, advantageous or otherwise, according to the fortune of war. * * There remained the original principle, that allegiance depended conditionally upon good treatment, and that an appeal might be *lawfully* made to arms against an oppressive government. Nor was this, we may be sure, left for extreme necessity, or thought to require a long-enduring forbearance. In modern times, a king, compelled by his subjects' swords to abandon any pretension, would be supposed to have ceased to reign; and the express recognition of such a right as that of insurrection has been justly deemed inconsistent with the majesty of law. But ruder ages had ruder sentiments. Force was necessary to repel force; and men accustomed to see the king's authority defied by a private riot, were not much shocked when it was resisted in defence of public freedom."—3 *Middle Ages* 240-2.
5. Hume, Appendix 2.
6. Crabbe's *History of the English Law*, 236.
7. Coke says, "The king of England is armed with divers councils, one whereof is called *commune concilium*, (the common council,) and that it the court of parliament, and so it is *legally* called in writs and judicial proceedings *commune concilium regni Angliae* (the common council of the kingdom of England). And another is called *magnum concilium*, (great council;) this is sometimes applied to the upper house of parliament, and sometimes, out of parliament time, to the peers of the realm, lords of parliament, who are called *magnum concilium regis*, (the great council of the king). * * Thirdly, (as every man knoweth,) the king hath a privy council for mat-

ters of state. * * The fourth council of the king are his judges for law matters."—1 Coke's *Institutes*, 110a.

8. The Great Charter of Henry III, (1216 and 1225,) confirmed by Edward I, (1297,) makes no provision whatever for, or mention of, a parliament, unless the provision, (Ch. 37,) that "Escuage, (a military contribution,) from henceforth shall be taken like as it was wont to be in the time of King Henry our grandfather," mean that a parliament shall be summoned for that purpose.
9. The Magna Carta of John, (Ch. 17 and 18,) defines those who were entitled to be summoned to parliament, to wit, "The Archbishops, Bishops, Abbots, Earls, and Great Barons of the Realm, * * and all others who hold of us in chief." Those who held land of the king in chief included none below the rank of knights.
10. The parliaments of that time were, doubtless, such as Carlyle describes them, when he says, "The parliament was at first a most simple assemblage, quite cognate to the situation; that Red William, or whoever had taken on him the terrible task of being King of England, was wont to invite, oftenest about Christmas time, his subordinate Kinglets, Barons as he called them, to give him the pleasure of their company for a week or two; there, in earnest conference all morning in freer talk over Christmas [*22] cheer all evening, in some big royal hall of Westminster, Winchester, or wherever it might be, with log fires, huge rounds of roast and boiled, not lacking malmsey and other generous liquor, they took counsel concerning the arduous matters of the kingdom."
11. Hume, Appendix 2.
12. This point will be more fully established hereafter.
13. It is plain that the king and all his partisans looked upon the charter as utterly prostrating the king's legislative supremacy before the discretion of juries. When the schedule of liberties demanded by the barons was shown to him, (of which the trial by jury was the most important, because it was the only one that protected all the rest,) "the king, falling into a violent passion, asked, *Why the barons did not with these exactations demand his kingdom? * * and with a solemn oath protested, that he would grant such liberties as would make himself a slave.*" * * But afterwards, "seeing himself deserted, and fearing they would seize his castles, he sent the Earl of Pembroke and other faithful messengers to them, to let them know *he would grant them the laws and liberties they desired.*" * * But after the charter had been granted, "the king's mercenary soldiers, desiring war more than peace, were by their leaders continually whispering in his ears, *that he was now no longer king, but the scorn of other princes; and that it was more eligible to be no king, than such a one as he.*" * * He applied "to the [*25] Pope, that he might by his apostolic authority make void what the barons had done. * * At Rome he met with what success he could desire, where all the transactions with the barons were fully represented to the Pope, and the Charter of Liberties shown to him, in writing; which, when he had carefully perused, he, with a furious look, cried out, *What! Do the barons of England endeavor to dethrone a king, who has taken upon him the Holy Cross, and is under the protection of the Apostolic See; and would they force him to transfer the dominions of the Roman Church to others? By St. Peter, this injury must not pass unpunished.* Then debating the matter with the cardinals, he, by a definitive sentence, damned and cassated forever the Charter of Liberties, and sent the king a bull containing that sentence at large."—Echard's *History of England*, pp. 106-7.

These things show that the nature and effect of the charter were well understood by the king and his friends; that they all agreed that he was effectually stripped of power. *Yet the legislative power had not been taken from him; but only the power to enforce his laws, unless furies should freely consent to their enforcement.*

32

Relation of the State to the Individual

Benjamin Tucker

Ladies and Gentlemen: Presumably the honor which you have done me in inviting me to address you today upon "The Relation of the State to the Individual" is due principally to the fact that circumstances have combined to make me somewhat conspicuous as an exponent of the theory of Modern Anarchism—a theory which is coming to be more and more regarded as one of the few that are tenable as a basis of political and social life. In its name, then, I shall speak to you in discussing this question, which either underlies or closely touches almost every practical problem that confronts this generation. The future of the tariff, of taxation, of finance, of property, of woman, of marriage, of the family, of the suffrage, of education, of invention, of literature, of science, of the arts, of personal habits, of private character, of ethics, of religion, will be determined by the conclusion at which mankind shall arrive as to whether and how far the individual owes allegiance to the State.

Anarchism, in dealing with this subject, has found it necessary, first of all, to define its terms. Popular conceptions of the terminology of politics are incompatible with the rigorous exactness required in scientific investigation. To be sure, a departure from the popular use of language is accompanied by the risk of misconception by the multitude, who persistently ignore the new definitions; but, on the other hand, conformity thereto is attended by the still more deplorable alternative of confusion in the eyes of the competent, who would be justified in attributing inexactness of thought where there is inexactness of expression. Take the term "State," for instance, with which we are especially concerned today. It is a word that is on every lip. But how many of those who use it have any idea of what they mean by it? And, of the few who have, how various are their conceptions! We designate by the term "State" institutions that embody absolutism in its extreme form and institutions that temper it with more or less liberality. We apply the word alike to institutions that do nothing but aggress and to institutions that, besides aggressing, to some extent protect and defend. But which is the State's essential function, aggression or defence, few seem to know or care. Some champions of the State evidently consider aggression its principle, although they disguise it alike from themselves and from the people under the term "administration," which they wish to extend in every possible direction. Others, on the contrary, consider defence its principle, and wish to limit it accordingly to the performance of police duties. Still others seem to think that it exists for both aggression and defence, combined in varying proportions according to the momentary interests, or maybe only whims, of those happening to control it. Brought face to face with these diverse views, the Anarchists, whose mission in the world is the abolition of aggression and all the evils that result therefrom, perceived that, to be understood, they must attach some definite and avowed significance to the terms which they are obliged to employ, and especially to the words "State" and "government." Seeking, then, the elements common to all the institutions to which the name "State" has been applied, they have found them two in number: first, aggression; second, the assumption of sole authority over a given area and all within it, exercised generally for the double purpose of more complete oppression of its subjects and extension of its boundaries. That this second element is common to all States, I think, will not be denied—at least, I am not aware that any State has ever tolerated a rival State within its borders; and it seems plain that any State which should do so would thereby cease to be a State and to be considered as such by any. The exercise of authority over the same area by two States is a contradiction. That the first element, aggression, has been and is common to all States will probably be less generally admitted. Nevertheless, I shall not attempt to re-enforce here the conclusion of Spencer, which is gaining wider acceptance daily; that the State had its origin in aggression, and has continued as an aggressive institution from its birth. Defence was an afterthought, prompted by necessity; and its introduction as a State function, though effected doubtless with a view to the strengthening of the State, was really and in principle the initiation of the State's destruction. Its growth in importance is but an evidence of the tendency of progress toward the abolition of the State. Taking this view of the matter, the Anarchists contend that defence is not an essential of the State, but that aggression is. Now what is aggression? Aggression is simply another name for government. Aggression, invasion, government, are interconvertible terms. The essence of government is control, or the attempt to control. He who attempts to control another is a governor, an aggressor, an invader; and the nature of such invasion is not changed, whether it is made by one man upon another man, after the manner of the ordinary criminal, or by one man upon all other men, after the manner of an absolute monarch, or by all other men upon one man, after the manner of a modern democracy. On the other hand, he who resists another's attempt to control is not an aggressor, an invader, a governor, but simply a defender, a protector; and the nature of such resistance is not changed whether it be offered by one man to another man, as when one repels a criminal's onslaught, or by one man to all other men, as when one declines to obey an oppressive law, or by all men to one man, as when a subject people rises against a despot, or as when the members of a community voluntarily unite to restrain a criminal. This distinction between invasion and resistance, between government and defence, is vital. Without it there can be no valid philosophy of politics. Upon this distinction and the other considerations just outlined, the Anarchists frame the desired definitions. This, then, is the Anarchistic definition of government: the subjection of the non-invasive individual to an external will. And this is the Anarchistic definition of the State: the embodiment of the principle of invasion in an individual, or a band of individuals, assuming to act as representatives or masters of the entire people within a given area. As to the meaning of the remaining term in the subject under discussion, the word "individual," I think there is little difficulty. Putting aside the subtleties in which certain metaphysicians have indulged, one may use this word without danger of being misunderstood. Whether the definitions thus arrived at prove generally acceptable or not is a matter of minor consequence. I submit that they are reached scientifically, and serve the purpose of a clear conveyance of thought. The Anarchists, having by their adoption taken due care to be explicit, are entitled to have their ideas judged in the light of these definitions.

Now comes the question proper: What relations should exist between the State and the Individual? The general method of determining these is to apply some theory of ethics involving a basis of moral obligation. In this method the Anarchists have no confidence. The idea of moral obligation, of inherent rights and duties, they totally discard. They look upon all obligations, not as moral, but as social, and even then not really as obligations except as these have been consciously and voluntarily assumed. If a man makes an agreement with men, the latter may combine to hold him to his agreement; but, in the absence of such agreement, no man, so far as the Anarchists are aware, has made any agreement with God or with any other power of any order whatsoever. The Anarchists are not only utilitarians, but egoists in the farthest and fullest sense. So far as inherent right is concerned, might is its only measure. Any man, be his name Bill Sykes or Alexander Romanoff, and any set of men, whether the Chinese highbinders or the Congress of the United States, have the right, if they have the power, to kill or coerce other men and to make the entire World subservient to their ends. Society's right to enslave the individual and the individual's right to enslave society are unequal only because their powers are unequal. This position being subversive of all systems of religion and morality, of course I cannot expect to win immediate assent thereto from the audience which I am addressing today; nor does the time at my disposal allow me to sustain it by an elaborate, or even a summary, examination of the foundations of ethics. Those who desire a greater familiarity with this particular phase of the subject should read a profound German work, "Der Einzige und sein Eigenthum," written years ago by a comparatively unknown author, Dr. Caspar Schmidt, whose nom de plume was Max Stirner. Read only by a few scholars, the book is buried in obscurity, but is destined to a resurrection that perhaps will mark an epoch.

If this, then, were a question of right, it would be, according to the Anarchists, purely a question of strength. But, fortunately, it is not a question of right: it is a question of expediency, of knowledge, of science; the science of living together, the science of society. The history of humanity has been largely one long and gradual discovery of the fact that the individual is the gainer by society exactly in proportion as society is free, and of the law that the condition of a permanent and harmonious society is the greatest amount of individual liberty compatible with equality of liberty. The average man of each new generation has said to himself more clearly and consciously than his predecessor: "My neighbor is not my enemy, but my friend, and I am his, if we would but mutually recognize the fact. We help each other to a better, fuller, happier living; and this service might be greatly increased if we would cease to restrict, hamper, and oppress each other. Why can we not agree to let each live his own life, neither of us transgressing the limit that separates our individualities?" It is by this reasoning that mankind is approaching the real social contract, which is not, as Rousseau thought, the origin of society, but rather the outcome of a long social experience, the fruit of its follies and disasters. It is obvious that this contract, this social law, developed to its perfection, excludes all aggression, all violation of equality of liberty, all invasion of every kind. Considering this contract in connection with the Anarchistic definition of the State as the embodiment of the principle of invasion, we see that the State is antagonistic to society; and, society being essential to individual life and development, the conclusion leaps to the eyes that the relation of the State to the individual and of the individual to the State must be one of hostility, enduring till the State shall perish.

"But," it will be asked of the Anarchists at this point in the argument, "what shall be done with those individuals who undoubtedly will persist in violating the social law by invading their neighbors?" The Anarchists answer that the abolition of the State will leave in existence a defensive association, resting no longer on a compulsory but on a voluntary basis, which will restrain invaders by any means that may prove necessary. "But that is what we have now," is the rejoinder. "You really want, then, only a change of name?" Not so fast, please. Can it be soberly pretended for a moment that the State, even as it exists here in America, is purely a defensive institution? Surely not, save by those who see of the State only its most palpable manifestation: the policeman on the street-corner. And one would not have to watch him very closely to see the error of this claim. Why, the very first act of the State, the compulsory assessment and collection of taxes, is itself an aggression, a violation of equal liberty, and, as such, initiates every subsequent act, even those acts which would be purely defensive if paid out of a treasury filled by voluntary contributions. How is it possible to sanction, under the law of equal liberty, the confiscation of a man's earnings to pay for protection which he has not sought and does not desire? And, if this is an outrage, what name shall we give to such confiscation when the victim is given, instead of bread, a stone, instead of protection, oppression? To force a man to pay for the violation of his own liberty is indeed an addition of insult to injury. But that is exactly what the State is doing. Read the "Congressional Record"; follow the proceedings of the State legislatures;

examine our statute-books; test each act separately by the law of equal liberty, you will find that a good nine-tenths of existing legislation serves, not to enforce that fundamental social law, but either to prescribe the individual's personal habits, or, worse still, to create and sustain commercial, industrial, financial, and proprietary monopolies which deprive labor of a large part of the reward that it would receive in a perfectly free market. "To be governed," says Proudhon, "is to be watched, inspected, spied, directed, law-ridden, regulated, penned up, indoctrinated, preached at, checked, appraised, sized, censured, commanded; by beings who have neither title nor knowledge nor virtue. To be governed is to have every operation, every transaction every movement noted, registered, counted, rated, stamped, measured, numbered, assessed, licensed, refused, authorized, indorsed, admonished, prevented, reformed, redressed, corrected. To be governed is, under pretext of public utility and in the name of the general interest, to be laid under contribution, drilled, fleeced, exploited, monopolized, extorted from, exhausted, hoaxed, robbed; then, upon the slightest resistance, at the first word of complaint, to be repressed, fined, vilified, annoyed, hunted down, pulled about, beaten, disarmed, bound, imprisoned, shot, mitrailleused, judged, condemned, banished, sacrificed, sold, betrayed, and, to crown all, ridiculed, derided, outraged, dishonored." And I am sure I do not need to point out to you the existing laws that correspond to and justify nearly every count in Proudhon's long indictment. How thoughtless, then, to assert that the existing political order is of a purely defensive character instead of the aggressive State which the Anarchists aim to abolish!

This leads to another consideration that bears powerfully upon the problem of the invasive individual, who is such a bugbear to the opponents of Anarchism. Is it not such treatment as has just been described that is largely responsible for his existence? I have heard or read somewhere of an inscription written for a certain charitable institution:

"This hospital a pious person built,
But first he made the poor wherewith to fill it"

And so, it seems to me, it is with our prisons. They are filled with criminals which our virtuous State has made what they are by its iniquitous laws, its grinding monopolies, and the horrible social conditions that result from them. We enact many laws that manufacture criminals, and then a few that punish them. Is it too much to expect that the new social conditions which must follow the abolition of all interference with the production and distribution of wealth will in the end so change the habits and propensities of men that our jails and prisons, our policemen and our soldiers, in a word, our whole machinery and outfit of defence, will be superfluous? That, at least, is the Anarchists' belief.

33

Freedom, Society, and the State: An Investigation Into the Possibility of Society without Government (excerpt)

David Osterfeld

A Political and Economic Overview

Libertarianism is a politico-economic philosophy of individualism. It is premised on the belief that every individual has an unalienable right to live his own life as he sees fit, provided he does not aggress against the equal rights of others. There are two distinct strains of libertarian thought: minarchism and anarchism. While this study focuses on the anarchist branch of libertarianism, the sole, although crucial, difference between the two factions resides in their views regarding government provision of police and proper function of court services. The minarchist believes that the only proper function of government is to protect individuals from aggression. Consequently, they argue for a "night-watchman" state[1] to operate solely in this area and believe that all of the other services currently supplied by government can be handled on the market. The anarchists, however, go even further and believe that government can be dispensed with entirely and that even police and court functions can be supplied better and at less risk of tyranny on the market. Because the anarchists propose that a definite economic institution, the market, replace the political institution of government, they have been referred to as "free market anarchists," "anarcho-capitalists," and "individualist anarchists." Since libertarianism is compatible with any voluntary, non-coercive, institutional arrangement of which the market is only one—albeit the most significant—of such arrangements, terms such as "free market anarchism" or "anarcho-capitalism" are overly restrictive. The term "individualist anarchists" will therefore be the term normally used to refer to those who oppose government entirely and advocate the market as the primary—in fact indispensable—mechanism for the voluntary coordination of social activity.

It should be pointed out in this context that a synthesis of anarchism and capitalism was regarded as impossible by traditional proponents of both doctrines. While the defenders of capitalism such as the classical liberals of the nineteenth century believed that government should be kept strictly limited and as much as possible handled by the market, it should not be though that they allied themselves with anarchism. On the contrary, it would not be too strong to describe classical liberalism's attitude toward anarchism as one of both contempt as well as fear. It was contemptuous because, as one classical liberal philosopher wrote, anarchism "would be practicable only in a world of angels" and the "liberal understands quite clearly" that one must be in a position to compel the person who will not respect lives, health, personal feelings, or private property of others to acquiesce in the rules of society."[2] And classical liberalism had feared anarchism because, while encompassing a broad spectrum of thought ranging from the rampant individualism of Max Stirner to the communism of Peter Kropotkin, the dominant strain of anarchism ostensibly placed it squarely within the socialist camp. Daniel Guerin put the matter succinctly. Anarchism, he says, "is really a synonym for socialism."[3] And, while acknowledging "Stirner's complete rejection of all political, moral, and traditional ties of the individual," Max Adler goes so far as to argue that Stirner cannot even be considered an anarchist since anarchism is only "a definite political trend within the socialist labor movement," and Stirner was not a socialist.[4]

Hence, not just the state but the capitalist economic system were the principal evils for the majority of anarchist thinkers of the nineteenth century. It was not accidental that in Kropotkin's delineation of the three cardinal aims of anarchist communism the first was an injunction against capitalism: "Emancipation from the yoke of capital; production in common and free consumption of all the products of common labor." Only after his exhortation to abolish capitalism does one find a call for "emancipation from government" and "emancipation from religion."[5] The views of the Italian anarchist, Errico Malatesta,[6] and the Britisher, William Morris,[7] were similar. Both equated anarchism with communism and called for the free distribution of all goods. Bakunin, while a collectivist rather than a communist, also advocated the liberation from capitalism.[8] Even in the writings of the more individualist-oriented anarchists one finds condemnations of capitalism coupled with panegyrics to socialism. In a striking phrase, Proudhon not only declared that "Property is theft," but also exclaimed "What is the capitalist? Everything! What should he be? Nothing!"[9] Similarly, the English anarchist, William Godwin, asserted that "it follows upon the principles of equal and impartial justice, that the good things of the world are a common stock, upon which one man has as valid a title as another to draw for what he wants."[10] And the American anarchist, Benjamin Tucker, contended that there were "two schools of Socialistic thought," the State Socialism of Karl Marx and the Anarchism of Proudhon and the American Josiah Warren. Tucker placed himself in the anarcho-socialist camp.[11] Thus, it is not surprising that anarchism was abhorrent to the classical liberals. "Liberalism," wrote Ludwig von Mises, "is not anarchism, nor has it anything to do with anarchism,"[12] and the twentieth-century followers of classical liberalism, the minarchists, have followed their mentors in rejecting anarchism.[13]

But while a quick glance at the major anarchist thinkers of Europe, England, and America would ostensibly indicate that all were firmly anti-capitalistic, a closer look will show that this is incorrect, for the term "capitalism" has been used in socialist literature in two contradictory manners. On the one hand, the term is used to denote production according to the dictates of the market, or in socialist terminology, "commodity production." On the other, capitalism is defined in terms of class relations, i.e., the ownership of the means of production by the "bourgeois," or ruling, class. The former may be termed the economic definition and the latter the sociological definition. If the economic definition is used, it follows that the more things are handled by the market, the more capitalistic the society. This means that price controls, tariffs, licensing restrictions, state unemployment compensation, state poor relief, etc., whether they are considered beneficial or not, must be classified as anti-capitalistic institutions since they constitute modifications or restrictions of the market. Since the state does not sell its services on the market, "state capitalism," according to the economic definition, is a contradiction in terms.

But if the sociological definition is used, the state becomes compatible with capitalism, for whatever serves to entrench the bourgeois class, the owners of the means of production, in power is, ipso facto, "capitalistic." Since both proponents and critics of capitalism were in general agreement that market competition would force the "rate of profit" to fall, the two definitions lead to mutually exclusive consequences. Since the economic or market definition posits pure laissez faire, any government intervention to protect the interests of the bourgeoisie is anathema. But that is precisely what is entailed in the sociological definition: state intervention to protect profits and institutionalize the position of the property-owning class. When the sociological definition is used, capitalism becomes incomprehensible without control of the state by the bourgeoisie. For with the power of the state behind them, the bourgeoisie are able to protect their privileged positions from the threat of competition by the establishment of tariff barriers, licensing restrictions, and other statist measures.

The proponents of capitalism, however, had only the economic definition in mind when they defended capitalism.[14] Far from intending to defend state intervention to preserve artificially high profits, it was, in fact, such pro-capitalist writers as Adam Smith who vehemently condemned such "mercantilist" arrangements and urged their replacement by free trade capitalism.[15] Since comparison can only be made when definitions tap the same domain, confusion occurred because of these definitional differences, and critics and opponents of capitalism talked past each other when many were in basic agreement. But if the economic spectrum is analyzed from the point of view of the economic definition only, then comparison can be made on the following basis: capitalism would be equated with the market, communism with the absence of the market, and mercantilism with a mixed or restricted market.

communism	mercantilism	capitalism
0: --	:------------------------------------	:100
non-market	restricted market	market

We are now in a position to reassess the anti-capitalism of the anarchists. What is evident in such a taxonomy is that while certain anarchists such as Kropotkin and Bakunin must certainly be classified as socialist or communist, others like Proudhon, Godwin and especially the native American anarchists such as Josiah Warren, Benjamin Tucker, and Victor Yarros, despite their characterization of themselves as socialists, must be placed within the capitalist camp. A closer look at the anarchists themselves will make this clear.

1. The Economic Spectrum of Anarchist Communism to Capitalism

a. Anarcho-communism. At one end of the anarchist spectrum we find those who, like Kropotkin and his followers, bleed anarchism and communism. The anarcho-communists oppose exchange, money, the division of labor, private property, and the wage system. Capitalism, they argue is just as "barbarous" as feudalism; only the forms have changed. "The worker is forced, under the name of free contract," says Kropotkin, "to accept feudal obligations. For turn where he will he can find no better conditions. Everything has becomes private property and he must accept, or die of hunger." Since the capitalist owns the means of production he can dictate wage rates. This puts the worker at a distinct disadvantage. The wage system therefore reduces the worker to poverty.

On the other hand, despite the advance in technology which has made a life of abundance possible for all, "the owners of capital constantly reduce the output by restricting production," thereby keeping prices high. Labor is further squandered—by the production of luxuries for the capitalist class, as well as by the money spent on armaments, salaries for judges, prison guards, policemen, etc. All money spent by government is useless, says Kropotkin, since there is a definite relationship between crime and poverty. Hence, if one eliminates capitalism poverty and thus crime would nearly disappear, and government would become unnecessary. Social behavior would be regulated by voluntary compliance to "unwritten customs." As Kropotkin's biographer, Martin Miller, put it, "the tradition of authority was to be replaced by the authority of tradition."[16] As for the "few anti-social acts that may still take place," says Kropotkin, "the best remedy will consist in loving treatment, moral influence, and liberty." And if that doesn't work then the aggressor can "of course be expelled from fellowship."[17]

Private property, whether that of capitalism or mercantilism, is likewise condemned. Since everything material as well as mental is a product of the contributions of countless individuals, past as well as present, it is impossible to determine the actual contributions of each. Consequently, argues Kropotkin, property cannot rightfully be private, but only common; all have a right to an equal share of all that is produced. Not only the means of production but also the product of production including houses, clothing and food, is to be communalized. The first principle of anarcho-communism, says Kropotkin, is that "the means of production being the collective work of humanity, the product should be the collective property of the race."[18] Since collectivism only wishes to collectivize the means of production while retaining individual ownership of its product, Kropotkin condemns it as simply a modification rather than the "negation of wage slavery."[19]

In the absence of the state, the cities will automatically transform themselves into "communistic communes." These communes will be large enough to be nearly or completely self-sufficient and at one point Kropotkin says that each commune would be populated by "a few millions of inhabitants."[20] Man, he further argues, is not naturally lazy. It is the private ownership system that "places a premium on idleness." But since under communism everyone would know that their subsistence is secured for them "they would ask nothing better than to work at their old trades." In fact, he says, the voluntary work of the new society "will be infinitely superior and yield far more than work has produced up to now under the goal of slavery, serfdom and wagedom." Kropotkin envisions the anarcho-communist society to be so productive, in fact, that he claims that each individual would only have to work five hours per day, and that only between the ages of twenty or twenty-two to forty-five or fifty.[21]

In short, for the anarcho-communist, not only private property, whether capitalist or mercantilist, but the entire market as well, has all to be abolished. The capitalist system is to be replaced by "fee communism" which "places the production reaped or manufactured in common at the disposal of all, leaving to each the liberty to consume as he pleases."[22]

b. Anarcho-collectivism. Slightly less communal-oriented than anarcho-communism is the collectivism of the Bakunist and capitalistic private property and exchange both begin to appear even if only in an extremely rudimentary way. After the revolution, says Bakunin in his "On the Morrow of the Social Revolution," the bourgeoisie will be expropriated: "The city proletariat will become the owner of capital and of implements of labor, and the rural proletariat of the land which it cultivates with its own hands."[23] The peasants, according to the prominent Bakuninist James Guillaume, will then have the option of either owning and working their plots individually or associating into collectives. Because of the advantages of the collective in creating "a communal agency to sell or exchange their products," it is expected that the collective will be the dominant form of organization, but no coercion will be used to compel individual peasants to join the collectives.[24] A similar arrangement is envisioned for industry. Large-scale production, of course, would entail collective ownership, but handicrafts and other small industry may well be individually owned. As for remuneration, whereas anarcho-communism intends to follow the formula "From each according to his ability to each according to his needs," the collectivists, at least initially, adhere to the much different maxim of "From each according to his means to each according to his deeds."[25]

To meet their needs it will be quite natural for the collectives to organize themselves into federations of collectives.[26] Then, as Guillaume describes the operation of the anarcho-collectivist society, "the workers' associations as well as the individual producers...will deposit their unconsumed commodities in the facilities provided by the Bank of Exchange, the value of the commodities having been established in advance by a contractual agreement between the regional cooperative federations and the various communes... The Bank of Exchange will remit to the producers negotiable vouchers representing the value of the products; these vouchers will be accepted throughout the territory included in the federation of communes."[27]

The important difference between anarcho-communism and anarcho-collectivism is that while for the former the wage-system and all other market phenomena will be abolished the collectivists retain not only a modified wage system but other exchange relationships as well. Guillaume, for example, acknowledges that so long as any products are in short supply they would have to be treated as commodities with their prices set by the Bank of Exchange according to the dictates of supply and demand. It should be pointed out, however, that the collectivists believe that collective labor will be so productive that all shortages will eventually disappear and with it the need of any type of price mechanism.[28] Once this plateau of plenty is reached, the structures of anarcho-communism and anarcho-collectivism will become practically indistinguishable.

c. *Anarcho-syndicalism.* Syndicalism is both an organizational structure and a method of overthrowing the capitalist system. As a method, syndicalism, as popularized by Georges Sorel,[29] is a movement premised on the "myth of the general strike" and the use of force. Violence, it is held, is necessary to overthrow both capitalism and the capitalist state. But to galvanize the workers into action, they must believe in the inexorable triumph of their cause. It is this function that the "myth" fulfills. For by believing that the general strike will produce the triumph of their cause, it brings into relief the class antagonisms of the capitalist system. In doing so it unites the proletariat, producing an "epic state of mind" which rouses the proletariat to acts of "heroism."[30] This triumph of the proletarian will eventually culminate in the overthrow of capitalism. Belief in the myth of their inevitable victory, in other words, produces a will to action that does, indeed, make their victory inevitable.[31] Such, briefly, is the method of syndicalism.

We are most interested, however, in the organizational framework that will prevail once syndicalism has triumphed. There is an important difference between syndicalism and communism on the question of the ownership of the means of production. While both aim to expropriate these from the capitalist, under communism, as envisioned by Kropotkin, all workers would collectively own all capital. Under syndicalism, however, only those workers in a particular industry would own the means of production within that industry. This bears an obvious resemblance to the collectivism of Bakunin, and Bakuninism may actually be seen as a variant of syndicalism, as can the mutualism of Proudhon.

The essential aspect of syndicalism is workers' control according to industry. While these syndicates or industrial organizations are to be autonomous, they are nevertheless to be loosely confederated, both geographically as well as functionally. The workers in each locality, according to Rudolph Rocker, will join the unions of their respective trades. All the unions in a given region will then be combined into Labor Chambers. It would be the responsibility of the Labor Chambers "to determine the needs of the inhabitants of their districts and organize local consumption." On the other hand, every trade union is to be "federatively allied with all the organizations of the same industry and then in turn with all related trades, so that all are combined in general industrial and agricultural alliances." It would "be the task of the Industrial and Agricultural Alliances to take control of all instruments of production, transportation, etc. and provide the separate producing groups with what they need." In short, workers are to be organized functionally through the Federation of Industrial Alliances, which would coordinate production, and geographically through the Federation of Labor Chambers, which would handle the problems of distribution and consumption.[32]

Anarcho-syndicates maintain that syndicalism would accomplish "the complete overthrow of the wage system."[33] But since the income of each worker-owner is directly tied not only to the physical output of his own industry but to the demand for that output, it would be more accurate to view syndicalism as a modification rather than the abolition of the wage system.[34] In fact, while it may be too strong to call it "workers' capitalism," it should be pointed out that its very structure forces the workers to be not only workers and owners but capitalists and entrepreneurs as well. But this means that each syndicate would have to decide such questions as whether to expand or curtail production in any given period, how much of its gross revenue to reinvest and how much to divide between the members of the syndicate, whether to cease operations in one area or begin them in another, whether to use more labor and less machinery or vice versa, etc. These are entrepreneurial decisions and are invariably made within an environment of uncertainty and risk. And just as some entrepreneurs make the correct decisions and succeed while others fail, under syndicalism some syndicates might prosper but others would surely fail, for no system can eradicate the uncertainty of the future. Not only may tastes change, for example, but an invention may render a particular syndicate obsolete.

Not only would syndicalism have to make entrepreneurial decisions, just as is done under capitalism, but one must question whether "workers' control" is even possible. The crucial problem for syndicalism is whether or not the individual members of the syndicates would be permitted to sell their shares to other individuals or syndicates. Either way creates a dilemma for the concept of workers' control. For if they are not permitted to sell their shares then they cannot be said to really own their portion of the industry. Since sociologically ownership is defined as the power to dispose of property, that individual or group within the syndicate with the power to prevent the worker from selling "his" share to whom he wishes is the actual owner and controller. Rather than workers' control, there has merely been a change in form: one set of owners has replaced another. But if individuals within each industry really own a share of that industry then they must be permitted to dispose of their shares as they see fit. This means that they can sell their shares to those outside of the industry. But such a policy would entail an end to "workers' control" and a reemergence of the separation of ownership and labor which it was the aim of syndicalism to overcome. Similarly, the same dilemma presents itself if the original workers-owners of the more prosperous syndicates decide to hire workers as simple wage earners and not as part owners of the industry. To prevent them would be a denial of worker control; but so too would adoption of such a policy. Again, things would tend to return to the pre-syndicalist, i.e., capitalist, state of affairs.

Thus, while syndicalism may aim to eliminate private ownership of the means of production, the wage system, the market, and economic inequality, the structure of syndicalism itself forces a return to the paraphernalia of the market, if only in a somewhat modified for.[35]

d. Mutualism. Despite his famous remark that "property" is theft" Proudhon was, in fact, a staunch defender of the small property owner. He distinguished between property, in effect absentee ownership, and possession. His argument was that, the land really belonged to those who worked it and hence "possession," or "occupancy," "negated property."[36] He not only defended private ownership but the rights of barter, sale and hereditary property as well, and felt that individual liberty could be protected only if property were subject to no restrictions but that of size.

The three cornerstones of Proudhon's ideal society are contract, exchange, and property. The state is to be abolished and all relations between individuals and collectives are to be handled by contract. "The notion of contract precludes that of government," writes Proudhon. And again, "Instead of laws we would have contracts. No laws would be passed either by majority vote or unanimously. Each citizen, each commune or corporation, would make its own laws."[37] The corollary of contract is exchange; people contract with each other to exchange their products. Accordingly, Proudhon defines mutualism as "service for service, product for product..."[38] Proudhon was not so much an opponent of the capitalistic market system as of industrialism. He envisioned a society of numerous small and independent producers, voluntarily contracting to exchange their products on an equitable basis. Where the nature of production makes such a framework impossible, Proudhon advocates a syndicalist arrangement where the workers in each such industry would own the means of production in that industry. Relations between the syndicates and other syndicates or individual producers are to be handled in the same way as relations between individual producers: exchange and contract. But for contract and exchange to be meaningful there must be private ownership; one cannot exchange what one does not own. Proudhon, in fact, proclaims that property "is the only power that can act as a counter weight to the State..." Thus, property he says, "is the basis of my system of federation."[39] It is not surprising to find, therefore, that Proudhon was in fact a bitter opponent of communism, which he defined as "the exploitation of the strong by the weak." Any society failing to recognize the right of private property, he felt, must inevitably breed a stultifying rigidity and uniformity that is incompatible with "the free exercise of our faculties...our noblest dreams,...our deepest feelings."[40]

On the question of crime in an anarchist society, Proudhon thought that contract was the *sine qua non* of justice, and that a fully contractual society would be a fully just one. And he further believed, perhaps naively, that a just society would alleviate much of the tendency toward and need for criminal behavior. The occasional antisocial individual, Proudhon thought, could be handled through the method of voluntary reparation. The criminal would be asked to make reparation to his victim, and the threat of being the target of public disapprobation if he refused would all but insure compliance. And since reparation accords the criminal "as much respect as he lost through his crime...[h]is reparation is also a rehabilitation." Finally, anyone regularly violating the norms of the society, and refusing to make reparation, what Proudhon terms the "hopelessly obdurate scoundrel," can legitimately be subjected to physical suffering and even death.[41]

In short, despite Proudhon's famous statement on property and his regular condemnations of "capitalism," the essential components of mutualism are private property, exchange, and contract. With the one significant exception of his stricture concerning the size of property, mutualism is, in most other respects, not incompatible with capitalism.[42]

e. Godwinism. H. N. Brailsford says of Godwin that, "intensely equalitarian, he permits property only that it may be given away."[43] A close look at William Godwin, however, reveals that despite his repeated condemnations of "accumulated property" he was probably an even more vigorous defender of private ownership than Proudhon. The idea of property, says Godwin, "is a deduction from the right of private judgment." Thus, he continues, property is, "in the last resort, the palladium of all that ought to be dear to us, and must never be approached but with awe and veneration."[44] In fact, while otherwise eschewing violence, Godwin even goes so far as to remark that the "right of property, with all its inequalities...should be defended if need be by coercion... Godwin views property according to "three degrees." The first and most fundamental it that a person may own property provided "a greater sum of benefit or pleasure will result, than could have arisen from their being otherwise appropriated." From this he believes it follows "that no man may, in ordinary cases, make use of my apartment, furniture or garments, or of my food,...without first having obtained my consent." The crucial function of the "first degree of property" is that if everyone is granted a certain sphere of property, no one would be subject to the whims of another. Hence property will provide everyone with a sphere of action where he can exercise his judgment free form the influence of others.

The second degree of property is the right of every man "over the produce of his own labor." While this is less fundamental than the first degree, the latter does not automatically take precedence. Instead, the first degree can only be attained by persuasion and the force of public opinion.

The third degree is any system "by which one man enters into the faculty of disposing of the produce of the labor or another man's industry." Accumulated property, of which inheritance is one form, enables one to exercise power over another man's labor and is in "direct contradiction to the second." But even though Godwin terms this degree of property "wrong," it is significant that he opposes any active measures to abolish the system: "If by positive institutions the property of every man were equalized today...it would become unequal tomorrow. The same evils would spring up with a rapid growth...." In fact, the cure, he says, since it would be effected by coercion, would be worse than the evil.

The only effective way Godwin sees to alter the prevailing structure of property is through the same method that he envisions antisocial behavior being handled: "a revolution on opinions." Mankind is not naturally vicious, but has been corrupted by the unnecessarily complex institutions of political authority. "Simplify the social structure," he argues. And the resulting freedom will stimulate the gradual development of individual responsibility which, in turn, means that "we may expect the whole species to become reasonable and virtuous." It would then be sufficient for local juries, operating in Platonic fashion by judging each case on its own merits, simply to make public recommendations. Godwin is confident that no physical enforcement would be necessary, for "where the empire of reason was so universally acknowledged," any offender resisting the public reprimand of the jury "would feel so uneasy, under the unequivocal disapprobation, and the observant eye of public judgment," as either to finally comply or "to remove to a society more congenial to his errors."[45] And just as public opinion would be sufficient to regulate antisocial behavior, so, Godwin believes, it would be equally capable of regulating the abuses of property. If in any society "accumulation and monopoly be regarded as the seals of mischief, injustice and dishonor, instead of being treated as titles to attention and difference, in that society the accommodations of human life will tend to their level, and inequality of conditions will be destroyed."[46]

Since Godwin, like Proudhon, calls for the abolition of the state, it is not the property of mercantilism but of capitalism that he defends. Despite the fact that Godwin heaps moral condemnation upon the process of capital accumulation, it is most significant that he flatly rejects any coercive attempts to prevent evil than the resort to coercion. Thus his views on property are, in fact, largely compatible with the capitalist system.

f. Egoism. The essence of Max Stirner's anarchism was each individual's uniqueness. "Ownness," he wrote, "is my whole being and existence, it is I myself. I am free from what I am rid of, owner of what I have in my power or what I control."

Since egoism opposes the subjection of the individual to any external authority, Stirner flatly rejects not only the state, but all moral codes as well.[47] However, it does not follow that egoism entails either the isolation of the individual, as some have implied,[48] or a war of all against all, producing a Hobbesian world where life is "nasty brutish and short." On the contrary, Stirner claims that contemporary society is not a genuinely human society, for only when the human being acts *qua* human being, i.e., unencumbered by external social restraints, can his actions be considered truly human. And since contemporary society is maintained in part through the compulsions of State and Church, it follows that it is not a genuine society.[49] It is unfortunate that Stirner, in propounding what may be termed the "philosophy of the pure individual," was not more specific in outlining his alternative socio-political order. But his scattered remarks on the subject make it quite clear that he did not believe that a stateless and amoral society would be either chaotic or brutish.

Since every individual is dependent upon others in varying degrees for the satisfaction of his physical needs for food, shelter and clothing, as well as his psychological needs for love and companionship, individuals, acting purely out of a regard for their own self-interests, would be motivated to cooperate with one another. Groups of like-minded egoists, says James Martin, "would be drawn together voluntarily but the attraction of their mutual interests" to form a truly human association, i.e., what Stirner terms a "Union of Egoists."[50] Since insecurity is a most unpleasant sensation, the members of nearly every Union would agree to forego the use of force, and any member failing to abide by this rule could presumably be physically punished or expelled from the Union. And further, while there are neither rights nor duties, and power is the be all and end all, so that one owns only what he has to power to control, it is clear that Stirner believes that the utility of a secure property structure would encourage the Unions to protect that institution. "Unions will," he writes, "multiply the, individual's means and secure his assailed property."[51]

As in other types of anarchism, the egoistic writings of Stirner contain a sustained condemnation of capitalism and "legal property." A closer view, however, makes it evident that what Stirner opposes is actually the mercantilist, or state capitalist, system.

Thus he writes that "the State is a commoner's [merchant's] State..." "Under the regime of the commonality," he says, "the laborers always fall into the hands of the possessors—i.e., of those who have at their disposal some bit of the State domains,...especially money and land; of the capitalist therefore." And again: "The commoner" is what he is through the protection of the State, through the State's grace."[52] These statements, in themselves, are compatible with free-market capitalism. Further, Stirner was such a bitter opponent of any type of communism that Karl Marx wrote that Stirner's "egoistical property...is nothing more than ordinary or bourgeois property sanctified."[53] So while he was vague concerning what role the market and private property would play in a

Stirnerite society, Charles Madison accurately captures the thrust of Stirnerism when he remarks that "ironically enough, the hard selfishness of this individualist anarchism was admirably adapted to the 'rugged individualism' of modern capitalism."[54] It might also be pointed out that such prominent exponents of egoism as John Babcock and John Henry Mackay considered private property sacrosanct and reserved a central role for voluntary contract and exchange for mutual benefit. But both, it should be noted, were also heavily influenced by the prominent individualist or "philosophical" anarchist, Benjamin Tucker.[55]

g. Philosophical Anarchism. What is usually termed the philosophical anarchist tradition received its fullest expression in the writings of the nineteenth-century American anarchists, and in particular Benjamin Tucker and Victor Yarros. Tucker, like other anarchists, couched his arguments in socialist terminology. Yet an examination of his ideas, as well as those of his followers, place them squarely within the capitalist framework. He was an ardent opponent of communism, and a staunch defender of the free market, private property, and the wage system, and advocated what may be termed "laissez-faire socialism." As in the case of Stirner and Proudhon, what Tucker condemned was not free market capitalism but State capitalism or mercantilism. "The only reason why the banker, the stockholder, the manufacturer, and the merchant are able to extract usury from labor," he argued, "lies in the fact that they are backed by legal privilege, or monopoly." The way to eliminate these monopolies is "by subjecting capital to the natural law of competition, thus bringing the price of its use down to cost." He would apply freedom of competition to "the money monopoly, the land monopoly, the tariff monopoly and the patent and copyright monopoly." The first, felt Tucker, would eliminate interest, the second rent, the third and fourth profits. The elimination of these monopolies by means of total laissez faire would insure that the laborer would get the full value of his labor.[56]

A fundamental difference between the philosophical anarchists and all of the other types discussed thus far is their great faith in the ability of the market to control spontaneously the problem of power in society. This is clearly illustrated in Tucker's position on the proper handling of trusts. Since every individual has the right to dispose of his property as he sees fit, and since, Tucker argued, trusts are simply groups of individuals, they have the same rights as isolated individuals. Hence, the trust, "endeavoring to do collectively nothing but what each member of the combination rightfully may endeavor to do individually, is, per se, an unimpeachable institution." So long as the trust is not supported by legal privileges it can only remain in operation by selling more cheaply than any actual or potential competitor, which, of course, makes it a beneficial institution. If it is not beneficial, it will succumb to the challenge of competition, and fall apart.[57] According to the Tuckerites, everything, including police protection, should be handled on the market and be subject to the rigors of competition. Despite the fact that Tucker couches his position in socialist terminology, his "laissez faire socialism" falls squarely with the capitalist system.

h. Individualist Anarchism. The contemporary individualist anarchists such as Murray Rothbard agree with the overall structure of the Tuckerites: the state is to be abolished and everything is to be handled by, or at least open to the possibility of, competition on the free market. There is one significant difference, however. While Tucker, adhering to the labor theory of value, felt that competition would reduce price to cost, thereby eliminating profits, rents and interest, the individualist anarchists reject the labor theory of value and adopt, in its place, the subjective value-marginal utility approach. Free competition would indeed tend to reduce prices and raise wages, they say, but the Tuckerites are in error in believing that this means that profits and interest would also disappear. Instead, their maintenance is seen as a requisite for economic rationality, and even society itself.[58]

2. The Political Spectrum of Capitalism: Anarchism to Hyperarchism

A brief overview of the economic spectrum of anarchism revealed a wide array of economic arrangements. Similarly, the proponents of capitalism traverse the entire political spectrum from anarchism to what may be called "hyperarchism." Only by viewing this array of groups and then comparing the political spectrum of capitalism with the economic spectrum of anarchism can the relative positions of the individualist, or free market, anarchists be ascertained.

a. Individualist Anarchism. The previous discussion of individualist anarchism focused on its place in the anarchist school. Its position within the capitalist spectrum still needs to be discerned. The sanctity of private property and the market lie at the heart of laissez-faire capitalism. From a logical point of view, the more things are handled by the market, the more capitalistic the society. Consistently applied, argue the individualist anarchists, capitalism leads to anarchism. Hence, they argue, the minarchists, or limited-government libertarians, place themselves in a contradiction for, while believing that property rights must be protected and the market maintained, they also believe that these services—the police and court functions—are by their nature collective and cannot be provided by the market. Thus, they are forced to rely on an agency outside the market, i.e., the government. The minarchists, it is argued, are placed in the contradictory position of relying on a non-market institution to defend the market. Further, since to meet operating expenses a government is forced to collect taxes, which constitutes a forcible transfer of wealth from its rightful owners to others and therefore is a violation of property rights, the minarchists are also in the embarrassing position of relying, for the protection of property rights, on an institution that by its very nature entails the invasion of property rights.

The individualist anarchist then proceeds to push the anti-statist elements in libertarianism to their logical extreme: the elimination of government and total reliance on the market. The whole concept of "collective goods" is rejected.[59] All goods and services, including those supplied by government, can be broken down into marginal units and sold on the market. Thus, runs their argument, government can be completely dispensed with and its functions performed, voluntarily, by defense agencies, court companies, road companies, etc. Not only can these services be supplied better, more efficiently and less expensively on the market, they argue, but more importantly, the perennial threat of tyranny resulting from government monopoly of the use of force would be eliminated.

The limited-government however, maintains that the libertarian anarchist has placed himself in a dilemma. For permitting the market to operate in the choice of such things as police protection and legal codes means that justice will be determined by the highest bidders. But this, in turn, means that a libertarian legal code will emerge from an anarchist society only if the society, itself, is overwhelmingly libertarian. But if there were sufficient demand for, say, the suppression of nude swimming or marijuana smoking, an individualist anarchist society would produce laws prohibiting such activities as well as defense agencies willing to enforce them.

Thus, an individualist anarchist community contains the distinct possibility that economic classes, such as the poor, or minorities, such as blacks, redheads, ladies of the evening and the like, would find themselves being subjected to restrictive measures that squarely contradict the principles of libertarianism, In short, the dilemma of individualist anarchism, argue it's critics, is that its very *structural framework* renders it incapable of protecting the *substantive libertarian principles* it purports to cherish.[60, 61] Whether individualist anarchism is beset by such an internal contradiction will be examined in greater depth in a later chapter. Suffice it to be said at this point that if true, this would constitute a telling blow, indeed, for the Rothbardian, or natural rights, variant of individualist anarchism.

b. Ultraminarchism. Remarkably close to the individualist anarchists are the views of philosopher John Hospers. While Hospers' outline of his ideal social order is sketchy, certain aspects of it are clear. First of all, everyone is held to have such "human rights" as those to life, liberty and property.[62] The sole function of government is the protection of these rights, and a government is legitimate so long as it restricts its activities to this sphere; but as soon as it exceeds this sphere it becomes an aggressor. Second, since an absolutely fundamental right is that to property—Hospers denies that there can be any rights in the absence of property rights[63]—and since taxation is a clear violation of property rights, there would be no taxation by a Hosperian government.

The government, he believes, could support itself through a fee-for-service policy. The only time anyone would pay anything to a government agency would be when, and to the extent that, he chose to avail himself of a government service. No one, however, would be forced to receive or pay for any service he didn't desire. Thus, an individual would be free to interact with others, including signing a contract. However, if one desired to insure himself against the possibility of contractual default he could upon signing the contract pay a fee to the government granting him access to the courts in the event of any contractual dispute. This fee—which Hospers reluctantly terms a "contract tax"—would be voluntary: people would only pay the fee if they found it is their interest to do so. However, since a Hosperian state would be so miniscule, and since "most people would find it to their interest to pay the fee," he is confident that the government could be supported in this manner.[64]

A very similar arrangement is suggested for police protection. While Hospers feels that statutory law, and thus a government, is necessary to insure a rule of law, he sees no reason why the government would have enforce its own law. In fact, he acknowledges that private police forces are doubtless much more efficient than those run by government.[65] There is therefore an economic advantage to permitting police protection to be handled entirely by the market. The only restriction that would be necessary to impose upon these private police companies—a restriction that Hospers feels would be impossible to impose in anarchist society—is that "they should be able enforce only the law of the land..."[66] Beyond this, police companies would have complete freedom to compete against one another just like firms in any other field. Anyone desiring police protection could purchase from the firm of his choice. And while no one would be compelled to purchase protection, only those paying the protection fee would receive protection. "If you want police protection you have to pay a fee to obtain it, but of course you are free not to want it or pay for it, in which case," Hospers continues, "you will not have the protection even if you need it."[67]

In short, Hospers maintains that while "laws should...be enacted by the state,...the enforcement of them might be left to private agencies."[68] The provision of both police and court services would handled on a fee-for-service basis, with individuals free to purchase or not to purchase these services as they see fit, but unable to purchase the services any maverick police agency or court which adhered to norms at variance with those laid down by the state.

It is interesting to note that since a Hosperian state would render protection only to those purchasing it, it does not meet the criterion of a minimal state which, by definition, must provide protection for everyone within its territorial boundaries regardless of payment. We may, therefore, borrow a term coined by philosopher Robert Nozick, and refer to Hospers as "ultraminarchist."

But it is possible that even this appellation is too strong. One of the essential criteria of a "state" is that it must be generally recognized as exercising a legitimate monopoly on the use of force within a given area.[69] But since, in a Hosperian society, the use of force would presumably be handled not by the "government" but entirely by private police agencies, this raises the question of whether the Hosperian framework meets this monopoly criterion. Hospers might, of course, argue that his entire system—the legislature plus fee-for-service courts and the private police agencies—constitutes a "state."

But however one may resolve such definitional problems this still leaves open the really crucial question of how, if the use of force is to be left up to private police agencies, could the Hosperian proviso that these agencies must only enforce the legislature's statutory laws be enforced? What would happen if one, or two or a dozen enforcement agencies started enforcing norms that conflicted with the laws enacted by the legislature? There are, so far as I can see, two possible scenarios. First, Hospers might contend that since these maverick agencies would clearly be acting illegally either they would not receive public patronage and so go out of business, or other police agencies, perceiving the threat of the illegals, would join forces to crush them. But since these are exactly the same measures Rothbardian anarchists rely on to insure the enforcement of their common law, Hospers' ultraminarchism becomes all but indistinguishable from Rothbardian anarchism. But Hospers might argue for a second course: that of permitting the public legislature to diversify into the provision of police services. The public agency might then not only enact laws but have enough force at its disposal to punish or crush any maverick agency. But since Hospers admits that private agencies are much more efficient than public ones it is difficult to see why anyone would purchase protection from the latter. Consequently, the only ways the public agency could remain in business would be either by outlawing not just maverick, but all, private police agencies, or by charging every police agency a fee sufficiently high to cover the public agency's losses. Since the public agency would now hold an effective monopoly on the use of force it would meet the criteria for a state, although if it continued to operate on a fee-for-service basis it would remain a less than minimal state. But, it must be noted, neither of these options can be reconciled with libertarian principles. The outlawing of all private agencies would constitute a restriction on peaceful activities, while the fee charged every agency would be neither voluntary[70] nor paid in exchange for services rendered. It would therefore be a tax in the full sense of that word.

In short, Hospers is placed in a dilemma: either he must accede in some restriction on peaceful activities and/or taxation, thereby violating his libertarianism, or he must rely for the enforcement of his "statutory law" on non-monopolistic mechanisms, thereby abandoning his archism. Thus, Hosperian ultraminarchism appears to contain a serious internal contradiction which would logically compel it to move either to complete anarchism or full-fledged minarchism.

c. Minarchism. Those who do not believe that a market for protection services would be either economically viable or morally permissible must therefore endorse some sort of state. And those within that group who maintain that the provision of such services is the only proper function of government must therefore advocate a minimal, or completely laissez faire, state. The "minarchist" position has received its most recent and perhaps ablest—at any rate most ingenious—expression in the "invisible hand" argument of philosopher Robert Nozick.

Nozick begins with a discussion of a hypothetical free market anarchist society. But protective services, he says, differ from other types of services in that they employ the use of coercion. Therefore, in defending their respective clients they would come into conflict with each other, the result being that one, dominant protective agency would eliminate its competition and emerge as the single such agency in a particular geographical region. This, says Nozick, would constitute an "ultraminimal state," which differs from the minimal state of the classical liberals in that the former, by the law of supply and demand, eliminates its competition in a particular area, hereby maintaining "a monopoly over the use of force" but providing "protection and enforcement services only to those who would purchase its protection and enforcement policies."[71] The classical liberal state, on the other hand, held a legal monopoly over the use of force and supplied protection services to all its citizens.

But, argues Nozick, the "ultraminimal state" will soon transform itself into a minimal state, for under an "ultraminimal state" individuals would still be free to extract "private justice." But "the knowledge that one is living under a system permitting this, itself, produces apprehension," with individuals never knowing how or when they may receive "retribution" from a private agent. Fear will pervade the entire society.

Thus private justice constitutes "a public wrong." To protect its clients, the dominant protective agency may then "prohibit the independents from such self-help enforcement." This will not mean that the independents will be left defenseless for, contends Nozick, according to the "principle of compensation" "the clients of the protective agency must compensate the independents for the disadvantages imposed upon them by being prohibited self-help enforcement of their own rights against the agency's clients." Undoubtedly, the least expensive way to compensate the independents would be to supply them with protective services to cover those situations of conflict with the paying customers of the protective agency. This will not lead to "free riders," he insists, for "the agency protects these independents it compensates only against its own paying clients on whom the independents are forbidden to use self-help enforcement. The more free riders there are, the more desirable it is to be a client always protected by the agency."[72]

While believing that this argument has justified the state, Nozick then proceeds to point out that given natural rights—which he admits he merely assumes rather than demonstrates[73]—anything beyond the minimal state, including taxation, entails the violation of those rights, since it means the initiation of force against peaceful individuals. Hence, "the minimal state is the most extensive state that can be justified."[74]

While this is a most intriguing argument, it is not at all clear that Nozick has, in fact, succeeded in justifying the minimal state. For a minimal state, he notes, must (a) exercise, or come close to exercising, a monopoly on the use of force within a given territory, and (b) provide everyone within its domain with protection.[75] But while the dominant protection agency would prohibit self-help enforcement among its own clients and between independents and clients, its domain, Nozick says in a significant passage, "does not extend to quarrels of non-clients among themselves."[76] Nozick's dominant protection agency therefore falls short of his own criteria for a minimal state. In fact, since independent agencies could continue to operate so long as they didn't confront the dominant agency, it is not even clear that the latter would constitute an ultraminimal state, which requires the provision of protection services by a single agency.[77] Nozick, it should be noted, is aware of this difficulty and reacts to it by simply relaxing his criteria. He then refers to the dominant agency as a "state-like entity" instead of simply a "state."[78]

There is, however, the potential for an additional problem. Suppose, theorizes Roy Childs, that in the midst of an established minimal state an agency arises which uses procedures identical to those of the state's agents. Since, under this condition, the incipient agency could not be any more risky than the state, a state operating on Nozickian principles would have no grounds for prohibiting its activities. But, continues Childs, since the state was already compensating those who would have patronized agencies using risky procedures, the new agency would not have to assume this burden and could therefore charge lower prices for the same quality service. This would, in turn, create an economic incentive for people to subscribe to the new agency, thereby forcing the minimal state to abandon its own compensation policy. But this would mean that the minimal state had reverted to the ultraminimal state. But, continues Childs, provided the new agency continued to win new clients, and other entrepreneurs, seeing the success of the new agency, entered the field themselves, the ultraminimal state would degenerate into a mere dominant agency, and eventually that into "simply one agency among many." In short, Childs argues, there is no reason, *on strictly Nozickian grounds*, why the invisible hand could not strike back.[79]

But regardless of how it is justified, the minarchist advocates a single agency with a monopoly on the use of force in society and whose sole function is the protection of individual rights.

d. Evolutionary Individualist Anarchism. An interesting view, which proposed a minimal state for the present, while espousing an anarchist society for the future, was that advanced by the nineteenth-century English philosopher, Herbert Spencer, and the French economist, Frederic Bastiat. Both condemned any extension of government beyond the minimum necessary to protect the natural rights of every individual. Spencer argues that "every man has freedom to do as he wills, provided he infringes not the equal freedom of every other man." From this it follows, he believed, that if government does anything more than protect individual rights "it becomes an aggressor instead of a protector."[80] Thus Spencer was an ardent opponent not only of regulation of commerce, religion, health, education, etc., but of taxation as well. Indeed, Spencer goes even further and declares that the individual has a "right to ignore the state." His reasoning is instructive: "If every man has freedom to do all that he wills, provided that he infringes not the equal freedom of any other man, then he is free to drop connection with the state—to relinquish its protection, and to refuse paying toward its support. It is self-evident that in so behaving he in no way trenches upon the liberty of others.... It is equally self-evident that he cannot be compelled to continue as one of a political corporation...seeing that citizenship involves payment of taxes; and taking away a man's property against his will, is an infringement of his rights."[81] Having laid the philosophical groundwork for anarchism, Spencer goes a step further. "The power of self-government," he says, "can be developed only by exercise."[82] The more man is forced to accept responsibility for his own actions the more responsible and far-sighted he will become. And the more he so becomes, the less he will transgress the rights of others. Thus, "It is a mistake to assume that government must necessarily last forever. The institution marks a certain stage of civilization—is natural to a particular phase of human development." But, "as civilization advances," he says, "does government decay."[83]

Very similar to the writings of Herbert Spencer are those of Frederic Bastiat. Each of us "has a natural right...to defend his person, his liberty, and his property" and as soon as government exceeds this protective function it becomes an agency of "legal plunder" and the law, "instead of checking injustice, becomes the invincible weapon of injustice."[84] Like Spencer, Bastiat also goes a step further. While weak and frail now, "mankind is perfectible." Provided society is free and government is the oppressor, and not the agent, of plunder, then natural law will prevail and the consequences of each individual's action will redound upon himself. If they are pleasurable he will repeat them; if painful, he ceases. Further, since individuals have intellects, they are capable of transmitting to others what they have learned.[85] While Bastiat refrains from clearly stating the logical conclusions of his analysis, the components of evolutionary anarchism are present: government's only proper function is to suppress crime; but by the "law of responsibility" crime will eventually disappear: thus man will one day live in harmony and without government.

There is one fundamental difference between the individualist anarchists and the evolutionary anarchists. While both are ardent supporters of the market, the latter did not consider extending market analysis into the realm of police and the courts. Anarchism, for Spencer and Bastiat, would be possible only when man has progressed to the point of self-government, not before. The key question, of course, is whether that state of moral perfection is an attainable one.

e. Objectivism. The objectivists, headed by Ayn Rand, may be viewed as a variant of minarchism. Not only do they advocate a minimal state but, also like the minarchists, oppose taxation as a form of involuntary servitude.

The starting point for the objectivists is the cognition that life in society presupposes the repudiation of the initiatory use of violence. But, says Rand, "if physical force is to be barred from social relationships, men need an institution charged with the task of protecting their rights under an objective code of rules."[86] And an "objective code of rules," she believes, precludes the possibility of competition in this area. It is this fundamental incompatibility of force and production that is ignored by the anarchists. Suppose, says Rand in her critique of what she calls the anarchist theory of "competing governments," that

> Mr. Smith, a customer of Government A, suspects that his next-door neighbor, Mr. Jones, a customer of Government B, has robbed him; a squad of Police A proceeds to Mr. Jones's house and is met at the door by a squad of Police B, who declare that they do not accept the validity of Mr. Smith's complaint and do not recognize the authority of Government A. What happens then? You take it from there.[87]

But while a government, defined as "an institution that holds exclusive power to enforce certain rules of social conduct in a given geographical area," is absolutely necessary, its only proper function is the protection of individual rights.[88] Moreover, since the right to property is a most fundamental right, taxation would be immoral, and Rand therefore opts for what she terms "voluntary government financing."[89] The wealthy strata who would have the most to lose if there were no agency to protect individual rights would, she maintains, contract to contribute to the maintenance of this function. And since she believes that police protection is a collective good, "those on the lowest economic levels...would be virtually exempt—though they would still enjoy the benefits of legal protection." The great merit of this arrangement, she says, is that it would keep government to a minimum. "Men would pay voluntarily for insurance protecting their contracts. But they would not pay voluntarily for insurance against the danger of aggression by Cambodia."[90]

Beyond these rather vague and cursory remarks, Rand has written very little to further clarify her concept of "proper government." Some attention should therefore be paid to the series of articles by the objectivist, Paul Beaird, purporting to delineate and expand upon the Randian views on government.[91] According to Beaird, the crucial distinction between the Rothbardian-anarchist and the Randian-objectivist proposals for the rendering of police protection is that the latter is predicated upon the concept of territorial jurisdiction, while that notion is completely absent in the former. Because Rothbardian anarchism "lacks the geographical definition of jurisdiction," competing defense agencies, offering different policies and enforcing different laws, will operate on the same terrain. The result will be that "a person cannot be safe from the potential interference of unchosen defense agencies, even on his own territory."[92] The concept of jurisdiction solves this problem by establishing a single enforcement agency with "exclusive power" to enforce rules of conduct within a clearly demarcated territory. The extent of any government's jurisdiction, he says, would be determined by the individual decision of each property owner. "The area of a proper government's authority extends no further than the property lines of the lands owned by its citizens. When a person subscribes to a proper government, his land is added to its jurisdiction." This, he claims, insures that a government will always be based on the "consent of the governed." For the moment any property owner is no longer satisfied with "his government" he can secede from it and proceed "to contract with another government, or provide his own, or provide for none." Consequently, the application of objectivist principles may well "result in a map of a government jurisdiction looking like a patchwork, with the patches being separated from each other by the lands governed by other governments."[93]

This is a most curious piece indeed, for while it purports merely to propound and clarify the Randian position on government, it clearly conflicts with that position on three fundamental points. According to the logic of the Beairdian analysis, every property owner would have the right to contract with the government of his choice. But this can only mean that all governments would operate on a fee-for-service basis. For any government endeavoring to provide free protection for the poor would be forced to raise its premiums to cover the subsidy. But this, of course, would encourage its patrons to seek protection from other governments not providing a subsidy and therefore in a position to offer lower rates. Thus, under the Beairdian proposal only those paying for protection would receive it. But this is clearly at odds with Rand's assertion that under an objectivist government everyone, including the poor, would receive protection.[94] Thus, while Rand opts for a minarchist state, Beaird's proposal would be consistent with, at most, an ultraminarchist state.

Secondly, Rand's major criticism of "free market anarchism" is its failure to solve the problem of jurisdiction. Beaird, of course, reiterates this criticism and maintains that this would not be a problem under his proposal since "only one government" would have "authority on a plot of land at a time." But surely this would not be sufficient to alleviate the jurisdictional problem. Ironically, Rand's criticism of anarchism would apply with equal if not greater force, to this Rand-à la-Beaird proposal. For it would certainly be possible for a Beairdian society to be confronted with a situation in which "Mr. Smith, a customer of Government A, suspects that his...neighbor, Mr. Jones, a customer of Government B, has robbed him," and neither Government recognizes the other as legitimate. In fact, if every property owner were free to subscribe to the government of his choice, the number of governments would be likely to increase enormously—theoretically there could be as many governments as property owners—thereby magnifying the potential for the type of jurisdictional problems Rand is so anxious to avoid.

Finally, it is interesting that Rand calls the idea of "competing governments"—the idea that "every citizen" should be "free to 'shop' and to patronize whatever government he chooses,"—a "floating abstraction" and a "weird absurdity." But how else could one classify the Beairdian proposal except in terms of "competing governments" and the right of "every citizen...to 'shop' and to patronize the government of his choice"?

In short, while Beaird purports to be merely delineating the Randian views on government, there are fundamental conflicts between Rand's and Beaird's interpretation of Rand. Rand is a minarchist, while Beaird is, at most, an ultraminarchist.

Whether this indicates a flaw in the objectivist philosophy, or simply a misinterpretation of objectivism by Beaird, is both an interesting and difficult question to answer. Fortunately, since we are simply trying to get a fix on the relative positions of competing philosophies, this question need not be answered here.

f. Classical Liberalism. While relying on the market for most things, the classical liberals felt that there were various services that could be supplied only by the state. What they opted for was limited government and representative democracy. The classical liberals can be subdivided into two branches: the doctrinaire or uncompromising liberals who come very close to the contemporary minarchists, and the moderate liberals who would permit state extension into areas beyond that of police and the courts.

Probably only a few writers can be said to have been pure or doctrinaire liberals. Among the foremost are Wilhelm von Humboldt and Ludwig von Mises.[95] The argument of the doctrinaire liberals has most clearly been stated by Mises. "The essential teaching of liberalism," he says, "is that social cooperation and the division of labor can be achieved only in a system of private ownership of the means of production, i.e., a market society of capitalism." All of the other principles of liberalism, including democracy, he says, "are consequences of this basic postulate."[96] Thus, while the dogmatic liberal feels that the state should be completely democratized, he also believes that the sphere of state activity should be severely restricted: "As the liberal sees it, the task of the state consists solely and exclusively in guaranteeing the protection of life, health, liberty and private property. Everything that goes beyond this is an evil."[97] In a sense, the doctrinaire liberal places himself in a dilemma. He is ardently in favor of both the free market and democracy. Yet, the only way the market can remain completely unimpeded is if the scope of government is so circumscribed that its sole function is to protect individual rights. In that case issues subject to democratic control will be relatively meaningless. But if government expands and more areas are subject to vote, the scope of the market becomes progressively more restricted. Of this problem, Mises can merely hope that the majority will exercise such self-restraint that government will remain miniscule.[98]

The doctrinaire liberal also faces another dilemma. On the one hand he is passionate in defending the right of the individual to run his life as he deems fit. Mises, as we have seen, terms the extension of government beyond the protection of rights an "evil." But since government is necessary, and since it must have revenue, "taxes are necessary."[99] If it is evil to confiscate part of the earnings of individuals for some things, however, why is it not just as evil to confiscate them for other things such as court and police services? To this Mises can merely say that "the expenditure caused by the apparatus of a liberal community is so small" that it will be of little burden to the individual.[100] But the dilemma remains: taxation, whether large or small, constitutes a violation of the principles of liberalism so cherished by men like Mises.

In short, while what government exists is to be democratic, the doctrinaire liberal desires to restrict government activity as much as possible; he is a pro-capitalist first and a democrat second. The positions are reversed, however, for the moderate liberal, for he is prepared to see, and in fact often advocates, the extension of government into areas that the dogmatic liberal would consider anathema. The prototype of this group, which would include the bulk of the classical liberals, is John Stuart Mill. "The purpose for which power can rightfully be exercised over any member of a civilized community against his will," says Mill, "is to prevent harm to others. His own good…is not a sufficient warrant."[101] With such a statement Mill appears to fall into the dogmatic liberal tradition. But as George Sabine wrote of Mill, he was uncompromising in the abstract, "but having stated the principle, he proceeded to make concessions and restatements until in the end the original theory was explained away without any new principle being put in its place."[102]

Thus the state may if it wishes, he says, regulate trade as well as the hours of taverns. It may even "confine the power of selling these commodities…to persons of vouched-for respectability of conduct." The state has the duty to enforce "universal education" and to help to pay the school fees of the poorer classes of children although parents should be able "to obtain the education where and how they pleased." Mill also sanctions the prohibition of actions which may constitute "a violation of good manners" and "offences against decency." Presumably, this could entail regulation of dress in public, the selling of "pornographic" literature, as well as a host of other activities. "Compulsory labor" would be permitted to force parents to fulfill their obligations to their children. The state could also forbid marriage between two consenting adults if they cannot demonstrate "that they have the means of supporting a family."[103] And in his principles of political economy, Mill admits of "state protection of children, lunatics, and animals; state interference with joint stock companies; compulsion in the sphere of labor and industry; state charity; state supervision and control of colonization; state promotion of goods such as culture, science, research, etc."[104] As H. J. McCloskey says, Mill "allows a great deal of activity by the state towards promoting goods, and in restricting and preventing immoralities."[105]

One of the foremost contemporary exponents of moderate liberalism is F. A. Hayek. Like Mill, Hayek argues for the market and the supremacy of the individual. Yet he quickly modifies this by admitting a host of government activities. He permits state control of "most sanitary and health services" and "the construction and maintenance of roads…" He also adds that "there are many other kinds of activities in which the government may legitimately wish to engage…[106]

The distinction between the doctrinaire and moderate liberals is clear. Both profess to favor the market on the one hand and democracy on the other. But for the doctrinaires, so much would be handled by the market that the scope of issues falling under the state would be so small as to render democratic control most feeble. On the other hand, the moderates would grant much broader state jurisdiction. But as more and more areas are regulated by the state, the scope of the market is restricted and democratic control assumes primary importance. The distinction can be seen in an area like education. (The doctrinaire classical liberals believed that education is a good to be purchased on the market like any other good or service.) Under such a system there can be no question of democratic control of education since it would be entirely outside of the scope of government. Individuals would simply purchase the type, quantity and quality of education they desired. But if education is to be handled democratically then educational policy will be determined, not by the individual purchaser, but by the voting majority. Quite clearly, far from democracy being the counterpart of the market, as thought by the classical liberals, the two are incompatible. Thus the classical liberals placed themselves in a dilemma in advocating both democracy and the market. It is not surprising therefore to find classical liberalism divided into two factions: the dogmatic classical liberals such as Mises who are market proponents first and democrats second, and the moderate liberals such as Mill who are democrats first and market proponents second.

g. Conservatism. There is one final category that falls into the capitalist or free market spectrum: capitalist-hyperarchism. While this would entail fairly severe government regulation, it would be limited to the social sphere, such as press and speech, while leaving the market to function freely. Probably conservatism is the group that best fits into this category.

The founder of modern conservatism was Edmund Burke, and his followers today would include such figures as Russell Kirk, William F. Buckley and James Burnham. Conservatives are most reluctant to define precisely what they mean by conservatism, yet certain principles are discernable. They believe that true values manifest themselves over time via the emergence of traditions, and consequently that it is the duty of society to preserve and protect these traditions.[107] As a corollary, conservatives are distrustful of human reason. This view was eloquently expressed by Edmund Burke:

> You see, Sir, that in this enlightened age I am bold enough to confess, that we are generally men of untaught feelings; that instead of casting away all our old prejudices, we cherish them to a very considerable degree, and, to take more shame to ourselves, we cherish them because they are prejudices; and the longer they have lasted, the more we cherish them. We are afraid to live and trade each on his own private stock of reason; because we suspect that this stock in each man is small, and that the individuals would do better to avail themselves of the general bank and capital of nations, and of ages... Prejudice renders a man's virtue his habit; and not a series of unconnected acts. Through just prejudice, his duty becomes a part of his nature.[108]

One of the conservative traditions is the reluctance to rely on the government to solve social evils. Hence, conservatives opt for a limited government and a generally laissez-faire economic system. But not only do they not oppose the use of force to protect those "true values" that are viewed as necessary to maintain the social order; they feel it's one's duty to use force for such ends. Thus, force is advocated against such things as pornography, prostitution, labor unions, communism, and the like. Another fact of conservatism is that it consciously eschews delineating a positive program, which it condemns as abstract theorizing. Instead, its overriding characteristic is its resistance to "the enemies of the permanent things."[109] The most feared enemy is communism. The conservatives feel that it is man's moral duty to oppose communism by any means necessary and therefore advocate the use of government coercion in this regard. "The communists," argues noted conservative writer, James Burnham, "are serious and...are irrevocably fixed on their goal of a monopoly of world power... Because the communists are serious, they will have to be stopped...by superior power and will. Just possibly we shall not have to die in large numbers to stop them; but we shall certainly have to be willing to die."[110]

But, as has often been pointed out by their critics, conservatives place themselves in a serious dilemma. First, while they are in general opposed to government power and endorse a market economy, their willingness to use government force to protect "the permanent things" necessitates restrictions on the market that are far from minimal. Further, the fear of "the worldwide communist menace," has meant their endorsement of a military large enough "to defend the West against all challenges and challengers."[111] Not only is it difficult to see how the requirements of such a large military can be reconciled with their espousal of a minimal state, but a huge military can only be financed by massive taxation which, itself, constitutes further restrictions of the market. Thus while the conservatives generally endorse a market economy they are also perfectly willing to restrict its operations for goals they consider more important. In the insightful comment of L. T. Sargent, "The conservative seems to be in the unfortunate position of opposing government power except when it is on his side."[112]

It is also difficult to define the political position of the conservatives with any degree of precision. While earlier conservatives such as Burke and de Maistre were opposed to democracy, modern conservatives such as Kirk and Buckley have appeared to reconcile themselves to such a system. Nevertheless, their attachment to democracy seems to be strictly conditional: democracy is permissible so long as it does not endanger "the permanent things," the traditions and customs that hold society together. Authority and tradition are viewed as "pillars of any tolerable social order," which it is man's sacred duty to preserve at all costs.[113] While the conservatives have never squarely confronted the issue, this presumably means that at any time democracy comes into conflict with the permanent things, democracy must be abandoned for the sake of the latter. It is the acknowledgement that government is an indispensable social institution coupled with the reluctance to "accept the verdict of democracy's tribunal,"[114] that results in the marked authoritarian streak that runs throughout conservative thought.

The conservative sees society as an organic whole.[115] If democracy should conflict with the maintenance of the "permanent things," it becomes his duty to defend, and if necessary to sacrifice himself and others, for the sake of the preservation of the social order. Thus, the conservative's commitment to democracy is strictly conditional and masks a deeper authoritarianism that may, at times, border on fascism.[116]

3. Summary

Anarchism encompasses a wide range of economic positions ranging from anarcho-communism to individualist anarchism. Similarly, the capitalistic economic system is compatible with a spectrum of political structures ranging from anarchism to hyperarchism. The relationship between these two spectrums as well as their relationships to other philosophies can be seen in the following diagram. The political spectrum, ranging from anarchism on the left to hyperarchism on the right, runs across the top. The economic spectrum, ranging from capitalism at the top to communism at the bottom, runs down the page. The unbroken horizontal line across the top indicates the political range of capitalism; the unbroken vertical line indicates the economic scope of anarchism.[117]

Box [1] entails both a capitalistic economic system and an anarchistic political structure. This would include the contemporary individualist anarchists such as Rothbard and Friedman as well as the philosophical anarchists such as Tucker and Spooner. Still squarely within the anarchist spectrum but moving slightly away from capitalism would be Stirner and Godwin. On the other hand, somewhat less anarchistic but still ardently capitalistic would be the ultraminarchists such as Hospers.

Box [2] entails a limited form of government coupled with a capitalistic economic structure. This would include the minarchists, like Nozick, the evolutionary anarchists, like Spencer and Bastiat, as well as the objectivists. Also included in this category would be the doctrinaire classical liberals such

The Political/Economic Spectrum

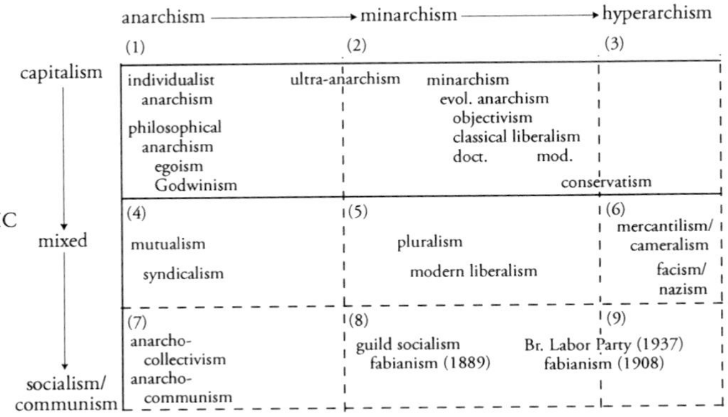

as Humboldt and Mises, and their more moderate counterparts like Mill and Smith and, more currently, Hayek.

Box [3] entails a highly interventionist state coupled with a market economy. Such a state would restrict its interventionist activities to the social realm, regulating speech, press, drug use, and the like, while permitting the market to function freely. While this category is, perhaps, of rather limited empirical import, probably the closest thing to capitalist-hyperarchism would be the conservatism of Burke and de Maistre and, more currently, Buckley, Kirk and Burnham.

Box [4] entails an anarchist political framework as in Box [1], but a less capitalistic economic structure than prevailed in Boxes [1-3]. There would still be much market phenomena and individual ownership, however some form of collectivism or workers control is also envisioned. This would include the mutualism of Proudhon and Warren and, while somewhat more collectively oriented, the syndicalism of Sorel, Rocker, and Goldman.

Box [5] entails the limitation of the market by interest group democracy which extends government into areas that under Boxes [1-3] would be handled by the market. This includes the modern exponents of pluralism and the partisans of contemporary liberalism and the welfare state such as John Rawls.

Box [6] entails severe limitations on the market. Democracy is also rejected in favor of rule by elites. It includes the mercantilists and cameralists of the eighteenth century, and the extreme conservatives as well as the exponents of facism and nazism such as Rockwell and Gentile.

Box [7] entails the rejection of the state coupled with a pronounced movement toward a marketless economy. This would include the anarcho-collectivism of Bakunin, and the more extreme anarcho-communism of Kropotkin.

Box [8] entails a socialist economy coupled with some form of limited statism. It would include the quasi-anarchistic Guild Socialism with its reliance on functional representation, where the only role for the state is to mediate between the functional groups when controversies could not be otherwise resolved. Close to this would be Fabianism (1889) with its emphasis on universal suffrage and municipal or local control of industry.

Box [9] entails a socialist or communist economic framework with planning to be done through the instrumentality of the state. This would include the British Labor Party (1937) with its call for nationalization of industry and a "general state plan." Close to this is Fabianism (1908) with emphasis on nationalization of such industries as water works, the mines, and the harbors, as well as a large dose of state planning. Also included in this category would be Marxism, which advocated a planned economy, but one in which all individuals participated in both the planning and the execution of the plans, and the elite-planned socialist technocracies outlined by Saint-Simon and Edward Bellamy.

If the foregoing is correct, the traditional view that anarchism is incompatible with capitalism is clearly incorrect. Both anarchism and capitalism traverse a wide spectrum of thought, and while some variants of anarchism are incompatible with some variants of capitalism, other types are quite compatible. Moreover, the place of the individualist anarchists in both the economic and the political spectrums has been pointed out, and the initial groundwork has been laid for the study of individualist anarchism.

Notes

1. One may distinguish between "states" and "governments." For example, John Sanders says that "states are not taken to be the same as governments... They are communities-with-governments." Government, therefore, is a necessary but not a sufficient condition for a state. Since Sanders defines government "in terms of coercion," and since government is a necessary condition for a state, the state too is inherently coercive. See John T. Sanders, *The Ethical Argument Against Government* (Washington, D.C.: University Press of America, 1980, pp. xi-xiii. Since the purpose of this study is to present and analyze a particular voluntary model of social organization and to compare it with the coercive model, unless otherwise noted, I will use the terms "government" and "state" interchangeably.
2. Ludwig von Mises, *The Free and Prosperous Commonwealth: An Exposition of the Ideas of Classical Liberalism* (Princeton: D. Van Nostrand, 1962), pp. 26-37.
3. Daniel Guerin, *Anarchism, from Theory to Practice* (New York: Monthly Review Press, 1970), p. 12.
4. Max Adler, "Max Stirner," *Encyclopedia of the Social Sciences* (New York: Macmillan, 1948), *Encyclopedia of Philosophy* (New York: Macmillan, 1967), vol. 1, pp. 111-14, and especially p. 113 where Stirner is described as being on the "dubious fringe" of anarchism.
5. Peter Kropotkin, "Anarchist Communism," *The New Encyclopedia of Social Reform*, eds. William Bliss and Rudolph Binder (New York: 1908), p. 47.
6. George Woodcock, *Anarchism, A History of Libertarian Ideas and Movements* (Cleveland: Meridian Books, 1969), pp. 163 and 204.
7. William Morris, *News From Nowhere* (London: 1891).
8. Mikhail Bakunin, "Stateless Socialism: Anarchism," *The Political Philosophy of Bakunin*, ed. G. P. Maximoff (New York: Free Press, 1953), pp. 298-99. Also see Woodcock, *Anarchism, A History*, p. 129.
9. Pierre Joseph Proudhon, "What is Property?" *Socialist Thought*, eds. Albert Fried and Ronald Sanders (New York: Doubleday, 1964), p. 202; and Woodcock, *Anarchism, A History*, p. 129
10. William Godwin, *Enquiry Concerning Political Justice* (Middlesex, England: Penguin, 1976), p. 705.
11. Benjamin Tucker, "State Socialism and Anarchism," *State Socialism and Anarchism, and Other Essays* (Colorado Springs: Ralph Myles, 1972), pp. 12-16.
12. Mises, p. 37.
13. John Hospers says that "my own option is for limited government." *Libertarianism* (Santa Barbara, Calif.: Reason Press, 1971), p. 417. Ayn Rand asserts that "anarchy as a political concept is a floating abstraction," and that "capitalism is incompatible with anarchism." *Capitalism: The Unknown Ideal* (New York: Signet Books, 1962), pp. 125 and 334. And Leonard Read writes that "the enemy of the free market is not the state... This formal agency of society, when organized to keep the peace, to uphold a common justice under law, and to inhibit and penalize fraud, violence, misrepresentation, and predation is a necessary and soundly principled ally of the free market." *The Free Market and Its Enemy* (Irvington-on-Hudson, N.Y.: Foundation for Economic Education, 1965), pp. 27-28.

14. "To point out the advantages which everybody derives from the working of capitalism is not tantamount to defending the vested interests of the capitalists. An economist who forty or fifty years ago advocated the preservation of the system of private property and free enterprise did not fight for the selfish class interest of the then rich." Ludwig von Mises, *Omnipotent Government: The Rise of the Total State and Total War* (New Rochelle: Arlington House, 1969), p. iii.
15. See Adam Smith, *The Wealth of Nations* (New Rochelle: Arlington House n.d.), especially vol. 2.
16. Martin Miller *Kropotkin* (Chicago: University of Chicago Press, 1976), p. 183.
17. Quoted in Paul Eltzbacher, Anarchism (New York: Chips, n.d.), pp. 101 and 106. Alan Ritter terms these methods "anarchist censure" as opposed to the "legal sanction" imposed by government. See his *Anarchism: A Theoretical Analysis* (Cambridge: Cambridge University Press, 1980). Also see his "The Modern State and the Search for Community: The Anarchist Critique of Peter Kropotkin," *International Philosophical Quarterly* (March 1976), especially pp. 24-28.
18. Peter Kropotkin, *The Conquest of Bread* (New York: Benjamin Blum, 1968), p. 15.
19. Ibid., p. 75.
20. Peter Kropotkin, "Fields, Factories and Workshops," *The Essential Kropotkin*, eds.. E. Caporya and K. Tompkins (New York: Liveright, 1975), pp. 270-72.
21. Eltzbacher, pp. 112-13.
22. Kropotkin, "Communist Anarchism," p. 45. Reasons of space permit only a brief presentation of the major representative figures of each anarchist type. Thus only Kropotkin was dealt with here. However, Leo Tolstoy and Paul Goodman could also be classified as "anarcho-communists." For a good summary of Tolstoy's views see Eltzbacher, pp. 149-81. Also see Paul and Percival Goodman, *Communitas* (New York: Vintage, 1960). On the similarities between Kropotkin and Paul Goodman see William Merill Downer, "Kropotkin in America: Paul Goodman's Adaptation of the Communitarian Anarchism of Peter Kropotkin" (Paper Presented at the 1977 Midwest Political Science Convention, April, 1977). Also in the Kropotkinian tradition is Murray Bookchin. See his *The Limits of the City* (New York: Harper, 1974).
23. Mikhail Bakunin, "On the Morrow of the Social Revolution," *The Political Philosophy of Bakunin*, ed. G.P. Maximoff (New York: Free Press, 1953), p. 410.
24. James Guillaume, "On Building the New Social Order," *Bakunin on Anarchy*, ed. Sam Dolgoff (New York: Alfred A Knopf, 1971), p. 360.
25. Woodcock, *Anarchism, A History*, p. 164. Witness Bakunin's remark that any persons who, though robust and of good health, do not want to gain their livelihood by working shall have the right to starve themselves to death…" "On the Morrow of the Social Revolution," p. 412.
26. According to Bakunin, the collectives will form themselves into federations, the federations into regions, the regions into nations and, ultimately, the nations into what he terms an "international fraternal association." See Bakunin, "Stateless Socialism: *Anarchism*," p. 298.
27. Guillaume, p. 366.
28. Ibid., p. 368.
29. It should be pointed out that the anarcho-syndicalist, Rudolph Rocker, explicitly repudiates Sorel and maintains that Sorel neither "belonged to the movement, nor had…any appreciable influence on its internal development." See Rudolph Rocker, "Anarchism and Anarcho-Syndicalism," appendix to Paul Eltzbacher, *Anarchism* (New York: Chips, n.d.), p. 250.

30. George Sorel, *Reflections on Violence* (New York: Doubleday, 1941), p. 294.
31. See Mulford Sibley, *Political ideas and Ideologies* (New York: Harper and Row, 1970), p. 547.
32. Rocker, pp. 253-55.
33. Emma Goldman, "Syndicalism," *Liberty and the Great Libertarians*, ed. Charles T. Sprading (New York: Arno Press 197 2), p. 507; quotation of Hins in Rocker, p. 247.
34. A critic of syndicalism, Ludwig von Mises writes that, "In the syndicalist society the citizen is made up of the yield from his property and the wages of his labor." *Socialism* (London: Jonathan Cape, 1969), p. 274.
35. See especially ibid., pp. 270-75.
36. Proudhon, pp. 546-48.
37. Pierre Joseph Proudhon, *Selected Writings of P. J. Proudhon*, ed. Stewart Edwards (New York: Doubleday, 1969), pp. 96-99.
38. Ibid., p. 59.
39. Ibid., pp. 140-41.
40. See George Woodcock, *Pierre Joseph Proudhon* (New York: Shocken Books, 1972), pp. 49-50.
41. For a good summary of Proudhon's ideas on handling antisocial activity in an anarchist society see Alan Ritter, "Godwin, Proudhon and the Anarchist Justification of Punishment," *Political Theory* (February 1975), especially pp. 81-84. An excellent presentation of Proudhon's views on justice and law can be found in William O. Reichert's "Natural Right in the Political Philosophy of Pierre-Joseph Proudhon," *The Journal of Libertarian Studies* (Winter 1980), pp. 77-91.
42. Proudhon was not a terribly consistent writer. Thus, despite his attacks on large-scale property, one also finds Proudhon writing that, "Once the land has been freed by the apparatus of the revolution and agriculture liberated, feudal exploitation will never be re-established. Let property then be sold, bought, circulated, divided, and accumulated, becoming completely mobile... It will no longer be the same institution. However, let us still call it by its own name, so dear to the heart of man and so sweet to the peasant's ear: PROPERTY." Proudhon, *Selected Writings*, p. 73.
43. H. N. Brailsford, "William Godwin," *Encyclopedia of the Social Sciences* (New York: Macmillian Co., 1948), vol. 6, p. 686.
44. Godwin, pp. 710-24.
45. Ibid., pp. 225-56. A good summary of Godwin's justification of punishment is found in Ritter, "Godwin, Proudhon," p. 72-79. Also useful is Eltzbacher, pp. 31-33, as is John P. Clark, *The Philosophical Anarchism of William Godwin* (Princeton: Princeton University Press, 1977), especially pp. 710-24.
46. Godwin, pp. 710-24.
47. See, for example, Stirner's statements that "Morality is incompatible with egoism," and "the State and I are enemies..." Max Stirner, *The Ego and His Own* (New York: Dover, 1973), p. 179.
48. See, for example, James Forman's sarcastic remark that "As far as Stirner was concerned, two people acting in concert were a crowd." James D. Forman, *Anarchism* (New York: Dell, 1975), p. 74. Incredibly, Forman also claims that Stirner was, through Nietzsche, a precursor of Nazism.
49. Stirner, pp. 34-36.
50. Ibid., p. 179, fn. Also see Woodcock. Stirnerite egoism, he points out, "does not deny union between individuals. Indeed, it may well foster genuine and spontaneous union. For the individual is unique, not as a member of a party. He unites freely and separates again," *Anarchism, A History*, pp. 100-02.

51. Stirner, p. 258.
52. Ibid., pp. 114-15, Emphasis in original.
53. In Paul Thomas, "Karl Marx and Max Stirner," *Political Theory* (May 1975), p. 169.
54. Charles Madison, "Anarchism in the United States," *Journal of the History of Ideas* (January 1945), p. 48.
55. The compatibility of egoism and the free market is especially apparent in the address of the egoist, John Babcock, "Slaves to Duty," reprinted in *Libertarian Analysis* (September 1971), pp. 15-39. On the views of Mackay see Thomas Riley, "Anti-Statism in German Literature, *Modern Language Association Publications* (September 1947), pp. 828-43.
56. Benjamin Tucker, "The Attitude of Anarchism Toward Industrial Combinations," *State Socialism and Anarchism, and Other Essays* (Colorado Springs: Ralph Myles, 1972), pp. 13-21.
57. Ibid., pp. 27-34.
58. For a succinct statement of the similarities and differences between the two schools of anarchism on the subject of profits and interest, see Murray Rothbard, "The Spooner-Tucker Doctrine: An Economist's View," *Egalitarianism as a Revolt Against Nature, and Other Essays* (Washington, D. C.: Libertarian Review Press, 1974), pp. 125-32.
59. Murray Rothbard, *Man, Economy and State, A Treatise on Economic Principles*, 2 vols. (Los Angeles: Nash, 1970), 2:883-90. Also see Sanders, pp. 97-192.
60. See, for example, Paul Beaird, "On Proper Government, *Option* (January 1976), p. 20; John Hospers, "Will Rothbard's Free-Market Justice Suffice? No," Reason (May 1973), pp. 18-23. Also see Jeffrey Paul, "Anarchism and Natural Rights" (Paper Presented at the Association for the Philosophic Study of Society, October 6, 1977).
61. David Friedman is one of the few individualist anarchists to recognize the distinction between libertarianism and anarchism, and he extricates himself from this possible dilemma by refusing to classify himself as a libertarian. See his *The Machinery of Freedom* (New York: Harper and Row, 1973), pp. 173-78.
62. John Hospers, "What Libertarianism Is," *The Libertarian Alternative*, ed. Tibor Machan (Chicago: Nelson-Hall, 1974), p. 13.
63. Ibid., pp. 7-8; and Hospers, *Libertarianism*, pp. 61-62.
64. Hospers, Libertarianism, pp. 386-87.
65. John Hospers, "Rothbard's Free-Market Justice," p. 21.
66. Ibid.
67. Hospers, *Libertarianism*, p. 387.
68. Hospers, "Rothbard's Free-Market Justice," p. 21.
69. See, for example, Max Weber, *Law in Economy and Society*, ed. Max Rheinstein (New York: Simon and Schuster, 1954), pp. 338-39.
70. It would certainly be stretching the point to maintain that the fee would be voluntary since consumers could forego purchasing protection altogether, and those providing protection could enter a new line of work, if either objected to the fee. This is tantamount to arguing that the obligation to pay income tax is "voluntarily" assumed when the individual "chooses" to earn a living.
71. Robert Nozick, *Anarchy, State and Utopia* (New York: Basic Books, 1974), pp. 15-26.
72. Ibid., pp. 110-13.
73. Ibid., pp. 33-5.
74. Ibid., p. 156.

75. See ibid., pp. 22-25.
76. Ibid., p. 109 (emphasis in original).
77. See John Sanders, "The Free Market Model Versus Government: A Reply to Nozick," *The Journal of Libertarian Studies* (Winter 1977), pp. 35-44.
78. Nozick, p. 118.
79. Roy Childs, "The Invisible Hand Strikes Back," *The Journal of Libertarian Studies* (Winter 1977), pp. 23-33.
80. Herbert Spencer, *Social Statics* (New York: D. Appleton, 1892), p. 125.
81. Herbert Spencer, *The Right to Ignore the State* (Cupertino, Cal.: Caymen Press, 1973), p. 5.
82. Spencer, *Social Statics*, p. 84.
83. Spencer, *Right*, p. 14.
84. Frederic Bastiat, *The Law* (Irvington-on-Hudson, N.Y.: Foundation For Economic Education, 1972), pp. 6-11.
85. Frederic Bastiat, *Economic Harmonies* (Princeton: D. Van Nostrand, 1964), p. 533.
86. Rand, *Capitalism*, p. 331.
87. Ibid., p. 335.
88. Ibid., p. 332. Rand also states, however, that the source of the government's authority is "the consent of the governed" (p. 332). But this introduces a tension—of the same sort found in John Locke and Herbert Spencer—between natural rights on the one hand and consent on the other. Would an individual be obliged to obey a government enforcing only "natural rights" even if he had not consented to it?
89. Ayn Rand *The Virtue of Selfishness* (New York: Signet, 1961), pp. 116-20. Interestingly, Rand also outlines a scheme for the payment of court services through a Hosperian-like fee-for-service arrangement, while Hospers, in turn, says he would have no objections to a Randian-donation policy.
90. Ibid., p. 118-19.
91. Paul Beaird, "Of Proper Government, I, II, and III," *Option* (January 1976, April 1976, and May-June 1976), pp. 19-20 and 28, 12-14 and 26-27, and 22-26.
92. Beaird, "Of Proper Government, III," p. 24.
93. Beaird, "Of Proper Government, II," p. 12. Beaird defends his consent doctrine by recourse to "tacit consent." This, of course, makes it very similar to the Lockean position, and it is therefore open to the same criticisms. While the landowner consents to a government by the positive act of subscribing to it, a traveler, a renter, etc., is claimed to be automatically consenting to a government simply "by entering land" over which a particular government has been given jurisdiction by the owner. But surely such a strained use of the term robs if of any real meaning.
94. It is true that Rand does mention the possibility of a fee-for-service arrangement for "one of the needed services" rendered by government, i.e., "the protection of contractual agreements among citizens." But not only does Beaird extend this to all government services, he also ignores Rand's disclaimer that "this particular plan is mentioned here only as an illustration of a possible method of approach to the problem…not as a definitive answer…" Rand, *Selfishness*, p. 117. She also mentions the possibility of lotteries, but Beaird has preferred to ignore this suggestion. Moreover, this fee-for-service suggestion, especially when extended beyond the area mentioned by Rand, would conflict with her goal of providing everyone, including the poor, with police and court services.
95. Wilhelm von Humboldt, *The Limits of State Action* (London: Cambridge, 1969); Mises, *Free and Prosperous.*
96. Mises, *Omnipotent Government*, p. 48.

97. Mises, *Free and Prosperous*, p. 52.
98. Mises, *Human Action* (Chicago: Henry Regnery, 1966), p. 150 Much, but not all, of the "Public Choice" literature also expresses the fear that democratic government, under the impetus of responding to the will of the electorate, will expand, with disastrous consequences, into areas that had traditionally been left to the market. This is especially evident in the writings of James Buchanan and Gordon Tullock, whose proposal for an "optimal majority"—a requirement of a two-thirds majority for most issues—was advanced as a device for controlling this tendency of democratic government to expand. See their *The Calculus of Consent* (Ann Arbor, Michigan: University of Michigan Press, 1962). For an intriguing contrasting view, also in the "Public Choice" vein, see Anthony Downs, "Why the Government Budget is Too Small in a Democracy," *World Politics* (July 1960), pp. 541-63.
99. Ibid., p. 807.
100. Mises, *Socialism*, p. 491.
101. Mill, *On Liberty* (Chicago: Henry Regnery, 1955), p. 13.
102. George Sabine, *A History of Political Theory* (New York: Henry Holt, 1937), p. 665.
103. Mill, pp. 140-60.
104. H. J. McCloskey, "Mill's Liberalism," *Essays in the History of Political Thought*, ed. Isaac Kramnick (Englewood Cliffs: Prentice Hall, 1969), p. 381.
105. Ibid., p. 379.
106. F. A. Hayek, *Constitution of Liberty* (Chicago: Henry Regnery, 1960), p. 223. Also see Chapter 15, pp. 220-33.
107. On the emergence of traditions as true values see Eric Vogelin, *The New Science of Politics* (Chicago: University of Chicago Press, 1952); Michael Oakeshott, *Rationalism in Politics* (New York: Basic Gooks, 1962); and Russell Kirk, *The Conservative Mind* (Chicago: Henry Regnery, 1967).
108. Edmund Burke, *Reflections on the Revolution in France* (New Rochelle: Arlington House, n.d), pp. 100-01.
109. See Kirk, *Conservative Mind*; and the same author's *Enemies of the Permanent Things* (New Rochelle: Arlington House, 1969).
110. James Burnham, *Suicide of the West* (New Rochelle: Arlington House, 1964), pp. 290-91.
111. Ibid., p. 288.
112. L. T. Sargent, *Contemporary Political Ideologies* (Homewood, Ill.: Dorsey Press, 1972), p. 99.
113. Kirk, *Enemies*, p. 282.
114. Burnham, p. 139.
115. "Conservatives respect the wisdom of their ancestors... They think society is a spiritual reality, possessing an eternal life but a delicate constitution: it cannot be scrapped and recast as if it were a machine." Kirk, *The Conservative Mind*, p. 6.
116. For analyses that point out the authoritarianism of conservatism see Edith Effron, "Conservatism: A Libertarian Challenge," *The Alternative* (October 1975), pp. 9-13; Murray Rothbard, "Conservatism and Freedom: A Libertarian Comment," *Modern Age* (Spring 1961), pp. 217-20; Murray Rothbard, "Confessions of a Right-Wing Liberal," Ramparts (June 15,1968), pp. 47-52. The contemporary sociologist Robert Nisbet sees at least the traditional conservatism of Burke, Lemmenais and DeBonald not only as highly pluralistic but as a bulwark against political central and the authoritarian state. See his "Conservatism and Libertarians: Uneasy Cousins," *Modern Age* (Winter 1980), pp. 2-8; "Conservatism and Sociology," *The American Journal of Sociology* (September 1952), pp. 167-75; and "DeBonald and the Con-

cept of the Social Group," *Journal of the History of Ideas* (June 1944), pp. 315-31. In emphasizing the role that the "social group" and tradition played in impeding the growth of centralized power, Nisbet has highlighted an important and unjustly neglected aspect of conservatism. But this still doesn't negate the authoritarian streak in much of conservative thought.

117. Two things should be mentioned regarding the "political spectrum." First, it might be argued that there is an inverse relationship between the economic and political spheres—as one increases the other must decrease—so that both spectrums are merely measures of the same thing. This, however, not only overlooks the large body of thought that felt that the reverse was true—that the market presupposed a highly interventionist and authoritarian state—Marx, for example, and Kropotkin—but also ignores that group which desired neither the market nor the state—Kropotkin, Bakunin and Berkman, to name just a few. It seems to me that while a free market presupposes some restraints on the state, the reverse is not true. A limited state does not necessarily entail the free market.

Second, one should not jump to the conclusion that the "political spectrum" is some sort of "freedom index." This spectrum classifies political frameworks according to the degree of state interventionism. Since there would be no state under anarchism, state intervention would, of course, be zero. But except in the sense in which freedom is defined in terms of the limits on the state there is no one-to-one relationship between the absence of state intervention and freedom. This is the major flaw in the analytical frameworks advanced by David Nolan and Randy Barnett. (See David Nolan, "Classifying and Analyzing Politico-Economic Systems," *The Individualist* (January 1971), pp. 5-11; and Randy Barnett, *In Defense of Political Anarchism* (Unpublished Manuscript, 1974), pp. 1-10.) For the state is not the only obstacle to freedom. One of the greatest fears by such thinkers as Mill and Tocqueville was of democracy's potential for repression by public opinion. Since many anarchists—Proudhon and Godwin to name but two—would rely, for the maintenance of order in their communities, on the force of public opinion, this introduces the possibility of the "tyranny of public opinion" in anarchist as well as democratic societies. Thus, "authoritarian-anarchism" is at least a theoretical possibility. Moreover, modern liberals, beginning with T. H. Green, have always maintained that state intervention is required to overcome the obstacles to freedom, such as poverty, ignorance, discrimination, and the like. Thus, a highly interventionist state, they hold, is necessary to increase freedom. This group mayor may not be correct, but things are hardly as simple as the analytical frameworks of Nolan and Barnett imply.

Section IV: Historical Case Studies of Non-Government Law Enforcement

34

Are Public Goods Really Common Pools? Considerations of the Evolution of Policing and Highways in England

Bruce Benson

I. Introduction

Policing and highways are frequently cites as "important examples of production of public goods," and it is often contended that "private provision of these public goods will not occur," as in Samuelson and Nordhaus (1985, 48-49 and 713). According to Tullock (1970, 83-84) and Samuelson and Nordhaus (1985, 49), for instance, private-sector production of policing and/or highways generates non-exclusionary external benefits for which private suppliers are unable to charge, thus creating free-rider incentives and non-cooperative behavior. I offer an alternative explanation for this lack of cooperation, however, which fits the historical evolution of public policing and highways in England. The fact is that public policing and highways evolved because of changes in property rights, which undermined private incentives to cooperate in the provision of these services. Indeed, these services are like the television signals discussed by Minasian (1964), in that different institutional arrangements create different incentives for the allocation of resources.[1] However, my presentation goes beyond simply providing two supporting examples for Minasian's (1964, 77) contention that the "public goods" concept is misleading, by proposing a more appropriate analytical toll for at least some allocation issues labeled as public-good/free-rider problems.

In the case of policing, for example, before English kings began to concentrate and centralize power, individuals had rights to a very important private benefit arising from successful pursuit and prosecution: victims received restitution. Effective collection of restitution required the cooperation of witnesses, and of neighbors to aid in pursuit; but anyone who did not cooperate with victims could not obtain similar support when victimized, and therefore could be excluded from this very important benefit of law enforcement. Policing was carried out by neighborhood associations and free riding did not appear to be a problem because anyone who did not cooperate was ostracized by the group. In other words, policing was not a public good in medieval England: the primary benefits were private and/or internal to small groups and non-contributors were excluded. One consequence of the development of monarchical government was the creation of criminal law as a source of royal revenues. Criminalization took away the private right to restitution and significantly reduced the incentives to voluntarily cooperate in law enforcement. A very different set of institutions evolved as a consequence. Today, rights to many attributes of public policing still require a substantial commitment of private resources, including victim and witness cooperation.[2] Incentives for individuals to under-invest in the commons are substantial relative to incentives to invest in the production of any private benefits that remain. In other words, policing is not a public good today either: its publicly produced aspects are generally treated as free-access common pools and private individuals under-invest in their maintenance. As demonstrated below, the same is true of highways.

It might be argued that "non-excludable public goods" and "free-access common pools" are simply two terms for the same concept. However, as Minasian (1964, 77) explains, the public goods terminology often is "asserted" to imply that non-excludability is an intrinsic problem that cannot be resolved without coercing free riders into paying for the good. The common pool terminology emphasizes that incentives arise because of the definition of property rights and, therefore, that another property rights assignment can alter such incentives. Beyond that, a property rights approach actually explains both the historical evolution and modern production of policing and highways better than public goods analysis.

The incentive structure underlying a hypothetical restitution-based legal system with private sector policing is discussed in section II below. Section III then examines an actual example of such a system: Anglo-Saxon law in England prior to the development of strong kings. This is followed in section IV, by an exploration of the incentives leading to the withdrawal of restitution and the development of public policing in England. Section V returns to the contention that public policing should be characterized as a common pool problem rather than as a public good by exploring some of the characteristics of modern law enforcement. It is contended in section VI that a similar, and indeed closely linked evolutionary process shaped the transition from a system of voluntary maintenance of roads in England to a system of public common-pool highways, as the taking of private property rights undermined the incentives to privately produce and maintain a system of highways. For instance, royal law would not allow private groups to charge tolls: this right was reserved for the king or those to whom he sold the privilege. Concluding comments appear in section VII.

II. Restitution and Incentives to Cooperate in Law Enforcement

The current institutional arrangement for criminal law, wherein individuals have common access to police services and criminals are punished by the state, is the only institutional arrangement that is possible for the production of law enforcement. To see this, assume that the rules of law now considered as crimes against persons or property are in the nature of torts. That is, if an accused offender is determined to be guilty of violations of some victim's rights, the "punishment" is restitution in the form of a fine or indemnity to be paid to the victim. Furthermore, as is generally the case with tort law, assume that the aggrieved party must pursue prosecution. Pursuit and prosecution are much more effective, however, if several people cooperate in their production. Cooperation of non-victim witnesses can be essential for prosecution, for example. Furthermore, pursuit by the victim alone is less likely to succeed than pursuit by a large group, or by trained specialists hired by a group. First, the offender is more likely to elude a single pursuer or a non-specialist, and second, the offender is more likely to violently resist an individual than a large group or a specialist.

Individuals never know if they will be the victim of an offense in the future, but they assign some positive probability to being victimized. Furthermore, an individual does not know whether an offender will be physically, politically or economically strong enough to apprehend and prosecute. Cooperation is desirable, but if each opportunity for pursuit of an offender mistreated as a one-shot game by victims, witnesses, and others in a position to aid in pursuit and prosecution, then cooperation is unlikely because only the victim gains from the cooperative exchange. As Buchanan and Tullock (1962, 37) point out, however, such a "collective choice is a continuous process, with each unique decision representing only one link in a long-time chain of social action." That is, most individuals in a group are involved in various long-term relationships, so they are in a repeated-game setting with finite but uncertain horizons, and when each individual has some probability of being a victim at some point, then cooperation becomes possible, à la Axelrod (1984). Under these circumstances, individuals may have incentives to voluntarily "exchange" obligations to support one another in pursuit of prosecution. Of, course, if individuals can express a willingness to cooperate and obtain benefits from the cooperative arrangements but then not actually reciprocate when called upon, such an arrangement will either fail to develop or break down if established. In a repeated game, however, a commitment can be made credible if there is a credible potential response by the other player; that is, if the tit-for-tat response is sufficient punishment for the cheater.

Even a repeated-game situation involves weaker incentives to cooperate than those which exist in groups wherein each individual enters into several different repeated games with different players. In fact, these games need not have anything to do with policing. For instance, they may involve team production, trade, religion, or any number of other day-to-day types of interaction, including road maintenance, as explained below. To the extent that reputation travels from one game to another, so that refusal to cooperate within one game can limit the person's ability to enter into other games, the potential for a credible response is expanded. Various forms of social pressure or ostracism can be brought to bear to induce cooperation in law enforcement.[3]

Indeed, individuals who do not fulfill obligations to support others in pursuit and prosecution can be excluded from *all* forms of social interaction with other members of the group (e.g., trade, religious activities). In other words, because each individual has invested in establishing a position in the community and building a reputation within the group, that investment can be "held hostage" by the community, à la Williamson (1983), to insure that the commitment to cooperate is credible. Under these circumstances, Milgrom et al. (1990) and Schmidtz (1991, 102) explain that the dominant strategy is to behave as expected in all games, repeated and on-shot alike. Indeed, there clearly is a simultaneous development of cooperation in law enforcement and other forms of interaction, since as Benson (1989) notes, most interactions require some degree of certainty about legal obligation.

This discussion of an alternative institutional arrangement for law enforcement is not just hypothetical. It describes a number of historical, anthropological, and modern legal systems. The makeup of such groups, including the institutional arrangement that produces the reputation effects and repeated-game interactions, may reflect family and/or religion as in Benson (1991), geographic proximity as described by Klein (1990), Ellickson (1991) and Benson (1992), functional similarity as detailed in Benson (1989) and Milgrom et al. (1990), or contractual arrangements as discussed by Friedman (1979) and Umbeck (1981a). One example is Anglo-Saxon England.

III. Policing in Anglo-Saxon England[4]

As Stephen (1883, 53) explains, there were no "crimes" against the state, under early Anglo-Saxon law, but a large proportion of the offenses that appear in a modern criminal code were defined as illegal. Indeed, Anglo-Saxon laws were very concerned with protection of individuals and their property; offenses such as homicide, assaults, rape, indecent assaults, and theft were extensively treated, but these offenses were treated as torts.

Institutions of Cooperative Policing

The Germanic tribes from which the Anglo-Saxons descended were divided into pagi, each of which was made up of vici. Lyon (1980, 59) suggests that a pagus apparently consisted of one hundred men or households, while the vici was a subdivision of the pagus responsible for policing.[5] Conceivably, these vici were bound by kinship. Successful pursuit of an offender resulted in payment of restitution defined by a system of wergeld or man-price (wer). As Baker (1974, 10) emphasizes, anyone who did not cooperate could be "put outside the protection of the community." The invaders carried this system to England. By the tenth century, there was a clearly recognized legal institution called the "hundred." Stephen (1883, 66) explains that these voluntary groups provided "the police system of the country." Indeed, Blair (1956, 232) points out that the two primary purposes of these organizations were to facilitate cooperation in rounding up stray cattle and in pursuing justice.[6] When a theft occurred, for example, the several "tithings" that made up the hundred were informed: they had a reciprocal duty to cooperate in pursuit and prosecution. A tithing was apparently a group of neighbors, many of whom probably were kin.

Private Benefits and Incentives to Cooperate

A primary reason for recognizing reciprocal duty in the tithings and hundreds was that these organizations produced a number or private benefits, such as the return of stray cattle, and significantly, as Stephen (1883,62) explains, restitution to a victim. Pollock and Maitland (1959, vol. 2, 50) and Stephen (1883, 58) both note that economic payments could be made for *any* first time offender. Pollock and Maitland (1959, vol. 2, 451) point out that "A deed of homicide," for example, "can be paid for by money...the offender could buy back the peace he had broken." The members of each tithing were clearly in a position to interact repeatedly on several dimensions, so that reputation effects were important. Thus, cooperation in pursuit and prosecution, as well as in other dimensions, such as rounding up stray cattle, and dispute settlement, evolved to capture various private benefits.

As Umbeck (1981a; 1981b) stresses, the threat of violence underlies any private property rights system. Thus, in the case of Angle-Saxon tithings and hundreds, as Stephen (1883, 62) observes, refusal to pay restitution to a member of the community in good standing put the offender outside the protection of the law. Physical retribution against an outlaw became the responsibility of the entire hundred, and there were also similar cooperative arrangements between different hundreds.[7] Likewise, Pollock and Maitland (1959, vol. 1, 47-48) emphasize that refusing to accept restitution and seeking physical revenge meant that the initial victim became an outlaw. Outlawry implied that physical attacks on the outlaw were legal and the potential for a "blood-feud" arose.[8] The community-wide threat of outlawry and physical revenge generally induced the reluctant offender, but without the backing of the community, this was relatively unlikely. Of course there were also common benefits to policing, such as localized deterrence, so individuals living in the area might benefit even if they refused to cooperate in policing or other kinds of team production. Indeed, these associations also produced other benefits common to the group as a whole, such as road maintenance as explained below, but cooperation in the production of such common benefits was an investment in reputation that allowed the individuals to consume the important team-produced private benefits as well. In fact, if someone was reputed to be uncooperative and therefore not a member of a tithing, he would be a relatively attractive target, and probably would have been victimized more often than members of effective tithings. Furthermore, the individual was ostracized by the community and therefore would not have access to the community's dispute resolution arrangements or other benefits of community interaction, such as the gathering of his stray cattle, religious rights, trade, etc. The cost of non-cooperation was high, even though exclusion may not have been possible for some common access benefits such as road use, and perhaps deterrence.

Pollock and Maitland (1959, vol. 2, 48) explain that early codes make it clear that "the ealdor man, and the king at need, may be called in if the plaintiff is not strong enough himself." Thus, even the most respected members of the

Anglo-Saxon community were involved in the cooperative arrangements used in posing the threat of outlawry. In fact, perhaps as a further threat to deter resistance to payment of restitution, or perhaps as an inducement to ealdormen to cooperate with the community, the restitution system was expanded: if a victim had to call upon an ealdorman or king for support, a guilty offender would not only have to pay *wer* to the victim or his kin, but he also would have to make a payment of *wite* to the ealdorman or king. Ealdormen and kings had no sovereign powers to coerce compliance, however, as Pollock and Maitland (1959, vol. 2, 40-41) explain. They simply supported someone who, due to insufficient strength of his own support group arrangements relative to the strength of the accused offender, could not get his cause heard in his own hundred. Nonetheless, this institutionalization of ealdormen's and king's role in the justice process, and in particular a *wit* as a payment for performing this role, was one of the first steps in what would soon be a rapid extension of the king's role in law. Kingship did not develop for the purpose of establishing internal law and order, however. Rather, as explained in Blair (1956, 196-198) and Benson (1990, 26-30; 1993), monarchial government evolved due to external conflict, as groups attempted to take land from other groups or to protect existing holdings.[9] But during the centuries of warfare kingship also acquired important legal ramifications.

IV. Justice for Profit: The Development of English Criminal Law

As Anglo-Saxon kings consolidated their power, they recognized that law and law enforcement could be used as a direct source of royal revenues. Well before the Norman conquest, for instance, Pollock and Maitlan (1959, vol. 1, 49) observe that outlawry began to involve "forfeiture of goods to the king." More significantly, they note (1959, vol. 1, 49) violations of certain laws began to be referred to as violations of the "king's peace," and punishment involved fines to the king rather than restitution.

The concept of the "king's peace" traces directly to Anglo-Saxon law in the sense that every freeman's house had a "peace"; if it was broken, the violator had to pay. Initially, the king's peace simply referred to the peace of the king's house, but as royal power expanded, the king declared that his peace extended to other places. First, it was applied to places where the king traveled, then to churches, monasteries, highways, and bridges. Eventually, as Lyon (1980, 42) notes, it would be "possible for royal officers such as sheriffs to proclaim the king's peace wherever suitable. Even included were festivals and special occasions." Violations of the king's peace required payment to the king, so the expansion in places and times protected by the king's peace meant greater potential for revenue. Pollock and Maitland (1959, vol. 1, 31-32) explain that the populace did not accept these changes gracefully, however: "There is a constant tendency to conflict between the old customs of the family and the newer laws of the State."

Royal profits from justice probably were only a small component of total income for Anglo-Saxon kings. However, they were an increasingly important component for at least two reasons. First, such income was relatively liquid. The potential for taxation was modest, for example. By far the largest component of royal income came from the king's land holdings, but this income was largely in the form of agricultural produce, which could not easily be transported or sold. Indeed, kings and their households traveled from estate to estate throughout the year, consuming each estate's output before moving to the next. This lack of liquidity contrasts sharply with fines collected through the king's evolving legal functions. Second, marginal changes in royal revenue could be made relatively easily by mandating changes in the law, in the form of extensions of the king's peace to other offenses, and increasing the *wite*, as compared to most other sources of revenue. Indeed, through confiscation of outlaws' property, kings expanded their land holdings, creating new sources of perpetual income.

Law enforcement and its profits also became something the king could exchange in the political arena. As Pollock and Maitland (1959, vol. 2, 453-454) stress, "pleas and forfeitures were among profitable rights which the king could grant to prelates and thegns. A double process was at work; on the one hand the king was becoming supreme judge in all causes; on the other hand he was granting out jurisdiction as though it were so much land." Ealdormen were granted special status as royal representatives within shires; Lyon (1980, 62-63) notes that they received "one-third of the fines from the profits of justice" and other duties levied by the king. In exchange, the ealdormen mustered and led men into combat, represented the king in shire courts, and executed royal commands. By the tenth century, a few powerful families provided all the ealdormen in England, and they had a great deal of national political power. As single earls evolved to represent the king in groups of shires, the office of sheriff also evolved in each shire. A sheriff received grants of land from the king and the right to retain some of the profit from the royal estates he supervised. Furthermore, as explained in Lyon (1980, 65), "by the reign of Edward the Confessor judicial profits had come to be lumped in with the farm of the royal manors and all these had to be collected by the sheriff" in exchange for part of the profit.

Norman Rule: The End of Restitution

Pollock and Maitland (1959, vol. 1, 94) emphasize that following their successful invasion of 1066, the Normans quickly established "an exceedingly strong kingship," and as Lyon (1980, 163) notes, one focus of this power was the use of law and law enforcement to generate revenues. In this regard, Pollock and Maitland (1959, vol. 1, 53) observe that one of the earliest and most significant changes the Normans made in English law was replacement of what remained of the Anglo-Saxon's restitution-based system's payments of clearly defined *wer* with a system of fines and confiscations for the king, along with corporal and capital punishment. Most offenses under the early Normans were still defined by Anglo-Saxon customary law, but elimination of the *wergeld* system meant that those offenses considered to be violations of the king's peace were significantly expanded, and the Normans continually added offenses of this kind. A significant factor in the growth of this list of offenses, as Lyon (1980, 189) stresses, was the king's "need of money; to increase his income the king only needed to use his prerogative and throw his jurisdiction over another offense." The Norman kings also brought the concept of felony to England, by making it a feudal crime for a vassal to betray or commit treachery against a feudal lord. Feudal felonies were punishable by death, and all the felon's property was forfeited to the lord. Soon, felony developed a broader meaning described by Lyon (1980, 190): "Again royal greed seems to be the best explanation for the expansion of the concept of felony. Any crime called a felony meant that if the appellee was found guilty his possessions escheated to the king. The more crimes called felonies, the greater the income, and so the list of felonies continued to grow throughout the twelfth century." During Henry I's reign, an attempt was made to translate the codes of the Saxon king, Edward. Three other law books were added to the translations. Pollock and Maitland (1959, vol. 1, 106) conclude that, "These law books have…one main theme… An offense, probably some violent offense, has been committed. Who then is to get money, and how much money, out of the offender." Revenues from law enforcement and their allocation were obviously the most important consideration in royal law at this time.

With the Norman's undermining of the Anglo-Saxon restitution-based legal system, one of the most powerful positive incentives to cooperate in law enforcement disappeared. Common-access benefits, such as deterrence, remained, as did some private benefits, such as the potential for revenge. But the remaining private benefits apparently were not sufficient to induce voluntary cooperation, particularly given other disincentives discussed below. Many of the hundreds ceased functioning altogether under William, for example, although other local associations took over some of the non-policing functions of the hundreds, such as road maintenance as noted below.[10] Thus, Norman kings were forced to attempt to establish new incentives and institutions in order to collect their profits from justice. The Normans instituted a local arrangement called the frankpledge, with similar functions to an Anglo-Saxon tithing. Based on coercively mandated requirements rather than positive incentives, the frankpledge ordered to pursue offenders and ensure the appearance of members in court where the victims were to prosecute so the king could collect his fines. If a frankpledge failed, the group could be fined. Thus, the incentives to cooperate under the restitution system were replaced with threats of punishment. These incentives were apparently much less effective, however: Lyon (180, 196) notes that frequently, entire communities were fined.

Many institutional foundations of the modern English system of law were laid during the reign of Henry II, a man who Berman (1983, 439) describes as "hungry for political power, both abroad and at home." Pollock and Maitland (1959, vol. 1, 153) explain that when Henry II came to power, he consolidated and expanded his revenue-collecting system. By 1168, for example, circuit tax collectors who were also the itinerant judges had become a "great subdivision" of the royal court.[11] The itinerant justices conducted royal inquests regarding financial issues and issues of justice, and they transmitted royal commands to counties and hundreds. The justices also amerced frankpledge groups that failed to or refused to take their policing duties, fined communities that did not form all men into frankpledge groups, and amerced both communities and hundreds that failed to pursue offenders or to report all violations of the king's peace through inquest juries.[12] Such amercements were increasingly important.

Pollock and Maitland (1959, vol. 1, 141) observe that Henry and his judges defined an ever-growing number of actions as violating the king's peace. These offenses came to be known as "crimes" at about this time, and as Laster (1970, 75) explains, the contrast between criminal and civil causes developed, with criminal causes referring to offenses that generated revenues for the king or the sheriffs rather than payment to the victim. Indeed, Lyon (1980, 295) notes that "the king got his judicial profit whether the accused was found guilty or innocent." If guilty, hanging or mutilation and exile, plus forfeitures of all goods to the crown were typical punishments; if the accused was found innocent, the plaintiff was heavily amerced for false accusation. This further reduced the incentives of crime victims and frankpledge groups to report crimes, of course.

Laster (1970, 76) stresses that the loss of restitution and its accompanying incentives, and the potential for amercement for false accusation, meant that English citizens had to be "forced" into carrying out their policing functions. In addition to efforts to mandate formation of frankpledge groups, Laster (1970, 76) details a long series of legal changes, such as declaring that the victim was a criminal if he obtained restitution prior to bringing the offender before a king's justice where the king could get his profits, and creation of the crime of "theftbote," making it a misdemeanor for a victim to accept the return of stolen property or to make other arrangements in exchange for an agreement not to prosecute. In delineating the earliest development of misdemeanors, Pollock and Maitland only discuss "crimes" of not cooperating in policing, suggesting (1959, vol. 2, 521-522):

> A very large part of the justices' work will indeed consist of putting in mercy men and communities guilty of neglect of police duties. This, if we have regard to actual results, is the main business of the eyre...the justices collect in all a very large sum from hundreds, boroughs, townships and tithings which have misconducted themselves by not presenting, or not arresting criminals...probably no single "community" in the county will escape without amercement.

Laster (1970) explains that more laws were added. For instance, civil remedies to a criminal offense could not be achieved until after criminal prosecution was complete; the owner of stolen goods could not get his goods back until after he had given evidence in a criminal prosecution; and a fine was imposed for advertising a reward for the return of stolen property, no questions asked. Coercive efforts to induce victims and communities to cooperate in pursuit and prosecution were not sufficient, however, and crime was on the rise.[13] Thus, a public component to policing and prosecution inevitably developed.

Public Institution for Policing and Prosecution

An early development in the evolution of public policing and prosecution was the creation of the office of justice of the peace (JP) in 1326. Stephen (1883, 190) notes that at the time, JPs were simply "assigned to keep the peace," but in 1360 they were empowered "to take and arrest all those they may find by indictment or suspicion and put them into prison." JPs were appointed by royal commission for each county; and Langbein (1974, 5) observes that as with much of the local apparatus of justice, these men were expected to perform their functions without monetary compensation. Lanbeing (1973, 334; 1974, 66) also explains that over thirty statutes were issued from the late fourteenth to the middle of the sixteenth centuries, establishing various functions for JPs in the criminal process. For instance, while victims or frankpledge groups continued to be responsible for pursuing criminals and prosecuting most cases, after a 1555 statue, JPs were obliged to take active investigative roles in felony cases; to organize cases for prosecution, including examination of documents; to assist the assize judge in coordinating the prosecution at trail; to bind over for appearance all relevant witnesses, including the accusers and the accused; and to act as a backup prosecutor when a private citizen was not available.

The declining incentives of citizens and victims to pursue and prosecute left a gap that JPs were intended to fill. However, the growing duties of JPs, particularly in urban areas, meant that "voluntary" JPs were not willing to fulfill the need. In fact, Beattie (1986, 59-65) stresses that one of the deterrents to private prosecution was the difficulty in finding a JP willing to perform the criminal justice functions assigned to them by various statues. These duties were becoming increasingly time consuming and the rewards (the various fees a JP could collect, the prestige of the position) were clearly not sufficient to compensate for the time and inconvenience of the job. Thus, in 1729, the central government chose to financially support one Middlesex JP to provide criminal investigative and prosecutorial services; he became known as "the court JP." Middlesex was the seat of government officials and parliamentarians were located there. The self-interest motives of these government officials in transferring the cost of law enforcement onto taxpayers certainly comes into question. They were the first to benefit from such expenditures at any rate.

Little record of the first court JP remains, but Langbein (1983, 63) explains that the second, Henry Fielding, along with his brother John who succeeded him in the position, appears to have had a dramatic effect on policing and prosecution in the Middlesex-London area.[14] For instance, George II began paying Middlesex and some London watchmen with tax monies.[15] Then, as Langbein (1983, 67) notes, Henry Fielding began organizing a force of quasi-professional constables in the early 1750s, known as the "Bow Street Runners," to seek out and apprehend suspects, assist in the retaking of goods, patrol, and infiltrate criminal gangs. Fielding was court JP so this group had some "public" status, but they were not a true public police force because their income came from rewards for criminal apprehensions.[16] Wooldridge (1970, 119-120) stresses that "Fielding continuously agitated for governmental financial assistance so his platoon could be regularly salaried...(but) Englishmen opposed on principle the idea of public policing during Fielding's lifetime. They feared the relation between police and what is known now as the police state."

In 1822 Robert Peel was appointed Home Secretary. According to Post and Kingsbury (1970, 13), Peel believed that "you cannot have good policing when responsibility is divided," and that the only way to consolidate responsibility was through government. But it took Peel some time to actually set up a publicly financed police force. Even after 1829 when Parliament gave Peel the authority and financing to form a London metropolitan police department, including Middlesex, of course, there was substantial opposition from the populace. Citizen concerns were apparently justified. Between 1829 and 1831, for example, Rocks et al. (1981, 6) observe that 3,000 of 8,000 public police officers referred to as "Peel's bloody gang" or "blue devils" who had been hired were fired. But support gradually increased in the face of cyclical upsurges in crime.[17] And, as Beattie (1986, 67) notes, once powerful individuals and groups began to see that they could shift part of the cost of their own protection to taxpayers, special interest support for public police began to grow. Some London merchants had organized and paid a police force to patrol the Thames River docks, for example, and the metropolitan police department absorbed this function, thereby reducing the merchants' costs. Public police also began to gain political power and expand its scope by, for instance, performing prosecution.[18] Distrust of public police persisted for much of the century, however.

V. Common Pool Problems in Modern Public Policing

The fact that the restitution-based system was replaced by a system dominated by public policing is not a reflection of the superior efficiency of government in production of a public good. Indeed, a clear implication of the analysis is that by taking the private right to restitution and increasing the private cost of cooperation, the only primary benefits of policing that remained for general citizens were common-access benefits. The one exception appears to be revenge. Another benefit was royal revenues, of course, but these revenues were not likely to benefit any victim or witness in any noticeable way, and as Benson (1992; 1993) explains, they ultimately disappeared under the pressures of interest groups politics. Consider two widely cited consequences of common property: (1) inefficient overuse or congestion of the common-access resources and (2) under-investments by individuals in privately provided resources used to produce common-access attributes. Both clearly apply to criminal law enforcement in the United States, which inherited much of its legal system from Great Britain, including the crime/tort distinction.

Common Access and Congestion

When resources are available in common pools, individuals do not bear the full cost of personal use, so they tend to overuse the resources. An example of the seriousness of the commons problem with public police resources is evident in the direct links that individuals and businesses have between alarm systems and the police. Most studies of such systems find a false alarm rate of well over 95 percent. Kakalik and Wilhorn (1971, 29) report that in Beverly Hills, California, for example, a survey of 1,147 alarm calls to which police responded found that 99.4 percent were not warranted. These false alarms have been attributed to several factors, including problems with equipment and subscriber error, but the argument here suggests another reason. Those using alarm systems do not pay the cost of each police response so they have no incentive to minimize those costs. And the real cost of these false alarms are the alternative, more valuable uses which are crowded out or must wait for attention-response to real emergencies, crime deterrence. More generally, if policing is a pure public good, then the demands of one individual would not prevent another individual from consuming the same services. In fact, however, the tremendous number of competing demands for police services means that many demands are crowded out. This is actually the type of "free" good that Minasian (1964, 78) is referring to when he notes that "explicit prices are not allowed to operate as either signaling or rationing devices, but resources *are* consumed in their production." The congestion that results means that individual police officers and police departments as a whole decide which laws to attempt to enforce and the magnitude of the effort made for each of those laws. This allocation decision results in selective enforcement, as some crimes are crowded out, receiving very little consideration or none at all, while other consume all the police resources.[19]

Under-Investment by Victims

Inputs to policing must include privately provided resources. Victims are particularly important inputs in the crime control process. As McDonald (1977, 301) observes, a huge portion of all crimes that come to the attention of police are those reported by victims. Very few arrests for property or violent crimes result from police initiated investigations or actions. Furthermore, without victim testimony, a very substantial portion of the criminals that are arrested would never be successfully prosecuted. Thus, successful production of the commonly shared benefits of crime control such as deterrence requires that an investment be made in providing the victim input. Victims themselves bear the cost of this investment, however, and they therefore have incentives to under-invest in the commons. Non-reporting can be viewed as a decision not to invest in crime control, for instance, and over 60 percent of the FBI Index crimes are not reported to police. One survey, reported by research and Forecasts, Inc. (1983, 105), concludes that 60 percent of personal larceny cases with no contact between thief and victim go unreported and that less than half of all assaults, less than 60 percent of all household burglaries, less than 30 percent of household larcenies, and only a little over half of all robberies and rapes are reported. Non-reporting is a natural reaction to the high cost of victim involvement with the criminal justice system relative to the private benefits obtained. It is not an example of free riding to consume benefits without paying. By definition, deterrence has not worked if there is a victim, so to obtain any benefits, they must bear costs.[20]

Under-Investment by Potential Victims

Non-victim witnesses and victims' neighbors are also important inputs into policing, but they have to incur costs of involvement themselves and their private benefits are virtually non-existent. A widespread popular perception is that large numbers of witnesses and others who could provide evidence regarding crimes choose "not to become involved." One tangential piece of evidence provides some insights in regard to the magnitude of their under-investment. As Sherman (1983, 158) emphasizes, private patrols and neighborhood watches are quite effective at crime prevention. Yet, such voluntary arrangements are not particularly widespread. A gallop poll reported by Sherman (1983, 145) indicates that organized participatory crime prevention efforts, including but not exclusively consisting of such patrols and watches, were only in place in the neighborhoods of 17 percent of the Americans surveyed. And non-participation is a problem for many of these organizations. After all, even without participating, individuals cannot access public police services or the deterrence arising from private patrolling of public streets.

This under-investment is crime control by witnesses, neighbors, etc. Obviously fits the idea of public good free riding better than the under-investment by victims, discussed above, but as Minasian (1964, 77) stresses, even this kind of situation does not mean that an alternative institutional arrangement cannot create a different set of incentives: "The concept of a *public good* has mislead people to infer the need for collective action for its production and allocation." Increases in private benefits from control, such as an expectation of restitution for potential future victims, or privatization of streets to allow exclusion, as discussed in Benson (1990, 209-211 and 243-244), could create incentives for cooperation, either in participatory watches or in hiring specialists. Indeed, Benson (1990, 211-213) explains that there were over twice as many private police in the United States today as there are public police, and a substantial majority of these private police are employed as watchmen or security officers in order to prevent crime. They may produce common pool benefits for others in the vicinity, but in fact, deterrence from watching actually tends to be localized, as it probably was with the Anglo-Saxon tithing. At any rate, the private benefits of such crime prevention clearly must also be substantial.[21]

Even if the deterrence aspect of policing might be labeled as public goods, perhaps because non-payers cannot be excluded from public streets, it is not clear that public police effectively produce it. After all, legislators do not enjoy a clear information source like prices when determining how to allocate publicly employed resources, so they often use some statistical representation of the "quality" of work being done. The number of crimes deterred cannot be determined, for example, but as Sherman (1983, 156) notes, arrests is a natural measure of police output, and this is a primary measure that police focus on in their lobbying efforts for expanded budgets. Given this emphasis on arrest statistics, police have incentives to wait until a crime is committed in order to make an arrest, and indeed, after an extensive study of police performance, Sherman concludes (1983, 149): "Instead of *watching to prevent crime*, motorized police patrol [is] a process of merely *waiting to respond* to crime." In fact, Sherman (1983, 151) explains that about half of an officer's time is spent in preventative patrolling, presumably to produce the public good of deterrence, but systematic observation indicates that such time is largely occupied with conversations between officers, personal errands, and sitting in parked cars on side streets. In other words, police manpower is being allocated to focus on measurable outputs in the form of arrests while sacrificing unmeasurable outputs in the form of crime prevention, just as Lindsay (1976) explains other bureaucracies do. An increase in the probability of arrest does not deter some crime, of course—see Benson et al. (1992) for example. The suggestion made here and in Sherman (1983), however is that a more effective way to deter crime would be for police to actively watch. As Minasian (1964, 77) emphasizes, the "real problem" is the choice between alternative intuitional arrangements, and although none "will reside in the ideal world of Pareto," some will come closer to maximizing the value of scarce resources than others will. When a private security firm is hired to protect a neighborhood or business, for example, the price that consumers are willing to pay measures effectiveness, and that firm has incentives to deter crime through watching and wariness.

VI. Highways

The public-good free-rider argument is an ex post rationalization for public provision of policing rather than an ex ante explanation for its development. The same is apparently true of highways, as Albert (1972, 3) explains: "In England the various transport sectors developed gradually and were controlled almost entirely by private enterprise." Direct evidence of the extent and quality of roads in Britain between the Roman occupation and the twelfth or thirteenth century is almost non-existent, but a good deal can be inferred from various travel records.[22] For instance, Gregory (1932, 94) and Parkes (1925, 5) observe that records of military marches demonstrate that at least some roads were in good condition. Similarly, Hindle (1982, 193) explains that Anglo-Saxon and early Norman kings and their courts "also moved incessantly around the kingdom," thus requiring passable roads to carry what Stenton (1936, 6) notes was a "very sizable company." Representatives of the king, including tax collectors and judges, and of the church with its widespread holdings, also traveled extensively. Furthermore, as Gregory (1932, 95) and Willan (1976, 13) both point out, England had fairly steady advances in population and in culture during this period, and internal trade was expanding, all requiring increasingly extensive internal communications. Clearly, as Stenton (1936, 21) concludes, the road network in medieval England was adequate for "the requirements of an age of notable economic activity, and it made possible a centralization of national government to which there was no parallel in western Europe." However, the roads were not created nor maintained by the state.

While considerable long-distance travel occurred in the early medieval period, Beresford and St. Joseph (1979, 273) note that "most medieval roads were entirely local in purpose with an ambition no higher than to serve the villagers' immediate wants. There was need for lanes to provide access to holdings in the fields; to take loaded wagons to the windmill or the watermill in the meadows; to reach the woodland with its timber, its fruit and its pannage for swine; to take the flock to the common pastures and heaths." Indeed, most of the benefits of were internal to a hundred. According to Webb and Webb (1963, 5), there is no actual documentation of local road maintenance and production before manorial records began to be produced in the twelfth and thirteenth centuries, but several inferences can be drawn from customary law. First, as Webb and Webb (1963, 6-7) observe, those with customary obligations to maintain roads were primarily responsible for removing any impediments to travel such as overhanging trees, hedges, logs, and water through a drainage ditch and/or building up of the roadway. Second, some of the property rights to the land over which a road passed belonged to the owner of the land on either side of the road: Pawson (1977, 66) also stresses that one customary Anglo-Saxon right to that property was assigned to the commons: "The right of passage was a communal right." Indeed, Jackman (1966, 5) explains that the concept of the "highway" referred to this customary right of passage rather than to the roadway or path itself. Third, Jackman (1966, 4) also points out that the manorial records indicate that all landowners were obliged to the hundred, and later to the parish, to watch over the roads on their land and keep them clear of obstructions. Thus, as Jackman (1966, 33) explains, the hundred and/or parish was responsible for seeing that its members maintained the roadways over their land, although Bodey (1971, 14) notes that the actual need for enforcement was rare. Individuals apparently cleared roads in recognition of the many benefits of neighborhood cooperation outlined above and of other factors discussed below.

As long distance travel increased, particularly by merchants and by representatives of the church and government, the need for good connections between different communities' road networks increased. But most local communities had relatively little interest in building and maintaining connecting arteries and bridges.[23] Of the three groups most in need of good inter-community connections, however, it was the church and the merchant community that took up the task, not the government.

Merchants and Monasteries

Jackman (1966, 15-16 and 30-32), Gregory (1932, 97-98) and Pawson (1977, 72-73) provide numerous examples of merchant organizations contributing to the construction and/or maintenance of roads, and especially bridges. Indeed, some guilds and wealthy benefactors continued supporting bridges and roads well into eighteenth century, as Pawson (1977, 73) explains:

> Many private improvements were, of course, carried out purely in self-interest. New roads were built to promote the exploitation of mineral wealth within estates, and to enable landowners to divert existing highways... Sometimes an economic interest led to improvements in the surrounding area, benefiting everyone... However, when there was little direct return to those involved in private schemes, there efforts were primarily for the social good. It was illegal for a toll to be charged on a public highway without the consent of parliament so it was not possible to charge those who benefited from such works except by voluntary means.

However, there were actually some very important rewards for such local benefactors in the form of local prestige and respect. After all, as Hindle (1982, 207) stresses, roads played a very significant role in determining the success of a town and its established markets, so other members of the community would tend to be very grateful to someone who aided the community in this way. Building and maintaining roads and bridges was an investment in reputation, not unlike advertisers who pay for television programming to be broadcast free of charge as discussed in Minasian (1964).[24] And for Christians, even more significant personal benefits were anticipated.

The medieval church had considerable demands for long-distance travel. The church encouraged pilgrimages and maintained frequent tours by peripatetic preachers and friars. Perhaps the most significant source of church travel was the monasteries, however: as Gregory (1932. 95) and Jackman (1966, 8) both note, the monasteries' scattered estates required constant visits. Thus, Jackman (1966, 8) emphasizes that the church promulgated the belief that care of the roads was "a work of Christian beneficence, well pleasing to God." This created incentives for private citizens to aid in the maintenance of roads and bridges and Jackman (1966, 16) observes that the bishops' registers throughout England provide ample evidence of such activity. Indeed, Jackman (1966, 15) and La Mar (1960, 13) both find that it was not uncommon for bequests to be left for the construction or maintenance of a road or bridge. More importantly, as Jackman (1966, 30-31) stresses, the monks were assigned, by custom, the responsibility of maintaining the roads and they willing took on the task because it "was a pious work highly to be commended." Furthermore, by promulgating such beliefs, the church hierarchy created incentives for local parishioners to maintain roads throughout the country, thus explaining the longstanding customary obligation that local parishes had for road maintenance, as Jackman (1966, 30) and Pawson (1977. 68) explain.[25] Indeed, with the breakdown of the hundreds under the Normans, the parishes apparently took on the major obligations of road maintenance, with the aid, encouragement, and where necessary, supervision of the monasteries and bishops.

The various groups and individuals who maintained roads in England and prior to 1500 were apparently quite effective, as suggested in Darby (1973, 174 and 287), given the technology available. The system of voluntary road maintenance, based on the cooperation of the monasteries and parishes, was ultimately undermined, however, by the almost continuous struggle for power between the English kings and the church. As Jackman (1966, 29) points out, Henry VIII finally dissolved the monasteries in 1536-1539, divided their properties, and transferred them to "a class of rapacious landlords who would be slow to recognize any claim upon their rents for the maintenance of roads…the inevitable result would be a rapid decadence of many highways which had hitherto been in common use"; also see Gregory (1932, 93) and Parkes (1925, 7) for similar observations. While various individuals and guilds continued to provide support for some roads and bridges, the undermining of the incentives of the church to encourage its parishioners to maintain roads in general was apparently quite significant. The customary right of passage that had evolved, primarily as a right for members of local communities, apparently was, for some of those communities, creating a common pool problem that could not be alleviated without the monasteries. Indeed, Jackman (1966, 30-31) contends that the dissolution of the monasteries was the primary reason for passage of the "Statute for Mending of Highways" in 1555 mandating that parishes establish very specific road maintenance institutions.

The Mandate Parish System

Under the 1555 statute, two surveyors of highways were to be chosen by the JPs from a list provided by each parish. The surveyors were obliged to travel the parish at least three time a year to inspect the roads and bridges, see to it that landowners kept the roads and ditches clear of impediments, organize annual maintenance procedures for parishioners, watch for and stop wagons drawn by more than an allowed number of horses or oxen, and announce before the church meeting any violators of the statute. They were also required to collect and account for the fines, compositions, and commutations that arose in conjunction with highway maintenance or lack thereof. The JPs were to audit the surveyors' accounts, hear pleas of excuse for non-fulfillment of the statute's labor requirements, levy fines and order seizures for violations, and when necessary, collect a tax from the parish residents to cover an extraordinary expense. Furthermore, both JPs and surveyors were to perform their tasks gratuitously. All manual labor, tools, horses and carts needed for repairing the roads were to be provided gratuitously by the parishioners for four eight-hour days, and then six after 1563, chosen by the surveyors.[26]

In much of the country the mandated obligations of the highway statue of 1555 were probably unnecessary and in the rest of the country they were unsuccessful. It appears that roads were not deteriorating significantly in most rural areas where the benefits and costs of road maintenance were largely internal to the parish because through traffic was minimal. This accounted for perhaps 80 to 85 percent of the roads in the country. On the other hand, the mandated obligations were not sufficient for the maintenance of many of the major arteries of long-distance travel, particularly in the area of London and some other trading centers. As Parkes (1925, 6-7) explains, these were the roads over which government officials and merchants traveled, and where traffic by heavy wagons, long pack trains, and herds of cattle "kept the roads in a perpetual slough." It is recognized in Parkes (1925, 8), Albert (1972, 8), Darby (1973, 290 and 372), Webb and Webb (1963, 29), and Pawson (1977, 68-69) that parishioners were unwilling to invest in maintenance when the road was, in effect, a free-access common pool whose benefits were bring consumed by outsiders. Indeed, as Parkes (1925, 9) explains, the mandated investments were often made even higher because the best time of year for road repairs was also the busiest time of year for most parishioners. Many parishioners did not show up for the mandated work, others sent their children or a substitute instead, and as Parkes (1925, 9) reports, those who did present themselves, "often poor men who could ill afford wageless days—would spend most of their time in standing still and prating, or asking for largesse of the passers-by...so that they became known as The King's Loiterers, in derision of their earlier title, the King's Highwaymen." Thus, Willan (1976, 3) finds that JPs were obliged to collect large numbers of fines from those who were unwilling to work.

A long series of statutes followed in an attempt to create sufficient negative incentives for the parishioners and surveyors to do their mandated statutes in maintaining the common pool highways. Ultimately, as Pawson (1977, 71) and Webb and Webb (1963, 20-21) explain, none worked and the system of fines developed into commutations, relieving parishioners' obligations and allowing JPs to hire laborers to work under surveyor supervision. These funds proved inadequate, however, as noted by Webb and Webb (1963, 36): "Indeed, what with the lack of any definite valuation roll or fixed assessment, the complications and uncertainty of the law, and the unwillingness of both Surveyors and Justices to be at the trouble of legal proceedings against their neighbors, it is plain that under the commutation system the greatest inequality and laxness prevailed." Thus, commutations were supplemented with a general highway tax after the mid-seventeenth century. However, Wenn and Webb (1963, 51-61) also emphasize that an even more important source of funds was generated by criminal fines levied through presentment or indictment of the parish as a whole for the non-repair of its highways. They (1963, 53-54) observe that some parishes were perpetually under indictment, and "At varying dates in the different Counties, but eventually...nearly all over England, it became the regular thing for a parish periodically to find itself indicted at the Sessions for neglecting to keep it's highways in repair." Parishioners chose to pay substantial fines rather than repair roads. Despite these sources of revenues, however, Parkes (1925, 30) and Jackman (1966, 48-49) both conclude that the quality of road and bridge construction and repair did not compare to conditions that had existed under the monk's supervision and encouragement.

Alternative Institutions: Tolls and Turnpike Trusts

Roads obviously do not have to be treated as common pool resources. Tolls can be charged and non-payers can be excluded, given appropriate property rights. However, in England, the right to charge a toll was severely restricted. Landowners could charge for the right to pass through private grounds, given that a customary right of passage had not been established, and Pawson (1977, 73-74) points out that enterprising landowners began to establish and charge tolls on "private roads," allowing travelers to avoid the "ill-repaired public highways." Furthermore, the king, and later parliament, could grant the power to collect tolls, and Jackman (1966, 9-11) explains that there is evidence that the merchants who formed local governments of several market centers, the burgesses, had requested and been granted the right to collect tolls as early as 1154. Tolls were, in fact, an important source of royal revenues, as Jackman (1966, 11) notes, but those who collected them often could retain some portion for their own purposes, including for road and bridge maintenance.

The destruction of the monasteries and the failure of the parish system to maintain the major long-distance arteries of the country left the government with few options. One was an attempt to ration the commons through various restrictions on how it could be used, such as weight limits, limits on number of horses, and so on, as detailed in Pawson (1977, 74-75). The local officials expected to enforce these laws were reluctant to do so, however. The second and more important approach was to loosen the central government's control over and claim to tolls so that charges for actual road users could be made by local groups. A long series of Acts were passes beginning in 1663 which established local *ad hoc* bodies known as "Turnpike Trusts." It must be emphasized, as in Albert (1972, 12), that these turnpike trusts were not a central government innovation, however. Members of local parishes, burdened by high road maintenance costs under the parish system, began to petition parliament for the right to charge tools.[27]

After about 1700 the process became increasingly standardized. Moyes (1978, 406) explains that a group of local landowners and/or merchants would accumulate the money necessary to fund a Turnpike Act in parliament and to carry the cost of the trust through its startup period. Most Turnpike Acts established a Turnpike Trust made up of a large number of important parishioners. The trustees were unpaid and forbidden to make personal profit from the trust. They were responsible for erecting gates to collect tolls, and for appointing collectors, a surveyor to supervise repairs, a clerk, and a treasurer. The funds collected could only be applied to the road named in the Act. These roads were usually existing highways, although there were some cases of new roads, particularly after 1740. The trusts were granted monopoly power over the road, generally for twenty-one years, so the common property attributes of the road were substantially reduced. As explained below, however, significant common property attributes remained.

Turnpike formation really began to accelerate during the 1740s and 1750s as Moyes (1978, 407) notes, and by 1770 Trusts controlled almost 75 percent of the eventual 22,000 miles of turnpikes. In Darby (1973, 374, 502 and 454) it is noted that the turnpikes were maintained using the same techniques as the monasteries and parishes had employed before, that only about one-fifth of the nation's roads became turnpikes, and that in general, the parish roads were not in any worse condition than the turnpikes. This does not mean that the same expense and effort was required to maintain the parish and turnpike roads, of course. Turnpikes developed into the parishes where the commons problems of overuse and under-investment by long-distance travelers were the greatest, while the roads in the remaining parishes were primarily used for local travel. Thus, at least initially, the turnpikes used conventional methods of repair, but as Pawson (1977, 107) stresses, the turnpikes used these methods far more intensively. However, some trusts hired paid surveyors who developed expertise in road maintenance, and after 1750 some specialists engaged in considerable experimentation and innovation.

The turnpike era came to and end due to a combination of at least two political economy factors. First, the structure and characteristics of the trusts created significant principle-agent problems. The Trustees were not allowed to earn a profit. The toll gates were farmed out, and while trustees were suppose to monitor the gatekeepers and surveyors, their incentives to do so were very weak. Furthermore, the Trusts had monopoly rights and there was no threat of takeover. With little monitoring and no competition, Hindly (1971, 63) notes that corruption was rampant "and only a small part of the money collected for the upkeep of the road was in fact used for that purpose." Second, there was significant political opposition to the trusts, from those involved in competitive transportation modes such as the river and canal barges, from trade centers that already had effective transportation connections and feared competition from other centers where road connections were to be improved, from some landowners and farmers who feared that better roads would make it easier for their low-wage laborers to be attracted away and from those farmers supplying local markets who feared that improved roads would bring in competition from distant suppliers. Therefore, Albert (1972, 12 and 24-29) demonstrates that successful Turnpike Acts always reflected significant political compromise, including long lists of toll-exemptions for some of the powerful individuals and groups who opposed each Act. Jackman (1966, 260-261) observes that large-scale agricultural interests and, in some areas, industrial groups, were particularly effective at obtaining exemptions. Often those who obtained exemptions were some of the worst abusers of what to them remained a common pool resource. Jackman (1966, 261) stresses that exemptions grew over time and seriously reduced the revenues of the trusts.

The combination of principle-agent problems and political exemptions meant that trusts were unable to fully finance road maintenance. Rather than solving the underlying incentive problems, however, the government began to empower the trusts to draw on "statute labor"—the labor parishioners were mandated to provide under the 1555 highway statute. Initially, the trusts were required to pay wages fixed by parliament, but Hindley (1971, 62) notes that later some labor was required without payment. Some trusts could even appropriate materials. Opposition to turnpikes grew, and turnpike riots occurred throughout the country: Albert (1972, 26) explains that the rioters were usually parish laborers required to work without pay, and farmers, miners and carriers who were not influential enough to obtain exemptions but who wanted free access to carry large loads over the turnpikes. Hindley (1974, 63) sums up the view of many regarding these events, concluding that, "What was needed, of course, was some mechanism of national road policy." Indeed, Hindley (1971, 73) goes on to state that, "Whatever other thoughts may be provoked by a study of the history of English roads during the eighteenth century at least we may be led to doubt whether the Englishman's much-vaunted love for personal liberty is not quite simply a dislike of efficiency and a scarcely secret love of violence. The refusal to countenance the expenditure of public money on road-building, or on a central and effective police force, guaranteed him a road system that was among the least serviceable and most dangerous in Europe." While there are numerous parallels between the development of public policing and public roads, the common pool perspective suggests a different conclusion than Hindley's for both services. Recognizing that these are common pools reinforces Minasian's (1964, 79) point that the outcomes reflect existing property-rights arrangements and that "alternative exclusion and incentives systems" would produce different results.

VII. Conclusions

According to Samuelson (1969), there is "a knife-edge pole of the private good case, and with all the rest of the world in the public good domain by virtue of involving some consumption externality," but a "slippery slope between private and common property" might be a better analogy. Indeed, when stacked against the reality of historical institutional evolution, the public goods concept appears to be little more than an ex post justification for claiming that the *only* efficient policy is publicly providing various goods and services, such as policing and highways, at zero money prices. In contrast, common pool analysis emphasizes that incentives arise because of the definition of property rights, and, therefore, it suggests an array of possible policy prescriptions involving the internalization of various costs and benefits through privatization of rights. Furthermore, this property rights perspective provides an accurate description of the historical evolution from private to public arrangements for the production of both policing and highways, something that the public goods concept cannot do; after all, as Samuelson and Nordhaus (1985, 713) explain, public goods could not have been produced by private institutional arrangements. A series of property rights alterations and limitations made by the government of England undermined the incentives of individuals to cooperate in the production of both policing and road maintenance, creating significant common pool problems that government production has not been able to overcome. Suggesting that these services are now public goods, even up to the point where crowding sets in, is analytically empty because, as Minasian (1964, 79-80) explains, "the theory generates economic analysis which is not based on the opportunity cost notion." Rationing of scarce resources cannot be avoided by declaring that no one can be excluded; such a declaration simply means that first-come first-served and the inevitable reality of congestion costs determine who gets what, or that regulations establishing non-price rationing mechanisms must be established.

Notes

1. Minasian (1964) criticizes the theory of public goods by examining the allocation of resources in production of television services, another of Samuelson's examples of a pure public good. Similarly, Coase (1974) demonstrates the fallacy of the lighthouse as a public good, explaining that historically, private provision was the norm in England (interestingly, Coase quoted and refuted the 6th edition of Samuelson's economics, but the quoted passage is unchanged in the 12th edition), and Klein (1990) explains that private associations produced highways in early America.
2. Barzel (1989, 64) emphasizes that a good or service can have many attributes and the bundle of rights associated with it can assign some benefits to particular individuals while other attributes are held in common. "Police services" clearly can be so characterized, for example. In fact, as demonstrated in Benson (1990, 201-213) many of the private attributes of policing, such as protection and property recovery, can be and are privately produced.
3. See Benson (1993) for an extensive discussion of the theoretical potential for cooperation under these and other circumstances, and Benson (1989; 1990-1991; 1992; 1993), Friedman (1979), Milogram et al. (1990), and Klein (1990) for specific examples.
4. The following description of Anglo-Saxon legal institutions is certainly not universally accepted by legal historians, in part because the written records from the period are quite sketchy, and in part because of the theory of legal positivism underlying many of the alternative views, wherein law is assumed to require a system of top-down command. See Benson (1993) for a detailed examination and rejection of alternative views, citations to relevant literature, and extensive support of the view presented here based on theoretical predictions, empirical analogy provided by contemporaneous legal systems in Ireland and Iceland as well as more recent anthropological evidence, and the admittedly sketchy historical date from this period of Anglo-Saxon history.
5. These groups had other functions as well. For instance, Lyon (1980, 83) notes that membership involved a surety responsibility, and Baker (1971, 10) explains that the groups provided dispute resolution. For more details, see Benson (1990; 1992; 1993), from which some parts of sections III and IV are drawn.
6. They also produced the functions suggested in note 5, and road maintenance, as explained below. They have been incorrectly characterized as an innovation of Anglo-Saxon kings by Lyon (1980, 84) and others, but see Blair (1956, 235) and Benson (1990; 1992; 1993) for counterarguments.

7. Institutions were developed to avoid violence even when a person was unable to pay restitution. Pollock and Maitland (1959, vol. 2, 441 and 449) explain that an offender was apparently given up to a year to pay a large debt, for example, and debts could be worked off through indentured servitude.
8. Some historians, such as Lyon (1980, 84) view outlawry and the blood-feud as the primary legal sanction prior to efforts by kings to force acceptance of economic restitution. Given the incentives and institution arising in this legal system and others like it, as described by Friedman (1979) and Benson (1990, 1991; 1993), however, blood-feud was clearly acceptable only after and attempt to go to trial, long before kings became active in law.
9. Blair (1956, 196) explains that Saxon and Jutish chieftains that led raiding parties into Britain were war leaders whom freeman chose to follow. Warfare apparently was virtually permanent, as efforts were continually being made to expand landholdings. Military ability won a small group of entrepreneurial war chiefs prestige and land, and their accumulated wealth allowed some to set themselves apart as kings. If a warleader king's successor was endowed with military ability, his kingdom would last; and if the king could establish a blood descendant as his successor, precedent for a hereditary dynasty would be established. Most Anglo-Saxon kings apparently did not presume to be lawmakers, however, and law enforcement remained in the hands of the hundreds and tithings.
10. Other private benefits arising from local cooperation also began to disappear due in part to Norman takings, so it should not be inferred that the end of restitution was the only relevant factor in undermining the hundred. For instance, the Normans seized much of the land in England and granted large tracts to Barons and the Church in exchange for support, and as noted in Darby (1973, 85), enclosure of some land soon followed. The land held directly by the lords, called the demesne, could be enclosed. Other types of land were controlled by freeholders who paid rent to the lord, and by the villiens who provided labor to the lords. Estimates from the Hundred Rolls of 1279 indicate that the demesne involved about 32 percent of the arable land at that time, as indicated in Darby (1973, 86). The Statute of Merton (1236) also permitted the lords to enclose large portions of the "waste," the high woodlands and unimproved pastures that lay in clumps around the arable lands, and as noted in Darby (1973, 98-99), grazing was significantly restricted in the vast royal forests and parks "in the interest of the chase." With increasing enclosure, the potential for straying cattle was diminishing. Then in the 1400s, as wool prices rose relative to grain prices, the lords evicted large numbers of tenants and enclosed large tracts of land, converting it to sheep pasture from crops and stubble fields upon which cattle grazed. Hundreds of local villages were abandoned, as explained in Darby (1973, 210-211).
11. The reduced incentives to participate in law enforcement meant that the king could not count on the hundred and country courts to collect his profits from justice. Thus, royal courts developed quite quickly. Pollock and Maitland (1959 vol. 1, 109-110) explain that the first permanent tribunal representing the king, beyond the king's own council, consisted of Henry I's financial administrators. The itinerant justices were another aspect of the king's effort to take on many of the functions of the county and hundred courts.
12. Henry II used inquisitional juries extensively, requiring them to inform the king's justices on various matters and make accusations. Sheriffs arrested and jailed those accused by the juries.
13. Indeed, the incentives for victims themselves to avoid the pursuit and prosecution functions were growing, so the failure of non-victims to cooperate is not very surprising. As noted above, unsuccessful prosecution was a finable offense, for

example. Furthermore, when a victim filed a complaint before a justice of the peace, he might have to pay for subpoenas and warrants if his witnesses and the suspect were not present. Beattie (1986, 41) explains that other fees were incurred for the recognizances in which he and witnesses were bound over for trial, for the clerk of the peace or of the assize for drawing up the indictment, for the officer of the court who swore the witnesses, for the doorkeeper of the courtroom, for the crier, and for the bailiff. Beyond these fees, the level of the cost of attending court was uncertain, because the length of the wait for an appearance before a grand jury and the timing of the trial were not known. A victim often had to bear costs of food and lodging for both himself and his witnesses.

14. Beattie (1986, 226) emphasizes that international military involvement served as a major impetus for the development of public prosecution and police during the eighteenth and nineteenth centuries: "The conclusion of wars...brought 'a great harvest of crime'...the peace brought back to England large numbers of disreputable men who had spent several years being further brutalized by service in the armed forces, without any provision being made for theirs reentry into the work force."
15. Parkes (1925, 35) notes that private watchmen had been employed for at least two centuries, and establishment of an unpaid watch had been mandated since Edward I.
16. Private rewards for the return of stolen property had been offered for some time, but beginning in 1692, public rewards for apprehension and conviction of criminals were offered in an effort to induce private sector pursuit, and a class of professional thief-takers or bounty hunters had developed. By 1792, seven other magistrate offices in the London area had operations similar to those in Middlesex.
17. The reason for the crime cycles in alluded to in note 14.
18. Public prosecution was also resisted for a long time, as Cardenas (1986, 361) emphasizes, because "a private prosecutorial system was necessary to check the power of the Crown. If not so limited, the power of criminal prosecution could be used for politically oppressive purposes." However, fear of public prosecution was primarily directed at the central government, so a localized bureaucracy was the natural organization to take on such duties. For more details on public police and prosecution, criminal courts, the end of "justice for profit" and other aspects of modern criminal law as they evolved, see Benson (1990, 43-83, 1992; 1993).
19. Participants in gambling, prostitution, and drug exchanges enter the transaction voluntarily, so victims are not demanding that the police correct specific offensive acts, and there is no direct evidence of crowding, such as files full of unsolved burglaries. There is, nonetheless, a common pool allocation system: demand filters through the political process. Some neighborhoods have no drug dealers or prostitutes walking their streets, for instance, while such activities are very visible in other neighborhoods. See Benson et al. (1992) for direct evidence of crowding. Also see Barnett (1986), Benson (1988; 1990) and Benson and Rasmussen (1991) for common pool analysis of policing.
20. There may still be some private benefits associated with public policing and prosecution, but they appear to be relatively insignificant. Stolen property is often not recovered, money loss is generally not restored, for example, and revenge is not very likely either. *Uniform Crime Reports* indicate that the portion of reported crimes cleared by arrest is less than 20 percent and declining, and only a small portion of arrests result in convictions.
21. As explained in Benson (1990), the private sector is still heavily involved in the production of policing services, of course, even though the close knit families and neighborhoods are generally not the institutional basis for cooperation. The fact is that contracting is another way to establish reciprocal relationships, and Benson

(1990, 357-364) stresses that a wide variety of additional private contractual arrangements can be anticipated, given expanded private benefits to crime control, such as restitution, thereby reducing the underinvestment incentives associated with policing services.

22. The Romans built "great military highways" in Britain, as Jackman (1966, 1) notes, and there is little doubt that these roads, largely constructed with "public" funding, were important transportation arteries for centuries. However, Jackman (1966, 4) goes on the explain that the Roman road system "was by no means so good nor so complete" as the road system in later periods. Also see Gregory (1932, 94) for a similar observation.
23. Some bridges were built and maintained by hundreds, however: Webb and Webb (1963, 107) note that the term. "Hundred Bridges" continued in use into the eighteenth century.
24. See Klein (1990) for an excellent discussion of the interplay between self-interests and social pressures in the private development of highways in the early history of the United States.
25. Religious beliefs were significant in the Anglo-Saxon legal system as well. When the guilt or innocence of the accused could not be determined from the evidence, the hundred turned to God as an arbitrator. Both parties would agree to perform an ordeal and accept the outcome as a decision, and the superhuman arbitrator revealed a decision by the failure of one of the parties to survive the ordeal unharmed. Without strong religious beliefs or modern sources of evidence, blood feuds might have been more common.
26. See Webb and Webb (1963, 14-26) for more details on this statute and others which followed.
27. For extensive discussion of the Turnpike Trusts, see Pawson (1977), Webb and Webb (1963), and Albert (1972).

References

Albert, William. *The Turnpike Road System in England, 1663-1840.* Cambridge: Cambridge University Press, 1972.

Axelrod, Robert. *The Evolution of Cooperation.* New York: Basic Books, 1984.

Baker, J. H. *An Introduction to English Legal History.* London: Buttersworth, 1971.

Barnett, Randy E. "Pursuing Justice in a Free Society: Part Two-Crime Prevention and the Legal Order." *Criminal Justice Ethics*, Winter/Spring 1986, 30-53.

Barzel, Yoram. *Economic Analysis of Property Rights.* Cambridge: Cambridge University Press, 1989.

Beattie, J. M. *Crime and the Courts in England, 1660-1800.* Oxford: Clarendon Press, 1986.

Benson, Bruce L. "Corruption in Law Enforcement: One Consequence of 'The Tragedy of the Commons' Arising with Public Allocation Processes." *International Review of Law and Economics*, June 1988, 73-84.

———. "The Spontaneous Evolution of Commercial Law." *Southern Economic Journal*, January 1989, 644-61.

———. *The Enterprise of Law, Justice Without the State.* San Francisco: Pacific Research Institute, 1990.

———. "An Evolutionary Contractarian View of Primitive Law: The Institutions and Incentives Arising under Customary Indian Law." *Review of Austrian Economics*, 5(1), 1991, 65-89.

———. "The Development of Criminal Law and Its Enforcement: Public Interest or political Transfers." *Journal des Economistes et des Etudes Humaines*, March 1992, 79-108.

———. "The Evolution of Law: Custom Versus Authority." Photocopy, Florida State University, 1993.

Benson, Bruce L., and David W. Rasmussen. "The Relationship Between Illicit Drug Enforcement Policy and Property Crimes." *Contemporary Policy Issues*, October 1991, 106-15.

Benson, Bruce L., Iljoong Kim, David W. Rasmussen, and Thomas W. Zuehlke. "Is Property Crime Caused by Drug Use or Drug Enforcement Policy?" *Applied Economics*, July 1992, 679-92.

Beresford, M. W., and J.K.S. St Joseph. *Medieval England: An Aerial Survey.* Cambridge, Cambridge University Press, 1979.

Berman, H. J. *Law and Revolution: The Formation of Western Legal Tradition.* Cambridge, Mass. Harvard University Press, 1983.

Blair, Peter Hunter. *An Introduction to Anglo-Saxon England.* Cambridge, England: Cambridge University Press, 1956.

Bodey, Hugh. *Roads.* London: B.T. Batsford, Ltd., 1971.

Buchanan, James M., and Gordon Tullock. *The Calculus of Consent.* Ann Arbor: University of Michigan Press, 1962.

Cardenas, Juan. "The Crime Victim in the Prosecutional Process." *Harvard Journal of Law and Public Policy*, Spring 1986, 357-98.

Coase, Tonald H. "The Lighthouse in Economics." *The Journal of Law and Economics*, October 1974, 357-76.

Darby, H. C., ed. *A New Historical Geography of England.* Cambridge: Cambridge University Press, 1973.

Ellickson, Robert C. *Order Without Law, How Neighbors Settle Disputes.* Cambridge, Mass.: Harvard University Press, 1991.

Friedman, David. "Private Creation and Enforcement of Law: A Historical Case." *Journal of Legal Studies*, March 1979, 399-415.

Gregory, J. W. *The Story of the Road from the Beginning Down to A.D. 1931.* New York: Macmillan Co., 1932.

Hindle, Paul B. "Roads and Tracks," in *The English Medieval Landscape*, edited by Leonard Cantor. Philadelphia: University of Pennsylvania Press, 1982, 191-210.

Hindley, Geoffrey. *A History of Roads.* London: Peter Davies, 1971.

Jackman, W. T. *The Development of Transportation in Modern England.* New York: Augustus M. Kelley, Publishers, 1966.

Kakalik, James S., and Sorrel Wildhorn. *Private Police in the United States: Findings and Recommendations.* Santa Monica Calif.: The RAND Corporation, 1971.

Klein, Daniel B. "The Voluntary Provision of Public Goods? The Turnpike Companies of Early America." *Economic Inquiry*, October 1990, 788-812.

La Mar, Virginia A. *Travel and Roads in England.* Washington: The Folger Shakespeare Library, Folger Booklets on Tutor and Stuart Civilization, 1960.

Langbein John H, "The Origins of Public Prosecution at Common Law." *American Journal of Legal History*, 17, October 1973, 313-35.

———. *Prosecuting Crime in the Renaissance: England, Germany and France.* Cambridge, Mass., Harvard University Press, 1974.

———. "Shaping the Eighteenth Century Criminal Trial: A View from the Ryder Sources." *University of Chicago Law Review*, Winter 1983, 1-135.

Laster, Richard E. "Criminal Restitution: A Survey of Its Past History and Analysis of Its Present Usefulness." *University of Richmond Law Review*, Fall 1970, 71-80.

Lindsay Cotton M. "A Theory of Government Enterprise." *Journal of Political Economy*. October 1976, 1061-77.

Lyon, Bruce. *A Constitutional and Legal History of Medieval England*, 2nd ed. New York: W.W. Norton, 1980.

McDonald, William F. "The Role of the Victim in American," in *Assessing the Criminal: Restitution and the Legal Process*, edited by Randy. E. Barnett and John Hagel III. Cambridge, Mass.: Ballinger Press, 1977, 295-307.

Milogrom, Paul R., Douglass C. North, and Barry R. Weingast. "The Role of Institutions in the Revival of Trade: The Law Merchant, Private Judges, and the Champagne of Fairs." *Economics and Politics*, March 1990, 1-23.

Minasian, Jora R. "Television Pricing and the Theory of Public Goods." *Journal of Law and Economics*, October 1964, 71-80.

Moyes, A. "Transport 1930-1900," in *An Historical Geography of England and Wales,* edited by R. A. Dodgshon and R. A. Butlin. London: Academic Press, 1978, 401-29.

Parkes, Joan, *Travel in England in the Seventeenth Century.* London: Oxford University Press, 1925.

Pawson, Eric. *Transport and Economy: The Turnpike Roads of Eighteenth-Century Britain*. London: Academic Press, 1977.

Pollock, Sir Fredrick, and Fredrick W. Maitland. *The History of English Law.* Washington, D.C.: Lawyers Literary Club, 1959.

Post, Richard S., and Arthur A Kingsbury. *Security Administration*. Springfield Ill.: Charles C. Thomas, Publishers, 1970.

Research and Forecasts, Inc. *America Afraid: How Fear of Crime Changes the Way We Live.* New York: New American Library, 1983.

Ricks, Truitt A., Bill G. Tillett, and C. W. Van Meter. *Principles of Security.* Cincinnati: Anderson Publishing, 1981.

Samuelson, Paul A. "Pure Theory of Public Expenditures and Taxation," in *Public Economics: An Analysis of Public Production and Consumption and Their Relations to the Private Sectors*, edited by J. Margolis and H. Guitton. London: Macmillan, 1969, 98-123.

Samuelson, Paul A., and William D. Nordhaus. *Economics.* New York: McGraw Hill, 1985.

Schmidtz, David. *The Limits of Government: An Essay of the Public Goods Argument.* Boulder, Colo.: Westview Press, 1991.

Sherman, Lawrence W. "Patrol Strategies for Police," in *Crime and Public Policy*, edited by James Q. Wilson. San Francisco: Institute for Contemporary Studies Press, 1983, 145-63.

Stephen, Sir James. *A History of the Criminal Law of England*. New York: Burt Franklin, 1883; 1963 reprint.

Stenton, Sir Frank. "The Road System of Medieval England." *Economic History Review*, November 1936, 1-21.

Tullock, Gordon. *Private Wants, Public Means: An Economic Analysis of the Desirable Scope of Government.* New York: Basic Books, 1970.

Umbeck, John. *A Theory of Property Rights with Application to the California Gold Rush*. Ames, Iowa: Iowa State University Press, 1981a.

———. "Might Makes Right: A Theory of the Foundations and Initial Distribution of Property Rights." *Economic Inquiry*, January 1981b, 38-59.

Webb, Sidney, and Beatrice Webb, *The Story of the Kings Highway: English Local Government*, Volume 5. Hamden, Conn.: Archon Books, 1963.

Willan, T. S. *The Inland Trade, Studies in Internal Trade in the Sixteenth and Seventeenth Centuries.* Manchester: Manchester University Press, 1976.

Williamson, Oliver E. "Credible Commitments: Using Hostages to Support Exchange." *American Economic Review*, September 1983, 519-40.

Wooldridge, William C. *Uncle Sam the Monopoly Man.* New Rochelle, New York: Arlington House, 1970.

35

Property Rights in Celtic Irish Law

Joseph R. Peden

"The laws which the Irish use are detestable to God and so contrary to all laws that they ought not to be called laws..."—Edward I of England (1277)

"Leviathan in swaddling clothes"—D. A. Binchy on the Irish Tuath

Introduction

It is impossible at the present time to present a systematic, coherent description of the ancient Irish law of property. The reason is that considerable portions of the sources have not been published in modern scientific textual editions and translations. The principal sources used repeatedly by historians in the 19th and early 20th centuries are the multi-volumed editions of the old Irish law tracts edited and translated by Eugene O'Curry and John O'Donovan and published posthumously by other editors between 1864 and 1901. While both these pioneer scholars were competent in their understanding of Middle and early Modern Irish, the language of the glosses and commentaries, neither was able to cope too successfully with the archaic and very technical terminology of the early Irish texts of the law—the oldest and most valuable strata for understanding Irish legal concepts and principles. The later editors of the O'Curry-O'Donovan transcriptions and translation were, with one exception, almost wholly ignorant of the Irish language, and the result was that their footnotes were misleading and inaccurate, their introductory essays teemed with misinterpretations, and the printed texts themselves were full of glaring errors.[1]

Scientific study of the Irish law tracts had to await the development of Celtic philology. This was begun in the early 20th century through the interest of the German Celticist Rudolph Thurneysen, the English linguist Charles Plummer and the Irish historian Eoin Mac Neill. These three undertook the first really competent study of the difficult Old Irish texts, and more importantly, they trained and encouraged younger scholars to pursue the very difficult linguistic, historical and juristic studies which would prepare them for further study of the law tracts.

Unfortunately, many historians not specializing in the study of the ancient Irish law tracts have been unaware of the textual inaccuracies of the O'Curry-O'Donovan translations and have continued to incorporate their older unscientific work, and that of their editors, into their own work. For example, one of the most commonly cited sources for early Irish history is Patrick Joyce's *A Social History of Ancient Ireland*, first published in 1906 and republished in 1913 and again as late as 1968.[2] This work is notoriously inaccurate; it has no sense of the fact that a chronology of at least 1000 years is being covered during which some changes in social and legal institutions took place. Joyce's book was used between 1914-1918 when the great French historian P. Boissonade was preparing his epochal history of social life and work in medieval Europe. Thus Boissonade speaks of "the soil of Ireland (belonging) to 184 *tribes or clans*...the clans held the land in common...no man held individual property save his household goods, and each held only the right of usufruct over his strip of *tribal* domain...in each *district* of Ireland the free population lived *communistically* in immense wooden buildings...they lived and fed in common, seated on long benches, and all the families of the district slept there upon beds of reeds...." One can see immediately that the writer is using the words "tribe," "clan," "tribal domain," "district" and "population" equivocally, leading to great confusion. Almost every part of this passage is incorrect or very misleading.[3]

We might ignore Boissonade's errors except they are typical of many other secondary sources including the *Cambridge Economic History*, whose editor Eileen Power, incidentally, translated Boissonade's work into English in 1927. Worse yet, this translation was reprinted as a Harper Torchbook in 1964 and circulates widely in American colleges, perpetuating errors dating back more than 60 years.

Even when native Irish authors like lawyer Daniel Coghlan attempted to write a systematic description of land law under the ancient law tracts, his work was described by a scholarly reviewer as "inaccurate and unreliable, of little value."[4] Despite nearly 50 years of persistent and rewarding scientific study of the Irish law tracts by professionally competent philologists and jurist-historians, a recent historical work appeared which ignores all that has been published on the problem of Irish land law in the ancient law tracts, and in a chapter entitled "Celtic Communism" repeats all the inaccuracies of Joyce.[5]

Under these circumstances, conscious of my own lack of knowledge of the Irish language, and keenly aware of the shoals that await the historian who is not expert in this highly specialized field of study, I have deliberately avoided all reliance upon authorities who are not themselves trained in Irish language and history. I am not presenting a coherent systematic review of the Irish law of property; I am presenting a review of what the most competent Irish scholars of the last half century have discovered since they applied modern scientific philological and historical standards of criticism to the ancient Irish Law tracts.

My survey of the literature indicates that (1) private ownership of property played a crucial and essential role in the legal and social institutions of ancient Irish society; (2) that the Irish law as developed by the professional jurists—the brehons—outside the institutions of the State, was able to evolve an extremely sophisticated and flexible legal response to changing social and cultural conditions while preserving principles of equity and the protection of property rights; (3) that this flexibility and development can be best seen in the development of the legal capacity and rights of women and in the role of the Church in assimilating to native Irish institutions and law; (4) that the English invasion, conquest and colonization in Ireland resulted in the gradual imposition of English feudal concepts and common law which were incompatible with the principles of Irish law, and resulted in the wholesale destruction of the property rights of the Irish Church and the Irish people.

I

Irish law is almost wholly the product of a professional class of jurists called *brithim* or brehons. Originally the Druids and later the *filid* or poets were the keepers of the law, but by historic times jurisprudence was the professional specialization of the brehons who often were members of hereditary brehonic families and enjoyed a social and legal status just below that of the kings. The brehons survived among the native Irish until the very end of a free Irish society in the early 17th century. They were particularly marked for persecution, along with the poets and historians, by the English authorities. The statutes of Kilkenny (1366) specifically forbade the English from resorting to the brehon's law, but they were still being mentioned in English documents of the early 17th century.[6]

The absence from the function of lawmaking of the Irish kings may seem startling. But Irish kings were not legislators nor were they normally involved in the adjudication of disputes unless requested to do so by the litigants. A king was not a sovereign; he himself could be sued and a special brehon was assigned to hear cases to which the king was a party. He was subject to the law as any other freeman. The Irish polity, the *tuath*, was, one distinguished modem scholar put it, "the state in swaddling clothes." It existed only in "embryo." "There was no legislature, no bailiffs or police, no public enforcement of justice...there was no trace of State-administered justice." Certain mythological kings like Cormac mac Airt were reputed to be lawgivers and judges, but turn out to be euhemerized Celtic deities. When the kings appear in the enforcement of justice, they do so through the system of suretyship which was utilized to guarantee the enforcement of contracts and the decisions of the brehon's courts. Or they appear as representatives of the assembly of freemen to contract on their behalf with other *tuatha* or churchmen. Irish law is essentially brehon's law—and the absence of the State in its creation and development is one of the chief reasons for its importance as an object of our scrutiny.[7]

The bulk of the Irish law tracts were committed to writing in the late seventh and early eighth centuries, and though influenced somewhat by the impact of Christianity, they are basically reflective of the social and legal principles, practices and procedures of pagan Irish society. In the early ninth century, the oldest texts were being glossed because the original meaning was no longer certain, or practice had in fact undergone developmental change. By the 10th century elaborate commentaries were being added which indicate that the texts were either so obscure to the new generation as to be inexplicable, or change had become so marked that the commentaries often contradict the text itself. Part of this confusion was due to the very archaic and technical language of the earliest texts and the subsequent change in the Irish language from what we call now Old Irish to Middle Irish. If we recall the marked differences between the English of Chaucer and that of Shakespeare, we will understand the difficulties of the brehon jurists over a comparable period of time.[8]

To complicate matters further, the earliest Irish texts reflect the existence of several different schools of law, each producing its own particular code or tract. While all the tracts are recognizably Irish in character, they do reflect local, perhaps regional differences; if the evidence were fuller, several local schools might be identified. As of now it appears that a northern and a southern regional affinity can be detected. The fact that in later historical times certain families of brehons were associated with specific *tuatha* or regions suggests that local variations in specific procedures and penalties were almost inevitable. But from the tenth century, the legal fiction arose that the Irish law was a unity and all contradictions were to be explained away by the commentaries. The multiple and competing law systems of the early period were now subjected to homogenization to produce what was considered to be a uniform law for the whole island. And this fiction, like the equally unhistorical claim that there was a single High-King of Ireland—the King associated with Tara—retained its hold on historians down to the application of modern textual criticism in the 20th century.[9]

The conversion of the Irish to Christianity begun in the fifth century was bound to affect profoundly Irish life and institutions. The Christian church was already very Romanized in its institutional and cultural conceptions. It was urban-oriented and, thanks to St. Augustine, had reconciled itself to the Roman conception of the State as part of the natural (if sinful) order of the world. In Ireland Romanized Christians found a wholly rural-oriented society with a barely embryonic conception of the State, and a well-developed legal tradition in which lawmaking was the special function of essentially private persons—a professional class of jurisconsults and arbitrators known as the brehons. Law and order, and the adjustment of conflicting interests, were achieved through the giving of sureties rather than State-monopolized coercion. The Church could not depend upon the Irish kings to compel their people to convert to Christianity nor could they use the State to impose Christian law on an unwilling population. Significantly, the conversion of the Irish was undertaken without State-directed compulsion and not a single martyrdom is associated with the Church's triumphant success.[10]

Without the instrumentality of the State to enforce its commands, the Church's impact on Irish law was still very weak in the sixth century; canonical texts of this period forbid Christians to make use of the brehon's court against one another. They are to resort to the clergy to arbitrate among them as in the pre-Constantinian Church. But the collapse of the Roman empire in the West, and the isolation from Roman influences, coupled with the rise of a wholly native clergy during the period, forced the Irish Church to integrate itself more fully into the native Irish institutions and culture.[11]

In legal tracts dating from the late seventh and early eighth centuries, the clergy are recognized in their seven ranks, with appropriate honor-prices, and other rights and obligations under the law. The right of free men to bequeath property to the Church under certain conditions was recognized, and the right of women to give gifts was also approved by the jurists. St. Patrick had mentioned the practice of newly baptized women placing their gold bracelets upon the altar as a gift, and his practice of returning them. He may have done so to avoid litigation as to their right to make such a gift at this early period when their legal capacity was dubious. The law also ruled out deathbed bequests to the Church as invalid due to possible mental impairment, and the laws on marriage and other sexual relations remained wholly pagan.[12]

The failure of the Church to impose its own will upon the Irish law is best appreciated if one considers the fact that the Church was compelled to create its own legal codes in which a wide variety of criminal and moral practices were outlawed and appropriate penalties assigned. The so-called penitentials of the Irish Church were later carried by Irish missionaries to the continent and became a vital part of the judicial structure of the entire Western Christian Church. Penalties ranged from set periods of prayer, fasting, abstinence, pilgrimage, hermitage, exclusion from the sacraments, and other spiritual acts, to a fixed scale of monetary commutations of these penalties. The influence of Irish secular law, with its dependence upon monetary compensation for offenses under law, seems clear.[13]

One way in which the Church did influence Irish law was by seeking to have the Irish kings and assemblies accept a specific written code of law composed by an outstanding ecclesiastic. The Annals of Ulster for A.D. 778 record that Bresal, Abbot of Iona, and Dunnchad, King of Southern O'Neill "confederacy," had agreed to accept the laws of St. Columcille, founder of Iona, as binding upon their peoples. This was something akin to a treaty or compact governing internal and external relations. The compact publicly committed the people represented here by their king to obey the new law. This is the closest that the Irish got to legislating a system of law. The law codes, always attributed to some saint, represent the intrusion of Christian moral practices into the customary law of the land—the brehons' law. They were largely concerned with ensuring better protection for the persons and property of the clergy, their households, clients, servants, tenants, and ordinary women and children. There were also efforts to impose Sabbath laws. But these new ecclesiastic-inspired codes were thoroughly Irish in structure and principles. As Kathleen Hughes has put it: "The general effect of Christianity upon Irish law was to modify it without dislocating it; its rigidity was reduced and the result was a strengthening of native institutions."[14]

The study of the law texts and the canonical texts has suggested to at least one historian that the existence of two competing law systems in medieval Gaelic Ireland reflected a more subtle tendency in Irish jurisprudence and practice to conceive of *Ecclesia* and *Tuath* as separate and alternate entities with each having its own rights, and relations between the two governed by contract. For example, a study of the development of the Church's manner of holding land suggests that it seems to have controlled some of its property as a sovereign entity—outside and apart from the authority of any king and the jurisdiction of any *tuath.* Some churches were very clearly held under lay proprietorship—the proprietor being a layman with the right of patronage. In other cases the land was given away without any restrictions at all—public or private—into absolute allodial ownership by an ecclesiastical corporation. In some cases familial land was donated with the consent of all the kindred but the abbot or cleric holding the benefice had to be chosen from the kindred of the donor. For example, ten of the first eleven Abbots of Iona were kinsmen of the founder, St. Columcille. Lastly, royal land—land which was attached to the public office of the kingship—was donated to the church with the consent of the assembly of the *tuath* in return for the clergy performing spiritual offices without fee among the people. These lands were apparently freed of all public obligations to billet troops, answer a call to arms or give tribute to the king.[15]

The Church continually pressed to free itself of all obligations to lay owners or public authorities. This effort accelerated during the 11th and early 12th century as part of the Gregorian reform movement and the investiture controversy. But as early as the 6th century, many monasteries were operating as virtual ecclesiastical *tuatha* ruled by their abbots. Daughter houses were established which recognized the abbot of the founding house as their "overlord" and the many houses and properties, tenants, clients and unfree dependents located over wide areas of the British isles and Ireland appear to be ecclesiastical principalities dealing with the secular *tuatha* as equals rather than subjects. By the early seventh century the Archbishopric of Armagh heads a federation of churches spread across the north and west of Ireland, while the bishoprics of Kildare, and probably Cork and Emly in the south, are following suit. Armagh claimed overlordship over any church that was free of obligations to an existing overlord—be he king, lay proprietor or abbot. By the 8th century the bishops of Armagh and Kildare, and the Abbots of Iona, Clonmacnois and Bangor were rulers over vast ecclesiastical principalities free of the rule of any secular authority.[16]

This situation continued in those parts of Ireland not subjected to English rule. For example, when the native Irish archbishop of Armagh, Nicholas mac Moel Iosa, received the notorious papal bull *Clericis laicos* asserting the most extreme papal claims to immunity from State control (issued by Boniface VIII in 1296), he called a meeting of the kings of all the *tuatha* within his jurisdiction, explained the implications of the papal bull, and asked for their oaths of affirmation. Apparently without any great conflict, they agreed to respect the immunity of the clergy, their property, tenants and artisans from any lay impositions—fiscal, alimentary or servile, and undertook to respect the right of the clergy to have all cases involving their delicts, debts or contracts heard in the bishop's court rather than the brehon's. They further undertook the obligation of acting as sureties to the church for the apprehension of anyone in their jurisdiction who failed to appear before the episcopal courts.[17]

While the Archbishop had no difficulty in getting the Irish kings to recognize the immunities of the Church, he ran into grave difficulties with the English king Edward I whose rule extended over parts of the province of Armagh. He was accused by Edward's officials in Ireland of wholesale usurpation of the King's rights over the Irish Church. He had appropriated to himself the custody of the temporalities—properties—of vacant bishoprics and abbacies; he had consecrated new prelates for these offices without the king's license; he had heard pleas in his court that by right belonged to the King's court, to the detriment of the royal prerogatives and revenues. Archbishop Nicholas defended himself by arguing that he had acted in accordance with the ancient rights (under Irish law) of his Church as in the days before the conquest, rights which the English king Henry II had sworn to uphold. Edward replied to that argument by imposing a heavy fine and ordering that his officials make sure no Irishman ever was elected again as Archbishop of Armagh.[18]

This is but one clear instance in which the property rights and the freedom the Irish church achieved under Irish law were to be radically reduced under the impact of English feudal and common law traditions. By the 14th century, the antagonism of the two peoples was so great that the English government forbade any religious order, monastery, collegiate church or cathedral to admit to its membership anyone of Irish nationality. Moreover, anyone who was Irish presenting himself for ordination to clerical orders in a diocese under the English king's jurisdiction was presumed to "have lived continuously among evil people and to come from an evil background," and was to be denied sacred orders. Thus were the native Irish dispossessed of their own churches in their own land to give places to foreign invaders.[19]

II

Let us now examine in some detail the character of Irish law and the role of in legal and social institutions.

Irish society was a precisely stratified, class-conscious society in which rank had legal and economic foundations, The earliest law tracts divide the population into two legal classes: the free and the unfree. The free are the kings, nobles and commoners—all those who own land and thus enjoy the franchise, a place in the assembly of *tuath*, and have a legal capacity to make contracts in their own right or through their father, husband or male kinsmen. Possibly under the influence of the Church, which had seven orders of clergy, the jurists subdivided the kings into three grades, the nobles and commoners into seven each. The grade or rank of a man was determined by the amount of property he owned and the number of clients he had. Since the clients varied according to his available wealth (see below), wealth was the principal basis for a man's rank in Irish society. The unfree were those who did not own land, thus did not have the franchise, and were usually household retainers or tenants at will of a landowner.

What is somewhat surprising is the fact that these ranks and categories were not fixed. The law texts say that "the free may sit in the seat of the unfree" and "the unfree may sit in the seat of the free." "Everyone may become free by his wealth and unfree by his lips." The free who become unfree are those who sell all their land or rights or body in service to another (slavery). The unfree in the seat of the free are those who buy land or the right to the franchise by their art (skilled craftsmen), their talent (bards), or by husbandry (tenants at will). This social mobility is reflected in the legal maxim: A man is better than his birth. The only class excluded permanently from recovering their free statues were those who had forfeited their lives for some crime, but were ransomed and kept as servile tenants by some freeman, But generally, wealth, talent or skilled craftsmanship were enough to make free status possible. In effect, economic self-sufficiency was the hallmark of free status.[20]

While some historians have been dubious as to the reality of the fine distinctions in grade or rank which the law tracts reveal when applied to the actualities of everyday life, I do not share their view. Admittedly medieval intellectuals in general, and the Irish jurists in particular, show a marked predilection for making numerically ordered distinctions in all sorts of situations. But it must be remembered here that the assessment of a man's property—its character and value (land, chattels, clients)—was absolutely necessary if he was to participate in the very elaborate system of suretyship which was the basic mechanism by which all law was enforced. And it also was vital to assess his honor-price—another essential part of the Irish system of justice.[21]

The honor-price (*dire* or *enclann*) was the payment due to any free man if his honor or rights were injured or impugned in any fashion by another person. It might be invoked for the violation of any contract, any act of violence to his person or that of his dependents, any trespass on his rights or property, or even a malicious use of "satire" without cause which damaged his reputation (usually the work of a bard or poet). In the oldest texts, honor-price varied in amount according to the rank of the victim, and the penalty for the offense varied, being fixed according to the seriousness of the offense at the amount of his honor-price or some multiple or fraction thereof. At a later stage of legal development, the jurists established fixed penalties for specific crimes and enforced them equally regardless of the rank of the victim. But in addition, the offender still had to pay the honor-price appropriate to the victim's rank.

Honor price was also essential in the workings of the surety system by which means all judgments of the brehons' courts were enforced. Since law enforcement was not a function of the state or king in the Irish *tuath*, it was entirely dependent upon each party in an action or suit providing himself with sureties who would guarantee that the judgment of the brehon's court would be honored. If a person was about to bring suit, he sought sureties to help him in persuading the defendant to submit to peaceful adjudication of the dispute; this might involve applying the law of distraint in which the plaintiff seized some movable property of the defendant and impounded it under lawful procedures until the defendant gave surety that he would submit to adjudication. If he refused to do so, the community would consider him an outlaw—and he and his property would lose the protection of the law.[22]

There were three kinds of surety: first, a surety might offer the plaintiff to join him in enforcing his claim against the defendant. Since Irish law did not distinguish between tort and criminal actions, all crimes or suits were punished by payment of fines and honor-prices. Thus the plaintiff—if he won his suit—became a creditor, the defendant became a debtor. The surety guaranteed payment by pledging his own honor-price. A second form of surety (*aitire*) had the surety pledge his person and freedom as a guarantee. If the party defaulted on his obligations, the surety had to surrender himself to the aggrieved party and then begin to negotiate his freedom by paying the debt and also the honor-price of the creditor for this new injury. Once freed he could of course try to recover his losses from the defaulter.[23] A third type of surety (*rath*) guaranteed that in the event the debtor defaulted the creditor would be paid out of the surety's own property. If the surety was subjected to loss, the debtor must pay his honor-price. If he defaulted, his honor-price was forfeited and he lost his legal status.

Because of the vital role that it played in the surety system, honor-price was one of the chief attributes of a person's rank and only men of full legal capacity possessed it in their own right. Wives, children and sons living in their father's house were protected by the honor-price of their husbands, fathers or male guardians. Sureties and compurgators—persons who gave oaths as to the truthfulness of contestants in a legal dispute—had to have their honor-price assessed because they were for-bidden to pledge payment of any debt beyond the value of their honor-price which was, of course, assessed on the basis of their rank which was in its turn based upon an assessment of their wealth. Thus ownership of property in all its forms was the basis of a man's legal status and marked the extent of his participation in and protection within the legal system.

The Irish law recognized three distinct kinds of contract: *sochor*, *dochor* and *michor*. A *sochor* was a "good contract" which had three qualities: it was a contract between two or more free men; these free men were legally capable to act (not insane or minors or otherwise restricted in legal capacity); and lastly, the objects exchanged were of "equal profitableness." In contrast is the *dochor* or "bad contract" in which the first two qualities are present, but the third is lacking. Here the seller has suffered some loss of value in the exchange. What appears to be present here is the intrusion of the Christian concept of the "just price," perhaps an early influence of the Church upon the law. But what is most significant is that, while failure to exchange at a just price renders a contract "bad," it does *not* render it invalid. An invalid contract—called *michor*—is one which is illicit or void because one or more of the parties had not the legal capacity to act in his own right or was not a free man. The moral dubiousness of the *dochor* is not the issue and has no direct legal impact. However, as we shall see, the legal distinction did have legal impact in cases where women executed contracts in the absence of their husbands, or men without the consent of their wives in some instances.[24]

As in so many ancient societies, in Ireland many economic transactions took place under the guise of a contractual relationship known as clientship. In Irish law, clientship was of two distinct types—free and base—distinguished from one another by the type of services required by each. Free clientship (*soer-celsine*) was the grant by a king or noble to another free man of livestock in return for the payment of a "rent" of 1/3 of the value of the livestock to be paid annually for 7 years. At the end of that time, the client became sole and absolute owner of the livestock and his clientship terminated. All classes of free men were eligible to become free clients without any loss of legal status, franchise or honor-price. The only other obligations were that the free client did homage to his "lord" or creditor by standing in his presence and by attending him on certain ceremonial occasions. Since a noble's or a king's rank depended in part on the number of clients that he had attending him, the Irish upper classes invested a large part of their assets in acquiring as many clients as they could afford. This gave them increased social and legal status, and probably increased their political power in the assemblies as well. It also raised the value of their honor-price, thereby increasing their capacity to act as sureties and compurgators.

The base client was also a free man, an owner of some land, but usually a commoner. He received a grant of either stock or land from a person of higher rank in return for the payment of an annual rent in kind (a food-rent) proportionate in value to the value of the borrowed land or stock. In addition he owed specified labor services to his "lord" or creditor, and this is why his clientship was "base."

The Irish apparently considered that laboring for another man somehow impugned one's honor because the "lord" had to pay the base client upon the initiation of the contract the value of his honor-price. In return the "lord" was entitled to receive a percentage of the base client's honor-price and other compensation paid to him if he sustained any injury or violence resulting in a legal settlement. The base client thus remained a free man and could terminate his base clientship at any time upon returning the "lord's" property and compensating him for any possible losses.[25]

The Anglo-Norman invasion of Ireland in the late 12th century and the subsequent partial conquest of its territory was to have a detrimental effect upon the status and legal rights of the Irish clients, particularly on those who were base. Neither form of Irish clientship was equivalent to Anglo-Norman vassalage. Free clientship was essentially a form of commercial contract in which the purchaser bought livestock on a deferred time payment system. He remained free in legal status and the contract was terminable at the end of seven years or even earlier if paid in full. No one could mistake this for a feudal bond of vassalage or a fief despite the free client's minimal social obligations to his creditor. But base clientship, where manual labor services were required along with an annual food-rent, was more easily misunderstood by the Anglo-Normans as equivalent to English villeinage or serfdom.[26]

In Irish law among the ranks of the unfree were a specific class—the *sen-chleithe*—who are the legal equivalent of the English villeins. They are hereditary holders of a parcel of land in return for uncertain service and pass as appurtenances of the land should it be alienated or sold. They are included as part of the owner's property for purposes of assessing his honor-price and rank. Another class of the unfree are the *fuidir* who are not "villeins" in Irish law but are tenants at will bound to uncertain services. However, they are free to move or abandon their holding upon due notice to their landlord, and may rise in social status or fall to the rank of *sen-chleithe* if they have had ancestors living on the same land for nine generations—an unlikely situation.[27]

With the English occupation both the *fuidir* and the base clients were reduced to serfdom under English law. They are called *betaghs* or *betagius* in the English documents from the 12th century onwards. The *fuidir* lost the right to leave his holding and the possibility of rising in status. The base client lost his personal status as a free man, his right to the ownership of his own land and moveable property, and the right to bequeath his property to the Church or others. Even the free clients seem to have suffered some loss in status as the distinction between them and the base clients was often ignored by the English in their efforts to seize the properties of the conquered Irish. Thus the English conquest meant a vast displacement and dispossession, and loss of status for most of the Irish landholding classes and tenantry as well.[28]

As we have already indicated, one of the most persistent myths of Irish history is the belief that a form of primitive communism prevailed in landholding. Due in part to the failure of the translators and editors of the law tracts published in the 19th century to use such words as "tribe," "clan" and "sept" precisely, later writers, particularly those dependent upon Patrick Joyce's work as a source, confused the lands of the *tuath* with those of the *fine* or family. In addition, Irish law recognized joint-ownership and co-tenancy as well as co-operative work ventures. All of these have been vaguely described in different places as "communal ownership" or communism.

In a very detailed critique of Joyce's work, Eoin MacNeill, one of the first professional historians who was also able to read and interpret the law tracts from their manuscripts with competency in Old Irish, pointed out that there was no evidence whatever to suggest that the lands of the *tuath* were held in common or periodically redistributed. Quoting Sir Henry Maine who had admitted that "all the Brehon writers seem to have had a bias towards private as distinguished from collective ownership," MacNeill wryly comments that it was hardly a bias—it was a reality. It was a myth of collective ownership that was the product of bias. There are only two kinds of land which seem to have been viewed as being without owners: mountain peaks and woodlands or forests which were not partitioned or appropriated. There was also the land that belonged to the king by reason of his office. But since the kingship was normally hereditary within a kindred or *derbfine*—four generations of males of which one had been a reigning king—even the royal domains had a semi-private character as they circulated in usufruct within the royal dynasty.[29]

The English government encouraged Irish rulers to surrender their *tuath* and its landed territory to the English Crown which would then re-grant it in feudal tenure to the Irish king who thenceforth would be a feudal vassal. The result of such a transaction in effect would be to transfer ownership of all lands from the allodial Irish owners to the English king and then as a fief to the new Irish vassal—dispossessing the people to the benefit of the Crown and the Irish former king. Needless to say, such Irish kings were swiftly repudiated by their people.[30]

Ownership of property in Ireland was generally absolute; but some instances of limitations were recognized in the law tracts. For example, there were three instances in which the rights of ownership were subject to adversative prescription. If two successive generations of landowners failed to challenge the right of a millrace to cross their land without receiving some form of compensation for the infringement, the millrace became the absolute property of the mill owner(s). The same rule applied to the construction of a fishing weir across a stream or estuary and the right of way of a bridge or plank roadway across a stream or bog. Also, the law recognized that certain personal "necessities" suspended private property rights in particular instances: a man might take a single salmon from a stream or a single drawing of a net from a river or lake without infringing on the property rights of the owners; he could also cut a sapling for a riding crop or the shaft of a spear or commandeer a wagon to carry home a corpse. The gathering of nuts or kindling from woodlands was free to all equally, provided the woodlands were not partitioned or appropriated for private use. Seaweed could be taken also under the same restrictions. As for wild beasts, they belonged to whoever killed them.[31]

A very common form of property holding was joint-tenancy. This was especially common where the kindred were acting as a close economic unit in livestock raising or tilling the soil. In a pastoral enterprise where summer and winter pasture were needed and large herds of cattle, sheep or kine required only a few persons to attend them in the fields, co-tenancy was a reasonable solution involving both division of labor and maximum utilization of land. The

Irish took a dim view of trespassing and neighbors were required to give each other sureties against trespass; in co-tenancy of land, the repair and maintenance of fencing was the responsibility of each co-tenant along the outer boundary of his own land; failure to keep it properly fenced compelled him to pay a fine to his co-tenants, and he probably forfeited his surety to his neighbor for trespass as well. Each tenant was required to supply some tool which was stored in a common place; each morning he was required to appear at a fixed time when the day's work on the fencing would begin. If late, another might take his tool for the day and he paid a fine. The co-tenants also took turns in guarding their livestock. To protect themselves against suit for negligence, the co-herders set limits to their personal liability before witnesses and gave sureties to each other. The losses due to attacks by wolves, gorings, and wanderings into bogs were provided against by these contracts and individual responsibility for loss thus established.[32]

A form of joint-ownership was used in the construction of mills. The owners were usually monasteries, kindred groups or individual joint owners. If a mill was wholly within the lands of a single landowner that would obviate the need for joint-ownership. But frequently the water for the millrace and pond had to be diverted from a distant lake or stream. This meant that the owners of the source of the water, and the landowners through whose land the millrace ran, had to be compensated for the infringement of their property rights. This might be done by payment of a single sum to the owners of the land or water resource, or else recognizing them as joint-owners with specific rights of use of the mill for set periods in varying proportions. The owner of the mill and pond and the owner of the source of the waters got the largest share, with the landowners of the land through which the millrace passed getting proportionately less. (It was noted elsewhere that the landowners had to allow the millrace and could lose their rights to compensation after two generations).[33]

The climate of Ireland is such that drainage is a major problem. Thus ditches abound for drawing off water, and for keeping cattle impounded. The occurrence of drownings was apparently so common that the jurists waived the liability of owners for drownings in ditches, or other accidental deaths in ditches surrounding cattle pens, homesteads, churches, or grave mounds, or in millraces and ponds, peat bogs or from footbridges. But if an accident was due to the failure to fence one's fields, the owner was liable to be fined.[34]

One of the more difficult problems in studying the Irish law of land ownership is the property of a family or kindred group. Mac Neill admits that here we may have "communal" ownership. By this he means that certain land cannot be sold without the consent of the *derbfine*—all males descended from a common great-grandfather to the third generation. Thus this group is also the normal range of inheritors and also entitled to the compensation for homicide for any of its members. While each member held and disposed of the fruits of his own parcel of land, some residual control was exercised by the kinsmen. When the land was redistributed is not clear, but some division must have taken place when a young man came of age, perhaps his share of his father's patrimony was transferred at this time. If he died without sons, it probably was redivided among his brothers. Sons were the normal and equal heirs of their fathers, and their mothers.[35]

Whether land was distributed in proportional share upon the death of any kinsman amongst all the kinsmen seems dubious. The fractionalization would seem very much against the interest of orderly management. Some writers imply this was the case, but may have been misled by a law tract dealing with the division of compensation due a dead man levied on his murderer by an armed raid into another *tuath*. In this tract, the deceased's compensation is obviously movable—it had been captured and taken from another territory. Also, it was divided first into three thirds—one went to the king and nobles of every grade above the deceased's; a second third to the members of the hosting other than the above; and the last third to the deceased's kindred. This last third was then divided by a series of apportionments by fractions among the kinsmen according to the closeness of their relationship to the dead man. This legal rule for a specific type of bloodletting should not be assumed to be the norm for the division of ordinary property. Thus the actual distribution of landed property may well have been confined normally to the immediate male issue, while the more distant kinsmen retained residual rights of inheritance in case of failure of direct issue.[36]

One result of the English conquest was the displacement of the Irish law of inheritance. Under the feudal customs of England the law of primogeniture prevailed and was also applied to Ireland. Certain 16th-century legal agreements have Irishmen trying to preserve the old system of equal sharing among sons, but these were not recognized in English courts, thus disinheriting the normal Irish heirs.[37]

One last look at Irish concepts of property right may be revealing. A 17th-century manuscript reveals a poetic dialogue between two contestants before a brehon. The first, representing the "men of Munster," claims they own the Shannon River and its resources on three grounds; the Shannon was conquered in the 11th century by the Munster king Brian Boru from the Vikings; that the river in its lower courses runs through their lands; and that in a previous case Brian's rights were upheld. The poet representing the "men of Connacht" bases his claim on the fact that the river was always recognized as theirs from the time of Patrick to that of Brian; that the passage of a river through the land of Munster does not make it the property of Munster, any more than a man traveling through Munster becomes thereby a Munsterman; that the judgment in favor of Brian was invalid because made by a foreigner (thus unfamiliar with Irish law); and lastly that the river belonged to Connacht because it had its source in that land.

The brehon decided in favor of the poet of Connacht. He held that "just as the offspring of every father belongs to the father and inherits his patrimony, the natural father of every stream is every unexhausted well from which it springs forth first." As the Shannon has its source in Connacht, it and its resources belong to the men of Connacht. The previous judgment on behalf of Brian is interesting also, and not repudiated explicitly. Brian as presumptive owner of the river claimed ownership of a jewel found in the gullet of a fish taken from the river by a trespassing fisherman. He won his claim since the fish in a lake or river belonged to its owner.

Rivers and streams and waters in Ireland are still held in private ownership—but by descendants of the English feudalists.[38]

III

A fair test of the sophistication of any legal system might be to examine the extent to which women enjoy legal capacity and property rights. By this standard Irish law in the 8th century may have had more sophistication than English law in the days of Queen Victoria.

Irish law was typically Indo-European in that it was patriarchal in character at the dawn of the historical period. In all the oldest legal texts women have no legal capacity to act or own property in their own right. They are under the tutelage of some male—father, brother, husband or son—just as if they were children.

Yet even under this burden, women were in practice straining to break the bonds of the law. The early law tracts found it necessary to mention that a husband has the right to rescind any contract made by his wife in his absence, even if she had found sureties to support it. The contract was deemed invalid, and the sureties as well. But the clear implication is that women were in fact making contracts in their husband's name in his absence, and the jurist who composed the tract must have been under some pressure to acknowledge the practice, for he specified that such an invalid contract could be validated if the husband neglected to repudiate it within 15 days of his return home or of his being notified of its existence.[39]

The legal incapacity of women is also evident in the earliest forms of marriage contract in which the wife is under her husband's tutelage. But already a concession to her appears. If she is of rank equal to him, she may interpose to prevent him making a *dochor*, a "bad" or disadvantageous contract (see above). Her intervention does not invalidate the contract; it merely suspends its coming into force until her son or husband's kinsmen can be informed and given time to act. The implication is that her husband is about to alienate property that is not fully his to dispose of. Even if she is only betrothed, a woman can intervene in some instances to prevent her future husband from acting, at least temporarily.[40]

Another somewhat important breach which opened the way for extending women's legal capacity was recognition of her right to give a gift of a value no greater than her honor-price—normally half that of her husband. Gift-giving is not a contractual act, but it implies the capacity to own property in one's own right. Specifically she had the right to give the "product of her own hands" to the Church.[41]

The greatest departure from the system of male tutelage over women is found in the law tract called the *Senchus Mor* composed in the early 8th century and reflecting the teachings of a school of law operating in Northern Ireland. There, as in so many other cases, one of the pressure points for granting women wider legal capacity was the natural desire of sonless fathers to wish to bequeath their property to their daughters. In the *SM* daughters are recognized as having the right to a life interest in the landed property of their father if he left no sons, or presumably grandsons of the male line. But at the daughter's death, the land, which appears to have been familial, reverted to the natural male heirs of the father's *fine* or kindred. As an heiress to such property, the daughter logically had to have the means to protect it; therefore she was recognized as having a variety of legal rights including the right to sue and be sued, to engage in distraint and even to make legal entry on disputed or unoccupied land by almost the same procedure as was open to males in the same circumstances. Recognition of life interest in familial land in certain circumstances also implied that she had full ownership of the product of that land, and the right to dispose of it freely. The older form of marriage contract in which the woman was under her husband's tutelage did not lend itself to such a situation, and it now gave way to a new form of marital contract which soon became the norm among the propertied classes. Called a marriage of "mutual portions," it required that each partner to a marriage bring to it a set portion of property which was to be held jointly by husband and wife, its profits being divided proportionately between them. In this joint ownership-partnership, no contract was valid without the consent of each partner, except when the contract "advanced their common well-being." If either party made a *dochor* or disadvantageous contract, it could be rescinded within 15 days of the other partner returning home or receiving notification of its having been made. Specific types of contracts mentioned in the texts include the hire of land, the purchase of livestock, the purchase of necessary household equipment or supplies, and agreement between kinsmen for joint tillage of fields. No object whose lack was disadvantageous to the joint household could be sold without mutual consent.[42]

In addition to the property which the marriage partners held jointly, each could own additional property, including the profits of their joint holding, in absolute single or sole ownership. The only restriction on the profits of their joint enterprise was that the wife could dispose of her share only to the value of her honor-price which was half that of her husband. This may have had some further restriction as to time limit but the texts are silent on it. The husband's share of the profits of their joint household was his sole property, but in certain instances his wife could dispose of it without his consent. She could alienate it to his advantage, but was subject to a fine if she acted without his consent. If he incurred any loss in the transaction, and she somehow made a gain, she could be sued by her husband for theft. This rule seems to envision embezzlement or fraud among partners.[43]

A woman could inherit property from her mother if there were no sons, but normally the sons were the natural heirs to their mother's as well as their father's property. If childless, a woman's property reverted to her nearest male kinsmen—not her husband—or she could bequeath it to the Church.

One of the most startling aspects of the Irish law was its treatment of the rights of women in various sexual relationships outside Christian marriage and their right to divorce. In one legal tract no less than ten different kinds of sexual union between males and females are legally recognized—each having a very precise legal character, each partner enjoying specific property rights and obligations. From a Christian viewpoint, some of these relationships are clearly polygamous, others irregular, some even casual or violent. Most legal systems in Christian Europe denied these women legal status and rights, and extended these deprivations to the children unless the father recognized them. The Irish law recognized rights of maintenance and support which vary in degree and amount according to the character of the sexual union. For example, in a marriage of mutual portions the cost of "fostering" or rearing a child is shared equally by the parents; but if the child is born of a bondwoman, or as a result of rape, or in secret, the father is responsible solely for its rearing costs. In some instances the male has some control over the woman's property rights and a right to share in her honor-price; in others she controls some of his property rights and shares in his honor price. The detail, extensiveness, balance and proportionality with which the rights and obligations of each partner are assigned in these very unchristian couplings is unique in the law tracts of Christian Europe.[44]

Although it has been suggested that this is another instance of the archaic and unreal character of the Irish law tracts, which could not have had validity in a Christianized Ireland, the evidence suggests otherwise. Throughout the medieval period, both Irish clerical and foreign commentators frequently denounce the Irish for their failure to suppress sexual promiscuity and adhere to the marriage laws of the Church and "civilized" societies. It is most unlikely that the Irish were more promiscuous than other peoples; but it was their unique practice of continuing to separate canon law from civil law that seemed so scandalous to other Europeans.[45]

Similarly, the Irish law recognized the right of divorce. A man might repudiate his wife for dishonoring him, doing him some injury or willful abortion. But, incredibly, the wife could initiate a divorce action against her husband! She could charge consanguinity, incurable infirmity, sterility, cruelty evidenced by lasting injury, slanderous remarks as to her character, abandonment for another woman, willful neglect in supplying the necessities of life, or abandonment by reason of his entering a monastery. None of the above except consanguinity was grounds for annulment in canon law. There were also some eleven categories of legal separation with respective property rights and obligations regarding the care of children and distribution of property. That these laws were not "obsolete" can be shown in the marital history of Gormflath. Wife first of Olaf, Viking king of Dublin, widowed, she married Malachy, king of Meath and High-King of Tara A.D. 980. Malachy repudiated her, and she later married and divorced Brian Boru, who also won the High-Kingship by replacing Malachy. Thus she had two ex-husbands still living when she became betrothed to a third, Sigurd, Earl of Orkney.[46]

While the history of Irish law between the 8th and 17th centuries is very sketchy due to the lack of surviving historical materials, occasional references indicate that women continued to enjoy an exceptional standing in law with regard to their property rights down to the end of native Irish culture and independence in the early 17th century. In the early 14th century there is reference to a woman acting as an agent for an English proprietor whose cattle have been "stolen" by some Irishmen. She is commissioned to mediate for their return—the Irish having in their law invoked the law of distraint on the Englishmen's cattle. There is even a reference to a woman sitting as an arbitrator along with a brehon in a suit. In the early 17th century the English observer Sir John Davies in his book investigating why the Irish were so hard to conquer remarks that the Irish are so savage that "the wives of Irish lords and chieftains claim to have sole property in a certain portion of the goods during coverture with the power to dispose of such goods without the assent of their husbands; (therefore) it was resolved and declared by all the (English) judges that the property of such goods should he adjudged to be in the husbands and not in the wives as the (English) common law is in such cases."[47] This is but another example of the destructive and retrogressive effect of the imposition of English common law on the legal status and property rights of the Irish people.

Conclusion and Summary

While a comprehensive survey of the Irish law of property and property rights cannot yet be written, we can already see that the idea of private ownership permeates those aspects of the law which have been subjected to recent study. The Irish frankly and openly used assessments of property as the criterion for determining a man's social and legal status, the extent of his capacity to act as a surety or compurgator, and to fix the amounts of compensation due him as a victim of crime or any kind of injury. Ownership of land determined a man's status as free or unfree and his right to participate in the public assembly. The needs of the Church modified but did not alter the basic character of native Irish institutions and law. While it secured for itself almost total freedom from lay ownership and secular obligations, it was never able to fully destroy the essentially secular character of Irish law as exemplified in the laws on marriage and divorce. The legal capacity of women showed exceptional development and gave women property rights in the 8th century that were centuries ahead of those enjoyed by English women. The fact that Irish law was the creation of private individuals who were professional, even hereditary, jurists, gave to the law both a conservative yet flexible and equitable character. Their power rested upon the free consent of the community in choosing them as arbitrators in disputes; and this made equity and justice more likely than in royal courts where the interests of the State and its rulers are paramount. The invasion and conquest of Ireland, the work of over 400 years before it was completed, was eventually fatal to the Irish system of law and the culture and civilization it expressed. The English State was incompatible with the Irish *tuath*; the English common law was totally incompatible with the Irish law. Ireland from the 12th century was a single land in which two nations and two laws and two cultures engaged in a constant struggle for survival. The end came in the early 17th century with the flight of the last Irish kings from Ulster and the new plantation of that region by Protestant Scots sent by James I—that most absolute of English Kings.

As for the native Irish and their ancient culture, the English official Sir Davies thought he said it all:

> For if we consider the Nature of the Irish Customes, we shall finde that the people that doeth use them, must of necessity be Rebelles to all good government, destroy the commonwealth wherein they live, and bring Barbarisme and desolation upon the richest and most fruitfull Land of the world.[48]

Notes

1. *The Ancient Laws of Ireland*, 6 volumes, 1865-1901. The most complete evaluation of the law tracts by a competent Irish philologist and jurist is D. A. Binchy's Rhys Memorial Lecture before the British Academy entitled *The Linguistic and Historical Value of the Irish Law Tracts* (London, 1943). Also, Binchy, "Ancient Irish Law," *Irish Jurist* NS 1 (1966), 84-92.
2. Patrick W. Joyce, *A Social History of Ancient Ireland* (Dublin, 1906), 2 vols. Reprinted in 1913 and 1968.
3. P. Boissonade, *Life and Work in Medieval Europe*, trans. by Eileen Power (London, 1917). Harper Torch book edition (New York, 1964). See pp. 78-79 of the latter.
4. See the review of Daniel Coghlan's *Ancient Land Tenures of Ireland in Irish Law Times and Solicitors' Journal* (March 10, 1934) Further comments in July 14 and Sept. 15 issues. The reviewer is anonymous.
5. P. Beresford Ellis, *A History of the Irish Working Class* (London, 1972). The author ignores all modern scholarship on the subject and rejects MacNeill's criticism of Joyce because he was pro-capitalist!
6. Binchy, *Historical Value of Irish Law Tracts*, 22 Also, Gearoid Mac Niocaill, "Notes on Litigation in Late Irish law," *Irish Jurist* NS 2 (1967), 299-307, and G. J. Hand, "The Forgotten Statutes of Kilkenny," *Irish Jurist* NS 1 (1966), 301.
7. D. A. Binchy in *Early Irish Society* (Dublin, 1954), 56-58. Also, Myles Dillon and Nora Chadwick; *The Celtic Realms* (London, 1967), 93 -98.
8. Binchy, *Irish Jurist* NS 1 (1966), 84-92.
9. Ibid. See also, Eoin MacNeill, "Prolegomena to a Study of the Ancient Laws of Ireland," *Irish Jurist* NS 2 (1967), 106-115.
10. The most authoritative recent study of the Irish church in the pre-conquest period is Kathleen Hughes, *The Church in Early Irish Society* (London, 1966). See chapters 4 and 5 in particular here.

11. Ibid. Chapter 12, pp. 123 -133 and Chapter 5, pp. 45-55.
12. Ibid. Also, for St. Patrick, see R.P.C. Hanson, *St. Patrick: His Origins and Career* (New York, 1968), 139.
13. Ludwig Bieler, "The Irish Penitentials," *Scriptores Latini Hiberniae* (Dublin, 1963).
14. Hughes, Chapter 14, pp. 143-156. See especially 149-153.
15. See paper given to Columbia University Faculty Seminar in History of Legal and Political Thought (1966) by Prof. Charles Donohue of Fordham University: *On the Senchas Mor, an early 8th century tract including material on Church–State Relations.* Also, Hughes, 161.
16. Hughes, Chapter 8, pp. 19-90 in monastic *paruchiae* and Chapter 11, 111-122 on Armagh.
17. J. A. Watt, *The Church and the Two Nations in Medieval Ireland* (Cambridge, England, 1970). 160- 169.
18. Ibid.
19. Ibid., 206-207 and 211.
20. Eoin Mac Neill, "The Law of Status or Franchise," *Proc. Royal Irish Academy* 36C (1921-24), 265-316. See here p. 273.
21. Binchy expressed some doubt on this in his *Historical Value*, p. 33.
22. See Dillon and Chawick, *Celtic Realms* (London 1967), 98-99. Also, see Mac Neill, op. cit.
23. Ibid.
24. Rudolf Thurneysen, "*Socher* and *Docher*," *Essays and Studies in Honor of Professor Eoin Mac Neill*, edited by John Ryan S. J. (Dublin, 1940), 158-159.
25. For a discussion for clientship, see D. A. Binchy, *Crith Gablach* (Dublin, 1941), pp. 78, 80, 96-97 and 107. Also, Dillon and Chadwick, 95-96.
26. Gearoid Man Niocaill, "The Origins of the Betagh," *Irish Jurist* NS 1 (1966), 292-298. Liam Price disagrees with Mac Nicoaill in ***Eriu*** 20 (1966), 185-190, but J. A. Hand is convinced by Mac Niecaill's analysis in his *English Law in Ireland 1290-1324* (Cambridge, 1967), 213.
27. Binchy, *Crith Gablach*, 105.
28. On *fuidir,* ibid., 93 Otherwise, see op. cit.
29. Eoin Mac Neill, *Celtic Ireland* (Dublin, 1921), 144-151.
30. On the policy if "surrender and re-grant" under Henry VIII see J. C. Becket, *The Making of Modern Ireland* (London, 1966), 18-19.
31. D. A. Binchy, "Irish Law Tracts Re-edited: Coibnes Uisci Thairidne (AL IV, 206-222)," *Eriu* 17 (1955), see p. 81 n. 9 52ff. Also, Mac Neill, *Celtic Ireland*, 170 ff.
32. *Ancient Laws*, IV, p. 372 ff.
33. Op. cit.
34. Ibid., 71-72
35. Mac Neill, *Celtic Ireland*, 152-176. Also, Mac Neill, "The Irish Law of Succession," *Studies* 8 (1919), 367 ff.
36. Mac Neill, *Studies* 8 (1919, 376-377. Also, Kuno Meyer, in *Eriu* 1 (1904), 214-215.
37. J. Otway-Ruthven, "The Native Irish and English Law in Medieval Ireland," *Irish Historical Studies* 8 (1950), 1-16.
38. Brian O' Cuiv, "The Poetic Confrontation about the Shannon River," *Eriu* 19 (1962), 89-105. The poem is dated to the 15th century.
39. D. A. Bunchy, ed. *Studies in Early Irish Law* (Dublin, 1936). This is the most complete study of the Irish law and the product of a seminar conducted by Rudolph

Thurneysen, the distinguished Celtist. See here D. A. Bunchy, "The Legal Capacity of Women in Regard to Contracts," *SEIL*, pp. 207-234, especially 211-216.

40. Bunchy, *SEIL*, 226-228.
41. Ibid., 226-227 and on 209 note 1. Women could act as sureties under certain limitations, see pp. 232-234. On gifts see Myles Dillon, "The Relationship of Mother and Son, Father and Daughter and the Law of Inheritance," *SEIL*, 129-179 *passim*.
42. Binchy, *SEIL*, 226-228.
43. Ibid., 227-230. Some texts indicate daughters may inherit some kinds of chattels from their fathers, Dillon, *SEIL*, 171, n3.
44. Nancy Power, "Classes of Women Described in the Senchas Mor," *Studies in Early Irish Law (SEIL)*, 81-108.
45. For a discussion of Irish marriage law and 12th century criticisms of it, A. Gwynn, "The First Synod of Cashel," *Irish Ecclesiastical Review* 66 (1945), 81-92; 67 (1946), 109-122.
46. August Knoch, "Die Eheschudung in alter Irischen Recht," *Studies in Early Irish Law*, 235-268. For Gormflath, see Edmund Curtis, *A History of Ireland* (Dublin, 1950), 28-30.
47. A quotation from Sir John Davies on "The Irish Custome de Gravelkind" in a review of *Studies in Irish Law* edited by D. A. Binchy in *The Irish Law Times*, 15 August, 1936.
48. Sir John Davies, *A discovery of the true causes why Ireland was never entirely subdued* (London, 1612), 165.

36

Private Creation and Enforcement of Law—A Historical Case

David Friedman[1]

> Iceland is known to men as a land of volcanoes, geysers and glaciers. But it ought to be no less interesting to the student of history as the birthplace of a brilliant literature in poetry and prose, and as the home of a people who have maintained for many centuries a high level of intellectual cultivation. It is an almost unique instance of a community whose culture and creative power flourished independently of any favouring material conditions and indeed under conditions in the highest degree unfavourable. Nor ought it to be less interesting to the student of politics and laws as having produced a Constitution unlike any other whereof records remain and a body of law so elaborate and complex, that it is hard to believe that it existed among men whose chief occupation was to kill one another.—James Bryce, *Studies in History and Jurisprudence* 263 (1901)

I. Introduction[2]

The purpose of this paper is to examine the legal and political institutions of Iceland from the tenth to the thirteenth centuries. They are of interest for two reasons. First, they are relatively well documented; the sagas were written by people who had lived under that set of institutions[3] and provide a detailed inside view of their workings. Legal conflicts were of great interest to the medieval Icelanders: Njal, the eponymous hero of the most famous of the sagas,[4] is not a warrior but a lawyer—"so skilled in law that no one was considered his equal." In the action of the sagas, law cases play as central a role as battles.

Second, medieval Icelandic institutions have several peculiar and interesting characteristics; they might almost have been invented by a mad economist to test the lengths to which market systems could supplant government in its most fundamental functions. Killing was a civil offense resulting in a fine paid to the survivors of the victim. Laws were made by a "parliament," seats in which were a marketable commodity. Enforcement of law was entirely a private affair. And yet these extraordinary institutions survived for over three hundred years, and the society in which they survived appears to have been in many ways an attractive one. Its citizens were, by medieval standards, free; differences in status based on rank or sex were relatively small;[5] and its literary output in relation to its size has been compared, with some justice, to that of Athens.[6]

While these characteristics of the Icelandic legal system may seem peculiar, they are not unique to medieval Iceland. The wergeld—the fine for killing a man—was an essential part of the legal system of Anglo-Saxon England, and still exists in New Guinea.[7] The sale of legislative seats has been alleged in many societies and existed openly in some. Private enforcement existed both in the American West[8] and in pre-nineteenth-century Britain; a famous character of eighteenth-century fiction, Mr. Peachum in Gay's "Beggar's Opera," was based on Jonathan Wild, self-titled "Thief-Taker General," who profitably combined the professions of thief-taker, recoverer of stolen property, and large-scale employer of thieves for eleven years, until he was finally hanged in 1725.[9] The idea that law is primarily private, that most offenses are offenses against specific individuals or families, and that punishment of the crime is primarily the business of the injured party seems to be common to many early systems of law and has been discussed at some length by Maine with special reference to the early history of Roman law.[10]

Medieval Iceland, however, presents institutions of private enforcement of law in a purer form than any other well-recorded society of which I am aware. Even early Roman law recognized the existence of crimes, offenses against society rather than against any individual, and dealt with them, in effect, by using the legislature as a special court.[11] Under Anglo-Saxon law killing was an offense against the victim's family, his lord, and the lord of the place whose peace had been broken; wergeld was paid to the family, manbote to the crown, and fightwite to the respective lords.[12] British thief-takers in the eighteenth century were motivated by a public reward of £40 per thief.[13] All of these systems involved some combination of private and public enforcement. The Icelandic system developed without any central authority comparable to the Anglo-Saxon king;[14] as a result, even where the Icelandic legal system recognized an essentially "public" offense, it dealt with it by giving some individual (in some cases chosen by lot from those affected) the right to pursue the case and collect the resulting fine, thus fitting it into an essentially private system.

In the structure of its legislature, Iceland again presents an almost pure form of an institution, elements of which exist elsewhere. British pocket boroughs, like Icelandic godord, represented marketable seats in the legislature, but Parliament did not consist entirely of representatives from pocket boroughs. All godord were marketable and (with the exception, after Iceland's conversion to Christianity, of the two Icelandic bishops) all seats in the lögrétta were held by the owners of godord, or men chosen by them.

The early history of Iceland thus gives us a well-recorded picture of the workings of particularly pure forms of private enforcement and creation of law, and of the interaction between the two. Such a picture is especially interesting because elements of both have existed, and continue to exist, in many other societies, including our own.

There are three questions in the economics of law which I believe this history may illuminate. The first is the feasibility of private enforcement.[15] The second is the question of whether political institutions can and do generate "efficient" law. The third is the question of what laws are in fact efficient. All three involve formidable theoretical difficulties; in the body of this paper I limit myself to sketching the arguments, describing how the Icelandic institutions worked, and attempting to draw some tentative conclusions. Appendix A gives some numerical information on the scale of punishments in Iceland, and Appendix B suggests how the Icelandic system might be adapted to modern society.

II. The Modern Literature

Some years ago, Becker and Stigler pointed out that a system of private enforcement of law, in which the person who caught a criminal received the fine paid by the offender, would have certain attractive characteristics;[16] in particular, there would be no incentive for bribery of the enforcer by the criminal, since any bribe that it paid the criminal to offer it would pay the enforcer to refuse.[17] The argument was criticized by Landes and Posner; they argued that since the level of fine determined both the "price" of criminal activities to the criminal and the "price" of enforcement activities, it could not in general be set at a level which would optimize both criminal and enforcement activities.[18] They further argued that enforcement had a positive externality (raising the probability of catching a criminal, hence lowering total crime) which would not be internalized by the enforcer; this effect by itself would tend to lead to suboptimal enforcement.

The first argument may well be correct; since government enforcement also provides no guarantee of optimality, it leaves open the question of which system is superior, as Landes and Posner pointed out. This is an empirical question and one on which the Icelandic case may provide some evidence. Landes and Posner's second argument shows insufficient ingenuity in constructing hypothetical institutions. If "enforcers" contract in advance to pursue those who perpetrate crimes against particular people, and so notify the criminals (by a notice on the door of their customers), the deterrent effect of catching criminals is internalized; the enforcers can charge their customers for the service. Such arrangements are used by private guard firms and the American Automobile Association, among others. The AAA provides its members with decals stating that, if the car is stolen, a reward will be paid for information leading to its recovery. Such decals serve both as an offer to potential informants and as a warning to potential thieves. Under medieval Icelandic institutions, who was protected by whom was to a considerable degree known in advance.

Another difficulty with private enforcement is that some means must be found to allocate rights to catch criminals—otherwise one enforcer may expend resources gathering evidence only to have the criminal arrested at the last minute by someone else. This corresponds to the familiar "commons" problem. One solution in the literature[19] is to let the right to prosecute a criminal be the private property of the victim; by selling it to the highest bidder he receives some compensation for the cost of the crime. This describes precisely the Icelandic arrangements.

Posner has asserted at some length[20] that current common law institutions have produced economically efficient law. I will argue that while that may or may not be true of those institutions, there are reasons why the Icelandic institutions might be expected to produce such law. Two specific features of "efficient" law in the Icelandic system which I will discuss are efficient punishment and the distinction between civil and criminal offenses.

III. History and Institutions

In the latter half of the ninth century, King Harald Fairhair unified Norway under his rule. A substantial part of the population left;[21] many went either directly to Iceland, which had been discovered a few years before, or indirectly via Norse colonies in England, Ireland, Orkney, the Hebrides, and the Shetland Islands. The political system which they developed there was based on Norwegian (or possibly Danish[22]) traditions but with one important innovation—the King was replaced by an assembly of local chieftains. As in Norway (before Harald) there was nothing corresponding to a strictly feudal bond. The relationship between the Icelandic godi and his thingman (thingmenn) was contractual, as in early feudal relationships, but it was not territorial; the godi had no claim to the thingman's land and the thingman was free to transfer his allegiance.

At the base of the system stood the godi (pl. godar) and the godord (pl. godord). A godi was a local chief who built a (pagan) temple and served as its priest; the godord was the congregation. The godi received temple dues and provided in exchange both religious and political services.

Under the system of laws established in A.D. 930 and modified somewhat thereafter, these local leaders were combined into a national system. Iceland was divided into four quarters, and each quarter into nine godord.[23] Within each quarter the godord were clustered in groups of three called things. Only the godar owning these godord had any special status within the legal system, although it seems that others might continue to call themselves godi (in the sense of priest) and have a godord (in the sense of congregation); to avoid confusion, I will hereafter use the terms "godi" and "godord" only to refer to those having a special status under the legal system.

The one permanent official of this system was the logsogumadr or law-speaker; he was elected every three years by the inhabitants of one quarter (which quarter it was being chosen by lot). His job was to memorize the laws, to recite them through once during his term in office, to provide advice on difficult legal points, and to preside over the lögrétta, the "legislature."

The members of the lögrétta were the godar, plus one additional man from each thing, plus for each of these two advisors. Decisions in the lögrétta were made, at least after the reforms attributed to Njal, by majority vote, subject apparently to attempts to first achieve unanimity.[24]

The laws passed by the lögrétta were applied by a system of courts, also resting on the godar. At the lowest level were private courts, the members being chosen after the conflict arose, half by the plaintiff and half by the defendant—essentially a system of arbitration. Above this was the thing court or "Varthing," the judges[25] in which were chosen twelve each by the godar of the thing, making thirty-six in all. Next came the quarter-thing for disputes between members of different things within the same quarter; these seem to have been little used and not much is known about them.[26] Above them were the four quarter courts of the Althing (althingi) or national assembly—an annual meeting of all the godar each bringing with him at least one-ninth of his thingmen. Above them, after Njal's reforms, was the fifth court. Cases undecided at any level of the court system went to the next level; at every level (except the private courts) the judges were appointed by the godar, each quarter court and the fifth court having judges appointed by the godar from all over Iceland.[27] The fifth court reached its decision by majority vote; the other courts seem to have required that there be at most six (out of thirty-six) dissenting votes in order for a verdict to be given.[28]

The godord itself was in effect two different things. It was a group of men—the particular men who had agreed to follow that godi, to be members of that godord. Any man could be challenged to name his godord and was required to do so, but he was free to choose any godi within his quarter and to change to a different godord at will.[29] It was also a bundle of rights—the right to sit in the lögrétta, appoint judges for certain courts, etc. The godord in this second sense was marketable property. It could be given away, sold, held by a partnership, inherited, or whatever.[30] Thus seats in the lawmaking body were quite literally for sale.

I have described the legislative and judicial branches of "government" but have omitted the executive. So did the Icelanders. The function of the courts was to deliver verdicts on cases brought to them. That done, the court was finished. If the verdict went against the defendant, it was up to him to pay the assigned punishment—almost always a fine. If he did not, the plaintiff could go to court again and have the defendant declared an outlaw. The killer of an outlaw could not himself be prosecuted for the act; in addition, anyone who gave shelter to an outlaw could be prosecuted for doing so.

Prosecution was up to the victim (or his survivors). If they and the offender agreed on a settlement, the matter was settled.[31] Many cases were settled by arbitration, including the two most serious conflicts that arose prior to the final period of breakdown in the thirteenth century. If the case went to a court, the judgment, in case of conviction, would be a fine to be paid by the defendant to the plaintiff.

In modern law the distinction between civil and criminal law depends on whether prosecution is private or public; in this sense all Icelandic law was civil. But another distinction is that civil remedies usually involve a transfer (of money, goods, or services) from the defendant to the plaintiff, whereas criminal remedies often involve some sort of "punishment." In this sense the distinction existed in Icelandic law, but its basis was different.

Killing was made up for by a fine. For murder a man could be outlawed, even if he was willing to pay a fine instead. In our system, the difference between murder and killing (manslaughter) depends on intent; for the Icelanders it depended on something more easily judged. After killing a man, one was obliged to announce the fact immediately; as one law code puts it: "The slayer shall not ride past any three houses, on the day he committed the deed, without avowing the deed, unless the kinsmen of the slain man, or enemies of the slayer lived there, who would put his life in danger."[32] A man who tried to hide the body, or otherwise conceal his responsibility, was guilty of murder.[33]

IV. Analysis

One obvious objection to a system of private enforcement is that the poor (or weak) would be defenseless. The Icelandic system dealt with this problem by giving the victim a property right—the right to be reimbursed by the criminal—and making that right transferable. The victim could turn over his case to someone else, either gratis or in return for a consideration.[34] A man who did not have sufficient resources to prosecute a case or enforce a verdict could sell it to another who did and who expected to make a profit in both money and reputation by winning the case and collecting the fine. This meant that an attack on even the poorest victim could lead to eventual punishment.

A second objection is that the rich (or powerful) could commit crimes with impunity, since nobody would be able to enforce judgment against them. Where power is sufficiently concentrated this might be true; this was one of the problems which led to the eventual breakdown of the Icelandic legal system in the thirteenth century.[35] But so long as power was reasonably dispersed, as it seems to have been for the first two centuries after the system was established, this was a less serious problem. A man who refused to pay his fines was outlawed and would probably not be supported by as many of his friends as the plaintiff seeking to enforce judgment, since in case of violent conflict his defenders would find themselves legally in the wrong. If the lawbreaker defended himself by force, every injury inflicted on the partisans of the other side would result in another suit, and every refusal to pay another fine would pull more people into the coalition against him.

There is a scene in *Njal's Saga* that provides striking evidence of the stability of this system. Conflict between two groups has become so intense that open fighting threatens to break out in the middle of the court. A leader of one faction asks a benevolent neutral what he will do for them in case of a fight. He replies that if they are losing he will help them, and if they are winning he will break up the fight before they kill more men than they can afford![36] Even when the system seems so near to breaking down, it is still assumed that every enemy killed must eventually be paid for. The reason is obvious enough; each man killed will have friends and relations who are still neutral—and will remain neutral if and only if the killing is made up for by an appropriate wergeld.

I suggested earlier that one solution to the externality problem raised by Landes and Posner was to identify in advance the enforcer who would deal with crimes committed against a potential victim. In Iceland this was done by a system of existing coalitions—some of them godord, some clearly defined groups of friends and relatives. If a member of such a coalition was killed, it was in the interest of the other members to collect wergeld for him even if the cost was more than the amount that would be collected; their own safety depended partly on their reputation for doing so. This corresponds precisely to the solution to the problem of deterrence externality described above.

How well do the Icelandic laws fit the ideas of "economically efficient" law in the modern literature?[37] In Appendix A, I give some quantitative calculations on the value of various fines. Here I will discuss two qualitative features of Icelandic law which seem to correspond closely to the prescriptions of modern analysis.

The first is the prevalence of fines. A fine is a costless punishment; the cost to the payer is balanced by a benefit to the recipient. It is in this respect superior to punishments such as execution, which imposes cost but no corresponding benefit, or imprisonment, which imposes costs on both the criminal and the taxpayers.[38]

The difficulty with using fines as punishments is that many criminals may be unable to pay a fine large enough to provide adequate deterrence. The Icelandic system dealt with this in three ways. First, the offenses for which fines were assessed were offenses for which the chance of detection was unity, as explained below; it was thus sufficient for the fine to correspond to the cost of the crime, without any additional factor to compensate for the chance of not being caught.[39] Second, the society provided effective credit arrangements. The same coalitions mentioned above provided their members with money to pay large fines. Third, a person unable to discharge his financial obligation could apparently be reduced to a state of temporary slavery until he had worked off his debt.[40]

The second feature is the distinction between what I have called civil and criminal offenses. Since civil offenses were offenses in which the criminal made no attempt to hide his guilt, a reasonably low punishment was sufficient to deter most of them. High punishments were reserved for crimes whose detection was uncertain because the criminal tried to conceal his guilt. A high punishment was therefore necessary to keep the expected punishment (at the time the crime was committed) from being very low.[41] Further, the difference between the two sorts of offenses provided a high "differential punishment" for the "offense" of concealing one's crime, an offense which imposed serious costs—both costs of detection and the punishment costs resulting from the need to use an inefficient punishment (since no payable fine, multiplied by a low probability of being caught, would provide a sufficiently high deterrent).

V. Generating Efficient Law

Is there any reason to expect the Icelandic system to generate efficient law? I believe the answer is a qualified yes. If some change in laws produced net benefits, it would in principle be possible for those who supported such a change to outbid its opponents, buy up a considerable number of godord, and legislate the change. A similar potential exists in any political system; one may think of it as the application of the Coase theorem to law. The effect is limited by transaction costs—which were probably large even in the Icelandic system but, because the godord was legally marketable, smaller than under other political arrangements.[42]

A second reason is that inefficient laws provided, in some cases, incentives for individual responses which could in turn make changes in the laws Pareto desirable (without side payments). Suppose, for example, that the wergeld for killing was too low—substantially below the point at which the cost of an increase to an individual (involving the possibility that he might be convicted of a killing and have to pay) balanced the advantages of increased security and higher payments if a relative were killed. The individual, functioning through the coalition of which he was a member, could then unilaterally "raise" the wergeld by announcing that if any member of the coalition were killed, the others would kill the killer (or some other member of his coalition, if he were not accessible) and let the two wergelds cancel. This is essentially what happens in the famous "killing match" in *Njal's Saga*, where Hallgerd and Bergthora alternately arrange revenge killings while their husbands, Njal and Gunnar, pass the same purse of silver back and forth between them.[43] Once such policies became widespread, it would be in the interest of everyone, potential killers, potential victims, and potential avengers, to raise the legal wergeld. And even before the legal wergeld was raised, killers would begin offering higher payments (as part of "out-of- court" settlements) to prevent revenge killings.[44]

Conclusion

It is difficult to draw any conclusion from the Icelandic experience concerning the viability of systems of private enforcement in the twentieth century. Even if Icelandic institutions worked well then, they might not work in a larger and more interdependent society. And whether the Icelandic institutions did work well is a matter of controversy; the sagas are perceived by many as portraying an essentially violent and unjust society, tormented by constant feuding. It is difficult to tell whether such judgments are correct. Most of the sagas were written down during or after the Sturlung period, the final violent breakdown of the Icelandic system in the thirteenth century. Their authors may have projected elements of what they saw around them on the earlier periods they described. Also, violence has always been good entertainment, and the saga writers may have selected their material accordingly. Even in a small and peaceful society novelists might be able to find, over the course of three hundred years, enough conflict for a considerable body of literature.

The quality of violence, in contrast to other medieval literature, is small in scale, intensely personal (every casualty is named), and relatively straightforward. Rape and torture are uncommon, the killing of women almost unheard of; in the very rare cases when an attacker burns the defender's home, women, children, and servants are first offered an opportunity to leave.[45] One indication that the total amount of violence may have been relatively small is a calculation based on the Sturlung sagas. During more than fifty years of what the Icelanders themselves perceived as intolerably violent civil war, leading to the collapse of the traditional system, the average number of people killed or executed each year appears, on a per capita basis, to be roughly equal to the current rate of murder and nonnegligent manslaughter in the United States.[46]

Whatever the correct judgment on the Icelandic legal system, we do know one thing: it worked—sufficiently well to survive for over three hundred years. In order to work, it had to solve, within its own institutional structure, the problems implicit in a system of private enforcement. Those solutions may or may not be still applicable, but they are certainly still of interest.

Appendix A: Wages and Wergelds

Two different monies were in common use in medieval Iceland. One was silver, the other wadmal (va*d*mal), a woolen cloth. Silver was measured in ounces (aurar) and in marks; the mark contained eight ounces. Wadmal was of a standard width of about a meter, and was measured in Icelandic ells (alnar) of about 56 centimeters.[47] The value of an ounce (eyrir) of silver varied, during the twelfth and thirteenth centuries, between 6 and 7 1/2 ells.[48] The "law ounce" was set at 6 ells;[49] this appears to have been a money of account, not an attempt at price fixing.

Gragas, the earliest book of Icelandic written law, contains a passage setting maximum wages—presumably an attempt to enforce a monopsonistic cartel agreement by the landowning thingmen against their employees.[50] The passage is unclear. Porkell Johannesson estimates from it that the farm laborer's wage, net of room and board, amounted to about one mark of silver a year and cites another writer who estimates it at about three-quarters of a mark.[51] Porkell Johannesson also states that wages (net of room and board) seem to have been low or zero at the time of settlement but to have risen somewhat by the second half of the tenth century. He dates Gragas to the second half of the twelfth century, or perhaps earlier; Conybeare gives its date as 1117.

These figures give us only a very approximate idea of Icelandic wages. The existence of maximum wage legislation suggests that the equilibrium wage was higher than the legislated wage.[52] But wages, as Porkell Johannesson points out, must have varied considerably with good and bad years; the legislation might be an attempt to hold wages in good years to a level below equilibrium but above the average wage.

I have attempted another and independent estimate of wages, based on the fact that one of the two monetary commodities was woolen cloth, a material which is highly labor intensive. If we knew how many hours went into spinning and weaving an ell of wadmal, we could estimate the market wage rate; if it takes y hours to produce one ell, then the wage of the women making cloth (including the value of any payment in kind they receive) should be about l/y.

I have estimated y in two ways—from figures given by Hoffman for the productivity of Icelandic weavers using the same technology at later periods,[53] and from estimates given me by Geraldine Duncan, who has herself worked with a warp-weighted loom and a drop spindle, the tools used by medieval Icelandic weavers.[54] Both methods lead to imprecise results: the first because reports disagree and also because the sources are vague whether the time given is for weaving only or for both weaving and spinning, the second because Mrs. Duncan did not know the precise characteristics of wadmal, or precisely how the skill of medieval Icelandic weavers compared with her own. My conclusion is that it took about a day to spin and weave an ell of wadmal; this estimate could easily be off by a factor of two in either direction. If we assume that, in a relatively poor society such as Iceland, a considerable portion of the income of an ordinary worker went for room and board, this figure is consistent with that given in Gragas.

A rough check on these estimates of wages is provided by the fact that the logsogumadr received an annual salary of 200 ells of wadmal, plus a part of the fines for certain minor offenses. While his position was not a full-time one, it involved more than just the two weeks of the Althing; he was required to give information on the law to all comers. Since the man chosen for the post was an unusually talented individual, it does not seem unreasonable that the fixed part of his salary (which, unlike the wages discussed before, did not include room and board) amounted to five year's wages, or an amount of wadmal which would have taken about ten months to produce. Thus, this figure is not inconsistent with my previous estimate of wages.

It is interesting to note that during the Sturlung period, when wealth had become relatively concentrated, the richest men had a net worth of about three to four hundred year's production of wadmal—or about a thousand cows. The former figure would correspond today to about six million dollars, but the latter to only a few hundred thousand—wages having risen considerably more, over the last millennium, than the price of cattle.

Table 1 gives values for a number of things in ounces, ells, years of production of wadmal, and years of wages. The ounce is assumed to be worth six ells, the year's production of wadmal to be three hundred ells (three hundred days at one ell/day) and the year's wages to be one mark of forty-eight ells.

Wergeld for a thrall, the price of a thrall, and the manumission price of a thrall were all equal, as might be expected. The price of a thrall presumably represents the capitalized value of his production net of room and board. It seems at first surprising that this should amount to only a year and a half of wages (also net of room and board), but we must remember that wages, according to Thorkell Johanneson, were lower in the early period, when thralldom was common; thralldom disappeared in Iceland by the early twelfth century, about when Gragas was being written.

It is worth noting that the wergeld for a thrall was considerably lower than for a free man. This is to be expected. The wergeld for a thrall was paid to his

Table 1

	Ounces	Ells	Years Production of Wadmal	Years Wages	Source
Normal Price of Male thrall	12	72	.24	1.5	Carl O. Williams, supra note 4, at 29
Manumission price of thrall	12	72	.24	1.5	Sveinbjorn Johnson, supra note 4, at 225
Wergeld for thrall	12	72	.24	1.5	Id.
Wergeld for free man	100	600	2	12.5	Njal's saga, supra note 3, at 108
Wergeld for free man[a]	400	2400	8	50	Id.
Wergeld for important man	200	1200	4	25	Id. at 225 ns.
Wergeld for important man[a]	800	4800	16	100	Id.
Law-speaker salary		200+	.8+	5+	Vigfusson & Powell, supra note 1, at 348
Wealth of very rich man (Sturlung Period)		120,000	400	2500	Einar Olafur Sveinsson, supra note 44, at 45
Wealth of very rich man (Sturlung Period)		96,000	320	2000	Id.
Price of Cow (c. A.D. 1200)		90–96	.3–.32	1.9–2	Id. at 56

[a]Magnusson & Palsson (Njal's Saga, *supra* note 3, at 63, trans. n.) interpret the ounce by which compensations are measured as probably meaning "an ounce of unrefined silver...worth four legal ounces." Williams, *supra* note 4, at 31, interprets it as the legal ounce.

master and it was his master, not the thrall, who had some part in the political bargaining process by which, I have argued, wergelds were set. The value of a thrall to his master would be the capitalized value of his net product. But the value of a free man to himself and his family includes not only his net product but also the value to him of being alive. Food and board, in other words, are expenses to the owner of a thrall but consumption to a free man. Furthermore, one would expect that the costs of the thrall to the owner would include costs of guarding and supervision that would not apply to the free man's calculation of his own value.

If we interpret the "ounce" of Njal's Saga as a legal ounce, the usual wergelds for free men again seem somewhat low, ranging from 12 1/2 year's wages for an ordinary man to twice that for a man of some importance.[55] Here again we must remember that there is considerable uncertainty in our wage figures. Twelve and a half years' wages might be a reasonable estimate of the value of a man to his family, assuming a market interest rate of between 5 and 10 percent, but it hardly seems to include much allowance for his value to himself. If we accept the interpretation in Magnusson and Palsson[56] of the ounce in which the wergelds of *Njal's Saga* are paid as an ounce of unrefined silver, worth four legal ounces, the figures seem more reasonable.

Appendix B

The first step in applying the Icelandic system of private enforcement to a modern society would be to convert all criminal offenses into civil offenses, making the offender liable to pay an appropriate fine to the victim. In some cases, it might not be obvious who the victim was, but that could be specified by legislation. The Icelanders had the same problem and took care to specify who had the right to pursue each case, even for procedural offenses.[57] For some minor offenses anyone could sue; presumably, whoever submitted his case first would be entitled to the fine. It must be remembered that specifying the victim has the practical function of giving someone an incentive to pursue the case.

The second step would be to make the victim's claim marketable, so that he could sell it to someone willing to catch and convict the offender. The amount of the claim would correspond approximately to the damage caused by the crime divided by the probability of catching the criminal.[58] In many cases it would be substantial.

Once these steps were taken, a body of professional "thief-takers" (as they were once called in England) would presumably develop and gradually replace our present governmental police forces.

One serious problem with such institutions is that most criminals are judgment proof: their resources are insufficient to pay any large fine. The obvious way to deal with this would be some variation on Icelandic debt-thralldom. An arrangement which protects the convicted criminal against the most obvious abuses would be for every sentence to take the form of "so many years or so many dollars." The criminal would then have the choice of serving out the sentence in years or accepting bids for his services. The employer making such a bid would offer the criminal some specified working conditions (possibly inside a private prison, possibly not) and a specified rate at which the employer would pay off the fine. In order to get custody of the criminal, the employer would have to obtain his consent and post bond with the court for the amount of the fine. In order for the private-enforcement system to work, it would be necessary for most criminals to choose to work off their sentences instead of sitting them out (since their fines provide the enforcer's incentive). This could be arranged by appropriately adjusting the ratio between the number of years and the number of dollars in the sentence.

There might be some crimes, such as murder, for which the appropriate fine would be so high that the convicted killer would be unable to work it off, however unattractive the alternative. For such cases the system would break down and would have to be supplemented by some alternative arrangement—perhaps a large bounty paid by the state for the apprehension and conviction of murderers.

It would be beyond the scope of this article to argue the advantages and disadvantages of such a system, or to compare at length its potential abuses with those of our present system of enforcement and punishment; it would be beyond my competence to discuss the legal problems, and in particular the constitutional objections, that might be raised to its introduction.

Notes

1. I would like to especially thank Professor Jere Fleck of the Germanic Languages Department at the University of Maryland for answering innumerable questions and Julius Margolis for his initial encouragement. Thanks are also due to Juergen Backhaus, for the difficult feat of translating an Icelander's German, and to Geraldine Duncan. Finally, I am grateful to the authors and translators of Njal's Saga, Egils Saga. Haralds Saga, Gisla Saga, and the Jomsvikinga Saga.
2. I have been hampered in this work by my unfortunate ignorance of Old Norse. In particular Gragas, the earliest compilation of Icelandic law. seems never to have been translated into English, save for a few fragments in *Origines Icelandicae* (Gudbrand Yigfusson and F. York Powell, trans., 1905) (hereinafter cited as Yigfusson & Powell). A Norse scholar willing to correct that lack would do a considerable service to those interested in the legal institutions of this extraordinary society.
3. Most of the principal sagas were written down in the second half of the thirteenth century, or at the latest, the first half of the fourteenth. Prior to 1262 the institutions seem to have been relatively close to those established in the tenth century, although their workings may have been substantially different as a result of the increased concentration of wealth and power which led to their final collapse.
4. Magnus Magnusson and Hermann Palsson, trans., *Njal's Saga* (Penguin ed., 1960) (hereinafter cited as *Njal's Saga*).
5. Sveinbjorn Johnson, *Pioneers of Freedom* (1930). A partial exception is the status of thralls, although even they seem freer than one might expect; in one saga a thrall owns a famous sword, and his master must ask his permission to borrow it. Carl O. Williams, in *Thraldom in Ancient Iceland* 36 (1937), estimates that there were no more than 2000 thralls in Iceland at any one time, which would be about 3 percent of the population. Williams believes they were very badly treated, but this may reflect his biases; for example, he repeatedly asserts that thralls were not permitted weapons despite numerous instances to the contrary in the sagas. Stefansson estimates the average period of servitude before manumission at only five years but does not state his evidence. Vilhjalmur Stefansson, "Icelandic Independence," *Foreign Affairs*, January 1929, at 270.
6. C. A Vansittart Conybeare, *The Place of Iceland in the History of European Institutions* 6-8 (1877).
7. *New York Times*, Feb. 16, 1972, at 17, col. 6. For an extensive survey of wergeld in Anglo-Saxon and other early societies, see Frederic Seebohm, *Tribal Custom in Anglo-Saxon Law* (1911).
8. Terry L. Anderson and P. J. Hill, "An American Experiment in Anarcho-Capitalism: The Not So Wild, Wild West" (1978) (staff paper in economics, Montana State University at Bozeman, Ag. Econ. & Econ. Dept.).
9. Marilyn E. Walsh, *The Fence* 17-23 (1977).

10. H. S. Maine, *Ancient Law* 355-71 (1963).
11. *Id.* at 360-61.
12. Seebohm, *supra* note 6 at 330-335: and Naomi D. Hurnard, *The King's Pardon for Homicide before A.D. 1307*, at 1-5 (1969).
13. Walsh, *supra* note 8, at 18-19.
14. "In no part of Anglo-Saxon England and at no time in its history is any trace to be found of a system of government knowing nothing of the rule of kings." P. H. Blair, *An Introduction to Anglo-Saxon England* 194 (2nd ed. 1977).
15. This question is discussed at some length in modern libertarian or anarcho-capitalist writings. See David Friedman, *The Machinery of Freedom* (1973); and Murray N. Rothbard, *For a New Liberty* (1973).
16. Gary Becker and George Stigler, "Law Enforcement, Malfeasance, and Compensation of Enforcers," 3 *J. Legal Stud.* I (1975).
17. This is not quite true, since the trial process might impose costs on the criminal, such as uncertainty and unreimbursed time, he might be willing to pay the enforcer more than the expected value of the fine. In this case bribery is an efficient substitute for the court process.
18. William M. Landes and Richard A. Posner, "The Private Enforcement of Law," 4 *J. Legal Stud.* I (1975).
19. *Id.* at 34.
20. Richard A. Posner, *Economic Analysis of Law* (2nd ed., 1977).
21. Some estimates put it at about 10 percent.
22. Barthi Guthmundsson, *The Origin of the Icelanders* (Lee M. Hollander, trans., 1967), argues that the settlers were in large part Danes who had colonized in Norway and thus brought Danish institutions with them to Iceland.
23. In the northern quarter there were twelve godord; the rules for membership in the lögrétta and the appointment of judges were modified to compensate for this fact, so that the northern quarter had the same number of seats as each of the other three quarters. I shall ignore the resulting complications (and some other details of the system) in the remainder of the description. I shall also ignore the disputed question of which features were in the original system and which were added by modifications occurring between A.D. 930 and c. A.D. 1000.
24. Conybeare, *supra* note 5, at 95 ns.; and I Vigfusson & Powell, *supra* note 1, bk. 2, § 3, at 343-344.
25. The Icelandic judges correspond more nearly to the jurymen of our system than to the judge, since it was up to them to determine guilt or innocence. Conybeare, *supra* note 5 at 146. There was no equivalent of our judge; individual experts in the law could be consulted by the court. According to Sigurdur A. Magnusson, *Northern Sphinx* 14 (1977), "Since every breach of the law had a fixed fine, the judges merely had to decide whether the culprit was guilty or innocent." The lögrétta had the power to reduce sentences.
26. Conybeare, *supra* note 5, at 48.
27. *Id* at 50-51 at 50-51. But Sveinbjorn Johnson, *supra* note 4, at 64; and James Bryce, *Studies in History and Jurisprudence* 274 (1901), state that the judges of the quarter court were appointed only by the godar of that quarter.
28. Magnusson *supra* note 24, at 14; and Conybeare, *supra* note 5, at 95 ns., both interpret the requirement for the lower courts as no more than six dissenting votes. If this was not achieved, the case was undecided and could be taken to a higher court. While there does not seem to have been anything strictly equivalent to our system of appeals, claims that a case had been handled illegally in one court could be resolved in a higher court. In a famous case in Njalssaga the defendant tricks the prosecution into prosecuting him in the wrong court by secretly changing his

godord, and hence his quarter, in order to be able to sue the prosecutors in the fifth court for doing so. *Id.* at 93-94; *Njal's Saga*, *supra* note 3, at 309-310. Similarly, if a private court was unable to reach a verdict, or in cases of "contempt of court, disturbance of the proceedings by violence, brawling, crowding, etc.," or if the plaintiff was unwilling to submit the case to a private court, it went to the appropriate public court instead. Conybeare, *supra* note 5, at 77.

29. *Id.* at 33-34, 47; Bryce, *supra* note 26, at 268-69.
30. Conybeare, *supra* note 5, at 28.
31. But according to Johnson, *supra* note 1, at 112, for certain serious offenses the plaintiff was liable to a fine if he compromised his suit after it had been commenced.
32. Quoted by Conybeare, *supra* note 5, at 78 ns., from the Gulathing Code.
33. For a discussion of the contrast between Icelandic and (modern) English ideas of murder, see *id.* at 78-81.
34. For examples, see *Njal's Saga*, *supra* note 3, at 75, 151.
35. The question of why the system eventually broke down is both interesting and difficult. I believe that two of the proximate causes were increased concentration of wealth, and hence power, and the introduction into Iceland of a foreign ideology—kingship. The former meant that in many areas all or most of the godord were held by one family and the latter that by the end of the Sturlung period the chieftains were no longer fighting over the traditional quarrels of who owed what to whom, but over who should eventually rule Iceland. The ultimate reasons for those changes are beyond the scope of this paper.
36. "But if you are forced to give ground, you had better retreat in this direction, for I shall have my men drawn up here in battle array ready to come to your help. If on the other hand your opponents retreat, I expect they will try to reach the natural stronghold of Almanna Gorge...I shall take it upon myself to bar their way to this vantage ground with my men, but we shall not pursue them if they retreat north or south along the river. And as soon as I estimate that you have killed off as many as you can afford to pay compensation for without exile or loss of your chieftaincies, I shall intervene with all my men to stop the fighting; and you must then obey my orders, if I do all this for you." *Njal's Saga*, *supra* note 3, at 296-97. A similar passage occurs *id.* at 162-63.
37. See especially Posner, *supra* note 19; and Gary Becker, "Crime and Punishment: An Economic Approach," 76 *J. Pol. Econ.* 169 (1963). Also, Gordon Tullock, *The Logic of the Law* (1971).
38. I am here comparing the direct costs and benefits of different sorts of punishment. Both execution and fine have the additional indirect "benefit" of deterrence. Execution has the further indirect benefit of preventing repetition of the crime.
39. Some additional punishment might be required to compensate for the chance that a guilty person would be acquitted on a technicality, as sometimes happened. The advantage of private enforcement for acts where detection is easy is discussed by Landes & Posner, *supra* note 17, at 31-55, in the context of modern law.
40. My only source for this is Williams, *supra* note 4, at 117-121. The system seems to have differed from the later English imprisonment for debt, which served as an incentive to pay debts but not as a means of doing so.
41. This may be only an approximate statement. The sagas describe many miscarriages of justice, including outlawry based on relatively minor offenses. Here as elsewhere I am trying to distinguish what the rules were from how they may sometimes have been applied, partly because I believe that misapplications probably became common only in the later years, as part of the general collapse of the system described in the Sturlung sagas. Since most of the sagas were written during or shortly after the Sturlung period, I regard their description of that period as accurate and their

description of the earlier "saga" period as somewhat exaggerating the resemblance between the two periods. They portray the Sturlung period as one in which justice was less common than in the saga period, and much less common than in the period between the two.

42. For a description of a very different system of private production of law (by lawyers), see Maine, *supra* note 9, at 32-41. There seems no obvious reason to expect the Roman system he describes to generate efficient law.
43. *Njal's Saga*, chs. 36-45, at 98-119.
44. One common procedure was for the defendant to offer the plaintiff "self-judgment"—the right to set the fine himself.
45. Einar Ólafur Sveinsson, *The Age of the Sturlungs* 68, 73 (Johann S. Hannesson, trans., 1953) (Islandica vol. 36); *Njal's Saga* 266.
46. *Id.* at 72 gives an estimate of three hundred and fifty killed in battle or executed during a fifty-two-year period (1208-1260). The population of Iceland was about seventy thousand. For the U.S. figures, see Michael S. Hindelang et al., *Sourcebook of Criminal Justice Statistics—1976*, at 443 (1977).
47. Marta Hoffman, *The Warp-Weighted Loom* 213 (1964).
48. Knut Gjerset, *History of Iceland* 206 (1924).
49. *Njal's Saga* 41, trans. n. Also Þorkell Johannesson, *Die Stellung der Freien Arbeiter in Island* 37 (1933).
50. *Id.* at 207-208.
51. *Id.* at 211.
52. The existence of maximum wage legislation raises a problem for my thesis that the Icelandic system generated efficient law. The simplest answer is that I do not expect to see perfectly efficient law. Maximum wage legislation can most naturally be interpreted as a cartel arrangement among the landowners; such an arrangement may well be in their interest, provided that the farm workers are unable, for organizational reasons connected with the public-good problem, to combine in order to bribe the landowners to repeal the legislation or, within the Icelandic system, to buy sufficient godord to repeal it themselves.
53. Hoffman, *supra* note 46, at 215-16.
54. Private communication.
55. In comparing this figure with current sentencing levels for murder or manslaughter, one must remember that killing, in Icelandic law, was distinguished from murder by the fact that the killer "turned himself in." Thus, even if the average sentence served by the convicted killer in our society were as high as 12 1/2 years—which it surely is not—the corresponding expected punishment would be much higher in the Icelandic case.
56. *Njal's Saga*, *supra* note 3, at 63.
57. Vigfusson & Powell, *supra* note 1, bk. 2, at 340, 356, 358-59.
58. This is only a first approximation; the optimal fine must make allowance for enforcement costs—part of the cost of a crime is the cost of catching the criminal—and for the net cost of collecting the fine. This is a complicated subject and beyond the scope of this paper.

37

The Role of Institutions in the Revival of Trade: The Law Merchant, Private Judges, and the Champagne Fairs

Paul Milgrom, Douglass North, and Barry Weingast

How can people promote the trust necessary for efficient exchange when individuals have short run temptations to cheat? The same question arises whether the traders are legislators swapping votes, medieval merchants exchanging goods, or modem businesspeople trading promises about future deliveries. In each of these situations, one of the important ways in which individuals ensure one another's honest behavior is by establishing a continuing relationship. In the language of economics, if the relationship itself is a valuable asset that a party could lose by dishonest behavior, then the relationship serves as a *bond*: a trader would be unwilling to surrender this bond unless the gain from dishonest behavior was large.

Variants on this basic idea are found throughout the literatures of economics (Klein and Leffler, 1981; Shapiro, 1983; Shapiro and Stiglitz, 1984), politics (Axelrod, 1984, 1986; Calvert, 1989) and game theory (Abreu, 1988; Aumann, 1985; and Fudenberg and Maskin, 1986). Even in a community in which any particular pair of people meet rarely, it is still possible (as we show) for an individual's reputation in the group as a whole to serve as a bond for his good and honest behavior toward each individual member. This illustrates the important fact that a reputation system may sometimes work only when it encompasses sufficiently many traders and trades, that is, there are economies of scale and scope in reputation systems.

These conclusions about the potential effectiveness of a reputation system however, leave us with a puzzle: If informal arrangements based on reputations can effectively bond good behavior, then what is the role of formal institutions in helping to support honest exchange? The legal apparatus for enforcing business contracts in many ages and many parts of the world, the suppliers' organizations that negotiate contracting patterns among modern Japanese firms, the complex institutional structure that facilitates agreements among U.S. Congressmen,[1] the notaries that recorded agreements in the Italian city-states in the Middle Ages, and the organization of international trade via the Champagne Fairs are all examples of institutionalized arrangements to support trade and contracting.

All involve the creation of specialized roles which would not be necessary if reputations alone could be an adequate bond for trade. But, why can't a simple system of reputations motivate honest trade in these various settings? And, what role do formal institutions play when simple reputational mechanisms fail?

We embed our study of these questions in the time of the revival of trade in Europe during the Early Middle Ages. At that time, without the benefit of state enforcement of contracts or an established body of commercial law, merchants evolved their own private code of laws (the *Law Merchant*) with disputes adjudicated by a judge who might be a local official or a private merchant. While hearings were held to resolve disputes under the code, the judges had only limited powers to enforce judgments against merchants from distant places. For example, if a dispute arose after the conclusion of the Champagne Fair about the quality of the goods delivered or if agreements made at the Fair for future delivery or for acceptance of future delivery were not honored, no physical sanction or seizure of goods could then be applied.

The evolution and survival for a considerable period of a system of private adjudication raises both particular versions of our general questions and new questions about the details of the mechanism. What was the purpose of the private adjudication system? Was it a substitute for the reputation mechanism that had worked effectively in earlier periods (Greif, 1989)? Also, if there was no state to enforce judgments, how did they have any effect? How could a system of adjudication function without substantial police powers?

The practice and evolution of the Law Merchant in medieval Europe was so rich and varied that no single model can hope to capture all the relevant variations and details. Our simple model is intended to represent certain universal incentive problems that any successful system would have to solve. It abstracts from many of the interesting variations that are found across time and space as well as from other general problems, such as the spatial diversion of traders and trading centers and the interactions among competing trading systems.

We begin in section 1 with a discussion of the medieval Law Merchant and related institutions. We set the theoretical context for our analysis in section 2. It is well known, as we have explained above, that in long-term, frequent bilateral exchange, the value of the relationship itself may serve as an adequate bond to ensure honest behavior and promote trust between the parties. We argue in section 2 that even if no pair of traders come together frequently, if each individual trades frequently enough within the community of traders, then transferable reputations for honesty can serve as an adequate bond for honest behavior *if members of the trading community can be kept informed about each other's past behavior.* Well-informed traders could boycott those who have violated community norms of honesty, if only they knew who the violators were. It is the costliness of generating and communicating information—rather than the infrequency of trade in any particular bilateral relationship—that, we argue, is the problem that the system of private enforcement was designed to overcome.

In section 3, we introduce our basic model of a system of private enforcement and develop our core thesis that the role of the judges in the system, far from being substitutes for the reputation mechanism, is to make the reputation system more effective as a means of promoting honest trade. The formal system is more complex than the simple informal system of reputations that preceded it, but that was a natural outcome of the growing extent of trade. In a large community, we argue, it would be too costly to keep everyone informed about what transpires in all trading relationships, as a simple reputation system might require. So the system of private judges is designed to promote private resolution of disputes and otherwise to transmit *just enough* information to the right people in the right circumstances to enable the reputation mechanism to function effectively for enforcement. In order to succeed, such a system must solve a number of interconnected incentive problems: Individual members of the community must be induced to behave honestly, to boycott those who have behaved dishonestly, to keep informed about who has been dishonest, to provide evidence against those who have cheated, and to honor the decisions of the judges. All of these problems can be resolved by the system if certain institutional constraints are satisfied, as we show in section 3. Briefly, the costs of making queries, providing evidence, adjudicating disputes, and making transfer payments must not be too high relative to the frequency and profitability of trade if the system is to function successfully.

Intuitively, the system of private judges accomplishes its objectives by bundling the services which are valuable to the individual trader with services that are valuable to the community, so that a trader pursuing his individual interest serves the community's interest as well. Unless a trader makes appropriate queries, he cannot use the system to resolve disputes. The requirement that the traders make queries provides an opportunity for the judge to collect payments for his services even if no actual disputes arise. As applied to the Champagne Fairs, the local lord or his agents could appoint honest judges, register transactions, and tax them.

In section 4, we make a brief digression to assess how *efficiently* the system of private judges accomplishes its task. We argue that no system can restore the effectiveness of the community reputation mechanism without incurring costs that are qualitatively similar to those incurred by the system of private judges, and moreover that the latter system seems to have been designed in a way that kept these transaction costs low.

Our analysis in section 3 gives the judge a passive role only. In section 5, we study the possibility that the judge may threaten to sully the reputations of honest traders unless they pay bribes. We show how the system can survive some such threats, though we do not attempt a comprehensive evaluation of all the kinds of bribes and extortion that might be tried in such a system.

Concluding remarks, relating our model to a broader institutional perspective, are given in section 6.

1. The Medieval Law Merchant

The history of long-distance trade in medieval and early modem Europe is the story of sequentially more complex organization that eventually led to the "Rise of the Western World." In order to capture the gains associated with geographic specialization, a system had to be established that lowered information costs and provided for the enforcement of agreements across space and time. Prior to the revival of trade in the Early Middle Ages, few institutions underpinned commercial activity; there was no state to enforce contracts, let alone to protect merchants from pirates and brigands. In contrast, modern Western economies possess highly specialized systems of enforcing contracts and protecting merchants, resulting in widespread geographic specialization and impersonal exchange. The story of this evolution has been told elsewhere (e.g., Lopez, 1976; North and Thomas, 1973). Our purpose in this section is to suggest the outlines of an important step in this evolution, namely the early development of commercial law prior to the rise of large-scale third-party enforcement of legal codes by the nation-state.

A large number of problems had to be resolved in order to support the expansion of trade. First, as trading communities grew larger, it became harder within each community for merchants to monitor one another's behavior. New institutions were required to mitigate the types of cheating afforded by the new situation. Second, as trade grew among different regions, institutions were needed to prevent reneging by merchants who might cheat in one location, never to be seen again.

In response to these problems, a host of institutions arose and evolved over time. Towns with their own governments became homes for merchants who developed their own law separate from the traditional feudal order (Pirenne, 1925; Rorig, 1967). Merchant gilds arose to provide protection to foreign merchants away from their homes, but also protection to local merchants against fly-by-night foreign merchants who might never be seen again (DeRoover, 1963; Thrupp, 1948). Key to understanding the ability of merchants from widely varying regions to enforce contracts was the evolution of the *Lex Mercatoria* or Law Merchant—the legal codes governing commercial transactions and administered by private judges drawn from the commercial ranks. While practice varied across time and space, by the end of the 11th century, the Law Merchant came to govern most commercial transactions in Europe, providing a uniform set of standards across large numbers of locations (Benson, 1989). It thereby provided a means for reducing the uncertainty associated with variations in local practices and limited the ability of localities to discriminate against alien merchants (Berman, 1983; Trakman, 1983). Thus, "commercial law can be conceived of as coordinating the self-interested actions of merchants, but perhaps an equally valuable insight is gained by *viewing it as coordinating the actions of people with limited knowledge and trust*" (Benson, 1989, p. 648, emphasis added).

While the governments of towns supported the development of markets and were intimately involved in developing merchant law (Pirenne, 1925; Roria, 1967), they often could not provide merchants protection outside their immediate area.[2] Nor could they enforce judgments against foreign merchants who had left town prior to a case being heard. Thus, merchant law developed prior to the rise of a geographically extensive nation-state. But this raises a key problem in the theory of enforcement, for what made these judgments credible if they were not backed up by the state? Ostracism played an important role here, for merchants that failed to abide by the decisions of the judges would not be merchants for long (Benson, 1989; DeRoover, 1963; Trakman, 1983).

The Law Merchant and related legal codes evolved considerably over time. In addition to providing a court of law especially suited for merchants, it fostered significant legal developments that reduced the transaction costs of exchange (North, 1989, ch. 13). As agency relationships became common—whether between partners on different locations or between a sedentary merchant who financed a traveling one—a new set of rules governing these agreements and insurance. Here, we note the development of law covering agency relations (DeRoover, 1963; Greif, 1989), bills of exchange, and insurance (North, 1989, ch. 13).

The benefits of all these developments, however, could only be enjoyed as long as merchants obeyed the Law Merchant. Moreover, since disputes arise even among honest merchants, there needed to be a system for hearing and settling these disputes. To see how these feats of coordination might have been accomplished, we developed a game theoretic model of the judicial enforcement system—a model inspired by the Law Merchant and by the Champagne Fairs. The latter played a central role in trade in the 12th and 13th centuries (DeRoover, 1963; North and Thomas, 1973; Verlinden, 1963), and included a legal system in which merchants could bring grievances against their trading partners. However, it is not clear why such a system would be effective. What prevents a merchant from cheating by supplying lower quality goods than promised, and then leaving the fairs before being detected? In these circumstances the cheated merchant might be able to get a judgment against his supplier, but what good would it do if the supplier never returned to the Fairs? Perhaps ostracism by the other merchants might be an effective way to enforce the payment of judgments. However, if that is so, why was a legal system needed at all?

Another part of the inspiration for our formal model is the system of notaries that was widely used to register the existence of certain types of contracts and obligations. Typically, notaries were used for long-tern contracts such as those for apprenticeships, sales of land, and partnerships (Lopez and Raymond, 1955). The extensive use of notaries in certain areas to register agreements suggests that reputation via word of mouth alone was insufficient to support honest behavior and that a third party without any binding authority to enforce obligations was nonetheless quite valuable for promoting honest exchange.

2. Community Enforcement without Institutions

With the exception of barter transactions, in which physical commodities are exchanged on the spot, virtually all economic transactions leave open the possibility of cheating. In the Champagne Fairs, where merchants brought samples of their goods to trade, the quantities they brought were not always sufficient to supply all the potential demand. Then, the merchants sometimes exchanged promises—to deliver goods of like quality at a particular time and place, or to make payment in a certain form. Promises, however, can be broken.

To represent the idea that cheating may be profitable in a simple exchange, we use the Prisoners' Dilemma (PD) game as our model of a single exchange transaction. Although this PD model is too simple to portray "the richness of even simple contracts, it has the advantage" that it is very well known and its characteristics in the absence of institutions have been thoroughly studied, so that the incremental contribution made by the Law Merchant system will be quite clear. Moreover, the PD game represents in an uncluttered way the basic facts that traders have opportunities and temptations to cheat and that there are gains possible if the traders can suppress these temptations and find a way to cooperate.

The Prisoners' Dilemma game that we employ is shown below, where $\alpha > 1$ and $\alpha - \beta < 2$.

	Honest	Cheat
Honest	1, 1	$-\beta$, α
Cheat	$\alpha - \beta$	0, 0

Each player can choose to play one of two strategies: Honest or Cheat. As is well known, honest behavior maximizes the total profits of the two parties. However, a trader profits by cheating an honest partner ($\alpha > 1$) even though cheating imposes still a still larger loss on his honest partner ($1 - (-\beta) > \alpha - 1$).

It is clear that if this game is played only once, it is in each player's separate interest to play Cheat, since that play maximizes the player's individual utility regardless of the play chosen by the competitor. Consequently, the only *Nash equilibrium* of the game is for both to play Cheat. Then both are worse off than if they could somehow agree to play Honest.

Now suppose that the players trade repeatedly. Let α_{it} represent the action taken by player *i* in period *t*; let $\pi_i(\alpha_{1t}, \alpha_{2t})$ represent the resulting payoff earned by player *i* in period *t*; and let δ be the discount factor applied to compute the present value of a stream of payoffs. If trade is frequent, then δ is close to one; if trade occurs only once (or is quite infrequent), then δ is (close to) zero. A player's time weighted average payoff over the whole sequence of trades is given by:

$$\bar{\pi}_i = (1-\delta)\sum_{t=0}^{\infty}\delta^t \pi_i(a_{1t}, a_{2t}) \qquad (1)$$

In this repeated trading relationship, if the players can condition their actions in each period on what has transpired in the past, then they have an instrument to reward past honest behavior and to punish cheating. For the PD game, Axelrod (1984) has shown that for δ close enough to 1 there is a Nash equilibrium in which each player adopts the Tit-for-Tat (TFT) strategy—according to which that player chooses Honest play at $t = 0$ and for any later t plays whatever his partner played in the immediately preceding period (that is, at $t - 1$).

To see this, suppose that there are N traders and that there is some rule M that matches them at each stage. Let h_t be the history of trade through date t and let $M(h_t, i)$ be the identity of the trader who is matched with trader i at date t + 1 at history h_t. Consider the Adjusted Tit-for-Tat (ATFT) strategy according to which player i plays Honest at date 0 and then plays Cheat at date $t + 1$ if two conditions hold: (1) i made the play at date t that was specified by his equilibrium strategy and (2) $M(h_t, i)$ did not make the play at date t that was specified by his equilibrium strategy. If either condition fails, then the ATFT strategy calls for i to play Honest. The ATFT strategy formalizes the idea that a trader who cheats will be punished by the next merchant he meets if that merchant is honest, even is that merchant is not one who was cheated.

One might wonder what reason the merchant who was not cheated has to carry out the punishment. Within the PD model, the answer is twofold: First, punishing the cheater is directly profitable, because the punishment is delivered by playing Cheat. Second—and this is the reason that applies even in more general models—a merchant who fails to deliver a punishment, say by participating in a boycott, when he is supposed to do so is himself subject to punishment by the community of merchants. The community, in its turn, will carry out the punishment for the very same reasons. Theorem 1 below verifies that this system is in fact sometimes an equilibrium, that is, no merchant could gain at any time by deviating from its rules provided he expects other merchants to adhere to the rules in all future play.

Theorem 1. For δ near enough to one—specifically if

$$\delta \geq \text{Max}\,[\beta/(1+\beta), (\alpha - 1)/(1+\beta)] \tag{2}$$

—the adjusted Tit-for-Tat strategies are a subgame perfect equilibrium in the community trading game for *any* matching rule M.

Proof. By the Optimality Principle of dynamic programming, it suffices to show that there is no point at which player i can make a one-time play different from the equilibrium play that raises his total payoff. By inspection of the strategies, it is clear that the player may face one of four decision situations according to whether condition (1) only is satisfied, condition (2) only is satisfied, or both or neither of (1) and (2) are satisfied. If just condition (1) or condition (2) (not both) is satisfied, then a current period of deviation by player i is unprofitable if:

$$(1-\delta)[\alpha - \delta\beta] + \delta^2 \cdot 1 \leq (1-\delta) \cdot 1 + \delta \cdot 1 \tag{3}$$

which holds if and only if $\delta \geq (\alpha - 1)/(1 + \beta)$. If (1) and (2) are both satisfied, deviation is unprofitable if:

$$(1 - \delta)[0 - \delta\beta] + \delta^2 \cdot 1 \leq (1 - \delta) \cdot 1 + \delta \cdot 1 \quad (4)$$

and this is satisfied for all ≥ 0. If neither (1) nor (2) is satisfied, then deviation is unprofitable if:

$$(1 - \delta)[0 - \delta\beta] + \delta^2 \cdot 1 \leq (1 - \delta) \cdot \beta + \delta \cdot 1 \quad (5)$$

which only holds if and only if $\delta \geq \beta(1 + \beta)$.

Our formal analysis verifies that it is not necessary for any pair of traders to interact frequently—that is, for traders to establish client relationships—in order for the boycott mechanism to be effective. However, that simple conclusion relies on the condition that the members of the community are well enough informed to know whom to boycott. This condition is probably satisfied in some communities, but it is more problematical in others. For example, merchants engaged in long-distance trade could not be expected to know, of their own knowledge, whether another pair of merchants had honored their mutual obligations. Unless social and economic institutions developed to fill in the knowledge gap or unless other means of enforcement were established, honest behavior in a community of self-interested traders could not be maintained. Our model in the next section shows how a particular institution could have resolved this problem.

3. The Law Merchant Enforcement System

We now consider in more detail a model of trade in which outsiders cannot readily observe what has transpired in a given bilateral trade. While "disputes" may arise in which one party accuses the other of cheating, none of the other players have a method of freely verifying the parties' claims. Even if the dispute itself can be observed by others, they cannot costlessly determine whether cheating by one has actually occurred or whether the other is opportunistically claiming that it did.

In our model, we suppose that choices in each bilateral exchange are known only to the trading pair, so that each individual possesses direct information *solely about his own past trading experiences.*[3] To capture the idea that traders know little of their partners' past trading behavior, we use an extreme model of matching due to Townsend (1981). In Townsend's matching model, there is an infinity of traders indexed by ij where $i = 1$ or 2 and is an integer which may be positive or negative. At period t, trader $1j$ is matched with trader $2,j + t$.[4] In particular no two traders ever meet twice and no trader's behavior can directly or indirectly influence the behavior of his future trading partners. In the absence of institutions, players possess *no information* about their current partner's past behavior.

Under these conditions, the opportunities available to a player in any period cannot depend in any way on his past behavior. Strategies such as TFT and ATFT become ineffective. So, in our Prisoners' Dilemma game, it can never be in the players' interest to be honest. We have established the following:

Theorem 2. In the incomplete information Prisoners' Dilemma with the Townsend matching rule, the outcome at any Nash equilibrium is that each trader plays Cheat at every opportunity.[5]

With limited information about the past behavior of trading partners and no institution to compensate, there are no incentives for honest behavior. It is evident that incentives could be restored by introducing an institution that provides full information to each trader about how each other has behaved. Such an institution, however, would be costly to operate. Moreover, efficient trade does not require that every trader know the full history of the behavior of each other trader. For example, in the ATFT strategy considered in the preceding section, a trader need only know his own history of behavior and whether his partner has defected in the immediately preceding period to determine his own current behavior. One part of the problem is to arrange that the traders are *adequately* well informed so that they can sanction a Cheater when that is required.

However, there is a second problem that the institutions must overcome: Traders may not find it in their individual interests to participate in punishing those who cheat. As one simple example, if trade is expected to be profitable, a trader will be reluctant to engage in a trade boycott. The institutions must be designed both to keep the traders adequately informed of their responsibilities and to motivate them to do their duties.

In the model we develop below, this second problem has multiple aspects. First, traders must be motivated to execute sanctions against Cheaters when that is a personally costly activity. Second, traders must be motivated to keep well enough informed to know when sanctions are required, even though information gathering activities may be personally costly and difficult to monitor. In effect, one who keeps informed about who should be punished for past transgressions is supplying a public good; he deters the traders from cheating against *others.* Moreover, in our model, no other trader except his current partner will ever know if a trader does not check his partner's past history, so the trader could avoid supplying the public good without facing any sanction from future traders. Third, traders who are cheated must be motivated to document the episode, even though providing documentation may be personally costly. After all, from the cheated trader's perspective, what's lost is lost, and there may be little point in "throwing good money after bad." But if players who are cheated are unwilling to invest in informing their neighbors, then, just as surely as if the neighbors are unwilling to invest in being informed, the Cheater will profit from his action and Honest trade will suffer. These are the problems that the trading institution in our model must solve.

The institution that we model as the resolution of these problems is based on the presence of a specialized actor—a "judge" or "law merchant" (LM) who serves both as a repository of information and as an adjudicator of disputes.

The core version of our model is based on the following assumptions. After any exchange, each party can accuse the other of cheating and appeal to the LM. Any dispute appealed to the LM is perfectly and honestly adjudicated at cost C to the plaintiff. (We consider the case of a dishonest LM later.) The LM's pronouncements include the ability to award damages if the defendant is found to have cheated the plaintiff. However, payment of the damage award is *voluntary* in the sense that there is no state to enforce payment. Finally, we assume that any party can visit the LM prior to finalizing a contract. At that time, for a cost of Q, the party can *query* the LM for the records of previous judgments about any other player. Without querying the LM, players have *no* information about their current partners' trading history.

By structuring this sequence of events around the basic trade transaction, we create an "extended" state game called the *LM system game* with the following sequence of play:

(a) Players may query the LM about their current partner at utility cost $Q > 0$. In response to a query, the LM reports to the traders whether a party has any "unpaid judgments." Whatever transpires at this stage becomes common knowledge among the LM and the two partners.
(b) The two traders play the (Prisoners' Dilemma) game and learn the outcome.
(c) Either may appeal to the LM at personal cost $C > 0$, but only if he has queried the LM.
(d) If either party makes an appeal, then the LM awards a judgment, J, to the plaintiff if he has been Honest and his trading partner has Cheated (we call this a *valid appeal*); otherwise, no award is made.
(e) If a judgment J is awarded, the defendant may pay it, at personal cost $f(J)$, or he may refuse to pay, at cost zero.
(f) Any unpaid judgments are recorded by the LM and become part of the LM's permanent record.

The players' utilities for the extended stage game are determined as the sum of the payments received less those made. For example, a player who queries, plays Honest, is Cheated, and appeals, receives $-Q - \beta + -CJ$ if the other party pays the judgment and $-Q - \beta - C$ if he does not.

The function f: $\Re^+ - \Re^+$ represents the utility cost of paying a given judgment. We naturally assume that f is increasing and continuous. Thus, the greater the size of the judgment, the greater the cost to the defendant. We also assume that $f(x) \geq x$: The cost of paying a judgment is never less than the judgment itself. This excludes the possibility that the payment of judgments adds to the total utility of the players. The desired behavior of the parties in various contingencies under the Law Merchant system is fully described by the *Law Merchant System Strategy* (LMSS) as follows.

At substage (a), a trader queries the Law Merchant if he has no unpaid judgments on record, but not otherwise.

At substage (b), if either player has failed to query the Law Merchant or if the query establishes that at least one player has an outstanding judgment, then both traders play Cheat (which we may interpret as a refusal by the honest trader to trade); otherwise, both play Honest.

At substage (c), if both parties queried at substage (a) and exactly one of the two players Cheated at substage (b), then the victim appeals to the LM; otherwise, no appeal is filed.

At substage (d), if a valid appeal was filed, the LM awards damages of J to the aggrieved party.

At substage (e), the defendant pays the judgment J if and only if he has no other outstanding judgments.

Theorem 3. The Law Merchant System Strategy is a symmetric sequential equilibrium strategy of the LM system game if and only if the following inequality holds:

$$(1 - Q)\delta / (1 - \delta) \geq f(J) \geq \max[\alpha - I), f(C)]$$

If this condition is satisfied, then the average payoff per period for each player (at the equilibrium) is $1 - Q$.

Remark. The condition in Theorem 3 can be satisfied only if $1 - Q$ is positive (because the right-hand-side is at least $\alpha - 1 > 0$).

Proof. To establish that the LMSS is a symmetric sequential equilibrium strategy, we again appeal to the Optimality Principle of Dynamic Programming. If we show that there is no point at which a single change in the trader's current action only (followed by later adherence to the LMSS) can raise the trader's expected payoff at that point, then there is no point at which some more complicated deviation can be profitable, either.

In evaluating his expected payoffs, the player must make certain conjectures about what other players have done in the past in order to forecast what they will do in the future. To verify the equilibrium, we may assume that the trader believes that all other traders have played according to the LMSS in all past plays except those where the trader has actually observed a deviation. We may also assume that the trader believes that all others will adhere to the LMSS in all future plays. To derive the conditions under which the LMSS is an equilibrium strategy, we work backward through a typical extended stage game.

First, we check when it "pays to pay judgments," that is, under what conditions a player will find it more profitable to pay any judgment rendered against him than to refuse to pay. (We ignore the sunk portion of the payoff which is unaffected by later behavior.) Paying the judgment J yields an additional payoff of $-f(J)$ in the current period. In future periods, the player will spend Q to query the LM and earn a trading payoff of 1, for a total of $1 - Q$. In terms of lifetime average payoff, paying the judgment leads to $-(1 - \delta)f(J) + \delta(1 - Q)$. If the trader refuses to pay the judgment, then his current period payoff is zero and, given the system, his payoff is about zero in every subsequent period.

Therefore, it "pays to pay judgments" is and only if $-(1-\delta)f(J)+\delta(1-Q)\geq 0$, or equivalently,

$f(\mathrm{J})\ (1-Q)\delta/(1-\delta)$. (7)

Second, does it pay the victim to appeal to substage (c), incurring personal cost C? Given the strategies, the trader expects the judgment to be paid. So he will appeal if and only if $J \geq C$. It is convenient to write this condition as:

$f(J) \geq f(C)$. (8)

If there are no unpaid judgments and the LM has been queried, does it pay the trader to play Honest? If he does, then his current period payoff will be $1-Q$. If he Cheats, and later adheres to the strategy (which entails paying the judgment), then his payoff will be $-Q+\alpha-f(\mathrm{J})$. Equilibrium requires that the former is larger, that is:

$f(J) \geq \alpha - 1$. (9)

Does it pay the trader otherwise to play Cheat? With the given strategy, his future opportunities do not depend on his play in this case, and Cheat always maximizes the payoffs for the current period, so the answer is that it does pay, regardless of parameter values.

Does it pay the players to query the LM if neither has an outstanding judgment? If a player does so, his current period payoff is expected to be $1-Q$. If not, it will be zero. In both cases, his payoffs per periods for subsequent periods are expected to be $1-Q$. So it pays off only if

$Q \leq 1$. (10)

However, condition (10) is redundant in view of conditions (7) and (9).

Does it pay a party with an outstanding judgment to query? No, because the party's expected payoff is $-Q$ if he queries and 0 if he does not.

Thus, regardless of the circumstances wrought by past play, there is no situation in which a one-time deviation from the Law Merchant System Strategy that is profitable for a trader provided that conditions (7)-(9) hold. These are the conditions summarized in formula (6).

Corollary. There is a judgment amount J which makes the LMSS a symmetric sequential equilibrium strategy (that is, satisfying formula (6)) if and only if

$(1-Q)\delta/(1-\delta) \geq \max[\alpha-1, f(C)]$. (11)

Conditions (7)-(10) show the relationship among various parameters for the LM system to support the efficient cooperation. Each corresponds to one of the problems we described in introducing the model. Condition (7) requires that Cheating and then paying a judgment not be profitable; put simply, the judgment must be large enough to deter Cheating. Condition (8) requires that judgments excess the cost of an appeal, that is, the judgment must also be large enough to encourage the injured party to appeal. Otherwise, information about Cheating will never reach the LM and Cheating will go unpunished. The two previous conditions require that the judgment be large enough, but condition (9) requires that it not be so large that the Cheater would refuse to pay, for then the injured party would not expect to collect, and so would find it unprofitable to appeal. Notice that the feasibility of satisfying all these conditions simultaneously depends on the technology of wealth transfer summarized by f. If the traders live at great distances from one another and if their principle asset holdings are illiquid (such as land and fixed capital, or reputation and family connections), then wealth transfers may be quite costly, $(f(J)/J$ may be large) and the fines required by the LM system then will not work.

Finally, condition (10) requires that it be worthwhile for the traders to query the LM. In our model, this condition is implied by the others, but that need not be true for extension of the model. If traders do not query the LM, then they will have insufficient information to administer punishments, so once again Cheating will go unpunished. The LM institution encourages queries by making them a condition for appealing the LM, and, as we have seen, querying deters Cheating. At equilibrium, traders who fail to query are constantly cheated by their trading partners.

If condition (6) fails, then the LMSS is not an equilibrium strategy. However, the condition is satisfied for a wide range of plausible parameter values. Table 1 below gives some acceptable values for the parameters. In it, we assume that $f(x) = x/(1 - p)$ where p is the percentage of value that is lost when assets are transferred. The LMSS is an equilibrium strategy for some J with the given combinations of parameters and for any other combination with lower transaction costs (lower p, Q and C), less temptation to cheat (lower α) and more frequent trade (higher δ). In the table, $J = C/(1 - p) = \alpha - 1$ is the judgment which is just sufficient to provide the incentives for not cheating and for complaining about being cheated.

For example, in the last line of Table 1, Cheating is seven times more profitable than playing Honest at each current round, the cost of querying the LM consumes one-third of the profits of Honest venturers, the cost of complaining is three times the profits of the venture, and half of any assets transferred in settlement of a judgment are lost. The judgment itself is six times what the Cheater could expect to earn from Honest trade with his next partner (nine times net of transaction costs). Nevertheless, if the inter-trade discount factor is at least 0.9, the LM system is in equilibrium and supports honest behavior, filing valid complaints, and payment of judgments.

4. Minimizing Transaction Costs

Theorem 3 shows that the LM system restores cooperation even when the players know little about their partners' histories. There are transaction costs necessary to maintain this system, however: That the average payoff per period is $1 - Q$ reflects the transaction cost of Q per period incurred by each trader to support the Law Merchant system.

Notice that the costs, C, of making and investigating a claim and cost $f(J) - J$ of making the transfer do not appear in the expression of the average payoff. These costs appear in condition (6): The Law Merchant system is not viable if the cost of making and investigating a claim or the cost of paying a judgment is too high, for then the traders cannot reasonably expect that the others will make

Table 1
Sample Parameters for Which the Law Merchant Strategy is a Sequential Equilibrium Strategy

Transaction Costs Parameters			*Tempted to Cheat*	*Discount Factor*	*Penalty or Judgement*
Q	*C*	*p*	*a*	*d*	*J*
0.50	*0.5*	*50%*	*2.0*	*0.67*	*1.0*
0.50	*1.0*	*50%*	*3.0*	*0.80*	*2.0*
0.33	*3.0*	*50%*	*7.0*	*0.90*	*6.0*

claims and pay judgments when they should. However, once these costs are low enough that the threat to file claims with the Law Merchant is credible, they act only as a deterrent: These costs are never actually incurred at equilibrium in our model of the Law Merchant system.

Is the Law Merchant system the least expensive way to induce Honest behavior from traditional traders at every stage? Theoretically, any institution that restores incentives for honest trading by restoring the effectiveness of decentralized enforcement must inform a player when his partner has cheated in the past. If the temptation to Cheat is small and the value of continued trading is high, then this information need not be perfect, as in our model. So it may be possible to induce honest behavior using a less costly information system—one that costs only $q < Q$ to inform a trader adequately well—and correspondingly to increase the traders' average payoffs from $1 - Q$ to $1 - q$.[6] However, using imperfect information to economize on information costs calls merely for a refinement of the Law Merchant system—not for something fundamentally different. It is not possible to provide correct incentives without incurring some information cost of this kind and, as we have seen, the LM system avoids the unnecessary costs of dispute resolution and loss on transfers.

In operation, the Law Merchant system would appear to be a low cost way to disseminate information, for two reasons. First, the LM system centralizes the information system so that, for information about any partner, a player need only go to one place. He need not incur costs trying (i) to establish who was his current partner's previous partner, and (ii) to find the partner to make the relevant inquiry. Second, for the Prisoners' Dilemma, it is not sufficient to know only one period's history, but several.[7] The LM system not only centralizes this information but provides it in a very simple form: all that needs to be communicated is whether there are any outstanding judgments. For large communities, locating each of one's partner's previous partners and asking them for information is likely to be more expensive than the centralized record-keeping system of the Law Merchant.

Given the lack of quantitative evidence about the full costs of running different kinds of institutions, it is not possible to write down a convincing formal model to establish that the LM system minimizes costs in the class of feasible institutions. What we can say confidently is that the kind of costs incurred by the LM system are inevitable if Honest trade is to be sustained in the face of self-interested behavior and that the system seems well designed to keep those costs as low as possible.

5. Dishonest Law Merchants

Our analysis in section 2 proceeded on the assumption that the Law Merchant has no independent interest in the outcome of his decision. In addition, he is diligent, honest, and fair.

One need not look far in history (or, for that matter, in the modem world) to see that judges are not always so perfect. Within our model, there are many small amendments that could be made to insert opportunities for bribery and extortion. Although we do not provide a systematic treatment of these, we shall give a brief development of one of them to emphasize the simple idea that the Law Merchant business is itself valuable and that LMs may wish to maintain their reputation for honesty and diligence in order to keep the business active.

The most obvious problem with this reputation based account is that it seems to presume that a trader who is extorted by the Law Merchant can somehow make his injury widely known to the community of traders. It might be that the Law Merchant is a more sedentary merchant than the long-distance traders whom he serves, so that idea is perhaps not so far-fetched. Nevertheless, we shall argue that even if, in the spirit of our earlier analysis, there is no way for the trader to inform others about his injury, it may still be an equilibrium for the LM to behave honestly, due to the "client" incentives in the long-term relationship between the LM and each individual trader. More precisely, we will show that there is an equilibrium of the system in which every trader expects that if he pays a bribe he will be subjected to repeated attempts at extortion in the future; this dissuades the trader from paying any bribe. Then, a Law Merchant who commits to his threat to damage the reputation of a trader succeeds only in losing business, so he does not profit from making the threat.

To set the context for the formal extension, we modify the Law Merchant system stage game to regard the Law Merchant as a player. In the original version, the LM was allowed no choices, but let us nevertheless suppose that the LM earned a payoff of $2e > 0$ per contract, which is paid for as part of the $2Q$ that the parties spend to query the LM.

Next, we create a Modified Law Merchant System game in which our basic model is altered to allow the LM to solicit bribes. Initially, we consider only one kind of bribe that extorted from a trader with no unpaid judgments by an LM who threatens to report falsely that there *are* unpaid judgments. Thus, we assume that before the traders make their queries, the LM may demand that one of the traders who has no unpaid judgment pay a bribe, $B \geq O$. The amount B demanded is chosen by the LM. If the bribe is not paid and the query is made, the LM is committed to report falsely that the trader has an unpaid judgment.[8]

The trader next decides whether to pay the bribe. The stage game then continues as previously described. When a bribe of B is paid, the LM's payoff is increased by B and the victim's payoff is reduced by an equal amount.[9]

Now consider the following variation of the Law Merchant System Strategy for the traders. If a player has no unpaid judgments and no bribe is solicited from him at the current stage, then he plays the LMSS as previously described. If the player has never before paid a bribe and a bribe is solicited, then he refuses to pay the bribe and does not query the LM in the current period. If the player has ever before paid a bribe, then he pays any bribe up to $\alpha - Q$ that is demanded of him. A player who has paid a bribe at the current round plays Cheat at that round and refuses to pay any judgment made against him. We call this specification the Extended Law Merchant System Strategy (ELMSS).

The Law Merchant's expected behavior is specified by the LM's Bribe Solicitation Strategy (BSS). If one of the present traders has no unpaid judgment but has previously paid a bribe, then the LM demands a payment of $\alpha - Q$. Otherwise, the LM does not demand any payment.

Theorem 4. If condition (6) holds and, in addition,

$$\alpha \leq 1 + (1 - Q)(2\delta - 1)/(1 - \delta)$$

then there is a sequential equilibrium of the Modified Law Merchant System game in which each trader adopts the strategy ELMSS and the Law Merchant adopts the strategy BSS.

Proof. Once again, we check that there is no contingency after which a onetime deviation by any player is profitable, when each player expects that the others have adhered to the strategy except where deviations have been explicitly observed, and each expects that all will adhere to it in the future. As before, we begin again from the last stage and work forward.

Consider a trader who has paid a bribe and cheated, and been assessed a judgment of $J > 0$. He expects a zero future payoff in each future period if he pays the judgment (because he will be extorted again and again). He expects the same zero payoff if he does not pay, since he will then have an unpaid judgment on his record. Since $-f(J) < 0$, he will find it most profitable to refuse to pay the judgment.

Having paid a bribe B, a trader expects to earn x this period and zero in the future if he cheats today, or 1 this period and zero in the future in he does not. Since $\alpha > 1$, cheating is most profitable.

Given that a player has paid a bribe before, if a bribe B is demanded today, then the profits from playing the bribe, querying, and cheating are expected to be $\alpha - Q - B$; not paying leads to profits of zero. Hence, it is at least as profitable to pay the bribe whenever $B \leq \alpha - Q$.

If a trader has paid a bribe before, the strategy specifies that he will pay any bribe up to $\alpha - Q$ in the current period. In this case, according to the strategies, no trader's play in future periods will depend on whether the LM demands a bribe or on the amount of the bribe, so his most profitable play is to demand $\alpha - Q$.

Suppose a trader has not paid a bribe before and a bribe, B, is demanded currently. If the trader pays the bribe then, according to the strategy, he will cheat and refuse to pay the judgment. The resulting payoff is $\alpha - B - Q$ in the current period and, as a trader with an unpaid judgment, zero in future periods. If he refuses to pay the bribe, then his expected payoff is zero in the current period and $1 - Q$ in subsequent periods. So, it is most profitable for him to refuse to pay if

$$(1 - \delta)(\alpha - B - Q) + \delta \cdot 0 \leq (1 - \delta) \cdot 0 + \delta \cdot (1 - Q),$$

which is equivalent to condition (12).

Finally, when facing a trader who has never before paid a bribe, the LM expects that any demand for a bribe will be refused and that the trader will also not query in the current period, leading to a loss of revenues of e, with no effect on play in future periods. Hence, it is most profitable for the LM not to demand any bribe in this case.

Theorem 4 pertains to a model in which only one kind of dishonest behavior by the LM is possible. The problem of discouraging other kinds of dishonest behavior may require other strategies. From our preliminary analysis, it appears that the most difficult problem is to deter the LM from soliciting or accepting bribes from traders who have an unpaid judgment but wish to conceal that fact. By concealing the judgment, cheating, and refusing to pay the new judgment, the trader could "earn" $\alpha - Q$ and a portion of that might be offered as a bribe to the LM. As we add richness to the possibilities for cheating, it is natural to expect that the necessary institutions and strategies must respond in a correspondingly rich way.

6. Conclusion

We began our analysis by studying an environment in which private information about behavior in exchanges is a potential impediment to trade. Under complete information, even if meetings among particular pairs of traders are infrequent, informal norms of behavior are theoretically sufficient to police deviations. But when information is costly, the equilibrium may potentially break down and informal means may not be sufficient to police deviations.

The Law Merchant enforcement system that we have studied restores the equilibrium status of Honest behavior. It succeeds even though there is no state with police power and authority over a wide geographical realm to enforce contracts. Instead, the system works by making the reputation system of enforcement work better. The institutions we have studied provide people with the information they need to recognize those who have cheated, and it provides incentives for those who have been cheated to provide evidence of their injuries. Then, the reputation system itself provides the incentives for honest behavior and for payment by those who are found to have violated the code, and it encourages traders to boycott those who have flouted the system. Neither the reputation mechanism nor the institutions can be effective by themselves. They are complementary parts of a total system that works together to enforce honest behavior.

Our account of the Law Merchant system is, of course, incomplete. Once disputes came to be resolved in a centralized way, the merchants in Western Europe enhanced and refined their private legal code to serve the needs of the merchant trade—all prior to the rise of the nation-state. Without this code and the system for enforcement, trade among virtual strangers would have been much more cumbersome, or even impossible.[10] Remarkably, the Law Merchant institution appears to have been structured to support trade in a way that minimizes transaction costs, or at least incurs costs only in categories that are indispensable to any system that relies on boycotts as sanctions.

Our model is a stylization, not set in a particular locality at a particular date. Necessarily, then, it omits many important elements that some historians will argue are essential to understanding the institutions that are found there and then. However, our core contention that institutions sometimes arise to make reputation mechanisms more effective by communicating information seems almost beyond dispute. The Mishipora, described in the Hebrew Talmud, according to which those who failed to keep promises were punished by being publicly denounced; the use of the "hue and cry" to identify cheaters in medieval England; the famed "Scarlet Letter," described in Hawthorne's famous story; and the public stocks and pillories of 17th century New England, which were sometimes used to punish errant local merchants, are all examples of institutions and practices in which a principal aim is to convey information to the community about who has violated its norms.

It is our contention that an enduring pattern of trade over a wide geographical area cannot be sustained if it is profitable for merchants to renege on promises or repudiate agreements. In the larger trading towns and cities of northern Europe in the 10th through 13th centuries, it was not possible for every merchant to know the reputations of all others, so extensive trade required the development of some system like the Law Merchant system to fill in the gap.

Many of the key characteristics of our model correspond to practices found at the Champagne Fairs. While merchants at the Fairs were not required to query prior to any contract, the institutions of the Fair provided this information in another manner. As noted above, the Fairs closely controlled entry and exit. A merchant could not enter the Fair without being in good standing with those who controlled entry, and any merchant caught cheating at the Fair would be incarcerated and brought to justice under the rules of the Fair. So anyone a merchant met at the Fair could be presumed to have a "good reputation" in precisely the sense of our model. It did not indicate that all free merchants had never cheated in the past; but it did indicate that anyone who had been convicted of cheating had made good on the judgment against him. Moreover, because merchants might disappear rather than pay their judgments, judges at the Fairs had to balance the size of their judgment so that the value of being able to attend future Fairs exceeded the award.

According to Verlinden (1963, p. 132): "At the end of the 12th century and during the first half of the 13th, the Champagne Fairs were indeed the centre of international commercial activity of the western world." This is a long time for a single fair to maintain such dominance, but the Champagne Fair had two advantages over its potential competitors. First, it had an effective system for enforcing exchange contracts. Second, as we observed earlier, there are important economies of scope and scale in reputation mechanisms. Other, smaller fairs that tried to compete with the Champagne Fairs on an equal footing would have to contend with merchants who participated only long enough to make a profitable cheating transaction and then return to the Champagne Fairs where their participation rights were intact.

Despite this observation, it must be counted a weakness of the model that it does not fully account for trade outside of a single trading center. Even if the Law Merchant and related systems were effective underpinnings for local trade, how was information about a trader's dishonesty in one location transmitted to another? The model in this paper is too simple to handle this problem, but we hope to extend our approach to the institutions that developed during the Middle Ages to protect against the added problems raised by spatial separation. This includes the merchant gilds in northern Europe, the consulates of the Italian city-states, and the organization of alien merchants into colonies (like the Steelyard in medieval London) with local privileges and duties. These institutions can also be understood from the perspective developed in this paper—they are designed to reinforce reputation mechanisms that alone are insufficient to support trade.

The Law Merchant system of judges and reputations was eventually replaced by a system of state enforcement, typically in the late Middle Ages or the early modern era in Western Europe. Enforcement of the private codes by the state added a new dimension to enforcement, especially in later periods when nation-states exercised extensive geographic control. Rather than depend for punishment upon the decentralized behavior of merchants, state enforcement could seize the property of individuals who resisted paying judgments, or put them into jail. If judgments could be enforced this way, then, in principle, the costs of keeping the merchants well informed about one another's past behavior could be saved. To the extent that the costs of running state adjudication and enforcement were roughly similar to the costs of running the private system and to the extent that taxes can be efficiently collected, a comprehensive state-run system would have the advantage that it eliminates the need for each individual to pay Q each period. As the volume of trade increased in the late Middle Ages, the cost saving from that source would have been substantial.[11] Thus our approach suggests that the importance of the role of the state enforcement of contracts was not that it provided a means of enforcing contracts where one previously did not exist. Rather, it was to reduce the transaction costs of policing exchange.[12]

In closing, we return to the broader implications of our work for the study of institutions. In complete information settings, institutions are frequently unnecessary because decentralized enforcement is sufficient to police deviations. However, this conclusion fails in environments where information is incomplete or costly. In the context of our model, the Adjusted Tit-for-Tat strategy requires that a trader know his current partner's previous history. When such information is difficult or costly to obtain, decentralized enforcement mechanisms break down. Institutions like those of the Law Merchant system resolve the fundamental problems of restoring the information that underpins an effective reputation system while both economizing on information and overcoming a whole array of incentive problems that obstruct the gathering and dissemination of that information.

Notes

1. Either by facilitation coordination (Banks and Calvert, 1989) or by preventing reneging on agreements (Weingast and Marshall, 1988).
2. Of course, considerable variation existed across locations, especially between northern and southern Europe. In the latter area, city-states arose, providing law and protection beyond the immediate area of the city. Further, over time, as the nature of governments changed, so too did their involvement in the legal enforcement process.
3. This is also the premise of the game-theoretic analysis of Kandori (1989).
4. This matching rule is often called the "Townsend Turnpike," for Townsend suggested that one way to think of it is as two infinitely long sets of traders moving in opposite directions.
5. Kandori (1989) has shown that there exist other matching rules for which, despite the absence of sufficient bilateral trade and each player's ignorance about what has happened in trades among other players, there may be nevertheless be a cue of behavior that supports efficient exchange. However, as Kandori argues, the resulting system is "brittle" and leads to a breakdown of honest trade when these are even minor disturbances to the system. Both Kandori (1989) and Okuno-Fujiwara and Postlewaite (1989) consider other institutional solutions to this problem.
6. And, given that our model has a fixed starting state, there is really nothing to be learned from the initial query, so that could be eliminated with some small cost savings. However, this is just an artifact of our desire for modeling simplicity and not an inherent extra cost of the system.
7. Kandori (1989) shows that in the repeated Prisoners' Dilemma, players must know at least two periods of history for each partner to sustain an equilibrium with Honest behavior.
8. If the Law Merchant cannot commit to this action, then it is easy to show that there is an equilibrium in which the trader ignores the threat and the LM does not carry it out. It is no doubt true that some threats are disposed of in just this way—the victim simply calls the LM's bluff. We are interested in showing that the reputation mechanism can sometimes function even when the LM's threat must be taken at face value.
9. If we assumed that transfers are costly here, as in the case of judgments, then the victim would become more reluctant to pay and bribery would be less likely to succeed.
10. Of course, merchants could and did communicate extensively, writing letters, engaging in trial relations, and checking the credentials of their trading partners.

Where possible, they also relied on family members and client relationships to provide reliable services. But with geographic specialization in production, these devices alone could not allow merchants to escape the need to rely on the promises of individuals with whom they were not well acquainted.

11. Historically, the successful state enforcement came in a series of stages. As suggested above, state enforcement began with the adoption of the legal codes by a wide range of cities and towns. Some of these evolved over time into large city-states (e.g., Venice or Genoa) or, later, became part of a larger nation-state (e.g., London). For a discussion of the evolution of legal codes underpinning merchant trade, see North (1989).
12. As we emphasized in section 4, however, a full evaluation of state enforcement must also assess the potential for corruption in the enforcement mechanisms of state enforcement.

References

Abreu, Dilip, 1988, "On the Theory of Infinitely Repeated Games with Discounting," *Econometrica* 39, 383-96.

Aumann,Robert, 1985, "Repeated Games," in George Feiwel (ed.), *Issues in Contemporary Microeconomics and Welfare*, Macmillan Press, London, 209-42.

Axelrod, Robert, 1984, *The Evolution of Cooperation*, Basic Books, New York.

Axelrod, Robert, 1986, "An Evolutionary Approach to Social Norms," *American Political Science Review* 80, 1095-1111.

Banks, Jeffrey and Randall Calvert, 1989, "Equilibria in Coordination," Garnes, MS, University of Rochester.

Benson, Bruce, 1989, "The Spontaneous Evolution of Commercial Law," *Southern Economic Journal* 644-61.

Berman, Harold, 1983, *Law and Revolution: The Formation of Western Legal Tradition*, Harvard University Press.

Calvert, Randall, 1989, "Reciprocity Among Self-interested Actors," in Peter C. Ordeshook (ed.), *Models of Strategic Choice in Politics*, Michigan University Press.

DeRoover, Raymond, 1963, "The Organization of Trade," in M. M. Postan and E. E. Rich (eds.), *Cambridge Economic History of Europe*, Vol. III.

Fudenberg, Drew and Eric Maskin, 1986, "The Folk Theorem in Repeated Games with Discounting or with Incomplete Information," *Econometrica* 54, 533-554.

Greif, Avner, 1989, "Reputation and Coalitions in Medieval Trade," *Journal of Economic History* 49, 857-82.

Jones, William Catron, 1961, "The Settlement of Merchant Disputes by Merchants: An Approach to the Study of the History of Commercial Law," Ph.D. dissertation, University of Chicago.

Kandori, Michihiro, 1989, "Information and Coordination in Strategic Interaction Over Time," Ph.D. dissertation, Stanford University.

Klein, Benjamin and Keith Leffler, 1981, "The Role of Market Forces in Assuring Contractual Performance," *Journal of Political Economy* 89, 615-41.

Lopez, Robert S., 1976, *Commercial Revolution of the Middle Ages, 950-1350*, Cambridge University Press, Cambridge.

Lopez, Robert S. and Irving W. Raymond, 1955, *Medieval Trade in the Mediterranean World*, Columbia University Press, New York.

Mitchell, W., 1904, *Essay on the Early History of the Law Merchant*, Cambridge University Press, Cambridge.

North, Douglass, 1989, "Institutions, Transactions Costs, and the Rise of Merchant Empires," in James Tracey (ed.), *The Economics of the Rise of Merchant Empires*, Vol. 2.

North, Douglass, 1989, "Institutions, Institutional Change, and Economic Performance," Book MS, Washington University.
North, Douglass and Robert Thomas, 1973, *Rise of the Western World*, Cambridge University Press, Cambridge.
Okuno-Fujiwara, M. and Andrew Postlewaite, 1989, "Social Norms in Random Matching Games," mimeo, University of Pennsylvania.
Pirenne, Henri, 1925, *Medieval Cities: Their Origins and the Revival of Trade*, Princeton University Press.
Rorig, Fritz, 1967, *The Medieval Town*, University of California Press, Berkeley.
Scutton, Thomas E., 1909, "General Survey of the History of the Law Merchant," in *Select Essays in Anglo American Legal History*, compiled by the Association of American Law Schools.
Shapiro, Carl, 1983, "Premiums for High Quality Products as Returns to Reputations," *Quarterly Journal of Economics* 98(4), 659-679.
Shapiro, Carl and Joseph Stiglitz, 1984, "Equilibrium Unemployment as a Worker Discipline Device," *American Economic Review* 74(3), 433-444.
Thrupp, Silvia, 1948, *The Merchant Class of Medieval London*, University of Chicago Press, Chicago.
Townsend, Robert M., 1981, "Models of Money with Spatially Separated Agents," in J. H. Kareken and Neil Wallace (eds.), *Models of Monetary Economies*, Federal Reserve Bank, Minneapolis.
Trakman, L, 1983. *The Law Merchant*, Littleton, Rothman and Co.
Verlinden, C., 1963, "Markets and Fairs," *Cambridge Economic History of Europe*, Vol. III.
Weingast, Barry R. and William Marshall, 1988, "The Industrial Organization of Congress: or Why Legislatures, like Firms, are not Organized as Markets," *Journal of Political Economy* 96, 132-163.

38

Legal Evolution in Primitive Societies

Bruce Benson

The anthropological literature on primitive legal systems has attracted considerable attention from economists in recent years. These systems are of interest because they apparently represent examples of law and order without a state government (Posner 1980, 1981). Economic theory explains human behavior by considering how individuals react to incentives and constraints in various institutional settings, and the following examination will emphasize institutions and incentives which influence legal evolution. Such an economic perspective has been applied to primitive legal systems by Demsetz (1967) who explained the incentives to establish property rights and applied his analysis with examples from American Indian history. Johnsen (1986) explored the consequences of such incentives for the formation and protection of property rights among the Kwakiutl Indians. Similarly, Baden et al. (1981) examined the resource management incentives of various American Indian tribes. The presentation below extends these studies by emphasizing the process and institutions of legal change (property right formation and change) in order to focus on an argument recently resurrected by Posner (1980, 1981). Posner clearly demonstrated that examination of primitive legal systems from the perspective provided by the economic approach reveals that formal institutions of government are not needed in order to have a system of effective law and law enforcement. However, he emphasized the "customary" character of primitive law and described it as a "complex, slowly changing system of exact rules" (1981, p. 178). Indeed, Posner maintained that primitive law had no means of changing rules quickly.

Posner is not, by any means, the only legal scholar to express the opinion that primitive law lacked a method of rapid legal change. In fact, this opinion is frequently traced to Sir Henry Maine (1864). Maine wrote that "the rigidity of primitive law...has chained down the mass of the human race to those views of life and conduct which they entertained at the time when their usages were first consolidated into a systematic form" (1864, p. 74). Yet, anthropologist E. A. Hoebel proposed that, "If ever Sir Henry Maine fixed an erroneous notion on modern legal historians, it was the idea that primitive law, once formulated, is stiff and ritualistic" (1954, p. 283). Similarly, Popisil (1971, pp. 194 and 206) argued that those who view primitive law as static have simply "assumed" that tribal laws have existed forever. He suggested that most anthropologists have just not been interested in studying legal change, but when they do the process of change is easy to detect.

The presentation which follows will provide a theoretical description of the process of legal evolution in the absence of government legislation by pulling together the insights of economists (e.g., Smith, Hayek) and legal theorists (e.g., Fuller). The implications of the theory will then be illustrated with a brief description of examples of legal change among the Kapauka Papuans of West New Guinea, who were extensively observed by Popisil (1971).

1. Evolution of Customary Law

Malinowski (1926) defined law from an anthropologist's perspective as "the rules which curb human inclinations, passions or instinctive drives; rules which protect the rights of one citizen against the concupiscence, cupidity or malice of the other." This definition suggests that a society in which customs and social mores are widely accepted and obeyed has a legal system even with no state government, written constitution or codes. "Morality" and law would appear to be synonymous. Legal theorist Lon Fuller, however, differentiated between these concepts:

> Morality, too, is concerned with controlling human conduct by rules...how, when we are confronted with a system of rules, [do] we decide whether the system as a whole shall be called a system of law or a system of morality. The only answer to that question ventured here is that contained in the word "enterprise" when I have asserted that law, viewed as a direction of purposive human effort, consists in the "enterprise of subjecting human conduct to the governance of rules." (Fuller 1964, p. 130)

Thus, Fuller's definition of law includes more than simply the existence of "social mores" defining rules of behavior. There must be an "enterprise," and it is "precisely because law is a purposeful enterprise that it displays structural constancies..." (Fuller 1964, p. 151) The enterprise of law generates the mechanisms of enforcement, dispute resolution, *and* change.[1]

In the absence of the coercive power of government, customary law must take its "authority" from another source. In this regard, Hayek explained that law can be articulated through dispute resolution by arbitrators who have no state backed coercive authority. In such cases:

> The questions which they will have to decide will not be whether the parties have abused anybody's will, but whether their actions have conformed to expectations which other parties had reasonably formed because they correspond to the practices on which the everyday conduct of the members of the group was based. The significance of customs here is that they give rise to expectations that guide people's actions, and what will be regarded as binding will therefore be those practices that everybody counts on being observed and which thereby condition the success of most activities. (Hayek 1973, pp. 96-97)

This view of "authority" also characterizes Fuller's concept of law since he wrote "there is no doubt that a legal system derives its ultimate support from a sense of its being 'right'...this sense, deriving as it does from tacit expectations and acceptances..." (1964, p. 138)

Primitive cultures generally had clearly determined systems of private property (e.g., see Goldschmidt 1951; Popisil 1971; Benson 1990). The emphasis on private property may seem surprising to some who think of tribal society as some sort of socialist or communal system. On the contrary, however, private property rights are a common characteristics of primitive societies—they constitute the most important primary rules of conduct.[2] After all, the authority of customary law arose through voluntary recognition, and enforcement involved voluntary reciprocal arrangements for adjudication and ostracism sanctions (e.g., see Goldschmidt 1951; Popisil 1971; Barton 1967; Hoebel 1954; Popisil 1971; Benson 1990). Voluntary recognition of laws and participation in their enforcement is likely to arise only when substantial benefits from doing so can be internalized by each individual. That is, individuals require incentives to become involved in the legal process. Incentives can involve rewards (personal benefits) or punishment. Punishment is frequently the threat which induces recognition of law established by a coercive government, but when there is no government, incentives are largely positive. Individuals must expect to gain as much or more than the costs they bear from voluntary involvement in the legal system. Protection of their personal property and individual rights was apparently a sufficiently attractive benefit to induce voluntary participation among primitive societies.

Laws and procedures for adjudication and enforcement among primitive groups have been well documented, but actual examples of changes in such law aren't nearly so well documented. Popisil explained that, "Since many societies have been studied for a relatively brief period (one or two consecutive years), and since many investigators have been heavily influenced by the early sociological dogma that divorces the individual from the 'social process,' it follows that there are very few accounts of volitional innovations [in primitive law]" (1971, p. 215). However, existence of rules of adjudication, in turn, implies rules of change, since adjudication of a dispute often leads to articulation of a new law, or at least clarification of existing unwritten law in the context of an unanticipated circumstance. As Fuller explained:

> Even in the absence of any formalized doctrine of state decisis or res judicata, an adjudicative determination will normally enter in some degree into litigants' future relations and into the future relations of other parties who see themselves as possible litigants before the same tribunal. Even if there is no statement by the tribunal of the reasons for its decision, some reason will be perceived or guessed at, and the parties will tend to govern their conduct accordingly. (Fuller 1981, p. 90)

Arbitrators or mediators in primitive societies were likely to, on occasion, make new rules just as today's judges set precedents that become part of the law.

There is, in fact, a more fundamental reason to expect that the laws of primitive groups could and did change. After all, those laws were not imposed on these societies by some sovereign. They developed or evolved internally and were accepted voluntarily. Clearly most primitive societies consisted of very homogeneous groups by the time their laws and legal procedures had advanced to the level observed by anthropologists, but this homogeneity had to develop in conjunction with an evolving process of interaction and reciprocity facilitated by customary law. Law had to come from some place. Carl Menger (1963) proposed that the origin, formation and the ultimate process of all social institutions including law is essentially the same as the spontaneous order Adam Smith (1776) described for markets. Social institutions coordinate interactions. Markets do this and so does law, as Fuller (1981, p. 213) stressed. Indeed, he described customary law as a "language of interaction." Social institutions such as customary law develop the way they do because, perhaps through a process of trial and error, it is found that the actions they are intended to coordinate are performed more effectively under one system or process than under another. The more effective institutional arrangement replaces the less effective.

Under customary law, traditions and habits evolve to produce the observed "spontaneous order," to use Hayek's term. As Hayek (1967, p. 101) explained, however, while Smith's and Menger's insights regarding the evolution of social order "appear to firmly establish themselves [in several of the social sciences] another branch of knowledge of much greater influence, jurisprudence, is still almost wholly unaffected by it." In particular, the legal positivist view holds that law is the product of deliberate design rather than an evolutionary undersigned outcome of a process of spontaneous growth.

In the case of primitive societies, the earliest kinship groups probably proved to be an effective social arrangement for internalizing reciprocal benefits from legal, religious and external protection arrangements relative to previously existing arrangements. Others saw those benefits and either joined existing groups or copied their successful characteristics and formed new groups. In the process the arrangements may have been improved upon, becoming more formal (contractual) and effective. It is perfectly conceivable that neither members of the earliest groups nor those which followed even understood what particular aspect of the contract actually facilitated interactions that led to an improved social order—they may have viewed a religious function to be their main purpose and paid little attention to the consequence of their legal functions, for instance. At any rate, customary law and society develop coterminously. Those customs and legal institutions that survived were relatively efficient because the evolutionary process is one of "natural selection" where laws or procedures that serve social interaction relatively poorly are ultimately replaced by improved laws and procedures.

Many legal scholars and economists have described the growth of judge-made common law in much the same way (Landes and Posner 1979; Leoni 1961; Rubin 1977, 1980, 1982; Priest 1977; Hayek 1973). Indeed, the replacement of relatively poor rules with relatively superior ones is the characteristic of common law that such theorists have found to be desirable. They attribute this characteristic, in large part, to the fact that common law is judge-made law. But common law, assuming away legislative interference by non-judges (e.g., kings, legislators, bureaucratic administrators) and outright authoritarian legislation discretionarily imposed by judges themselves, would grow and develop in a fashion similar to the way customary law grows and develops. In particular, it would grow as a consequence of the mutual consent of the parties affected. Suppose, for example, that a dispute arises between two members of a primitive kinship group. The parties agree to call upon a recognized arbitrator (e.g., see Goldsmidt 1951; Popisil 1971) or mediator (e.g. see Barton 1967; Hoebel 1954) to help lead them to a solution and avoid a violent confrontation (Benson 1990). The solution only affects those parties in the dispute, but if it turns out to be an effective one and the same type of conflict arises for these parties or others within their kinship group, it will be voluntarily adopted by others. In this way it becomes part of customary law and the customary law grows. In effect, the private arbitrator/mediator has no authority over anyone beyond what individuals voluntarily give them by requesting a particular decision and adopting it after it is made. The decision carries no weight for others unless it is a good one in the sense that it facilitates interaction, and it is likely to be perceived as useful only if it fits well within previously accepted customary law.[3]

This process of growth may be one reason for widespread belief that primitive law was largely stagnant. Since many anthropological studies have involved only one or two years of observation, the evolving rules of customary law may have been difficult to recognize. (Of course, when a new rule proved especially beneficial it could be adopted very quickly,[4] but since most primitive societies were quite stable, the likelihood of observing rapid legal changes was probably quite small.) Contrast this with the way that government made law grows, for instance. Legislation imposed by a coercive authority (king, legislature, bureaucracy, supreme court) can make major alterations in law, rather than extensions which fit well within existing expectations, because the coercive authority does not require the voluntary consent of all parties affected. It becomes enforceable law for everyone in the society whether it is a useful law or not, and it takes effect immediately.[5] Thus, legal change as perceived in modem nation-states is very different than legal change under customary law. It is obviously much easier to observe, and beyond that, when researchers' expectations are conditioned on the rapid application of legal change arising from the modern legislative process, it is not surprising that they might fail to observe the relatively gradual spread of new law as it becomes applicable in evolving customary law.[6]

In order to illustrate the basic process of legal change in customary primitive law, let us briefly consider two examples from Popisil's (1974) detailed study of the Kapauka Papuans, in which he explicitly discussed the process of legal change.

2. Evolutionary Law: The Kapauku Papuans of West New Guinea

The Kapauku Papuans were a primitive linguistic group of about 45,000 individuals living by means of horticulture in the western part of the central highlands of West New Guinea well past the middle of this century. Certain basic characteristics of the society require mention before the process of legal change can be discussed. The Kapauku's reciprocal arrangements for support and protection were based on kinship. However, members of two or more patrilineages typically joined together for defensive and legal purposes, even though they often belonged to different sibs. These "confederations" often encompassed from three to nine villages with each village consisting of about fifteen households.

The Kapauku had no formal government with coercive power. Most observers have concluded that there was a virtual lack of leadership among these people. One Dutch administrator noted, however, that "there is a man who seems to have some influence upon the others. He is referred to by the name *tonowi* which means 'the rich one.' Nevertheless, I would hesitate to call him a chief or a leader at all; *primus interpares* (the first among equals) would be a more proper designation for him" (quoted in Popisil (1971, p. 65). In order to understand the role and prestige of the *tonowi* one must recognize two "basic values" of the Kapauku: an emphasis upon 1) individualism, and 2) physical freedom (Popisil 1971, p. 65). The emphasis on individualism manifested itself in several ways. For instance, a detailed system of private property rights was evident. In fact, there was absolutely no common ownership. "A house, boat, bow and arrows, field, crops, patches of second-growth forest, or even a meal shared by a family or household is always owned by one person. Individual ownership...is so extensive in the Kamu Valley that we find the virgin forests divided into tracts which belong to single individuals. Relatives, husbands and wives do not own anything in common. Even an eleven-year-old boy can own his field and his money and play the role of debtor and creditor as well" (Popisil 1971, p. 66).

The paramount role of individual rights also was evident in the position of the *tonowi* as a person who had earned the admiration and respect of others in the society. He was typically "a healthy man in the prime of life" who had accumulated a good deal of wealth (Popsil 1971, p. 67). The wealth accumulated by an individual in Kapauku society almost always depended on that individual's work effort and skill, so anyone who had acquired sufficient property to reach the status of *tonowi* was generally a mature, skilled individual with considerable physical ability and intellectual experience. However, not all *tonowi* (wealthy men) achieved respect that would induce others to rely upon them for leadership. "The way in which capital is acquired and how it is used makes a great difference; the natives favor rich candidates who are generous and honest. These two attributes are greatly valued by the culture" (Popisil 1971, p. 67).[7] Generosity was a major criterion for acceptance of a particular *tonowi* in a leadership role because, in large part, followers were obtained through contract.

Each individual in the society could choose to align himself with any available *tonowi* and then contract with that chosen *tonowi*. Typically followers would become debtors to a *maagodo tonowi* (a "really rich man") who was considered to be generous and honest. In exchange for the loan the individual agreed to perform certain duties in support of the *tonowi.* The followers got much more than a loan, however:

> It is good for a Kapauku to have a close relative as headman because he can then depend upon his help in economic, political, and legal matters. The expectation of future favors and advantages is probably the most potent motivation for most of the headman's followers. Strangers who know about the generosity of a headman try to please him, and people from his own political unit attend to his desires. Even individuals from neighboring confederations may yield to the wishes of a *tonowi* in case his help may be needed in the future. (Popisil 1971, pp. 68-69)

Tonowi authority was given, not taken. This leadership reflected, to a great extent, an ability to "persuade the unit to support a man in a dispute or to fight for his cause" (Popisil 1971, pp. 69-70). Thus, the *tonowi* position of "authority" was not, in any way, a position of absolute sovereignty. It was achieved through reciprocal exchange of support between a *tonowi* and his followers, support that could be freely withdrawn by either party (e.g., upon payment of debt, or demand for repayment).[8]

What happened if a *tonowi* proved to be ineffective or dishonest in his leadership role? First of all, honesty and generosity were prerequisites for a *tonowi* to gather a following. However, if someone managed to do so and then proceeded to be a bad "leader" he simply lost his following. In legal matters, for instance, "Passive resistance and refusal of the followers to support him is…the result of a decision [considered unjust]" (Popisil 1971, p. 94). Clearly, change in the legal authority was possible; indeed; one purpose of Kapauku legal procedure discussed below, which involved articulation of relevant laws by the *tonowi*, was to achieve public acceptance of his ruling. As Fuller noted, one source of "the affinity between legality and justice consisted simply in the fact that a rule articulated and made known permits the public to judge its fairness" (1964, p. 159).

The informal and contractual characteristics of Kapuku leadership led many western observers to conclude that Kapauku society lacked law, but clear evidence of recognized rules of obligation, as well as procedures for enforcement, adjudication, and change can be demonstrated within the Kapauku's legal system. A "mental codification of abstract rules" existed for the Kapauku Papuans, so that legal decisions were part of a "going order" (Popisil 1971, p. 80). Recognition of law was based on kinship and contractual reciprocities motivated by individual rights and private property. Grammatical phrases and/or references to specific customs, precedents or rules were present in all adjudication decisions Popisil observed during his several years of studying the Kapauku. He concluded that, "not only does a legal decision solve a specific case, but it also formulates an ideal—a solution intended to be utilized in a similar situation in the future. The ideal component binds all other members of the group who did not participate in the case under consideration. The authority himself turns to his previous decisions for consistency" (Popisil 1971, p. 80). The authority of the law is obvious in this statement, as is the drive for legal uniformity. Legal decisions had the status of modern legal precedents.

Adjudication Procedures and Sanctions

The Kapauku "process of law" appears to have been highly standardized almost to the point of ritual (but standardized, ritualistic procedure does not imply static, unchanging law, as explained below). It typically started with a loud quarrel where the plaintiff accused the defendant of committing some harmful act while the defendant responded with denials or justification. The quarrel involved loud shouting for the purpose of attracting other people, including one or more *tonowi.* The close relatives and friends of those involved in the dispute would take sides, presenting opinions and testimony in loud emotional speeches. The *tonowi* generally simply listened until the exchange of opinion approached the point of violence, whereupon he stepped in and began his argument. If he waited too long an outbreak of "stick fighting" or even feuds could occur, but this was rare. Popisil (1971, p. 36) observed 176 dispute resolutions involving "difficult cases"; only five led to stick fights and one resulted in a feud. The *tonowi* began his presentation by "admonishing" the disputants to have patience and then proceeded to question various witnesses. He would search the scene of the offense and/or the defendant's house for evidence if it was appropriate. "Having secured the evidence and made up his mind about the factual background of the dispute, the authority starts the activity called by natives boko duwai, the process of making a decision and inducing the parties to the dispute to follow it" (Popisil 1971, p. 36). The *tonowi* would make a long speech, summing up the evidence, appealing to the relevant rules and precedents, and suggesting what should be done to end the dispute.[9]

When judged to be guilty a Kapauku was punished. The specific sanction for a case was suggested by the *tonowi* if the dispute required his intervention, and if the dispute was settled it meant the guilty offender agreed to accept that sanction. Sanctions in this society varied considerably depending on the offense. They included economic restitution and various forms of physical punishment. Despite the use of a wide array of sanctions, however, the Kapauku's paramount concern for individual freedom precluded certain types of widely used punishments in western societies. There was no such thing as imprisonment, for instance, and neither torture nor physical maiming were permitted (both have been common in western nation-states, of course—see Benson [1990, chapter 11]). Moreover, capital punishment was not the normal sanction for even violent crimes: "Economic sanctions are by far the most preferred ones among the Kapauku" (Popisil 1971, p. 93). Restitution was the most important sanction among the Kapauku, as in fact it was in primitive societies in general (e.g., Benson 1990; Barton 1967; Goldsmidt 1951; Hoebel 1954, 1967).

The Kapauku did resort to physical punishment at times, nonetheless. In fact, defendants often had a choice between an economic sanction or a physical sanction, frequently choosing the latter. Nonetheless, an offense was occasionally considered too severe to warrant economic payment. "A heinous criminal or a captured enemy would be killed but never tortured or deprived of liberty" (Popisil 1971, p. 65). In keeping with the emphasis on individual freedom, for instance, the killing generally took place through an ambush with bow and arrow: "A culprit...would always have the chance to run or fight back" (Popisil 1973, p. 65).[10]

A third type of sanction was also applied by the Kapauku—psychological sanctions. "The most dreaded and feared of the psychological and social sanctions of the Kapauku is the public reprimand... The Kapauku regard this psychological punishment as the most effective of their entire inventory of sanctions" (Popisil 1971, p. 93).[11] Furthermore, punishment by sorcery or through the shaman's helping spirits was also employed when the offender was strong enough to resist a *tonowi*'s decisions. "Disease and death are the ultimate [psychosomatic] effect of this 'supernatural' punishment" (Popisil 1971, p. 94).

This suggests one solution to the problem that might arise when a defendant refused to submit to the sanction proposed by a *tonowi*, an infrequent but possible outcome of the Kapauku legal process (and, of course, a possible outcome of any legal system—resisting arrest, refusal to cooperate during a trial, attempted prison breaks, etc. are common today). As Fuller (1964, pp. 143-144) explained, one form of punishment in primitive societies has often been "an exercise of magical powers on the offender to purge to community of uncleanliness. A similar purging was accomplished through the generous use of ostracism." In fact then, the use of magic was simply one form of ostracism, and another, the most important in primitive societies, was ostracism by all members of a confederation.[12]

Legal Change

Popisil documented two ways that Kapauku law could change. First, very simply, as custom changed, new law could become articulated through the dispute resolution process. One example of such an occurrence had to do with the Kapauku adultery laws. It was customary up until a few years prior to 1954 that an adulterous woman would be executed by her husband. However, men, and particularly relatively poor men, came to realize that such a sanction was too costly because of the high price paid for a wife. As a result, some individuals wished to change the punishment to beating or perhaps wounding the adulteress. Punishment had to be approved through the formal dispute resolution process and when the less harsh (more economical) punishment was proposed by relatively poor men it was initially resisted by rich Kapauku. However, the new customary sanction was upheld by *tonowi* in four adultery cases observed by Popisil during the 1954-55 period. Thus, the new sanctions became part of customary law (Popisil 1971, p. 205). In a similar fashion, of course, a law which at one time is applied can loose its popular support and effectively be abolished.

A second procedure for legal change was also observed among the Kapauku. A change in one lineage's laws of incest resulted from "successful legislation" by a sublineage *tonowi*: "He succeeded in changing an old rule of sib exogamy into a new law that permitted intrasib marriages as close as between second cousins" (Popisil 1971, p. 110). This legislation was not authoritarian in the sense that its passage forced compliance by others, of course. Rather, its acceptance spread through voluntary recognition. First it was adopted by the *tonowi*, then by more and more young men in his sublineage, and ultimately by *tonowi* of other sublineages within the same lineage. The head of the confederacy, a member of that lineage, also ultimately accepted the new law, but other lineages in the same confederacy did not. Thus, incest laws varied across lineages within the same confederacy.[13] The characteristic that distinguishes this legal change from the previous one is that it was an intentional legal innovation initiated by a leader rather than developing as a result of dispute resolution. Its adoption was still voluntary, however. Popisil obtained descriptions of the legal change that was initiated in 1935, and observed its subsequent and considerable effects on Kapauku society over a nine-year period from 1954 to 1963.

Awiitigaaj, a sublineage *tonowi*, wished to marry his third paternal parallel cousin who belonged to his own sib. Kapauku law was quite explicit regarding incest, holding that "to marry one's sibmate is tabooed." Nonetheless, Awiitigaaj broke taboo and eloped with the girl. Relatives pursued the couple and the girl's father, Ugataga, also a *tonowi*, proposed that both be executed in accordance with Kapauku law. Awiitigaaj intended to purposefully challenge the law. Thus, he hid in the forest expecting that family members and the girl's father would soon tire of the search, and that the father might, once his temper cooled, be willing to forgo the physical punishment in exchange for a high bride price. After all, the personal disadvantages of killing his daughter and forfeiting a bride price made it likely that Ugataga would show great anger in public and make numerous expeditions into the forest, but eventually he would accept the inevitable, after preserving the public's opinion of his morality, and seek an unusually large bride price.

The role of "public opinion" was important to the outcome. The ultimate outcome had to be generally acceptable. Thus, the family members put up a pretense of searching until the *tonowi* of the two noninvolved confederacy lineages called for a peace settlement Then, at the suggestion of Awiitigaaj's maternal relatives who acted as go-betweens, Ugataga very reluctantly gave in to "the public pressure" and asked Awiitigaaj's paternal relatives for a bride price. This action constituted an implicit recognition of this particular incestuous marriage as legal. However, Awiitigaaj could not afford to be regarded as a lawbreaker, so he promulgated a new law, making it permissible to marry within the same sib, lineage, and even sublineage, as long as the couples were at least second cousins.

This new law was actually a fairly easy one to establish and understand, since similar legal precedent applied to nonsib marriage. Kapauku law prohibited marriage between first cousins even when they belonged to different sibs, so this new "legislation" simply made the same rule apply within a sib. Over the course of the next twenty years Awiitigaaj married three second paternal parallel cousins and eighteen other marriages in his sublineage involved what would have previously been incestuous unions. Furthermore, one such marriage took place in another sublineage within the confederacy. Ultimately the new law was accepted in three of the confederacy's sublineages.

These changes in the law of incest had a substantial impact on the Kapauku lifestyle beyond marriage relationships. As intrasib marriages became more prevalent, Awiitigaaj's village was divided into two halves, consisting of those who were related as first cousins or closer. Marriage then could only occur "across the line" which divided the village. Prior to this the village was simply a loose, irregular cluster of houses. As the incest boundary developed, the village began to take on a lineal form with houses in single lines divided by the boundary. Dutch pacification of the area in 1956 occurred before the lineal pattern was completely adopted, however. Other changes in Kapauku society due to this legal change also were on the horizon at the time of pacification. The status of women, for instance, was being elevated due to more intravillage marriages. Prior to this, all marriages involved women from other villages who would, after the marriage, have no immediate support from local relatives. As intravillage marriages became prevalent, local support for women's legal rights developed. Such developments were not intended consequences of the new law of incest, of course, but rather, an example of the evolutionary nature of customary law. Law and its impacts were constantly evolving among the Kapauku just as culture itself was evolving and changing. The same is true of primitive systems in general (Popisil 1971, p. 348).

Conclusions

One might argue that the evolutionary process of the customary law of primitive society has no relevance today, since the simple procedures described above could never be effective in a more complex society. Even if this argument is true, however, there are some very significant reasons to study primitive systems of governmentless law and order. As Lon Fuller explained, for instance, "if we look closely among the varying social contexts presented by our own society we shall find analogs of almost every phenomenon thought to characterize primitive law" (1981, p. 243). An understanding of these relatively simple systems may lead us to a clearer understanding of our own.

Furthermore, by studying the incentives and institutions of primitive law, including the process of legal evolution, it becomes evident that precisely the same kinds of governmentless legal systems have existed in considerably more "advanced," complex societies, ranging from Medieval Iceland (Friedman 1979), Ireland (Peden 1977; Rothbard 1973) and Anglo-Saxon England (Benson 1990 and references cited therein) to the development of the Medieval Law Merchant and its evolution into modern international commercial law (Benson 1989, 1990; Trackman 1983; and references cited in each) and even to the western frontier of the United States during the 1800s (Anderson and Hill 1979; Umbeck 1981; Benson 1986, 1990). The fact is that much of the law that guides today's modern complex American society actually evolved from or is simply a reflection of precisely the same customary law sources as those underlying primitive legal systems.

Notes

1. Fuller's concept of law corresponds more closely to the view of law from the anthropology literature proposed by Redfield, for example, than to Malinowski. Redfield defined law as "a system of principles and of restraints of action with accompanying paraphernalia of enforcement" (1967, p. 3). The "paraphernalia" Redford referred to clearly constitutes the "structural constancies" that are the manifestations of Fuller's legal enterprise.
2. Hayek explained that it is an "erroneous idea that property had at some late stage been 'invented' and that before these had existed an early state of primitive communism. This myth has been completely refuted by anthropological research. There can be no question now that the recognition of property preceded the rise of even the most primitive cultures, and that certainly all that we call civilization has grown up on the basis of that spontaneous order of actions which is made possible by the delimination of protected domains of individuals and groups. Although the socialist thinking of our time has succeeded in bringing this insight under suspicion of being ideologically inspired, it is well demonstrated a scientific truth as any we have attainted in this field" (1973, p. 108).
3. Fuller explained the procedure of such changes in customary law, as follows, noting that change like this is quite common, and can occur quite quickly:

"Where by his actions toward B, A has (whatever his actual intentions may have been) given B reasonably to understand that he (A) willin the future in similar situations act in a similar manner, and B has, in some substantial way, prudently adjusted his affairs to the expectation that A will act in accordance with this expectation, then A is bound to follow the pattern set by his past actions toward B. This creates an obligation by A to B. If the pattern of interaction followed by A and B then spreads through the relevant community, a rule of general customary law has been created. This rule will normally become part of a larger system, which will involve a complex network of reciprocal expectations. Absorption of the new rule into the larger system will, of course, be facilitated by the fact that the interactions that gave rise to it took place within limits set by the system and derived a part of their meaning for the parties from the wider interactional context within which it occurred.

Where customary law does in fact spread we must not be mislead as to the process by which this extension takes place. It has sometimes been thought of as if it involved a kind of inarticulate expression of group will; the members of group B perceive that the rules governing group A would furnish an apt law for them; they therefore take over those rules by an act of tacit collective adoption. This kind of explanation abstracts from the interactional process underlying customary law and ignores their ever-present communicative aspect... Generally we may say that where A and B have become familiar with a practice obtaining between C and D, A is likely to adopt this pattern in his actions toward B, not simply or necessarily because it has any special aptness for their situations, but because he knows B will understand the meaning of his behavior and will know how to react to it" (Fuller 1981, pp. 227-228).

4. As Fuller explained, the view that customary law changes very slowly is "too simple a view of the matter...in part because of mistaken implications read into the word customary, and in part because it is true that normally it takes some time for reciprocal interactional expectations to "jell." But these are circumstances in which customary law (or a phenomenon for which we have no other name) can develop almost overnight" (1981, p. 229). See Benson (1989), for example, where the rapid evolution of customary commercial law during the medieval period is discussed.
5. The same is true of judge-made common law precedent. These precedents are backed by the coercive power of the state, and therefore, they take on the same authority as statute law whether they are good laws or not.
6. The fact that customary law changes relatively slowly as compared to state-made law is not an indication of relative inefficiency of customary law, by the way. In fact, precisely the opposite applies. When authoritarian legislation makes a major change in property rights assignments that affect many parties, negative externalities are generated. Leoni (1961, p. 17) explained it well when he noted:

   "Legislation may have and actually has in many cases today a negative effect on the very efficacy of the rules and on the homogeneity of the feelings and convictions already prevailing in a given society. For legislation may also deliberately or accidentally disrupt homogeneity by destroying established rules and by nullifying existing conventions and agreements that have hitherto been voluntarily accepted and kept. Even more disruptive is the fact that the very possibility of nullifying agreements and conventions through supervening legislation tends in the long run to induce people to fail to rely on any existing conventions or to keep any accepted agreements. On the other hand, the continual change of rules brought about by inflated legislation prevents it from replacing successful and enduringly the set of nonlegslative rules (usages, conventions, agreements) that happen to be destroyed in the process."

   "Inflated legislation" tends to destroy the respect for law in general, besides creating considerable uncertainty about the permanence of property rights. When negative externalities arise in the process of production of some good or service, too much of the good or service is being produced. This is true of legislation as well.
7. Other criteria were important as well, including the ability and willingness to speak in public (Popsil 1971, p. 67).
8. One group of a *tonowi*'s followers was especially faithful and dependable, as well as always being available when a need for support arose. They were called *ani jokaani* or "my boys," and consisted of a group of young men who were "adopted" by the *tonowi* and became his "students." They come to live with the rich man to learn especially how he transacted business, to secure his protection, to share his food, and, finally, to be granted a substantial loan for buying a wife. In return they offer their labor in the fields and around the house, their support in legal and other disputes, and their lives in case of war. The boys may be from different sibs and

confederacies, or they may be relatives: "However, this contractual association is quite loose. Both parties are free to terminate it at any time and the boy is never treated as an inferior by the rich man" (Popisil 1971, p. 69).

9. Rules of adjudication among the Kapauku were much more detailed than suggested in this brief discussion. For instance, there were clearly specified, detailed jurisdictional delineations (Popisil 1971, p. 111; Benson 1990).
10. Interestingly, in many of these cases "the punishment was carried out by a close patrilineal relative of the culprit... Employment of patrilineal relatives to participate in the killing was a clever cultural device to prevent internal strain and feuds" (Popisil 1971, p. 92). Another form of physical sanction was beating the head and shoulders of the offender with a stick. Again the individual was not constrained so he could fight back, but in each instance observed by Popisil they submitted without raising a defense. Individual defendants apparently chose to submit to the beating rather than make a payment to the victim.
11. Other psychological sanctions were also employed. A private warning given by a *tonowi* for a minor violation of a taboo or for lying would cause the guilty party to suffer "a loss of face once it becomes known that he was punished in such a way" (Popisil 1971, p. 93).
12. Primitive societies' laws were enforceable because there was an effective threat of total ostracism by the entire community—an extreme form of a boycott sanction (e.g., see Goldsmidt 1951; Barton 1967; Hoebel 1954, 1967; Benson 1990). If someone refused to submit to arbitration/meditation, or refused to accept what was perceived to be an appropriate judgment, be became an outcast or "outlaw," which meant that anyone could kill him without any liability for the killing. The community at large recognized and backed such threats through various personal benefits of such arrangements because: 1) individuals recognized the potential personal benefits of such arrangements (e.g., the potential future need for justice and the similar support of the rest of the community), and 2) individuals and families realized that if the system failed, violent forms of dispute resolution would probably arise and such violence tended to spread to families and neighbors—violence is a costly form of dispute resolution which members of primitive communities tried to avoid (Benson 1990).
13. This was possible due to the detailed jurisdictional rules that applied in Kapauku law (see note 9).

References

Anderson, T. and Hill, P. J. (1979), "An American Experiment in Anarcho-Capitalism: The Not So Wild, Wild West," *Journal of Libertarian Studies*, 3, 9-29.

Baden J., Stroup, R., and Thurman, W. (1981), "Myths Admonitions and Rationality: The American Indian as a Resource Manager," *Economic Inquiry*, 19, 399-427.

Barton, R.F. (1967), "Procedure among the Ifugao," pp. 161-182 in Paul Bohanan (ed.), *Law and Warfare*, Garden City, NY.

Benson, B. L. (1986), "The Lost Victim and Other Failures of the Public Law Experiment," *Harvard Journal of Law and Public Policy*, 9, 399-427.

———. (1989), "The Spontaneous Evolution of Commercial Law," *Southern Economic Journal*, 55, 3, 644-661.

———. (1990), *The Enterprise of Law: Justice without the State*, San Francisco.

Demsetz, H. (1967), "Toward a Theory of Property Rights," *American Economic Review*, 57, 347-359.

Friedman, D. (1979), "Private Creation and Enforcement of Law: A Historical Case," *Journal of Legal Studies*, 8, 399-415.

Fuller, L. L. (1964), *The Morality of Law*, New Haven.

———. (1981), *The Principles of Social Order*, Durham, N.C.
Goldsmidt, W. (1951), "Ethics and the Structure of Society: And Ethnological Contributions to the Sociology of Knowledge," *American Anthropologist*, 53, 506-524.
Hayek, F. A. (1967), *Studies in Philosophy, Politics and Economics*, Chicago.
———. (1973), *Law, Legislation and Liberty*, Vol. 1, Chicago.
Hoebel, E. A. (1954), *The Law of Primitive Man*, Cambridge, Mass.
———. (1967), "Law—Ways of the Comanche Indians," pp. 183-204, in Paul Bohanan (ed.), *Law and Warfare*, Garden City, NY.
Johnsen, D. B. (1986), "The Formation and Protection of Property Rights among the Southern Kwakiutl Indians," *Journal of Legal Studies*, 15, 41-67.
Landes, W. M. and Posner, R. A. (1979), "Adjudication as a Private Good," *Journal of Legal Studies*, 8, 235-284.
Leoni, B. (1961), *Freedom and the Law*, Los Angeles.
Maine, Sir. H. S. (1864), *Ancient Law*, 3rd American from 5th English Edition, New York.
Malinowski, B. (1926), *Crime and Custom in Savage Society*, London.
Menger, C. (1963), *Problems of Economics and Sociology*, translated by Franas J. Nook, Urbana, ID.
Peden, J. R. (1977), "Property Rights in Celtic Irish Law," *Journal of Libertarian Studies*, 1, 81-95.
Popisil, L. (1971), *Anthropology of Law: A Comparative Theory*, New York.
Posner, R. A. (1980), "A Theory of Primitive Society, with Special Reference to Primitive Law," *Journal of Law and Economics*, 23, 1-53.
———. (1981), *The Economics of Justice*, Cambridge, Mass.
Priest, G. L. (1977), "The Common Law Process and the Selection of Efficient Rules," *Journal of Legal Studies*, 6, 65-82.
Redfield, R. (1967), "Primitive Law," pp. 3-24 in Paul Bohanan (ed.), *Law and Warfare*, Garden City, NY.
Rothbard, M. N. (1973), *For a New Liberty*, New York.
Rubin, P. H. (1977), "Why is the Common Law Efficient?" *Journal of Legal Studies*, 6, 51-64.
———. (1980), "Predictability and the Economic Approach to Law: A Comment on Rizzo," *Journal of Legal Studies*, 9, 319-334.
———. (1982), "Common Law and Statute Law," *Journal of Legal Studies*, 11, 203-224.
Smith, A. (1937), *An Inquiry into the Nature and Causes of the Wealth of Nations*, New York.
Trakman, L. E. (1983), *The Law Merchant: The Evolution of Commercial Law*, Littleton, Colo.
Umbeck, J. (1981), *A Theory of Property Rights with Application to the California Gold Rush*, Ames, Iowa.

39

An American Experiment in Anarcho-Capitalism: The *Not* So Wild, Wild West

Terry L. Anderson and P. J. Hill

The growth of government during this century has attracted the attention of many scholars interested in explaining that growth and in proposing ways to limit it. As a result of this attention, the public choice literature has experienced an upsurge in the interest in anarchy and its implications for social organization. The work of Rawls and Nozick, two volumes edited by Gordon Tullock, *Explorations in the Theory of Anarchy*, and a book by David Friedman, *The Machinery of Freedom*, provide examples. The goals of the literature have varied from providing a conceptual framework for comparing Leviathan and its opposite extreme to presenting a formula for the operation of society in a state of anarchy. But nearly all of this work has one common aspect; it explores the "*theory* of anarchy." The purpose of this paper is to take us from the theoretical world of anarchy to a case study of its application. To accomplish our task we will first discuss what is meant by "anarcho-capitalism" and present several hypotheses relating to the nature of social organization in this world. These hypotheses will then be tested in the context of the American West during its earliest settlement. We propose to examine property rights formulation and protection under voluntary organizations such as private protection agencies, vigilantes, wagon trains, and early mining camps. Although the early West was not completely anarchistic, we believe that government as a legitimate agency of coercion was absent for a long enough period to provide insights into the operation and viability of property rights in the absence of a formal state. The nature of contracts for the provision of "public goods" and the evolution of western "laws" for the period from 1830 to 1900 will provide the data for this case study.

The West during this time often is perceived as a place of great chaos, with little respect for property or life. Our research indicates that this was not the case; property rights were protected and civil order prevailed. Private agencies provided the necessary basis for an orderly society in which property was protected and conflicts were resolved. These agencies often did not qualify as governments because they did not have a legal monopoly on "keeping order." They soon discovered that "warfare" was a costly way of resolving disputes and lower cost methods of settlement (arbitration, courts, etc.) resulted. In summary, this paper argues that a characterization of the American West as chaotic would appear to be incorrect.

Anarchy: Order or Chaos?

Though the first dictionary definition of anarchy is "the state of having no government," many people believe that the third definition, "confusion or chaos generally," is more appropriate since it is a necessary result of the first. If we were to engage seriously in the task of dismantling the government as it exists in the U.S., the political economist would find no scarcity of programs to eliminate. However, as the dismantling continued, the decisions would become more and more difficult, with the last "public goods" to be dealt with probably being programs designed to define and enforce property rights. Consider the following two categories of responses to this problem:

1) The first school we shall represent as the "constitutionalist" or "social contractarian" school. For this group the important question is "how do rights re-emerge and come to command respect? How do 'laws' emerge that carry with them general respect for their 'legitimacy'?"[1] This position does not allow us to "'jump over' the whole set of issues involved in defining the rights of persons in the first place."[2] Here collective action is taken as a necessary step in the establishment of a social contract or constitutional contract which specifies these rights. To the extent that rights could be perfectly defined, the only role for the state would be in the protection of those rights since the law designed for that protection is the only public good. If rights cannot be perfectly well defined, a productive role for the state will arise. The greater the degree to which private rights cannot be perfectly defined, the more the collective action will be plunged into the "eternal dilemma of democratic government," which is "how can government, itself the reflection of interests, establish the legitimate boundaries of self-interest, and how can it, conversely carve out those areas of intervention that will be socially protective and collectively useful?"[3] The contractarian solution to this dilemma is the establishment of a rule of higher law or a constitution which specifies the protective and productive roles of the government. Since the productive role, because of the free rider problem, necessarily requires coercion, the government will be given a monopoly on the use of force. Were this not the case, some individuals would choose not to pay for services from which they derive benefits.

2) The second school can be labeled "anarcho-capitalist" or "private property anarchist." In its extreme form this school would advocate eliminating all forms of collective action since all functions of government can be replaced by individuals possessing private rights exchangeable in the market place. Under this system all transactions would be voluntary except insofar as the protection of individual rights and enforcement of contracts required coercion. The essential question facing this school is how can law and order, which do require some coercion, be supplied without ultimately resulting in one provider of those services holding a monopoly on coercion, i.e., government. If a dominant

protective firm or association emerges after exchanges take place, we will have the minimal state as defined by Nozick and will have lapsed back into the world of the "constitutionalist." The private property anarchist's view that markets can provide protection services is summarized as follows:

> The profit motive will then see to it that the most efficient providers of high quality arbitration rise to the top and that inefficient and graft-oriented police lose their jobs. In short, the market is capable of providing justice at the cheapest price. According to Rothbard, to claim that these services are "public goods" and cannot be sold to individuals in varying amounts is to make a claim which actually has little basis in fact.[4]

Hence, the anarcho-capitalists place faith in the profit-seeking entrepreneurs to find the optimal size and type of protective services and faith in competition to prevent the establishment of a monopoly in the provision of these services.

There are essentially two differences between the two schools discussed above. First, there is the empirical question of whether competition can actually provide the protection services. On the anarcho-capitalist side, there is the belief that it can. On the constitutionalist or "minimal state" side, there is the following argument.

> Conflicts may occur, and one agency will win. Persons who have previously been clients of losing agencies will desert and commence purchasing their protection from winning agencies. In this manner a single protective agency or association will eventually come to dominate the market for policing services over a territory. Independent persons who refuse to purchase protection from anyone may remain outside the scope of the dominant agency, but such independents cannot be allowed to punish clients of the agency on their own. They must be coerced into not punishing. In order to legitimize their coercion, these persons must be compensated, but only to the extent that their deprivation warrants.[5]

The second issue is more conceptual than empirical, and hence, cannot be entirely resolved through observation. This issue centers on the question of how rights are determined in the first place; how do we get a starting point with all its status quo characteristics from which the game can be played. Buchanan, a leading constitutionalist, criticizes Friedman and Rothbard, two leading private property anarchists, because "they simply 'jump over' the whole set of issues involved in defining the rights of persons in the first place."[6] To the constitutionalist the Lockean concept of mixing labor with resources to arrive at "natural rights" is not sufficient. The contractarian approach suggests that the starting point is determined by the initial bargaining process which results in the constitutional contract. Debate over this issue will undoubtedly continue, but even Buchanan agrees that "if the distribution or imputation of the rights of persons (rights to do things, both with respect to other persons and to physical things) is settled, *then away we go*. And aside from differences on certain specifics (which may be important but relatively amenable to analysis, e.g., the efficacy of market-like arrangements for internal and external peace-keeping), I should accept many of the detailed reforms that these passionate advocates propose."[7]

Our purpose in this paper is to discuss, in a historical context, some of the important issues that Buchanan says are amenable to analysis. We do not plan to debate the issue of the starting point, but will be looking at the "efficacy of market-like arrangements for internal...peacekeeping."[8] It does seem, for the time period and the geographical area which we are examining, that there was a distribution of rights which was accepted either because of general agreement to some basic precepts of natural law or because the inhabitants of the American West came out of a society in which certain rights were defined and enforced. Such a starting point is referred to as a Schelling point, a point of commonality that exists in the minds of the participants in some social situation.[9] Even in the absence of any enforcement mechanism, most members of the western society agreed that certain rights to use and control property existed. Thus when a miner argued that a placer claim was his because he "was there first," that claim carried more weight than if he claimed it simply because he was most powerful. Tastes, culture, ethics, and numerous other influences give Schelling point characteristics to some claims but not to others. The long period of conflicts between the Indians and the settlers can be attributed to a lack of any such Schelling points. We concentrate, however, on arrangements for peacekeeping and enforcement that existed among the non-indigenous, white population.

In the following pages we describe the private enforcement of rights in the West between the period of 1830 and 1900. This description does allow one to test, in a limited fashion, some of the hypotheses put forth about how anarcho-capitalism might function. We qualify the test with "limited" because a necessary feature of such a system is the absence of a monopoly on coercion.[10] Various coercive agencies would exist but none would have a legitimized monopoly on the use of such coercion. The difficulty of dealing with this proposition in the American West is obvious. Although for much of the period formal government agencies for the protection of rights were not present, such agencies were always lurking in the background. Therefore, none of the private enforcement means operated entirely independent of government influence. Also, one has to be careful in always describing private agencies as "non-government" because, to the extent that they develop and become the agency of legitimized coercion, they also qualify as "government." Although numerous descriptions of such private agencies exist, it is oftentimes difficult to determine when they are enhancing competition and when they are reducing it.

Despite the above caveats, the West is a useful testing ground for several of the specific hypotheses about how anarcho-capitalism might work. We use David Friedman's *The Machinery of Freedom* as our basis for the formulation of hypotheses about the working of anarcho-capitalism because it is decidedly non-utopian and it does set out, in a fairly specific form, the actual mechanisms under which a system of non-government protective agencies would operate. The major propositions are:

1) Anarcho-capitalism is not chaos. Property rights will be protected and civil order will prevail.

2) Private agencies will provide the necessary functions for preservation of an orderly society.
3) Private protection agencies will soon discover that "warfare" is a costly way of resolving disputes and lower-cost methods of settlement (arbitration, courts, etc.) will result.
4) The concept of "justice" is not an immutable one that only needs to be discovered. Preferences do vary across individuals as to the rules they prefer to live under and the price they are willing to pay for such rules. Therefore, significant differences in rules might exist in various societies under anarcho-capitalism.
5) There are not significant enough economies of scale in crime so that major "mafia" organizations evolve and dominate society.
6) Competition among protective agencies and adjudication bodies will serve as healthy checks on undesirable behavior. Consumers have better information than under government and will use it in judging these agencies.

Cases From the West

Before turning to specific examples of anarcho-capitalistic institutions in the American West, it is useful to examine the legendary characterization of the "wild, wild West." The potential for chaos is a major objection to trust in the market for enforcement of rights and many histories of the West seem to substantiate this argument. These histories describe the era and area as characterized by gunfights, horse-thievery, and general disrespect for basic human rights. The taste for the dramatic in literature and other entertainment forms has led to concentration on the seeming disparity between the westerners' desire for order and the prevailing disorder. If the Hollywood image of the West were not enough to taint our view, scholars of violence contributed with quotes such as the following: "We can report with some assurance that compared to frontier days there has been a significant decrease in crimes of violence in the United States."[11]

Recently, however, more careful examinations of the conditions that existed cause one to doubt the accuracy of this perception. In his book, *Frontier Violence: Another Look*, W. Eugene Hollon stated that the he believed "that the Western frontier was a far more civilized, more peaceful, and safer place than American society is today."[12] The legend of the "wild, wild West" lives on despite Robert Dykstra's finding that in five of the major cattle towns (Abilene, Ellsworth, Wichita, Dodge City, and Caldwell) for the years from 1870 to 1885, only 45 homicides were reported—an average of 1.5 per cattle-trading season.[13] In Abilene, supposedly one of the wildest of the cow towns, "nobody was killed in 1869 or 1870. In fact, nobody was killed until the advent of officers of the law, employed to prevent killings."[14] Only two towns, Ellsworth in 1873 and Dodge City in 1876, ever had five killings in any one year.[15] Frank Prassel states in his book subtitled "A Legacy of Law and Order," that "if any conclusion can be drawn from recent crime statistics, it must be that this last frontier left no significant heritage of offenses against the person, relative to other sections of the country."[16] Moreover, even if crime rates were higher, it should be remembered that the preference for order can differ across time and people. To show that the West was more "lawless" than our present day society tells one very little unless some measure of the "demand for law and order" is available. "While the frontier society may appear to have functioned with many violations of formal law, it sometimes more truly reflected community customs in conflict with superficial and at times alien standards."[17] The vigilance committees which sprang up in many of the mining towns of the West provide excellent examples of this conflict. In most instances these committees arose after civil government was organized. They proved that competition was useful in cases where government was ineffective, as in the case of San Francisco in the 1850s,[18] or where government became the province of criminals who used the legal monopoly on coercion to further their own ends, as in Virginia City, Montana Territory in the 1860s.[19] Even in these cases, however, violence was not the standard *modus operandi.* When the San Francisco vigilante committee was reconstituted in 1856, "the group remained in action for three months, swelling its membership to more than eight thousand. During this period, San Francisco had only two murders, compared with more than a hundred in the six month before the committee was formed."[20]

To understand how law and order were provided in the American West, we now turn to four examples of institutions which approximated anarcho-capitalism. These case studies of land claims clubs, cattlemens' associations, mining camps, and wagon trains provide support for the hypotheses presented above and suggest that private rights were enforced and that chaos did not reign.

a. Land Clubs

For the pioneer settlers who often moved into the public domain before it was surveyed or open for sale by the federal government, definition and enforcement of property rights in the land they claimed was always a problem. "These marginal or frontier settlers (squatters as they were called) were beyond the pale of constitutional government. No statute of Congress protected them in their rights to the claims they had chosen and the improvements they had made. In law they were trespassers; in fact they were honest farmers."[21] The result was the formation of "extra-legal" organizations for protection and justice. These land clubs or claims associations, as the extra-legal associations came to be known, were found throughout the Middle West with the Iowa variety receiving the most attention. Benjamin F. Shambaugh suggests that we view these clubs "as an illustrative type of frontier extra-legal, extra-constitutional political organization in which are reflected certain principles of American life and character."[22] To Frederick Jackson Turner these squatters' associations provided an excellent example of the "power of the newly arrived pioneers to join together for a common end without the intervention of governmental institutions…"[23]

Each claims association adopted its own constitution and by-laws, elected officers for the operation of the organization, established rules for adjudicating disputes, and established the procedure for the registration and protection of claims. The constitution of the Claim Association of Johnson County, Iowa offers one of the few records of club operation. In addition to president, vice president, and clerk and record, that constitution provided for the election of seven judges, any five of whom could compose a court to settle disputes, and for the election of two marshals charged with enforcing rules of the association. The constitution specified the procedure whereby property rights in land would be defined as well as the procedure for arbitrating claims disputes. User charges were utilized for defraying arbitration expenses.

> In such case of the place and time of holding such court and summons all witnesses that either of the parties may require the court made previous to their proceeding to investigate any case require the plaintiff and defendant to deposit a sufficient sum of money in their hands to defray the expenses of said suit or the costs of said suit. And should either party refuse to deposit such sum of money the court may render judgment against such person refusing to do...[24]

As a sanction against those who would not follow the rules of the association, violence was an option, but the following resolution suggests that less violent means were also used.

> *Resolved*, that more effectually to sustain settlers in their just claims according to the custom of the neighborhood and to prevent difficulty and discord in society that we mutually pledge our honors to observe the following resolutions rigidly. That we will not associate nor countenance those who do not respect the claims of settlers and further that we will neither neighbor with them... Trade barter deal with them in any way whatever....[25]

That the constitutions, by-laws, and resolutions of all claims clubs were not alike suggests that preferences among the squatters did vary and that there were alternative forms of protection and justice available. The most common justification for the clubs was stated as follows: "Whereas it has become a custom in the western states, as soon as the Indian title to the public lands has been extinguished by the General Government for the citizens of the United States to settle upon and improve said lands, and heretofore the improvement and claim of the settler to the extent of 320 acres, has been respected by both the citizens and laws of Iowa...."[26] Other justification "emphasized the need of protection against 'reckless claim jumpers and invidious wolves in human form,' or the need 'for better security against foreign as well as domestic aggression.'"[27] Some associations were formed specifically for the purpose of opposing "speculators" who were attempting to obtain title to the land. The constitutions of these clubs as evidenced by the Johnson County document specifically regulated the amount of improvements which had to be made on the claim. Other associations, however, encouraged speculation by making no such requirements. These voluntary, extra-legal associations provided protection and justice without apparent violence and developed rules consistent with the preferences, goals, and endowments of the participants.

b. Cattlemen's Associations

Early settlement of the cattle frontier created few property conflicts, but as land became more scarce, private, voluntary enforcement mechanisms evolved. Initially "there was room enough for all, and when a cattleman rode up some likely valley or across some well-grazed divide and found cattle thereon, he looked elsewhere for range."[28] But even "as early as 1868, two years after the first drive, small groups of owners were organizing themselves into protective associations and hiring stock detectives."[29] The place of these associations in the formation of "frontier law" is described by Louis Pelzer.

> From successive frontiers of our American history have developed needed customs, laws, and organizations. The era of fur-trading produced its hunters, its barter, and the great fur companies; on the mining frontier came the staked claims and the vigilance committees; the camp meeting and the circuit rider were heard on the religious outposts; on the margins of settlement the claim clubs protected the rights of the squatter farmers; on the ranchmen's frontier the millions of cattle, the vast ranges, the ranches, and the cattle companies produced pools and local, district, territorial and national cattle associations.[30]

As Ernest Staples Osgood tells us, it was "the failure of the police power in the frontier communities to protect property and preserve order," which "resulted over and over again in groups who represented the will of the law-abiding part of the community dealing out summary justice to offenders."[31]

Like the claims associations, the cattlemen's associations drew up formal rules governing the group, but their means of enforcing private rights was often more violent than the trade sanctions specified by the claims associations. These private protection agencies were quite clearly a market response to existing demands for enforcement of rights.

> Expert gunmen—professional killers—had an economic place in the frontier West. They turned up wherever there was trouble... Like all mercenaries, they espoused the side which made them the first or best offer....[32]

> Just why, when, and how he hooked up with the cattlemen around Fort Maginnis, instead of with the rustlers, is a trifle obscure, but Bill became Montana's first stock detective. Raconteurs of the period seem agreed that Bill's choice was not dictated by ethics, but by the prospect of compensation. At any rate, he became a hired defender of property rights, and he executed his assignments—as well as his quarry—with thoroughness and dispatch.[33]

The market-based enforcement agencies of the cattlemen's frontier were different from modern private enforcement firms in that the earlier versions evidently enforced their own laws much of the time rather than serving as simply an extension of the government's police force. An often expressed concern about this type of enforcement is that 1) the enforcement will be ineffective or 2) the enforcement agencies will themselves become large-scale organizations that use their power to infringe upon individual rights. We have argued above that there is little reason to believe that the first concern is justified.

It also appears that the second concern is not supported by the experience of the American West. Major economies of scale did not seem to exist in either enforcement or crime. Although there are numerous records of gunslingers making themselves available for hire, we find no record of these gunslingers discovering that it was even more profitable to band together and form a super-defense agency that sold protection and rode roughshod over private property rights. Some of the individuals did drift in and out of a life of crime and sometimes did form loose criminal associations. However, these associations did not seem to be encouraged by the market form of peace keeping, and in fact, seemed to be dealt with more quickly and more severely under private property protective associations than under government organization.

There were a few large private enforcement organizations, in particular the Pinkerton Agency and Wells Fargo, but these agencies seemed to serve mainly as adjuncts to government and were largely used in enforcing state and national laws. Other large-scale associations, e.g., the Rocky Mountain Detective Association and the Anti-Horse Thief Association, were loose information providing and coordination services, and rarely provided on-the-spot enforcement of private rules.[34]

c. Mining Camps

As the population of the U.S. grew, westward expansion was inevitable, but there can be little doubt that the discovery of gold in California in 1848 rapidly increased the rate of expansion. Thousands of Easterners rushed to the most westward frontier in search of the precious metal, leaving behind their civilized world. Later the same experience occurred in Colorado, Montana, and Idaho and, in each case, the first to arrive were forced into a situation where they had to write the rules of the game.

> There was no constitutional authority in the country, and neither judge nor officer within five hundred miles. The invaders were remitted to the primal law of nature, with, perhaps, the inherent rights of American citizenship. Every gulch was filling with red-hot treasure hunters; every bar was pock-marked with "prospect holes"; timber, water-rights, and town-lots were soon to be valuable, and government was an imperative necessity. Here was a fine field for theorists to test their views as to the origin of civil law.[35]

The early civil law which evolved from this process approximated anarcho-capitalism as closely as any other experience in the U.S.

In the absence of a formal structure for the definition and enforcement of individual rights, many of the groups of associates who came seeking their fortunes organized and made their rules for operation before they left their homes. Much the same as company charters today, these voluntary contracts entered into by the miners specified financing for the operation as well as the nature of the relationship between individuals. These rules applied only to the miners in the company and did not recognize any outside arbitrator of disputes; they did not "recognize any higher court than the law of the majority of the company."[36]

As Friedman's theory predicts, the rules under which the companies were organized varied according to tastes and needs of the company. "When we compare the rules of different companies organized to go to the mines, we find considerable variation."[37] In addition to the rules listed above, company constitutions often specified arrangements for payments to be used for caring for the sick and unfortunate, rules for personal conduct including the use of alcoholic spirits, and fines which could be imposed for misconduct, to mention a few.[38] In the truest nature of the social contract, the governing rules of the company were negotiated, and as in all market transactions unanimity prevailed. Those who wished to purchase other "bundles of goods" or other sets of rules had that alternative.

Once the mining companies arrived at the potential gold sites, the rules were useful only insofar as questions of rights involved members of the company; when other individuals were confronted in the mining camps, additional negotiation was necessary. Of course, the first issues to arise concerned the ownership of mining claims. When the groups were small and homogeneous, dividing up the gulch was an easy task. But when the numbers moving to the gold country reached the thousands, the problems increased. The general solution was to hold a mass meeting and appoint committees assigned to drafting the laws. Gregory Gulch in Colorado provides an example.

> A mass meeting of miners was held June 8, 1859, and a committee appointed to draft a code of laws. This committee laid out boundaries for the district, and their civil code, after some discussion and amendment, was *unanimously* adopted in mass meeting, July 16. 1859. The example was rapidly followed in other districts, and the whole Territory was soon divided between a score of local sovereignties.[39]

The camps could not live in complete isolation from the established forms of government, but there is evidence that they were able to maintain their autonomy. In California, military posts were established to take care of Indian troubles, but these governmental enforcement organizations did not exercise any authority over the mining camps. General Riley in an 1849 visit to a California camp told the miners that "all questions touching the temporary right of individuals to work in particular localities of which they were in possession, should be left to the decision of the local authorities."[40]

> No alcalde, no council, no justice of the peace, was ever forced upon a district by an outside power. The district was the unit of political organization, in many regions, long after the creation of the state; and delegates from adjoining districts often met in consultation regarding boundaries, or matters of local government, and reported to their respective constituencies in open-air meeting, on hillside or river-bank.[41]

Moreover, the services of trained lawyers were not welcomed in many of the campus and even forbidden in districts such as the Union Mining District.

> *Resolved*, that no lawyer be permitted to practice law in this district, under penalty of not more than fifty nor less than twenty lashes, and be forever banished from this district.[42]

In this way, the local camps were able to agree upon rules or individual rights and upon methods for enforcement thereof without coercion from U.S. authorities. When outside laws were imposed upon the camps, there is some evidence that they increased rather than decreased crime. One early Californian writes, "We needed no law until the lawyers came," and another adds, "There were few crimes until the courts with their delays and technicalities took the place of miners' law.[43]

While the mining camps did not have private courts where individuals could take their disputes and pay for arbitration, they did develop a system of justice through the miners' courts. These courts seldom had permanent officers, although there were instances of justices of the peace. The folk-moot system was common in California. By this method a group of citizens was summoned to try a case. From their midst they would elect a presiding officer or judge and select six or twelve persons to serve as the jury. Most often their rulings were not disputed, but there was recourse when disputes arose. For example, in one case involving two partners, after a ruling by the miners' court, the losing partner called a mass meeting of the camp to plead his case and the decision was reversed.[44] And if a larger group of miners was dissatisfied with the general rulings regarding camp boundaries or individual claim disputes, notices were posted in several places calling a meeting of those wishing a division of the territory. "If a majority favored such action, the district was set apart and named. The old district was not consulted on the subject, but received a verbal notice of the new organization. Local conditions, making different regulations regarding claims desirable, were the chief causes of such separations."[45] "The work of mining, and its environment and conditions, were so different in different places, that the laws and customs of the miners had to vary even in adjoining districts."[46] When disputes did arise and court sessions were called, any man in the camp might be called upon to be the executive officer. Furthermore, any one who was a law-abiding citizen might be considered for prosecutor or defender for the accused.

In Colorado there is some evidence of competition among the courts for business, and hence, an added guarantee that justice prevailed.

> The civil courts promptly assumed criminal jurisdiction, and the year 1860 opened with four governments in full blast. The miners' courts, people's courts, and "provisional government" (a new name for "Jefferson") divided jurisdiction in the mountains; while Kansas and the provisional government ran concurrent in Denver and the valley. Such as felt friendly to either jurisdiction patronized it with their business. Appeals were taken from one to the other, papers certified up or down and over, and recognized, criminals delivered and judgments accepted from one court by another, with a happy informality which it is pleasant to read of. And here we are confronted by an awkward fact: there was undoubtedly much less crime in the two years this arrangement lasted than in the two which followed the territorial organization and regular government.[47]

This evidence is consistent with Friedman's hypothesis that when competition exists, courts will be responsible for mistakes and the desire for repeat business will serve as an effective check on "unjust" decisions.

d. Wagon Trails

Perhaps the best example of private property anarchism in the American West was the organization of the wagon trains as they moved across the plains in search of California gold. The region west of Missouri and Iowa was unorganized, unpatrolled, and beyond the jurisdiction of the United States law. But to use the old trapper saying that there was "no law west of Leavenworth" to describe the trains would be inappropriate. "Realizing that they were passing beyond the pale of the law, and aware that the tedious journey and the constant tensions of the trail brought out the worst in human character, the pioneers...created their own law-making and law-enforcing machinery before they started."[48] Like their fellow travelers on the ocean, the pioneers in their prairie schooners negotiated a "plains law" much like their counterparts' "sea law."[49] The result of this negotiation in many cases was the adoption of a formal constitution patterned after that of the U.S. The preamble of the constitution of the Green and Jersey County Company provides an example.

> We, the members of the Green and Jersey County Company of Emigrants to California, for the purpose of effectually protecting our persons and property, and as the best means of ensuring an expeditious and easy journey do ordain and establish the following constitution.[50]

From this and the other constitutions which have survived it is clear that these moving communities did have a basic set of rules defining how "the game would be played" during their journey. Like the rules of the mining camps, the wagon train constitutions varied according to the tastes and needs of each organization, but several general tendencies do emerge. Most often the groups waited until after they have been on the trail for a few days and out of the jurisdiction of the United States. One of the first tasks was to select officers who would be responsible for enforcing the rules. For the Green and Jersey County Company, which was not atypical, the officers included a Captain, Assistant Captain, Treasurer, Secretary, and an Officer of the Guard. The constitutions also included eligibility for voting and decision rules for amendment, banishment of individuals from the group, and dissolution of the company. Duties for each officer were often well specified as in the case of the Charleston, Virginia, Mining Company.[51] In addition to these general rules, specific laws were enacted. Again, the introduction of the Green and Jersey County Company is illustrative.

> We, citizens and inhabitants of the United States, and members of the Green and Jersey County Company of Emigrants to California; about starting on a journey through a territory where the laws of our common country do not extend their protection, deem it necessary, for the preservation of our rights, to establish certain wholesome rules and regulations. We, therefore, having first organized a constitution of government, for ourselves, do now proceed to enact and ordain the following laws; and in so doing we disclaim all desire or intention of violating or treating with disrespect, the laws of our country.[52]

The specific rules included organization of jury trials; regulation of Sabbath-breaking, gambling and intoxication; and penalties for failing to perform chores, especially guard duty. In certain cases there were even provisions for the repair of road, building bridges, and protection of other "public goods."[53]

It has been argued that "these ordinances or constitutions...may be of interest as guides to pioneers' philosophies about law and social organization, [but] they do not help answer the more essential question of how, in fact, not in theory, did the overland pioneer face problems of social disorder, crime, and private conflict."[54] Nonetheless, it is clear that the travelers did negotiate from Schelling points to social contracts without relying upon the coercive powers of government. And these *voluntary* contracts did provide the basis for social organization.

The Schelling points from which the individuals negotiated included a very well accepted set of private rights especially with regard to property. One might expect that upon leaving the legal jurisdiction of the U.S. with its many laws governing private property that the immigrants would have less respect for others' rights. Moreover, since the constitutions and by-laws seldom specifically mentioned individual property rights, we might infer that these were of little concern to the overlanders. In his article, "Paying for the Elephant: Property Rights and Civil Order on the Overland Trail," John Phillip Reid convincingly argues that respect for property rights was paramount. Even when food became so scarce that starvation was a distinct possibility, there are few examples where the pioneers resorted to violence.

> Indeed, it is no exaggeration to say that the emigrants who traveled America's overland trail gave little thought to solving their problems by violence or theft. We know that some ate the flesh of dead oxen or beef with maggots while surrounded by healthy animals they could have shot. Those who suffered losses early in the trip and were able to go back, did so. The disappointment and embarrassment for some must have been extremely bitter, but hundreds returned. They did not use weapons to force their way through. While a few of those who were destitute may have employed tricks to obtain food, most begged, and those who were "too proud to beg" got along the best they could or employed someone to beg for them. If they could not beg, they borrowed, and when they could not borrow they depended on their credit.[55]

The emigrants were property minded. The fact that the constitution contained few references to individual property rights may well reflect the significance of private property Schelling points.

When crimes against property or person did occur, the judicial system which was specified in the contracts was brought into play. "The rules of a traveling company organized at Kanesville, Iowa, provided: 'Resolved, that in case of any dispute arising between any members of the Company, they shall be referred to three arbiters, one chosen by each party, and one by the two chosen, whose decision shall be final.'"[56] The methods of settling disputes varied among the companies, but in nearly all cases some means of arbitration were specified to insure "that the rights of each emigrant are protected and enforced."[57]

In addition to the definition and enforcement of individual rights, the overlanders also were faced with the question of how to solve disputes involving contractual relations for business purposes. For all of the same reasons that firms exist for the production of goods and services, individuals crossing the plains had incentives to organize into "firms" with one another. Scale economies in the production of goods such as meals and services such as herding and in the provision of protection from Indians provided for gains from *voluntary* and collective action. Again markets seemed to function well in providing several types of contractual arrangements for this production and protection.

A common form of organization on the overland trail was the "mess." Similar to share-cropping arrangements in agriculture, the mess allowed individuals to contribute inputs such as food, oxen, wagons, labor, etc. for the joint production of travel or meals. In this way, the mess, which allowed the property to remain privately owned, differed from the partnership where property was concurrently owned. Since mess property was available for use by all members of the mess, the potential for conflict was great. When the conflicts occurred, renegotiation of the contract was sometimes necessary. When new agreements could not be reached, the mess would have to be dissolved and property returned to individual owners. Since ownership remained private, division was not difficult. Moreover, since there were gains from trade to be obtained from combining inputs, it was usually possible to renegotiate when violations in the contract occurred. There were, however, cases where renegotiation seemed impossible, as in the following example of a mess which found one of its members unwilling to do his share of the chores.

> [W]e concluded the best thing we could do was to buy him out and let him go which accordingly we did by paying him one hundred doll[ar]s. He shoulder[ed] his gun, carpet bag, and blanket and took the track to the prairie without saying good by to one of us.[58]

While other cases of dissolution of messes occurred, there is no evidence that coercive power was used to take property from rightful owners. If an individual left one mess he could usually join another.

The other common type of organization on the overland routes was the joint stock company. In this organization members contributed capital and other property which was held concurrently. The Charlestown, Virginia, Mining Company provides an example of such a company and its constitution attests to the establishment of rules governing use of concurrent property.[59] Again it should be emphasized that these rules were voluntary though coercion was used within the organization to enforce them.

Like the mess, when disagreements occurred within the joint stock company, renegotiation was necessary. However, since the property was held concurrently this process was more complicated. In the first place, an individual could not simply leave the company. Most often withdrawal could only occur with the consent of a percentage of other members. But even then withdrawal was complicated by the need to divide the property. In at least one case this problem was solved by dividing all of the property and reorganizing into messes.

> When the original joint stock company of sixty men dissolved, there was no mention of individual ownership. The property was parceled by assigning it to traveling units already in existence. However, in executing the second division, the smaller group found it possible—perhaps even necessary—to utilize the concept of personal property. In order to accomplish their purpose, the men first transmuted the common stock from "company" or partnership property into private property. Then, by negotiating contracts, goods they briefly had held as individuals, were converted back into partnership or mess property.[60]

All of this occurred in the absence of coercion.

Perhaps an even more revealing example of anarcho-capitalism at work is found in the dissolution of the Boone County Company. When the eight members of the company fell into rival factions of 3 and 5, dissolution became imminent. Negotiations continued for some time until all the company property (note that none of the private property was divided) was divided between the two groups. When negotiations appeared at an impasse because of the indivisibility of units and differences in quality, prices were assigned to units and the groups resolved the issue by trade. However, a $75 claim of the majority group proved even harder to resolve. The claim resulted from the fact that a passenger who owned two mules and a horse and who had been traveling with the company chose to take his property and go with the minority. The disadvantaged majority demanded compensation. Unable to settle the dispute, arbitration came from a "private court" consisting of "3 disinterested men," one chosen by each side and a third chosen by the two. Their decision follows.

> [W]e can see no just cause why the mess of 3 men should pay anything to the mess of 5 men. It being...a mutual and simultaneous agreement to dissolve the original contract. The fact that Abbott joins in with the 3 men does not alter in our opinion the matter of the case—for the dissolution being mutually agreed upon, all the parties stand in the same relation to each other which they did, before any contract was entered into. And Abbott might or not just as he chose unite with either party. If he chose to unite with neither party, then clearly neither could claim of the other. If he united with a foreign party then who could think of claiming anything of such a party.[61]

The important point of this example is that when the Boone County Company could not renegotiate its initial contract the members did not resort to force, but chose private arbitration instead. The many companies which crossed the plains "were experiments in democracy and while some proved inadequate to meet all emergencies, the very ease with which the members could dissolve their bonds and form new associations without lawlessness and disorder proves the true democratic spirit among the American frontiersmen rather than the opposite."[62] Competition rather than coercion insured justice.

While the above evidence suggests that the wagon trains were guided by anarcho-capitalism, it should be noted that their unique characteristics may have contributed to the efficacy of the system. First, the demand for public goods was probably not as great as found in more permanent communities. If nothing else, the transient nature of these moving communities meant that schools, roads, and other goods which are publicly provided in our society were not needed, hence there was no demand for a government to form for this purpose. Secondly, the short-term nature of the organization meant that there was not a very long time for groups to organize to use coercion. These were "governments" of necessity rather than ambition. Nonetheless, the wagon trains on the overland trails did provide protection and justice without a monopoly on coercion, did allow competition to produce rules, and did not result in the lawless disorder generally associated with anarchy.

Concluding Remarks

From the above descriptions of the experience of the American West, several conclusions consistent with Friedman's hypotheses appear.

1) The West, although often dependent upon market peacekeeping agencies, was, for the most part, orderly.
2) Different standards of justice did prevail and various preferences for rules were expressed through the market place.
3) Competition in defending and adjudicating rights does have beneficial effects. Market agencies provided useful ways of measuring the efficiency of government alternatives. The fact that government's monopoly on coercion was not taken as seriously as at present meant that when that monopoly was poorly used market alternatives arose. Even when these market alternatives did become "governments" in the sense of having a virtual monopoly on coercion, the fact that such firms were usually quite small provided significant checks on their behavior. Clients could leave or originate protective agencies on their own. Without formal legal sanctions, the private agencies did face a "market test" and the rate of survival of such agencies was much less than under government.

The above evidence points to the overall conclusion that competition was very effective in solving the "public goods" problem of law and order in the American West. However, this does not mean that there were no disputes that would cause one to doubt the efficacy of such arrangements. Two examples of civil disorder are often mentioned in Western history and they must be dealt with.

The first is the very bitter feud between the Regulators and the Moderators in the Republic of Texas in the 1840s.[63] What started as a disagreement between two individuals in Shelby County escalated until it involved a significant number of people in a large area of east Texas. In 1839 a loosely organized band, later to be known as the Moderators, was issuing bogus land papers, stealing horses, murdering, and generally breaking the "law" of Shelby County, Texas. To counter this lawlessness a vigilance committee was formed under the name of Regulators. Unfortunately, "bad elements soon infiltrated the Regulators, and their excesses in crime later rivaled those of the Moderators. The situation evolved into a complexity of personal and family feuds, and complete anarchy existed until 1844."[64] One citizen described the situation in a letter to a friend:

> Civil war, with all its horror, has been raging in this community. The citizens of the county are about equally divided into two parties, the Regulators and Moderators. It is no uncommon sight to see brothers opposed to each other. Every man's interest in this county is seriously affected.[65]

During the period eighteen men were murdered and many more wounded. Only when President Sam Houston called out the militia in 1844 did the feuding stop. Thus, for whatever reasons, in this case it appears that dependence upon non-governmental forms of organization was not successful.

Another major civil disruption that should be considered is the Johnson County War in Northern Wyoming in 1892. A group of stockgrowers and their hired guns entered Johnson County with the express purpose of wiping out the rustlers they believed to be prevalent there. The citizens of the county, feeling they were being invaded by a foreign army, responded en masse and for a short period of time a "war" did result. However, in this case the disorder seems to have been more a battle between two "legitimized" agencies of coercion, the state and the local government, than between strictly private enforcement agencies. The invaders, while ostensibly acting as a private party, had the tacit approval of the state government and used that approval to thwart several attempts by the local authorities to secure state or federal intervention. Those who responded to the invasion were under the leadership of the Johnson County sheriff and felt very much that they were acting appropriately under the existing laws of that time.[66] Thus this incident sheds little light on the efficacy of market arrangements for maintaining order.

In conclusion, it appears in the absence of formal government, that the western frontier was not as wild as legend would have us believe. The market did provide protection and arbitration agencies that functioned very effectively, either as a complete replacement for formal government or as a supplement to that government. However, the same desire for power that creates problems in government also seemed to create difficulties at times in the West. All was not peaceful. Especially when Schelling points were lacking, disorder and chaos resulted, lending support to Buchanan's contention that agreement on initial rights is important to anarcho-capitalism. When this agreement existed, however, we have presented evidence that anarcho-capitalism was viable on the frontier.

Notes

1. James M. Buchanan, "Before Public Choice," in G. Tullock, ed., *Explorations in the Theory of Anarchy* (Blacksburg, Va.: Center for the Study of Public Choice, 1972), p. 37.
2. James M. Buchanan, "Review of David Friedman, *The Machinery of Freedom: Guide to Radical Capitalism*," *The Journal of Economic Literature*, Vol. XII, No. 3 (1974), p. 915.
3. E.A.J. Johnson, *The Foundations of American Economic Freedom* (Minneapolis: University of Minnesota Press, 1973), p. 305.
4. Laurence S. Moss, "Private Property Anarchism: An American Variant," in G. Tullock, ed., *Further Explorations in the Theory of Anarchy* (Blacksburg, Va.: Center for the Study of Public Choice, 1974), p. 26.

5. James M. Buchanan, *Freedom in Constitutional Contract* (College Sta., Tex.: Texas A&M University Press, 1977), p. 52.
6. Buchanan, "Review of *Machinery of Freedom*," p. 915.
7. Ibid., emphasis added.
8. Ibid.
9. For a longer discussion of Schelling points, see Thomas C. Schelling, *The Strategy of Conflict* (Cambridge: Harvard University Press, 1960), pp. 54-58; Buchanan, "Review of *Machinery of Freedom*," p. 914; and David Friedman, "Schelling Points, Self-Enforcing Contracts, and the Paradox of Order" (unpub. Ms., Center for the Study of Public Choice, Virginia Polytechnic Institute).
10. David Friedman, *The Machinery of Freedom: Guide to Radical Capitalism* (New York: Harper & Row, 1973), p. 152.
11. Gilbert Geis, "Violence in American Society," *Current History*, Vol. LII (1976), p. 357.
12. Eugene W. Hollon, *Frontier Vio1ence; Another Look* (New York: Oxford University Press, 1974), p. x.
13. Robert A. Dykstra. The *Cattle Towns* (New York: Alfred A. Knopf, 1968), p. 144.
14. Paul I. Wellman, *The Trampling Herd* (New York: Carrick and Evans, 1939), p. 159.
15. Hollon, *Frontier Violence*, p. 200.
16. Frank Prassel, *The Western Peace Officer* (Norman, Okla.: University of Oklahoma Press, 1937), pp. 16-17.
17. Ibid., p. 7.
18. See George R. Stewart, *Committee on Vigilance* (Boston: Houghton Mifflin Co., 1964); and Alan Valentine, *Vigilante Justice* (New York: Reynal and Co., 1956).
19. Thomas J, Dimsdale, *The Vigilantes of Montana* (Norman, Okla.: University of Oklahoma Press, 1953).
20. Wayne Gard, *Frontier Justice* (Norman, Okla.: University of Oklahoma Press, 1949), p. 165.
21. Benjamin F. Shambaugh, "Frontier Land Clubs, or Claim Associations," *Annual Report of the American Historical Association* (1900), p. 71.
22. Ibid., p. 69.
23. Frederick Jackson Turner, *The Frontier in American History* (New York: Henry Holt and Co., 1920), p. 343.
24. Shambaugh, "Frontier Land Clubs," p. 77.
25. Ibid., pp. 77-78.
26. Quoted in Allan Bogue, "The Iowa Claim Clubs: Symbol and Substance," in V. Carstensen, ed., *The Public Lands* (Madison, Wisc.: University of Wisconsin Press, 1963), p. 50.
27. Ibid.
28. Ernest Staples Osgood, *The Day of the Cattleman* (Minneapolis: University of Minnesota Press, 1929), p. 182.
29. Ibid., p. 118.
30. Louis Pelzer, *The Cattlemen's Frontier* (Glendale, Calif.: A.H. Clark, 1936), p. 87.
31. Osgood, *Day of the Cattleman*, p. 157.
32. Wellman, *Trampling Herd*, p. 157.
33. Robert H. Fletcher, *Free Grass to Fences: The Montana Range Story* (New York: University Publishers, 1960), p. 65.
34. Prassel, *Western Peace Officer*, pp. 134-141.

35. J. H. Beadle, *Western Wilds and the Men Who Redeem Them* (Cincinnati: Jones Brothers, 1882), p. 476.
36. Charles Howard Shinn, *Mining Camps: A Study in American Frontier Government* (New York: Alfred A. Knopf, 1948), p. 107.
37. Ibid.
38. John Phillip Reid, "Prosecuting the Elephant: Trials and Judicial Behavior on the Overland Trail," *BYU Law Review*, Vol. 77, No. 2 (1977), pp. 335-336.
39. Beadle, *Western Wilds*, p. 477, emphasis added.
40. Quoted in Shinn, *Mining Camps*, p. 111.
41. Ibid., p. 168.
42. Quoted in Beadle, *Western Wilds*, p. 478.
43. Quoted in Shinn, *Mining Camps*, p. 113.
44. Marvin Lewis, ed., *The Mining Frontier* (Norman, Okla.: University of Oklahoma Press, 1967), pp. 10-18.
45. Shinn, *Mining Camps*, p. 118.
46. Ibid., p. 159.
47. Beadle, *Western Wilds*, p. 477.
48. Ray Allen Billington, *The Far Western Frontier, 1830-1860* (New York: Harper & Bros., 1956), p. 99.
49. David Morris Potter, ed., *Trail to California* (New Haven: Yale University Press, 1945), pp. 16-17.
50. Reprinted in Elizabeth Page, *Wagon West* (New York: Farrar & Rinehart, 1930), Appendix C.
51. Constitution reprinted in Potter, *Trail to California*, Appendix A.
52. Page, *Wagon West*, p. 183.
53. Ibid., p. 119.
54. David J. Langum, "Pioneer Justice on the Overland Trail," *Western Historical Quarterly*, Vol. 5, No. 3 (1974), p. 424, fn. 12.
55. John Phillip Reid, "Paying for the Elephant: Property Rights and Civil Order on the Overland Trail," *The Huntington Library Quarterly*, Vol. XLI, No. 1 (1977), pp. 50-51.
56. Reid, "Prosecuting the Elephant," p. 330.
57. Quoted in Reid, "Prosecuting the Elephant," p. 330.
58. Quoted in John Phillip Reid, "Dividing the Elephant: The Separation of Mess and Joint Stock Property on the Overland Trail," *Hastings Law Journal*, Vol. 28, No. 1 (1976), p. 77.
59. See Potter, *Trail to California*, Appendix A.
60. Reid, "Dividing the Elephant," p. 85.
61. Quoted in Reid, "Dividing the Elephant," p. 85.
62. Owen Cochran Coy, *The Great Trek* (San Francisco: Powell Pub. Co., 1931), p. 117.
63. See Gard, *Frontier Justice*; Hollon, *Frontier Violence*; and Hugh David Graham and Ted Robert Gurr, eds., *The History of Violence in America: Historical and Comparative Perspectives* (New York: Prager, 1969).
64. Hollon, *Frontier Violence*, p. 53.
65. Quoted in Gard, *Frontier Justice*, pp. 35-36.
66. See Helen Huntington Smith, *The War on the Powder River: The History of an Insurrection* (Lincoln, Neb.: University of Nebraska Press, 1966).

40

Order without Law: How Neighbors Settle Disputes (excerpt)

Robert C. Ellickson

The Resolution of Cattle-Trespass Disputes

Trespass by cattle, the subject of Coase's Parable of the Farmer and the Rancher, is a common event in ranching country. A complex body of law, much of it of unusually ancient lineage, formally applies to these occurrences. In Shasta County, the rules of trespass law vary between open- and closed-range districts, and the location of district boundaries has been the focus of intense political controversy. Nevertheless, it turns out, perhaps counter-intuitively, that legal rules hardly ever influence the settlement of cattle-trespass disputes in Shasta County.[1]

Animal Trespass Incidents

Each of the twenty-eight landowners interviewed, including each of the thirteen ranchette owners, reported at least one instance in which his lands had been invaded by someone else's livestock. Hay farmers grow what cattle especially like to eat and can thus expect frequent trespasses. For example, John Woodbury, an alfalfa grower, suffered almost weekly incursions in 1973. Woodbury's situation later improved when many traditionalist cattlemen declined to renew their grazing leases on mountain forest,[2] but he was still experiencing a couple of cattle trespasses a year in the early 1980s. Another hay farmer, Phil Ritchie, could identify six neighbors whose cattle had trespassed on his lands in recent years. Owners of large ranches are also frequent trespass victims because they cannot keep their many miles of aging perimeter fence cattle-tight. Thus, when a rancher gathers his animals on his fenced pastures each spring, he is hardly startled to find a few head carrying a neighbor's brand.

Because beef cattle eat feed equal to about 2 ½ percent of their body weight each day,[3] a trespass victim's vegetation is always at risk. Nevertheless, a victim usually regards the loss of grass as trivial, provided that the animals are easy to corral and the owner removes them within a day or two. Trespassing livestock occasionally do cause more than nominal damage. Several ranchette owners reported incidents in which wayward cattle had damaged their fences and vegetable gardens; one farmer told of the ravaging of some of his ornamental trees.

The most serious trespasses reported were ones involving at-large cattle or bulls. A ranchette owner described how mountain cattle had once invaded his house construction site, broken the windows, and contaminated the creek. The part-time horse breeder Larry Brennan told of buying seven tons of hay and stacking it on an unfenced portion of his fifty-acre ranchette, where it was then eaten by cattle that Frank Ellis had let roam free.

Rural residents especially fear trespasses by bulls. In a modern beef cattle herd, roughly one animal in twenty-five is a bull, whose principal function is to impregnate cows during their brief periods in heat.[4] Bulls are not only much more ornery but also much larger than other herd animals. A Hereford bull has a mature weight of 2000 pounds. By contrast, a mature Hereford cow weighs only 1100-1200 pounds, and Hereford steers (castrated males) are typically slaughtered when they weigh between 1000 and 1150 pounds.[5] Several ranchers who were interviewed had vivid memories of bull trespasses. A farmer who owned irrigated pasture was amazed at the depth of the hoof marks that an entering bull had made. A ranchette owner and a rancher told of barely escaping goring while attempting to corral invading bulls.[6] Because an alien bull often enters in pursuit of cows in heat, owners of female animals fear illicit couplings that might produce offspring of an undesired pedigree. Although no cow owner reported actual damages from misbreeding, several mentioned that this risk especially worried them.

Animal Trespass Law

One of the most venerable English common law rules of strict liability in torts is the rule that an owner of domestic livestock is liable, even in the absence of negligence, for property damage that his animals cause while trespassing. In the memorable words of Judge Blackburn:

> The case that has most commonly occurred, and which is most frequently to be found in the books, is as to the obligation of the owner of cattle which he has brought on his land, to prevent their escaping and doing mischief. The law as to them seems to be perfectly settled from early times; the owner must keep them in at his peril, or he will be answerable for the natural consequences of their escape; that is with regard to tame beasts, for the grass they eat and trample upon, though not for any injury to the person of others, for our ancestors have settled that it is not the general nature of horses to kick, or bulls to gore; but if the owner knows that the beast has a vicious propensity to attack man, he will be answerable for that too.[7]

This traditional English rule formally prevails in the closed-range areas of Shasta County.[8] In the open-range areas of the county—that is, in the great bulk of its rural territory—the English rule has been rejected in favor of the pro-cattleman "fencing-out" rule that many grazing states adopted during the nineteenth century.[9]

In 1850, just after California attained statehood, an open-range rule was adopted for the entire state. In that year the legislature enacted a statute that entitled a victim of animal trespass to recover damages only when the victim had protected his lands with a "lawful fence."[10] This pro-cattleman policy grew increasingly controversial as California became more settled and field crops became more common. During the latter part of the nineteenth century, the California legislature enacted a series of statutes effectively closing the range in designated counties, thereby granting more protection to farmers who had not built fences.[11]

The closed-range exceptions eventually began to swamp California's traditional open-range rule and triggered a comprehensive legislative response. In the Estray Act of 1915,[12] the legislature adopted for most of California the traditional English rule that the owner of livestock is strictly liable for trespass damage.[13] This statute, however, retained the open-range rule in six counties in the lightly populated northern part of the state, where the tradition of running cattle at large remained strong, The six counties were Shasta, Del Norte, Lassen, Modoc, Siskiyou, and Trinity.[14]

In 1945 the legislature enacted two amendments that dealt exclusively with Shasta County, the least rural of the six exempt counties. The first stated that a prime agricultural area just south of Redding was "not…devoted, chiefly to grazing"—a declaration that the legislature had decided to close the range in that small area of the county.[15] The second amendment empowered the Board of Supervisors of Shasta County to adopt ordinances designating additional areas of the county as places no longer devoted chiefly to grazing. A board action of this sort would make cattlemen strictly liable for trespass damage occurring in those locations.[16] Between 1945 and 1974 Shasta was the only California county to possess this special authority,[17] As a result Shasta County today has a crazy quilt of open- and closed-range areas that no other California county can match.[18]

The distinction between open range and closed range has formal legal significance in Shasta County trespass disputes. In closed range, the English rule governs and an animal owner is strictly liable for trespass damage to property.[19] In open-range areas, by in contrast, even a livestock owner[20] who has negligently managed his animals is generally not liable for trespass damage to the lands[21] of a neighbor.

Even in open range in Shasta County, however, an animal owner is legally liable for animal-trespass damages of three significant sorts. First, owners of goats, swine, and vicious dogs are strictly liable for trespass throughout Shasta County.[22] Second, when a cattleman's livestock have trespassed in the face of a "lawful fence" that entirely enclosed the victim's open-range premises, the cattleman is also strictly liable.[23] (A California statute, unamended since 1915, defines the technological standard that a fence must meet to be "lawful.")[24] Third, common law decisions make a livestock owner liable for *intentional* open-range trespasses. Thus when Frank Ellis actively herded his cattle across the unfenced lands of his neighbors, he was legally liable for trespass. According to some precedents, he would also have been liable had he merely placed his cattle on his own lands in a way that would make it substantially certain that they would venture onto his neighbor's pastures.[25]

When the law of either open or closed range entitles a trespass victim to relief, the standard legal remedy is an award of compensatory damages.[26] (In part because evidence of damage to forage is fleeting, some states, although currently not California, authorize the appointment of disinterested residents of the area to serve as "fence viewers" to assess the amount of the damages.)[27] A plaintiff who has suffered from continuing wrongful trespasses may also be entitled to an injunction against future incursions.[28] California's Estray Act additionally entitles a landowner whose premises have been wrongly invaded by cattle to seize the animals as security for a claim to recover boarding costs and other damages. A trespass victim who invokes this procedure must provide proper notice to the state director of agriculture; if certain statutory requirements are met, the animals can be sold to satisfy the claim.[29]

The formal law provides trespass victims with only limited self-help remedies. A victim can use reasonable force to drive the animals off his land,[30] and is arguably privileged to herd them to a remote location he knows is inconvenient for their owner.[31] In addition, as just noted, a trespass victim willing to give the animals proper care can seize strays and bill the costs of their care to their owner. But a victim is generally not entitled to kill or wound the offending animals. For example, a fruit grower in Mendocino County (a closed-range county) was convicted in 1973 for malicious maiming of animals when, without prior warning to the livestock owner, he shot and killed livestock trespassing in his unfenced orchard.[32] In this respect, as we shall see, Shasta County mores diverge from the formal law.

The distinction between open range and closed range has formal relevance in public as well as private trespass law. Shasta County's law enforcement officials are entitled to impound cattle found running at large in closed range, but not those found in open range.[33] Brad Bogue, the county animal control officer, relies primarily on warnings when responding to reports of loose animals. Regardless of whether a trespass has occurred in open or closed range, Bogue's prime goal is to locate the owner of the livestock and urge the prompt removal of the offending animals. When talking to animal owners, he stresses that it is in the owner's self-interest to take better care of the livestock. When talking to ranchette owners living in open range who have called to complain about trespassing mountain cattle, Bogue informs them of the cattleman's open range rights. He asserts that this sort of mediation is all that is required in the usual case. In most years, Bogue's office does not impound a single head of cattle[34] or issue a single criminal citation for failure to prevent cattle trespass.[35]

Knowledge of Animal Trespass Law

The Shasta County landowners interviewed were quizzed about their knowledge of the complex legal rules of animal trespass law reviewed above. The extent of their knowledge is relevant for at least two reasons. First, Coase's parable is set in a world of zero transaction costs, where everyone has perfect knowledge of legal rules. In reality, legal knowledge is imperfect because legal research is costly and human cognitive capacities are limited. The following overview of the working legal knowledge of Shasta County residents provides a glimpse of people's behavior in the face of these constraints. Data of this sort have implications for the design of legal rules to achieve specific instrumental goals, because rules cannot have instrumental effects unless they are communicated to the relevant actors. Second, my research revealed that most residents resolve trespass disputes not according to formal law but rather according to workaday norms that are consistent with an overarching norm of cooperation among neighbors. How notable this finding is depends in part on how many residents know that their trespass norms might be inconsistent legal rules.

Lay Knowledge of Trespass Law

To apply formal legal rules to a specific trespass incident, a Shasta County resident would first have to know whether it had occurred in an open-range or closed-range area of the county. Ideally, the resident would either have or know how to locate the map of closed-range areas published by the county's Department of Public Works. Second, a legally sophisticated person would have a working command of the rules of trespass law, including how they vary from open to closed range.

I found no one in Shasta County—whether an ordinary person or a legal specialist such as an attorney, judge, or insurance adjuster—with a complete working knowledge of the formal trespass rules just described. The persons best informed are, interestingly enough, two public officials without legal training: Brad Bogue, the animal control officer, and Bruce Jordan, the brand inspector. Their jobs require them to deal with stray livestock on almost a daily basis. Both have striven to learn applicable legal rules, and both sometimes invoke formal law when mediating disputes between county residents. Both Bogue and Jordan possess copies of the closed-range map and relevant provisions of the California Code. What they do *not* know is the decisional law; for example, neither is aware of the rule that an intentional trespass is always tortious, even in open range. Nevertheless, Bogue and Jordan, both familiar figures to the cattlemen and (to a lesser extent) to the ranchette owners of rural Shasta County, have done more than anyone else to educate the populace about formal trespass law.

What do ordinary rural residents know of that law? To a remarkable degree the landowners interviewed *did* know whether their own lands were within open or closed range. Of the twenty-five landowners asked to identify whether they lived in open or closed range, twenty-one provided the correct answer, including two who were fully aware that they owned land in both.[36] This level of knowledge is probably atypically high.[37] Most of the landowner interviews were conducted in the Round Mountain and Oak Run areas. The former was the site in 1973 of the Caton's Folly closed-range battle. More important, Frank Ellis' aggressive herding had provoked a furious closed-range battle in the Oak Run area just six months before the landowner interviews were conducted. Two well-placed sources—the Oak Run postmaster and the proprietor of the Oak Run general store—estimated that this political storm had caught the attention of perhaps 80 percent of the area's adult residents. In the summer of 1982, probably no populace in the United States was more alert to the legal distinction between open and closed range than were the inhabitants of the Oak Run area.[38]

What do laymen know of the substantive rules of trespass law? In particular, what do they know of how the rules vary from open to closed range? Individuals who are not legal specialists tend to conceive of these legal rules in black-and-white terms: either the livestock owners or the trespass victims "have the rights." We have seen, however, that the law of animal trespass is quite esoteric. An animal owner in open range, for example, is liable for intentional trespass, trespass through a lawful fence, or trespass by a goat. Only a few rural residents of Shasta County know anything of these subtleties. "Estray" and "lawful fence," central terms in the law of animal trespass, are not words in the cattlemen's everyday vocabulary. Neither of the two most sophisticated open-range ranchers interviewed was aware that enclosure by a lawful fence elevates a farmer's rights to recover for trespass. A traditionalist, whose cattle had often caused mischief in the Northeastern Sector foothills, thought estrays could never be seized in open range, although a lawful fence gives a trespass victim exactly that entitlement. No interviewee was aware that Ellis' intentional herding on his neighbors' lands in open range had been in excess of his legal rights.

As most laymen in rural Shasta County see it, trespass law is clear and simple. In closed range, an animal owner is strictly liable for trespass damages. (They of course never used, and would not recognize, the phrase "strict liability," which in the law of torts denotes liability even in the absence of negligence.) In open range, their basic premise is that an animal owner is never liable. When I posed hypothetical fact situations designed to put their rules under stress, the lay respondents sometimes backpedaled a bit, but they ultimately stuck to the notion that cattlemen have the rights in open range and trespass victims the rights in closed range.

Legal Specialists' Knowledge of Trespass Law

The laymen's penchant for simplicity enabled them to identify correctly the substance of the English strict-liability rule on cattle trespass that formally applies in closed range. In that regard, the laymen outperformed the judges, attorneys, and insurance adjusters who were interviewed. In two important respects the legal specialists had a poorer working knowledge of trespass and estray rules in Shasta County than did the lay landowners.[39] First, in contrast to the landowners, the legal specialists immediately invoked *negligence* principles when asked to analyze rights in trespass cases. In general, they thought that a cattleman would not be liable for trespass in open range (although about half seemed aware that this result would be affected by the presence of a lawful fence), and that he would be liable in closed range *only when negligent.* The negligence approach has so dominated American tort law during this century that legal specialists—insurance adjusters in particular—may fail to identify narrow pockets where strict liability rules, such as the English rule on cattle trespass, formally apply.[40]

Second, unlike the lay rural residents, the legal specialists knew almost nothing about the location of the closed-range districts in the county.[41] For example, two lawyers who lived in rural Shasta County and raised livestock as a sideline were ignorant of these boundaries; one incorrectly identified the kind of range in which he lived, and the other admitted he did not know what areas were open or closed. The latter added that this did not concern him because he would fence his lands under either legal regime.

Four insurance adjusters who settle trespass-damage claims in Shasta County were interviewed. These adjusters had little working knowledge of the location of closed-range and open-range areas or of the legal significance of those designations. One incorrectly identified Shasta County as an entirely closed-range jurisdiction. Another confused the legal designation "closed range" with the husbandry technique of keeping livestock behind fences; he stated that he did not keep up with the closed range situation because the fence situation changes too rapidly to be worth following. The other two adjusters knew a bit more about the legal situation. Although neither possessed a closed-range map, each was able to guess how to locate one. However, both implied that they would not bother to find out whether a trespass incident had occurred in open or closed range before settling a claim. The liability rules that these adjusters apply to routine trespass claims seemed largely independent of formal law.[42]

The Settlement of Trespass Disputes

If Shasta County residents were to act like the farmer and the rancher in Coase's parable, they would settle their trespass problems in the following way.[43] First, they would look to the formal law to determine who had what entitlements. They would regard those substantive rules as beyond their influence (as "exogenous," to use the economists' adjective). When they faced a potentially costly interaction, such as a trespass risk to crops, they would resolve it "in the shadow of"[44] the formal legal rules. Because transactions would be costless, enforcement would be complete: no violation of an entitlement would be ignored. For the same reason, two neighbors who interacted on a number of fronts would resolve their disputes front by front, rather than globally.

The field evidence casts doubt on the realism of each of these literal features of the parable. Because Coase himself was fully aware that transactions are costly and thus that the parable was no more than an abstraction, the contrary evidence in no way diminishes his monumental contribution in "The Problem of Social Cost." Indeed the evidence is fully consistent with Coase's central idea that, regardless of the content of law, people tend to structure their affairs to their mutual advantage. Nevertheless, the findings reported here may serve as a caution to law-and-economics scholars who have underestimated the impact of transaction costs on how the world works.[45]

Norms, Not Legal Rules, Are the Basic Sources of Entitlements

In rural Shasta County, where transaction costs are assuredly not zero, trespass conflicts are generally resolved not *in* "the shadow of the law" but, rather, *beyond* that shadow. Most rural residents are consciously committees to an overarching norm of cooperation among neighbors.[46] In trespass situations, their applicable particularized norm, adhered to by all but a few deviants, is that an owner of livestock is responsible for the acts of his animals. Allegiance to this norm seems wholly independent of normal legal entitlements. Most cattlemen believe that a rancher should keep his animals from eating a neighbor's grass, regardless of whether the range is open or closed. Cattlemen typically couch their justifications for the norm in moral terms. Marty Fancher: "Suppose I sat down [uninvited] to a dinner your wife had cooked?" Dick Coombs: It "isn't right" to get free pasturage at the expense of one's neighbors. Owen Shellworth: "[My cattle] don't belong [in my neighbor's field]." Attorney-rancher Pete Schultz: A cattleman is "morally obligated to fence" to protect his neighbor's crops, even in open range.

The remainder of this chapter describes in greater detail how the norms of neighborliness operate and how deviants who violate these norms are informally controlled. The discussion also identifies another set of deviants: trespass victims who actually invoke their formal legal rights.

Incomplete Enforcement: The Live-and-Let-Live Philosophy

The norm that an animal owner should control his stock is modified by another norm that holds that a rural resident should put up with ("lump") minor damage stemming from isolated trespass incidents. The neighborly response to an isolated infraction is an exchange of civilities. A trespass victim should notify the animal owner that the trespass has occurred and assist the owner in retrieving the stray stock. Virtually all residents have telephones, the standard means of communication. A telephone report is usually couched not as a complaint but rather as a service to the animal owner, who, after all, has a valuable asset on the loose. Upon receiving a telephone report, a cattleman who is a good neighbor will quickly retrieve the animals (by truck if necessary), apologize for the occurrence, and thank the caller. The Mortons and the Shellworths, two ranching families in the Oak Run area particularly esteemed for their neighborliness, have a policy of promptly and apologetically responding to their neighbors' notification of trespass.[47]

Several realities of country life in Shasta County help explain why residents are expected to put up with trespass losses. First, it is common for a rural landowner to lose a bit of forage or to suffer minor fence damage. The area northeast of Redding lies on a deer migration route. During the late winter and early spring thousands of deer and elk move through the area, easily jumping the barbed-wire fences.[48] Because wild animals trespass so often, most rural residents come to regard minor damage from alien animals not as an injurious event but as an inevitable part of life.

Second, most residents expect to be on both the giving and the receiving ends of trespass incidents. Even the ranchette owners have, if not a few hobby livestock, at least several dogs, which they keep for companionship, security, and pest control. Unlike cattle, dogs that trespass may harass, or even kill, other farm animals. If trespass risks are symmetrical, and if victims bear all trespass losses, accounts balance in the long run. Under these conditions, the advantage of reciprocal lumping is that no one has to expend time or money to settle disputes.

The norm of reciprocal restraint that underlies the "live-and-let-live" philosophy also calls for ranchers to swallow the costs of boarding another person's animal, even for months at a time. A cattleman often finds in his herd an animal wearing someone else's brand. If he recognizes the brand he will customarily inform its owner, but the two will often agree that the simplest solution is for the animal to stay put until the trespass victim next gathers his animals, an event that may be weeks or months away. The cost of "cutting" a single animal from a larger herd seems to underlie this custom. Thus, ranchers often consciously provide other people's cattle with feed worth perhaps as much as $10 to $100 per animal. Although Shasta County ranchers tend to regard themselves as financially pinched, even ranchers who know that they are legally entitled to recover feeding costs virtually never seek monetary compensation for boarding estrays. The largest ranchers northeast of Redding who were interviewed reported that they had never charged anyone or been charged by anyone for costs of that sort. Even when they do not know to whom a stray animal belongs, they put the animal in their truck the next time they take a load of animals to the auction yard at Cottonwood and drop it off without charge so that the brand inspector can locate the owner.[49]

Mental Accounting of Interneighbor Debts

Residents who own only a few animals may of course be unable to see any average reciprocity of advantage in a live-and-let-live approach to animal trespass incidents. This would be true, for example, of a farmer whose fields frequently suffered minor damage from incursions by a particular rancher's livestock. Shasta County norms entitle a farmer in that situation to keep track of those minor losses in a mental account, and eventually to act to remedy the imbalance.

A fundamental feature of rural society makes this enforcement system feasible: Rural residents deal with one another on a large number of fronts, and most residents expect those interactions to continue far into the future. In sociological terms, their relationships are "multiplex," not "simplex."[50] In game-theoretic terms, they are engaged in iterated, not single-shot, play.[51] They interact on water supply, controlled burns, fence repairs, social events, staffing the volunteer fire department, and so on. Where population densities are low, each neighbor looms larger. Thus any trespass dispute with a neighbor is almost certain to be but one thread in the rich fabric of a continuing relationship.

A person in a multiplex relationship can keep a rough mental account of the outstanding credits and debits in each aspect of that relationship.[52] Should the aggregate account fall out of balance, tension may mount because the net creditor may begin to perceive the net debtor as an overreacher. But as long as the aggregate account is in balance, neither party need be concerned that particular subaccounts are not. For example, if a rancher were to owe a farmer in the trespass subaccount, the farmer could be expected to remain content if that imbalance were to be offset by a debt he owed the rancher in, say, the water-supply subaccount.[53]

The live-and-let-live norm also suggests that neighbors should put up with minor imbalances in their aggregate accounts, especially when they perceive that their future interactions will provide adequate opportunities for settling old scores. Creditors may actually prefer having others in their debt. For example, when Larry Brennan lost seven tons of baled hay to Frank Ellis' cattle in open range, Brennan (although he did not know it) had a strong legal claim against Ellis for intentional trespass. Brennan estimated his loss at between $300 and $500, hardly a trivial amount. When Ellis learned of Brennan's loss he told Brennan to "come down and take some hay" from Ellis' barn. Brennan reported that he declined this offer of compensation, partly because he thought he should not have piled the bales in an unfenced area, but also because he would rather have Ellis in debt to him than be in debt to Ellis. Brennan was willing to let Ellis run up a deficit in their aggregate interpersonal accounts because he thought that as a creditor he would have more leverage over Ellis' future behavior.

The Control of Deviants: The Key Role of Self-Help

The rural Shasta County population includes deviants who do not adequately control their livestock and run up excessive debts in their informal accounts with their neighbors. Frank Ellis, for example, was notoriously indifferent about his reputation among his neighbors. In general, the traditionalists who let their animals loose in the mountains during the summer are less scrupulous than the modernists are in honoring the norms of neighborliness. This is likely due to the fact that traditionalists have less complex, and shorter-lived, interrelationships with the individuals who encounter their range cattle.

To discipline deviants, the residents of rural Shasta County use the following four types of countermeasures, listed in escalating order of seriousness: (1) self-help retaliation; (2) reports to county authorities; (3) claims for compensation informally submitted without the help of attorneys; and (4) attorney-assisted claims for compensation. The law starts to gain bite as one moves down this list.

Self-help. Not only are most trespass disputes in Shasta County resolved according to extralegal rules, but most enforcement actions are also extralegal. A measured amount of self-help—an amount that would serve to even up accounts[54]—is the predominant and ethically preferred response to someone who has not taken adequate steps to prevent his animals from trespassing.

The mildest form of self-help is truthful negative gossip. This usually works because only the extreme deviants are immune from the general obsession with neighborliness. Although the Oak Run-Round Mountain area is undergoing a rapid increase in population, it remains distinctly rural in atmosphere. People tend to know one another, and they value their reputations in the community. Some ranching families have lived in the area for several generations and include members who plan to stay indefinitely. Members of these families seem particularly intent on maintaining their reputations as good neighbors. Should one of them not promptly and courteously retrieve a stray, he might fear that any resulting gossip would permanently besmirch the family name.

Residents of the Northeastern Sector foothills seem quite conscious of the role of gossip in their system of social control. One longtime resident, who had also lived for many years in a suburb of a major California urban area, observed that people in the Oak Run area "gossip all the time" much more than in the urban area. Another reported intentionally using gossip to sanction a traditionalist who had been "impolite" when coming to pick up some stray mountain cattle; he reported that application of this self-help device produced an apology, an outcome itself presumably circulated through the gossip system.

The furor over Frank Ellis' loose cattle in the Oak Run area induced area residents to try a sophisticated variation of the gossip sanction. The ranchette residents who were particularly bothered by Ellis' cattle could see that he was utterly indifferent to his reputation among them. They thought, however, that as a major rancher, Ellis would worry about his reputation among the large cattle operators in the county. They therefore reported Ellis' activities to the Board of Directors of the Shasta County Cattlemen's Association. This move proved unrewarding, for Ellis was also surprisingly indifferent to his reputation among the cattlemen.[55]

When milder measures such as gossip fail, a person is regarded as being justified in threatening to use, and perhaps even actually using, tougher self-help sanctions. Particularly in unfenced country, a victim may respond to repeated cattle trespasses by herding the offending animals to a location extremely inconvenient for their owner.[56] Another common response to repeated trespasses is to threaten to kill a responsible animal should it ever enter again. Although the killing of trespassing livestock is a crime in California,[57] six landowners—not noticeably less civilized than the others—unhesitatingly volunteered that they had issued death threats of this sort. These threats are credible in Shasta County because victims of recurring trespasses, particularly if they have first issued a warning, feel justified in killing or injuring the mischievous animals.[58] Despite the criminality of the conduct (a fact not necessarily known to the respondents), I learned the identity of two persons who had shot trespassing cattle. Another landowner told of running the steer of an uncooperative neighbor into a fence. The most intriguing report came from a rancher who had had recurrent problems with a trespassing bull many years before. This rancher told a key law enforcement official that he wanted to castrate the bull—"to turn it into a steer." The official replied that he would turn a deaf ear if that were to occur. The rancher asserted that he then carried out his threat.

It is difficult to estimate how frequently rural residents actually resort to violent self-help. Nevertheless, fear of physical retaliation is undoubtedly one of the major incentives for order in rural Shasta County. Ranchers who run herds at large freely admit that they worry that their trespassing cattle might meet with violence. One traditionalist reported that he is responsive to complaints from ranchette owners because he fears they will poison or shoot his stock. A judge for a rural district of the county asserted that a vicious animal is likely to "disappear" if its owner does not control it. A resident of the Oak Run area stated that some area residents responded to Frank Ellis' practice of running herds at large by rustling Ellis' cattle. He suggested that Ellis print tee shirts with the inscription: "Eat Ellis Beef. Everyone in Oak Run Does!"

Complaints to public officials. The longtime ranchers of Shasta County pride themselves on being able to resolve their problems on their own. Except when they lose animals to rustlers, they do not seek help from public officials. Although ranchette owners also use the self-help remedies of gossip and violence, they, unlike the cattlemen, sometimes respond to a trespass incident by contacting a county official who they think will remedy the problem.[59] These calls are usually funneled to the animal control officer or brand inspector, who both report that most callers are ranchette owners with limited rural experience. As already discussed, these calls do produce results. The county officials typically contact the owner of the animal, who then arranges for its removal. Brad Bogue, the animal control officer, reported that in half the cases the caller knows whose animal it is. This suggests that callers often think that requests for removal have more effect when issued by someone in authority.

Mere removal of an animal may provide only temporary relief when its owner is a mountain lessee whose cattle have repeatedly descended upon the ranchettes. County officials therefore use mild threats to caution repeat offenders. In closed range, they may mention both their power to impound the estrays and the risk of criminal prosecution. These threats appear to be bluffs; as noted, the county never impounds stray cattle when it can locate an owner, and it rarely prosecutes cattlemen (and then only when their animals have posed risks to motorists). In open range, county officials may deliver a more subtle threat: not that they will initiate a prosecution, but that, if the owner does not mend his ways, the Board of Supervisors may face insuperable pressure to close the range in the relevant area. Because cattlemen perceive that a closure significantly diminishes their legal entitlements in situations where motorists have collided with their livestock, this threat can catch their attention.[60]

A trespass victim's most effective official protest is one delivered directly to his elected county supervisor—the person best situated to change stray-cattle liability rules. Many Shasta County residents are aware that traditionalist cattlemen fear the supervisors more than they fear law enforcement authorities. Thus in 1973 the alfalfa farmer John Woodbury made his repeated phone calls about mountain cattle not to Brad Bogue but to Supervisor John Caton. When a supervisor receives many calls from trespass victims, his first instinct is to mediate the crisis. Supervisor Norman Wagoner's standard procedure was to assemble the ranchers in the area and advise them to put pressure on the offender or else risk the closure of the range. Wagoner's successor, Supervisor John Caton, similarly told Frank Ellis that he would support a closure at Oak Run unless Ellis built three miles of fence along the Oak Run Road. If a supervisor is not responsive to a constituent's complaint, the constituent may respond by circulating a closure petition, as Doug Heinz eventually did in Oak Run.

The rarity of claims for monetary relief. Because Shasta County residents tend to settle their trespass disputes beyond the shadow of the law, one might suspect that the norms of neighborliness include a norm against the invocation of formal legal rights. And this norm is indeed entrenched.[61] Owen Shellworth: "I don't believe in lawyers [because there are] always hard feelings [when you litigate]." Tony Morton: "[I never press a monetary claim because] I try to be a good neighbor." Norman Wagoner: "Being good neighbors means no lawsuits." Although trespasses are frequent, Shasta County's rural residents virtually never file formal trespass actions against one another. John Woodbury, for example, made dozens of phone calls to Supervisor John Caton, but never sought monetary compensation from the traditionalists whose cattle had repeatedly marauded his alfalfa field. Court records and conversations with court clerks indicate that in most years not a single private lawsuit seeking damages for either trespass by livestock or the expense of boarding estrays is filed in the county's courts.[62] Not only do the residents of the Northeastern Sector foothills refrain from filing formal lawsuits, but they are also strongly disinclined to submit informal monetary claims to the owners of trespassing animals.[63]

The landowners who were interviewed clearly regard their restraint in seeking monetary relief as a mark of virtue. When asked why they did not pursue meritorious legal claims arising from trespass or fence-finance disputes, various landowners replied: "I'm not that kind of guy"; "I don't believe in it"; "I don't like to create a stink"; "I try to get along." The landowners who attempted to provide a rationale for this forbearance all implied the same one, a long-term reciprocity of advantage. Ann Kershaw: "The only one that makes money [when you litigate] is the lawyer." Al Levitt: "I figure it will balance out in the long run." Pete Schultz: "I hope they'll do the same for me." Phil Ritchie: "My family believes in 'live and let live.'"

Mutual restraint saves parties in a long-term relationship the costs of going through the formal claims process. Adjoining landowners who practice the live-and-let-live approach are both better off whenever the negative externalities from their activities are roughly in equipoise. Equipoise is as likely in closed range as in open. Landowners with property in closed range—the ones with the greatest formal legal rights—were the source of half of the quotations in the prior two paragraphs.

When a transfer *is* necessary to square unbalanced accounts, rural neighbors prefer to use in-kind payments, not cash. Shasta County landowners regard a monetary settlement as an arms' length transaction that symbolizes an unneighborly relationship. Should your goat happen to eat your neighbor's tomatoes, the neighborly thing for you to do would be to help replant the tomatoes; a transfer of money would be too cold and too impersonal.[64] When Kevin O'Hara's cattle went through a break in a fence and destroyed his neighbor's corn crop (a loss of less than $100), O'Hara had to work hard to persuade the neighbor to accept his offer of money to compensate for the damages. O'Hara insisted on making this payment because he "felt responsible" for his neighbor's loss, a feeling that would not have been in the least affected had the event occurred in open instead of closed range. There can also be social pressure against offering monetary settlements. Bob Bosworth's father agreed many decades ago to pay damages to a trespass victim in a closed-range area just south of Shasta County; other cattlemen then rebuked him for setting an unfortunate precedent. The junior Bosworth, in 1982 the president of the Shasta County Cattlemen's Association, could recall no other out-of-pocket settlement in a trespass case.

Trespass victims who sustain an unusually large loss are more likely to take the potentially deviant step of making a claim for monetary relief. Among those interviewed were adjusters for the two insurance companies whose liability policies would be most likely to cover losses from animal trespass. The adjusters' responses suggest that in a typical year these companies receive fewer than ten trespass damage claims originating in Shasta County. In the paradigmatic case, the insured is not a rancher but rather a ranchette owner, whose family's horse has escaped and trampled a neighboring homeowner's shrubbery. The claimant is typically not represented by an attorney, a type of professional these adjusters rarely encounter. The adjusters also settle each year two or three trespass claims that homeowners or ranchette owners have brought against ranchers. Ranchers who suffer trespasses virtually never file claims against others' insurance companies. An adjuster for the company that insures most Shasta County ranchers stated that he could not recall, in his twenty years of adjusting, a single claim by a rancher for compensation for trespass damage.

Attorney-assisted claims. The landowners, particularly the ranchers, express a strong aversion to hiring an attorney to fight one's battles. To hire an attorney is to escalate a conflict. A good neighbor does not do such a thing because the "natural working order" calls for two neighbors to work out their problems between themselves. The files in the Shasta County courthouses reveal that the ranchers who honor norms of neighborliness—the vast majority—are not involved in cattle-related litigation of any kind.

I did uncover two instances in which animal-trespass victims in the Oak Run-Round Mountain area had turned to attorneys. In one of these cases the victim actually filed a formal complaint. Because lawyer-backed claims are so unusual, these two disputes, both of them bitter, deserve elaboration.

The first involved Tom Hailey and Curtis McCall. For three generations, Hailey's family has owned a large tract of foothill forest in an open-range area near Oak Run. In 1978 Hailey discovered McCall's cattle grazing on some of Hailey's partially fenced land. Hailey suspected that McCall had brought the animals in through a gate in Hailey's fence. When Hailey confronted him, McCall, who lived about a mile away, acted as if the incursion had been accidental. Hailey subsequently found a salt block on the tract—an object he could fairly assume that McCall had put there to service his trespassing herd. Hailey thus concluded that McCall had not only deliberately trespassed but had also aggravated the offense by untruthfully denying the charge. Hailey seized the salt block and consulted an attorney, who advised him to seek compensation from McCall. The two principals eventually agreed to a small monetary settlement.

Hailey is a semi-retired government employee who spends much of his time outside of Shasta County; he is regarded as reclusive and eccentric—certainly someone outside the mainstream of Oak Run society. McCall, a retired engineer with a hard-driving style, moved to Shasta County in the late 1970s to run a small livestock ranch. The Haileys refer to him as a "Texan"—a term that in Shasta County connotes someone who is both an outsider and lacks neighborly instincts.

The second dispute involved Doug Heinz and Frank Ellis. As described in Chapter 2, Heinz had the misfortune of owning a ranchette near Ellis' ranch. After experiencing repeated problems with Ellis' giant cattle herds, Heinz unilaterally seized three animals that had broken through his fence. Heinz boarded these animals for three months without notifying Ellis. Heinz later asserted he intended to return them when Ellis next held a roundup. According to Heinz, Ellis eventually found out that Heinz had the animals and asked for their return. Heinz agreed to return them if Ellis would pay pasturage costs. When Ellis replied, "You know I'm good for it," Heinz released the animals and sent Ellis a bill. Ellis refused to pay the bill, and further infuriated Heinz by calling him "boy" whenever Heinz brought up the debt.

On January 8, 1981, Heinz filed a small-claims action against Ellis to recover $750 "for property damage, hay and grain ate [sic] by defendant's cattle, boarding of animals."[65] Acting through the attorney he kept on retainer,

Ellis responded eight days later with a separate civil suit against Heinz.[66] Ellis' complaint sought $1,500 compensatory and $10,000 punitive damages from Heinz for the shooting deaths of two Black Brangus cows that Ellis had pastured on Bureau of Land Management lands; it also sought compensation for the weight loss Ellis' three live animals had sustained during the months Heinz had been feeding them. The two legal actions were later consolidated. Heinz, who called Ellis' allegation that he had killed two cows "100 percent lies" and "scare tactics," hired an attorney based in Redding to represent him. This attorney threatened to pursue a malicious prosecution action against Ellis if Ellis persisted in asserting that Heinz had slain the Black Brangus cows. In December 1981, the parties agreed to a settlement under the terms of which Ellis paid Heinz $300 in damages and $100 for attorney fees. Ellis' insurance company picked up the tab. By that time Heinz was spearheading a political campaign to close the range Ellis had been using.

The Heinz-Ellis and Hailey-McCall disputes share several characteristics. Although both arose in open range, in each instance legal authority favored the trespass victim: Hailey, because McCall's trespass had been intentional; and Heinz, because Ellis' animals had broken through an apparently lawful fence.[67] In both instances the victim, before consulting an attorney, had attempted to obtain informal satisfaction but had been rebuffed. Each victim came to believe that the animal owner had not been honest with him. Each dispute was ultimately settled in the victim's favor. In both instances, neither the trespass victim nor the cattle owner was a practiced follower of rural Shasta County norms. Thus other respondents tended to refer to the four individuals involved in these two claims as "bad apples," "odd ducks," or otherwise as people not aware of the natural working order. Ordinary people, it seems, do not often turn to attorneys to help resolve disputes.[68]

Notes

1. My field research relied heavily on face-to-face interviews. In all, seventy-three interviews were conducted, most of them in the summer of 1982. They were arranged with two sorts of people: landowners in the Oak Run-Round Mountain area, and a somewhat larger number of specialists—such as attorneys, claims adjusters, and government employees—thought likely to be knowledgeable about how rural residents resolve stray-cattle disputes. Various government records were also consulted, partly to have a crosscheck on the landowners' version of history. The techniques used are more fully described in the Appendix.
2. See infra Chapter 6, text following note 9.
3. Division of Agric. Sci., Univ. of Cal., Leaflet No. 21184, *Beef Production in California* 12-13 (Nov. 1980).
4. Cf. Cal. Agric. Code 16803 (West 1968) (cattlemen grazing herds on open range must include at least one bull for every thirty cows). The refinement of artificial insemination techniques has enabled some ranchers to increase the ratio of cows to bulls in herds kept behind fences.
5. *Beef Production in California*, supra note 3, at 3, 5.
6. None of the landowners interviewed mentioned an instance in which trespassing cattle had caused personal injury. Two insurance adjusters, who frequently had been called upon to settle dog-bite claims, could remember, between them, only

one personal-injury claim arising from cattle—an instance in which a cow had stepped on someone's foot.

7. *Fletcher v. Rylands*, I L.R.-Ex. 265, 280 (1866) (dictum) (Blackburn, J.). See also 3 William Blackstone, *Commentaries* *211 ("A man is answerable for not only his own trespass, but that of his cattle also"). This rule was established in England by 1353 at the latest. I *Select Cases of Trespass from the Kings Courts, 1307-I399* lxxviii (Morris S. Arnold ed. 1985). The details of animal-trespass law are explored more fully in Ellickson, "Of Coase and Cattle: Dispute Resolution among Neighbors in Shasta County," 38 *Stan. L. Rev.* 623, 659-667 (1986).
8. See, e.g., *Montezuma Improvement C. v. Simmerly*, 181 Cal. 722, 724, 189 P. 100, 101 (1919). A trespass victim's own misconduct, such as failing to close a cattle gate or breaching a contractual duty to build a fence, may diminish or bar his recovery. See Glanville L. Williams, *Liability for Animals* 178-181 (1939). In California, misconduct by a plaintiff does not typically operate as a complete defense in a strict liability action. *Daly v. General Motors Corp.*, 20 Cal. 3d 725, 575 P.2d 1162, 144 Cal. Rptr. 380 (1978) (products liability case).
9. Many authorities assert that the western states have been the chief followers of "fencing-out" rules. See, e.g., 2 Fowler V. Harper and Fleming James, *The Law of Torts* 14.10 (1956). Nineteenth-century treatises on fence law reveal, however, that in that era, fencing-out was the dominant rule throughout the United States, particularly in the northern states. See W. W. Thornton, *The Law of Railroad Fences and Private Crossings* 8-10 (1882) (identifying thirteen states following the English rule and twenty-one states having fencing-out regimes); Ransom H. Tyler, *The Law of Boundaries, Fences, and Window Lights* 361-512 (1874) (state-by-state review of fence law, indicating, at 451, that Michigan, for example, enacted a fencing out statue in 1847).
10. 1850 Cal. Stat., ch. 49, 131. See *Comerford v. Dupuy*, 17 Cal. 308 (1861); *Waters v. Moss*, 12 Cal. 535 (1859) (dictum). Because lawful-fence statutes are consequently suited to enforcement by law "fence viewers," described infra note 27. For a more extended analysis of the merits of alternative rules of cattle-trespass liability, see infra Chapter 11, text accompanying notes 3-11.
11. See Note, "Torts: Trespass by Animals upon Unenclosed Lands in California," 7 *Cal. L. Rev.* 365 (1919).
12. 1915 Cal. Stat. 636 (current version at Cal. Agric. Code 17001-17128 (West 1968 & Supp. 1986)).
13. Although the 1915 statute nominally dealt with only a trespass victim's rights to take up estrays (strays) California case law has consistently held that a statutory right to seize estrays on unfenced land carries with it the right to recover trespass damages under the traditional common law rule of strict liability. See, e.g., *Montezuma Improvement Co. v. Simmerly*, 181 Cal. 722, 189 P.100 (1919); *Williams v. Goodwin*, 41 Cal. App 3d 496, 116 Cal. Rptr. 200 (1974) (dictum).
14. 1915 Cal. Stat. 636 (current version at Cal. Agric. Code 17123-17126 (West 1968)). Subsequent amendments repealed the exemptions applicable in all of Del Norte County, and in parts of Shasta and Trinity counties. See Cal. Agric. Code §§17123-17I26 (West 1968). Cal. Agric. Code §17124 (West 1968) authorizes the board of supervisors of *any* county to convert closed-range areas to open range. Responding in part to lobbying efforts by local cattlemen's associations, an increasing number of California's foothill counties have "opened" parts of their mountain forest. See, e.g., Amador County, Cal., Ordinance 590 (Apr. 26, 1977); Placer County, Cal., Ordinance 2017-B (June, 1976).
15. 1945 Ca. Stat. 1538-39 (current version at Cal. Agric. Code 17126 (West 1968)).

16. 1945 Ca. Stat. 1539 (current version at Cal. Agric. Code 17126 (West 1968 & Supp. 1986)).
17. In 1974 the state legislature granted similar authority to the Board of Supervisors of Trinity County, Shasta's neighbor to the west. 1974 Cal. Stat. 409 (current version at Cal. Agric. Code §17127 (West Supp. 198)). A number of other western states that generally adhere to an open-range regime also authorize substrate entities to "close" parts of their range. See, e.g., *Maguire v. Yanke*, 99 Idaho 829, 590 P.2d 85 (1978) (describing Idaho procedure through which landowners can petition to close range on a district-by-district basis); Wash. Rev. Code Ann. §16.24.010 (1962) (counties without townships granted power to close range).
18. A map issued by the Shasta County Department of Public Works in 1981 showed twenty-eight separate areas the Board of Supervisors had closed by ordinance since 1945. Although most of the closed areas were located near Redding, there were areas of closed range in the hinterland in every direction from the city.
19. Defenses based on the trespass victim's misconduct are discussed supra note 8.
20. Persons other than the animal's owner could conceivably be held liable for an animal's damage. The California courts (at least until the late 1980s) were as expansive as any state's in imposing tort liability. They would have been likely to hold a landlord who had leased land for grazing liable were he negligently to have abetted trespasses by a lessee's livestock. Cf. *Uccello v. Laudenslayer*, 44 Cal. App. 3d 504, 118Cal. Rptr. 741 (1975) (residential landlord who knew of tenant's vicious dog and had the power to have it removed owed a duty of care to tenants' invitees and could be liable for negligence to dog-bite victim). But cf. *Blake v. Dunn Farms, Inc.*, 274 Ind. 560, 413 N.E.2d 560 (1980) (landlord not liable for damages stemming from escape of tenants horse that he knew little about).
21. Other rules may apply when livestock have caused personal injury or damage to chattels. In closed range, a cattle owner is strictly liable for foreseeable personal injuries that his livestock have caused. See *Williams v. Goodwin*, 41 Cal. App. 3d 496, 116 Cal. Rptr. 200 (1974). But cf. *Restatement (Second) of Torts* §504 (1977) (denying possessor of unfenced land in open-range recovery for personal injuries on a strict liability theory). In both open and closed range, the owner of a trespassing animal would be strictly liable if that animal were to kill animals belonging to the owner of the premises invaded. See Cal. Civ. Code §3341 (West 1970).
22. See Cal. Agric. Code. §17128 (West 1968) (excepting owners of "goats, swine, or hogs" from benefits of open-range rule); Shasta County Ordinance Code §3306 (declaring it "unlawful" to permit "any vicious dog or other dangerous animal" to run at large).
23. Section 17122 of the Agricultural Code reads: "In any county or part of a county devoted chiefly to grazing and so declared pursuant to this article, a person shall not have the right to take up any estray animal found upon his premises, or upon premises to which he has the right of possession, nor shall he have a lien thereon, *unless the premises are entirely enclosed with a good and substantial fence.*" Cal. Agric. Code §17122 (West 1968) (emphasis added). Judicial decisions construe this sort of provision as also denying a person without such a fence the right to recover damages for callie trespass. See supra note 13.
24. "A lawful fence is any fence which is good, strong, substantial, and sufficient to prevent the ingress and egress of livestock. No wire fence is a good and substantial fence within the meaning of this article unless it has three tightly stretched barbed wires securely fastened to posts of reasonable strength, firmly set in the ground not more than one rod [16 ½ feet] apart, one of which wires shall be at least four feet above the surface of the ground. Any kind of wire or other fence of height,

strength and capacity equal to or greater than the wire fence herein described is a good and substantial fence within the meaning of this article..." Cal. Agric. Code §17121 (West 1968). This statutory definition of a lawful fence has remained essentially unchanged since 1919. Compare 1919 Cal. Stat. 1150. The definition is technologically obsolete because, at least in Shasta County, cattlemen customarily use at least four strands of barbed wire in their boundary fences. California's statutory definitions of lawful fences before the invention of barbed wire are described in R. Tyler, supra note 9, at 482-484 (some samples: stone walls 4 ½ feet high; rail fence 5 ½ feet high; a 5-foot-high hedge).

25. In some states an open-range cattleman has been held liable for the trespass damages only when he has deliberately driven his livestock onto the lands of another. See, e.g., *Garcia v. Sumrall*, 58 Ariz. 526, 121 P.2d 640 (1942); *Richards v. Sanderson*, 39 Colo. 270, 89 P. 769 (1907). In other states, the entry of a cattleman's livestock has also been regarded as intentionally tortious when he has left them on a range from which it was substantially certain that they would enter the plaintiff's lands. See, e.g., *Lazarus v. Phelps*, 152 U.S. 81 (1894); *Mower v. Olsen*, 49 Utah 373, 164 P. 482 (1917). Two reported California decisions deal with the issue of intentional trespass by livestock owners; in both, applicable statutes prohibited the "herding" of livestock on the lands of others. The more recent decision, *Cramer v. Jenkins*, 82 Cal. App. 269, 255 P. 877 (1927), supports the proposition that leaving animals in a range from which they are substantially certain to trespass constitutes tortious misconduct. But cf. *Logan v. Gedney*, 38 Cal. 579 (1869) (implying that active herding may be required). The California Supreme Court's pro-plaintiff predilections during the early 1980s would have inclined it to follow the *Cramer* approach.
26. Some early California statutes authorized cattle-trespass victims to recover double damages in certain situations. See, e.g., 1850 Cal. Stat. 131 (victim enclosed by lawful fence can recover double damages for defendant's second offense). See also Nev. Rev. Stat. Ann. §569.440(l) (1986) (entitling trespass victim situated behind a lawful fence to recover double damages for second offense if the animal owner had been negligent).
27. See, e.g., Wash. Rev. Code Ann. §16.60.015 (Supp. 1989) ("damages [shall be] assessed by three reliable, disinterested parties and practical farmers, within five days next after the trespass has been committed..."). See generally 35 *Am. Jur. 2d* Fences §§24-32 (1967). The practice of delegating valuation issues to fence viewers was widespread in the nineteenth century and before. See R. Tyler, supra note 9, at 395, 399, 459, 476 (describing statutes in New York, Maine, Wisconsin, and Kansas); William Cronon, *Changes in the Land: Indians, Colonists, and the Ecology of New England* 135 (1983) (colonial Massachusetts). At least one of the early California fence statutes provided for the appointment of fence viewers. See 1860 Cal. Stat. 142 (viewers' role is to assess the contributions that each adjoining landowner should make to build a sufficient partition fence).
28. See *Montezuma Improvement Co. v. Simmerly*, 181 Cal. 722, 189 P. 100 (1919); *Blevins v. Mullally*, 22 Cal. App. 519, 135 P. 307 (1913).
29. See Cal. Agric. Code §§17041. 1742, 17091-17095, 17122 (West 1968 & Supp. 1986). The animal owner may contest the propriety of the victim's invocation of this self-help remedy. See *Yraceburn v. Cape*, 60 Cal. App, 374, 212 P. 938 (1923) (victim wrongly invoked power to seize animals). The distraint procedure also poses potentially thorny state action and due process issues. Cf. *Flagg Brothers, Inc. v. Brooks*; 436 U.S. 149 (1978) (warehouseman's sale of entrusted goods). The "right to distrain animals damage feasant" has deep roots in the English common law. See 3 William Blackstone, *Commentaries* 8211; G. Williams, supra note 8, at 7-123.

30. *People v. Dunn*, 39 Cal. App. 3d 418, 114 Cal. Rptr. 164 (1974) (dictum).
31. On the issue of whether this represents a reasonable exercise of self-help, compare *Gilson v. Fisk*, 8 N.H. 404 (1836) (trespass victim who drove herd three miles away held liable in damages for death of eight sheep), with *Wells v. State*, 13 S.W. 889 (Tex. Ct. App. 1890) (victim of intentional trespass did not violate criminal statute when he drove cattle three to four miles a field). Shasta County trespass victims sometimes adopt this time-honored self-help strategy. See infra note 56.
32. *People v. Dunn*, 39 Cal. App. 3d 418,114 Cal. Rptr. 164 (1974). See also Annot., 12 A.L.R.3d 1103 (1967) (liability for accidentally or intentionally poisoning trespassing stock). But see *Hummel v. State*, 69 Okla. Crim. 38, 99 P.2d 913 (1940) (rancher was privileged to castrate a bull that threatened to impregnate pure-bred cows grazing on open range).
33. See Shasta County Ordinance Code §3306 (habitual animal trespasses declared to be a public nuisance, "provided that this section shall not apply to livestock upon the open range").
34. The Shasta County Animal Control Office's Monthly Reports for 1980-1982 indicate that the office impounded one "bovine" during that period—a stray animal that Bogue said had been found within one block of the office's animal shelter. This figure understates the number of public impoundments because the brand inspector occasionally hauls stray cattle to the Cottonwood Auction Yard, which is better equipped than the animal shelter to board livestock.
35. Robert Baker, the county district attorney from 1965 to 1979, could not recall a single criminal prosecution for cattle trespass on private lands. Gary Glendenning, the livestock specialist in the detective's division of the county sheriff's office, affirmed that criminal trespass actions were "never" brought. Criminal proceedings have been initiated against owners of stray livestock, however, when the stray animals have repeatedly posed serious risks to motorists. See infra Chapter 5, note 41.
36. Eleven correctly stated they lived in open range; eight correctly stated they lived in closed range; one gave a flatly wrong answer; one, a partially wrong answer; and two "didn't know."
37. Two interviewees involved in open-range politics had obtained copies of the Department of Public Works' closed-range map.
38. However, of eleven respondents asked, only three stated that they had known when buying their land what kind of "legal range" it lay in.
39. This finding can be attributed to the fact, documented below, that trespass and estray claims are virtually never processed through the formal legal institutions of Shasta County.
40. Some legal specialists may also believe that the negligence principle is in every application normatively superior to the principle of strict liability.
41. In addition, neither of the two fence contractors interviewed had any notion of these boundaries. The county tax assessor assigned to the Oak Run-Round Mountain area was also unfamiliar with the closed-range map.
42. In his study of the settlement of automobile-liability claims, Ross found the law in action to be simpler and more mechanical than the formal law, but he did not find it to be quite as disconnected as animal-trespass law is in Shasta County. See H. Laurence Ross, *Settled Out of Court* 134-135, 237-240 (rev. ed. 1980).
43. The scholars involved in the Civil Liability Research Project have attempted to standardize the vocabulary of dispute resolution. They use "grievance" to describe a perceived entitlement to pursue a claim against another, "claim" to describe a demand for redress, and "dispute" to describe a rejected claim. See, e.g., Richard E. Miller and Austin Sarat, "Grievances, Claims, and Disputes: Assessing the

Adversary Culture," 15 *Law & Soc'y Rev.* 525, 527 (1980-81). The usage of this book is not precise.

44. This now-familiar phrase originated in Robert H. Mnookin and Lewis Kornhauser, "Bargaining in the Shadow of the Law: The Case of Divorce," 88 *Yale L. J.* 950 (1979).
45. Law-and-economics scholars often employ models that explicitly assume that actors have perfect knowledge of legal rules. See infra Chapter 8, text accompanying notes 10-13.
46. Although the rural landowners were emphatic about the importance of neighborliness and could offer many specific examples of neighborly behavior, they never articulated a general formula for how a rural resident should behave. Chapter 10 puts forward the hypothesis that the norms they honored served to maximize their objective welfare.
47. A trespass victim who cannot recognize the brand of the intruding animal—a quandary more common for ranchette owners than for ranchers—may telephone county authorities. Calls of this sort are eventually referred to the brand inspector or animal control officer who then regards the main priority to be the return of the animal to its owner.
48. One rancher reported that during the winter he expects to find thirty to forty deer grazing in his hayfield each night. The owner of a particularly large ranch estimated that about five hundred deer winter there, a condition he welcomes because he regards deer as "part of nature." John Woodbury, a key lobbyist for the passage of the Caton's Folly ordinance, stated that elk and deer had eaten more of the grass in his alfalfa field than mountain cattle ever had.
49. Brand Inspector Bruce Jordan estimated that ranchers drop off approximately three hundred head of stray livestock at the auction yard each year, and that these ranchers typically decline to seek compensation from the owners of the strays.
50. See Robert L. Kidder, *Connecting Law and Society* 70-72 (1983). The phrase *multiplex relationship* was first coined in Max Gluckman, *The Judicial Process among the Barotse of Northern Rhodesia* 19 (1955).
51. The law-and-society literature has long emphasized that law is not likely to be important to parties enmeshed in a continuing relationship. For example, Marc Galanter has observed: "In the American setting, litigation tends to be between parties who are strangers. Either they never had a mutually beneficial continuing relationship, as in the typical automobile case, or their relationship—marital, commercial, or, organizational—is ruptured. In either case, there is no anticipated future relationship. In the American setting, unlike some others, resort to litigation is viewed as an irreparable breach of the relationship." Marc Galanter, "Reading the Landscape of Disputes: What We Know and Don't Know (and Think We Know) about Our Allegedly Contentious and Litigious Society," 31 *UCLA L. Rev.* 4, 24-25 (1983). See also infra Chapter 10, text at notes 35-49 (discussion of close-knit groups).
52 Cf. Arthur J. Vidich and Joseph Bensman, *Small Town in Mass Society* 34 (rev. ed. 1968): "To a great extent these arrangements between friends and neighbors have a reciprocal character: a man who helps others may himself expect to be helped later on. In a way the whole system takes on the character of insurance. Of course some people are more conscious of their premium payments than others and keep a kind of mental bookkeeping on what they owe and who owes them what; which is a perfectly permissible practice so long as one docs not openly confront others with unbalanced accounts."
53. See Oliver E. Williamson, *Markets and Hierarchies* 256-257 (1975) (a participant in a continuing relationship seeks to achieve a favorable balance in the overall set of interactions, not in each separate interaction).

54. Even-Up strategies arc discussed infra Chapter 12, text accompanying notes 39-48.
55. See supra Chapter 2, note 14.
56. Two residents stated in interviews that they had done this. For some scattered precedents on the legality of this practice, see supra note 31.
57. Cal. Penal Code §597 (a) (West Supp. 1989); *People v. Dunn*, 39 Cal. App. 3d 418, 114 Cat. Rptr. 164 (1974).
58. Violent self-help—occasionally organized on a group basis as vigilante justice—was a tradition in the nineteenth-century American West. "The laws (in Wyoming) appeared to require that a farmer fence his land to keep cattle out, but many a farmer preferred to save the cost of a fence, then wait until cattle came in his land, and with a shot or two secure a winter's supply of beef." Daniel J. Boorstin, *The Americans: The Democratic Experience* 30 (1973). See also Ernest Staples Osgood, *The Day of the Cattleman* (1929), at 157-160 (lynching of horse thieves); at 242 (killing of trespassing cattle); and at 252-253 (describing how large cattle companies mobilized an army to invade Johnson County, Wyoming, to prevent small ranchers from using violent self-help against the companies' cattle).
59. The role of complaints to public officials is explored in M. P. Baumgartner, *The Moral Order of a Suburb* 80-82 (1988) (New York suburb), and David M. Engel, "Cases, Conflict, and Accommodation: Patterns of Legal Interaction in an American Community," 1983 *Am. B. Found Research J.* 803, 821 (rural Illinois county).
60. See infra Chapters 5 and 6.
61. Norms against litigation are discussed more generally infra Chapter 14, text accompaning notes 36-43.
62. In the Central Valley Justice Court, no small claims for the August 1981 to June 1982 period were provoked by animal trespass, and the civil clerk who had worked there for eleven years could not remember any. The court's index of defendants for the 1975-1982 period indicated that Frank Ellis had been the only large rancher to become the target of any kind of legal action. In the Burney Justice Court, the small-claims files for 1980 showed no animal trespass cases, and the clerks could recall no such cases in their four years on the job.
63. There were several reports that others had informally settled claims for the costs of boarding estrays. Only one rancher told of paying such a claim; he regarded the claimant's pursuit of the money as a "cheap move."
64. This pattern poses a puzzle for transaction-cost economists, because in-kind transfers tend to be more costly to defect than cash transfers. But see infra Chapter 13, text accompanying notes 14-17 (in-kind exchange among members contributes to a group's cohesion).
65. *Heinz v. Ellis*, No. 81 SC 7 (Cent. Valley Just. Ct., filed Jan. 8, 1981).
66. *Ellis v. Heinz*, No. 81 CV 6 (Cent. Valley Just. Ct., filed Jan. 16, 1981).
67. Heinz had technically imperiled his statutory claim for damages under the Estray Act when he failed to notify the proper public authorities that he had taken up Ellis' animals. See Cal. Agric. Code §§17042, 17095 (West 1967 & Supp. 1986).
68. See also William E. Nelson, *Dispute and Conflict Resolution in Plymouth Colony, Massachusetts, 1725-1825* (1981) (Plymouth's particularly litigious individuals during the 1725-1774 period tended to be people who were poorly socialized); Harry F. Todd, Jr., "Litigious Marginals: Character and Disputing in a Bavarian Village," in *The Disputing Process: Law in Ten Societies* 86, 118 (Laura Nader and Harry F. Todd, Jr. eds. 1978) (socially marginal people were disproportionately represented in civil and criminal litigation).

About the Editor

Edward P. Stringham is an associate professor of economics at San Jose State University and a research fellow at the Independent Institute. He is president of the Association of Private Enterprise Education, editor of the *Journal of Private Enterprise*, editor of *Anarchy, State, and Public Choice* (2006), and author of dozens of articles in scholarly journals including the *Journal of Institutional & Theoretical Economics*, *Quarterly Review of Economics & Finance*, *Journal of Labor Research*, *Quarterly Journal of Austrian Economics*, *Review of Austrian Economics*, *Journal of Libertarian Studies*, and *Independent Review*. His work has been discussed in the *San Francisco Chronicle*, *San Jose Mercury News*, *Oakland Tribune*, *Miami Tribune*, and dozens of other newspapers.

Stringham earned his Ph.D. from George Mason University in 2002, and has won Paper of the Year Award from the Association of Private Enterprise, Best Article Award from the Society for the Development of Austrian Economics, Second Place in the Independent Institute Garvey Contest, and Distinguished Young Scholar Award from the Liberalni Institut and the Prague School of Economics.

About the Contributors

Terry L. Anderson is executive director of the Property and Environment Research Center, senior fellow at the Hoover Institution at Stanford University, and professor emeritus at Montana State University.

Randy Barnett is the Austin B. Fletcher Professor of Law at Boston University.

Bruce Benson is DeVoe L. Moore Professor and Distinguished Research Professor of Economics at Florida State University.

Edmund Burke (1729-1797) was an Anglo-Irish statesman and political theorist who served for many years in the British House of Commons.

Bryan Caplan is an associate professor of economics at George Mason University.

Roy A. Childs, Jr. (1949-1992) was the editor of *Libertarian Review Magazine* and the lead book reviewer for Laissez Faire Books.

Voltairine de Cleyre (1866-1912) was an anarchist, feminist essayist, and orator.

Tyler Cowen is the Holbert C. Harris Chair of Economics at George Mason University and director of the James Buchanan Center and the Mercatus Center.

Alfred G. Cuzán is a professor of political science the University of West Florida.

Robert C. Ellickson is Walter E. Meyer Professor of Property and Urban Law at Yale Law School.

David Friedman is a professor at Santa Clara University Law School.

David Hart is the director the Liberty Fund's Online Library of Liberty and is the founding editor of *Humane Studies Review*.

John Hasnas is an associate professor of business at Georgetown University where he teaches courses in ethics and law.

P. J. Hill is George F. Benett Professor of Economics at Wheaton College.

Randall G. Holcombe is DeVoe Moore Professor of Economics at Florida State University.

Hans Hoppe is a professor of economics at the University of Nevada, Las Vegas, and editor-at-large of the *Journal of Libertarian Studies*.

Jeffrey Rogers Hummel is an assistant professor in the Department of Economics at San Jose State University.

Anthony de Jasay is an independent scholar and author living in Paluel, France.

Don Lavoie (1951-2001) was the David H. and Charles G. Koch Chair of Economics at George Mason University.

Peter Leeson is an assistant professor of economics at West Virginia University.

David Lipscomb (1831–1917) was a Church of Christ preacher and editor of the weekly paper the *Gospel Advocate*.

Roderick Long is an associate professor of philosophy at Auburn University and is the editor of the *Journal of Libertarian Studies*.

Paul Milgrom is a professor of economics and the Shirley and Leonard Ely Professor of Humanities and Sciences at Stanford University.

Gustave de Molinari (1819-1912) was a Belgian-born economist and the editor of the *Journal des Économistes*.

Douglass North is the Spencer T. Olin Professor in Arts & Sciences at Washington University Saint Louis and is winner of the 1993 Nobel Prize in Economic Science.

Robert Nozick (1938-2002) was a chair of the department of philosophy and the Pellegrino University Professor at Harvard University.

David Osterfeld (1950-1993) was a professor of political science at St. Joseph's College, Indiana.

Joseph R. Peden (1933-1996) was a professor of history at City University of New York, Baruch College.

Murray Rothbard (1926-1995) was the S.J. Hall Distinguished Professor of Economics at University of Nevada, Las Vegas and the founding editor of the *Journal of Libertarian Studies* and the *Review of Austrian Economics*.

Andrew Rutten is a lecturer in political science at Stanford University.

Lysander Spooner (1808-1887) was an American individualist anarchist, abolitionist, and legal theorist.

Daniel Sutter is a professor of economics at University of Texas Pan American.

Morris Tannehill (1926-1989) and *Linda Tannehill* (1939-) wrote their one book on political economy as independent scholars.

Benjamin Tucker (1854-1939) was an American individualist anarchist author who edited the periodical *Liberty*.

Barry Weingast is the Ward C. Krebs Family Professor in the Department of Political Science at Stanford University.

Index

CPSIA information can be obtained at www.ICGtesting.com
Printed in the USA
BVOW081850111212

307880BV00003B/7/P